EVERYMAN'S LIBRARY
EDITED BY ERNEST RHYS

REFERENCE

THE
EVERYMAN ENCYCLOPÆDIA
EDITED BY ANDREW BOYLE
VOLUME SEVEN

I WILL
MAKE
A BRIEF
OF IT
IN
MY NOTE
BOOK

MERRY WIVES
OF WINDSOR

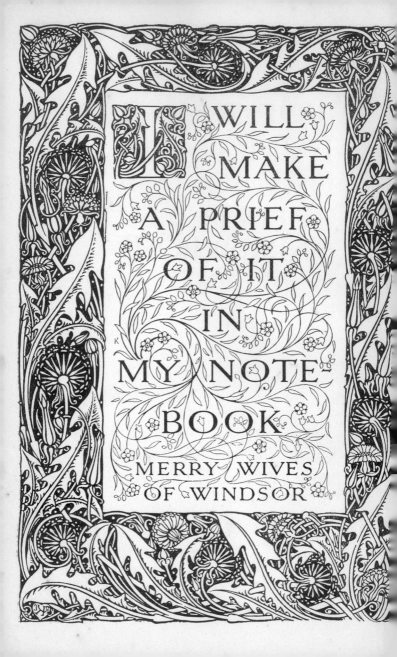

I WILL MAKE A PRIEF OF IT IN MY NOTE-BOOK

MERRY WIVES OF WINDSOR

THE ENCYCLOPÆDIA
EVERYMAN
ENCYCLOPÆDIA
EDITED BY
ANDREW BOYLE
VOLUME 7
GRA=INL

LONDON: PUBLISHED
by J·M·DENT·&·SONS·L^{TD}
AND IN NEW YORK
BY E·P·DUTTON&CO

THE

LIST OF ABBREVIATIONS

ac., acres.
A.D., after Christ.
agric., agricultural.
ambas., ambassador.
ann., annual.
arron., arrondissement.
A.-S., Anglo-Saxon.
A.V., Authorised Version.
b., born.
B.C., before Christ.
Biog. Dict., Biographical Dictionary.
bor., borough.
bp., birthplace.
C., Centigrade.
c. (circa), about.
cap., capital.
cf., compare.
co., county.
com., commune.
cub. ft., cubic feet.
d., died.
Dan., Danish.
dept., department.
dist., district.
div., division.
E., east ; eastern.
eccles., ecclesiastical.
ed., edition; edited.
e.g., for example.
Ency. Brit., Encyclopædia Britannica.
Eng., English.
estab., established.
el seq., and the following.
F., Fahrenheit.
fl., flourished.
fort. tn., fortified town.
Fr., French.
ft., feet.
Ger., German.
Gk., Greek.
gov., government.
Heb., Hebrew.
Hist., History.

i.e., that is.
in., inches.
inhab., inhabitants.
Is., island, -s.
It., Italian.
Jour., journal.
Lat., Latin.
lat., latitude.
l. b., left bank.
long., longitude.
m., miles.
manuf., manufacture.
mrkt. tn., market-town.
Mt., mts., mount, mountain, -s.
N., north ; northern.
N.T., New Testament.
O.T., Old Testament.
par., parish.
parl., parliamentary.
pop., population.
prin., principal.
prov., province.
pub., published.
q.v., which see.
R., riv., river.
r. b., right bank.
Rom., Roman.
R.V., Revised Version.
S., south ; southern.
sev., several.
Sp., Spanish.
sp. gr., specific gravity.
sq. m., square miles.
temp., temperature.
ter., territory.
tn., town.
trans., translated.
trib., tributary.
U.S.A., United States of America.
vil., village.
vol., volume.
W., west ; western.
yds., yards.

THE ENCYCLOPÆDIA

Grand-Combe, La, a com. of France, in the dept. of Gard and the arron. of Alais. There are coal mines, glass works, and zinc mines. Pop. 11,300.

Grandee (Sp. *grande*), the highest title of nobility which can be borne by a Spaniard. The term includes all members of the royal house. They held special privileges, such as freedom from taxation and arrest. They could also remain covered in the presence of the king.

Grand Falls: 1. Cataracts of the Hamilton, or Grand R., in Labrador, situated about 250 m. from the mouth of the river. There are two falls, each having a clear drop of 300 ft. or more. 2. A city on Exploits R., Newfoundland, founded in 1905, and engaged in the manufacture of paper.

Grand Forks: 1. A city of N. Dakota, U.S.A., and cap. of Grand Forks co. It is situated on the west bank of the Red R., opposite the mouth of Red Lake R.; it is served by two railways, and is about 75 m. N. of Fargo. The surrounding district is a rich wheat valley, and a trade in wheat and flour is carried on. There are saw-mills, breweries, and iron-works. Pop. (1910) 12,478. 2. A city of British Columbia on the Kettle R. with extensive smelting plant. Pop. 3000.

Grand Haven, a city of Michigan, U.S.A., and the cap. of Ottawa co. It is situated on Lake Michigan opposite Milwaukee, and 30 m. from the Grand Rapids. It possesses medical springs, and does a shipping trade in fruit (peaches), lumber, etc. There are saw-mills, shingle works, and manufactures of engines. Pop. 5856.

Grand Island, a tn. of Nebraska, U.S.A., and the cap. of Hall co., situated on the Platte R., and served by three railways. It has an extensive trade in cattle and grain, and possesses a college. Pop. (1910) 10,326.

Grand Junction, a city of Colorado, U.S.A., in Mesa co., of which it is the cap. It forms an important railway junction. In the neighbourhood gold, silver, and coal are mined. It is about 200 m. W.S.W. of Denver. Pop. (1910) 7754.

Grand Manan, an island at the entrance of the Bay of Fundy in the co. of Charlotte, New Brunswick. Well known as a holiday and health resort. Its greatest length is about 16 m., and its greatest breadth 6 m. Pop. 2700.

Grand Pré, or Lower Horton: 1. A post vil. in Nova Scotia, situated in King's co., 15 m. from Windsor. Stands in the midst of very fertile country. Has been made famous as the scene of Longfellow's poem *Evangeline.* Pop. 900. 2. A French tn. in the Ardennes.

Grand Rapids, a city of Michigan, U.S.A., situated in Kent co., of which it is the cap. It stands on the Grand R. The chief industries are the lumber industry and the quarrying of gypsum. It manufactures paper, flour, hosiery, and tobacco. It is the seat of both a Catholic and Protestant bishop. Pop. 112,571.

Grand River, The, Canada, rises in Grey co., flows S. and then S.E., entering Lake Erie after a course of 150 m. It can be used for navigation for 70 m. up, and communicates with Lake Ontario by the Welland Canal. 2. One of the head streams of the R. Colorado, U.S.A.; it rises in the Rocky Mts., and joins the Green in Utah, flowing through a very mountainous district. Length 348 miles. 3. Rises in the co. of Jackson in Michigan, one of the U.S.A., and after flowing first in a westerly, then a northerly direction, directs its course once more westward, emptying its waters into Lake Michigan at Grand Haven. It is about 300 m. long. 4. Rises in Missouri, U.S.A., and eventually joins the Missouri at Brunswick. Length 300 m.

Grand, Sarah (*b.* 1862), an English novelist, born in Ireland. She became famous through her first novel *Ideala,* 1888. She has also written *The Heavenly Twins,* 1893; *The Beth Book,* 1897; and *Babs the Impossible.* She is a distinctly original writer with a strong vein for painting romantic situations.

Grand Serjeanty. In the feudal system of land holding tenure by G. S., or per *magnum servitium*, meant that the vassal held his land on condition of rendering special services to the king instead of serving the king generally in time of war. The services were always free, but were uncertain in nature. Instances of such services were carrying the king's banner or lance when he went to war, filling the post of butler, champion (the officer whose duty it was to ride fully armed into Westminster Hall and challenge to single combat any one who should deny the king's title to the crown), or other officer at his coronation. In most other respects tenure by G. S. was assimilated to tenure by knightservice; but a tenant by G. S. was not compelled to pay aids or scutage, and where a tenant by knight-service paid £5 for taking up a knights fee (relief) as heir, the tenant by G. S. paid only one year's value of his land. In contradistinction to G. S. was the tenure by *petit serjeanty*, where the duties or services were of a somewhat servile nature. (*See* PETIT SERJEANTY.) A somewhat similar tenure was that by *cornage*, where the tenant's duty consisted in winding a horn to give men warning of the coming of the Scots or other enemies.

Grandson, see GRANSON.

Grand Theatre, Islington, London, was erected in 1870, and was the first of the London music halls. It became in the course of time famous for opera bouffé. Twelve years after its first opening it was burnt down, but was reopened in the next year. Since then it has twice suffered destruction by fire, in 1887 and 1900.

Grandville, the pseudonym of the celebrated caricaturist **Jean Ignace Isidore Gérard** (1803-47). He was born at Nancy. Quite early in life a series of caricatures, which portrayed the woes of the small proprietor, gained him a certain amount of popularity. He was also well known as a book illustrator; he illustrated editions of *Gulliver's Travels, Don Quixote,* and *La Fontaine's Fables.* His political caricatures also came in for much praise. He died in a lunatic asylum at the age of forty-four.

Grange, or **Grange-over-Sands,** a par. and vil. on Morecambe Bay, N. Lancashire, situated about 10 m. N.W. of Carnforth. A well-known watering-place, especially popular among the inhabitants of Lancashire and Yorkshire. Pop. 2232.

Grangemouth, a seaport tn. in Scotland, in Stirlingshire, at the entrance of the Forth and Clyde Canal, about 3 m. N.E. of Falkirk. Coal is mined in the immediate vicinity. There are saw-mills and shipyards. The chief exports are pig-iron, iron ore, and timber. It has direct communication with the Continent. New docks (93 acres) were opened in 1905. Pop. (1911) 9840.

Granger, James, Rev. (1723-76), born at Shaston, Dorset, and took orders. He became vicar of Shiplake, in Oxfordshire. He is remembered for the *Biographical History of England* which he published, and which went from the 8th to the end of the 17th century. The striking feature of this biographical history was the collection of portraits with which he illustrated his work. A continuation of his work appeared in 1806.

Grangers, the name given in U.S.A. to a farmers' trade union, founded in 1867 under the name of the National Grange of Patrons of Industry. It promoted the education of the farmer on the technical side, and advised co-operation in the sale of seeds, machinery, etc. It used its influence to agitate for the removal of railway monopolies. It was founded by a man named Kelley at Washington, D.C.

Granicus (Mod. Bigha Chai), a river in Asia Minor. Its source is in Mt. Ida, and it flows into the Sea of Marmora. Here Alexander the Great defeated the Persians in 334 B.C., and it was also the scene of the defeat of Mithridates in 73 B.C. by Lucullus.

Granier de Cassagnac, see CASSAGNAC.

Granite, a group name for several plutonic rocks which form the great bulk of the igneous rocks of all ages, and consist of a completely crystalline mixture usually of quartz, felspar, and muscovite. This last substance may be wholly or partly replaced by several other minerals, *e.g.* hornblende or biotite, or in rarer cases by augite. Accessory minerals are always found, the most common being apatite, garnet, zircon, or sphene, with varying quantities of plagioclase. Sections of G. show considerable diversity of detail, but usually it is found that the quartz is a colourless transparent allomorphic substance filling the interstitial spaces between the other crystals. The orthoclase, which is the general type of felspar present, will have a clearly marked outline, and is generally translucent, on account of more or less decomposition. The muscovite will show definite cleavage cracks, and in large crystal specimens separate flakes can be easily removed. The presence of biotite is generally indicated by glistening black particles which are readily flaked. In some specimens the crystals can only be distinguished under the microscope, and such are said to possess a *micro-granitic* structure. Although G. possesses at least three essential minerals, yet there are related rocks which possess two of the constituents. *Greisen* is composed of quartz and muscovite, while *aplite* is made up of quartz and orthoclase. There is hardly any extensive region of the world in which granitic masses do not occur. To mention but a few sites: N.W. Portugal, S.W. Spain, between Dresden and Görlitz, in the Grampians of Scotland, the Lofodens off Norway, Corsica, Sardinia, S. chain of the Urals, S.E. across France from St. Malo towards Avignon, along the E. coast of Brazil, plateaus of S. Africa, etc. The great value of the rock is as a building material, and the fact that masses of the rock of great magnitude can be procured of perfect continuity is one of the many reasons for its popularity. For vast and massive structures intended to resist weather and violence most Gs. are admirably adapted, though in the case of those rich in potash felspar they are less valuable against weathering. The Egyptian obelisks consist of porphyries and syenitic Gs. The Aberdeen quarries yield massive blocks of stone of excellent quality in which the chief felspar is albite (soda-felspar). The ultimate result of the disintegration of G. is to yield soils rich in plant food, and also to yield a long list of compounds of which the kaolin (china clay) of Dartmoor, etc., is specially noted. See Harris' *Granite and the Granite Industries.*

Granite City, a city of Madison co., Illinois, situated on the Mississippi, about 3 m. N.N.E. of St. Louis. Iron and steel goods are manufactured here. Pop. 9903.

Granja, La, or **San Ildefonso,** a Spanish tn. in the prov. of Segovia, Old Castile, Spain, situated about 7 m. E.S.E. of the town of Segovia. Philip V., the first of the Bourbon kings of Spain, built a summer resort here, which is situated at an elevation of 4150 ft. His tomb is here. The town is well known as a summer resort. Pop. 4000.

Granollers, a Spanish tn. in the prov. of Barcelona, in Catalonia, Spain, situated about 20 m. N.E. of the tn. of Barcelona. Its principal manufs. are iron and woollen goods. Pop. about 7000.

Granophyre, an igneous rock of porphyritic structure. In appearance it is very similar to granite, but is much finer grained. The rock is usually found in offshoots of masses of granite rock. In Great Britain they are chiefly found in the Highlands of Scotland, the Lake District, N. Wales, and Cornwall. See Harker's *Petrology,* 1897.

Gran Sasso d'Italia, a mountain group in the Apennines, reaches an elevation of 9585 ft. in Monte Corno, which is the highest point in the whole mountain chain.

Granson, or **Grandson,** a Swiss tn. in the canton of Vaud, situated near the S.W. end of Lake Neuchâtel. It has a fine castle. Here the Swiss defeated Charles the Bold in 1476. Pop. about 2000.

Grant, in English law, a term which, in its widest sense, is a synonym for any transfer of property. In a narrower sense, it is interchangeable with ' assurance,' as meaning a conveyance by deed of lands. In this sense it connoted not only such old forms of conveyance as feoffment, and bargains and sales, but also all such existing forms as leases, charges, and settlements. In this sense, too, it was contrasted with transfer by ' livery of seisin,' *i.e.* by delivery of possession; practically, all real property is now conveyed by deed, but formerly corporeal hereditaments in possession were transferable by mere delivery of possession, whereas incorporeal hereditaments (reversions, remainders, advowsons, tithes, rights of way, franchises, annuities, rents, etc.), not being physically capable of delivery, were said to lie in G., *i.e.* they were transferred by deed. In relation to *personalty,* G. is used as opposed to *gift* (*q.v.*), which latter term implies a transfer without consideration (*q.v.*).

Grant, Albert (1830-99), born at Dublin, being the son of V. Gottheimer of London; he was usually known as Baron Grant. His early attempts at company promoting were enormously successful, and in 1874 he purchased Leicester Square, which at that time was practically waste land. He had this land laid out properly and presented it to the metropolitan Board of Works for the benefit of the public. He was twice member of parliament for Kidderminster. His later speculations were not fortunate, and he died comparatively a poor man.

Grant, Sir Alexander (1826-84), a leading British educationalist, born in New York, and educated at Harrow and Oxford. He distinguished himself at the university, and from 1849-60 he was a fellow of Oriel. In 1857 he published a book, *Ethics.* He was an examiner for the Indian Civil Service, and in 1859 went to India, where he became a professor at Elphinstone, and later vice-chancellor of Bombay University and Director of Public Instruction for the Bombay Presidency. In 1868 he became principal of Edinburgh University. Here he remained until his death.

Grant, Anne (*née* **M'Vicar**) (1755-1838), a Scottish authoress, was the daughter of Duncan M'Vicar, a British officer, born in Glasgow. Her youth was spent in America, from whence the family returned in 1768. She married, eleven years later, the Rev. James Grant. She published *Poems* in 1803, two years after the death of her husband. She received a pension of £100 in 1825. Amongst her other works may be mentioned, *Letters from the Mountains*, and *Superstitions of the Highlanders*.

Grant, Charles, Baron Glenelg (1778-1866), an English politician, born in Calcutta and educated at Magdalen College, Cambridge, where in 1801 he graduated as fourth wrangler. He entered parliament in 1807, and was the representative of Inverness county from 1811-35, when he became a peer. He held high office during his political career, being Chief Secretary for Ireland under Lord Liverpool, President of the Board of Trade under Canning, and President of the Board of Control under Grey. During Melbourne's ministry he held the portfolio of Colonial Secretary, but approving of the Canadian policy of Lord Durham, was compelled to resign. As has been already mentioned, during his tenure of the latter office he was raised to the peerage.

Grant, Sir Francis (Lord Cullen) (1658-1726), a Scottish judge, born at Ballentomb, Morayshire. In 1691 he became an advocate, and sixteen years later became a lord of session. He contributed much to the literature dealing with the Scottish Church, and was a strong supporter of the Protestant succession and of the Union.

Grant, Sir Francis, P.R.A. (1803-78), a Scottish portrait painter, born at Edinburgh. He was educated at Harrow and Edinburgh University, and was intended for the bar. He, however, almost immediately began his career as a painter, and at the age of twenty-one had already exhibited in the Academy. He became an R.A. in 1851, and fifteen years later became president of the Royal Academy, and in the same year was knighted. Amongst the more famous of his portraits were: An equestrian portrait of the Queen and Prince Consort, The Marchioness of Waterford, Palmerston, Macaulay, and Russell.

Grant, James (1743-1835), a Scottish advocate, an advanced exponent of Liberal political principles who numbered amongst his friends many of the most learned and advanced men of the day, *e.g.* Sir James Mackintosh. He wrote *An Essay on the Origin of Society*, 1785; and *The Origin and Descent of the Gael*, 1814.

Grant, James (1822-87), a British novelist, born at Edinburgh. He was taken to Newfoundland when a boy, but returned at the age of seventeen and entered the army. After four years' service he resigned and took up literature instead. In 1846 he published the *Romance of War*, which gained some reputation for him. This was, however, but the beginning of a long series of historical and military novels which illustrated principally the military history of Scottish regiments. In 1875 he was received into the communion of the Roman Church. Amongst his works may be mentioned: *Adventures of an Aide-de-Camp; Frank Hilton; Bothwell;* and *Old and New Edinburgh*.

Grant, James Augustus, Colonel, C.B., F.R.S. (1827-92), born at Nairn. He was educated at the Marischal College, Aberdeen, and entered the army. He saw service at Gujerat, and was actively employed during the Mutiny and the expedition to Abyssinia. He gained distinction for his services in both expeditions. Between the years 1860-63 he accompanied the explorer Speke in his expedition to the sources of the Nile. Amongst the works which he published were : *A Walk across Africa,* and *The Botany of the Speke and Grant Expeditions.*

Grant, Sir James Hope (1808-75), a British general. Brother to Sir Francis G., born at Kilgraston, Perthshire, and entered the army. He was first on active service in China, and from here he went on to the Sikh wars, where he greatly distinguished himself. He was of great service during the Mutiny, taking part in the relief of Cawnpore, and the retaking of Lucknow. After the Mutiny had been broken he commanded the army which finally settled India. He also took part in the Chinese War which followed the Mutiny. From 1861-65 he was commander-in-chief of the army in Madras. See *Life* by Knollys, 1894.

Grant, Sir John Peter (1807-93), a British administrator, born in London, and entered the Bengal Civil Service at the age of twenty-one, and became, some twenty-two years later, the permanent secretary in the Home Department of the Indian government. From 1859-62 he was lieutenant-governor of Bengal, having previously occupied a similar position in the Central Provinces. As a member of the council he was a strong advocate of the annexation of Oudh and the legalising of the remarriage of Hindu widows. He was for seven years governor of Jamaica (1866-73).

Grant, Sir Patrick (1804-95), a British field-marshal, born at Auchterblair, Inverness-shire. Entered the Bengal native infantry as an ensign, and became a captain in 1832. He rose fairly rapidly in the service, and was present at the battle of Maharajpur (1843), Moodkee (1845), and Sobraon (1846). In 1849 he saw still more active service, and was made A.D.C. to the queen. He served under Sir C. Napier in 1851, and from 1856-61 he was commander-in-chief of the Madras army. In 1857 he took over the command of all troops in India, and directed the operations against the mutineers until the arrival of Sir Colin Campbell. In 1861 he left India. He became successively K.C.B. (1857), G.C.B. (1861), lieutenant-general (1862), governor of Malta (1867-72), G.C.M.G. (1868), field-marshal (1883). From 1874-95 he was governor of the Royal Hospital at Chelsea.

Grant, Robert (1814-92), an astronomer of some note, born at Grantown, Morayshire, Scotland. He received the gold medal of the Royal Astronomical Society in 1856 for a work entitled *A History of Physical Astronomy*. In 1859 he became professor of astronomy in Glasgow University. He published, in 1883, *A Catalogue of* 6415 *Stars*, and nine years later, *A Second Catalogue of* 2156 *Stars*.

Grant, Ulysses Simpson (1822-85), an American general, and 18th president of the U.S.A. He was descended from a Scottish family which had settled in Massachusetts in the 17th century. He was born at Clermont, Ohio, and was brought up on a farm there. He was, however, sent to Key West to the Military Academy there, and entered the army of the U.S.A. In 1844 he went to Lousiana with his regiment, and later he served as a second lieutenant under General Taylor with the army in Texas. He was present at the battles of Palo Alto, Resaca de la Palma, and at the capture of Monterey. He was also with Scott at the capture of Mexico. After this latter war he returned to the States, resigned his commission, and lived for some time on a farm at St. Louis, Missouri. On the outbreak of war in 1861 he offered his services to the Federals, and was appointed as a lieutenant-colonel to a Missouri infantry regiment. He soon, however, proved his ability as a soldier, and was made a brigadier-general. He fought at the battle of Belmont, and made a great attack in 1863 on Vicksburg. He finally drove the enemy into the town and sat down and besieged it. He was ultimately successful in forcing the besieged to surrender, and took over 31,000 prisoners. In 1864 he was made lieutenant-general and given supreme command of the U.S.A. army. He concentrated his forces and moved against the enemy. He succeeded, after a three days' battle in the ' Wilderness,' in defeating General R. E. Lee, and moving on still against the enemy, he succeeded in forcing a whole division to surrender. On April 9, 1865, Lee surrendered the whole of his army. This practically ended the war. In the next year G. was made general, and two years later was elected president. At the expiration of his term of office he was again elected. Probably the greatest event of his presidency was the peaceful settlement of the Alabama claims. When he retired from his presidency he accepted a position as a partner in a banking firm, which, however, in 1884 suspended payment, the two other partners having defrauded G. and absconded, ruining the ex-president. In the same year he commenced to write his autobiography to earn money for himself and his family. He died in the following year of cancer of the tongue. Before his death, however, he was restored to his rank of general, which he had to resign on becoming president. See *Personal Memoirs*.

Grantham, a municipal and parl. bor. of Lincolnshire, England, situated on the R. Witham, and forms an important junction on the Great Northern Railway. The parish church of St. Wulfran is a most magnificent building. It is mainly Early English and Decorated, and shows also many other styles of architecture. Two libraries of the 16th and 17th century are preserved in the church. There are many other old and interesting buildings of note. The main hotel of the town, the Angel, was originally a hostel of the 15th century, and its architecture preserves many traces of its antiquity. The chief industries of the town are the manufacture of implements for agricultural use and malting. The town is mentioned in the Domesday Book, and was originally governed by the bailiff of the lord of the manor. A mayor and alderman were granted it early in the reign of Edward IV. It has returned a member to parliament since 1467. In fact until 1885 it returned two members, but by the Redistribution Bill of that year the number was reduced to one. Pop. (1911) 20,074.

Grantham, Sir William (1835-1912),

an English judge, born at Lewes, and educated at King's College School, London. In 1860 went as a student to the Inner Temple, being called to the bar three years later. Took silk in 1877. He achieved success on circuit, but made no great mark in London. Politics were his chief interest, and in 1885 he was returned as a Conservative for Croydon. In 1886 he was made a judge of the Queen's Bench Division, and knighted.

Grantia, the name of a genus of chalk-sponges belonging to the family Grantiidæ; *G. compressa* is the commonest species.

Grant Land, a ter. situated in the Polar regions between the parallels 81° and 83°. It was discovered in 1875 by Hayes, Hall, and Nares. Nares spent the winter in exploring it, and set up at that time a record for the most northerly of any encampment.

Granton, a port of Edinburgh, Scotland, situated on the Firth of Forth, 2¾ m. N.W. of Edinburgh, with timber yards, and printing ink and chemical works. G. was made a head port in 1860. It is the ferry station of the N. British Railway, and the headquarters of several steamboat lines. There is a large tobacco bonding warehouse.

Grantown-on-Spey, a tn. and par. of Elginshire, Scotland, situated in Cromdale on the R. Spey. It is a noted health resort, and has whisky distilleries, also a cattle market. Pop. (1911) 1451.

Granulation, the action of forming into grains. The process by which a metal is reduced into grains is brought about by melting the metal and then pouring it in a thin stream into cold water. The metal divides itself into grains which are each practically perfect spheres. Metals which are easily melted are often poured in a molten state into a wooden box and violently shaken. This results in the metal granulating into much finer portions.

Granulite, a name used by petrographers for two distinct classes of rocks. By French geologists it is regarded as synonymous with muscovite-biotite granite. German petrologists give the term to a schistose metamorphic rock consisting essentially of small irregular crystals of quartz and orthoclase with minute pale red garnets; these last may be accompanied by kyanite, zircon, sillimanite, etc. The second use of the term is more common in England and America. Saxony is a typical region for Gs. which are here for the most part igneous; the 'moine gneisses' of N. Scotland related to these were originally sediments.

Granvella, Antoine Perrenot, Car- dinal de (1517-86), born at Besançon, his father being a lawyer, who afterwards became Chancellor of the Empire under Charles V. He studied law and divinity at Padua and Louvain, and at the age of about twenty-three became Bishop of Arras. The influence of his father not unnaturally created for him some considerable influence in the councils of the empire, and he was entrusted with several very delicate pieces of diplomacy. He showed himself a past master of the art of diplomacy, and became, in 1550, Secretary of State. He helped to draw up the treaty of Passau (1552), and when the emperor abdicated he transferred his services to Philip III. He negotiated the marriage with Mary of England, and the treaty of Cateau-Cambrésis. He became archbishop in 1560, and cardinal in 1561. For a short time he was forced to withdraw from the Netherlands, but was called from his retirement to go on a mission to Rome, the result of his mission was the alliance which overthrew the Turks at Lepanto. He presided over Naples for some time, and had just been raised to the archbishopric of Besançon when he died. He was buried in his native town near his father.

Granville: 1. A port and watering-place of France in the dept. of La Manche. It is situated at the mouth of the Bosq, on the English Channel, and is fortified. The harbour is accessible to the largest vessels, and there is regular communication with the Channel Islands. Vegetables, fruit, fish, oysters, etc., are exported, and shipbuilding and the manuf. of brandy, cod-liver oil, etc., are carried on. Pop. 12,000. 2. A tn. of New South Wales, Australia, situated in Cumberland co., 12 m. W. of Sydney. Has flour mills, iron works, etc. Pop. 5000.

Granville, George Leveson-Gower, second **Earl** (1815-91), eldest son of the first earl, was educated at Eton and Christ Church, Oxford, and in 1836 was returned to parliament as the Whig member for Morpeth. He married Lady Acton, widow of Sir Richard Acton. From 1841-46 he sat in the House of Commons as member for Lichfield. In the latter year he succeeded his father. He was now looked upon as a rising man of the Whig party and had already declared himself a staunch Freetrader. He was vice-president of the Board of Trade in 1848, and became king's secretary in place of Palmerston in 1851. In the ministry of Lord Aberdeen he also held the office of Chancellor of the Duchy, and in the administration of Lord Palmerston he occupied the position of president of the council. He had shown great interest in the educational problems of the day, and was in 1856 elected chancellor of the University of London. Another question in which he showed great interest was the Women's Movement. He was invited to form a ministry in 1859, but was unable to do so, but served again as president of the council in the administration of Lord Palmerston. When Lord John Russell became a peer, the leadership of the Upper House which he had held for some time past, was taken up by Russell who had on the death of Palmerston succeeded to the office of Prime Minister. He married again in 1865. In 1868 he served as Colonial Secretary in the first administration of Gladstone. He was Foreign Secretary in the Liberal administrations from 1870-74 and from 1880-85. This was the most important side of his career, but the policy pursued by his party was colourless and often weak, and his career as Foreign Minister does not add much to his fame as a politician. He followed Gladstone on the question of Home Rule, but was superseded by Rosebery at the Foreign Office. He became for a short period Colonial Secretary, but in 1886 he retired from political life. Five years later he died. As a politician and diplomat he had great influence, but his tenure of the Foreign Secretaryship gives him no marked place amongst the great statesmen of the time.

Granville Barker, Harley (*b.* 1877), an English dramatist and actor-manager, born in London, and made his first appearance on the stage in 1891. After playing many parts in the provinces and London, he, in partnership with Mr. J. E. Vedrenne, became manager, in 1904, of the Court Theatre, Sloane Square, London. Here, and later still at the Savoy Theatre, he produced and acted in many new plays, including several by his master, Mr. G. Bernard Shaw. Although G. belongs to the school of dramatists headed by Mr. Shaw, he has a distinct style of his own, and is considerably less didactic than the latter. His plays include : *The Marrying of Ann Leete*, 1901; *The Voysey Inheritance*, 1905, perhaps his greatest play; *Waste*, 1907, which the Censor of Plays refused to license for public performance; and *Madras House*, 1910. In collaboration with Mr. Berte Thomas he has written *The Weather Hen*, and is part author with Mr. Laurence Housman of *Prunella*. He has published the above plays and a book on *A National Theatre*, written by Mr. William

Archer and himself. G. B. who is one of the pillars of the Stage Society, took an active part in the agitation which led to the modification of the dramatic censorship. As a producer he excels, but his methods have given rise to considerable controversy, many holding that he does not leave sufficient to the initiative of the actors. In 1906 G. B. married Miss Lillah McCarthy, who has, in conjunction with her husband, or independently, staged many ' advanced ' pieces.

Grao, or **Villanueva del Grao,** a maritime tn. of Spain, in the prov. and dist. of Valencia, situated on the Mediterranean, and is the port of Valencia ; it also has a fine beach, suitable for bathing. Pop. 6000.

Grape, *see* VINE.

Grape-fruit, *see* SHADDOCK.

Grape-Hyacinth, or *Muscari racemosum*, a species of Liliaceæ which occurs in Great Britain. The inflorescence is a raceme of beautiful flowers of which the uppermost are sterile.

Grapeshot, a form of projectile. This consisted of a number of loose shot sewn into a bag made of canvas and inserted into a gun. The projectile when fired did much damage by bursting and spreading. G. has now been superseded by shrapnel.

Graphic, The, an illustrated weekly newspaper, founded in 1869, of independent political principles, and appealing to the popular taste by reason of its photographs and original drawings of incidents in current events, reproductions of masterpieces of painting or drawing, and excellent serials, illustrated by notable artists of the day. Both in the past and present, many leading novelists have written serials or other literary contributions for the G., the haunting story of *Tess of the D'Urbervilles*, by Mr. Thomas Hardy, first appearing in the G., and other no less distinguished contributors have been : Meredith, Charles Reade, Mr. Barrie, and Mr. Kipling. Some of its most distinguished artists have been : Randolph Caldecott, who contributed Christmas pictures portraying sprightly scenes of hunting squires and hounds, and stagey highwaymen, and finely executed sketches of life at Monte Carlo; Arthur Boyd Houghton, serial illustrator; J. E. Penwell, the water-colour painter; Sir Hubert von Herkomer, whose ' Chelsea Pensioners ' originally appeared as a drawing in the G.; E. J. Gregory; Sir Luke Fildes, who early in his career was a notable wood-designer, and whose Royal Academy picture, ' Applicants for a Casual Ward,' appeared first as a wood-cut in the G.; George du Maurier, and Phil May. At the present day some of its best drawings are Mr. Lewis Baumer's artistic skits on contemporary social life, the topical pictures of Mr. Reginald Cleaver, and the broadly farcical caricatures of Mr. E. T. Reed. The G. has always been remarkable for distinguished war-artists, the most notable, perhaps, being Frederic Villiers, while there have recently (April 1913) appeared some striking impressionist pictures of the Balkan War by George Scott, pupil of Edouard Detailles, under the title of ' Mud, Blood, and Silence.'

Graphical Methods of Representation, as the name implies, are methods by which varying values or estimates are placed side by side, so that their changes and fluctuations may be readily seen. Suppose, for example, we are considering the yearly average price of wheat per quarter for the past twenty years. Take for convenience a piece of squared paper

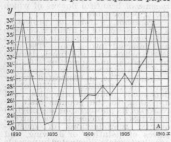

and draw two lines Ox and Oy at right angles to each other. Let each point of division along Ox represent one year, beginning with 1890 at O to 1910 at A. Then taking any convenient length as a standard, measure off along Oy and the successive perpendiculars to Ox, lengths representing the average prices for each year in turn. By joining up the points so obtained the yearly change may be followed much more readily than from any table of figures. In a similar way the changes in any series of values taken at intervals may be graphically represented ; and the method is particularly convenient in the case of economic, political, and meteorological statistics, where returns are made at regular intervals and comparison with previous returns are most important. So long as we are considering estimates for which there is one definite value for each year, the graph is obviously a complete record of fluctuations ; but where we have a value which changes from day

to day, for which observations are only made at longer intervals, the graph made up of a series of short straight lines is no indication of values at any time during an interval. In cases where it is practicable, where, in fact, the values do not fluctuate too abruptly, we can obtain a fair estimate of values for intermediate positions by joining the points by as smooth and continuous a curve as is possible (*see* INTERPOLATION). The most complete form of graphical representation is obtained in the barograph, which traces out mechanically, in one line on specially ruled paper, every slight variation in the height of the barometer throughout the day. A drum covered with ruled paper is made to revolve regularly by means of clockwork, while a pencil, rising and falling with changes of atmospheric pressure traces out a continuous line.

Graphic Granite, the name given to a special formation of granite, which consists of angular patches of clear quartz, distributed through a dull striated matrix of felspar. It is so called because the quartz areas bear resemblance to primitive inscriptions. In polarised light, the separate areas of each mineral extinguish simultaneously, so proving that they have the same optical orientation.

Graphic Statics deals with the determination of stresses, tensions, etc., of frameworks and systems in equilibrium, by geometrical methods of construction. A force is completely determined when its magnitude, direction, sense, and point of application are known. It may, therefore, be represented by a straight line of definite length, drawn in a given direction through a point with an arrow head to determine the sense. This line is called the *vector*. It is proved that the resultant of two forces acting on a particle may be found by representing the forces by two straight lines OA, OB (Fig. 1),

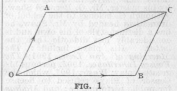

FIG. 1

drawn through a point O, and by completing the parallelogram OACB. Then the diagonal OC represents the resultant in magnitude and direction. It is evident that the three sides of the triangle OBC represent the three forces in magnitude and direction, though BC does not represent the point of application. Thus, if we are not concerned with the point of application, the proposition (known as the *Triangle of Forces*) may be stated thus: If two forces acting at a point are represented in direction, magnitude, and sense by two sides of a triangle OB, BC, then the third side OC similarly represents the resultant.

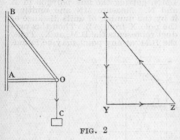

FIG. 2

Further, the three forces OB, BC, and CO, if acting at a point are in equilibrium. This may be extended to the *Polygon of Forces* which states that the resultant of forces represented by the lines AB, BC, CD, DE....HK taken in order is represented by the line AK which closes the polygon. Consider first the simple case of a load supported by a simple wall crane consisting of two bars, considered weightless (Fig. 2). The pin at O is

the line of action of the resultant of any number of forces of given magnitudes acting on a body in given straight lines. Let p, q, r, s, t be the lines of action (Fig. 3) of the given forces. Draw the vector AB to scale to represent the force along p. Similarly, draw BC, CD, etc., parallel to q, r, etc., and proportional to the forces along them. Join AF and take any point O called the pole. Join OA, OB, etc. On p take any point P, draw PV parallel to AO, PQ parallel to BO, cutting q in Q. Through Q draw QR parallel to CO, and so on, finally drawing TV parallel to OF. Then the straight line through V, parallel and equal to AF, completely determines the resultant. This may be proved from the polygon of forces. The two figures are known as the *link or funicular polygon* and the *vector polygon* respectively. When the vector polygon is closed, the forces are either in equilibrium or are equivalent to a couple. When the link and vector polygons are both closed the forces are in equilibrium. To find the stresses in the bars of a roof truss of the shape shown in Fig. 4, where the joints M, N, and P are loaded, and to determine the reactions at the supports L and Q. Here the vector polygon becomes a straight line called the line of loads. Draw the load line AD, AB, BC, and CD, being respectively proportional to the loads at M, N, and P. Take any pole X and join XA, XB, XC, XD. Take any point T on the

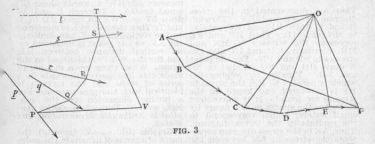

FIG. 3

kept in equilibrium by three forces acting along OA, OB, and OC. Draw the load line XY, vertically, to some given scale, say 1 in. to 1 ton. Through X and Y draw lines XZ and YZ parallel to BO and AO. Measure YZ and ZX and find the weights their lengths represent, and hence are found the pull which BO exerts on the pin O, *i.e.* the tension in BO, and the force of compression in AO.

To determine the magnitude and

vertical through L, and draw TU, UV, etc., successively parallel to XA, XB, etc., and join TY. Through X draw XO parallel to TY. Then OA and DO represent the reactions at the supports L and Q. For the stress diagram, consider first the forces at L; OA represents the vertical force. Through O and A draw lines OE and AE parallel to LR and LM respectively. Then EO and AE measured according to the scale will give the stresses in LR and LM. The former is in tension and the latter in compression. Consider now the point Q. In a similar way ODK is the stress diagram and OK and KD measure the stresses in QS and QP. It is now possible to consider the points M and P. At M we know already the vertical force and the stress in LM.

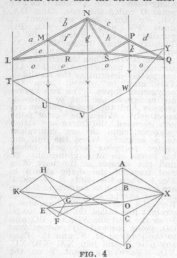

FIG. 4

They are represented in the stress diagram by AB and EA. Through B and E draw BF and EF parallel to MN and MR. Then BF and FE represent the stresses in MN and MR. Similarly, KH and HC give the stresses in SP and PN. For the point N draw HG and FG parallel to NS and NR. Finally, by joining GO which is parallel to RS, the stress in RS is measured and hence all the stresses are found. It is convenient to denote the spaces on the figure by small letters, which correspond to the capitals in the stress diagram. Thus, AE in the stress diagram represents the stress in LM between the spaces a and e.

The shearing force (S.F.) and the bending moment (B.M.) at any section of a beam or bridge are defined as being the sum and the sum of the moments respectively of all the external forces perpendicular to it. To draw the S.F. and B.M. diagrams for the case of a beam or bridge loaded with a given weight at one point. The method here given will hold equally well for any number

of loads. Let PQ (Fig. 5) represent the bridge drawn to scale, and R the position of the given load. Draw the load line AB for the vector polygon. Let X be the pole at a definite distance from AB. Construct the link polygon CDE, closing it by joining CE. Through X draw XO parallel to CE, thus determining the re-actions at the ends. Through any point L on PQ draw a vertical line LMN, cutting the link polygon in M and N. Measure MN and multiply it by the number of units distance of the pole X from AB. Then this product represents the B.M. at X. Thus, the B.M. at any point may be found.

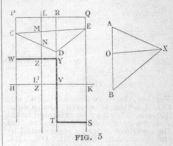

FIG. 5

To determine the S.F. draw any horizontal line HK to intersect the verticals PC and QE at H and K. From K measure off KS downwards along QE equal to OB, and from H measure off HW upwards along CP equal to OA. Through S and W draw ST and WY to meet RD in Y and T. Then the S.F. at L is measured by the vertical line L^1Z, and similarly the S.F. at any point is measured by its vertical distance between HK and the line WYTS, thickened in the figure. When there are a number of loads this line moves upwards in a series of steps and the method is identical with the present one. For a further discussion on the subject, *see* G. C. Turner's *Graphics Applied to Arithmetic Mensuration and Statics*.

Graphis (Gk. γραφίς, drawing), the name of a genus of lichens in the order Graphidaceæ, given to them because of the curious form of their apothecia. They are often called vulgarly scripture-worts.

Graphite, *see* BLACK-LEAD.

Graphotype, a process invented in 1860 by Dr. Clinton Hitchcock, an American. The process consisted of drawing the design to be printed on specially prepared French chalk. The outlines were drawn in special ink and were raised into relief by brushing away the chalk in between. From these chalk blocks electrotypes and stereotypes were then obtained. The process has long been superseded by other more modern and successful methods.

Grapple-Plant, or *Harpagophytum procumbens*, a species of Pedaliaceæ found in S. Africa. It is a trailing plant with purple flowers, and the fruit is provided with pointed grapples which aid in its distribution by animals.

Grapsus (Gk. γραψαῖος, a crab), the name of a genus of crustaceans belonging to the family Grapsidæ; they are marine crabs and are very numerous on the shores of the Mediterranean. Frequently they are found on exposed rocks, over which they travel at a very rapid pace.

Graptolites, a group of fossil remains of extinct marine animals which floated about hanging to the underside of sea-weeds, or in some cases were anchored to the seabottom. They are usually found in great abundance in the Palæozoic rocks extending from the Cambrian to the Carboniferous. The most common form is a central stem which bore rows of minute pockets in which the polypes lived, though many varieties of shapes have been found. Those remains obtained from limestone rocks generally show considerably less recent flattening than the specimens obtained from the bedding planes of black shales where they are particularly numerous.

Graptophyllum, a genus of Acanthaceæ found only in Australasia. The species do not number half a dozen in all; they are evergreen shrubs with red flowers, and *G. hortense* is frequently cultivated on account of its foliage.

Gras, Félix (1844-1901), a Provençal writer, born at Malemort in the dept. of Vaucluse. He made a distinguished appearance as author in 1876, by publishing a work called *Li Carbounié*. An epic dealing with the topic of Simon de Montfort and the Albigensians appeared in 1882, and five years later he published his celebrated collection of Provençal ballads, *Lou Roumancero Provençal*. In 1891 he published a series of stories dealing with the Hungarian popes under the title of *Li Papalino*. His three great novels on the revolutionary period have been translated into English by C. A. Janvier—*The Reds of the Midi*, *The Terror*, and *The White Terror*.

Graslitz, a tn. of Bohemia, Austria, situated near the Saxon frontier, and 32 m. N.E. of Eger. The manufs. are: musical instruments, articles made of mother-of-pearl, and embroidery. Pop. 13,825.

Grasmere, a small lake situated in Westmorland. It lies 4 m. N.W. of Ambleside, between Thirlmere and Windermere. It drains through to Windermere by the Rothay. Its length is about a mile. To the N. of the lake the village of G. lies. The church of this village has been made famous by the description of it given by Wordsworth in the *Excursion*. The poet himself lived much in the immediate vicinity, and lies buried, together with his daughter and sister, in the churchyard there. Pop. 876.

Grasscloth, a material manufactured principally in China from the fibres of a plant called Bœhmeria. The plant is also found in some parts of India, and in N. and Central America.

Grasse, a tn. of France in the Alpes-Maritimes dept., about 20 m. S.W. of Nice. It stands well over 1000 ft. above sea-level, and is situated in such a way as to be sheltered from the cold winds of the N. and open to the S. The vegetation produced is typical of Southern Europe, and many acres of land are devoted to the cultivation of flowers. The town is the centre of the manuf. of perfumes. Pop. of commune, 20,300.

Grässe, Johann Georg Theodor (1814-85), a German historian, born at Grimma, Saxony. He was the royal librarian and head of the museum of porcelain at Dresden for the greater part of his life. He retired in 1882. The greatest of his works was: *Lehrbuch einer allgemeinen Litterärgeschichte aller bekannten Völker der Welt*, 1837-60. He translated *Gesta Romanorum*, 1842; and wrote *Beiträge zur Litteratur und Sage des Mittelalters*, 1850; *Handbuch der alten Numismatik*, 1853.

Grasses (natural order Graminaceæ). These form one of the largest orders in the vegetable kingdom, and some of its members are of great service to man. They are evergreen, annual or perennial herbs, though bamboos sometimes reach a height of 100 ft. All G. either flower on a spike upon the same model as wheat, or upon a panicle such as oats; some are awned or bearded like barley. Each spikelet, whatever the inflorescence, consists of one to five flowers arranged alternately on a short axis, and beneath the lowest flower there are usually two (or more) empty bracts known as glumes. Each flower is sessile in the axil of a bract termed the outer palea or flowering glume, and there is an inner palea, opposite to, and higher than, the outer one; these two paleæ completely enclose the flower. In some species both stamens, usually one to three in number, and pistil are in the same flower, but more commonly the flowers are unisexual. The stem is generally characterised by swollen or tumid nodes to which the sheathing leaf-bases contribute; the long internodes are hollow, and a membraneous ligule is developed at the junction of leaf-base and lamina. The ovary is one-chambered and one-ovuled, and the fruit or grain, technically known as a caryopsis, is entirely filled by the seed. G. are abundant on land, and a few species inhabit fresh water, but there are no marine forms. In the tropics they acquire a much greater height than in colder regions, but those species of a 'social' habit, constituting turf, are found only in temperate regions. The cereal G., wheat, oats, barley, rye, maize, rice, and various millets, cultivated for the sake of their grain, are the most valuable members of the order to mankind. Among the most esteemed fodder G. are rye G. (*Lolium perenne*); cock's-foot G.; timothy G. (*Phleum pratense*); the sweet-scented vernal G., which gives much of its fragrance to new-mown hay; and various species of *Poa* and *Festuca*. The tussack G. (*Dactylis cæspitosa*) of the Falklands is also much liked by cattle. Sugar is extracted from the stems of the sugar cane, *Saccharum officinarum*, a native of South-eastern Asia, but now cultivated throughout the tropics; and to a smaller extent from those of the guinea corn, *Sorghum saccharatum*. Other useful products of the family are bamboo; a valuable material for paper making, obtained from esparto G. (*Macrochloa tenacissima*); aromatic 'G. oils,' such as verbena, citronella, and geranium or ginger G., much used in perfumery.

Grasshoppers, insects belonging to the families Locustidæ and Acridiidæ, which have very long hind legs with strong thighs, enabling them to jump great distances. The Locustidæ or

GRASSHOPPER

green G., have very long antennæ, four-jointed tarsi or feet, a long ovipositor, and the stridatory organ in the wings; while the Acridiidæ (to which family the 'locusts,' the true G., belong) have short antennæ, no ovipositor, feet with three joints, and the stridatory organ in between the

hind leg and the wing. These insects inhabit woods, thickets, and fields, and feed on vegetables and plants, but some eat flies and caterpillars as well. They generally fly about in the twilight, and being of a green or brown colour can easily hide themselves among the foliage. They lay their eggs either in the earth or in a dry stem; these hatch in spring and produce the young G., which moult six times before they become full grown. The 'chirp' is produced by the friction of the hind legs against portions of the wings or wing-covers in the Acridiidæ, but in the Locustidæ by scraping one wing against the other. The common British type is the *Locusta viridissima*, which has a body about an inch long, but the *Decticus verrucivorus* (so called because the Swedish peasants use it to cure their warts) is also found.

Grassmann, Hermann Gunther (1809-77), mathematician and Sanskrit scholar, born at Stettin. He studied philosophy, theology, and mathematics at Berlin, and succeeded his father as professor of mathematics at the Gymnasium at Stettin. In 1844 he published his mathematical work, *Die Wissenschaft der extensiven Grössen oder die Ausdehnungslehre*, which did not at first meet with a favourable reception. At the age of fifty-three he began his study of Sanskrit, and made a great reputation. He published on this subject *Wörterbuch zum Rig-Veda* and a translation of *Rig-Veda*. Among his other scientific works are: *New Theory of Electro-dynamics*, *Theory of the Mixture of Colours*, and treatises on arithmetic and trigonometry. He enunciated, in 1863, the linguistic law which bears his name.

Grass-moth, a small moth, allied to the clothes-moth, which inhabits pastures. It is generally brown in colour, and long and narrow in shape, with a pointed head.

Grass of Parnassus, or *Parnassia palustris*, a species of Saxifragaceæ, which is found in damp places of Britain. The flower consists of five sepals, petals and stamens, and there are also five staminodes; the petals are white, and the plant is of graceful appearance. It is fabled to have appeared first on Mt. Parnassus, hence its name.

Grass Oil, a name under which several volatile oils derived from widely different plants are grouped. Ginger G. O. derived from the Indian plant *Andropogon nardus*, and geranium oil from *Pelargonium radula*, are very similar in properties, and are used for adulterating oil of roses. Turkish G. O. and lemon G. O. or citronella oil are both obtained from

India; the latter has an odour resembling citron, and is largely used for scenting soap.

Grass Snake (*Tropidonotus natrix*), a ringed snake found in England and in all the countries of Europe except Scotland and Ireland. It is of a brownish colour and differs from the common viper or adder in that it has not the zigzag black line down its back. There are two yellow or white spots behind its head which make it easy to recognise. The usual length is 3 ft. or a little over; it rarely reaches 4 ft. The snake hisses and strikes out with its head when attacked, but does not bite. It inhabits moist places, and feeds chiefly on frogs, toads, and fishes. It lays its eggs (which resemble a dove's in size and shape) in mould or under damp leaves. These vary in number and are glued together.

Grass-tree and **Black-boy**, names given to a liliaceous plant found in Australia, and called technically *Xanthorrhœa hastilis*. The plant exudes a resinous substance used in the manufacture of varnish, and is hence sometimes termed the grass gum-tree. The leaves are long and grass-like, and the white flowers are arranged in a bulrush-like spike.

Grassum, in Scots law, means a fine paid in consideration of a right which is to last for a term of years. It is money down as opposed to a periodical payment. In more recent Scots law payment of G. is practically confined to leases.

Grass Valley, a tn. in Nevada co., California, U.S.A., 55 m. N.E. of Sacramento. It is noted for its gold mines. Pop. 4520.

Grass-wrack, or **Eel-grass**, the name given to the two species of *Zostera* found on British shores. *Z. marina* and *Z. nana*, species of Potamogetonaceæ, are submerged plants with creeping roots and grass-like leaves.

Grateloupia, the name given to a genus of lamellibranchiate molluscs belonging to the family Veneridæ. They are fossil forms, found in the Tertiary strata, and have a solid, equivalve shell with three cardinal teeth. *G. irregularis* is the chief species.

Gratian, or **Gratianus**, was born at Chiusi in Tuscany at the beginning of the 12th century. The greater part of his life was spent in the monastery at Bologna, but he also taught in the University. He is famous as the founder of the science of canon law, and for his book, *Concordia discordantium canonum* or *Decretum Gratiani*.

Gratianus, Augustus (359-383 A.D.), Roman emperor, son of Valentinian and Severa, born at Sirmium in Pannonia. In 366 he was made consul, and the following year received the title of Augustus. On the death of his father in 375, the troops proclaimed Valentinian II., his half brother, emperor. G. divided the provinces, but the real authority remained in his hands. In 378 he defeated the Lentienses at Argentaria, and in 379, with the help of Theodosius, drove the barbarians out of the Balkans. The first years of his rule were marked by energy and success, but later in life he became indolent and pleasure-seeking. This aroused the contempt of the Roman troops, and they elected Maximus, who was then in Britain, as emperor. He at once crossed to Gaul and defeated G. near Paris. G. fled to Italy but was overtaken near Lyons and killed.

Gratiola, a genus of scrophulariaceous plants, is world-wide in distribution. The best-known species is *G. officinalis*, the common hedgehyssop, which was formerly used in medicine.

Gratry, Alphonse (1805-72), French author and theologian, born at Lille. He was vicar-general of Orleans in 1861, professor of ethics at the Sorbonne in 1862, and in 1867 a member of the French Academy. He was one of the principal opponents of papal infallibility, and wrote *Mgr. l'évêque d'Orléans et Mgr. l'archevêque de Malines*, which contains historical arguments against this doctrine. He also wrote *La Morale et la loi de l'histoire*, in which he approves of the principles of the French Revolution; *De la connaissance de Dieu; La Philosophie du crédo; Commentaire sur l'évangile de Saint Matthieu.*

Grattan, Henry (1746-1820), an Irish statesman, and the greatest of Irish orators, born in Dublin. He was educated at Trinity College, Dublin, and gave himself up to the study of the classics, especially the great orators of antiquity. At the age of twenty-one he entered the Middle Temple, London, but took little interest in his law studies, availing himself of every opportunity to listen to debates in the House of Commons. In 1772 he was called to the Irish bar, and in 1775 entered the Irish parliament as member for the borough of Charlemont. The nation was then suffering from the loss of market that followed the war with America, and from the restrictions upon trade which dated back to William III.; G. championed the cause of Irish independence, and in 1779 got a total repeal of all the restriction Acts. His next step was to move a declaration for the independence of the Irish parliament; it was granted, and his countrymen voted him £50,000. This independence, however, was only nominal without reform, and for this G. pressed. He was also in favour of Catholic emancipation, and in 1785 supported Pitt's commercial propositions for establishing free trade between Great Britain and Ireland. In 1792 he succeeded in carrying an Act conferring the franchise on the Roman Catholics, and in 1794 introduced a Reform Bill; but his mild measures promoted more extreme opinions, and the country drifted into rebellion and G. retired from parliament in 1797. He, however, returned to take his seat for Wicklow in the last session of the Irish parliament and fought the Union Bill. He was member for Malton, Yorkshire, in 1805, and for Dublin in 1806. His last years were devoted to the cause of Catholic emancipation, but, though supported by Canning and other statesmen, did not live to see his triumph. He was buried in Westminster Abbey beside Fox. G. was famous for his remarkable eloquence and incorruptible patriotism.

Gratuitous Deed, in Scots law, a deed transferring the ownership of real or personal property and made without consideration or value given by the transferee. Such a deed is perfectly valid, unless made to the prejudice of the creditors of the transferer, or of those to whom he happens to be under legal obligations at the time of making the deed. *See also* INSOLVENCY.

Grätz, a tn. in Prussia about 26 m. W. of Posen. Pop. 5812.

Grätz, in Austria, *see* GRAZ.

Graubünden, *see* GRISONS.

Graudenz, a tn. of Prussia in the prov. of W. Prussia, situated on the r. b. of the Vistula, 18 m. S.S.W. of Marienwerder. It has communication by boat with Dantzig, and many manufactures. The fortress was built by Frederick the Great in 1772-76, and was a little to the N. of Graudenz. The remains are now used as barracks and prison. Pop. 40,313.

Graun, Carl Heinrich (1701-59), a German musical composer, born at Wahrenbrück in Saxony. He studied under Johann Schmidt, and at an early age composed a number of sacred cantatas. He always had a beautiful voice, and when a boy was in the choir at Dresden, but later, when his voice changed to a tenor, made his début at the opera of Brunswick. He rewrote much of the music he had to sing and was commissioned to write an opera for the next season. This piece, *Polydorus*, made him famous throughout Germany, and he was engaged by Frederick the Great for his private chapel at Rheinsberg. He composed twenty-eight operas, of which *Merope* is the best, as well as cantatas and pieces for the church service; his oratorio, *The Death of Jesus*, is perhaps his greatest achievement.

Gravel, a collection of small stones formed by the action of water upon rock, which is found in rivers and on the seashore. It varies much in character and appearance; when the fragments are small the deposit is sand, when large it is called shingle. It consists of pieces from all kinds of rock, but pebbles of quartz and quartzite are most common. When first deposited the G. is loose, but after a time it forms a hard rock known as ' puddingstone.' There are various kinds, the best being the ' Kensington,' a pit G. consisting of large quantities of oxide of iron which makes it binding (a quality essential for a good G.), and gives it a rich colour. Other kinds are the ' Dorset Pea,' composed of flinty pebbles about the size of a pea; the ' Lyming-ton,' a flint G. which comes from Hampshire; the ' Sussex Pea,' and ' Sussex Bean,' and the ' Shell G.,' found on the coasts of the Channel Is.

Gravelines, a port and tn. of France, in the dept. of Nord and the arron. of Dunkirk. It is situated about 11½ m. S.W. of Dunkirk, and 48 m. N.W. of Lille. The harbour is 75 acres in extent, with a depth of 16 and 18 ft. The cod and herring fisheries are important, and an export trade with England is carried on in fruit, vegetables, eggs, and fish. Pop. 6500.

Gravelot, Hubert François d'Anville (1699 - 1773), a French engraver and designer, born in Paris. He was an excellent draughtsman, and made designs for ornaments and drawings of ancient buildings with great taste. He etched several plates for books, his chief being those for Hanmer's and Theobald's editions of Shakespeare. He also executed in England drawings for Vertue's monuments, but his best plate is a large engraving of Kirkstall Abbey.

Gravelotte, a tn. in Alsace-Lorraine, Germany, about 6½ m. W. of Metz. A famous battle was fought in the neighbourhood of this town in 1870, in the Franco-German War, resulting in the defeat of the French under Marshal Bazaine. Pop. about 2500.

Graves, Clotilde Inez Mary (*b.* 1864), a British journalist, novelist, and dramatist, born at Barracks, Buttevant co., Cork. Among her plays are the Drury Lane pantomime *Puss in Boots*, and *The Bond of Union*, 1906. Her best known novel is *The Dop Doctor*, written under the *nom de plume* of Richard Dehan, and she has recently published *Between*

Two Thieves, 1912, under the same pseudonym.

Graves, Richard (1715–1804), a poet and novelist, born in Gloucestershire. He was educated at the grammar school, Abingdon, and at Pembroke College, Oxford, where he became very friendly with Shenstone, whose life he afterwards wrote. At an early age he compiled verses for the magazines, and some of his poems appeared in the collections of Dodsley and Pearch. He, however, attained greater popularity by his novels, all of which are now forgotten except the *Spiritual Quixote*.

Graves, Robert James (1796-1853), an Irish physician, born in Dublin. He studied in Dublin, London, and Edinburgh, and showed a great faculty for languages. In 1821 he was elected physician to the Meath Hospital, and was one of the founders of the Park Street School of Medicine. He reformed the abuses of the hospital, but is chiefly famous for his *Clinical Lectures*, which were published in 1843. He was president of the Irish College of Physicians in 1843 and 1844, and was elected a fellow of the Royal Society in 1849. One of his greatest reforms was that ' He fed fevers.'

Graves, Thomas, Lord (c. 1725-1802), an admiral, entered the navy at an early age and served in many famous expeditions, among which may be mentioned the engagement in Chesapeake Bay in 1781, and the operations against the French in Hudson Bay. He was also appointed to command the Channel fleet, under Lord Howe, when war broke out with France in 1793.

Graves, Sir Thomas (c. 1747-1814), an admiral; the first cousin once removed of Admiral Thomas Lord G. He entered the navy at an early age, and in 1770 was lieutenant of the *Arethusa*. In 1773 he went on a voyage of discovery in the Arctic Seas with Lord Mulgrave, and in 1774 went to N. America with his uncle, and was in charge of a small schooner employed for the prevention of smuggling. He was in command of the *Bedford* during the action in Chesapeake Bay, and was present in the engagement at St. Kitts. In 1783 he fought the French frigate *Sybille*, in 1801 went to the Baltic with Sir Hyde Parker, and later in the year was third in command under Lord Nelson at the battle of Copenhagen.

Gravesend, a municipal bor., river port, and market tn. in Kent on the r. b. of the Thames. It is defended by three forts on the Kentish coast, and Tilbury fort on the Essex side. It is the boundary of the port of London, and a place where troops and passengers embark for long voyages. It is also a noted holiday resort, and many people visit Rosherville and Springhead. Cobham Hall, the seat of the Darnley family, is here. Pop. 28,117.

Graville St. Honorine, a tn. in France in the dept. Seine-Inférieure, about midway between Havre and Harfleur. It has copper, zinc, and lead mines. Pop. 13,300.

Gravina, a tn. of Southern Italy in the prov. of Bari, about 32 m. from the tn. of Bari. The town is surrounded with walls and towers, and a castle of the Emperor Frederick II. rises above the town. Pop. 18,700.

Gravina, Giovanni Vincenzio (1664-1718), a jurist, born at Rogiano, near Cosenza in Calabria. He was first educated under the direction of his uncle, Gregorio Caloprese, but afterwards studied civil and canon law at Naples. In 1689 he went to Rome and was mainly responsible for the formation of the Academy of Arcadians, but in consequence of a dispute he withdrew from this and founded the Academy of Quirina. In 1699 he occupied the chair of civil law in the college of La Sapienza, and in 1703 that of canon law. He wrote : *Origines juris civilis*, which established his reputation as a jurist; *De Romano imferio; Della Ragion Poetica*, and several tragedies.

Gravitation, a term used in physical science for the mutual attraction between masses of matter. The full statement of Newton's law of gravitation is: *Every particle of matter in the universe attracts every other particle with a force whose direction is that of the line joining the two, and whose magnitude is directly as the product of the masses and inversely as the square of their distance from each other.* In order to marshal the evidence for this great generalisation it is convenient to consider it under the following heads: (*a*) The direction of the force between the particles; (*b*) the law of inverse square of distances; (*c*) the universality of the law of inverse squares; (*d*) the proportionality of the force of attraction to the product of the attracting masses.

Newton based his investigation into the law of gravitation on the three laws deduced by Kepler from the astronomical observations of Tycho Brahe. Kepler's laws are purely kinematical. They completely describe the motions of planets, but they say nothing about the forces by which these motions are maintained. Their dynamical interpretation was discovered by Newton. *Law* 1: Each planet describes an elliptical orbit. The sun occupies one focus of the ellipse. *Law* 2: The radius vector of each planet sweeps out equal areas in equal times. *Law* 3: The square of the periodic time (in an elliptical orbit) is proportional to the cube of the major axis of the ellipse.

(a) As an immediate consequence of Law 2, Newton showed that the direction of the attraction of the sun for a planet must be that of the line joining them. For twice the area described by the radius vector of a planet in one second is numerically equal to the moment of its velocity about the centre of the sun. Hence, as the moment of the velocity of the planet is constant, the moment of each successive increase of velocity must be zero. Hence these increments in velocity (*i.e.* the accelerations) must be directed towards the sun. But the direction of the acceleration must coincide with the direction of the force which causes the acceleration. Therefore the force of attraction must be directed towards the sun.

(b) The acceleration of the planet can readily be calculated to be $4\pi^2 \dfrac{a^3}{T^2} \cdot \dfrac{1}{r^2}$, where a is the semi-major axis of its elliptical path, T the periodic time, r the distance of the planet from the sun. Hence the acceleration of the planet is inversely proportional to the square of its distance from the sun. Therefore the force of attraction due to the sun varies inversely as the square of the distance.

(c) Kepler's third law states that $\dfrac{T^2}{a^3}$ is the same for all planets. Hence it is the same gravitation, diminishing as the square of the distance increases, which acts on each one of the planets. In other words, the force of attraction due to the sun does not pay any attention to the quality of matter. The inverse square law is universally true for every kind of matter.

(d) The expression $4\pi^2 \dfrac{a^3}{T^2} \cdot \dfrac{1}{r^2}$ shows that the acceleration of a planet towards the sun depends only on its distance r from the sun, since $\dfrac{T^2}{a^3}$ is constant for all planets. Hence the force acting on a planet due to the sun's attraction is proportional to the mass of the planet. Since action and reaction are equal, each planet reacts on the sun with a force equal and opposite to that exerted by the sun or the planet. Hence each planet acts with a force proportional to its own mass and inversely as the square of the distance away. We must therefore conclude that the sun, which is a planet of great magnitude, also acts with a force proportional to its own

mass. Hence the force acting on a planet due to the sun is (1) proportional to the mass of the planet; (2) proportional to the mass of the sun, *i.e.* the force is proportional to the product of the attracting masses. In the above discussion the dimensions of the sun and planets have been considered as inappreciable compared with their distances apart. Measurement shows that they are approximately spherical; is, then, the attraction exerted due to the attracting body as a whole, or is it due to its separate particles each acting independently? Newton attacked the question by assuming the law of gravitation for the separate particles of a body, and thence finding the law of attraction for the body as a whole. He thus arrived at two exceedingly beautiful theorems: (1) A spherical shell of uniform matter exercises no attraction on a particle inside it. (2) A spherical shell of uniform matter attracts an external particle as if its whole mass were concentrated at the centre.

An obvious corollary from the second theorem is that a sphere made up of uniform concentric shells attracts, and is therefore attracted by all external bodies, as if its whole mass were concentrated at its centre. Since the planets behave as if their masses were concentrated at their centres, and since their departures from this behaviour can all be accounted for by their want of sphericity, there is very strong presumption that the attraction is the resultant of all the attractions, each particle of mass m of one body exercising on a particle of mass n of another body, an attractive force of $\dfrac{Gm \times n}{d^2}$, where d is the distance between the two particles, and G is a constant—the constant of gravitation. The law of gravitation is unique among the laws of nature, in the fact that it is unaffected by any condition or cause whatsoever. The force of attraction between two electrified charges is modified by the medium intervening between them, and also by their relative or absolute motions. But no conditions to which matter has ever been subjected have been found to affect its gravitation in the slightest degree.

Determination of the mass of the earth and the mass of the sun.—Astronomical observations enable us to compare the masses of the various members of the solar systems. For example, the acceleration of the earth towards the sun is about 0·6 cm. per sec. per sec.; the distance between the two is 15×10^{12} cms. The acceleration of the moon towards the earth is about 0·27 cms. per sec. per sec., and the distance between them is 4×10^{10} cms. If S is the mass of the sun, E the mass of the earth, M the mass of the moon, then $·6 = \dfrac{GS}{(15 \times 10^{12})^2}$ and $·27 = \dfrac{GE}{(4 \times 10^{10})^2}$, therefore the ratio $\dfrac{S}{E} =$ 300,000 approximately. To determine S and E in terms of the terrestrial standards of mass, the kilogramme and the pound, recourse must be had to experiments with terrestrial masses. A body of mass m suspended at the earth's surface is attracted by a force $\dfrac{G \times E \times m}{R^2}$, where E is the mass of the earth. But if g is the acceleration of a body falling freely under the influence of the gravitational force of the earth, the value of this force is also expressed by mg. Then $mg = \dfrac{G \times E \times m}{R^2}$ or $E = \dfrac{gR^2}{G}$. To determine G the force F between two artificially prepared masses M_1 and M_2 at a distance apart d is measured, and since $F = \dfrac{GM_1 \times M_2}{d^2}$ we get at once $G = \dfrac{Fd^2}{M_1 M_2}$. $\therefore E = \dfrac{g \times R^2 \times M_1 \times M_2}{Fd^2}$.

Cavendish's experiment.—An experiment for determining the force of attraction between two artificial masses was first planned by the Rev. John Mitchell who did not live to begin work on the apparatus which he had designed and completed. After Mitchell's death, the apparatus came into the hands of Henry Cavendish who largely reconstructed it but adopted Mitchell's original plan. The attracted masses consisted of two small balls, A and B, an inch or two in diameter, connected by a stiff wooden beam suspended at its middle point E by a long fine wire.

The whole of this part of the apparatus was enclosed in a case, carefully coated with tinfoil to secure, as far as possible, a uniform temperature within the case. Irregular distribution of temperature would have resulted in convection currents of air which would have had a serious disturbing effect on the suspended system. To the beam was attached a small mirror with its plane vertical. A small glazed window in the case allowed any motion of the mirror to be observed by the consequent deviations of a ray of light reflected from it. The attracting masses consisted of two equal, massive, lead spheres, so mounted that they could be made to move from the positions C_1 D_1 to the positions C_2 D_2 or C_3 D_3. Cavendish found that the suspended system was never at rest. The equilibrium position was determined by the method usually employed when weighing with a delicate balance. When the large masses were placed at C_2 D_2, the oscillations were practically due to the torsion of the wire. If T is the period of vibration for this position of C and D, and I the moment of inertia of the suspended system, then $\mu = \dfrac{4\pi^2 I}{T^2}$, where μ is the couple required to twist the lower end of the wire through tortion relatively to the top end. The angle θ through which the beam was deflected when

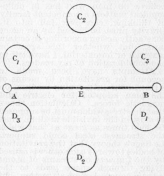

the attracting masses were moved from the positions C_1 D_1 to the positions C_3 D_3 was measured. Then $\mu\theta = \dfrac{2G \times M \times m}{d^2} \times l$, where l is the length of the beam and d the distance between the centres of the attracting and attracted masses. Whence $G = \dfrac{\mu\theta d^2}{2M \times m}$ $= \dfrac{2.\pi^2 I.\theta.d^2}{T^2.M.m}$. The experiment has been repeated by Reich, Bailey, Cornu, Boys, and Braun. Cavendish obtained for the value of G $6·6 \times 10^{-8}$ dynes, Reich $6·613 \times 10^{-8}$, Bailey $6·685 \times 10^{-8}$, Boys $6·6576 \times 10^{-8}$, Braun $6·65786 \times 10^{-8}$. The remarkable agreement between the results of these experiments, which were performed at different times and at different places on the earth's surface, provides a powerful confirmation of the truth of the law of gravitation.

Cause of gravitation.—The cause of gravitation remains undiscovered. Newton, in his celebrated *Letters to Bentley*, says: ' You sometimes speak of gravity as essential and inherent to matter. Pray do not ascribe that notion to me; for the cause of gravity is what I do not pretend to know, and therefore would take more time to consider it. It is inconceivable that inanimate brute matter should, without the mediation of something else which is not material, operate on and affect other matter without mutual contact, as it must do if gravitation in the sense of Epicurus be essential and inherent in it. . . . That gravity should be innate, inherent, and essential to matter so that one body may act upon another at a distance through a vacuum, without the mediation of anything else, by and through which their action and force may be conveyed from one to the other, is to me so great an absurdity, that I believe no man who has in philosophical matters a competent faculty of thinking, can ever fall into it. Gravity must be caused by an agent constantly acting according to certain laws; but whether this agent be material or immaterial, I have left to the consideration of my readers.'

Attempts have been made to account for gravitation by means of stress in the intervening medium on the plan adopted for electric and magnetic forces. Calculation shows that the stress which must be supposed to exist in the invisible medium must be 3000 times as great as that which the strongest steel could support. Le Sage's theory that the gravitation of bodies towards each other is caused by the impacts of streams of atoms flying through space leads to the inverse square law of attraction, but it demands that the rate at which the energy of the bombarding atoms is spent in order to maintain the gravitating property of a single pound, is at least millions of millions of foot pounds per second. In fact, all the theories which have been advanced to account for gravitation imply the existence of stresses or the presence of stores of energy absolutely gigantic in comparison with anything hitherto observed or even suspected to exist in the universe.

Gravity, Centre of, see CENTRE OF GRAVITY.

Gravity, Specific, see SPECIFIC GRAVITY.

Gravosa, the fortified harbour of Ragusa in the prov. of Dalmatia in Austria. It is a seaport and fishing-town. Pop. 1500.

Gray, a com. of France, on the l. b. of the Saône in the dept. of Haute-Saône. Pop. 6700.

Gray, Asa (1810-88), an American botanist, born in Paris, New York. He received only an ordinary education and at the age of sixteen began his collection and study of plants. In 1842 he accepted the Fisher professorship of natural history at Harvard University and devoted himself to the establishment of a herbarium and a

library there, giving up his own collection of plants to the former and his books to the latter. He made a special study, with Dr. Torrey, of the *Flora* of N. America, and two volumes were published on this subject in 1838 and 1843, respectively. He was also an enthusiastic supporter of Darwin's theory of evolution. His *Manual of the Botany of the Northern United States* is his most important work, but he also published a *Botanical Text-book, How Plants Grow, How Plants Behave, Synoptical Flora,* and the *Botany of Japan in Relation to North America,* which is in point of originality and far-reaching results, his *opus magnum.*

Gray, David (1838-61), a Scottish poet, born at Merkland, near Glasgow. He was educated at Glasgow University for the Church, but at an early age began to write verses. He became intimate with the poet Robert Buchanan, with whom he went to London in 1860. There he became acquainted with Lord Houghton who gave him some literary work and endeavoured to get his poem *The Luggie* published in *The Cornhill Magazine.* This poem, a reminiscence of the scenes and events of his childhood, is his chief work, but he also wrote a series of sonnets, *In the Shadows,* which have a beauty all their own.

Gray, Elisha (1835-1901), an American inventor, born at Barnesville, Ohio. He studied for a time at Oberlin College, but afterwards took up the subject of telegraphy, and in 1867 patented a telegraphic switch. He also experimented with the telephone, which he claimed to have invented, his application for a patent being received only a few hours after Mr. Alexander Bell's. He was engaged for some time in the manufacture of telegraphic apparatus, and was the electrical expert of the Western Electric Company of Chicago. Among his inventions are the multiplex telegraph by which eight messages can be sent at a time, and the telantograph by which handwriting can be transmitted.

Gray, John Edward (1800-75), an English naturalist, born at Walsall. He assisted his father in the preparation of his *Natural Arrangement of British Plants* in 1821, and in 1824 entered the British Museum as assistant in the Natural History department. In 1840 he was appointed keeper of the Zoological collections and made them the most complete in the world. He wrote many books, the most important being his catalogues of the British Museum collections.

Gray, Thomas (1716-71), an English poet, born in London, and educated at Eton and Peterhouse College, Cambridge. Of a studious and reserved nature, he formed few intimate friendships, but these were lasting ones. The story of his life is simple and colourless, the outstanding event in it being his tour on the Continent with Horace Walpole, 1739-41. Their unfortunate quarrel, late in this tour, which was not healed for three years, was the only break in a life-long attachment. Returning to England, G. found his father dying and his mother only moderately provided for. After residing with her for a while at Stoke Pogis he went back to Cambridge, where, except for brief intervals, he spent the rest of his life. He had always a tendency to melancholy, the best cure for which would have been plenty of exercise and cheerful company; of the former, however, he took little, and the latter he was too reserved to enjoy freely. Yet he was naturally very humorous, and his letters, charming in their mixture of fun, sincere friendliness, and wise criticisms of men and books, are worthy to stand with those of Lamb. His learning was immense, not only in the classics, but also in art and natural science. He holds an honourable place in English literature, though his works are small in quantity, and in quality do not attain the highest rank, even the immortal *Elegy* owing its fame to exquisite expression and natural pathos rather than to greatness or originality of thought. But if this, the Odes, and the translations from the Norse be compared with anything written by his immediate predecessors (except Thomson), it will be seen that G. was a pioneer, a true poet in a prosaic age, and the forerunner of Goldsmith and Cowper in breaking away from the monotonous artificiality of early 18th century verse. No wonder that Johnson, who condemned *Lycidas*, failed to appreciate *The Progress of Poesy* and *The Bard*, but it is quaint to find the author of *Rasselas* complaining of the ' cumbrous splendours' of G., and elsewhere of his ' dullness.' Other contemporaries called him obscure. G. was one of the first to celebrate the glories of mountain scenery. While other writers were still shuddering at ' horrid precipices ' and ' frightful solitudes ' he was enthusiastic in his admiration of the Alps, and later of the Grampian and Cumbrian peaks. *See* Gosse's *Gray's Works,* 1884, and *Life,* 1889; *Poems and Letters* (Everyman's Library),and Matthew Arnold's fine essay on Gray.

Grayling, a fresh-water fish of the salmon family having a long many-rayed dorsal fin. It is found in the N.

of Europe, Asia, and N. America. The British G. generally inhabits rivers with a rocky or gravelly bottom, and is in best condition when trout are out of season.

GRAYLING

Grayling Butterfly (*Hipparchia semele*), a butterfly widely distributed over the British Isles. It has dark-brown wings with two black eye-spots on each of the fore-wings and one black eye-spot centred with white on the hind-wings. It is found on heaths and in dry stony places, especially on chalk and in clearings in woods.

Gray's Inn, *see* INNS OF COURT.

Gray's Thurrock, a par. and tn. of Essex, England, situated on the Thames, 3 m. N.W. Tilbury,and 12 m. S.E. of Romford. There are two training ships, and a trade in cement, lime, and bricks. Pop. (1911) 16,003.

Graz (Grätz until 1843), a tn. of Austria, capital of Styria, on the Mur, at the head of the valley's expansion round the foot of the hill, Schlossberg. There is railway communication both N. and S. across the Mur's valley, and E. by the valley of the Raab. It is a bishop's see, and has numerous buildings of interest. Amongst these are the university (1586, new buildings 1890-95); 15th century Gothic cathedral (with fine altar - pieces and glass - paintings) ; mausoleum of Ferdinand II. with sarcophagi of his parents, the Archduke Charles and his wife ; 13th century Gothic parish church of the Teutonic knights; Landhaus (1569), in Renaissance style; the Joanneum with natural history library, given by the Archduke John (1811); arsenal (1644); 11th century castle. The Castle Hill was fortified till 1809, and there is a curious clock-tower on the Schlossberg. There are cold mineral springs at Radegund near by, and the health-resort, Tobelbad. A polytechnic was opened 1888, and there are other educational institutions. Manufs, include machinery, rails, ironwares, paper, leather, soap, beer, hats, and wine. The lignite of Kainach valley, the chief mineral fuel deposit of the Alps, is important. Population 151,688. *See* Gsell Fels, *Gratz und seine Umgebung,* 1897.

Grazalema, a tn. of Spain, in the

prov. of Cadiz. It is situated 45 m. N.E. of Jerez, and is difficult of access, as it stands on a steep rock on G. Sierra de Penar at an altitude of 4200 ft. The manufs. are flannel, shawls, quilts, cloth, etc. Pop. 5600.

Grazzini, Antonio Francesco (1503-83), an Italian poet and dramatist, founder of the Accademia degli Umidi (Florentine Academy), 1540, assuming the name ' Il Lasca ' (mullet, or barbel). He was also later chief founder of the Accademia della Crusca (1550), formed to perfect the Tuscan language. His works include a collection of tales in the style of Boccaccio's *Decameron*—*La prima e la seconda Cena* (selections appearing as *Le Cene*, 1756); sonnets, satirical poems, and comedies; *Gelosia*, 1568; *La Spiritata*, 1561; *I Parentadi, La Pinzochera*. His works were considered ' testi di lingua ' by the Della Cruscan Academy. See Fanfani's ' Vita del Lasca ' in *Le Cene ed altre prose*, 1857, and edition of the *Commedie*, 1859; Ginguené, *Histoire Littéraire d'Italie*, 1810-24.

Grease, a term generally applied to oily and fatty substances. In its special application it has reference to fatty matters which have been rendered impure by dirt, so that they are not fit to be used in making candles or in other manufactures which require pure materials. G. is used to oil machinery of all sorts as well as for the wheels of carriages, but the inferior kind mixed with tar is used for carts and waggons, etc. A great quantity of G. is used on the English railways for the goods trains, but palm-oil is generally employed for passenger trains. *See* LUBRICANTS.

Great Barrier Island, an island of New Zealand, on the E. coast of North Island. To the W. is a small island known as Little Barrier Island.

Great Barrier Reef, a series of coral reefs off the E. coast of Australia, about 1250 m. in length. In its widest part it is 100 m. broad and is 150 m. from the coast, but towards the N. it comes nearer the land, and in some places is only 10 m. distant. The reef can be seen at low tide, but can always be distinguished by the breakers which wash over it. The reef is not continuous, but is broken up by many deep channels the chief of which are the Bligh Entrance, the Olinda Entrance, the Raime Entrance, and Flinders Passage. The channel between the reef and the coast is a valuable route of communication for steamers owing to the calmness of the sea, but careful navigation is necessary, especially at night when the reef can scarcely be discerned, hence sailing vessels only use the route by

day. The most valuable products of the reef are pearls, pearl shells, and trepangs.

Great Barrington, a tn. in the Berkshire co. of Massachusetts, U.S.A. on the Housatonic R. about 12 m. from the S.W. corner of the state. It is a manuf. tn. and summer resort. Pop. (1910) 5926.

Great Basin, a large region of drainage in the U.S.A. which includes nearly all Nevada, Utah, Oregon, and California, and lies between the Sierra Nevada on the W., and the Wasatch Mts. on the E. Mountains run from N. to S. of it, and rise to a height of 4000 ft. above the plateau. The soil is fertile where irrigation can be applied, but the hills are barren. It has numerous lakes, most of which are salt, the chief being Great Salt Lake, Lake Utah, Lake Sevier, Lake Walker, and Lake Carson. The mountains are rich in minerals, especially silver ore.

Great Bassa, or **Grand Bassa**, a port of Liberia, W. Africa, situated about 55 m. S.E. of Monrovia.

Great Batanga, a river of W. Africa, flowing S.W. into the Atlantic, at 3° 18′ N. The English and German factories of Little Batanga are at its mouth.

Great Bear Lake, *see* BEAR LAKE, GREAT.

Great Britain. The Act of Union (1707) made England and Scotland one united nation under the name of G. B., and the accession of George I. in 1714 is a convenient point to commence the history of that nation. The Protestant succession in 1714 was the final step in the Revolution of 1688; the vindication of the principles of Protestantism, and election of the monarch by parliament. Further, it marked very distinctly a new era in the constitution. The king was a foreigner, and a figurehead; the real power had passed from the hands of the crown into the hands of the parliament, and during the 18th century that meant that the power remained in the hands of the great Whig families. These families had been responsible for the Revolution of 1688, and for the peaceful succession of George I., but they were inspired by no feelings of loyalty, rather they regarded the matter as a financial speculation, and supported the Hanoverians because, whilst a Protestant sat on the throne, their funds were safe. The first two Hanoverian kings had little, if any, doubt as to the exact feelings of their subjects. The first event of importance during the reign of George I., was the Jacobite Rebellion of 1715, which was really of little importance and which stirred the absolute apathy of the nation at large. During that rebellion the Septennial Bill was passed, prolonging the duration of parliament to seven years instead of three. This was obviously an Act passed in order to prevent an election during these troublous times, and was but a temporary expedient. It lasted, however, down to the passing of the Preamble to the Parliament Bill of 1910, which reduced the duration of parliament to five years. One important development also took place. The king no longer attended cabinet councils, his place was taken by a first or prime minister. The system of party government had been developed previously, but now the entire personal element of the crown was eliminated. Under kings who simply regarded England as a source of revenue the plan worked well, but under more ambitious kings it was apt to become a trifle irksome. The mania for speculation which broke out during this reign and was really one of the results of the treaty of Utrecht, culminated in the South Sea Bubble which broke, rendering many people in England penniless. The ministry could not entirely exonerate themselves, but financial matters were put right by the genius of Walpole. From 1721-42 Walpole ruled the country. This period of office was a period of stagnation, nothing happened, affairs dragged themselves quietly along, other countries took part in wars, England stood aloof, and prospered. Walpole was intensely fond of power and could brook no rival, hence we find during his period of office the Whigs themselves began to be divided, and the discarded rivals of Walpole led the opposition. The Patriots and the Bays were two such parties. In 1727 George I. had died and his son had succeeded. George II. had no love for Walpole, but guided by his wife, Caroline of Anspach, he continued Walpole in office, and affairs assumed the usual even tenor of their way. In 1733 Walpole introduced his famous excise scheme, a scheme which was years ahead of his time, but withdrew it rather than enforce it at the point of the bayonet. In 1739 he declared war with Spain, the War of Jenkins' Ear, which ran on into the War of the Austrian Succession, and in 1742, finding his majorities continually dwindling, he resigned. It is important to notice during this century that in every war which we fought we either were in direct opposition to France or ranged amongst the allies on the opposite side. Also the wars were no longer European wars solely,

but struggles for colonial and maritime supremacy. The European wars were repeated in India and America, and often even, when the two countries were at peace at home, war was going on in the colonies. During the War of the Austrian Succession, the second and last Jacobite rising too place. Again it illustrated the apathy of the country at large, but this time, owing to more efficient leadership, England was invaded and the Pretender reached Derby. That day has since been known as Black Friday. The government were seriously upset, the only person who scoffed at the danger being the king himself. But from Derby the Pretender had to retreat and was finally defeated at Culloden, and after many adventures got safely out of the country. One other point deserves notice here, and that the battle of Dettingen in 1743, when for the last time a British sovereign led his troops in person. The War of the Austrian Succession ended with the treaty of Hachen (1748), and eight years later began the Seven Years' War. During this war William Pitt the Elder became Minister for War, and owing to his genius the war was the most successful that we had yet waged. He set himself to conquer India and America on the plains of Germany. He instituted a system of financing the English allies, keeping France busy in that way on the Continent, and attacking at the same time India and America. During this war we definitely established the beginnings of an empire in India, and Canada also passed into our hands. France had been defeated in both countries. Before the end of the war George II. died. He had not been unpopular, and he was certainly respected throughout the country. He was succeeded by his grandson, George III., the eldest son of Frederick Prince of Wales, who had predeceased his father. George III. (*q.v.*) was ambitious and had been dangerously educated. He, however, proudly proclaimed that he gloried in the name of Briton. Before he had been on the throne long, Bute, his tutor, was in possession of the premiership. Pitt had resigned and a peace had been signed, by which we obtained much, but not so much as would have been obtained with a competent man at the head of affairs. The early part of the reign resolved itself into a struggle between the king and the Whigs. The king desired personal rule, and ultimately he, for a short time, obtained it. One of the indirect results of the cession of Canada to Britain was the outbreak of war with the colonies. The English parliament declared itself capable of taxing the colonies. The colonies protested that taxation went with representation. The government, under Grenville, remained obstinate; the king regarded the colonists as rebels from the first. Conciliation was tried, but it was useless conciliating with one hand and irritating with the other, and finally, in 1775, war broke out and in the following year the Americans declared their independence and became a republic. By 1778 the war was extended and England found herself fighting practically the rest of Europe. In America she was defeated at York-town, and the surrender of Corn-wallis there in 1781 sealed the fate of America. Against France and Spain she was more successful, and the victories of Rodney in the W. Indies, and the failure of the Spaniards to recover Gibraltar enabled England to come out of the war with flying colours, but, nevertheless, at a lower pitch of power than she had reached before in the century. America's independence was of course recognised. The disasters of the American War put a period to the personal power of the king, although he was still able to influence events by the use of the body of politicians known as the king's friends. That series of changes in the economic world, usually known as the industrial revolution, began to become prominent just about this time. Change seemed to be in the air. The fiscal system was altered; the influence of Adam Smith's *Wealth of Nations* was felt; Free Trade began to be seriously spoken of; parliamentary reform found some bold and strenuous advocates, and then came the greatest event of all—the French Revolution. For over four years that revolution remained disregarded by this country, save in as far as it found some supporters but more enemies. The peace of Europe was held to be unaffected by it. Pitt himself declared the year before the outbreak of war that peace with France had never been so secure. Then, in 1793, Louis XVI. was executed, and the international treaties of Europe torn up by France. The republic desired to fight Europe, and speedily Europe found that the fight was not so unequal after all. But the enthusiasm of the Revolution calmed down, the natural genius of the people slowly returned, and step by step they were led by Napoleon (*q.v.*) until the republic was a consulate and then an empire. Still the menace of imperial France was as great as that of republic France, and certainly it is due to the fact that it was impossible to invade

and conquer England that Europe was saved. Every other country in Europe suffered from actual invasion, but as Pitt said, England saved herself by her courage and Europe by her example. Waterloo decided the fate of Europe, and Napoleon was sent to the island of St. Helena. Undoubtedly the victory had been due to a very great extent to the resources of England, without her manufactures even her enemies could not exist. The Berlin decrees failed owing to the number of exceptions which Napoleon had to make. During the reign of George III. England had changed to a very great extent from an agricultural to an industrial nation. The new manu-factures had led to new roads and new means of transit; it was obviously necessary to obtain quick transit for goods, and necessity was the mother of invention. Roads were better con-structed, canals were made all over the country, and finally came the steamship and the steam-engine. The period which followed the great war was one of great distress. Economic troubles took place all over the country. The new machinery was attacked, and the increasing numbers of soldiers returning from the war made affairs worse. In 1819 the great riots broke out, and at Manchester the mob was charged by the military and a number of the rioters were killed; this event is known as the Manchester Massacres or Peterloo. In the meantime the demand for reform had continued, but the Re-volution had stopped all chance of immediate reform. Anything savour-ing of reform was regarded as re-volutionary, and anything revolu-tionary was anathema with the vast majority of the people of the country. Catholic emancipation had been mooted at the time of the Union (1800) (*see* IRELAND—*History*), but the king had refused to hear of it, and Pitt, rather than break his promise to the Irish, resigned. The king, who had now for some considerable time been incapable of ruling, died in 1820, weak, old, blind, and insane. His son, the Prince Regent, became king as George IV.

The death of George III. in 1820 makes practically no difference in the history of the nation. The king had long been imbecile and blind, and the accession of the regent made but little change. Almost immediately the trouble between George IV. and his wife came to a head and the queen was brought up for trial. It is im-possible here to discuss in detail the events of the century which has almost passed since the accession of George IV. The effect of the Revolution in France, however, was tremendous, and this intellectual awakening, stimulated by and stimulating the movement which we know as the Industrial Revolution, brought in its train results of the highest significance. There has probably been more real progress packed into the years of the 19th and early 20th centuries than into the whole of the preceding history of the world. Democracy, hitherto an ideal which could not be attained, became not only a possibility but, during the later years, a reality. During the reign of George IV., toleration became a real thing in spite of violent opposition, the Test and Corporation Acts were repealed, and a Bill for the relief of the Catholics was passed as well. These changes seem nowadays but small and necessary ; to the age which passed them they were practically revolutionary. It is necessary also to remember that the close of the Napoleonic wars had been followed by a reaction in almost every country in Europe, and in spite of this revolutionary measures were passed in G. B. In 1830 George IV. died, and was succeeded by his brother, William IV. To what extent the principles which were then called Radical had supplanted the solid and, to a certain extent, unreasoned Toryism of the previous century may be gauged from the measures that were passed during this reign. The agitation for a Reform Bill at last had its reward in the passing of the great Reform Act of 1832 ; to the aristocracy of the time, the beginning of the end of all things. Slavery was abolished, a Poor Law was passed, legislation for the protection of the worker passed and municipalities received attention also. In 1837 William IV. died, and was succeeded by his niece, Queen Victoria, whose long reign witnessed so much change and progress. The reign can be well divided into three distinct periods: the early Victorian— an age of constant turmoil and bustle, during which Europe was agitated by countless revolutions : an age which regarded monarchies, to a certain extent, as necessary evils. Of the second period all that need be said of it is that it was Mid-Victorian— an epithet that carries its own condemnation ; and the last period an age of transition, of preparation for a great awakening, during which loyalty seems to be tinged almost with a maudlin sentiment which passed for pious reverence. The early period witnessed the repeal of the Corn Laws and the great Chartist agitations, together with the beginning of the great Irish question. The year 1848 was called the year of the Revolution,

all Europe was in a state of unrest, and every side of the social fabric seemed to be agitated. The Forties witnessed the Scottish Disruption movement and the Oxford movement, both indications of the state of unrest. Commercially G. B. was prospering and progressing by leaps and bounds. The great European wars had left her the workshop of the world, and for a time she had no competitors at all. Politically her progress was equally great, while the great parties still remained fairly true to the old ideas, nevertheless the Liberals who represented the Whigs, and the Conservative who represented the Tories were both being gradually tinged with the democratic spirit. The people were at last being recognised as a real factor in political existence, but this fact must not be overestimated. The power of the Crown and of the landed proprietors was as great as ever, but were skilfully disguised. The power of the House of Lords, although still great, was not great enough to compete with the Lower House, and gradually from this period the power of the House of Commons increased until it is now recognised as the greatest power in the legislature. It will perhaps be best here to review as briefly as possible the main political events of the period from 1830 to the present time. The Reform Bill of 1832 stands out as the great event of the ministry of Lord Grey, and before this ministry relinquished office they had attempted the reform of the Poor Laws and had introduced the first Factory Act. Melbourne became Prime Minister in 1834, and although the ministry was dissolved by the king, the Tory minister, Peel, after trying to hold office with a minority in the House of Commons, resigned, and Melbourne continued in office until 1841. In 1839, defeated on a question of the affairs of Jamaica, he resigned, and Peel was again sent for, this time by Queen Victoria, who had succeeded in 1837. The question of the change in the ladies of the bed-chamber, however, roused such difficulty that Melbourne was again induced to accept office. In 1841 he finally dissolved parliament, and a Tory majority was returned. On the whole the ministry had not been very successful, they had passed the Municipal Corporation Act, and had introduced Penny Postage, but their policy in Canada and Jamaica had been bad, and the zeal for reform seems to have left the Whig party. The great event of the ministry of his successor, Peel, was the repeal of the Corn Laws (1846). His financial measures were a great success, but were overshadowed by the great measure of repeal. The Irish famine forced his hand, and the head of a nominal Protectionist ministry introduced the greatest measure of Free Trade which the country had yet been given. The 'betrayal of the party,' as many Conservatives considered it, was bitterly attacked by a young politician, Benjamin Disraeli (*q.v.*), the future leader of the Conservative party. Peel was almost immediately defeated on the question of a Coercion Act for Ireland, and resigned, never to hold office again. The Tory party was split up by this measure, and the Peelites, chief among whom were Gladstone and Aberdeen, ultimately joined forces with the Whigs, whilst the Protectionists, under Bentinck and Disraeli, ultimately formed the Conservative party. Peel was succeeded by Lord John Russell, whose greatest difficulty during this period was the quelling of the Chartist riots. The Chartist demands were : manhood suffrage, vote by ballot, annual parliament, payment of members, abolition of the property qualification, and equal electoral districts. The great plan of the leader of this movement was the presentation of a monster petition to the House of Commons, but the procession failed, and almost half the total number of signatures in the petition were found to be forged. In 1851 Palmerston's somewhat cavalier methods of conducting affairs at the Foreign Office led to his resignation, and in 1852 he threw the ministry out by defeating them on the Militia Bill. The ministry was succeeded by Lord Derby's Irish administration, and this, after a short period of office, was succeeded by a coalition ministry under the leadership of Lord Aberdeen. Its chief ministers were : Aberdeen, Gladstone, Russell, and Palmerston. It lasted only for three years, and Disraeli remarked, ' England does not love coalition.' During its tenure of office, however, Gladstone definitely abolished all the remaining protective duties, and England became altogether a Free Trade country. Nevertheless this ministry's utter mismanagement of the Crimean War led to its overthrow in 1855. During the next ten years the outstanding figure in English politics was Palmerston. After two years' office he was defeated, but appealed to the country and was returned by a splendid majority, and later in 1858 his Conspiracy to Murder Bill was thrown out, and Lord Derby formed his second administration, which lasted only for fifteen months, after which Palmerston again came into power. From this time until his death Palmerston was all supreme. The main events

of importance were those concerned with foreign affairs, the position of France and the ambition of Napoleon III. made many very apprehensive of France. Gladstone who was by this time a Liberal, was rapidly making a name for himself as a great financial minister. The invasion scare of 1858 led to the formation of the volunteers, and in 1861 the Prince Consort died. In 1865 Palmerston died and was succeeded by Lord John Russell, who attempted to pass a Reform Bill but was so bitterly attacked by many members of his own party that he resigned, and was succeeded by Lord Derby. In 1867 Disraeli introduced a Reform Bill, and ' educating his own party' up to it, passed it. It was described by Lord Derby as ' a leap in the dark,' and contained many amendments accepted from Gladstone. From 1867, almost to the end of the century, the field of politics is almost entirely occupied by the duel between Gladstone and Disraeli. Seldom have two statesmen of such genius been opposed to one another, or so entirely different in character. In 1868 Disraeli became Prime Minister in succession to Lord Derby, but was defeated in the general election of that year and resigned before the end of the year. Disraeli was succeeded by Gladstone, who during the five years of his ministry passed more measures than almost any previous one. Education became compulsory, Trade Unions were legalised, the Ballot Act was passed. Under Cardwell the army was reformed, and the linked battalion method adopted. The Irish Church Act and a Land Act for Ireland were passed, and the state of Ireland at the time also necessitated Coercion Acts. But the ministry gradually became unpopular—even those sections of the community that would benefit most from the measures of the ministry turning against it—whilst the foreign policy of the government was decidedly unpopular, G.B.'s action towards Russia during the Franco-Prussian War, and towards the *Alabama* claims of the U.S.A., being decidedly weak. In 1874 Gladstone resigned, and the Conservatives were returned to power, having for the first time since 1841 a real majority in the House of Commons. The ministry formed by Disraeli was a brilliant one, and the Opposition was for a time weakened by the withdrawal into private life of Gladstone. The great question of Home Rule was gradually forcing itself to the front, and the Irish tactics in the House became obstructive. It was at this time that Disraeli put forward his imperial policy, and the ministry is chiefly

noticeable for its attitude on foreign and imperial affairs. The Bulgarian atrocities led to the intervention of Russia and to the Congress of Berlin, from which England issued in 1878 with 'peace with honour.' Affairs in Africa and India also attracted much attention ; the title of Empress of India was taken by the queen, and the majority of the shares of the Suez Canal became the property of Britain. In 1880, however, Disraeli, or Beaconsfield as he was now called, resigned, and was badly defeated at the polling booths. The renewed enthusiasm of the Liberals on the re-appearance of Gladstone, and the ' swing of the pendulum,' account to a large extent for this. Gladstone now formed his second administration. He again remained in power for about five years. During that time he was much troubled by the Irish question, and the agrarian outrages in that country led to the passing of fresh Coercion Acts. In 1882 Lord Frederick Cavendish was murdered. In 1880 the Boers were, after the defeat at Majuba, granted independ-ence, and in 1885 the Egyptian ques-tion, which had necessitated the bom-bardment of Alexandria in 1882, was marked by the murder of Gordon at Khartoum. In 1881 the second Irish Land Bill was passed, and in 1884 the Reform Bill became law. In 1885 Gladstone resigned and was suc-ceeded by Salisbury, but he held office only for a short time. In 1886 at the general election the Liberals were again returned to power. Glad-stone formed his third ministry, but his majority was dependent on the Irish. In 1886 he determined at last to introduce a Home Rule Bill, which led to grave dissensions in his own party. On a division on the second reading he was deserted by Harting-ton, Chamberlain, and Bright, and was defeated by a majority of thirty. He appealed again to the country, and was defeated. Lord Salisbury now formed his second administration. From 1886-1906, broken only by a short administration of the Liberals, the Conservatives were constantly in power. The introduction of the Home Rule Bill had seriously split the Liberal party, and later, at the retire-ment of Mr. Gladstone, differences became still more marked. The dis-sentient Liberals called themselves Liberal-Unionists, and refused at first to co-operate with the Conservatives. The chief members of the second Salisbury administration were Lord Randolph Churchill, Sir Michael Hicks-Beach, and Mr. Balfour. The Liberal-Unionists, however, gradually became willing to accept office, and in 1887 Mr. Goschen succeeded Lord

Randolph Churchill as Chancellor of the Exchequer. In 1892 the Liberals succeeded to office, but after a second Home Rule Bill had been introduced and thrown out in the House of Lords, Mr. Gladstone definitely retired and was succeeded by Lord Rosebery. In 1895 the Conservatives again came into power, and the Liberal-Unionists formed a coalition with them, the Duke of Devonshire (Hartington), Lord Lansdowne, and Mr. Chamber-lain accepting office. Mr. Chamberlain quickly made a name for himself as Colonial Secretary. In 1899 the Boer War broke out and was concluded in 1902. In 1902, after the Conservatives had again been returned to power at the ' Khaki ' election (1900), Lord Salisbury died, and was succeeded by Mr. Balfour. During this administra-tion the highly controversial Educa-tion Act was introduced, and in 1903 Mr. Chamberlain put forward the Tariff Reform scheme which succeeded in breaking up the Conservative party and led to the overwhelming victory of the Liberals at the election of 1906. It is too early to comment on the measures of the Liberal adminis-trations which followed. Sir Henry Campbell-Bannerman formed the first administration, and was succeeded shortly before his death by Mr. Asquith (1908). The rejection of the Budget in 1909 by the House of Lords led to the introduction of the measure for the curtailment of the power of that House, and after a conference of the parties had failed, the Parliament Bill of 1911 was introduced and finally, after a great struggle, passed, since the Prime Minister obtained from the king a promise to create enough peers to swamp the Tory majority in the House of Lords if the Bill were thrown out. The Parliament Act pro-vides that the veto of the House of Lords shall only be suspensory, and at the end of three years from the first introduction of the Bill, provided that the Bill has been introduced three separate times in three separate sessions, it shall become law despite the action of the House of Lords. Since the passing of this Act the gov-ernment have introduced and passed through the Commons a Home Rule Bill and a Bill for the Disestablish-ment of the Church in Wales, both of which have been rejected by the Lords and reintroduced in the Commons.

Great Central Railway, was estab-lished in 1849 and was then known as the Manchester, Sheffield, and Lin-colnshire Railway. Until 1897 the line had no connection with London, and had to be dependent on other com-panies, particularly the Great North-ern, to distribute the enormous sup-plies of fish from Grimsby. This was

a very sore point, and in 1897 an extension was constructed from Annesley in Nottinghamshire to Quainton Road in Buckinghamshire, which enabled the company to bring its line to London by the Metropolitan Railway. After this it was known as the Great Central Railway, and its chief London station is at Maryle-bone. The main line runs to Rugby, Nottingham, Leicester, Sheffield, and Manchester, and the former main line from Manchester and Sheffield E. to Retford, thence serving Grimsby and Hull, with branches to Lincoln, etc.

Great Circle, or **Tangent, Sailing,** was known at least as early as the 16th century; for John Davies refers to it in his *Seaman's Secrets* (1594). A navigator who sails along the arc of a great circle reaches his destination by the shortest route. A 'great circle' on a sphere is one whose centre corre-sponds with the centre of that sphere; in the case of the earth the equator and all meridians are imaginary great circles. An amateur consulting the map of the world as it is erroneously represented on Mercator's projection, would naturally imagine that a ship's shortest course is along the 'rhumb' line, that is the straight line joining the two places concerned, more especially as the graph of the great circle, when plotted on such a map, must of necessity be represented by a curve. But this is not so. On Mercator's map the curve of the great circle will always come on the polar side of the rhumb line. This explains why the curved course is really the shorter: the difference of latitude is the same for the curved and for the straight tracks, but the former, being on a higher circle of latitude, has the advantage of shorter degrees of longi-tude. Thus the nearer the voyage is to the polar regions, the greater will be the difference between the tracks. As a matter of fact sailors cannot take advantage of this in the Arctic and Antarctic regions, as other conditions, such as the existence of ice, make navigation unsafe. Thus if they wish to go from Australia to the Cape of Good Hope, they must follow what is called a 'composite' great circle in order to avoid the dangerous lati-tudes. In place of the 'vertex,' that is, the point on the great circle track which is farthest from the equator, they must substitute the most southerly latitude they dare touch. In practice it is impossible to keep the vessel always along the great circle: what happens is that it is steered in a series of courses, which are, roughly speaking, tangents to that circle, and it therefore follows that the greater the number of those courses, or, in other words, the shorter

the tangents, the more nearly will the actual course approximate to the theoretical. Thus the ship is never headed direct for her destination till the latter is actually in sight, and traverses the meridians each time at different angles. A vessel steering a rhumb line crosses all meridians at practically the same angle. A rough means of discovering the great circle is to stretch a piece of string tightly between the places of arrival and departure on the earth's globe, and so locate a few points on the circle: an accurate measurement involves a knowledge of spherical trigono-metry.

Great Dane, The, a large dog which became popular in England about forty years ago. It is very muscular and strongly built, but its movements are easy and graceful. It is faithful and trustworthy, and when first intro-duced into England was a favourite companion of both ladies and gentle-men ; but when the order came into force commanding all dogs to be muzzled, this hound, having a will of its own, rebelled against being held in check, and being very strong, could not easily be kept under control, so had to be abandoned as a companion. It is now chiefly used as a show dog, but in the middle ages it was a sport-ing dog, and was employed to hunt the wild boar, and chase the deer, being very suitable for this owing to its great activity, muscular develop-ment, and power. It has been called by various names, 'German boar-hound,' 'Great Dane,' 'Ulmer Dog,' or 'German Dogge,' and some say it originated in Germany. Anyhow, it was very popular there, and Prince Bismarck had a G. D. as companion, and owned specimens for sixty years. One of his hounds, Tyras, is said to have attacked the Russian Prime Minister, Gortschakoff, when he was holding a spirited conversa-tion with his master. Tyras was slate coloured, a type very popular in Germany, but the recognised colours for the English show dog are bluish grey, red, black, pure white, or white with patches of colour. The dog has a long head, which it carries high, broad muzzle, blunt at the point, a large nose, small eyes deeply set, and very small ears. Its neck is rather long and well arched, the legs strong and straight terminating in large round feet. The tail is long and has a slight curl at the end, and its hair is very short. The dog should not be less than 30 in. in height, and its minimum weight should be 120 lbs.

Great Dividing Range, a mountain system in Australia, which extends from N. to S., near the E. coast, then turns W., terminating a little to the

E. of the western frontier of Victoria. The highest summit is 7349 ft.

Great Eastern, a great ship planned in 1852 by Brunel and Scott Russell, and which was the largest in existence at that time. It was completed at Millwall in 1857, and was originally intended for the route to Australia round the Cape. In 1859 the ship was launched, but an explosion took place off Hastings and a trip across the Atlantic had to be abandoned. In 1860 the vessel reached New York in eleven days, and from 1869 the G. E. laid some of the telegraph cables across the Atlantic. She was broken up in 1888.

Great Eastern Railway, founded in 1862 from the Eastern Counties Railway incorporated in 1836, started with a bad reputation. People sixty years ago were in the habit of ridiculing the Eastern counties and styled the railway ' the scapegoat of the companies '; indeed *Punch* making fun of the line remarks, ' On Wednesday last a respectably-dressed young man was seen to go to the Shoreditch terminus of the Eastern Counties Railway and deliberately take a ticket for Cambridge. No motive has been assigned for the rash act.' This reputation was extremely difficult to overcome, but Lord Salisbury championed the cause of the Great Eastern in 1867 when he was chairman, and the directors received a grant from parliament. After that time the company rapidly developed, and in 1891 a six - wheeled - coupled goods engine, weighing over 67 tons, was erected in the space of ten hours at the railway works at Stratford. The company also turned out the Sinclair single-wheel outside-cylinder passenger engine which took the late King Edward and Queen Alexandra to Sandringham on their wedding-day, as well as the ' Petrolea ' which pulls an express train practically without the help of coal. The line runs from Liverpool Street station to Cambridge, Peterborough, Newmarket, Ely, Norwich, Yarmouth, Lowestoft, and has a joint-line with the Great Northern from March to Lincoln and Doncaster; it also travels to Chelmsford, Colchester, Ipswich, and Harwich, and sends steamers from this port to the Hook of Holland, Rotterdam, Antwerp, etc. The company has a considerable traffic in coal; indeed carries anything in the shape of passengers and goods. It is essentially the workmen's railway, and when the Cheap Trains Act was passed in 1883 acted in a very generous way, and was pronounced by the London County Council in 1892 to be especially the workmen's London railway. It is significant that during the coal strike in England in 1912 the Great Eastern was one of the few railways which did not reduce its staff to a minimum.

Greater Punxsutawney, a bor. in the Jefferson co. of Pennsylvania, U.S.A., about 62 m. from Pittsburg. Coal is mined here. Pop. (1910) 9058.

Great Falls, a city in the Cascade co. of Montana, U.S.A., in the Missouri R., about 10 m. from the G. F. of the Missouri, from which it derives its name. It is in the centre of a rich mining district, and is an important shipping point for wool, live-stock, and cereals. Copper-smelting is carried on to a large extent. Pop. (1910) 13,948.

Great Fish Bay, an inlet of the Atlantic in Portuguese W. Africa, 20 m. long.

Great Fish River : 1. In Cape of Good Hope, rises in the Sneeuwbergen Mts., and enters the Indian Ocean after a course of 230 m. It is only navigable for small boats owing to the bar at its mouth. 2. Or **Back River**, in Canada, rises close to Lake Aylmer and flows into the Arctic Ocean. It has a wide estuary, and Montreal Island stands at its mouth, where relics of Sir John Franklin's expedition were discovered.

Great Grimsby, see GRIMSBY.

Great Harwood, an urban dist. in the Darwen parl. div. of Lancashire, about 3 m. from Accrington. There are collieries in the vicinity, and the manufacture of cotton is carried on. Pop. (1910) 13,817.

Greathead, James Henry (1844-96), a British engineer, born at Grahamstown in Cape Colony. He migrated to England in 1859, and became a pupil of Barlow, from whom he learned the shield system of tunnelling, which he made use of in the construction of the Thamés Tunnel. After this he devoted his time to the improvement of his ' shield,' and it was used in the tunnelling of the tube railway, now known as the City and South London. He was also engaged on the Waterloo and City, and the Central London Railways.

Great Kanawha, a river of N. Carolina, Virginia, and W. Virginia, U.S.A. Rising in the Blue Ridge, N. Carolina, in its upper course it is called the New R. The direction of its course is generally N.W., through ranges of the Alleghanies and along valleys, having a course of over 450 m., while the area of its basin is 10,800 sq. m. It eventually enters the Ohio at Mt. Pleasant, Mason co., W. Virginia, and is navigable for about 100 m. from its mouth.

Great Lakes, The, the fresh-water inland seas of Lakes Superior, Michigan, Huron, St. Clair, Erie, and

Ontario, lying between Canada and the U.S.A. They are drained by the St. Lawrence, which flows into the Atlantic, and are navigable for large vessels from the head of Lake Superior to Buffalo, at the foot of Lake Erie, a distance of 1024 m. S. of Lake Erie are large coalfields; round Lake Michigan and W. of Lake Superior are grain-growing plains, while both N. and S. of Lake Superior are the most extensive iron mines in the world. Wheat, too, is extensively grown, and all these products are shipped on the G. L. Fish of commercial value is also found; in Lakes Superior and Huron salmon-trout and white fish; in Lake Erie, white fish and sturgeon; while speckled trout is found in the R. Nipigon, and black bass in Georgian Bay. The greatest area of the lakes is 98,500 sq. m., and their elevation varies from 600 ft. (Lake Superior) to 250 ft. The difference of level between Montreal and Lake Ontario is overcome by a series of nine canals, with a length of 42 m. Between Lakes Ontario and Erie there is a drop of 326 ft. (167 ft. being at the Niagara Falls); the Welland canal overcomes this by twenty-seven locks in a course of 28 m. This canal once passed, the whole of Lakes Erie, Huron, and Michigan are accessible. Another canal between Huron and Ontario is being constructed (1913). The chief ports are Toronto, Chicago, Duluth, Milwaukee, Toledo, Detroit, Cleveland, Erie, Buffalo, Hamilton, and Kingston.

Great Marlow, *see* MARLOW.

Great Northern, The, forming with the North-Eastern and North British lines the ' East Coast ' express route between England and Scotland, was started in 1846, and owes its origin to the amalgamation of the London and York and Direct Northern Railways. It goes from London (King's Cross) to Peterborough, Doncaster, York, Darlington, Newcastle, Edinburgh, Perth, Aberdeen, and Inverness, and has numerous branches that serve London and the suburbs, that spread over the eastern counties and Yorkshire, that penetrate into Wales, and that go to Derby and across the country to Manchester and Liverpool. The company do a great traffic in agriculture and dairy produce, and also carry a quantity of coal, in fact ' carry anything from a queen to a blackbeetle.'

Great Northern and City Tube Railway, *see* LONDON TRAFFIC.

Great Northern, Piccadilly, and Brompton Tube Railway, *see* LONDON TRAFFIC.

Great Northern Railway of Ireland, one of the principal Irish railroads,

including the Dublin and Belfast Junction and the Ulster Railway (one of the oldest in the British Isles, opened 1839). The Dublin and Drogheda Railway was also amalgamated in 1875, four other lines being added the next year, and the whole being known as the Great Northern of Ireland Railway. It is conducted by methods closely resembling those of English railways. The total length is about 687½ m. (1913), and like most Irish railroads it has a gauge of 5 ft. 3 in. It serves the N. half of Leinster and much of Ulster. The main line runs from Dublin to Belfast; branches connect with Londonderry and Donegal *via* Armagh, Enniskillen, and Omagh. There are also branches to Dundalk, Drogheda, Navan, and Oldcastle from Dublin, and to Lisbon, Killebegs, and Ballyshannon from Belfast and Donegal. The Great Northern is half owner of the County Donegal Joint Railway. The company's capital (1913) is £8,485,702; expenditure 59 per cent. of total receipts. They own numerous passenger and goods' vehicles, 164 locomotives, several electric tramcars and steam rail motor-cars. The head office is at Dublin.

Great North of Scotland Railway, opened in 1846, has since absorbed several other lines. The main line runs from Aberdeen to the Highland Railway at Elgin, and at Boat of Garten Junction, Inverness-shire. It runs chiefly near the E. coast, branches connecting with Ballater, Peterhead, Fraserburgh, and Banff. The total length is about 331 m. The authorised capital is about £7,585,030, expenditure 51 per cent. of the total receipts (1913). The head office is at Aberdeen.

Great Ormes Head, a limestone headland of Wales, situated on the E. side of Conway Bay, N.E. Carnarvonshire. There are interesting ruins, and a 5½ m. marine drive; also a lighthouse, whose light is visible at 20 m.

Greatrakes, Valentine (c. 1629-83), the ' touch doctor,' born in co. Waterford, Ireland. He served as a soldier for some years, and was also for a time a magistrate. He believed himself to have the gift of curing the king's evil, and in 1666 published a *Brief Account* of himself and his cures.

Great Rift Valleys, a depression stretching from Palestine to Central Africa. These rift valleys have their origin in the valleys of the Jordan and Dead Sea, extend through the Red Sea, and from thence across French Somaliland and Abyssinia to Lake Rudolf. They then divide, one branch extending in a southerly direction through Lake Manyara, and the other in a westerly direction through the Albert Nyanza, and then taking a southerly course to Lake Tanganyika. These valleys are parallel cracks in the earth's crust, and in Central Africa have walls between 4000 and 5000 ft. above sea-level.

Great Salt Lake, in Utah, U.S.A., is 80 m. long and 32 m. broad, and has an area of from 2000 to 3000 sq. m. It lies 4218 ft. above sea-level, and is situated in the E. part of the Great Basin near the foot of the Wasatch Mts. The lake is from 10 to 50 ft. deep, but its depth, like its area, changes greatly. It is fed by the Bear, Ogden, Weber, and Jordan rivers, all of which are too small for navigation, but the lake has no outlet. Its waters contain chloride of sodium, chloride of magnesia, and sulphate of soda to a large extent, and the lake is a popular bathing resort; indeed, owing to the greatness of the specific gravity of the water the human body will not sink in it. The manufacture of salt is an important industry. Glauber's salt occurs in large quantities in some parts of the lake. Antelope Is., the largest island, is 18 m. long.

Great Seal of England, see SEAL.

Great Slave Lake, a large lake in Canada, in the North-West Territories, about 300 m. long and 60 m. wide. It has an area of 10,000 sq. m., and forms two large bays, McLeod's Bay in the N. and Christie's Bay in the S. It is connected with Artillery Lake, Clinton-Golden Lake, and Aylmer Lake, and the Mackenzie R. flows out from it on the W. It contains trout, salmon, and other fish.

Great Slave River, in the North-West Territories, Canada, flows from the W. of Lake Athabasca, and enters Great Slave Lake by a large delta. It is navigable for sea-going steamers to the rapids near Fort Smith, and above this for river steamers.

Great Southern and Western Railway of Ireland, one of the longest railways of Ireland, 1121 m. (1913). Originally established in 1844 to connect Dublin and Cashel, it now serves the S. of Leinster, all Munster, and part of Connaught. Branches connect with Cork, Waterford, Limerick, and Sligo. The company's capital is £14,453,601 (1913); expenditure, 60 per cent. of total receipts. The head office is at Kingsbridge, Dublin.

Great Western Railway, one of the first built of our lines, was opened from London to Bristol in 1841 at a cost of about five millions. It stretches from London to Bristol, goes down to Weymouth, and has a boat-service to the Channel Is. It also goes to Devonshire and Cornwall, striking away to Barnstaple on the W., to

Exeter and Torquay in the S., on to Plymouth, Falmouth, and Penzance, and by boat to the flower-growing Isles of Scilly. The great line, too, makes its way N. to Gloucester, Birmingham, Chester, Liverpool, and Manchester, and runs through S. Wales from Newport to Milford. The G.W.R. has always been active and enterprising, and even in its early days people always journeyed in comfort in the roomy carriages; and in spite of the broad-gauge line, and trains travelled at a good speed. An express ran from Paddington to Didcot, a distance of 53 m., in forty-eight minutes. The broad-gauge was abandoned in 1892, and the G.W.R. now holds the record for the longest run without stopping. The Plymouth Express goes from Paddington to Plymouth, a distance of 246 m., at the rate of 55 m. per hour.

Greaves, see ARMOUR.

Greaves, John (1602-52), an English mathematician, born in Hampshire. He was educated at Balliol College, Oxford, and in 1630 was appointed professor of geometry in Gresham College, London. He was a great traveller, and visited Egypt in 1637, and made a very accurate survey of the Pyramids, of which he published a description in 1646. He also collected manuscripts, especially those relating to astronomy, gems, medals, and other remains of antiquity. In 1643 he was appointed to the Savilian professorship of astronomy at Oxford, but was expelled from both this and the post at Gresham College in 1648 because he was a royalist.

HEAD OF GREAT CRESTED GREBE

Grebes, diving birds (Pygopodes) which usually frequent rivers and fresh-water lakes in the summer and the sea in the winter. They have broad, flat feet, and the toes are lobed, and bear separate membranes which are only joined at the base. The wings are short and rounded, and there is practically no tail. The legs are placed far back and the birds stand upright like the penguins. The best-known British species is the Little G. or Dabchick, which is found also in Scotland and Ireland. The

HEAD AND FOOT OF LITTLE GREBE

Great Crested G., the Red-necked G., the Horned G., and Black-necked G. are also found at definite seasons of the year. G. are useful for their plumage, but are so timid that they are extremely difficult to catch.

Grecian Architecture, see ARCHITECTURE—*Greece.*

Greece, a European kingdom situated in the S. extremity of the Balkan Peninsula. The Greeks of classical times called themselves Hellenes, and their country Hellas. But the appellation Hellenes, designating the inhabitants of the peninsula as opposed to Barbarians in general, is of a comparatively late origin. In the Homeric epos the Hellenes are a people of Phthiotis in S. Thessaly. The names Græci and Græcia, as universal names for the people and country of G., were solely used by the Romans, who extended to the whole country the name of the first tribe they encountered on the Greek mainland —the inhabitants of Dodona in Epirus. In its widest and loosest application, Hellas signified in ancient times the abode of the Hellenes, and thus embraced mainland and colonies alike. More specifically, Hellas was the land which, prior to the Macedonian conquests, lay S. of the Cambunian and Ceraunian Mts., and included the following districts: Epirus, Thessalia, Acarnania, Ætolia, Doris, Locris, Phocis, Bœotia, Attica, and Megaris (in N. Greece), and Corinthia, Sicyonia, Phliasia, Achaia, Elis, Messenia, Laconia, Cynuria, Argolis, and Arcadia (in S. Greece). The demarcation of the frontiers of the modern kingdom has been provocative of fierce and protracted contention. In July 1832, by the settlement concluded at Constantinople between Great Britain, France, Russia, and Turkey, the N. boundary line of G. was drawn from the Gulf of Arta to the Gulf of Volo. The Cyclades, the island of Eubœa, and the N. Sporades were included in the kingdom. Great Britain ceded the Ionian Islands in 1864. The proposal of the Berlin Conference in 1880 to transfer to G. Thessaly and S. Epirus was rejected by the Turks. In 1881 the boundary line was drawn from Platamona to Mts. Kritiri and Zygos, whence it followed the R. Arta to its mouth. A slight readjustment of the boundary was effected in 1897, by which G. ceded to Turkey about 578 sq. m. of her northern frontier lands. The decision of the Great Powers with regard to the allocation of land at the close of the contemporary war in the Balkan states will considerably affect Greek area and population. The limits of Albania, the fate of Crete and the Ægean Islands, and the status of Mount Athos have not yet been determined. The area of G. in 1908 was 24,400 sq. m. The population in 1907 was 2,631,952.

Physical features.— The character of the Hellenic race and the influence which it has exerted on the world's history have been conditioned to a great extent by the geographical configuration of the land, and its singular endowments. Occupying the most central position of the ancient world, G. enjoyed facile communication with the Orient and Occident. The islands of the Ægean and Ionian Seas were stepping-stones to maritime enterprise. Broken by innumerable harbours, creeks, and bays, the coast-line is phenomenal, its total length being out of all proportion to the area of the interior. The determining feature of the country is the mountain system. The great Pindus chain forms the backbone of Northern G., and its ramifications interlace the whole area. The mountains of Morea (Peloponnesus) are an independent system, and radiate in all directions from the central plateau of Arcadia. It is the partial submergence of these mountain systems that has produced the deep indentations of the coast-line of G. and the fringes of systematically grouped islands. The basis of these mountains is hard limestone, hence the precision of outline and the parallelism of the ridges. The nature of the drainage system is peculiar, owing to the unique character of the mountain system. The course of the rivers is short and torrential, and only the longer streams, such as the Alpheus, Peneios, and Spercheius, posses a perennial water supply. No river of G. is navigable. The mountains closely hem in the lake basins, from which the waters find no outlet, except by subterranean passages. G. in her early history was subject to severe volcanic action. In modern times visitations of earthquake are frequent.

Climate.—The mountains have also important effects on the climate, tempering the vehemence of the southern sun and aerating the country with refreshing breezes. The exceptional variety in elevation also effects rapid transitions from heat to cold. Spring in G. is a season of short duration. The Etesian winds blow steadily in early summer, but these delightful breezes are replaced later by the inclement blasts of the Sirocco. Autumn is humid and unhealthy, and accompanied in low-lying districts by visitations of malarial fever. Winter is crisp and temperate.

Flora.—The flora of G. is not so exuberant and varied as that of Italy and Syria. The geological structure, of which limestone and metamorphic marbles are the predominating features, is not favourable to rich vegetation. Four zones are usually recognised: (1) Below 1500 ft., olives, cypress, myrtle, oranges, dates, almonds, figs, poplar, tobacco, cotton, pomegranates, etc.; (2) Below 3500 ft. and above 1500 ft., forest zone, oak, chestnut, etc.; (3) Below 5500 ft. and above 3500 ft., the region of the beech and pine; (4) Above 5500 ft., Alpine zone, small shrubs and mosses.

Industry.—Agriculture is the staple industry of G. The chief products are wine, currants, olive oil, and tobacco. Sheep and goats are pastured in great numbers in the peninsula. Peasant proprietorship predominates. The celebrated mines at Laurion in Attica yield iron, manganese, lead, and zinc. Other mining products are magnesite, lignite, sulphur, alum, emery, and baryta. Marble is found in Paros, Attica, Thessaly, and the Cyclades.

History.—According to the Greek historians the earliest inhabitants of Hellas were the so-called Pelasgians, but the information afforded by the ancients on the subject is scant and vague. There is mention of the name Pelasgian in Homer, but it appears to be merely a tribal name designating the inhabitants of Thessaly, Epirus, and Crete. For our knowledge of the inhabitants and civilisation of pre-historic G., we are therefore dependent on the more certain witness of archaeology, and in recent years Greek archaeological evidence has been supplemented to a remarkable extent. Excavations at Cnossus in Crete have revealed to us the civilisation of the Minoan age of Greek history. This civilisation is the oldest of which we have knowledge. It flourished about 2000 B.C. Prehistoric Cnossus was a city of massive structure in which the fine arts flourished and had reached a remarkably high stage of development (specimens of Minoan pottery are of exceptional beauty and grace) and in which the art of writing was known. This last fact is of great importance as until recently the art of writing in G. was supposed to be post-Homeric. The next age of Greek civilisation on which archaeology has concentrated its searching light is the Mycenaean (*fl. c.* 1600-1100 B.C.). The Mycenaean civilisation is revealed to us by excavations in the sites of Mycenae, Tiryns, etc. The characteristic feature of these splendid cities is their massiveness and solidity. Pausanias relates that tradition attributed the building of Tiryns and Mycenae to the Cyclopes (hence the expression ' Cyclopean walls ' used to denote structures of this massive type), thus testifying to the gigantic edifices of prehistoric times as contrasted with the masonry of a later date. The jewellery, pottery, and weapons excavated from these ancient cities are of rare beauty. Iron was practically unknown in the Mycenaean age. Its use is more extensive in the Homeric age, and therefore Homeric civilisation is probably post-Mycenaean. But vast invasions swept over G., and a ruder civilisation displaced this early culture. In the latter half of the 11th century B.C. the Dorians ravaged G. They were a coarser, hardier stock than the peoples they conquered, but they brought to G. a new vigour and a new robustness, which when toned and harmonised by the finer influences of the land produced that civilisation which is the world's marvel for all time. These great migrations which swept over G. created a congestion of the population which was eventually relieved by widespread colonisation. The Æolian migrations established settlements in Lesbos, Tenedos, and the Mysian mainland. The Ionian migrations from N. Peloponnesus colonised Chios, Samos, the Cyclades, and the centre of the Lydian coast of Asia Minor. The Dorians also pushed their frontiers and occupied Crete, Melos, Rhodes, Cos, etc. During the 8th and 7th centuries B.C. great changes took place in Greek civilisation. Various communities became federalised and some states (notably Athens and Sparta) began to exert a formidable supremacy over neighbouring states. Religious union found expression in the institution of *Amphictyonies*, national games (*e.g.* the Olympian), and the pan-Hellenic dictatorship of the Oracles. Greek commerce began to out-rival Phoenician enterprise. In maritime activity the Corinthians were the foremost state. The Æginetan system of weights and measures was adopted, and the coinage of money was introduced from Lydia, two epoch-making innovations which are attributed to Pherdon, King of Argos (*c.* 748 B.C.). During this period monarchies were displaced in most states by oligarchies, which again were displaced by tyrannies. The constitution of Sparta developed by a unique process; it continued to be a monarchy but subordinated all interests to militarism. In the 6th century B.C. the waves of commercial and intellectual development among the Ionians reached its zenith and quickly receded. In the Greek mainland new economic evils appeared. The quick development of mercantile activity caused a violent displacement of occupations, and debtors suffered enslavement. As champions of these debtors the tyrants in most states first established their power. Thus, in Athens, Solon attempted to alleviate the distress of the citizens by his famous legislation (594-593 B.C.), but the real object of his life-work (the confirmation of the political freedom of the Athenians) was reversed when his relative, Peisistratus, just ruler though he was, established himself tyrant of Athens (561 B.C.). In 514 B.C., however, Harmodius and Aristogeiton freed the city of tyrant sway. Cleisthenes in 507 B.C., by an equable distribution of the people in tribes for voting purposes, paved the way for the great Athenian democracy. The 5th century B.C. was the most momentous period of Greek history, for during this period the East came into decisive conflict with the West for the dominion of the ancient world. At the beginning of the century the Ionians revolted from the 'Great King' Darius. This ill-organised revolt resulted in the destruction of Miletus and the subjection of the Asiatic Greeks by the Persians. Athens, being an Ionian city, had sent aid to her trans-Ægean kinsmen, and Darius resolved to punish Greek interference and make an example of the Athenian state. The Persian army destroyed Naxos and Eretria, but landing in Attica the ill-armed, ill-organised hosts of barbarians were no match for the little band of finely trained Attic hoplites, and the plain of Marathon

was strewn with the Persian hosts (490 B.C.). The palm of victory was won for Athens by the genius of her leader, Miltiades. Darius heard with consternation of the annihilation of his vast army. In the midst of his preparations for a second invasion the great king was cut off (485 B.C.). But Xerxes, his son, mustered soldiery from all parts of his extensive dominions, and the combined forces of the East were arrayed once more against the West. The overwhelming numbers of the barbarians terrified the Thessalians, Locrians, and Bœotians into offering earth and water as tokens of submission; but Athens and Sparta stood firm. A small force under Leonidas, King of Sparta, was despatched to guard the Pass of Thermopylæ, and kept the countless hosts at bay till, through the treachery of the miscreant Ephialtes, the little body of Spartans was surprised from the rear and was slaughtered to a man (480 B.C.). But it was the genius of Themistocles that saved G. and inspired Athens to seek her own safety and the safety of her country in her fleet. In the narrow Strait of Salamis the Greek fleet encountered the unwieldy ships of the Persians, and the defeat of the barbarians was so severe that Xerxes resolved to quit G., leaving Mardonius, his captain, to complete the campaign (480 B.C.). In the spring of 479 the Persians devastated Attica and razed Athens, but suffered decisive defeat at Platæa. In the summer of the same year the united fleets of Athens and Sparta destroyed the remnant of the Asiatic fleet at Mycale. Thus, by the sustained courage of Sparta and the altruistic intrepidity of the Athenians by land and by sea, the powers of the East were broken. By this war, as never before, G. learned her own potentialities, and her several states were forced to combine and recognise their true unity. The example of high moral calibre exhibited by the Greek leaders during the war became a great inspiration in the art and politics of G. The Greeks having expelled the Persian invaders, freed their kinsmen across the Ægean from subjugation to Persia, and received them into alliance. Pausanias, the Spartan victor of Platæa, at first commanded the combined fleets, but his deflection to 'Medism' aroused distrust and suspicion, and the command passed into the hands of the Athenians. In 477 B.C. Athens formed the Delian League, and the treasury of the allies was kept at Delos. The cities of the league were required to furnish ships or the equivalent in money towards the maintenance of the combined fleet. The formation of this allegiance was the nucleus of the Athenian empire. Sparta, meantime, still retained her position as leader of the Peloponnesian confederacy. Thus the Greek powers united by the common danger of the Persian invasion became divided through the antagonism of the rival confederacies for the supremacy. Within the city of Athens the tides of democracy were rising fast. Themistocles was the champion of this popular movement, first organised by the genius of Cleisthenes. The mantle of Cleisthenes had then fallen on the shoulders of Ephialtes, who diminished the ancient prestige of the Areopagus, the pillar of aristocracy. By the policy of Pericles this dictatorial court was robbed of all but nominal powers. By the removal of the confederate treasury to Athens and the appropriation of the funds for civic purposes, the relation of the Athenians towards their allies became avowedly autocratic. By the five years' peace (451 B.C.) and the thirty years' peace (446 B.C.) an attempt was made to defer the inevitable war with Sparta, but the peace policy miscarried and the conflagration burst forth in 431 B.C. During the period immediately preceding the war, when the reins of government were in the hands of Pericles, Athens reached the zenith of her literary and artistic glory. In the galaxy of great names, Æschylus, Sophocles, Euripides, Cratinus, Aristophanes, Pindar, and Pheidias shine supreme. The city beautiful was a veritable haunt of the Muses. The Peloponnesian War was not merely a decisive dual between two rival cities, it became a racial conflict between Ionians and Dorians, and a political conflict between democratic and oligarchic principles. It drained G. of her resources and left her weak and spiritless, an easy prey to the uncorrupted vigour of the barbarians. The war raged from 431 B.C. to 404 B.C. and terminated in the destruction of Athens. The chief causes which brought about the final disaster were the unscrupulousness and temerity of the popular leaders, among whom Alcibiades was chief offender, the Quixotic scheme of the Sicilian empire which resulted in the destruction of the Athenian armament, and the exhausting intestine strife which reached a climax in the outrages of the Four Hundred. The final victory of Sparta was due to an ignominious and traitorous allegiance with the Persian Cyrus. The destruction of the Long Walls of Athens and the surrender of her fleet (404 B.C.) were the final throes of her tragic fall. It was as champion of Greek freedom against the despotic presumptions of the 'tyrant' city that Sparta had won the confidence of her allies, but when at the close of the war she devoted her victory to private aggrandisement, the forces of disintegration began to act. A combination was formed during the succeeding decade to lay the power of Sparta low, but the efforts of the hostile coalition were abortive, in spite of assistance from the Persians, who overthrew Spartan naval supremacy at Cnidus (394 B.C.). Sparta, however, once more enlisted Persia among her supporters, and by the peace of Antalcidas became the supreme land power in G. But the price of the peace was the surrender of the cities on the Asiatic coast. The dominion, however, of Sparta was not destined to stand for long. Thebes suddenly, under her dauntless leader Epaminondas, confronted the Greek powers and irrevocably destroyed the Spartan supremacy at Leuctra (371 B.C.). The subversion of Sparta's ascendency was a fatal blow to the oligarchic governments of Greece, and democracies were re-established in many states. By the restoration of the Messenians Epaminondas further incapacitated Sparta. The domination of Thebes was for the moment indisputable, invincible. But the death of Epaminondas on the field of Mantinea (362 B.C.) left Thebes without a leader and opened the gates for the Macedonian invaders. Philip, King of Macedon, a barbarian, fired with the ideals of Hellenism and a staunch believer in militarism, having organised an army on his own 'phalanx' scheme, awaited an opportunity to interfere in the domestic variances of the rival Greek powers. As champion of the Delphic cause, he devastated Thessaly, sacked Olynthus, and overran Phocis. Bribing here, subduing there, he gradually won over the Greek states, and even the eloquence of Demosthenes could not avail to arrest the victor's progress. In 338 B.C. the victory of Chæronea made Philip the indisputable master of G. It is a strange irony of events that the unity of G., which the great Grecian powers, Athens, Sparta, and Thebes, had spilled their life-blood to create, was only realised by the sword of a semi-barbarian king, and at a time when the glory of the country's prime had irredeemably departed. As G. was exhausted as a field of military enterprise, Alexander, son and successor of Philip, resolved to devote his indefatigable energies to the conquest of the East. Having made an example of the recalcitration of Thebes, the Macedonian turned his back on G. and conquered the great Persian empire. He then penetrated into the heart of India, spreading effectually the language and civilisation of the Greeks over the conquered lands. His schemes were gigantic. He intended to follow up the subjugation of the East with the conquest of Italy, Carthage, and the further powers of the West. But death interrupted his victorious course. He died at Babylon 323 B.C., aged thirty-two. No successor was found competent to shoulder the responsibilities of his Olympian dominions, and his vast empire fell into disintegration. The Greek states, realising Macedonia's hour of weakness, made several attempts to reassert their independence. The revolt was headed by the Athenians and the Ætolians, but in 322 B.C. the insurgents sustained a decisive defeat at Crannon. Antipater, the Macedonian leader, changed the constitution of Athens to an oligarchy, and disfranchised and deported the poorer classes. Macedonia recovered her prestige under Antigonus Gonatus, who in the Chremonidean War (266-262 B.C.) once more subdued G. in spite of the formidable opposition of Athens and Sparta. The Achæan League, renewed in 281 B.C., became gradually enlarged and consolidated, its main object being the restoration of Greek independence. Under Aratus, the celebrated Sicyon general, Sicyon and Corinth were persuaded to join the league, which soon became the chief political power in G. But the league, now extending its power over Peloponnesus, came into collision with Sparta. A succession of victories over the league by Cleomenes, King of Sparta, prompted Aratus to invite Macedonian assistance, and thus the primary object of the combination was defeated. During the Social War the Achæan League was assisted by Philip V. of Macedon against the Ætolian League, but the wider interests of both parties at stake in the second Punic War called for a cessation of hostilities. Philip himself made a treaty with Hannibal (215 B.C.). Rome in revenge sowed seeds of dissension among Philip's Greek dependencies, and when Zama (202 B.C.) brought the second Punic War to a satisfactory close, she turned her attention to the Greek delinquents. Philip's forces were utterly crushed at Cynoscephalæ. Peace was made on generous terms, and the freedom of the Greek cities was proclaimed at the Isthmian games (194 B.C.). At the battle of Pydna (168 B.C.) Æmilius Paulus defeated Perseus, King of Macedon, and brought the Macedonian kingdom to an end. In 147 B.C. the Achæan League made an abortive attempt to throw off the Roman yoke, but Metellus defeated the Achæans at Scarphea, and Nummius, his successor, made a bitter example of Corinth, dismantling her glorious edifices and transporting her priceless treasures. The Roman administration in G. was, on the whole, tolerant and beneficial. Greek ascendency in thought and letters caused Rome to treat her dependency with exceptional leniency. Peace was, however, broken in 88 B.C. Mithridates, King of Pontus, incited Athens, Achaia, Bœotia, and Laconia to support him against Rome. Archelaus, Mithridates' general, was defeated by Sulla with immense loss at Chæronea, and Orchomenos (86 B.C.) and the Greek cities which conspired against Rome were treated with extreme severity. During the civil war between Cæsar and Pompey, the Athenians sided with Pompey, but when Pompey was finally vanquished, Cæsar treated his opponents with his characteristic clemency and generosity. Their gratitude was, however, short lived, for Athens affiliated herself to Brutus and Cassius, seeing in Cæsar's murderers champions of freedom comparable to her own heroes, Harmodius and Aristogeiton. During the struggle between Octavian and Antony, the Athenians offered their partisanship to Antony, and consequently the victorious Octavian ruled them with a firm hand. Not till the time of Vespasian, however, did the internal administration of Athens suffer fundamentally through Roman interferences, but that emperor deprived the Athenians of their gilded show of liberty and brought them under the iron rigidity of Roman institutions and law. Adrian, however, entertained a warm admiration and affection for the country, and made a generous attempt to restore the glory and splendour to the citadel of the muses, and revive its literary and artistic genius. But the work of vandalism had already begun. Incursions of the Goths swept over G., leaving destruction in their train, and the history of the Greek states becomes as shifting sand. In the 13th century Athens fell into the hands of Baldwin. Subsequently it was governed by Delves of the house of Aragon, and at his death it fell into the hands of Bajazet, Emperor of the Turks. It was afterwards held by the Spaniards and the Venetians, but in 1460 the peninsula was entirely subjugated by the Turks. The Venetians invaded G. towards the close of the 17th century, recovered Athens from the Turks, and occupied a considerable portion of the mainland and some of the islands. But the Venetian central power was not strong enough to maintain its control, and in 1718 G. passed once more under the Ottoman yoke. Peter the Great projected a campaign to free the oppressed states, but did not live to carry out his schemes. The assistance sent by Catherine was inadequate and ineffectual. The succession of Ali Pacha made the condition of the Greek people more hopeless than before. In 1814 a society of young Greek patriots, called the Hetairia, was formed at St. Petersburg. The objects of this society were ostensibly literary but were really political, and it was this society that was largely instrumental in fanning the flames of rebellion throughout G. In 1821 Jusuff Pacha defeated the insurgents at Galatz, and in the same year the sacred battalion, under the dauntless leader, Jordaki, was annihilated. But in the Morea the cause of freedom was attended with greater success. In September 1821, a constitution was formulated by the independent party at Missolonghi, applicable to Western Hellas; later a similar constitution was drafted at Salona, embracing the eastern states, and in December the constitution of Peloponnesus was framed. In 1823 a final constitution comprehending the whole of G. was adopted by the National Assembly convened at Astro. But the Ottoman powers made a desperate effort to annul the decrees, and in 1825 an Egyptian army, under Ibrahim Pasha, was despatched to the Morea. In a few months the work of the patriotic party was all but subverted, and only the combined intervention of European powers rescued the tottering standard of liberty. Ibrahim Pasha haughtily repudiated the claims of the Powers, and the crisis came when, in the decisive battle of Navarino (October 1827), the allies destroyed the Turkish and Egyptian fleet. By the protocol of 1830 G. was declared an independent kingdom and her boundaries were defined. The arrangement was in many respects unsatisfactory; it excluded Acarnania from Greek territory and a great part of Ætolia and Thessaly; a Turkish barrier interrupted communication between G. and the Ionian Islands, while Candia, Samos, etc., were not comprehended. The liberated state was at first governed by a national assembly, but the president, Count Capo D'Istrias, assumed autocratic powers, and sedition culminated in his assassination. Subsequently the Powers offered the throne of G. to Prince Leopold (after-

wards King of Belgium), but the offer was refused. The crown was then given to Otho, son of Louis I. of Bavaria. Throughout his reign discontent was rife, and an insurrection in 1862 resulted in the deposal of the king. George, second son of the King of Denmark, was then chosen king, and the Ionian Islands, at that time under British protection, were ceded unconditionally to the kingdom. By the Berlin Congress of 1878, G. was promised a modification of her frontier, and in 1881 a readjustment was accepted. Thessaly, S. of the northern watershed of the Salambria, was ceded to G. and the tract of land bordered by the Arta R. The allocation proved distasteful to the Hellenes, who demanded Crete, and hostilities commenced with Turkey in 1897. The war was short-lived, and was disastrous to the Greeks, and on the intervention of the Powers an armistice was concluded. By the Treaty of Constantinople, G. was constrained to pay an indemnity to submit to the readjustment of her frontier, and to accept the control of the Powers in financial affairs. In October 1912, war broke out in the Balkan states (see BALKAN WAR). The permanent effects on the Greek frontier, owing to the Hellenic participation in the victory over the Turks, are not yet determinable. The demarcation of the frontiers of the new kingdom of Albania, the allocation of Crete and the Ægean Islands, and the status of Salonica and Mt. Athos, all deeply affect Greek interests, and depend on the decision of the Great Powers, which will shortly be divulged. George, King of the Hellenes, was assassinated in Salonica by a maniac named Schinas in March 1913. The perpetrator of the crime subsequently committed suicide. The new ruler of G. is the late king's eldest son, who was proclaimed King Constantine XII.

Greek literature is conveniently divided into six periods, viz.: (1) Early literature, ceasing about 475 B.C., and embracing epic and lyric; (2) Attic literature, ceasing about 300 B.C., and including the development of drama and prose; (3) Alexandrian literature, ceasing about 146 B.C., and producing miscellaneous works of a learned and artificial type ; (4) Græco-Roman literature, ceasing about 529 A.D., and occupied mainly with critical and historical treatises ; (5) Byzantine literature, ceasing about 1453 A.D., and yielding principally scholastic works ; (6) Modern Greek literature, excelling chiefly in lyric and ballad.

Greek literature attained perfection in all its branches without extraneous influence, and therefore its history affords a unique study of the natural order and development of the divers species of poetic and prose composition. The first department of Greek letters to reach maturity was epic, which arose from selection and unification of loose ballads and folk songs. This branch of literature may be classified as objective and uncritical. Lyric came next in order of development. In theme it is distinguished by subjectiveness and emotional intenseness; in form it makes for artificiality and crystallisation. The lyric epoch was followed by the rise of the Greek drama. The Athenian drama was democratic and individualistic in outlook. In style its tendency was towards naturalness, and thus, while preserving the character of poetry, it assimilated some of the qualities of prose. Lastly, Greek prose developed, in style it advanced from the accidental rhythms of the early writers to the carefully systematised cadences and metrical graces of the later writers. While ancient Greek literature developed in many and divers directions it nevertheless maintained throughout its entire career certain characteristics which reflect the distinctive genius of the Greeks as a nation apart from all other nations. As in her art and in her ethics, the keynote of the literature of G. is beauty and power in restraint. This moderation which is to be carefully distinguished from mediocrity is an essential feature of the 'classical spirit.' True Greek chastity never permitted in artistic conceptions the intrusion of sentimentality, effusiveness, and superelaboration. There is always perfect harmony and balance in thought and expression, in content and form.

The great epics of G. are the *Iliad* and the *Odyssey*, whose authorship is traditionally attributed to the blind bard Homer, and which were composed about 900 B.C. In 18th century criticism the unity of the Homeric authorship was called into dispute, and a highly composite authorship was assumed. The limits of this article prohibit a detailed discussion of the Homeric question, and it must suffice to say that the *Iliad* and the *Odyssey* were undoubtedly inspired by the folk songs of the ballad epoch, and that their respective unity of thought and perfection of structure compel us to admit that each must have taken its final form from the magic hand of a great poet. The wellspring of the poems is a cycle of ancient Achæan ballads. The Æolic bards of Asia Minor transfigured and transformed these rude songs, but their final form bears the impress of

Ionic genius. The poems are written in hexameter verses, a metre of unknown antiquity, and occurring in most ancient Delphic oracular responses. The so-called 'cyclic poems' continue the epic history. They complete the story of Troy, but are inferior in conception and design in the Homeric epos.

The poems of Hesiod (*fl. c.* 735 B.C.), the next great poet in the history of Greek literature, form a striking contrast in subject and treatment to the Homeric epics. The Homeric heroes seem almost to enjoy participation in the blithe life of the gods; the atmosphere is clear, the prospect luminous. The hand of fate does indeed loom over gods and man, but the inevitable decrees are accepted with calm and unperturbed submission. But in Hesiod the world is rough and rugged, and the heavens are afar off. Nature is a hard task-mistress demanding of man toil unceasing. Hesiod's gospel is veritably a gospel of work. Xenophanes, Parmenides, and Empedocles, the early natural philosophers, continued the tradition of didactic poetry.

The so-called Homeric hymns do not synchronise with the composition of the *Iliad* and *Odyssey*. They belong to the 6th century, and are probably preludes which were sung by rhapsodists at the recitals of the Homeric epics at the Panathenæa.

Greek lyric, like Greek epic and Greek philosophy, was primarily the inspiration of the Greek colonists of Asia Minor, the period of colonisation being marked with phenomenal activity in all spheres of thought and action. The chief lyric species were elegiac and iambic. The distinguishing feature of Greek elegiac verse is its universal range of application. Thus Callinus (690 B.C.) and Tyrtæus (640 B.C.) adapt it to martial themes, Mimnermus (620 B.C.) to erotic, Solon (600 B.C.) and Theognis (550 B.C.) to gnomic, and Archilochus (690 B.C.) and Simonides (530 B.C.) to funereal. Iambic verse approximates more closely to a colloquial form, and hence is best adapted to a satiric and controversial vein. The instrumental accompaniment which had originally been indispensable to elegiac and iambic verse gradually fell into disuse and melic verse (or verse inseparable from an instrumental accompaniment) was represented by two new orders, viz. Æolian and Dorian. The Æolian mode was monodic and personal; the Dorian was choral and civic. The greatest achievements in Æolian verse were attained by Sappho; her poetry excels in intensity of passion and beauty of melody. Unsurpassed in the Dorian mode is Pindar, whose odes are inimitable in majesty of thought and grandeur of expression.

Tragedy was gradually differentiated from the dithyramb, a triumphant hymn to Dionysus. Arion and Stesichorus are shadowy names in the early history of the dithyrambic chorus, but the name of Thespis brings us to the fringe of history. Thespis first introduced an actor or answerer (ὑποκριτής), and thus dialogue between the leader of the chorus and the actor was now effectuated. Phrynicus, author of the historical plays, the *Capture of Miletus* and the *Phœnissæ*, employed without alteration the dramatic framework invented by Thespis, and no further innovation was made till the daring genius of Æschylus (b. 525 B.C.) startled the Athenian audiences. According to Aristotle (*Poetics*, iv. 13), ' Æschylus first introduced a second actor; he reduced the importance of the chorus and apportioned the principal part in the dialogue.' This new departure, providing two actors in addition to the leader of the chorus, enabled the dialogue to become more complex, for an actor might take more than one rôle. The leading thoughts in the great drama of Æschylus are bold and emphatic. There is a power manifest in the universe which makes for righteousness, and by putting himself in harmony with its tendencies man wins his happiness. Through suffering man learns the will of the gods, but an insolent and overbearing attitude brings sorrow even unto the third and fourth generation. To Sophocles (b. 496 B.C.), a younger contemporary of Æschylus, are also ascribed technical improvements in the production and construction of tragedy. Tradition attributes to him the introduction of a third actor, and the invention of scene painting. The motive idea in the tragedies of Sophocles is less vast than the motive idea in the tragedies of Æschylus. The chief interest in the dramas of Æschylus is in the ultimate and universal problems; the central issue in the dramas of Sophocles is concerned with individual ethics and psychology. In the elder tragedian man is engaged in a titanic struggle with destiny; the religious conceptions of the younger dramatists have ripened to a mellower loveliness. With the third of the great tragic writers of Athens the dramatic atmosphere has quite altered. The sublime elevation and stately repose have vanished before the ferment of moral perplexity and religious doubt. The aim of Euripides is occasional effect rather than sustained excellence.

Emasculate sentiment and tempestuous passion refract the clear rays of spirituality. Instead of the natural being transformed into the supernatural, the supernatural is transformed into the natural. There is discord in the plays of Euripides, a discord between character and environment, between rationalistic thought and mythical setting, between the movement of the plot and the function of the chorus. These are faults of a transition period, for Euripides was too far in advance of his age to harmonise his thoughts with its artistic conventions. But in his humanity Euripides reaches heights undreamed of by his great predecessors. He sympathises with the slave, the barbarian, and the weak. His portraiture of women is characterised by a tenderness and sympathy that are strangely modern. In the *Alcestis* he abandons the dramatic traditions and introduces lisping children into his tragedy. If the Euripidean drama, as a whole, is unequal, unsymmetrical, there are, nevertheless, passages whose loveliness and beauty are unapproached by anything in Greek literature.

Greek comedy like Greek tragedy had its origin in the cult of Dionysus. The occasion of harvest thanksgiving gave rise in extempore farces, which in due time took literary shape. Aristotle in the *Poetics* says that comedy sprung from the phallic choruses of these festivals. Such choruses were probably abusive and derisive, and were directed against such personages as were conspicuous enough to excite the interest of the assemblage. The temperament of the Sicilians was especially conducive to the development of comedy, and in Sicily comedy first reached literary excellence and acquired permanent value. Epicharmus of Cos (b. c. 535 B.C.) was the greatest of the early Sicilian comedians. The earlier writers had produced the comedy of situation, but Epicharmus created comedy of plot and character. Political satire is, however, absent from Sicilian comedy, which ridicules the type rather than the man. The chorus is altogether absent. Attic comedy is divided into three divisions: the Old, the Middle, and the New. The Old Comedy flourished from 450 to 390 B.C., and was characterised by broad and undisguised raillery of contemporary events and living personages. It was a product of the political independence and fearlessness of the Athenian democracy. When the democratic constitution of Athens was annulled comedy ceased to be personal. Middle Comedy flourished from 390 to 320 B.C. It satirises movements and factions, but personal satire has practically disappeared. Philosophy, literature, and other contemporary arts are caricatured. In this type of comedy the chorus has practically disappeared. The New Comedy flourished from 320 to 250 B.C. It is distinctly a comedy of manners and character ; domestic intrigue takes the place of political situation, and the ' sock ' is worn by the man in the street instead of the statesman. Aristophanes far eclipses contemporary writers of the Old Comedy. His belief in the high calling of his art saved him from the grotesqueness and coarseness which before his time seemed inseparable from comedy. He was, above all, a patriot, and it is his pride in the ancient institutions of history of his country that impels him to use his ridicule as a scourge against adventitious experiments and innovations in civil government and morality. Conservative in his ethics he vehemently attacks the disquieting influence and negative teaching of the Sophists. Socrates' intellectual and philosophical empirics he regarded as a public danger worthy of reprobation and exposure. The charm of his style is unrivalled, except in the Attic idiom of the dialogues of Plato. But Aristophanes is a poet as well as a comedian. Passages of exquisite beauty and sentiment are intermingled with the mockery and the raillery. The gradations of the transition to the Middle Comedy are not clearly defined. In some of the plays of Aristophanes the political licence and overt criticism are already abandoned. Thus in the *Plutus* he discards concrete censorship, and adopts symbolical farce. For examples of the New Comedy we were for long dependent on the Latin imitations of Terence, but the recently discovered fragments of Menander now put within our reach a representative body of that dramatist's original work. Menander excels in his delicate delineation of character, the subtle construction of his plot and the consummate chastity of his idiom.

Greek prose, as is the natural course of things, attained complete development at a much later date than Greek poetry. The earliest examples of prose in G. belong to the 6th century B.C., and these are chiefly records and chronicles quite unpretentious with regard to style and expression. The Ionian philosophers made considerable advances, but their aim also was mainly didactic, and where style is studied it is in the interests of lucidity. Herodotus, the historian (b. 484 B.C.), is the first conscious prose stylist. The structure of

his history is almost dramatic. His inspiration was the momentous drama of the Persian wars. He traces the conflict of the East and West up to its great crisis, marking the intricate chain of cause and effect with insight worthy of an evolutionist, but he abandons the rôle of critical and scientific historian in his acceptance and narration of legends whose value is purely dramatic and artistic. It is the unity of his design and the dramatic graphicness of his narrative that won Herodotus the title of 'the Homer of historians.' In the architecture of his sentences Herodotus adopted the loose style. Thucydides, the next great writer of Greek history after Herodotus, is a contrast to his predecessor, both in conception and design. The field of Thucydides' activity is the Peloponnesian War. He wrote when G. was no longer self-assured and buoyant in her national glory and victory. She was torn by intestine strife, and the sport of unprincipled statesmen and generals. The scene presented much food for reflection and moralisation. The history of Thucydides is no heroic epos. Incisive, sedulous, judicial, the genius of Thucydides as a pure historian is undeniable. He makes no parley whatever with seductive legends and traditions irreconcilable with a calmer rationality. He sifted evidence meticulously, and indefatigably consulted all available documents relative to his subject. Only in his speeches did he allow himself freedom. These he meant to be true to the spirit and not to the letter. His style, too, is illustrative of his mental character. He builds his sentences on the periodic system, lucid, pregnant, and severe. His idiom is pure and unadulterated Attic. Xenophon (b. c. 429 B.C.) was essentially a man of action. He therefore excels in brilliancy, vividness, and freshness, but both in intellectuality and style he falls far below the level of Thucydides. His finest work is perhaps the *Anabasis;* racy, virile, dramatic, the narrative compels interest, but it is not trustworthy nor convincing. Political economist, historian, philosopher, the range of Xenophon's activities is wide, but he is lacking in intellectual power and thoroughness. As a stylist Plato is as great a stylist as he is a philosopher, and praise can go no higher. Richness without satiety, grace without elaborateness, and charm without conceit make the dialogues of Plato models of literary excellence for all time.

Though eloquence was appreciated and cultivated in G. as far back as the time of Homer, oratory as a science and art was only first formulated at the time of the Peloponnesian war. The chief reason for the lateness of the development of the rhetorical art is that oratory depends on the study and cultivation of prose composition, and prose composition itself attained literary merit in G. at a much later period than poetry. It was in Sicily that the first treatises on rhetoric were written, the demand for such systems being caused by the need of effective speech in the innumerable law-suits which arose during the re-distribution of land on the overthrow of the Syracusan tyranny. Corax and Tisias were the earliest of the Sicilian rhetoricians, but their theories were rudimentary, consisting chiefly in the differentiation of the various parts of a speech. The argument from pro-bability had a conspicuous place in their evidence. Gorgias of Leontini, sent from his native city in 427 B.C. as an ambassador to Athens, attracted the admiration of the Athenian audiences by the splendour and brilliancy of his oratory, and hence the art was transplanted to Attic soil. The style of Gorgias was distinguished by its floridness and luxuriance. The Alexandrian critics selected ten Attic orators as being of the foremost rank. Each orator exemplified a peculiar excellence in style. The perfect harmony and balance of all the ex-cellences of style was attained by Demosthenes, the greatest of the Attic orators, who blends perfectly the virtues of his predecessors and reproduces none of their excesses. But the secret of Demosthenes' enormous power of eloquence was a moral force generated from the soul and quickening to vital potency the technical graces and devices which he commanded. Alexander, after the sack of Thebes, demanded the sur-render of the Athenian orators, and Greek liberty and Greek oratory perished side by side. Robbed of its political significance oratory in the Macedonian age degenerated into declamation, and style into ornament. Asiatic affectation conquered Attic purity.

But the victories of Alexander diffused Greek letters and Greek culture over half the world. Greek became the ' common tongue,' and thus the spread of Christianity was facilitated by the victories of the pagan sword. It was in Egypt that the scattered Hellenic seeds produced the most exuberant growth. Alex-andria became the capital of the intel-lectual world. But the new Greek literature was vastly different from the autochthonous literature of free G. The spirit of Alexandrianism was cosmopolitan and not patriotic. The promoters of the new literature were

courtiers and grammarians, and their work is characterised by learning and artificiality. Genuine inspiration and high seriousness are lacking in the poetry of Apollonius, Rhodius, Aratus, Lycophron, and Callimachus. But the Sicilian Theocritus (fl. 270 B.C.), although enticed to the Alexandrian court by the lavish patronage of Ptolemy Philadelphus, never lost the freshness and warmth of sentiment that the rural surroundings of his youth had inspired. His idylls of Sicilian pastoral life are representa-tions of genuine rustic character and incident, and are clothed in the rich sweetness and charming simplicity of the Doric idiom. Moschus (fl. c. 150 B.C.) and Bion (fl. c. 100 B.C.) con-tinued the pastoral tradition at Alex-andria, but though their elegies excel in grace and delicacy, in naïveté and spontaneity, they pale before the Theocritan idyll.

When compared with the noon-day splendour and effulgence of the litera-ture of free G., the afterglow that lingered during the Græco-Roman period seems pale and crepuscular. But though the Græco-Roman period produced no literary work of the highest merit, it nevertheless gave proof of a vigorous intellectual activity, which is all the more re-markable in face of the crucial national calamities. The historian Polybius (b. c. 204 B.C.), in spite of the immense scope of his work and the wide field of his activities, is a sane and reliable thinker, and the style of his *General History* was much admired, though it exemplified post-classical innovations in vocabulary and phraseology. Plutarch's *Lives* will live on account of its dramatic and atmospheric power. The wit and satire of Lucian are always lively and refreshing. Longinus' work (*On the Sublime*) shows a singular apprecia-tion of beauty and keenness of critical insight.

The Byzantine literature was purely retrospective, and produced nothing of permanent value. Among the Byzantine historians are Procopius (fl. 550 A.D.), Porphyrogenitus (fl. 940 A.D.), Zonaras (fl. 1120 A.D.), and Critobulus (fl. 1450 A.D.). The most famous critics of Byzantium were Photius (fl. 850 A.D.), Suidas (fl. 950 A.D.), and Eustathius (fl. 1170 A.D.).

Neo-Hellenic poetry is chiefly bucolic. The first poet writing in modern Greek who attained literary eminence was Theodorus Prodromus (fl. 1200 A.D.). Drimiticos (fl. 1625 A.D.) wrote a pastoral entitled *The Fair Shepherdess*, which contains passages of touching beauty. In 1824 Fauriel made his famous collection of modern Greek ballads. These spirited ballads deal for the most part with the Klephts, who so heroically raised the standard of Greek independence. In more recent times the patriotic lyrics of Rhigas captivated the ears of Byron. The amorous Anacreontics of Christopoulous have considerable charm and beauty. The brothers Soutsos show considerable lyric power. Rangaris is, perhaps, the greatest of modern Greek lyricists. The lyrics of Calvos and Salomos are graceful, but slight.

Greek philosophy originated in the Ionian colonies of the East. The cults of the Greek mainland were essentially local, and so the early colonists left their gods behind them in the motherland, and settled in their new home with minds free for speculative inquiry. The Ionian philosophers of the 6th century B.C., were principally physicists and cosmologists. They sought to reduce the universe to a first principle, or single element. Thus Thales postulated that the origin of all things was water. Anaximander took for his first principle ' the infinite,' which he conceived as being intermediate between the elements. Anaximines selected air as the primary substance, from which he held the universe was evolved by the processes of rarefaction and condensation. Heracleitus, the last of the Ionian school, adopted fire as his basic element. He was also the originator of the theory that the universe is in perpetual flux. The philosophical teachings of Pythagoras of Samos were of a psychological and religious character. The theory of numbers played an important part in the Pythagorean doctrines. Harmony was built on numbers, and was, according to Pythagoras, the key to the universe. Among the religious tenets of the sect the doctrine of metempsychosis had a foremost place, and inspired the brotherhood to observe a life of religious asceticism. The Pythagorean philosophy was largely influenced by the Orphic mysteries, in which immortality and spiritual purification were the leading ideas. Xenophanes was the founder of the Eleatic school. He was the first Greek rationalist, boldly attacking the uncompromising anthropomorphism of the Greek Pantheon. His theory of the universe is based on ' the one ' as opposed to ' the many,' *i.e.* on an essential unity as opposed to an essential plurality. Parmenides is the author of the apothegm, ' The " ent " (ὄν) is, the " nonent " (μὴ ὄν) is not.' He identifies the ' ent ' with truth, knowledge, and the ' one.' His disciple Zeno, to disprove ' the many,' invented some famous paradoxical arguments relative to space and time.

A reaction followed in favour of ' the many ' as opposed to ' the one.' Empedocles held that the evolution of the universe was conditioned by the segregation and aggregation of the four elements under the influences of hate and love. Anaxagoras postulated ' atoms ' and a ' governing mind.' Democritus and the atomists conceived the universal as generated from atoms falling in space. They postulated the power of deflection in the atom, and hence made aggregation possible.

The sophistry of the humanists was a complete reaction from the natural philosophy of the physicists. In the teachings of the new school the macrocosm was of secondary importance as compared to the microcosm. Though the Greek sophists had no doctrine in common, they all based their speculations on an initial scepticism. Their influence was negative, rather than positive, and destructive rather than constructive. The famous aphorism of Protagoras is characteristic of the sophists' mode of thought —' Man is the measure of all things, of what is, that it is, and of what is not, that it is not.' The empirics of the sophists did not immediately benefit Greek thought and morality, but they paved the way for the advent of Socrates.

Though Socrates is justly called the father of critical philosophy, he never committed his doctrines to writing. Our knowledge of his theories and principles is derived from two of his disciples—Xenophon and Plato. Formerly Xenophon was regarded as the more trustworthy authority, but in recent years there is evidence of a reaction in favour of Plato. Socrates followed the sophists in basing his theories on a primary scepticism or agnosticism; he was also at one with the sophists in applying empiricism as a final infallible test to all theories. The dialectical method of philosophical inquiry was the invention of Socrates. He himself assumed ignorance, and by deferential interrogation he elicited from some bystander an opinion on the subject he wished to investigate. Starting with this dogmatic assertion of the respondent, he proceeded by a systematic series of questions and answers to lead his victim up to a consequence inconsistent with his primary proposition. This was the so-called ἔλεγχος, or destructive process; the false opinion has been swept away, and the mind is now unprejudiced for the receipt of a substitute. The new opinion was reached by induction, from the respondent's admissions in a fresh series of interrogations. Most often the object of this philosophical research was a definition, and the mass of definitions attained formed Socrates' ethical system. Virtue, he held, consisted in the knowledge of such definitions and opinions, for right action, he conceived, was the logical consequence of right knowledge. Virtue is knowledge and knowledge is the 'good.' The proof and justification of these Socratic axioms were found in utility.

Until recently the doctrines of Plato were treated as a reaction from, rather than a development of, those of his master Socrates. Plato was regarded as a pure idealist, and Socrates was classified as an uncompromising empiricist. The great point of departure was the Platonic theory of ideas. But critics are veering round. The extremists not only find in the Socratic final definition an adumbration of the Platonic theory of final ideas but also credit Socrates with the full-fledged theory. Thus the modern tendency is to emphasise Socrates' indebtedness to the abstractions of the Pythagoreans rather than his indebtedness to the empirics of the sophists. But be that as it may, the ideal theory is chiefly associated with Plato's expositions. The Platonic hypothesis is, briefly, that transcending the plural phenomena which are mutable, imperfect, temporal, generated, and opined there are single ideas which are immutable, perfect, eternal, ungenerated, and known. Beyond the ideas is the idea of ideas, the 'supreme good.' The ideal life is the philosophical life of approximation to, and contemplation of, the ideas. The soul is akin to the eternal ideas ; the body is related to the ephemeral phenomena.

Aristotle bodily rejects Plato's theory of ideas. His philosophy is inductive. According to Aristotelian conceptions, it is the species which exists and can be known. From the species his metaphysical and transcendental hypotheses are derived. Aristotle's system of ethics is based on empiricism. Man's chief end is the attainment of true happiness, and happiness consists in an energy of the soul, which accords to virtue. Virtue is of two grades, moral and intellectual. Moral virtue is attained when man's rational being correctly governs this appetitive and emotional being. The prime virtues are nine, of which seven are moral and two are intellectual. The moral virtues are courage, temperance, liberality, munificence, magnanimity, self-respect, gentleness, justice. These virtues are really ' means ' between immoral ' extremes,' e.g. courage is a mean between rashness on the one hand and cowardice on the other.

Towards the attainment of these virtues a sufficiency of the world's goods contributes. The intellectual virtues are judgment and wisdom. The highest life consists in the exercise of the intellectual virtues, and is the philosophical life of contemplation. The moral life consists in social action, and is inferior only to the contemplative life.

The Academic school founded by Plato and the Peripatetic school founded by Aristotle are the principal philosophical orders of G. The minor schools which arose diverged from the two rival systems, and became extravagantly metaphysical or extravagantly material.

Epicurus dismissed the abstractions of the speculative idealist, and founded a new philosophy on the sensations of the practical materialist. The senses were regarded as infallible, and the chief good in life was happiness. But happiness is of two kinds. There is exciting carnal pleasure, and there is also tranquil mental pleasure. The latter Epicurus pronounced supreme. In his theory of the universe Epicurus revived the atomism of Democritus. All that is is corporeal and composed of atoms ; soul itself is but a harmonious combination of finest atoms.

The Stoic school was founded by Zeno ; its doctrines are largely eclectic. Antisthenes, an immediate follower of Socrates, had founded the Cynic school, whose chief aim was an austere asceticism. The Cynics taught that virtue was alone worthy, and happiness was madness. A minimum of the world's goods was essential for the practice of the virtuous life. These tenets Zeno at first embraced, but latterly modified with views borrowed from various antithetical systems. The Stoic doctrines gravitated round two central and corresponding ideas—the unity of the macrocosm, or universe, and the unity of the microcosm, or man. The macrocosm was conceived as a living organism, governed by intelligence, which underwent transformation from, and reabsorption into, its primitive substance or being. The microcosm also is governed by intelligence, survives death, and attains thereby true being. The basis of Stoic ethics is harmony between the microcosm and the macrocosm. Such harmony is attainable by man when he leads a life of moral virtue. There are no gradations between good and evil. The ideal man of the Stoic philosophy is self-sufficient, free, misled neither by error nor emotion, and in no wise inferior to a god. But while the Stoics emphasised self-sufficiency, they did not neglect the duties of social life. All men, whether Greek or barbarian, bond or free, were citizens of the world-city of God. The humanity inspired by these doctrines tempered the exclusiveness and rigidity of Greek patriotism, and brought comfort during the stress of national calamities. Stoicism was in complete harmony with the finer Roman ideals. Its most beautiful and noble interpretation is the book of *Meditations* by the Roman emperor, Marcus Aurelius. Throughout the empire's long nights of blackness it was the one spiritual lamp that burned steadily upwards.

Greek art is conveniently considered under three heads: painting, architecture, and sculpture. The architectural and sculptural remains are considerable and representative, but extant examples of painting are scant, and, for the most part, belong to the periods of immaturity and decline. Specimens of Greek vase-painting are, however, plentiful, but they possess the disadvantage of giving us no adequate idea of the development of the use of colours. Excavations in Cnossus and Mycenæ have revealed examples of Greek vase-painting which belong to the millennium 2000-1000 B.C. The vases are exceedingly beautiful in shape, and the painting is of a very vigorous and free type. There are some examples of geometrical and conventional designs, but the finest specimens exhibit free drawings of plants, animals, and human figures, which can bear comparison with the most beautiful products of the Hellenistic age. The Dorian conquests checked the development of Mycenæan or pre-historic Greek art, and the art of vase-painting was arrested with the sister arts. The earliest specimens of Attic art are of the geometric type; the figures are rigid and the balance is laboured. Prior to the 6th century B.C. light red clay was used and the figures were painted in rich black glaze. Lines of physiological and ornamental detail were incised on the black with a fine point. Other colours were frequently superimposed after the firing of the black—notably white and purple. But the effect of these black silhouettes on the light background was always grotesque, and not seldom ludicrous. In the 6th century B.C. a complete reversal of this arrangement was effected. The figures were left in the light ground-colour, and the background was superimposed in black glaze. Details in the figures were then drawn in fine lines of glaze. The red-figure vases comprise the most beautiful specimens of Attic vase painting. In the period of the decline white

washes were frequent in the red-figure vases, and simplicity of design was abandoned for elaborate detail. Our knowledge of Greek mural and easel painting is mainly derived from critical comments scattered through classical authors. There are, indeed, extant specimens of Greek prehistoric wall-painting found at Mycenæ and Cnossus, and, like the vase-painting of the same period, they show a remarkable beauty of conception and freedom in execution. Polygnotus was the first great Athenian mural painter. He flourished during the inspiring epochs of the Persian wars. He is especially commended for his treatment of human expression, and his skill in representing drapery. At the close of the 5th century, mural painting was succeeded by easel painting. Perspective was studied more carefully by the younger school, and the effect aimed at was emotional and sentimental. Zeuxis is the representative painter of the period. He was most successful in his delineation of the female figure, especially in the nude. The ' Helen ' of Zeuxis in the temple of Hera at Croton, was his most perfect achievement. The Attic school was characterised by its free naturalness, and the representative names are Euphranor and Nicias. Apelles, the greatest of all the ancient painters belonged to the Ionic school, and flourished about 350 B.C. His works were chiefly portrait paintings—a new departure in Greek art, which flourished under Macedonian court patronage. The ideal element entered into his portraiture, through the addition to his subject of mythological or symbolical motives. Thus he painted equestrian portraits of Alexander the Great, in company with the Dioscuri, and leading War in chains behind him. His most famous picture was, however, a mythological subject entitled ' Aphrodite Anadyomene.' It represented the goddess in the nude, rising from the sea and wringing the water from her hair. The descriptions of this picture give us some conception of that peculiar ' charm ' by which the ancients characterised the works of Apelles. In conception sentimentality and in treatment superelaboration vitiate the art of the decline; in subject genre paintings predominate.

Prehistoric Greek architecture, as revealed to us by excavations in Cnossus, Mycenæ, Tiryns, and Troy, was of a very massive and substantial type. A characteristic feature was the so-called ' Cyclopean walls ' whose giant structure the imagination of the ancients attributed to the Cyclopes. The stone walls of domestic buildings in these sites only reached an elevation of a few feet, the superstructures consisting of wood and cement work. The column had already differentiated itself in Mycenæan architecture.

Mycenæan civilisation disappeared during the general upheaval that followed the Dorian invasion. With these Dorian invaders is connected the differentiation of the Doric order in Greek architecture, one of the three characteristic architectural orders of G. The column is the distinguishing feature of these orders, and was itself, no doubt, evolved from the tree-trunk props of primitive structures. In G. the column was fluted and tapered slightly upwards, thus producing the combined effect of stability and grace. The Doric column is the boldest, simplest, and most impressive. The fluted shaft rests directly on the foundation step or floor with no intervening base, and is capped by a simple square abacus. In the noble beauty and perfect proportions of the Parthenon at Athens, the Doric order finds its most sublime expression. The architecture of the Ionic order gains in delicacy, but loses in sublimity. The shaft of the Ionic column is also fluted, but the flutes, being separated by flat fillets, do not intersect, as in the Doric pattern. The shaft rests on a plinth or base, and culminates in the characteristic volute. The finest examples of the Ionic order are the remains of the temple of Nike Apteros, and the Erechtheum at Athens, whose chaste beauty and symmetry are incomparable. The Corinthian order is more susceptible to elaboration and embellishment. Tradition ascribes its invention to Callimachus, who drew his inspiration from a votive basket filled with the twining leaves of the Acanthus plant. The Corinthian column follows the Ionic in all detail except the capital, which represented a cluster of Acanthus leaves. The finest specimen of the order is the Olympieum at Athens. This order, unlike its sisters, admitted superfluous detail and enrichment, and with variations was almost exclusively adopted by the Romans.

The finest work of the Greek architects was devoted to the building of the temples. The temples of G., like the temples of the Hebrews and other nations, were, for the most part, built upon hill-tops. The primary function of the Greek temple was to enshrine the statue of the deity. The statue was placed in the main chamber or *vaòs*, whose great doors faced E., and which was flanked with colonnades. The *vaòs* was divided into two chambers. The whole was surrounded by an external ambulatory, termed

the Peristyle, which was also flanked with columns. The temple was adorned with magnificent sculpture and mural decoration.

Greek architecture is characteristic of Greek genius. At its best it is strong but not stern, simple but not plain, noble but not overwhelming; it is beautiful yet chaste, restrained yet powerful, clearly definite yet infinitely suggestive. Here there is nothing in excess, but the realisation of that mean of means, neither too little nor too much.

Greek sculpture was closely associated with temple architecture. The temples enshrined the statues of their respective gods and the metopes were adorned with the choicest achievements of glyphic art. Faithfulness in nature, combined with the worshipful and dedicatory spirit of idealism, are the essential qualities of Greek statuary. The ideal and the inspiration came from the gods, whose perfections the Greek sculptors sought to portray, but the type and model were derived from the palæstra, where Greek athleticism had moulded the human physique to superb proportions. Thus was the ideal realised and at the same time the real idealised.

Just as the temple column was evolved from the rude tree trunk that propped the primitive dwelling, so the perfect statue was evolved from a rough shapen trunk, which represented some deity. Several examples of this block type of wooden image existed in classical times. A rough wooden block in the Parthenon was revered as being the most ancient statue of the goddess Athena. Herodotus refers to similar representations of the Dioscuri, and the Hermes busts which stood in classical times at the cross-roads mark the transition stage from limbless block to perfect statue. In the early stages of the art the pose is simple and the arrangement of the members is absolutely symmetrical, the legs being stiff and close together, and the arms hanging straight and rigid. The drapery of these early types falls in stiff perpendicular folds, showing no indication of the form beneath. Muscles and other physiological details are but imperfectly rendered. One of the finest productions of this early period is the famous ' Charioteer ' from Delphi (c. 480 B.C.). The stiffness of the drapery and the simplicity of the pose are indications of the archaic conventions, but the suggestive poise of the head and the slight backward bend of the body give to the attitude a forcible truth which harbingers greater developments. The works of Pythagoras and

Myron bring us to the very threshold of sculptural maturity. These sculptors were most successful in representing athletic types. The celebrated ' Discobulus ' of Myron is a most complex pose, but there are indications of archaism in the lack of suppleness and flexibility.

Pheidias, the greatest sculptor of ancient G., was born in about 450 B.C. He thus flourished in the period when G., flushed with her victories against the Persians, realised for the first time her infinite potentialities. It was an age of great inspiration, an age which produced Pericles, Pindar, Æschylus, Sophocles, Euripides, and a galaxy of lesser stars. The colossal works of Pheidias were the gold and ivory statue of ' Athena Parthenos,' the bronze statue of ' Athena Promachos,' and the gold and ivory statue of Zeus at Olympio. Unfortunately these statues have all perished. The ' Athena Parthenos ' represented the goddess wearing the ' ægis,' and bearing in her right hand a statuette of victory. In the great bronze statue of the Acropolis the goddess was represented in full armour ; the figure dominated the city and was a landmark to ships at sea. Pheidias drew his inspiration for his colossal Zeus from Homer's description of the thunderer (*Iliad* i. 527). The power of this statue has this ancient tribute, ' Let the man who is sick and weary of soul, who has suffered much sorrow and tribulation, and whose pillow is visited not by kindly sleep, but stand before the image, and he will, I deem, forget all the terrors and troubles of human life.' From the sculptures of the Parthenon we derive our first-hand knowledge of the works of Pheidias and his school. The eastern and western pediments contained the finest sculptures. The ' Theseus ' (of the eastern pediment) is a nude figure in repose, yet the very calmness is suggestive of power and potentiality. The so-called ' Three Fates ' (also of the eastern pediment) is a harmoniously balanced group of singular beauty, the draperies fall in soft and clinging folds exquisitely revealing the physiological details of the figures. Pheidias' works thus represent the sublimest achievements of Greek sculpture. Polycleitus of Argos (*c.* 452-412 B.C.) as an artist approached most nearly to an equality with Pheidias. The characteristic feature of the works of Pheidias was sublimity; nobility is the distinguishing quality of the works of Polycleitus. The massive and splendid figure of the ' Doryphorus ' is characteristic. This statue became known as the ' Canon,' as embodying a perfect representation of the ideal human figure.

Characteristic of the transition period is the ' Eirene with Infant Plutus ' of Cephisodotus. The stiff folds of the drapery are archaic survivals, but the sentiment in the poise of the head and expression of the faces are indicative of the coming age of emotion and sentiment.

The representatives of the new school are Scopas, Praxiteles, and Lysippus. In this school representations of the human figure and the minor deities predominate. The restraint and repose of the Pheidian school have given place to the emotional, the sentimental, and the sensational. Scopas was particularly successful in representing motion and frenzy. The works of Praxiteles chiefly represented the minor deities, and these in their more sensuous aspects. His ' Cnidian Aphrodite ' was a nude figure of the goddess about to enter the bath. The flesh was tinted to a most life-like hue, and the effect of the statues was vividly realistic. His statue of Hermes with the infant Dionysus, though exceedingly beautiful, has indications of that softness and sensuality that ran rampart in the decline. Lysippus is the last representative of the loftier traditions of Greek sculpture, and he is not guilty of the sentimentality already visible in Praxiteles. His sculpture is rather of the bold virile leonine type, as his ' Apoxyomenus ' witnesses.

In the 3rd century B.C. the chief centres of Greek art were Pergamum and Rhodes. Exaggeration and sensationalism are characteristic of the schools, exaggeration of muscle and sinews in male figures, and of softness and rondure in female figures ; sensationalism in the choice of dramatic and harrowing subjects. Representative of the former school is the figure of the ' Dying Gaul,' representative of the latter school is the ' Laocoon ' group. These show great technical power.

In the Græco-Roman period the art of sculpture is mainly imitative and reproductive. The period, however, produced some beautiful works, which a fine eclectic spirit, if not genuine creative genius, inspired. The loveliest of these are the ' Venus of Melos,' the ' Apollo Belvedere,' and the ' Diana of Versailles.'

Bibliography. — GEOGRAPHICAL AND GENERAL : Philippson's *Der Peloponnes*, 1892; *Thesalien und Epirus*, 1897 ; *Inselwelt*, 1901 ; Leake's *Travels in Northern Greece ; Travels in the Morea ;* Wordsworth's *Greece, Pictorial, Descriptive, and Historical*, 1882; Lolling's *Hellenische Landes-*

kunde und Topographie ; Bursian's *Geographie von Griechenland.* HIS-TORICAL: Grote's *History of Greece ;* Thirlwall's *History of Greece ;* Holm's *History of Greece ;* Busolt's *History of Greece ;* Bury's *History of Greece ;* Ridgeway's *Early Age of Greece ;* Mahaffy's *Social Life in Greece ;* Curtius' *History of Greece* (Eng. trans.); Jebb's *Modern Greece ;* Rickford-Smith's *Greece under King George ;* Phillip's *The Greek War of Independ-ence.* LITERARY: *Histories of Greek Literature* by Mure (5 vols.), Jevons, and Gilbert Murray; M. Croiset, *Histoire de la Littérature Grecque ;* W. R. Hardie, *Lectures on Classical Subjects ;* Butcher, *Some Aspects of the Greek Genius ;* Jebb, *Growth and Influence of Greek Poetry ;* Haigh's *Tragic Drama of the Greeks ;* Rhan-gabé's *Histoire de la Grèce Moderne ;* Nicolai's *Geschichte der neugrie-chischen Litteratur.* PHILOSOPHICAL: Ritter et Preller, *Historia Philo-sophiæ Græco-Romanæ ;* Zeller, *Die Philosophie der Griechen ;* Jowett's *Plato* and *Politics of Aristotle ;* A. C. Pearson, *Fragments of Zeno and Cleanthes.* ART: Anderson and Spiers, *Architecture of Greece and Rome ;* Rayet et Collignon, *Histoire de la Céramique Grecque ;* Tarbell, *History of Greek Art ;* Gardner, *Handbook of Greek Sculpture ;* A. S. Murray, *Manual of Archæology.*

Greek Archipelago, a collection of islands in the Ægean Sea, belonging to Greece. There are some 300 of them, and they are divided into the following groups: the Eubœa and the Sporades, covering an area of 2216 sq. m., with a pop. of 115,500, the chief island being Skyros ; and the Cyclades, covering 923 sq. m., with a pop. of 134,750. These latter are of vol-canic origin, and number some 200, of which the most important are Naxos, Syra, Andros, Milos, and Paros.

Greek Church, more correctly spoken of as ' Eastern Church,' and described officially as ' The Holy Orthodox Catholic Apostolic Eastern Church,' is the historical representa-tive of the churches of the ancient East, and consists of fourteen self-governing churches, all of whom possess the same faith, the same bases of worship, and the same principles of government. These are: (1) The Ecumenical Patriarchate of Con-stantinople, (2) the Patriarchate of Alexandria, (3) the Patriarchate of Antioch, (4) the Patriarchate of Jerusalem, (5) the Archiepiscopate of Cyprus, (6) the Church of Russia, (7) the Church of Greece, (8) the Metro-polis of Carlovics, (9) the Church of Roumania, (10) the Church of Servia, (11) the Archiepiscopate of Monte-negro, (12) the Metropolis of Her-mannstadt, (13) the Metropolis of Bukowina and Dalmatia, (14) the Holy Monastery of Sinai. All these adopt the doctrinal decisions of the seven œcumenical councils, together with the canons of the Concilium Quinisextum or second Trullan council (692), and entirely reject the pope's supremacy. They express their faith by the Creeds, except that they object to the ' Filioque ' clause, saying that the Holy Ghost proceeds from God the Father alone, and believe that their communion is the only true Church of Christ. Moreover, they differ from the Roman Church in that they deny Purgatory and the doctrine of the Immaculate Con-ception of the Blessed Virgin.

As regards their rites they adopt the Julian calendar, beginning their ecclesiastical year on September 1, and have four great fasts, the most strictly kept being Lent, and a number of feasts, which they divide into three classes: great, middle, and lesser days. Easter is ' the feast,' then follow sixteen other great feasts, all of which relate to Our Lord or the Blessed Virgin. The middle feasts are those which relate to certain chief saints and apostles, and all the other days are the lesser feasts. The first Sunday of Lent is the feast of Ortho-doxy, which was founded in memory of the restoration of the holy pictures after the second Council of Nicæa, the Sunday after Whit Sunday (our Trinity) is All Saints, and there are two All Saints' days, the Saturdays before Sexagesima and Whit Sunday. The stronghold and centre of the whole worship is the Liturgy, of which two types are used: that of Basil the Great, recited on fixed days, and that of Chrysostom, which is usual throughout the year. The liturgy of the pre-sanctified or the ' Dialogos ' is only employed in Lent. Preaching of the divine word, which formed a part of the worship, has now disappeared, and is only to be found in some Russian churches. There are eleven chief service books, but no compendium like the Roman breviary, and the service is conducted in ' Old Greek,' or ' Old Slavonic,' not in an unknown tongue. There is plenty of singing, though no instru-mental music, and no images except the crucifix are allowed, only ikons of the saints are found in the churches. The vestments are numerous, and correspond with those of the Church of Rome. Other characteristics are of the Eastern Church; they baptize by immersion, rarely hear confessions, give Holy Communion under both kinds, confirm by the priest immedi-ately after baptism, ordain by laying on one hand only, crown the spouses at marriage, and anoint not only the sick but even people in good health.

The principles of church government are supported by the holy canons, by the fathers, and by the administrative laws of the emperors referring to the Church and completing the canons. According to their principles the head of the Orthodox Church is Christ, and believers are divided into two classes, *clergy* (consisting of archpriests, priests, and deacons) and *laity*. Monastic life, which is an important feature of the Eastern Church, is a single organism resting upon the monastic arrangements of Basil the Great, reduced to order by means of legal commands of ecclesiastical and political legislation. The monks, except those of the imperial monasteries and those of the ' stanropegia,' are subject to their local bishops. The centre of each church is the bishop, but the basis of administration is the Synodical system, all questions on ecclesiastic subjects and discipline being solved in regular or periodically convoked synods. And not only spiritual questions which affect ecclesiastical life are regulated by Church law, but also many relations of social life which are bound up closely with those of the Church, such as questions of marriage, divorce, etc. The estrangement between the Eastern and Western Churches was of gradual growth, but the final rupture may be traced to the increasing claims of the Roman bishops and to Western innovations in practice, and in the doctrine of the Holy Spirit, accompanied by an alteration of creed. In the early church there were three great bishops of importance, those of Rome, Alexandria, and Antioch, and the rivalry between the churches seems to have begun when the seat of the empire was transferred from Rome to Constantinople. For this left the head of the Church of Rome free from the interference of the court and meddling statesmen, and this, added to the fact that the Eastern patriarchates were engaged in violent disputes, did much to increase his power. But it was not to be expected that the pope's pre-eminence would be acknowledged in the East, and to press it upon the patriarchs in times of irritation must result in schism. The Eastern theology had its roots in Greek philosophy, while a great deal of Western theology was based on Roman law. This gave rise to misunderstandings, and finally led to two different ways of defining one important doctrine, the procession of the Holy Spirit from the Father and the Son. Political jealousies aggravated the disputes, and at last the final break came in 1054 when Pope Leo IX. excommunicated Cerularius and the whole of the Eastern Church. The separation was now final, and the ostensible cause was the introduction of the word ' Filioque ' into the creed, and it is this addition which was and is still the permanent cause of separation.

Greek Fire, a name applied in general to the different kinds of liquid fire employed in the middle ages, but specifically used of a preparation of ' wet fire ' invented by an architect named Callinicus, who lived in the reign of Constantine Pogonatus (648-685). He is said to have fled from Heliopolis in Syria to Constantinople, and his ' wet fire ' was used at Cyzicus to set fire to the Saracen ships. Exactly what the mixture was is unknown, but Lieut.-Col. H. W. L. Hime, after a careful study of all available evidence, decided that it differed from the other preparations of the kind in having quicklime as an ingredient, which, when mixed with sulphur, naphtha, etc., took fire spontaneously when wetted.

Greeley, a city of N. Colorado, U.S.A., and the cap. of Weld co. It is situated on a feeder of the S. Platte river in a fertile valley, and is served by the Denver Pacific Railway. There is a trade in flour and lumber. Pop. (1910) 8717.

Greeley, Horace (1811-72), an American journalist and politician, born at Amherst, New Hampshire. His family became very poor, and the boy worked as a day labourer until he was apprenticed in the office of the *Northern Spectator* in Vermont. After many hardships G. found his way to New York. In 1833, with the partnership of a fellow-workman, F. V. Story, he published the first cheap paper in New York, called the *Morning Post.* This paper failed, and after many adventures among several newspapers, G. established his reputation as an editor of the *Jeffersonian,* the *New Yorker,* and the *Log Cabin.* In 1841 he founded the *Tribune,* a paper which largely influenced public discussions of the time. He was among the first to advocate violently the emancipation of slaves; it is said that he influenced Lincoln to issue his proclamation of emancipation. After the conclusion of peace, when the Civil War was ended, he lost much of his popularity by offering himself as bail for Jefferson Davis. He was an exceedingly capable and intellectual man; during his life he was a target for his foes and for the ignorant, but after his death he became publicly acknowledged as a leader of public thought and opinion. He published many works, among them *History of* *the Struggle for Slavery Extension,* 1856; *Hints Towards Reforms,* 1850.

Greely, Adolphus Washington (*b.* 1844), an American Arctic explorer, born at Newburyport, Mass. He served in the Union Army during the Civil War, and became attached to the signal service in 1868. In 1881 he was appointed to command the Arctic expedition, with the purpose of establishing a chain of thirteen stations about the N. pole for scientific and meteorological observations. He sailed from St. John's, Newfoundland, in the *Proteus,* with twenty-four men. A detachment of his expedition under Brainwood and Lockwood penetrated to a higher latitude than any had attained before. G. and his companions suffered incredible hardships. Three separate relief expeditions were sent after him, the third, commanded by W. Scott Schley in 1884, arrived at Cape Sabine and found G. and six of his companions out of the twenty-four on the point of starvation ; the rest had perished. His scientific records were saved, and a valuable collection of specimens. He published *Three Years of Arctic Service,* 1885; *American Explorers,* 1894, etc.

Green, John Richard (1837-83), an English historian. He was born at Oxford, and educated at Magdalene College School and at Jesus College, where he won an open scholarship. In 1860 he took holy orders and became a curate in London. In 1866 he was appointed incumbent of St. Philip's, Stepney. He studied history, and at this time wrote frequently for the *Saturday Review.* His health broke down ; his views on the teaching of the Church of England changed, and he retired from the Church, and accepted the post of librarian at Lambeth. He thus devoted himself to history. In 1874 he published his *Short History of the English People,* a brilliant picture of the social and economic evolution of English life, in contrast to the usual political histories. This became exceedingly popular. His style is vivid, interesting, and accurate, and he made the reading of history a pleasure to thousands who had regarded it as tedious and dry before. In 1882 he wrote the *Making of England,* and in 1883 *The Conquest of England.* On his death his wife was left to finish the last book. It has been said that *Robert Elsmere,* by Mrs. Humphrey Ward, is partly a portrait of him. Mrs. G. (Alice Stopford) helped considerably in her husband's work, and has also written valuable historical works, especially relating to the early history of Ireland.

Green, Mary Anne Everett (1818-95), an English historian, born at Sheffield. She married in 1845 George Pycock G., the artist, and her first literary work appeared in 1856, when she edited the *Diary of John Rous* for the Camden Society. The following year she edited the *Life and Letters of Henrietta Maria,* and this was followed by over forty volumes of *Calendars and Domestic State Papers* belonging to the house of Stuart.

Green, Michael (1825-77), a German philologist, born at Hesse-Kassel; became librarian at, Kassel in 1865 and in 1870 at Marburg. Three years later he became a professor at Marburg. He studied principally ancient German literature and Anglo-Saxon. His most important works were : *Bibliothek der angelsächsischen Poesie,* 1857-64 ; *Bibliothek der angelsächsischen Prosa,* 1872; *Hildebrandslied,* 1858; *Beowulf,* 1867.

Green, Thomas Hill (1836-82), an English philosopher, born at Birkin in Yorkshire, of which his father was rector ; educated at Rugby and Balliol College, Oxford ; elected fellow, 1860. He spent his life in teaching, chiefly by lectures on philosophy as fellow and tutor of his college and as Whyte's professor of Moral Philosophy, from 1878 till his death. His influence on the philosophy school at Oxford both during his life and in succeeding years has been great and has stamped the final honours examination of Literæ Humaniores, with his Hegelian and Kantian idealism. His published works were few ; apart from his Introduction to the standard edition of Hume (J. H. Green and T. H. Grove), his philosophy is stated in the *Prolegomena to Ethics,* 1883, edited by H. C. Bradley, and the *Principles of Political Obligation;* his collected works were published and edited, with Memoir, in three volumes, by R. L. Nettleship. *See also* W. H. Fairbrother, *Philosophy of J. H. Green,* 1896; J. H. Muirhead, *The Service of the State, Four Lectures on the Philosophy of J. H. Green,* 1908.

Greenaway, Kate (1846-1901), an English artist and illustrator of books in London. Her father was John G., an engraver and draughtsman. She studied at South Kensington and at the Slade Schools. In 1868 she first exhibited water-colour drawings at the Dudley Gallery, London. In 1873 she began to illustrate for *Little Folks,* and commenced her series of Christmas cards for Marcus Ward ; they were full of quaint beauty and charm, and became extremely popular. In 1877 she began to draw for the *Illustrated London News.* The charming freshness of her illustrations in her books, one of which, *Under the Window,* sold to the extent of 150,000 copies, made her famous. Her drawings of children dressed in the style of the early 19th century, are full of artistic grace and delicate quaintness. Among her best known illustrated books are: *A Birthday Book for Children, The Pied Piper of Hamelin, Mother Goose,* and *Little Ann.*

Greenbacks, the popular name of the legal tender circulating notes of the U.S.A., so called because the back is printed with green ink. Treasury notes were first issued of necessity to provide funds for the Civil War in 1862; there were three of these issues, the first in February, the next in July, 1862, and the last in March 1863. The notes soon depreciated in value and fell to 35 cents on the dollar. An Act of March 1878, restoring specie payments, had the effect of fixing the amount then current as the regular circulation, and G. have never fallen below par.

Green Bay: 1. A city of Wisconsin, U.S.A., and cap. of Brown co., situated at the head of G. B., near the mouth of Fox R. It is 114 m. N. of Milwaukee, and 240 m. N. of Chicago. It is a centre of the lumber trade, and has an export trade in shingles, staves, etc. There are iron works, flour-mills, breweries, etc., and the fisheries are important. Pop. (1910) 25,236. 2. A large arm of Lake Michigan, upon which the above city stands. It is 100 m. long, and from 15 to 35 m. wide.

Greenburg, a township and vil. of New York, U.S.A., in Westchester co., situated on the Hudson R., 5½ m. from Yonkers. Pop. (1910) 23,193.

Greenbush, a tn. of New York, U.S.A., situated in Rensselaer co., on the Hudson R. It is opposite Albany, with which it is connected by a railway bridge. There are sawmills, a tannery, colour work and manufs. of tools. Pop. (1910) 7500.

Greenbushes, a post tn. of Western Australia, and also a dist., which is chiefly notable as being one of the chief tin-bearing districts of W. Australia.

Green Cloth, Board of, a committee of the British royal household taking its name from a green covered table at which it has long been a custom for the board to sit when transacting business, which is to examine and pass all the household accounts. At one time they also had the power to punish offenders within what was known as the ' verge of jurisdiction,' or the precincts of the palace. The Board is presided over by the Lord Steward, and consists of the leading officials of the royal household.

Greene, Maurice (1695-1755), an English musical composer, born in London. The son of a city clergyman, he commenced his musical career as a chorister in St. Paul's Cathedral, becoming in 1718 the cathedral organist. Nine years later he was appointed organist at the Chapel Royal, and in 1730 was elected to the chair of music at the University of Cambridge, and had the degree of doctor of music conferred on him. He was the composer of a great deal of church music of which the best known works are *Forty Select Anthems,* and *Catches and Canons for Three or Four Voices.* He also wrote several oratorios, a masque, and a pastoral opera. He was a friend of Handel and Buononcini, and sided with the latter in their famous quarrel and so lost the friendship of the German master. In conjunction with Michael Christian Festing, the violinist, and others, he founded the Society of Musicians for the help of poor artists and their families.

Greene, Nathaniel (1742-86), an American general, born at Potowomut in the township of Warwick, Rhode Island. He came of Quaker stock, and was not originally intended for the army, but in 1775, having been for a year in the militia, he was given the command of the Rhode Island contingent of troops, and joined the American forces at Cambridge. His able generalship won him Washington's confidence, and his promotion was rapid. He took part in many successful engagements, distinguishing himself especially at Trenton and Princetown. In 1780 he was given the command of the Southern army, which was opposed to a far superior force under Lord Cornwallis. His masterly strategy during the retreat from Catwaba to the Dan, was such that it enabled him not only to survive the two defeats of Guilford Court House (March 1781) and Hobkirk Hill (April 1781), but eventually to win the victory of Eutaw Springs and drive the British out of S. Carolina. At the end of the campaign he was offered the post of Secretary of War, but he refused, and in 1785 he settled on the Georgia estate, Mulberry Grove, where he died the following year. See *Life of Nathaniel Greene,* by his grandson, George W. Greene (3 vols.), 1867-71 ; and *Biography* (New York), 1893, by Brig.-Gen. F. V. Greene in the Great Commander series.

Greene, Robert (1560-92), an English dramatist and writer, born at Norwich; it is not certain who his father was. In 1575 he went to St. John's College, Cambridge, as a sizar, where he took his B.A., and in 1583 he became an M.A. from Clare Hall. According to his own account, his life at the university was utterly disreputable. In 1585 he married, and deserted his wife after the birth of their child, then he went to London, where he soon became famous as a playwright and writer of love fantasies. Before his death he became sunk in every kind of vice, and quite dependent on the charity of very poor persons. The story of his death was disgusting yet pitiful. One of his pamphlets, entitled *A Groat's-worth of Wit bought with a Million of Repentance*, 1592, appears to hold an attack on Shakespeare, part of the quotation being : ' Is in his own conceyt the only Shakescene in a country.' Among his other writings are : *Orlando Furioso*, 1594 ; *The Honourable History of Friar Bacon and Friar Bungay*, 1594. His *Pandosto*, the *Triumph of Time*, 1588, formed the foundation for Shakespeare's *Winter's Tale*. In 1599 he produced *Alphonsus, King of Aragon* and *George-a-Greene, the Pinner of Wakefield*. His works were filled with wit and charming romance, and contain much good verse. *See* Churton Collins, *Plays and Poems*, with introduction (2 vols.), 1905.

Greene, Sir William Conyngham (*b.* 1854), a British diplomatist, born in Ireland. He entered the diplomatic service and held appointments at Athens (1880), Stuttgart (1883-87), the Hague (1889-91), and Brussels (1891-93). In 1893 he was made Secretary of Legation at Teheran, then chargé d'affaires, and he remained there until 1896, when he was appointed British agent and chargé d'affaires for the Transvaal, a post which he held until 1899, the year in which the Boer War broke out. In 1900 he was made a K.C.B., and the following year went to Roumania as British minister.

Green Earth, a mixture of magnesian, ferrous, and aluminium silicates of uncertain composition found in cavities and veins of basaltic igneous rocks. It is evidently a secondary product resulting from altered pyroxene, amphibole, etc., and may resemble serpentine or chlorite. *Glauconite* is a form of it met with in some of the sandstone of the Cretaceous system.

Greenfield, a city of Massachusetts, U.S.A., and the cap. of Franklin co. It is situated near the R. Connecticut, 34 m. N. of Springfield. There are manufs. of cutlery, tools, and machinery. Pop. (1910) 10,427.

Greenfinch, or **Green Linnet** (*Ligurinus*, or *Chloris*), a common European bird, to be found also in parts of Asia and in New Zealand ; it is also an occasional visitor to Palestine. It abounds in the British Isles, having a preference for wooded districts. The cock is one of the brightest coloured

of the common British birds, its plumage being of a light yellowish-green, with the breast of yellow.

Greengage, the name given to a certain kind of small round plum, grown especially for dessert. It is less hardy than some kinds, and requires shelter and a good deal of care in cultivation, which follows the same lines as those of the plum.

Greenheart, or **Bibiru,** the popular name given to the species of Lauraceæ technically known as *Nectandra Rodiæi*. It is a native of America, and is a tree which yields a useful timber; the bark is employed for medicinal purposes. The term of G. is also applied to *Calyptranthes Chytranculia*, a species of Myrtaceæ, and to *Colubrina ferruginea*, a species of Rhamnaceæ.

Greenhithe, an ecclesiastical par. and vil. of N.W. Kent, England, situated on the Thames, 2¼ m. N.E. of Dartford. It was the starting point of the ill-fated Franklin expedition in 1845. There are chalk quarries, a trade in lime and cement, brick-fields, and market-gardens. Ingress Abbey, which formerly belonged to Dartford Abbey, was occupied by Queen Caroline. Pop. 2000.

Greenhouse, *see* HOTHOUSE.

Greenland, an island continent belonging to Denmark, the larger part of which lies within the Arctic circle. It is bounded on the E. by the N. Atlantic and the Norwegian and G. seas, with the Denmark Strait dividing it from Iceland. On the W., Davis Strait and Baffin Bay separate G. from Baffin Land. Cape Farewell is the most southerly point, 59° 45′ N. The length of G. is about 1650 m., and at the northerly part, where it is widest, the breadth is about 700 m. The interior is covered with a vast glacier of ice and snow, deep enough to bury the mountains and fill the valleys. This inland stretch of ice rises to 9000 ft. and more, leaving only occasional isolated rocks uncovered. The glacier slopes gradually down to the coast, discharging icebergs, which float down the Atlantic and travel S. of Newfoundland. The coast is indented with deep fjords, and numerous small islands lie close to the land. Of these Disco is the largest, having an area of 3005 sq. m.; native iron is found here, also coal of a poor quality. The only other mineral of any economic importance is cryolite, found and worked at Ivigtut in the Arsuk fjord on the S.W. coast. The climate varies a great deal from bright sunshine to dense snow and fog; in the warmest month, July, the heat never exceeds 32° F., and in the coldest month, January, it may drop to - 22° F. and below, while inland it may descend to - 90° F. The climate on the E. coast is more Arctic than on the W., and the land more deeply covered with snow. The plant life of G. is of the Arctic type. There are no forests; the dwarf willow and birch are the chief trees; flowering mosses flourish, and the yellow poppy, etc. Gardening is difficult, but in the S. a few vegetables are grown, chiefly radishes and turnips. The chief wild animals are the white polar wolf, the polar bear, the polar fox, the Arctic hare, and the reindeer, although hunted to extinction in the S., still abounds in the more northerly districts. There are several varieties of birds, among them the eider-duck, guillemot, and the ptarmigan. The fisheries are very important, including cod, caplin, halibut, sea trout, etc. The whaling industry, though not as flourishing as formerly, still continues, and the sealing is very important. Narwhal and walruses are also caught. The population is about 12,000, and consists mainly of Eskimos; the Europeans number about 300, chiefly Danes. The trade is only with Denmark, it being a monopoly of the Danish crown since 1774. The principal exports are seal and whale oil, fox, bear, reindeer, and seal-skins, eider-down, feathers, and cryolite. For purposes of government the country is divided into two inspectorates, Godthaab and God-havn, ruled by two governors responsible to the board at Copenhagen. Each inspectorate is divided into districts. These districts have a chief settlement and various outlying hunting stations, of which there are about sixty. Trading is carried out on a system of the government giving low prices for the produce, and selling European necessities at the smallest possible rate. The inspectors are magistrates as well as trade superintendents, but crime is very rare. The Danish inhabitants usually live in houses built of imported wood, covered with pitch, while the Eskimo dwell in huts built of stone and turf, entered by a little tunnel. Godthaab is the principal settlement in the S.; Christianshaab is one of the best settlements of the N. Apernavik in the cap. of N. Greenland. The history of G., as we know it, began in 982, when the Norwegian, Eric the Red, sailed from Iceland to find the country which one Gunnbjorn declared he had seen and stayed at. Eric discovered the country and called it G., hoping by this name to persuade people to colonise there; two colonies were formed, one called Osterbygd in the district of Julianehaab, and another in the district of Godthaab.

Remains of these Northmen have been found and numerous ruins. Christianity was introduced in 1000 A.D. by Leif Ericsson; the colonists built twelve churches and a monastery. From 1261 to 1814 G. belonged to Norway, after which it became Danish. Several Arctic explorers have visited G. The first person to give a trustworthy report of the coast was the Scottish whaler, Captain William Scoresby, in 1822. After this several other expeditions of exploration were made by Germans, Danes, and Englishmen. Nansen, in 1888, travelled along a part of the coast. In 1905 the Duke of Orleans' expedition discovered that the farthest N.E. point was an island. See Hans Egede, Description of Greenland ; H. Rink, Danish Greenland, 1877; H. Mohn and F. Nansen, The First Crossing of Greenland, 1890.

Greenland Sea, that part of the Arctic Ocean lying between Spitzbergen on the N. and Greenland and Jan Mayen on the S. In places it is 2500 fathoms in depth, and its greatest width, between Norway and Greenland, is 700 m. The temperature is variable, owing to the current from the Polar Sea, which runs along the E. coast of Greenland in a southerly direction.

Greenlaw, a small tn. of S. Berwickshire, Scotland, on the Blackadder. Antiquarian remains are found, including a camp and several cairns. The chief manufs. are woollens and agricultural implements. Pop. (1911) 744.

Greenlet Island, an island of Canada, situated in the Strait of Belle Isle, in lat. 51° 34′ N., and long. 56° 36′ W. It was proposed that here should be the landing-place of a Canadian Atlantic cable, extending from Clew Bay in Ireland.

Greenock, a municipal and police burgh and seaport tn. in Renfrewshire, Scotland. It is situated on the S. bank of the Clyde, and is 23 m. by rail W. of Glasgow by the Caledonian and the Glasgow and South-Western Railways. The town stretches along the water for nearly 4 m., and the harbour works are extensive, including the Victoria and Albert harbours, the James Watt dock, and the Garvel graving dock. The town possesses some fine public buildings; notably the municipal buildings, after the style of the Italian Renaissance, with a tower 244 ft. high ; the county buildings (1867), which also possess a tower 112 ft. high ; the custom house (1818) in classic style, with Doric portico; the Watt Institution founded in 1837 by James Watt (whose birthplace G. is), containing the public library (1783), the Watt scientific library, presented by the founder,

and the statue of James Watt by
Sir Francis Chantry. The North
Parish Church, a Gothic building
dating from 1591, contains windows
by William Morris, and the churchyard is the resting-place of Burns'
'Highland Mary,' and also of James
Galt, the novelist. The chief industries are shipbuilding and sugar
refining, also iron foundries, paper
mills, and a variety of other industries, and there are large fishing
fleets for the home waters and Newfoundland. G. has a town council
with provost and bailies, and returns
one member to parliament. Pop.
(1911) 75,160.

Greenore, a watering-place of co.
Louth, Ireland, situated on Carling-
ford Lough. It has grown considerably since the establishment of a
steam-packet service by the London
and North-Western Railway Company, which has also laid out golf
links and owns the hotel. G. affords
beautiful scenery, and has a raised
beach, about 10 ft. above sea-level.
Pop. 400.

Greenough, George Bellas (1778-
1855), an English geologist, born in
London. While studying law at
Göttingen, he attended Blumenbach's
lectures, and became interested in
natural history; he then went to
Frieburg and studied mineralogy
under Werner, and continued to
travel and pursue his study of science.
In 1807 he became interested in
politics and entered parliament,
where he represented Gatton until
1812. This did not hinder his
geological studies, however, and
he was elected F.R.S., and that
same year was one of those who
founded the Geological Society of
London, of which he was the first
president. He published : *A Critical
Examination of the First Principles
of Geology*, and the famous *Geological
Map of England and Wales*, in six
sheets, and a geological map of
India.

Greenough, Horatio (1805-52), an
American sculptor, born at Boston.
He evinced a taste for art while still
at Harvard, and designed the Bunker
Hill monument. In 1825 he went to
Rome and became a pupil of Thorwaldsen. The following year he returned for a time to Boston and did
busts of Quincy Adams, and other
well-known men, after which he went
to Florence and was commissioned
by Fenimore Cooper to do a group
of Chanting Cherubs. The American
government selected him to execute
the colossal statue of Washington in
the city of that name, which was un-
veiled in 1843; and later he also
executed a group representing the
struggle between the Anglo-Saxon

and Indian races, ' The Rescue.' The
gallery of the Boston Athenæum
contains a bust of Lafayette by him,
and the 'Medora' and 'Venus
Victrix.' In addition to being a
sculptor he was also an author, and
wrote both prose and verse. *See*
H. T. Tuckerman, *Memoir of Horatio
Greenough* (New York), 1853; and
Letters, ed. by F. B. Greenough, 1887.

Green Point, a suburb of Cape
Town, Cape of Good Hope.

Green River, a river of the U.S.A.
It forms one of the two great streams
which alternately go to form the
Colorado. It rises in the Wind River
Mts. in W. Wyoming and joins the
R. Grand. It has a total length of
about 720 m. and flows through deep
cañons, which it cuts out for itself
through the rocks of the Uinta Mts.
2. Another American river, which
is the largest tributary stream of the
Ohio. It rises in Kentucky and joins
the Ohio near Evansville, Indiana.
Length 300 m.

Greenroom, the waiting-room built
close to the stage of a theatre for the
use of actors and actresses during the
intervals of a play. Actors suffer from
' stage-glare ' caused by the artificial
lighting of a theatre, and the colour
green is a good antidote to this
affection of the eyes, therefore the
waiting-room walls were coloured
green, hence the name. See *The
Green Room Book* (a directory of
prominent people connected with the
stage, published annually), also *The
Secret History of the Greenrooms . . .
in the Three Large Theatres*, 1790-93
(vol. i., Drury Lane; vol. ii., Covent
Garden; vol. iii., The Haymarket).

Greensand, so named from the
colour of some of its beds due to the
presence of glauconite, consists largely
of the internal casts of the chambers
of Foraminifera. It was divided by
Webster (1824) into Upper Greensand
and Lower Greensand; the former in
the Upper Cretaceous system (*q.v.*),
and the latter in the Lower, being
separated from one another by the
Gault. The terms are unsatisfactory,
and the name *Vectian* is now frequently applied to the Lower, which
is more frequently yellow or brown
than green, while the Upper with
Gault forms the *Selbornian*. The
Lower Greensand can be traced in
England at intervals from the Isle of
Wight, through Dorset and Oxfordshire, to Lincolnshire, but it largely
centres on the Weald. The Upper
Greensand in England is deposited
on a V-shaped area from Kent and
Sussex to Dorset, back to Norfolk,
with a continuation in Lincolnshire
and Yorkshire. Many local names
exist for G. In Surrey the deposit
known as ' firestone ' and ' hearth-

stone ' · in Hampshire as ' malm-stone.' The scythe stones and whet-stones known as ' Devonshire bats ' come from the Upper Greensand, while the concretions of carbonate of lime from the Lower are used in the manufacture of cement. Other pro-ducts are glass sands and Fuller's earth. In the Weald important corre-lations exist between these deposits and local scenery, village sites, and industries.

Greensboro, an American city of N. Carolina, U.S.A., situated in Guild-ford co., of which it is the capital. There are three colleges here, viz. Greensborough Female College (1846), Bennett College, and the State Agri-cultural College. The surrounding country produces tobacco and fruit, and the town is famous for its cotton mills and blast furnaces. Iron and copper are mined in the neighbour-hood. Pop. 15,895.

Greensburg: 1. A city in the co. of Westmoreland, Pennsylvania, U.S.A., situated in the centre of a coal-min-ing district, and is slightly less than 30 m. E.S.E. of Pittsburg. It manufs. glass, iron, and steel. Pop. (1910) 13,012. 2. An American city in Decatur co., Indiana, U.S.A., 47 m. S.E. of Indianapolis. Its chief indus-tries are flour milling, quarrying, and lumber. Pop. 5420.

Greenshank (*Totanus canescens*), a bird of greenish colour, which be-longs to the sandpiper class. It is migratory, leaving Great Britain at the end of July and reappearing at the end of April. It is found princi-pally in the N. and W. of Scotland.

Green Sickness, in reality the dis-ease chlorosis, (*q.v.*) but was formerly known by the name given above. It is a form of anæmia which occurs in young females, and is caused by con-stipation.

Greenstick Fracture. This can best be described as a bending of the bone and not an actual fracture ; not un-naturally it occurs principally in the very young.

Greenstone, a name formerly used quite generally for weathered igneous rocks, *e.g.* basalt, gabbro, diabase, etc., in which a development of chlorite or serpentine had caused them to become dark green. The term has now been replaced by more definite names dependent on actual analyses. *See* GREEN EARTH.

Greenville: 1. A city and co. seat of Washington co., Mississippi, U.S.A., on the Mississippi R., 76 m. from Vicksburg. It is in the centre of a large cotton-producing region, and its industries are largely connected with that staple, in which it has an extensive trade. Pop. (1910) 9610. 2. A city and co. seat of Darke co., Ohio,

U.S.A., on Greenville Creek, 35 m. N.W. of Dayton. It has a foundry, lumber mills, and machine shops, and is the trade centre for a large and fertile agricultural district, producing cereals and tobacco. Here General Wayne concluded the Treaty of Greenville with the Indians, 1795. Pop. 5530. 3. A parl. bor. in Mercer co., Pennsylvania, U.S.A., about 52 m. S.E. of Erie. The trade of the town is considerable, as it is the commercial centre of a large section of Mercer county and places near in Ohio. The coal, oil fields, and stone quarries in the vicinity add to its industries, which are chiefly the manufacture of flour, woollen goods, machinery, and carriages and wagons. There are also foundries, saw and planing mills, and railway works. Pop. (1910) 5909. 4. A city and co. seat of Greenville co., South Carolina, U.S.A., 100 miles N.W. of Columbia. It is in the centre of an extensive cotton-growing and cotton-manufacturing district, and its chief industry is therefore connected with that staple, but it has also carriage and wagon works, iron works, and flour mills. The city is the seat of Furman Uni-versity, Chicora College for girls, and Greenville Female College. Pop. (1910) 15,741. 5. A city and co. seat of Hunt co., Texas, U.S.A., about 50 m. N.E. of Dallas. It is a trade centre for a rich agricultural district, and is also an important cotton market, having cotton compresses, and a large cotton seed oil refinery. There are also flour mills, machine shops, stock yards, and brick yards. It is the seat of Burleso College. Pop. (1910) 8850.

Greenweed, or Dyer's Greenweed, the popular name of the leguminous plant *Genista tinctoria*. It is so called from the dye obtained from the flowers, which is mixed with woad, and gives a green colour.

Greenwell, Dora (1821-82), an Eng-lish writer. She became known as an essayist and a writer of religious poetry. She was compared, because of her religious feeling and expression, with Thomas à Kempis and Fénelon. In 1869 she published *Carmina Crucis*, and in 1871 *Colloquia Crucis.* She published her essays (1866), and a *Life of Lacordaire,* 1867.

Greenwich: 1. A parl. bor. in the co. of London; situated on the Thames some 4 m. S.E. of the city of London. It is situated on the S. side of the river, and there are two tunnels under the river which connect it with the N. side. One is for foot passengers, and the other, called the Blackwall Tunnel, is used by vehicular traffic passing to the India Docks. The town is celebrated for its observatory and hospital. The observatory is built on the point through which passes the first meridian. G. time, which is telegraphed each day to all parts of Great Britain, is the standard time. The observatory stands in lat. 51° 21′ 38″ N. The borough returns one member to parliament. Pop. 95,977. 2. An American tn., Fairfield co., Connecticut, U.S.A., situated on Long Island Sound, about 30 m. N.E. of New York. It is a well-known health resort. Pop. 16,463.

Greenwich Hospital, as it is still called, though since 1873 a Royal Naval College, occupies the site of an ancient royal palace called Greenwich House, which was a favourite royal residence as early as 1300. It was, however, granted by Henry V. to Thomas Beaufort, Duke of Exeter, and in time passed to Humphrey, Duke of Gloucester, who gave it the name of ' Placentia.' It reverted to the crown in 1447 at his death, and was enlarged by Edward IV.; by Henry VIII., who made it one of his principal residences; by James I.; and by Charles I., who built the ' Queen's House ' for Henrietta Maria. It was occupied by the Protector at the Revolution, and after the Restoration by Charles II., who had it pulled down. He, however, started to erect another building, which was granted, in the reign of William III., as an asylum for disabled seamen of the navy. The most notable rooms of the hospital are a chapel with rich marble carved work, and a painting by West of the shipwreck of St. Paul; and a spacious hall, 106 ft. long and 56 ft. broad, which is decorated with representations of sea-fights, statues, portraits, and relics of naval heroes. Formerly 2700 retired seamen were boarded in the hospital, but now the building is utilised for the Royal Naval College, the greater number of the seamen residing with their friend and receiving pensions for personal use. The management of the revenue is vested in commissioners under the Admiralty.

Greenwich Royal Naval College, a naval school established by the Admiralty for the purpose of giving special technical training to intending officers of the British marine services. It occupies the greater part of the Royal Hospital at Greenwich. The college is open to students for the navy, the Royal Marines, the Indian Marines, the merchant service, and all sides of naval education are cultivated. A course of naval construction is taken; the subalterns of the Royal Marines take this course here as part of their qualifying training.

Greenwood : 1. A co. tn. of the co. of the same name in S. Carolina, U.S.A.

Its chief manufs. are cotton and cotton-seed oil. Pop. (1910) 6614. 2. The cap. of Leflore co., Mississippi, U.S.A., about 90 m. N.E. of Vicksburg. It manufs. cotton. Pop. (1910) 5836.

Greenwood, Frederick (1830-1909), an English journalist. He began life in a printing-house, but his contributions to various periodicals gained him a reputation, and in 1862 he became, with G. H. Lewes, joint editor of the *Cornhill*, and sole editor in 1864. In this paper he published his novel *Margaret Denzil's History*. In 1865 he became first editor of the *Pall Mall Gazette*, which soon acquired a powerful influence upon Conservative politics. It was due to G. that Great Britain bought the Khedive's shares in the Suez Canal (1875). In 1880 when the *Pall Mall* changed into the hands of a Liberal proprietor, G. resigned and accepted the editorship of a new paper, the *St. James's Gazette*, over which he ruled for eight years. In 1891 he launched the *Anti-Jacobin*, which, however, was unsuccessful. He continued to exercise his influence in the political sphere, by contributing to such papers as the *Westminster Gazette, Cornhill, Blackwood, Pall Mall,* etc. His chief publications are *The Lover's Lexicon,* 1893, and *Imagination in Dreams,* 1894.

Greet, Ben, an English actor-manager. He revived the practice of giving Shakespeare's plays outdoors, and had several companies of ' Woodland Players.' He co-operated with Mr. W. Peel, the founder of the Elizabethan Stage Society, and together they produced the old morality play *Everyman.*

Greetland, a tn. and par. of West Riding of Yorkshire, England, situated some 2 m. S.W. of Halifax. Pop. (1911) 4490.

Greg, William Rathbone (1809-81), an English essayist, born in Manchester, being the son of a merchant. He was educated at Edinburgh University, and for a time managed his father's mill at Bury. His first literary attempt was an essay on ' Agriculture and the Corn Laws,' and after this he gradually devoted himself to literary work. In 1851 he published his *Creed of Christendom,* and in the following year appeared many essays in the quarterly reviews from his pen. He was greeted with universal praise and was given first a commissionership of the Customs and later the comptrollership of the Stationary Office. He wrote principally on political and social subjects. His best known works are *The Enigmas of Life,* 1872, and *Rocks Ahead,* 1874.

Gregale, a wind which comes from

the N.E., and is extremely unhealthy. During the spring and early summer it blows over Malta. It is exceedingly dry and cold.

Gregarina, a parasitic protozoon, which is found principally in the alimentary canal of arthropods, such as lobsters. The creature is enveloped in a strong sheath, and has, when full grown, a single cell. Its food is absorbed throughout the whole area of its body since it has no mouth. Its reproduction is not of a necessity a result of the union of the sexes. A sub-class of these, the Gregarinida, are common to all invertebrates, but do them no harm.

Grégoire, Henri (1750 – 1831), a French statesman and ecclesiastic, born near Lunéville, and educated for the church. He took orders and for a time lectured at a Jesuit College. On the outbreak of the Revolution he went as a representative of the clergy to the States-general. He was by nature a Democrat and quickly identified himself with the Thiers Etat, taking a prominent part in the chief movements of the Revolution. He became the constitutional bishop of Loir-et-Cher. He acted, however, a moderate part throughout the Revolution, and did his best to prevent the execution of the king. He refused to recognise the change in religion of the revolutionaries, and remained true to Christianity and the Church until the Concordat with Rome was made. From this time until his death he remained outside the Church. He published *L'Eglise Gallicane,* and early in his career, *Essai sur la Régénération de l'Eglise. See* his *Mémoires* (Life by Carnot, 1831), and *Studies* by Krüger, 1838.

Gregorian Calendar, *see* CALENDAR.

Gregorian Chant, *see* PLAIN-SONG.

Gregorio, Rosario (1753-1809), an archæologist, born at Palermo. He was educated for the Church, took holy orders, and became professor of theology at Palermo. He also devoted himself to the study of archæology, and was commissioned by the king to superintend the opening of the tombs in his native city. He afterwards studied Arabic, and published in this tongue a history dealing with the subject of Sicily under the Arabs (this work was also issued in Latin). In 1789 he was made professor of public rights in Palermo University. His greatest work is *Considerazioni sulla storia della Sicilia dai tempi dei Normanni sino al presente,* but he also published many old chronicles.

Gregorovius, Ferdinand (1821-91), a German historian, born at Neidenburg and educated at Königsberg. After spending some time as a teacher he finally took up his residence in Italy where he soon made the history of that country his special study. The result of his long-continued residence in Rome was the publication of his great work, *Geschichte der Stadt Rome im Mittelalter.* This work, which has been translated both into English and Italian, deals with the history of Rome from about the year 400 to the death of Pope Clement VII. in 1534. It is written in marvellous detail and traces the history of the empire and the papacy during that time, showing that the connection between the two was greater than was usually imagined. He published numerous other works, amongst which may be mentioned, *Geschichte der Kaisers Hadrian und seiner Zeit ; Lucrezia Borgia ; Die Grabdenkmaler der Papste ; Geschichte der Stadt Athen im Mittelalter.*

Gregory, the name of sixteen popes : *Gregory I.* (*c.* 596-604), surnamed the Great, was born in Rome about 540 A.D. He entered a monastery (*c.* 575), and became one of the seven Legionary Deacons of Rome. Pelagius II. appointed him 'Apocrisiarius' at Constantinople (*c.* 579-*c.* 586), and on his return to Rome, abbot of St. Andrew's Monastery. On the death of Pelagius, he was unanimously elected pope, and consecrated Sept. 3, 590. He showed remarkable ability and wisdom in his administration of the Church. He sent Augustine to Christianise Britain, reconciled Spain to the faith, and abolished simony among the clergy of Gaul. He regulated the services and ritual, and wrote many of the old chants of the Roman Catholic Church. His works, printed in Migne's *Patrologia Latina* (vols. lxxv.-lxxix.) and in folio (4 vols., 1705), include *Moralia, Regulæ pastoralis liber,* and *Dialogorum liber.* Consult studies by Barmby, 1892; F. H. Dudden, 1905; Kellet, 1889, and Gasquet, 1904.

Gregory II. (715-31) was born about 669. He sent Boniface as a missionary to Germany and did all in his power to promote Christianity among the heathen. By his conflict with Emperor Leo the Isaurian, concerning sacred images, as well as on the question of heavy taxation, he greatly increased the political power of the popes.

Gregory III. (731-41) was born in Syria. He excommunicated the Iconoclasts; he was unsuccessful in his attempt to obtain the help of Charles Martel against the Lombards.

Gregory IV. (827-44) recognised the supremacy of the Frankish emperor, and sided with Lothair in his quarrel with Louis the Pious. He instituted, it is said, the feast of All Saints.

Gregory V. (996-99). During his pontificate John XVI. was set up as an anti-pope (996-97).

Gregory VI. (1045-46) bought the pontificate from his godson, Benedict IX., and was deposed on a charge of simony in the following year. Hildebrand (afterwards Gregory VII.) accompanied him to Germany, where he died in 1047.

Gregory VII. (1073-85), Hildebrand, was born at Soana, in Tuscany, about 1020, and was educated in the monastery of St. Maria, on the Aventine, and afterwards at Cluny. He accompanied Leo IX. to Rome (1049), and entered holy orders He succeeded Alexander II. as pope, and laboured to remedy the evils that existed within the Church. He aroused the imperial displeasure for prohibiting the abuse of investiture, and was formally deposed by Henry IV. in 1076, whereupon Gregory inflicted a sentence of excommunication and ultimately made him submit to a humiliating penance at Canossa in 1077. In 1080 Henry again deposed Gregory, appointing in his place the anti-pope Clement III. and laid siege to Rome (1081-84). Gregory was relieved by Robert Guiscard, and withdrew to Salerno, where he died. Consult studies by Bowden, 1846; Stephens, 1886; Villemain (Eng. trans. 1873); Vincent, 1896; and Mathew, 1910.

Gregory VIII. (Oct. 21 to Dec. 17, 1187) was born in Benevento. He made peace with Henry VI., and reconciled the Pisans and the Genoese. He died at Pisa while inaugurating a new crusade to recover Jerusalem.

Gregory IX. (1227-41) was born of noble family at Anagni, and studied at Paris and Bologna. He excommunicated Frederick II. for refusing to take part in the crusades, who was absolved in 1230, but was again excommunicated in 1239. The emperor marched on Rome (1241), but Gregory died before the siege began. He made rules against the heretics and systematised the Inquisition. Consult his 'Letters' in *Monumenta Germaniæ historica*, 1883, and a *Life* in Italian by Balan, 1872-73.

Gregory X. (1271-76) was born at Piacenza in 1208. During his pontificate a temporary union was brought about between the Greek and Roman Churches, and the constitution of the conclave was determined upon (1274).

Gregory XI. (1370-78) was born at Limousin in 1330. He reformed the monastic orders, tried to make peace between England and France, and transferred the papal see from Avignon back to Italy (1377).

Gregory XII. (1406-15) was born of noble family at Venice about 1326. He held a general council with the anti-pope, Benedict XIII., at Savona (1408), but on his election of new cardinals, his former cardinals left him, and both popes were deposed (1409) in favour of Alexander V. Gregory retaliated by banning Benedict and Alexander as schismatical, but was banished from Naples in 1411 and sent in his resignation to the Council of Constance (1415). He became cardinal-bishop of Porto, and died at Recanati in 1417.

Gregory XIII. (1572-85) was born at Bologna in 1502. He took part in the Council of Trent (1562-63). He denounced heresy, helped the Irish against Elizabeth, subsidised Philip II. in his wars against the Netherlanders, and supported the Catholic League in France. He promoted the work of the Jesuits, and established the Collegium Germanicum in Rome. On Feb. 24, 1582, he brought about the reform of the calendar.

Gregory XIV. (1590-91) was born at Cremona in 1535. He was under the influence of Philip II., and excommunicated Henry of Navarre.

Gregory XV. (1621-23) was born at Bologna in 1554. He founded the Congregation of the Propaganda, and helped Ferdinand II. in the Thirty Years' War.

Gregory XVI. (1831-46) was born at Belluno in 1765. He entered the order of the Camaldoli, and in 1800 joined the Academy of the Catholic Religion. He was a great patron of learning and spent money lavishly on architecture. He wrote *Il Trionfo della Santa Bede*, 1799. Consult *Life* by Sylvain, 1889; Wiseman's *Recollections of the Last Four Popes*, 1858; and Nielsen, *History of the Papacy in the 19th Century*, 1906; also see H. K. Mann's *Lives of the Popes;* L. Pastor's *History of the Popes* (Eng. trans. 1899); M. Creighton's *History of the Papacy*, 1899, and Ranke's *History of the Popes*.

Gregory, the name of a Scottish family, distinguished in mathematics and medicine:

James Gregory (1638-75), a native of Aberdeen, and educated at the Grammar School and Marischal College of that city. He invented the Gregorian reflecting telescope, described in his *Optica Promota*, 1663. While studying at Padua University he published *Vera circuli et hyperbolæ quadratura*, 1667; *Geometriæ Pars Universalis*, 1668; and *Exercitationis Geometricæ*, 1668. He was elected F.R.S. and professor of mathematics at St. Andrews (1669) and Edinburgh (1674).

David Gregory (1661-1708), the nephew of above, born in Aberdeen.

He was appointed professor of mathematics at Edinburgh (1683-91), and Savilian professor of astronomy at Oxford (1691-1708). He was a friend and admirer of Newton. Chief publications: *Exercitatio Geometrica de Dimensione Figurarum*, 1684; *Astronomiæ Physicæ et Geometricæ Elementa*, 1702, and an edition of Euclid, 1703.

John Gregory (1724-73), the grandson of James G., born at Aberdeen. He studied medicine at Edinburgh and Leyden, becoming professor of medicine at Aberdeen (1755), and at Edinburgh (1766-73). His works include *A Comparative View of the State and Faculties of Man*, 1765; and *Elements of the Practice of Physic*, 1772; his collected *Works* were edited by Tytler (1788).

James Gregory (1753-1821), son of John G., and a native of Aberdeen. After studying at Edinburgh, Oxford, and abroad, he became professor of medicine at Edinburgh (1776). He wrote *Conspectus medicinæ theoreticæ*, 1788; and *Literary and Philosophical Essays* (2 vols.), 1792.

William Gregory (1803-58), son of the preceding. He became professor of chemistry at Glasgow (1837), Aberdeen (1839), and Edinburgh (1844). He was among the first to advocate Liebig's theories in Great Britain, and translated Liebig's *Principles of Agricultural Chemistry*, 1855. He also wrote *Outlines of Chemistry*, 1845, and *Elementary Treatise on Chemistry*, 1853. Consult A. G. Stewart, *The Academic Gregories* (Famous Scots series, 1896).

Gregory, Olinthus Gilbert (1774-1841), an English mathematician, born at Yaxley, Huntingdon. He acted as sub-editor of the *Cambridge Intelligencer*, subsequently teaching mathematics in schools at Cambridge and Woolwich. He wrote a *Biography of Robert Hall*, 1833; *Memoir of John Mason Good*, 1828; and *Mathematics for Practical Men*, etc. He was one of the founders of the Royal Astronomical Society.

Gregory, St., called 'The Illuminator' (*fl.* 3rd and 4th centuries), was of the royal race of the Arsacidæ. His father, Anak, murdered the king of Armenia, for which crime the whole family was destroyed, except G., who was rescued at the age of two years by his nurse. She brought him up as a Christian at Cæsarea in Cappadocia. About 286, while doing mission work in Armenia, he was thrown into a pit where he was kept for fourteen years, but on healing King Terdat of an affliction, he was released and became head of the Armenian Church, which flourished under his care. He died in a cave about 340. *See* Malan's translation of Vertabed Matthew's *Life*, 1868.

Gregory Nazianzen, St. (329-89), a father of the Eastern Church, born at Arianzus, near Nazianzus, in Cappadocia. He studied at Athens, where he made the friendship of Basil (afterwards bishop of Cæsarea) and Julian (afterwards emperor). He was ordained about 361, and nearly ten years later was elected bishop of Sasima, in Cappadocia. In 378 he was asked to champion the cause of the adherents to the Nicene doctrine at Constantinople, and became archbishop of that city in 380. His promotion causing jealousy in certain quarters, he resigned and retired to his native place, where he lived an ascetic life, largely devoted to literary pursuits. He left many poems, orations, and epistles. His works have been published by Hervagius (1550), and by the Benedictines (1778-1840). *See* monographs, Ullmann (Eng. trans. 1857), and Bénoit (1877).

Gregory of Nyssa, St. (*c.* 331-*c.* 396), a younger brother of Basil, bishop of Cæsarea, who was his teacher. G. showed great talent as a teacher of rhetoric, but was persuaded by G. Nazianzen to enter the church, and, though married, was consecrated bishop of Nyssa, in Cappadocia, by St. Basil about 371. In 375 during the reign of Valens, having roused the dislike of the Arians, he was deposed by the synod of Ancyra on a charge of wrongful expenditure of church money; but he returned from exile (378) on the death of Valens, and took a prominent part in the councils of Constantinople (381 and 394). He was a speculative theologian and wrote *Twelve Books against Eunomius*, *Ten Syllogisms*, *Hexaëmeron*, etc. *See* complete editions of his works in Migne's *Patrologia* (new edition. 1855-61). *See also* studies by Rupp (1834), Heyns (1835), and Stigler (1857).

Gregory of Tours, St. (538-94), a Frankish historian, born at Averni (now Clermont) in Auvergne. He was educated by his uncle, Gallus, bishop of Clermont, and in 563 was ordained a deacon. Ten years later he was elected bishop of Tours, and in the Civil War helped Sigbert against Chilperic. He is chiefly remembered as the author of *Historiæ sive Annalium Francorum libris*, which covers a period from the creation of the world to the end of the 6th century, and is of great value to the student of early European history. Consult the edition by Arndt and Krusch (1885). His complete works may be found in Migne's *Patrologia Latina*, lxxi. *See* Kurth, *Grégoire de Tours*, 1878, and Mark Pattison's *Essays*, i., 1889.

Gregory Thaumaturgus, St. (*c.* 210-

70 A.D.), an apostle of Christianity in Pontus, born at Neocæsarea, in Pontus, where he became a disciple of Origen. He was consecrated bishop of his native town in 240. His treatises, including a *Confession of Faith*, and a *Panegricus* on Origen, may be found in Galland's *Bibliotheca Patrum*, iii., and in an edition by Bengel (1722). Consult Ryssel, *Gregorius Thaumaturgus* (Leipzig), 1880.

Gregory, Lake, a large salt lake in Southern Australia, E. of Lake Eyre.

Gregory's Powder, a mild aperient administered for the relief of slight stomachic trouble. It is composed of rhubarb, magnesia, and ginger, and acts as a mild aperient, and is administered in doses of one or two teaspoonfuls. Water is added gradually to the powder.

Greif, Martin (1839-1911), the pseudonym of Friedrich Hermann Frey, a German dramatist. He was born at Speier, and educated at Munich. His lyrics, which are beautiful and full of noble sentiment, are collected in *Gedichte*, 1868, and *Neue Lieder und Mären*, 1902. His dramatic pieces include *Nero*, 1877; *Marino Falieri*, 1879; *Konradin*, 1888; *Agnes Bernauer*, 1894; *General York*, 1899, and *Schiller's Demetrius*, 1901. *Hans Sachs*, 1866 (recast 1894), appeared under his own name.

Greifenberg, a Prussian tn. in prov. of Pomerania, situated just over 40 m. N.E. of Stettin; manufs. bricks, machines, and stoves. Pop. 7770.

Greifenhagen, a Prussian tn. in prov. of Pomerania, situated 12 m. S.S.W. of Stettin; great centre of the cattle trade. Pop. 7259.

Greifswald, a tn. in the prov. of Pomerania, Prussia, about 3 m. from the Baltic, and 70 m. N.W. of Stettin. It is a university town, having been founded in 1456. There are iron foundries, and railway carriages are made here. During the greater part of its history it has been a Swedish town, and only became German in 1815. Pop. 21,680.

Greigia, the name of a genus of plants indigenous to Chile, and belonging to the Bromeliaceæ. *G. sphacelata*, or hardy bromelia, the only species, bears pinkish flowers.

Greisen, a substance resembling pale granite, from which it differs by the absence of felspar and biotite. It consists essentially of quartz and muscovite ; the latter mineral giving the hand specimen a silvery appearance. Accessory minerals are topaz, fluorspar, apatite, etc. Containing small amounts of tin oxide, it is worked as a source of this metal in Cornwall, Saxony, and Tasmania.

Greiz, a German tn., cap. of princi-

pality of Reuss, situated about 50 m. from Leipzig, and is in the middle of the White Elster valley. It manufs. cashmeres, merinos, and other fabrics. There are large dye-works here. Pop. 23,245.

Grenada, an island of the W. Indies which belongs to Great Britain, situated amongst the Caribbees at the southernmost point. It is 21 m. in length, and about 12 m. in breadth. The island is volcanic, having many craters, the highest of which is St. Catherine, which is about 2750 ft. The Grand Étang (alt. 1740 ft.), one of the features of the island, is in reality an extinct crater which has become filled with water and has a circumference of about 2 m. The rainfall is usually excessive, being often more than 200 in. per annum. The capital of the island is St.George, a coaling station for the British fleet, situated on a very fine harbour. The chief export is cocoa. The history of the island is extremely interesting. It was discovered in 1498 by Columbus, who named it Conception. In 1756 it was a French possession, but was captured in 1762 by the British. Again it fell into the hands of the French, but by the Treaty of Versailles (1783) it was ceded to Britain. Pop. 75,000.

Grenade, a ball of iron which is made hollow and filled with explosive material. By means of a lighted fuse the ball is exploded. Hand Gs. were at one time carried by soldiers and thrown amongst the enemy, hence the term grenadiers. Gs. played an important part in the Japanese attacks on the trenches at Fort Arthur in 1904.

Grenade-sur-Garonne, tn. of France, in the dept. of Haute-Garonne, situated on the R. Garonne, in the arron. of Toulouse, and 14 m. N.N.W. of that town. Pop. 3500.

Grenadier, originally a soldier trained to throw hand-grenades, who had to be distinguished by his height and strength. Subsequently the word was applied to a member of the first company of a battalion. It is now only used of the G. Guards, formerly the first regiment of foot guards.

Grenadines, a chain of small islands belonging to the W. Indies, in the Windward group. They extend between St. Vincent and Grenada, for 60 m., and are of volcanic origin. Carriacou, Union, and Canaguan are the largest, and they yield coffee, cotton, sugar, and indigo. Pop. 8000.

Grenelle, a suburb of Paris, France, on the Seine, famous for its artesian well, which supplies water to the upper part of the city. The well has a depth of 1704 ft. and a temperature at the bottom of 82°-85° F.

Grenfell, Bernard Pyne (b. 1869), an English Egyptologist, born in Birmingham, educated at Clifton College and at Queen's College, Oxford. In 1894 he began excavations in Egypt, and, in collaboration with Mr. Hunt, published his important discoveries of ancient papyri, including *Sayings of our Lord* and *New Sayings of Jesus*. Mr. G. is a fellow of the British Academy, and since 1908 professor of papyrology at the Oxford University. His publications include: *The Revenue Laws of Ptolemy Philadelphus*, 1896; *An Alexandrian Erotic Fragment*, 1896, and in conjunction with Mr. Hunt, *The Geneva Fragment of Menander*, 1898; *The Amherst Papyri*, 1900-1; *The Tebtunis Papyri*, 1902, and *The Hibeh Papyri*, 1906.

Grenfell, Francis Wallace, Baron (b. 1841), a British general, born in London. He was educated at Blandford, and entered the army in 1869, attaining the rank of captain in 1871. He served in the Kaffir War (1878), and in the Zulu War (1879). During the war in the Transvaal (1881-82) he served as assistant quartermaster-general under Sir Evelyn Wood. He distinguished himself in the Egyptian War, fighting at Tel-el-Kebir in 1882. He took part in the Nile Expedition (1884), and was appointed sirdar of the Egyptian army from 1885 to 1892. He commanded the operations at Suakin (1888), and won the battle of Toski (1889). From 1894 to 1897 he was at the War Office as inspector-general of auxiliary forces. In the latter year he again took command in Egypt, and was appointed commander-in-chief and governor-general of Malta (1899-1903). He commanded the 4th Army Corps (1903-4), and the forces in Ireland (1904-8). He was created first Baron of Kilvey in 1902, and made field-marshal in 1908.

Grenfell, George (1849-1906), an English explorer and missionary, born at Lancred in Cornwall. In 1874 he went to Kamerun under the Baptist Missionary Society, and with Comber explored the country. Four years later he went to the Congo to make an extensive survey, and in 1885 explored the Ubangi R. During 1891-92 he served on a commission as a delegate of the Congo Free State to determine the boundary line between that country and the Portuguese territory. Consult Johnston, *George Grenfell and the Congo*, 1908, and Hawker, *Life of George Grenfell*, 1909.

Grenoble (ancient *Gratianopolis*), the former cap. of the Dauphiné, now a first-class fortress and chief city of the dept. of Isère in S. France, 60 m. S.E. of Lyons. Its bishopric was founded in the 4th century; there are many interesting buildings, including the 15th century cathedral of Notre Dame and the Gothic palais de justice. The town has a university of three faculties, with a magnificent library. The chief manufactures are kid gloves, liqueurs, paper, cement, hats, and artificial flowers, and considerable trade is done in walnuts, grain, and cheese. See Pitot's *Histoire de Grénoble*, 1843-46. Pop. 73,000.

Grenville, George (1712-70), an English statesman, educated at Eton and Christ Church, Oxford. He sat in parliament as member for Buckingham from 1741 till his death. After having held various offices, he became Secretary of State, 1762; First Lord of the Admiralty, 1762-63; Chancellor of the Exchequer, First Lord of the Treasury, and Prime Minister, 1763-65. His ministry is especially remembered for the prosecution of Wilkes and the passing of the American Stamp Act, 1765. Consult *The Grenville Papers*, 1852-53, and E. D. Adams, *Influence of Grenville on Pitt's Foreign Policy*, 1904.

Grenville (or Greynville), Sir Richard (c. 1541-91), a famous English seaman, of an ancient Cornish family. He commanded Raleigh's expedition to Virginia of 1585-86, and was in command of the *Revenge* in the fight with the Spanish fleet of Flores in the Azores, and died on board the enemy's flag-ship, *San Pablo*. Consult Sir Walter Raleigh, *The Truth of the Fight about the Iles of Azores*, 1591; Gervase Markham, *The Most Honourable Tragedie of Sir Richard Grinvile, Knight*, 1595; Froude's essay in *Short Studies on Great Subjects;* and Tennyson's ballad, *The Revenge*.

Grenville, Richard (1797-1861), see Buckingham and Chandos, Richard Plantagenet Temple Nugent Brydges Chandos Grenville, Duke of.

Grenville, William Wyndham, Baron (1759-1834), an English statesman, son of George G. He was educated at Eton and Christ Church, Oxford, and entered parliament as member for Buckingham in 1782. He became secretary to his brother, Earl Temple, then Lord - Lieutenant of Ireland, and Paymaster - General of the Army under his cousin, William Pitt. He was appointed in succession Speaker of the House of Commons, 1789; Secretary of State for the Home Department, 1789; Foreign Secretary, 1791. Pitt and his colleagues resigned office in 1801, on George III.'s refusal to pass the Catholic Emancipation Bill. G. formed part of the short-lived government of ' All the Talents,' 1806-7. He edited Chatham's letters to his nephew, 1804, and wrote *Nugæ Metricæ*, 1824.

Gresham, Sir Thomas (1519-79), an

English merchant, founder of the Royal Exchange. He was apprenticed to his uncle, Sir John G., a London mercer, and in 1543 was admitted a member of the Mercers' Company. He held the post of ' king's merchant ' in Antwerp from 1551 to 1567. For a short while he acted as Queen Elizabeth's ambassador at Brussels (1559). During 1566-71 he erected the Royal Exchange on the model of the one in Antwerp, and left a large sum of money to endow a college with seven lectureships. His house in Bishopsgate Street was converted to this purpose, and in it lectures were given from 1597 to 1768. Consult Dean Burgon, *Life and Times of Sir Thomas Gresham* (2 vols.), 1839.

Gresham's Law was first so called by Macleod in 1857, on the understanding that the principle ' bad money drives out good ' was first expounded by Sir Thomas Gresham to Elizabeth in 1558. Early economic writers, such as Copernicus, had, however, already explained it. The principle is that the worst form of currency will be most used in circulation, and the more valuable tending to disappear. Thus, if there are two metals in circulation, the one which costs least in production will predominate. The law also applies where there is debased coinage in circulation with full-weight coinage, and metallic currency with inconvertible paper money.

Gresset, Jean Baptiste Louis (1709-77), a French poet and dramatist, born at Amiens, where he was brought up by Jesuits. In 1725 he was sent to the Collège Louis le Grand in Paris, and subsequently received an appointment as master in a college at Rouen. In 1734 he published his delightful poem, *Vert Vert*, of a convent parrot, who, having fallen among profane wayfarers, shocks the nuns and is returned in disgrace to his original convent. There he repents of his sins and is forgiven. G.'s reputation was made, and he returned to Paris, where he published a second poem, *La Chartreuse*, followed by *Carême im-promptu*, and *Lutrin Vivant*. He produced a tragedy, *Edouard III.*, 1740, and two comedies, *Le Méchant* and *Sidnei*, 1745. He was expelled from his order for the ridicule he poured on monks and nuns in *Vert Vert*, and bitterly repented its publication. He was admitted to the Academy, 1748. Consult A. A. Rénouard's edition of his poems, 1811, and his *Life* by St. Albain Berville, 1863, and by Jules Wogue, 1894.

Greta Hall is situated in the Vale of Keswick, Cumberland, and consists of two houses under one roof. Coleridge took up his residence (1800-3) in one half, and in 1803 Southey occupied the other till his death in 1843.

Gretna Green, a vil. in Dumfries-shire, Scotland, 9 m. N.N.W. of Carlisle. It was formerly notorious for the clandestine marriages which were, after the abolition of Fleet marriages (1754), held here, as being the nearest place within the Scottish border line. In 1856 a law was passed requiring one of the parties to reside in Scotland for three weeks previously. *See* P. O. Hutchinson's *Chronicles of Gretna Green*, 1844.

Grétry, André Erneste Modeste (1741-1813), a French operatic composer; comedy was his forte, and his efforts in this direction won for him a very wide contemporary reputation which has, however, diminished considerably, although he is regarded by musical historians as the originator of the modern type of French comic opera. His operas number about fifty, the best being : *Le Tableau Parlant*, 1769; *L'Amant Jaloux*, 1778; *Le Caravane de Cairo*, 1783 ; and, perhaps his finest achievement—certainly his most popular one—*Richard Cœur de Lion*, 1784. He also made some early attempts at symphonic works, and later published sundry writings on musical and dramatic æsthetics and a treatise on harmony, all of which met with the small success they deserved.

Greuze, Jean Baptiste (1725-1805), a French genre and portrait painter, born at Tournus, near Mâcon, in Burgundy ; studied in the Academy at Paris. His first picture, ' Le Père de famille expliquant la Bible à ses enfants,' was so good that his teachers doubted whether it was his sole production. His success, however, was followed up, and he won great popularity, especially for his pretty heads of young girls. He was elected to the Academy in 1769. His chief works are : ' Aveugle trompé,' 1755; ' La Jeune Fille à l'agneau ': ' La Jeune Fille qui pleure le mort de son oiseau,' etc. See *Monograph* by Normand, 1892.

Greve, a com. of Tuscany, Italy, in the prov. of Florence. It is situated on the G., 13 m. S.E. of the city of Florence. Pop. 14,000.

Greven's Fejde (' Count's Feud '), applied to the struggle for the Danish crown in the first half of the 16th century. Christian II. went into exile in 1523, when his uncle, Frederick of Holstein, seized the throne. On the death of the latter (1533) his son, Duke Christian of Holstein, claimed the crown, but was opposed by Count Christian of Oldenburg, who invaded Denmark ostensibly to restore the exiled King Christian II. The Duke of Holstein was nominated Christian III.

by the State Council in 1534. In the following year Oldenburg was defeated at Helsingfors, and in 1536 the struggle ended in the victory of Christian III.

Greville, Charles Cavendish (1794-1865), an English diarist; educated at Eton and at Christ Church, Oxford. He became private secretary to Earl Bathurst and clerk of the Council in Ordinary (1821-60), during which time he made excellent use of his opportunities for studying court and political life. He left his journal to Mr. Henry Reeve, with the request that it should be published soon after his death. Accordingly, instalments appeared in 1875, covering the years 1820-37; in 1885, covering 1837-51; and the third portion, 1852-60, in 1887. These *Memoirs* are of great value to students of 19th-century history. G. also wrote, and published anonymously, *Past and Present Policy of England to Ireland*, 1845, in which he advocated payment of Roman Catholic clergy in Ireland.

Greville, Sir Fulke, Lord Brooke (1554-1628), an English poet, born at Beauchamp Court, Warwickshire. He was educated at Cambridge and Oxford, and travelled abroad; entered the court of Queen Elizabeth in 1577. He was a friend of Sir Philip Sidney, whose *Life* he wrote (posthumously published in 1652). G. wrote a tragedy, *Mustapha*, in 1609, some sonnets, and a considerable number of laboured didactic poems. He was Chancellor of the Exchequer from 1614 to 1621, and was killed in a quarrel with his serving-man. *See* Grosart, *The Friend of Sir Philip Sidney*, 1894; and his edition of *Greville's Collected Works*, 1870.

Gréville, Henry, *see* DURAND, MADAME ALICE.

Grevillea (after Charles Francis Greville, vice-president of the Royal Society, 1809), the name of a large genus of trees and shrubs belonging to the Proteaceæ, and indigenous to Tasmania and Australia. They are tall and graceful, with red or yellow flowers, and are often grown in Europe under glass. *G. robusta*, the silky or silver oak, is the commonest species, and *G. striata*, the silvery honeysuckle, is another.

Grévy, François Paul Jules (1807-91), President of the French republic, born at Mont-sous-Vaudrey, Jura, and studied law in Paris, becoming an advocate in 1837. In 1848 he was elected by the republicans of his department to the constituent assembly, of which he became vice-president. He vigorously opposed the second empire under Louis Napoleon, and confined his attention to the bar till 1868, when he was returned

as deputy for the Jura, and was elected president of the national assembly in 1871, being re-elected in 1876, 1877, and 1879. On the resignation of Marshal MacMahon in 1879, he was elected president of the republic. In 1885 he was re-elected for a further period of seven years, but, on the discovery of his son-in-law Daniel Wilson's dishonest traffic in the decorations of the Legion of Honour, he was obliged to resign office. *See* his *Discours politiques et judicaires*, edited by L. Delabrouse (2 vols.), 1888; and his *Life* by Barbou, 1879, and by Bertrand, 1892.

Grewia, a genus of Liliaceæ, contains about 100 species which inhabit Asia, Africa, and Australia, and have various useful properties. *G. oppositifolia* is employed in making ropes in the Himalayas: *G. elastica* has a strong and elastic wood; the leaves of *G.'didyma* are given as food to cattle.

Grey, Albert Henry George, fourth **Earl** (*b.* 1851), Governor-General of Canada, the son of General Hon. Charles G. He was educated at Harrow and at Trinity College, Cambridge, and entered parliament as Liberal member for S. Northumberland in 1885. In 1896-97 he was Administrator of Rhodesia, where he was associated with Cecil Rhodes. He was director of the British South Africa Company (1898-1904), and Lord-Lieutenant of Northumberland (1899-1904). He succeeded the Earl of Minto as Governor-General of Canada (1904-11). He has published *Hubert Hervey, a Memoir*, 1899.

Grey, Charles, second Earl (1764-1845), an English statesman, born at Falloden, Northumberland, and educated at Eton and Cambridge. In 1786 he was returned by Northumberland to parliament in the Whig interest; he vigorously opposed the policy of William Pitt, associating himself with Fox, Burke, and Sheridan, as one of the managers of the impeachment of Warren Hastings. On Burke's supporting the government in declaring war upon France during the Revolution, G. remained faithful to his leader. He was one of the founders of the Society of the Friends of the People, and asserted that parliament did not represent the nation. He moved the impeachment of Pitt (1797), and took part in the secession of the Whigs as a protest against his policy. On the formation of the Fox-Grenville ministry, he was appointed First Lord of the Admiralty (1806), and, on the death of Fox, Foreign Secretary and leader of his party. During his ministry, Wilberforce's Act abolishing African slavery was passed (1807). In that year his ministry retired and he led the Opposition till 1830, when he became Premier and First Lord of the Treasury. During this term of office the great Reform Bill went through all its readings, and passed the House of Lords in 1832. In 1834 he resigned office on the Irish question, and retired from public life. Consult his *Correspondence with William IV.*, 1867; *Correspondence with Princess Lieven*, 1890; and the *Life*, written by his son, Charles Grey, 1861.

Grey, Sir Edward (*b.* 1862), an English statesman, the grandson of Sir George G., Gladstone's colleague. He was educated at Winchester and at Balliol College, Oxford, and entered parliament in 1885, representing Berwick-on-Tweed in the Liberal interests. During the Rosebery administration (1892-95), he was appointed Under-Secretary for Foreign Affairs. In 1905 he became Foreign Secretary in Sir Henry Campbell-Bannerman's cabinet, and has retained this office during Mr. Asquith's premiership. In 1897 he went out to the W. Indies, acting as chairman of a commission to report on the economic conditions of those islands. Sir Edward G. is a keen sportsman, and is well-known as an amateur champion tennis-player, and as an angler. Author of *Fly-fishing*, 1899.

Grey, Sir George (1799-1882), an English statesman, the nephew of Earl Grey, the Liberal statesman. He was born at Gibraltar, and was educated at Oriel College, Oxford. He represented Devonport in parliament from 1832 to 1847, and became Under-Secretary for the Colonies in 1834. He was appointed Judge-advocate (1839), Chancellor of the Duchy of Lancaster (1841), and, during Russell's ministry, Home Secretary (1846). He was not a brilliant speaker, but showed much practical ability during the Chartist riots and the Fenian activity in Ireland. He carried successively through parliament the Crown and Government Security Bill and an Alien Bill; he remodelled the ticket-of-leave system, amended the Parliamentary Oath Act, helped to stamp out the cattle plague, and for a time secured the suspension of the Habeas Corpus Act in Ireland. Under Lord Palmerston he was Home Secretary (1855), Chancellor of the Duchy of Lancaster (1859), and Home Secretary again in 1861. See *Memoirs* by Creighton (1884).

Grey, Sir George, K.C.B. (1812-98), Governor of New Zealand. He was born at Lisbon, and was educated at the Royal Military College, Sandhurst. He entered the army in 1829, and attained his captaincy in 1837,

when he sent in his papers. From 1837 to 1840 he explored the N.W. region of Australia for the Royal Geographical Society, publishing the results of his travels in *Journals of Discovery in Australia*, 1841. In 1841 Lord John Russell appointed him governor of S. Australia. He reduced the public expenditure, and showed such wisdom in his government of the young colony that in 1846 he was sent as governor to New Zealand, in order to conciliate the Maori chieftains, who were at the time in open rebellion. He succeeded in establishing peace and won the admiration of the natives. In 1854 he was appointed governor and commander-in-chief of

SIR GEORGE GREY

the Cape of Good Hope, and had to use all his tact and firmness in allaying the discontent left after the Kaffir War. In 1858, however, the Colonial Office objected to some measures of G., who thereupon resigned office. Feeling in his favour was high at the Cape, and he resumed office. In 1861 he was a second time sent to New Zealand to bring the native war to an end. He resigned in 1867 on some point of difference between himself and the Colonial Office, and entered the New Zealand Legislature in 1874, becoming Premier in 1877. He advocated many reforms, including manhood suffrage, and had great influence with all parties. His publications include *Polynesian Mythology*, 1855, and *Proverbial Sayings of the Ancestors of the New Zealand Race*, 1858. Consult his *Life* by Rees, 1892, and J. Collier, 1909.

Grey, Henry George, third Earl (1802-94), an English statesman, born at Howick, in Northumberland. As Viscount Howick he entered the House of Commons, representing Winchelsea (1826), Northumberland (1831), and Sunderland (1841-45) in succession. He was appointed Under-Secretary for the Colonies (1830), and Secretary for War (1835). He resigned from both offices, in the former case on the slavery question, and in the latter objecting to the reforms advocated by some of his colleagues. He became Colonial Secretary (1846-52) in Russell's cabinet, and published a defence of his colonial policy, entitled *Colonial Policy of Lord John Russell's Administration* (1853). He also wrote weighty letters to the *Times*, and an *Essay on Parliamentary Government as to Reform*, 1858, and edited his father's *Correspondence with William IV.*, 1867.

Grey, Lady Jane (1537-54), the 'nine days' queen' of England, and great-granddaughter of Henry VII. She was born at Bradgate in Leicestershire. In 1553 Lord Northumberland forced her into marrying his fourth son, Lord Guildford Dudley. On the death of Edward VI. she was proclaimed Queen Jane on July 10, 1553. Meanwhile, Mary advanced upon London, and Northumberland was too faint-hearted to oppose her. On July 19 Jane found herself a prisoner in the Tower, and on Feb. 12, 1554, was beheaded on Tower Hill on a charge of high treason. She was an exceedingly accomplished scholar, was well versed in feminine accomplishments, and was of a happy and gentle disposition. Consult J. G. Nichols' edition of *The Chronicles of Queen Jane*, 1850; J. A. Taylor, *Lady Jane Grey and her Times*, 1908; and R. Davey, *The Nine Days' Queen*, 1906.

Greybeards, stoneware drinking jugs used chiefly in the 16th and early part of the 17th centuries. They obtained their name from the fact that on the neck of the jar was depicted in relief a head with a beard. These heads were made with a likeness to Cardinal Bellarmine with the object of ridiculing him.

Greyfriars, a church in Edinburgh which dates back to the 15th century. It was the scene of the betrothal of the Prince Royal of Scotland (afterwards James IV.) to Cecilia of England, 1474; and the National Covenant was first subscribed here, 1638, when the aggressive measures of Charles I. roused to arms the whole of Scotland. The church was desecrated by Cromwell's soldiers in 1650, and in 1679 its burying-ground was used as a prison for some of the unhappy Covenanters, the Martyr's monument bearing witness to the fact. A new church, since denominated New G., was built in 1721. Among distinguished incumbents was William Robertson, the eminent historian, who was appointed in 1761, and Scott, who from youth to manhood was a sitter in Old G., in his novel *Guy Mannering*, introduces this old church, and relates how when Colonel Mannering came to Edinburgh to consult Councillor Pleydell, the latter conducts him 'to the Greyfriars, to hear our historian of Scotland, of the Continent, and of America preach.' Old G. was destroyed by fire in 1845, but has since been repaired at a considerable cost. Its burying-ground contains the tombs of George Buchanan, George Heriot, Allan Ramsay, James Borthwick, Duncan Ban MacIntyre, and Sir Walter Scott's family.

Greyhen, the name given to the female of the black grouse (*Lyrurus tetrix*), the male being called the black cock.

Greyhound, a breed of dogs of great antiquity, found from the earliest times in Eastern Europe and Asia, while many Egyptian monuments are ornamented with unmistakable representatives of the modern G. They are characterised by their long and narrow muzzles, slight build, and elongated limbs, and small ears falling at the tips, but they differ greatly in the length of their hair. They hunt almost entirely by sight, the sense of smell being defective. The long, slender skull points to affinity with the wolf. The English G. is the best-known of the group, and has sometimes been regarded as the parent of the others. It can readily be distinguished from all other dogs by its slender form, smooth hair, and rat-like tail, as well as by its comparatively large size. It is thoroughly adapted for extreme speed, the long rat-like tail being used as a balance for the body during quick turns, while the slender limbs with wire-like muscles give the greatest possible length of stride and offer the least possible resistance to the air. The favourite colour is a uniform sandy or pale grey tone, but the colour is of very little importance in comparison with the capacity for speed. The Italian G. is kept purely as a pet and is a miniature of the English variety; its proportions are most elegant and its speed considerable, but it is so delicately made that it is almost unable to pull down even a rabbit. The eyes are larger and softer than in the English type, and the most valued are a golden-fawn in colour. The Scottish deerhound is a larger and heavier variety of the

English G., with rough and shaggy hair; it used to be employed both for coursing and deer-stalking, and the twofold use has given rise to different strains of the breed. The Irish wolf-dogs are now extinct, but seem to have had characteristics of the G. Other varieties are the Grecian, Persian, and Russian Gs., and several Oriental types characterised by their silky hair.

Grey League, the name of the ' Ober Bund,' the second in date of the three leagues of Grisons, Switzerland. Originally formed in 1395 by the Abbot of Disentis, the men of the Lugnetz Valley and the lords of Räzuns and Sax, and strengthened by the Counts of Werdenberg in 1399, the freemen of Rheinwald and Schams in 1424, and the Val Mesocco in 1480. *See* GRISONS.

Greymouth, a tn. and seaport of New Zealand in Grey co., 105 m. N.W. of Christchurch. It is noted as the port of a gold and a coal field, and there are three government railway wharves. The depth of the bar is 17 ft. at high water and 7 ft. at low water. Pop. 4600.

Grey Powder, the name given to a drug prepared by rubbing together mercury and chalk until the metallic globules have disappeared. It is the mildest preparation of mercury, and is largely used for children during teething or derangement of the stomach, a little rhubarb often being added.

Greytown: 1. Called also **San Juan del Norte,** a tn. and port of Nicaragua on the Caribbean Sea, at the mouth of the San Juan R. It is a port of call for mail packets, and monopolises the import and export trade of the country. Pop. 2500. **2.** A tn. of Natal in the Umvoti Valley, 65 m. S.W. of Pietermaritzburg. Pop. 2400.

Greywacke, or **Grauwacke,** *i.e.* grey earthy rock, a term of loose usage, formerly largely quoted by English geologists to include dark-coloured, impure, and coarse-grained gritty rocks, belonging to the Palæozoic Age. Some of them are coarsely pebbly, even resembling conglomerates, others are finer grained and approach shales and vary in colour from yellow through brown to black. Typical greywackes are found in the Silurian and Cambrian formations in Wales, N. Ireland, S. Scotland, and the Lake District of England. They are also found in Germany and the Ardennes, etc., and in some districts they indicate that they have been cleaved by pressure. Though generally deficient in fossils, they contain a great variety of materials, *e.g.* quartz, felspars, micas, chlorite, chert, schists, shale, slates, graphite, etc., while the cementing material may be siliceous, argillaceous, or more rarely calcareous.

Grey-wethers, or less commonly **Grey Weathers,** are exposed blocks of Eocene sandstone left on the modern surface of the land in Wiltshire and N. France. The first name is due to their likeness at a distance to a flock of sheep. The term *Sarsen stones* is also applied to them. They are sometimes of a considerable size (10 to 15 ft. long), as in the blocks comprising the outer ring of the Stonehenge druidical remains. They undoubtedly represent the harder concretionary portions of a stratum which once extended over all the area where they are now abundant, though the greater portion has been removed by the transporting and solvent action of rain water.

Grias, a genus of Lecythidaceæ found in tropical countries. There are only four species, and of these *G. cauliflora*, the anchovy pear, is the best known. It is a tall tree with oblong leaves, large white flowers, and a brown ovate berry. The plant is cultivated in Jamaica for this edible fruit.

Griboyedov, Alexander Sergievitch (1795-1829), a celebrated Russian poet and dramatist, born at Moscow. He served for a time in the army, but entered the civil service in 1817, and was appointed secretary of the Russian legation in Persia in 1818. In 1828 he became minister-plenipotentiary to Persia, but in 1829 the populace of Teheran, incensed against the Russian embassy, attacked the house and assassinated the minister. He began his literary work with a comedy, *The Young Spouses,* in 1816, but his great work, *Goré ot uma,* or *Misfortune from Intelligence* (Eng. trans. 1857), a satirical comedy upon Russian society, was rejected by the censorship, and was not published until 1833. He left unfinished a romantic drama, *A Georgian Night.*

Grieg, Edward Hagerup (1843-1907), a Norwegian composer and pianist. His music is intensely national in character and is mostly lyrical. The piano concerto, Op. 16, is perhaps his best composition. His works for pianoforte solo include a great number of lyric pieces, an early sonata, a ballade in variation form, and the famous ' Holberg ' suite. In chamber-music he has written two indifferent string quartets; three sonatas for violin and piano, of which the later two rank amongst his finest achievements; and an excellent sonata for 'cello and piano, whilst, of his numerous songs, the settings, particularly of Hans Andersen and Björnson, are exquisitely poetic.

Grierson, George Abraham (b. 1851), a scholar and authority on the languages of India, born near Dublin. He was appointed a member of the Indian Civil Service (1873), and after holding various government offices became director (1898-1903) and superintendent of the Linguistic Survey of India. Among his publications are: *Grammar and Chrestomathy of the Maithili Language; Seven Grammars of the Bihári Dialects*, 1883-84; *Bihar Peasant Life*, 1885, with some valuable illustrations; *Modern Vernacular Literature of Hindustan*, 1889; *The Satsaiya of Bihári*, 1896; *Essays on Kashmiri Grammar; Linguistic Survey of India*, 1898-1904; *Pisaca Languages of North Western India*, 1906, and *Manual of the Kashmiri Language*.

Grierson, Sir Robert (1655-1733), Laird of Lag, was the great persecutor of the Covenanters. He was especially active in helping to put down conventicles, and in enforcing the Test Act, using all kinds of severity to gain his ends. He succeeded, in fact, in making his name a byword for all that was cruel. He was also one of these to condemn the Wigtown martyrs. In 1685 he was made a Nova Scotia baronet. After the Revolution he was several times fined and imprisoned. He is the original of Scott's *Sir Robert Redgauntlet. See* Lt.-Colonel Alexander Fergusson's *Laird of Lag*, 1885.

Griesbach, Johann Jacob (1745-1812), German biblical critic, born at Butzbach in Hesse-Darmstadt. He studied theology at Tübingen; at Halle, where he became acquainted with Semler who influenced his whole subsequent life; and at Leipzig. He acted for some time as 'privat-docent' at Halle, and in 1773 was appointed to a professorship there, which he left for one at Jena in 1776. The great work with which his name is associated is his critical version of the text of the N.T. (1774-75), the most remarkable feature of which was his division of the MSS. into three groups : (1) The Alexandrine recension; (2) the Latin or Western recension; (3) the Byzantine or Eastern recension. His other works are: *Synopsis Evangeliorum*, 1774-75 ; *Populäre Dogmatik*, 1779, and *Opuscula Academica* (ed. Gabler, 1825). See *Life* by Köthe, 1812 ; *also* BIBLE.

Griesheim : 1. A small market tn. of Germany, situated in the Grand-duchy of Hesse-Darmstadt, about 5 m. W. of Darmstadt. Pop. 6842. 2. A small tn. of Prussia, in the prov. of Hesse-Nassau, situated on the Main, about 4 m. W. of Frankfort-on-the-Main. Pop. 11,474.

Griffenfeld, Peder, Count (1635-99),

a Danish statesman, born at Copenhagen. After travelling in various countries he became, in 1663, director of the royal archives and royal librarian, appointments given him by Frederick III., and was instrumental in claiming absolute power for the king. Under Christian V., successor to Frederick, he also obtained preferment, being knighted and becoming a privy councillor. In 1673 he was made chancellor. These honours, however, caused him to have many enemies, and in 1676 he was accused of treason and condemned to death. His sentence, however, was commuted to imprisonment which lasted for over twenty years, at Munkholm near Trondhjem.

Griffin, a city of Georgia, U.S.A., 40 m. S. of Atlanta, and the cap. of Spalding co. Here is situated the state agricultural experiment station, and there is an important cotton and fruit trade. Pop. (1910) 7478.

Griffin, or **Griffon**, a mythological beast used in architectural decoration and as a charge in Heraldry (q.v.). It is the oldest and most common of the outlandish monsters used in heraldic devices, having the hinder parts of a lion with the fore-parts, head and shoulders, wings and fore-legs of an eagle. When the head alone is borne it can be distinguished from that of the eagle by the long tuft under the beak, and the pointed ears. The 'griffin rampant' was taken as a quartering by the family of Montague at a very early date.

Griffin, Gerald (1803-40), an Irish novelist and dramatic writer, born at Limerick. He early began to write for the papers, and in 1821 edited a newspaper in Limerick. Having written a tragedy, *Aguire*, which was highly praised by his friends, he came to London in 1823 ' to revolutionise the dramatic taste of the time.' After great hardships he succeeded with *The Nayades*, an opera entirely in recitative, in bringing himself into public notice. His tragedies were entirely unsuccessful, but he attained great popularity by the *Holland Tide Tales*, 1827, followed by *Tales of the Munster Festivals*, 1827 ; and the fine novel, *The Collegians*, 1829, which Dion Boucicault adapted for the stage under the title of *The Colleen Bawn*. Among his other novels are, *The Invasion*, 1832 ; *Tales of my Neighbourhood*, 1835 ; *The Duke of Monmouth*, 1836, and *Talis Qualis, or Tales of the Jury-room*, 1842. In 1838 he joined the Society of the Christian Brothers at Dublin, whence he removed to the North monastery, Cork, where he died of typhus.

Griffin, Sir Lepel Henry (1838-1908), an Anglo-Indian administrator, born at Watford, Herts. He entered the Indian Civil Service and was appointed assistant commissioner in the Punjab (1860). After holding various offices in the state he was appointed permanent chief secretary to the Punjab in 1878. G. had before this shown his literary abilities in his *Punjab Chiefs,* 1865; *Law of Inheritance to Sikh Chiefships previous to the Annexation,* 1869, and the *Rajas of the Punjab,* 1870. In 1880 he was appointed by the viceroy as special superintendent of negotiations at Kubla, where his tact and skill was largely instrumental in establishing friendly relations between England and Afghanistan. He retired in 1889.

Griffith, Sir Samuel Walker (*b.* 1845), a chief justice of Australia, born at Merthyr-Tydvil, Wales, and educated at Sydney, Australia. He was called to the bar in Queensland, 1867, and also in New South Wales and Victoria, appointed Q.C. in 1876, Attorney-General of Queensland, 1874-78, 1890-93; Secretary for Public Instruction, 1876-79, 1883-84; Secretary for Public Works, 1878-79; Premier of Queensland, 1883-88, 1890-93; Colonial Treasurer, 1887-88; President of the Federal Council of Australasia, 1888, 1891, 1893; Chief Justice of Queensland, 1893-1903; Chief Justice of Australia since 1903. He has published *Queensland Criminal Code,* and a translation of Dante's *Divina Commedia.*

Griffith, William (1810-45), an English botanist, born at Petersham, Surrey. He studied for the medical profession at University College where he was a pupil of Dr. Lindley. His first public work appeared in Dr. Wallich's *Plantæ Asiatica rariores* in 1832; in the same year he sailed for India, and was appointed assistant-surgeon in the service of the East India Company. In 1835 he formed one of an expedition to inspect the tea-forests of Assam, which was the first of many such journeys and resulted in enormous additions to the botanical and geological knowledge of less known districts of India, Burmah, Assam, Khorassan, Afghanistan. His most important papers were published in the *Transactions of the Linnean Society,* and his books, *Icones Plantarum Asiaticarum, Itinerary Notes, Palms of British East India,* and *Notulæ ad Plantas Asiaticas,* were published by Mac-Clelland after G.'s death.

Griffiths, John Norton, F.G.S., F.Z.S. (*b.* 1871), Conservative M.P. for Wednesbury since 1910. He was educated privately, and became an engineer and public works contractor. He is managing director of Griffiths & Co., Ltd., contractors, London,

and president of the Norton Griffiths Steel Construction Co., Canada; Griffiths & Co., Australia; Griffiths & Co., Russia; and Griffiths & Co., Africa. In 1896-97 he served in the Matabele War, and in 1896 was in command of scouts in Rhodesia. He is a member of the Institute of Mining and Metallurgy, and of the Institute of Mining Engineers.

Griffith's Valuation, the main authority for the adjustment of rents under the Irish Land Act. Mr. (afterwards Sir) Richard Griffith was called upon to assist in a bill of the general valuation of Ireland; it was passed in 1826, and he was appointed commissioner of valuation, in which capacity he acted until 1868. His valuation was long regarded as the most exact and minute basis for equitable taxation.

Griffon Bruxellois, a toy dog of terrier extraction bred in Belgium, with a rough coat, the smooth dog of the same breed being the 'petit Brabançon.' It was introduced into England in 1895. The points of the G. B. are: General appearance, intelligent, sprightly, robust, and of compact appearance; head large and rounded, covered wth rather coarse, rough hair; ears semi-erect when not clipped; eyes very large and black; eyelashes and eyebrows finished with long, stiff black hair; nose short, black, surrounded with hair and converging upwards to meet the hair round the eyes; lips edged with a black moustache; chest rather wide and deep; legs of medium length and very straight; tail upwards, colour red; harsh and wiry coat; weight, small size, maximum, 5 lbs., large size, 10 lbs. *See* James Watson, *The Dog Book,* 1906.

Grig, or Glut (*Anguilla latirostris*), a small and very lively species of eel. It is widely distributed, being found on British and European, Chinese, W. Indian, and other coasts.

Grignan, a tn. of France, in the dept. of Drôme and the arron. of Montelimar, situated 20 m. N.E. of Orange. It possesses a noted castle, where resided Madame de Sévigné during the last part of her life, and which contains souvenirs of this lady and her daughter. Pop. 2500.

Grigoresco, Nicolæ Ion (1838-1907), a Roumanian painter, born near Titu, N.W. of Bucharest. He became famous during the Russo-Turkish War (1877-78) by his fine military pieces, notably 'The Storming of Smârdan,' which is in the town hall at Bucharest, and ' Provision Transport in Bulgaria,' in the museum of Bucharest. His portrait of ' Carmen Sylva ' is a fine, spirited achievement.

Grigoriopol, a tn. of Southern

Russia, in the government of Kherson. It is situated on the Dniester R., 80 m. N.W. of Odessa. There is a trade in wine, fruit, and tobacco, and fine leather is manufactured. Pop. 9000.

Grille, a grating or screen made usually of metal and used as a protection for a window, tomb, or some sacred place. Properly speaking, the G. should be made of hammered and punched metal. The term is also applied, however, to bars placed across a door for the purpose of communication without the door being opened, and also to the grating in the ladies' gallery in the House of Commons.

Grillparzer, Franz (1791-1872), the greatest dramatic poet of Austria, born at Vienna. In 1813 he was appointed a clerk in the Lower Austrian Revenue administration. In 1818, through the influence of the Minister of Finance, he was appointed poet to the Hofburg Theatre, and was promoted to the Hofkammer (Exchequer). In 1832 he was made director of archives of the Hofkammer, from which he retired with the title of 'Hofral' in 1856. He first attracted attention by his tragedy *Die Ahnfrau*, 1817, a ' fate-drama,' in the trochaic measure of the Spanish drama. In 1818 appeared *Sappho*, a drama in the classic spirit of Goethe's *Tasso*, followed by the trilogy *Das goldene Vliess*, 1821, comprising *Das Gastfreund*, *Die Argonauten*, and *Medea*, all noble pieces of work, modern in sentiment, and classical in design. His historical tragedies *König Ottokars Glück und Ende*, 1823, and *Ein treuer Diener seines Herrn*, 1826, first brought G. into conflict with the censor, a struggle which helped to embitter all this period of his life. With *Des Meeres und die Liebe Wellen*, 1831, a dramatisation of the story of Hero and Leander, he returned to the classical themes and the style of *Sappho* with an even greater measure of the Spanish grace of expression which he borrowed mainly from Calderon. *Der Traum, ein Leben*, 1834, is his technical masterpiece, and the first of his dramas without a tragic ending. His only attempt at comedy, *Weh dem, der Lügt*, 1838, in spite of its brilliance, failed to meet the popular taste, and disgusted him for ever with the Austrian theatre. Three unpublished tragedies, *Die Jüdin von Toledo*, *Ein Bruderzwist im Hause Habsburg*, and *Likussa*, were found among his papers after his death. Although essentially a dramatist, his lyric poetry is of fine quality, and he left one prose masterpiece, *Der arme Spielmann*, 1848. *See* H. Laube,

Franz Grillparzers Lebengeschichte, 1884; A. Ehrhard, *Franz Grillparzer*, 1900; G. Pollak, *F. Grillparzer and the Austrian Drama*, 1907.

Grilse, *see* SALMON.

Grimaire (*cf.* Eng. *gramarye*, magic), the French name for the book of invocations by which the sorcerers called up demons; hence it came to mean gibberish. The older forms of the word *grammaire* and *gramare* approximate to the Low Latin *gramma*, a letter.

Grimald, Nicholas (1519-62), an English poet and theologian, born in Huntingdonshire, and educated at Cambridge. He became a probationer fellow of Merton College, Oxford, in 1541, and chaplain to Bishop Ridley in 1547. His connection with Ridley led to his imprisonment, and he is said to have escaped only by recanting. It was at Ridley's desire that G. translated Laurentius Valla's book, the alleged *Donation of Constantine*, also Æneas Sylvius' *De Gestis Basilionsis Concilii*. He is best remembered by his contributions to Tottel's *Songs and Sonettes*, 1557, although for some reason thirty of his forty poems were suppressed in the second edition. His poetry was modelled on Surrey's, but is inferior to it. There are two Latin tragedies of G.'s still extant: *Archipropheta sive Johannes Baptista*, 1548, and *Christus Redivivus*, 1543 ; and translations of Cicero's *De Officiis*, and Virgil's *Georgics*.

Grimaldi, Francesco Maria (1619-63), an Italian Jesuit and natural philosopher, born at Bologna. He wrote a valuable work entitled *Physico-mathesis de Lumine, Coloribus, et Iride alliisque annexis*, 1665, which contains accounts of numerous experiments relating to the interferences of the rays of light. This phenomenon of interference was at the time enunciated as a proposition: ' That a body actually enlightened may become obscure by adding new light to that which it has already received.' He was also the discoverer of ' diffraction ' of light, afterwards designated ' inflexion ' by Newton, who also corrected his theories of the different refrangibilities of the rays.

Grimaldi, Giovanni Francesco (1606-80), an Italian architect and landscape painter, surnamed ' Il Bolognese ' from his birthplace. He was a relative and pupil of the Caracci. He became architect to Pope Paul V., and was employed by Cardinal Mazarin and Louis XIV. upon architectural designs and fresco-painting in the Louvre.

Grimaldi, Joseph (1779-1837), the most famous of English clowns, born in London, and was the son of an

Italian actor. He first appeared at Sadler's Wells as an infant dancer in 1781, and in the same year he took part in the pantomime at Drury Lane. He obtained his greatest success as clown in the pantomime of *Mother Goose* at Covent Garden in 1806; a part which he constantly revived until his retirement in 1828. *See* his *Memoirs*, ed. by Charles Dickens (1838).

Grimm, the name of two brothers, distinguished German philologists and storiologists, both born at Hanau, and fellow students in law at Marburg University. They were devoted friends, serving each other's interests and collaborating in many literary labours.

Jacob Ludwig Grimm (1785-1863), began his literary career at Paris (1805) as assistant to Professor Savigny, a celebrated German jurisconsult, the founder of the ' historical school ' in Germany. This work enabled G. to gain valuable insight into the ' scientific method ' he later pursued in his investigations of the

JACOB GRIMM

Teutonic languages, which led to his becoming the founder of scientific philology and to his epoch-marking discovery known as *Grimm's Law* (*q.v.*), enunciated in his *Deutsche Grammatik*, the greatest work of the age in philology. While librarian at Wilhelmshöhe and then at Cassel he was able to carry on his favourite studies of philology and old and mediæval German poetry. In 1811 he published his first work in the latter subject, *Ueber den Altdeuschen Meistergesang*. During 1827-37 he was lecturer in the German language, literature, and antiquities at Göttingen University. The brothers G. were among the seven professors who

signed a protest against the innovations introduced into the constitution by the king of Hanover, and both suffered banishment. In 1841 he became lecturer at Berlin University. His *Kinder-und-Hausmärchen*, collected and published with his brother, made fairy tales popular throughout Europe, and gave rise to the investigations which established the modern science of *Folklore*. His *Deutsche Recht-Altersthümen* and *Mythologie* treat of the society and religious superstitions of Central Europe in the middle ages. G. stands out among famous scholars for his stupendous learning and for the noble disinterestedness of his life and work.

Wilhelm Karl Grimm (1786-1859) was assistant librarian at Cassel and professor extraordinary at Göttingen. At Berlin he collaborated with his brother. He wrote independently *Die Deutsche Heldensage*, *Kœmpe-Viser*, and many treatises on German literature and antiquities.

Grimm, Friedrich Melchior, Baron von (1723-1807), a witty German writer, born at Ratisbon, and educated at Leipzig. He accompanied the young Count de Schönburg to Paris, and became reader to the young Duke of Saxe-Gotha. In 1749 he made the acquaintance of Rousseau, and became closely associated with the Encyclopædists. In the musical war between the partisans of French and Italian music, G. sided with the latter and wrote in their defence a witty pamphlet, *Le petit Prophète de Boehmischbroda* (1753), followed by *Lettres sur la Musique Française*. On becoming secretary to the Duke of Orleans he wrote, in conjunction with Diderot and Abbé Ragnal, the literary bulletins containing acute criticism on French literature. In 1776 he was appointed minister to the French court by the Duke of Gotha, and in 1795 as minister of Russia to Hamburg by the Empress Catherine. His *Correspondance Littéraire, Philosophique, et Critique* was published in 1812.

Grimm, Hermann (1828-1901), a German art critic and essayist, son of the philosopher W. Karl G., born at Cassel, and educated at Berlin and Bonn. After publishing two dramas, a volume of stories, and his successful novel, *Unäberwindliche Mächte*, he wrote chiefly on art, for which he had prepared himself by a long sojourn in Italy. He published: *Essays, Neue Essays, Zehn ausgewählte Essays zur Einführung in das Studium der modernen Kunst*, and *Fünfzehn Essays*. As professor at Berlin University, he gave some most interesting lectures on Goethe.

Grimma, a tn, situated in the kingdom of Saxony. It stands on the l. b. of the Mulde, and is about 17 m. S.E. of Leipzig. Here is the Fürstenschule, a school founded in 1550. The people are engaged in the manufacture of iron goods, and in agriculture. Pop. about 11,200.

Grimmelshausen, Hans Jakob Christoffel von (c. 1625-76), a German author, born at Gelnhausen in Hesse-Cassal. As a boy he was kidnapped by Hessian soldiers, and becoming a soldier himself fought on the Imperial side in the Thirty Years' War. At the end of the war he settled at Renchen in Baden, and entered the service of the Bishop of Strassburg, becoming ' Schultheiss' (magistrate) of Renchen in 1665. He devoted his leisure to literature and published several remarkable novels. In 1669 he published *Der abenteuerliche Simplicissimus*, one of the best novels of the 17th century. It is modelled on the picaresque romances of Spain, and is largely autobiographical in its descriptions of the stirring scenes of the hero's childhood. Among his other works are : *Simplicianische Schriften; Die Erzbetrügerin und Landstörtzerin Courasche* (c. 1669), *Der seltsame Springinsfeld* (1670), and *Das wunderbarliche Vogelnest* (1672). His satires and gallant novels, modelled on *Cyrano de Bergerac*, such as *Dietwald und Amelinde* (1670) are very inferior to *Simplicissimus*. See *Simplicissimus* (ed. by A. von Keller, 1854; H. Kurz, 1863-64).

Grimm's Law, an important phonetic law which states the changes in the consonants of words in the course of their development from the Primitive Aryan language into Low and High German. The various languages of the Indo - European family show that, as they developed from Primitive Aryan, each into its own special form, their consonants and vowels underwent change according to a certain law. Knowing this law, the philologist can take a word from Primitive Aryan and say beforehand in what form that word will be found in any one of the languages descended from it — in Sanskrit, Latin, Greek, Teutonic. The vowel or consonant of the word will have

undergone a regular and known metamorphosis. He could predict, for example, that *bhrâtr* in Sanskrit would be in Greek φράτηρ, in Latin *frater*, in Gothic *broþar*, in German *bruder*, and in English *brother*. The Teutonic languages, which Grimm investigated, differ from Primitive Aryan much more in their consonants than in their vowels, and these consonants it is with which G. L. is concerned. The Primitive Teutonic system of consonants is best seen in Gothic, the most ancient of the Teutonic languages, in Early, Low German, and in Early Scandinavian. The Primitive Aryan consonant system is seen, with little deviation, in Sanskrit, Greek, Latin, Lithuanian, Old Slavonic, and Old Keltic. The Teutonic languages underwent their characteristic changes at two more or less definitely marked epochs. The first, known as the *First Consonant Shifting*, took place in prehistoric times, the *Second Consonant Shifting* belongs to the 5th, 6th, and 7th centuries. In the latter, certain Primitive Teutonic consonants underwent a change as the words in which they occurred entered the High German dialects. A word beginning with a *t* in Gothic, for instance, would change this *t* for a *z* (pronounced *ts*) in High German. Gothic, which underwent only the first consonant shifting is the best representative of the Low German and Scandinavian dialects; Old High German the best representative of the other divisions of the Teutonic languages. The most important consonant changes by which Primitive Aryan developed into Teutonic, is summed up in the formula known as G. L., from Jakob Ludwig Karl Grimm (1785-1863), who first worked out the law which had already been suspected by Rask. This law, which takes into account the ' permutation of consonants ' of the first shifting, states that the Aryan *bh, dh, gh* (the ' voiced aspirates ') ultimately became in Teutonic *b, d, g* (' voiced stops ' or ' mediæ '), that *b, d, g* became *p, t, k* (' unvoiced stops ' or ' tenues ') and that *p, t, k* became *f, þ, h* (' unvoiced spirants '; the *h* is like *ch* in *loch*).

	Sanskrit.	Greek.	Latin.	Gothic.	Old High German.	German.	English.
bh	Bhrâte	φράτωρ	frater	prôþar	bruoder	Bruder	brother
dh	rudhira	ερυθρός	ruber	rands	rôt	rot	red
gh	stighnôti	στείχω	—	steigan	stigan	steigen	sty
b	—	—	tribus	þaúrp	dorf	Dorf	thorp
d	dam	δαμάω	domare	tamjan	zamjam	zähmen	tame
g	jánu	γόνυ	genu	kniu	kniu	Knie	knee
p	pad	πούς	pes	fôtus	fuoz	Fuss	foot
t	tri	τρεῖς	tres	þreis	drî	drei	three
k	kampata	κώπη	capere	hafjan	heffan	heben	heave

Whitney believes that these changes, so arbitrary in appearance, have a physiological basis. They arise in the course of what Max Müller calls 'dialectic growth,' similar to that instanced in the word *vat*, in wine-vat, which is the Old English form of the Northern English *fat*, a vessel, and in such a dialectical change as that of *he liveth* into *he lives*, where the aspirate dental *th* becomes *s*. *See* Morris, *Historical Outlines of English Accidence.*

Grimsby, or **Great Grimsby**, a seaport in Lincolnshire, on the S. bank of the Humber, 15 m. S.E. of Hull, is the largest fishing port in England. There are many fine old buildings, including a parish church and some interesting Roman remains. In the middle ages it was an important commercial centre, but the harbour became silted up and trade declined. In 1849 improvements were made, and there are now eight docks, covering 350 acres. Other industries carried on are tanning, brewing, and shipbuilding. There is a free grammar school (1547), a school for technical instruction, a mechanics' institute, and a free public library. The town returns one member to parliament. Cleethorpes, 3¼ m. S.E. of G., is a well-known health resort. A new dock has been made at Immingham, 5 m. N. of G. Pop. 74,663.

Grimsel Pass, situated in the Bernese Alps, Switzerland. It is over 7000 ft. high, and leads to the valley of the Aar, being crossed by a carriage road. At the foot of the pass is the Grimsel Hospice. It was here that the French were victorious over the Austrians in 1799.

Grimthorpe, Edmund Becket, Baron (1816-1905), a famous authority on architecture and horology, was the designer of Big Ben, the great Westminster clock. He was born at Carlton Hall, near Newark, educated at Eton and Cambridge, was called to the bar, and became a Q.C. in 1854. He was for some years a leader of the parliamentary bar. He was much interested in architecture, designed several churches, and was responsible for restoring St. Albans Cathedral. He also occupied the presidency of the British Horological Institute, and published many useful works of scientific interest, as well as articles on ecclesiastical law.

Grindal, Edmund (1519-83), Archbishop of Canterbury, was born at St. Bees, Cumberland. He took his degree at Cambridge, and after receiving several minor appointments in the church, became a prebendary of Westminster. But the favours he enjoyed under Edward VI. were withdrawn in Mary's reign, and he

left the country, returning on the accession of Elizabeth. He was made Bishop of London (1559), Archbishop of York (1570), and Archbishop of Canterbury (1575). He did not keep the confidence of the queen, who objected to his advanced views. After suspending him for six months she advised him to resign. Blind and in ill health he did so, but was reinstated before his death, which occurred at Croydon. His writings, which are unimportant, were published by the Parker Society.

Grindelia, a genus of Compositæ, is to be found in America and consists of two dozen species. They are all hardy plants and are often called gum-plants from their sticky nature.

Grindelwald, a vil. situated in the canton of Bern, Switzerland, and in the Bernese Oberland. Here are the Upper and Lower G. glaciers, and the beauty of the spot attracts a large number of visitors. Pop. about 3400.

Gringore (or **Gringoire**), **Pierre** (c. 1475 - c. 1544), a French poet and dramatist, born at Caen. He began his literary career by writing allegorical and moral poems, afterwards writing for the stage, his works containing satires on the politics of the time. He was for many years a member of the ' Enfants sans Souci,' a theatrical company of Paris, and in his comedies attacked all people, including the pope. The latter years of his life were spent in the service of the Duke of Lorraine, during which time he wrote religious poetry. His chief works are : *Le Jeu du Prince des Sots,* 1511, in which he satirised Pope Julius II.; *Le Mystère de Saint-Louis,* about 1524 ; *La Chasse du cerf des Cerfs,* about 1520 ; *Heures de Nostre Dame,* 1524. *See* Emile Badel, *Pierre Gringoire,* 1892.

Grinnel, a city of Iowa, U.S.A., in Powieshiek co., 55 m. N.E. of Des Moines. Manufs. include carriages, flour, gloves, etc. Pop. (1910) 5036.

Grinnell Land, a land in the N. Polar regions, lying between the latitudes of 79° and 81° 30' N., and bounded on the N. by Lady Franklin Strait, and on the S. by Hayes Sound. It is on the W. side of Kennedy Channel, the N. continuation of Smith Sound. It was discovered in the first Grinnell expedition by De Haven.

Grinstead, East, a tn. in the co. of Sussex, England, just over 30 m. to the S.E. of London, and about 14 m. N.E. of Horsham. Here are situated Sackville College and the St. Margaret sisterhood. Pop. (1911) 7090.

Grinstead, West, a vil. in the co. of Sussex, about 6 m. S. of Horsham. Pop. (1911) 1500.

Gripenberg, Oscar Casimirovitch

(*b.* 1838), a Russian general of German extraction. He entered the Russian army in 1854 and took part in the Crimean War (1855). He also saw active service in the Polish insurrection of 1863, and subsequently fought in Turkestan (1867), in the Russo-Turkish War (1877-78), and in the Russo-Japanese War (1904-5).

Gripes, or Griping, a popular name for attacks of pain in the abdomen, produced by colic or any similar disease. The usual treatment is hot fomentations.

Griqualand East, a district of Cape Colony, S. Africa, and lies to the S. of Natal. It has an area of over 7500 sq. m. Adam Kok, the Griqua chief, originally settled here, bringing with him 15,000 Griquas. Since 1875 it has been under the rule of Cape Colony. The chief town is Kokstad. Pop. about 222,000.

Griqualand West, situated to the N. of Cape Colony, is bounded E. and S. by the Orange R., and N. by Bechuanaland. It was annexed to Cape Colony in 1871, and is noted for its diamonds. The chief towns are Kimberley, which is the cap., Griqua Town, De Beers, and Barkly. The area is about 15,197 sq. m. Pop. about 100,000.

Grisebach, August Heinrich Rudolf (1814-79), a German botanist, born at Hanover. He studied at Göttingen and in 1836 took the degree of doctor of medicine, and became a professor in Göttingen University. He made a special study of the vegetation of America and the W. Indies, and published a work on the flora of the British West Indian Islands. He also wrote *Journey through Roumelia, Outlines of Systematic Botany,* and other scientific books. He died in Göttingen.

Griselda, a fictional character whose conduct typifies wifely obedience. She was a very beautiful Piedmontese peasant girl wooed by the Marquis of Saluzzo. She became his wife, and to assure himself of the worth and stability of her character he put her to the severest ordeals, through all of which she passed successfully. After which, confidence completely restored, they were reconciled and happy. The origin of the story was Boccaccio's *Decameron.* Petrarch also used it, and Chaucer in his *Clerke's Tale.* On all parts of the Continent versions of it are found, and it has formed the subject of several plays: French, German, and Early English.

Griselinia : 1. A genus of leguminous plants found in tropical countries, and is usually considered as synonymous with the Linnæan genus *Pterocarpus.* 2. A genus of Cornaceæ, con-

tains only two species, both of which are to be found in New Zealand. The plants are arborescent, have leathery leaves, and bear small flowers.

Grisi, Guilia, or Julia (1811-69), a famous soprano *prima-donna,* born at Milan. She studied at Bologna under Giacomo Giacomelli, and made her first public appearance there in the part of Emma, in Rossini's *Zelmira.* She visited Florence, Paris, and London, winning universal fame. Several operas were written especially for her, including Bellini's *Puritani ;* but the rôle in which she obtained her greatest triumphs was that of Norma. In 1856 she married Mario, a tenor, and toured with him in America. The tour was not a success, and she returned to Europe. She died at Berlin.

Gris-nez (Fr. 'grey ness'), a cape in the dept. of Pas de Calais, France, is the point on the French coast nearest to Britain. It is midway between Calais and Boulogne, and opposite Dover. Its lighthouse has a revolving light.

Grison, or *Galictis vittata,* also called **Huron,** a weasel found in S. America and Mexico. It is about the same size as a marten and a little larger than the European weasel. It lives on small animals and birds, and destroys poultry.

Grisons, the largest canton of Switzerland, is bounded on the E. and S. by the Tyrol and Lombardy. It is a wild mountainous district intersected by narrow valleys. It includes the upper valley of the Inn, the three main sources of the Rhine and several glacier groups. The valleys are fertile and cattle rearing and agriculture are the chief pursuits of the inhabitants. Iron, lead, and copper are found in small quantities, and there are mineral springs. The name (from Graubünden, the Grey League) is derived from the grey coat worn by the people of the canton who formed a league in the 15th century to resist the tyranny of the nobles. The capital is Chur, and Davos, St. Moritz, and Arosa, are popular pleasure resorts. Pop. 118,262.

Griswold, Rufus Wilmot (1815-57), an American editor and compiler, born at Benson in Vermont. He was apprenticed to a publisher, and became an assistant editor. Tiring of this, he took up the study of theology and entered the Baptist ministry, gaining the degree of D.D. He returned to journalism, 1841, and wrote for many of the New York weekly papers, editing the *International Magazine,* which afterwards amalgamated with Harper's. He compiled several anthologies, and edited Milton's prose works. In the capacity of literary executor, he wrote a biography for the first edition of the works of Edgar Allan Poe, which received much condemnation. He died in New York.

Grits, coarse sandstones, often very impure. Examples occur in the grey-wackes and the Torridonian sand-stones of Scotland and Wales. Mill-stone G. is the fourth member of the Upper Carboniferous series, and is situated between the Lower Coal Measures and the Pendleside group. It varies from 4000 ft. thick in Lan-cashire until it becomes very unim-portant in Scotland. In South Wales it consists of several layers, the top of massive sandstones termed ' Farewell Rock ' by the miners, because no workable seams of coal lie below it. Pennant G. of the same district is a hard grey felspathic sandstone, cut as a freestone, and used for building purposes. Kinderscout G., so named from the Peak of Derbyshire, is the lowest division of the Millstone G. of that area, while Rosslyn sandstone of Scotland is still another local development.

Groat (from the Dutch, ' great ' or ' thick '), the name applied in the middle ages to all large thick coins. The English G. was first issued in 1351, and discontinued in 1662. It was a silver coin equal in value to four pence. In 1836 a coin of similar value was struck, called a fourpenny-piece. The German equivalent of Gs. were *groschen*, worth 1½d., in circulation in N. Germany till 1876.

Grocyn, William (1446-1519), a Greek scholar, was the first Englishman to teach Greek publicly in Oxford Uni-versity. He was born at Colerne, Wiltshire, educated at Winchester College and New College, Oxford. He studied under Chalcondylas, and in-cluded among his friends, Erasmus and More. He was master of All Hallows, Maidstone, and held the livings of St. Lawrence Jewry, Shepperton, and E. Peckham. No authentic writings have been pre-served. He was buried at Maidstone in All Hallows Church.

Grodek, a tn. in Galicia, Austria, 16 m. W.S.W. of Lemburg, is a great flax growing centre. Pop. 13,382.

Grodno: 1. A gov. in the W. of European Russia, is bounded N. by Vilna, S. by Volhynia, E. by Minsk, W. by Poland, and covers an area of 14,900 sq. m. It is low and marshy, and there are extensive pine forests. The principal rivers are the Niemen, Bug, and Narev. Rye, flax, hemp, barley and potatoes are grown; the chief industries are cloth, leather, bricks, and tobacco manufactures. Pop. 2,000,000. 2. A tn., cap. of above gov., on the Niemen, 80 m. S.S.W. of Vilna. It contains two

castles, one dating from the 12th century; the other, quite modern, is now turned into a military hospital. Here the second partition of Poland was arranged, 1793, and in 1795 it was taken over by Russia. The chief manufactures are pottery, tobacco, soap, tallow, and machinery. Pop. 46,871.

Grog, a name given to a mixture of rum and cold water, without sugar. The name is supposed to be derived from a nickname (Old Grog) of Admiral Vernon, who about 1745 ordered his sailors to dilute their spirits with water. Admiral Vernon's nickname was in allusion to his habit of wearing breeches, or a cape, made of grogram, a fabric stiffened with gum, which was then worn.

Groin, an architectural term signi-fying the angular curve made by the intersection of two arches; when the intersecting arches have the same diameter and height, the G. is said to be regular; when one is semi-elliptical and the other semicircular, the G. is irregular. In Gothic architecture the Gs. are always ribbed.

Groix, an island off the coast of Brit-tany, France, in the dept. of Mor-bihan. It is 4½ m. long and 2 m. wide; deep-sea fishing is carried on. Pop. 5000.

Grolier, Jean, Viscount d'Aguisy (1479-1565), a French bibliophile and connoisseur of book bindings, was born at Lyons. He entered the diplo-matic service under Francis I. and spent some time in Milan and Rome. There he gradually collected a unique library of richly-bound volumes, de-voting a great part of his fortune to it. In 1675 the collection was sold publicly, realising very high prices. Part of it is in the National Library, Paris, and a few volumes are in the British Museum.

Gronau, a tn. in Westphalia, Prussia, is 30 m. N.W. of Münster, on the R. Dinkel. The chief industry is dyeing, and there are also large cotton factories. Pop. 10,079.

Groningen: 1. The most northerly prov. of the Netherlands, is bounded N. by the North Sea, S. by the Drente, E. by Hanover, and W. by Friesland. It is very low, and includes much reclaimed marshland. The soil is fertile and well cultivated, and agri-culture is the principal industry of the people. On the coast, fishing and shipbuilding are carried on. 2. The cap. of the prov. of G., on the Hunse, 92 m. N.E. of Amsterdam, is the most important town in the N. of Holland. Connected by canals with the Dollart and Zuyder Zee, it forms a good centre for trade. It possesses a uni-versity, botanical gardens, a museum and town hall, and is well laid out.

The chief industries are linen and woollen manufs., tobacco, and boat building.

Gronovius, the name of a family of scholars who settled in Holland. They were of German extraction — their name being Gronov — of which the above is a Latinised form. The principal members of this family were:

Johann Friedrich Gronovius (1611-71), born at Hamburg. He was at first a professor at Deventer (1642), and afterwards at Leyden (1658). His knowledge of the classics and of antiquities was profound. He edited Livy, Tacitus, Plautus, Cicero, and the works of many other writers.

Jacobus Gronovius (1645-1716), son of the preceding, was born at Deventer. He also was a great scholar, and was first a professor at Pisa and then at Leyden from 1679 till his death. His chief work was *Thesaurus Antiquitatum Græcarum*, 1697-1702, although he edited several of the classics.

Abraham Gronovius (1694-1775), son of the preceding, was librarian of Leyden University.

Johann Friedrich Gronovius (1690-1760), brother of the preceding, was a botanist, and writer of *Flora Virginica*, 1739-43, and *Flora Orientalis*, 1755.

Lorenz Theodor Gronovius (1730-77), brother of the preceding, was the author of *Museum Ichthyologicum*, 1754-56, and *Zoophylacium Gronovianum*, 1763-81.

Groome, Francis Hindes (1851-1902), an English author, son of Archdeacon G. of Suffolk. By 1877 he had embarked on a literary career, and is especially known as a student of gipsies, their life, language, and customs. He lived amongst them himself, winning their confidence and becoming steeped in their lore and history. G. wrote *In Gypsy Tents*, 1880; *Gypsy Folk-Tales*, 1899; and edited Borrow's *Lavengro*, 1900. He was one of the founders of the Gypsy Lore Society, and joint-editor of its *Journal* from 1888-91. Other works are: *A Short Border History*, 1887; *Two Suffolk Friends* (Archdeacon G. and E. FitzGerald); the novel *Kriegspiel*, 1896; and the editing of the *Ordnance Gazetteer of Scotland* . . ., 1882-85. G. was one of the editors of Chambers's *Encyclopædia*, 1885-92, and joint-editor of the *Biographical Dictionary*, 1897. See *Athenæum*, Nos. 2763, 3012.

Groot, Gerhard (1340-84), founder of the ' Brethren of the Common Life,' born at Deventer. In 1379 he became a travelling preacher and gathered together a number of people who agreed to have common goods. This was formed into the above-named brotherhood—which met with much opposi-

tion in clerical circles. *See* Gaston Bonet-Maury, *G. de Groote*, 1878.

Groote Eylandt, an island lying off the northern coast of Australia in the Gulf of Carpentaria. It is about 40 m. long, and 40 m. broad.

Gros, Antoine Jean, Baron (1771-1835), a French painter, born in Paris, was the son of a miniature painter. He studied first at David's studio, and afterwards travelled in Italy where he became acquainted with Napoleon Bonaparte, having been introduced by Josephine. He was given an official position by Bonaparte and became a military painter. In 1824 he was made a baron by Charles X. for his paintings in the Pantheon. He afterwards gave up the romantic style of painting and turned to the classic style. In this, however, he seems to have been unsuccessful, and committed suicide by throwing himself in the Seine. His best pictures are: ' Bonaparte at the Bridge of Arcole; ' ' Napoleon visiting the Plague-stricken at Jaffa; ' ' The Battle of Eylau; ' ' The Meeting of Charles V. and Francis I.;' and among his classic style, ' Hercules and Diomedes.'

Grosart, Alexander Balloch (1827-99), a Scottish ecclesiastic and writer, born at Stirling. He was a student at Edinburgh University, and in 1856 was appointed Presbyterian minister at Kinross. In 1865 he became minister of Prince's Park, Liverpool, and of Blackburn in 1868, giving up the ministry in 1892. His chief work was done in his editing of Elizabethan literature. He published the Fuller's Worthies Library, consisting of thirty-nine volumes, 1868-76, and in the latter year began the Chertsey Worthies Library, both of which publications included the works of many authors, among them George Herbert, Sir Philip Sidney, and Abraham Cowley. In addition to these, he edited the works of writers such as Edmund Spenser, Samuel Daniel, and a number of others.

Grosbeak, the name applied to some of the species of the family Fringillidæ, belonging to the order Passeriformes, and including the various kinds of finches. In these birds the beak is stout and very much developed. Among the species may be mentioned the Pine G. (*Pyrrhula enucleator*), found in the regions of the N., and the Hawfinch (*Coccothraustus vulgaris*), occasionally found in Britain.

Grose, Francis (c. 1731-91), an English antiquary, born at Greenford in Middlesex. He was at first a draughtsman, and exhibited his architectural drawings at the Academy, and from 1755-63 was Richmond herald. He spent a large part of his time in antiquarian research, and during this time became acquainted with Robert Burns. His chief works are : *Antiquities of England and Wales*, 1773-87; *Antiquities of Scotland*, 1789-91; *Classical Dictionary of the Vulgar Tongue*, 1785.

Grosnaya, or **Grosnyi**, a Russian tn., situated in Ciscaucasia in the Terek ter. It has refineries of petroleum. Pop. about 16,000.

Gross, Samuel David (1805-54), an American surgeon, born in Pennsylvania. After taking his degree in medicine at Jefferson College, Philadelphia, in 1828, he was appointed professor of pathological anatomy at Cincinatti, 1835. In 1840 he became professor of surgery at Louisville, and ten years later in New York, finally obtaining the same appointment in Jefferson College. Among his works are : *System of Surgery*, 1859 (6th ed. 1884) ; *Diseases of the Bones and Joints*, 1830 ; *Elements of Pathological Anatomy* (3rd ed.), 1857.

Grossbeeren, a Prussian vil., situated 12 m. S.E. of Berlin. It is memorable for a victory gained here in 1813 by the Prussians over the French. Pop. about 1400.

Grossenhain, a tn. of Germany, situated in the kingdom of Saxony to the N.W. of Dresden, and on the R. Röder. It manufs. silk and woollen goods, hosiery, and machinery. Pop. about 12,200.

Grosseteste Robert (*c.* 1175-1253), a Bishop of Lincoln, born at Stradbroke in Suffolk, and was of humble parentage. He was educated at Oxford, and seems also to have obtained some of his education in Paris. He became chancellor of Oxford University, and rector of the Franciscans in that town. After holding the offices of archdeacon of Northampton and then Leicester, he became, in 1235, Bishop of Lincoln. While holding this office he carried on a dispute from 1239 - 45 with the Lincoln chapter, finally gaining his point—the right of visitation. He also stood up for the rights of the Church against the State, thus involving himself in disputes with Henry III., and for his own church against that of Rome, thereby coming into conflict with the pope, as on the occasion of his refusing to appoint the pope's nephew in the Lincoln diocese. *See* Francis Seymour Stevenson, *Robert Grosseteste, Bishop of Lincoln*, 1899.

Grosseto : 1. An Italian prov. in Tuscany. 2. A tn. of Italy, cap. of the above prov., about 40 m. S.S.W. of Siena. It is an old fortified town, and has a beautiful cathedral which dates from 1294. Near to G. are the ruins of Rusellæ, an old Etruscan city. Pop. (commune) about 9599.

Grossglockner, *see* GLOCKNER, GROSS.

Grossgörschen, a vil. of Prussian Saxony, situated S. of Lützen. The battle of Lützen, in 1813, is often styled the battle of G.

Gross-Lichterfelde, a tn. and com. of Prussian Germany in the prov. of Brandenburg. It forms a suburb of Berlin, and is situated about 6 m. from the city. There is a royal cadet school. Pop. 42,510.

Grossmith, George (1847-1912), an English actor and public entertainer, son of a journalist. In 1866 he was a reporter for the *Times*, but soon gave it up for the stage. In 1870 he made his début at the Polytechnic as an entertainer, with comic songs and sketches at the piano. In 1877 he began a successful career as actor in *The Sorcerer*, later playing in many other Gilbert and Sullivan operas, and winning especial distinction as the Admiral in *Pinafore*. He was with the D'Oyly Carte company at the Savoy from 1881-89, and then resumed his individual recitals for a time. He played in *His Excellency*, 1894; *Young Mrs. Yarde*, 1898; and *The Gay Pretenders*, 1900. Again resuming his recitals for some years, he finally retired in 1909. His writings include : *The Reminiscences of a Society Clown*, 1888; *The Diary of a Nobody* (with his brother, Weedon G.), 1894; *Cups and Saucers*, and various songs. George G., junior, and Lawrence, are his sons.

Grossmith, Weedon, an English actor and artist, brother of George (*d.* 1912). He has exhibited at the Royal Academy. He first appeared on the stage in 1885 with Rosina Vokes's company at Liverpool. In her company on tour to America, he played in *A Pantomime Rehearsal* (Lord Pomeroy), 1885 ; *The Schoolmistress ; A Quiet Rubber ;* and *Caste*. His first London appearance was in 1887; in 1888 he was with Sir Henry Irving at the Lyceum, and under Tree at the Haymarket in 1889. He became lessee and manager of Terry's Theatre, 1894-96. In 1898 he appeared at the Pavilion as Jack Sheppard. Among his later rôles are : Hamilton Preedy in *Mr. Preedy and the Countess*, 1909; Billy in *Billy's Bargain*, 1910; Jimmy Jinks in *Baby Mine*, 1911; Frantz in *Money;* and Jones in *David Garrick* at the gala performances at Drury Lane and His Majesty's, 1911. His publications include : *A Woman with a History*, 1896; *A Commission; The Night of the Party*, 1901; *The Duffer*, 1905, and other plays.

Gross-Moyeuvre, a tn. of Alsace-Lorraine, Germany, in the circle of Diedenhofen, on the R. Orne, 10½ m. from Metz. Iron-ore is mined, and there are smelting works. Pop. 9556.

Gross-Rohrsdorf, a tn. of Saxony, Germany, in the circle of Kamenz, 18 m. S.W. of Bautzen. Pop. 6000.

Grossularite (Ca₃Al₂Si₃O₁₂), a lime-alumina garnet (*q.v.*) known as *gooseberry stone;* usually brownish-green and obtained from Siberia. Special varieties of it exist under the names *wiluite* (Siberia) and *romanzovite* (Finland).

Grosswardein (Hungarian *Nagyvárad*), an old tn. of Hungary, cap. of Bihar, on the Rapid Körös, about 150 m. S.E. of Budapest. It contains an old fortress and many public buildings, among them two bishops' palaces, as it is the seat of both Roman Catholic and Greek Catholic bishops. Near to this town are hot mineral springs. Pop. 64,169.

Grote, George (1794 - 1871), an eminent English historian and politician, author of a standard work on Greece. He was educated at Charterhouse School, and after spending thirty years of his life as a banker and ten as one of the members of parliament for London, he retired from parliament in 1831 and from business in 1843 to give his whole time to literature. He was, with Bentham and Mill, one of the group of ' Philosophical Radicals ' whose principles he actively supported in parliament; he was one of the chief advocates of the ballot. G. criticised Mitford's *History of Greece,* attacking its anti-democratic deductions, which he held to be based on misconception. His own *magnum opus* regards the government of Athens as that of an idealised democracy. G.'s *History of Greece,* characterised by deep learning and the method of the ' philosophical ' historian, superseded Mitford's and even the more scholarly work of Thirlwall. He wrote also *Plato and other Companions of Socrates,* and an unfinished work on Aristotle. See *Life* by Mrs. Grote.

Grotefend, Georg Friedrich (1775-1853), a German orientalist and classical philologist, educated at Göttingen. He held posts at the Frankfort gymnasium, 1797-1821, leaving to become director of the lyceum at Hanover, and retiring from public life, 1849. G. is most famous for contributing to the decipherment of old Persian (cuneiform) inscriptions, and is sometimes considered as the first to find the key, increasing the number of known characters from three to eleven. He first began this study in 1802, and directed his attention to the interpretation of the Lycian inscriptions.

His *Neue Beiträge zur Erläuterung der Persepolitanischen Keilschrift* appeared in 1837 ; . . . *zur Erläuterung der Babylonischen Keilschrift,* 1840. Other works are : *Anfangsgründe der deutschen Poesie,* 1815 ; *Rudimenta Linguæ Umbricæ,* 1835-38 ; *Rudimenta Linguæ Oscæ,* 1839 ; *Geographie und Geschichte von Altitalica,* 1840-42. He also revised Wenck's *Lateinische Grammatik,* 1823-24, and contributed to the *Encyclopædia* of Ersch and Gruber. *See* works of Sayce on *Ancient Monuments,* 1881-94.

Grotefend, Karl Ludwig (1807-74), a German classical scholar, born at Frankfort. He was a great writer on the subject of classical coins, and wrote many historical studies.

Grotesque (It. *grottesco,* from *grottesca,* style of painting found in ancient crypts, *crypta,* or *grotta*), in art, a capricious and incongruous style of decoration, in which human figures, animals, flowers, and fruit are all fantastically mingled in wild confusion. This style was used in the 13th century, and rediscovered during excavations made in the baths of Titus. It was very popular in the Renaissance period, but soon became debased. G. has come to be applied to any fanciful combination of ideas, or to any extravagant and absurd representation or appearance. *See* Florio's *Dictionary,* 1598 and 1611; *also* ARABESQUE, CARICATURE.

Groth, Klaus (1819-99), a German poet, born at Heide in Schleswig-Holstein, and educated at Tondern. He then became a teacher in his own native village, but afterwards went to Kiel in order to further continue his studies. His health, however, broke down, and for some time he was not able to go on. He finally took a degree as doctor of philosophy at Bonn, and settled in the town of Kiel. He wrote lyric and epic poetry, and although his poems do not reflect the expression of German country-life as well as the author on whom he modelled himself, nevertheless he has gained for himself a place amongst the German poets. His chief works are : *Quickborn : Drei Plattdeutsche Erzählungen ; Vertelln ; Volksleben im plattdeutschen Gedichten.*

Grotius, Hugo, otherwise known as **Huig von Groot** (1583-1645), a celebrated Dutch jurist, born at Delft, and educated at Leyden. Leaving here he entered the diplomatic service and was for a short time in service with an embassy to England. He became pensionary of Rotterdam, and supported the Armenians in their religious controversies. This gained for him the hatred of Prince Maurice, and he was arrested and condemned to imprisonment for life. By the aid of his wife he escaped, and took refuge in Paris. Here he was granted a pension by Louis XIII. (1621). He distinguished himself in every branch of literature and diplomacy. In 1625 he issued his celebrated work on international law, *De Jure Belli et Pacis*. He became the ambassador of Sweden at the French courts, and later proceeded to Stockholm. Returning from here he died at Rostock.

HUGO GROTIUS

He wrote much on theology, history, and law, whilst as a poet he published some respectable verse both in Latin and Dutch. Works: *Annales de Rebus Belgicis*, and *De Veritate Religionis Christianæ. Life* by Butler, 1827.

Grotius, William (1597-1662), a Dutch jurist and law writer, was the brother of the statesman Hugo, and son of John de Groot, who was curator of the University of Leyden. He published *Enchiridion de Principiis Juris Naturalis* as an introduction to Hugo's great work, *De Jure Belli et Pacis*.

Groton, a tn. in the U.S.A., co. of New London, Connecticut, on the R. Thames. Its chief industries are connected with engineering and tobacco. In 1781 the town played an important part in the American War of Independence, but the garrison was massacred. Pop. (1910) 6495.

Grotta del Cane (Grotto of the Dog '), a cave near Naples and bordering on Lake Agnano. The cave is filled with carbonic acid gas fumes of great strength. The name was given because little dogs when sent into the cave were almost suffocated, but revived on being taken out.

Grottaglie, an Italian tn. in the prov. of Lecce, situated some 30 m. S.W. of the port of Brindisi. It is the centre of a pottery district. Pop. about 12,000.

Grotte, a Sicilian tn., 13 m. N.E. of the tn. of Girgenti. It is the centre of the sulphur mining industry. Pop. about 11,000.

Grouchy, Emmanuel, Marquis de (1766-1847), a French general who was born in Paris. He first saw active service with the revolutionary armies in La Vendée. He was second in command of the army which was sent to invade Ireland, and was able to land in Ireland, although he accomplished little. He next proceeded to Italy where he helped Joubert. He showed great courage and ability during the battles of Eylau, Friedland, and Wagram, and was in command of the bodyguard of Napoleon during the Russian campaign. He fought at Leipzig, and covered the retreat of Napoleon to Paris. He was amongst the first to welcome Napoleon on his return to France. He fought and defeated Blucher at Ligny, but misjudged that general's tenacity of purpose. After attempting to hold together the French armies after Napoleon's second abdication, he fled to the U.S.A. He returned in 1819, and was restored to his rank in the French army in 1831. His *Memoirs* (5 vols.) were published by his grandson.

Ground Annual, in Scottish law, an interest in land in the nature of an annual rent or perpetual annuity. It is of two kinds: (*a*) Feu duties arising out of Church property parcelled out in lordships erected by the crown, such feu duties being the interest retained by the Lords of Erection after resigning their superiorities to the crown. The feu duties became perpetually payable because the crown never rendered any consideration (*q.v.*) for the power to redeem them. (*b*) Rents reserved for building lots in burghs where sub-feus are prohibited. Such G. A. is in the nature of a real burden laid on the lands of a fixed annual payment in lieu of price, and is usually accompanied with a personal obligation on the part of the building speculator that he and his representatives in a sale will not get rid of the G. A.

Ground-base, in music, a bass, consisting of a few notes or bars, unceasingly repeated, and each time accompanied by a new or varied melody. *See* Beethoven's *Sonate Pathétique*, Op. 13, first movement, *molto allegro*.

Ground-ice, *see* ANCHOR-ICE.

Ground Ivy, or *Nepeta glechoma*, a species of Labiatæ closely allied to the cat-mint. It is a small trailing plant with rough leaves, and the flowers are small and purple.

Groundling (*Cobitis tænia*), a fish of the loach variety. It is rarely found nowadays, but occurs in English waters occasionally. It is very small.

Ground-nut, a term often applied to the edible parts of the roots of various plants. Amongst the best known may be mentioned the earth nut (*Bunium esculentum*) and the roots of the *Apios tuberosa*.

Ground Pigeon, a pigeon of the Peristerinæ family. They have longer legs than the usual type of pigeon. Turtle-doves belong to this family.

Ground Rent, the rent reserved by a landowner to himself in consideration of allowing buildings to be erected on his land. The customary arrangement in speculative building operations is for the landowner not to grant a lease at all until the buildings are part of the buildings are completed, but to enter into a binding agreement with the builder to reserve a total G. R. on his land to be subsequently apportioned to the houses as and when they are completed. As each house or integral building is completed the landowner grants a lease in which he reserves the G. R. on the site covered by such house or building. The interest of the builder in the land therefore ends with the sale of the houses built, unless, as often happens, he buys the G. R. himself. As the builder thus drops out of the transaction, the liability on the covenants becomes severable. Each purchaser being liable only for breaches in respect of his own lease and house.

Groundsel, or *Senecio vulgaris*, a composite herb found in Britain. The head contains many little yellow florets, none of which are ray-florets, and they are much appreciated by cage-birds.

Groups, Theory of, the study in higher mathematics which deals, not with actual quantities, but with operations. Certain operations in elementary work are familiar, *e.g.* multiplication, the squaring of a number, the rotating of a figure about an axis, and differentiation. If A is any operator which operates on any quantity F, the result is usually expressed AF. If A operates again on the result, this becomes AAF or A^2F; if again, A^3F, and so on. When the result of two successive operations in any order leaves the subject of the operations unchanged, the operators are then said to be *inverse*. The successive application of an operator and its inverse is known as the *identical* operation. Thus if X and Y are two such inverse operators, XYF =F and YXF=F ; ∴ XY=1 and YX=1, and hence it is found convenient to write X^{-1} for Y. Thus $XX^{-1}=1$ and $X^{-1}X=1$. Thus the result of the inverse operation of X on F is $X^{-1}F$, and the result of a second operation is $X^{-2}F$, and so on. Let A, B, C be three operations capable of operating on the same set of objects, of which the result of any two in any order equals the third, *e.g.* AB=C, then A, B, C and their inverses are said to form a group. And generally any number of such operations of which the result of the successive application of any two is equivalent to a third, form with their inverses a group. The number of operations in a group may be finite or infinite. When it is finite, the number is called the order of the group. For example, A^2, A, 1, A^{-1}, A^{-2} form a group, which in this case is said to be cyclical.

Grouse and Grouse-shooting. G. is a name which is in the exact sense applicable to all the members of the sub-family Tetraonidæ ; as commonly used the word refers only to the Red G. In addition to this species, the Black G. (*Tetrao tetrix*) and the

BLACK GROUSE

Wood G. (*T. urogallus*) are found in Great Britain ; these are better known by the names respectively of Blackcock and Capercailzie, and reference should be made to articles under those headings. Among the other species of G. may be named the Pinnated G. (*T. cupido*), peculiar to America; the Dusky G. (*T. obscurus*), which inhabits the Rocky Mountains; the Canadian G. (*T. Canadensis*), found in Canada and the United States ; the Hazel G. (*Bonasa sylvestris*) of N. Europe ; the Ruffed G. (*B. umbellus*) of N. America ; the Sand G. (*Pterocle*) and the Prairie Hen (*Syrrhaptes*), which are found in the Asiatic table-lands, constitute another family (the Pteroclidæ). For the White G. (*Lagopus mutus*, or *vulgaris*) *see under* PTARMIGAN. The Red G. (*L. Scoticus*), also called the Moorcock or Moor-fowl, is considered to be a variety of the willow G. (*L. albus*), which is found in Northern Europe, Asia, and America. It is found in the N. of England, particularly in Yorkshire, Lancashire, Derbyshire, and Durham; in Wales, Ireland, and the Scottish islands, and in most abundance in the Highlands of Scotland. The species is peculiar to the above-mentioned localities, and differs from the other members of the same genus in the fact that it does not turn white in the winter. G. shooting, as generally used, refers exclusively to the Red G., and under that heading the habits, etc., of the bird will be treated.

Grouse-shooting.—The Red G. is monogamous; the pairing takes place early in the spring. The female lays from five to fifteen eggs, which require twenty-four days to hatch. The young birds are strong and hardy after the first fortnight, which is a somewhat critical period. The principal enemy of the birds is the G. disease (*Strongylus pergracilis*), an epidemic disease which occasionally causes great ravages among the birds, and in a very bad season will practically preclude shooting over the moors affected. All through the summer the young birds follow the parent birds; in the autumn they ' break up ' until the winter, when they come together again in flocks (known as ' packs '), numbering, on the average, about thirty or forty, though sometimes as many as sixty are found. In order that a G. moor should furnish an abundance of birds, the latter must have a good supply of food and drink. The first requisite for a moor is therefore an abundant supply of pure water, and as the young shoots of the heather and wild ling form the chief food of the birds at certain seasons, the heather must be made to produce such shoots. This is effected by skilful periodical burning of the heather in tracts, as old heather will not provide the required shoots. There are two methods of shooting G., over dogs, or by driving. The former method, usually only practised on small moors, is impossible after the birds have begun to pack. The most important thing in G.-shooting over dogs is the direction of the wind. When a G. is disturbed, it will fly down the wind, and if the sportsman is also coming down the wind, his chance of a good shot will be small. If the G. is made to breast the wind as it rises, it will turn and fly down the wind as soon as

it has a sufficient velocity, and as it turns there will be the best chance of a shot. A moderate breeze blowing across the line taken by the shooting party is the best, and the most favourable weather is clear and sunny. If the weather is wild and wet, the best of dogs and shots do not stand much chance of a heavy bag. The dogs used are pointers or setters, the former being better if there is a plentiful supply of birds, otherwise the latter. The G. are ' driven ' towards hidden ' butts,' or ' batteries,' in which are the ' guns '; and which are situated about 80 yards apart. It is obvious that upon the site of the ' butts ' depends much of the success of the shooting. The beaters are spread out in the form of a crescent; and are provided with flags to show the line of flight. The flanks must be well protected, the usual line of flight of the birds, and the peculiarities of the district must all be taken into account. The birds are shot as they fly towards the butts; their flight is so very rapid that it requires a first class shot to kill with both barrels. From Dec. 11 to Aug. 11 (inclusive) is the ' close time ' for G.; ' the Twelfth,' is the abbreviation by which the opening of the season is generally known. For G. diseases *see* the papers of Prof. Young in the *Proceedings of the Natural History Society of Glasgow* (T.P. 225), and Dr. Klain's work on the subject. See *Grouse Shooting*, 1893; T. Cank, *Forty Years Mingled in Game, Fur, and Feather*, 1891; C. Dixon, *The Game Birds and Wild Fowl of the British Isles*, 1893.

Grove, Sir George (1820-1900), an English writer who is principally remembered for his contributions to the literature of music. He was at first an engineer, and spent his early days in works of engineering in the West Indies. In 1849 he became secretary to the Society of Arts and later to the Crystal Palace. Here he was largely responsible for the institution of those concerts which have had so much to do in the education of the British public in music. In 1868 he became editor of *Macmillan's Magazine*, and between the year 1878-1889 he edited the *Dictionary of Music*. He was the first director of the Royal College of Music, and was knighted on his appointment. See *Life* by Charles L. Graves.

Grove, Sir William Robert (1811-96), a scientist and lawyer, born at Swansea, he was educated by private tutors and at Brasenose College. He was called to the bar in 1835, and then for a time devoted himself to scientific studies. He invented a voltaic cell that is called the Grove Cell, and by this and by an anticipation of the methods of electric lighting, he made a great name for himself in the realm of science. He published in 1846 a book called the *Correlation of Physical Forces*. In 1866 he was president of the British Association. His legal work had not been neglected, and in 1853 he became a Q.C., and was later made a judge of the Court of Common Pleas.

Grove's Cell, see CELL, VOLTAIC.

Growler, a fish found chiefly in the fresh waters of N. America. It usually measures 2 ft. or more, and is allied to the perch family (*Percidæ*). This fish is edible.

Groyne, The, see CORUNA, LA.

Grub, the term applied to the larvæ of coleopterous insects. It is also erroneously given to the maggots, or larvæ of Diptera, which differ from the true Gs. in having no distinct head; and to the caterpillars, or larvæ of Lepidoptera, which differ in having rudimentary legs; the G. of a bee or beetle generally has a distinct head, but no legs. The so-called sheep-grub is the larvæ of the gad-fly, which sometimes deposits its eggs in the nostrils of animals.

Grub, George, LL.D. (1812-92), born in Old Aberdeen and educated at the university there, where he ultimately became first a lecturer at Marischal, and afterwards professor of civil law at the university. He was greatly interested in Scottish ecclesiastical history, and edited several Scottish historical works. His great work was *The Ecclesiastical History of Scotland*, 1861, which was written from the Anglican point of view. For his Life see Walker, *Three Churchmen*. 1893.

Grubber, an agricultural implement which consists of an iron framework, in which curved teeth, or ' tines,' are fixed, and which is mounted on wheels. The teeth penetrate the earth in an oblique direction when the machine moves forward, and the depth at which they work is regulated by an apparatus attached to the wheel. The G. is supposed to be an improvement on the harrow (*q.v.*), and is also called a ' cultivator ' or a ' scarifier.'

Grubenhagen, an old principality of Germany. It was in the prov. of Hildesheim and formed part of the kingdom of Hanover, being divided into two districts—the Eastern and Western—having the Harz Mts. as a dividing line. The chief town was Eimbeck, situated on the Ilm. Pop. about 80,000.

Gruber, Johann Gottfried (1774-1851), a German author and historian, was born at Naumburg. He was educated in his native town and at the University of Leipzig, after which he visited many of the other universities of Germany. At Weimar he enjoyed for a time the friendship of Goethe. He became a professor at the University of Wittenberg, and was largely instrumental in bringing about the union of that university with Halle. With Prof. Ersch he edited the *Allgemeine Encyklopädie der Wissenschaften und Künste*, a work which he continued after Ersch's death. He was also responsible for the editing of the *Allgemeine Literaturzeitung*. The whole of his works were very numerous.

Grub Street, now called Milton Street, in honour of the poet whose home was near it, was famous in the 17th century, for the reason given in Dr. Johnson's interesting definition in his *Dictionary:* ' Originally the name of a street near Moorfields in London. much inhabited by writers of small histories, dictionaries, and temporary poems, whence any mean production is called *Grub Street*.' The name has also been applied, since this time, as a collective term to struggling hack writers.

Gruel, an article of food usually given to invalids on account of its nutritious and digestive properties. It is made by placing a teacupful of oatmeal in a pint of water. After standing for some twenty minutes the water is poured off and any impurities in the meal rejected. The meal is then boiled for about twenty minutes and the G. is then ready. This preparation is held by expert medical advice to be far more nourishing than arrow-root or kindred preparations.

Grün, Anastasius, see AUERSBERG, ANTON ALEXANDER, COUNT OF.

Grunberg, a tn. of Prussia in the prov. of Silesia, 33 m. from Glogau. It has manufactures of woollens, machinery, straw hats, leather, and tobacco, and the vine is cultivated to a large extent, and wine and champagne exported. Pop. 23,162.

Grundtvig, Nicolai Frederick Severin (1783-1872), a Danish antiquarian, poet, preacher, and reformer, born at Udby, Zealand, and educated at Copenhagen. He was pastor of Præsto from 1821-22. when he became chaplain of the Church of the Saviour, Copenhagen. In 1825 he made a vehement protest in his *Kirkens Gjenmæle* against ' rationalism ' in the church. This raised a storm of bitter controversy, and G. was deprived of ecclesiastical office. He championed the cause of civil and religious freedom, advocated the separation of church and state, and helped to bring about many reforms. As a member of the *Folksthing* he collaborated in the drawing up of the Liberal constitution of 1849. He was reinstated and made a bishop in 1861.

G. studied and wrote upon the ancient Norse traditions and translated the *Saxo Grammaticus, Snorri Sturluson,* and the *Beowulf.* In connection with his antiquarian studies he was charged with three missions to England to collect the remains of the ancient Anglo - Saxon literature. He published a volume of the ancient popular songs of Iceland, *Popular Danish Songs,* collected among the Danish peasantry who sang them to him, *Kort Begreb af Verdens Krönike i Sammenhœng,* several volumes of poems, and a system of philosophy, *Mind and Liberty.*

Grundtvig, Svend Hersleb (1824-83), son of the preceding, a Danish philologist. His father educated him, teaching him especially Greek, Danish, Old Norse, and English, and transmitting to him his own great enthusiasm for the Danish ballads and literature. His greatest work is *Danmarks gamle Folksviser* (5 vols.) in which are reproduced the ancient texts of popular songs together with their subsequent forms collected orally. He also translated English and Scottish popular songs.

Grundy, Mrs., the name given to an imaginary character, who may well be described as the presiding deity of English respectability. She appears first in English literature in a play called *Speed the Plough,* where she is continually referred to as an authority on the proprieties. Her name has become a household word, but the cult of Mrs. G. is rapidly becoming less.

Grundy, Sydney (b. 1848), a dramatic author, born at Manchester. He was educated at Owen's College, Manchester, and after leaving, studied law and practised as a barrister in his native town from 1869 to 1876. His first play, *A Little Change,* was produced at the Haymarket Theatre in 1872, and in 1887 he made a great success with *The Bells of Haslemere,* written with Mr. Pettitt. He had, however, previous to this production, become well known as an adapter of plays, having brought out *The Snowball,* taken from *Oscar, ou le mari qui trompe sa femme,* by Scribe and Duverque, in 1879, and *In Honour Bound,* from Scribe's *Une Chaine,* in 1880. The years 1889 and 1890 saw the production of the comedies, *A White Lie* and *A Fool's Paradise,* and these were followed by *Sowing the Wind,* 1893 ; *An Old Jew,* 1894 ; and *A Bunch of Violets,* 1894, taken from Feuillet's *Montjoye.* But the most successful of his adaptations was *A Pair of Spectacles,* 1890, taken from *Les Petits Oiseaux* of Labiche and Delacour. Others were : *A Marriage of Convenience,* 1897 ; *The Silver Key,* 1897 ; and *The Musque-*

teers, 1899, all of which were taken from the works of Dumas ; *Frocks and Frills,* 1902; *The Garden of Lies,* 1904; *Business is Business,* 1905; and *The Diplomatists,* 1905. He also produced *The New Woman* and *The Slaves of the Ring* in 1894; *The Greatest of These* in 1895, played by Mr. and Mrs. Kendal; and *A Fearful Joy,* 1908.

Gruner, Wilhelm Heinrich Ludwig (1801-82), a German engraver, born at Dresden. He became the director of the Royal Museum at Dresden, and made a great name for himself as an engraver of many fine Italian masterpieces. In 1850 he published *Specimens of Ornamental Art* and *The Terra-cotta Architecture of North Italy,* 1867.

Grus, see CRANE.

Grus (' the Crane '), a southern constellation near Aquarius and Piscis Australis, introduced by 16th-century mariners. Near by are the constellations of Indus and Phœnix, on either side.

Gruter, John (1560-1627), a classical scholar, born at Antwerp. He studied at the universities of Cambridge and Leyden and was appointed professor of several universities, among them Heidelberg, and when the latter town was besieged he lost his library. His works contain editions of many of the Latin classics in addition to: *Inscriptiones Antiquæ Totius orbis Romani in corpus Absolutessimum redactæ,* 1602-3; and *Lampas sive Fax Artium Liberalium, hoc est, thesaurus criticus,* etc., 1603-34.

Grütli, or **Rutli,** a meadowland of Switzerland, situated in the canton of Uri, near Lake Lucerne. The Swiss League was founded here against Austria by the peasant leaders, Stauffacher, Arnold, Melchtal, and Walter Fürst. The meadow is now the property of the state, having been purchased by the school children of Switzerland. *See* Schiller, *Wilhelm Tell,* ii. 2.

Gruyère, a dist. and tn. of Switzerland in the canton of Freiburg, and 16 m. S.W. of that town. It is noted for its cheese. Pop. 1375.

Gryllidæ, the name of a family of Orthoptera, belonging to the section Saltatoria, and typified by *Gryllus,* the cricket genus. All members of this family are characterised by a cylindrical body, long, slender antennæ, and, in the females, a long curved ovipositor. There are several genera, which are widely distributed, *G. domesticus,* the common house-cricket, being found in the Old World and in N. America. The name grasshopper is often applied to *G. campestris,* and *Nemobius sylvestris,* two species of field-crickets.

Gryllus, the genus to which the

crickets belong. This order is distributed all over the world, but there are only four British varieties.

Gryphæa, the name given to a genus of fossil oysters belonging to the family Ostræidæ, and noted for their thick unequal valves.

Gryphius (or Greif), Andreas (1616-64), a German lyric poet and dramatist. His early life was a series of disasters, but nevertheless he managed to obtain a good classical education. In 1634 Georg von Schönborn became his patron, and did much to advance his genius. After the death of his patron he went to Leyden. Here he fell under the influence of the Dutch school of dramatists, and after an exhaustive tour in Europe he settled down to the drama himself. His chief works are : *Absurda comica ; Die gelsible Dornose ;* and *Kirchhofsgedanken.* The latter is the greatest of his lyrics. As a dramatist he was a good comedy writer, but became too lurid and wild when he attempted serious drama.

Gryphius, Sebastian (1493-1556), a printer, born at Reutlingen in Swabia. He settled at Lyons in 1528, and from that date onwards printed about 300 books, including Hebrew, Greek, Latin, Italian, and French. He was especially distinguished for the beauty of his Greek and Hebrew types, and his French and Latin books are still highly esteemed. Among the most noted of his works are the fine Latin Bible of 1550, and Dolet's *Commentaria Linguæ Latinæ.*

Gsell-Fels, Theodor (1819-98), a guide-book editor, born at St. Gall in Switzerland. He originally practised medicine, but later devoted most of his time to the compilation of guide books, chiefly for Italy and Switzerland. Among them may be mentioned : *Ober Italien und die Riviera,* 1898; *Unteritalien und Sizilien,* 1902 (4th ed.).

Guacharo, or **Oil-bird** (*Steatornis caripensis*), first found at Caripe in Venezuela. It constitutes the family Steatornithidæ, but is allied to the Nightjars. It is about the size of a crow, and lives chiefly in caverns near the sea, only coming out in the evening in search of food, which consists largely of fruit. The young birds are used as food, and from them also is obtained an extremely useful oil. They are natives of S. America.

Guadagnini, the name of a family of violin makers in Italy. *Lorenzo,* who, between 1695 and 1742, resided at Milan among other places, was a pupil of Stradivarius. His son, *Giovanni Battista* (1711-86), resided at Milan and Turin, both of them making instruments which are among the best of their kind.

Guadalajara : 1. Prov. of New Castile, Spain, bounded N. by Segovia, Soria, and Saragossa, E. by Teruel, S. by Cuenca. W. by Madrid. It is watered by tributaries of the Tagus, and yields agricultural produce. Area 4676 sq. m. Pop. 208,447. 2. Cap. of above on the Henares, 33 m. N.E. of Madrid. Among its chief noted buildings are the palace of the Mendozas and the Pantheon containing their tombs, the cloister of San Francisco, and a military engineering academy. There are textile and flour mills, and some serge and flannel are manufactured. Pop. about 11,000. 3. Cap. of Jalisco State, Mexico, founded about 1530, second largest city of the republic. It is the seat of an archbishop. The 17th-century cathedral contains an ' Assumption ' by Murillo. There are also a university, art academy, and mint. Its manufs. of cottons, woollens, pottery, metal wares, glass, and confectionery are noted. Pop. 118,799.

Guadalaviar, a river of Eastern Spain, which rises in a small lake in the Sierra of Albaracin. Its course, amidst beautiful scenery, is generally S. and S.E. for 180 m. until it reaches the Mediterranean Sea at Valencia.

Guadalcanal, a tn. of Spain in the prov. of Seville, 68 m. N.N.E. of Seville. It is situated in a silver, lead, copper, and iron mining district. Pop. 6000.

Guadalcanar, an island belonging to the Solomon group in the South Pacific, 100 m. long and 34 m. wide. It is mountainous and densely wooded. Aola and Lunga are the chief towns.

Guadalcazar, a tn. of Mexico in the state of San Luis Potosi, and 40 m. N.E. of that place. There are noted mines of quicksilver in the vicinity. Pop. 12,500.

Guadalquivir (ancient *Bœtis*), a river of Spain. It rises in the Sierra del Pozo Morena, and at first flows N.E. and then alters its course, assuming a south-westerly direction through Andalusia, entering the Atlantic about 20 m. N. of Cadiz. It is navigable as far as Seville, below which town it divides, forming the islands of Isla Mayor and Isla Menor. It is about 350 m. long.

Guadalupe : 1. A river of Texas, rising in Kerr co. and flowing into the bay of San Antonio. It is about 250 m. long. 2. A com. of Mexico, in the state of Zacatecas, and situated 10 m. S.E. of the town of Zacatecas. Pop. about 8800.

Guadalupe Hidalgo, a tn. of Mexico, situated between 2 and 3 m. N. of Mexico. It is the site of a church which is much visited by pilgrims, and it was in this town that the treaty was made between the United

States and Mexico in 1848, giving New Mexico and Upper California to the United States. Pop. *c.* 5500.

Guadarrama, Sierra de, a range of mountains in Spain, separating Madrid and Segovia, and situated between the Douro and the Tagus. The highest points in the range rise to about 8700 ft. Among them may be mentioned Sierra de Ayllon and the Pico de Penalara.

Guadéloupe, an island of the W. Indies and a French possession. It is really formed of two islands, Basse-Terre and Grande-Terre, separated by the Rivière Salée. Basse-Terre is of volcanic formation, the largest volcano being Soufrière, while Grande-Terre is comparatively flat. The climate is hot and the soil fertile, producing sugar, coffee, bananas, and rice, while Basse-Terre is covered with large forests. The dependencies of G. are : Marie Galante, St. Barthélemy, Désirade, Les Saintes, and part of St. Martin. The island is ruled by a governor, and is represented in the French parliament. The capital is Basse-Terre. The island was discovered by Columbus in 1493, and after being in the possession of the French and English alternately, was given to the former nation about 1814. Pop. (with dependencies) about 200,000.

Guadiana, a river of Spain, the Zancara, which rises in the prov. of Cuenca, being its head stream. Not far from the Zancara are the lakes known as Los Ojos. The G. flows westward through La Mancha and Estremadura to Badajos, where it assumes a southerly direction forming a boundary between Spain and Portugal. The river is about 500 m. long, its chief tributaries being the Javalón, Zujar, and Ardila.

Guadix, a city of N. Spain in Granada, situated on the R. Guadix. There are mulberry plantations, and in the vicinity are the warm mineral springs of Graena. Pop. 12,700.

Guaduas, a tn. of Colombia, S. America, situated 45 m. N.W. of Bogota. Pop. 11,000.

Guagua, a tn. and com. of the island of Luzon, Philippine Is. It is situated in the province of Pampanga. Pop. 10,500.

Guaiacum, a genus of Zygophyllaceæ, is indigenous in America, and contains only four species. The most remarkable of these is *G. officinale,* from which the hard, compact, black-green wood called *lignum vitæ* is obtained; it also produces the gum-resin known in medicine as G.

Guaira, La *see* LA GUAIRA.

Gualdo Tadino, a com. of Italy in the prov. of Perugia, situated about 58 m. from Ancona on the road leading to

the Furlo Pass. It possesses a noted cathedral. In the vicinity, Totila was defeated by Narses in 552. Pop. 9000.

Gualeguay, a tn. in the prov. of Entre Rios, Argentina, about 8 m. from Porto Ruiz. It contains a library, theatre, and slaughterhouses, thus being enabled to carry on a trade in meat. Pop. about 9000.

Gualeguaychu, a river port in the prov. of Entre Rios, Argentina, situated on the R. Gualeguaychu, about 9 m. from its confluence with the Uruguay. This town has a considerable amount of commerce in meat extracts. Pop. about 15,000.

Guam, Guahan, or Guajan, the largest and most southern of the Ladrone Is. The surface is mountainous, the coast being surrounded by coral reefs. The best harbour is Apra on the W. Rice and sugar are cultivated on the island, which, since 1898, has been the property of the United States. Cap. Agaña. The area is about 200 sq. m. Pop. about 10,000.

Guamo, a tn. of Colombia, situated to the S.W. of Bogota. Pop. *c.* 11,000.

Guan, a bird belonging to the family Cracidæ, sub - family Penelopinæ, native of Central and S. America. These birds are characterised by bare throats and wattles. They are gregarious birds, and are usually to be found in forests. Their colour is olive-green or brown, and several of the species are capable of being domesticated.

Guanabacoa, a tn. of Cuba, 3 m. E. of Havana. It is built on high land and is well provided with public buildings. Pop. about 14,000.

Guanacaste, a prov. of Costa Rica, including the peninsula of Nicoya. The surface of the province is covered by large forests, and is well provided with land suitable for grazing. The capital is G., or Liberia. Pop. (province) about 24,500; (town) about 3500.

Guanaco, a wild species of the camel family, the llama and alpaca being the domesticated varieties. It is of a reddish-brown colour, and is a native of S. America, found particularly on the Andes, and generally living in herds.

Guanajay, a tn. in the prov. of Pinar del Rio, Cuba. It lies 35 m. S.W. of Havana, and is noted as a health resort. Pop. 8800.

Guanajuato : 1. A state of Mexico, bounded on the N. by San Luis Potosi, on the S. by Michoacan, on the W. by Jalisco, and on the E. by Queretaro, with an area of about 10,950 sq. m. This state lies in the central plateau of Mexico, and its surface is very mountainous, the Sierra Gordo and Sierra de G. being the highest ranges. The chief river is the Nerona, and the capital G. This state is exceedingly rich in minerals. Pop. about 2,000,000. 2. The cap. tn. of the state of G., situated to the N. W. of Mexico. This city has steep and winding streets, well-built houses, and a generally Oriental appearance. Among its chief buildings are the Alhóndiga, a cathedral, mint, university, and theatre. In addition to the silver and gold mines which are near, G. manufs. pottery, chemical, and other articles. Pop. about 41,500.

Guanare, the cap. of the state of Zamora, Venezuela. It is noted for its trade in cattle. Pop. about 11,000.

Guanches, or **Guanchos**, the race originally found in the Canary Is. They were finally conquered by the Spaniards at the end of the 15th century, and at the present time are nearly extinct. The character of their skull—low forehead and projecting jaw—shows a likeness to the Cro-Magnon race of France, while their language and inscriptions point to a connection with the Berbers of Northern Africa. See Sabin Berthelot, *Antiquités Canariennes ou Annotation sur l'Origine des Peuples qui occupèrent les Iles Fortunées depuis les premiers Temps jusqu'à l'Epoque de leur Conquête*, 1879.

Guanes, a tn. in Cuba, situated in the centre of flourishing tobacco, cotton, and coffee plantations. It is 120 m. S.W. of Havana in the prov. of Pinar del Rio. Pop. 10,500.

Guanine ($C_5H_5N_5O$), a highly nitrogenous base containing the uric acid nucleus found in guano and other animal products. It forms a white insoluble powder which is converted by nitrous acid into xanthine, a substance present in tea.

Guano (derived from the Peruvian word *huano*, dung), the excrement of certain sea-fowl, *e.g.* gulls, cormorants, and penguins, together with other animal remains such as feathers and bones. It is used largely as a manure, its value as such depending on the fact that it is a general fertiliser yielding all the constituents of plant food in a condition that can be readily assimilated. The chemical composition is extremely complex, and varies according to the locality and age of the deposit. The main constituents are nitrogenous (uric acid) and phosphatic (calcium phosphate) compounds together with various potassium and ammonium salts and a nitrogenous substance, guanine (*q.v.*). There are three classes of G.: (1) Those that come from a hot and rainless climate, the nitrogenous matter being preserved in its original state, *e.g.* Peruvian G.; (2) those from damp climates which have lost a large part of their soluble constituents, *e.g.* Ichaboe, Bolivian, and Chilian Gs.; (3) those consisting merely of the phosphatic remains contaminated with sand, *e.g.* African, Patagonian, and Australian Gs. The most highly nitrogenous and therefore most valuable G. (containing nitrogen from 13 to 14 per cent., and phosphoric acid to the same amount) has been imported since 1840 from the Chincha Islands off Peru. According to Boussingault, one ton of this is equal to about thirty tons of farmyard manure or cow-dung. The best supplies of G. are now practically exhausted, and low quality grades are now 'fortified' with ammonium sulphate. In 1850 the import was 117,000 tons, rising to 280,000 tons in 1870, but it has now fallen to about 20,000 tons. Fish Gs. and other artificial fertilisers have now taken the place, to a large extent, of the natural material. These are made by drying and pulverising the bones and heads of fish, often together with superphosphate of lime.

Guantanamo, a tn. in the chief coffee-growing district of Cuba, 13 m. N. of Caimanera, its port, and 49 m. E. of Santiago de Cuba. One of the four naval stations ceded to the United States by Cuba in 1901. Exports sugar and lumber. Pop. 8500.

Guapai, or **Rio Grande**, a river in Bolivia rising in the dept. of Cochabamba. Tributary of the Mamore, into which it runs after a circuitous course of 550 m.

Guapore, or **Itenez**, a navigable S. American river rising in the W. of the Matto Grosso State, Brazil, and forming for a considerable distance on its course the boundary between Brazil and Bolivia. It unites with the Mamore after a distance of 800 m.

Guarana, or **Brazilian Cocoa**, a medicinal preparation or dried paste made from the powdered seeds of the S. American *Paullinia sorbilis* (N.O. Sapindaceæ). G. bread is made by the Guaranis and other Brazilian tribes. It is a brownish substance, like chocolate in appearance, used both as food and medicine. It contains an alkaloid (4 or 5 per cent.) called 'guaranine,' the same as caffeine or theine. The cocoa has a somewhat astringent, bitter taste, and is used as a stimulant and cure for headache.

Guarani, **Guaranys**, or **Guaranies** (' warriors '), S. American aborigines, one of the chief groups of S. American Indian tribes, who lived between Parana R. and the Atlantic. The name is also applied to a great linguistic family, Tupi-Guarani, which formerly occupied Paraguay, Uruguay, and Brazil, with branches also in Bolivia and Peru. These numerous tribes were distinguished by the same language and similar customs. They cultivated the manioc and other plants, and had developed various peaceful arts. They were usually friendly with the whites and easily subdued. The modern population of Paraguay are largely descendants of the G. and the Spaniards with whom they intermarried. The Jesuits established important missions among them. The Guarany language has Mongolian characteristics, and was early adopted by missionaries as the 'lingoa geral.' *See* Martius, *Ethnographie und Sprachenkunde Amerikas,* 1867; Brinton, *The American Race,* 1891.

Guarantee, or Contract of Suretyship, a promise to be collaterally responsible for the debt or default of another person, the principal debtor. It is to be distinguished from an indemnity (*q.v.*) because no liability arises until the principal debtor has made default. A G. is within the Statute of Frauds (*see* FRAUDS, STATUTE OF), and hence is unenforceable unless evidenced by writing; but the writing need not contain any statement of consideration (*q.v.*) given to the surety in return for his G. The practical effect of this is that a surety cannot be successfully sued if he can prove that there has been no consideration, but that where consideration has been given, it is no defence that it is not stated in writing. There is practically no limit to the transactions, the performance of which may be guaranteed, although the majority relate to mercantile matters. Gs. are also frequently given to secure the fidelity or honesty of some person newly appointed to some office. A valid contract of suretyship must be made with the creditor, and the guarantor must be under no liability in the principal contract. For example, if a husband and wife go to a furrier, and on the wife buying furs the husband tells the furrier he will see him paid *in any event,* such words may make the husband liable on the contract of sale jointly with his wife, or even solely liable; if, however, he tells the furrier he will pay if his wife declines, that would probably imply a G. A surety who has contracted jointly with other sureties is entitled to contribution from his co-sureties if he pays the whole debt; but he cannot, in the absence of agreement with the creditor or to the contrary, compel the latter to sue his co-sureties with him. It is doubtful whether a surety can compel the creditor to sue the debtor before having recourse to him. Any fraudulent concealment or wilful misrepresentation on the part of the

creditor inducing the G. will entitle the guarantor to repudiate the G., and if the creditor alters the terms of the G. without the consent of the surety, the latter is discharged, as also if he takes a new security from his debtor in substitution for the original security. On payment of the debt the surety has the right not only to recover from the principal debtor the full amount of the debt with interest, and costs reasonably incurred in disputing the claim, but to be subrogated to all the rights, equities, and securities given by the principal debtor to the creditor.

Guarantee Associations, associations or insurance companies which issue policies guaranteeing the assured against the default or insolvency of his debtors; or, specifically, fidelity policies or bonds to guarantee the assured against dishonesty of a servant or employee. Contracts to issue such policies are within the Statute of Frauds (*see* FRAUDS, STATUTE OF), and must therefore be in writing. In the case of fidelity bonds, the employer is bound to disclose to the G. A. any knowledge he may have respecting previous defalcations on the part of the employee whose integrity is the subject of the policy or bond. It is a defence to an action on a fidelity policy that the assured has been negligent in supervising the employee. If during the currency of a fidelity policy the employee is guilty of any dereliction of duty which would justify his dismissal, the assured must give notice to the G. A., even although the conduct of the employee has given rise to no claim upon the policy. Speculation or gambling on the part of the employee must also be disclosed where the policy contains a condition to the effect that the employer must give notice on becoming cognisant of such fact. Guardians of the poor may accept policies of G. A. as securities for the faithful performance by collectors of poor rates and other poor law officers, of the duties of their office. Guarantee policies against insolvency or default of debtors must be distinguished from ordinary contracts of guarantee. (*See* GUARANTEE.) Full disclosure must be made as in the case of fidelity bonds, whereas in ordinary guarantees such disclosure is not essential. The G. A. is discharged from liability, generally speaking, if the creditor consents to any alteration in the liability of the debtor.

Guarayos, aborigines of S. America. They are found chiefly in the forest lands of Bolivia. They have never been fully civilised, and all attempts to bring them under the permanent influence of civilisation have been frustrated by their fierce and barbarous habits. They cultivate maize and plantains.

Guarda, the name of a tn. and dist. in Portugal. The district forms part of the prov. of Beira. The town is fortified and is the seat of a bishop. It is situated just over 70 m. N.E. of Coimbra. Pop. (1900) 6092.

Guardafui, the N.E. extremity of E. Africa, 11° 50′ N., and 51° 21′ E., situated at the southern entrance of the Gulf of Aden.

Guardi, Francesco (1712 - 93), a Venetian painter. His greatest works are to be found in the Manfrini Palace at Venice. He was a pupil of Canaletto, whose style he followed closely.

Guardiagrele, a city in the prov. of Chieti, Italy, 18 m. S.W. of Ortona, and possessing mineral springs. Pop. (commune) 10,000.

Guardian, The, a newspaper founded in 1846 by R. W. Church (afterwards Dean) and Frederick Rogers (afterwards Lord Blatchford), and a few other enthusiasts, to keep the flag flying after the secession of Newman. The first editor was Martin Richard Sharp, ' a model editor, shrewd, practical, courteous, and an admirable judge of men.' He was succeeded in 1883 by D. C. Lathbury, who continued till 1899; next, Canon Walter Hobhouse (1900-5), followed by J. Penderel-Brodhurst (1905 to present date). The paper made an early success, enlisting distinguished contributors from the first, and has long been accepted as the representative journal of the English Church. The price was lowered from 6d. to 3d. in 1898, and to 1d. in 1910, resulting in a great increase in circulation. It has always been marked by literary ability, scholarship, and scrupulous fairness, whilst holding definitely Tractarian views; and it still enjoys that reputation.

Guards (Household Troops) (from Fr. *garde*). G. form the oldest part of established armies, in fact it is probably from the G. that the army, as we know it, is derived. Formerly it was customary for the sovereign to depend upon the national levy for his soldiers, but gradually there grew up the nucleus of a standing army in the formation of bodies of personal G. for the king. In England these took the form of the house carles, a body probably first brought into England by Cnut. History gives us many examples of G. playing an important part in the history of their country. In this respect we may mention the house carles of Harold who died to a man practically round his body at Hastings; the Swiss G.

of Louis XVI., who perished defending their king, and the Old Guard of Napoleon, the veterans upon whom he depended when all else had failed. These are but a few examples. The G. of the king at the present time may be distinctly divided into two groups: The first, those gentlemen and retainers who form a purely *personal* bodyguard, and secondly, those regiments which are brought into closer contact with the sovereign than usual, but who form part of the active army as well. To the first division belong the Honourable Corps of Gentlemen-at-Arms, the Yeomen of the G., together with the Royal Company of Archers, who form the King's Scottish bodyguard. The two former owe their origin to the Tudor monarchs. The oldest of all these bodies is the Yeomen of the G., founded by Henry VII. Next came the Honourable Company of Gentlemen-at-Arms, founded at the accession of Henry VIII. The Scottish Company of Archers was founded by Act of the Privy Council of Scotland during the reign of Charles II. The second section of G. consists of certain regiments from the active army. These, again, may be divided into two sections: the Household Cavalry and the Foot G. The Household Cavalry was founded at the Restoration. There are three regiments of Household Cavalry which were, originally at the Restoration, the King's Troop, the Queen's Troop (formerly the Lord-General's Troop), and the Duke of York's Troop. Later, the name of the Life G. was given to the first two troops (1685) and finally was raised a third troop, known variously as the Duke of York Blues, the Royal Horse G. Blue, and finally as the Royal Horse G. (the Blues). The Foot G. of the Household Troops consist of four regiments : the Grenadiers, the Coldstreams, the Scots G., and the Irish G. The Grenadiers served with Charles II. and James, Duke of York, during their exile and returned at the Restoration. The Coldstreams were originally a regiment raised by General Monk, and they received their name from the village on the borders of England and Scotland. The Scots G. were raised and maintained in Scotland at the time of the Restoration, and were added to the strength of the British army at the Restoration. The Irish G. were formed at the conclusion of the South African War, as a mark of the appreciation of the sovereign of the services which they rendered during that war.

Guardship, the name applied to a ship which is posted at some port to act as guard. Usually she is the headquarters of the various coastguard districts, and is stationed at a certain point with a nucleus crew. The crew can easily, however, be brought up to strength, and can then proceed immediately to action. The name of guard boat is also applied to a boat which sails round an anchored fleet at night in order to see that proper watch is being kept. Formerly the term was applied to that ship of the fleet which received the men from the press-gangs.

Guarea, a genus of Meliaceæ, is found in tropical America and in Africa. There are between seventy and eighty species characterised by having the stamens so completely fused as to form a tube.

Guarico, the name of a state of Venezuela. It was formed in 1901 from a portion of the state of Miranda. It has an area of about 25,500 sq. m., and its capital is Calabozo. Pop. about 180,000.

Guarini, Giovanni Battista (1537-1612), a poet, born at Ferrara, and was employed by the duke of that place in various diplomatic missions. He visited Rome, and Venice, and was sent also as envoy to the emperor. He is, however, strictly remembered for his drama, *Il Pastor Fido*, which he wrote under the influence of Tasso. The poem has been translated into English. *See* Monograph by Rossi, 1886.

Guarino (c. 1370-1460), a scholar, born at Verona. He studied .Greek at Constantinople and returned to teach it in Europe. His instructor was the famous Manuel Chrysoloras. He taught in Verona, Padua, Bologna, and Ferrara. He is chiefly remembered owing to the fact that he helped greatly to establish the texts of many of our classics. He translated Strabo and some of the lives of Plutarch. See *Life* by Sabbadini, 1891.

Guarneri, the surname of a famous Italian family of violin-makers who lived and worked at Cremona:

Andrea Guarneri (1626-98), a pupil of Nicholas Amati, whose marriage he witnessed in 1641. Many of his violins are of the Amati pattern, but are inferior to those of his master; his 'cellos possess fine acoustic properties.

Giuseppe Guarneri (1666-1739), son of Andrea G., introduced a narrow-waisted and more boldly curved instrument, with the sound-holes set lower down, and in its power of sound is superior to his father's.

Pietro Guarneri (c. 1690 - 1728), second son of Andrea G., introduced greater width between the sound-holes; his varnish was of exquisite gold and pale red tints.

Pietro Guarneri (c. 1725-60), a son

of Giuseppe G., who produced some very fine instruments.

Giuseppe Antonio Guarneri (1683-1745), a nephew of Andrea G., and greatest genius of the family. His violins are of bold and massive build, with grand sonority of tone, and some of his finest date from about 1740.

Guarroman, a tn. in prov. of Jaen, and 28 m. N. of town of same name, Spain. A lead-mining centre. Pop. 3500.

Guastalla, an ancient city of Northern Italy, situated on the R Po., about 20 m. N.E. of Parma. It has a cathedral and a school of music. It is the seat of a bishop. Pop. 11,000.

Guatemala : 1. Republic of Central America. The name is probably of Aztec origin, and is said to mean ' land of the eagle ' in its original form of Quauhtematlan. It is divided into five regions, the lowlands of the Pacific coast, the volcanic mountains of the Sierra Madre, the plateaux N. of these, the mountains of the Atlantic versant, and the plain of Peten. It is richly watered and there are several extensive lakes. The bird life of the country is rare. The climate is healthy, save on the coast, where fever is prevalent. The country is very rich in minerals and in rubber, as well as in vegetable products. No part of Central America contains a greater diversity of tribes. There are eighteen languages spoken. The chief town is Guatemala la Nueva. The prevailing form of religion is Roman Catholic, but the state recognises no distinction of creed. No convents or monasteries are allowed. For the white and mixed population military service is compulsory. Guatemala was conquered by the Spaniards under Pedro de Alvarado, between 1522 and 1524. Pop. 1,992,000, or more than one-third of the entire population of Central America. 2. Capital of the Republic. Guatemala (sometimes written Guatemala la Nueva and formerly Santiago de los Caballeros de Guatemala), until 1821 capital of the Spanish captaincy-general of G., which comprised Chiapas in Mexico and all Central America except Panama. G. is built more than 5000 ft. above sea-level, in a wide table-land traversed by the Rio de las Vacas, or Bow R., so called from the cattle introduced here by Spanish colonists in the 16th century. The edge of the table-land is marked by deep ravines. Beyond it are lofty mountains, the highest peaks being on the S., where the volcanic summits of the Sierra Madre exceed 12,000 ft. It has a station on the trans-continental Railway from Puerto Barrios on the Atlantic (190 m. N.E.) to San Jose on the Pacific (75 m. S. by W.).

It is three times the size of any city in the republic, and has a corresponding commercial superiority. Its archbishop is the primate of Central America (excluding Panama). Like most Spanish-American towns it is laid out in wide and regular streets which are often planted with avenues of trees, and it has large suburbs. Though usually only of one story, the houses are solidly and comfortably constructed. Many of them have large gardens and courts surrounding them. The chief of the open spaces is the Plaza Mayor which contains the cathedral. This was built in 1730; then there is the archiepiscopal palace, the government buildings, the mint, and other public offices; and the more modern Reforma Park and Plaza de la Concordia, now the favourite resort of the inhabitants. There are a number of schools for both sexes, besides hospitals and an orphanage. Many of the principal buildings in the place were originally convents. In 1858 a theatre was founded. This is one of the best in Central America. A museum founded in 1734 is maintained by the Sociedad Economica, which in various ways has done great service to the city, and to the country. There are a couple of fortresses. The Castello Matamoros, built by Rafael Carrera, and the Castello San Jose. Water is brought from a distance of about 8 m. by two old aqueducts from the towns of Mixco and Pinula; fuel and provisions are largely supplied by the Pokoman Indians of Mixco. The general prosperity of G. has secured for it the name of the Paris of Central America. It is lit by electricity. The foreign trade is largely controlled by Germans. Pop. (1905) 97,000.

Guatemala Antigua (old Guatemala) is situated 20 m. S.W. of the present cap. It was once a splendid city, but it has been destroyed several times by earthquakes. Pop. 6000.

Guatusos, aborigines of Central America, a southern branch of the Chorotegans, whose home is in Costa Rica. They are generally a peaceful race, and still retain their primeval tribal arrangements and their independence.

Guava, or *Psidium Guajava,* a species of Myrtaceæ found in tropical America. It is a tree which bears white flowers, followed by a succulent edible yellow fruit which is often used in making jellies and preserves. The black G. is *Guettarda argentea,* a species of Rubiaceæ.

Guaviare, or **Guabiare,** a river of Colombia, which rises in the Andes. It is navigable only for small craft, but for a distance of 600 m. It joins the Orinoco. Length, 700 m.

Guayama, a tn. of Porto Rico. The tn. is situated in the centre of the cane-growing industry, and has a large trade in molasses, sugar, and rum. Pop. about 8000.

Guayaquil, the chief port of Ecuador, S. America. It is the cap. of the prov. of Guayas, and is 40 m. from the mouth of the river of that name. The climate is extremely unhealthy, and the town is badly built. The newer part of the town where the richer residents live is far better than the old. The streets are dirty and badly paved. The town is the seat of a bishop, and has a cathedral, a bishop's palace, a university, and a technical school. The chief exports are cacao, Panama hats, cotton, tobacco, and coffee. It has also large shipbuilding yards. Pop. about 90,000.

Guayaquil, Gulf of, an inlet of the Pacific Ocean on the W. coast of S. America.

Guayas, a stretch of ter. on the S.W. coast of Ecuador forming a prov. of that country. The land is generally low-lying and is extremely fertile. The chief products are coffee, tobacco, sugar cane, and rice. Area 11,500 sq. m.; pop. 100,000.

Guaycurus, aborigines of S. America. They are found to-day chiefly in the Gran Chaco. They are of Guarani stock.

Guaymas, a Mexican seaport situated on the Gulf of California in the State of Sonora. The chief exports are pearls and silver ore. Pop. 8600.

Guayra, La, *see* LA GUAIRA.

Guazuma, a genus of sterculiaceous plants found in the W. Indies and tropical America. There are ten species, and *G. ulmifolia* is well known in Britain as a cultivated plant.

Gubat, a small port on the E. coast of Albay prov., Luzon, Philippine Is. Exports copra and hemp. Pop. 16,500.

Gubbio, a city of Central Italy, 27 m. S. of Urbino in the prov. of Perugia, delightfully situated on the slopes of the Apennines. It has a picturesque mediæval appearance with its 13th-century cathedral, a communal palace of the 14th century, and many old convents and churches. G. was celebrated for its majolica ware, which is still imitated in a few factories. The famous Eugubine Tables are kept here. Since its incorporation in the duchy of Urbino (1384) the pop. has dwindled from 30,000 to less than 5000.

Guben, a walled manufacturing tn. in Prussia on the Neisse, 28 m. S. of Frankfort-on-the-Oder. Industries: woollen, linen stuffs, hats, machinery, earthenware, dolls. Pop. 37,300.

Gubernatis, Angelo de, *see* DE GUBERNATIS, ANGELO.

Gude, Hans Frederic (1825-1903), a Norwegian painter, pupil of the Düsseldorf Academy (1841), and professor there (1854). He went to England (1862), and became professor at Karlsruhe arts school (1864), and at Berlin Academy (1880-1901). He is perhaps the finest Norwegian landscape painter, and has won numerous medals in Europe and America. Among his chief works are: ' Early Morning in the Mountains of Norway,' exhibited 1873 ; ' A Scotch Landscape,' exhibited 1878; ' Bridal Procession on Hardanger Fjord,' 1848; ' Calm Sea '; ' Fishing by Night '; ' Fishermen Landing '; ' A Viking Ship '; ' After the Storm '; ' Harbour of Christiania,' 1881. *See* Atkinson, *Art Tour to the Northern Capitals of Europe ;* Dietrichson, *Af H. Gude's Liv og Værker*, 1899.

Guden-Aa, the chief river of Jutland, Denmark, about 80 m. long. It flows N.E., joining the Kattegat by an estuary 1 m. wide, about 16 m. N.E. of Randers.

Gudgeon (Gk. κωβιός), a small fish of the carp family (Cyprinidæ), common in the streams of Europe, resembling the chub and the barbel. The *Gobio fluviatilis* abounds in English rivers, especially in those with gravelly bottoms. They swim in shoals, feeding on worms and small animals. They are easily caught and prized as food.

Gudrun, or Kudrun, a heroine of a Middle High German 13th - century epic (author unknown), the German *Odyssey*, next important in Early German literature to the *Nibelungenlied*. She was the daughter of King Hettel of Hegelingen (Friesland). The epic deals with legends mainly of the North Sea coasts and Normandy. Martin's edition (1902) is the best modern one. There are modern German versions by Simrock (1843), Freytag (1888), Lemmermayer (1890), Legerlotz (1900), and others. *See* Wilmann's *Die Entwickelung der Kudrundichtung*, 1873.

Guebres, Guebers, Gabers, or **Ghebres** (Persian *ghebr. Cf.* Giaour), a name (meaning infidels) applied in Persia to the adherents of the ancient religion, Fire-worshippers, Zoroastrians, or Parsis. They number about 8000 or 10,000, and call themselves Beh-Dinân (' those of the Good Faith '). *See* Tylor, *Prim. Cult.*, ii., 1871 ; Lovell's trans. of *Thevenot's Trav.*, 1687.

Guelderland, *see* GELDERLAND.

Guelder-rose, or *Viburnum Opulus,* a beautiful species of Caprifoliaceæ, a marsh shrub common to N. Europe and to Britain. The petals are large and when cultivated the flowers are neuter; because of its white balls of flowers the G. is called also the snowball tree.

Guelma, a tn. in Algeria, situated 38 m. S.S.W. of Bona in Constantine dept. Has a college, mosque, and fine museum. Pop. 10,000 (Europeans 3600).

Guelph, a city of Ontario, Canada, cap. of Wellington co., on the Speed. It is built on a number of hills, 45 m. W. by S. of Toronto by rail. An inland port of entry and seat of the Ontario Agricultural College. Manufs. sewing machines, pianos, organs, and woollen goods. John Galt, the Scottish author, founded the town. Pop. 12,300.

Guelphs and Ghibellines. These names are the Italianised forms of the German words Welf and Waiblingen, although one tradition says that they are derived from Guelph and Gibel, two rival brothers of Pistoia. Another theory derives Ghibelline from Gibello, a word used by the Sicilian arabs to translate Hohenstaufen. A more popular story tells how, during a fight round Weinsberg in Dec. 1140, between the German king, Conrad III., and Welf, Count of Bavaria, a member of the powerful family to which Henry the Lion, Duke of Saxony and Bavaria, belonged, the soldiers of the latter raised the cry ' Hie Welf,' to which the king's troops replied with, ' Hie Waiblingen,' this being the name of one of Conrad's castles. The rivalry between Welf and Hohenstaufen, of which family Conrad was a member, was anterior to this event, and had been for some years a prominent fact in the history of Swabia and Bavaria, although its introduction into Italy, in a modified form, dates from the time of the Italian expeditions of the Emperor Frederick I. Chosen German king in 1152, Frederick was not only nephew and heir of Conrad, he was related also to the Welfs; yet although his election abated to some extent the rivalry between Welf and Hohenstaufen in Germany, it opened it upon a larger and fiercer scale in Italy. During the period covered by Frederick's Italian campaigns, his enemies became known as Welfs, while his partisans seized upon the term of Waiblingen or Ghibelline, and the contest between the two parties was carried on with a ferocity unknown even to the inhabitants of Southern Germany. The story of the contest between Guelph and Ghibelline is nothing less than the history of Italy in the middle ages. At the opening of the 13th century the contest was intensified by the fight for the German and Imperial thrones between Philip, Duke of Swabia, a son of Frederick I., and the Welf, Otto of

Brunswick, afterwards the Emperor Otto IV. A fight waged in Italy as well as in Germany. Then, as heir of Philip of Swabia, Frederick II. was forced to throw himself into the arms of the Ghibellines, whilst his enemies, the popes, ranged themselves definitely among the Guelphs, and soon Guelph and Ghibelline became synonymous with supporter of pope and emperor. After the death of Frederick II. in 1250, the Ghibellines looked for leadership to his son, the German king, Conrad IV., and then to his natural son, Manfred, whilst the Guelphs called the French prince, Charles of Anjou, to their aid. The combatants were nearing exhaustion, and after the execution of Conrad in 1268, this great struggle began to lose force and interest. Guelph and Ghibelline were soon found representing local and family, rather than papal and imperial interests. In the 15th century the two names began to die out of current politics. When Louis XII. of France conquered Milan at the beginning of the 16th century, the old names were revived. The French king's supporters were called Guelphs, and the friends of the Emperor Maximilian I. were referred to as Ghibellines. The Guelph party meant the burghers of the consular communes, the men of industry and commerce, and the Ghibelline party meant the men of arms and idleness. Dante was a Ghibelline and Petrarch was a Guelph.

Guéméné Penfao, a vil. of France, 34 m. N.N.W. of Nantes in a picturesque region of the dept. of Loire-Inférieure. Pop. 6850.

Guenon, the popular French name for several species of Old World monkeys belonging to the genus *Cercopithicus;* they are also called green monkeys.

Guerande, a picturesque old French tn., situated 47 m. W. by N. of Nantes in the dept. of Loire-Inférieure. It is near the sea, and has a handsome mediæval church. Pop. 7000.

Guercino (' squint-eyed '), the nickname of **Giovanni Francesco Barbieri** (c. 1591-1666), born at Cento, in Ferrara. He belongs to the class of self-taught geniuses, and his works are distinguished by three different styles, which he followed at different periods of his life. He first followed the school of the Zenobrosi, which is conspicuous for its daring contrast of light and shadow; his second style was a modification of this, and was more refined and elevated, his masterpiece, 'St. Petronilla,' is in this style; in his third he became a follower of Guido and lost his own original power. He painted numerous pictures which are mostly in oil.

Guéret, a tn. in France, cap. of the dept. of Creuse, which grew up round an abbey founded in the 7th century. Its chief industries are brewing, leather-making, the manuf. of basket-work and wooden shoes. Pop. 8000.

Guericke, Heinrich Ernst Ferdinand (1803-78), a German theologian, born at Wettin, in Saxony. He studied at the University of Halle, and was appointed professor in 1829. He was very much against the union between the Lutheran and the Reformed Churches, and in 1833 definitely took the side of the Old Lutherans. He wrote a life of *August Hermann Francke; A Church History* (which has been translated into English); *Christliche Symbolik;* and a *Manual of the Antiquities of the Church.*

Guericke, Otto von (1602-86), a German physicist, born at Magdeburg. He studied at Leipzig and Leyden, visited France and England, and in 1636 became engineer-in-chief at Erfurt. In 1646 he was mayor of Magdeburg and a magistrate of Brandeburg. He is famous for his discoveries on the nature of air and electricity, as well as for his researches in astronomy, which are contained in *Experimenta Nova.* He was the inventor of the air-pump, 1650.

Guerillas, the name given to bands of armed men who carry on an irregular warfare on their own account. They belong peculiarly to Spain, and in 1808-14 they fought against the French. Some joined Wellington and rendered him service, but when peace was concluded formed themselves into robber bands.

Guerilla Warfare, the term used to denote war carried on by bands in an unorganised manner. In the Basque provinces at the time of the civil wars of Spain, G. W. was frequent. The subject was dealt with at the Hague Conference in 1899, and the rules made were reaffirmed in 1907.

Guérin, Eugénie de (1805-48), was the sister of Maurice de Guérin, for whom she had a peculiar affection. She is especially known for her *Journal* and *Letters*, which were first published in 1855 under the title *Reliquiæ*, but re-edited in 1862, and appeared as *Eugénie de Guérin; Journal et lettres.* She was a woman of remarkable character, and a fervent Catholic, and her love for her brother was the predominant element of her life.

Guérin, Georges Maurice de (1810-39), born at La Cayla, Languedoc, and educated at the College Stanislas, Paris, intending to study for the Church of Rome, but coming temporarily under the influence of Lamennais at La Chênaie (near Dinan) he renounced that intention (1833). On his return to Paris he became for a short time teacher at his own college. His marriage, in 1838, to a young, beautiful, and rich creole, placed his time at his disposal, until his death, from consumption, eight months later. George Sand's warm appreciation in the *Revue des Deux Mondes* (May 1840) was the first public recognition of his genius. His *Reliquiæ*, letters, poems, etc., were published in 1860, edited by G. S. Trébutien; to this edition appeared as preface the famous critique of Sainte-Beuve, who regards him as a spiritual kinsman of Bernardin de Sainte-Pierre. G. seems to have been incapable of the deep passions of love; there is a platonic serenity about him which reminds one of Fogazzaro, but his writings, although not wholly devoid of a tendency to morbid sentimentalism, are unique in their exquisite appreciation of the pagan beauty, the harmony and pathos of Nature. *See* Matthew Arnold's *Essays in Criticism*. *See* GUÉRIN, EUGÉNIE DE.

Guérin, Pierre Narcisse, Baron (1774-1833), a French historical painter, born in Paris. He studied under Regnault, and in 1797 obtained one of the three prizes at a competition. In 1799 he exhibited his ' Return of Marcus Sextus,' in which he reached the highest point of his art. In 1803 he received the cross of the Legion of Honour, and in 1816 was appointed director of the French school at Rome. G.'s paintings in their own style are very beautiful, but his earlier productions are more vigorous than his later ones. His chief works are: ' Hippolytus and Phædra'; ' Pyrrhus and Andromache '; ' Æneas and Dido '; ' Clytemnæstra '; ' The Revolt of Cairo '; ' Ulysses '; ' Death of Marshal Launes.'

Guernica, a small tn., situated on the Mundaca, in the prov. of Vizcaya, Spain. It was the seat of the diet of Vizcaya until the abolition of the fueros. Pop. 3300.

Guernsey, the second in size of the Channel Isles, lies 30 m. from the coast of Normandy. It is triangular in form, with an area of 25 sq. m., and its surface slopes from S. to N. The climate is mild and healthy, and the soil, when manured, is very fertile. The chief crops are vegetables, wheat, barley, and apples for cider, but oranges, melons, and figs are also grown, as well as large quantities of grapes and tomatoes. The island, too, produces a famous breed of cows, and a special sort of granite, almost unrivalled for paving, is exported from St. Sampson's. The chief town is St. Peter's Port. Pop. (1911) 44,997.

Guernsey Lily, or *Nerine Sarniensis,*

a Cape plant belonging to the order Amaryllidaceæ. The flowers are of a delicate pink colour.

Guerrazzi, Francesco Domenico (1804-73), an Italian author, born at Leghorn. He studied law in Pisa University, and practised for a time at Leghorn, but soon abandoned this in order to devote himself to literature and politics. His first published work was *Battagli di Benevento*, 1827, an historical novel which is remarkable for its exquisite expression; his *Assidio di Firenze* was written while he was in prison at Ponto-ferrato, 1834. This is perhaps his most important work, and tells of the downfall of the republic of Florence. G. was frequently engaged in republican conspiracies and imprisoned, and was the most powerful Liberal leader at Leghorn. In 1848 he became a minister, and in 1849, when the grand duke of Tuscany fled, he was proclaimed member of the provisional government, and subsequently dictator. On the restoration, however, he was imprisoned for three years, but released in 1852 and banished to Corsica. His other works are : *Apologia*, his defence ; *Isabella Orsini; Beatrice Cenci.*

Guerrero, a coast state of Mexico, between the R. de las Balzas-Mexcala and the Pacific. It is very mountainous, and has great mining capabilities, the minerals found here being silver, gold, mercury, lead, iron, coal, sulphur, and precious stones. The agricultural products are cotton, coffee, tobacco, and cereals. Pop. 605,437.

Guesclin, Bertrand du (*c.* 1320-80), a constable of France, born in Brittany. He was of a persistent and turbulent character, and was renowned for his prowess even when a boy. He fought for Charles de Blois at Vannes in 1342, when he was contesting for the dukedom of Brittany, and distinguished himself against the English at Rennes, 1356, and Dinan, 1357. In 1359 he took Melun and freed the Seine from the English, and in 1364 won the battle of Cocherel against Charles the Bad, but was taken prisoner by Sir John Chandos at Auray. On being released he fought against Pedro the Cruel, but was defeated and taken prisoner by the Black Prince, 1367. Being ransomed he defeated and captured Pedro in 1369, and in 1370 was made constable of France by Charles V., with the result that in a few years nearly all the English possessions were in the hands of the French.

Guest, Lady Charlotte, afterwards **Schrieber** (1812-95), the daughter of the ninth Earl of Lindsay, was famous as a collector of fans and china. She presented some fine china and earthenware to the South Kensington Museum. She published several volumes containing pictures of her most notable fans, and the playing cards of all nations, as well as several old Welsh manuscripts, one of which *Mabinogion*, appeared in 1849.

Guest, Edwin (1800-80), an historical writer, born at King's Norton, Worcestershire. He was educated at King Edward VI.'s Grammar School, Birmingham, and Caius College, Cambridge, and was made a fellow of Caius in 1824. He afterwards went to Weimar and made the acquaintance of Goethe. His first published work was the *History of English Rhythms*, in 1838, the second edition of which appeared in 1882, edited by Professor Skeat. G. was practically the founder of the Philological Society, and was secretary in 1842. He was elected F.R.S. in 1839, and master of Caius College in 1852. His writings are of great value in the study of Roman-British history, and include *On Julius Cæsar's Invasion of Britain; The Campaign of Aulus Plautius in Britain*, etc.

Guettarda, a genus of rubiaceous plants, consists of forty species of evergreen shrubs. All occur in tropical America but *G. speciosa*. *G. argentea* is known as the black guava.

Gueux Les, or The Beggars, the name assumed by the malcontents who opposed the introduction of the Inquisition into the Netherlands. They formed themselves into an association in 1565, and presented a petition to the regent, Margaret of Parma, 1566. The regent being at first afraid, one of her councillors asked her what she had to fear from 'beggars' (*gueux*). The word was remembered, and the party adopted it. They maintained a vigorous warfare against Philip for some time, but were finally suppressed by the Duke of Alva. 'The Beggars of the Sea,' under Count de la Marck did much damage to the Spanish fleet, and captured Briel in 1572, a victory which ultimately resulted in the independence of the Netherlands in 1648.

Guevara, Antonio de (c. 1490-1545), a Spanish theologian and historian, born at Viscaya. His early years were passed at the court of Isabella, but in 1528 he entered the Franciscan order and subsequently became historiographer and court-preacher to Charles V. In 1529 he published his *Dial for Princes*, a didactic novel professing to be a life of Marcus Aurelius. This work has been translated into Latin, Italian, French, and English, and reprinted several times in Spanish. He also wrote *Lives of*

the Ten Cæsars, and *The Golden Letters*—this, too, has been translated into English. G. had considerable influence upon the Spanish prose of the 16th century, and his bombastic style may be compared with the euphuism of Lyly, who may have taken G. as his model.

Guevara, Luis Velez de (1570-1644), a Spanish dramatist and novelist, born at Ecija in Andalusia. He practised as an advocate for some years, but came under the notice of Philip IV., and was appointed court chamberlain. He wrote a great number of plays, of which *Reinar despues de morir*, *Más pesa el rey que la sangre; La Luna de la Sierra* are the best; but he is chiefly famous for his fantastic novel, *El Diablo Cojuelo* (the limping devil), which is the basis of Le Sage's *Diable Boiteux*.

Guglielmi, Pietro (1727-1804), an Italian musical composer, born at Massa Carrara. He studied under Durante, and produced his first operatic work at Turin in 1755. In 1762 he went to Dresden to conduct the opera there, and some years afterwards appeared in London. In 1793 he became musical director at the Vatican. He was a writer of operas, both comic and serious, as well as of oratorios and orchestral pieces. His best operas are *La Didone; Enea e Lavinia; I due Gemelli; La Pastorella Nobile; La Bella Pescatrice.*

Guiana, see BRITISH, DUTCH, and FRENCH GUIANA.

Guiana Bark, French, the bark of *Portlandia hexandra*, also called *Conteria speciosa*, a tree, a native of Guiana, belonging to the natural order Cinchonaceæ, which has opposite ovate leaves, and corymbs of large purple flowers. It is used as an antidote in cases of fever.

Guibert of Nogent (1053-1124), an historian and theologian, born at Clermont-en-Beauvoisis. In 1104 he was chosen head of the abbey of Notre Dame de Nogent. He wrote his *Autobiography*, which contains some very fine pictures of the customs in his day; and a history of the First Crusade, *Gesta Dei per Francos.*

Guicciardini, Francesco (1483-1540), the celebrated Italian historian and statesman, born at Florence. Marsilio Ficino held him at the font. He came of a noble and illustrious family. After the usual education of a boy, his father sent him to the universities of Ferrara and Padua, where he stayed till 1505. The death of an uncle who had occupied the see of Cortona, caused the young man to hanker after an ecclesiastical career. He saw the scarlet of a cardinal awaiting him. His father checked the ambition, declaring that the Church was too corrupt to receive any of his sons. The youth then turned his attention to law, and at twenty-three was appointed to read the Institutes in public. Soon after he became betrothed to the daughter of Alamanno Salviati. He was then practising at the bar, where he won distinction and was entrusted with an embassy to the court of Ferdinand the Catholic. Thus he entered upon the real work of his life as a diplomat and a statesman. He was ambitious, a time-server, and a place-seeker. In 1515 Leo X. took him into service and made him governor of Reggio and Modena. In 1521 Parma was added to his rule; and in 1523 he was appointed vice-regent of Romagna by Clement VII. These rendered him virtual master of papal states beyond the Apennines. In 1526 Clement gave him still higher rank as lieutenant-general of the papal army. In 1531 he was advanced to the governorship of Bologna. This post he resigned in 1534, preferring to follow the fortunes of the Medicean princes. Though he served popes through twenty years, his hatred of the papacy was great. He did not hesitate to place his powers at the disposal of the most vicious members of the house of Medici, for the enslavement of Florence. When he returned to inhabit it in 1534 it was as the creature of the dissolute Alessandro de' Medici. After the murder of Duke Alessandro in 1537, he espoused the cause of Cosimo de Medici, who, displaying the genius of his family for politics, dismissed him, and he retired in disgrace to his villa, where he spent his last years in the composition of the *Storia d'Italia*.

Guiccioli, Countess Theresa (1802-73), a daughter of Count Gamba of Ravenna, and wife of Count G., whom she married in 1818. She was a great admirer of Lord Byron, and wrote *My Recollections of Lord Byron*, 1869, in which she gives her hero undue praise.

Guicowar, Garkwar, or **Gáckwár,** the title of a powerful Mahratta prince, ruler of the state of Baroda in western India. It was originally a family name, and is derived from the word meaning cow, though the family are not of low caste, but belong to the Mahrattas proper. The dynasty was founded in the first half of the 18th century by Damaji I., Pilaji, who gradually acquired authority over Gujarat, and Damaji II., who threw off his allegiance to the Peishwa.

Guide-books have not long been in existence. The first were Ebel's *Anleitung* for Switzerland, 1793; Boyce's *Belgian Traveller*, 1815, and Mrs. Mariane Starke's *Directions for Travellers in Italy*, 1820; but the most

famous writer of a G. is Wordsworth, whose *Guide to the English Lakes* was published in 1822. In 1836 Murray published his handbook for Holland, Belgium, and North Germany, and this was followed by Baedeker's German guide to Holland and Belgium. Baedeker's G. are now numerous, and can be used by all travellers, English as well as foreign, for translations are available. Other notable G. are those of Yoanne, for France, Gsell Fels, for Italy, Tonsberg, for Norway, as well as those published by A. and C. Black, Ward, Lock & Co. (Illustrated Guide Books), Stanford (Tourists' Guides), Macmillan (Highways and Byways), Adams (Bradshaw's Illustrated Handbooks).

Guides. In the British army, the name of The G. is applied to the corps of G. of the Punjab Frontier Force, consisting of six troops of cavalry and eight companies of infantry, and known as ' Queen's Own Corps of Guides.' Their permanent headquarters is at Hoti Mardan in the Peshawar district of the N.W. Frontier Provinces.

Guidi, Carlo Alessandro (1650-1712), an Italian poet, born at Pavia. He is important as being the chief founder of the academy called L'Arcadia. He is essentially a lyric poet, his songs being written with singular force and charm. The most beautiful perhaps is *Alla Fortuna*. He also wrote *Amalasunta in Italy*, a lyric tragedy; and *Daphne* and *Endymion*, two pastoral dramas.

Guido d'Arezzo, or **Guido Aretinus** (c. 990-1050), a musician of the 11th century, who has been called the father of modern music. He was a monk in the Benedictine monastery of Pomposa, where he taught singing, and invented the principle in which the stave is based. He introduced the names, ut, re, mi, fa, sol, la, for the first six notes of the scale, adopting them from a hymn in honour of St. John the Baptist. He is also said to have introduced the F clef. His doctrines are explained in *Micrologus* and *Antiphonarium*.

Guido Reni, commonly called **Guido** (1575-1642), an Italian painter, born at Calvenzano, near Bologna. He studied under Denis Calvaert, but afterwards entered the studio of the Carracci, one of whom he accompanied to Rome. Here he came under the influence of Caravaggio, and also began to study the works of Raphael, and soon afterwards painted ' Aurora preceding the Chariot of Apollo,' which is usually considered his greatest work. He also painted ' St. Cecilia,' ' The Crucifixion of St. Peter,' ' St. Michael,' and ' Ariadne and Fortune,' while in Rome. He spent some time in Naples in 1621, and began his famous picture the ' Nativity,' and also visited Bologna and the other towns of N. Italy. As a painter he is remarkable for the purity of his colouring and his dramatic force, while as an engraver he was bold and free in execution; and his works in this direction are as graceful as his pictures. It was only in his later years that his work declined, and this was owing to rapidity of execution.

Guienne, or Guyenne, the largest of the ancient provinces of France, which in the 12th century formed with Gascony the duchy of Aquitaine. It came into the hands of the English when Henry II. married Eleanor of Aquitaine, but was finally united to France by Charles VII. in 1451.

Guignes, Joseph de (1721-1800), a French Orientalist, born at Pontoise. In 1741 he was appointed interpreter to the French king, chiefly on account of his thorough knowledge of Chinese. In 1753 he was elected a member of the Academy of Belles Lettres, and in 1757 made professor of Syriac at the College Royal. All his works are characterised by research and industry, his chief being *L'Histoire Générale des Huns, Turcs, Mogols, et autres Tartares occidentaux.*

Guildford : 1. A municipal bor. and cap. of Surrey, England, 30 m. S.W. of London, at the E. end of the Hog's Back, on R. Wey. It has stations on the London and South-Western Railway, South-Eastern Railway, London, Brighton, and South Coast Railway, and water communication with the Thames and with Godalming. Its first known charter dates from 1256, and there are many interesting old buildings. Chief is the Norman keep of the royal castle (c. 1150). The grammar school dates from the 16th century (Edward VI. foundation); Trinity Hospital was founded by Archbishop Abbot in 1619; there is a ruined 14th century chapel, and the town-hall dates from 1683. The Church of St. Mary contains some curious frescoes. G. is the seat of the suffragan-bishop of Winchester, and was a royal residence in Plantagenet times. It is noted as a grain-market. Pop. (1911) 23,823. 2. A tn. of W. Australia, on Swan R., 10 m. from Perth. Pop. about 1400 (district, 4000).

Guildhall, an important public building of London, the place of assembly for various courts (court of common council, court of aldermen, chamberlain's court). Originally begun in 1411, the building was partly destroyed by the fire of 1666, receiving its present form in 1789, with G. Dance for architect. It has an ancient crypt. (*See* Loftie, *London City*, 1891.) It is famous for civic conclaves and banquets, being first used for this purpose in 1500, when Sir J. Shaw gave the Lord Mayor's feast. (*See* Price, *Guildhall*, 1886.) In a general sense, G. is the hall where guilds and corporations usually meet, corresponding to a town-hall.

Guilds, or Gilds. The origin of gilds, which played so important a part in mediæval city life, dates back to very early times, when small family groups, united solely by kinship, became merged in larger communities. We find among the Anglo-Saxons ' frith-gilds,' associations of freemen for mutual aid. London had a union of such societies, with the ' Knighten-gild ' at their head, and there were ' Thane-gilds ' at Cambridge and Canterbury. Even before the Norman Conquest the lithsmen or shippers' gild of London had considerable importance, but religious and merchant gilds only came into prominence later, as trade and wealth increased The former often undertook a good deal of secular work, acting as benevolent and insurance societies, and sometimes providing roads, bridges, and schools. The *gilda mercatoria* became in many instances so important that some historians have asserted that the ' gild-merchant ' formed practically the municipal government, but this does not seem to be correct. Burgesses might or might not be gildsmen, and the gild did not govern the borough. But each controlled its own trade, having within its proper area a monopoly granted by charter. In time the craftsmen grew jealous of the traders and formed gilds of their own, master-craftsmen often belonging to both fraternities. As early as 1180, under Henry II., eighteen such gilds were fined for having been formed without special permission. Merchant gilds, especially in the larger cities, gradually found themselves supplanted by the new order, and by the end of the 14th century, the craft-gilds were victorious. They were as great monopolists as their predecessors, every ' misterie' being a close corporation, with very strict rules against competition, and also as to the hours of labour, and the amount and quality of the work. These misteries held charters from the government, and were assigned distinctive liveries ; from them are descended the Livery Companies of to-day. Before long the craft-gilds themselves subdivided, the journeymen setting up companies of their own to contest the question of hours, wages, etc., with their masters, thus becoming the forerunners of modern trade-unions. The contest was much fiercer in Germany than in England, as the merchants there had organised themselves on very autocratic lines, and the struggle was not merely for improvement of labour conditions, but for general liberty. Most craft-gilds had religious associations, each having its own chapel and patron saint. In England these were abolished under Edward VI. *See* Smith's *English Gilds ;* Gross, *The Gild Merchant;* Loftie's *London,* etc.

Guillemin, Amédée Victor (1826-93), a French scientific writer and critic, educated in Paris, becoming a mathematical teacher. He has written many popular books on scientific subjects, including *Le Ciel,* 1864; *Les Mondes, causeries Astronomiques,* 1861; *La Lune,* 1865; *Les Phénomènes de la Physique,* 1867; *Les Applications de la Physique aux Sciences,* 1873; *Le Soleil,* 1873; *Les Comètes,* 1874; *Les Etoiles,* 1877; *Le Monde Physique,* 1880-85; *Petite Encyclopédie populaire,* 1886-91.

Guillemots (*gull* and *mew*), a genus of diving birds of the auk family (Alcidæ), and the genera Cepphus and Uria. There are about eight species in the Arctic and N. temperate zones. The common or ' foolish ' G. (*Uria troile*) breeds in Britain. The bill is long and straight, the wings and tail short, the feet three-toed and webbed, the legs being placed very far back. In colour G. are mostly brownish-black on top and white underneath. The dark throat becomes white or mottled in winter. They build no nests, but breed on rocky coasts. One pear-shaped egg is laid at a time. They are numerous round Flamborough Head (Yorkshire), the eggs being sought after chiefly for their albumen, which is used to clarify wine, and in the preparation of patent leather. The black G. (*Cepphus grylle*) is less common, but found in N. Scotland, and is smaller. A third British species (*U. Bruennichi*) is rare. *See* Howard Saunders, *Manual of British Birds.*

Guillim, John (*c.* 1565-1621), an English heraldic official, educated at Oxford. He was red cross herald-in-ordinary at the London College of Arms for most of his life. He was editor of *A Display of Heraldrie,* 1610 (reprinted 1724), from Dean Barkham's collections, according to Dugdale and Wood (17th century). Ballard, Bliss, and Moule think it was chiefly G.'s own work. *See* Fuller's *Worthies,* 1662; Duncumb, *Herefordshire ;* Wood's *Athenæ Oxon.* (edited by Bliss, 1813-20), ii.; Moule's *Bibliotheca Heraldica; Notes and Queries* (2nd series), vi.-viii.

Guillotine, an instrument for inflicting capital punishment, intro-duced into France at the time of the Revolution. It consists of two upright posts surmounted by a cross-beam and grooved so as to guide an oblique-edged knife, the back of which is heavily weighted to make it fall swiftly and with force, when the cord by which it is held aloft is let go. Some say that the machine was invented by the Persians, and previous to the time when it became known by its present name, it was used in Scotland, England, and various parts of the Continent. In a museum in Edinburgh there is still preserved the ' Maiden,' as it is called. Until 1650 there existed in the forest of Hardwick, in England, a mode of trial and execution called the gibbet law, by which a felon convicted of theft, within the liberty, was sentenced to be decapitated by a machine called the Halifax gibbet. In Germany the machine was in general use during the middle ages, under the name of the Diele, the Hobel, or the Dolabea. From the 13th century it was used in Italy, under the name of Mannaia, for the execution of criminals of noble birth. Dr. Guillotin, who first suggested its use in modern times, was born at Saintes in 1738. In 1789 he brought forward two propositions regarding capital punishment, one being that it should be by means of a machine, and the other, that all, gentle and simple, who were sentenced, should be executed in the same way, as swiftly and painlessly as possible. The idea was adopted on Oct. 6, 1791. A German named Schmidt furnished a machine for each of the departments in France. Experiments were first made with dead bodies from hospitals. A highwayman was the first to be thus executed; this was in 1792. Some doubt seems to have at first existed as to whether death was instantaneous, and the case of Charlotte Corday is instanced in support of the theory that it was not. It is said that when the executioner lifted her head and struck it, after execution, the countenance blushed.

Guimarães, an ancient fortified tn. of Portugal, in the prov. of Minho. It is picturesquely situated on the R. Avc, and possesses hot sulphurous springs. Knives, leather, paper, etc., are manufactured, and table linen is woven. Pop. 9000.

Guimaras, a small island belonging to the Philippine group, and situated between Negros and Panay. Its surface is rough and hilly, but without high mountains. Cocoanut palms are abundant, and the climate is extremely healthy. Pop. 20,000.

Guimbal, a tn. situated in the island of Iloilo, belonging to the Philippine group. Pop. 11,500.

Guinea, a former gold current coin of Great Britain, first struck in Charles II.'s reign (1664), and so called because originally made from gold obtained from the Guinea Coast. ' Spade Gs.' were those which had a spade-shaped shield on the reverse with the royal arms. It was the chief English gold coin, till replaced by the sovereign in 1817. Its value varied considerably from 30s. in 1695 to 21s. in 1717—the value now understood by the word, though no current coin of the name still exists. Professional fees, subscriptions, prices of pictures, etc., are often estimated in Gs.

Guinea, a large section of the W. coast of Africa, generally considered to extend from the mouth of the Senegal to Cape Negro. The name came into general use in the 15th century. It is divided into two parts, Upper and Lower G., and comprises many states and political territories, viz. Senegal (a French colony), the English settlements on the Gambia; Birrajos (Portuguese territory); Sierra Leone (British); the Ivory and Gold Coasts (French and British); the Slave Coast (French, German, and British); the British Protectorate of Southern Nigeria, etc., etc. The coast-line is uniform and flat, interspersed with shallow lagoons. Inland the country rises to the central plateau of Africa, and the rivers are usually precipitated in cataracts and rapids. The coast is hard of access from the sea, owing to the dearth of good havens and the roughness of the surface. The climate of G. is very unhealthy, if not deadly. The Portuguese were the first to explore and trade along the coast, tempted by the gold deposits, and later by the opportunities of slave-trading.

Guinea, Gulf of, a gulf of the Atlantic Ocean on the W. coast of Africa, between Capes Palmas and Lopez. On the N. and E. are two open bays—the Bights of Benin and of Biafra—separated by the delta of the Quorra or Niger. The gulf contains the islands of Fernando Po, Prince's (Principe) Is., St. Thomas (São Thomé), and Annobon. It receives the counter-equatorial current crossing the Atlantic near the equator, and sends out the equatorial current which flows in the opposite direction, finally giving rise to the Gulf Stream. For explorations there, see *Scot. Geog. Mag.*, 1888.

Guinea-fowl (*Numida*), a genus of African birds of the pheasant family (Phasianidæ). There are about a dozen different species in the Ethiopian region, extending E. to Madagascar and S. to Natal. They are now naturalised and domesticated in most countries, but prefer a warm climate.

Gs. are inclined to be quarrelsome in a poultry-yard, but are much valued for their flesh and eggs, which command high prices. The common pintado (*Numida meleagris*), sometimes called ' Come-back ' from its frequent harsh cry (probably the *Meleagris* or *Gallina Numidica* of the Romans), has dark-grey plumage with round white spots, a horny ' casque ' on the head, and fleshy wattles on the cheeks. Other species are the *Guttera cristata* of W. Africa, and the *Phasidus niger* of equatorial W. Africa (very rare), the males having spurs like pheasants. The birds are mostly gregarious and ground-feeders, but roost in trees. They were probably reintroduced to Europe by the Portuguese explorers of Africa in the 16th century. *See* Gesner, *Paralipomena*, 1555; Elliot, *Monograph of the Phasianidæ;* Darwin, *Animals and Plants under Domestication*, 1875.

Guinea-grass, or *Panicum maximum,* a species of Gramineæ in the same genus as the millets. It is a perennial plant growing in a tropical climate, and is used as a fodder plant.

Guinea Pepper, or **Bell Pepper,** a name given to the seeds or dried fruit of several plants of W. Africa, such as the *Capsicum grossum, Capsicum frutescens, Piper Clusii,* and *Xylopia Æthiopica.* Malaguetta (Malagheta) pepper and Ethiopian pepper are often considered equivalent to G. P. It was much used as a vegetable and for pickling in the East (till replaced by Eastern peppers in the 18th century), and the trade in it resulted in the settlements of Grand Bassa and Cape Palmas. *See* CAPSICUM, CUBEBS.

Guinea-pig, or **Cavy** (**Cavia**), a genus of small rodents native to S. America, but now domesticated in most countries. Sometimes considered as a separate species (*Cavia cobaya*), the familiar common cavy is probably a domesticated form of the *Cavia aperea* of Guiana and Brazil, introduced by the Dutch into Europe in the 16th century. The domesticated kinds are mostly white, or marked with yellow and black, or tawny-coloured. They have short limbs, the fore-feet having four toes, the hind feet only three. Their ears are short and rounded, and they have no tails. Gs. are very prolific, producing young five or six times a year. They are much used in bacteriological laboratories for the study of germ-diseases. The popular name is strictly very incorrect. The animals are rather rabbit-like rats than pigs. ' Guinea ' may perhaps be a corruption of ' Guiana,' or merely mean ' foreign.'

Guinea-worm, found in the tropics under the human skin, especially of the legs The worms are the thickness of horse hairs, and measure from one or two to six feet in length. The eggs of the worm occur in water; they are swallowed by men, pass out of the stomach and migrate. The males die in the journey from the stomach to the skin. This is first raised into a pimple in which the female worm is found gradually working its way out. It is gently drawn out little by little for a week or so, for if the worm is broken, severe inflammation is set up. The G. is said by some authorities to be the 'fiery serpent' of Mosaic history.

Guinegate, a vil. of arron. Saint-Omer, dept. Pas-de-Calais, France. The site of two important battles: (1) In 1479, when the Austrians defeated the French; and (2) in 1513 (Aug. 16), when the English, under Henry VIII., and the Imperialists, under Maximilian I., put the French to flight so precipitately that the engagement was called the 'Battle of Spurs.'

Guines: 1. A city of Havana prov., Cuba, on R. Mayabecque, 34 m. S.E. of Havana. The town is flourishing, with many modern institutions, and stands in a fertile plain. Pop. 8149. 2. A tn. of arron. Boulogne, dept. Pas-de-Calais, France, 7 m. S. of Calais. Near this town in 1520 Francis I. of France and Henry VIII. of England met on the 'Field of the Cloth of Gold.' Pop. 4400.

Guinevere, Guinever, or **Guenever,** a corrupt form of Guanhumara (Welsh *Gwenhwyfar*), an ancient British queen, daughter of King Leodograunce of Camelyard, and wife of King Arthur. She was the most beautiful of women, and cherished a guilty love for Sir Launcelot of the Lake, one of the Knights of the Round Table. According to Geoffrey's *History of Britain*, during King Arthur's absence against Leo, King of Rome, she married his nephew Modred, who had usurped the kingdom left in his charge by Arthur. Arthur returned and defeated Modred at Cambula, a battle fatal to both leaders, while G. fled from York to the nunnery of Julius the Martyr at Newport in S. Wales. According to Malory, Arthur had gone to Brittany to punish Launcelot when Modred usurped the kingdom and attempted to marry G. She, however, shut herself up in the Tower of London, and on hearing of Arthur's death went into a nunnery at Almesbury. Tennyson, in the *Idylls of the King*, makes Modred discover the relationship between Guinevere and Launcelot. The latter flung Modred to the ground and took to horse, while the queen fled to Almesbury where Arthur came to take leave of her.

Guingamp, cap. of arron. in the dept. of Côtes-du-Nord, France, on the R. Trieux, 52 m. W. of St. Malo. From the 14th to the 17th century it was the capital of the duchy of Penthièvre. The mediæval church of Notre Dame de Bon Secours is a great resort of pilgrims. Pop. 9233.

Guinicelli, Guido (c. 1230-76), an Italian poet, born in Bologna, where he studied and practised law. In 1274 he was exiled as one of the Ghibelline Lambertazzi party, and died in exile. Only seven canzoni and five sonnets by him are extant, the best known being the canzone, *The Gentle Heart* (translated by G. D. Rossetti), which is praised by Dante. They are printed in a collection published at Florence by Nanucci in 1843.

Guinness: 1. *Arthur* (d. 1855), a brewer; head of the firm of Arthur Guinness & Sons, of Dublin. He married Anne, daughter of Benjamin Lee. 2. *Sir Benjamin Lee* (1798-1868), third son of the above, born in Dublin, and succeeded his father as head of the firm, which he managed with the greatest success. In 1851 he became first lord mayor of Dublin, and during 1860-65 restored St. Patrick's Cathedral at a cost of £150,000. In 1863 he was made an LL.D. of Dublin University; in 1865 was elected M.P. for the city in the Conservative interest, and in 1867 was created a baronet. 3. *Sir Arthur Edward* (b. 1840), eldest son of the above, succeeded to the baronetcy, and in 1880 was created Lord Ardilaun. 4. *Edward Cecil* (b. 1847), third son of Benjamin Lee, was created a baronet in 1885, Baron Iveagh in 1891, and Viscount Iveagh in 1905.

Guinobatan, a tn. and com. in Albay prov., Luzon, Philippine Is. It is situated on the R. Inaya, and hemp is extensively cultivated. Pop. 20,000.

Guipuzcoa, a maritime prov. of Northern Spain, situated on the Bay of Biscay, with an area of 728 sq. m. There are numerous mineral springs —salt, sulphurous, and ferruginous— which are greatly frequented by visitors. The industries are carpets, glass, paper, chemicals, soap, cannon, etc. San Sebastian is the capital. Pop. 225,271.

Guiraud, Ernest (1837-92), a composer, born at New Orleans, of French parentage; studied at Paris and Rome. He served in the Franco-German War (1870-71), and in 1876 became professor of harmony and accompaniment at the Conservatoire. His operas include : *Le roi David*, 1852; *Sylvie*, 1864; *En Prison*, 1869; *Le Kobold*, 1870 ; *Mme. Turlupin*, 1872 ; *Gretna Green*, 1873 ; *Piccolino*, 1876

Le galante aventure, 1882 ; *Gli avventurieri*, and *Brunhilde* (edited and produced posthumously). He also wrote several cantatas, overtures, masses, etc.

Guiraud, Paul (*b.* 1850), a French historian, born at Cenne-Monestiès, dept. Aude, and educated at the Ecole normale. In 1884 he was appointed professor of history at Tolouse, and two years later became lecturer on ancient history in Paris. Since 1888 he has been professor at the Sorbonne. His works include: *Differend entre César et le Sénat*, and *Les Assemblées provinciales de l'Empire romain*, the latter of which was ' crowned ' by the institute.

Guiraut de Borneil (*c.* 1138-*c.* 1220), a Provençal troubadour, born at Excideuil (modern *Dordogne*), and accompanied Richard I. of England to the third crusade. About eighty love poems by him, written to a lady of Gascony, are extant, and are distinguished by simplicity and directness. He was known as ' Master of the troubadours,' and is mentioned in Dante's *Divina Commedia*. Some of his poems were edited by Kolsen in 1894, but no complete edition exists.

Guisborough, a market tn. of N. Riding, Yorkshire, England, situated in the valley of Cleveland, 9 m. E.S.E. of Middlesbrough. Iron is largely obtained in the neighbourhood, and there are breweries and tanyards. There is a sulphurous spring in the vicinity. Pop. 7000.

Guiscard (or **Wiscard**), **Robert** (1015-85), first Norman Duke of Apulia and Calabria, born near Coutances, Normandy; the son of Tancred de Hauteville. He went to Italy as a pilgrim, and raised a band of adventurers to fight the Greeks and Calabrians. He was soon joined by many Normans, and was very successful. In 1060 he captured Reggio and Cozenza, and accordingly obtained from Nicholas II. the investiture of Apulia and Calabria. He and his brother, Roger, were the papal champions in S. Italy and Sicily against the Greeks and Saracens. In 1081 he invaded the Byzantine empire and defeated the emperor, Alexius Comnenus, at Durazzo. He hurriedly returned to Italy to protect the pope, Gregory VIII., from the Emperor Henry IV., and later went back to the E., dying in Cephalonia.

Guischard, Carl Gottlieb (1724-75), a military writer, born at Magdeburg. He served in the armies of Holland and Prussia, being greatly favoured by Frederick the Great. His works include : *Mémoires Militaires sur les Grecs et les Romains*, 1757, and *Mémoires critiques et historiques sur plusieurs Points d'Antiquité Militaire*.

Guise, a tn. of arron. Vervins, dept.

Aisne, France, on the R. Oise, 16 m. N.E. of St. Quentin. It has important ironworks and manufactures of textiles, and contains a communistic labour colony. It was fortified in the 11th century and has stood many sieges. It gives its name to the duchy of G., founded 1528. Pop. 7298.

Guise (or **Guyse**), **Dukes of**, a ducal family of Lorraine, France, named from the town of Guise (*q.v.*). *Claude of Lorraine* (1496-1550), the first duke born at the Château of Condé, being the fifth son of René II., Duke of Lorraine. He became a French citizen; married Antoinette de Bourbon about 1514; joined the army and fought at Marignano (1515), and was created Duke of G. by Francis I. for suppressing the peasant revolt in Lorraine in 1527. *Francis of Lorraine* (1519-63), the second duke, was the son of Claude, and became a great military commander and leader of the Catholics. In 1552-53 he defended Metz against Charles V. of Germany; in 1554 fought at Renti, and in 1556 commanded the expedition against Naples. In 1557 Henry II. made him lieutenant-general of the kingdom, and in 1558 he took Calais from the English and brought about the treaty of Cateau-Cambrésis in 1559. He and his brother, Charles, Cardinal of Lorraine, were active in suppressing the Protestants, and defeated the conspiracy of Amboise, taking its leader, the Duke of Condé, captive at Dreux in 1562. He was assassinated by a Huguenot at the siege of Orleans. He left valuable memoirs. *Henry of Lorraine* (1550-88) (Balafre), the third duke, was the son of Francis and succeeded him as an opponent of Protestantism. He fought at Poitiers, Jarnac, Moncontour (1569), and Dormans; was concerned in the massacre of St. Bartholomew (1572), and in the murder of Coligny. In 1576 he became head of the Catholic League. Becoming too ambitious, he was assassinated at Blois by the order of Henry III. *Charles IV. of Lorraine* (1571-1640), fourth duke, was imprisoned at Tours at the assassination of his father, Henry, in 1588. He escaped in 1591 and entered the service of Henry IV., gaining a victory at Marseilles in 1596. He was banished by Richelieu in 1631. *Henry II. of Lorraine* (1614-64), fifth duke and Prince of Joinville, born at Blois, son of Charles IV. In 1629 he became Archbishop of Rheims, and in 1640 succeeded to the dukedom. In 1641 he joined the conspiracy of the Count de Soissons against Richelieu and was condemned to death, but escaped to Flanders. In 1647 he joined the Neapolitan revolt of Masaniello against Spain, but was taken as a prisoner to Madrid. He escaped in 1652, again attempted to win Naples in 1654, and became High Chamberlain of France in 1655. The ducal line became extinct at the death of *Francis Joseph of Lorraine* (1670-75), the seventh duke.

Guiseley, a par. and vil. of W. Riding, Yorkshire, England, 2 m. S.W. of Otley. Tweeds and other woollen goods are manufactured. Numerous ancient stone coffins have been discovered. Pop. 4925.

Guitar (Sp. *guitarra*), a stringed musical instrument. It has a flat soundboard, made of pine, with a large sound-hole; a flat back, made of maple, ash, or cherry-wood, and joined to the soundboard by ribs and curving sides. There are six strings, three of gut and three of wire-covered silk, which extend from the bridge, which is of ebony, to the end of the finger-board, from which the head is bent back at an obtuse angle. The strings are tuned to the notes E, A, D, G, B, E in the treble clef, but they are produced an octave lower than written. The instrument is played by plucking at the strings with the thumb and three fingers of the right hand, while the fingers of the left hand press the strings to regulate the intervals.

Guittone of Arezzo (*d.* 1294), an Italian poet, born in Tuscany; fought in the wars between Florence and Pisa, and in 1267 became a brother of the military order known as the Fratelli Gaudenti. He founded the Camaldolese monastery, Degli Angeli, at Florence, but died before it was completed. As a poet, he ranks high as one of the founders of Italian literature, being the first to give polish and regularity to the sonnet, while his prose style also had considerable influence for good. He is mentioned by Dante and Petrarch. His poems mostly appear in old collections of Italian poetry, such as *Antichi Poeti* (Venice), 1532. His prose writings and letters were published by Bottari at Rome in 1745.

Guiuan, a city of Samar Island belonging to the Philippine group. It is situated in the S. of the Archipelago. Pop. 12,000.

Guizot, François Pierre Guillaume (1787-1874), a French historian and statesman, born at Nîmes, of Protestant family. His father died on a scaffold during the Revolution, and the family fled to Geneva, where G. was educated. In 1805 he went to Paris to study law, but met with literary people who fired his aspirations, and seven years later he became modern history professor at the University of France. The same year saw the publication of his translation of Gibbon's *History*. In 1815 he became Secretary for the Interior, and was promoted the following year to the State Council. During the next few years he led the 'Doctrinaire' party, but on the break-up of the Duc Decazes ministry (1821) he was stripped of office, and a year or two later was forbidden even to lecture. During this period he produced his *History of the English Revolution* (vols. i.-ii.), 1826-27; *History of Civilisation in Europe*, 1828; and the *History of Civilisation in France*, 1829-32; all of which have appeared in English translations. In 1830 he again took to public life as deputy for Lisieux (Normandy), and after the July Revolution became a cabinet minister, being finally promoted, when the cabinet was re-organised (1832), to Minister of Education. In 1840, when his rival Thiers became Foreign Minister, G. came to London as ambassador, and was very cordially received, but returned to Paris after a very brief sojourn. The next task which he attempted was the complete reconstruction of the French ministry and reorganisation of public administration, which occupied him until the 1848 Revolution. In 1847 he became Prime Minister, but at once involved himself in a disgraceful intrigue over the 'Spanish Marriages' question; he aimed at Palmerston's foreign policy in this, but succeeded only in causing bad feeling between England and France. The Revolution was largely due to his iron-handed firmness in carrying out his schemes; after this he took no further part in political life, but retired to his home at Lisieux and concentrated on literary work. The first eight years of his retirement were occupied in the completion of his *History of the English Revolution* (vols. iii.-viii.), 1850-56 ; his *Mémoires* appeared in nine volumes (1858-68), and his daughter, Madame de Witt, published his *Child's History of France* (5 vols.), 1870-75; his only remaining work of importance is the remarkable biography of Washington (1840). G. is considered to be the founder of historical science, as opposed to the old style of chronicle pure and simple. His writings leave much to be desired in point of form and style, but are highly suggestive, well reasoned, and full of value in ideas.

Gujerat, or Guzerat : 1. A northern maritime prov. of Bombay presidency, British India. It includes the peninsula of Kathiawar, and a large district along the Rann of Cutch and the Gulf of Cambay. The political division of G., under direct British rule, is included in it, as are also several feudatory states, such as Baroda. The district contains parts of the Western Ghats, and the Vindhya and Satpura Mountains, and is watered by the Tapti, Nerbudda, Mahi, and Sabermutti rivers. The soil is fertile, but the climate unhealthy. Area, 70,038 sq. m. Pop. 11,500,000. 2. A cap. tn. of above dist., 72 m. N.W. of Lahore. Has important industries of brass vessels, footwear, inlaid articles, and textiles. Pop. 19,048.

Gujranwala, a dist. and tn. of the Punjab, British India. The tn. is situated on the Grand Trunk Road and Northern State Railway, 40 m. N. of Lahore. There are manufs. of silk scarves, jewellery, and brass goods. Pop. 30,000.

Gulden, a silver coin, current in Austria, equivalent to about 2s. English money. The Dutch 'guilder' is worth about 1s. 8d., and previous to 1876 a G. of that value was current in the S. German states. In the middle ages there were also gold German Gs., imitated from the Florentine florin.

Gulek-Boghaz, or **The Cilician Gates,** a pass in the S.E. of Asiatic Turkey. From earliest times the main road from all parts of the plateau has been through here.

Gules, in heraldry, the colour scarlet, the most honourable of the heraldic colours (Lat. *gula*, the throat).

Gulf : 1. A tract of the sea extending into the land, similar to, but larger than, a bay. 2. A term applied at Cambridge to that section of an examination list coming between the creditable passes and the complete failure.

Gulfport, the port for the Pearl river customs dist., situated in Mississippi, U.S.A., 13 m. from Biloxi. The dredging of a channel between G. and Ship Island (finished in 1906), gave a great impetus to the trade of the former. Pop. (1910) 6386.

Gulf Stream. An ocean current in the North Atlantic. It issues from the Gulf of Mexico, which gives it its name, being formed from the warm waters of the equatorial current, and flows out northward through the Gulf of Florida and along the E. coast of N. America, from which it is separated by the 'Cold Wall,' a narrow strip of cold water. It is early joined by another current coming from outside the W. Indies. When leaving the gulf, the G. S. is from 50 to 100 m. wide, and 2000 ft. deep, and moves with an average velocity of 80 m. a day. Its temperature is then about 80° F., but as it flows northwards, the temperature drops, and the current becomes broader and less rapid. At a point off Newfoundland it merges into the 'G. S. Drift,' which flows

eastward across the Atlantic, and later divides into two branches, which flow N. and S. respectively.

Gulfweed, the popular name of a floating seaweed, the correct designation of which is *Sargassum bacciferum* belonging to the Phæophyceæ. In form it is branched, and bears hollow, bladder-like floats, which have the appearance of berries. It is found in large quantities in the Sargasso Sea, between 40° and 75° W., and 20° and 35° N., where it was observed by Columbus in 1492. It is carried out of the Gulf of Mexico by the Gulf Stream for some distance northward.

Gull (Welsh *gwylan*), the name applied to a group of sea-birds, members of the division Larinæ of the family Laridæ. Under the most recent classification, forty-nine species of gulls are admitted, and these are placed in five genera : *Pagophila* (the ivory gull), and *Rhodostethia* (which has a small bill and wedge-shaped tail), in each of which there is only one specie, *Rissa* (in which the hind toe is wanting), and *Xema* (the members of which have forked tails), each containing two species, and *Larus* (with square tails), in which are a large number of varying species. Among the most common are the black-headed gull (*L. ridibundus*), which frequents marshy coasts; the herring gull (*L. argentatus*), a large and handsome variety; the common gull (*L. canus*) ; the lesser black-backed gull (*L. fuscus*) ; the greater black-backed gull (*L. marinus*), which is one of the largest species ; and the glaucous gull (*L. glaucus*), which is circumpolar in its distribution. The smallest species are the *L. minutus*, and the *L. philadelphia*.

Gull, Sir William Withy (1816-90), a physician, born in Essex ; educated at Guy's Hospital, London ; graduated as M.B. in 1841 and M.D. in 1846. From 1847 to 1849 he was Fullerian professor of physiology at the Royal Institution of Great Britain; and from 1856-65 a physician and lecturer at Guy's Hospital. He was elected a fellow of the Royal College of Physicians in 1848, and in 1871 attended the Prince of Wales during his attack of fever. For his services in this respect he was made a baronet, and appointed physician to the queen in 1872. His numerous works, which have been edited by Dr. Acland, include : *Gulstonian Lectures on Paralysis ; Report on Cholera ; Hypochondriasis ; Abscesses of the Brain.*

Gullet, or **Œsophagus,** a tube lined with mucous membrane which is separated by cellular tissue from its muscular foundation. The muscular fibres are striped in the upper portion and unstriped in the lower. The mucous membrane is thrown into a number of longitudinal pleats to allow of stretching. Compound racemose glands secrete a viscid mucus, and occur throughout the whole length of the G., though they are most numerous at the bottom. In man the tube is 9 to 10 in. in length, and from ¼ to 1 in. in diameter, and extends from the lower part of the pharynx, passes along the front of the spine, and terminates with about 1 in. of it in the abdomen at the cardiac end of the stomach. Among certain mammalia, *e.g.* ruminants, a layer of voluntary muscle in the G. allows of antiperistaltic movements being induced by which food can be regurgitated into the mouth.

Gully, John (1783-1863), an English sportsman and politician. He was prominent as a boxer and owner of race horses, and during 1832-37 was M.P. for Pontefract. In 1862 he bought the Wingate Grange Collieries.

Gully, William Court, Viscount Selby (1835-1909), an English statesman, born in London; educated at Cambridge; in 1860 was called to the bar at the Inner Temple. After contesting two unsuccessful elections, in 1880 and 1885, he was elected as Liberal M.P. for Carlisle in 1892. In 1895, on the resignation of Mr. Speaker Peel, he became Speaker of the House of Commons. He filled this difficult post with impartiality, dignity, and courtesy, and the only unfortunate incident of his career was the forcible removal of several Irish members who refused to leave their seats after a division had been called in March 1901. This lost him the confidence of the Irish party. He resigned office in 1905, and was created Viscount Selby on his retirement.

Gulo, the name given to a genus of carnivorous quadrupeds belonging to the family Mustelidæ. It contains a single species, *G. luscus*, the glutton or wolverene.

Gum. Gs. are the solidified exudations of different parts of plants (branches, stems, fruits, etc.), or are contained in the plant juices themselves. They belong to the carbohydrate group, are odourless, tasteless, amorphous substances which on treatment with water form either clear solutions or gelatinous liquids. The following are the principal kinds met with commercially: *Gum arabic,* obtained from various species of *Acacia,* sometimes known as G. acacia, is probably a calcium potassium salt of gummic acid (first prepared by dialysis by Graham). The G. occurs in rounded lumps which in some cases are almost transparent, while in others opaque owing to the large number of minute cracks. When treated with water it swells up and eventually dissolves, giving a solution with marked adhesive properties. On treatment with dilute sulphuric acid it gives galactose, and on oxidation a mixture of mucic and saccharic acids together with oxalic and tartaric acids. It is used in the ' dressing ' or finishing of fabrics such as silks and calicoes, and, when mixed with glycerine, for making ' gummed ' labels. *Gum senegal* is closely allied to G. arabic, and is often used to adulterate the latter. It is derived from *Acacia Verek*. *Gum tragacanth,* sometimes known as G. dragon, is obtained from different species of *Astragalus* which flourish in Persia, Syria, and Kurdistan. G. tragacanth forms curious horny translucent masses which swell slowly when treated with water, yielding a thick mucilage of low adhesive power. It is mainly used in the dressing of fabrics and in calico-printing, but is also employed in the manufacture of metallic-filament lamps for electric lighting. G. tragacanth probably belongs to the bassorin group of Gs. The Gs. exuding from cherry, plum, and apricot trees form a group apart. On hydrolysis they yield arabinose, and on oxidation oxalic acid. Under the term G. resins are included the juices of certain plants which are mixtures of Gs. and resins. On treatment with water, partial solution of the G. takes place and the resin is held in suspension. The best-known specimens of this class are: G. ammoniacum, G. euphorbium, G. galbanum, gamboge, and myrrh. Possibly caoutchouc and gutta-percha might find place in this group.

Gumal Pass, or Gomal, a mountain pass of Afghanistan, and the chief on the Indian frontier, between the Khyber and the Bolan. It forms a connection between Dera Ismail Khan and the Gomal valley.

Gumbinnen, a gov. dist. and tn. of E. Prussia, Germany. The town is situated on the Pissa, 72 m. E. of Königsberg; it is a flourishing industrial centre. The manufactures are machinery, beer, brandy, and hosiery; the weaving of woollen, cotton, and linen is also carried on. Pop. 14,539.

Gumboil, a small abscess situated at the socket of a tooth, and usually due to decay in the tooth. It readily yields to any treatment which brings about free discharge of the contents.

Gummersbach, a tn. of Prussia, Germany, situated in the Lower Rhine prov., 24 m. E. of Cologne. There are manufactures of woollen and cotton goods. Pop. 16,050.

Gumming, a contagious disease which

commonly attacks the vine and the plum, cherry, pear, peach, and other trees. It is due to the ravages of a fungus, *Coryneum beijerinckii*, which converts the cells of the host into gum. It is best to destroy the diseased tree, but the treatment consists in frequent washings. Excess of manure is often the cause.

Gumti, a river of the United Provinces and Oudh, India, rising 520 ft. above sea-level. Its course is generally S.E. for 365 m., until it enters the Ganges, 25 m. from Benares.

Gümürjina, a tn. of Turkey in Europe, situated in Adrianople, on the R. Karaga. Wheat, barley, maize, etc., are grown, copper and antimony are mined, and there is a trade in wine and silk. Pop. 8500.

Gun, the name applied generally to a weapon from which is discharged by means of an explosive a projectile. The word is, nowadays, applied almost entirely to the weapons used for sport, the military weapons, such as a musket or a rifle, being described as small arms. Originally, however, the G. was employed for purely military purposes; it was not until very much later that the weapon began to be generally used for sport. The origin of the name G. does not seem to be generally known. The generally accepted derivation, however, is that it is an abbreviation of the Gunhilda. This derivation has received the support of the late Professor W. W. Skeat, and is given also by the *New English Dictionary*. Other dictionaries give the derivation as from the Old French word *mangonnel*. The name is applied really only to the tubular weapon together with its stock as used for hand firing, but in common is often called a G. The hand G. was in fairly general use by the middle of the 15th century, but at this time was of very rude construction. It consisted simply of a tube of brass or iron which had a touch hole at the top and a straight stock which was placed under the armpit when the weapon was to be fired. The soldiers carried long matches made of cotton soaked in a strong solution of saltpetre. Horse soldiers also carried this type of G. which was suspended by a cord over their shoulders, and which when about to be fired was placed on a forked rest, which when not in use hung down beside them. During the early Tudor period an improvement in the shape of a matchlock G. was invented. This had a cock at the side of the G. which held the match, and by means of a trigger the match was brought into contact with the gunpowder. Almost at the same time we find a number of improvements in the weapon used, the stock of the G.

being made bent, and also provided with a broad butt end which could be more or less comfortably placed against the right breast. This was generally termed an arquebus and was a lighter weapon than the later musket, since it did not need a rest, and could be more easily carried. A smaller weapon was at the same time used, constructed on much the same principle, but which may be regarded as the forerunner of the later pistol. The next improvement in G.-making was the invention of the wheel lock, a weapon which carried a wheel at the side of the priming pan. This wheel was wound tightly up and could only be released by the trigger. When the trigger was pulled the wheel revolved, and by means of its rapid action on a piece of iron pyrites on which it rested gave forth a number of sparks which ignited the powder. This weapon, however, did not come into general use, since its mechanism was somewhat involved, and therefore naturally expensive. At the same time it was liable to get out of order in a very short space of time, and hence it is not at all to be wondered at that it was not generally used. Nevertheless, it remained in use until the reign of Charles II. About the middle of the 16th century the musket was invented by the Spaniards. This weapon was much heavier than the Gs. previously used and carried a much heavier shot. It necessitated the use of a forked rest, but proved of such great value that it was generally adopted throughout Europe. It was made on the matchlock principle, and it carried a ball of about 1½ oz. During this period the snaphance was invented in Germany. During the early part of the 17th century the firelock or flintlock was produced. This was a great improvement on previous weapons, since it did away with the necessity for filling the priming pan either from a flask of powder which was carried for that purpose, or by biting off the top of the cartridge as was the later practice. This weapon when at first invented was of little use, but gradually, during the 17th century, it was improved upon and began to be generally used in the European armies. From William III.'s time, for example, the raising of regiments of fusiliers, dates. These were regiments which carried a fusil or musket made on the principle of the firelock or flintlock. This weapon was of the type of the famous Brown Bess used during the War of the Spanish Succession by the troops under the command of Marlborough. During the 18th century continual improvements went on, and this weapon continued in general use until the middle of the 19th century. This type of weapon, however, did not fulfil all its functions equally well, and whereas it increased the rapidity of artillery fire, nevertheless, at the same time, it was always liable to misfire, since the priming could not always be guarded from the wet. To obviate this difficulty, early in the 19th century percussion caps were invented, but were not used in the army until some considerable time later. By the end of William IV.'s reign, however, we find them in fairly general use, and after a prolonged trial by the army authorities, they were adopted for use in the army. In 1842 the last improvement took place in the weapons of the Brown Bess type, but these were within ten years replaced by the use of rifles in the British army. Rifles did not at first altogether replace the percussion musket, but with the improvement of the rifle the use of muskets was abandoned altogether (1855). The rifle was a form of musket in which by means of grooves in the bore the bullet was made to rotate before leaving the barrel. The effect of this rotation is to ensure a more accurate flight of the projectile. The grooves in the bore were usually spiral in form, although some seem to have been made with straight grooves. The great difficulty which had to be overcome was the manner in which the bullet was to be introduced into the rifle. The principle of rifling was discovered early in the 16th century, but does not seem to have been generally used except for purposes of amusement. We do, however, come across occasional examples of its use, and by the end of the 18th century the idea of its general use had been adopted. Some rifle regiments were formed both in France and in England, but the difficulty of loading, and the waste of time which it entailed, prevented the general adoption of this method of warfare. Various experiments were tried, but they all either allowed too much windage, or else, owing to the means adopted to force them into their place, were erratic in flight. The difficulty, however, was gradually being overcome, and by 1835 a regiment of riflemen had been raised and armed with rifles made on the percussion principle. This, in fact, was the first recognition by the army authorities of Forsyth's invention of the percussion cap. In 1835 Greener produced an expansive bullet which was rejected by the army authorities on the ground that it was a compound bullet. It had, however, shown the advantage of rifle fire over musket fire, and had also shown that the

difficulty of windage and the erratic flight of the bullet could be overcome. In 1851 the Minie bullet was adopted by the British military authorities, and this Minie rifle was used during the Crimean War. In 1855 the Enfield rifle was invented, and was adopted by the authorities, being used in the later stages of the Crimean War, and taking the place of the Minie rifle. The Enfield rifle was in general use until the adoption of the breech loader in 1867. During the American Civil War, breech loading Gs. were used by the Federal cavalry, and in 1867 Snider's method of converting the muzzle loading Enfield into a breech loader was adopted by the military authorities of Great Britain. The adoption of the breech loading rifle became at this time fairly general throughout Europe, although the type of rifle adopted were by no means the same. The celebrated needle G. of the Prussians which caused such a sensation and was of such great value during the short Austrian War, had been adopted some time previously; in fact, the Russians were the first to thoroughly appreciate the value of a breech loading bolt action weapon. In 1871 the breech loading Martini-Henry rifle was adopted by the British military authorities. The calibre of this rifle was ·433 in., and it had bolt action. The authorities of Europe about this time generally adopted rifles of similar pattern. Various improvements were continually being made until a great step forward was made by the invention of a magazine G. Russia was again to the fore in the adoption of this new invention, and in 1884 it adapted the Mauser rifle to the magazine rifle. Not unnaturally France followed suit in a similar action in the following year, but adopted a rifle of different pattern. In the meantime, after a series of experiments and exhaustive commissions, the British War Office adopted a new rifle in the shape of the Lee-Metford Mark I. rifle in 1888. In 1891 the Lee-Metford Mark II. was adopted, this being a six cartridge magazine carbine with bolt action and firing smokeless powder, which had come into general use in 1890. This rifle was subsequently still further improved, and became known as the Lee-Enfield rifle. Cordite was introduced as a smokeless explosive adapted to both the Lee-Metford and Lee-Enfield type of rifle, both of which took cartridges made from cordite. Both these rifles also were small bore magazine rifles, the whole length of whose barrel was protected by a wooden handgrip. The length of the barrel was 21 in.

In 1900 Great Britain had adopted a rifle of the bolt action type, but had rejected the multiple loader by means of a charger. This adopted weapon was given up in 1903 when the short rifle came into prominence. Up to 1903 the principle adopted by the musketry regulations had been to use the rifle as a single loader whenever possible and to reserve magazine fire for special emergencies. By the adoption of a similar rifle in 1903, as already mentioned, this principle was given up and the principle of magazine fire was adopted in the British army. The most serious difficulty to be overcome as far as the short rifle was concerned was the loss of five inches when the bayonet was used. In 1908 this was made up for by the adoption of a bayonet five inches longer than the previous one. The long Lee-Metford and Lee-Enfield rifles were fitted out with a charge-loading apparatus and issued to the infantry territorials. One of the chief reasons which had been urged for the adoption of the short rifle was the fact that when the cavalry was armed with this weapon they could compete on more equal terms with the infantry when they were fighting dismounted. Many experiments have been made with a view to improving the modern rifle, but probably the next great change made will be the adoption of an automatic weapon of some description. The automatic principle has already been applied to pistols and to machine Gs. It now remains for an invention to be made whereby a G. of real use under active service conditions and on the automatic principle should prove itself of real value to infantry. The chief objection to the experimental weapons already put forward are that they are too heavy for the infantry to carry; they approximate too closely to the ordinary machine G., and also that under active service conditions they have yet to prove of value. Up to the present time no power has adopted an automatic rifle, principally for the reasons already given. For Cannon, see ARTILLERY.

Gunboat, the main principle which underlies the construction of a boat of this type is, that she shall to all intents and purposes be simply a floating gun-carriage. The earliest type of G., constructed about the middle of the 19th century, was of about 180 tons, 75 ft. long with a speed of about 6½ knots. Various improvements were made on this type of boat, until at the present time we have specially constructed Gs., which are used to a very great extent for river service and which have a displacement tonnage of about 700 tons. The average speed is just over 12 knots an hour, and they carry two 4-in. quick-firing guns, four 12-pounders, and ten machine guns. The boat is steel built and copper sheathed, and about 2½ times as long as the earliest type of G. Boats of this type are used a great deal on the R. Nile.

Gun-carriage, the support of a very large piece of ordnance. It is built in order to be able to stand very heavy strains. It has to withstand the shock caused by firing the piece, and it has also to be of great stability in order to be able to stand the strain of being drawn at a rapid pace over broken or rocky ground. There is a special department in the arsenal at Woolwich which attends to the manufacture of Gs. This department is of special importance since the G. must of a necessity be neither too heavy nor too lumbersome to be easily moved.

Gun-cotton, regarded usually as a nitrate of cellulose, but probably a mixture of nitrates. It is produced, briefly, by the action of strong nitric acid or cellulose. Early in the 19th century the action of concentrated nitric acid on fibrous or woody bodies was noted, and finally Pelonze made the discovery that cotton when treated with concentrated nitric acid became a highly explosive body. Following on these experiments Schönbein commenced his discovery of G. proper, i.e. cotton which had been treated with nitric acid and which had then become an exceedingly explosive substance. The modern method of manufacture is based essentially upon the method discovered by Schönbein. Cotton waste which has been carefully cleaned and dried is treated with a mixture of concentrated sulphuric and nitric acid. The sulphuric acid is used in quantities in excess of the nitric, and its chief use is to absorb the water produced during the process and to keep the nitric acid constantly concentrated. The process takes place at the ordinary temperature and lasts for from three to four hours. The product is then carefully washed and cleaned, since there is always present a certain amount of cellulose which has not been treated, and certain impurities in the cellulose give rise to the formation of sulphates, these sulphates are one of the causes of the not infrequent instability of the G. The G. is now pulped and either compressed into blocks, or dried in its ordinary state. It still retains the appearance of ordinary cotton waste, and does not explode save under confined conditions. The chemical formula is $C_6H_7O_2(NO_3)$.

Gundagai, a tn. of New South Wales, Australia, situated in Clarendon co.,

95 m. N.E. of Albury, in the vicinity of the goldfields. Pop. 1600.

Gundamuk, see GANDAMAK.

Gundelia Tournefortii, a species and genus of Compositæ with purple florets. It is to be found in Asia Minor and in Persia.

Gungl, Josef (1810–89), a Hungarian composer and conductor, born at Zsámbék; was a bandmaster in the Austrian army (1835-43); in 1843 established an orchestra, with which he toured in Europe and America. He became director of music to the King of Prussia in 1849, and to the Emperor of Austria in 1858. He composed numerous popular dances, marked by easy and rhythmical melody.

Gunib, a fortified tn. of Daghestan, Caucasia, 75 m. N.W. of Derbent. It stands at an alt. of 4020 ft. close to Gunib Peak (7718 ft.) and was the last refuge of Shamil, the Circassian chief who surrendered to Russia in 1859. Pop. 1000.

Gun-metal, an alloy consisting of about 9 parts copper, 1 part tin, together with small quantities of lead and zinc. It is a tough reddish metal, much used for making castings for bearings and other engineering purposes, and formerly used for making ordnance. It requires careful casting as the constituents are somewhat liable to separate in the process.

Gunnel, or Butterfish, a kind of blenny (*Pholis gunnellus*), found in the N. Atlantic, and notable for its covering of a thick mucous secretion.

Gunnery, the science which governs the employment of firearms. The science is itself very detailed, since a knowledge of it requires a knowledge of the metals from which the guns are made, the method of their manufacture, and an ability to calculate the strain to which proper use will subject the weapon. Again the science must calculate the probable effect of the missile upon the object fired at, and velocity of the projectile when fired and the effect of the forces which will be brought to bear upon the missile both before and after it leaves the gun. The subject has been frequently treated in various books which have been published from time to time. The earliest book which we find on this subject was published fairly early in the 16th century, but literature on the subject increased enormously during the 19th century and is increasing almost every day. The science is to-day far more exact than it has ever been, and the calculations which are made in gun testing and gun making are abstruse in the extreme. Calculating tables and instruments have been produced, and have reached such a pitch that it is possible nowadays to calculate before a shot is fired the range of a gun, where elevations and calibre are known, and usually such calculations are well within the mark. The intricate calculations and the beautiful mechanism, both of the modern gun and of the modern instruments, are such that G. may now be regarded as an exact science. *See* Tartoglia, *Nova Scientica*, 1537; Galileo, 1638; *The Official Textbook of Gunnery*, 1902; *Ordnance and Gunnery*, 1907.

Gunnigfeld, a com. and small tn. of Prussia in Westphalia, situated in the gov. of Arnsberg. Pop. 9901.

Gunning, Elizabeth, Duchess of Hamilton and of Argyll (1734-90), a celebrated beauty, daughter of John G. of Castle Coote, Co. Roscommon, Ireland. In 1751, she and her sister Maria (*q.v.*) went to London, and attracted great attention as ' the handsomest women alive.' In 1752 Elizabeth married James, sixth Duke of Hamilton, and in 1759 John Campbell, Marquis of Lorne, who was afterwards fifth Duke of Argyll. She and her sister were frequently painted, and numerous engravings of the portraits exist.

Gunning, Maria, Countess of Coventry (1733-60), a celebrated beauty, said to have been more handsome than her sister Elizabeth (*q.v.*). She was once mobbed by a crowd in Hyde Park, and the king accordingly gave her a guard. In 1752 she married George William, sixth Earl of Coventry.

Gunning, Susannah (*née* Susannah Minifie) (1740-1800), an English novelist. She married John G., brother of Elizabeth and Maria G. (*q.v.*), an officer in the army. She and her daughter Elizabeth were compelled to leave home on account of their flirtations, and the affair, known as ' the Gunningiad,' became very notorious. Her novels were numerous, but unimportant. Her daughter also wrote, and later married Major James Plunkett.

Gunnison, a riv. of Colorado, U.S.A. Its source is in the N. of Saguache co., and its course is W. and N.W., until it enters the Grand R. at Grand Junction, about 25 m. E. of the western borders of Colorado. There are numerous cañons.

Gunny-bags, bags used for rice, sugar, etc., made from a coarse cotton or jute cloth. The material was originally spun by hand by the natives of India in the districts where the jute was grown, mainly within a radius of about 200 m. round Dacca, and was known as *chotee*. As material and labour were plentiful, Gs. were cheap and greatly in demand. They are now chiefly made by power in the neighbourhood of Calcutta, and also in Dundee, Scotland.

Gunpowder, an explosive composed of charcoal, sulphur, and saltpetre. This substance has had an enormous influence on the history of the world; it revolutionised the art of war, and has not been without its effect upon the arts of peace. It is, perhaps, scarcely possible to speak about the discovery of G., since if it was discovered, we have no definite proof of the fact, and what facts we have at our command seem rather to prove that it was but the development which went on for some considerable time. The names, however, of Friar, Roger Bacon, and the German, Schwartz, have usually been associated with its discovery. Schwartz is supposed by the greater number of authorities to be the inventor of G., but we have proof that G. and cannon existed previous to the date when Schwartz is *supposed* to have invented it. Bacon himself does not appear to have been aware of many of the properties of G., although he certainly was the first person in England to make it. He, however, regarded it to a very great extent as an explosive which was to be used for purposes of diversion. He knew, however, of its explosive properties and probably realised that it could be used for blowing people up. Many references to the existence and use of cannon and G. are found between the years 1327-40. Edward III. is supposed to have used cannon against the Scots in the early wars of his reign, whilst we find another reference to the existence of G. in England in 1338. In Richard II.'s reign it was in fairly common use, and Henry V. ordered that G. should not be taken out of the country without license. Henry V. used it before Harfleur, but it did not become really effective until the end of the 15th century.

Gunpowder Plot, a conspiracy to blow up the Houses of Parliament and the king (James I.) who was to be present to open parliament on Nov. 5, 1605. It was contrived by a number of Roman Catholics, with Robert Catesby at their head, and seems to have been brought to a head by the revival, in 1604 and 1605, of measures of repression against the Roman faith in England. It is known that Catesby was conceiving a plan in May 1603, and in January 1604 some details were arranged between himself, Robert Winter, and John Wright. They were later joined by Guy Fawkes, brought by Winter from Spain, Thomas Percy, Thomas Winter, John Grant, Ambrose Rokewood, Robert Keyes, Sir Everard Digby, Francis Tresham, and Thomas Bates,

a servant of Catesby's, while two Jesuit priests, Greenway and Garnet, were also involved. In May 1604 the conspirators hired a house adjoining the House of Lords, and in December began to work a mine from the cellar. In March 1605 they obtained possession of a vault under the House of Lords, and stored in it thirty-six barrels of gunpowder. In May they separated to make arrangements for the carrying out of the plot subsequent to the explosion. The plot was discovered through an anonymous letter, for which Tresham was probably responsible, sent to Lord Monteagle on Oct. 26. On Nov. 4, a thorough search was made, and Guy Fawkes was arrested at his post in the cellar. The efforts of Catesby to bring about the arranged rising were fruitless.

Güns (Hungarian *Köszeg*), a tn. of Hungary, in the co. of Vas, situated on the Gyöngyös. It has an extensive wine and fruit trade, and there are manufs. of earthenware and cloth. There is a noted castle. Pop. 8423.

Gunst, Pieter van (1667-1724), a Dutch portrait engraver, born at Amsterdam. His work is neat and careful, but sometimes weak in drawing. Among his best engravings are those of A. Houbraken's drawings from Vandyck; of Brandon's ' William III. and Queen Mary '; of Holbein's ' Erasmus '; of Van der Werf's ' Duke of Marlborough '; of Kneller's ' Queen Anne '; of Riley's ' Dryden ' ; and of Greenhill's ' Locke.'

Gunter, Archibald Clavering (1847-1907), an American novelist and dramatist, born in England, but went as a child to California, where he studied in the School of Mines. After working as an engineer, a chemist, and a stockbroker, he took up literature, and became the proprietor of the Home Publishing Company. His best plays are *Prince Carl;* and *Mr. Barnes of New York;* and among his novels are *Mr. Barnes of New York*, 1887; *Mr. Potter of Texas*, 1888; *That Frenchman*: 1889; *Jack Curzon*, 1899; *A Manufacturer's Daughter*, 1901; and *My Japanese Prince*, 1904.

Gunter, Edmund (1581-1626), an English mathematician, born in Hertfordshire; educated at Westminster and Oxford. In 1619 he became professor of astronomy at Gresham College, London. He was the inventor of several useful mathematical devices, including Gunter's chain, used in land surveying, which is 22 yds. long and divided into 100 links; Gunter's line, being a logarithmic line laid down upon scales, etc.; Gunter's quadrant, used for finding times and altitudes; and

Gunter's scale, employed in navigation and trigonometry. He published several mathematical treatises.

Günther, Albert Karl Lewis Gotthilf (b. 1830), a German zoologist, attended Tübingen, Berlin, and Bonn Universities. From 1856 to 1895 he worked in the zoological department of the British Museum, and for twenty years (1875-95) was keeper of that department. During a busy life, he has identified himself with many learned societies, acting as vice-president of the Royal Society during 1875-76, and as president of the Linnean from 1898-1901. From 1858-70 he published ten volumes of catalogue of the reptiles and fishes in the Museum. *Fische der Südsee*, 1873-1910, and *Reptiles and Batrachians of Central America*, 1885-1902, are two of his many original contributions to zoology.

Günther, Johann Christian (1695-1723), a German poet, belongs to the Silesian school of poetry, of which, indeed, he is the last representative of talent. Unfortunately, however, a youth of brilliant promise was wrecked by a deplorable lack of self-control, a deficiency which soon precipitated him down the path of drunkenness and mind-destroying dissipation. His poem on the peace of Passarowitz and his lyrics, which reveal a deep emotionalism and a fine imaginative range, won Goethe's praise.

Guntur, see GANTUR.

Gurdaspur, the name of a tn. and dist. of British India, in the Lahore div. of the Punjab. The town, which was captured after a long siege by the Moghuls in 1712, has a population of 5764. The district (1889 sq. m.) has a pop. of 940,334.

Gurgaon, a tn. and dist. in the Delhi div. of the Punjab, British India. The district rebelled during the Mutiny. The commerce is chiefly in corn, hardware, and minerals. Pop. of town is 4765, and of district (1984 sq. m.) 746,208.

Gurhwal, see Garhwal.

Guriev, or **Guriev Gorodok,** a dist. and tn. on the r. b. of the Ural, 11 m. from the Caspian Sea in the government of Uralsk, S.E. Russia. Pop. 10,000.

Gurjun Balsam, or **Wood-oil,** obtained from a Dipteracea, which flourishes in the Andaman Islands. Father Damien used gurjun-oil to give relief to the lepers of Molokai, but the liquid is chiefly used in the East as a timber preservative against the attacks of ants and as a boat varnish. As it shares the medicinal properties of Copaiba Balsam, it is used as a substitute for the latter, especially in Indian hospitals.

Gurkhas, see GHURKAS.

Gurnall, William (1617 – 79), an English divine, is remembered as the author of *The Christian in Compleat Armour : a Treatise of the Saints' War against the Devil*, 1655-62. It is a volume of practical theology based on the 6th chapter of Ephesians, and may be described as a spirited exposition of a devout thinker's faith; its value is enhanced by what is now an old-world flavour.

Gurnard, or *Trigla*, a genus of fish belonging to the family of mailed-cheeks (*Triglidæ*). Gs. are bottom-fish, and are best caught, therefore, with a trawling net; they keep near the coast and are represented by as many as forty species in temperate and tropical seas. Along British shores the most common are the grey and red G. (*Trigla gurnardus* and *T. pini*). The head of a G. is angular and bony, but tne two most characteristic features are three detached finger-like rays, projecting beneath its mouth, which are at the same time organs of motion and of touch, and the pectorals which, when expanded, make a young fish look like a butterfly.

Gurney, Edmund (1847–88), an English psychologist, devoted his life to the serious and scientific study of what is known as ' Psychical Research.' At Trinity College, Cambridge, he obtained a good classical degree, and later turned his attention to music, medicine, chemistry, and physics. In his *Power of Sound*, he discussed the philosophy of music, but his fame rests on his psychological writings, including : *Hallucinations*, an essay, and *Phantasms of the Living*. The latter was a mass of data collected by G., Myers, and Podmore during their experiments in hypnotism and thought-transference for the Society of Psychical Research. G. was led to believe in telepathy by the weight of the evidence he amassed.

Gurney, Sir Goldsworthy (1793-1875), an inventor, began life by practising as a surgeon, and disappointed his patients when, shortly after 1823, he gave up the practice of medicine altogether. Faraday has acknowledged his indebtedness to G.'s course of scientific lectures, which were published in 1823. G.'s first invention was the oxy-hydrogen blowpipe; later he discovered the splendid light obtained by the fusion of magnesia and lime (the ' Drummond light '), and soon afterwards the high pressure steam jet, which was to revolutionise locomotion, and was also invaluable in the purification of sewer gas. The systems of lighting and ventilation in the present

Houses of Parliament were devised by G.

Gurney, Joseph John (1788-1847), a philanthropist; became a minister of the Society of Friends, and in social work supported the unselfish efforts of Zachary, Macaulay, and Wilberforce. The two causes, into which he threw his best endeavours, were the abolition of slavery and the improvement of prisons. In the latter he worked side by side with his sister, Elizabeth Fry. In *Prison Discipline*, 1819, he unfolds his schemes of reform, whilst a Quaker's opinion of his own sect is revealed in his *Religious Peculiarities of the Society of Friends*, 1824.

Gussets, in engineering, are triangular pieces of plate iron which are riveted to box girders, etc., inside to strengthen their angles. G. stays are plated stays used for connecting the areas of the flat ends of Lancashire and Cornish boilers, above the furnace flues to the shell. They are thin, and riveted with double angles to put the rivets into double shear.

Gustavus I. (Vasa), King of Sweden (1523-1560), born at Lindholm in 1496, the son of Erik Johansson of Rydboholm and Cecilia Mansdatter. In 1514 he was sent to the court of his cousin, Sten Sture, and bore the Swedish standard in the battle of Brännkyrka (1518), when Sture defeated Christian II. of Denmark. During the subsequent negotiations he was one of the Swedish hostages, and was treacherously carried off by the Danes and imprisoned at Kalö. He escaped and returned to Sweden in 1520. In 1520, roused with the rest of the nation by the news of the Stockholm massacre, he organised the revolt of the yeomen of Dalecarlia. The Danes were driven out and Gustavus was proclaimed king by the parliament of Strengnas and crowned in 1523. The task which faced him in establishing the independence of Sweden was full of difficulties, as the country was in great poverty and there was an utter lack of capable statesmen. He made a treaty with the Danes at Malmo in 1524, but never felt safe with regard to them. His projects for the strengthening of the national monarchy were in constant danger from the Swedish peasantry, and between 1525 and 1542 he put down four rebellions. For political reasons he severed Sweden's connection with Rome, and introduced the Reformation at the parliament of Westeras in 1527.

Gustavus II. (Adolphus) (1611-32), King of Sweden, was born at Stockholm in 1594, the son of Charles IX. and Christina. He was carefully educated in languages, politics, military achievement, and Protestant principles, and succeeded to the throne in 1611 as a capable and practical ruler. In 1613 he terminated the war with Denmark by the peace of Knäröd, and in 1617 the peace of Stolbova closed the Russian war and gave Karelia and Ingria to Sweden. In 1621 he resumed the war with Poland, of which the chief events were the capture of Riga and Mitau in 1621, the capture of Kokenhusen and the invasion of Lithuania in 1625, the battle of Walhof, completing G.'s conquest of Livonia, the occupation of Pillau, the conquest of Ermeland, the surrender of Elbing and Marienburg, and the blockade of Danzig in 1626,

GUSTAVUS ADOLPHUS

the disastrous campaign of 1627, and the defeat of G. by Koniekpolski at Stuhm in 1629. The war ended with the truce of Altmark. G. then joined in the Thirty Years' War, partly from a sincere desire to help the German Protestants, but still more from a fear that the emperor might acquire the Baltic ports and so menace Sweden. The Swedish fleet set out in 1630, and the army disembarked at Peenemunde in June. A successful campaign in Pomerania followed, and later in the year Magdeburg declared in favour of G. This city was invested by the imperialists, and early in 1621 G. advanced to relieve it. The suspicions and timidity of the electors of Brandenburg and Saxony frustrated his designs, and Magdeburg fell in May. In September the elector of Saxony definitely threw in his lot with G., and the allies defeated Tilly at Breitenfeld, near Leipzig. G. then marched towards the Rhine, took Marienburg and Frankfort, and wintered in Mainz (1631-32), and then resumed the pursuit of Tilly. In April he forced the passage of the Danube and the Lech, and finally defeated Tilly at Ingolstadt. In July Wallenstein united with Maximilian of Bavaria, and G., attempting to reach Saxony, was confronted with the allied army and defeated at Nuremberg in September. Wallenstein then retired southwards, but was overtaken by G. at Lützen. A terrible battle was fought on Nov. 16, during which G. was killed, while Wallenstein was forced to retire upon Leipzig. G. was a wise and popular ruler, and succeeded in bringing the wealthy nobles and the lower classes into the working of a harmonious scheme. The government was reorganised upon a bureaucratic basis, and the prosperity increased by the building of towns and the promotion of commerce. G. married Marie Eleonora, sister of the Elector of Brandenburg, in 1620, and had one daughter, Christina, who succeeded him. *See* C. R. L. Fletcher, *Gustavus Adolphus*, 1892.

Gustavus III. (1771-92) King of Sweden, was born in 1746, the son of King Adolphus Frederick and Louisa Ulrica of Prussia. In 1766 he married Sophia Magdalena, daughter of Frederick V. of Denmark. In 1768, during his father's interregnum, he compelled the ' Caps ' to summon a diet which he wished to execute some monarchical reforms, but these were defeated by the ' Hats.' During the early part of 1771 he spent some time in Paris, where he was very popular, on a diplomatic mission. On his accession he attempted to mediate between the opposing ' Hat ' and ' Cap ' factions, which were leading the country into a position of great danger, but only succeeded in breaking the power of the oligarchical ' Caps ' by the *coup d'état* of Aug. 19, 1772. The greater part of his reign was occupied in organising many useful reforms. In 1774 the liberty of the press was provided for ; the army and navy were enlarged ; in 1777 the ' currency realisation ordinance ' righted the national finances ; free trade in corn was promoted, and religious liberty was proclaimed. In 1786 the mutinous attitude of his Diet caused him to adopt an attitude of absolutism, which he maintained throughout the war with Denmark and Russia (1788-90). He was assassinated at Anckarstrom.

Gustavus IV. (1792-1809), King of Sweden, was born at Stockholm in 1778, the son of Gustavus III. and Queen Sophia Magdalena. In 1797 he married Frederica Dorothea, daughter of the Grand Duke of Baden. His character was marked by an abnormal seriousness and piety, which, added to a hatred and fear of Jacobinism, led him to act in a most mistaken way in several directions, notably with regard to the foreign policy of the country. In 1800 he joined the armed neutrality of the northern powers ; in 1803 joined the Bourbon cause, and later allied himself with the coalition against Napoleon. In 1807 he refused the terms offered him by Napoleon, and thus lost Rügen and Stralsund, while Napoleon persuaded Russia to invade and annex Finland. By the end of 1808 it was obvious that G. was insane, and in May 1909 he was deposed. He died in Switzerland in 1837.

Gustavus V., King of Sweden, was born at Drottningholm in 1858, the son of Oscar II. of Sweden and Norway, and Sophia Wilhelmina; entered the army and travelled considerably. In 1881 he married Victoria, daughter of the Duke of Baden. He succeeded to the throne of Sweden in 1907, the union between Norway and Sweden having been dissolved in 1905.

Güstrow, a tn. in the grand duchy of Mecklenburg-Schwerin, Germany. It stands on the Nebel, about 20 m. from Rostock and contains several interesting old buildings, among them a cathedral, church, castle, and town hall. The manuf. of machines and other articles is carried on, and also a large trade in wool. Pop. 17,809.

Gut, technically used in zoology as the equivalent to the alimentary canal. Three parts have to be distinguished: (*a*) The fore-gut or stomodæum lined by the outer layer or ectoderm; (*b*) the mid-gut or mesenteron lined by the inner layer or endoderm ; (*c*) the hind-gut or proctodæum lined by the ectoderm. These three typical parts, thus distinguished according to their origin, vary greatly in size and function in different classes, but the mid-gut is the most important on account of its digestive function, and because of its outgrowths (liver, etc.) in higher animals. In vertebrate anatomy the pharynx, gullet, and stomach are sometimes called fore-gut; the small intestine, mid-gut; the large intestine, hind-gut. In a human adult the small intestine is from 22 to 25 ft. long, and the large intestine, which is wider but much shorter, is connected to the small intestine at the ileo-cæcal valve.

Gut of Canso, a strait of Canada, situated between Nova Scotia and Cape Breton Island. It is 20 m. in length, and from 1 to 2 m. wide.

Gutenberg, Johann Gensfleisch, or Henne (*c.* 1397 - 1468), a German printer, was born at Mainz. He is said to have been the inventor of the art of employing movable types in printing. About 1424 he settled in Strassburg, where he stimulated the art of block-printing by the invention of a press for the multiplying of impressions. At the end of 1444 he returned to Mainz and was occupied until 1450 trying to perfect his art. In that year he entered into partnership with a rich burgher named Faust or Fust, who lent him the money to set up a printing press. This partnership, however, was dissolved in 1455 when Faust brought an action against G. to recover his money, and in consequence of the verdict Faust secured the press. G., however, continued his work, but was not very successful commercially. The works ascribed to him are: *The Bible of 42 Lines*, which was sold in 1873 for £3400; *The Bible of 36 Lines;* and the *Catholicon.*

Gütersloh, a tn. in the prov. of Westphalia, Prussia, which is famous for its rye-bread (*pumpernickel*). It also manufs. silk and cotton goods, and has a large trade in Westphalian hams and sausages. Pop. 8334.

Guthlac, St. (c. 673-714), the son of wealthy parents of the Middle Angles. At the age of twenty-four he became a monk, but in 699 left the monastery for Crowland in the Fens, where he led a hermit's life until his death.

Guthrie, the cap. of Oklahoma, U.S.A., and the county seat of Logan co. It was founded in 1889, and in 1890 made the capital of the territory, becoming the state capital in 1907, when Oklahoma was made a state. It has considerable trade with the surrounding country, and manufs. cotton-seed oil, cotton goods, flour, cereals, cigars, lumber, brooms, and furniture. Pop. 11,654.

Guthrie, Sir James (b. 1859), a Scottish painter, born at Greenock. He first studied under John Pettie in London, but afterwards went to Paris. On his return he joined the young Glasgow painters, and did a good deal of work in the open air. His pictures show him to have been a keen observer of nature, and are remarkable for their realism. His first pictures, ' The Gipsy Fires are Burning, for Daylight is Past and Gone,' and the ' Funeral Service in the Highlands,' are rather highly coloured, but his later ones are better. ' Schoolmates ' is in the Ghent Gallery. He has also painted portraits, some of his best being Mr. Galloway, Major Hotchkiss, and Professor Jack. He was president of the Royal Scottish Academy in 1902 and knighted in 1903. He is also an hon. member of the Royal Academy, London.

Guthrie, Thomas (1803 – 73), a Scottish preacher and philanthropist, born at Brechin, Forfarshire. From 1815-25 he was at the University of Edinburgh, but in 1826 went to study in Paris. In 1830 he was ordained minister of the parish of Arbilrot, near Arbroath, and while here started a savings bank, a Sunday school, and a parish library. In 1837 he became one of the ministers of Old Greyfriars Church, Edinburgh, and in 1840 was appointed to St. John's parish there. He supported Dr. Chalmers in 1843, who was against the intrusion of civil authority into church government, and his eloquence did much for the cause. He was also one of the first in Scotland to advocate compulsory education, and his name is associated with the cause of Scottish ragged schools, his *Plea for Ragged Schools* being published in 1847. Other works of his are : *The Gospel in Ezekiel; The City, its Sins and Sorrows; The Way to Life; Christ and the Inheritance of the Saints.* G. was also the first editor of the *Sunday Magazine.*

Guthrie, Thomas Anstey, *see* ANSTEY, F.

Guthrie, William (1708-70), a miscellaneous writer, born at Brechin, Forfarshire. He went to London in 1730, and was engaged in reporting parliamentary debates for the *Gentleman's Magazine.* He made a reputation as a political writer. Some of his works are : *History of England from the Invasion of Julius Caesar to* 1688; *A General History of the World;* and *Geographical, Historical, and Commercial Grammar.*

Guthrum (d. 890), one of the leaders of the Danish host which encamped near Reading in 871, and fought against Æthelred and Alfred. He was finally defeated by Alfred at Ethandun in 878, and a treaty was made at Wedmore whereby G. pledged himself to withdraw from Alfred's kingdom. He afterwards occupied E. Anglia, and was baptised at Aller, Alfred standing godfather to him.

Guthry, Henry (c. 1600-76), Bishop of Dunkeld, born at Cupar-Angus. In 1632 he was presented by Charles I. to the Parish Church of Stirling, but opposed the king, in 1836, when he was about to introduce a liturgy. In 1665 he was translated to the bishopric of Dunkeld. He was the author of *Memoirs of Scottish Affairs, Civil and Ecclesiastical, from the year* 1637 *to the Death of Charles I.*, a book which is of value as a contemporary account.

Guts Muths, Johann Christoph Fredrich (1759 – 1839), a German teacher, born at Quedlinburg. He was educated at Halle University, and in 1785 became a teacher of geography and gymnastics at Schnepfenthal. He introduced a new method of teaching geography, and it was largely owing to him that gymnastics became so popular in the schools of Germany. His handbooks explain his methods: *Gymnastik für die Jugend; Handbuch der Geographie;* but he also published *Deutsches Land und Deutsches Volk.*

Gutta-percha, the name applied to the dried milky juice of trees found mainly in the islands of the Malay Archipelago. These trees belong to the order Sapotaceæ, and often reach a height of 100 ft., and have trunks varying from 2 to 3 ft. in diameter. The name G. is Malay *getah,* meaning gum, and *pertja* being the name of the tree. The substance, which is similar to india-rubber, was formerly obtained by cutting down the tree, and then stripping off the bark, but now the less destructive method of tapping the trees is employed. The milky juice soon coagulates on exposure to the air, and is then kneaded under a supply of running water, and rolled into sheets to expel the air and to enable it to dry quickly. It is afterwards put into a masticator, which is heated, and revolved until it is fit for use. There are various kinds of G., but that from Singapore is considered the best. The substance has long been known to Europeans, having been imported in the form of native shoes, etc., but it was not until 1843 that they realised its value, or knew of its nature and usefulness. Dr. William Montgomerie, of the Indian Medical Service, first noticed that the Malays used it for making handles to their knives, etc., and conceived the idea of employing it for medical instruments. After this it was imported to a great extent, and used for coating marine electric telegraph wires (although it has now been superseded by india-rubber), for making golf-balls, overshoes, beltings for machinery, tubing, etc., as well as for stopping teeth. It is also used by surgeons for splints, but it is chiefly employed now for electrical purposes because of its inability to conduct electricity. When imported, G. appears in hard cakes of a reddish brown colour, and when cut has a peculiar cheese-like smell. It becomes soft when put into hot water, and can be drawn out into threads, but hardens on cooling, and is not brittle. It is not affected by alkaline solutions or by dilute acids, but rapidly deteriorates when exposed to air and light. It differs from india-rubber in being non-elastic.

Gutta Serena, another term for Amaurosis (*q.v.*).

Guttiferæ, a group of polypetalous (*i.e.* petals free from one another) plants which have their flowers regular, with their floral leaves in whorls, and their stamens are usually indefinite. *Hypericaceæ,* the St. John's wort family, is the only British order of the group, and includes the single genus *Hypericum,* of which there are numerous species. *H. calycinum* is common in shrubberies; *H. androsœmum,* the tutsan, and *H. perforatum,* the common St. John's wort, are the best known.

Gutzkow, Karl Ferdinand (1811-78), a German dramatist, born at Berlin. He studied theology at the University of Berlin, but the publication of his *Forum der Journalliteratur,* in 1831, began his literary career. The same year he joined Menzel in Stuttgart, and worked on the *Litteraturblatt,* and in 1832 published *Maha-Guru,* a satirical romance. In 1835 his *Wally, die Zweiflerin* appeared, for the publication of which he was imprisoned, having shown himself in this book to be an advocate of the ' Young Germany ' movement. On his release he went to Frankfort and Hamburg,' where he wrote his tragedy *Richard Savage,* 1839. Other plays of his are : *Zopf und Schwert,* 1844; *Das Urbild des Tartüffe,* 1847; *Der Königsleutnant,* 1849, all three of which are comedies; and *Uriel Acosta,* a blank verse tragedy. In 1847 he became director of the Court Theatre, Dresden. He was also a writer of novels, *Seraphine* appeared in 1838 and *Blasedow unde seine Söhne,* a satire on the education of the day. His *Die Ritter vom Geiste* was published in 1850-52, and *Der Zauberer von Rom,* a picture of Roman Catholic life in S. Germany, 1858-61. G. works contain some very fine character drawing, and are of interest for the glimpses they afford of the conflicts and intellectual problems of his time, but they are marred by the fact that he could not subordinate his political opinions to art.

Gützlaff, Karl Friedrich August (1803-51), a German Chinese scholar and missionary, born at Pyritz in Pomerania. He worked for the Netherlands Missionary Society at Java, and afterwards visited Singapore, Bangkok, Macao, and Hong Kong. He was joint Chinese secretary to the English commission in 1835, and rendered valuable service during the opium war of 1840-42 ; he was also the founder of an institute for training native missionaries. He translated the Bible into Chinese, and published several books in Chinese and in English.

Guy, Thomas (1644-1724), the founder of Guy's Hospital, born in

Southwark. He was educated at Tamworth, and in 1660 was apprenticed to a bookseller, but in 1668 set up in business for himself. By his trade, chiefly in bibles, and his investments, especially in the South Sea Company, he amassed a large fortune, and in 1695 became member of parliament for Tamworth, where he had founded an almshouse in 1678 for six poor women. He also built a town-hall for Tamworth in 1701, which is still standing. In 1709 he contributed largely for the poor refugees from the palatinate, and in 1712 subscribed to the fund for Bowyer, the printer, after his great loss by fire. In 1704 he became governor of St. Thomas' Hospital, and in 1707 built three new wards at a cost of £1000, and contributed yearly towards their support. In 1722 he began the erection of Guy's Hospital, on which he spent £18,793, and when he died left for its endowment £200,000. He endowed Christ's Hospital with £400 a year.

Guyenne, see GUIENNE.

Guy of Warwick, the hero of a middle English romance, versions of which existed in French in the 13th century. The story is an account of Guy's foreign wars and of his marriage to Félice, daughter and heiress of the Earl of Warwick. His pilgrimage to the Holy Land is also related, and his defeat of the giant Colbrand, by whose death Winchester was delivered from the invading northern kings.

Guyon, Mme. (*née* Jeanne-Marie Bouvier de la Motte) (1648-1717), a French mystic, born at Montargis. She was acquainted with the duchesse de Béthune, and was also very friendly with Father Lacombe, who was imprisoned for his mysticism in 1687. She preached her doctrine of quietism at Turin, Grenoble, Nice, Genoa, Vercelli, and Paris, where she settled in 1686, but was arrested in 1688 for having taught heretical opinions, and for having corresponded with Molinos, the leader of quietism in Spain. After her release she became acquainted with Fénelon, who supported her teaching and conduct in a controversy with Bossuet. She was again imprisoned in 1695 and not released till 1702. Madame G.'s works, in 40 vols., including the *Autobiography*, were published, 1767-91.

Guyon, Richard Debaufre (1803-56), a general in the Hungarian army, born at Walcot, Bath. He entered the Hungarian Hussars in 1823, but left the Austrian service on his marriage in 1838. He distinguished himself in the Hungarian Revolution, 1848, in command of the Honveds at the battles of Sukoro and Schewechat. In 1852 he entered the service of the sultan, and rendered great service in

the campaign against the Russians in Asia Minor (1854-55).

Guyot, Arnold Henry (1807-84), a Swiss geologist, born near Neuchâtel, Switzerland. He was very friendly with Louis Agassiz, at whose suggestion he undertook the study of glaciers. He was professor of history and physical geography at Neuchâtel, 1839-48, when he removed to Cambridge, Massachusetts; his lectures given in America being embodied in *Earth and Man*, published in 1853. From 1854-84 he was professor of geology and physical geography at Princeton. He published: *Meteorological and Physical Tables; A Memoir of Louis Agassiz; Creation, or the Biblical Cosmogony in the Light of Modern Science;* and *Lectures on Comparative Physical Geography in its Relation to the History of Mankind.*

Guyot, Yves (*b.* 1843), a French journalist, publicist, and statesman, born at Dinan (Côtes-du-Nord); became editor of *L'Indépendant du Midi*, published at Nîmes, in 1868. In 1892 he was attached to *Le Siècle*, and has been editor of *Le Journal des Economistes* since 1909. He has always been a Liberal in policy, and is an ardent Free Trader. During the S. African War he was temerous enough to side with Great Britain, and was one of the first to take up the cudgels on behalf of Dreyfus. His attacks upon the Police des Mœurs and their methods of dealing with prostitution, caused him to be imprisoned for some months. He was a member of the Chamber of Deputies (1885-92), and Minister of Public Works (1889-92). His works, principally on political economy and labour questions, include the following: *The Sugar Question,* 1901; *Conflits du Travail et leur Solution,* 1903; *La Science économique* (3rd ed. 1903); *La Tyrannie protectionniste,* 1905; *Le Commerce,* 1909; *Les Préjugés économiques,* 1909; *Les Chemins de fer et la Grève,* 1911. In collaboration with M. Raffalovich he published *Le Dictionnaire du Commerce, de l'Industrie et de la Banque,* 1901.

Guyton de Morveau, Louis Bernard, Baron (1737-1816), a French chemist, born at Dijon. He studied law in the university at Dijon, and became a member of the legislative assembly in 1791, and was a member of the national assembly in 1792 and 1795. From 1800-14 he was master of the mint, and was made a baron in 1811. He contributed largely to the scientific periodicals of the day, and also published *Méthode d'une nomenclature chemique;* and *Traité des moyens de désinfecter l'air,* which describes the disinfecting powers of chlorine and of hydrochloric acid gas.

Guzerat, see GUJARAT.

Guzman-Blanco, Antonio (1830-99), a president of Venezuela, born at Caracas. He was banished from his country for taking part in political disturbances, but returned and became vice-president in 1863. He was expelled from his office in 1868, but headed a revolution which restored him to power in 1870, and from that year to 1889 was virtual dictator of the country. During this period he opened a railway in Venezuela, and did all he could to promote education.

Guzmania, a genus of Bromeliaceæ, consists of five species, all of which occur in tropical S. America. They are epiphytic plants, and *G. tricolor* is cultivated in Britain.

Gwadur, a port of Baluchistan, situated on the Makran coast, 290 m. W. of Karachi. The steamers of the British India Navigation Company call here. Pop. 5000.

Gwalior, one of the largest native states of Central India, lies between the United Province and the Central Provinces. The state consists of hilly country and plains, and is, to a great extent, sterile and stony. The climate is extreme. The hilly part contains the small district of Amighera. Area 29,000 sq. m.; pop. 3,000,000. The capital is G., or Lashkar; it is strongly fortified, the fortress being on a rock 340 ft. high. From 1854 to 1885 it was in British hands. Pop. 120,000.

Gweedore, a holiday resort of Ireland, in co. Donegal, situated on the Clady, which river affords good trout and salmon fishing.

Gwelo, the central tn. of Southern Rhodesia, S. Africa. It is situated midway between Salisbury and Buluwayo, being 113 m. N.E. of the latter town by rail. The white pop. is about 400.

Gwersyllt, a par. and tn. of Denbigh, Wales, 2½ m. N.N.W. of Wrexham, situated in a colliery district, with iron works. Pop. (1911) 4600.

Gwynn, Nell (1650-87), an English actress and the mistress of Charles II. Of her early history very little is known, but when quite young she sold oranges somewhere near Drury Lane. She afterwards joined the acting profession and made her first appearance in 1665 as Cydaria in Dryden's *Indian Emperor*, and afterwards in many other witty parts, being a general favourite with the public. Her two sons by Charles were Charles, made Duke of St. Albans, and James Beauclerk, who died while young.

Gwynne, H. A. (b. 1866), editor of the *Morning Post*, born at Kilvey, and educated at Swansea Grammar School and abroad. In 1893 he acted as correspondent for the *Times* in the Balkans, and in 1896 accompanied Lord Kitchener's expedition to Dongola as Reuter's chief war correspondent, following the operations of the Turkish-Greek war in 1897 in the same capacity. In 1899 he sailed for S. Africa, and organised Reuter's war service for the Boer War, taking part in many of the minor operations. He became editor of the *Standard* in 1904, but resigned in 1911. He has published *The Army on Itself*.

Gyangze, a fortified tn. of Tibet, situated on the trade route between Lhassa and Darjiling. In 1904 the English entered this town when on an expedition.

Gyaros, Ghiura, or **Giura**, one of the Cyclades Is., about 10 m. from Syra. This island was used as a Roman place of banishment.

Gyges, King of Lydia, was the founder of the Mermnad dynasty in the 7th century B.C., having put to death Candaules, his predecessor and last of the previous dynasty. During his kingship he captured Smyrna, Colophon, and other cities, and was successful against the Cimmerians. After helping the Egyptians against the Assyrians, he was again attacked by the Cimmerians, who took Sardis and put him to death.

Gylippus, son of Cleandridas, an exile from Sparta, was a Spartan general. In 414 B.C. G. was appointed commander of the Syracusans against the Athenians, and in this he was entirely successful—Nicias being defeated. Afterwards, however, he was entrusted by Lysander with treasure from Athens, and on being found guilty of appropriating some, was exiled as his father had been.

Gyllembourg-Ehrensvärd, Thomasine Christine (1773-1856), a Danish writer, born at Copenhagen. When quite young she (then named Buntzen) married Peter Heiberg and became the mother of Johan Ludvig Heiberg. She was afterwards divorced, and then married Baron Ehrensvärd. Her first novel, *Familien Polonius*, appeared in 1827 in the journal known as the *Flyvende Post*. Among her other works are: *En Hversdage historie*, 1828; *To Tidsaldre. See* J. L. Heiberg, *Peter Andreas Heiberg og Thomasine Gyllembourg*, 1882.

Gyllenborg, Count Carl (1679-1746), a Swedish statesman, born at Stockholm. He obtained an appointment in London, being attached to the Swedish legation there, and in 1717 was connected with a plot against the Stuarts. On returning to Sweden he became chancellor and spent some of his time in political writing.

Gyllenstjerna, Johan (1635-80), a Swedish statesman. After travelling in various countries, he returned to Sweden and took an active part in politics there. He sided with the country against the aristocrats, to whom he belonged, putting the national interests before all others. About the year 1675 he became the adviser of Charles XI., and obtained an influence over him which lasted throughout his reign. In 1679 he was the chief promoter of peace at the Congress of Lund.

Gymkhana (probably through Hindustani *gend-khana,* racquet court) was originally some public place where athletics could be indulged in, but the word is now applied to a display of sports.

Gymnadenia, a genus of Orchidaceæ usually included in the genus *Habenaria. G.* (or *H.*) *conopsea,* the scented orchis, is found in mountainous and hilly pastures of Britain.

Gymnastics, a term signifying physical exercises practised for recreation or for promoting health. The gymnasium of the Greeks was originally the school where competitors in the public games received their training, and was so named from the circumstance that the competitors exercised naked (γυμνός). Athletic contests formed part of the social life of the Greeks from earliest times. The victor in any such contest was rewarded with the honour and respect of his fellow-citizens, and a victory in any of the religious festivals, was looked upon as an honour to the whole state, for religious festivals were marked by contests and games. In these circumstances the training of athletics became a matter of public concern, accordingly, special buildings were provided by the state, and their management was entrusted to public officials. Men were paid to look after the youths who were training for public contests, to conduct the games at the great Athenian festivals, to exercise general supervision over the morals of the youths, and to adorn and keep up the gymnasium. This office was one of the public services, and great expense was entailed on the holders. Under them were the *sophronistæ,* whose duty was to watch the conduct of the youths at all times, and especially to be present at all their games. The practical teaching and selection of suitable exercises for each youth were in the hands of the *pædotribæ* and *gymnatæ,* the latter of whom also superintended the effect on the constitution of the pupils, and prescribed for them when they were unwell. The *aleiptæ* oiled and rubbed dust on the bodies of the youths, acted as surgeons, and administered any drugs prescribed. According to Galen there was also a teacher of the various games of ball. The gymnasia, built to suit these various purposes, were large buildings, which contained not merely places for each kind of exercise, but also a stadium, baths, covered porticos for practice in bad weather, and outer porticos where the philosophers and men of letters read public lectures and held disputations. The gymnasium of the Greeks did not long remain exclusively devoted to athletic exercises. It soon began to be put to other even more important uses. The gymnasium became connected with education on one side and medicine on the other. Due training of the body, and maintenance of health and strength of children, were the chief part of the earlier Greek education. The education of boys was conducted in the gymnasia, save that part devoted to letters and music. As they grew older, philosophers and sophists attended to talk and to lecture in the gymnasia. In Athens there were three great public gymnasia—Academy, Lyceum, and Cynosarges, each of which was consecrated to a special deity with whose statue it was adorned; Plato's teaching in the Academy has given that gymnasium immortality. Aristotle conferred lustre on the Lyceum, and Cynosarges was the resort of the Cynics. Plato, when treating of education, devotes much time to G. Prodicus is said to have first pointed out his connection between G. and health. The Greek institution of the gymnasium never became popular with the Romans, who thought such training was conducive to idleness and immorality, and of little use from a military point of view, though at Sparta G. training had been chiefly valued as promoting bodily strength, such as was needed for the use of weapons and the endurance of hardship. The first public gymnasium at Rome was built by Nero, and another by Commodus. Rousseau in his *Emile* was the first in modern times to call attention to the serious consequences of neglecting G. And Pestalozzi and Froebel, the German educational reformers, emphasised the need for systematic physical training. It was not till the end of the 19th century that G. were regarded in England as more than recreation, and at present the larger public schools and universities are supplied with elaborate gymnasia, and even the children in the council schools are taught simple G. exercises. In Germany the state not only controls the practice of G., but makes it compulsory for every child and adult to undergo such training; in France, too, such training is under government control. In Sweden, Denmark, Switzerland, Italy, and Russia, systems are more or less distinct and enjoy a wide popularity.

Gymnema, a genus of Asclepiadaceæ, consists of twenty-five species of evergreen shrubs growing wild in tropical countries. *G. lactiferium* is noted for its milky juice, and *G. sylvestre* for the gymenemic acid contained in its leaves.

Gymnocladus, a genus of leguminous plants, contains two species which flourish in China and N. America. The better known of these is *G. Canadensis*, the Kentucky coffee-tree or stumptree. The branches have a dead appearance in winter, showing no buds; the wood is hard and compact, and is used in cabinet-making.

Gymnops (Gk. γυμνός, naked, and ὤψ, eye), the name of a genus of passerine birds, of which the chief species is *G. tricolor*.

Gymnosophists (Gk. γύμνός, naked, σοφιστής, sages) was the name given by the Greeks to those Hindu philosophers who practised the most rigorous asceticism, regarding food and clothing as hindrances to purity of thought. They often lived as hermits in forests, and some, like Kalanus, even burned themselves to death to enter a state of purer being.

Gymnosperms (plants with naked seeds), one of the two divisions of phanerogams or flowering plants. It differs from the other group, the angiosperms, in the fact that there is no closed ovary in the female flower at the time of pollination. When this process takes place the cone scales are separated from one another sufficiently to leave an open passage down to the ovules, and it is upon the micropyle of the ovule itself that the pollen falls. Thus there is no need for a stigma and style. After pollination the scales close up so as to shelter the developing seeds, opening again when the latter are ripe, so as to allow them to escape. The flowers are all unisexual, and are generally without a perianth. The plants of this class are all perennial trees and shrubs, for the most part evergreen; they are classified into the three natural orders Cycadaceæ, Coniferæ, and Inetaceæ.

Gymnostachyum, a genus of Acanthaceæ, to be found in tropical Asia. There are fifteen species in all, and these are herbaceous plants bearing white flowers.

Gymnotus, *see* ELECTRIC EEL.

Gymnura, a genus of Erinaceidæ, a family of insectivorous mammals. *Gymnura rafflesii* inhabits Malaysia and is characterised by a long and rough tail.

Gympie, a tn. of Queensland, Aus-

tralia, lying 107 m. N. by W. of Brisbane, and the centre of a goldmining district. Pop. about 12,000.

Gynæcology, the name given to that department of medicine which deals with diseases peculiar to women.

Gynandria (Gk. γονή, female, ἀνήρ, male), a term which was used in the Linnæan system of classification of plants to include those bearing gynandrous flowers, *i.e.* flowers in which the stamens are adherent to the carpels, as in all orchids.

Gyndes, an ancient river of Assyria. It has been identified with various modern rivers, among them the Diala and the Mendeli.

Gynerium, a genus of Gramineæ, consists of three species which grow in a tropical or warm climate. *G. argenteum* is the well-known Pampas grass often cultivated as an ornamental plant in Britain. The flowers are borne in panicles, and the plant is diœcious.

Gynocardia odorata, a species of Flacourtiaceæ found in tropical Asia and constitutes a genus in itself. It is of medical value and yields Chaulmoogra oil.

Gynophore, in botany, a prolongation of the flower axis or thalamus which takes place between the insertion of the stamens and the pistil in certain plants. It occurs in some Cruciferæ and in some of the gentians.

Gynura, a genus of Compositæ, contains about two dozen species. They are all to be found growing wild in tropical Asia and Africa, and some will flourish when carefully cultivated in Britain.

Gyoma, a vil. situated in the prov. of Békés, on the Körös, Hungary. Pop. about 11,669.

Gyöngyös, a tn. in the co. of Heves, Hungary. This town possesses a Franciscan monastery, and trades in dairy produce and wine. Pop. about 16,450.

Gyp, pseudonym of **Gabrielle Sybille Marie Antoinette Riquetti de Mirabeau, Comtesse de Martel de Janville** (b. 1850), a French novelist, born at the château of Koëtsal in the Morbihan. She began by writing stories for the *Figaro* and the *Vie Parisienne*, but afterwards published numerous other novels in which she describes the society of Paris. In 1882 *Petit Bob* appeared; in 1883 *Autour du Mariage*, which has run through over ninety editions. Other notable works are: *L'Education d'un prince*, 1890; *Ohé ! la grande vie*, 1891; *Mariage Civil ; Le Bonheur de Ginette ; Trop de Chic ; Un Ménage dernier cri ; Maman ; Le Cœur de Pierrette ; Bijou ; Journal d'un Casserole l'âge du Toc ; La Bonnefortune de Toto ; La Meilleure Amie.*

Gyp holds an important position among the writers of her class, and her works are remarkable for their humour (especially the dialogues) and for the types which illustrate the luxurious manners of the 19th century.

Gypaëtus, a genus of birds of the sub-family Gypætinæ, family Falconidæ. They are birds of prey, and are natives of the mountain regions of Africa and Asia, also some parts of Europe. Among them may be mentioned *G. barbatus* (lammergeier).

Gypogeranus, *see* SECRETARY BIRD.

Gypsies, or **Gipsies**, a wandering race scattered over the world, and found throughout Europe, in Western Asia and Siberia, Egypt, Northern Africa, America, and Australia. It is impossible to estimate their numbers exactly. Their total number in Europe is probably over 900,000. They are in greatest numbers in Hungary, Roumania, and Turkey. The figures for Hungary have been given as 280,000 (in 1910), for Roumania as about 250,000, for European Turkey 117,000 (in 1903), and for Asiatic Turkey about 80,000. Austria has over 16,000, and France and Germany about 2000 each. For the British Isles it is estimated that there are some 12,000 G. It would be mere guesswork to state how many thousands of these nomads are settled or are wandering in America, Africa, and Australia.

The word G. is a corruption of Egyptian, and is found in different forms throughout Europe: *Gyptenaer* in the Netherlands; *Aegypter* in Germany (16th century); *Gitano* in Spain; and *Gyphtos* in modern Greece. The name no doubt arose from the tale which they spread on their first appearance in Europe, that, for refusing to apostatise, they had been driven by the Saracens out of ' Little Egypt,' by some supposed to be a confusion between Little Armenia and Egypt, and by others identified with Epirus. The other name of the G. is *Atzigan*, or *Atzingan*, derived, according to Miklosich, from the *Athinganoi* (' not to be touched '), a heretical sect formerly inhabiting parts of Asia Minor. This name appears in Roumania under the form of *Tsigan*, in Turkey *Tshingian*, in Hungary *Czigany*, in Germany *Zigeuner*, in Italy *Zingari*, and in Spain *Zincali*. G. have also been known as *Faraon* and *Phárao-Nephka*, again indicating their supposed Egyptian origin, *Heydens* or *Heïdens* (' heathens '), Saracens, Bohemians, and Tartars. They have, too, been called Greeks, Germans, Flemings, etc., apparently from the country from which they happened to have come last. The G.

call themselves *Rom* (feminine *Romni*), which may be derived from *Droma*, Indian, or more likely from *Romanoi*, the name applied to themselves by the Byzantines of the Grecian empire.

The Athinganoi mentioned above were magicians, soothsayers, and serpent charmers who lived in Asia Minor as early as 810 A.D. According to one tradition they were the descendants of Samer, an outcast, since he fashioned the Golden Calf for the Israelites in the desert. The G. cannot definitely be identified with these Athinganoi, but it is known that G. passed into Europe from the further side of the Bosphorus in the early 14th century, and traces of people with peculiarities not unlike those of the G. may be found in Eastern Europe and Asia Minor prior to that century. In the rhymed paraphrase of the Genesis, written before 1122 (ed. Ditmar, 1862), there is a passage referring to the ' Ishmaelitish folk,' descended from Hagar's son. The writer calls them *Chaltsmide* (' iron-workers '), and says of them, ' They have neither house nor country; every place is the same to them. They roam about the land, and abuse the people by their knaveries. It is thus they deceive folk, robbing no one openly.' It is certain that as early as the 10th century there were itinerant smiths or tinkers, who sold their wares in many countries. The *Komodromoi* (' village-roamers ') mentioned by Theophanes as hailing from Italy in 554, were probably smiths of the same order as the Chaltsmide. Even if G. may not with certainty be identified with these vagrant pedlars, it is extremely probable that they assimilated them in large numbers. *Atkinkan*, ' sorcerers and famous rogues,' lived at Constantinople about 1050, and an unnamed race, who ' wander like a cursed people,' and dwell in ' little, oblong, black, low tents, like those of the Arabs,' are mentioned in Friar Simon's *Itinerarium* as living in Crete in 1322. It is certain that G. existed in Corfu before 1326, and twenty years later they were reduced to a state of serfdom by the Empress Catherine de Valois. There can be no doubt that by the 15th century they had been settled for a long time in the Balkan Peninsula and in many of the countries N. of the Danube. They had possibly already made their way further W., but there is no very good authority for their appearance in Western Europe before the beginning of the 15th century. In 1414 a troupe of G. is said to have arrived in Hesse. In 1417 a large company of them, bearing letters of protection from the Emperor Sigismund, who declared that they were Christian penitents engaged on a seven years' pilgrimage, and were well received by various western towns. Some had reached Hamburg, Wismar, and Lübeck in 1417; others arrived in Switzerland, Leipzig, and Frankfort-on-the-Main in 1418; they entered Bologna on their way to Rome in 1422; and reached Paris in 1427. In 1423 a second immigration followed, led by Ladislaus, *Woiwode* (' count ') of the Cigani, who also was furnished with letters of protection by Sigismund, and who appears to have hailed from Hungary. Between 1438 and 1512 the G. came in hordes, swarming over Germany, Italy, and France. They probably reached England and Scotland about 1500. The exodus of the G. from Rumelia and the eastern countries is generally accounted for by incursions of Turks who subdued the kingdoms of Greece, Servia, and Bulgaria. *The Constitutions of Catalonia* (1512) speaks of the G. as Greeks, which shows that they continued for a time to live in Greece under Turkish rule. The most nomadic of the tribes probably first moved to Walachia and Transylvania, and then, as others followed in ever increasing numbers, moved further and further westwards.

From the earliest description of G., it is evident that they then possessed those peculiarities of physique and mode of life which distinguishes them to-day. The G. who settled in Germany in 1417 are described by Krantzius in his *Saxonia*, and subsequently by Münster in *Cosmographia*. Most of them bivouacked in the fields, while their count and knights sometimes put up for the night in an inn. Some of them rode on horseback, others following on foot, while the women and children travelled in waggons. They had no honest means of livelihood, but practised palmistry and fortune-telling, and before very long became notorious for dishonest dealings and for theft. In appearance they were described as being black and dirty. At first they were well received, if not welcomed by the chief towns of Europe. At Utrecht, in 1429, they were given pots of ale, bread, and a hundred herrings, probably because they had a ' written permission from the pope to visit the Christian land,' and in the following year twenty schellings was paid from the public purse of Middelburg to a count of ' Litill Egypt.' In 1505, James IV. of Scotland gave Antonius Gaginus, a count of Little Egypt, letters of recommendation to the King of Denmark. They were entertained by the Earl of Surrey in Tendring Hall, Suffolk, in 1519, and

were given ' two towers for their residence ' by Sir William St. Clair, whom they had delighted by their dancing and acting. But before very long their popularity had waned. Middelburg, which had previously given generous hospitality to the wandering strangers, in 1460 sent Constantine, Count of Egypt, a bribe of ten schellings that his troupe might not visit the town. Country-folk had been gulled by these wily, insinuating visitors, and small farmers and owners of barns looked forward with dread to any repetition of their visits. Those in authority found it impossible to legislate for people who had gone as soon as they had come and might reappear as suddenly, and consequently classed them wholesale as vagabonds and outlaws, and treated them accordingly. In 1560 an ordinance of the states of Orleans enjoined all Bohemians or Egyptians to quit the kingdom under pain of death, and similar edicts had been and continued to be issued in many European countries. At Durham, in 1592, five men were hanged ' for being Egyptians,' and at Edinburgh, in 1611, four met with the same punishment ' for abyding, within the kingdome, they being Egiptienis.' In Hungary and Germany G. were racked and tortured as late as the 18th century. They were also accused of definite malpractices and crimes, often without any foundation. As early as 1424 they were thought to be emissaries of the Turks, probably on account of their dark, foreign faces, and strange tongue. Certainly they were used as spies by Frederick the Great. But far more dreadful crimes than treachery and stealing were attributed, most unjustly, to the G. In 1692 four Estremadura G. were taken captive, and under the torture of the Inquisition confessed that they had devoured a friar, a pilgrim, and a woman of their own race, and were in consequence put to a painful death. The charge of cannibalism was first made in 1547. In Hungary, in 1782, forty-five G. were hanged, drawn, and quartored on a charge of having eaten the victim of a supposed murder. The case was subsequently inquired into and the charge was proved false, for there had been no murder. Since the beginning of the 17th century G. have frequently been charged with kidnapping children, and many lurid tales have been told and written on the subject. In 1872 forty-seven G. were imprisoned in Germany for child-stealing, but the charge was afterwards proved false. G. have frequently been deported from one country to another, as from Scotland to the Barbadoes, and other American colonies in 1665 and 1715, and from the Basque country to N. Africa in 1802. Even in the 20th century German legislation has been busy with the G. problem. In Roumania and Eastern Europe, a certain class of G., called *Robi*, were deprived of their liberty, bought, sold, and exchanged, and treated as slaves. They were granted freedom in Hungary and Transylvania between the years 1781-82, and in Moldavia in 1856. The Empress Maria Theresa interested herself on their behalf, and ordered those G. in her states to be instructed in agriculture with a view to their permanent settlement. A great improvement became evident in their character and bearing, and in 1866 they were declared Roumanian citizens with full political rights. The G. of Bulgaria have not enjoyed similar privileges, and in 1906 held a congress at Sofia, protesting against their political status and demanding their recognition as citizens.

G. from the beginning of their history, have shown great versatility in turning their hands to any kind of work. In Roumania and Turkey a large proportion of the settled, nationalised G. are bricklayers. In Hungary and Transylvania many of them follow some regular trade and have fixed habitations. They wash gold from the sand of the rivers, and they work iron or copper ; some are horse-dealers, others are carpenters and turners, and some even keep wine-shops or public-houses. In England, they are generally thought of as hawkers, tinkers, knife-grinders, showmen, and basket-weavers. The nomadic G. still carry on the traditional craft of metal-work, while some make sieves and traps. They also have cast bells, the church bell (1726) of Edzell in Forfarshire being their work. In Scotland, they were engaged during the 18th century on pewter, copper, and lead work, and also executed some engravings and paintings in somewhat primitive fashion. They were also known by the bullets and cannons they fashioned in Hungary, and had an iron-foundry at Little Carron in Scotland. They make excellent farriers and good horse-dealers. They are far-famed for their musical talent. The G. musicians, it is thought, originally belonged to the serf class, and were kept within the precincts of courts and palaces to provide entertainment. The women were regarded as particularly graceful dancers, and danced to the accompaniment of the fiddle. In 1530 we hear that they ' dansit before the king in Holyrudhouse ' in Scotland. They won a

high reputation in Wales as harpists, and in Hungary as fiddlers. In fact, Liszt declared, though his theory has been hotly disputed, that the Hungarian national music originated in them. G. show special talent in singing or reciting old ballads and folksongs, often to the accompaniment of the guitar. They have, too, a great aptitude for telling fairy stories. These tales do not appear to belong to their own tribe, but to have been picked up in the various countries which they have visited, and are passed on by word of mouth from one generation to another. In this connection their extraordinary gift of speaking in foreign languages may be mentioned. The G. women are famous fortune-tellers. They seldom repeat their charms and incantations in their own tongue, but in Greek or Roumanian in a Romanised dialect. They tell fortunes not only by palmistry but by playing cards. They use the Tarock, a special set of cards, each card having a mystical meaning of its own, the secret of which they keep within their own tribes. It is quite possible that playing-cards were first brought into Europe by the G., and were originally only used for telling fortunes and for lotteries, later being employed for games and gambling. G. were formerly despised for their looks ; the writers probably being unable to recognise their undoubted beauties behind the dirt. They are dark-skinned, with dark, lustrous eyes, thick dark hair, often coarse and frizzled, and gleaming white teeth. They show off their darkness by wearing bright Oriental colours. The women bind their hair with gaudy silk handkerchiefs, and show an inordinate love of jewellery. Though paying great attention to their clothes, they are at the same time shabbily and untidily dressed, and are slovenly in their habits. Their great moral defects are probably due to the vagrant life the race has lived from its beginning. G. as a whole have no sense of responsibility, and have not the same sense of honour as other European races. They are not religious by nature, but frequently adopt the prevailing religion of the country in which they travel. Many of them still retain old superstitions, probably the remnants of a religion they have lost. Some of these superstitions, such as the worship of trees and serpents, may be found in their folk-tales and songs. G. seldom go to church, except to baptise their infants, to marry, and to bury their dead. They are fatalists, and have the philosophy of the open highroad. To their friends they are loving and lovable, and generous to excess, but they mostly dislike and despise all who dwell in houses.

Language. — The G. language (*Romani chiv*) is split up into very many dialects, those of the E. and W. of Europe being so different from each other that an English G. would have great difficulty in understanding a Greek G., and possibly could not understand him at all. But there is no doubt that originally there was only one G. tongue, and that the existing differences in the dialects are due to the adoption of words and idioms of the different peoples with which this remarkable race has come into contact. The researches of Ruediger (1782) and Grellmann (1783) in Germany, and of Marsden (1783) in England proved that the language of the G. was unmistakably connected with some Indian language. Some of the words in the G. language have a more archaic form than those of modern Indian dialects, and it is impossible to determine to which of them it is most closely allied. The speech of the Armenian G., however, shows more resemblance to Prakrit than does the speech of the European G., and that the speech of the Asiatic or Syrian G. is peculiar in itself, and entirely different from any other dialect. These facts have led scholars to think that the G. originally came from India; that there must have been at least two great movements westward, the first horde of G. making their way to Greece, and the second horde moving southwards to Syria and Northern Egypt. The route taken can be determined in part from the elements other than Indian present in the G. vocabulary. Now, there is in it a large percentage of Persian words, but, according to Miklosich (1878), no Arabic element. This shows that the G. could not have resided in Persia long after the Mohammedan conquest to have been so completely unaffected by the language of the conquerors, and that they must have made their way to Europe *viâ* Persia and not through Arabia. That is to say, the movements from the East must have taken place before the middle of the 7th century A.D. The G. tongue possesses far more Greek than Persian words, so that it may safely be concluded that their stay in Greece was more prolonged than it had been in Persia. Some scholars have thought that they lived in Greece from very early times, but this theory cannot be accepted, for the G. vocabulary contains no old forms of Greek and no archaic forms of Slavonic words. The G. of Wales and of Turkey speak the purest gypsy, and retain the oldest forms. The language

of English G. shows an almost complete loss of grammatical inflections and an adoption of English forms and idioms. In Spain, Italy, Norway, and other countries the same process of levelling has been taking place, and in many cases the original inflections have been superseded by those in use among their neighbours. Consequently the language has deteriorated in grammar, but from the earliest times its vocabulary has been enriched by the adoption of foreign words. Modern legislation has tended to crush the national spirit of the G. In a country like England, where attendance at the national schools is compulsory, where G. children are brought into daily contact with English children, and are obliged to learn and speak English, where every step is taken to suppress vagrancy, the denationalisation of the G. and their assimilation with the land of their adoption must gradually take place.

Bibliography.—Leland, *A Collection of Cuttings . . . relating to Gypsies,* 1874-91; Grellmann, *Die Zigeuner,* 1783 (English translation by Roper, 1787); A. F. Pott, *Die Zigeuner in Europa und Asien* (2 vols.), 1844-45; Miklosich, *Beiträge zur Kenntnis der Zigeuner-Mundarten,* 1874-78; Morwood, *Our Gypsies,* 1885; MacRitchie, *Scottish Gypsies under the Stewarts,* 1894; Dumbarton, *Gypsy Life in the Mysore Jungle,* 1902; G. Smith, *Gipsy Life;* G. Borrow, *The Zincali, or an Account of the Gipsies of Spain,* 1841; and his novels *Lavengro* and *Romany Rye;* Palmer and Tuckey, *English Gipsy Songs in Romany, with metrical English Translation,* 1875; H. von Wlislocki, *Märchen und Sagen der transsilvanischen Zigeuner,* 1886; Groome, *Gypsy Folk-Tales,* 1899; the *Journal* (3 vols., 1888-92) of the Cosmopolitan Gypsy Lore Society, revived in Liverpool, 1907; C. G. Leland, *The Gypsies,* 1882, *Gypsy Sorcery and Fortune-Telling,* 1891, *The English Gypsies and their Language,* 1873, *The Gipsies [of Russia, Austria, England, America,* etc., 1882; Beames, *Comparative Grammar of the Modern Aryan Languages of India* (3 vols.), 1872-79; Grierson, *The Pi'sāca Languages of North-Western India,* 1906; Kalina, *La Langue des Tsiganes slovaques,* 1882; Smart and Crofton, *The Dialect of the English Gypsies* (2nd ed.), 1875, etc.

Gypsophila, a genus of caryophyllaceous plants, consists of fifty herbaceous species occurring in Europe and Asia. The flowers are small and are insect-pollinated. *G. elegans* is a well-known British species.

Gypsum, hydrated calcium sulphate ($CaSo_4.2H_2O$), which occurs in large monoclinic crystals sometimes known as selenite. Marggraf in 1750 showed that *gypsum artefactum*, obtained from sulphuric acid and lime, was identical with the naturally-occurring mineral. When G. is heated to 120° a hemihydrate, $2CaSO_4.H_2O$, is obtained, and on further heating the anhydrous calcium sulphate results. In this state the product is almost insoluble in water, and is identical with natural anhydrite. Another modification, soluble anhydrite, is obtained from G. by dehydration *in vacuo* over phosphoric anhydride. When G. is heated moderately there results a product known as plaster of Paris (G. was formerly worked in Montmartre, to the N. of Paris), which, according to Le Chatelier, consists mainly of the hemihydrate above mentioned. On addition of water this dissolves in part, forming a saturated solution which is, however, supersaturated with respect to the dihydrate, $CaSO_4.2H_2O$. Consequently some of the dissolved salt separates as G., and the solution can then dissolve more of the soluble form. By repetition of this process all the hemihydrate is converted into G., which separates in interlacing crystals forming a solid mass. In the original burning of the G. care must be taken that too great heat is not applied, otherwise the product refuses to take up water at all, or at least very slowly. In this state it is said to be 'dead-burnt.'

Gypsywort, or *Lycopus Europœus*, a species of Labiatæ which is commonly found in Britain. It is an aquatic plant and bears whorls of pink flowers.

Gyracanthus (Gk. γυρός, round, and ἄκανθα, spine), the name given to a genus of fossil fishes found in devonian and carboniferous strata.

Gyrocarpus, a genus of Hernandiaceæ, contains a single species, and was formerly incorrectly classed under Lauraceæ. It grows in a tropical climate as a large tree with cordate leaves and whitish-coloured wood.

Gyrodus, the name of a genus of fossil fishes of the family Pychodontidæ, found in the Jurassic strata.

Gyroscope and Gyrostat, mechanical instruments used to illustrate the curious principles of rotating bodies. The ordinary form of gyroscope (Fig. 1) consists of a heavy wheel A mounted on an axis BC, which is fixed in a ring BDCE. This ring in turn is capable of rotation about the axis DE, which is fixed in another ring also capable of rotation, about the axis FG. The instrument is supported by a heavy stand. The whole is arranged so that the three axes of rotation in any position pass through a fixed point, which is the centre of gravity of the wheel.

The wheel is thus capable of rotation about three mutually perpendicular axes, and its axis may thus take up any direction. If the wheel is rotated rapidly, it is found that a very considerable push is required to change the direction of the axis of rotation. In the absence of any external forces, the rotating axis will preserve a fixed direction in space. This was used originally by Foucault to prove the rotation of the earth. Thus, if the axis is initially pointed to some star and the wheel kept rotating rapidly, the axis will remain pointing at the star irrespective of the earth's rotation. Thus, it will appear to an ob-

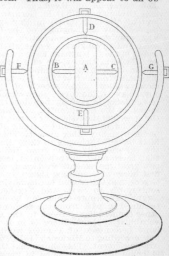

FIG. 1

server to turn about an axis parallel to the axis of the earth, and follow the star as it rises and sets. It is on this principle that the G. compass is made. So long as the rotation of the wheel can be kept up, the axis, if originally pointed to the pole star will remain in that direction. By means of several rapidly rotating wheels a telescope stand has been constructed, which will remain fixed irrespective of the motion of a ship. Perhaps the most important practical application of the theory is seen in the torpedo. It is of immense importance that the original direction should be kept after the torpedo has been fired, and so the steering gear is connected with a G. by means of a slide valve. The wheel is set rotating very rapidly at the moment of fire, and the axis of rotation remains fixed in direction. Thus, if the torpedo shows any deviation in course, the connection between the rudder and the G. at once produces a steadying effect. So long as the rotation remains very rapid, it is found that the general line of fire is accurately kept. The G. has also been applied to the mono-rail by Louis Brennand, an English inventor, the stability of the train being secured

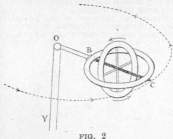

FIG. 2

by two gyroscopic wheels revolving in vacuo at a high speed. A more simple form of the G. is sold as a toy. It consists of a wheel set on an axis in a ring, like the wheel A and the ring BDCE in Fig 1. This ring is fixed on an axis in the same straight line as BC, the end of which fits into a small cup on the top of a stand provided. In Fig. 2, let O represent the cup, and let CBO be the position of the axis as it is placed in the cup after the wheel has been rapidly rotated. It is found that the whole instrument revolves about the vertical axis OY, the end C gradually dropping lower and lower, as the rotation of the wheel gradually dies away. This turning about the axis OY is known as *precession*. Another motion of an oscillatory character, known as *nutation*, also exists, but this is so small as often to be hardly perceptible. The reason for precession may be seen from the following: Let ABCD be a wheel rotating about an axis through O perpendicular to the plane of the paper, and also turning about the axis BD. Let any particle of mass m move in the circle from P to Q in a short time τ. Then if ω_1 is the angular velocity of the wheel, $PQ = \omega_1\tau$. If ω_2 is the angular velocity about BD, P is also moving up out of the plane of the paper with velocity $\omega_2.PM$ when PM is the perpendicular on BD. At Q the velocity out of the paper has increased to $\omega_2.QN$, *i.e.* it has increased by $\omega_2.QL$. PQ may be considered a

straight line since the time τ is very small, and its length is $OP.\omega_1\tau$. Hence this increase of velocity $= \omega_1.PQ.\cos\theta = \omega_2.OP.\omega_1\tau\cos\theta = \omega_1\omega_2\tau.OM$. Hence the momentum of the particle upwards out of the paper increases at the rate $m\omega_1\omega_2OM$, *i.e.* proportional to its distance from AC. It must, therefore, be acted upon by a force $m\omega_1\omega_2OM$ upwards out of the plane of the paper. Similarly, particles on the arc AB are acted upon by an upward force, whilst those on AD and DC are acted upon by a similar downward force. Thus the rotation about BD is due to a couple which would turn the wheel, when not rotating, about the axis AC. Generally, the effect of a couple on a rapidly spinning wheel is to produce displacement of the axis of rotation perpendicular to the plane of the couple. Hence in Fig. 2 the effect of the force of gravity and the support at O results in a turning about a vertical axis. Though the terms G. and gyrostat are often used for one another, the distinction usually made is that the gyroscopic flywheel rotates about an axis of which one point is fixed, whilst the gyrostat is free to move on a plane. The common model of a gyrostat consists of a flywheel enclosed in a case, slits being left for the string to set the wheel in motion. When the wheel is

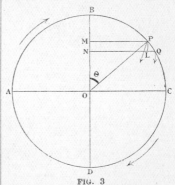

FIG. 3

rotated, the instrument may be placed on a table on its point (in the same straight line as the axis of the wheel) or on any point of the bearing edge (in the plane of the wheel itself, and usually consisting of a regular sixteen-sided figure). In the former case the motion is exactly that of a spinning-top, which is the most simple practical form of gyrostat. Other common forms are a hoop, and the two-wheels of a bicycle. The general properties of a rotating wheel hold equally well for these cases. Thus the precession of a spinning top, the circular path of a hoop moving with its plane inclined to the vertical, and the turning of the handle-bars of a bicycle to preserve equilibrium, are to be explained by methods similar to that employed in Fig. 3. In the construction of an aeroplane, where the engine wheel and the propeller are rotating rapidly, the gyroscopic effect has to be considered. The barrels of guns and rifles are fitted with spiral grooves to give the projectile a rapid rotation on its axis, thus tending to keep the direction of the axis unchanged. The rotation of the earth about its axis makes its action very much like that of a top suspended by a string, and corrections for precession and nutation have to be made in astronomical calculations. Many other cases may be quoted.

Gythium, one of the old seaports of Greece, situated on the Gulf of Laconia. The Spartan fleet was stationed here, and consequently, during the time of the wars against Athens, it suffered many vicissitudes. At the present day the larger part of it is sunk in the sea.

Gyula, the chief tn. of the co. of Békés, Hungary. It carries on a considerable trade in cattle, and manufs. spirits, wine, and oil. Pop. about 22,000.

H

H, the eighth letter of our alphabet as it was of the Phœnician, from which it is derived. It was formerly written ⊢ or ⊟, and was called *heth* or *cheth*. Semitic scholars explain that the Phœnicians used it not only as a strong aspirate, which is the modern use, but also as a continuous guttural pronounced like the *ch* in the German *lachen*. The Greeks, of course, borrowed it with the rest of the symbols, and, curiously enough, early made use of it to represent a long *e* sound, ῆτα, to distinguish it from the short. Still the right and left halves of the letter were used for smooth and rough breathings, the latter being the aspirate (⊢ and ⊦), so that the *h* passed into the Roman alphabet. Yet by 240 B.C. it was quite neglected by the common people just as it is to-day, so that Catullus pokes fun at Arrius, who tried to be correct, but always succeeded in getting his aspirates in the wrong place, so that he said *hinsidias* for *insidias*, etc. In modern Italian the *h* has quite disappeared, and it is fast becoming obsolete in French. Sometimes it represents other sounds ; for example, the Spanish *h* is often a substitute for the Latin *f* (*hijo*, from *filius*), but it is not pronounced. In English it is not infrequently put for *c* and *s*. Thus the prefix *hyper-* corresponds to *super-* ; the first syllable of *hex*-agon corresponds with *six*, whilst *hun*-dred and *cen*-tury are real doublets. In English the *h* may be anything from a strong aspirate to a cipher. Thus it is very pronounced in *history*, less so in *when*, and not at all in *hour*.

Haag, Carl (*b.* 1820), a naturalised British painter, born in Bavaria, and trained at the academies of Nurnberg and Munich. He began as an illustrator and as a painter, in oils, of portraits and architectural subjects, but on settling in England, in 1847, he devoted himself to water-colours. He was elected member of the Royal Society of Painters in Water-Colours in 1853, and is now court painter to the Duke of Saxe-Coburg-Gotha. He travelled much in the East and painted Eastern subjects.

Haakon or Haco (Old Norse *Hákon*), the name of as many as seven kings of Norway :

Haakon I. (*d.* 961), called ' the Good,' was brought up as a Christian by Asthelstan, King of England, but failed in his efforts to convert his own people from their pagan rites. His foster-father gave him ships in 933, and he sailed home and was soon proclaimed king. The sons of Erik, H.'s half-brother, were constantly rebelling, but H. came off victor.

Haakon IV. (1204-63), called ' the Old,' put to death Earl Skule in 1239, as the latter had become the centre of intrigue. His hold over the Hebrides was secured by a victory at Largs over the Scots. In 1262 the chiefs of Iceland finally acknowledged the suzerainty of Norway's king.

Haakon V., or *Haakon Longlegs* (1299-1319), was the son of Magnus Law Mender, and became king after Eric, his brother. He was the last male descendant of his line. His daughter, Ingeborg, was successfully married to Duke Erik (1312), who, however, was soon starved to death by his father, King Birger of Sweden.

Haakon VII. (*b.* 1872), the present King of Norway, was a Danish prince, the son of Frederick VII. of Denmark. He married Maud, the youngest daughter of Edward VII. of England, and his only son, Prince Olaf, was born in 1903. In 1905 Norway separated from Sweden, and in the following year H. was crowned king.

Haan, a vil. of Rhenish Prussia, 10 m. E. of Düsseldorf, with manufs. of silk and wool. Pop. (1910) 9841.

Haarlem, the chief tn. of the prov. of N. Holland in the Netherlands, is 11 m. distant from Amsterdam. It has a through communication to Zandvoort, Leyden, Amsterdam, and Alkmaar by means of electric and steam trams. It presents the appearance of a typical Dutch city, with its long, narrow canals and gable-roofed houses. The principal buildings are situated in the market-place, which is a large space in the centre of the city ; here are to be found the Flesher's Hall (built in 1603 and containing the archives), the town hall, the Stadsdoelen, and the Groote Kerk, or Great Church, also called St. Bavon, dating from the close of the 15th century. This church has a famous organ consisting of four keyboards, sixty-four registers, and 5000 pipes, and was constructed by Christian Müller. The statue of L. Koster, the founder of the movable printing type, stands in the market-place. Cotton manufacture, dyeing, printing, and type-founding form the chief industries of H. The city carries on an extensive horticultural trade, rearing the celebrated Dutch bulbs, especially the hyacinth and tulip. H. has played no inconsiderable part in the history of Holland; it took part in the revolt of the Netherlands against the Spanish tyranny in 1572, and was forced to submit to Alva's son, Frederick, in 1573; it owed its final deliverance to William of Orange, who rescued it in 1577. H. is the birthplace of the celebrated Dutch painters, Ostade, Berghem, Ruisdael, and Vanderhelst. Pop. 69,410.

Haarlem, Lake, or Haarlemmer Meer, in the prov. of N. Holland in the Netherlands, a triangular-shaped expanse of now fertile land reclaimed by dint of unremitting industry in 1840-53 from a sheet of water called Haarlemmer Meer formed by the great inundation of the 16th century. It lies between Amsterdam, Haarlem, and Leyden, and has an area of about 72 sq. m. It communicates through the River Y with the Zuider Zee.

Habakkuk, one of the twelve minor prophets of the O.T. Nothing is known of him historically, though legend, as embodied in such works as *The Lives of the Prophets,* has much to say of him. The book bearing his name can be separated into two distinct parts at the end of the second chapter. The third chapter is a psalm ascribed to the prophet H., but which internal evidence shows to be certainly post-exilic. Its text is somewhat corrupt, but not so much so as is that of the first two chapters. In each division valuable emendations have been made by Wellhausen. The problem of the earlier chapters is more difficult. The book opens with a lament to Jehovah (or Yahweh) asking why the iniquity of the wicked is suffered to continue (vv. 2-4), and the prophet receives an answer that Yahweh is about to raise up the Chaldeans as an instrument of vengeance. Then follows another complaint (vv. 12-17) and in chap. ii. 2 comes Yahweh's answer. Then follows the song of triumph of the nations over their oppressor. Many critics hold that the world-power over which the nations should exult is Assyria, and that the difficulties which arise in this interpretation are due to the editors of the 5th or 4th centuries B.C. Others have held that the prophecy was primarily directed against the Chaldeans themselves. The date of the original composition was towards the end of the 7th century B.C. (c. 615). *See* Commentaries by Delitsch, Davidson, Nowack, and Driver (*O.T. Lit.*).

Habberton, John (b. 1842), an American author, born at Brooklyn. He has been successively printer, soldier, merchant, and journalist.

From 1865-72 he was connected with Harper Brothers; he was on the editorial staff of the *New York Herald* in 1877, and of *Godey's Magazine* in 1893. His most popular work is *Helen's Babies,* 1876. He has also written: *The Jericho Road,* 1877; *Other People's Children* (new ed. 1903); *Life of George Washington; All He Knew,* 1890; *Some Boys' Doings; The Tiger and the Insect,* 1902. His play, *Deacon Crankett,* 1880, had a two years' run.

Habeas Corpus, in law, a writ directed to a person having custody of a prisoner commanding him to produce the body (*habeas corpus*) of the prisoner before the court, with a statement of the day and cause of his detention. The personal liberty of the subject has ever in England been the subject of jealous regard by the people, and as early as Magna Charta the principle underlying the writ of H. C. was solemnly enacted. But up to 1679 the constantly recurring acts of repression in the name of the king, notably in the heyday of the notorious Star Chamber, demonstrated the need for a far more stringent system of procedure. The culminating point was reached in the history of the variations of this celebrated writ when, in the reign of Charles I., the subservient judges decided that they had no power, upon such a writ, either to bail or hand over a prisoner, although committed to prison without assigned cause, when he was in custody by the special command of the king. Such a decision obviously struck at the root of the whole substantive law on the liberty of the subject, and the Petition of Right explicitly settled the question that in future the orders of the sovereign were not a sufficient ground for incarcerating his subjects. But after the historic arrest of Jenks in 1676, when the judges decided that a change of prison quarters fully exonerated the prison governor from all liability for failure to produce the prisoner, the famous Habeas Corpus Act of 1679 was passed to meet the new difficulty. Briefly, the Act provides: (1) That a writ of H. C. may be claimed by any prisoner except one committed for treason or felony from a judge in term or vacation, the writ to be returnable immediately before the judge granting it with a statement of the cause of the commitment; (2) prisoners committed for treason or felony are to be brought up for trial at the next ensuing assizes, unless the crown witnesses cannot be produced so soon; (3) heavy penalties for shifting the custody of the prisoner from one prison to another without sufficient reason or authority, or for neglecting to give the prisoner a true copy of the warrant of commitment; (4) penalties of £500 for sending persons to prison beyond the seas or re-committing them after delivery by H. C. The flaws in this Act were that there were no safeguards against (a) excessive bail, (b) a false return, or (c) illegal *civil* detention. The Bill of Rights remedied (a), and an Act passed in 1816 extended the Act of 1679 to cases of civil detention, and remedied (b) by empowering the judges themselves to examine the truth of the return. The Habeas Corpus Act of 1679 has occasionally been suspended in times of rebellion and civil commotion, *e.g.* during the Jacobite rebellions of 1714 and 1745, and the agitations excited out of sympathy for the French revolutionaries at the end of the 18th century. The writ has been used before now to restrain the rights of a parent over a child, and of a guardian over his ward; and again, the mother of an illegitimate child can claim the custody of such a child as against the reputed father by suing out a writ of H. C. On the person detained being produced before a judge, the latter has three courses open to him. He may either make no order at all, discharge the prisoner, or release him on bail.

Habelschwert, a tn. of Prussia in Silesia, situated at the entrance of the Weistritz into the Neisse, 10 m. S. of Glatz, and 58 m. S.S.W. of Breslau. Pop. 6156.

Habenaria, a genus of Orchidaceæ, is found in tropical and temperate lands, and is represented in Britain by five species. *H.* (or *Cœloglossum*) *viridis,* the frog - orchis, grows in pastures; *H.* (or *Platanthera*) *bifolia,* the lesser butterfly-orchis, in heathy places; and *H. chlorantha,* the great butterfly-orchis, in moist woods and thickets.

Habere Facias Possessionem, a judicial writ directed to the sheriff commanding him to put the person who has succeeded in an action for the recovery of a chattel interest in land into possession. Chattel interests or chattels real include all leasehold interests or other interests less than freehold (*see* ESTATE, FEE, FEE SIMPLE), *e.g.* tenancy by elegit, tenancies by sufferance (*i.e.* on expiry of a lease) and at will (*i.e.* without a specified term of years). The name was often used interchangeably with *habere facias seisinam,* though such use was scientifically inaccurate. The term ' writ of possession ' is now the appropriate name for both writs.

Habere Facias Seisinam, a judicial writ directed to the sheriff commanding him to put the recoveror of

a freehold interest in lands into possession. In the execution of the writ, as well as of the writ of *habere facias possessionem,* the sheriff may break open doors if the possession be not quietly delivered up (*see* EXECUTION). Such writ is usually known at the present time as a ' writ of possession ' simply. A writ of *fi. fa.* for the amount of the mesne profits (rents, etc.) and costs may be joined in the writ for possession.

Habergeon, or **Haubergeon,** *see* HAUBERK.

Habington, William (1605-54), an English poet, born at Hendlip in Worcestershire. He belonged to a Catholic family, and his father and uncle were both implicated in Babington's plot. Having resisted the pressure brought to bear upon him to become a Jesuit, he went to Paris and married Lucy Herbert, daughter of the first Lord Powys, whom he immortalised in *Castara,* 1634, a volume of lyrical poems, some of which are of great sweetness and marked by unusual purity. He also wrote: *Historie of Edward the Fourth,* 1640; *The Queene of Arragon,* 1640, a tragi-comedy; and *Observations upon Historie,* 1641.

Habit, in physiology. It is well known that every time a certain stimulus gives rise to a specific reflex, the response to the stimulus comes more easily, so that if the cycle is repeated often enough it becomes automatic and even unconscious, and thus a H. is formed. When any nerve ending is stimulated, a current passes along its specific nerve fibre until the spinal cord is reached. In the cord there is a choice of several paths up to the brain, or directly to the nerve fibres passing out of the cord (*see* diagram). It is not known what makes the current take one of these courses more than another for the first time. The direction must depend upon conditions of tension and of *block* existing at the moment in the nervous system. But once a stimulus has travelled along a certain path, it becomes the easiest path, and will always be used unless there is a block in the path from some other cause. The process is often, and very fairly, compared to the making of ruts in a road. Modern psychologists are agreed that it is primarily due to the physical properties of the matter of which the nervous system is composed. Most Hs., *e.g.* walking, swimming, cycling, etc., are complex, and involve the co-ordination of various groups of muscles. In fact, the growth of a H., in the physiological sense, can be very well seen in the baby ' feeling its feet ' and learning to walk, or in a boy learning to swim. Actions which at first occupy the whole attention, which are laborious, irregular, and varied, become more and more uniform, and less and less conscious, until they can be continued for long stretches of time without any effort of the will. Persons with a neurotic temperament contract Hs. far more readily than lethargic individuals. It is this fact

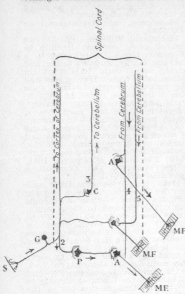

Spinal Cord

To Cortex of Cerebrum

To Cerebellum

From Cerebrum

From Cerebellum

A

3
C 4 5

MF

G 2

S P A

MF

MF

DIAGRAM TO ILLUSTRATE SOME OF THE PATHS THAT A STIMULUS TO AN AFFERENT NERVE MAY TAKE

S, Surface at which sensory impulse is received ; G, cell of posterior root ganglion; P, cell of posterior horn; C, cell of Clarke's column ; A, cell of anterior horn; MF, muscle fibre.

1, Fibre of posterior columns ; 2, fibre of coma tract ; 3, fibre of tract of Flechsig; 4, fibre of pyramidal tract ; 5, fibre of tract of Loewenthal.

that explains *habit spasms*, the well-known *tics*. The movement of the *tic* is at first the reflex to an irritation, such as ill-fitting, uncomfortable clothes, some irritation of the eyes, etc., but owing to the peculiarly irritable state of the nervous system at the time, the action rapidly gets beyond the control of the will.

Alcoholism and drug Hs. can be explained in the same way. The law of H. applies equally to mental and bodily functions, and is of vital importance to educationists, for education may be described as the development of Hs. The greater the number of mental processes reduced to the realm of H., the more is the brain set free for further thought, so that the aim of the educationist is to create good Hs. and many.

Habit and Repute, in Scots law, a phrase indicating the inference of a legal relationship or fact of which the law takes cognisance from the *general belief* that such relationship exists or that such event has happened. It is especially applicable to the presumption of marriage from evidence of general reputation as husband and wife coupled with cohabitation. Erskine states that the repute in such a case must be that of substantially all who have an interest to inquire. The term also has a special significance in regard to the condition of a person accused of theft. According to Horne (*Commentary on the Law of Scotland Respecting Crimes*), it is an aggravation of the crime of theft to be a thief by H. and R., but apparently such H. and R. could only be supported by proof that the accused made a trade of theft, and lived wholly or partially on the proceeds of his thefts; and, again, the evil reputation must have existed for at least a year without interruption and down to the date of incarceration (Erskine). Apparently, the accused never gets notice that his reputation will be put before the jury in aggravation, it being the practice now not to ' libel ' (include in the indictment) the H. and R.

Habitual Drunkards, *see* DRUNKENNESS.

Habsburg, *see* HAPSBURG.

Hachette, Jean Nicolas Pierre (1769-1834), a French mathematician, born at Mézières, and educated at the College of Rheims. Through the influence of Gaspard Monge he obtained the post of assistant professor in the newly-established Ecole Polytechnique (1794), becoming professor of descriptive geometry in 1797. In 1816 he lost his chair on the accession of Louis XVIII., and failed to obtain election to the Académie des Sciences owing to royal opposition until after the Revolution in 1831. His chief works are : *Deux Suppléments à la Géométrie descriptive de Monge*, 1811; *Eléments de Géométrie à Trois Dimensions*, 1817; *Traité de Géométrie descriptive*, 1822; *Traité élémentaire des Machines*, 1811.

Hachette and Company, a French house of publishers and booksellers, established in Paris in 1826 by Louis Christophe François H. (1800-64). At first the firm published only a series of books designed to improve the system of school instruction, especially the classics, but in 1850 they extended their publications to include books of almost every type, as well as magazines, a directory-guide to Paris, *Paris Hachette*, and a popular annual.

Hachinohe, a tn. of Japan, situated about 49 m. S.E. by E. of Awomori. Pop. 10,600.

Hachioji, a tn. of Hondo, Japan, 30 m. W. of Tokyo, with an extensive silk industry. Pop. 24,000.

Hackberry, *see* NETTLE TREE.

Hackbut, *see* FIREARMS.

Hackee, another name for the chipmunk.

Häckel, Ernst, *see* HAECKEL.

Hackensack, a tn. of New Jersey, U.S.A., and the cap. of Bergen co. It is situated on the R. Hackensack, 12 m. N. by rail of Jersey City, and 14 m. N.W. of New York, and is served by four lines of railway. It is chiefly a residential town, but in the vicinity are many factories and silk mills. Pop. (1910) 14,050.

Hackert, Philipp (1737-1807), a German landscape painter, born at Prenzlau in Prussia. About 1768 he visited Rome, and passed the rest of his life in Italy. He was commissioned by the Empress Catherine of Russia to paint six pictures of Count Onlow's naval victory over the Turks in 1770. In 1786 he was appointed painter to the King of Naples, but left Naples for Florence in 1799. His paintings, the chief merit of which consists of their close imitation of nature, include, 'View of Rome,' 'Views in the Vicinity of the Villa Horace,' and many seaports of Italy. *See* Goethe's memoir, *P. Hackert: Biographische Skizze.*

Hacket, John (1592-1670), an English ecclesiastic, born in London and educated at Westminster and Trinity College, Cambridge. In 1618 he was appointed chaplain to the Bishop of Lincoln, and in 1624 vicar of St. Andrew's, Holborn, and Cheam, Surrey; the former living was sequestered in 1645. In 1661 he was consecrated Bishop of Lichfield and Coventry. He wrote a comedy, *Loiola*, which was twice performed before James I.; a volume of sermons, and an excellent biography of his patron, Archbishop Williams, 1693.

Hackländer, Friedrich Wilhelm von (1816-77), a German novelist and dramatist, born at Burtscheid, near Aix-la-Chapelle. He served an apprenticeship to business, and served for some time in the Prussian artillery, but began his literary career with

Bilder aus dem Soldatenleben im Frieden, 1841. In 1843 he became secretary to the Crown Prince of Würtemberg. *Wachstubenabenteuer*, 1845, was followed by *Bilder aus dem Soldatenleben im Kriege*, 1849, the fruits of a campaign in Piedmont. A tour in Spain in 1854 resulted in *Ein Winter in Spanien*, 1855, and in 1857 he founded, with Zoller, the illustrated weekly *Über Land und Meer*. Among his novels the best are, *Namenlose Geschichten*, 1851; *Eugen Stillfried*, 1852; *Krieg und Frieden*, 1859; and his best comedies are, *Die Geheime Agent*, 1850, and *Magnetische Kuren*, 1851. *See* H. Morning, *Erinnerung au F. W. Hackländer*, 1878.

Hackney, a north-eastern metro-politan bor. of London, 3 m. N.N.E. of St. Paul's. The borough is in three divisions (North, Central, and South, each returning one member), and includes Clapton, Homerton, Dalston, and part of Kingsland. The R. Lea flows to the E., and Victoria Park lies partly within the borough limits. The ancient Gothic church of St. Augustine is the only important historic build-ing. H. was once a fashionable place of residence, but is now a poor district. John Howard (d. 1790) and Daniel Defoe (d. 1731) both resided here. Pop. (1911) 222,533.

Hackney Carriages are carriages, other than omnibuses, used for the conveyance of passengers, and in-clude hansom cabs, four-wheeled cabs, and motor or taxi-cabs. The forerunner of the cab (*cabriolet de place*) was the hackney coach; the hansom cab was invented by J. A. Hansom in 1834. H. C. in London are regulated by a variety of statutes, and regulations may be made by the Home Secretary at his discretion. Every cab must have an annual licence from the Home Secretary, which is issued by the chief com-missioner of police, and costs £2. It must have the number of persons it is licensed to carry painted on the back, and must bear a light from one hour after sunset to one hour before sunrise. The driver of a cab must pass an examination in topography of London and pay 5s. for his licence. The hiring of a cab may be by time or distance, but no driver is com-pelled to go for more than 6 m. or longer than one hour. Inside the radius (4 m. from Charing Cross) the fare is 1s. up to 2 m. for an ordinary cab, with extras for luggage, more than two passengers, and waiting; for taxicabs the rate is 8d. a mile.

Hackney Coach (Fr. *haquenée*, Lat. *equus*, an ambling horse or mare, kept especially for the use of ladies). From the hiring-out of 'hackneys' the word came to be associated with letting out coaches, etc., for hire. The H. C. was a conveyance with four wheels and two horses let out for hire generally after being discarded by some owner among the nobility. Some authorities derive the name from 'Hackney,' formerly a suburb of London, from which the first hired coaches were accustomed to start.

Hadad, a descendant of Esau, the son of Behad. He defeated the Midianites in the field of Moab, and became king of Edom in the place of Hushan. He is mentioned in Gen. xxxvi. 35-36.

Hadad, an Edomite, who fled while young into Egypt to escape from Joab, King David's commander-in-chief. He became a favourite of Pharaoh, and remained with him until he heard of the death of Joab and David. He was an enemy of Solomon. *See* 1 Kings, xi. 14-21.

Haddington, a royal municipal and police bor. and the co. tn. of Haddingtonshire, Scotland. It lies on the Tyne, 18 m. E. of Edinburgh. The chief building is the ruined St. Mary's Church, a cruciform Decorated building in red sandstone, the nave of which is sufficiently repaired to serve as parish church. Other buildings are the county buildings (1833), the corn exchange (1854), the town hall (1748 - 1831), and the Knox Memorial Institute (1880). Famous natives of the town were John Knox, John and Samuel Brown, Samuel Smiles (1816-1904). The town has suffered from fires in 1216 and in 1244, floods in 1775, and the great siege of the English by the Scots in 1549. The chief industries are the manufactures of agricultural implements, woollen goods, and sacking, and brewing and tanning. Pop. (1911) 4135.

Haddingtonshire, or **East Lothian,** a south-eastern maritime co. of Scotland, bounded by the Firth of Forth and the North Sea, and the counties of Berwick and Edinburgh. Its surface is generally hilly, with the Lammermuirs (1500 ft.) in the S., and the scattered peaks of Traprain Law (724 ft.), North Berwick Law (612 ft.), and Garleton Hill (590 ft.). The only important river is the Tyne (28 m.). Coal and iron are mined and limestone quarried in various districts, but the chief industries are agricultural, Haddingtonshire having long been famous for the richness of its grain and green crops. Fishing is also largely followed. The county returns one member to parliament. The chief towns are Haddington, Dunbar, North Berwick, and Prestonpans. Area 267 sq. m. Pop 43,253. *See* EAST LOTHIAN.

Haddock, or *Gadus æglefinus,* a species of Gadidæ, a family of marine carnivorous fishes; it is found on all coasts in the N. Atlantic Ocean, and is abundant everywhere round Great Britain. There is a strong resemblance between the H. and *G. morrhua,* the cod, both having three dorsal and two anal fins of an elongated form; the H. is distinguished by a black lateral line and a black spot behind each of the pectorals. The H. is also smaller, as it never exceeds a length of 3 ft., some of the largest specimens being found in Dublin Bay. Its colouring is brown, and silvery underneath, the black markings on the pectorals sometimes extending to the middle of the back; tradition ascribes the origin of these spots to the finger and thumb of St. Peter, and alleges that the H. was the fish from whose mouth he took tribute money. The H. lives largely on molluscs, and the bait used in catching them consists generally of mussels; trawl-nets are also employed in H. fishery. These fish are gregarious and inhabit deep waters, travelling to the coast to spawn during March and April. They are sometimes cured by salting, but the usual method is to dry and smoke them; the familiar Finnan H. is so named after the fishing village of Findon, Kincardineshire.

Haddon, Alfred Cort (*b.* 1855), an English anthropologist, born in London. He was appointed professor of zoology at the Royal College of Science, Dublin, in 1900; university lecturer in ethnology at Cambridge, 1900-9; lecturer in ethnology in the University of London, 1904-9; and fellow of Christ's College, Cambridge, since 1901. His publications include: *Introduction to Embryology,* 1887; *Evolution in Art,* 1895; *Study of Man,* 1898; *Head Hunters : Black, White, and Brown,* 1901; *Magic and Fetishism; The Wanderings of Peoples,* besides numerous papers and memoirs on anthropological subjects.

Haddon Hall, one of the most famous old English baronial mansions, stands on the R. Wye, 2 m. S.E. of Bakewell in Derbyshire, and 23 m. N.N.W. of Derby. The styles of the architecture range from the Norman to the 16th and 17th centuries. Before the Conquest it was the property of the crown, but William I. granted it to William Peveril. It has been successively in the families of Avenell, Vernon, and Rutland. It is referred to by Scott in *Peveril of the Peak. See* S. Rayner, *History and Antiquities of Haddon Hall,* 1836; G. Le Blanc Smith, *Haddon, the Manor, its Hall, its Lords and Traditions,* 1906.

Hade, *see* DISLOCATION, ORES, and DEPOSITS.

Haden, Sir Francis Seymour (1818-

1910), an English surgeon and etcher, born in London; his father, C. Thomas H., was a well-known doctor. He was educated at University College School and University College, London. He took his degree (1840) in Paris, after studying at the Sorbonne. He became a member of the College of Surgeons (London) in 1842. His career as a surgeon was very distinguished. Amid his many interests and hard work in the world of science he found time to pursue seriously his favourite art of etching. His love for this branch of art and his strenuous labours rapidly placed him as the first artist etcher in England. He founded the Royal Society of Painter-Etchers and Engravers (1880), and as president practically revived a dying art. In 1847 he married a sister of J. A. M. Whistler. He made his art very perfect, his work was filled with a freedom of treatment and original beauty that is entirely his own. Among his many famous works are: 'The breaking up of the Agamemnon,' 'Early Morning, Richmond,' 'A By-road in Tipperary,' 'Shere Mill-pond, Surrey,' etc. He also practised mezzo-tint, 'An Early Riser' being one of many beautiful examples.

Hadersleben, or Haderslev, a sea-port and tn. of Prussia, in Schleswig-Holstein, situated on the H. Fiord, an inlet communicating with the Little Belt. A considerable export trade is carried on in grain, seeds, hides, etc., and among the industries are iron foundries, engineering works, tanneries, and tobacco factories. Pop. 13,050.

Hades, in Greek mythology, was the name applied to the kingdom of the underworld, the place of the departed spirits or shades. It is the Greek translation of the Hebrew *sheol*, which is frequently referred to in the N.T. H. was also the personal name of the king of the underworld, Dis or Pluto (*q.v.*), who is sometimes represented as seated on a throne of sulphur from which issued the streams of Lethe, Cocytus, Phlegethon, and Acheron, which traversed the kingdom of the dead. For the legend of Dis's rape of Persephone, *see* PROSERPINE.

Hadfield, a par. and vil. of Derbyshire, England, on the Cheshire border, 2 m. N.W. of Glossop. The cotton industry is carried on. In the Catholic church are some noted pictures, including a 'Transfiguration' by Raphael. Pop. (eccl. dist.) 6500.

Hading, Jane (*b.* 1859), a French actress, whose real name was Jeanne Alfrédine Tréfouret, born at Marseilles. The daughter of an actor, she was trained for the stage, and became one of the leading actresses of her day,

her first engagement being in 1873 for the theatre at Algiers. From there she went to Cairo, and her voice having attracted attention she returned to Marseilles and sang in operetta. She made her appearance in Paris at the Palais Royale in *La Chaste Suzanne*, and in 1883 made a great hit at the Gymnase in *Le Maitre de Forges*. The following year she married the manager of the theatre, Victor Koning, but divorced him in 1887. In 1888 she toured America with Coquelin, and on her return played at the Vaudeville in London with great success, establishing her world-wide reputation.

Hadj, or Hajj, the Arabic word, meaning literally ' a setting out,' is used for the greater pilgrimage of Mohammedans to Mecca which takes place from the 8th to the 10th of the twelfth month of the Mohammedan year, and which every Mohammedan whose wealth and health will permit of it must perform once at least in his lifetime. The term is used more loosely to include the ' umrah ' or lesser pilgrimage to Mecca, a Mohammedan's pilgrimage to any shrine or sacred place, and also to the pilgrimages of Eastern Christians to Jerusalem. The title of Hadji is given to all Mohammedans who have performed the greater pilgrimage. *See* MECCA and MOHAMMEDANISM.

Hadleigh, a tn. in the co. of Suffolk, England, situated 9½ m. W.S.W. of Ipswich. It is a very old-fashioned and old-world town, and contains many quaint houses. It is chiefly noted for the possession of a very fine church. Pop. (1911) 3200.

Hadley, a par. and vil. of Shropshire, England, situated in the Wellington div., 10 m. E. of Shrewsbury. Coal and iron are found, and the works of the Shropshire Iron Company are here. Pop. (1911) 3108.

Hadley, James (1821-72), an American philologist, born at Fairfield, Herkimer co., New York. An accident in childhood made him lame for life. He graduated at Yale (1842), and took up the study of Sanskrit under Edward Elbridge Salisbury, which resulted in his turning his attention to languages. He knew Greek, Latin, Sanskrit, Hebrew, Arabic, and Armenian, in addition to all the modern European languages and several Celtic languages. He was professor of Greek at Yale from 1851 until his death. He published a *Greek Grammar* 1860 (revised 1884), and wrote an essay on the ' History of the English Language ' for Webster's *Dictionary*. *See* sketch by his son A. T. Hadley in *Biographical Memoirs of the National Academy of Sciences*, vol. v., 1905, pp. 247-54.

Hadley, John (1682-1744), an English mathematician and mechanician. He greatly improved the reflecting telescope, and in 1731 he invented a reflecting quadrant or sextant. His claim to the invention was disputed, a glazier in Philadelphia named Thomas Godfrey (1704-49) having invented a similar instrument, but it was satisfactorily proved that each had worked independently.

Hadramaut, or Hadramut, a dist. on the S. coast of Arabia, bounded W. by Yemen, E. by Oman, and N. by the Dehna desert; modern Arab geographers restrict the name to the district between 48° and 51° E. It consists of a plateau, cut into deep ravines, between a strip of coastland and the range of hills which bound the interior desert. The climate is dry but healthy, the inhabitants mainly of S. Arabian stock, and the chief pursuits agriculture, cattle-breeding, date, indigo, and tobacco cultivation. The chief towns are Shibam, Saiyun, Tariba, and Terim. Pop. (estimated) 150,000. *See* L. Van der Berg, *Le Hadramut et les Colonies arabes*, 1885; J. T. Bent, *Southern Arabia*, 1895.

Hadrianopolis, *see* ADRIANOPLE.

Hadrian's Villa, near Tivoli (Tibur), Italy, about 17 m. E.N.E. of Rome, a country residence of the Emperor Hadrian, a magnificent building with gardens, temples, a palace, theatres, and a stadium, all miniatures of the most celebrated places in the provinces, and filled with art treasures.

Hadrian's Wall, the name generally given to the remains of the Roman fortification stretching from Wallsend on the Tyne to Bowness on the Solway, probably built by command of the Emperor Hadrian in A.D. 122 as a turf wall. It was repaired and partly rebuilt in stone by Septimus Severus in A.D. 209. The fortification consists of (1) a stone wall to the N. with a ditch on its N. side to act both as a barrier against the Caledonian tribes and as a line of military strategy; (2) a series of forts, blockhouses, and towers along the rampart; (3) an earthwork to the S., fenced with stakes, and called the Vallum, of uncertain use. *See* J. C. Bruce, *The Roman Wall* (3rd ed. 1867).

Hadrianus, Publius Ælius (A.D. 76-138), generally called Hadrian, Emperor of Rome, A.D. 117-38. In A.D. 85 or 86 he was placed under the guardianship of Ulpius Trajanus (afterwards the Emperor Trajan) at Rome. He held various public offices in Rome; distinguished himself in the Dacian campaigns; was ' legatus praetorius ' of Lower Pannonia in 108, ' legatus ' in the Parthian campaign (113-17). When the emperor fell ill in the East, he formally adopted Hadrian as his successor, and left him as commander in Syria. Hadrian was proclaimed emperor on Aug. 11, 117, and promptly proceeded to simplify the difficulties which besieged him at home and abroad by adopting a peaceful policy. He made peace with the Parthians, abandoning Mesopotamia and Assyria to them; appeased the Roxolani who had invaded Mœsia, and sent Marcius Turbo to pacify Mauritania. In 118 he hastened back to Rome to remove the unfavourable impression produced by the execution of some conspirators who had plotted his assassination. In 119 he began his celebrated travels through the empire, visiting Gaul, Germany, Britain, Spain, Mauritania, and Egypt. From 125-26 he was in Athens; in 130 on the Nile where he lost his beloved Antinous; in 134 he returned to Rome, and passed the remainder of his life between the capital and his beautiful villa at Tibur. Hadrian was a capable and just ruler, and, except during his last illness, when he was subject to fits of violent cruelty and severity, succeeded in endearing himself to his subjects, and at the same time remaining a strict disciplinarian. He introduced various constitutional reforms at Rome, and was a patron of poets and scholars, while his magnificent buildings, especially in Athens and Rome, have been the admiration of succeeding centuries. *See* Gregorovius's *The Emperor Hadrian* (Eng. trans. 1898).

Hadrosaurus (Gk. ἁδρός, thick, and σαῦρος, lizard), the name given to a genus of extinct fossil reptiles belonging to the Dinosauria; they are found abundantly in the Cretaceous strata of N. America. Most of them are of enormous size, *H. Mirabilis* measuring 38 ft., and in many respects they closely resemble the iguanodon. They have curious spoon-shaped bills, and the hind-limbs are much larger than the fore-limbs.

Haeckel, Ernst Heinrich (*b.* 1834), a German biologist, born at Potsdam. He studied medicine and science at Würzburg, Berlin, and Vienna under Müller, Virchow, and Kölliker. He began to lecture at the University of Jena in 1861, and was professor of zoology there from 1862-1909, with short intervals spent in travelling in search of zoological specimens. He is equally famous for his detailed zoological researches and for his generalisations on biological themes. In the former he has confined himself mainly to the Invertebrata, and has published *Die Radiolarien*, 1862; *Die Kalkschwämme*, 1872, on calcareous sponges; *Das System der Medusen*, 1879-81, on jelly-fishes, and numerous smaller works, as well as his contributions to the *Challenger* reports—on *Deep-sea Medusæ* (1882), on *Siphonophora Keratosa*, and *Radiolaria* (1889), all beautifully illustrated with superb plates which show the author's supreme skill in draughtsmanship. In the work of generalisation in biology his greatest achievement is *Generelle Morphologie* (2 vols.), 1866, a treatise on animal morphology in the two sections of tectology and promorphology, much of which he subsequently re-wrote in his *Natural History of Creation*, 1868. H. was one of the first to attempt to draw up a genealogical tree (Stammbaum) exhibiting the relationship between the various orders of animals with regard both to one another and their common origin, and his theory that the life history of the individual is more or less a recapitulation of its historic evolution, embodied in his *Studies on the Gastræa Theory*, 1873-84, has been generally accepted as the basis of all modern zoological classifications. H.'s more popular works are very brilliantly written, but he is not always so careful in statement as Darwin, while his monist theories result in a materialistic tendency in his writings. His *Anthropogenie*, 1874 (translated into English as *The Evolution of Man*, 1879), and his *Lectures on Development and Evolution*, 1878-79, are very widely read. Extending his theory of evolution from zoological subjects, H. applied it to problems of philosophy and religion, embodied in *Die Welträtsel*, 1899 (Eng. trans. *The Riddle of the Universe*, 1901); *Die Lebenswunder*, 1904 (Eng. trans. 1904). His other works include: *Ursprung des Menschen*, 1898 (Eng. trans. *The Last Link*, 1899); *Insulinde*, 1901; *Wanderbilder*, 1905; *Das Menschenproblem und die Herrentiere*, 1907; *Das Weltbild von Darwin und Lamarck*, 1909. See *Biography* by Bölsche (in German), 1900, and by M'Cabe (in English), 1906.

Hæmatite, or Hematite, diferric trioxide (Fe₂O₃), obtains its common name in allusion to its usual colour. In its crystalline condition it may be almost black, but even then its characteristic blood-colour is given on the streak plate. It crystallises in the rhombohedral system, and is isomorphous with corundum. *Elba Iron Ore* or H. from Rio Marina often possesses a brilliant metallic lustre which may be iridescent; this particular form receives the name of *specular iron ore*, and has a hardness of 6, and sp. gr. of 5·2. Recent volcanic rocks, as lavas of Auvergne, Eifel, etc., sometimes contain small thin scales of specular ore (*micaceous iron ore*). One form of micaceous iron ore is worked in Devonshire under the name of *shining ore*.

H. may also exist in fibrous or granular conditions, and an impure earthy form, *red ochre*, is an economic product. The hard fibrous form from Spain is used by bookbinders, goldsmiths, and others as a burnisher. In the N. of England fibrous H. often occurs in concretionary masses, it then receives the name of *kidney ore*, in recognition of its appearance on fracture. H. is widely distributed, and has been known since very remote days, having been occasionally cut and polished as an ornamental stone by the Assyrians, etc. The modern use of the mineral is as an ore of iron, and being remarkably free from phosphorus it is particularly suitable for the manufacture of steel. Analyses of certain specimens have closely approached the theoretical 70 per cent. of iron for this oxide. Important mines occur in Elba, Spain (Bilbao), and Scandinavia on the Continent. Large deposits also occur near Lake Superior. In Britain the chief supplies are in W. Cumberland, and N. Lancashire. Apart from the uses mentioned above, ground H. is used largely in paint manufacture.

Hæmatocele, a blood tumour in the tunica vaginalis. It may be the result either of a blow causing rupture of a blood vessel or a diseased vessel may burst. Its importance consists in the fact that it may be the first indication of a new growth. As new growths in this part are extremely dangerous, care should be taken to have an expert opinion as to its cause at the earliest possible moment.

Hæmatococcus, the name of a genus of plants belonging to the Algæ. It is so called because of the red-coloured cells of its species.

Hæmatomesis, blood vomiting, from changes originating in the stomach wall, as in cases of ulcer, the result of long-continued dyspepsia. The hæmorrhage may be sudden and unexpected in cases in which the dyspepsia has lasted so long that individuals regard it as their normal condition, to which they have become accustomed. H., however, may also occur suddenly and unexpectedly on account of liver trouble.

Treatment.—Until the bleeding has ceased, and its cause has been certainly decided upon, it is inadvisable to take anything, bite or sup, but to remain absolutely at rest, sucking pieces of ice and spitting out the water. In this way the thirst is relieved, but care should be taken to prevent anything whatever entering the stomach.

Hæmatopus, the name given to a genus of Charadriidæ, birds which breed on the plains of E. Europe and

Asia, but migrate in winter to Palestine and N. Africa. *H. ostralegus*, the oyster-catcher, is common to Great Britain, and because of its black and white plumage is sometimes called the sea-pie.

Hæmatoxylin, a colouring extracted from logwood (*Hæmatoxylon campeachianum*). Its chemical formula is $C_{16}H_{14}O_6$, and is in itself a crystalline substance and nearly colourless, but when combined with oxygen becomes a reddish colour, forming a substance known as hæmatein. H. is used for dyeing, principally to produce blue and black colourings.

Hæmatozoa (literally, a blood animal), worms of the genus *Filaria* that inhabit the blood. In humans, these animals only breed in the tropics. They cause the legs to swell until they attain a considerable size and have the straight up-and-down appearance of an elephant's legs. Hence the condition is known as elephantiasis. Various other symptoms are produced, but these are less characteristic than the appearance under the microscope of the worms in the blood.

Hæmaturia, blood in the urine. This may come from the urethra or bladder, from injury, ulceration, or tumours. It may occur as simply trickling or preceding the voidance of urine, as clots, or oozing at the end of the act. It may be derived from the kidney, when it causes a smoky colour, or it may be in such minute quantities that it can only be detected by the microscope, or by chemical tests. Blood from the kidneys is found as a complication in various diseases, originating in the kidneys, and also in fevers and general diseases. Other causes of H. are stones in the bladder or kidneys, rupture of vessels in these parts or, at and after middle life, of the prostate. It occurs in tubercle, in which, however, it is usually a late symptom, and also appears in inflammation of the bladder. When, on account of clots, or from other cause, there is pain, the application of heat, by fomentations or hip baths, is indicated.

Hæmodoraceæ, an order of Monocotyledons, was established by Dr. Robert Brown in 1810, and consists of over thirty Australian, African, and American species. The flowers are hermaphrodite and in parts of three, the stamens are epiphyllous, the carpels are united and have several ovules in each loculus; the fruit is a capsule. The chief genera are *Lachnanthes* and *Wachendorfia*.

Hæmoglobin, a protein occurring in the red blood-corpuscles which pos-

sesses the property of combining with oxygen and again yielding up the same when the concentration of oxygen sinks below a certain amount (*see* BLOOD). H. gives a definite absorption spectrum which is quite different from that of oxyhæmoglobin (the oxygenated product). In colour it is purplish-red, whilst oxyhæmoglobin is bright red. This difference in colour may be noticed by comparing venous and arterial blood. H. also has the power of combining with carbon monoxide, giving a compound which has a much brighter red colour than oxyhæmoglobin. The poisonous character of carbon monoxide is due to this property of forming with H. a more stable compound than oxyhæmoglobin; H. is easily decomposed into a pigment hæmatin which contains iron, and a proteid globin which seems to belong to the group of histones.

Hæmophilia, literally, a tendency to blood. This is also known as the hæmorrhagic diathesis. Patients suffering from this are known as 'Bleeders.' H. is a condition in which the blood clots very slowly, and consequently, from the slightest injury, hæmorrhage persists for some considerable time, and even the smallest wound may be fatal. The condition is of great interest, as it is distinctly hereditary, being inherited by women, but most common in men. Tooth drawing and other operations are much dreaded by dentists and surgeons, as except for the tendency to bleed, there is no other sign or indication of disease. The bleeding may be internal, under the skin, when the slightest injury causes extensive discoloured bruises. In joints slight injuries result in bleeding into them, so that they swell to considerable size and become useless. A fall on the head may result in bleeding in the brain, which may be fatal. A popular fallacy that a bleeder has a skin too little originated in the official statement that this was what a distinguished personage, with this disease, was suffering from.

Hæmoptysis, spitting of blood, that is, hæmorrhage from the lungs or air passages; a common, if not the most frequent, cause of tuberculosis, of which it is often the first symptom. It has consequently come to be unduly feared, because looked upon as identical with consumption, whereas it may be beneficial as an indication of a condition which, when treated early, results in complete recovery and the restoration of good health. On the other hand, in the course of consumption, unexpected bleeding may occur and cause death by choking. The main lines of the treatment of H. are: To keep the patient absolutely flat on the back, with perfect rest of mind and body. Warm drinks should be avoided and all food taken cold, or even nothing taken at all, except sucking small pieces of ice.

Hæmorrhage, bleeding. This may occur from an artery, when the blood spurts out in jets synchronous with the pulse beat and contraction of the heart. From a vein the blood is scarlet and flows in a continuous steady stream. Oozing, or capillary bleeding, is intermediate in tint between the two former ones. It is more readily controlled than the others, though in a place where the bleeding spot cannot be reached, as in the nose, it may continue for a considerable time. The main art of the surgeon is to perform an operation with as little bleeding as possible, and to control the H. in cases of injury. Thus, to fully discuss bleeding would be to write a treatise on surgery. The main points, however, are: To apply pressure on the bleeding spot; this is usually sufficient in a case of oozing, such as occurs in small cuts, when no large vessels are severed. In venous bleeding, the parts should be raised. In cases of arterial bleeding, pressure should be applied in the course of the artery, between the wound and the heart, or a bandage tied round the part sufficiently tight to check the H.

Hæmorrhoids, *see* PILES.

Hæmulon, the name given to a genus of Teleostei belonging to the family Pristipomatidæ; they are rather small marine fishes, and are sometimes called ' grunts ' because of the noise they make. Many species are found on the coasts of tropical America, but are unknown to Europe and Asia; some are known to enter fresh water. *H. plumieri*, the commonest species, is distinguished by having narrow blue stripes across the head.

Haffkine,Waldemar Mordecai Wolff (*b.* 1860), a pupil of the celebrated French chemist and microscopist, Pasteur; held for some time the post of professor of physiology at the Geneva Medical School. From thore he went to India, and was made director-in-chief of the government laboratory at Bombay. He was the first to produce a vaccine for the treatment of cholera, his first inoculation being made at Agra in 1893. Four years later he introduced a fluid for inoculation against plague. He was later appointed bacteriologist to the Indian government.

Haffs (Danish *hav*, sea), the term applied to lagoons in the Baltic Sea. These lagoons are separated from the sea by *nehrungs*—strips of sand. The

chief ones are Pommersches or Stettiner Haff, Frisches Haff (50 m. long and over 10 ft. deep), and Kurisches Haff (60 m. long).

Hafiz, the *nom-de-plume* of **Khwájá Shamsuddin Mohammad,** the greatest Persian lyric poet, ' the most Persian of the Persians ' (Fitzgerald). The date of his birth is doubtful; his death is variously given as 1388, 1391, and 1394. Little is known of his life except that it was mainly spent in Shiraz under the successive patronage of the governor Shah Ishák, Shah Shujá, and the vizier Kawámuddin, at whose college he lectured on the Koran; of this his knowledge was unrivalled, and he is credited with having written a great commentary. His verses, which reveal an extraordinarily brilliant technical accomplishment, are expressed in terms of typical oriental hedonism — wine, roses, and lovely maidens; he has been called the Anacreon of Persia. But his writings had a deeper mystic significance, and expressed symbolically the religious idealism of the Sufis (*q.v.*). H. was apparently a Sufi by training, and a realist by temperament. The famous *Diwán,* a series of ghazals collected by one of his pupils, is his best-known work, but no satisfactory complete translation has yet appeared. The most important European study of H. was written late in the 17th century by a Bosnian, Sudi. English translations are: Robinson (1875), Love (1877), and Sir Wm. Ouseley (1797-98); Cowell's translation of the Odes (1854); and Abdul Majid and Cranmer Byng's *Rubaiyat* (Murray's Wisdom of the East series, 1910).

Hagar (Gen. xvi.), an Egyptian slave of Sarai, the wife of Abraham. She was evidently the companion as well as the servant of Sarai, and at the latter's wish became the concubine of Abraham, to whom she bore a son, Ishmael. Motives of jealousy then led Sarai to drive her out into the wilderness, where she received the oracle as to the future fate of the Ishmaelites.

Hagberry, *see* BIRD CHERRY.

Hagbut, *see* FIREARMS.

Hagedorn, Friedrich von (1708-54), a German poet, born at Hamburg. The son of a Danish minister, he became unpaid private secretary to the Danish ambassador in London, where he stayed until 1731. For two years after his return to Hamburg he suffered great privations, but was eventually appointed secretary to the ' English Court ' (Englischer Hof), an old English trading company. His poems have considerable charm, his love songs are delicate and fanciful, and his tales and fables in verse compare not unfavourably with La Fontaine, whom he took as his model. His poems were edited by Eschenburg (1800) in 5 vols. *See* H. Schuster, *F. von Hagedorn* (Leipzig), 1882.

Hagelberg, a vil. in the prov. of Brandenburg, Prussia, 22 m. S.W. of Potsdam. Noted historically for the victory obtained by the allies, under Hirschfield, over the French, August 1813.

Hagen, a tn. in the Prussian prov. of Westphalia, Germany, 15 m. N.E. of Elberfeld. It is one of the most flourishing industrial centres of Westphalia, and possesses some fine public buildings, including a technical school with a special engineering branch. There are large iron and steel works, and woollen, cotton, leather, paper, etc., are manufactured; there are also breweries and distilleries. In the neighbourhood there is an alabaster quarry, and limestone is also worked. Pop. 88,631.

Hagen, Friedrich Heinrich von der (1780-1856), a German philologist, born at Schmiedeberg in Brandenburg. He studied law at the Halle University, and was given a state appointment at Berlin, which he resigned in 1806. Four years later he was made professor extraordinarius of German literature at the Berlin University, and in 1811 went to Breslau to take up a similar appointment, returning again to Berlin in 1821. His chief work was research into Old German literature, and he succeeded in rousing an interest in Old German poetry. His works include the *Nibelungenlied* (4 eds.), 1810-42; the *Minnesinger* (4 vols.), Leipzig, 1838-50; *Gottfried von Strassburg*, Berlin, 1823; and *Gesamtabenteuer*, a collection of Old German tales (3 vols.), Stuttgart, 1850.

Hagenau, a tn. in the imperial prov. of Alsace-Lorraine, Germany. It is about 16 m. N. of Strassburg in the middle of the Hagenau Forest. It possesses two fine old churches dating from the 12th and 13th centuries, besides other public buildings. The main industries are wool and cotton spinning; boots, soap, wine, and oil are manufactured; and there are also breweries and potteries. It is a garrison town and dates from the 12th century, when the dukes of Swabia had a hunting-lodge there. In 1154 the Emperor Frederick I. gave it town rights and built walls round it, and an imperial palace. In 1257 Richard of Cornwall, King of the Romans, made it an imperial city. Later it fell into the hands of the French, passing into the possession of Germany, 1871. Pop. 18,868.

Hagenbach, Karl Rudolph (1801-74), a Swiss theologian, born at Basel. His interest in theology started at an early date, and while at Bonn he came under the influence of G. C. F. Lücke, and later at Berlin that of Schleiermacher and Neander. In 1823 he returned to Basel and made a stir by his trial dissertation, *Observationes historico-hermeneuticæ circa Origenes methodum interpretendæ sacræ Scripturæ*. In 1824 he became professor extraordinarius and five years later professor ordinarius of theology at Basel. His works were numerous, and include: *Encyclopädie u. Methodologie der theol. Wissenschaften*, 1833; *Lehrbuch der Dogmengeschichte*, 1840-44 (Eng. trans. 1850); *Vorlesungen über die Geschichte der alten Kirche*, 1853-55. Church history was his strong point, but he also published some biographies and poems.

Hagerstown, a city and the co. seat of Washington co., Maryland, U.S.A., about 86 m. by rail N.W. of Baltimore. It is situated in a valley overlooked by the North and South Mountains, and contains the Kee Mar College (1852) for women. It is a large manufacturing centre; flour, shirts, automobiles, agricultural implements, etc., being some of its products. Pop. (1910) 16,507.

Hag-fish, or **Borer**, the name applied to all members of the Myxinidæ, marine fishes belonging to the Cyclostomata; they occur off all the coasts of W. Europe and off the E. American coast as far as Cape Cod. Their bodies are eel-shaped, with no lateral fins, and a slight median fin at the extremity; the head is equipped with four pairs of sharp tentacles, with which the H. attack cod, haddock, etc., devouring all the flesh and leaving only the skeleton of their prey. Shoals of fish are often destroyed by the various species of *Myxine* which, when not seeking food, lives in mud-beds at the bottom of the sea; *M. glutinosa* and other species secrete a thick glutinous slime. *Bdellostoma* contains two species which occur in the S. Pacific.

Haggada, *see* EXEGESIS, TALMUD.

Haggai (either ' born on a feastday ' or ' feast of Yahweh '), a prophet contemporary with Zechariah whose prophecies are contained in the book of the O.T. which bears his name. Little is known about the prophet himself, but from chap. ii. 3 of his work we may gather that he was already an old man when he began to prophesy, being one of those who had seen the temple ' in its former glory.' His book contains four short prophecies all delivered in the latter part of the second year of Darius the king (520 B.C.), the first three dealing with the restoration of the temple, the last being a special promise to Zerubbabel.

Haggard, Lieut. - Col. Andrew Charles Parker, D.S.O. (*b.* 1854), an author, novelist, historian, and poet, born at Bradenham Hall, Norfolk, and educated at Westminster School. In 1873 he joined the King's Own Borderers 25th Regiment and served in India, Aden, and Egypt. In 1884 fought at the battle of Samai and commanded the 1st Battalion of the Egyptian army in operations on the Nile (1885-86), was mentioned in despatches, and obtained medal and star D.S.O. His publications include : *Tempest Torn; Under Crescent and Star; Sporting Yarns; A Canadian Girl; The Amours of Henri de Navarre and Marguerite de Valois; Louis XI. and Charles the Bold*, etc.

Haggard, Sir Henry Rider (*b.* 1856), an English novelist, born at Bradenham Hall, Norfolk. At nineteen years of age he went to S. Africa as secretary to Sir Henry Bulwer, governor of Natal. In 1877 he was a member of the staff of Sir Theophilus Shepstone, special commissioner for the Transvaal, and in 1878 became Master of the High Court of the Transvaal. He married Miss Margitson, of Norfolk, in 1879. He takes a deep interest in rural and agricultural questions, being an exceedingly practical farmer and gardener on his own estate. In 1902 he published *Rural England*, a valuable study of rural conditions and of agriculture. In 1905 the Colonial Office commissioned him to inquire into the Salvation Army settlements in the United States, his report being published in 1905 as *The Poor and the Land*, with a scheme for national land settlements. As a novelist Sir H. Rider Haggard has been writing since 1882: *Cetywayo and his White Neighbours* appeared first. Among the most popular are: *King Solomon's Mines*, 1886, one of the best written and most thrilling of romances; *She*, 1887; *Allan Quatermaine*, 1888 ; *Jess*, 1887 ; *The World's Desire*, 1890, written with Andrew Lang; and many others. He received the honour of knighthood in 1912.

Haggis, an ancient Scottish dish, called by Burns ' great chieftain o' the puddin' race.' The stomach bag of a sheep having been well washed, turned inside out and salted, is filled about half full (room being left for expansion) with the heart, liver, and lungs of the animal, all minced, together with a large onion, half a pound of oatmeal, a pound of suet, salt, pepper, and half a teaspoonful of mixed spice; the addition of the juice of a lemon and some good stock is often found to be an improvement.

The bag is then securely sewn up and left to boil for about three hours. It was common in England until the 18th century.

Hagi, a tn. on the W. coast of Hondo, Japan, 145 m. N.E. of Nagasaki, which took a prominent part in the national movement for the abolition of feudalism. Pop. 21,000.

Hagiographa, The (' sacred writings '), a name sometimes given to the miscellaneous books of the O.T. which are not grouped either with the Law or with the Prophets. Among these are the various poetical books, such as the Psalms, Lamentations, and Canticles, and the other three books, Ruth, Ecclesiastes, and Esther, which, with the two last, form the Megilloth or Rolls.

Hagiology, the name of the body of literature dealing with the lives of Christian saints and martyrs. The oldest collection is *The Assembly of the Ancient Martyrs* by Eusebius. In the Greek Church these collections of lives of the saints are called menologies (Gk. $\mu\acute{\eta}\nu$, month), and they can be traced from the 9th century. Among those of the Western Church, perhaps the most famous is the *Legenda Aurea* (Golden Legend) of Jacobus de Voragine. The founder of hagiologic criticism was a Flemish Jesuit, Heribert Rosveyde (*d.* 1629), who published, among other works, the *Vitæ Patrum* (Antwerp), 1615. He also arranged a great systematic collection of the lives of the saints, resulting in the *Acta Sanctorum*, and the foundation of the Belgian Society of Bollandists, now occupied in the critical publication of the *Acta Sanctorum* (*q.v.*).

Hagonoy, a tn. of the prov. of Bulacan, Luzon, Philippine Islands, on Manila Bay. It produces rice, Indian corn, sugar, and coffee. The chief industries are alcohol distilling and the weaving of native fabrics. Pop. 21,304.

Hague, Cap de la, a cape in France at the N.W. extremity of the Cotentin peninsula, in the dept. Manche, between Cherbourg and the island of Alderney, on the English Channel. It must be distinguished from La Hogue, which is a roadstead lying on the E. side of the peninsula, where the French fleet, which was sent to the support of James II., was defeated by the English and Dutch fleets in 1692. The Channel Islands are visible from Cap de la Hague.

Hague, The (in Dutch, *'s Gravenhage* or *Den Haag*), the official capital of the Netherlands, situated about 2 m. from the North Sea. It is the usual residence of the court, and the seat of the States-general, though Amsterdam is still the commercial cap. of the Netherlands. Many of its streets are intersected by canals, bordered with rows of trees, and in the centre of the city is the artificial lake known as Vijver. The fashionable quarter of the city lies in the N., and here the principal buildings are to be found; the royal palace, purchased by the states in 1595; a large monument by Jacquet commemorating the jubilee of the restoration of Dutch independence in 1813; the museum, Meermanno-Westreenianum, which contains some interesting specimens of early typography, and the royal library which contains over half a million books, as well as coins and medals, antique gems, and some interesting manuscripts. Besides these, there are the government buildings situated in the Binnenhof, which was once surrounded by a moat, and was founded in 1249 by William II., Count of Holland, whose son made it his residence; the prison, where the brothers De Witt were killed by the mob in 1672; the law courts, the building containing the state archives, and the Mauritshuis, which was built in 1633-44, and contains the famous picture gallery of the H. The city, too, contains numerous churches, the Groote Kerk of St. James, which dates back to the 14th century and is Gothic in style; the Nieuwe Kerk, containing the tombs of the brothers De Witt, and of the philosopher Spinoza, and many others. There is also a picturesque town hall, built in 1565, a fine modern railway station erected in 1892, and the famous royal villa 'Huis ten Bosch,' built in 1645, where the International Peace Conference was held in 1899. The H. was the birthplace of the astronomer Huygens, the physician Boerhaave, and the place where Spinoza, to whom a monument has been erected, died, 1677. Here, too, the Triple Alliance between England, Sweden, and the Netherlands, 1688, was signed; the Hague Convention was assembled, 1899 and 1907, and the Palace of Peace designed by Cordonnier is to be completed. The chief industries are printing, cannon founding, copper and lead smelting, iron casting, gold and silver decorations, and the manufacture of furniture and carriages. Pop. 280,515.

Hague Conference, a peace conference initiated by the Tsar Nicholas II. in 1899, with the object of ' a possible reduction of the excessive armaments which weigh upon all nations,' to be effected by ' putting a limit to the progressive development of the present armaments.' But it was not found practicable either in 1899 or in 1907 (the second conference) to achieve anything in this direction. The conference of 1899 established a permanent judiciary system ready to be called into action whenever two or more states desire a matter in difference to be settled. The convention provided for the conduct of good offices and mediation, inquiry by commissions into disputed matters of fact, the constitution of a permanent court, with an international office at the Hague. The provision for commissions of inquiry did good service in 1904, during the Russo-Japanese War, when a Russian fleet opened fire upon the Hull fishing fleet off the Dogger Bank. The second conference, 1907, passed an amended convention for the settlement of international disputes. Other matters discussed were the laws and customs of war, e.g., guerilla warfare, etc., and the application to naval warfare of the principles of the Geneva Conference. Rules, too, were made at the first conference against the throwing of missiles from balloons, the use of missiles intended to diffuse suffocating gases, and the use of expanding bullets. To this latter Great Britain did not accede at first, but acted upon it shortly afterwards in the S. African War, and formally acceded to it at the conference of 1907. It is significant that in the congress of 1907, the republics of S. and Central America were represented, as well as the empire of Japan.

Hahnemann, Samuel Christian Friedrich (1755 - 1843), a German physician and founder of homœopathy, born at Meissen, in Saxony. He studied medicine at Leipzig and Vienna, and took his degree in 1779 at Erlangen. He practised first at Dresden, then, in 1789, settled at Leipzig. He was not satisfied with the state of the science of medicine and in 1796 advanced a new principle, ' the law of similars,' i.e. that diseases should be treated by those drugs which produce symptoms similar to them, in the healthy. Four years later he published his doctrine on a system of smaller doses of drugs. In 1810 his chief work was printed, *Organon der rationellen, Heilkunde,* explaining this system, which he named homœopathy. The hostility of the apothecaries forced him to leave Leipzig and find protection with the Grand - duke of Anhalt-Cothen. Fourteen years afterwards he went to Paris and practised homœopathy with great success. *See* Bradford, *Hahnemann's Life and Letters* (Philadelphia), 1895; *see also* MEDICINE (*Homœopathy*).

Hahn-Hahn, Ida, Countess von (1805-80), a German author, born at Tressow in Mecklenburg-Schwerin, daughter of Count Karl Friedrich von H. She married her cousin, Count Adolf von Hahn-Hahn, and divorced him in 1829. She published some volumes of poems, and in 1838 her first novel appeared, *Aus der Gesellschaft*. Several other novels followed, dealing chiefly with aristocratic society. In 1852 she retired to the convent of Angers, and shortly afterwards founded a nunnery at Mainz, where she continued her literary work. Her novels were popular though very sentimental. Among them are *Ulrich*, *Gräfin Faustine*, *MariaRegina*, etc.

Hai-Cheng, a tn. in the prov. of Liao-tung, Manchuria, Russia, 20 m. S.E. of Newchang. It was the scene of a Japanese victory over the Chinese in 1894, and over the Russians in 1904.

Haidarabad, or **Hyderabad**: 1. The principal native state of India, and occupies a large portion of the Deccan, the central plateau of Southern India. It is also called the Nizam's Dominions, and has an area of 82,698 sq. m. and a pop. of 11,150,000. The Nizam of H. is the chief Mohammedan ruler in India. The Nizam has been under the protection of the British government since 1799, and in 1902 in a treaty made by Lord Curzon, the district of Berar was assigned in perpetuity to Great Britain, whilst the Hyderabad contingent was incorporated into the British army. H. is very mountainous and densely wooded in some parts, whilst in other districts it is flat and undulating. There are two principal tracts called Jelingana and Marath-wala. The chief rivers watering the district are the Godavari, Dudna, Manjira, Pranhita, Wardha, and Kistna, with their tributaries. The chief products are oil seeds, rice, cotton, and the sugar cane. The mineral wealth of the country is indifferent, but there is a huge coal mine at Singareni. 2. The name of the cap. of the above state, and is situated on the r. b. of the R. Musi and is the fourth largest city in India. It possesses many fine buildings, chief amongst which are the British residency, the Mecca Mosque, and the Char Minar or Four Minarets. The city is surrounded by a stone wall with thirteen gates, and resembles a parallelogram in shape. The beautiful grounds of the residency and many fine buildings were devastated by floods caused through the overflow of the R. Musi in 1908. Pop. 500,623. 3. The name of a city in British India, was formerly the cap. of Sind in the Presidency of Bombay. It stands on a hill, which serves as an excellent natural fortress. Pop. 70,000.

Haidar Ali, or **Hyder Ali** (1728-82),

an Indian ruler and commander, the second son of a Mohammedan chieftain. He was turned out by his father to seek his own fortunes. His brother commanded a brigade in the Mysore army and Hyder occasionally acted for him, but spent most of his time in studying French army tactics. He induced his brother to purchase artillery and firearms, and enrol European sailors as gunners. In 1749 he obtained an independent command, and during the next twelve years became complete master of the Rajah of Mysore and his kingdom. By the conquest of Kanara he gained the treasures of Bednor, and his destruction of the military caste of Nairs on the Malabar coast caused the government of Madras to send Colonel Smith with a small force to check his advance; a fierce battle was fought at Chengam, 1767, and Hyder was defeated; his terms of peace were rejected, and collecting a larger army he came within five miles of Madras. A treaty was arranged providing for mutual aid in defensive war. The British broke faith and Hyder commenced to revenge himself; in one encounter Colonel Baillie's force of 2800 men was utterly destroyed. Finally Sir Eyre Coote defeated him in three different battles, and the British fleet seized Negapatam. He sent his son Tippoo, to gain help from the French, but died suddenly before his return. This man could neither read nor write, was a mere adventurer, yet became the most formidable rival the British encountered in India, and threatened the extinction of the East India Company.

Haiduks, or **Hayduks** (in Hungarian, 'drovers'), a term originally applied to brigands and outlaws, still used in this sense in Servia and Bulgaria. In Hungary the name was given to a class of mercenary foot soldiers, distinguished for courage and fidelity to the Protestant cause. They received titles and land in a district on the left bank of the R. Theiss, afterwards known as the Haiduk region. Later the word was applied to a male servant or footman, also an attendant in the court of law. The Hungarian light infantry were called H. in the 18th century.

Haiduong, or **Haizuong**, the cap. of a prov. of the same name in Tongking, French Indo-China, 32 m. E.S.E. of Hanoi, and largely in ruins. Pop. (prov). 1,100,000, (town) 8000.

Haifa, or **Khaifa**, a seaport of Palestine, on the S. of the Bay of Acre, 9 m. S.W. of Acre, and at the foot of Mount Carmel. Since 1890 it has rapidly developed and is now connected with Damascus by railroad. Egyptian cotton is being successfully cultivated, and the exports of grain and oil amount to about £180,000 annually. There is a small colony of Germans belonging to the Unitarian sect of the Templars (founded 1869); the rest of the population consists of Moslems, Christians, and Jews, estimated at 12,000. *See* Laurence Oliphant, *Haifa*, 1887.

Haifong, *see* HAIPHONG.

Haik, *see* ARMENIA.

Hai-K'ou, *see* HOI-HAU.

Hail and Hailstorms. In old text-books hail used to be described as frozen rain, but its production is now ascribed to more complex atmospherical conditions than were then supposed. Volta suggested that when two clouds, charged respectively with positive and negative electricity, lie one above the other, hail is produced by electric discharges passing up and down through the moisture-laden atmosphere But a more modern theory is that whirling movements, caused by the uprush of heated air to mingle with colder and denser strata moving transversely above, bring down nuclei of ice from the higher clouds; these as they descend congeal upon themselves layers of softer ice from the moisture around, and are again driven upward, such movements continuing till at length the hail falls to the ground. In most cases electricity is generated, with flashes of lightning. Another theory is that hailstones are due to the congelation of water at a great height, that the ice-fragments thus produced are shattered by electric discharges and then re-congealed, this being many times repeated. True hail is rarely seen except in summer, is most frequent in warm countries, and is usually associated with thunderstorms. Hailstones vary greatly in shape and size, but rounded and conical pellets are the most common. There is always a kernel, surrounded by layers, sometimes alternately transparent and opaque. Professor Sylvanus Thomson says the kernel has occasionally been known to consist of stony matter containing iron. Hailstones have been found which took the curious form of plano-convex lenses, like magnifying glasses. The very large specimens sometimes met with may be produced by the conglomeration of smaller pellets. Darwin tells of a storm in S. America, when 'hail as large as small apples, and extremely hard, fell with such violence as to kill most of the wild animals' round about. In the Rhone Valley, July 7, 1875, Monsieur Collodon found hailstones with kernels 60 to 100 millimetres in diameter (2¼ to 4 in.) and weighing 300 grammes, *six hours* after

the fall. In July 1788 a hailstorm passed over France in two parallel belts, each only about 9 m. wide, one 500 m. and the other 600 m. in length. In the interval between them, 15 m. wide, rain fell in torrents. It has been asserted that in districts which have been largely disafforested, hailstorms become more prevalent, owing to the bare earth, when heated by the sun, sending up a much greater rush of hot air than would arise from a cool forest region.

Hail Mary, *see* AVE MARIA.

Hailes, Lord, *see* DALRYMPLE, SIR DAVID.

Haileybury College, in Hertfordshire, England. One of the big public schools: it was founded by the East India Company, in 1806, as a training college for Civil Service cadets. Originally it occupied Hertford Castle, but in 1809 the college was removed to its present site, 2 m. S.E. of Hertford. In 1862 the present school was established and incorporated by royal charter in 1864. *See* Higgens, *Old and New Haileybury*, 1887.

Hailsham, a market tn. in the Eastbourne parl. div. of Sussex, England. It possesses a fine example of Perpendicular architecture in the Church of St. Mary, and close by is the Augustinian priory of Michelham, with an old gatehouse and crypt. Ropes and matting are manufactured, and there is a good agricultural trade. Pop. 4197.

Haimura, a fresh-water fish of Guiana which belongs to the group Erythrinina. From 3 to 4 ft. in length, it has powerful jaws with large strong teeth. It is extremely voracious, and abounds near the rapids in the Guiana rivers; the Indians eat large quantities.

Hainan, an island off Kwang-tung prov., China, separated from the mainland by H. Strait, and lying between the China Sea and the Gulf of Tongking. Area about 16,000 sq. m. The central and southern portions are traversed by granitic mountains, reaching an altitude of nearly 7000 ft., while the northern portion is an undulating plain, broken by isolated hills. The island is well watered and produces timber, rice, sugar, cotton, etc. Chief town, Kiungchow (harbour, Hoihow) on the N. coast, which is a treaty port. Pop. estimated at 2,500,000.

Hainau, or **Haynau,** a tn. in the prov. of Silesia, Prussia, about 10 m. W.N.W. of Liegnitz. It is chiefly engaged in tanning and the manuf. of gloves and agricultural implements. There are also iron foundries in the town. Pop. about 10,459.

Hainaut, or **Hainault,** a prov. of Belgium, bounded on its southern side by France, is traversed by the Ardennes Mts. and watered by the Sambre, Scheldt, and other rivers, as well as several canals. There are extensive coal-fields here, and iron is produced in large quantities. The manufacture of textile goods is also carried on. The capital is Mons. In 1433 H. was given to Burgundy, and in the 17th century parts of it were acquired by France. Area about 1437 sq. m. Pop. about 1,200,000.

Hainburg, a tn. in Lower Austria on the R. Danube, 27 m. E.S.E. of Vienna. It is a very fine old town, surrounded by walls with a gate guarded by two ancient towers. There are numerous Roman remains, and water is brought to the town by a Roman aqueduct. In 1477 it was besieged by the Hungarians, and five years later was captured by Matthias Corvinus, King of Hungary, and in 1683 it was sacked by the Turks. There is an historical old castle known in German tradition as Heimburc, which the Emperor Henry III. took from the Hungarians in 1042. It possesses one of the largest tobacco factories in Austria, and also a needle factory. Pop. 7304.

Hainichen, a tn. of Saxony on the Little Striegis, 28 m. W.S.W. of Dresden, and 40 m. S.E. of Leipzig. There are collieries in the neighbourhood, and manufs. of cotton and linen goods; it is also a centre of the flannel manufacture. Pop. 7863.

Hain Steamship Company, established in the year 1878, is under the management of Edward Hain & Son, of St. Ives, Cornwall. This company, which was registered in 1901, owns thirty vessels.

Haiphong, or Haifong, a tn. and port of Tongking, French Indo-China, situated on the Cua-Cam, one of the branches of the Song Koi delta, about 20 m. from the Gulf of Tongking. It is the second port of French Indo-China and a naval station, having communication by canal, river, and railway. There is a sandy bar which prevents ships drawing more than 13 ft. from entering the harbour. Shipbuilding, cement works, and cotton spinning are the chief industries. Pop. 22,000.

Hair, an outgrowth of the skin. The human body, with the exception of the palms of the hands and the soles of the feet, is covered in short, fine Hs. or down, but on the scalp and, in the case of men, on the cheeks, etc., H. tends to grow both thick and long.

Physiology of human hair.—A H., like a nail, is built up from the corneous cells of the epidermis. It is shut up in a bag, called a H. sac, or 'follicle,' at the bottom of which is a 'papilla.' The superficial epidermic cells surrounding the papilla become horny and coalesce into a 'shaft,' which is finally thrust out above the surface skin by new growths from below. When it has reached its natural height it dies, but not before a fresh papilla and sac have been formed so as to send up another H. to replace the old one. Each H. shaft has an elaborate structure. In the centre is 'medullary' matter, which may contain air. This is wrapped round with a 'cortical' substance, composed of elongated horn cells. Enveloping the latter

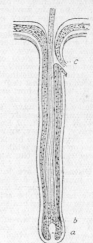

A HAIR IN ITS FOLLICLE

a, Papilla ; *b,* newest part of the hair growing on the papilla ; *c,* mouth of a sebaceous gland.

is an outer 'cuticle' made of flat corneous plates fitting transversely round the shaft. The cuticle in its turn is enclosed in the epidermis of the H. sac which corresponds to the integument, just as the dermis of the H. sac, which is the last coating, corresponds to the dermis of the integument. In these superficial layers of the follicle are the root-sheaths, which, as their name suggests, contain the root of the H. A fatty liquid, which lubricates the H., is secreted from the sebaceous glands, whose ducts open into the H. follicle. The phenomenon called 'goose-skin,' when H. stands erect, usually through alarm or horror, is produced by the involuntary contraction of tiny H. muscles.

Growth of hair.—A crop of head H. lasts from two to four years, but normally its loss is imperceptible as a new one has meanwhile arisen to take its place. Baldness results when the powers of renewal are unequal to the loss. It is a natural process for H. to turn grey with age, but there are many curious cases on record where, under the influence of violent emotion, like inconsolable grief or panic, H. has turned grey in a night or even in a few hours. This misfortune is supposed to have happened to Marie Antoinette. In some families white patches, or premature blanching of the hair, are hereditary. Length of H. varies very considerably. There are records of crops 6 ft. long, but 2¼ ft. is an average length for a good growth of women's H.

Hair and anthropology.—H. is an important anthropological criterion. There are four kinds, whether superficial or structural distinctions be taken into account. Most negroes have jet-black H., which is short and curly, and popularly described as 'woolly.' The yellow races have straight, coarse, lank, and, generally speaking, the longest H. The H. of Europeans is either wavy, or glossy, and smooth, the colour varying from black to very fair browns or yellows, whilst 'frizzy' H. is characteristic of the Australian aborigines, etc.

Hair, Diseases of, are intimately related to many skin diseases, such as eczema, and in general the condition of the hair may be said to be symptomatic of bodily health. Children especially are liable to vermin in their hair, and an inflamed, itching scalp and a verminous head often lead to eczema, in which case a sulphur or an ammoniated mercury ointment should be smeared over the diseased parts. If a child suffers from ringworm, which is a highly contagious and troublesome skin disease, his hair will break off or fall out and bald circular patches be left. This disorder is due to a fungus which grows between the true skin and the scarf, and the safest remedy is to shave off the hair and then to apply some chemical agent, such as oil of cade or pitch mixed with glycerine, to kill the parasite. Constitutional weakness and many forms of debility may cause the forking, or splitting, or excessive shedding of the hair. Such evils may be checked by regular cutting, which undoubtedly strengthens the hair, but the best way to deal with them is to try to remove the much more serious bodily weakness, which lies at their root. There are endless prescriptions for saving the hair and preserving it in good condition, but many of them emanate from quacks, and on the whole it is unwise to adopt any, unless recommended to do so by a properly qualified practitioner. Some aver that a drachm of balsam of Peru, well mixed with an ounce of simple cerate (melted), makes an excellent local application. Baldness is probably the most common of all hair diseases, and one which still continues obstinately to resist most treatments. Adults of the male sex are in particular prone to baldness, and are often faced quite early in life with the problem how to deal with it. General diseases such as fever, or a chronic constitutional malady like tuberculosis, may give rise to it, whilst other causes are excessive perspiration, which invariably weakens the epidermis, and a decrease in the supply of blood to the scalp, which often accompanies old age. Applications containing Spanish blistering flies or cantharides are often effective in stimulating the skin and thus encouraging the growth of another crop; perspiration on the head may be diminished by ventilation when under cover, and also by covering the head as little as possible; shaving two or three times in succession may promote another growth when the hair has fallen out after some serious illness, but should the misfortune be due to an eruptive disease, the patient should apply to his doctor, who will probably try some soothing and medicinal treatment. There is no cure for the baldness of grey hairs or old age. This article may be closed with the mention of a disease which seems endemic only in Poland. A peculiar glutinous sweat exudes and renders the hair disagreeably matted and almost succulent. One symptom is shocking irritation of the scalp.

Hair, Trade in, is very considerable in Great Britain, but it is difficult to get statistics up to date as '·hair' is usually included with 'hides,' etc., in all tables of imports and exports. Peasant girls of France, Belgium, and Italy sell their hair to agents especially appointed for collecting it. Auburn and golden hues fetch a much higher price than browns, because of their comparative rarity. Great Britain obtains fair hair from Scandinavia and Germany, whilst coarser kinds are imported from India and China. Human hair 8 in. long is worth 1s. an ounce. Wigs, artificial fronts, etc., are produced both from long tresses and 'combings' of human hair. In 1888 about 20,000 cwt. of horse-hair were shipped from Russia, Germany, Australia, and S. America, etc., and 95,000 cwt. of cow-hair. Hair industries and manufactures are manifold and various. Long tail hair of horses is imported into this country from Russia and S. America to be woven into hair-cloth. Short horse-hair is curled and freely used for stuffing chairs and sofas. The hair of cows is utilised in the manufacture of roofing and boiler felts, and also of coarse rugs and blankets: plasterers employ it to bind the mortar applied to walls of houses; and the tail hair of oxen is suitable for stuffing cushions and making barristers' wigs. Russian pigs' bristles are in great demand for toilet and decorators' brushes, whilst artists' brushes are made from camels' hair. Even the tail hair of elephants has been turned to account, and is worked up into bracelets in Nyassaland.

Hair Balls, see GEOLOGY.

Hair-dressing has continued, since the beginning of things down to the 20th century, to exercise and to tax to the utmost human ingenuities. Babes and young children are usually allowed to wear their hair as it grows, and negroes for the most part leave their luxuriant and tousled masses as nature made them. But, speaking generally, a comparison of different tribes and nations brings out an extraordinary diversity in H., a diversity, moreover, which is hardly less remarkable, when note is taken of the multiplicity of fashions which at one time or another have held an individual people in their grip. Perhaps savages have been most fertile in the invention of hair contortions. Such tribes of American Indians as the Dakotas and Iroquois wear a picturesque head-dress of gaily-coloured feathers. All kinds of plumes and feathers are variously worn by different tribes all over the world, whilst Papuans wear .bones; Maoris, sharks' teeth; Polynesians, flowers and cocoa-nut leaves; Dana-kils, porcupine quills; and Niam niams, cowries for ornament. Some men in the New Hebrides proudly twist their hair into as many as 600 whip-cords, a process which takes years to complete, and certain natives of Southern Tropical Africa are at great pains to stiffen some strands into a screw-like tuft by means of fat, and then to decorate the same with an ostrich feather. Shaving, frizzing, greasing, and plaiting are devices everywhere practised for forcing the hair into fashionable shapes. A Chinaman shaves his scalp in front and wears his fine black pigtail behind. Japanese ladies coil their glossy hair into an elaborate chignon, secured by a great pin and made smooth with the aid of a bandoline. Moslems have been known to clip away all their hair save a small clump, which in time will serve as a handle to raise them up to Heaven. In England early Britons were remarkable for their long, bushy hair, whilst Danes and Saxons also wore it long. In Edward I.'s reign men wore their hair in large curls, which stood out at the sides, whilst ladies confined theirs in a caul of gold-network, or, as later, in a ponderous turban. In the days of Henry V. men cropped their hair hideously close, whilst in Tudor times they parted it in the centre, combed it down on either side, and turned it under all round. Cavaliers, during the Stuart period, wore their hair in curls over the shoulders until the Restoration, when the huge powdered perukes were borrowed from France together with other eccentric modes. In modern times short cutting for men has become universal. The acme of extravagant and vicious taste in ladies' coiffures was reached in the 18th century, when, indeed, the trade of barber was elevated to a high art. The hair and was gathered over a mighty erection of tow, which was profusely adorned with pearls, glass beads, and all manner of jewels, mostly false, and with endless varieties of curls, plumes, ribbons, and bobs. If a court lady were economical, she would make one dressing suffice for three weeks, and often she would be obliged to go to the barber some days before a ball, if she wished to ensure a new and extensive hair-dress. At all times false hair, powders, pomatum, hair washes, and frames of every size and description have been in vogue. To-day the modes of H. for women are still legion, but they are one and all free from the incredible mon-strosities of the Georgian era.

Hair Dye has been used from earliest times by savage tribes, and among civilised nations is still fashionable with certain classes at the present day. The Chinese colour hair with the juice of the *Hibiscus Trionum*, but chemical compounds are now in greatest demand. Women may obtain golden tresses by bleaching their hair with hydrogen peroxide, which is also recommended for matching white hairs with requisite shades of grey. The most permanent and deepest black is procurable as follows: The hair is saturated with a solution of potassium sulphide and, after drying, dipped in a solution of silver nitrate, the strength of which depends on the colour desired.

Hair-eel, or **Hair-worm,** the name applied to various species of Nema-thelminthes, and particularly to those of the genus *Gordius* (*q.v.*) because of their thread-like shape;

according to a popular superstition, these worms are produced from horse hairs.

Hair-grass, the name applied to several species of *Aira*, grasses found in Britain and other temperate climates and belonging to the order Gramineæ. *A. cæspitosa*, the common tufted hair grass, reaches a height of 2 or 3 ft., and is frequently found in moist pastures.

Hair Powder was used by the aristocracies of Europe during the two centuries preceding the French Revolution, and is still employed by a few footmen as a badge of their office. It is made of pulverised starch, and accordingly is white in colour.

Hairs in Plants are natural excrescences from epidermal cells. They are many in kind : root hairs are one-celled tubes ; stinging hairs, with a drop of poison on the top are attached to the nettle order (Urtica), and glandular hairs, the glands being either at tip or base, characterise the order of sun-dew (Drosera). Ferns have scaly hairs: bristles are merely hairs made rigid with silica, etc., and the prickles of rose trees and brambles are hairs grown firm and woody. Externally they grow on any part of the plant, whilst in a few species they cover inner surfaces. The function of hair underground is to absorb food, *i.e.* water and minerals, and above ground to afford protection from frost, cold, or excessive radiation.

Hair-Tail (*Trichiurus*), a sea fish, which is found generally near land, with a long ribbon-shaped body which ends in a long whip-like tail. The dorsal fin extends the whole length of the back, and the ventral fins are in the form of a pair of scales. There are several species, most of which occur in the tropics, but some are occasionally found off the English coast.

Haiti, Santo Domingo, or **Hispaniola,** an island in the W. Indies, lying in the centre of the chain, and second in size to Cuba. Since the discovery of the island by Columbus in 1492 there has been no generally accepted designation for it. Columbus called it Española (Hispaniola), 'Little Spain,' whereas the native name for it was Hayti (Haiti), 'Highlands,' and after the first settlement the island received the name of San Domingo. In 1677, when Spain ceded the western section to France, the name Haiti was reserved for the western part of the island, San Domingo for the eastern, and the whole land was known as Hispaniola. The island has a length of 400 m., with an extreme breadth of 162 m., and a total area of 28,000 sq. m. It is essentially a mountainous region, and the steep escarpments run right down to the shores. The highest point is Mt. Loma, 10,300 ft., which is situated N.W. of the city of San Domingo. It has a coast-line of 1250 m., which has some good harbours, the Samana inlet containing one 30 m. in length. There are four large rivers, the Yaqui, the Neyba, the Yuna, the Artibonite, as well as smaller ones, but the mouths of all are obstructed by shallows, so that they are only navigable for light river craft. H. has a wider range of climate than any other part of the Antilles, owing to the great diversity of its relief. The yearly rainfall is abundant, but is badly distributed, the uplands are constantly bathed in dense mists or heavy dews, while other districts have hardly any rain. The mountains are densely wooded, and such valuable species as rosewood, mahogany, satinwood, pines, cedars, oaks, and ironwood are found. All tropical fruits, too, arrive at perfection, the coffee shrub yielding heavy crops, and no other region is better suited for tobacco and sugar culture. Several ores exist in abundance, gold, silver, copper, tin, etc., but the mines are no longer worked. The republic of H. owns the western part of the island, and has an area of 10,204 sq. m. At its head is a president, assisted by two chambers. This constitution dates back to 1889, and provides for freedom of worship, trial by jury, freedom of the press, etc. The population is almost entirely composed of negroes who speak a *patois* of French origin known as Creole; but French is the official language. The chief towns are Port-au-Prince (cap.), Haitien, Les Cayes, Gonaïve, Port de Paix ; and Plaisance, Gros Morne, and La Croix des Bouquets in the interior.

Hai-Yun-Tau, or **Hai Yan Tao, Battle of,** was a battle of the Chino-Japanese War of 1894-95. It was fought on Sept. 17, 1894; the Chinese fleet was commanded by Admiral Ting, and the Japanese by Vice-Admiral Ito. The battle resulted in a Japanese victory, by which they obtained the command of the sea in that quarter.

Haja-Hya, *see* COW TREE.

Hajdu-Böszörmeny, *see* BÖSZÖRMENY.

Hajdu-Dorog, a com. and market tn. of Hungary, in the prov. of Hajduken, situated 20 m. N.W. of Debreczin. Pop. 10,000.

Hajdu-Hadhaz, a tn. of Hungary, in the prov. of Hajduken, 12 m. N.E. of Debreezen. Pop. 9000.

Hajdunanas, a tn. and magistracy of Hungary, in the prov. of Hajduken, situated 20 m. S. of Tokay. Pop. 16,000.

Hajduszoboszlo, a tn. of Hungary,

in the prov. of Hajduken, 12 m. S.W. by W. of Debreczin. Pop. 15,000.

Hajipur, a tn. of Bengal, India, on the Little Gandak at its junction with the Ganges, in the Muzaffarpur dist. It has considerable water traffic. The old fort there was taken by the imperial troops in 1572 and 1574. Pop. 22,000.

Hajj, *see* HADJ.

Hakata, a seaport tn. of Japan on the N.W. coast of Kinshin Is., 70 m. N.N.E. of Nagasaki, with important manufs. of silk. Pop. 23,000.

Hake (*Merluccius*), a fish of the cod family, which has an elongated body, two dorsal fins, one short and one long, and a very long anal fin. The head is flattened, and the mouth has no barbels. It varies in length from 3 to 4 ft., and has a dark grey back, but is much lighter at the sides and underneath. It is found in the British seas, and off the coasts of Europe, and Eastern N. America, and large quantities are consumed as food, the flesh being white and flaky. The spawning season is from March to June, and during these months the fish keeps near the bottom and has to be caught by trawl-nets ; at other times it is taken by lines.

Hake, Thomas Gordon (1809-95), an English poet was born at Leeds and came of an old Devonshire family. His mother's maiden name was Gordon. He entered the medical profession, studying at St. George's Hospital and at Edinburgh, but he abandoned medicine for literature. He met with a friend in Dante Gabriel Rossetti, who keenly interested himself in his literary efforts. When he was thirty years of age he published a prose epic called *Vates*, which was reprinted as ' Valdarno ' in *Ainsworth's Magazine*. His poems were reviewed by Rossetti in the *Academy* and *Fortnightly Review*. His chief productions are *Madeline*, 1871; *Parables and Tales*, 1872; *The Serpent Play*, 1883; *New Day Sonnets*, 1890, and *Memoirs of Eighty Years*, 1892. A civil list literary pension was bestowed upon him in 1893, which he lived to enjoy for only two years.

Hakim, an Oriental word commonly used in Mohammedan countries with two distinctive meanings. A H. is both a judge or the administrative authority of a district, and a sage, or, in modern times, a physician. The word is Arabic.

Hakim-ibn-Allah, *see* AL-HAKIM-IBN-OTTO.

Hakkas (' guests ' or ' strangers '), a people of China found chiefly in Kwang-Tung, Fu-Kien, and Formosa. They differ from the Chinese in disposition, appearance, and customs, and speak a distinct dialect. They are very industrious and have great intelligence, and serve as intermediaries between the Chinese and European traders and natives. They have been persecuted by the native population for over 2000 years, but at the invasion of Kublai Khan, they distinguished themselves by their bravery on the Chinese side.

Hakluyt, Richard (1552-1616), a geographer; took holy orders and became a prebendary of Bristol, 1586, and seven years later Archdeacon of Westminster. He wrote several books on his favourite study. In 1582 he published *Divers Voyages touching the Discovery of America*, and six years afterwards issued his *Principall Navigations, Voyages, and Discoveries of the English Nation* (reprinted) 1903-5. His last work was a translation from the Portuguese, known as *Virginia Richly Valued*, 1609. The *Principall Navigations* has always been highly esteemed, and is an invaluable work. Froude called it ' the prose epic of the English nation.' H. is buried in Westminster Abbey.

Hakluyt Society was founded in 1846 for printing rare and unpublished voyages and travels. More than 150 volumes have now been issued by the society, which include *Divers Voyages*, 1850 ; *Principall Navigations;* C. R. Beazley's edition of Carpini, Rubruquis, and other mediæval texts from Hakluyt, including his *Galvano*, edited by Admiral Bethune in 1862. The society also issued Purchas's *Pilgrimes*, 1903-5.

Hakodate, or **Hakodadi,** a seaport tn. of Japan on the island of Yezo; it was formerly the capital of the island until supplanted by Sapporo. It is frequently compared with Gibraltar on account of its position. There is daily steamboat traffic with Aomori, and also passages to Yokohama, etc. The exports are edible seaweed, dried fish, fish manure, furs, sulphur, beans, pulse, etc., but foreign trade is of small account. Pop. 90,000.

Hakon, *see* HAAKON.

Hakone, a dist. and vil. of Japan in the island of Honshiu, 8 m. W.S.W. of Odawara and 58 m. S.W. of Tokio. It is noted for its scenery and its warm sulphurous and mineral waters.

Hal, or **Halle,** a tn. and com. of Belgium in prov. of S. Brabant, and the arron. of Brussels. It is situated on the Senne, and has manufs. of sugar and chicory. Pop. 13,000.

Halas, or **Kiskunhalas,** a tn. of Hungary, situated on Lake Halasto, 75 m. S.S.E. of Budapest. There is a trade in wine. Pop. 19,000.

Halberd, or **Halbert,** a weapon, which consists of a combined spear and axe, *i.e.* a wooden staff about 5¼ ft. long, surmounted by an axe-blade, the opposite end of the staff furnishing a spear. This weapon was much used during the 15th and 16th centuries, and while similar in make, Hs. varied a little in shape; some blades were extremely narrow, while others were flat, broad, and double-edged. The H. originated in Germany and Scandinavia, and later was used by the Swiss, French, and English. Now the H. is carried by yeomen of the guard on ceremonial occasions, being a mere symbol of authority.

Halberstadt, a tn. of Prussia in Saxony, situated at the base of the Harz Mts., on the R. Holzemme, a tributary of the Bode, 30 m. S.W. of Magdeburg. It is extremely quaint, many houses dating from the 15th century and decorated with fine carving. The cathedral (13th to 15th century) is Gothic and, viewed from the interior, is particularly lofty and majestic. The poet Gleim lived here, and the house where he died in 1803 was converted into a museum in 1899. Another interesting building is the 12th century Lieb-frauenkirche, or Church of Our Lady. The town has manufs. of gloves, sugar, etc., and there are railway works, paper mills, and breweries. Pop. 46,397.

Halcyon Days, *see* ALCYON.

Halcyonidæ, *see* KINGFISHER.

Haldane, James Alexander (1768-1851), a Scottish preacher, born at Dundee. When a man he settled in Edinburgh (1794) and established the Society for Propagating the Gospel at Home (1797). In this work he was aided by his brother, Robert, and friends. He seceded from the Church of Scotland and founded in Edinburgh in 1799 the first Congregational church in Scotland, and became its pastor. He wrote numerous controversial treatises, but more important are his itinerant evangelistic tours throughout Scotland. His brother built for him a great ' Tabernacle ' in Leith Walk, Edinburgh. *See* Alexander Haldane's *Lives of Robert and James A. Haldane*, 1852.

Haldane, Robert (1764-1842), a Scottish propagandist, brother of James H., born in London. He was educated at Edinburgh University, and spent some years in the navy, being present at the relief of Gibraltar, but in 1783 retired to Airthrey, near Stirling. Here he devoted himself to the advancement of Christianity, and in 1797 founded, with his brother and others, the Society for the Propagation of the Gospel at Home. He also built chapels, supported missionaries, and maintained institutions for students. He visited Geneva in 1816, and Montauban in 1817, lecturing and holding personal intercourse with theological students. Here he procured the printing of two editions of the Bible in French, and circulated a French translation of his *Evidences and Authority of Divine Revelation* (one of his most important works). He returned to Scotland in 1819. He also wrote *The Authenticity and Inspiration of the Scriptures*, and *Exposition of the Epistle to the Romans*.

Haldane of Cloan, Rt. Hon. Richard Burdon Haldane, Viscount (*b.* 1856), a British Liberal statesman and philosopher, born in Edinburgh. He was educated at the universities of Edinburgh and Göttingen, and called to the bar in 1879, becoming Queen's Counsel in 1890. He entered parliament in 1885 as member for Haddingtonshire, and retained his seat until 1911. In 1893 he was appointed a commissioner to inquire into the Featherstone Riots, and in 1903 spoke against Mr. Chamberlain's fiscal policy, his speeches having far-reaching results. He has also taken an interest in the political position of women. He has always been known as one of the ablest men of the Liberal party, and during the Boer War of 1899-1902 was conspicuous as a Liberal Imperialist, being vice-president of the Liberal League in 1901. In 1905 he was Secretary for War in Sir H. Campbell-Bannerman's cabinet, and was responsible for the scheme of replacing the militia and volunteer forces by the territorial force. He was made Viscount of Cloan in 1911, being the first to hold that title, and in 1912 succeeded Lord Loreburn as Lord High Chancellor of Great Britain. He has also made a name as a philosopher and has great knowledge of Hegelian metaphysics. From 1902-4 he was Gifford lecturer in St. Andrews University, and is now rector of Edinburgh University and chancellor of the University of Bristol. His publications include: *Essays in Philosophical Criticism* (with Professor Seth); *Life of Adam Smith;* a translation of Schopenhauer's *World as₄ Will and Idea* (with Mr. Kemp); *Education and Empire; The Pathway to Reality.*

Halde, Jean Baptiste du (1674-1743), a Jesuit, born in Paris. For many years he was occupied in adapting the letters and reports of the missionaries for publication, and from this source derived his material for his great work, *Description Geographique, Historique, etc., de la Chine*, published in 1735. This book has been translated into many languages, including English, and was long regarded as the standard work of reference on the subject of which it treats.

Haldimand, Sir Frederick (1718-91), a British general, born at Neuchâtel, Switzerland. He entered the British army in 1754 and subsequently became naturalised as an Englishman. He served in America, being present at the taking of Montreal in 1760, and became governor-general of Canada. He returned to England in 1785 and died at Neuchâtel.

Hale, a par., tn., and vil. of Cheshire, England, about 2 m. S.S.E. of Altrincham and 7 m. W.S.W. of Stockport. The parish has an acreage of 3724, and contains the Altrincham Girls' Home, established in 1883, which has accommodation for sixty girls. Pop. 8351.

Hale, Edward Everett (1822-1909), an American Unitarian minister and author, born at Boston, Massachusetts, and educated at Boston Latin School and Harvard. He was licensed to preach in 1848, and from 1846-56 was pastor of the Church of the Unity, Worcester, Massachusetts. In 1856 he became pastor of the South Congregational Society in Boston, a Unitarian church. He was a popular preacher and a successful organiser of humanitarian societies. His literary work was voluminous. He founded and edited *The Christian Examiner* and *Old and New,* and among his works were : *Elements of Christian Doctrine; The Ingham Papers; The Fortunes of Rachel; They Saw a Great Light; The New Harry and Lucy; Fifty Years; Poems; Historic Boston; Memories of a Hundred Years.* A collected edition of his works appeared in 1901.

Hale, Horatio (1817-96), an American lawyer and philologist, born in New Hampshire, son of Mrs. Sarah J. Hale (*q.v.*), graduated at Harvard in 1837. His great work, *Ethnology and Philology,* contains a large amount of valuable philological data, and met with considerable commendation. He also edited *The Iroquois Book of Rites.*

Hale, John Parker (1806-73), an American statesman, born at Rochester, New Hampshire, and admitted to the bar in 1830. In 1834 he was appointed district attorney for New Hampshire, and in 1843 returned to Congress as a Democrat. He was an opponent of slavery and of the annexation of Texas. In 1846 he was Speaker of the House of Representatives of New Hampshire, and in 1847 elected senator for that state by a combination of anti-slavery Democrats and Whigs. He was nominated for the presidency by the Liberty party in 1852. He was re-elected a senator in 1855 and again in 1859.

Hale, Sir Matthew (1609-76), an English lawyer and judge, was born at Alderley in Gloucestershire. He was called to the bar in 1637, and in 1653 became judge in the Court of Common Pleas. In 1655 he sat in Cromwell's parliament, but on the Restoration (1660), he was made chief baron of the Exchequer, and received the order of knighthood. In 1671 he was made Lord Chief Justice, but resigned in 1676 owing to ill-health. It is significant that while H. was neither a good speaker nor a bold pleader he rose to the head of his profession, but he owed his success to the fact that he steered a middle course, realising that a judge and lawyer can best serve his country who holds himself aloof from partisanship. He wrote *History of the Pleas of the Crown,* and *History of the Common Law of England.* H. was also noted for his poetry, and was the author of *Contemplations, Moral and Divine,* and numerous other books on religious subjects.

Hale, Nathan (1756-76), an American soldier, born at Coventry, Connecticut. He joined the army in 1774, and was made a captain in 1776, after participating in the siege of Boston. He volunteered to obtain information from the British lines on Long Island and in New York, but was captured by the British and executed as a spy.

Hale, Sarah Josepha (*née* Buell) (1790-1879), an American author and editor, born in Newport, New Hampshire; married David H. in 1813 and was left a widow with five children in 1822. From 1828-37 she was editor of the Boston *Ladies' Magazine,* and from 1837 of *Godey's Lady's Book.* Her best-known work is *Woman's Record; or Sketches of all Distinguished Women,* 1853.

Haleb, *see* ALEPPO.

Halebid, a vil. of Mysore, India, and the site of the ancient Dorasamudra. There are the ruins of two temples which were never completed, but which are regarded as masterpieces of Hindu architecture.

Halenia, a genus of Gentianaceæ, flourishes in cold and mountainous districts of Asia and America. Self-pollination is common among the twenty-five known species.

Halepa, *see* CANEA.

Hales (Doctor Irrefragabilis), *see* ALEXANDER OF HALES.

Hales, Alexander, *see* ALESIUS.

Hales, John (1584-1656), an English scholar and theologian, often called ' the Ever-memorable,' was born at Bath. He was educated at Corpus Christi College, Oxford, and in 1612 became public lecturer on Greek to the university. He was present at the Synod of Dort in 1618, and his reports are included in his *Golden Remains.* In 1836 he wrote a tract, *Schism and Schismatics;* this fell into the hands of Laud, who made H. one of his chaplains, and obtained for him a canonry at Windsor. In 1642 he was deprived of his office, and retired to Eton.

Hales, Stephen (1677–1761), an English philosopher, physiologist, and inventor, born at Beckesbourn; educated at Cambridge and Oxford; was curate of Teddington from 1709. He invented artificial ventilators, and other contrivances. His valuable researches in vegetable physiology were published in *Vegetable Staticks* (1727) and in animal physiology in *Statical Essays* (1733). He also wrote *Philosophical Experiments* (1739). He was a F.R.S. in 1718, Copley medallist in 1739, and vice-president of the Society of Arts in 1755, and clerk of the closet to the Princess Dowager, and chaplain to her son in 1751.

Halesia, a genus of Styracaceæ, contains about half a dozen species found in E. Asia and N. America; these are trees with drooping white flowers and a winged fruit. *H. tetraptera,* the snowdrop tree, grows in S. Carolina and attains a height of 20 ft.; it is a handsome plant with a hard wood.

Halesowen, a par. and market tn. of Worcester, England, situated in the Oldbury parl. div. The parish has an acreage of 12,439, and the town lies in a fertile valley, watered by the Stour and its feeders. There are extensive iron and steel works and manufactures of anchors, gun barrels, perambulators, agricultural implements, etc. William Shenstone, the poet is buried here. The ruins of a Premonstratensian abbey, founded in 1215, are to be seen S.W. of the town. Pop. (1911) 4121.

Halesworth, a par. and market tn. of Suffolk, England, situated on the Blyth, 2 m. N.E. of Ipswich. There are a few breweries. Pop. (1911) 2258.

Halévy, Fromental (Jacques François Fromental) (1799–1862), a French operatic composer of Jewish descent; entered Paris Conservatoire at the age of eleven, and became the pupil and friend of Cherubini, by whose musical purism he was greatly influenced. After a few still-born early works, he first gained recognition with the excellent opera, *La Juive,* 1835, adding later to his reputation by *La Reine de Chypre,* 1841; *Prometheus Bound,* 1849, and *The Tempest,* written the following year for a London production. In 1854 he was appointed secretary to the Academy of Fine Arts. His music, which consists almost entirely of

lyrical dramas, is brilliant and charming, rather than great or profound; he has been called the French Verdi. Sainte-Beuve relates that H. was a man of genial disposition and wide culture, an elegant poet, and an accomplished linguist.

Halévy, Joseph (1827–1908), a French Semitic scholar, was born at Adrianople. He has written numerous books on Semitic, Berber, Indian, and Babylonian subjects, and for some time was professor of Ethiopian at the Ecole des Hautes Etudes in Paris. In 1868 he made a journey to Northern Abyssinia to study the religion of the Jewish Falashas, and in 1869 went to Yemen in quest of Sabacan inscriptions, collecting as many as 860. His chief works are: *Etudes Berberes; Mission archéologique dans le Yémen; Recherches critique sur l'Origine de la Civilisation Babylonienne; Essai sur l'Origine des Ecritures Indiennes; Nouveau Essai sur les Inscriptions Proto-Arabes,* and *Essai sur la Langue Agaon, le Dialect des Falachas.*

Halévy, Léon (1802-83), a French man of letters, brother of Fromental H., the composer. He was born at Paris, where he studied law and became adjunct professor of literature at the Ecole Polytechnique (1831-37). In the latter year he was appointed chief of the bureau of historical monuments in the Ministry of Instruction, a post which he held for sixteen years. He wrote *Résumé de l'Histoire des Juifs,* 1827-28; *Poésies Européennes,* 1837; *Recueils de fables,* 1844 ; *La Grèce Tragique,* 1845-61, besides a *Life* of his brother, and several dramatic pieces.

Halévy, Ludovic (1834–1908), a French dramatist, was born in Paris. From his early years he was connected with the stage, his uncle Fromental H. being associated with the opera, and his father Léon H. being a dramatist. In 1855 he became acquainted with Offenbach, and wrote *Entrez, messieurs, mesdames* for the opening night of his theatre in the Champs Elysées. Other works followed, and he became famous by the production of his *Orphée aux enfers,* a musical parody (a translation of which was produced at His Majesty's Theatre, London, in 1911 by Tree). About 1860 he met Henri Meilhac, and the two collaborated, producing operettas, farces, and comedies. Their works met with extraordinary success, both being endowed with wit, humour, and observation of character. The most celebrated were: *La Belle Hélène; Barbe Bleu ; La Grande Duchesse de Gérolstein;* and *La Périchole.* Their attempts at more serious drama were not so successful, but *Froufrou,* 1869, made a great hit. Of their lighter comedies, the best known are: *Les Sonnettes; Toto chez Tata; Le Roi Candaule; La Cigale; Madame attend Monsieur.* H. has also made a name as a novelist, and was elected to the French Academy in 1884, his *L'Abbé Constantin*, 1882, being a great favourite, containing as it does such delightful characters, in direct contrast to those of Zola. Other works of his are: *La Famille Cardinal; Criquette; Mariette; Karikari; Deux Mariages.*

Halfa, *see* ESPARTO.

Half-blood, related through one parent only. When two persons are born of the same father, but not of the same mother, they are said to have a consanguinean relation one to the other, but if they have the same mother, and not the same father, their relationship is said to be uterine. In the succession to real or landed property a kinsman of the H. inherits next after a kinsman of the whole blood in the same degree, and after the issue of such kinsman when the common ancestor is a male, but next after the common ancestor when such ancestor is a female. So that brothers consanguinean inherit next after the sisters of the whole blood and their issue ; and brothers uterine inherit next after the mother.

Half Dome, or **South Dome,** a granite mountain of California, situated near the eastern end of the Yosemite Valley. It is separated from North Dome by the cañon of the Tenaya Fork, and rises 8800 ft. above the sea level.

Halford, Sir Henry (1766-1844), a physician, born at Leicester, was the son of Dr. James Vaughan. He studied at Christ Church, Oxford, and then went to Edinburgh. In 1793 he was elected physician to the Middlesex Hospital, and fellow of the Royal College of Physicians in 1794. He changed his name from Vaughan to Halford in 1809 on coming into a large fortune, and the same year was created a baronet by George III. He was president of the College of Physicians in 1820, and it was chiefly owing to him that the college was removed from Warwick Lane to Pall Mall East in 1825. He was appointed physician extraordinary to George III., and also attended George IV., William IV., and Queen Victoria. He published *Essays and Orations delivered at the Royal College of Physicians; Nugœ Metricœ.*

Half-pay, an allowance given in the British army (corresponding to the French *demi-solde*) to commissioned officers who are not actively employed, and is most commonly granted to those who have been promoted to higher rank when there is no vacancy for them. Officers, as a rule, can be put on H. at their own request or if suffering from illness, but can only continue on the list for five years, after which period they must resign, permanent H. having been abolished in 1884. They are then placed on ' retired pay,' and are liable to be called upon to serve in case of great emergency, or when the country is in peril.

Half-pike, the name of a weapon, a small variety of pike (*q.v.*) of about half the usual length. H. were subdivided into ' spontoons,' which were used by the infantry officers, and ' boarding pikes,' used in the navy for repelling boarders of vessels.

Haliartus, an ancient tn. of Greece in Bœotia, situated on a hill overlooking Lake Copais. It was burnt down by Xerxes (480 B.C.) and rebuilt. In 395 B.C. the Thebans defeated Lysander in front of H. It was finally destroyed in 371 B.C. by the Romans.

Haliburton, Thomas Chandler (1796-1865), an author, was born in Nova Scotia. Called to the bar there, he eventually rose to be chief justice, to which high office he was appointed in 1828. He retired in 1856, when he came to England, where he resided until his death. He was the author of many books, including histories of his native province; but it is for his writings under the pseudonym of ' Sam Slick ' that he became best known. The three series of *The Clockmaker, or Sayings and Doings of Sam Slick of Slickville,* 1837-40, were reprinted in England and attracted much attention. His wit was racy, and the rigour of his outspokenness was only gilded by the humorous coating under which he disguised it. There is a memoir by F. Blake Crofton (1889).

Halibut, or **Holibut,** so called because it was commonly eaten on holy days, is the name given to *Hippoglossus vulgaris,* a species of Pleuronectidæ, or flat-fishes (*q.v.*). It has both eyes on the right side, which is brown with deeper coloured markings, the under side being white; the mouth is symmetrically placed and very capacious; the body is smooth and covered with small oval scales. The H. attains considerable size, specimens 7 or 8 ft. in length being common on the coasts of N. America, but the flesh of smaller fishes is more highly esteemed; these are abundant on all the Atlantic coasts, though infrequent in the English Channel.

Halicarnassus, an ancient Greek city of Asia Minor, on the site of the modern Budrun, situated on the S.W. coast of Caria on the Ceramic Gulf. Originally it was built partly on the island of Zephyria, but the latter became united to the mainlaid during the course of time, and the city consequently was extended. It was founded by the Dorians who settled there from Trœzen, and was in 334 B.C. almost destroyed by the Macedonians. In 352 B.C. the Mausoleum—the tomb of Mausolus—was erected, which was regarded as one of the seven wonders of the world. It consisted of a basement 142 ft. by 92 ft., a pedestal, Ionic columns, a pyramid, and a chariot group. Herodotus and Dionysius were born in the city.

Halicz, or **Galicz,** a tn of Galicia, Austria, situated on the Dniester, 48 m. W.S.W. of Tarnapol and 70 m. S.S.E. of Lemberg. Salt and soap are manufactured, and a trade in lumber is also carried on. Pop. 4957.

Halidon Hill, a hill situated 2 m. N.W. of Berwick-on-Tweed, England. It is noted for a battle fought, in 1333, between the English and Scots, when the latter were defeated.

Halifax, a municipal co. and bor. of W. Riding, Yorkshire, England, situated on the Calder, 7 m. S.W. of Bradford, 16 m. S.W. of Leeds, and 194 m. N.N.W. of London. It is served by the Great Northern Railway and the Lancashire and Yorkshire railways. It ranks with Bradford, Leeds, and Huddersfield in the woollen and worsted manufacture; carpets are a special feature. The cotton industry is also carried on, and in the vicinity are important coal-mines and iron and steel works; stone is also quarried. The town is chiefly modern, and contains some noteworthy buildings, including the town hall, museum and art gallery, and mechanics' institute. The Parish Church dates from the 12th century; the Piece or Cloth Hall, erected in 1799, is now used as a market. Pop. (1911) 101,553.

Halifax, a city and cap. of Nova Scotia, Canada, situated on the E. coast on a fortified eminence on Chebucto Bay. The harbour is 6 m. long and 1 m. wide, and is open all through the year, having splendid anchorage. It has two entrances which are formed by McNab's Island, situated in the mouth, and in the N. it is connected by a narrow channel with Bedford Basin, which is deep enough for the largest vessels. Until 1905 this was the sole point in Canada with a garrison of British regular troops. It is the Atlantic terminus of the Intercolonial, Canadian Pacific, and other railways. The exports are fish, lumber, fruit, etc., and the imports are sugar, rum, and British manufs. Pop. 53,000.

Halifax, Charles Lindley Wood,

second **Viscount** (b. 1839), born in London; educated at Eton and Christ Church, Oxford. From 1862-70 he was groom of the bedchamber to the Prince of Wales, and in 1886 served on the Ecclesiastical Commission for England. In 1867 he became president of the English Church Union, and in 1895 visited Rome as representative of the extreme High Church party, in an unsuccessful attempt to obtain a papal acknowledgment of the validity of Anglican orders and sacraments. The only result was considerable discussion in the press and ecclesiastical circles.

Halifax, Charles Montagu, Earl of (1661-1715), an English statesman and poet, born at Horton in Northamptonshire. He was educated at Westminster School and Trinity College, Cambridge, and assisted Newton in forming the Philosophical Society of Cambridge. In 1687 he wrote (with Matthew Prior) *The Country Mouse and the City Mouse* (a parody on Dryden's *Hind and Panther*), which secured him a great reputation. In 1689 he entered parliament as member for Malden; in 1692 was made Lord of the Treasury, and introduced the national debt by raising a loan of £1,000,000. In 1694 he introduced a bill for the incorporation of the Bank of England, following out Paterson's idea, and was for this made Chancellor of the Exchequer. In 1695 he took measures to remedy the currency, and in 1697 was made First Lord of the Treasury. In 1698 and 1699 he acted as one of the council of regency during the king's absence from England, and in 1699 accepted the auditorship of the Exchequer. He was impeached for malpractices in 1701 and 1703, and continued out of office during the reign of Queen Anne, but became First Lord of the Treasury on the accession of George I. He is especially famous as being a minister of finance.

Halifax, George Montagu, second **Earl of** (1716-71), assumed the title Dunk on his marriage, in 1741, to Anne Richards, the heiress of Sir Thomas Dunk. In 1748 he was made president of the Board of Trade, and helped to found Halifax, Nova Scotia. In 1757 he entered the cabinet, and in 1761 was appointed Lord Lieutenant of Ireland, and First Lord of the Admiralty. In 1762 he became Secretary of State for the Northern Department under the Earl of Bute.

Halifax, George Savile, Marquis of (1633-95), an English statesman, born at Thornhill, Yorkshire. In 1660 he was elected member for Pontefract, and in 1668 was created Baron Savile of Eland and Viscount

Halifax. He took an active part in passing through parliament the Test Act of 1673; in 1680 was instrumental in getting the Exclusion Bill rejected, and in 1688 took the popular side on the occasion of the trial of the bishops. On the accession of William III. he was made Lord Privy Seal, and had considerable influence. H. was a great statesman and consistent in his principles, although he was not appreciated in his own day, earning for himself the title of 'Trimmer,' which he defended in *Character of a Trimmer*

Halifax Law, properly known as the Gibbet Law, was a curious custom enacted at an early period of the woollen manufacture to protect the trade. By this law the inhabitants were empowered to execute any one taken within their liberty who had stolen property of the value of 13½d. or above. The accused were tried by the frith-burghers, and if found guilty were executed on a gibbet (an instrument similar to a guillotine) outside the town on a market-day. The last execution took place in 1650.

Haliotis, a genus of gasteropods, belonging to the family of Haliotidæ, and to the sub-order Rhipidoglossa of the order Aspidobranchia. The H. is found all over the globe: it lives in the littoral zone and fastens itself on to rocks like limpets. The shell has a wide mouth, and from its shape is often referred to as the 'ear shell' (*cf.* the French name *oreille de mer* and the English contraction *ormer*). The outer margin is perforated with holes, which are useful for containing the pallial folds, but are closed up after growth. Not only the shell but the animal, too, are splendidly iridescent; the 'Nacre' or 'mother of pearl' is much sought after for ornament.

Halitherium, *see* Dugong.

Halkirk, a vil. of Caithness, Scotland, on the Thurso. Flagstones are quarried and exported, and there is a distillery. Pop. (1911) 2158.

Hall, in architecture, a term used in several senses: 1. A large room in a private or public building. Thus the *tepidarium* of the Roman baths, and the interior of Egyptian temples are spoken of as Hs. In the middle ages the H. was the most important room in the residence of an English nobleman. It may be said, in fact, that it was the only important room. Here all the inhabitants of the house, the lord, the ladies, the family, and the retainers, met for their meals, and here many of the latter slept. The prominence of the college Hs. at the universities is a survival of this system, and their presence shows who the mediæval H. retained its im-

portance even after the multiplication of private rooms. The mediæval Hs. were simple in plan, consisting generally of a low, oblong apartment lighted from side windows. The public H. is a large room built for lectures, meetings, concerts, entertainments, or some such purposes. The name is often extended to the entire building, as especially in the town H. and the music H. 2. In Britain the term H. is applied to a large and important mansion, more especially in country districts. 3. In recent times it has also been given to the vestibule of a building when it is large enough to merit it. Generally, the title is given if the room or passage into which the outer doors open is large enough to contain some furniture, but the term is often used very loosely.

Hall, a health resort of Austria in the Tyrol, situated on the R. Inn at an elevation of 1835 ft., 5 m. from Innsbruck. It has noted mineral and brine springs, and 7 m. N. of the town are the Salzberg salt mines. Pop. 7519.

Hall, or **Bad-Hall**, a watering-place of Upper Austria, 10 m. W. of Steyer and 25 m. S. of Linz. It is famous for its saline and iodine springs, which have been known since the 8th century; they belong to the government; and the iodine waters are exported. Pop. 1000.

Hall, or **Schwäbisch-Hall**, a tn. of Germany in Würtemberg, situated on the R. Kocher, 35 m. N.E. of Stuttgart, and 34 m. E. of Heilbronn. It is noted as a health resort, possessing brine springs. Salt is produced, and other industries are the manuf. of metal ware, machines, soap, starch, etc.; there are iron foundries and tanneries. Pop. 9321.

Hall, Anna Maria (*née* Fielding) (1800-81), an Irish authoress, born at Dublin; came to London in 1815, and in 1824 married Samuel Carter H. (*q.v.*). She was prominent in charitable work and assisted in the foundation of Brompton Consumption Hospital. Her works include: *Sketches of Irish Character*, 1829; *Tales of Woman's Trials*, 1834; *The French Refugee* (a play), 1837; *Lights and Shadows of Irish Life*, 1838; *Tales of the Irish Peasantry*, 1840; *Marian, or A Young Maid's Fortunes*, 1840; *Midsummer Eve*, 1848; *A Woman's Story*, 1857; *Can Wrong be Right*, 1862; and *The Flight of Faith*, 1868-69.

Hall, Basil (1788-1844), a British naval officer, born at Edinburgh. He entered the navy in 1802, and was present at the battle of Corunna in 1809, on board the *Endymion*. In 1816 he went to China with Lord

Amherst's embassy, and described the incidents of the commission and the explorations in the Eastern seas, etc., in his *Account of a Voyage of Discovery to the West Coast of Corea and the Great Loo-Choo Islands*, 1818. He also published *Philosophical Transactions; Extracts from a Journal written on the Coasts of Chili, Peru, and Mexico;* and *Fragments of Voyages and Travels*, which contains, besides the subject-matter of the title, some interesting accounts of the navy in the early part of the 19th century. In 1842 H.'s mind gave way, and he ended his days in Haslar Hospital.

Hall, Charles Francis (1821-71), an American Arctic explorer, born at Rochester, New Hampshire. He was for some time a journalist, but offered his services to the American Geographical Society in 1859 to go in search of Franklin. He sailed in 1860 on board a whaler, but was icebound and lived among the Eskimos for two years. He described his experiences in *Arctic Researches, and Life among the Esquimaux*, 1864. He made another expedition in 1864 and was more successful, finding out some information respecting Franklin's crew. In 1871 he went on a North Polar expedition in the *Polaris* and reached 82° 11′ N. latitude, the highest point hitherto attained.

Hall, Chester Moor (1703-71), an English optical inventor, born in Essex; was a bencher of the Inner Temple in 1763. In 1733 he anticipated Dolland in the invention of the achromatic telescope.

Hall, Christopher Newman (1816-1902), an English Congregational minister, born at Maidstone, graduated at the University of London. From 1842-54 he was minister of Albion Chapel, Hull, in 1854 became minister of Surrey Chapel or Christchurch, Blackfriars Road, London, originally founded by Rowland Hill. He was a very popular preacher, and in 1876 a new church was opened for him in Kennington Road, Lambeth, where he remained till 1892. He was the author of numerous devotional works, many of which had a large sale.

Hall, Edward (c. 1499-1547), an English historian, born in London; educated at Eton and Cambridge. He was a common sergeant of law in 1532, and a reader at Gray's Inn in 1533 and 1540, and in 1540 a judge of the sheriff's court. He became M.P. for Bridgnorth in 1542 and a commissioner to enquire into Transgressions of the Six Articles (1541-44). His *Union of the Noble and Illustre Famelies of Lancastre and York* (1542) was followed by Shakespeare.

Hall, Edwin Thomas (b. 1851), an architect, educated at S. Kensington. He has been the architect for a large number of public buildings in London, including Plaistow Hospital, Camberwell Infirmary, and Dulwich College Library. He was at one time vice-president of the R.I.B.A., and has held various other appointments, being also the author of several works such as *Flats, British and Foreign*, 1907.

Hall, Professor Francis J., D.D. (b. 1857), a professor of theology in Western Theological Seminary, Chicago, educated at Racine College, New York, and Western Theological Seminary, Chicago. In 1898 he was granted the degree of D.D. by Kenyon College, and in 1910 by the General Theological Seminary. In 1886 he was ordained priest and appointed to his present position as professor of theology. He has written: *Theological Outlines*, 1892-95; *The Being and Attributes of God*, 1909; *The Trinity*, 1910.

Hall, James (1811-98), an American geologist, born at Hingham, Massachusetts; educated at Rensselaer School, Troy, under Amos Eaton. In 1837 he became one of the state geologists of New York and commenced the survey of the western part of the state; in 1855 he was appointed chief state geologist of Iowa; in 1858 of Wisconsin, and in 1866 of New York. His *Palæontology of New York* (3 vols., 1847-59) contains the results of his researches in Silurian fossils.

Hall, Joseph (1574-1656), an English satirist, born at Ashby-de-la-Zouch, Leicestershire. He was educated at Emmanuel College, Cambridge, and while here wrote his *Virgidemiarum*, 1597, in which he claims to be the first English satirist. For this he was attacked by Marston in 1598, and the works of both were burnt in 1599. In 1608 he became chaplain to Prince Henry; in 1616 Dean of Worcester, and in 1627 Bishop of Exeter. His religious views corresponded with those of Charles I., but he was frequently blamed by Laud for his lenience to the Puritans. He defended the English Church in *Episcopacy by Divine Right*, and *Remonstrance to the High Court of Parliament*, which latter produced a reply from the Puritans in the shape of 'Smectymnuus.' Thus began a long controversy in which Milton took part, attacking H. for his early satires. In 1641 he was translated to Norwich, but at the end of the year was expelled from office and suffered imprisonment under the Long Parliament. When released he retired to Higham. He is best known by his early work.

Hall, Marie (b. 1884), a violinist, born at Newcastle-on-Tyne. At the age of ten she studied under Sir Edward Elgar for a year, and then under Max Mossel in Birmingham for three years. She has also been taught by Professor Johann Kruse and Sevcik, and made her début in 1902 at Vienna when only eighteen. Since then she has visited England, America, Canada, New Zealand, Australia, S. Africa, India, etc., her first appearance in London being at St. James' Hall in 1903. She is considered one of the finest players of the day.

Hall, Marshall (1790–1857), an English physiologist, born near Nottingham; graduated M.D. at Edinburgh in 1812, and visited foreign medical schools, 1814-15. He practised in Nottingham (1817-25), and in London (1826-53). His speciality was nervous diseases, and his main contributions to medical science are his discovery of reflex action, his rational treatment of epilepsy, and his introduction of methods of resuscitation in asphyxia and drowning. He published numerous medical and scientific works.

Hall, Owen (c. 1848-1907), the penname of James Davis, a dramatic author. He practised as a solicitor from 1874-86, but abandoned law for literature, and edited the *Bat*, 1885-87; the *Phœnix*, 1899 (which he started), and assisted in the editorship of the *Messenger*. He also contributed to *Truth*, *The World*, *The Illustrated London News*, and *The Ladies' Pictorial*. But he is chiefly famous as a writer of musical comedy, his chief plays being: *A Gaiety Girl; An Artist's Model; The Geisha; A Greek Slave; Florodora; The Silver Slipper; The Girl from Kay's;* and *The Medal and the Maid.* He was also part author with James Tanner of *All Abroad*, and wrote four novels: *Eureka; Jetsam; The Track of a Storm;* and *Hernando.*

Hall, Robert (1764-1831), an English Baptist minister, born at Arnsby, Leicestershire ; educated at Bristol and Aberdeen. In 1785 he became assistant to Caleb Evans at Broadmead Chapel, near Bristol, and in 1791 succeeded Robert Robinson at the Baptist church in Cambridge. He was temporarily insane during 1804-6. In 1807 he took charge of Harvey Lane Church, Leicester, remaining there till 1826, when he returned to Bristol. His published sermons and other works rank high.

Hall, Samuel Carter (1800-89), an editor and critic, born at Waterford, Ireland; came to London in 1821; was literary secretary to Ugo Foscolo (1822), and a reporter in the House of Lords, 1823. In 1826 he founded *The Amulet*, and edited it till 1837; from 1830-6 was connected with the *New Monthly Magazine ;* from 1839-80, edited the *Art Union Monthly* (' Art Journal ') and published several books.

Hallam, Arthur Henry (1811-33), an English poet, son of Henry H., historian, born in Bedford Place, London. He was educated at Eton and Trinity College, Cambridge. In 1829 he visited Italy with his parents, and on his return wrote some excellent Italian sonnets. He entered the Inner

ARTHUR HENRY HALLAM

Temple, 1832, but his health broke down, and whilst travelling on the Continent with his father, he died in Vienna. He was an intimate friend of Tennyson who commemorated his death in *In Memoriam.*

Hallam, Henry (1777-1859), an historian, was one of the first English historians of importance to go to original documents for his material. The result of this careful research work is that his books, in spite of the investigations of his successors, still hold a place as standard authorities. He was not a brilliant writer, but he was impartial, and he was usually accurate. His first great work, published in 1818, was *A View of the State of Europe in the Middle Ages*, and this at once gave him a recognised position. It was followed nine years later by *The Constitutional History of England from the Accession of Henry VII. to the Death of George II.*, and his third important book appeared in 1837-39, *The Introduction to the Literature of Europe during the*

Fifteenth, Sixteenth, and Seventeenth Centuries.

Hallamshire, a dist. of W. Riding, Yorkshire, England, which comprises the parishes of Sheffield and Ecclesfield. Its character is that of forest and moorland.

Halland, a maritime län of Gotaland, Sweden. Said to have been acquired by the Danish hero ' Dan ' in the 6th century; ceded to Sweden at peace of Bromsebro, 1645. Area 1900 sq. m. Pop. 146,000.

Halle, or **Halle-an-der-Saale**, a tn. on the Saale, 18 m. E. by S. of Eisleben, connected by railway with Leipzig, Berlin, Frankfort, Hanover, and Magdeburg, in the province of Saxony, Prussia. Its university was founded in 1694, and considerably augmented in 1817, when it was amalgamated with that of Wittenburg. Among the many buildings of interest may be mentioned the Gothic Marienkirche and the cathedral, now in the hands of the Calvinists (16th century); the mediæval town hall in the market square, where stands a bronze statue of Handel, who was born in Halle, and the 12th century St. Moritzkirche. The chief industries are paraffin and sugar refining, and the manufacture of machinery, spirits, cocoa, cement, etc. The commercial prosperity depends largely on lignite beds in the vicinity. Close by are important salt works controlled by a non-German people who still preserve distinctive dress and customs. In 806 A.D. H. was fortified by Charlemagne's son; in 965 it came under the control of the Archbishop of Magdeburg, and later it became an influential Hanse town. Pop. (1910) 180,551.

Hallé, Sir Charles (1819-95), an Anglo-German pianist, born at Hagen in Westphalia. In 1836 he went to Paris, where he became friendly with Cherubini, Chopin, Liszt, De Musset, and George Sand, but was compelled to leave France in 1848 and came to London. Here he started pianoforte recitals, and it was mainly due to him that Beethoven's sonatas became so well known in England. He frequently performed at concerts, and in 1853 was director of the Gentlemen's Concerts in Manchester. In 1888 he married Madame Norman-Neruda, the violinist, and toured with her in 1890 and 1891. H.'s band was one of the best in England, and his pianoforte playing was remarkable for its precision and clearness of tone as well as for its faithful interpretation of the composer's idea.

Hallé, Lady (Madame Wilma Maria Francisca Norman-Neruda) (1839-1911), a violinist, born in Moravia.

At an early age she began to play the violin, and excited great admiration in 1846, at Vienna, by her fine rendering of one of Bach's sonatas. She rapidly became famous, appearing in the London Philharmonic Concerts, as well as in France and Russia, and in 1901 was appointed violinist to Queen Alexandra. In 1908 she played at the concert in London in memory of Joachim, with whom she had been very friendly. She was remarkable for technique, and was the first of the women violinists to compare with men in fulness of tone.

Halleck, Fitz-Greene (1790-1867), an American poet, born at Guildford, Connecticut; became a clerk in New York, and in 1832 secretary to John Jacob Astor, who left him an annuity, upon which he retired in 1849. His first poems which attracted attention appeared in 1818-19 in the New York *Evening Post*, under the signature of ' Croaker & Co.,' designating himself and J. R. Drake. His work includes *Fanny* (1820), a satire upon contemporary literature, fashions, and politics, and *Marco Bozzaris*. His complete works appeared in 1868-69, edited by J. G. Wilson.

Halleck, Henry Wager (1815-72), an American general, born at Westerville, New York. From 1841-46 he was employed on the defence works at New York, and in 1845 visited the principal military establishments in Europe. On his return he lectured on the science of war, publishing them under the title of *Elements of Military Art and Science*. He served in Mexico in 1846, and in 1849 helped to frame the state constitution of California. In 1862 he was made commander-in-chief of the federal forces. He wrote: *International Law; The Mining Laws of Spain and Mexico*, etc.

Hälleflinta (Swedish), an extremely hard rock consisting of a mixture of quartz and felspar, but chlorite, mica, iron ores, and other minerals are frequently present, and many examples are striated. It is of a white, grey, yellow, green, or pink colour, and when seen under a microscope is very finely crystalline. It is found with gneisses and schists in the Scandinavian Peninsula, but rocks very similar occur in the Tyrol, in Galicia, and Eastern Bohemia.

Hallein, a tn. of Salzburg, Austria, on R. Salzach, 8 m. S.E. of Salzburg. Has famous salt mines and brine baths. Pop. 7128.

Hallelujah (Heb. ' Praise ye Jevovah '), a term which is used as a doxology by both Jews and Christians, the custom dating from very early times. It is not used in the penetential seasons, being essentially a song of gladness, and in the time of St. Augustine was only sung from the feast of Easter to that of Pentecost. Later, however, it was only omitted in Advent and Lent and on the vigils of the principal festivals. The word was inserted in the Prayer Book after the first Gloria Patri in 1549, and in 1552 was translated to ' Praise ye the Lord.'

Haller, Albrecht von (1708-77), a Swiss poet, anatomist, and physiologist, born at Bern. His poem *Die Alpen*, written in 1729, which was the result of a journey through the Alps, is important historically as being one of the first written in appreciation of the Alps, and his other poems, lyrical and didactic, show him to be among the regenerators of German poetry. He at first practised as a physician at Bern, gaining a name for his anatomical investigations, as well as for his botanical researches, and in 1736 he was appointed professor of medicine, etc., at the University of Göttingen, but resigned in 1753. His chief works are: *Icones Anatomicæ; De Respiratione; Opuscula Pathologica ; Enumeratio Stirpium Helveticarum ;* and *Gedichte.*

Haller, Johann (*c.* 1792-1826), a German sculptor, was born at Innsbruck. He studied at the Royal Academy, Munich, where he attracted the attention of King Ludwig. He was responsible for the huge statues in front of the Glyptothek, and was commissioned to execute the statuary for the gable end of the same to be done in Rome. He was unable to finish it owing to ill-health. He came home and died in his thirty-fifth year. Among his works are the busts of several well-known men.

Hallett, Holt S. (1845-1911), an engineer and author, was employed (1860-68) in building railways through Lancashire and Cheshire, and for the twelve years following (1868-80) was in the service of the Public Works Department in India. The Indian and Burmese railway systems were constructed largely at his suggestion and in accordance with his practical recommendations. In 1883-84 he discovered the source of the Menam and made a preliminary survey for a branch line to Bangkok. He advised the annexation of Upper Burmah, and his *Joint Report on Railway Connection of Burmah and China*, which was drawn up with a personal knowledge of those countries, was submitted by request to the Foreign and War Offices. H. wrote a great deal on social and economic questions affecting India.

Halley, Edmund (1656-1742), an astronomer, was born at Haggerston, London. In 1676 he went to St. Helena

to observe the stars, earning for himself the title of the ' Southern Tycho.' In 1682 he began his study of the moon, and the important problem of gravity, which resulted in the publication of Newton's *Principia* (1698-1700). He studied the variation of the compass in the Atlantic, and published his results in a *General Chart of the Variation of the Compass* in 1701. In 1703 he was made Savilian professor of geometry at Oxford, and in 1720 succeeded Flamsteed as astronomer-royal, and carried out a complete observation of the moon through a period of eighteen years. He is famous for having detected the ' long equality ' of Jupiter and Saturn, for his method of determining the solar parallax by means of the transits of Venus, for his prediction of the return of the comet of 1682, which occurred in 1759, and his discovery of the proper motions of the fixed stars, etc.

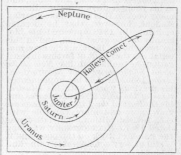

Halley's Comet, the name of the most celebrated of the periodic comets, taking its name from Edmund Halley (*q.v.*), who, in 1705, predicted that the comet of 1682 would return in 1759. This prediction proved true, and the comet has since returned in 1835 and 1910, its period being seventy-five years. Halley thought that the comets of 1531 and 1607 were identical with his own, and it may be taken as practically certain that the comet of 1066, depicted on the Bayeux

BAYEUX TAPESTRY COMET

Tapestry, is H. C. It is also quite possible that it is the same as the comets mentioned in the Chinese records as having been seen in 87 B.C. and 240 B.C. At aphelion H. C. is thirty-three times more distant from the sun than the earth is.

Hallgrimsson, Jonas (1807-45), an Icelandic poet and critic. After 1832 he lived mainly in Denmark, but was one of the chief agents in the reformation of Icelandic poetry. His chief poem, *Gunmarsholmi*, has been translated into English by D. Leith (1897). His views on literature were largely disseminated in the paper *Fjölnir*, and he also wrote numerous independent critical papers.

Halling, a par. and vil. in Kent, England, situated on the Medway, 3½ m. S.S.W. of Rochester. The chief industry is connected with Portland cement. Pop. (1911) 2337.

Halliwell-Phillipps, James Orchard (1820-89), a biographer, was all his life a collector of books and MSS., and in his younger days was the editor of many books. It is as a Shakespearian student, however, that he became eminent. In 1848 appeared his biography of the great poet, and in this he brought to light much new material. As the result of further investigation he published his *New Boke about Shakespeare and Stratford-on-Avon*, 1850. In 1863 he supplemented his previous works with his *Illustrations of the Life of Shakespeare*, and his *Outlines of the Life of Shakespeare* grew more and more valuable with each revised edition. The latest was dated 1887. His biography was long the standard work on the poet, and it is still of very considerable value and interest.

Hall-marks, or **Plate-marks.** There are a great number of Acts going back to the reign of Henry VI. relating to the assaying of gold and silver plate and the marking of the same. An Act of 1738 provided that no gold plate should be made, or in any way commercially dealt with, unless marked as of 22 carats, and no silver plate unless marked as of 11 oz. 2 dwt. per lb. troy. By a later Act the gold standard was reduced to 18 carats, and a still later Act permitted gold plate of any standard to be wrought, provided not less than one-third part was fine gold. By the combined operation of the Acts of 1700 and 1739 all gold and silver wares must, before being sold or exported, be marked with : (1) The initials of the worker or marker. (2) The assay mark or mark appointed to be used by one of the assaying towns, York, Exeter, Bristol, Chester, Norwich, and Newcastle-on-Tyne. Most of these assay marks have fallen into disuse. If not made in an assaying town, then with the arms of the town where made. (3) A *variable* mark or letter in Roman character to denote the year in which the plate was made. Gold ware of 22 or 18 carats' fineness must in addition to the above marks, bear the *standard* mark of a crown and the figure 22 or 18 respectively; and silver of 11 oz. 10 dwt. and 11 oz. 2 dwt. fineness, the standard marks of *Britannia* and a lion *passant*. The other mark of the Company of Goldsmiths, the leopard's head, is no longer necessary. By an Act passed in 1790, the following articles need not be marked: (1) Chains, necklace beads, lockets, filigree work, shirt buckles or broaches (*sic*), stamped medals, or spouts to china, stone, or earthenware teapots of any weight whatsoever; (2) tippings, mounts or swages under 10 dwt. in weight, except necks and collars for castors, cruets, or glasses appertaining to any sort of stands or frames; (3) articles of silver under 5 dwt. in weight, but the following must be marked: Necks, collars, and tops for castors, cruets, or glasses appertaining to any sort of stands or frames, buttons, solid sleeve buttons and studs not having a bissilled edge soldered on, wrought seals, blank seals, bottle tickets, shoe clasps, patch boxes, salt spoons, salt shovels, salt ladles, tea spoons, tea strainers, caddy ladles, buckles (shirt buckles or broaches before mentioned excepted), and pieces to garnish cabinets, or knife cases, or tea chests, or bridles, or stands, or frames. Rings were exempted by the Act of 1734, but now gold wedding rings must be marked as gold plate. Plated goods and makers of Sheffield, or districts within a radius of 100 m. of Sheffield, are entitled to mark their goods with their firm's name. An Act of 1904 provides for the compulsory hall-marking of all foreign imported plate, except ornamental plate made before 1800. Gold foreign watch-cases stamped at any assay office in Great Britain must be marked ' Foreign,' together with a cross-shaped shield; silver cases with an octagonal-shaped shield.

Halloween, Halloweven, or **All Hallowe'en,** the name given to the 31st of October, the eve of All Saints or Hallowmas. The day was observed in very early times, and it was generally believed that it was the time of all others when supernatural influences prevailed, indeed this day is still called the ' Vigil of Saman ' (Saman being the lord of death) in some parts of Ireland. In Scotland and England, H. was long observed by fireside revelries which were chiefly concerned with divination of the future. These revelries are admirably described by Burns in his poem *Hallowe'en*.

Hallstatt, a small tn. in the Salzkammeraut, in the extreme S.W. of Upper Austria, on the W. shore of the Hallstättersee or Lake of Halstatt 16 m. N.E. of Radstadt. The town is picturesquely built, connecting stairways taking the place of streets to a large extent and stands in a district noted for its salt mines and its archæological interest, being rich in pre-Roman antiquities. The lake on which it stands is about 6 m. long and from 400-650 ft. deep. Alt. 1620 ft. It abounds in fish, and is noted for its wild and gloomy scenery. Pop. of town about 1000.

Hall-Stevenson, John (1718-85), an author; was a friend of Laurence Sterne, and the ' Eugerius ' of that writer's works. He wrote an imitation of *Tristram Shandy* and a continuation of *A Sentimental Journey*. His principal book is *Crazy Tales*, 1762, a collection of clever verses, disfigured, as all his writings are, by coarseness of expression and thought. He entertained 'at his seat, Skelton Castle, a club called The Demoniacs, of which Sterne was a member. There is an account of him in Melville's *Life and Letters of Sterne*, 1911.

Hallström, Per (*b.* 1866), a Swedish writer, and a native of Stockholm. For some years he worked as a civil servant in the post-office, but he definitely resigned his position in 1897. In spite of his humorous vein, which reveals to him the comic side of life, H. ranks in literature with the idealists. Laughter and sorrow are inextricably blended in his novels as in life, but it is the purity and charm of his prose which his countrymen especially single out for praise. Among his works are : *Vilsna Fåglar*, 1894 ; *Purpur*, 1895; *Våren*, 1898; *Thanatos*, 1901 ; and *Döda Fallet*, 1902.

Hallucination (from Lat. *alucinari*, to wander in mind ; Gk. ἄλη, wandering), the perception of an object which does not exist, while illusion consists in a wrong interpretation of the sensory object. H. may or may not involve delusion, *i.e.* belief in the reality of the object falsely perceived. Sane people can recognise almost at once that their brains are playing them tricks, whereas the insane or those under the influence of hypnotism are not able to do so. Hs. of all the senses occur, but those connected with sight and hearing are the most common, the human figure and the human voice being the objects most frequently perceived. Nearly every healthy person is able to confess that he has experienced one H., *i.e.* has

seen the figure of one with whom he is acquainted quite clearly defined, or has heard his voice, when he himself has been fully awake, and has only been able to recognise the unreality of the figure by its noiseless movements and disappearance. This H. in the ' waking ' state has been investigated by the Society of Psychical Research, and many theories have been put forward to account for it, especially for what is known as ' veridical ' H., *i.e.* that which is apparently caused by actual occurrences, *e.g.* the death of a person at the time of the appearance of his wraith, the results being published in *Phantasms of the Living*, etc. It has not, however. yet been proved that ' forces ' exist in nature to cause this, and indeed no one has ever yet heard or seen anything which he had not previously heard or seen, which points to the fact that H. is a brain phenomenon. Every impression on the senses is conducted through the nerves to the cells of the brain, and the person is then conscious of the thing heard, or seen, or felt, and an image is registered if the impression is repeated or lasting. This image can be conjured up at any time, and often seems as real as the original impression. But it generally depends upon the condition of the brain whether a person suffers from H. or not; if he is in a semi-conscious state, or insane, or under the influence of drugs, or hypnotism, his brain cannot work properly, and the result is he thinks he actually sees something of which he is thinking, *i.e.* he suffers from H.

Halluin, a tn. of France, in the dept. of Nord, and the arron. of Lille, on the Lys, 11 m. N.N.E. of Lille. It is an important industrial town, with manufs. of cottons and linens, oil, bricks, etc. Pop. 16,500.

Halmstad, a seaport at the mouth of the Nissa, on the E. shore of the Cattegat, 70 m. N.W. of Christianstad, in the district (län) of Halland, Sweden. The chief exports are granite (to Germany), timber, butter, and hats, whilst in the town are manufactories of beer, wood-pulp, jute, and paper. Both the salmon fisheries and potato crops are profitable. Pop. (1910) 18,342.

Halmyros, or **Kirtsinion**, a tn., 18 m. S.W. by W. of Volos, in the prov. of Larissa, Greece. Pop. 7000.

Halo, a word applied to any luminous ring, such as that sometimes seen around the sun or moon, or depicted about the heads of saints ; probably derived from ἅλος, a threshing floor, on account of the circular path traced out by the oxen threshing the corn. In physical science, Hs. are coloured circles which appear around the sun and less frequently about the moon. They are formed by refraction of light by ice crystals floating in the atmosphere. It is necessary to distinguish between Hs. and coronæ. Hs. are at definite distances (22° and 46°) from the sun, and are coloured red on the *inside*, being due to refraction ; coronæ surround the sun at variable distances, and are coloured red on the *outside*, being due to diffraction. Hs. are very common in northern regions and are not rare in our climate. The H. which is most commonly seen has an angular radius of 22°. Manolle explained the phenomenon by the existence of ice crystals in the atmosphere. Crystals of ice occur in numerous forms, but one crystalline form occurs more frequently than all others ; this is the form of a hexagonal prism which may be elongated like a needle or very flat like a thin flake. Three different refracting angles are possible in a hexagonal prism. Two adjacent faces are inclined at 120°, alternate faces at 60°, and the base of the prism forms an angle of 90° with the sides. To explain the H. of 22°, suppose the air contains ice crystals distributed in all directions in space, there must occur prisms whose edges will be perpendicular to the plane drawn through the luminary and the observer's eye. The minimum deviation for a ray of light passing through a prism of ice of refracting angle 60° is exactly 22°. Therefore, since the changes of deviation are slowest near a minimum or maximum, a maximum of light will be seen in all directions making an angle of 22° with the line joining the eye and the luminary. Also, since red rays are deviated less than blue rays, the H. will be coloured red on the inside and violet on the outside. Cavendish attributed the H. of 46° to the refraction of light across faces inclined to each other at 90°. Calculation shows that for such a refraction through an ice prism the minimum deviation is 46°. Thus the formation of the H. and the order of the colours is explained just as before. The impurity of the colours in Hs. is due to two causes : first, the superposition of the spectra produced by light coming from different points on the luminary ; secondly, oblique refraction. As a rule, only the red is at all pure, a mere trace of blue or green is seen, the external portion of each H. being nearly white.

Halo, or Nimbus, the disc or glory encircling the head of saints and holy personages in sacred art, used in the West as a symbol of sanctity from about the 5th century. It had a pagan origin, being known to Hindu, Oriental, and Classical art. In the East it was regarded as the ' attribute of power,' figuring in Byzantine art in representations of Satan and other great powers of evil. Many of the Roman emperors are represented with radiating diadems or Hs. The usual form of the nimbus is circular, sometimes it is formed by concentric circles, or indicated by a straight line or by rays diverging from the head.

A triangular or cruciform H.— ☧ or

☧, the Constantinian monogram or labarum—marked one of the three persons of the Trinity. A square nimbus denoted that the person represented was still living. The nimbus was usually of gold, but sometimes of other colours. After the Renaissance it became lighter, almost melting away into the picture. An illumination surrounding the whole figure was called an ' aureole.'

Halogens, or Salt-producers (Gk. ἁλς, salt), a group of four non-metallic elements, viz. fluorine, chlorine, bromine, and iodine (*q.v.*), which have properties similar to one another but graduating in the order given above. The halides or haloids are the metallic salts of the H. acids, and may be formed in most cases by the direct combination of the metal and the H.

Haloragidaceæ, a dicotyledonous order, closely related to Onagraceæ, contains nearly 100 herbaceous species, many of which inhabit watery places and all of which have minute inconspicuous flowers. The flowers are either hermaphrodite or unisexual, in parts of four, with or without a perianth, the stamens are one to eight in number, the ovary is inferior and consists of one to four united carpels with one ovule in each of the many loculi ; the fruit is a drupe or a nut. The chief genera are *Haloragis* and *Hippuris.*

Hals, Dirk (*c.* 1589-1656), a Dutch genre painter, brother of Frans (*d.* 1666), pupil of A. Bloemaert. Examples of his work are at Amsterdam and Copenhagen. His pictures can be traced from 1624-53, usually representing cavaliers, women, and young people drinking, dancing, listening to music, or talking, as in ' A Party of Ladies and Gentlemen,' ' Three Musicians, and Two Persons Dancing.' His pictures have recently been highly appreciated.

Hals, Frans, the Elder (*c.*1580-1666), a Flemish portrait and genre painter, born at Antwerp. In 1616 he settled at Haarlem, where his brother Dirk was born and died. He was perhaps a fellow-pupil of Rubens under van Noort before 1600, or studied under van Mander the Elder.   Reputed second only to Van Dyck as a portrait painter, H. was the pioneer in the Dutch school of free, broad brush-work, noted for his masterly juxta-position of flesh-tints and portrayal of laughter and merriment (*see* his ' Laughing Cavalier ' in the Wallace Collection, London). He worked largely in Haarlem and Delft, but the Louvre, London National Gallery, and Scottish National Gallery also have examples of his paintings. Fine works are : ' St. George's Guild Banquet ' (' St. Joris' Doelen,' 1616 and 1639), at Haarlem ; ' F. Hals and Lysbeth Reyniers,' 1624 ; ' Hille Bobbe,' 1650 ; ' Regenten of the Old Men's Almshouse,' 1664. Many of his sons were minor artists. *See* Davies, *F. Hals*, 1902, 1905; Bode, *F. Hals und seine Schule*, 1871 ; Knackfuss, *F. Hals*, 1896.

Halsbury, Hardinge Stanley Giffard, first Earl of (created 1898) (*b.* 1825), an English statesman, educated at Oxford, graduating 1855. He became a barrister of the Inner Temple, 1850 ; Q.C., 1865 ; Solicitor-General under Disraeli, 1875-80 ; M.P. (Conserva-tive) for Launceston, 1877-85. H. was Lord High Chancellor of England from 1895-1905, first appointed under Lord Salisbury's administration (1885-86), then in his second government (1886-92), again in the Unionist government (1895-1900), and also in Balfour's first administration (1902-5). Like Lord Mansfeld he has done much as judge to adapt English common law to the changing con-ditions of life and circumstances. He was engaged in the famous Overend and Gurney and Tichborne cases. He was created Viscount Tiverton in 1898, a title now borne by his son and heir. Lord H. has been high steward of Oxford University since 1896. He is president of the Royal Society of Literature, and senior grand warden of English Freemasons. He was fore-most among the Diehards who opposed the passing of the (1911) Parliament Bill through the House of Lords. He edits *The Laws of England*. Consult Atlay, *Victorian Chancellors*, ii., 1908.

Halsingborg (a tn. in Sweden), *see* HELSINGBORG.

Halstead, or Halsted, a par. and market tn. of Essex, England, Mal-don div., on R. Colne, 6 m. from Braintree. It is on the Great Eastern Railway. Its church contains ancient monuments. Silk and crepe are manu-factured. Pop. (1911) 6265.

Haltwhistle, a market tn. and par. of Northumberland, England, 14 m. from Hexham, on the North-Eastern Railway. It lies in the valley of S. Tyne, with Hadrian's Roman wall 1½ m. S., and Featherstonehaugh Castle near by. Coal and clay in-

dustries are carried on, and coarse baize is manufactured. Pop. about 3000 (rural dist. 8520).

Halver, a tn. of Prussia, West-phalia prov., 15 m. from Barmen ; has iron manufs. Pop. 10,227.

Halyards, Halliards, or Haulyards, probably a later form of ' hallier ' (one who hales or hauls). The ropes, tackle, or purchase used for hoisting or lowering sails, yards, spars, or flags, on their respective masts, stays, or gaffs. All yards have them except the lower yards and lower topsail-yards. The H.-rack is a wooden framework for keeping the running part coiled. Jeers answer the same purpose for the mainsail, foresail, and mizen.

Halyburton, Thomas (1674-1712), a Scottish divine, travelled to Rotter-dam (1682), then became minister of Ceres, Fifeshire (*c.* 1700), for eleven years, and professor of divinity at St. Andrews (1710). His works, once very popular in Scotland, include : *Natural Religion insufficient and Revealed necessary to Happiness*, 1714 ; *The Great Concern of Salvation*, 1722 ; *Ten Sermons . . .*, which were mostly written against the deists. See *Auto-biographic Memoirs*, 1714 ; *Works* (published by Dr. Burns), 1835 ; Leland, *View of Deistical Writers ;* Chalmers, *Biog. Dict.*

Halysites (Gk. ἅλυσις, chain), a genus of fossil ' chain-corals ' found in the Ordovician and Silurian (Palæo-zoic) rocks of N. America, Europe, and Australia, showing a chain-like figure in cross-section. Two species, *H. catenularius* and *H. escharoides*, are common in N. America and Eng-lish Silurian coral-reefs.

Ham, a com. of Somme dept., France, on the Oise-Somme Canal, Péronne arron., 12 m. from St. Quentin. Its famous old fortress serves as a state prison. Among its most celebrated prisoners were Charles X.'s ministers (1830) and Prince Louis Napoleon (1840-46). Pop. 3200.

Ham (connected with Lat. *camur*, crooked), properly the hind-part or angle of the knee, usually applied to the cured thigh of hogs or sometimes of sheep or oxen. H. curing and bacon curing are important industries, per-formed in various ways according to the country and district. Salting and smoking are essential operations. The meat is rubbed with salt, and later with a mixture of salt, saltpetre, and sugar. Smoking is carried on in smok-ing-houses, the meat being hung high, and the fire kept smouldering with wood for five or six weeks. Wet salt-ing requires three weeks, dry salting about four weeks. Beef and mutton Hs. are cured largely in N. England,

and Dumfriesshire, Scotland ; pork-curing thrives at Chicago.

Ham, according to Gen. x., one of the three sons of Noah, and ancestor of the Ethiopians, Egyptians, Babylonians, etc. The narrative in Genesis shows traces of much alteration, and it is clear that in ver. 22 (chap. ix.) the present verse originally had Canaan instead of H., Noah's three sons thus being Shem, Japheth, and Canaan. At this period, the division between the three was considered as referring to Palestinian groups, but it was later extended to the surrounding nations. The name H. is usually derived either from an ancient name for Egypt signifying ' black,' or from the name of an early Babylonian king.

Ham, East, see EAST HAM.

Ham, West, see WEST HAM.

Hamada, a maritime tn. and open port of Japan, on S.W. coast of Honshiu (Hondo), 180 m. from Kobe, 200 m. from Nagasaki. Much timber is exported. Pop. about 3000.

Hamadan, a tn. of Persia in Irak Ajemi, 165 m. S.W. of Teheran, at the base of Mt. Elvend. It has an elevation of about 6000 ft. It is a trading place of considerable importance, being one of the routes from Bagdad to Teheran and Ispahan. It has extensive bazaars and caravan-saries. The chief objects of interest are the tomb of Avicenna, near the great mosque, resorted to by pilgrims, and the reputed tomb of Esther and Mordecai, a structure of black wood. The principal industries are carpet-weaving and tanning. Pop. 40,000.

Hamadryad, King Cobra, or **Giant Cabra,** one of the Oriental cobras of a large and poisonous variety, found from Southern India to China and the Philippines, sometimes reaching a length of 13 ft., and one of the longest and most venomous of snakes. It is of a yellow colour, with black cross-bands ; of a fierce disposition, and feeds wholly on other snakes.

Hamadryads, the eight daughters of Hamadryas, in Greek mythology. They were nymphs attached to particular trees, from which they received their names, and with which they were supposed to come into existence and die. They did not possess immortality, thus differing from other nymphs. They were also known as dryads and oreads and lived in forests from which they never emerged.

Hamamatsu, a coast tn. of Hondo, Japan, 120 m. W.S.W. of Yokohama. Pop. about 12,000.

Hamamelidaceæ, an order of dicotyledonous plants, contains subtropical trees and herbs which yield good timber, and some resin, but have no known useful properties. The infloresence is racemose, the flowers are hermaphrodite or unisexual, the sepals, petals, and stamens are typically in four to five free parts, the ovary is formed from two united carpels and is trilocular with one ovule or more in each loculus ; the fruit is a capsule. The chief genera are *Hamamelis, Liquidambar,* and *Fothergilla.*

Haman ('Full of Grace'), see ESTHER.

Hamann, Johann Georg (1730-88), a German author, sometimes called the ' Magician of the North ' from the originality of his thought, born at Königsberg, Prussia. He lived a somewhat chequered life, trying various callings, but finally devoted himself to the study of ancient languages, and Oriental literature. He knew many eminent authors and largely influenced Goethe and Herder, though his own writings were little esteemed by his contemporaries. H. wrote *Sokratische Denkwürdegkeiten* and *Krenzzüge des Philologen.* His complete works were published by Roth, and Gildemeister wrote his biography. See Claassen's *Hamanns Leben und Werke.*

Hamar, a tn. in Norway, 59 m. from Christiania, on Lake Mjösen. It is the seat of a bishopric, and has breweries, and metal and iron foundries. Pop. 6003.

Hamasah, or **Hamâseh** (Arabic *hamasah,* bravery, from *hamisa,* to be firm), a famous collection of Arabic poetry compiled by Abu Temmam, and divided into ten books (*c.* 807-846). The first (dealing with the heroes of pre-Islamic times) is the longest book, and the remaining nine deal with various subjects. The collection is of great historical value, and is taken from extempore works chiefly. There are three editions of the Arabic, viz. Freytag's, Bulak's, and the Calcutta edition, 1856. See Lyall, *Ancient Arabic Poetry,* 1885.

Hamath (' fortress,' or ' enclosed place '), or **Hamah,** a city situated on the banks of the Orontes, chief city of the Hittites, and capital of the surrounding territory. In several places of the O.T. (*e.g.* Num. xxxiv. 8, Judges iii. 3) it is spoken of as the northern boundary of the kingdom of Israel. It later came under the suzerainty of Solomon, on whose death it became independent. It then finally came under the dominion of Assyria, and was entirely destroyed by Sargon. It was known to the Greeks and Romans as Epiphaneia.

Hambach, a com. and vil. of the Bavarian Rhine Palatinate, Germany, 2 m. S. of Neustadt. The ' Hambacher Fest,' a great German Liberal meeting, was held here in 1832, proclaiming 'the sovereignty of the people,' as the foundation of organised government. Pop. 2270.

Hambato, or Ambato (Hambald), a tn. of Ecuador, cap. of Tunguragua prov., about 78 m. S. of Quito, between Chimborazo and Cotopaxi. Destroyed in 1698 by an eruption of Cotopaxi, and by an earthquake in 1796; it became very flourishing later on. It trades in grain, cochineal, and sugar, and has shoe manufactories. Pop. about 12,000.

Hamborn, a rural com. of Rhenish Prussia, in the dist. of Düsseldorf. Noted for coal and iron industries. Pop. 103,372.

Hamburg, a city of the German empire, chief tn. of the independent state of Hamburg, situated on the N. bank of the Elbe. It is the largest seaport on the Continent, and the third largest in the world. The greater part of the harbour is a free port, and, with the two new docks completed in 1904, the total water area amounts to 1260 acres. H. is one of the chief continental ports for the embarkation of emigrants from Europe. The city consists of two radically different parts, the central part, reconstructed since the fire of 1842; and the ancient ramparts, separating the old city from the adjacent suburbs. The beauty of the city is much enhanced by the large sheets of water formed by the Alster. The canals in the city are spanned by over sixty bridges, and there are numbers of steam ferries. There are many fine public buildings; notably the Exchange, with its commercial library of over 110,000 volumes; the Rathaus, completed in 1897; the Deutsches Schauspielhaus, completed in 1900; the marine office (Seewarte), and numerous museums of arts, crafts, botany, natural history, etc. H. has also many fine churches, viz. St. Michael, St. Peter, St. Nicholas, and St. Catherine's, dating from the 15th century. The streets of H. are well paved and kept very clean, the principal thoroughfare being the Jungfernstieg. The Epidemic Hospital of H, opened in 1894, is considered one of the best in the world. There are many large and excellent private schools, as well as over 200 public schools, in addition to gymnasiums, a school of art, and a conservatoire. In 1888, H. became a member of the German Customs Union, which did much to stimulate its trade. Among its chief industries are cigar making, spirit and sugar refining, machine and shipbuilding, brewing, flour-milling, and the manufacture of furniture, musical instruments, mechanical and optical instruments, leather, ivory, etc., etc. It is also one of the largest coffee marts in the world. Raw materials, foodstuffs, and manufactured articles are the chief imports. The city-state has a democratic constitution, and is administered by an executive senate of eighteen life members. The legislative power is confined to the House of Burgesses, 160 members, elected for six years, one half of whom retire every three years. In 1910, the pop. of the state was 1,015,707, second only to Berlin. H. seems to have been founded early in the 9th century by Charlemagne, who built a citadel and church as a defence against the Slavs. In 831 an episcopal see was erected and H. rapidly became a centre of civilisation for Northern Europe. It was frequently devastated by Danes and Slavs, but in 1189 was granted important commercial privileges by Frederick Barbarossa, and by treaties with Lübeck and Bremen in 1241 and 1249 respectively, formed the Hanseatic League. It was formally acknowledged as an imperial city in 1618. Owing to the immunity of its position, its prosperity increased during the Thirty Years' War, and in the following century, commercial relations with N. America were developed owing to the American and French revolutions and the wars between England and France. In 1815, it became an independent state of the German federation, and its trade and importance have increased ever since. It united with the German empire as a free city state in 1871. H. occupies a distinguished place in the history of German literature and the drama. It was the home of Heine, Lessing, Klopstock, Schröder, and other noted writers. H. is practically the biggest commercial city of Europe, and next to London has the largest money-exchange transaction on the Continent, the Bank of H. being founded in 1619. As a commercial centre, its only rivals are London, Liverpool, Antwerp, and New York. In 1865 5186 vessels entered the port, and by 1900 this number had risen to 13,100, with a gross burden of 8,000,000 tons; 30 per cent. of the vessels entering being British. In 1909, H.'s imports were valued at £183,000,000, and her exports at £140,000,000. H. has commercial transactions of great magnitude with Great Britain, the United States, the countries on the W. and E. coast of S. America, France, Holland, and Belgium, Central America, Russia, the East Indies, China, and the E. and W. coasts of Africa. *See* Gallais, *Geschichte der Stadt Hamburg* (3 vols. Hamburg), 1856 ; Wichmann, *Hamburgische Geschichte in Darstellung aus alter und neurer Zeit* (Hamburg), 1889 ;

Shaw, *Municipal Government in Continental Europe* (New York), 1897; Maltbie, *Municipal Functions* (New York), 1898.

Hamburg - American Line, dates from 1847, and owns the largest steamship service in the world. It has altogether 408 ships employed in 68 different services, with a total tonnage of 1,200,000, and its steamers ply between Hamburg and New York. They also visit the chief ports of England, France, Canada, the United States, South and Central America, the W. Indies, the East, and the Mediterranean. In the evolution of the steamship of the N. Atlantic it is interesting to notice that the *Borussia* (1856) owned by the Hamburg-American Line was the first to carry United States mails, that the *Fürst Bismarck* was the first to accomplish its journey from Southampton under six and a half days, that the *Deutschland* (1900) was the fastest ocean steamer to date, and that the *Imperator* (1913) has a displacement of 70,000 tons, is 919 ft. long, 98 ft. beam, and 62 ft. deep.

Hamburger Nachrichten, Die (*The Hamburg News*), established in 1792: a moderate Liberal, and at one time a very influential paper. Prince Bismarck attacked through its columns the government of William II.

Hamburg-South American Steamship Line, was established in 1871, and possesses 56 steamers with a total tonnage of 251,000. Some of its latest boats are *Cap Finisterre* (1911), with a speed of 17 knots and a tonnage of 14,503; *Bahia Blanca* (1912), and *Buenos Aires* (1912).

Hamden, a tn., Newhaven co., Conn., U.S.A., 6 m. N.N.E. of Newhaven. Pop. (1910) 5850.

Hameln, a tn. in prov. of Hanover, Prussia, on the Weser, 33 m. S.W. of Hanover. There are many ancient houses here, but the only public buildings of any interest are the Minster Church, restored in 1872, and a town house. It has a gymnasium, two hospitals, district prison, etc. Is famed as being the scene of Robert Browning's famous legend of the Pied Piper. Pop. 22,054.

Hamerling, Robert (1830-89), an Austrian poet, born at Kirchenberg-am-Walde in Lower Austria, in humble circumstances. He was educated at the University of Vienna, and became a teacher at the gymnasium at Trieste in 1855. In 1866 he was obliged to retire on the grounds of health, and spent the rest of his life as an invalid at Gratz. In 1860 he published his first volume of lyrics, *Sinnen und Minnen*, which was followed by *Amor und Psyche* (1882) and *Blätter im Winde* (1887). *Ahasver*

in *Rom* (1866) and *Der König von Sion* (1869), two powerful satiric epics, are his masterpieces. Consult his *Life* by Rabenlechner (1896 and 1901) and Polzer (1890).

Hamerton, Philip Gilbert (1834-94), an English writer, born at Laneside in Lancashire. He worked at landscape painting in Scotland, but in 1858 settled in France and devoted his life to art criticism. He contributed to the *Saturday Review* and *Fine Arts Quarterly*, and in 1870 established an art journal, *The Portfolio*, which he edited till his death. His publications include: *A Painter's Camp in the Highlands*, 1863; *Etching and Etchers*, 1866; *Contemporary French Painters*, 1868; *Painting in France after the Decline of Classicism*, 1869; *The Graphic Arts*, 1882; and *Landscape*, 1885. Of his more general literary works the chief are *The Intellectual Life*, 1873, and *Human Intercourse*, 1884. His *Autobiography* and a *Memoir* by his wife were published in 1896.

Hamesucken, in Scots law, means the felonious seeking and invasion of a person in his dwelling-house. It consists essentially in the co-existence of entry with intent to commit an assault and actual personal violence. The entry may be either by terrifying those within or by artifice, or by secretly entering and lying in wait for an opportunity of assault. Formerly H. was punishable with death, but since the Criminal Procedure Act, 1887, penal servitude or other imprisonment has been substituted.

Hamheung, a walled tn. of Korea, situated near the E. coast of the peninsula in lat. 39° 56' N. Pop. 70,000.

Hami, Kamel, or **Khamil,** a tn. of S.W. Mongolia, situated about lat. 42° 50' N., and long. 93° 28' E. It is an important trading centre. Rice and fruit are grown in the neighbourhood.

Hamilcar, the name of several Carthaginian generals, the chief of whom was *Hamilcar Barca* (d. 229 B.C.). During the First Punic War he was in command of the Carthaginian forces in Sicily (247), where he maintained his position on Mt. Herctè, near Panormus. After the Roman victory at the Ægatian Is., which brought the war to an end, he returned to Carthage, where he suppressed a revolt of mercenaries (240-238). In the latter year he went with his young son Hannibal to Spain, and began the conquest of that country, much of which he accomplished during the following nine years. He fell in battle against the Vettones.

Hamilton: 1. A tn. and parl. bor. of Lanarkshire, Scotland, on l. b. of Clyde, 10 m. S.E. of Glasgow. It stands in the centre of a rich coal and iron field and has large foundries and cotton mills, as well as fine public buildings, extensive barracks, and a good race-course. Here also is the ducal palace of the house of Hamilton, with its park, part of old Cadzow Forest, where wild white cattle are still preserved, and the ruins of Cadzow Castle. Pop. (1911) 38,644. 2. The city and port of entry of Ontario, Canada, cap. of Wentworth co., 40 m. S.W. of Toronto, and 56 m. W.N.W. of Niagara Falls. It is an important railway centre in the midst of a populous and highly-cultivated fruit district, and possesses a large number (over 400) of factories engaged in the manufacture of cotton and woollen goods, iron, brass, steel, glass-ware, furniture, boots, etc. It was laid out and settled in 1813 on a plateau at the foot of ' the Mountain,' where lies the business quarter. It contains many fine residences, public buildings, wide streets, and is the seat of an Anglican and of a Roman Catholic bishop. Pop. 90,000. 3. The cap. of Butler co., Ohio, U.S.A., on Great Miami R., and Miami and Erie Canal, 25 m. N. of Cincinnati. It has paper and flour mills, foundries, breweries, manufactories of farming implements, machinery, woollen goods, and trades in grain, hay, vegetables, and tobacco. Pop. (1910) 35,279. 4. The chief tn. of the counties Dundas and Normanby, Victoria, Australia. It is situated on the Grange Burne Creek, 50 m. from Portland, and 198 m. W. of Melbourne. Sheep-farming is carried on in the district, and there are meat-preserving works : frozen mutton is exported. Pop. 4200. 5. The cap. of the Bermudas, W. Indies. It is situated on the largest island of the group, Great Bermuda, or Main Island. Pop. 2300. 6. A vil. in Northumberland co., New South Wales, Australia. It is a suburb of Newcastle which lies 3 m. to the E.

Hamilton, a famous Scottish family, who trace their descent back to Walter FitzGilbert (*fl.* 1295), son of Gilbert de Hameldone, who is mentioned in a charter of 1272. Walter owned lands in Lanarkshire, and for a time swore fealty to Edward I. of England. After the battle of Bannockburn, however, he joined King Robert Bruce, and was subsequently knighted and granted the barony of Cadzow in Lanarkshire, receiving lands forfeited by adherents to the English crown. His elder son, David, was the first to assume the surname Hamilton. His younger son, John, was the father of Alexander H., whose descendants acquired the lands of Priestfield, one Thomas becoming Lord Priestfield in the reign of Queen Mary. Sir David H. of Cadzow,

already mentioned, was taken prisoner at the battle of Neville's Cross in 1346, but was ransomed, and sat among the barons in the Scottish parliaments of 1368, 1371, and 1373. Sir David died in 1392. Little is known of his son, Sir John H., except that he was twice taken prisoner in England. His grandson, Sir James H. of Cadzow, was likewise taken captive into England, and from him are descended the Hs. of Silvertonhill and of Dalzell. His eldest son, also called James, was created Lord H. in 1445. He was the first layman to found a college in Scotland; as well as endowing a college at Glasgow (1460), he also founded the collegiate church of Hamilton. He was connected, by his marriage with the widow of the fifth earl, with the powerful family of Douglas, whom he assisted in their struggle against James II. About 1455 he changed sides, and on the death of his wife, being now in royal favour, married Princess Mary, sister of James III. and widow of the Earl of Arran. His only son, James, by Mary, negotiated the marriage between Margaret Tudor and James IV. of Scotland. In 1503 this James, second Lord H., was created Earl of Arran and succeeded to lands on his mother's side. He died in 1529, and his heir, James, second Earl of Arran (by Janet Beaton, niece to the cardinal), on the death of James V. (1542) was appointed regent of Scotland and governor to the young Queen Mary. In 1549 he was granted the duchy of Châtelherault by Henry II. of France, and resigned from his governorship in favour of Mary of Guise, the queen-mother, in 1554. His eldest son, James, who succeeded to the title in 1575, was proposed at different times as husband for Queen Mary and for Queen Elizabeth, but he lost his reason in 1562 and died in 1609. His brother, Lord John H., created Marquis of H. in 1599, administered his estates until his own death in 1604, when his son James became second marquis. James was created Earl of Cambridge (1619), and died in 1625. The third marquis, James, was created by Charles I. Duke of H. (1643) for the signal services he had rendered in the struggle with the Scottish Covenanters. He headed a Scottish army against the Parliamentarians, but was defeated by Cromwell at Preston in Lancashire, and was beheaded at Westminster in 1649. His brother William, created Earl of Lanark (1639), succeeded to the dukedom. He negotiated with Charles I. at Newcastle (1646), and signed the ' Engagement' at Carisbrooke Castle (1647), fleeing with other Royalists to Holland in 1648. He returned with Prince Charles in 1650, and died in the following year from wounds received at the battle of Worcester. The second Duke of H. was succeeded by his niece, Lady Anne, whose husband, William Douglas, Earl of Selkirk (1635-94), was created Duke of H. for life only (1660). The Duchess Anne resigned her titles in 1698 in favour of her eldest son, James Douglas, Earl of Arran, who was formally created Duke of H. In 1711 he was granted a British peerage, being created Duke of Brandon. In the following year he fought the famous duel in Hyde Park with Charles, Lord Mohun (see Thackeray's Esmond), the principals being killed. His son, James (1703-43), became fifth duke, and he was succeeded by his son James (1724-58), who married the famous beauty, Elizabeth Gunning. The seventh duke, James George (1755-69), succeeded to the title at the age of three. In 1761, by the death of the Duke of Douglas, the titles of his family devolved on the Hs. The seventh duke was succeeded by his brother Douglas (1756-99), who sat in the House of Lords. He died childless, the title passing to his uncle Archibald (1740-1819), whose son Alexander, tenth duke (1767-1852), was ambassador at St. Petersburg in 1806-7. The eleventh duke was William Alexander (1811-63), who married Princess Marie Amélie, a cousin of Napoleon III. His son William Alexander (1845-95) received the ancient title of Duke of Châtelherault, granted to his ancestor in 1549. The thirteenth duke, Alfred Douglas (b. 1862), is descended from Claud H., the third son of the fourth duke. From this Claud are descended the dukes of Abercorn, whose eldest sons are styled by courtesy Marquis of Hamilton.

Consult Gilbert Burnet, Memoirs of the Lives and Actions of James and William, Dukes of Hamilton and Chatelherault, 1677; John Anderson, The House of Hamilton, 1825; S. R. Gardiner, The Hamilton Papers relative to 1638-1650 (for the Camden Society), 1880; and Appendix vi. of the Eleventh Report of the Historical MSS. Commissioners, 1887. There is a Briefe Account of the Family of Hamilton by Dr. James Baillie (early 17th century) in manuscript in the Advocates' Library, Edinburgh. See also Scots Peerage (vol. iv.), 1907.

Hamilton, Alexander (1757-1804), an American statesman and economist, born on the island of Nevis in the W. Indies. On the outbreak of hostilities with England, H., then a young student at King's (now Columbia) College, New York, wrote two very influential pamphlets in defence of the colonies, and was given the command of an artillery regiment (1775). He became aide-de-camp to Washington (1777), and distinguished himself for his gallantry at Yorktown (1781). He was returned to Congress (1782); was prominent in the deliberations at Annapolis (1786); became Secretary of the Treasury in the new government (1789); and was one of the founders of the National Bank. He resigned office in 1795, but throughout his life wielded great influence over American politics. His works were published by his son in 7 vols., 1851, and by Lodge in 12 vols., 1904. See his Life by Morse, 1876, and Lodge, 1882; and studies by Shea, 1877 and 1879, and Oliver, 1906.

Hamilton, Count Anthony (c. 1646-1720), an author; led a most adventurous life during his early years. As a lad he served in the French army, but later held an English commission, and fought in Ireland for James II. After the battle of the Boyne he escaped to France. He wrote several contes, and about 1705 began to compose the memoirs of his brother-in-law, the Comte de Grammont. The memoirs, which give an admirable picture of the court of Charles II., were published anonymously in 1713. H. is especially remarkable as an Englishman who wrote, and wrote extraordinarily well, in French. He is the only Englishman who has become a French classic, with the exception of his collateral descendant, William Beckford, the author of Vathek.

Hamilton, Sir Bruce Meade (b. 1857), a British general, entered the army in 1877. He has served in the Afghan War (1880), South African War (1881), and in Burmah (1885) and Ashanti (1895). He particularly distinguished himself in the South African War of 1900, after which he was created K.C.B. He was placed in command of the 2nd division of the First Army Corps (1904-9), and was promoted to the rank of lieutenant-general in 1907. He was given the Scottish Command in 1909.

Hamilton, David (1768-1843), a Scottish architect, born in Glasgow. He was awarded one of the four £500 premiums for his designs of the new houses of parliament. He designed and executed many of the modern buildings in Scotland, including the Western Clubhouse and the Exchange at Glasgow, the Duke of Hamilton's place in Lanarkshire, Toward Castle, and Lennox Castle.

Hamilton, Sir Edward (1772-1851), a British admiral. While in command of the Surprise he succeeded in capturing eighty privateers (1797-98), and cut out the *Hermione* from the batteries of Puerto Cabello. He was for a time taken prisoner by the French (1800) but was exchanged, and in the following year blockaded the N. coast of France. He was promoted to the rank of admiral in 1846.

Hamilton, Elizabeth (1758-1816), a Scottish authoress, born at Belfast. On the death of her father she was adopted by his sister, Mrs. Marshall, and brought up in Stirling. She subsequently lived in Bath, Harrogate, and London, and died in Edinburgh. Her works include: *Letters of a Hindoo Rajah*, 1796; *Memoirs of Modern Philosophers*, a satire on the enthusiasts of the French Revolution; *Life of Agrippina*, 1804; and *The Cottagers of Glenburnie*, 1808, which shows her at her best in depicting domestic life in rural Scotland. Consult Miss Benger, *Memoirs of Mrs. Elizabeth Hamilton*, 1818.

Hamilton, Emma, Lady (*née* Emma Lyon) (*c.*1761-1815), was of humble origin, and in early days was a nursemaid. Her extraordinary good looks brought her many admirers, and she lived under the protection, first, of Sir Harry Fetherstonhaugh, and then of the Hon. Charles Greville. She made the acquaintance of Romney, who painted the well-known pictures of her. From 1786 she lived with Sir William H., the ambassador, and married him five years later. While still living with her husband, she became the mistress of Nelson about 1798, and in 1801 gave birth to a child, Horatio, of which the sailor was the father. H. and Nelson remained on good terms until the former's death in 1803. In later days Lady H. fell upon evil times, was imprisoned for debt, but contrived to escape to Calais, where she died in obscurity. There are biographies by Jeaffreson, 1887, and Sichel, 1905.

Hamilton, Gavin (1730–97), a Scottish painter and antiquary, born at Lanark. He studied painting under Massuchi at Rome, where he principally lived. While in London he joined the committee whose object it was to found a royal academy (1755). He painted classical subjects, scenes from the *Iliad* being his favourites. His excavations at Hadrian's villa at Tivoli, at Civita Vecchia, and elsewhere, rendered great service to art. His marbles are in the Louvre; his collection of busts and bas-reliefs in the Museo Pio-Clementino in the Vatican. In 1773 he published *Schola Italica picturæ*.

Hamilton, Lord George Francis (*b.* 1845), a British statesman, a younger son of the first Duke of Abercorn. He was educated at Harrow. In 1868 he was returned to parliament by the county of Middlesex, and subsequently represented the Ealing division (1885-1906). He received an appointment in the India Office as Under-Secretary of State (1874-78) from Disraeli, which he exchanged for that of vice-president of the Council of Education (1878-80). He has twice been First Lord of the Admiralty, in 1885-86 and 1886-92. In Mr. Balfour's ministry he was Secretary of State for India, but resigned office in 1903 on the fiscal question. He was chairman of the Poor Law Commission (1905-9).

Hamilton, General Sir Ian Standish Monteith (*b.* 1853), a British soldier, born at Corfu. He was educated at Wellington, entering the army in 1873. He served in the Afghan War (1878-80) and the Boer War (1881), and took part in the Nile expedition (1884-85), when he was awarded the Khedive's star. He also saw service in the Burmese expedition (1886-87) and with the Chitral relief force under Sir R. Low (1895). In 1897-98 he commanded the third brigade during the Tirah campaign, and was despatched to S. Africa in 1899 on the outbreak of war with the Boers. He was appointed head of the staff of the Natal field force under the generalship of Sir George White, and was present at the battle of Elandslaagte. He fought with conspicuous gallantry during the defence of Ladysmith, and was subsequently promoted to the rank of major-general. In 1901-2 he was appointed chief of the staff of S. Africa to Lord Kitchener, and was put in command of the mobile columns in the western district of the Transvaal. He fought with the Japanese troops in Manchuria (1904-5) as a representative of the Indian army. In 1905 he was given command of the Southern Command, and in 1910 became commander-in-chief of Malta. His chief publications are : *A Jaunt in a Junk*, 1884; *A Ballad of Hadji*, 1887; and *A Staff-Officer's Scrap-Book during the Russo-Japanese War*, 1906.

Hamilton, James (1769-1831), an educationist. In early life he was engaged in mercantile pursuits, and set up a business in Paris which was ruined by the war. Having been taught German at Hamburg by an original method which discarded a grammar-book, using instead literal word for word translation, H. began teaching languages in the United States (1814-23) and in England (1823), and attained great success. He taught that the laws of a foreign language could only be learnt by observation, setting forth his theories in *The History, Principles, Practices, and Results of the Hamiltonian System*, 1829.

Hamilton, John M'Lure (*b.* 1853), an English artist, born in Philadelphia. He studied in Philadelphia, Paris, and Antwerp, and finally settled in London in 1878. He is chiefly a portrait painter, but in his early work he painted subjects such as 'The Syren,' 'The Heiress,' etc. His principal portraits are two of Gladstone (in the Pennsylvania Academy of Fine Arts, and the Luxembourg, Paris), Professor Tyndall (National Portrait Gallery), Cardinal Manning, Herbert Spencer.

Hamilton, Patrick (*c.* 1504-28), 'the protomartyr of the Scottish Reformation.' He graduated M.A. at Paris in 1520, and three years later became a member of Aberdeen University. But he came under suspicion on account of his Lutheran sympathies, and fled to Germany. On his return to Scotland (1527), he began to preach at Kincavel and attended a conference at Aberdeen. In 1528 he was brought to trial on a charge of heresy, and was burned at the stake on Feb. 29. His *Loci communes*, or 'Patrick's Places,' setting forth the doctrine of justification by faith, is included in Foxe's *Acts and Monuments*. See *Life* by Lorrimer, 1857.

Hamilton, Robert, L.L.D. (1743-1829), a Scottish mathematician and political economist, born at Pilrig, Edinburgh, where he was educated at the University. He abandoned a career in a banking-house for the rectorship of Perth Academy (1769), and became professor of natural philosophy at Aberdeen (1779). His *Essay on the National Debt*, 1813, exposed the weaknesses of the sinking-fund scheme. He also wrote: *Introduction to Merchandise*, 1779 ; *On War and Peace*, 1790; and *The Progress of Society* (published 1830).

Hamilton, William (*c.*1665-1751), of Gilbertfield, a Scottish poet, born at Ladyland, Ayrshire. His fame rests on his abridged and modernised edition of Blind Harry's *Wallace*, 1722. He contributed to Watson's *Choice Collection*, 1706, and his 'Willie was a Wanton Wag' was included in the *Tea-Table Miscellany* of Allan Ramsay, with whom he had a verse correspondence, included in Ramsay's *Works* as 'Seven Familiar Epistles which passed between Lieutenant Hamilton and the Author,' 1719.

Hamilton, William (1704-54), a Scottish poet, born at Bangour, in Linlithgowshire. He espoused the cause of Prince Charlie, and was consequently obliged to seek refuge in France, but returned to Scotland in 1749, succeeding to the family estates at Bangour in 1750. He contributed

to Allan Ramsay's *Tea-Table Miscellany*, 1724. His finest poem is 'The Braes of Jarrow.' The first edition of his poetry appeared in 1748, and a second in 1760. He died at Lyons, and was buried in the Abbey Church of Holyrood House, Edinburgh. Consult James Paterson, *The Poems and Songs of William Hamilton*, 1850.

Hamilton, Sir William (1730-1803), a British ambassador and archæologist, grandson of the third Duke of Hamilton. He sat in parliament as member for Midhurst (1761-64) until he was sent as ambassador to the court of Naples (1764-1800). He was elected to the Royal Society in 1766, and was made Knight of the Bath in 1772. He took an active interest in volcanic observations, on which subject he published various treatises: *Observations on Mount Vesuvius*, 1772; *Campi Phlegræi*, 1776-77, etc. He married Emma Lyon, the mistress of Nelson.

Hamilton, William (1751-1801), a Scottish artist, born in London. He studied at a very early age under Zucchi, the painter of ornaments, at Rome. On his return to England he was engaged on various public works, including the Shakespeare Gallery, Macklin's Bible, etc. He chiefly excelled in ornament, his designs being rich and classical.

Hamilton, Sir William (1788-1856), a Scottish philosopher, born at Glasgow. His father and grandfather had held the chairs of anatomy and botany in Glasgow University. In 1807 he entered Balliol College, Oxford, as a Snell exhibitioner, and graduated with first-class honours (1811), taking M.A. degree in 1814. He was called to the Scottish bar (1813), but devoted his whole time to reading and research. In 1816 he made good his claim to the title of the Hamiltons of Preston, which had not been used since 1688. He was appointed professor of history (1821) and of logic and metaphysics (1836) at Edinburgh, and in 1829 began his literary career with a criticism of Cousin's *Cours de Philosophie*, entitled 'Philosophy of the Unconditioned,' in the *Edinburgh Review*. To this paper he continued to contribute, publishing his essays in 1852-53 under the title *Discussions in Philosophy, Literature, and Education*. His influence was great, not only upon his own countrymen, but in Germany and France. His lectures were published posthumously by Professors Mansel and Veitch (1859-61). Sir William H. published an edition of Reid with seven dissertations (1846), and an edition of Dugald Stewart (9 vols.), 1854-55, but in all his work he was hampered by ill-health, his right side having been struck with paralysis (1844). He invented the doctrine of the ' quantification of the predicate,' urged that the philosophy of common sense is the highest human speculation, and distinguished reasoning in the quantity of extension from reasoning in the quantity of comprehension. Consult a memoir by Veitch (1869), and a study by Monck (1881).

Hamilton, William Gerard (1729-96), an English statesman, born in London. He was educated at Winchester and Oriel College, Oxford. He chose a political career and entered the House of Commons as member for Petersfield, Hants. On Nov. 13, 1754, he made his maiden speech in the House. Apparently he never followed up his initial success, and was consequently nicknamed ' Single-speech Hamilton.' He became chief secretary to Lord Halifax, lord-lieutenant of Ireland (1761), and Chancellor of the Irish Exchequer (1763-83).

Hamilton, Sir William Rowan (1805-65), a celebrated mathematician. He came of a Scottish family that had settled in Ireland, and was born in Dublin. He was a precocious boy, reading Hebrew at seven and having good knowledge of thirteen languages at the age of thirteen. In later life he read Sanskrit and Persian for recreation. In his early teens he showed extraordinary mathematical ability, and when twenty-three years of age, Dr. Brinkley, the astronomer, said of him, ' This young man, I do not say *will be*, but *is*, the first mathematician of his age.' H.'s *Theory of Systems of Rays* was published by the Royal Irish Academy in 1828, and made a great sensation among European mathematicians, and he gained in reputation by his subsequent works, which include: ' A General Method in Dynamics,' in *Philosophical Transactions*, 1834-35 ; *Theorem in the Separation of Symbols in Finite Differences ; Algebra as the Science of Pure Time.* Consult *Life* by Graves (new ed. 1903).

Hamilton Group, the middle div. of the upper Devonian strata of New York; its deposits are of limestones, sandstones, and shales.

Hamilton Mount, California, U.S.A., 41 m. S.E. by E. of San Francisco, with the Lick Observatory, containing the largest refracting telescope ever made. Alt. 4209 ft.

Hamilton, Port, a group of little islands off S. coast of Korea, occupied by the British, 1885-87.

Hamilton, or Grand, River, in Canada, issues from Lake Petchikapou, flows through a chain of lakes below which are the Grand Falls, about 2000 ft. high, and enters the Atlantic through Labrador at Hamilton Inlet.

Hamites, the name given to a genus of cephalopod molluscs belonging to the family Ammonitidæ; they are characterised by a long body, with narrow ribbed whorls, terminating in a single or double hook. The species are found in Europe, India, and S. America.

Hamlet, the hero of one of Shakespeare's greatest tragedies which is founded upon a legend in the *Historia Danica* of Saxo Grammaticus (13th century). Shakespeare, however, owed little but the outline of his plot to Saxo, whose hero, Amleth, only feigned his madness and plotted a deliberate vengeance a year before carrying it out. For a discussion of Shakespeare's play and its sources, see *Shakespeare;* also Latham's *Dissertations on Hamlet*, 1872; Simrock's *Quellen des Shakespeare*, 1870 ; and Hansen's *Legend of Hamlet*, 1887.

Hamley, Sir Edward Bruce (1824-93), a British general and author, born at Bodmin, Cornwall. He entered the Royal Artillery in 1843, served in Gibraltar, and through the Crimean campaign, where he won special distinction at Inkerman. His articles in *Blackwood's Magazine* brought him literary recognition and led to his appointment as professor of military history at Sandhurst in 1859. His lectures were afterwards published as *The Operations of War*, 1867. H. was commandant at the Staff College (1870-77), and commander of a division in Egypt (1882), where he took part in the battle of Tel-el-Kebir. He publicly expressed his dissatisfaction at what he considered lack of recognition of his services. From 1885-92 he was M.P. for Birkenhead. *See* Innes Shand, *Life of Hamley*, 1895.

Hamlin, Hannibal (1809-91), an American statesman, born at Paris, Maine. He was admitted to the bar in 1833, and soon entered the political arena as an anti-slavery Democrat. He was a representative in Congress from 1843-47, and a member of the United States Senate, 1848-56, 1857-61, 1869-81. In 1856 he broke with the Democrats on the question of slavery and joined the Republican party, who elected him governor of Maine in the same year. From 1861-65, during the Civil War, he was vice-president of the United States under President Lincoln. He was minister to Spain, 1881-83. *See* C. E. Hamlin's *Life and Times of Hannibal Hamlin*, 1899.

Hamm, a tn. of Westphalia, Prussia, at confluence of Lippe and Alse, 22 m. S.E. of Arnsberg. It has an important iron industry, and near it are thermal brine springs. Pop. 43,658.

Hammamet, a seaport of Tunis, N. Africa, on the Gulf of Hammamet, a bay of the Great Syrtis, 42 m. S.E. of Tunis. The harbour is insecure. Pop. 5000.

Hammam-Rirha, a watering-place in Algeria in a beautiful mountain district, having saline and ferruginous springs, near the ruins of Aquæ Calidæ. Pop. 18,000.

Hamme, a tn. in E. Flanders, Belgium, on branch of R. Scheldt, 19 m. E.N.E. of Ghent. Pop. 14,000, engaged in agriculture and manufacture of lace, ribbon, etc.

Hammer, an implement consisting of a heavy head, usually of metal, but sometimes of wood or stone, set crosswise on a handle and used for striking blows; the name is also applied to heavy masses of machinery in which a block of metal is used for the same purpose (*see* STEAM and POWER HAMMERS). Hs. of stone have been found among antiquities and are still in use among barbarous peoples. The H., more often under its French name of *martel-de-fer*, was a common weapon in war throughout mediæval times. The word is applied to many objects which resemble the common H. in appearance or use, as, for instance, the ' striker ' in a clock or in a bell, a part of the sounding mechanism of a pianoforte, the part of a gun which, by its impact on the cap, explodes the charge. It has also been used as a nickname for noted fighters, *e.g.* ' Hammer of the Scots ' for Edward I.

Hammer, Sir Thomas Bartholomew (1677-1746), an English statesman and scholar; received his education at Westminster and Christ Church, Oxford. He entered into political life in 1701, being elected M.P. for Suffolk, and twelve years later he rose to the position of Speaker in the House of Commons. In 1727 he retired from public life, and gave up his time to the study of literature. He published an edition of Shakespeare in 1744.

Hammer - cloth, an ornamental cloth covering for the box-seat of a carriage. The word occurs as early as 1465, and its origin is explained by the carrying of a hammer and other tools in the box-seat for repairs.

Hammerfest, a tn. of Finmarken prov., Norway, on the Kval-oe, or Whale Island, 60 m. S.W. of the North Cape. It is the northernmost town of Europe, lying in lat. 70° 40′ 11″ N. There is a good fortified harbour. Fishing is the main industry, and there is a large export trade. The climate is often oppressive in summer and mild in winter. The sun remains above the horizon for two months. Pop. 2298.

Hammer-head, or **Hammer-headed Shark,** a shark of the family Sphyrnidæ or Zygænidæ, of which the common species *Zygæna malleus* occurs in almost every latitude. It is generally from 11 to 15 ft. in length, and is so called from the peculiar shape of its head, which resembles a double-headed hammer laid flat, on the flattened ends of which the eyes are placed. Specimens over 13 ft. in length have been captured round the British coasts, and they abound in all the warmer seas.

Hammerich, Peter Frederick Adolf (1809-77), a Danish theologian and author, born at Copenhagen. In 1845 he became pastor of a church in Copenhagen, and in 1859 was appointed professor of theology at the university of that town. His principal historical works are: *Danmark i Valdemarernes Tid*, 1847; *Danmark under Adelsvaelden*, 1854-59; *Danmark under de tre Nordiske Rigers Forening*, 1849-54. He also published some popular national songs in *Skandinaviske Reiseminder*, 1840.

Hammer-Purgstall, Joseph, Baron von (1774-1856), an Austrian Orientalist and historian, born at Graz. He entered the diplomatic service in 1796, and was interpreter at Constantinople from 1799-1806. In 1807 he returned to Vienna and was made a privy councillor. His knowledge of Oriental matters was rather superficial, but he was considered an authority in his own day. His chief works are: *Geschichte der Assassinen*, 1818; *Geschichte des Osmanischen Reiches* (new ed. 1840; Eng. trans. 1854); *Geschichte der Osmanischen Dichtkunst*, 1836-38; *Litteraturgeschichte der Araber*, 1850-56. See *Life* by Schlottmann, 1857.

Hammersmith, a western metropolitan bor. (formed 1899), Middlesex, England, on the R. Thames, 5 m. W. of St. Paul's. H., with Fulham, was the winter camp of the Danish invaders in 879, and formed part of the parish of Fulham until 1834. Old H. Bridge (1824) was the first suspension bridge near London, but was insecure and replaced in 1887. St. Paul's School, originally founded by Dean Colet in 1509 under the Cathedral church, was moved to its present site in Hammersmith Road in 1883. Other buildings are: Wormwood Scrubs Prison; Olympia, with its huge arena under a glass roof; the ' White City ' buildings and grounds, originally occupied by the Franco-British Exhibition of 1908; and the W. London Hospital. Kensal Green Roman Catholic cemetery, in which Cardinal Manning is buried, is also within the borough. Thomson wrote his *Seasons* in H. and William Morris also lived there. Chief industries are iron and dye works, lead and oil mills, boat-building yards, motor works, and distilleries. Pop. (1911) 121,603.

Hammock, a swinging bed or couch, apparently of W. Indian origin, from the 'hamack' tree, the bark of which was used by the natives to make the nets in which, slung from trees, they slept. They were common among the natives of America at the time of Columbus, and are still much used in warm climates, made of grasses or small cords. A sailor's H. is made of canvas, about 6 ft. long by 3 ft. broad, threaded through eyelet holes with strong cords, called ' clews,' which are gathered together in iron rings and fastened on to hooks under the deck.

Hammond, a city in Lake co., Indiana, U.S.A., 20 m. S.E. of Chicago. Its chief industries are meat-packing, flour-milling, and steel spring and chemical manufs. Pop. (1910) 20,925.

Hammond, Henry (1605-60), an English divine, born at Chertsey in Surrey, and educated at Eton and Magdalen College, Oxford. In 1633 the Earl of Leicester presented him with the living of Penshurst in Kent, and in 1643 he was made Archdeacon of Chichester. At the outbreak of the Civil War he joined the king at Oxford and attended him as chaplain during his captivity. He was deprived of his subdeanery of Christ Church by the parliament, and died in retirement at Westwood, Worcestershire. At Oxford he published his *Practical Catechism* in 1644, but as an author he is best remembered by his *Paraphrase and Annotations on the New Testament*, 1653. See Life by Bishop Fell, prefixed to H.'s *Miscellaneous Theological Works* (Anglo-Catholic Library), 1847-50.

Hammond, James (1710–42), a poet and politician, second son of Anthony H. (1668-1738). When about eighteen he was introduced to Lord Chesterfield, and subsequently became one of the clique who surrounded Frederick, Prince of Wales. In 1741, by the influence of the prince, H. was elected M.P. for Truro, but, according to Walpole, was a failure as an orator. Popular tradition said that he died of a love for Kitty Dashwood, one of Queen Charlotte's maids of honour, whom he addressed as Neæra or Delia in *Love Elegies by Mr. H—nd* (written 1732, with preface by the E. of C—d in 1743), written in imitation of Tibullus.

Hammond, James Bartlett (b. 1839), an inventor, a native of Boston,

U.S.A. He served as a newspaper correspondent during the Civil War, but afterwards left journalism to turn his attention to inventions. In 1880 he patented the typewriter which bears his name.

Hammond, Robert (1621–54), a soldier, first in the service of the royalists and later in the army of the parliament. In the struggle between the army and the parliament in 1647, H. sided with the former, but retired from active service in the same year and was appointed governor of the Isle of Wight, in which capacity he was in custody of the king from November 1647 to November 1648.

Hammond, William Alexander (1828-1900), a surgeon-general in the United States army, born at Annapolis, Maryland. He entered the U.S.A. Army Medical Service in 1849 ; was appointed professor of anatomy in the University of Maryland in 1860, but returned to the army on the outbreak of the Civil War, and was appointed surgeon-general in 1862. He was subsequently professor at the University of New York. He edited the *Journal of Psychological Medicine*, and published numerous medical works.

Hammonton, a tn. in Atlantic co., New Jersey, U.S.A., 28 m. S.E. of Philadelphia. It is a popular summer health resort on account of its mineral springs. There are manufs. of cut-glass, shoes, and aluminium. Pop. (1910) 5088.

Hammurabi (also written Khammurabi and Ammurapi, and Amraphel in Genesis xiv. 1), the son of Sin-muballidh, a ruler of Babylonia. He became ruler in 2370 B.C., and within thirty years succeeded in throwing off the supremacy of the Elamites and driving them out of Babylon. He then added Larsa and Tamutbal to his kingdom and formed Babylonia into a single monarchy. A great revival of literature seems to have followed and have been encouraged by the ruler, and he drew up a noted code of laws. *See* BABYLONIA.

Hamoaze, *see* PLYMOUTH SOUND.

Hamond, Sir Andrew Snape (1738-1828), an English naval captain, born at Blackheath, Kent. He entered the navy in 1753; took part in the battle of Quiberon Bay in 1759, and distinguished himself during the American War of Independence, especially in the defence of Sandy Hook (1778), for which he was knighted. In 1780 he was appointed governor of Nova Scotia and commander-in-chief at Halifax. In 1793 he was appointed a commissioner of the navy, becoming comptroller of the navy in 1794, which post he retained, at the special request of Mr. Pitt, until his retirement in 1806. From 1796-1806 he was M.P. for Ipswich.

Hamond, Sir Graham Eden (1779-1862), an English admiral, born in London, only son of Sir Andrew Snape Hamond, Bart. He was entered on the books of the navy in 1785; served in Lord Howe's flagship at the battle of the First of June 1794 ; took part in the Baltic campaign; and was present at the battle of Copenhagen, 1801. He was made rear-admiral in 1825, and was commander-in-chief of the S. American station, 1834-38. He became an admiral in 1847, and admiral of the fleet in 1862.

Hampden, John (1594 – 1643), a statesman, entered parliament at the age of twenty-seven, but first came into prominence in 1626, when he was imprisoned for declining to pay the forced loan raised in that year. He was a leader of the opposition to the king, and a

JOHN HAMPDEN

firm and stalwart objector to ship-money and other methods of raising money, which he regarded as illegal. As a matter of principle he refused to pay the small sum at which he was assessed in respect of his property, but in the courts the judgment went against him. In 1642 he was impeached, but contrived to escape arrest when the king in person came to the House of Commons on Jan. 4 in that year. He took an active part in organising the parliamentary army, but early in the Civil War was mortally wounded at Chalgrove Field. His untimely death was a great blow to his party. There are biographies by Lord Nugent (1831), which occasioned Macaulay's famous article, and by John Forster (1837).

Hampden, Renn Dickson (1793-1868), an English divine, born in Barbados. He was appointed principal of St. Mary's Hall, Oxford, in 1833, professor of moral philosophy in 1834, and, in spite of violent opposition, regius professor of divinity in 1836. His Bampton lectures, delivered in 1832, on ' The Scholastic Philosophy considered in its relation to Christian Theology,' in which he upheld the theory that the authority of Scriptures is of greater weight than that of the Church, resulted in a charge against him of unorthodoxy, and a violent controversy ensued. His appointment as Bishop of Hereford in 1847 was the signal for another outbreak. His chief works are : *Work of Christ and the Spirit*, 1847 ; *Lectures on Moral Philosophy*, 1856 ; and *Fathers of Greek Philosophy*, 1862. See *Memorials* by his daughter, Henrietta Hampden, 1871.

Hampole, Richard Rolle (known as the Hermit of Hampole), *see* ROLLE, RICHARD.

Hampshire, Hants, or County of Southampton, a southern maritime co. of England, bounded by Dorset, Wilts, Berks, Surrey, Sussex, and the English Channel. The coast is broken by the great inlets of Langston and Portsmouth Harbours (divided by Hayling and Portsea Islands), Southampton Water, Christchurch and Poole Bays. The Isle of Wight is separated from the mainland by the Solent and Spithead. The surface of the county is diversified by the Downs, rising to 940 ft. in Sidown Hill, and 1011 ft. in Inkpen Beacon, the highest chalk-down in England. The south-western portion of the county, cut off by Southampton Water, is occupied by the New Forest (*q.v.*), while in the E. are remains of the forests of Bere, Woolmer, and Waltham Chase. The chief rivers are the Avon, the Test, and the Itchen. The chief industries are agriculture and market-gardening, while Hampshire pigs are famous. The manufactures are unimportant except those connected with the government establishments at Portsmouth. The county is very rich in Roman remains, and there are many notable monastic buildings and old castles, including Porchester Castle, Carisbrooke Castle in the Isle of Wight, Netley and Beaulieu Abbeys. H. (exclusive of the Isle of Wight) returns five members to parliament, and Portsmouth, Southampton, Winchester, and Christchurch are parliamentary boroughs. Other important towns are Aldershot, Andover, Basingstoke, Bournemouth, and Romsey. Area (including the Isle of Wight) 1,048,916 acres. Pop. (1913) 915,503. See Victoria County History, *Hampshire*, and Ball and Varley's *Hampshire*, 1909.

Hampshire, a British armoured cruiser of the *Devonshire* type (naval estimates 1901-2), with two torpedo tubes, 21,000 horse power; 22·5 maximum speed.

Hampstead, a parl. and metropolitan bor. and residential suburb of N.W. London. In the early part of the 18th century it was famous for its medicinal springs. On the top of a hill (430 ft.) is Hampstead Heath (480 acres), a favourite resort of Londoners, which affords a splendid view and most bracing air. An old house on the Heath, now a private residence, was the meeting-place of the Kit-Kat Club, frequented by Steele, Addison, Richardson, and Walpole. Other famous names connected with H. are Pitt, Constable, Du Maurier, Keats, Joanna Baillie, and Leigh Hunt. The chief institutions are the Orphan Working School, the General and Fever Hospitals, New and Hackney Colleges. The borough includes the greater part of Primrose Hill to the N. of Regent's Park. H. returns one member to parliament. Area 2265 acres. Pop. (1911) 85,510. See Baine's *Records of Hampstead*, 1890, and C. A. White's *Sweet Hampstead*, 1901.

Hampton, the cap. of Elizabeth co., Virginia, U.S.A., at mouth of James R., 70 m. S.E. of Richmond. A strongly fortified naval station and a shipping point for fish and oysters. Pop. (1910) 5505.

Hampton, a par. in Uxbridge div. of Middlesex, England, on R. Thames 15 m. S.W. of London, on the London and South-Western Railway. It contains many fine private residences, and near it is the old royal palace and park of Hampton Court. The palace was partly built by Wolsey and contains some beautiful paintings. Pop. (1911) 9221.

Hampton, Wade (1818-1902), an American soldier and statesman, born at Columbia, S. Carolina; educated at S. Carolina University. In early life he served in the legislature of S. Carolina, but his views as a Union Democrat were unpopular. He enlisted at the beginning of the Civil War, and formed and equipped the command of infantry, cavalry, and artillery known as 'Hampton's Legion' which served with distinction at Bull Run and Seven Pines. Wade was prominent at Gettysburg, in the Shenandoah Valley, and in command of J. E. Johnston's cavalry. He was governor from 1876-78, and a senator from 1878-91.

Hampton Court Conference, a conference between the bishops and the Puritans which took place at Hampton Court Palace in 1604. James I., on his way to London, after his accession, was presented with the Millenary Petition by the Puritan clergy, demanding the reformation of certain abuses in the church and the relaxation of certain penalties directed against themselves. James, whose dislike of the Scottish Presbyterians was extended to the English Puritans, had no intention of complying with their demands, which would have involved changes in the Prayer Book unacceptable to the mass of the clergy and a large proportion of the people, and called a conference in which the High Church element so preponderated over the Puritan that the rejection of the latter's demands, with a few trifling exceptions, was a foregone conclusion. See *Political History of England*, vii.

Hampton Court Palace, on the Thames, 15 m. S.W. of London, was built by Cardinal Wolsey in 1515, and was presented by him to Henry VIII. in 1526. Henry VIII. enlarged it and formed a fine deer park around it; and Jane Seymour died here at the birth of her son, Edward VI. Mary, Elizabeth, Cromwell, and the Stuarts used it as a residence; the Hampton Court Conference was held here in 1604, and Charles I. was imprisoned in the palace. William III. partly rebuilt it from the designs of Sir Christopher Wren, and laid out the park and gardens in the Dutch style. It was used as a royal residence till the reign of George II., since when it has been lent in suites to well-born pensioners of the crown. The state apartments are open to the public, and the picture gallery contains some valuable works of Italian art and other masterpieces. The palace is one of the finest extant examples of Tudor architecture, and the park and grounds are of great beauty. In one of the greenhouses is the famous vine planted in 1768. N. of the palace is the royal demesne of Bushey Park (1000 ac.). See Law's *Hampton Court in Tudor, Stuart, Orange, and Guelph Times*, 1885-91; *Masterpieces of the Royal Gallery of Hampton Court*, 1904; and Julia Cartwright's *Hampton Court*, 1909.

Hampton Roads, a channel between Chesapeake Bay and the estuary of the James R., Virginia.

Hampton Roads, Battle of. Two notable naval engagements took place in Hampton Roads during the Civil War. In 1862 the Confederate ironclad, *Virginia* (' Merrimac '), destroyed the Federal frigates *Cumberland* and *Congress*, the other Union vessels (*Minnesota, St. Lawrence*, and *Roanoke*) escaping. Returning the next day to crush these also, the *Virginia* found the Federal ironclad *Monitor* awaiting her. This was the first engagement between the iron-clads, and the *Virginia* was forced to retire. *See* MONITOR.

Hampton Roads Conference, an in-formal conference held in the cabin of the *River Queen*, near Fort Monroe, in 1865, brought about by Blair to try and arrange peace between N. and S. President Lincoln and Seward, Secre-tary of State, represented the U.S.A. government, while vice-president Stephens, Senator Hunter, and Camp-bell, Assistant Secretary of War, represented the Confederates. Lin-coln would only consider peace pro-positions which ensured complete restoration of the Union, and ac-cepted the Emancipation Proclama-tion. He disapproved of a joint attack upon the French in Mexico, and the conference broke up without reaching any definite conclusion. *See* Davis, *Rise and Fall of the Confederate Government*, ii., 1881 ; Nicolay and Hay. *A. Lincoln* . . ., x., 1890 ; *Camb. Mod. Hist.*, vii., 1903.

Hampton Wick, a tn. of England, in the co. of Middlesex, 15 m. S.W. of London. Pop. (1911) 2417.

Hamster (*Cricetus*), a genus of rodent animals of the Muridæ family. There are in all nine species, of which the most important is the Common H., occurring in certain districts of Germany, and in parts of Europe and Asia. The H. has a stoutish body with thick glossy coat, short legs and tail, and is about one foot in length.

HAMSTER

It breeds twice during the year. During the winter it hibernates, living upon its store of food consisting of roots, grains, and fruits. The H. is a great pest to the farmers of the countries where it abounds, and is very destructive to their crops. The male H. is very pugnacious, and will defend itself to the last gasp.

Hamsun, Knut (*b.* 1860), a Nor-wegian writer. Brought up in the Lofoden Isles, he early showed a powerful and original genius, which was developed by a wandering life. After running away to sea, he became successively a schoolmaster, a stone-breaker, a tramway-conductor in America, and a journalist. The publication of his novel *Sult*, 1888 (English trans. *Hunger*, 1899), won him fame and recognition. Other works are: *Lars Oftedal*, 1889; *Mys-terier*, 1893; *Pan*, 1894; *Redaktör Lynge*, 1898; *Siesta*, 1897; *Kratskow*, 1904, and dramas. *Norn*, written in 1894, contains beautiful descriptions of scenery and forest life.

Hamun, a huge shallow trough in Seistan, on the borders of Persia and Afghanistan, is about 100 m. long. It is generally dry, excepting after heavy rains. Two large lakes receive the Helmund, Furrah-Rud, and Harud, at the N. end. The water is for the most part salt.

Han, a river of Korea, flows W. to the Yellow Sea, is navigable to vessels of shallow draught to 100 m. above Söul, where there are rapids.

Hanaper, an office in the Court of Chancery, now abolished, under an officer called the clerk of the ' hanaper ' (Med. Lat. *hanaperium*), a wicker basket or hamper, in which writs and other documents were kept, hence the derivation of the name. The office still survives in Ireland, and from the H. are issued writs for the return of members of parliament. The Comptrollers of the Hanaper were abolished in 1842.

Hanau, a tn. in the prov. of Hesse-Nassau, Prussia, 13 m. N.E. of Frank-fort, at the confluence of the Kinzig and the Main. There is an old and new town; Protestant refugees founded the latter in 1597, when they came from Holland and Belgium, and introduced woollen and silk manu-factures. Other manufactures are carpets, leather, gloves, porcelain, paper, and machinery. Diamond cutting is also carried on, and there are government powder works near. Napoleon defeated the Austrians and Bavarians here in 1813 on his retreat from Leipzig. It is the birthplace of the brothers Grimm. Wilhelmsbad, a watering-place noted for its mineral springs, is in the neighbourhood. Pop. 34,411.

Hanbourdin, a tn. in France, dept. of Nord, 4 m. S.W. by W. of Lille. Pop. about 6200.

Hanbury, Sir James Arthur (1832-1908), an English army surgeon, graduated at Dublin, obtained M.R.C.S., and entered the Army Medical Department. He served in China, India, and was under Lord Roberts in Afghanistan, receiving a bronze star and C.B. after the march to Kandahar. He also served in the Egyptian War, after which he received K.C.B.

Hanbury, Rt. Hon. Robert William

(1845-1903), an English statesman and politician. He took up politics in 1872, entering the House of Commons as M.P. for Tamworth. From 1878-80 he was member for N. Stafford, and from 1886-1903 sat for Preston. In 1895 he was chosen Financial Secretary to the Treasury. A number of reforms in connection with the army and civil service were accomplished owing to his initiative. In 1899, he carried through the post-office scheme of telephone communication, representing the Postmaster - General in the House of Commons. He was made president of the Board of Agriculture in 1900, by Lord Salisbury, and continued to occupy this office under Mr. A. J. Balfour in 1902.

Hancock, a vil. in Houghton co., Michigan, U.S.A., on the N. of Portage Lake, 1 m. N. of Houghton. A ship-canal connects it with Lake Superior. In the neighbourhood are rich copper mines, in connection with which there are smelting furnaces and machine shops. Pop. (1910) 8981.

Hancock, Winfield Scott (1824-86), a famous American soldier, born in Montgomery co., Pa. In 1844 he graduated from the United States military academy and served for two years with the Sixth Infantry in the Indian country. In the Mexican War he fought with credit, and in 1847 was made first lieutenant ' for gallant and meritorious conduct ' at Contreras and Churubusco. He served successively as regimental adjutant and quartermaster from 1848 to 1855, and in that year was appointed captain and assigned duty in Florida. At the outbreak of the Civil War, H. was appointed brigadier-general of volunteers, and fought with distinction at Williamsburg, Fredericksburg, Chancellorsville, and Gettysburg. In 1866 he received his commission as majorgeneral in the regular army. In 1880 he was made the democratic nominee for president of the U.S.A., but was defeated. *See* Walker, *General Hancock,* 1894.

Hand, *see* MANUS.

Hand, in heraldry, is termed either ' dexter,' right, or ' sinister,' left, and when seen in the escutcheon, signifies equity, fidelity, and friendship.

Handcuffs, instruments for securing prisoners under arrest, known in the 15th and 16th centuries as swivels, or manacles. They generally consist of two divided metal rings, connected by a short chain, adjustable to wrists of different sizes, and of recent years several improvements have been made in their construction. A long chain is used to remove gangs of prisoners from one prison to another, connecting the separate

H. by which each prisoner is secured, and made fast at both ends by what are known as ' end-locks.' Some H. are made so that they can be placed on the wrist and immediately secured by a single movement. There are several appliances, of recent invention, resembling handcuffs, employed by the police, such as ' snaps,' ' nippers,' ' twisters,' etc., differing from H. in that they are meant for one wrist only, the handle part being held by the officer conveying the prisoner.

Handeck, a waterfall in Switzerland in the canton of Bern, is on the R. Aar. It has a magnificent fall of 240 ft. into a dark chasm.

Handel, Georg Friedrich (1685-1759), born at Halle of unmusical parentage, was destined for law, but showed such remarkable proclivity for music that he was finally permitted to adopt it for a career. He studied under the famous organist, Zuchau, and made

GEORG FRIEDRICH HANDEL

rapid progress in composition, the organ, harpsichord, and violin. He became organist at Halle Cathedral in 1702 ; the following year he was engaged as second violin in Keiser's orchestra at Hamburg, where he shortly produced his first operas, *Almira* and *Nero.* He next visited Florence, Venice, Rome, and Naples (1706-10), producing operas with considerable success. Similar good fortune awaited him in London, where he produced *Rinaldo* (1711). From this time until his death, H. practically remained in England, his closest friends including such men as Pope, Fielding, Arne, and Hogarth; and he was subsequently naturalised in 1726. The death of his admiring patron, Queen Anne, the stoppage of his pension (awarded him in recognition of his fine *Utrecht Te Deum*), and the succession of the Elector of Hanover, whom he had offended by leaving, caused him much anxiety; but he was restored to favour in 1715, and afterwards became choir-master to the Duke of Chandos. This post he retained until 1720, composing, meanwhile, the famous serenade *Acis and Galatea*, many anthems, and some harpsichord pieces. His first oratorio in English, *Esther*, was also produced with great success (1720). The same year saw the foundation of an operatic company under the management of H. and his rival Bononcini; for its productions, H. wrote over a dozen operas, including *Ottone*, 1722; *Tamerlano*, 1724, and *Scipione*, 1726. On the company's failure (1728) H. organised a similar affair, for which he wrote another dozen operas or more, including *Arianne*, *Deborah*, and *Athaliah*, all 1733, and *Alcina*, 1735. The failure of this venture (1737) brought on an attack of paralysis, and he was forced to go to Aix-la-Chapelle. Shortly after his return in 1739 he forsook opera and turned to oratorio, and from that time until blindness overtook him (1752) he wrought, in fifteen oratorios of unique, unprecedented splendour, the reformation and development of choral composition on which his claim to greatness principally rests, commencing with *Saul*, 1739 ; *Israel in Egypt*, 1739, his finest work, but neglected ; and *L'Allegro*, 1740. The year 1742 witnessed the production at Dublin of the wonderful *Messiah*, which shares with Mendelssohn's *Elijah* the greatest popularity of any oratorio ever written. His chief subsequent works were, *Samson*, 1743; *Judas*, 1747; *Theodora*, 1750, a beautiful work which has never been appreciated, and, last of all, *Jephtha*, 1752. Although of German birth and saturated with Italian ideas, H. is remembered purely as an English composer, by reason of the tradition of big choral writing which he founded, a peculiarly English tradition, best exemplified to-day in Elgar and Granville Bantock. It was in England, unfettered by German and Italian conventions, that he could best express his ideas, dramatic and devotional. With the exception of J. S. Bach, H. far outshone his contemporaries. For the most part he adhered strictly to accepted forms; he had an excellent sense of balance; and his sure instinct for dramatic

values was a predominating feature in his operas and oratorios alike. His writings are marvellously fluent, and his skill in contrapuntal choral writing profound; his music is consequently rich in effects at once broad, massive, noble and inspiring: the ideals of classical oratorio. H. was a very fine performer on the organ and harpsichord ; and his instrumental music is still greatly appreciated, *e.g.* his *Suites pour le Clavecin*, and the *Concerti grossi*.

Handfasting, a custom at one time prevalent in Scotland by which a kind of temporary marriage was entered into by the joining of hands (A.-S. *handfœstan*, to pledge one's hand). Persons thus handfasted were joined together for a year and a day, after which period, they could either be formally united, or, if so desired, separate. Sir Walter Scott describes the custom in his book, *The Monastery*. It was the means of bringing about great evils in society, and many injunctions were directed against it by the clergy both before and after the Reformation.

Hand-glass, a portable glass cover used by gardeners for sheltering plants in winter, or to secure a uniform amount of moisture to young plants, and protect them from severe weather, without excluding light. They are often made with cast iron frames and movable tops.

Handicap, in games and sports is a disadvantage placed upon the abler competitors in order to reduce the participants to equality and thus afford a closer contest. There are many methods of handicapping, depending upon the nature of the contest. In foot races the best runner has to cover a greater distance, in billiards the better player to score a greater number of points. In yacht races a shorter time is allowed, while in shooting matches a greater range is fixed. In such games as draughts and chess the better player is deprived of some of his pieces, and loses one or more moves at the beginning of the game. Cricket matches are common in which one side takes the field with more than the usual number of men. Handicapping is general in horse - racing, where the weight a horse has to carry is fixed in proportion to his quality. This practice originated at the beginning of last century and at first took the form of a H. according to the horse's age. The handicappers are licensed by the Jockey Club, and upon the publication of the weight to be carried owners have the option of withdrawing their horses from the contest without losing their entrance money. The weight to be carried is carefully taken into account in estimating the chances of the horse winning the race.

Hands, Laying on of, a religious ceremony used to accompany various sacramental and other rites. Instances of the ceremonial imposition of hands are numerous both in the O.T. and N.T., and the custom has been continued to the Christian Church. In the Early Church, it accompanied confirmation, absolution, ordination, and a number of minor rites and benedictions. The Greek Church no longer retains it for confirmation, and the Roman Church does not make use of it in absolution.

Handsel, a term formerly used in England, denoting earnest-money, viz., part payment by way of a bargain. In Scotland it means the first of a series of business transactions, and is also employed to signify a present or gift made (generally to servants and children) on the first Monday in the year— hence, Handsel Monday.

Handspike, a bar, generally made of wood, used as a lever for raising weights or for heaving a windlass.

Handsworth: 1. A par. and vil. in the West Riding of Yorkshire, 4 m. S.E. of Sheffield : has quarries, nurseries, and collieries. Pop. (1911) 14,199. 2. In Staffordshire, is a suburb of Birmingham, between Birmingham and West Bromwich. Pop. (1911) 68,618.

Hand - tree, *see* CHEIROSTEMON PLATANOIDES.

Handwriting, *see* WRITING.

Hanford, a city in King's co., California, U.S.A., 20 m. W. of Visalia, is the centre of an oil district. It is also the shipping depôt for distributing agricultural produce. Pop. (1910) 4829.

Hang-Chau-fu (Hangchow-fu), cap. of Chekiang prov., China, on the Tsientang-kiang, which flows into Hangchow Bay. It is the Kinsai, Kingtse, or Quinsay of Marco Polo, at the S. terminus of the Imperial or Grand Canal. Noted for trade in silk manufactures, fans, and gold-embroidered stuffs, and as a literary centre, the port was opened to foreign commerce, 1896. H. was the capital of the S. Sung dynasty, 1127-1278, and was held by the Taipings, 1861-64. Near by is Lake Sihu. A railway to Shanghai (110 m. distant) and Ningpo is being constructed. The estuary tides below Hangchow, causing the 'Hangchow bore,' considerably hinder navigation. Pop. 350,000. *See* Moule, *Notes on Hangchow,* 1889; Scidmore, *China . . .,* 1900; *Marco Polo* (Yule's ed.), 1874.

Hanging, *see* CAPITAL PUNISHMENT.

Hanging Gardens of Babylon, a structure of ancient Babylon, famed as one of the Seven Wonders of the World. It was probably made by order of Nebuchadnezzar (604-561 B.C.) to please his Median queen, Amyitis. It appears to have been a kind of tower or pyramid rising in terraces over a square, about 4 acres in area. The terraces rested on arches supported by hollow pillars (75-300 ft. high), and were planted with trees, shrubs, groves, and flowers. Fountains and banqueting - halls were interspersed. Water was pumped up from the Euphrates for a reservoir at the top, from which the gardens were irrigated. The story ascribing them to Semiramis has no historical foundation. Probably the N. portion of the mound Amran ibn ali is on the site. *See* Diodorus, ii. 1; Strabo, xvi. 1, 5; Ward, *The Master of the Magicians ;* Rawlinson, *Ancient Monarchies,* ii. and iii.

Hangnest, a name for birds of the sub-family Icteridæ, sometimes called Troupials or Orioles, resembling finches. They are brilliant black and yellow in colour, and good songsters, found especially in the tropical parts of S. America, where the *Cassicus* and *Ostriops* genera abound, and in Baltimore, N. America, where they are known as hang-birds in many parts. Their purse-like nests, sometimes 2 ft. long, hang from branches, with an entrance near the bottom to one side. These passerine birds of America are related to the starlings and weaver-birds of the eastern hemisphere.

Hangö, a port and fashionable watering-place at N.W. extremity of the Gulf of Finland. It is a railway terminus and has an active trade by sea, being the only winter ice-free port in Finland. It imports coal, cotton, iron, and breadstuffs, and exports butter, fish, timber, and wood pulp. In 1714 a Russian fleet, with the Czar Peter as rear-admiral, won a victory off H. over the Swedes; while in the Crimean War (1854-56) the works near Hangö Head were several times engaged by British ships. Pop. about 5000.

Han-hai (' dry sea '), the Chinese name for a great tract of desert in Central Asia. It is an area of inland drainage, divided by hills into the basin of the Tarim and the desert of Gobi.

Han-kiang, or **Hang-kiang,** a riv. in China, rises in the mountains of Tsinling in the Shensi prov. It then flows through Hupé, and enters the Yangtse-kiang at Hankow. It is 900 m. long, and navigable for small boats for most of its course. The country it drains is rich in minerals, and thickly populated.

Hankow, Hankau, or **Han-keu,** a treaty port (since 1861) of Hu-peh prov., China, at the confluence of the

Han-kiang, and the Yangtse-kiang. Han-yang (with large ironworks) is opposite across the Han, and Wu-chang across the Yangtse. The city was walled round in 1863. It is the chief emporium of Central China, exporting tea, antimony, ore, hides, rhea, fibre, beans, silk, tobacco, wood-oil, and Chinese medicines. The railway between Hankow and Peking was completed in 1905, and a line to Canton has been surveyed. The town has been submerged (1866, 1869, and 1870), but structures to prevent the rise of the river have been built along the river frontage of the British settlement. Pop. about 826,000. H. was the scene of much fighting in the revolutionary uprising in Oct. 1911. *See* CHINA.—*History.*

Hanley, the centre of the potteries dist., Staffordshire, is situated 1 m. N.N.E. of Stoke-upon-Trent, it was made a municipal bor. in 1857, a parl. bor. with one member, in 1885, and a co. bor. in 1888. Large coal and iron mines are found in the neighbourhood, and extensive steel and iron industries are carried on. The manufacture of earthenware, for which the town is famous, includes some of the finest kinds of porcelain. Market days, Tuesday, Wednesday, and Saturday. Pop. of municipal bor. (1911) 61,600.

Hanna, William, LL.D., D.D. (1808-82), a theologian and biographer, was the son of a Presbyterian minister stationed at Belfast. He received his education at Glasgow and Edinburgh universities, and in 1835 was ordained to the parish of East Kilbride. While here he married Anna, daughter of Dr. Chalmers. Later he became colleague to Dr. Guthrie in St. John's Free Church, Edinburgh, and won considerable reputation as a preacher. His chief work was the *Life of Dr. Chalmers,* 1849-52, but he was also the author of many theological books.

Hannah, wife of Elkanah the Ephraimite (1 Sam. i.), to whom, in response to prayer, a son, Samuel, was given. She had vowed to devote her son to the Lord, and so the child was then taken to the temple at Jerusalem.

Hannay, James (1827-73), a Scottish author, was born at Dumfries. He entered the navy, was present at the blockade of Alexandria, and after five years' service was dismissed by court-martial for insubordination. He became a reporter for the *Morning Chronicle,* and editor of the *Edinburgh Evening Courant,* and published two naval stories, *Singleton Fontenoy* and *Eustace Conyers.* He also wrote essays to the *Quarterly Review,* and published a volume of *Lectures on Satire and Satirists.* He was appointed British consul at Brest, but

exchanged for Barcelona in Spain, where he died.

Hannay, Rev. James Owen (George Birmingham) (*b.* 1865), a novelist and ecclesiastic, born in Belfast; educated at Haileybury and Trinity College, Dublin. He became a priest in 1888 and rector of Westport, co. Mayo, in 1892. He was Donellar lecturer at Dublin University in 1901-2, and became a canon of St. Patrick's Cathedral in 1912. His novels include : *The Seething Pot,* 1904 ; *Spanish Gold,* 1908; *Lalage's Lovers,* 1911; *The Inviolable Sanctuary,* 1912: *The Red Hand of Ulster,* 1912 ; *Dr. Whitty,* 1913 ; and he has written two plays : *Eleanor's Enterprise,* and *General John Regan.*

Hannen, James Hannen, Lord (1821-94), an English judge, was the son of a London merchant, and was born at Peckham. In 1848 he was called to the bar at the Middle Temple, and he advanced rapidly in his profession. He was appointed judge of the Queen's Bench in 1868, and four years later was transferred to the Probate and Divorce Courts. He presided over the Parnell Special Commission in 1888, was made a Lord of Appeal in 1891, and appointed one of the British arbitrators in the Behring Sea fishery inquiry at Paris in 1892.

Hannibal, a city of Marion co., Missouri, U.S.A., situated on the r. b. of the Mississippi; it is an important railway centre and river port, and carries on an extensive trade in lumber, flour, cattle, cement, tobacco, etc. Pop. 12,780.

Hannibal, the name of a British battleship, with a displacement of 14,900 tons; it was launched at Pembroke in 1896.

Hannibal (247-183 B.C.), a celebrated Carthaginian general, the son of Hamilcar Barca. He was educated in his father's camp and trained in all the arts of military warfare. He was taken to Spain when only nine years old, and there made an oath to his father upon an altar of eternal hostility to Rome. On his father's death (229 B.C.), Hasdrubal, the son-in-law and successor of Hamilcar, placed him in command of the troops in Spain, and in 221, on the assassination of the Hasdrubal, he was unanimously proclaimed by the soldiers the ruler of Carthaginian Spain, his election being later ratified by Carthage. H. crossed the Tagus and subdued the Celtiberian tribes, and before 219 he had reduced all the country S. of the Iberus, with the exception of Saguntum. In the spring of that year he laid siege to Saguntum, which surrendered after a resistance of eight months. The Romans, having made an alliance with that city, regarded

H.'s action as an intended provocation to war, and demanded his surrender, which, being refused, war was formally declared between the two nations. H. prepared his army in the winter of 219, and left Spain in the following spring with some 90,000 foot, 12,000 horse, and 50 elephants (Polybius, iii. 34, 18). In the early summer he performed his brilliant march across the Alps, and on reaching Northern Italy, defeated Publius Scipio at Ticinus and at Trebia. After spending some months in winter quarters, he marched into Etruria early in 217 to the banks of the Arno.

HANNIBAL

The Carthaginian army endured great suffering from the unwholesome swamps, and H. himself lost the sight of one eye. The Roman army under Flaminius was encamped at Arretium, which H. passed by on his way S. Flaminius hurried in pursuit and fell into an ambush near Lake Trasimene, the Romans being practically wiped out and the consul slain. Rome now elected dictator Q. Fabius Maximus, who, on account of his caution, won the name of 'Cunctator.' He continually harassed the Punic forces, without risking a hand-to-hand engagement. H. marched S. to Capua and into Apulia. In 216 he encountered Æmilius Paulus and Terentius Varro, and inflicted a most crushing defeat

upon the Romans on the r. b. of the Aufidus, below Cannæ. He wintered in Capua, and several other southern towns revolted from Rome to his side. It has been said that the luxury prevailing in Capua enervated his troops; whether this be true or not, 216-215 mark the turning-point of his career. H. obtained some successes in the S., taking Tarentum in 212; but he did not feel himself strong enough to attack the stronghold of Rome until his army was reinforced. His brother, Hasdrubal, approached with his troops from Spain, but at the R. Metaurus met the Roman army under Livius and Claudius, and with most of his men was slain. H. maintained his ground in the wild, mountainous region of Bruttium from 207-203, in which year he was recalled to Africa on the success of the younger Scipio. In 202 he met Scipio at Zama, where he was defeated for the first time. He urged his countrymen to make peace with Rome and himself signed the treaty which forbade Carthage to wage war outside her own dominions without permission from Rome (201). The Romans continually urged the banishment of H., and it was felt in Carthage that the family of Barca was too great for the state. In 195, compelled by the jealousy of factions at home as well as by the enmity of Rome, he sought refuge with Antiochus III., King of Syria, who was allied with Egypt against Rome. Antiochus was defeated at Thermopylæ (191) and at Myonnesus (190), and H., fearing to be given up as a hostage of war, fled to the court of King Prusias of Bithynia. In 183 Rome sent Quintus Flamininus to demand the surrender of the fugitive, and, accordingly, to escape being placed in the hands of his enemy, H. took poison in 183. H. is a great figure in the history of the world. His army was composed of paid mercenaries of many nations—Africans, Spaniards, Gauls, and Italians—yet he retained their confidence during sixteen years of hardship and privation in a foreign land, never having a single mutiny in camp. He was an extraordinary organiser, and trained his mixed bands into a most efficient whole. The Second Punic War may more fitly be called the Hannibalic War, for he is the one prominent figure throughout it. For military strategy and statesmanship he can only be compared with another great hero of history, Napoleon Bonaparte. Consult Hennebert, Histoire d'Annibal, 1870-92; and Morris, Hannibal, 1897.

Hannington, James (1847-85), a bishop of Eastern Equatorial Africa, was born at Hurstpierpoint, near

Brighton. For a few years he helped his father in business, but abandoned the idea of a commercial career, went to Oxford, and graduated there in 1873. He was ordained, and was for seven years curate in his native parish church, built by his father. In 1882 he went to Uganda under the Church Missionary Society, but was forced to return almost immediately owing to ill-health. When that was restored he again offered himself as a missionary. He was appointed Bishop of Eastern Equatorial Africa, consecrated, and reached Mombasa in January 1885. In October, when heading an expedition to Lake Victoria Nyanza, he was murdered by King Mwanga.

Hanno, a Carthaginian navigator, who flourished about 500 B.C. H. undertook a voyage of exploration and colonisation with sixty ships along the W. coast of Africa, and on his return wrote an account, of which a Greek translation, *Periplus,* remains.

Hanno the Great (*fl.* 3rd century B.C.), the leader of the peace party at Carthage, and an opponent of Hamilcar and Hannibal. He was unsuccessful in his command over the rebellious Carthaginian mercenaries (241 B.C.), and after the battle of Zama (202 B.C.) went on a deputation to Scipio to sue for peace.

Hanno's Periplus, an extant Greek translation of an account, made by Hanno, the Carthaginian navigator (*q.v.*), of a coasting voyage he undertook along the W. coast of Africa. The date of the voyage has been assigned to about 470 B.C. Hanno founded colonies and trading stations, and explored the country. The original account was inscribed in Phœnician on a tablet and placed in the temple of Melkarth. The authenticity of *Periplus* has frequently been discussed. Consult Falconer's English translation (1797), Mer's *Mémoire sur le Périple d'Hannon,* 1885, and an essay by C. T. Fischer, 1893.

Hanoi, or **Ke-Cho,** cap. of Tong-king and French Indo-China, on the r. b. of the Song-koi or Red R., about 80 m. from its mouth in the Gulf of Tong-king. The modern town is European in appearance, and lies to the N. of the picturesque native quarter which is built round a lake. H. is in communication with Hai-Phong, both by rail and steamer, and by rail with the Chinese frontier. The chief industries are cotton spinning, brewing, and distilling, and the manuf. of tobacco, earthenware, and matches, with native metal-work, jewellery, and silk embroideries. Pop. about 150,000.

Hanotaux, Albert Auguste Gabriel (*b.* 1853), a French statesman and historian, educated at St. Quentin College. He won the notice of Gambetta by an article in *La République française,* obtaining a post in the Foreign Office, and later in the cabinet. He was deputy for Aisne, 1886-89, and Minister for Foreign Affairs, 1894-98. H. has written: *Henri Martin,* 1885 ; *L'énergie française,* 1902 ; *Du choix d'une carrière,* 1902; *Histoire du Cardinal Richelieu* (vols. i. and ii.), 1893-1903, which won the Gobert prize; *Histoire de la France contemporaine . . .,* 1903 (English translation by Tarver, 1903-5) ; *Etudes historiques sur le XVIᵉ et le XVIIᵉ Siècles en France ; La Paix Latine,* 1903 ; *Fachoda.*

Hanover (Ger. *Hannover*): 1. Formerly a separate kingdom in Northern Germany, was made a province of Prussia in 1866. It lies between Holland on the E., the R. Elbe on the W., the North Sea on the N., and Westphalia and Brunswick on the S. Its area is 14,800 sq. m., and its population (1910) 2,942,546. The inhabitants are nearly all Lutherans, but there are some 300,000 Catholics. The province is mountainous in the S., where the Harz Mts. rise to over 3000 ft., but elsewhere it is flat, and contains large stretches of moors and heath, including the great Lüneburg Heath between the Elbe and the Aller. Besides these two streams, it is also watered by the Weser, Ems, and Leine. Agriculture is carried on in the river valleys, where the soil is fertile; cattle-breeding on the heaths and marshes ; and mining in the Harz Mts., where coal, iron, zinc, lead, silver, copper, and salt are obtained. Shipbuilding and other sea-faring industries are carried on along the coast. The most important industries are the manufacture of iron and steel goods, textiles, glass, paper, machinery, chemicals. The islands of Nordeney and Borkum serve as seaside resorts. There is a university at Gottingen. The cap. is H. (*see below*). The history of H. was extremely disturbed until the year 1705, when George Lewis reunited the two duchies of H. and Celle. In 1714 he became king of England as George I., and the duchy belonged to the English kings until 1837, when, upon the accession of Queen Victoria, H. went to the next male heir, Ernest Augustus, Duke of Cumberland, fifth son of George III. In 1866 H. sided with the Austrians against Prussia, but its army was defeated and captured at Langensalza, and the duchy incorporated with Prussia. 2. The cap. of the prov., situated close to the Leine, a sub-tributary of the Weser, 82 m. S. of Hamburg and 162 m. W. of Berlin. It stands at the junction of the railway lines from Cologne to Berlin and from Hamburg to Frankfort. The town consists of the older portion, dating from the 15th and 16th centuries, with narrow streets and old-fashioned houses, and the modern additions to the N. and E. On the E. are the extensive woods of Eilenriede, while close to the town are the palace and grounds of Herrenhausen, which is open to the public. Apart from the old buildings, such as the old town hall (1439), the royal palace, and the house of Leibnitz, the town contains many fine modern buildings, the railway station being considered one of the finest in Germany, while the Kestner Museum of archæology, the town hall, and others are worthy of note. The industries are iron-founding, type-founding, india-rubber goods, machinery, hardware, linen, and brewing. During the 14th century the town was a member of the Hanseatic League, but subsequently declined in importance until the latter half of last century, when its manufactures developed. Pop. (1910) 302,384. 3. A magisterial dist. in N.E. prov. of Cape Colony. The chief town, H., 420 m. E.N.E. of Cape Town, and 40 m. S.E. of De Aar Junction, is known for its sulphur springs. 4. A bor. in York co., Pennsylvania, U.S.A., 42 m. N.W. of Baltimore. Manufs. of machinery, shoes, and cigars. Surrounded by rich agricultural region. Pop. (1910) 7057.

Hansard, Luke (1752 - 1828), a printer, born at Norwich, and educated at Boston Grammar School. He came to London and entered the office of John Hughs, printer to the House of Commons, as compositor. In 1774 he became a partner and acting-manager, and began to print the journals of the House of Commons. Subsequently, his two sons entered the business, and after their father's death they and their sons continued as printers to the House of Commons. Luke II. was buried in the parish church of St. Giles-in-the-Fields.

Hansa Steamship Line, founded at Bremen in 1880 : it does a considerable cargo trade between that port and India, Argentina, etc.

Hanseatic League, a mediæval federation of N. German cities which for centuries was of great commercial and political importance. Germany's foreign trade dates from very early times : in England, for example, Ethelred II. (978-1016) granted to ' the emperor's men ' equality with English merchants in trading privileges, and a 'Gildhalla Teutonicorum' was established in London by Rhineland merchants, under Henry II. The rent of this Gildhall (two shillings per

annum) was remitted by Cœur de Lion as an acknowledgment of the reception given him at Cologne on his way home from captivity. While the Cologners thus prospered in England, other Germans were busy elsewhere. Early in the 15th century Wisby (in Gothland) was the centre of a mercantile association which monopolised the Baltic trade, and extended its operations eastward to Novgorod and westward to England. In 1241 Hamburg and Lübeck formed a league to protect themselves against pirates, robber barons, and the tolls and exactions of feudal nobles. They were joined by other cities, and the H. L. (*Hansa*, a defensive alliance) soon absorbed the Wisby association, and not only became paramount in the Baltic, but rivalled the Cologners in England, obtaining from Henry III. permission to found a new settlement in London. After some years of contention the rivals amalgamated, and their Stafel Hof, or Steelyard (*q.v.*), became the centre of London's commerce, the Cologners retaining the chief interest. In Germany the league made Lübeck its capital city; all disputes were referred thither, and from 1260 onward a diet was held there every third year. About eighty-five cities joined the Hansa, and were arranged in four districts, with Lübeck, Cologne, Brunswick, and Dantzic as their centres. There were four great ' factories ' at London, Bruges, Bergen, and Novgorod, of which Bergen was said to be more German than Norwegian, Bruges more Hanse than the Hanse towns, and in London the Gildhalla, lending money to Edward III. and other kings, received from them valuable privileges and monopolies which led to serious quarrels with English merchants, especially as the latter had no corresponding advantages abroad. About the time of Henry VII. the league export of English cloth was forty times greater than that sent out in English ships. During the 14th and 15th century, the Hansa, though never formally recognised by the empire, was stronger than most of the rulers with whom it had dealings. It had its own financial system and courts of justice, enforcing its decrees by fines, and if necessary, by war. Strict discipline was maintained among its members, any recalcitrant city being liable to exclusion. Some monarchs who defied it were overwhelmed; for example, Waldemar of Denmark (1369). But several causes gradually tended to weaken its power: the discoveries of Columbus and Vasco da Gama diverted the course of trade, the Baltic fishery declined, and political changes in Germany made princes stronger and cities weaker. The Dutch after a hard fight secured much of the Baltic and North Sea trade, and S. Germany competed for the inland commerce, while the London monopoly was abolished by Elizabeth in 1598. A disastrous war against Scandinavia broke the power of the league, and in the 17th century it was finally dissolved. *See also* HANSE TOWNS.

Hansi, a tn. in the Hissár dist. of the Punjab, British India, 82 m. N.W. of Delhi; it has been in the possession of the British since 1802. Pop. 16,500.

Hansom Cab, *see* CABS.

Hansom, Joseph Aloysius (1803-82), an architect and inventor, was the son of a joiner, to which trade he himself was at first apprenticed. Showing an aptitude for design, he became assistant to a York architect: afterwards he entered the profession himself and designed many important buildings, chiefly Roman Catholic churches. The Birmingham town hall is his work. His name is remembered as the inventor of the patent safety cab, for which he received only £300.

Hansson, Ola (*b.* 1860), a Swedish author, born at Honsinge in S. Sweden. He went to Berlin, and his fanciful and dainty poems first attracted attention in 1884. In marked contrast to his contemporary, Strindberg, he idolises woman and his *Sensitiva amorosa,* 1887, inculcates a severe self-restraint. He married, in 1889, Laura Mohr, an authoress of advanced ideas who writes under the name of Laura Marholm. His work includes some excellent criticisms : *Der Materialismus in de Literatur,* 1892, and *Scher und Deuter,* 1894; he also wrote *Friedrich Nietzsche,* 1890 ; *Fru Ester Bruce* (a novel), 1893 ; *Amors Hœven,* 1894 ; and *Ung Ofegs Visor,* which was translated into English by George Egerton, 1895.

Hansteen, Christopher (1784-1873), a Norwegian astronomer, born at Christiania. He is especially noted for his researches in connection with terrestrial magnetism, and in 1816 he was appointed to the chair of astronomy and applied mathematics at the Christiania University. His first publication on the subject was in 1819, and was translated into German by P. T. Hanson with the title *Untersuchungen über den Magnetismus der Erde.* In furtherance of his studies, he travelled in Finland and also took charge of a government expedition to Western Siberia, on which he was accompanied by G. A. Erman. An account of the expedition was published in 1863. After his return he was made director of a new

observatory that had been built at Christiania (1833), and to which he had a magnetic observatory added in 1839. In 1837 he carried out the survey of Norway. He retired from active work in 1861, but continued to write and carry on his researches.

Hanswurst (Jack Sausage or Pudding), a conventional buffoon in Old German comedy. He was dressed in motley and provided with a cracking whip. He was vulgar, a braggart, and a great eater and drinker, and very boisterous. His familiar figure was seen less frequently after the revival of better plays, after 1700. He was sometimes called Pickelhering, and really corresponded to the Old English Jack Pudding.

Hanthawadi, or **Hanthawaddy,** a dist. in Lower Burma in Pegu div.; forms part of the valley of the Rangoon R. The capital is Rangoon.

Hants, *see* HAMPSHIRE.

Hanumân (' having large jaws '), in Hindu mythology, the monkey-king (*Semnopithecus Entellus*), a conspicuous figure in the epic *Rámáyana.* He assisted Ráma (Vishnu) in his war against Rávana, and was supposed to be of divine origin, and credited with superhuman powers, such as jumping from India to Ceylon, carrying the Himalayas through the air, etc. His exploits are favourite topics among the Hindus, paintings and temples for his worship being common, especially in the Maratha country. He is sometimes called son of Pavana (god of the winds), and was said to have colonised much of the Deccan with his followers. The Sanskrit drama *Hanumannataka* (10th or 11th century) deals with his adventures.

Hanway, Jonas (1712-86), a philanthropist, amassed a considerable fortune as a merchant, during the acquisition of which he travelled extensively in Russia and Persia. At the age of thirty-eight he retired from trade, settled in London, and published an account of his travels (1753). He now interested himself in social questions, and as a reward for his efforts in this direction, he was, in 1762, appointed commissioner of the victualling office. In 1756 he, with the co-operation of Sir John Fielding and others, founded the Marine Society, which was of great use in attracting recruits for the navy. Two years later he became a governor of the Foundling Hospital, and in the same year was instrumental in instituting the Magdalen Hospital. To him is due the invention and the introduction of the umbrella. Two years after his death a monument was erected to his memory in Westminster Abbey. There is a biography by John Pugh, 1787 (second and revised ed. 1798).

Hanwell, a par. in Middlesex, 7 m. W. of Paddington. H. Asylum, which serves for the county of Middlesex, is in the adjoining parish of Norwood. In the cemetery of St. Mary's Church, Jonas Hanway, traveller, who introduced the umbrella into England, is buried. Pop. (1911) 19,131.

Han-yang-fu, a city in China, in the prov. of Hupeh, on the r. b. of the Han Kiang, opposite Hankow. It has an arsenal and steel works. Pop. 100,000.

Haparanda (Aspen coast), a seaport tn. in Sweden in the prov. of Pitea, on the N. shore of the Gulf of Bothnia. Opposite is the Russian town Tornea. It has considerable trade, and has a meteorological station. Pop. 1600.

Haplodon, or Aplodon, a genus of primitive rodents, having the angular process of the lower jaw arising from the inferior surface of the socket of the incisor. They include two species known as 'sewellels,' natives of N. America, W. of the Rocky Mts. They are a burrowing family and partially aquatic, related structurally to the beaver and the squirrel. They are short of tail and limb, heavily built, and possess five - toed feet. The species Rufus is the longest known.

Hapsburg, or Habsburg, the imperial house of Austria - Hungary, called from the ancestral castle on the Aar in the Swiss canton of Aargan, built in the 11th century by Bishop Werner. At a later period, the owners of H. became Counts of H., and by degrees extended their territories. The first distinguished member of the race was Count Albert IV., whose son, Rudolph, became emperor in 1273, and it is to this line that the historical celebrity of the house is almost entirely due. Rudolph, Emperor of Germany, or Holy Roman Emperor, is the founder of the reigning house of Austria, the line of Hapsburg-Lorraine, and from him to Charles VI., the Austrian monarchs were of the H. male line. On the death of Charles VI. in 1740, his daughter, Marie Theresa, who succeeded him, married Francis Stephen of Lorraine, chosen Emperor of Germany in 1745, and the house of Hapsburg-Lorraine continued to provide emperors till 1806, when, with the establishment of the new empire, the title of ' Holy Roman Emperor ' was changed for that of Emperor of Austria. A Spanish dynasty was also descended from the Emperor Rudolph, beginning with the Emperor Charles V., who united Spain to the H. dominions, but in 1556 it was again placed under a separate ruler, and a

further attempt to place a H. on the Spanish throne after the death of Charles II. in 1700, met with no success. See Lichnowski, *Geschichte des Hauses Hapsburg.*

Hapur, a tn. of British India, 20 m. S. of Meerut, has considerable local trade in sugar, grain, cotton, and brass vessels. Pop. 18,000.

Hara-kiri, a method of suicide which became customary among the Japanese nobility during the middle ages. About five centuries ago it was recognised as a national institution, and was either voluntary or obligatory. A Samurai leader might choose this death rather than allow himself to be captured or disgraced ; or he might receive an intimation from court that he had incurred the death penalty for some offence, but was permitted to avoid the indignity of a public execution by disembowelling himself with the dagger which accompanied the message. Obligatory H. was abolished in 1868. On the death of the emperor, General Nogi committed H.

Harbin, a tn. in Manchuria, on the Sungari R., 325 m. N.E. of Mukden. It is situated at an important junction of the Siberian railway, since the construction of which it has made great progress. It has flour mills and breweries. Pop. 80,000.

Harbledown, a par. and vil. in Kent, 1 m. W. of Canterbury, was a well-known resting-place of Canterbury pilgrims. It contains an almshouse, formerly a hospital founded by Lanfranc for lepers, and close by is the old church of St. Nicholas. Pop. 971.

Harbour (Middle Eng. *hereberge,* from *here,* an army; and *beorg,* shelter; same root as Fr. *auberge,* an inn), a sheet of water, protected from the action of wind, etc., on the waves, and designed for the protection of ships. All Hs. may be classified either as havens for the protection of ships in storms, or as ports for commercial purposes; according to another classification all Hs. are either natural or artificial.

Natural harbours, as their name implies, are those Hs. which are sufficiently protected by their situation, without needing any artificial aid. In determining the value of such Hs., the geological and other physical peculiarities of the shore; the strength, direction, and range of tides ; the depth of water in the protected area; the angle at which the heaviest waves impinge on the coast-line ; the slope of the foreshore; and the width and shape of the entrance, must all be taken into account. Among the natural Hs. which possess most advantages may be mentioned the following: the Bay of Rio de Janeiro is one of the largest natural Hs. of the world, being 15 m. in length, from 2 m. to 7 m. in width, protected by headlands on either side, and having an entrance almost a mile in width; New York H. is protected by Long Island, as Southampton Water is sheltered by the Isle of Wight, both being very good Hs.; Milford Haven (' haven ' having the same significance as ' harbour ') has a minimum depth of eight fathoms, and combines facility of entrance with perfect security. At various places there are large enclosed areas which have openings to the sea, but these are as a rule very shallow, save in the main channels, and access is as a rule rendered difficult by the bar which forms at the mouth, where the ocean checks the outgoing current of the river. Among such Hs. may be named Venice, Poole, Wexford, and those at the mouths of various rivers; in many cases works have been carried out to prevent deterioration and increase the depth, when the Hs. more properly come into the category of artificial harbours.

Artificial harbours are those in which the natural resources of the coast are supplemented by breakwaters. Generally a H. is formed where shelter is provided to a certain extent by the natural configuration of the land, but requires to be made complete by one or more breakwaters. Where the exposure is from one direction only, and some shelter is given by a projecting headland, one breakwater at right angles to the shore, curving inwards slightly at its extremities, may be sufficient, as is seen at Newhaven. As a rule some abrupt projection from the coast is utilised to provide shelter from one quarter, and breakwaters enclosing the site complete the protection, as at Colombo. Naval Hs., which are required by maritime powers as stations for their fleets, and dockyards for the construction and repairs of ships, generally come within the class of artificial Hs. The Dover H. is purely artificial, for instance, the length of the breakwaters being over 2 m.

Harbours of refuge.—All Hs. can of course be used as Hs. of refuge when a ship is in need of shelter, but some Hs. are built more for the purpose of protection than for anything else. A refuge H. is occasionally constructed where a long expanse of stormy coast, which is near some route of ships, is without any natural shelter. In such cases breakwaters are carried out from the shore at a considerable distance apart, and converge to a central entrance of suitable width, to form the required shelter. Easy approach and a safe entrance, combined

with good anchorage, are requisite for a H. of refuge.

Commercial harbours are those designed primarily for commercial uses. On important trade routes commercial Hs. must be provided for the formation of ports within their shelter, or for the protection from the sea of the approaches of ports near the sea coast, or on large rivers. A greater latitude may be observed in the selection of a site for a H. of refuge or for a naval H. than for a commercial H. The docks of a commercial H. keep the water at the same level, for the discharge of cargo, etc. A good commercial H. should have an ample supply of machines for the removal and transport of goods, plenty of quay space, and good warehouse accommodation.

Situation of harbours, etc.—When the exposure of the H. is great, as when it is situated on a regular coastline, it is essential that there should be either a considerable internal area, or a separate basin, opposite the entrance to the inner basin, for the waves to spend their force. If possible such a basin should enclose a portion of the original shore for the waves to break upon; if this is impossible there should be a flat talus wall of a slope of at least 3 or 4 to 1. The same points which determine the value of a natural H. (*see above*) must be studied in the case of an outer H., the direction of the entrance in relation to the line of maximum exposure, etc. Mr. Stevenson drew up a formula for determining the reduction produced in the enclosed area on waves at any given distance not exceeding 50 ft. from the entrance:

$$x = H\frac{\sqrt{b}}{\sqrt{B}} - \frac{1}{50}\left(H + H\frac{\sqrt{b}}{\sqrt{B}}\right)\sqrt[4]{D}$$

H=height of wave at entrance; b= breadth of entrance; B=breadth of H. at place of observation; D=distance from mouth of H. to place of observation; x=height of reduced wave at place of observation; all in feet. If H is said to be equal to unity, then x equals a fraction representing the reductive power of the H.

In order to render tranquil Hs. of small reductive power, logs of timber called ' booms ' are used. Their heavy ends are secured by projecting into grooves cut in each side in the masonry; and they are warped down or fixed with an iron hasp at the coping course, in order to prevent the swell entering the H. from underneath. Thus a temporary wall is formed which checks the waves and prevents them from spreading into the interior basin. For further particulars on various points, *see* PIER, BREAKWATER, DOCKS, and COAST

PROTECTION. *See also* ' Researches in Hydrodynamics,' *Trans. Royal Soc. of Edinburgh*, xiv., 1837 ; Sir J. Rennie, *Theory of the Formation and Construction of British and Foreign Harbours*, 1854 ; Thos. Stevenson, *Design and Construction of Harbours*, 1874.

Harbour Grace, a port of entry and second most important town in Newfoundland, is situated W. of Conception Bay and 26 m. S. by W. of St. John's, with which it is connected by river. It does considerable trade in furs, fish, seal - skins, and cod - oil. Pop. 7000.

Harburg, a seaport in the prov. of Hanover, Prussia, situated on the Elbe, 6 m. S. of Hamburg. It does considerable trade in gutta-percha, linseed and cocoanut oil, jute, chemicals, etc. The town is a favourite holiday resort, one of its chief attractions being a castle on the river. Pop. 67,024.

Harcourt, Lewis Vernon (*b.* 1863), an English politician, eldest son of Sir William Vernon-Harcourt (*q.v.*) by his first marriage; was educated at Eton. He acted for many years as his father's private secretary during his tenure of the offices of Home Secretary and Chancellor of the Exchequer, and was closely connected with the organisation of the Liberal party during its period of opposition from 1895. In 1904 he was elected as Liberal member for N.E. Lancashire (Rossendale), which seat he has retained by large majorities. In Sir H. Campbell - Bannerman's first ministry, 1905-6, he was First Commissioner of Works, and became a cabinet minister in 1907, posts which he retained in Mr. Asquith's first cabinet, 1908, and in 1910, and then was promoted to the Secretaryship of State for the Colonies. He is an advanced Radical and a keen opponent of Woman's Suffrage. Though an admirable speaker and debater, he is rarely heard.

Harcourt, Sir William George Granville Venables Vernon (1827-1904), a statesman ; after a distinguished career at Trinity College, Cambridge, was entered at Lincoln's Inn in 1851, and three years later was called to the bar. He soon was in the enjoyment of an extensive practice, and made a name for himself at the parliamentary bar, the most lucrative branch of the profession. He had early begun to write for the *Morning Chronicle*, and was one of the original staff of the *Saturday Review*. He wrote, generally on international law, as ' Historicus ' in the *Times*. He took silk in 1866, and was appointed Whewell professor of international law at Cambridge, which position he

held from 1869 until 1887. As what may be called an Independent Liberal, he entered parliament in 1868. Five years later he became Solicitor-General in Gladstone's administration and was knighted. In the following year Disraeli came into office, and H. was in opposition. When Gladstone returned to office, H. became Home Secretary. In 1886 he became Chancellor of the Exchequer, and was looked upon as having the reversion to the leadership of the party. When Gladstone retired in 1894, H. expected to be his successor, but to the general surprise the queen sent for Lord Rosebery, under whom H. generously consented to serve. In that year he introduced his famous death-duties budget, which, although fiercely contested at the time, marked a new era in the country's financial policy. In the following year the government was defeated. In Dec. 1898, owing to want of support in the party, he resigned the leadership. He was a brilliant speaker, an excellent leader, and a most popular man.

Harda, a tn. in the dist. of Hoshangabad, British India, 64 m. S.S.W. of Bhopal. Pop. 13,500.

Hardanger Fjord, an inlet, 68 m. long, on the S.W. coast of Norway in the prov. of Bergen ; its greatest breadth is 3 m., but some of its branches are considerably narrower. The Hardanger Fjeld stretches away to the N.E., and the scenery throughout the whole length of the fjord is magnificent. The many islets and peninsulas divide the opening into various branches as the Sörfjord, Osefjord, Aakrefjord, Graverfjord, and Maurangerfjord.

Hardenberg: 1. A small tn. in the Netherlands, situated on the R. Vecht, in the prov. of Overyssel. Pop. 9778. 2. A com. of Rhenish Prussia, 8 m. E. of Düsseldorf, with manufs. of textiles, machinery, etc. Pop. 12,605.

Hardenberg, Georg Philipp Friedrich von, *see* NOVALIS.

Hardenberg, Karl August, Prince von (1750-1822), a Prussian statesman, in the service of Hanover and Brunswick, 1770-90. In 1791 he became a Prussian minister of state under Frederick William II., helping to conclude peace between Prussia and the French republic at the conference of Basel, 1795. Under Frederick William III. he became Prime Minister, 1803. At home he aimed at developing Prussia by various economic measures, abolishing serfdom, and improving the condition of the peasants generally, and providing for educational reforms and trade. His foreign policy was to oppose Napoleon, and he allied with

Russia (1805), but was soon driven from power by Haugwitz (1806). In 1810 he succeeded Stein as chancellor, and carried on the latter's reforms. H. took part in the war of liberation, and signed the first Treaty of Paris (1814). He was plenipotentiary at the Congress of Vienna (1815), and became president of the State Council (1817). See *Memoirs* (ed. by Ranke), 1877; Hennings, *Biographie des Fürsten und Staats-Kauzlers von Hardenberg*, 1824; Klose, *Leben C. A. Fürsten von Hardenberg*, 1851; *Cambridge Mod. Hist.*, ix., 1907; Wolf, *Geschichte des Geschlechts von Hardenberg*, 1824.

Harderwijk, a seaport of the Netherlands, situated in the prov. of Gelderland, on the S.E. shore of the Zuyder Zee, 31 m. E. of Amsterdam. It was a Hanseatic town, and from 1648 to 1811 the seat of a university. Herring-curing is the chief industry, with exports of wood and cereals. Pop. 7289.

Hardhead (a N. American fish), *see* MENHADEN.

Hardicanute, or **Hardacnut** (*c.* 1019-1042), son of Canute, King of England, and Emma of Normandy. On the death of his father the English crown was contested by his half-brother, Harold. The Queen Emma and Earl Godwine supported H., and Earl Leofric assisted Harold. The Witan met at Oxford, and decided that Harold should rule as regent in England and H. remain in Denmark. This was not agreed to, and H. joined Queen Emma and attacked Harold. Harold was elected king, and the queen was driven out. While H. was collecting another army Harold died, and he peacefully succeeded. His reign was cruel and oppressive. He burnt the city of Worcester for rebelling against an excessive tax. While present at a marriage feast he was seized with a fit and died a few days later.

Hardie, Charles Martin (*b.* 1858), a Scottish painter, born at E. Linton, Haddingtonshire. He studied at the Edinburgh School of Design and later at the Royal Scottish Academy (1877). Among his best works are: ' The Meeting of Burns and Scott,' 1893, and ' Burns Reading his Poems,' 1887.

Hardie, James Keir, M.P. (*b.* 1856), ex-miner, journalist, and politician, has a world - wide reputation as a Socialist, anti - militarist, woman suffragist, and temperance reformer. Born of working - class parents in Ayrshire, he had no schooling, but learned to read at home. At eight years old he was doing odd jobs, and at ten was working in a pit. Always thoughtful, Carlyle's *Sartor Resartus*

and the N.T. made deep impression on him in his early teens; he came under evangelical influence (his parents were agnostics) and joined the Good Templar movement. He was a voracious reader before he taught himself writing — longhand and shorthand — during meal-times in the pit. Trade Unionism claimed his attention, and he became honorary secretary of the newly formed Ayrshire Miners' Union, in which he was associated with Andrew Fisher, who became Prime Minister of the Australian Commonwealth. For this he was black-listed, which fact turned him into an agitator, and he devoted his life thenceforth to persuading his class to work out their own social salvation. In 1888 he contested Mid-Lanark unsuccessfully, but sat in parliament as Independent Labour member for S. West Ham from 1892-95. In 1900 was returned as Socialist and Labour member for Merthyr-Tydfil, and has retained his seat with increased majorities in three subsequent elections. In 1892 he founded with others the Independent Labour Party (I.L.P.) (*q.v.*), and was the first chairman of the Parliamentary Labour Party. Was editor of the *Cumnock News* from 1882 to 1886, and the following year founded and edited the *Miner*, afterwards the *Labour Leader*. He contributes to magazines, and has written considerably on Socialism and Labour topics, including a book on India, which he visited during a world-tour for health reasons in 1907-8. He is a lover of animals, is fond of gardening, has artistic tastes, and collects ballad literature. Though quiet and retiring by nature, he has gained from his enemies, by his outspokenness, the reputation of a political bravado. His followers look up to and revere him as a prophet. He married, in 1880, Miss Lillie Duncan, and has three children.

Harding, James Duffield (1798-1863), an English artist, born near London. He began painting in water-colours and became a member of the Water-Colour Society, 1821, giving up the exclusive use of transparent colours. He was the inventor of a tinted paper for sketching, and also attained fame as a lithographer, among his lithographs being: ' Park and Forest,' 1841, and ' Picturesque Selections,' 1861. Among his writings may be mentioned *The Principles and Practice of Art*, 1845.

Harding, Stephen (*c.* 1060-1134), an abbot of the monastery of Cîteaux, born at Sherborne in Dorsetshire. After travelling for some time, he joined the monks of Molême, near Dijon, and thence went to found the abbey of Cîteaux, of which he became abbot in 1110. In 1113 he was joined by S. Bernard and thirty other people, in spite of the fact that many had been driven away by the rigour of the order. He afterwards founded the abbey of Clairvaux. He drew up the constitution of the Cistercian order under the title 'The Charter of Charity.'

Hardinge, Henry, first Viscount Hardinge of Lahore (1785-1856), a British general, was born at Wrotham in Kent. After being gazetted as ensign, he was in active service in the Peninsular War. From 1809-13, he was connected with the Portuguese army, and was then appointed commissioner at the Prussian headquarters by Wellington, but being wounded at Ligny was unable to fight at Waterloo. After being Secretary for War in 1828, Secretary for Ireland in 1830, he became Governor-General of India in 1844, and in the following year took command in the Sikh War. After the peace of Lahore he was made a viscount, and in 1852 succeeded Wellington as commander-in-chief, being made a field-marshal in 1855.

Hardinge of Penshurst, Charles, first Baron (b. 1858), was educated at Harrow and Cambridge, and began his career in the diplomatic service in 1880, and received appointments at Teheran and St. Petersburg, becoming British ambassador at the latter place in 1904. In 1906 he became permanent Under-Secretary of State for Foreign Affairs, and in 1910 viceroy of India. In 1912 an attempt was made upon his life.

Hardingstone, a par. and vil. in the co. of Northampton, situated 2 m. S.E. of the town of that name. It contains the Northampton Cross—which is one of the Eleanor crosses. Near here, during the second half of the 15th century, a battle took place between the Earl of Warwick and Henry VI. Pop. (1911) 7568.

Hard Labour, see PRISONS and IMPRISONMENT.

Hardness, Scale of, in mineralogy. The H. of a mineral is measured according to its power of scratching other minerals. For this purpose Mohs arranged a series of minerals in definite order of H., to form a standard scale for comparative purposes. Those selected were : (1) Talc ; (2) gypsum ; (3) calcite ; (4) fluorspar; (5) apatite; (6) orthoclase; (7) quartz; (8) topaz; (9) sapphire; (10) diamond. In this scale each member will scratch all those with lower, and will be scratched by those with higher numbers. The test, which is only approximate, is best made with crystals or fragments having smooth, bright faces ; a collection of such pieces of the above minerals forms an important part of a mineralogist's equipment ; and by means of it the relative H. of two unknown specimens may be determined, which would otherwise be undistinguishable except by elaborate chemical tests. Minerals often differ in H. on different faces of their crystals, and the same face may also have different degrees of H. in different directions. More refined methods are necessary to detect these differences, and for this purpose the 'sclerometer,' an instrument in which a small point of steel or diamond is drawn across the surface under a definite pressure, is used. Useful tests may be made by quite simple means; thus talc (1) will mark paper or cloth; gypsum (2) is scratched by the finger-nail; calcite (3), fluorspar (4), apatite (5) are cut without difficulty by a steel knife; orthoclase (6) can just be scratched, and quartz (7) is harder than steel. Minerals which have a H. above (6), and cannot be scratched with a splinter of quartz, are rare, and are generally precious stones.

Hardoi, the chief tn. of a dist. of the same name in the United Provinces, India. It is situated about 60 m. N.W. of Lucknow. Pop. about 11,500

Hardouin, Jean (1646 - 1729), a French scholar, was born at Quimper in Brittany, and after becoming a Jesuit, was appointed librarian of the College Louis-le-Grand, Paris. His chief theory was that none of the old writings, except some of the works of Homer, Herodotus, Cicero, Pliny, Horace, and Virgil, were genuine, but had been written in the 13th century. He likewise denied the genuineness of all old coins and medals, and declared his disbelief in all councils of the Church held before that of Trent. In spite of these eccentricities, however, he was a great scholar. Among his works are an edition of the *Historia Naturalis* of Pliny (1685), and *Conciliorum collectio regia maxima*, 1715.

Hard Spelter, see SPELTER.

Hardt, a mountainous region of Germany, and is a continuation of the Vosges Mts. towards the N. Its culminating point is the Donnersberg (about 2250 ft. high). To the S. of it lies several valleys, among them the Queich.

Hardwar, Hurdwar, or Haridwari, a tn. in the dist. of Saharanpur, United Provinces, India. It stands on the r. b. of the Ganges, and is visited every year by a large number of pilgrims, owing to its sacred position. Sometimes there are as many as 300,000, especially when, every twelfth year, a greater festival is held. Pop. 26,000.

Hardwicke, Albert Edward Philip Henry Yorke, sixth Earl of (1867-1904), an English statesman, was in 1900 appointed Under-Secretary for India by Lord Salisbury. In 1902 he became Under-Secretary for War, and in the following year, until his death, was again Under-Secretary for India.

Hardwicke, Philip Yorke, first Earl of (1690-1764), an English lawyer and Lord Chancellor, was born at Dover. After spending some time in the office of a London solicitor, he was called to the bar in 1715. In 1719 he became a member of parliament, and in the following year was made Solicitor-General and knighted. In 1732 he became Lord Chief Justice, and four years later Lord Chancellor. In 1740 H. assisted in the government of the country, during the absence of the sovereign, and was also instrumental in settling affairs after the Jacobite rebellion in 1744. He was created Viscount Royston and Earl of H. in 1754.

Hardwicke Stakes, The, see RACE MEETINGS.

Hard-wood Trees, deciduous trees, as distinguished from evergreens (pines, firs, etc.). The name is especially applied to the oak and the ash and other trees of slow growth. In Australia the name is given to trees with timber like teak (*Backhousia Bancroftii*). The W. Indian shrub *Ixora ferrea* is another example. Ebony, walnut, maple, sycamore, and beech are also H. T.

Hardy, Alexandre (c.1560-c.1631), a French dramatist, was born in Paris. He was connected for some time with a travelling company of actors, and wrote plays for them. His plays, which he obtained mainly from Spanish and Italian sources, numbered probably about 600—the best being *Mariamne*. See E. Rigal, *Alexandre Hardy et le Théâtre Français à la fin du XVIᵉ et au commencement du XVIIᵉ Siècle*, 1889.

Hardy, Sir Charles (1716-80), an English admiral, entered the navy about 1730. In 1744 he was charged with the loss of a convoy to Newfoundland, but was eventually acquitted. In 1755 he was made governor of New York, and took part in the siege of Louisberg. In 1759 he was in command under Hawke at Quiberon Bay, and was made an admiral in 1770. He was appointed to be governor of Greenwich Hospital in 1771, and was given the command of the Channel Fleet in 1779.

Hardy, Thomas (b. 1840), an English novelist, born in Dorsetshire, and was in 1856 articled to an architect in Dorchester, and in 1862 studied architecture under Sir A. Blomfield in London until he left this profession for that of literature, his first publication appearing in *Chambers's Journal*, March 1865, under the title of ' How I built Myself a House.' This was followed by *Desperate Remedies*, 1871; *Under the Greenwood Tree*, 1872; and *A Pair of Blue Eyes*, 1873, after which time he finally adopted literature as a profession. His stories all show his thorough knowledge of Wessex life, language, and manners, while during the time that he was a student of architecture he made himself quite familiar with many villages and churches, all of which knowledge he used for his novels, some of the latter having been dramatised. Among a large number may be mentioned: *Far from the Madding Crowd*, 1874; *The Hand of Ethelberta*, 1876; *The Return of the Native*, 1878; *The Trumpet-Major*, 1880; *A Laodicean*, 1881; *The Mayor of Casterbridge*, 1886; *The Woodlanders*, 1887; *A Group of Noble Dames*, 1891; *Tess of the D'Urbervilles*, 1891; *The Well Beloved*, 1897. His poems, including the epic, *The Dynasts*, have been collected in a Wessex edition, 1912. See Miss Annie Macdonnell, *Thomas Hardy*, 1894, and Sir Bertram C. A. Windle, *The Wessex of Thomas Hardy*, 1901.

Hardy, Sir Thomas Duffus (1804-78), an English scholar, born at Port Royal, Jamaica. In 1861 he became deputy keeper at the New Record Office, and in 1869 acted for the Historical Manuscripts Commission. In 1848 he was the publisher of the *Monumentia Historica*, and he edited also many of the Rolls of early times. Among the other works which he edited are: *A Catalogue of the Lords Chancellors, Keepers of the Great Seal, Masters of the Rolls, and Principal Officers of the High Court of Chancery*, 1843; *Descriptive Catalogue of the Materials relating to the History of Great Britain and Ireland to the End of the Reign of Henry VII.*, 1862-71; *The Register of Richard de Kellawe*, 1873.

Hardy, Sir Thomas Masterman (1769-1839), an English vice-admiral, born in Dorsetshire. He entered the navy in 1781, and in 1793, after various appointments, was promoted a lieutenant of the *Meleager* frigate, and came under the immediate orders of Captain Nelson. In 1798, H. joined Nelson near Elba, and was present at the battle of the Nile. In 1803 he was flag-captain of the *Victory* with Nelson, and acted in that capacity in the battle of Trafalgar. H. was with Nelson on the quarter-deck of the *Victory* when he received his mortal wound, and at his funeral in 1806, bore the ' banner of emblems.' H. was created a baronet the same year. He joined the Board of Admiralty as first Sea Lord in 1830, and in 1837 became a vice-admiral. The last years of his life were spent in peaceful retirement.

Hardy, Sir William (1807-87), an archivist, born in the island of Jamaica, the younger brother of Sir T. D. Hardy. He was educated at Fotheringay and Boulogne, and in 1823 obtained an appointment at the Tower of London. Seven years later he held the post of keeper of the records of the duchy of Lancaster, and in 1839 was elected a fellow of the Society of Antiquaries. His work was connected with antiquarian, legal, and genealogical inquiries. While at the duchy of Lancaster, he was busily engaged on the records and calendars, and compiled a volume in 1845, entitled, *Charters of Duchy of Lancaster*. In 1878 he was made deputy-keeper of the Rolls, which post he was compelled to resign in 1886 on account of failing health.

Hardy, William John (b. 1857), an English legal and genealogical record searcher and translator, son of Sir William H., deputy keeper of the public records, born in London. He received a private education, and for a time assisted his father, later entering into partnership with Mr. Page, F.S.A. He is on the council of the Society of Antiquaries, and the editor of *Calendar of State Papers*, *Middlesex and Hertfordshire Notes and Queries*. Chief publications: *Lighthouses, their History and Romance; Book-Plates; Handwritings of the Kings and Queens of England*, etc.

Hardyng, John (1378-c. 1465), a rhyming chronicler belonging to a northern family, admitted into the household of Sir Henry Percy (Hotspur), whom he saw fall at the battle of Shrewsbury in 1403, at the early age of twelve. In 1405 he entered the service of Sir Robert Umfreville, and was made constable of Warkworth Castle. He took part in the battle of Agincourt in 1415, and served the crown in confidential missions to Scotland. Hardyng's *Chronicle* treats of the history of England from the earliest times down to the flight of Henry VI. from Scotland. The account contained in it of the Agincourt campaign has the interest of an eye-witness, but the *Chronicle* is poor history and poorer poetry.

Hare, the name of all rodent quadrupeds of the family Leporidæ, except rabbits, the two chief genera being *Lepus* and *Lagomys*. They have long ears and hind-legs, very short upturned tails, and a divided upper lip. Hs. construct 'forms,' or shallow nests on the earth's surface in the grass, and do not burrow like rabbits. They are extraordinarily swift in

leaping and running, and their colouring which much resembles their surroundings is protective. Hs. are solitary and nocturnal in habit, and feed on vegetable substances, grain, roots, and barks of young trees. They are common to most parts except Madagascar and Australasia, but abound chiefly in the N. hemisphere.

SKELETON OF HARE

Where the common *Lepus europæus* is not found, the smaller *L. timidus* (Alpine or mountain hare) generally replaces it. Two to five leverets are produced several times annually. *See* Coues and Allen, *Monograph of the Rodentia*, 1877; Thompson, *Wild Animals I have known*, 1898; Beddard, *Mammalia*, 1902. *See also* RABBIT.

Hare and Hounds, originally a schoolboy pastime in the form of a kind of paper-chase. Two chosen persons, called 'hares' have about 15 min. start (their 'law') and lay the 'scent' (usually fragments of paper). They are chased by the remainder, called 'hounds,' who have to track out their course. The one who is first to reach the goal wins. Rugby was the cradle of paper-chasing in the early 19th century. Since 1877 the game has developed into an organised sport, with recognised rules and clubs. Among noted clubs are the original 'Thames Hare and Hounds,' the South London, Blackheath, Spartan, Ranelagh, Finchley, Hampton Court, Epsom, Moseley, Highgate, Huddersfield, and Liverpool Harriers, the Essex Beagles and Oxford and Cambridge University Hare and Hounds. There is a national cross-country championship annually, held in the North, South, or Midlands of England.

Hare, Augustus John Cuthbert (1834-1903), an English author

nephew of the Churchmen Augustus William and Julius Charles H., born in Rome, educated at Harrow and Oxford. His works contain accounts of his travels, especially of the cities of Italy and France. They include: *A Winter at Mentone*, 1861; *Walks in Rome*, 1870; *Wanderings in Spain*, 1872; *Days near Rome; Cities of North and Central Italy*, 1875 ; *Walks in London*, 1877; *Cities of South Italy and Sicily*, 1882 ; *Sussex*, 1894 ; *Florence*, 1884; *South-Eastern France; North-Eastern France*, 1890 ; *North-Western France*, 1895; *The Rivieras*, 1896. He also wrote *Memorials of a Quiet Life*, 1872-76; a biography of his aunt and uncles; *Life and Letters of Maria Edgeworth*, 1894 ; *Story of my Life*, 1896-1900 ; *Story of Two Noble Lives*, 1893 ; *The Gurneys of Earlham*, 1895.

Hare, Sir John (b. 1844), an English actor and manager, son of Thomas Fairs, of London. His first appearance on the stage was at Liverpool, 1864. He came to the Prince of Wales's Theatre, London, 1865, acting under the Bancrofts, and winning a name in many of Robertson's comedies, especially as Lord Ptarmigant in *Society*. He was at the Prince of Wales' for about nine years, appearing in *Caste*, 1867; *School*, 1869; *Money*, 1872; *The School for Scandal*, 1874. H. became manager of the Court Theatre, 1875-79, producing *A Quiet Rubber*, 1876. He entered into partnership with Kendal at St. James's Theatre, 1879-88, and they introduced a number of Pinero's plays to the public. The Garrick was built for H. by W. S. Gilbert, and opened 1889 with *The Profligate*. *A Pair of Spectacles* was produced, 1890; Benjamin Goldfinch being now one of his most popular rôles. H. also played in *The Gay Lord Quex*, 1899; *A Scrap of Paper*, 1876, 1883; *Money* (at the command performance at Drury Lane), 1911. He has toured in America, and was knighted in 1907. *See* Pemberton, *John Hare, Comedian*, 1895; Scott, *The Drama of Yesterday and To-day*, 1899.

Hare, Julius Charles (1795-1855), an English theologian and writer, born in Italy. He was at Charterhouse, London, from 1806-12, and then went on to Cambridge, becoming assistant-tutor of Trinity College from 1822-32, after first travelling abroad. H. was ordained in 1826, and became rector of Hurstmonceaux, Sussex, in 1832, where he collected a splendid library. He was made Archdeacon of Lewes in 1840. H. was a leader of the Broad Church party, and became queen's chaplain in 1853. His works include: *Guesses at Truth by Two Brothers* (J. C. and A. W. Hare), 1827;

The Victory of Faith (3rd ed.), 1874; and *The Mission of the Comforter* (3rd ed.), 1876, sermons preached at Cambridge; and a series of vindications of Niebuhr (1829), Coleridge, Luther (1855), and others. See A. J. C. Hare, *Memorials of a Quiet Life*, 1872-76.

Hare, Robert (1781-1858), an American scientist. He invented the compound oxyhydrogen blow-pipe, for which the American Academy of Boston awarded him the Rumford medal (1801). From 1818-47 he was professor of chemistry at Pennsylvania University. H. invented a galvanic apparatus or 'calorimotor,' in 1816. The Smithsonian Institution has his collection of chemical and physical apparatus. He wrote *Chemical Apparatus and Manipulations*, 1836 ; *Spiritualism Scientifically Demonstrated*, 1855 ; and treatises for the *American Journal of Science* and other periodicals. See *Lives of Eminent Philadelphians*, 1859.

Hare, William, one of the Irish criminal body-snatchers. *See* BURKE, WILLIAM.

Harebell, the 'Scotch bluebell,' the name now usually applied to the charming perennial wild flower, *Campanula rotundifolia*, with delicate bell-shaped flowers, usually a lovely blue, but sometimes white. Hs., or 'witches' thimbles,' are found chiefly in the northern hemisphere, growing freely among bracken and heather on open downs and hills. The lower (radical) leaves only are heart-shaped, the others being linear (narrow blades). Lindley (1799-1865) tried to establish the spelling 'hairbell' with reference to the frail stalk, but it seems to be incorrect. H. was originally in England the *Scilla nutans* (wild hyacinth or bluebell). Always a favourite with poets, it is with them an emblem of purity. The juice yields a fine blue colour, sometimes used as ink.

Hareld (*Harelda glacialis*), or **Long-tailed Duck**, a species of sea-duck, also known as the 'calloo,' 'south southerly,' or 'old squaw' (*Clangula hiemalis*), common to the northern (Arctic) parts of both hemispheres. The male bird is variegated black and white in colour, and has a remarkably long tail. It has a loud but musical cry.

Harelip, a deformity of the human lip due to the imperfect development at an early stage of the barrier between mouth and nose cavities. The usual form is a cleft or vertical fissure in the upper lip, generally to one side of the median line (single H.), but sometimes on both sides (double H.). The latter is often accompanied by a defective roof to the mouth (cleft palate). H. can easily be cured by a slight operation during infancy if the child is healthy, but the operation for cleft palate should be performed four or five years later.

Harem, or **Haram** (Arabic *harīm*, prohibited, unlawful, sacred), the name given in the East to that part of the household set aside for the wives and concubines of a Mussulman, called also the ' seraglio,' ' zenana,' or ' andarūn.' The term is also used collectively for all the female members of the household. It is applied also to the mosques at Mecca and Medina, and to the sacred enclosure round a mosque. The H. system is of very ancient origin, and common to most Oriental communities, especially where polygamy is allowed. The Koran allows four wives to a Mohammedan (the sultan may have seven by unwritten law), but there is no limit to the number of concubines except ability to support them. The rules of the H. vary in the different countries, Turkey, India, Egypt, Arabia, Syria, Persia, Siam. Usually the ruler's mother reigns supreme in the royal Hs. Each wife has a separate suite of apartments, with female slaves and odalisques for attendants. Women must all be veiled in public; they have little occupation, and are supervised by eunuchs. No man, unless a near relative, may enter on pain of death. *See* Lott, *Harem Life in Egypt and Constantinople*, 1869; Hughes, *Dictionary of Islam;* Harvey, *Turkish Harems and Circassian Homes*, 1871 ; Denny, *Toward the Uprising;* Barnes, *Behind the Pardah*, 1897; Ramsay, *Everyday Life in Turkey*, 1897; Van Sommers and Zwerner, *Our Moslem Sisters*, 1907; Loti, *Les Désenchantées;* Driver, *The Englishwoman in India*, 1909.

Haren, a com. of Groningen prov., Netherlands, 3½ m. from Groningen. Pop. 5916.

Hares, N. American aborigines, a main branch of the Chippewas or Ojibways, themselves a subdivision of the Algonquins. They live chiefly in the regions above the Great Lakes, by the Mackenzie, Anderson, and Macfarlane rivers. They earn a living as trappers, and are often attached to the stations of the Hudson Bay Co. The H. are mostly quiet and inoffensive to strangers, though inclined to quarrel among themselves.

Hare's Ear, a name applied to certain umbelliferous plants, especially to species of *Bupleurum* (N.O. Umbelliferæ) and *Erysimum* (N.O. Cruciferæ), from the shape of their leaves (auricled). They are mostly hardy annuals, biennials, or herbaceous perennials. The flowers are generally in compound, many-rayed umbels.

VII

Harfleur (ancient *Harflevium* or *Harfloricum*), a seaport tn. of Seine-Inférieure, France, near the mouth of the Lézarde, about 3 m. from Havre. It has metallurgical works, potteries (for delft and faience-ware), distilleries, and a sugar-refinery. H. (the harbour on the channel) was captured by the English under Henry V. in 1415. The fine Gothic church is attributed to him. Alternately in the possession of France or England during the early 15th century, H. was finally recaptured by Charles VII. in 1450. Its former harbour was silted up by a stream, and Havre replaced it as an important centre. Pop. about 3000.

Hargreaves, Edmund Hammond (*c.* 1816-91), the discoverer of the Australian gold-fields, born in Hampshire, England. Settling in Australia in 1833, he was a sheep farmer at Sydney from 1834-49. He gained experience as a gold-digger in California in 1849, and struck by the similarity in geological formation between California and the Blue Mts. of New South Wales, determined to seek for deposits there also. He succeeded in finding gold near Macquarie R., at Lewis Ponds Creek (1851). He received a reward of £15,000 from the colonial government, and later a pension. H. wrote *Australia and its Goldfields*, 1855.

Hargreaves, James (*d.* 1778), an English operative of the 18th century. He earned his living as a weaver and carpenter, helping Peel to construct a carding-machine in 1760. About 1766 he invented the spinning-jenny used in the manufacture of cotton. His fellow-spinners, being strongly prejudiced against machinery and new methods, mobbed him and destroyed his frame. H. removed to Nottingham in 1768, and erected a spinning-mill there. *See* Howe, *Lives of Eminent American and European Mechanics;* Espinasse, *Lancashire Worthies*, 1874.

Haricot, a leguminous plant of the genus *Phaseolus*. The name is usually given to the dried seeds of the French bean, kidney-bean, or string-bean (*Ph. vulgaris*). They are much eaten in France, and contain a large proportion of starch and casein. *See* BEAN.

Häring, Georg Wilhelm Heinrich (*c.* 1797-1871), a German novelist, better known by his pen-name ' Willibald Alexis.' He studied law in Berlin and Breslau, but gave it up for a literary career. His first novel, *Walladmor*, 1823, purporting to be a translation of Sir Walter Scott, was very successful (*see* De Quincey's free English rendering, 1824). Other works were: *Die Geächteten*, 1825 ; *Schloss Avalon*, 1827 ; *Cabanis*, 1832 (one of his best productions); *Der falsche Woldemar*, 1842; *Hans Jürgen und Hans Jochem*, 1846; *Der Wärwolf*, 1848; *Isegrimm*, 1854; *Dorothé*, 1855. His *Gesammelte Werke* appeared in 1874; the historical romances, as *Vaterländischen Romane*, in 1884. *See* Brockhaus, *Conversations-Lexikon*; Schmidt, *Neue Bilder aus dem geistigen Leben unsrer zeit*, 1873; Stern, *Zur Literatur der Gegenwart*; *Bilder und Studien*, 1880; *Erinnerungen* (ed. by Ewert), 1899.

Harington, Sir John, *see* HARRINGTON.

Haringvliet, a channel of the Netherlands, between S. Holland and Overflakkee and Goeree Is., forming the entrance to the Hollandsch Diep, which receives the mouths of the Maas and the Waal (Rhine). Breadth about 2¼ m.

Harīrī (Hareeree), Abu Mohammed al-Kāsem (Qāsim) ibn 'Ali, surnamed **Al-Harīrī** (the silk-merchant) (c. 1054-1122), an Arabian writer, famed for his studies of the niceties of the Arabic language. He wrote two treatises on philology: *Mulhat-ul-'Irāb* (*see* Pinto's ed., Paris, 1885-89), and *Durrat-ul-Ghawvās* (*see* Thorbecke's ed., Leipzig, 1871). His chief work is the *Mācāmat* (Assemblies), fifty Maqāmas in prose and verse. It ranks in the East next to the Koran, and has influenced all the nations of Islam. *See* editions of *Mācāmat* by Silvestre de Sacy, 1822; by Steingass, 1896; German translation by Rückert, 1826; English translations by Preston, 1850, by Chenery and Steingass, 1867 and 1898. Consult Delatre, ' Hariri, sa Vie et ses Ecrits,' in *Revue Orientale*, 1853.

Hari-Rud, *see* HERI-RUD.

Harivansa, or **Harivansha,** the title of a Sanskrit epic poem (Hari's Race), purporting to be part of the *Mahābhārata*, but probably later, resembling a ' Purāna ' in some respects. *See* Langlois (French trans.), 1834; Bombay edition of the text, 1891.

Harlamoff (or Harlamov), Alexis (*b.* 1844), a Russian artist. He studied at St. Petersburg, becoming member of the Academy of Fine Arts, 1869. Later he settled in Paris, contributing regularly to the Salon, and becoming noted for his portraits (of Czar Alexander and other distinguished Russians), and pictures of children and young girls. *See* Walker's article in *Good Words*, 1889.

Harland, Henry (1861-1905), an American author, born in Russia, educated at Rome, Paris, New York College, and Harvard (U.S.A.). He wrote his early works under the pseudonym ' Sidney Luska.' These include : *The Land of ' Love*, 1887 ; *Grey Roses*, 1895 ; *Comedies and Errors*, 1898. With Beardsley and Lane, H. founded *The Yellow Book* (illustrated), and became editor in 1894. Its ultra-modern tone excited much discussion. Later works are : *The Cardinal's Snuff-box*, 1900 ; *The Lady Paramount*, 1902 ; *My Friend Prospero*, 1904.

Harlaw, a locality of Aberdeenshire, Scotland, 18 m. from Aberdeen, noted for the defeat of the Highlanders under Donald, Lord of the Isles, by the forces under the Earl of Mar, 1411.

Harlebeke, Harelbeke, or **Haerlebeke,** a com. and tn. of W. Flanders prov., Belgium, on the Lys, 3 m. from Courtrai. It has tobacco factories. Pop. about 7800.

Harlech, a coast tn., par., and ancient cap. of Merionethshire, Wales, 10 m. from Barmouth, on the Cambrian Railway. The castle was captured by the Yorkists from the Lancastrians (1468), the national Cambrian war-song ' March of the Men of Harlech ' perhaps originating during this siege. It held out long for Charles I. Its beautiful ruins still remain overlooking the sea. There are mines of manganese ore. Pop. about 1000.

Harleian Manuscripts, a collection of valuable MSS., books, and pamphlets (including the earliest known copy of Homer's *Odyssey*), originally made by Robert Harley, first Earl of Oxford (1661-1724), and increased by his son, Edward (1689-1741). Copies of the classics and of Early English poetry are included, as well as many unique illuminated MSS. A selection of rare pamphlets was published as *The Harleian Miscellany*, 1744-46, edited by Oldys (1696-1761), who also catalogued the Harleian Library. Much of the collection was acquired for the British Museum for £10,000, in 1753, from Lady Oxford. Consult *Life and Times of R. Harley, Earl of Oxford* (New York), 1902.

The Harleian Society was founded in 1869 (incorporated 1902) for publishing MSS. dealing with genealogy, heraldry, etc. Some forty volumes of transactions have been issued by it. Hon. Sec., W. B. Bannerman, 140 Wardour Street, W.

Harlem, a tn., Cook co., Illinois, now called Forest Park (*q.v.*).

Harlem, part of New York City, U.S., extending about 2 m. N. of Central Park, with East and Harlem R. on E. *See* Riker, *Hist. of Harlem* (new ed.), 1904.

Harlem River, in New York City, separates Manhattan Is. from the mainland to the E. and N. It is crossed by bridges, and is navigable, having a short ship canal, which provides a waterway between the Hudson and East rivers.

Harlequin (Fr. *arlequin*, It. *arlecchino*), equivalent to the English clown. The word is a survival from Greek and Roman comedy, the old Roman 'mimi' or mimes being players in ridiculous pieces or farces of a loose character. The character of the ancient H. was a mixture of extravagant buffoonery with great bodily agility, but in the middle of the 16th century his character changed, and he became a simple, ignorant servant, cowardly, and easily induced to commit tricks and knaveries. In English pantomime he has become a lover and magician, whose business it is to protect columbine from the clown and pantaloon.

Harlequin Duck (*Anas histrionica*), a species of Garrot inhabiting Northern Europe and Canada. It is found in Kamtchatka and Greenland, and inhabits the seashore and its inlets and river mouths, seldom being seen inland. In America it is found in Labrador, Hudson Bay, and Newfoundland, and advances southwards in winter to the United States. It receives its name from its variegated markings—white, grey, black, and brown.

Harless, Gottlieb Christoph Adolf von (1806-79), a German Lutheran theologian, born at Nuremberg. In 1836 he became professor of theology at Erlangen, and in 1845 at Leipzig. He was chief court preacher at Dresden in 1850, and exercised great influence on ecclesiastical affairs in Saxony. Two years later he was appointed president of the Protestant consistory at Munich. His chief publications are: *Theologische Encyklopädie und Methodologie*, 1837; *Die Christliche Ethik*, 1842; and his autobiography.

Harley, Robert, Earl of Oxford and Mortimer (1661-1724), son of Sir Edward H., whose family were Whigs in politics. Robert entered parliament first for the Cornish borough of Tregony, but in a short time was elected for New Radnor, which constituency he represented till 1711. In William III.'s reign he acted with the Whigs, but after the accession of Anne, in conjunction with his more celebrated colleague, St. John, afterwards Lord Bolingbroke, he deserted this party and became a leader of the Tories. He was Speaker of the House of Commons in 1701, and chief Secretary of State in 1704, which post he resigned four years later. In 1710 he was nominated Chancellor of the Exchequer, and in the following year he was invested with the office of Lord High Treasurer, and raised to the peerage with the title of Earl of Oxford. He was impeached of high treason in the early part of George I.'s reign, but subsequently acquitted.

Harlingen, a seaport in Holland in the prov. of Friesland, 16 m. W. by S. of Leeuwarden. It is intersected by numerous canals; has an excellent harbour, and carries on an extensive trade with Amsterdam, Norway, the Baltic, and Great Britain. The town was overwhelmed by an inundation in 1134 and in 1566, when a dyke was constructed for its future protection. H. exports butter, cheese, flax, bark, and salted hides, and imports grain, timber, tar, pitch, and hemp. Pop. 10,209.

Harlow, a market tn. in Essex, England, in the Epping div., 7½ m. from Ware, on the R. Lee and the Great Eastern Railway. Pop. 2600.

Harlow, George Henry (1787-1819), an English painter, born in London, the posthumous son of a China merchant. He went to Westminster School for a short time, but soon showed a strong predilection for painting, and was placed under the landscape painter, Henry de Cort. He also worked under Samuel Drummond, and finally entered the studio of Sir Thomas Lawrence, and from henceforward, devoted himself to painting. He pursued an original system of art education, and inveighed against all academical principles and rules. Among his principal paintings are 'Queen Elizabeth striking the Earl of Essex,' 'The Earl of Bolingbroke entering London,' and many portraits, graceful and pleasing in style, some of which have been engraved. *See* Cunningham's *Lives of the British Painters*.

Harmalin, a vegetable base occurring in the husk of the seeds of *Peganum harmala*, or Syrian hue, a shrubby plant growing in the steppes of Russia. The seeds are used for dyeing silk various shades of red.

Harman, Sir John (*d.* 1673), a British admiral, probably one of a family of shipowners, whose ships were engaged for the service of the state. He is first definitely mentioned as commanding a ship in the battle of Portland (1652-53), and in 1654 he accompanied Robert Blake to the Mediterranean. The following year he shared in Blake's brilliant achievement at Santa Cruz. In 1665 he was captain of the *Royal Charles*, carrying the Duke of York's flag in the battle of June 3, a few days after which he was knighted and promoted to the rank of rear-admiral. In 1666 he took a prominent part in the four days' fight off the North Foreland, in which he was severely wounded. In 1669 and 1670 he served in the expedition to the Straits, and in 1673 held the post of vice-admiral of the red squadron, dying shortly after his appointment. *See* Charnock's *Biog. Nav.* i. 396.

Harmattan, a hot E. wind blowing periodically from the interior parts of Africa towards the Atlantic Ocean. It is laden with clouds of reddish dust coming off the desert, and is usually accompanied with a fog and haze that conceals the sun for days at a stretch. It is characterised by extreme dryness, and no dew falls during its continuance—the grass, in consequence, becoming like hay, and vegetation withering. It affects the human body likewise, causing the skin to peel off, but cures skin diseases and checks infection. It prevails at intervals during December, January, and February, continuing sometimes for a fortnight, but more commonly from two to three days.

Harmer, Thomas (1715-88), a Protestant dissenting minister, born at Norwich and educated under Thomas Ridgley, D.D., and John Eames. H. began his ministry at the independent church at Wattisfield, Suffolk, before he was twenty, but was not ordained till 1735. He had much influence in the dissenting eastern counties, owing to his enterprise and studious research. He published *Some Account of the Jewish doctrine of the Resurrection, Remarks on the Ancient and Present State of the Congregational Churches of Norfolk and Suffolk*, etc.

Harmodius, an Athenian, who, in conjunction with his devoted friend, Aristogiton, formed a conspiracy in 514 B.C. to slay the brothers Hipparchus and Hippias, tyrants and joint rulers of Athens. They succeeded in killing Hipparchus, but not Hippias, who seized the reins of government alone, and revenged his brothers' death by imposing taxes, selling offices, and putting to death all of whom he entertained the least suspicion. H. was killed, but Aristogiton fled, only to be subsequently taken and executed. Afterwards, H. and Aristogiton came to be regarded as patriotic martyrs, and received divine honours from the Athenians, who raised statues to their memory.

Harmonica, a musical instrument invented in 1760 by Benjamin Franklin, the sounds of which are produced by the friction of the moistened fingers on cups or tubes of glass or metal. The H. found many admirers, and gave rise to a host of similar instruments by Chladni, Kaufmann, and others, none of them being very successful. The original H. was the instrument known as ' musical glasses,' for which Mozart and Beethoven composed. Forms of it were in use as early as the 17th century, but it has now become merely a toy.

Harmonical Progression, the name given to a series of quantities in which any three consecutive terms a, b, c are connected by the relation $\dfrac{a}{c} = \dfrac{a-b}{b-c}$. From this it may be easily proved that $\dfrac{1}{a} - \dfrac{1}{b} = \dfrac{1}{b} - \dfrac{1}{c}$, *i.e.* that $\dfrac{1}{a}$, $\dfrac{1}{b}$, $\dfrac{1}{c}$ are in arithmetical progression. Hence the reciprocals of the terms of an H. P. form an arithmetical progression. Thus $\tfrac{1}{1}$, $\tfrac{1}{2}$, $\tfrac{1}{3}$, $\tfrac{1}{4}$, . . . form an H. P. No general formula can be found for the sum of any number of terms, and questions on H. P. are solved generally by the use of the above property. The middle term of any three in H. P. is known as the harmonic mean of the other two, and hence the harmonic mean between a and c is $\dfrac{2ac}{a+c}$.

Harmonic Engine, an instrument invented by Edison, by means of which the energy of an electric current is used to sustain the vibrations of a large, heavily-weighted tuning-fork, the arms of which are connected with two pistons, which work a small pump. This pump compresses air, and is able to drive sewing-machines, etc.

Harmonic Motion, the general name given to motion of natural vibration and oscillation. Thus it includes the oscillation about the position of equilibrium of a weight supported by a spring or an elastic string, the small oscillations of the bob of a pendulum, the vibration of any point on the string of a musical instrument, and finally wave motion in general, of which the last example is a particular case. Thus, if a series of waves moves regularly over any surface, any point on the surface will move up and down with H. M. If equal and opposite waves move in opposite direction, certain points called *nodes* will remain fixed; and this is the case with the strings of a musical instrument fixed at two ends which are nodes. If a pencil moving vertically up and down with the simplest form of H. M. traced a locus on a piece of paper which moved horizontally with a uniform velocity, it would trace out the curve in the figure known as the *curve of sines*. It will be recognised by the student of trigonometry as the graph of sin x (Fig. 1). The most elementary form of H. M. is known as *Simple Harmonic Motion*. Let a point X (Fig. 2) move with uniform velocity along the circumference of a circle, and let XP be the perpendicular on any fixed diameter AB. Then P will move with simple H. M. It will be seen that P moves continually backwards and forwards along AB, coming to rest instantaneously and turning back again at A and also at B, and having

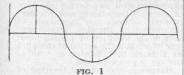

FIG. 1

its biggest velocity when passing through the centre O. The time taken over one complete journey backwards and forwards is called the *period*. The time to any position since last passing through the middle point O going in a direction previously fixed as positive, is called the *phase*, and OA is the *amplitude*. If ω is the constant angular velocity of OX, and t the time from C, the end of the perpendicular diameter to AB, to the point X; then the angle COX is ωt, and OP is $a \sin \omega t$, where a is the radius of the circle. Hence it may be seen why the locus traced in Fig. 1 is a curve of

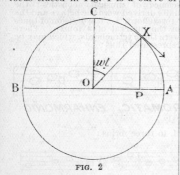

FIG. 2

sines. The period is the time for X to go once completely round the circumference, *i.e.* $\dfrac{2\pi}{\omega}$, and this result is seen to be independent of the amplitude a. Since X has a velocity $a\omega$ along the tangent to the circle, and by virtue of its circular motion an acceleration $a\omega^2$ along XO, it will be seen that P has a velocity $a\omega \cos \omega t$ along OA and an acceleration towards O, $a\omega^2 \sin \omega t$. *i.e.* ω^2XOP. Thus a point moving with simple H. M. has an acceleration directed towards the

centre, which varies directly as its distance from the centre. As the point P passes through O on its backward journey, the acceleration becomes a retardation and is still proportional to the distance from O. This very important property is sometimes taken as the definition of simple H. M. The more complicated forms of H. M. may be obtained by compounding two or more simple H. M.'s. Thus any point of a vibrating string fixed at its two ends, where the motion is made up of ten equal and opposite wave motions, moves with two equal and opposite simple H. M.'s in the same straight line. Another simple case occurs in the compounding of two simple H. M.'s of equal periods but different amplitudes a and b, along two lines Ox and Oy where the locus of the point is the ellipse $\dfrac{x^2}{a^2} + \dfrac{y^2}{b^2} = 1$.

Harmonicon, a musical instrument made of glass or metal plates supported on strings about one-fourth of the length of the free ends. Soft hammers strike the plates, which enter into transversal vibrations, varying in frequency according to the square of the length and the elasticity of the vibrating material. This name is also given to the toy musical instrument blown with the mouth, and composed of several free reeds in a case of a number of cells, two notes being produced by each cell — one by drawing in, and the other by breathing out, the breath.

Harmonics, or Partial Tones, as Helmholtz more correctly terms them in his *Sensations of Tone*, are the tones which sound over any pure musical note, their pitch being regular and governed by mathematical laws. If a taut string be plucked, for instance, vibrations are caused and a fundamental or predominating note is given; furthermore, not only does the whole string vibrate, but its aliquot parts also, each part having its corresponding sound according to the ' period ' of vibration. Half the same length of string gives a note an octave higher; one third, a fifth higher; one quarter, a sixteenth higher, and so on. These notes give the intervals of the common chord of the diatonic major scale, of which they are the theoretical basis. The production of harmonics on both stringed and wind instruments is used as a technical resource. Helmholtz showed that harmonics affect tone-quality.

Harmonists, *see* RAPP, GEORG.

Harmonium, a musical instrument invented in modern times which produces sounds similar to those of an organ by means of an arrangement known as the ' free vibrating reed,' acted upon by a current of air from a bellows worked by the feet. The invention is ascribed to Alexandre Debain of Paris, though he only perfected an instrument previously known, called the 'orgue expressif,' and the same principle followed in the construction of this kind of organ was applied to the H. The feet communicate a more or less rapid movement by the action of two pedals, according to the shades of expression which are to be brought out, and the air is made to impinge against thin tongues of metal, and sets them vibrating. Debain's invention of the H. in 1840 became more or less the model of all others that have followed. The H. is about 3 ft. 3 in. high and 4 ft. broad, and occupies little space. It has a compass of five octaves of keys from C to C, the keyboard being placed on the top, just below the lid. Under this is the bellows-board with the valves for each key, and the different rows of reeds are above the valves. A peculiarity of the free reed is that the pitch of the sound is not altered by the increase or diminution of wind-pressure, the volume being merely increased or decreased. Some Hs. are made with two rows of keys, with pedals for the feet, similar to organ-pedals, attached. This instrument may be had in various sizes and qualities, at prices ranging from £5 to £120. The best-known makers are the Alexandres and Mustel in France, and Bauer in England. A similar but inferior instrument is the 'seraphine,'

and Messrs. Mason and Hamlin in 1861 introduced a kind of H. called the 'American organ,' which acts by suction and works by exhaustion bellows instead of by force bellows. Since Debain's invention many improvements have been made to the H., the chief of which are the addition of a knee action, serving as an expression stop, or bringing into play at once all the stops; and the percussion action, the invention of Kaufmann of Dresden, which consists of the addition of a small hammer which aids the action of the wind by striking the vibrator as soon as the key is pressed down.

Harmony, the science treating of the laws which govern the relation of tones in chord-combinations and of the progressions between such combinations. The earliest attempt at H. seems to have consisted in adding a drone-bass, sustained as an accompaniment throughout a melody, somewhat in the style of the modern device of pedal-point, *e.g.* as in the bagpipes. The Greeks had some knowledge of theoretical H., although for some reason no practical application was attempted; and to understand the development of modern H. it is necessary to discuss in some detail the Greek. Pythagoras may be credited with the origination of the science of musical acoustics; the units derived were the octave and the 'tetrachord,' *i.e.* the division of tones in the interval of a fourth. There were three tetrachords, which may be represented thus:

DIATONIC CHROMATIC ENHARMONIC

FIG. 1

Of these only the diatonic has survived, in three forms:

DORIAN PHRYGIAN LYDIAN

FIG. 2

From these tetrachords the scales were derived. Fig. 3 shows the relation between these scales (or 'species') and the full Pythagorean scale, as far as the disposition of their intervals is concerned, the question of pitch being immaterial in practice, although absolute in theory.

From this system the elaborate mediæval church modes shown in Fig. 4 were derived; but the dif-

ference between Greek and ecclesiastic scales bearing the same name is worthy of note. Incidentally, too, whilst the intervals were read downwards in Greek, the modern practice of reading them upwards was used in church music at this time.

It is unnecessary here to do more than mention the hexachord system, which was later substituted in ecclesiastic music for the Greek tetrachord system. At this time also the addition of B flat to the scale made possible wider experiments in the direction of modulation. During the period when these changes were being evolved, an advance was made in the addition of

a single part, either in fourth, fifth, or octave, to a canto fermo; and in the 11th century the method of 'discantus' came into vogue, *i.e.* the singing together of two independent subjects or melodies, so constructed as

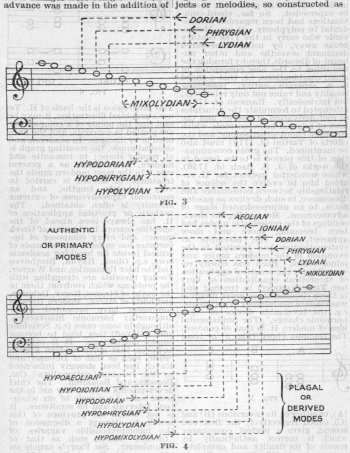

FIG. 3

FIG. 4

to produce two-part H. Other devices were tried in the course of the next two or three centuries: chords were grouped in some crude classification, and attempts made to formulate their progressional principles. The ' discantus ' had led to the reduction of subjects to regular rhythm, and had also laid the foundation of

counterpoint; and by the end of the 15th century polyphony (*i.e.* the contrapuntal weaving together of separate melodic parts) was on a fairly sound footing—four-part writing had been attained, and inversions, passing notes, discords, and chromatics had arisen. The 16th century was an age of brilliant achievement under such men as Josquin, Lassus, and Palestrina. But before further progress could be made it was necessary that the limitations and prejudices of the Græco-ecclesiastic modes, which still prevailed, should be superseded. So far, chord-combinations had been regarded as incidental to polyphony. It was Monteverde who early in the 17th century broke away, by using unprepared dominant sevenths and other unheard-of discords, thereby forming the transition to the new conception of chord-combinations, *i.e.* that a chord is a separate entity, possessing tonality and value not only relatively, but intrinsically. Rameau (*d.* 1764), attempted to formulate the principles of root-derivation of chords, and the laws of relation between roots which governed chord-progressions; and the efforts of Tartini (*d.* 1770) must also be mentioned. The great consummation of this period is to be found in the works of J. S. Bach (*d.* 1750), whose wonderful instinct for H. enabled him to evolve the science of relationship between consonance and dissonance, in such devices as passing notes, to an unprecedented stage of advancement. Meanwhile, the shortcomings of the ecclesiastic modes had been becoming more and more apparent, and the attempts at systematisation had resulted in the evolution of the modern major and minor scales. Bach was chiefly responsible for the practical application of theoretical equalisation of keys (*see* TEMPERAMENT) in tuning: and in these circumstances great progress was made in modulatory experiments, *e.g.* the invaluable device of ' enharmonic change.' The fundamental idea of modern H. is that of concord. The common chord (Fig. 5) or triad

FIG. 5

(A), or either of its inversions (B) and (C), called respectively the first and second, gives a perfect consonance which is correct æsthetically by reason of its finality and completeness, and scientifically according to the laws of harmonics (*see* Helmholtz, *Sensations of Tone*). As opposed to concords, we have discords, or dissonant chord-combinations, which must be resolved into their relative concords before a complete idea can be expressed ; unresolved discords leave a sense of incompleteness to the ear. The most familiar discord is the

dominant seventh, which is resolved into the triad of the tonic, *i.e.* of the keynote on which it is based: *e.g.*—

CLOSE OPEN

FIG. 6

This progression is the basis of H. To use a graphical illustration, it may be said that the points of a composition are plotted in concords, and the lines filled in by discords. In academic and classical music, the resulting graph is of regular shape ; in romantic and modern, less regular, as a general rule. In the most modern music the treatment of discord is carried to very elaborate lengths, and an emotional expressiveness of extreme intensity is often obtained. The æsthetic or practical application of H. has always been ahead of the scientific (except in the case of Greek music); and every composer of importance has suffered at the hands of critical jurists for breaking academic laws, *e.g.* Gluck, Haydn, Beethoven and the later Romantics, and Wagner. To-day theorists are struggling with the problems which confront them in the works of Strauss, Reger, Debussy, and hosts of others. Modern Russian composers have presented many noteworthy harmonic innovations, although in some cases (*e.g.* Scriabine and Rébikoff) they tend to become empty mannerisms. It is evident, however, that much modern French music, such as that of Debussy and Ravel, has been strongly influenced by the Russian ' nationalists ' Cui, Borodin, and Balakireff. The chief developments of H. to-day are in the tonal scale, *i.e.* a scale of six wholetone intervals and no semitones. It is not within the province of this article to attempt a discussion of the incomprehensible vagaries of ' futurist ' music, such as that of Schonberger. *See* Parry's article on ' Harmony ' in Grove's *Dict. of Music and Musicians ;* D. F. Tovey's in the *Ency. Brit.*, and works by numerous authors, amongst whom MacFarren and Stainer are prominent.

Harmony, a term used by Leibnitz to denote the relation existing between the monads or ultimate psychical units of his metaphysical system. He held that substance exists only in the form of atoms, each a self-contained individuality, and that the entire series are so constituted that each is at every moment in perfect H. with all the rest, though at the same time obeying the laws of its own self-determined development. This system pertains to the very highest and to the very lowest, and since God is the contriver of universal H., this world must be the best of all possible worlds. Leibnitz describes the relation of monads as ' a harmony pre-established by a contrivance of the divine foresight.'

Harmony of the Gospels, see NEW TESTAMENT.

Harmotome, or **Cross Stone,** found in metalliferous veins at Strontian, Old Kirkpatrick, and Campsie, in Scotland. Its prevailing colour is white, and it is translucent with a pearly lustre, and hard enough to scratch glass. When heated it fuses to a glass.

Harms, Claus (1778-1855), a German divine, born in Schleswig-Holstein. From 1816 to 1849 he was pastor of Kiel, and exercised a great deal of influence over the university students. In 1817 he wrote a memorial work in celebration of the tercentenary of the Reformation, which produced quite a sensation when published in Germany, and was widely read. It was entitled *Das sind die 95 Theses oder Streitsätze Luthers.* H. also published three volumes of *Pastoraltheologie* (3rd ed. 1878). *See* his *Autobiography* (new ed. 1888).

Harmsworth, Alfred Charles William, Baron Northcliffe (*b.* 1865), an English newspaper proprietor and journalist, born at Chapelizod, co. Dublin, and educated at Stamford Grammar School. He was the son of Alfred H., a barrister ; in 1888 he started the weekly periodical *Answers,* in conjunction with his brother Cecil H. ; this was the first of the ' snippet ' type of journal which proved so popular, and success attended it from the first. In 1894 he purchased the *Evening News,* and in 1896 the *Daily Mail* (*q.v.*) was started. Lord Northcliffe owns the *Daily Record,* Glasgow, and several provincial publications, amongst them the *Leeds Mercury* and the *Birmingham Gazette.* He is the head of the company which runs the various publications and periodicals associated with the name of Harmsworth and has great business aptitude. In 1894 he equipped the Jackson Arctic Expedition at his own expense; the volume on *Motors and Motor Driving* in the Badminton Library was edited by him. He married Miss M. E. Milner in 1888, was raised to a baronetcy in

1904, and created a peer as Baron Northcliffe, the first Baron of the Isle of Thanet, in 1905.

Harnack, Adolf (*b.* 1851), a German theologian and historian, born at Dorpat in Russia, where his father, Theodosius H., held a professorship of pastoral theology. In 1874 he became a lecturer in church history, and two years later a professor of the same subject. His lectures dealt with Gnosticism and the Apocalypse, and attracted considerable attention. In 1876 he began the publication, in conjunction with Von Gebhardt and Zahn, of an edition of the works of the apostolic fathers. In 1880 he went to Giessen as professor of church history, where he collaborated with Von Gebhardt in *Texte und Untersuchungen zur Geschichte der altchristlichen Litteratur,* a periodical containing essays on N.T. history. H. next published a work on monasticism, *Das Mönchtum, seine Ideale und seine Geschichte,* and then became joint-editor with Emil Schürer of the *Theologische Literaturzeitung.* The first volume of his epoch-making work, *Lehrbuch der Dogmengeschichte,* of which there is an English translation in seven volumes, was published in 1885. In this work H. traces the rise of dogma. In 1893 he published a history of early Christian literature down to Eusebius, entitled *Geschichte der altchristl. Litteratur bis Eusebius,* and in 1900 appeared his popular lectures, *Das Wesen des Christenthums.* He also wrote *Die Mission und Ausbreitung des Christenthums in den ersten drei Yahrhunderten* in 1902, and some interesting and important N.T. studies, which have been translated into English: *Luke the Physician,* and *The Sayings of Jesus.* H.'s distinctive characteristic is his claim for absolute freedom in the study of church history and the New Testament.

Harnes, a com. and vil. of France in the dept. of Pas-de-Calais. Pop. 5000.

Haro, a tn. in Spain in the prov. of Logroño, on the r. b. of the R. Ebro, noted for its wine. Pop. 7500.

Haro, The Cry of, an ancient form of appeal prevalent in Normandy and the Channel Is. It was thought to be an appeal to Rolf, first Duke of Normandy, but would seem to be derived from Old High German *hara,* here, a cry for aid.

Haroëris, an Egyptian deity, the brother of Osiris and ruler over heaven, identified with the sun-god, Apollo.

Harold, or **Harald** (850-933), first king over Norway, surnamed Harfagr (' beautiful haired '), son of Halfdan the Black. He vowed not to cut or comb his hair till he was sole king of Norway; ten years later he fulfilled his oath and exchanged the nickname of Shockhead for Beautiful Hair. In 866 he made his first conquests over the petty states that divided Norway, and in 872 found himself master of the whole kingdom. His opponents fled to the isles of the Orkneys, Shetlands, and Hebrides. Later he was forced to make an expedition against them. He secured the Scottish isles, and the remaining Vikings fled to Iceland and founded a commonwealth there. At the end of his reign his sons quarrelled over the succession; he assigned them lands and royal titles, leaving the chief power to his favourite son, ' Erik of the bloody axe.'

Harold (936-986), King of Denmark, surnamed Blue-tooth, son of Gorm the Old. He obtained the overlordship of Norway on the death of Harold Harfagr. He was baptised in 960, to conciliate the Emperor Otho, and tried to convert Denmark to Christianity. He was driven from his country by his son Sweyn I. (Svend-Forkbeard), the leader of the pagans. H. died during his flight.

Harold I. (d. 1040), surnamed Harefoot, the illegitimate son of Canute, King of England. On the father's death (1035) he claimed the crown with the support of Leofric, Earl of Mercia. The Witan at Oxford elected him regent, while the rightful king, Hardicanute, remained in Denmark; the latter stayed away so long that H. was crowned king in 1037. He died suddenly at Oxford while Hardicanute was preparing to invade England.

Harold II. (c. 1022-66), King of the English, second son of Earl Godwine. While still very young, he was made Earl of the E. Angles. He was outlawed and banished with his father in 1051, taking refuge with his brother Leofwine in Ireland. The family was recalled, and H. was restored to his earldom. On his father's death (1053), he succeeded to the earldom of the W. Saxons, becoming the first minister to the king. Edward the Confessor died in 1066, leaving his throne to H., who was immediately crowned. William Duke of Normandy challenged the crown, alleging that Edward left the English throne to him, and that H. was under an oath, extorted from him in Normandy during his exile. H. was now attacked on both sides: Duke William landed at Pevensey in Sussex, and Tostig of Northumberland, H.'s brother, with Harold Hardrada, King of Norway, sailed up the Humber and subdued York; they were defeated at Stamford Bridge, and while the two earls, Edwin and Morkere, kept back the northern invaders, H. marched south and engaged the Normans on the hill of Senlac (Bath), near Hastings. H. was defeated and slain with two of his brothers. He was the last of the Saxon kings.

Harold III., or **Harald** (1015-66), King of Norway, surnamed Hardraade, or Hardrada (' the ruthless '), son of King Sigurd and half-brother to Saint Olaf. When fifteen years old he fled from Norway after fighting at the battle of Stiklestad (1030), where King Olaf was slain. He found refuge in Novgorod, and then went to Constantinople, where he commanded the Varangian guard of the Empress Zoe; he won various victories in Italy and Northern Africa, and then decided to return home. On his way back he married Elizabeth of Novgorod. He now allied himself with Sweyn (Svend) of Denmark against his nephew Magnus, King of Norway, but accepted half Norway as a gift from Magnus, and strove to keep the peace. On the death of his nephew he became king and attempted to conquer Denmark; having failed he agreed to peace. He invaded England with Earl Tostig of Northumberland, and was defeated and slain at Stamford Bridge by the English Harold.

Harold's Cross, see DUBLIN.

Haroun al-Raschid, or **Harun ar-Rashid** (763-809), born near Teheran, and succeeded to the caliphate in 786. He made Barmecide Yahya his grandvizier, and left the entire administration of his extensive dominions to him and his four sons, in whose sagacity his confidence was well placed. Haroun, meanwhile, devoted himself to the pleasures of life, and his court at Bagdad became a brilliant centre of all the wit, learning, and art of the Moslem world. Towards the close of his reign he developed a hatred of the Barmecides, and caused the vizier and his four sons to be executed. His affairs immediately fell into confusion, and treason and rebellion broke out. Haroun marched against the rebels, but died at Tus of an apoplexy. A highly-coloured but false picture of his memory is found in the *Arabian Nights* stories. See Gibbon's *History.*

Harp (A.-S. *hearpe,* Old High Ger. *harfa*), a musical stringed instrument which was greatly esteemed by the ancients. It was known in Egypt from very early times, though there is no reason to suppose that they were its inventors. The Egyptian H. was bow-formed, had no front pillars, and was strung with catgut it was of great size, often standing over 6 ft. high, and the pedestal was profusely decorated with jewels and carvings; many varieties are found in ancient sculptures and paintings. The Assyrian H. resembled the Egyptian, except that the sound-body was placed uppermost. Nothing definite is known as to the shape of the Hebrew or biblical H., but it was probably a small hand instrument bearing more resemblance to the lyre. In the earliest records of Celtic history, the H. is given a prominent place; the old Scottish instrument was about 3 ft. high and had thirty strings. One of the earliest specimens, known as the *Clarsach Lamonach* or Lamont's clarschoe, was taken from Argyllshire by a lady of that family on her marriage, about 1460. The oldest and finest specimen of the beautiful Irish H. is contained in Trinity College, Dublin, and dates from the 14th century; there is a cast of it in S. Kensington Museum. The old Welsh H. resembled the Irish one, but the modern instrument is triple-strung. The ordinary Italian H. has two rows of wire-strings, but it is an imperfect instrument and now almost obsolete. A celebrated Bavarian musician, Hoch-bruker, invented pedals about 1730, but it is to Sebastian Erard that we owe the power and sweetness of the modern pedal instrument. For many years he worked at the invention of a double action pedal, and gained a great triumph on the production of his mechanism in Paris, 1810.

Harpagus, a general of Cyrus the Great, the Persian monarch. He conquered the Carians, Lycians, and Asiatic Greeks about 540 B.C.

Harpalidæ, a genus of beetles belonging to the family of Carabidæ (carnivorous ground beetles) and to the Pentamera group. All Pentamera have five joints to the tarsi of each leg. Members of this genus are small in size, with the pronotum as big as the abdomen. In colour they are sometimes bronze-green and sometimes blue or black. They kill vermin, such as millepedes, caterpillars, etc., and so are useful in the garden. The *Harpalus Æneus* and the *Harpalus ruficornis* are commonly found under stones, at the foot of trees, on paths, or in dry leaves.

Harpalus, a Macedonian who was treasurer, or receiver-general to Alexander the Great. His headquarters were at Babylon, and in the winter of 325-24, while the king was in India, he seems to have so betrayed the trust reposed in him as to have made him afraid to meet Alexander on his return. Taking 8000 mercenaries and treasure to the value of about a mil-

lion and a quarter sterling, he fled to Greece. By the orders of Demosthenes he was warned off the harbours of Attica, so he left his troops and part of the treasure at Tacnarum and proceeded to the Piræus alone to try and persuade Demosthenes to go to war with Alexander, which he refused to do. Meantime Antipater and Olympias sent to demand that H. should be given up. This Demosthenes declined to do, but he had him arrested and the treasure deposited in the Parthenon. H. escaped, but met his death soon after at the hands of one of his own officers (324 B.C.), and Demosthenes was fined and exiled from Athens on the plea that he had taken some of the treasure.

Harpe, Jean François de la, *see* LA HARPE.

Harpenden, par., vil., and urban dist., mostly residential, in Hertfordshire, England, 25 m. from London. Sir John Bennett Lawes began his systematic experiments in agriculture at Rothamsted (1843) near by, and in 1889 provided an endowment of £100,000 for the continuance of the experiments. Pop. (1911) 6173.

Harper and Brothers, New York printing and publishing firm, founded by James (1795-1869), John (1797-1875), Joseph Wesley (1801-70), Fletcher (1806-77), sons of Joseph H., farmer of Long Is., New York. They published some 200 books before altering the name to Harper Brothers in 1833. It was rebuilt after destruction by fire (1854), and is now an extensive establishment carried on by the descendants of the founders. The firm issues *Harper's Magazine* (monthly), 1850; *Harper's Weekly*, 1857; *Harper's Bazaar* (fashions), 1867; *Harper's Young People*, now *Harper's Round Table*, 1881. The firm was reorganised as a limited liability company in 1899.

Harper, William Rainey (1856-1906), an American scholar and educator, born at New Concord, Ohio; graduated at Muskingum College in 1870. From 1879-86 he was professor of Hebrew in Chicago Baptist Theological Seminary; from 1886-91 professor of Semitic languages at Yale; and from 1889-91 professor of Biblical literature at Yale. From 1885-91 he was principal of the Chautauqua College of Liberal Arts, and in 1891 became director of the Chautauqua system. In 1891 he was elected first president of the University of Chicago, where he was head of the department of Semitic languages and literature. He was editor of *Hebraica*, *The Old Testament Student*, *The Biblical World*, *The American Journal of Theology*, and *The American*

Journal of Semitic Languages and Literature, and wrote *Elements of Hebrew, Hebrew Method and Manual, Elements of Hebrew Syntax,* and *The Trend in Higher Education.*

Harper's Ferry, a tn. of Jefferson co., W. Virginia, U.S.A., situated at the confluence of the rivers Shenandoah and Potomac. In 1796 a United States armoury and arsenal was established there. This was seized in 1859 by John Brown, the abolitionist, but only held till next day. In 1862 the garrison under Colonel Miles surrendered after some fighting to Stonewall Jackson. The Federal loss amounted to 12,500 taken prisoners, and 13,000 small arms. Colonel Miles died of his wounds immediately after the surrender. Pop. (1910) 896.

Harpignies, Henri Joseph (*b.* 1819), a French landscape painter, born at Valenciennes. He studied with Achard in Paris, and then went to Italy, returning in 1850. Later he became a friend of Corot, and went with him to Italy, and in 1861 he made his first great hit at the Salon with his ' Lisière de bois sur les bords de l'Allier.' He is a fine draughtsman, and his work, though showing something of the influence of Corot, is distinctive. He obtained his first medal in 1886, for ' Le Soir dans la compagne de Rome,' but his most famous picture is perhaps ' Le Saut de Loup ' (1873), in the Luxembourg Gallery. In 1870 he showed a panel at the Salon, 'La Vallée Egérie,' done for the Paris Opera. He is also a painter in water-colours.

Harpocrates, *see* HORUS.

Harpocration, Valerius, a Greek grammarian. He wrote a lexicon, Λεξικὸν τωνδέκα, ῥηγόρων, containing notes on well - known people and events spoken of by the orators, with explanations of legal and commercial terms, and as most works of the kind have been lost this is of considerable value. He was of Alexandria, and may have been the Greek tutor to Antoninus Versus (2nd century A.D.), mentioned by Julius Capitolinus (*Life of Versus 2nd*), or if, as some authorities aver, he borrowed from Athenæus, his date would have been much later.

Harpoon, a weapon used to capture whales or other large fish, either thrown by hand or fired from a gun. Originally the head of the H. was a heavy flat piece of iron, triangular in shape and with sharp barbs on the outer edg   it was fastened to a wooden handle some 3 ft. long and having a long rope attached to it. The modern weapon has but one barb or sharp point, with a cross piece on a pivot that works in such a manner as to prevent the shaft being

withdrawn once in the whale, these are known as *toggle irons.* These weapons are not used to kill the whale but merely to effect its capture, the killing being done with a lance. H. guns which project a missile of the kind described above are used, some being fired from the shoulder, others being cannon-like guns mounted on pivots in the bow of the boats. In 1865-66 a Norwegian, Svend Foyn, invented an explosive H.; a hollow cap of iron, filled with blasting powder, is fixed to the point of the H. and a fuse attached which causes the bomb to explode within the whale. This method of killing them is used now in many places in preference to the spear.

Harp-shell (*Harpa*), a genus of gasteropod molluscs belonging to the family of Buccinidæ, or whelks. The shells, which are remarkable for their beauty, are found in tropical seas on soft or sandy floors. The name is derived from the smooth string-like markings on the large outer whorl.

Harpsichord, a musical instrument which was in vogue especially in the 16th and 17th centuries, and which developed into the invention of the modern grand pianoforte (*q.v.*). Outwardly it resembled that instrument in shape, though it was also made with two keyboards and stops, but instead of the hammer action of the piano the tones were produced by quills fixed in the centred tongues of wooden uprights called ' jacks,' which when the note was struck twanged or twitched the strings, thus emitting the sounds. The notes thus produced were of necessity sharp and metallic, and though lending themselves to brilliant technical performance it was difficult to make them expressive, but a good deal was done by means of stops and the double keyboard, especially that invented by Hans Ruckers about 1640, the Ruckers of Antwerp being the most famous H. makers. Handel possessed one made by this firm, which is now preserved at Buckingham Palace. In 1766, a maker named Tschudi made some beautiful instruments for Frederick the Great still to be seen in the New Palace, Potsdam. Through him and Kirckmann many great improvements were made, pedals being introduced for the first time. The ' harp ' stop and the ' swell,' a device worked by a pedal, were the inventions of Roger Plenius, who was the first to make a pianoforte in England. The older spinet and virginal belonged to the same family as the H., but the latter has as many as four strings to a note, while the others had only one. The H. held an important place in the orchestra of its time, being played always by the conductor, and it was first displaced by the composer Gluck.

Harpy, or Harpy Eagle (*Thrasaëtus harpyia*), a bird of prey which inhabits the tropical regions of S. America from Southern Mexico to Brazil, and which is variously referred by ornithologists to the hawk, buzzard, and eagle families. (*See* FALCONIDÆ.) Its salient features are its powerful talons, with which it pounces on monkeys, sloths. and fawns, and its enormous hooked beak. The H., so-called after the legendary vampire of the Greeks, has a white head, breast, and belly, save for one dark pectoral band; a black tail barred with grey, a black back and grey dusky wings. The face is owl-like, and the head crested. In flight it is slow and heavy, as the soft feathers and small wings would lead one to expect. Too much faith must not be set in the fabulous tales of its voracity told by the early naturalists.

Harpyiæ, or Harpies, originally personifications of sudden wind storms which snatched away people (*Iliad*, xvi. 150). Homer mentions one only, Pidarge, who in the shape of a mare carried to Zephyrus the horses of Achilles. Hesiod represents them as winged goddesses, but later writers describe them as spirits of evil, half-maidens, half-birds. In the story of the Argonauts the gods sent them to torment Phineus, by either defiling or carrying off his food. *See* J. C. Lawson's *Modern Greek Folklore*, 1910.

Harquebus, *see* ARQUEBUS.

Harraden, Beatrice (*b.* 1864), an English novelist, born at Hampstead, London. Her book, *Ships that Pass in the Night*, 1893, became very popular. *Untold Tales of the Past* (a book for children), 1897; *The Fowler*, 1899; *Katharine Frensham*, 1903; *The Scholar's Daughter*, 1906; *Interplay*, 1908; *Out of the Wreck I Rise*, 1912.

Harrar, or Harar, a tn., Abyssinia, the chief place in the Galla country, connected by railway with Jibuti, a French port, on the Gulf of Aden. It is built on slopes of a hill at an elevation of over 5000 ft. Exports include coffee, ghee, gums, wax, ivory, hides, and skins. The trade of H. is declining, owing to construction of a railway from Jibuti to Dirre Dawa, also to misgovernment and oppression of the Gallas. Pop. 50,000.

Harratin, a tribe of black Berbers of the Sahara. They dwell in Tidikelt and other Saharan oases. They are blacker than the average negro, of handsome appearance, and well-proportioned limbs.

Harrier, a breed of dog which hunts the hare by scent. In qualities and general appearance a H. closely re-sembles a foxhound, from which, indeed, it was probably at first derived. However, it is built on a smaller scale and usually is not taller than 22 in., whereas a foxhound frequently attains to 27 in. Hs. can hunt a much colder scent than their prototype, but are not so swift-footed. There are over 150 packs in the British Isles, and the Hs. are especially a feature of Irish country life where hare-hunting is a most popular sport.

Harrier (*Circus*), a genus of non-arboreal Falconidæ. Hs. are often called hen-harriers, because of their predilection for poultry as their prey. They have long legs and wings, insignificant beaks, an owl-like frill of thick-set feathers round the face, and soft plumage. They live on frogs, birds, snakes, and small mammals, and chiefly frequent marshy districts. At one time the *C. cyaneus*, or hen-harrier, and the *C. æruginosus*, or marsh-harrier, were common in the British Isles, but they are fast dying out. Hs., including the *C. cinereus* and the *C. cineraceous*, etc., are distributed all over the world.

Harriers, a name assumed by athletic clubs which go in for cross-country sports. Some of them are S. London, Blackheath, Spartan, Finchley, Liverpool, Huddersfield, and Moseley H. *See* ATHLETICS.

Harriman, Edward Henry (1846-1909), an American railroad magnate and capitalist, born at Hempstead In 1870 he became a member of the New York stock exchange, and was very prosperous financially. He was interested in American railways, and was made vice - president of the Illinois Central in 1887. In 1898 he began to organise railways, and by the aid of bankers rescued the Union Pacific out of bankruptcy, and made it an efficient line. He also did much for the Southern and Northern Pacific in 1901. He was bitterly censured by President Roosevelt in 1907 for the methods he employed to gain his marked successes, but whatever may be said of his ' means,' he certainly attained his ' end,' and created for America a vastly improved railway service.

Harrington, a par. and seaport on the W. coast of Cumberland, England, 2 m. S. of Workington. It has shipbuilding yards, coal mines, blast furnaces, and manufs. iron goods and fire-bricks. Pop. (1911) 4340.

Harrington, James (1611-77), an English political philosopher, born at Upton, Northamptonshire. He spent some time in the suite of Charles I. during his imprisonment, but on the king's death devoted himself to the composition of *Oceana*, a somewhat dull but very minutely worked-out scheme for an oligarchical republic. In 1559 he formed the ' Rota ' Club to try and push the practical application of his theories. In 1661 he was imprisoned by Charles II. on a charge of conspiracy. See *Works* (edited by John Toland in 1700).

Harrington (or **Harington**), **Sir John** (1561-1612), an English courtier and miscellaneous writer, born at Kelston, near Bath. He was a favourite with Henry VIII. and became a servant of Elizabeth, at whose court he was famous for his wit. By command of the queen he translated Ariosto's *Orlando Furioso,* 1591, and he entertained her at his house at Kelston in 1592, but in 1596 he fell into disgrace at court on account of an inuendo about the Earl of Leicester. In 1598 he accompanied Essex to Ireland and afterwards wrote an account of the campaign. He was appointed tutor to Prince Henry, eldest son of James I., for whose instruction he wrote *A Briefe View of the State of the Church,* pub. 1653. Among his other writings are : *A Tract on the Succession to the Crown,*1602; *The Englishman's Doctor,* 1608; *Nugæ antiquæ,* pub. 1779, and the collected *Epigrams,* pub. 1613.

Harrington, Timothy Charles (1851-1910), an Irish politician, born at Castletown Bere, Co. Cork, Ireland, and educated at Trinity College, Dublin. He was elected M.P. for co. Westmeath in 1883. and was M.P. for Dublin from 1885 until his death. He was called to the Irish bar in 1887, and was counsel for Mr. Parnell at the Special Commission (1888-89). He established the *Kerry Sentinel* in 1877; took a prominent part in the Land League and National League, and was Lord Mayor of Dublin in 1901.

Harriot (or **Hariot**), **Thomas** (1560-1621), an English mathematician and astronomer, born at Oxford. He became tutor to Sir Walter Raleigh, who appointed him to the post of geographer to the second expedition to Virginia (1585), an account of which voyage was published by Harris in 1588, and afterwards reprinted in Hakluyt's *Voyages* in 1600. H. virtually gave to algebra its modern form. *See* Wallis, *History of Algebra,* 1685 ; *also* Harriot's own *Ephemeris chrysometria,* and *Artis analyticæ praxis ad æquationes algebraicas resolvendas,* 1631 ; Stevens' *Thomas Hariot,* 1900, and *Harriot Papers* (edited by Rigaud, 1831).

Harris, a par. in the Outer Hebrides, Inverness-shire, Scotland, comprising the southern part of the island of Lewis, the adjacent islands of Killigray, Pabbay, Scarp, and Tarrensay, and the distant island of St. Kilda. Harris - Lewis is separated from the mainland by ' The Minch,' and to the S. is the Sound of H., the only navigable channel through the Hebrides. H. is separated from Lewis by a long range of hills, and is nearly cut in two by the lochs of Tarbert. The population is engaged in crofting, fishing, and sheep-farming; the wool-weaving connected with the latter is done on handlooms, and the material is the noted ' Harris Tweed.' Area 123,757 ac. Pop. (1911) 5448.

Harris, Sir Augustus Henry Glossop (1852-96), a theatrical manager, was the son of Augustus H., some time manager of Covent Garden. After gaining experience as an actor, he became, in 1879, lessee of Drury Lane theatre, where he was very successful as the producer of pantomimes and melodramas, in which elaborate scenic effects played a large part. He occasionally produced grand opera at Drury Lane, but from 1891 transferred that branch of his activity to Covent Garden. He was sheriff of London (1890-91), and in that capacity received the honour of knighthood.

Harris, Frank (*b.* 1856), a British journalist born in Galway. He was editor of the *Evening News* from1882-88, of the *Fortnightly Review* from 1888-93, and of the *Saturday Review* from1893-98. He founded and edited the *Candid Friend,* afterwards becoming editor of *Vanity Fair.* Among his publications are *Elder Conklin and other Stories,* 1894 ; *Montes the Matador,* 1900 ; *The Bomb,* 1908 ; *The Man Shakespeare,* 1909 ; and the play, *Mr. and Mrs. Daventry,* 1900.

Harris, George Robert Canning, fourth **Baron** (*b.* 1851), educated at Eton and Christ Church, Oxford, and early devoted his attention to politics, becoming Under-Secretary for India (1885-86), Under-Secretary for War (1886-89) and governor of Bombay (1890-95). He was a lord-in-waiting to Queen Victoria from 1895 to 1900, and assistant adjutant-general for Imperial Yeomanry in England in 1900, and in S. Africa in 1901. He is well known as a cricketer, and it is largely due to his efforts and influence that Kent occupies her present high position among the counties. He was elected president of the Marylebone Cricket Club (M.C.C.) in 1895.

Harris, Howel (1714-73), one of the founders of Welsh Calvinistic Methodism, born at Trevecca in Brecknockshire. In 1735 he began his work as an itinerant preacher, confining himself, for the most part, to S. Wales. In 1737 he was deprived of a school in which he taught and which was connected with the Establ-ished Church, after which he devoted himself entirely to preaching, and had founded thirty societies in S. Wales by the end of 1737. *See* his *Autobiography*, 1791, and Morgan, *Life and Times of H. Harris*.

Harris, James (1709-80), an English philologist and grammarian, born at Salisbury, and educated there and at Wadham College, Oxford. He became member of parliament for Christchurch in 1761, and was comptroller to the queen from 1774-80. He was a Lord of the Admiralty and a Lord of the Treasury under Lord Grenville in 1763, returning with him in 1765. He is chiefly remembered for his *Hermes*, 1751, a philosophical inquiry concerning universal grammar. His works, with a brief *Biography*, were collected and published by his son, the first Earl of Malmsbury, 1801.

Harris, James, first **Earl of Malmesbury** (1746-1820), a diplomatist; after holding minor positions in the service, became minister at Berlin in 1772, and five years later went as ambassador to St. Petersburg. At the Hague, from 1784, he rendered assistance in the revolution in favour of the House of Orange, and four years later took charge of the negotiations resulting in an alliance between Prussia and Holland. A friend of the Prince of Wales (afterwards George IV.), he had considerable influence over him. He was created baron in 1778, and earl in 1800. His *Diaries* were published in 1844.

Harris, James Howard, third **Earl of Malmesbury** (1807-89), a diplomatist, grandson of the first earl, succeeded to the peerage in 1841. He soon began to take interest in political matters, and especially in foreign affairs. In 1852 he held the office of Foreign Secretary in the administration of Lord Derby, and was again appointed to the same post under the same leader in 1858-59. In Derby's third ministry (1866) he was Lord Privy Seal, and remained in office when Disraeli became Prime Minister. He was again Lord Privy Seal when Disraeli came into power in 1874, but retired two years later owing to ill-health. He published his *Memoirs* in 1884.

Harris, James Rendel, an English Biblical scholar, born at Plymouth. He was educated at Plymouth Grammar School and Clare College, Cambridge, and became moderator and examiner for the mathematical tripos. He was professor at Johns Hopkins University from 1882-85, and at Haverford College, 1886-92. He has travelled much in the East, and in 1889 discovered an important Syriac manuscript of the 7th century in a convent on Mt. Sinai. He visited Armenia in 1896. He was lecturer in palæology at Cambridge University from 1893-1903, professor of theology at Leyden, 1903-4, and was made Haskell lecturer at Oberlin College in 1910. His publications include: *The Teaching of the Apostles and the Sibylline Books; Fragments of Philo; The Acts of Perpetua; The Apology of Aristides; Some Syrian and Palestinian Inscriptions; Lectures on the Western Text of the New Testament; Letters from Armenia; Double Text of Tobit; The Dioscuri in Christian Legend; Aaron's Breastplate*, 1908; *Side-lights on New Testament Research*, 1909; *The Odes and Psalms of Solomon*, 1910; and *An Early Christian Psalter*, 1910.

Harris, Joel Chandler (1848-1908), an American author, born at Eatonton, Putnam co., Georgia, U.S.A. He practised law for a short time, but soon took to journalism and joined the staff of the Savannah *Daily News*, 1871, and the Atlanta *Constitution* in 1876, becoming editor of the latter in 1890. His most noted contributions to these papers were his negro dialect stories, the first collection of which were published in 1880, as *Uncle Remus; his Songs and Sayings*. Among his other works are: *Mingo*, 1884; *Free Joe*, 1887; *On the Plantation*, 1889; *Daddy Jake, the Runaway*, 1890; *Little Mr. Thimblefinger*, 1894; *Mr. Rabbit at Home*, 1895; *Aaron in the Wildwoods*, 1897; *Aunt Minervy Ann*, 1899; and *Wally Wanderoon*, 1904, as well as a *Memoir of H. W. Grady*, 1890, and a history of *Georgia from the Invasion of De Soto to Recent Times*, 1899.

Harris, John (*c.* 1666-1719), an English scientific writer, divine, and topographer, born probably in Shropshire. He held the livings of Icklesham and Winchelsea in Sussex, St. Margaret Moses, and St. Mildred, Bread Street, and was a prebend of Rochester (1707). He was best known as the editor of the *Dictionary of the Arts and Sciences*, 1704, and as the compiler of a *Collection of Voyages and Travels*, 1705.

Harris, Thomas Lake (1823-1906), a founder of the religious sect ' Brotherhood of the New Life,' born at Fenny Stratford, Buckinghamshire, but his parents settled at Utica, New York, in 1828. When about twenty he became a Universalist preacher, then a Swedenborgian, but in 1850 became imbued with spiritualistic doctrines. He lectured on spiritualism in England in 1858, and on his return to America founded the ' Brotherhood ' at Wassaic, New York. Among his most notable disciples were Lady Oliphant and her son Laurence, who, although they broke away from H. himself in

1881, did not abandon his teaching. H. had no written creed or form of government, holding that 'government was inspired.' It is in reality a mixture of Swedenborgianism and Fourierism, while maintaining the sacredness of the Scriptures and the sanctity of marriage. He published: *Wisdom of Angels*, 1856; *The Arcana of Christianity*, 1857; *Modern Spiritualism*, 1860; *The Millenial Age*, 1861; and *Lyra Triumphalis*. See Laurence Oliphant's *Masollam;* also *Life* by A. H. Cuthbert, 1908; and Allen's *T. L. Harris the Seer*, 1897.

Harrisburg: 1. Cap. of Pennsylvania, U.S.A., on the Susquehanna R., 105 m. W.N.W. of Philadelphia. It is named after John Harris, Quaker, who settled here in 1704. The river is wide and flows through picturesque scenery, and it contains an abundant supply of water. Several railroad bridges cross it. Among the chief buildings in the city are the courthouse, government building, state arsenal, state asylum, opera-house, and several handsome public monuments. It became the capital of Pennsylvania in 1812, and was incorporated as a city in 1860. It is also the see of a Roman Catholic bishop. Coal and iron are extensively worked in the neighbourhood, and it has manufactories of railroad cars, carriages, typewriters, boilers, bricks, cotton and woollen goods, silks, etc. Pop. (1910) 64,186. 2. A banking post tn., cap. of Saline co., Illinois, 110 m. S.E. by E. of St. Louis, Missouri, on the Cleveland, Cincinnati, Chicago and St. Louis Railway. It has coal and iron mines, flour mills, and carriage factories. Pop. (1910) 5309.

Harrismith, a tn. in Orange River Colony, cap. of the H. district. Has an altitude of 5250 ft., and is connected by rail with Durban, Natal, 170 m. to the N.W. A prosperous trading centre and important health resort of S. Africa. Pop. 8300.

Harrison, a tn. in New Jersey, U.S.A., in Hudson co., adjoining Newark on the E., with which it is connected by bridges. Here is located the State Soldiers' Home. It has steel and iron works, and among its manufs. are cutlery, leather, refrigerators, electric incandescent lamps, cotton thread, cloth, etc. Pop. (1910) 14,498.

Harrison, Benjamin (1833-1901), the twenty-third president of the United States, born at N. Bend, near Cincinnati, Ohio. He was educated at Miami University, and pursued the study of law, being called to the bar in 1853. He took part in the Civil War, serving in the union army, and was breveted a brigadier-general

in 1865. After the war he resumed his legal work, and was reporter of the supreme court of Indiana from 1860-62 and 1864-68. He also took an interest in the campaign which resulted in the election of James Garfield as president, and in 1881 was elected a member of the United States senate. He was nominated for the presidency in 1888 by the Republican party, and elected, and after his term of office America was in a condition of prosperity and on friendly terms with foreign nations. The settlement of the Behring Sea fur-seal question with Great Britain, the negotiation of a Hawaiian annexation treaty, the passing of the McKinley Tariff Bill, the meeting of Pan-American Congress at Washington, were all events of his presidency. He was again nominated in 1892, but failed to secure election. In 1899 he was leading counsel in the Venezuela question, and was the member for the United States at the Hague Conference the same year. He wrote *This Country of Ours*, 1897; *Views of an Ex-President* 1901.

Harrison, Constance Cary, a novelist, born in Virginia. She married Burton H., a lawyer, and after her marriage left Virginia and settled in New York, where she now lives and writes her books, among them being: *Golden Rod*, 1880; *Bar Harbour Days*, 1887; *The Anglomaniacs*, 1887; *A Daughter of the South*, 1892; *A Son of the Old Dominion*, 1897; *Good American*, 1898; *A Triple Entanglement*, 1898; *A Princess of the Hills*, 1901.

Harrison, Frederic, an English author and philosopher, born in London in 1831. He was educated at King's College School, London, and Wadham College, Oxford, where he became a fellow and tutor. He was called to the bar in 1858, and was professor of jurisprudence and international law to Inns of Court (1877-89). He also worked at a codification of the law with Lord Westbury, and was placed upon the Trades Union Commission of 1867-69, becoming secretary to the Commisson for the digest of the law (1869-70). He was a follower of the positive philosophy, and was president of the English Positivist Committee (1880-1905), as well as editor of the Positivist *New Calendar of Great Men*, writing much on Comte, of whom he was a follower. He was Rede lecturer, Cambridge, in 1900; Washington lecturer, Chicago, in 1901; Herbert Spencer lecturer, Oxford, in 1905; and is now vice-president of the Royal Historical Society, and London Library. His publications include *Order and Progress*, 1875; *The Meaning of History*, 1862; *The Choice of Books*, 1886;

Oliver Cromwell, 1888; *Annals of an Old Manor House*, 1893; in which he gives an account of his home, near Guildford ; *William the Silent*, 1897; *The Millenary of King Alfred*, 1897; *Tennyson, Ruskin, Mill and others*, 1899; *Byzantine History in the Early Middle Ages*, 1900 ; *Life of Ruskin*, 1902; *Theophano*, 1904, a ' romantic spirit in Barebone's Parliament the monograph ' of the 10th century. *Nicephorus, A Tragedy of New Rome*, 1906; *The Creed of a Layman*, 1907; *My Alpine Jubilee*, 1908 ; *Autobiographic Memoirs*, 1911 ; *Among My Books*, 1912 ; *The Positive Evolution of Religion*, 1912. Mr. H. took a prominent part in the life of his time. His son, Austin H., (*b.* 1873) has been editor of *The English Review* since 1910.

Harrison, Jane Ellen (*b.* 1850), an English Hellenic scholar, born in Yorkshire. She was educated at Cheltenham and Newnham Colleges, Cambridge, where she became lecturer in classical archæology. She was a member of the Council Hellenic Society (1889-96), and a member of the committee of British School of Archæology at Athens in 1890. She has published *Myths of the Odyssey in Art and Literature*, 1882 ; *Introductory Studies in Greek Art*, 1885; *Mythology and Monuments of Ancient Athens*, 1890 (jointly with Mrs. Verrall) ; *Greek Vase Painting* (with Mr. MacColl), 1894 ; *Prolegomena to the Study of Greek Religion; Religion of Ancient Greece; Themis*, 1912.

Harrison, John (1693-1776), an English mechanician and inventor, born at Faulky, near Pontefract, Yorkshire. In 1715 he invented a clock with wooden wheels and in 1726 his famous ' gridiron pendulum ' which maintains its length unaltered in spite of changes of temperature. In 1762 he claimed the reward of £20,000 offered by the government for a satisfactory method of determining longitude when at sea. He invented a chronometer which, by means of the application of a compensation curb to the balance wheel, determined the longitude within 18 m. during a voyage to Jamaica. It was not until 1773 after the direct intervention of the king that H. received the £20,000. He was also the inventor of the recoil escapement.

Harrison, Mary St. Leger, daughter of Charles Kingsley (*q.v.*).

Harrison, Thomas (1606-60), a Puritan, signatory to the death-warrant of Charles I., was born at Newcastle-under-Lyme. In 1642 he enlisted in Essex's bodyguard, and was major in Fleetwood's horse at Marston Moor (1644). He entered the ' new model ' with Fleetwood, and was present at Naseby and Langport,

and at the captures of Winchester and Basing. From 1650-51 he held chief command in England during Cromwell's absence, and after the battle of Worcester (1651) was charged with the pursuit of the flying royalists. He assisted in expelling the Long Parliament in 1653, and was a leading spirit in Barebone's Parliament the same year. He was deprived of his commission in 1653 under the instrument of government, and suffered imprisonment, 1655-56 and 1658-59, for his relations with the Anabaptists. At the Restoration he was executed because he would neither leave the country, nor acknowledge the new monarch.

Harrison, Thomas (1744-1829), an architect, born at Richmond, in Yorkshire. He studied in Rome and was admitted to the academy of St. Luke, and awarded medals by Pope Clement XIV. In 1777 he was commissioned to build a bridge over the Lune at Lancaster, the first stone being laid in 1783, and the work completed in 1788. He also rebuilt Lancaster Castle in Gothic style, but his best-known works are Chester Castle, and the celebrated Grosvenor Bridge over the Dee at Chester, which consists of a single arch of 200 ft. span, a then unequalled dimension. In Liverpool he was the architect of the Athenæum, the Lyceum, the St. Nicholas tower, etc., and in Manchester of the Portico, the Exchange buildings, etc. He built Broomhall, Fifeshire, for Lord Elgin, and suggested to him that he should make a collection of Greek works of art.

Harrison, William (1534-93), an English historian and chronicler, born in London. He was rector of Radwinter in Essex from 1560 until his death, and also rector of Wimbish in Essex (1571-82) and canon of Windsor from 1586. His amusing *Description of England*, planned by Reginald Wolfe, was intended to form part of ' an universall cosmographie,' which was finally confined to the description and histories of England, Scotland, and Ireland, of which the topographical section was supplied by H., while Holinshed provided the historical. It was finally published in 1577 as *The Chronicles of England, Scotland, and Ireland*, and is an invaluable view of the life and customs of Elizabethan England. Dr. Furnivall quotes some extracts from H.'s *Chronologie*, as well as the ' Description ' in his *Shakespeare's England*, 1877-78.

Harrison, William Henry (1773-1841), the ninth president of the United States, born at Berkeley, Charles City co., Virginia. He entered the army in 1791 and served till 1798, when he was elected governor of the N.W. territory. In 1800 he was created governor of Indiana, but did not enter office until 1801; and while governor he tried to prevent the sale of alcohol to the Indians. Having had several fruitless conferences with the Indian chiefs, he advanced against them in 1811, and gained a complete victory at Tippecanoe. From 1811-13 he was actively engaged in the war with England. From 1819-21 he was a member of the Ohio senate, and of the United States senate from 1825-28. In 1841 he was elected president, but only acted for one month. One of his addresses survives in *A Discourse on the Aborigines of the Ohio.*

Harrison Steamship Line, a British line of steamers, established in 1830, headquarters, Liverpool, with a fleet of forty-three steamers, and a gross tonnage of 217,085. There is a regular passenger and cargo service between Liverpool and the W. Indies, United States, Mexico, Brazil, S.E. Africa, the E. Indies, and the S. of France. London offices: Dock House, Billiter Street, E.C.

Harrisse, Henri (*b.* 1830), a French geographical historian, born in Paris. He studied for the law and practised as a barrister in New York, but later settled in Paris and devoted himself to the study of bibliography and the history of discovery. Among his publications are: *John Cabot,* 1896; *Bibliotheca Americana Vetustissima,* 1866; *The Discovery of North America,* 1892; *The Diplomatic History of America,* 1897; *Découverte de Terre-Neuve,* 1900. His best-known work is *Christophe Colomb,* 1884 (Eng. trans. 1892).

Harrogate, a municipal bor., watering-place, and market tn. in the West Riding of Yorkshire, about 17 m. N. of Leeds. As a health resort it is famous for its springs, the first of which was discovered in Knaresborough forest by Slingsby in 1571. The waters are chalybeate, saline, and sulphurous, and some of the springs (eighty in all) possess all these qualities. They are used both for drinking and bathing purposes, the Royal Baths, which were erected at a cost of £200,000, and are unsurpassed by any in the country, affording facilities for every kind of bath and massage. There are also the Victoria Bath, and the town also has a large kursaal, public parks, such as the Valley Gardens and the Stray, several hospitals, including the Royal Bath Hospital, and a grand opera house. There are two parts to the town, Low H. and High H., and visitors can enjoy the bracing air of the latter, or the warm, more sheltered climate of the former. H. was incorporated in 1884,

and its borough extended in 1900. Pop. (1911) 33,706.

Harrow, an agricultural implement, usually formed of pieces of timber or bars of metal crossing one another and provided with iron teeth, which is drawn (usually by one corner) over ploughed land to break the earth clods and level it and to cover the newly sown seeds. *See* IMPLEMENTS and MACHINERY.

Harrow, or **Harrow-on-the-Hill,** an urban district in the Harrow parl. div. of Middlesex, situated about 19 m. N.W. of London. It is on a hill about 350 ft. high, and has a fine old church (St. Mary's), said to have been founded by Lanfranc, Archbishop of Canterbury, in William I.'s reign; at any rate traces of Norman work can be seen on the tower, and there are, too, some old monuments and interesting brasses (one of them to John Lyon). But the town is chiefly famous for its school which was founded in 1571 by John Lyon, to whom Queen Elizabeth granted a charter. It was originally intended for the education of poor boys of the parish, but the statute drawn up by the founder in 1590 provided also for the admission of ' so many foreigners as that place can conveniently contain,' which provision has led to the present position of the institution, one of the great schools of England. The building was first opened for scholars in 1611, and since then various new buildings have been added, the chief being the Second-pointed chapel, 1875, containing a glass in memory of the Harrovians who died in the Crimean War (a memorial has also been added for those who fell in the S. African War); the Vaughan Memorial Library, 1863 ; and the Speech-room, 1877, where a brilliant ceremony is held every summer term. The fourth form room is interesting, dating as it does from 1611, and because it contains the names cut in the panels of famous pupils, such as Byron, Robert Peel, R.B., Sheridan, and Lord Palmerston (Temple). Among celebrated headmasters may be mentioned Thackeray, Sumner, Butler, Longley, Christopher Wordsworth, and Vaughan, all of whom did much to make the school what it is. The education afforded is a general one, and includes the study of classics, mathematics (made compulsory in 1837), modern languages (introduced 1851-55), English literature and history (begun about 1869), etc. Archery, which was encouraged by the founder who instituted a prize of a silver arrow to be shot for annually on Aug. 4, has been abolished since 1776, and cricket, football, etc., have taken its place ; the cricket match played every year at Lord's between Eton and Harrow dating back to 1818. Since the passing of the Public Schools Act in 1868, the government of the school is in the hands of a council composed of the surviving members of the old board and six persons chosen by the Lord Chancellor, the Universities of Oxford, Cambridge, and London, the Royal Society, and the assistant masters of the school. Pop. (1911) 17,076.

Harry, Blind, or Henry the Minstrel (*fl.* 1470-92), a Scottish poet, was the author of a poem on William Wallace. He was blind from birth and earned his livelihood by reciting poems and historical tales about Wallace to the nobility. He is mentioned by William Dunbar in the *Lament for the Makaris* along with Sandy Traill, so he must have been dead when that poem was written, 1508, and his own work was probably composed about 1450-65, at any rate a manuscript dated 1488 is in the Advocates' Library, Edinburgh. It is written in the Lothian dialect, and is entirely devoted to a description of Wallace, but the poem is largely a translation from John Blair. It is not a great poem, but is interesting as being one of the earliest in Scottish written in the heroic couplet, and it is famous because it did much to create Scottish nationality. There have been numerous printed editions of it, and the modern Scottish version by William of Gilbertfield, 1722, was reprinted thirteen times, and became more familiar than the original. Gilbertfield's version is much praised by Burns. A good edition of the original was published by Dr. Jamieson, 1820, but a more accurate one appeared in 1885-86, edited by Mr. Moir. It has been said that the 'Wallace' was the work of John Ramsey, the transcriber, but there is very little evidence in support of this theory.

Hart, the name given to the male deer or stag, from about the age of six years, when the terminal snags or surroyals of the antlers begin to appear.

Hart, Charles Henry (*b.* 1847), a lawyer, art expert, and writer, born in Philadelphia. He was director of the Pennsylvania Academy of Fine Arts in his native city for twenty years, resigning in 1902. He was called to the bar in 1868 and practised till 1894, after which time he devoted himself to art and literature, and is recognised as an expert in historical portraiture in America, having exposed many frauds in portraits of celebrities. He has made a special study of Gilbert Stuart's work. His publications include, *Life Portraits of*

Great Americans ; Turner the Dream Painter ; Gilbert Stuart's Portraits of Women ; The Earliest Painter in America ; The Original Portraits of Washington ; Descriptive Catalogue of Miniatures owned by Lucy Wharton Drexel, 1911. He also selected and edited the illustrations for Elson's *History of the United States,* 1905; Lodge's *Story of the American Revolution ;* Tarbell's *The American Women,* 1910.

Hart, Sir Robert (1835-1911), an inspector-general of customs in China, born at Portadown, co. Armagh, Ireland. He was educated in Dublin and at Queen's College Belfast, and was nominated for the consular service in China in 1854. In 1855 he was assistant in the vice-consulate at Ningpo, and acted for some months as vice-consul, but in 1858 was transferred to Canton where after the Chinese War, terminating in the treaty of Tientsin, he was made secretary to the allied commissioners. In 1859 he joined the new Chinese imperial maritime customs service, and became inspector-general in 1863, a post he held nominally till his death, having resigned in 1906. H. was a friend of Gordon's, and was largely responsible for the reconciliation between Li Hung Chang and Gordon in 1864, and to him was due the settlement of China's troubles in Formosa, and on the Tong-king frontier with France in 1885. He published *These from the Land of Sinim,* a description of China and its people.

Hart, Soloman Alexander (1806-81), an English historical painter, born at Plymouth. He went to London in 1820 and became a student at the Royal Academy in 1823, his first exhibit being his father's miniature at Somerset House in 1826. In 1834 he exhibited in the Academy, ' The Quarrel Scene between Wolsey and Buckingham, and Richard Cœur de Lion and Saladin,' in 1835, becoming the same year an associate of the Academy. In 1839 he produced a picture of ' Lady Jane Grey at the Place of her Execution on Tower Hill,' and was made in consequence R.A. in 1840. He also painted pictures of Italian history and scenery, the chief of which are: ' Interiors of the Cathedrals at Modena and Pisa,' ' Milton visiting Galileo in Prison,' ' A Reminiscence of Ravenna,' as well as ' The Three Inventors of Printing.' H. succeeded Leslie as professor of painting at the Academy in 1854, and from 1865-81 acted as librarian of that institution.

Hart-Dyke, see DYKE, SIR WILLIAM HART.

Harte, Francis Bret (1839-1902),

an author, had, as a lad, an adventurous career, during which he served as a schoolmaster, a miner, and a compositor. His leanings, however, were always towards journalism, and at the age of eighteen he obtained an engagement on a San Francisco paper, to which he contributed his early stories. In 1864 he began to write his *Condensed Novels*, and four years later he founded the *Overland Monthly*, in which he printed his best-known short tales. Secretary of the Mint at San Francisco from 1864 until 1870, in 1878 he entered the government service again and went as United States consul to Crefeld, two years later being transferred to Glasgow. In 1885 he retired, and spent his remaining years in London. The *Condensed Novels* were much appreciated, and still rank as masterpieces of parody, his skit on Disraeli being second only to *Codlingsby*. The *Heathen Chinee* won him a high place as a humorous poet, but it is as the author of short sketches of mining life that he became famous and is still best remembered. He threw over the rough Californian life of those days a glamour that fascinated the whole world, and *The Luck of Roaring Camp; Meggles; The Outcast of Poker Flat;* and *Tennessee's Partner* are but a few of those that evoked high praise. While not disguising the evil in men, he had the gift of showing that even villains had good in them, and this he brought out without outraging nature or being mawkish. His later work was poor, but these stories will long keep his name fresh. There is a biography by T. Edgar Pemberton, 1903.

Harte, Walter (c. 1709-74), an English poet and divine, educated at Oxford. He was successively vice-principal of St. Mary Hall, Oxford (1740-45), travelling tutor to the son of the Earl of Chesterfield (1745-50), and canon of Windsor (1750). In 1730 he published *Essay on Satire,* and in 1735 *Essay on Reason,* both in imitation of and under the influence of Alexander Pope. In 1759 appeared his *History of Gustavus Adolphus, King of Sweden,* a book which, in spite of its execrable style, is full of valuable matter. His *Essays on Husbandry,* 1764, won the praise of both Johnson and Chesterfield. *See* Lord Chesterfield's *Letters* (ed. by Lord Mahon, 1853), iv. 193, 207, 263; also Boswell's *Johnson.*

Hartebeest, the Boer name applied throughout S. Africa to a large antelope of the genus *Bubalis,* on account of its fancied resemblance to a stag. It is characterised by its reddish colour, with black markings on the forehead and nose, long horns, which diverge from each other in the form of a V with tips turned backwards at right angles, and long face with a naked muzzle. It stands about 4 ft. at the withers, and is one of the swiftest of the antelope family. This antelope is really the *Bubalis* or *Alcelaphus cama,* and is found in S. Africa and as far N. as Mashonaland and Matabeleland, but the name is extended to include all the numerous members of the same genus found throughout Africa and even in Syria. *See* ANTELOPE.

Hartford: 1. State cap. and seat of H. co., Connecticut, situated on the Connecticut R., 60 m. from Long Island Sound. It is the head of navigation, and the distributing point for the Connecticut Valley, and is important as a centre of wholesale trade; it is also noted for its insurance business, being one of the leading centres in the world. There are various manufactures: firearms, including the Gatling guns, at the famous Colt Works, electric machinery and vehicles, bicycles, for which it is famous, cyclometers, steam-engines and boilers, typewriters, furniture, etc. The town has also one of the largest printing houses in New England, besides a large number of handsome and notable buildings. Pop. (1910) 98,915. **2.** Cap. of Blackford co., Indiana, U.S.A., situated about 60 m. N.E. of Indianapolis. The natural gas supply, the oil fields, and the products from the surrounding agricultural country, contribute largely to its commercial interests. The chief manufs. are iron, glass, and flour, paper. Pop. (1910) 6187.

Hartford Convention, a gathering held in 1814 to discuss measures for securing New England interests against the S. and W., especially with regard to the war of 1812. The Federalists opposed the war on several grounds, their chief objection being that it was destroying all American commerce in order to punish Great Britain for crippling a part of it. Thus, all through the war they harassed the government, but by 1814 the destruction of New England industries had become intolerable, and a convention was called. This met at Hartford, and George Cabot, of Massachusetts, was chosen president. Various proposals were made, but before anything definite could be arranged, a satisfactory peace was made, and all disasters were forgotten in the blaze of the battle of Orleans.

Hartha, a tn. in Germany, kingdom of Saxony, 19 m. N. of Chemnitz. Chief manufs. are mother-of-pearl goods, felt, and fustian. Pop. 6252.

Harthau, a vil. in Germany, kingdom of Saxony, 3 m. S. of Chemnitz. Pop. 6484.

Harting, James Edmund (b. 1841), an English scientist, born in London. He was educated at Downside College and the University of London, and practised for some time as a solicitor, retiring in 1878 to devote himself to the study of ornithology. In 1869 he promoted the passing of the Sea Birds Preservation Act, and in 1873 gave evidence before the Select Committee of the House of Commons on wild birds protection. He travelled through France, Holland, Belgium, Italy, Greece, and Thessaly, and visited Paris in 1889 to report on guns and rifles at the Paris Exhibition for *The Field.* In 1888 he was appointed librarian to the Linnean Society, and in 1893 went to Thessaly for the Board of Agriculture to report on the Vole plague. His publications include: *The Birds of Middlesex; The Ornithology of Shakespeare; A Handbook of British Birds* (new ed.), 1901; *White's Natural History of Selborne; Ostriches and Ostrich Farming; Hints on the Management of Hawks; Walton's Angler;* the volume on *The Rabbit,* in Fur and Feather Series, and *Recreations of a Naturalist.* He has also written for the *Encyclopædia of Sport* and *The Field,* and has edited *The Zoologist,* 1877-96.

Hartington, Lord, *see* DEVONSHIRE, DUKE OF.

Hartland, Edwin Sidney (b. 1848), an English author, and authority on folklore, registrar of county court, Gloucester, and district registrar of the High Court. Among his publications are: *English Fairy and other Folk-tales,* 1890; *The Science of Fairy Tales,* 1890; *The Legend of Perseus* (3 vols.), 1894-96, numerous papers, chiefly on archæological and anthropological subjects, and *Primitive Paternity,* 1910.

Hartlepool, a municipal bor., seaport, and bathing resort, about 18 m. E.S.E. of Durham in the co. of the same name, forming with W. Hartlepool a parl. bor. It has been noted as a port since the 12th century, standing as it does on a headland nearly surrounded by the sea, and an important trade is carried on in exporting coal, ships, machinery, woollens, and cot tons, and in importing timber, sugar, iron and copper ores, and eggs; the chief industries being shipbuilding, boiler and engineering works, flourmills, soap works, iron and brass foundries, paper, and paint factories. The old town of H. contains the parish church of St. Hilda, which dates back to the 13th century and has a high massive tower, and also a handsome borough hall in Italian style. W. Hartlepool, the new town, has some

handsome churches, an exchange, market hall, municipal buildings, and public library. Its municipal area includes Seaton Carew, Stranton, and Throston. Pop. of parl. bor. (1911) 84,550.

Hartley, a tn. in Southern Rhodesia, S. Africa, on the main route through the Tati hills, north-eastwards through Bulawayo and Umbanjin. H. Hill has an altitude of 3800 ft., and consists largely of rich iron deposits.

Hartley, Sir Charles Augustus (b. 1825), an honorary member of the Roumanian Academy of Arts and of the Canadian Society C.E., born at Heworth, in Durham. In 1855-56 he served in the Crimea as captain in the Anglo-Turkish contingent. In 1867 he reported to the Foreign Office on the engineering connected with the R. Scheldt, and designed plans for the enlargement of Odessa. In 1875 he was made a member of the Board of Engineers to report on the improvement of the Mississippi, and in 1879 sat in the Congress appointed to decide the best route for a ship canal across the Isthmus of Panama. In 1879 he was appointed by the Board of Trade umpire in a dispute between the Metropolitan Board of Works and the Conservators of the Thames. He was engineer-in-chief and consulting engineer to the European Commission of the Danube (1856-1907). He has published *Delta of the Danube, Public Works in the United States and Canada, Inland Navigations in Europe,* and *History of the Engineering Works of the Suez Canal.*

Hartley, David (1705-57), an English philosopher, born near Halifax. He was intended for the Church, and took up medicine, practising as a physician at Newark, Bury St. Edmunds, London, and Bath. He is chiefly remembered by his *Observations on Man* (1749), in which he upheld the theory that the phenomena of the mind, memory, emotions, and reasoning were the direct result of molecular nervous vibrations. See *Life* by his son, prefixed to the 1801 edition of his works ; also Leslie Stephen's *History of English Thought in the Eighteenth Century* (3rd ed.), 1902.

Hartlib, Samuel (c. 1600-c. 1670), an English writer on education and an agriculturist, the son of a Polish merchant, born at Elking in Prussia. He came to England about 1626, and became acquainted with Milton, who dedicated his *Tractate on Education* (1644) to Hartlib, and with Sir William Petty, of whose *Two Letters* (1647 and 1648) he was the occasion. See *Biographical Memoir,* by H. Dircks, 1865.

Hartmann, Alfred (1814-97), a

Swiss author, born near Langenthal, Berne, Switzerland. He practised law in Solothurn, but from 1845 was the editor of a comic periodical called *Postheiri*. He is best known by his Swiss romance, *Meister Putsch und seine Gesellen* (1858), but he also wrote *Junker und Bürger* (1865), *Schweizer novellen* (1877), *Fortunat* (1879), *Der Gerechte Branntwein-brenner* (1881), and *Lives* of Martin Disteli, the painter (1861) and H. J. von Staal (1861). See *Life* by Arx, 1902.

Hartmann, Jakob, Frieherr von (1795-1873), a German soldier, born at Maikammer, the Palatinate. He was educated in France at the military colleges of Bonn and St. Cyr. He entered the French army, and afterwards helped the Bavarians against Prussia. He became general in the Bavarian army and took part in the Franco-German War, attaining special distinction in the battle of Sedan.

Hartmann, Johann Peder Emilius (1805-1900), a Danish musical composer, born in Copenhagen. His first opera, *The Raven*, with words by H. C. Andersen, was produced in 1832, and was followed by *Die goldnin Hörner* (1834), *Die Corsaren* (1835), and *Liden Kirsten* (1846). He wrote, besides a great deal of incidental music for the theatre, choral works, including the cantata on the death of Thorwaldsen (1848), songs, symphonies, and pianoforte pieces. He became director of the Copenhagen Conservatorium in 1840.

Hartmann, Karl Robert Edouard von (1842-1906), a German philosopher, born at Berlin. He was educated for the army, but was obliged to quit the service in 1865, and turned his attention to philosophy. His first book, *The Philosophy of the Unconscious*, appeared in 1869, and met with great success, owing to the originality of its title, as well as its interesting contents. H.'s Unconscious is the Absolute of German metaphysicians, and is a combination of that of Hegel, Schopenhauer, and Shelling, his Unconscious playing the rôle of creator and providence. H. published books on ethical consciousness, the development of the religious consciousness and German æsthetics, as well as criticisms of contemporary philosophies and defences of his own system, among which may be mentioned *Ethical Consciousness*, 1879; *The Philosophy of Religion* (2nd ed.), 1888; *Æsthetics*, 1886-87; *Critical Grounds of Transcendental Realism; The Crisis of Christianity in Modern Theology*, 1880; *Judaism in the Present and the Future*, 1885; *Lotze's Philosophy*, 1888; *The Ghost Theory in Spiritism*, 1891; *The Fun-*damental Social Questions*, 1894. He was a pessimist as regards the inevitable misery of existence, thinking that happiness is neither attainable here, now, nor hereafter, but an optimist in that he was a champion of evolutionary progress.

Hartmann, von Aue (c. 1170-1210), a German poet, born in Swabia. He took part in a crusade in 1197, and is mentioned by Gottfried von Strassburg about 1210 as being alive, but both the date of his birth and that of his death are uncertain. He published four poems: *Erec*, which relates the legend reproduced in Tennyson's 'Enid' in *Idylls of the King; Iwein*, a better work than the former, and also taken from the Arthurian cycle; *Gregorius*, a narrative poem of the early life of Pope Gregory the Great; and *Der arme Heinrich*, one of the most delightful specimens of mediæval German poetry. His work was largely adapted from the French, *Erec* and *Iwein* being translations of epics by Chrétien de Troyes, and *Gregorius*, too, was taken from a French epic: but in spite of this fact, H. ranks high as a poet of the Middle High German period, and his works exhibit a delicacy of feeling and a beauty of diction rarely found in writers of the time.

Hartshorn, the horn of the common stag, which in composition differs from that of the ox, etc., being nearly identical with that of bone. The substances derived from the horns were the volatile liquor, salt, and oil, and the ash which remains when the horns are calcined in air. The fluid parts are got by distillation, and the salt formed is carbonate of ammonia. From this pure ammonia is obtained, which, when condensed in water, constitutes the spirit of H. The volatile alkali, or spirit of H., is now seldom obtained from that source; the ammonia sold in shops being obtained from gas-liquor, etc.

Hartshorn, Spirit of, the name for a solution of ammonia which used to be obtained from the horns of the stag, and which has now been replaced by carbonate of ammonia or sal-volatile.

Hartsœker, Nicholas (1656-1725), a Dutch optician and physicist, born at Gouda. He was educated for the Church, but abandoned the idea in order to study science. He became acquainted with Jean Dominique Cassini in Paris, who induced him to apply himself to the manufacture of telescopes, in which he was very skilful. In 1694 he published an essay on dioptrics, and in 1696 a treatise on physics. In 1699 he was made a foreign associate of the French Academy of Sciences, and in 1704 became professor of mathematics and natural philosophy at Düsseldorf. He fiercely opposed the system of Newton, thinking that it required the supposition of empty space between the heavenly bodies.

Hart's-tongue Fern, the common name given to ferns of the evergreen genus Scolopendrium, which is distinguished by its fructification, *i.e.* sori joined together in pairs. Only one variety is found in England in the wild state, viz. *Scolopendrium vulgare*, which has shining, undivided fronds.

Hartzenbusch, Juan Eugenio (1806-80), a Spanish dramatic poet, born at Madrid. He was educated for the Church, but abandoned the idea, and in 1830 joined the staff of the *Gaceta*. He began dramatic work by translating and recasting existing plays, but produced his own in 1837, which at once made him famous. The play was *Los Amantes de Teruel*. His next productions were *Doña Mencia*, 1839, and *Alfonso el Casto*, 1841; these were not so good as his first, but in 1845 he published *La Jura en Santa Gadea*, which was a great improvement on the other two, being equal to the first in excellence. He became director of the National Library at Madrid in 1862, and edited the plays of Triso de Motina, Calderon, etc. H. was a versatile writer, but somewhat lacking in inspiration.

Hartz Mountains, *see* HARZ MOUNTAINS.

Harun-al-Rashid, *see* HAROUN AL-RASCHID, and ABBASIDES.

Haruspices, a class of soothsayers of ancient Rome, who foretold events chiefly by the observation of the entrails of animals. They also interpreted all portents or unusual phenomena of nature, and were especially employed to deal with cases not mentioned in the pontifical or sibylline books, prescribing the offering necessary to expiate the god. They were of Etruscan origin, and were introduced into Rome by Romulus about 750 B.C. and abolished by Constantine in 337 A.D. As a class they ranked below the augurs, being paid, and although the art was of great importance, it never formed part of the state religion.

Harvard University, the oldest institution of learning in the United States, was founded in Cambridge, Massachusetts, by the general court at Boston in 1636. It received its name from John Harvard who bequeathed to it £750 and his library. The first building was erected in 1637, and the first graduating class was established in 1642. There were immense difficulties to be overcome at the time of the foundation of the college, especially those dealing with religion, but the authorities perse-

vered, and the heroic courage necessary was never found wanting. Between 1642 and 1782 Harvard College conferred only the degrees of bachelor and master of arts, but in 1782-83 three professorships of medicine were established, the first degree of bachelor of medicine being conferred in 1788 (the school is now removed to Boston). In 1817 the law school was established, and in 1819 the divinity faculty was organised (the Hollis professorship of divinity having been established in 1721). There is a good history school, and Abbott Lawrence Lowell, the present president, was professor of history at Harvard for many years. Harvard is famous for having encouraged the higher education of women, as well as for its movement to better the teaching of the English language and literature in the schools of America. The very name stands for culture and advanced thought. There are seven professors of English at Harvard. The Bussey Institution at Jamaica Plain was established in 1871, but reorganised in 1908, for research in agriculture and horticulture. The Graduate School of Applied Science (1906) and the Graduate School of Business Administration (1908) are successful innovations. The University institutions, too, include the Botanic Garden (1807); the Asa Gray Herbarium (1864); the Arnold Arboretum (1872); the Museum of Natural History founded by Louis Agassiz; the Peabody Museum of American Archæology and Ethnology (1866); the Semitic Museum (1889); the Germanic Museum (1902), etc. The annual baseball and football matches between Harvard and Yale are events of national interest. The library is one of the largest in the States.

Harvest and its Customs. Harvest (from the A.-S. *haerfest*, autumn) is the season for the gathering in of the crops, and has always been regarded as a time of rejoicing from time immemorial. The Jews celebrated the feast of Pentecost as their harvest festival, the Romans held feasts in honour of Ceres, and the Druids kept their feast on Nov. 1. Before the Reformation Aug. 1 or Lammas Day was generally considered the first day of the harvest festival in England, and was marked by the presentation of a loaf made of new wheat, in the churches, by every member of the congregation. Afterwards the feast of ingathering, known in Scotland as the 'kern,' was a peculiar secular method of celebrating the close of the harvest. This still survives in some places, but the modern general harvest festival is rapidly superseding it. It is recorded in the *Folk-Lore of*

North England, 1879, that in the northern part of Northumberland at the close of the harvest, when the last sheaf of corn is set on end, the 'kern' is celebrated. An image is crowned with wheat-ears and dressed in a white frock and coloured ribbons, and hoisted on to a pole. All the reapers then crowd round their 'kern-baby,' or 'harvest-queen,' and go to the barn where a supper awaits them. In Scotland the last sheaf is called the 'maiden,' and the youngest girl in the harvest-field is supposed to have the privilege of cutting it. But in the N.E. of Scotland, it is known as the 'cailleach' (old woman), and is dressed up as such, being placed at the head of the table at the harvest feast. Then there is the custom known as 'hollering largess.' The reapers form a ring in front of the house, bow their heads very low towards the centre of the circle saying, 'Hoo-Hoo-Hoo,' then jerk their heads backward shrieking 'Ah! Ah!' After this the leader of the band cries 'Holla largess,' which is echoed by the company. This is still done in E. Anglia when largess is asked for and obtained. In Herefordshire a final handful of grain was left uncut, but was tied up and given the name of a 'mare.' The reapers then threw their sickles at it to cut it down, the successful one crying out 'I have her,' 'A mare, a mare, a mare.' A similar practice to that of crying the 'mare,' was that of the 'cripple goat' in the Isle of Skye, and in Devonshire the last handful of the standing grain is still called the 'nack,' or 'neck.' The worship of the last sheaf seems to have been the main feature of the festival all over the world, and in Russia it is known as the 'bastard,' and a boy is wrapped in it, the woman who binds it being the 'corn-mother.' In America the 'Fête of the Big Sheaf' was held till quite recently, the last sheaf made large, being put on the last cart-load of grain as an emblem of abundance, and carried home with great rejoicing.

Harvest-bug, or Harvest-mite, the common name for mites of the family of Trombidiidæ, of the order Araci of the class Arachnida. At one time they were regarded as a distinct species (*Leptus autumnalis*), but are now known to be the six-legged larval forms of several species of the genus *Trombidium*. They are minute, scarlet, or rusty-brown mites, which are found in enormous numbers on gooseberry bushes, grass, and low herbage in the summer and autumn. They are parasitic, and especially liable to attack man, causing intense irritation by lodging in places where the skin is thin, such as behind the knees or between toes. After a certain time they leave their host and drop to the ground when they feed upon minute insects. The best remedy is to destroy them by applying turpentine, ammonia, or spirits of wine to the affected part. *See* MITES.

Harvest-fly, a species of *Cicada* (*q.v.*).

Harvest Moon. The full moon that occurs nearest to the autumnal equinox in September. At this season the moon's path is only very slightly inclined to the horizon, so that it rises for several nights in succession about the same time, thus yielding a series of moonlit evenings.

Harvest-spiders, or Harvest-men, so called on account of their abundance in the late summer or early autumn, are an order of Arachnids of the family Phalangiidæ. They can easily be distinguished from spiders because they have no waist between the cephalothorax and abdomen, and have extremely long thin legs. They feed upon small insects and spiders, and lay their eggs in autumn, which hatch out in the following spring or early summer. H. especially abound in temperate countries of the northern hemisphere, but are also common in India.

Harvey, a banking city of Cook co., Illinois, U.S.A., on the Illinois Central and other railroads, and a suburb of Chicago. Manufs. stoves, machinery, etc. Pop. (1910) 7227.

Harvey, Gabriel (*c.* 1545-1630), an English writer, born at Saffron Walden in Essex. In 1570 he was elected fellow of Pembroke Hall, Cambridge, when he became an intimate friend of Edmund Spenser, for whose Hobbinol in the *Shepheard's Calendar* he served as model. H. was an excellent scholar and an elegant Latin writer, but his bitter controversies with Greene and Nashe, the dramatist, who made him the butt of the brilliant satires, *Have with you to Saffron Walden* (Nashe), 1596, and *Quip for an Upstart Courtier* (Greene) brought on him general contempt. After H.'s retort to the former in the *Trimming of Thomas Nashe*, 1597, Archbishop Whitgift forbade all such books of satire. See *Works* (ed. A. B. Grosart), 1884-85, and Isaac Disraeli, *Calamities of Authors*, 1840.

Harvey, Sir George (1806-76), a Scottish painter, born at St. Ninians, Stirlingshire. He was apprenticed to a bookseller, but at the age of eighteen went to Edinburgh to study art and exhibited his first picture, 'A Village School,' in 1826 in the Edinburgh Institution, becoming an associate of the Scottish Academy the same year. He painted pictures illustrating the history and daily life of the Scottish nation, among which are: 'Covenanters Preaching,' 'The Curlers,' and 'Quitting the Manse.' He also did some important figure-pictures, e.g. 'Shakespeare before Sir Thomas Lucy,' 'A Castaway,' 'Dawn Revealing the New World to Colum-bus.' He was, too, famous as a painter of landscape, his finest being 'Ferragon,' 'Sheep-shearing,' 'In-vernarnon,' 'Loch Lomond.' In 1864 he was made president of the Scottish Academy and knighted, and in 1870 published his notes on the *Early History of the Royal Scottish Academy*.

Harvey, Sir Henry (1737-1810), a British naval officer, entered the navy in 1751. In 1773 he accom-panied Captain Phipps as lieutenant of the *Racehorse* on his voyage of dis-covery towards the North Pole. In 1776 he was present at the relief of Quebec; was commander of the *Ramillies* at Lord Howe's battle of June 1, 1794, and took part in the action off L'Orient and remained in command of the blockading squadron off Quiberon Bay, 1795. In 1797 as commander-in-chief in the Leeward Islands, he assisted Sir Ralph Aber-cromby in the capture of Trinidad. He became an admiral in 1804.

Harvey, John (1740-94), a British naval captain, entered the navy in 1755, and was commander of the *Panther* and employed in its defence during the early part of the siege of Gibraltar, 1779-80. He was present at the relief of Gibraltar, and in the engagement off Cape Spartel, 1782. He was in command of the *Bruns-wick*, under Lord Howe, at the battle of June 1, 1794, where he was en-gaged in a desperate struggle with the *Vengeur* and *Achille*, during which he was mortally wounded.

Harvey, John Martin (b. 1867), an English actor, born at Wyvenhoe, Essex. He was educated at King's College School, London, with a view to taking up naval architecture, but abandoned this for the stage, and studied elocution under John Ryder. He made his first appearance at the Old Court Theatre under John Clay-ton, but ultimately joined Sir Henry Irving, with whom he remained for many years. He has managed the Lyceum, the Prince of Wales, the Court, the Royalty, and Apollo theatres, and has appeared at the Court, the Avenue, Terry's, and the Garrick theatres. Among his pro-ductions are: *The Only Way; Ib and Little Christina; Eugene Aram; The Breed of the Treshams; Hamlet; The Corsican Brothers; Great Possessions; The World and his Wife; The Last Heir; An Idyl of Seven Dials; Richard III.*; and *Œdipus.*

Harvey, Sir Thomas (1775-1841), a British naval commander, entered the navy in 1787, and served as master's mate of the *Ramillies* in the battle of June 1, 1794; as lieutenant off L'Orient, June 23, 1795; and as commander of the *Pelican* at the reduction of Trinidad, 1797. He afterwards commanded in the frigates *Lapwing* and *Unité* on the Medi-terranean and W. Indian stations. In 1807 his ship, the *Standard*, was one of Sir John Duckworth's squad-ron in the destruction of the Turkish fleet at the entrance to the Dardan-elles. In 1837 he was promoted to vice-admiral and appointed commander-in-chief in the W. Indian station, where he died at Bermuda.

Harvey, William (1578–1657), a physician and discoverer of the cir-culation of the blood, born at Folke-stone, Kent. He was educated at Canterbury and Cambridge, and travelled through France and Ger-many to Padua, the most famous

WILLIAM HARVEY

school of physic of that time. In 1607 he was elected a fellow of the College of Physicians, and in 1609 was made assistant physician at St. Bartholomew's Hospital. In 1615 he was made Lumleian lecturer at the College of Physicians, where he made known his theory of the circulation of the blood, publishing his essay on the subject in 1628. In his essay he shows that the blood coming into the right auricle from the vena cava, and passing thence to the right ven-tricle, is pumped out to the lungs through the pulmonary artery, and comes thence by the pulmonary veins to the left ventricle. It is then pumped out to the body. It is carried out by arteries and comes back by veins, so performing a complete circulation. H. is famous for being the first to give an exact explanation of this theory.

Harvey-Gibson, Robert John, M.A., F.L.S. (*b.* 1860), professor of botany, and dean of the Faculty of Science in the University of Liverpool, born in Helensburgh. He has been a demonstrator at the Universities of Aberdeen and Edinburgh, and examiner to the Universities of Edinburgh, Glasgow, Durham, and Wales, and to the Pharmaceutical Society of Great Britain. He is still examiner in botany in the National University of Ireland. Publications: *Primer of Biology*; trans. Jost's *Plant Physiology*; 'Seaweeds' in *Chambers's Encyclopædia*, and papers in *Annals of Botany*, and for the Linnean Society, etc.

Harveyed Steel is steel which has been 'face-hardened' by a process invented by Mr. H. A. Harvey, which is chiefly applied to armour plates. The process is as follows : When the plate has been rolled out to the desired size and shape, in steel containing from ·10 to ·35 per cent. of carbon, such as Bessemer, or open-hearth steel, it is laid flat in a bed of finely powdered clay or sand, upon the bottom of a compartment erected within a furnace. The compartment is then fitted with granular carbonaceous material which is covered with a layer of sand and pressed down on the plate by rows of heavy fire-bricks. The furnace is then raised to an intense heat, the temperature being kept up for about 120 hrs., by which time the face of the steel has absorbed sufficient carbon to harden it, sometimes as much as 1 per cent. being thus taken up. The temperature of the furnace and duration of the process necessary for the maximum amount of hardening, depends upon the thickness of the plate, and the results are only assured by experience. When the surface of the plate has cooled down to a dull cherry-red colour, the superincumbent material is removed and the plate chilled by spraying with torrents of cold water, so as to uniformly harden the surface. A plate of steel 10½ in. thick, when treated in the above manner, is found to be supercarbonised to a depth of about 3 in., the depth depending to a large extent on the pressure exerted from above on its surface. Also, a plate of H. S. of the above thickness will withstand a hardened projectile of 6 in. diameter, weighing 100 lbs.,

and travelling with a velocity of 2000 ft. per second, the latter being shivered to fragments without scarcely penetrating the plate. Nickel steel when treated by the above process, yields a material which is even harder than H. S.

Harvie-Brown, John A. (*b.* 1844), a Scottish naturalist, born at Edinburgh, and educated there and at Cambridge. His researches in natural history have been mainly devoted to the Vertebrate Fauna of Scotland, Britain, and foreign countries, and to the migration of birds, for which studies he has travelled in Norway, Russia, and Transylvania, Faroe Is., and Rockall, as well as making a complete investigation of the Scottish coasts. Among his publications are : *The Capercaillie in Scotland*, 1879; *History of the Squirrel*, 1881; *Reports on the Migration of Birds; Vertebrate Fauna of Sutherland*, 1887; *Vertebrate Fauna of the Outer Hebrides*, 1888 ; *Vertebrate Fauna of the Orkney Islands*, 1891; *Fauna of the Moray Basin*, 1895, the last four in collaboration with Mr. T. E. Buckley; *The Wonderful Trout*, 1898; and *Travels of a Naturalist in Northern Europe*, 1905. See *Bibliography* of his writings, 1896.

Harwich, a municipal bor., seaport and market tn. in Essex, England, on a small peninsula at the confluence of the Stour and the Orwell, 70 m. N.E. of London. Dovercourt is the residential quarter of H., and is a favourite seaside resort. There is a large trade in shipbuilding, cement, and fish, and is one of the chief English ports for continental passenger traffic. It has been a fortified port since the time of James I., and was the scene of a naval engagement between the Dutch and English in 1666. It has been an important trading centre since the 14th century. Pop. (1911) 13,623.

Harwood, a tn. in the co. of Lancashire, England, 2 m. N.E. of Bolton. Pop. (1911) 13,817.

Harwood, Edward (1729–94), an English classical scholar and Biblical critic, born at Darwen, Lancashire. He was trained for the ministry, and from 1765-72 was minister in the Tucker Street Presbyterian Chapel, Bristol. He was an excellent Biblical critic and scholar, and among his publications are a *Translation of the New Testament*, 1768, with another volume by way of introduction, 1771; *A View of . . . editions of the Greek and Roman Classics*, 1775 ; *An Edition of the Greek Testament, with English Notes*, 1776; and *Biographica Classica* (new ed.), 1778.

Harzburg, a summer resort in the Harz Mts., Germany, at the N. foot of the Brocken in the Duchy of Brunswick. H. lies in the shadow of Burgberg (1520 ft.) 28 m. S. of the town of Brunswick, and includes the neighbouring hamlets of Neustadt, Bündheim, and Schlewecke. On the Burgberg are the ruins of a castle built in 1065 by the Emperor Henry IV., and the 'Canossa pillar,' erected in 1877 in honour of Bismarck. The town is now famous for its brine and carbon springs. Pop. (1910) 4728.

Harz Mountains, the most northerly mountain system of Germany, extending between the rivers Weser and Elbe. Their greatest length is 57 m., from S.E. to N.W.; their greatest breadth about 20 m., from N. to S.; and their total area about 784 sq. m. The range consists of an elevated plateau rising steeply on all sides, more especially on the N., and divided into the Upper and Lower Harz, with a general elevation of from 2000-3000 ft.; the Brocken, which separates them, belongs to the former, and reaches a height of 3750 ft. The range is heavily wooded, and its wild and melancholy beauty has given rise to numerous legendary tales in German folklore, the chief of which, connected with the Brocken (q.v.), has been immortalised by Goethe in his *Faust*. The Harz Mts. are a favourite summer resort of the Germans : Harzburg, Thale, Bode thal, Alexisbad, Hubertsbad, and other places having, in addition to their natural charm, the advantages of mineral springs, pine-needle and other baths, whey cures, etc. The district is particularly rich in metals and minerals, silver, lead, iron, copper, sulphur, arsenic, marble, granite, and gypsum all being found. The chief mining centres are St. Andreasberg and Klausthal, the 'Samson' mine, near the former being one of the deepest shafts (2790 ft.) in Europe. Vitriol is also manufactured, and there is a large timber industry. A rack-railway up the Brocken was opened in 1898, the observatory on the top of the mountain dating from 1895. *See* H. Hoffmann, *Der Harz*, 1899, and *Harzwanderung*, 1902.

Hasa, El, a dist. in the E. of Arabia, stretching for some 360 m. along the shore of the Persian Gulf. Politically El Hasa belongs to Turkey and is included in the vilayet of Basra. Its capital, Hofuf (pop. 20,000), is the headquarters of the sanjak of Nejd. Dates, rice, cotton, and indigo are cultivated, and camels are bred; it also shares in the valuable pearl fishery of Bahrein. Other towns are Katif, Uber or Ujer, the port of El Hasa, and Mubāriz, famous for its hot springs. Most of the pop. consists

of nomads, but it is estimated at about 150,000.

Hasbaya, or Hasbeya, a tn. in Syria, 22 m. E.S.E. of Sidon. In 1846 a Protestant mission was established here, and during the Druse massacre of 1860 the town was nearly destroyed, most of the Christians fleeing to Tyre or Sidon for refuge. Pop. numbers about 5600, 4000 of whom are Druse or Christians.

Hasbury, par. and vil. of Worcestershire, England, 5 m. S. of Dudley. Pop. (1911) 3400.

Hasdeu, Bogdan Petriceicu (b. 1838), a Roumanian historian and philologist, born near Khotin in Bessarabia. He was appointed professor at Bucharest in 1864, and keeper of the national archives. His *Critical History of the Roumanians* (2 vols., 1875) is valuable, chiefly on account of his broad and original views. Among his other publications are: *Cuvinte din Batrani* (2 vols.), 1878-81; *Etymologicum Magnum Romaniæ*, the chief dictionary of the Roumanian language (3 vols.), 1887-93, and *Strat și Substrat*, 1893, an account of the origin of the Balkan peoples.

Hasdrubal, the name of two Carthaginians: 1. (d. 221 B.C.) The son-in-law of Hamilcar Barca, on whose death in 229 he became leader of the Carthaginian forces in Spain. He founded the city of New Carthage, and agreed to the treaty with Rome which forbade him to pass the Iberus. He was assassinated by a slave, whose master he had killed. 2. (d. 207 B.C.) The son of Hamilcar Barca, the brother of Hannibal. When Hannibal set out with his troops for Italy (218), Hasdrubal was left in command in Spain, where he had to contend with the two Scipios. In 207 he marched into Italy with reinforcements for his brother, but was defeathed on the Metaurus by the consuls M. Livius Salinator and C. Claudius Nero. He was slain in battle, and his head thrown into Hannibal's camp.

Hase, Karl August von (1800-90), a German theologian, born at Steinbach in Saxony. In 1829 he was appointed professor of philosophy at the University of Leipzig, and professor of theology at Jena in the same year. His best known works are: *Die Leipziger Disputation,* 1827; *Leber Jesu,* 1829 (Eng. trans. 1881), in which he anticipated the arguments put forward by Strauss ; *Theologische Streitschriften,* 1834-37; *Die Tübinger Schule,* 1855; *Hutterus Redivivsus* (12th ed.), 1883; *Lehrbuch der Kirchengeschichte* (11th ed.), 1886 (Eng. trans. 1855); *Die Beiden Erzbischöfe,* 1839, and an edition of *Libri Symbolici Ecclesiæ Evangelicæ.*

See *Life* by Buerkner (in German), 1900.

Haselrig, Sir Arthur (also **Heselrige, Hazelrigg**), one of the five members whom Charles I. ordered to be arrested for high treason on Jan. 3, 1642. The other names were Pym, Hampden, Hollis, and Strode. The Commons refused to give them up.

Hashish, or **Hasheesh**, the Arabic name, meaning literally ' dried herb,' for the various preparations obtained from the flowering tops of the Indian hemp plant (*Cannabis indica*). It is used as an intoxicant in several Eastern countries (called ' bhang ' in India), and is either smoked, chewed, or drunk. It is valuable as a narcotic, and is sometimes employed in medicine as an anodyne. The English word ' assassin ' is probably derived from the Arabic ' hashishin,' *i.e.* hemp-eaters, who committed great excesses when under the influence of hashish. *See* HEMP.

Haskerland, a com. in the prov. of Friesland in the Netherlands. Pop. 7956.

Hasland, a par. and vil. in Derbyshire, England, 2 m. S.S.E. of Chesterfield. Pop. (1911) 7500.

Haslar Hospital, *see* GOSPORT.

Haslemere, a market tn. and par. of England in the co. of Surrey in the Guildford div., on the London and South-Western Railway, 10 m. from Farnham, and 8 m. from Godalming. Near by is Aldworth House, Tennyson's last home. The town is situated in very picturesque surroundings, and is healthy and salubrious, and a favourite residential place. Hindhead Common, with its celebrated Devil's Punch Bowl is quite close. Pop. (1911) 2600.

Haslingden, a market tn. and municipal bor. of England in the co. of Lancashire. It is in the diocese of Manchester, on the Lancashire and Yorkshire Railway, and has two stations, Haslingden and Helmshore. It has a church dating from the 13th century. It manufactures cottons, silks, woollens, and has stone quarries, coal mines, and iron works. Pop. (1911) 18,723.

Hasmoneans, *see* ASMONEANS, and MACCABEES.

Haspe, a tn. in Prussia, prov. of Westphalia, the seat of an important iron and steel industry, manufactures scythes, etc. Pop. (1901) 16,039.

Hassall, Arthur (*b.* 1853), an English historian, born at Bebington, Cheshire ; educated at Uppingham and Oxford. In 1880 he became a lecturer and tutor in history at Keble College, and in 1883 at Christchurch. His works include: *Life of Bolingbroke*, in the Statesmen Series, 1889 ; *Louis XIV.*, in the Heroes of the Nations

Series, 1895 ; *The Making of the British Empire*, 1896 ; *A Handbook of European History*, 1897 ; *The Balance of Power*, 1896 and 1898, in the Periods of European History Series, of which he is editor; *A Class Book of English History*, 1901 ; *History of France*, 1901 ; *The French People*, 1901 ; *Mazarin*, in the Foreign Statesmen Series, 1903 ; *History of France*, in the Temple Primers, 1903 ; *The Tudor Dynasty*, 1904 ; *A Brief Survey of European History*, 1906 ; *The Expansion of Great Britain*, 1907 ; *Castlereagh*, 1908 ; *The Great Rebellion*, 1909 ; *Modern Europe*, 1910 ; *The Great Napoleon*, 1911 ; *History of British Foreign Policy*, 1912.

Hassall, John (*b.* 1868), an English artist, son of the late C. C. Hassall, R.N. He received his education at Newton Abbott College, Devon, and Neuenheim College, Heidelberg, and began life farming in Manitoba. He abandoned this pursuit in 1891, and for three years studied art at Antwerp and Paris. His particular branch comprises posters, illustrations, book-covers, etc. He married in 1903, and has one son. He is a member of several clubs, including the Savage, Eccentric, and New Vagabond.

Hassan, a dist. of Mysore state, forming the N.W. part of the Ashtagram div. The chief tn. is H. in the centre of the dist., where the administrative headquarters are situated. H. is bounded on the S. partly by the state of Coorg, and on the S.W. by the Madras district of S. Kanara. Its area is 2547 sq. m. The district is divided into two portions, the Malnad, or hill - country, including some of the highest ranges of the Western Ghats, and the Maidan, or plain country, in the direction of Mysore to the S. Staple cultivation, dry and wet crops. Pop. (est.) 570,000.

Hassan and Hussein, sons of Ali and Mohammed's daughter Fatima:

Hassan (625-69) succeeded his father as Caliph at Kufa in 660, but in a few months retired in favour of his rival Moaweeyah, and went to live at Medina, where he attained a great reputation for piety. He is said to have been poisoned by one of his wives.

Hussein, or *Hosein* (629-80), succeeded his brother Hassan as Imam of the Shiites, and claimed the caliphate also. In attempting to depose the latter's troops at Kerbela. The two brothers are held in the greatest veneration by the Shiites, who hold an annual festival in their honour, at which their deaths are dramatically represented. *See* Elmacin's *Historia Saracenica ;* Weil's *Geschichte der Chalifen ;* Sir Lewis Pelly's *The*

Miracle-Play of Hasan and Hosein, 1879; and M. Arnold's ' A Persian Passion-Play ' (*Essays in Criticism*).

Hassan - ibn - Sabbah (1054 – 1124), called 'The Old Man of the Mountain,' was the founder of the sect of Assassins. A Shiite of Khorassan, he had studied the secret doctrines of Ismaili dais or religious leaders at Nishapur. However, he quarrelled with them, and was forced to leave their country. He collected a society round him in the fortress of Alamut in Persia, and here he instituted his abominable code of the doctrine of assassination. A band of youths called the Fedavis (the devoted) were appointed by him to assassinate, being first intoxicated by the hashish or hemp-plant; hence the term Hashishin=assassin (hempeaters). *See* ASSASSINS.

Hasse, Johann Adolf (1699-1783), a German dramatic composer. Born at Bergedorf, near Hamburg, educated first by his father, and then joined Keiser's operatic troupe, later obtaining an engagement at the Court Theatre of Brunswick. Here, in 1723, he produced his opera *Antigonus,* which was so successful that in 1724 the duke sent him to Italy, where he studied with Porpora and Scarlatte. In 1726 he produced at Naples *Sesostrato,* which brought him into prominent notice. In 1727 he went to Venice ; then became kapellmeister at Dresden, and in 1733 went to London, where he was asked to head an opposition to Handel. Here he produced *Artaserse,* first produced at Venice in 1730. From 1739-63 he was in court service at Dresden, and then retired to Vienna and Venice. His other operas include *Alcide al Bivio,* 1760, and *Ruggiero,* 1771.

Hasselguist, Fredrik (*b.* 1722), a Swedish naturalist. He studied under Linnæus at the University of Upsala in 1741, and afterwards travelled in Asia Minor, Palestine, and Egypt, making many valuable natural history collections. After his death in 1752, Linnæus paid tribute to his memory in a book called *Resa till Heliga Landet forattad fran ar 1749 till 1752.*

Hasselt (*Hasselholt,* hazel grove), the chief tn. of the prov. of Limburg in Belgium. It is 16 m. from Maestricht by rail. It has manufactures of linen fabrics, tobacco, and gin-distilleries. Chicory is largely cultivated in the surrounding district. Pop. (1900) 15,249.

Hassert, Ernst Emil Kurt, (*b.* 1868), a German geographer, was born at Naumburg on Saale. He holds the appointment of professor of commercial geography at the commercial high school in Cologne, and amongst his many valuable contributions to geo-graphy and science are his *Reise durch Montenegro,* 1893 ; *Beiträge zur Physische Geographie von Montenegro,* 1895 ; *Deutschlands Kolonien,* 1899-1902 ; *Polarforschung,* 1902 ; and *Landeskunde der Königsreichs Württemberg,* 1902.

Hasslinghausen, a tn. in Prussia, prov. of Westphalia, 8 m. W. by S. of Hagen. It has coal and iron mines. Pop. (commune) 8516.

Hassloch, a tn. of the Rhine Palatinate, Bavaria, 17 m. from Landan, on railway from Mannheim to Homburg. Pop. 7718.

Hastinapur, a ruined city of British India, in the Meerut dist.. United Provinces, on banks of former bed of Ganges. At one time it was the capital of the Pandava kingdom.

Hastings, a famous watering-place in Sussex, one of the Cinque Ports. and a parl. and municipal bor. On the S. it is open to the sea, but elsewhere surrounded by high cliffs. It is 62 m. S.S.E. of London, and 33 m. E. of Brighton. H. has an old and new town, the former chiefly inhabited by fishermen. The new town is large, and its resident population (1911) 61,146 is doubled in the holiday season. Both towns form one borough, fronted by a breezy, well-paved esplanade 3 m. in length. Being sheltered by the hills inland from easterly and northerly winds, H. is a well-known resort for pulmonary complaints in the winter and spring. The climate is dry, mild, and salubrious. There are two large piers and several public gardens, the chief of which is the extensive Alexandra Park.

Hastings : 1. A city of Nebraska, U.S.A., in Adams co. It has an altitude of 1947 ft., and is 130 m. W.S.W. of Omaha. Pop. (1910) 9338. 2. A post tn. of New Zealand, N. Island, in Hawkes Bayco., 11 m. S.S.W. of Napier. Its industries are of an agricultural nature. Pop. about 4600. 3. A city in Michigan, U.S.A., cap. of Barry co., on Michigan Central, and the Chicago, Kalamagoo. and Saginaw railways. Its chief manufs. are furniture, waggons, blinds, flour, felt, boots, etc. Pop. (1910) 4383.

Hastings, Battle of, the usual name given to the great battle at Senlac, near Hastings, where William, Duke of Normandy, defeated the English under Harold in 1066. The hill of Senlac overlooked the town of Hastings, and on its summit was firmly posted Harold's force—the Normans being ranged in three divisions, the centre one of which was commanded by the duke himself. The Normans were repeatedly driven back by the English, but at length, by a feigned flight, the latter were drawn from their stockade, and fell rapidly. *See* Freeman's *Norman Conquest*, vol. iii.

Hastings, Francis Rawdon (1754-1826), first Marquis of H. (1817), a British soldier and administrator, born in Ireland, the son of Sir John Rawdon of Moira; later Earl of Moira; educated at Harrow and Oxford, and entered the army. From 1775-82 he was on service in the American War, fighting at Bunker Hill, Brooklyn, White Plains, Camden, Charleston, etc., and was created a peer, as Baron Rawdon, on his return in 1783. In 1794 he fought against the French in Flanders; was appointed commander-in-chief in Scotland, 1803; became master-general of the ordnance, 1806; and governor-general of India in 1813. The chief events of his administration were the wars against Nepal (1814-16) and the Mahrattas and Pindaris (1817-18). He retired in 1823, and was appointed governor of Malta in 1824.

Hastings, Selina, *see* HUNTINGDON, SELINA, COUNTESS OF.

Hastings, Warren (1732-1818), a governor-general of India, went out in 1750 to Calcutta, where the influence of his uncle had secured for him a cadetship in the E. India Company's service. He rose rapidly, and became a person of such considerable importance that eleven years after his arrival in the country he, having already filled other posts with credit, was appointed a member of the Calcutta council. In 1764 he returned to England. Unlike most of his colleagues, he had made no attempt to amass a private income, and had nothing but his savings to live upon, and these were so inconsiderable that they were already exhausted when, in 1769, he accepted the Company's offer to go out to Madras as second in council. Two years later he was promoted to the governorship of Bengal. He now fulfilled the hopes of the directors at home, and proved himself a wise and far-seeing administrator. He instituted reforms, both in the government of the province and in the law courts, that were taken as models by his successors. He upheld treaty rights and removed abuses, but was bitterly opposed by some members of his council, his most bitter opponent being (Sir) Philip Francis, whom in 1780 he wounded in a duel. In 1785, having done magnificent work, he resigned his office and returned to England. At once an agitation was set on foot by Francis and others, who enlisted the support of Burke, and he was impeached in 1788 for corruption and cruelty. The trial dragged on for seven years, when he was acquitted on all counts. His expenses in con-

nection with it amounted to £70,000, his entire fortune. Thereupon the E. India Company, very rightly, but to the great indignation of Burke, granted him a handsome pension, which enabled him to fulfil his long-cherished dream of repurchasing the family estate of Daylesford. In later days, largely owing to the kindly influence of the Prince Regent (afterwards George IV.), he was reinstated in popular opinion, though his impeachment was never officially reversed. Mill, the historian of India, declared that ' few men would be found whose character would present a higher claim to indulgence than his, and this view is now generally accepted. There are biographies by Gleig, 1841, and by Trotter, 1878.

Hastings Beds or **Sands,** a part of the Lower Cretaceous series and a lower division of the Wealden beds. They vary in thickness from 500 to 1000 ft., and consist mainly of sand and sandstone with subordinate layers of clay. They have been deposited in shallow fresh water, and fine specimens of ripple marks are often to be seen in the sand. The strata, which differ only slightly from those of the overlying Weald clay, are highly fossiliferous and contain numerous saurian reptiles and the remains of several chelonians, besides the remarkable lepidotus and other fish belonging to the ganoid or placoid orders.

Haswell, a tn. in the co. of Durham, England, situated on the North-Eastern Railway, 6 m. E. of Durham. Pop. (1911) 5500.

Hat, The, like all articles of apparel, has a history, and it is very interesting to trace its gradual evolution from earliest times in the simple close-fitting cap to the many elaborate structures supplied by the demands of a 20th-century civilisation. The word H. comes from the A.-S. *hæt,* and German *Hut,* hat. The Anglo-Saxon *hæt* consisted of a woollen cap, and was worn by the higher class of the Anglo-Saxons. But centuries before this time caps or coverings for the head were worn amongst the Oriental nations, when they had a certain religious significance, as in the case of the ' pilos ' worn by the Jewish levitical priest. It is conjectured that the oldest head-covering was the circular close-fitting cap either plain or braided, which was worn by captives from Palestine in Assyria, and which also appeared on the heads of various deities among the heathen tribes. There were two kinds of head-covering worn by the Greeks in early times, the ' pileus ' and the ' petasus.' The pileus had no brim, whilst the petasus was made of felt, and had a wide brim to protect the wearer from the rays of the sun. The English felt H. may be said to be the direct descendant of the Greek petasus, but did not come into vogue in England till the year 1510. At the time of the Norman Conquest the Phrygian cap, flat bonnet, and brimmed H. were worn. With the advance of centuries new fashions crept in, adopted from intercourse with other nations. This is especially noticeable in Tudor times, where we meet with wide Hs. crowned with plumes and feathers, and with low-crowned caps with upturned brims. Beaver felts in many shapes came into vogue in Queen Elizabeth's reign, and were the common form of head covering for three centuries. To see what an important part the H. has played in the making of history, one has only to reflect upon the Civil War in Charles I.'s reign, when the distinguishing feature of the Roundheads or Puritans was the high-steepled H. of plain felt, whilst the Cavaliers' head covering was adorned with feathers. A century later the three-cornered cocked H. became the prevailing fashion, owing, no doubt, to the necessity of looping up the extravagant width of the brim. The felt H. of to-day is manufactured either of fur, of a mixture of fur and wool, or of wool only. At one time they were manufactured exclusively of beaver-fur, but the scarcity of this animal made it necessary to use other materials. The fur or hair of rabbits, beaver, musk-rat, and camel are used for the finer Hs., whilst sheep's wool is used for the inferior felted Hs. The cheapest kinds of felt are also made with wool mixed with cotton and other vegetable fibres; in this case they are not really felted, but cemented by varnish which helps to hold together the fibres and to stiffen the H. body. Other forms of H. have come into vogue, viz. the silk H. and the straw. The manufacture of silk Hs. began early in the 19th century in England. It was invented in Florence about 1760, but the fashion did not become popular till half a century later. The silk H. consists of a stiff body covered with a plush of silk, the body consists of calico, which first being stiffened with a varnish of shellac, is then cut into pieces sufficient for crown, side, and brim. The brim usually consists of three thicknesses of calico cemented together to give it the required stiffness. The Hs. are moulded on wooden blocks according to the prevailing fashion, when there are many processes such as dressing, polishing by means of damping and ironing, and veluring before the H. is complete. The only trimming for the silk H. is a silk braid on the edge of

the brim, and a silk band round the body to hide the joins. The felt H. trade is carried on chiefly at Denton and other villages near Manchester. London, Paris, Edinburgh, and New York manufacture excellent silk Hs. Hs. have undergone a variety of changes both in shapes and trimmings. The most usual forms of H. worn by men consist of the ordinary silk top H., the wide-awake or bowler, and the crush felt H. The variety of shape and size in the ladies' fashions is complex and multiform. The tight-fitting toque, the medium-sized beaver, and the gigantic, broad-brimmed H. are equally popular. Straw Hs. are worn by men and women during the summer months, and the chief places of industry are Luton and Dunstable in England. The Leghorn plaits and Tuscany plaits imported from Italy fetch a high price.

Hatch, Edwin (1835-89), an English theologian, was born at Derby and educated at King Edward's School, Birmingham. He first studied at Pembroke College, Oxford, and then went to America as professor of classics in Trinity College, Toronto. Returning to Oxford in 1867, he became principal of St. Mary's Hall (1867-85). In 1883 he obtained the living of Purleigh in Essex, and was appointed university reader in ecclesiastical history in 1884. He is noted for his treatises: *On the Organisation of the Early Christian Churches* (Bampton lectures), and *The Influence of Greek Ideas upon the Christian Church* (Hibbert lectures). He is a very liberal-minded and original thinker.

Hatchettite, a mineral found generally in rock-crevices or in fossil shells. It is a hydrocarbon, melting-point 46° to 47°, odourless, colourless, or faint yellow when first exposed, but darkening on exposure.

Hatching, *see* INCUBATION.

Hatchment, Achievement, or Funeral Escutcheon, derived from Fr. *achever* (*à chef venir*), to come to a head, or to accomplish. The word H. is the name given to the armorial shield suspended against the wall of a deceased person's house. Thus it is customary at Oxford and Cambridge to hang the H. of a deceased college authority above the entrance to his residence. *See* HERALDRY.

Hatfield, or **Bishop's Hatfield**, a market tn. of England in the co. of Hertfordshire, 6½ m. W.S.W. of Hertford and 5 m. E. by N. of St. Albans, on the Great Northern Railway, 18 m. by rail from London. Near by is Hatfield House, the seat of the Marquis of Salisbury, a fine specimen of Jacobean architecture, rich in historical manuscripts and portraits, built in 1611 by Sir Robert Cecil. Both Edward VI. and Elizabeth were living here when called to the throne. Pop. (1911) 8592. *See* Brewer's *English Studies*, 1881.

Hatfield Chase, a level tract of land in the N.E. of the Doncaster div. of the W. Riding of Yorkshire. It is about 8 acres in extent, and the fenny land has been drained and is now cultivated. *See* John Tomlinson, *The Level of Hatfield Chace*, 1882.

Hathaway, Anne (1556-1623), wife of William Shakespeare.

Hatherley, William Page Wood, **Baron** (1801-81), Lord Chancellor of England, born in London, educated at Winchester, Geneva, and Cambridge; called to the bar in 1824. In 1845 he became a queen's counsel; in 1847 was elected Liberal M.P. for Oxford; in 1849 was appointed vice-chancellor of the county palatine of Lancaster; and in 1851 became Solicitor-General and was knighted. In 1853 he was made a vice-chancellor, and in 1868 Lord Justice of Appeal. At the end of the same year he was appointed Lord Chancellor by Mr. Gladstone, being also raised to the peerage. He retired in 1872.

Hathor, an Egyptian goddess, *see* ATHOR.

Hathras, a tn. of British India in the United Provinces. An important commercial centre, ranking second to Cawnpur. Pop. 43,000.

Hatia, an island in British India, Bengal dist. The island is sometimes visited by storm-waves of a very destructive nature. In 1876 a cyclone completely submerged it, causing a loss of life estimated at 30,000. H. is low-lying and has an area of 185 sq. m.

Hatien, a seaport tn. of Cochin-China on the Gulf of Siam, in French Indo-China. Pop. 11,000.

Hatim-et-T'ai, who has been the subject of many poems among Oriental writers, was an Arab chief, remarkable for his greatness of disposition and generosity. He lived shortly before the advent of Mahommed.

Hatmatack, *see* LARCH.

Hats and **Caps**, the name given to two political parties in Sweden, which existed for a period of thirty-five years. The Hats, under Tessin, were in power in 1738, but were ousted by the Caps twenty-seven years later. The Caps then reigned for three years, from 1766 to 1769, when they had to make way again for the Hats. The Caps reconquered in 1771, but both parties were abolished in 1772.

Hatshepsu, or **Hatshepsut**, a queen of the eighteenth Egyptian dynasty, daughter of Thoutmosis I. and sole heiress to the Egyptian throne. For fifteen years she reigned in Egypt as regent for her nephew, Thoutmosis III., governing well and energetically. She was instrumental in building the temple of Deir El-Baharf at Thebes, as well as many other monuments.

Hatteras, Cape, in N. Carolina, U.S.A., at the end of a long sandbank or island separated by Pamlico Sound from the mainland. Violent storms often occur, producing a heavy sea, which makes the inlet dangerous to navigators.

Hattiesburg, cap. of Perry Co., Missouri, U.S.A. It has foundries, cotton-seed oil mills, machine works, etc. Pop. (1910) 11,733.

Hattin, a vil. in Palestine, 'Ziddim' in the O.T., 5½ m. N.W. of Tiberias. In 1187 Saladin defeated the Crusaders here, securing Jerusalem and Palestine to the Mussulmans.

Hattingen, an old tn. of Prussia in prov. of Westphalia, on the l. b. of the Ruhr. It has iron works and coal mines, and there are ruins of the mediæval castle of Isenburg near by. Pop. 12,765.

Hatto I., archbishop of Mainz, came of a Swabian family, and obtained his archbishopric under Arnulf, a German king, in 891. He was so popular with this monarch that he received the nickname of ' the heart of the king.' Upon the death of Arnulf, in 899, H. was appointed regent of Germany and guardian of the young king Louis. He exercised his power in a very arbitrary way, and was guilty of many crimes in the course of his career. This, no doubt, accounts for the legend of his being thrown into the crater of Mount Ætna. He died in 913.

Hatto II., was archbishop from 968-970; his name is associated with the legend of the Mouse Tower at Bingen, where he is reported to have been devoured by mice.

Hatton, John Liptrot (1809-86), an English musical composer, born at Liverpool. After holding many appointments as organist in Liverpool, he came to London in 1832; ten years later he was appointed conductor of Drury Lane Theatre, where his own operetta, *Queen of the Thames*, was produced. Some years later he was the accompanist of the St. James's Hall Ballad Concerts. He also composed the songs, *Goodnight Beloved*, *Simon the Cellarer*, and *To Anthea*.

Hatton, Joseph (1841-1907), a novelist, at an early age became a journalist, and between 1863 and 1868 edited several provincial papers. In the latter year he came to London, when he wrote for many periodicals and newspapers. In later days he contributed a causerie to the *People*, under the title of ' Cigarette Papers.' He wrote many novels, the best known of which were: *Clytie*, and *By Order of the Czar*. These, and others, were very popular, but they have no value as literature. H. was an intimate friend of Sir Henry Irving and J. L. Toole, and he edited Irving's *Impressions of America* and Toole's *Reminiscences*. He was for many years a notable figure at the Garrick Club and in Fleet Street.

Hatvan, a tn. of Hungary, 30 m. E.N.E. of Budapest. It has a large castle. Pop. 9707.

Hatzfeld (Hungarian *Zsombolya*), a market tn. of Hungary in Torontal. It is a flourishing town, and the rearing of horses is one of its industries. Pop. 10,152.

Hatzfeldt-Wildenbourg, Paul, Count von (1831-1901), a German diplomatist, born at Düsseldorf and entered the diplomatic service. After holding several minor posts, in 1883 he became Secretary for Foreign Affairs, and in 1888 was appointed German ambassador at the court of St. James. He continued in this position till his death. He was a great friend and favourite of Bismarck, and was prominent in the great national revival promoted by that statesman. See *The Hatzfeldt Letters*, 1905.

Hauberk, a twisted coat of mail extending as high as the neck and sometimes even forming a coif so that only the face was exposed. In the 14th century the H. was worn under plate-armour called ' Haubergeon.' This was short and sleeveless.

Hauch, Johannes Carsten (1790-1872), a Danish poet and dramatist, born at Frederikshald, Norway, of Danish parents; returned to Denmark in 1803 and in 1807 fought against the English invasion. In 1808 he entered the University of Copenhagen, and in 1821 took a doctor's degree in zoology. In 1846 he became professor of Scandinavian languages at Kiel; in 1848 returned to Copenhagen; in 1851 became honorary professor of æsthetics at Copenhagen University, and from 1858-60 was director of the Danish National Theatre. His works include some early dramatic poems and lyrical dramas, a group of unsuccessful tragedies produced in 1828-32; five romances, 1834-53; collections of *Poems*, 1842, and of *Lyrical Poems and Romances*, 1861; *Valdemar Seir*, 1862; an historial epic, and some very fine tragedies produced between 1841 and 1866, including *Svend Grathe*; *The Sisters at Kinnekulle*; *Marshal Stig*; *Honour Lost and Won*; *Tycho Brahe's Youth*; *The King's Favourite*, and *Henry of Navarre*.

Hauff, Wilhelm (1802-27), a German author, born at Stuttgart; educated at Blaubeuren and Tübingen. In 1824 he became tutor to the children of General Baron Ernst Eugen von Heigel. In 1825 he published *Der Mann im Monde*, a satire on the novels of Clauren, who brought and won an action for damages against H. He retaliated in *Kontroverspredigtüber H. Clauren und den Mann im Monde* (1826), which was most successful. In the same year he produced *Lichtensteen*, an historical novel which became very popular. His other work includes : *Memoiren des Satan*; *Bettlerin von Pont des Arts*; *Phantasien im Bremer Ratskeller*, and *Marchenalmanach auf das Jahr*, 1826, and some short poems. In 1827 he became editor of the Stuttgart *Morgenblatt*.

Haug, Martin (1826-76), a famous Sanskritist, entered the University of Tübingen in 1848, where he studied the Oriental languages. He went to India in 1859 as professor of Sanskrit at Poona. Besides writing *Essays on the Parsees*, he has published valuable material for all students of the literatures of Ancient India and Persia.

Haugesund, a seaport in Norway, 36 m. N.W. of the tn. of Stavanger. It has a harbour of a depth from 17 to 50 ft., the depth alongside of the small quays being 6 to 15 ft. Pop. 9144.

Haughton, William, an English dramatic writer of the 17th century who collaborated in many plays with Henry Chettle and Thomas Dekker. Philip Henslowe mentions in his diary how he helped to release H. from ' the Clink,' by a loan of ten shillings. He is supposed to have written the greater part of *The Patient Grissill*.

Haukal, Abul Kasem Mohammed Ibn, an Arabian traveller and geographer of the 10th century A.D., born at Bagdad. In 943 he left his native city and spent many years in travelling through the countries lying between the Indus and the Atlantic. About 975 he wrote a record of his journeys, called, *A Book of Roads and Kingdoms*, which is furnished with maps, and contains much valuable information.

Hauksbee, Francis, *see* HAWKSBEE.

Haulbowline, an island S. of co. Cork, Ireland, situated in Cork Harbour, opposite Queenstown. It has a convict station, artillery barracks, and various ordnance works.

Haunted Houses, the usual phenomena associated with H. H. consisted in apparitions, strange sounds, as banging of doors and moving about of furniture. The Rev. Samuel Wesley complained of disturbances in Epworth Rectory in 1717 when he felt himself pushed by some unseen presence. Very often houses were supposed to be haunted on account of some crime committed in them; ghosts of the victims appeared, or groans and sighs would be heard.

Haupt, Moritz (1808-74), a German-ist and classical scholar, studied at the Leipzig University. He became professor extraordinarius, first of the chair of German language and litera-ture at Leipzig, and then at Berlin. He was an able lecturer, wrote valu-able criticisms and edited many classical and Old German works.

Hauptmann, Gerhard (b. 1862), a German dramatist, born at Salz-brunn, Silesia; educated there and at the Realschule in Breslau. He worked for a time on a farm at Jauer, and then returned to Breslau to study art, continuing his education at Jena, and going to Italy in 1883-84. In 1885 he married and settled to literary work in Berlin. In 1891 he retired to Schreiberhaw, Silesia. He was awarded the Grillpazzer Prize in 1898, and in 1905 was made an honorary LL.D. of Oxford University. Among his dramas are: *Vor Sonnen-aufgang*, 1889, which was a pioneer of the movement towards realism; *Das Friendensfest*, 1890; *Einsame Men-schen*, 1891; *Die Weber*, 1892, which dealt with the rising of the Silesian weavers in 1844, and was banned by the Licenser of Plays; *Kollege Cramp-ton*, 1892; *Der Biberpelz*, 1893; *Hannele*, 1894; *Fuhrmann Henschel*, 1898, and *Der rote Hahn*, 1901.

Hauptmann, Moritz (1792-1868), a German composer, born at Dresden; in 1822 entered the orchestra at Cassel, and in 1842 became a pro-fessor of music at Leipzig. He wrote numerous masses, choral songs, and part songs, an opera, *Mathilde*, and sonatas, and wrote a treatise on music.

Haupur, *see* HAPUR.

Hauraki, a gulf of the Pacific in North Is., New Zealand, 70 m. long and 40 m. broad. It has several excel-lent harbours, the town of Auckland being situated on that of Waitemata, and it also contains many well-wooded islands. A good outer breakwater is formed by the Great Barrier Island.

Hauran (Heb. *chauran*, the hollow land, so called from its numerous caves), a dist. in Syria, comprising the mountainous plateau extending in the East, from the Jordan and the Sea of Tiberias. It consists of mountain ranges and large plains, with scattered eminences rising steeply from the valley of the Jordan to a height of about 2000 ft., above the Mediterranean. It is full of the remains of ancient cities and various monuments of the Greek and Roman periods. The whole country is inhabited only by wandering Bedouins and a few colonies of Druses.

Hauréau, Jean Barthélemy (1812-96), a French historian, born in Paris; was on the staff of the *National;* and in 1848 was elected a member of the National Assembly. From 1848-52 he was director of the MS. depart-ment of the Bibliotheque Nationale; from 1870-81 director of the National Printing Press, and in 1893 became director of the Fondation Thiers. His works include *Histoire littéraire du Maine*, 1834-52; and 1870-72 a con-tinuation of the *Gallia christiana*, 1856-70; *Histoire de la philosophie scolastique*, 1872-80, and contribu-tions to numerous learned works.

Hausas, Houssas, or **Haussa,** a W. African race, inhabiting a district of about 50,000 sq. m. in the W. and Central Sudan, from the R. Niger to Bornu. They represent a very high negro type, and have a strong ad-mixture of Arab and Fula blood. The skin is very black; but the lips less thick and the hair less woolly than in most negroes. The men are of medium height, heavily built, and of great physical strength and endurance. Their language, which has a very wide range, is notable for its rich vocabulary. It belongs to the Hamitic group, and a large proportion of the words are connected with Arab and Semitic roots, thus tending to verify the native tradition that the origin of the race was beyond Mecca, to the E. The language has been reduced to writing, in modified Arabic characters by the natives themselves, and there is a certain amount of native litera-ture. The H. are a most industrious people. They are excellent agricul-turists; have for long mined iron, tin, silver, lead, and salt; have developed numerous industries, including spin-ning, weaving, dyeing, and working in leather and glass; and their com-merce is flourishing, Kano, Katsena, and Yakoba being the chief centres. Their staple food is guinea corn. Though naturally peaceful, they make excellent soldiers. Most of the popu-lation, which numbers over 5,000,000, are heathen, but a large number are Mohammedans. *See* C. H. Robin-son's *Hausaland*, 1896.

Hauser, Kaspar, a mysterious Ger-man youth, who was found in May 1828, in Nuremberg, dressed as a peasant, and in a strange state of ignorance and bewilderment. From letters in his possession it appeared that he had been born in 1812, the son of a cavalry officer, and handed over to the charge of a labourer, who had taught him to read and write, but kept him in close confinement. He was educated by Professor Daumer.

In 1829 he was mysteriously wounded, and his case attracted the interest of Earl Stanhope, who sent him to be further educated at Ansbach. In 1833 he received another mysterious wound, from the effects of which he died.

Haussman, Georges Eugène, Baron (1809-91), a builder of modern Paris. Born in Paris ; was educated at Collège Henri IV., and studied for the law. In 1830 he became *sous-préfet* of Nérac ; from 1849-51 was successively prefect of Var, Yvonne, and Gironde, and in 1853 was made prefect of the Seine, by Louis Napoleon, who had vast schemes for the embellishment of Paris. The improvements carried out by H. have transformed Paris, but their cost, which amounted to £34,000,000, led to considerable opposition, and in 1870 he was forced to resign by the government of Emile Ollivier. In 1877 he became Bonapartist deputy for Ajaccia. See *Mémoires* (3 vols.), 1890-93.

Haussonville, a com. in Algeria, Africa. Algiers is 44 m. distant in an easterly direction. Pop. about 6300, of whom 250 are Europeans.

Hautbois, a musical instrument, *see* OBOE.

Hautefeuille, Jean de (1647-1724), a French mechanician, born at Orleans, the son of a baker. He took ecclesiastical orders, but devoted himself mainly to the physical science. He invented numerous ingenious and useful mechanical contrivances, and made some valuable improvements in the works of clocks and watches. He is best known for his invention of a spiral steel spring to regulate the oscillations of the balance-wheel of a watch. He exhibited this to the Academy of Science in 1674, and it was afterwards improved by Huggens. He wrote *Problèmes d'acoustique*, 1688 ; *Balance magnétique*, 1702 ; *Perfectionnement des instruments de mer*, 1716 ; *Problème d'horlogerie*, 1719, etc.

Haute-Garonne, a dept. of S.W. France, formed from parts of Languedoc and Gascony, and divided into four arrons. : Toulouse, Muret, Saint-Gaudens, and Villefranc. Cap. Toulouse. Area, 2457 sq. m. The S. is very mountainous, containing some of the highest peaks of the Pyrenees, including Mont Perdiguére (10,560 ft.). The intervening valleys are very fertile. The centre of the department is formed by a hilly plateau, with an altitude of 1150-1500 ft. Chief river, the Garonne, with its tributaries the Pique, Save, Salat, Ariège, and Hers. Oats, maize, beans, vines, and wheat are grown. Iron, marble, and rock-salt are mined, and there are mineral springs. Pop. 432,126.

Haute-Loire, a dept. of S.E. France, formed from parts of Languedoc, Lyonnais, and Lower Auvergne, and divided into three arrons., Le Puy (cap.), Brioude, and Yssingeaux. Area, 1931 sq. m. Situated on the central plateau of France, it is traversed by four mountain ranges running from N. to S., viz. the Vivarais and its continuation the Boutières Chain, the Massif du Mégal, the Velay Mts., and the Margeride Mts. There are numerous signs of volcanic activity. Chief rivers, the Loire, with its tributaries the Borne and Lignon, and the Allier. The climate is cold. Rye, oats, barley, wheat, lentils, peas, and root crops are grown, and cattle and goats are largely reared. Coal and antimony are mined, and there is a large lace-making industry. Pop. 303,838.

Haute-Marne, a dept. of N.E. France, formed from the S.E. part of Champagne, with parts of Burgundy, Lorraine, and Franche-Comté, divided into three arrons.: Chaumont, Langres, and Vassy. Area 2420 sq. m. The centre of the dept. is formed by the plateau of Langres, the highest point being Haut-du-Sec (1695 ft.) in the S.W. To the N.E. are the Monts Faucilles. The low country forming the remainder of the dept. is called the Bassigny. The district contains the upper basins of the Marne, Ourcq, and Aube, tributaries of the Seine, the Meuse, and some small tributaries of the Rhone. There is considerable forest land. The soil is mostly poor, but cereals and vines are produced in parts. There are valuable iron-mines and mineral springs. Cap. Chaumont, Pop. 214,765.

Haute-Saône, a dept. of N.E. France, formed from parts of Franche-Comté, and divided into three arrons. Vesoul, Gray, and Lure. Area 2062 sq. m. The surface is mainly a plateau gradually descending from the Vosges in the N. (highest point, Ballon de Servance, 3970 ft.) towards the S., and intersected by many valleys and depressions. Chief rivers, the Saône, with its tributaries the Coney, Lanterne, Durgeon, and Ognon, and tributaries of the Rhone and Doubs. There is much forest, and wheat, oats, rye, vegetables, and tobacco are grown. A little wine is produced. Coal, copper, manganese, and iron are mined, and there are mineral springs. Cap. Vesoul. Pop. 257,606.

Haute-Savoie, a dept. of S.E. France, formed from Savoy, and divided into four arrons.: Annecy, Bonneville, Thonon, and St. Julien. Area 1774 sq. m. The surface is exceedingly mountainous, the department containing Mont Blanc (15,780 ft.). Chief rivers the Arve, Dranse, Usses, and Fier, tributaries of the

Rhone. There is much forest land, wheat, oats, and hardy root crops are grown, and in the lower slopes orchard fruits, vines, and tobacco flourish. The most fertile region is the N. and N.W., where the elevation is under 1640 ft. There is excellent pasture. Manufs. are limited, but include textiles and watches and clocks. Cap. Annecy. Pop. 255,137.

Haute-Vienne, a dept. of S.W. France, formed from parts of Limousin, and divided into four arrons. Limoges (the capital), Bellac, Rochechouart, and St. Yrieix. Area 2119 sq. m. The surface is diversified, the department containing the mountains of Limousin, Ambazac, and Blond, with peaks of about 2500 ft. The chief river is the Vienne, with its tributaries the Maude, Briance, and Gartempe. The soil is poor, but rye, wheat, buckwheat, hemp, colza, and chestnuts are grown. Cattle and sheep are largely reared. The mineral wealth includes kaolin, granite, mica, serpentine, garnets, and emeralds. Limoges has an important porcelain industry. Pop. 384,736.

Hautes-Alpes, a dept. of S.E. France, formed from parts of Dauphiné and Provence, divided into three arrons.: Gap, Briançon, and Embrun. Area 2158 sq. m. The department is mountainous throughout, being traversed by the Cottian Alps, rising to about 13,500 ft. in Pelvoux, and the Pic des Ecrins. The chief river is the Durance, with its tributaries the Buech and Gail. The scenery is very fine, there being some beautiful valleys and the climate generally healthy. Agriculture is very little practised, but the lower slopes of the Alps are being re-afforested, and the mountain pastures produce fine sheep. Argentiferous lead, copper, iron, anthracite, and marble are mined. Capital, Gap. Pop. 105,083.

Hautes-Pyrénées, a frontier dept. of S.W. France, formed from parts of Gascony, and divided into three arrons.: Tarbes, Argelés, and Bagnères-de-Bigorre. Area 1749 sq. m. The southern part is very mountainous, containing ramifications of the Pyrenees, with the peaks of Vignemale (10,820 ft.), Pic de Néouville (10,145 ft.), and Pic du Midi de Bigorre (9440 ft.). Between the spurs are picturesque valleys, fertile in the lower parts. The hills gradually descend to a plain in the N. In the N.E. lies the desolate plateau of Lannemezan. The chief river is the Adour, with its tributaries the Arros and Gave de Pau. The Garonne is on the S.E. frontier. There is much forest land, and wheat, maize, vines, tobacco, flax, and chestnuts are grown. Marble is quarried, and there are mineral springs. Capital, Tarbes. Pop. 206,105.

Hautmont, a tn. of dept. Nord, France, on the R. Sambre, 18 m. S.E. of Valenciennes. The chief industries are brewing, iron-working, and sugar refining. Pop. 13,200.

Haut-Rhin, see BELFORT.

Haüy, René Just (1742-1822), a French physicist and mineralogist, born at St. Just, educated at the colleges of Navarre and Lemoine, and became a teacher at the latter. In 1781 he discovered the geometrical law of crystallisation associated with his name, which he afterwards expounded in his *Traité de Minéralogie*, 1801. For this he was elected to the Academy of Sciences in 1783. In 1794 he became curator in the School of Mines, and in 1802 professor of mineralogy at the Museum of Natural History. He suffered considerably during the Revolution. He also made valuable observations in pyro-electricity. His other works include *Traité élémentaire de Physique*, 1803, and *Traité de Cristallographie*, 1822. *See his Life by G. Cuvier, 1823.*

Haüyne, a rock-forming mineral, named after the French mineralogist, Haüy, consisting of silicates of aluminium and sodium, or aluminium and calcium, together with sodium and calcium sulphates. H. is a sky-blue vitreous, translucent substance, having a conchoidal fracture, a hardness of 5 to 5·5 and sp. gr. of 2·2 to 2·5. Nosean and sodalite are very similar to H., and lapis lazuli is a member of the same group. On heating in the blowpipe H. melts to a glass, whilst nosean only melts at the edges; both are, however, gelatinised with acids. H. is essentially of volcanic origin, and is found at Vesuvius, Albano, and the Laacher See near Coblentz.

Havana, the cap. of the island of Cuba, and one of the most important seaport towns. It has been called 'Lave del Nuevo Mundo ' (' the New World's Key '), on account of its important position. It occupies a peninsula, forming the entrance of a large harbour, averaging about 260 yds. in width and about 1400 yds. in length. This permits large vessels of all descriptions to come within the shelter of the harbour, which is divided into three distinct arms or bays, called Regla Bay, Guanabacoa Bay, and the Bay of Atarés. The lighthouse tower of the Morro commands the approach to the harbour on the left-hand side. Many improvements have been effected in H. since the United States military occupation, notably in the way of wider thoroughfares, better built houses, and general sanitation. Yellow fever, a very prevalent epidemic, was found to be caused through the sting of a mosquito (*Stegomzia*), and precautions were taken to remove the cause of offence. The chief trade of H. is the tobacco industry, and there are numerous cigar factories. Sugar is also one of the principal products. H. presents a picturesque appearance, for the S. and W. of the city is backed by an amphitheatre of hills, some of which are 1000 ft. high and crowned with fortifications, as the ' Castillo del Principe.' There are several important public buildings, such as the Palace, the Exchange (El Mueble), and the custom-house. H. has an extensive trade with the western side of Cuba. Pop. 32,526.

Havant, a tn. of Hampshire, England, near the head of Langstone Harbour. Near it is the island of Hayling. It has brewing and tanning industries, and manufactures parchment. Pop. (1911) 4093.

Havas Agency, or Agence Havas, a French news-distributing organisation founded by Charles Havas, born in Paris in 1785. He amassed a large fortune in business, which he employed in developing this agency for political news, and at his death the work was carried on by his son. It was in 1835 that the agency received a definite organisation. The service of news, which was supplied to journals for a monthly subscription, was translated from various foreign newspapers, and its scope was soon widely extended. In 1879 the H.A. was converted into a company with a capital of 8,500,000 francs, the subscribers including private persons as well as newspapers.

Havel, a riv. of Prussia, Germany, rising in Lake Dambeck, Mecklenburg, and flowing into the Elbe just above Wittenburg after a course of 221 m. Its course from the Lake is S. as far as Spandau, where it is joined by the Spree, then S.W. past Potsdam and Brandenburg to the Plauer Lake, where it turns N.W. It is navigable for 205 m., and has a total fall of only 158 ft. It is largely canalised and joined to other rivers and lakes by canals.

Havelberg, a tn. of Brandenberg, Prussia, on the R. Havel, 69 m. N.W. of Berlin. It was a bishop's see from 946-1548, and the 12th century Romanesque cathedral is still standing. In 1548 the bishopric was seized by the Elector of Brandenburg. Tobacco manufacturing, sugar-refining, and timber work are the main industries. Pop. 6171.

Havelock, Sir Henry, Bart. (1795-1857), a soldier, entered the army in 1815, and went to India with the 13th regiment eight years later. He served in the Burmese War (1824-26), and

was aide-de-camp to Sir Willoughby Cotton in the Afghan War of 1839. During the next years he rose steadily in his profession, and saw much active service. In the Indian Mutiny, during the last year of his life, he won worldwide renown. He recaptured Cawnpore in July, and was promoted majorgeneral; and in the next few months effected the relief of Lucknow. A few days later he died. He had in September been made K.C.B., and, before his death was known in this country, was created a baronet and granted a pension of £1000 a year. His biography was written by Marshman, 1860.

Havelock-Allan, Sir Henry Marshman (1830-97), a British army officer, born in India, the eldest son of Sir Henry Havelock. He served in the Indian Mutiny, and was conspicuous for his gallantry, twice saving the life of Outram, and winning the V.C. in 1858. He later took part in the Maori War (1863-64). From 1874-81 he was M.P. for Sunderland, and in 1885 became M.P. for S.E. Durham. He retired from the army in 1881 with the honorary rank of lieutenant-general. In 1880 he assumed the additional name of Allan. He was shot by a Khaibari on the Afghan frontier while on a visit to India.

Havelock the Dane, *see* ENGLISH LITERATURE.

Haven, *see* HARBOURS.

Haver, a term in Scottish law, used to denote a person who has custody of a document.

Havercamp, Sigebert (1683-1742), a classical editor, was born at Utrecht; he was appointed minister at Stadaan-'t Haringvliet, in the island of Overflakkee, but he left the church in 1721 to take the Greek chair at Leyden. He edited many Latin and Greek authors, amongst them Tertullian, Lucretius, Sallust, and others: he also wrote *Introductio in Historiam Patriæ*, 1739.

Haverfordwest, a seaport of Pembrokeshire, S. Wales, on W. Cleddau R., 6 m. N.E. of Milford. It is a contributory parl. and municipal bor. and a county of itself, having a Lord-Lieutenant. There are coal mines, and the town is still of considerable commercial importance, though it has declined from its former greatness. The town was settled by the Flemings in the reign of Henry I. Pop. (1911) 5920.

Havergal, Frances Ridley (1836-79), an English poetess, born at Astley, Worcestershire, daughter of the Rev. William Henry H. She was a talented child, and began to write verses at the age of seven. Her best work is religious, and is characterised by graceful expression, sympathetic feeling, and introspective insight. Many of her hymns are well established favourites, and are included in numerous collections for use in churches. Her works, originally published as *Ministry of Song*, 1870; *Under the Surface*, 1874; *Loyal Responses*, 1878, were collected in 1884 by her sister, who, in 1880, had published *Memorials of Frances Ridley Havergal*.

Haverhill: 1. A market tn. and par. on the borders of Essex and Suffolk, England, 18 m. S.E. of Cambridge, and 11½ m. S. by E. of Newmarket, on the Great Eastern Railway. It has a weekly market, and its chief manuf. is silk for umbrella covers. Pop. (1911) 4749. 2. A city in Essex co., Massachusetts, on l. b. of the R. Merrimac, 33 m. N. of Boston. It is connected with Bradford by a bridge. H. is the birthplace of the poet Whittier, who was educated at the academy in the town. The principal business of the place is the manuf. of boots and shoes, and it also manufs. bricks, flannel, hats, and caps. Pop. (1910) 44,115.

Havers, Clopton (*c.* 1655-1702), a British physician, educated at Catherine Hall, Cambridge, and became a doctor in London, obtaining his M.D. (Utrecht) in 1685, and becoming L.R.C.P. in 1687, and F.R.S. in 1686. In 1691 he published *Osteologia Nova*, a valuable anatomical work dealing with the structure of the bones. The 'Haversian Canal,' which he was the first to detect, is named after him.

Haverstraw, a vil. of New York, U.S.A., on the r. b. of the R. Hudson, 35 m. N. of New York, overhung by limestone cliffs. Pop. (1910) 5669.

Haviland, John (1790–1852), an English architect, born near Taunton, Somersetshire. In his youth he emigrated to the United States. Here he made a speciality of penitentiary buildings, and erected the Eastern State Penitentiary at Philadelphia, and prisons at Pittsburg, New York, Rhode Island, and Missouri. H. also designed the United States Mint, Philadelphia; Hospital for the Insane at Harrisburg, and many other public edifices. He published the *Builder's Assistant* (3 vols.), 1818, in conjunction with Hugh Bridport.

Havildar, the name applied to a noncommissioned officer of the highest rank among the native troops of India and Ceylon.

Havre, or **Le Havre,** a seaport in France, and is only second in importance to Marseilles. It is the cap. of the arron. in the dept. of Seine Inférieure, and is situated on the N. side of the estuary of the Seine, being distant 143 m. from Paris, and 55 m. from Rouen. The larger portion of the town stands on the level ground surrounding the estuary, but the richer quarter is situated on the heights of La Côte. The basins or docks of Le Havre form a triangle in shape, and are entered by means of the Outer Port. There are nine basins, the oldest dating back to the 17th century. In recent years another new entrance was made by means of two breakwaters, whilst the Tancarville Canal permits river-boats to approach the port direct, without attempting the estuary of the Seine. The chief basins are the Bassin Bellot, and the Bassin de l'Eure. This port trades with all the chief European ports, with America, Africa, and the W. Indies. Its chief imports are cotton, woollen goods, silk, wheat, sugar, and coffee, whilst its exports are French manufactured cloths, wine and spirits, and agricultural and dairy produce. H. possesses an extensive shipbuilding trade. Its name was originally Havre de Grâce, because a chapel was built in 1516, dedicated to Notre Dame de Grâce. The chief buildings are the hôtel-de-ville, the law courts, and the exchange. Pop. 136,159.

Havre-de-Grace, a city in Harford co., Maryland, U.S.A., on W. bank of Susquehanna R., 35 m. N.E. of Baltimore. Through it passes the Wilmington and Baltimore Railroad, which crosses the Susquehanna by a steam-ferry. Pop. (1910) 4212.

Hawaiian Islands, or **Hawaii,** formerly the **Sandwich Islands,** were discovered by Captain James Cook (*q.v.*) in 1778. These islands form a chain in the Pacific Ocean, eight being inhabited, and the rest uninhabited. The inhabited islands extend for about 380 m. from E.S.E. to W.N.W., whilst the uninhabited ones continue the chain for many hundreds of miles W.N.W. All the islands are of volcanic origin, and nearly all of them are surrounded by coral-reefs. The names of the inhabited islands are Hawaii, Maui, with two smaller islands, Kahoolawe and Lanai, Molokai, Oahu, Kauai, and Niihau. Hawaii Island is in the shape of an irregular triangle, the sides of which measure 90 m., 75 m., and 65 m. This island is the chief of the group, and it possesses the largest volcano in the world, the Mauna Loa (Great Mountain). This mountain has been the scene of many terrible eruptions, the last of which, in 1907, was attended by an earthquake. The mountain has a huge crater, called Mokuaweoweo, and is 13,675 ft. high. Maui lies 26 m. distant from Hawaii, and consists of two mountains connected by the isthmus Wailuku, about 8 m. long and 6 m. wide. The two small islands Kahoolawe and Lanai afford pasturage for sheep, and are private property. The island of Molokai has a famous leper settlement called Kalawao, which is a peninsula, shut off from the rest of the island by a rock wall, 2000 ft. high. The island of Oahu is surrounded by a coral reef, and lies 23 m. from Molokai. It is very mountainous, with remarkably beautiful valleys and tropical vegetation. There are several craters on the lower mountains near the coast. Kauai is 63 m. away from Oahu, and has been called the ' garden isle ' on account of its fertile ground. Nūhau completes the chain of inhabited islands, and is remarkable for its coral reef in the W. and for the large salt lagoons in the S. These islands all form a territory and were annexed by the United States in 1900. The natives of Hawaii were cannibals in earliest times, but they became more civilised with the influx of other races, and they owe their Christian religion and general education to missionaries (see DAMIEN, FATHER), the first to arrive coming from America in 1820. The population is very varied, consisting of Europeans, Chinese, Americans, and Japanese. The climate is most salubrious, and the cultivation of the sugar-cane forms the chief trade. Valuable timber is procured from the vast forests.

Hawarden, or Harden, a market tn. and par. of Flintshire, N. Wales, 7 m. W. of Chester, and 195 m. N.W. of London. It is connected by a railroad with the banks of the Dee. The town is large and well-paved, and contains a church, nearly destroyed by fire in 1857, but now restored. In the park is the ruined keep of a 13th-century castle, from which a fine view is obtained of the Dee. Mr. Gladstone's seat, Hawarden Castle, dates from 1572. H. has coal mines, clay fields, brick works, and potteries, and manufs. tiles, pottery, etc. St. Deiniol's Library and Hostel for theological students was founded at H. in 1895 by Gladstone. Pop. of parish (1911), 5732.

Haweis,Hugh Reginald (1838-1901), an author and preacher, born at Egham, Surrey, the eldest son of the Rev. J. O. W. Haweis, prebendary of Chichester Cathedral. He suffered from delicate health as a child, but grew stronger later on, and went to Trinity College, Cambridge, where he became a notoriety. He had great musical ability, and an aptitude for the violin, and wrote a good deal of verse and prose, showing an original strain of mind. In 1889 he graduated and then travelled for his health in Italy, where he arrived at the seat of war when Garibaldi was besieging Capua. He took holy orders in 1862 on his return to England, and in 1866 became incumbent of St. James',

Marylebone, where he remained till his death, and by his unconventionality and somewhat sensational methods, attracted a large and fashionable congregation. His best-known works are : *Music and Morals, My Musical Life, Old Violins, Thoughts for the Times, Christ and Christianity, Ideals for Girls, Realities of Life*, etc., for a time he also edited *Cassell's Magazine*, and Routledge's World Library. *See* Crockford, *Men of the Time*, 1899.

Hawes, a market tn. in N. Riding of Yorkshire, England, on the r. b. of the Ure. Coal is mined in the neighbourhood. Pop. (1911) 1600.

Hawes, Stephen (*d. c.* 1523), an English poet, probably a native of Suffolk. Educated at Oxford, and afterwards travelled in Europe. Was attached to the court of Henry VII., his knowledge of English poetry and literature procuring him an entry. His earliest and principal work is *The Passetyme of Pleasure, or History of Graunde Amoure, and la Bel Pucel, containing the Knowledge of the Seven Sciences and the Course of Man's Life in this Worlde*, an elaborate allegory in forty-six chapters. He also wrote *Wynkyn de Worde, The Temple of Glasse*, etc. *See* Ellis's *Early English Poets*.

Hawes-Water, a lake in Westmorland, England, 5 m. N. of Kendal, and forming a fine cataract on the road to Penrith. It is very narrow, but deep.

Hawfinch (*Coccothraustes vulgaris*), a species of the Grosbeak genus and Finch family, a good deal larger than the chaffinch. The male bird has brown and black markings on the head, black wing quills and a white tip to the tail, and the neck crossed at the back by a broad band of ash colour. It is a timid bird and perches on the topmost branches of trees, where it commands a good outlook, and is not easily discovered. The nest is built in lichen-covered trees, of twigs and mosses. Its food consists of the fruit of the pine, hornbeam, plum, cherry, hawthorn, laurel, holly, etc. It is abundant in Southern Europe, and is distributed in the temperate parts of Asia. It is not uncommon in some parts of England, but in Scotland is very rare.

Hawick, a par. in the S.W. of Roxburghshire, 52 m. by rail S.S.E. of Edinburgh, and 45 m. N.N.E. of Carlisle. Its greatest length is 15¼ m., breadth, 3½ m., and it covers an area of about 15,360 acres, rather more than one-fourth of which is in tillage. The town adapts its topographical arrangement to the course of the rivers Teviot and Slitrig, a handsome bridge being built across the former. H. is a place of great antiquity, traces of which are seen in the Moat, an artificial earthen mound, and in part of Tower Hill, at one time the peel-tower of the Douglas family, and later, a residence of the Duchess of Monmouth. H. is the seat of a woollen manufacture, the earliest branch seeming to be that of carpets, established in 1752. The fabrics principally made are hosiery, drugget, checks, tartan, etc. It also has considerable manufs. in the tanning of leather, and dressing of skins, etc. All the previously existing mills have been largely added to, and several new factories recently erected. Pop. (1911) 18,021.

Hawk, a term applied in a general way to all the diurnal birds of prey with the exception of vultures, eagles, and owls. Of the Hs. proper, the chief British species are members of the genus *Accipiter*, the goshawk and sparrowhawk. Hs. are distinguished by their short wings, and not particularly strong beaks.

Hawkbit (*Leontodon*), a genus of plants belonging to the natural order Compositæ. The autumnal H. is closely allied to the dandelion, and although later blooming, is very similar to this flower in appearance, having large yellow flowers with long petals. Its name is due to the deep tooth-like lacerations of the leaves. It has been naturalised in America, and several species are natives of Britain which, with some others comprised in the genus, are widely distributed throughout Europe and Russian Asia.

Hawk-Eagle, a species of hawk of smallish size, belonging to the genera *Spizaëtus* and *Morphnus;* natives of warm climates, and often very beautiful in form and colour. Some species are provided with well-developed crests which extend backwards from the crown of the head. An Indian species is called 'peacock-killer' and is exceedingly destructive to game-birds of every description; and in Africa there is a species 31 in. long. Hs. are often termed 'crested eagles,' the crest being best seen in a species of *Morphnus* from Guiana, though it is absent in a bird of the genus *Nisaëtus* in India.

Hawke, a British battle cruiser, completed in 1893. Has a displacement of 7350 tons; main armament, viz. number of guns and calibre, two 9·2 in., ten 6 in.; speed, 19 knots.

Hawke, Sir Edward, Lord Hawke of Lowton (1705-81), an English admiral, born in London; entered the navy in 1720, becoming commander in 1733. In 1744 he distinguished himself in the action off Toulon, commanding the *Berwick*, one of the few ships properly handled. In 1747 he became a rear-admiral, and gained a

victory over the French off Finisterre. For this service he was knighted and became M.P. for Bristol the same year. He became an admiral in 1757. His chief fame was gained in 1759 over his attack on Marshal Conflan in Quiberon Bay, which resulted in the destruction of the French fleet, and the collapse of their invasion scheme. In 1766 he was made First Lord of the Admiralty and created Baron H. for life. *See* Burrows' *Life of Hawke*, 1883.

Hawker, Robert Stephen (1803-75), an English poet and antiquary, born at Stoke Dameral, near Plymouth, Devonshire, eldest son of J. S. Hawker, vicar of Stratton, Cornwall. Educated at Cheltenham Grammar School and Pembroke College, Oxford. In 1827 he carried off the Newdigate prize, was ordained in 1831, and became vicar of Morwenstow on the Cornish coast in 1834. He laboured here for forty years, during which period he rebuilt the vicarage, restored the church, and built a school. His theological views were mainly those of the tractarians. H.'s ballads were direct and simple in style and composed in the true spirit of antiquity. None is better known than his spirited ballad based on the old Cornish refrain, 'And shall Trelawney die ?' Other of his poetical pieces are: *Tendrils by Rueben*, *Records of the Western Shore*, *Quest of the Sangrael*, *Footprints of Former Men in Cornwall*, *Reeds Shaken with the Wind*. *See* Lives by Baring Gould and the Rev. F. G. Lee, and Mortimer Collins' novel, *Sweet and Twenty*, in which H.'s character is delineated under the name of Canon Tremaine.

Hawkers and Pedlars, itinerant dealers engaged in the business of carrying their goods for sale from place to place. The trade is regulated under special supervision of the legislature, this being made necessary by the opportunities afforded dealers with no fixed domicile of evading responsibility and practising fraud. By the Act of 1871, a pedlar is a person who sells articles, travelling without a horse or other beast, and certificates are supplied to those desirous of carrying on the trade of a pedlar in good faith, by the chief officer of the police of the district for which they are asked, such certificated pedlar being deemed a licensed hawker. The Hawkers Act, 1888, defines a hawker as one who travels with a horse, or other beast, bearing or drawing a burden. A single act of selling does not constitute a pedlar, and persons who travel about seeking orders for goods, as agents, sellers of fish, fruit, victuals, and exposing goods for sale in a public market, do not come under the category. Neither in England nor the United States is the bagman, commercial traveller, or nomadic merchant, who sets up a temporary establishment for the purpose of selling goods, comprehended under the term pedlar or hawker. The fee for a pedlar's certificate is 5s., and a hawker's licence can be taken out at a cost of £2. H. and P. are obliged to take out licences under state laws and federal laws in the United States.

Hawkes Bay, or Wairoa, in New Zealand, North Is., between Auckland and Wellington, on the E. coast. It is enclosed on the N.E. by Mahia Peninsula, and extends S. to Cape Mata-mawi, a total distance of about 60 m. In 1769 Cook entered it in the *Endeavour*, and in 1848 it was occupied by Europeans. H. B. receives several considerable streams.

Hawkesbury, one of the chief rivers of New South Wales, flowing eastward and formed by the union of the Nepean and Grose Rivers. The united stream forms the N., W., and E. boundaries of Cumberland co., and after a course of about 60 m. eastwards, falls into Broken Bay. It is navigable for vessels of 100 tons, but is liable to great and rapid inundations, produced by the fall of rain on the Blue Mts. Its banks consist of fine alluvial soil. In 1889 railway connection between Adelaide and Brisbane was completed by a bridge over the river. Total length, 330 m.

Hawkesworth, John (*c.* 1715–73), a miscellaneous writer of humble parentage, born in London. In 1744 he succeeded Dr. Johnson as compiler of the *Gentleman's Magazine*. In 1752 he started with Johnson and others *The Adventurer*. H. was the editor, and of the 140 papers, wrote some seventy-two or so. In 1755 he published *The Works of Jonathan Swift*, with historical notes and explanations, and prepared the account of Captain Cook's first voyage, forming part of his own publication, *Voyages*. He also wrote *The Fall of Egypt*, several essays, and some plays.

Hawkhurst, a par. partly in Kent and partly in Sussex, England, 12 m. N.W. by W. of Rye, on the South Eastern Railway. Pop. 3500.

Hawking, *see* FALCONRY.

Hawkins, Anthony Hope (*b.* 1863), an author, writes over the name of 'Anthony Hope.' He began to write early, but though some of his first books attracted attention, it was not until he published *The Dolly Dialogues* (1894) that he became generally known. Since then he has published many books, the best of which are *The Prisoner of Zenda*, *The King's Mirror*, *Quisante*, and

Second String. A master of dialogue, he can tell a story well, and has designed a large portrait-gallery of interesting characters that ranges from music-hall singers to statesmen. He has sentiment in plenty, but it is always kept in check by the keen sense of humour that dominates all his work.

Hawkins, Cæsar Henry (1798-1884), an English surgeon, grandson of Sir Cæsar H., born at Bisley, Gloucestershire. Educated at Christ's Hospital, and then admitted as a student to St. George's Hospital. In 1821, became a member of the Royal College of Surgeons. Appointed surgeon to St George's Hospital in 1829, and, on his resignation in 1861, consulting surgeon. President of the Royal College of Surgeons in 1852 and 1861. Appointed sergeant-surgeon to the queen in 1862. Fellow of the Royal Society and trustee of the Hunterian Museum in 1871. Chief publications: *The Hunterian Oration*, 1849 ; *Lectures on Tumours ; Experiments on Hydrophobia ; On Excision of the Ovarium*, etc.

Hawkins, Sir Henry, Baron Brampton (1817-1907), a judge, born at Hitchin, Herts, and educated at Bedford School. In 1839 entered at the Middle Temple. Called to the bar in 1843 and joined the home circuit and Hertfordshire sessions. Took silk in 1858, and for the next eighteen years was one of the most prominent leaders of the bar. He was engaged in many important cases; his well-chosen language and lively intelligence succeeded in winning for him the verdicts of juries. In 1876 appointed judge of the High Court of Justice; knighted and transferred to the Exchequer Division the same year. H. figured in the Tichborne trials and many others of equal importance. As a criminal judge he had few equals.

Hawkins, Sir John (1719-89), an English lawyer, born in London. He retired from practice early in life and became one of the founders of the Madrigal Society. He was one of Dr. Johnson's executors, and wrote his life, which he published with an edition of Johnson's works in 1787. His chief work is, *A General History of the Science and Practice of Music*, 1776, which is of value at the present day.

Hawkins, or Hawkyns, Sir John (1532-95), an English seaman and naval commander, born at Plymouth. While quite a young man he made several voyages, and was the first Englishman to traffic in slaves. In 1573 he was made navy treasurer, and knighted as a reward for his services against the Armada in 1588. In the mustering of the English fleet to defend the country against the Spaniards, H. was captain of the *Victory*. While at Plymouth he served under Drake, and was a member of the council of war. In 1594 he served in an expedition ordered to the W. Indies under the command of Drake, to the Spanish Main, but died at sea off Porto Rico. He left one son, Sir Richard H., also a naval commander.

Hawk-moth, a species of Lepidoptera belonging to the family Sphingidæ, sometimes also known as 'sphinx-moth,' the name being derived from the resemblance shown in the caterpillar stage to the Egyptian Sphinx. The moths belonging to

SPURGE HAWK-MOTH

this family are all large and dull coloured, with a long proboscis, a small hinder pair of wings, and long and pointed body. The caterpillars are smooth and striped, and usually furnished with an erect horn at the hinder end. Allied species are the privet H., the pine H., the deaths-head moth, and the humming-bird H. See *The Moth Hawk Book*, 1903.

Hawks, Francis Lister (1798-1866), an American clergyman, born at New Berne, N.C., and educated at the university there. He first studied law, but became an Episcopal minister in 1827. From 1830-31 he was professor of divinity at Hertford, and subsequently became rector of churches in New York, Baltimore and Orleans. In 1844 he was elected bishop of the diocese of Holly Springs, Mississippi, but owing to opposition did not accept the bishopric. He contributed works on the Episcopal communion, wrote a history of N. Carolina, and the story of Commodore Perry's expedition, and edited Appleton's *Cyclopædia of Biography*.

Hawksbeard, a plant of the genus *Crepis*, of a perennial composite nature, allied to hawkweed. There are about 150 known species, but the commonest British one is the annual smooth yellow H., which blooms in the autumn. The strap-shaped florets and down-like pappus are the distinguishing features of H., and it has smooth pinnatifid leaves.

Hawksbee, or Hauksbee, Francis (*d. c.* 1713), an English natural philosopher, born in the latter half of the 17th century. In 1705 he was admitted a fellow of the Royal Society, and appointed curator of experiments. By his experiments in electricity he laid the scientific foundations of that branch of knowledge. He also improved the earlier airpumps of Boyle, Papin, and Hooke. Between 1704 and 1713, he contributed forty-three memoirs to the *Philosophical Transactions*, chiefly on chemistry and electricity. His chief work was *Physico-Mechanical Experiments on various Subjects, touching Light and Electricity, producible on the Attrition of Bodies*, published in 1709.

Hawkshaw, Sir John (1811-91), an English engineer, born in W. Riding of Yorkshire. He has constructed various docks, Holyhead Harbour, the Severn tunnel (1887), Charing Cross and Cannon Street Railway and bridges, and part of the Underground Railway of London. He was for a time engineer to the Manchester and Leeds Railway; and later on to the Lancashire and Yorkshire Railway.

Hawksley, Thomas (1807-93), an English engineer, born at Arnold, Nottinghamshire. In 1852 he left his native place for London, and devoted his energies to the problems of main drainage, and gas and water supply. He constructed drainage systems for Birmingham, Worcester, and many other large towns, and a constant water-supply system for Nottingham. He also supplied water systems to Oxford, Cambridge, Leeds, Liverpool, Sheffield, etc., etc.

Hawksmoor, Nicholas (1661-1736), an English architect, born at East Drayton, Nottinghamshire, and at the early age of eighteen obtained employment under Sir Christopher Wren. He became deputy-surveyor of the works at Greenwich Hospital in 1705. Through Wren he obtained the post of clerk of the works at Kensington Palace, an office which he held till 1715. He also assisted Wren in the erection of St. Paul's Cathedral from its commencement to its completion in 1710. Under Sir J. Vanbrugh he was also assistant surveyor at Blenheim Palace, Oxfordshire (1710-15). At Oxford H. was employed from an early period, and much of his work is seen there at the different colleges. At the close of Anne's reign he took a large part in the building of fifty new London churches.

Hawkweed, or *Hieracium*, a genus of plants of the natural order Compositæ. They are a perennial species of herbs, characterised by yellow, orange, or red flowers. The orange H., a native of Southern Europe, is frequently cultivated in gardens by reason of its handsome blooms. The plant is very hairy, having a tuft of oblong leaves at the base. It is quite a pest in the meadows and pastures of New York state, and can only be overcome by cultivation.

Hawkwood, Sir John de (*d.* 1394), an English soldier and captain, born at Sible Hedingham in Essex. He won both renown and riches as a condottiere in Italy, where he was known as Giovanni L'Acuto. He distinguished himself at Crecy and Poitiers, and was knighted by Edward III. From 1363 onward he fought in the Italian wars on different sides, and was finally persuaded to fight the battles of Florence for an annual pension. *See* Temple Leader and Marcotti's *Life* (Eng. trans. by Mrs. Leader Scott, 1889) and *Quarterly Review* (Jan. 1890).

Hawkyns, Sir John, *see* HAWKINS.

Hawkyns, Sir Richard (*c.* 1562-1622), an English naval commander, son of Admiral Sir John H. He served under Drake, and took part in the defeat of the Armada (Aug. 1588) and in the subsequent descent on the Portuguese coast in 1590. Three years later he sailed in the *Dainty* on a voyage round the world. He touched Brazil, passed the Straits of Magellan, and took and plundered Valparaiso, but was defeated and wounded after a hard fight in San Mateo Bay, and imprisoned in Spain till 1602, when he was ransomed and knighted. Later he became vice-admiral of Devon and second-in-command in Sir Robert Mansell's fleet against the Algerine pirates (1620-21). *See* his *Observations on his Voyage into the South Seas*, with biography by Sir C. R. Markham, 1878.

Haworth, a moorland vil. and par. in the W. Riding of Yorkshire in the Keighley div., 9 m. N.N.W. of Halifax, on the Midland Railway. It has an area of about 10,540 ac. Charlotte Brontë, the novelist (1816--55), and her sisters resided here from their earliest years, and descriptions of the moorland scenery are to be found in their novels, notably *Wuthering Heights* by Emily Brontë. The old church of H. has been ruthlessly demolished, but the graves of Charlotte and Emily Brontë are in the churchyard. Pop. of town (1911) 6505.

Hawse, that part of a vessel known as the bows, where the ' hawse-holes ' for the cables to pass through are made.

Hawser (Old Fr. *haucier, hausser,* to raise, to hoist; from Late Lat. *altiare,* to lift ; *altus,* high), a three or four-stranded rope or small cable used at sea for moving or warping large vessels made of steel. When a cable is made of three or more small ropes, it is said to be ' hawser-laid.'

Hawthorn (Old Eng. *haga-, hœg-,* or *hege-thorn*), a genus of shrub or small tree belonging to the species *Cratœgus,* numbering about fifty, bearing fruit resembling in miniature that of the apple, and therefore belonging to the natural order Rosaceæ, with spiny branches and alternate, simple, or lobed leaves, smooth and shining. The flowers are sweet-scented, white, with a sometimes reddish tinge, and grow in flat-topped clusters. The H. is a native of the N. temperate regions, especially America, and is represented in the British Isles by the H., whitethorn, or may. It thrives best in dry soils, and may be propagated from seeds or cuttings.

Hawthorne, Julian (*b.* 1846), an American author, son of Nathaniel H., born in Boston, Massachusetts. He studied at Harvard University, and then went to Dresden, where he devoted himself to engineering. For a brief period he worked in the dock department of New York, and then returned to Dresden, where he began to write for the newspapers. For some years he was correspondent of the New York *Journal,* and from 1901-3 literary critic of the Philadelphia *North American.* He wrote several novels, chief of which are *Idolatry, Garth, Fortune's Fool, Dust, An American Monte Christo,* and many short detective tales.

NATHANIEL HAWTHORNE

Hawthorne, Nathaniel (1804-64), a novelist, is by common consent the greatest of all American writers of fiction. His best-known works are *Twice-Told Tales* (two series, 1837,

1842), *Mosses from an Old Manse* (1846), *The Scarlet Letter* (1850), *The House with the Seven Gables* (1851), and *The Blithedale Romance* (1852). While his earlier work won the praises of the critics, it secured for the author no recognition from the public, which was first attracted to his books when he published *The Scarlet Letter*, a story of New England in the 17th century. The admirable picture of the place and the spirit of the age, the tragic story so well unfolded, was at once acclaimed as the masterpiece it is still acknowledged to be. It is dark and gloomy, as a tale of human frailty and sorrow must be, and it would be painful to read were it not that the author so clearly shows that there is light beyond. Admirable as are H.'s other books, and especially *The House of the Seven Gables*, *The Scarlet Letter* stands apart, and above, all his works. There are biographies by his son Julian (1885), Henry James (1883), and M. D. Conway (1890).

Hawtrey, Charles Henry (*b.* 1858), an English actor and dramatist, son of the Rev. J. Hawtrey, an Eton master. First appeared in 1881 in a play entitled *The Colonel*, and four years later adapted from a German source, *The Private Secretary*, which was successfully received. H. has achieved success in a number of plays, both here and in the U.S.A., among the best known of which are: *The Man from Blankneys, A Message from Mars, Jack Straw, The Little Damozel, The Naked Truth, Inconstant George, The Great Name*, and *General John Regan*. H. is among the first flight of actor-managers, and one of the finest comedians of the English stage. Always himself, yet always varying, he is a delightful actor.

Hawtrey, Edward Craven, D.D. (1789-1862), a headmaster and provost of Eton College, born at Burnham, near Eton. Entered the school, with which his family had been connected for nearly 300 years, in 1799. See *Life* by T. Thackeray, 1896.

Hay: 1. A market tn. and par. in Breconshire, Wales, 20 m. W. of Hereford, on the Wye, and 12 m. S. of New Radnor. Pop. (1911) 1603. 2. Post tn. and cathedral city of New South Wales, Waradgery co., in the middle of the Riverina dist., 70 m. N. of Deniliquin. Pop. about 3000. 3. A riv. of Alberta, Canada, descending from the E. side of the Rocky Mts., and flowing into the Great Slave Lake, 350 m. in length, and navigable for 140 m.

Hay, John (1830-1905), an American statesman and author, born at Salem, Indiana. Graduated from Brown University in 1858, and was admitted to the Illinois bar in 1861. H. was secretary to the U.S. legation at Paris (1865-67), Vienna (1867-69), and Madrid (1869-70). On his return to America he was on the staff of the *New York Tribune* for five years. In 1879-81 he became first Assistant-Secretary of State. In 1897, on the inauguration of President McKinley, H. was appointed ambassador to Great Britain, becoming subsequently Secretary of State. After the war with Spain of 1898, he directed the peace negotiations. As Secretary of State under Presidents McKinley and Roosevelt, H.'s guidance, during a rather critical period in foreign affairs, was invaluable. In literature, also, H. represented the best American traditions. He published: *Pike County Ballads*, 1871, of which the most famous are 'Little Breeches' and 'Jim Bludso'; *Castilian Days*, 1871; a volume of poems, 1890; *Abraham Lincoln*, in conjunction with G. Nicolay, etc. H. was also an excellent public speaker, one of his best addresses being 'In Praise of Omar.' See *Addresses of John Hay*, 1906.

Hay, Sir John Charles Dalrymple (*b.* 1821), a British admiral, and vice-president of the Institution of Naval Architects, born in Wigtownshire, N.B. He was educated at Rugby, and entered the navy in 1834, serving the two following years on the Cape of Good Hope station. He then served in the Channel squadron on the N. coast of Spain, on the S. American and Pacific station, and took part in the operations on the Syrian coast (1840-41). Later he saw service in China and the E. Indies, and in the operations in Borneo (1845-46), was flag-lieutenant with Admiral Sir Thomas Cochrane, Lord of the Admiralty from 1866-68. In 1870 he was made a rear-admiral and placed on the retired list. His publications include: *The Flag List and its Prospects, The Reward of Loyalty, Suppression of Piracy in the China Sea*, and *Our Naval Defences*, etc.

Hay and Ensilage. Hay is composed of the stems and leaves of grasses, mown and dried for use as fodder. The object of the farmer in haymaking is to preserve the hay for winter use in a condition most nearly resembling the grass in its natural state, so preserving its nutritive value. To ensure this, the mowing should be done when the plants contain the largest amount of gluten, sugar, and other soluble matter; this occurs when the grass is in flower. For the operation of mowing, dry sunny weather is required. Under the old plan, using the scythe, fork, and rake, three or four days are required to get the hay ready for stacking. The grass is tedded, that is, shaken evenly abroad over the ground, on the first day, and afterwards put into small heaps, or 'cocks' for the night. On the second day the whole must be thrown out again, to secure the most benefit from the action of the sun and wind, and then made up into larger cocks at night. After being shaken out into rows and turned on the next day, the hay will be ready for stacking, if the weather has continued propitious. The stacking is an operation requiring skill, and is carried out gradually, a certain quantity of hay being added to the stack daily. The

practice of using salt with the hay as a preservative is more usual in Scotland, though not unknown in this country; about 10 lbs. of salt are used to the ton; hay improves with age. A haymaking or 'tedding' machine, drawn by a horse, is adopted for use on a large farm, though it is not applicable to clover hay, which must not be violently agitated. For export, etc., hay is now so compressed that a ton occupies only about 70 cub. ft., being made up in small bales of about 150 lbs. The following table gives the average constituents of clover hay and meadow hay of average quality percentage in each case :—

Dry Matter.	Nitrogen.	Mineral Ash.	Phosphoric Acid.	Potash.
83·0	2·40	7·0	·57	1·5
84	1·5	6·5	·4	1·6

In 1890 the area of grass land in the United Kingdom was 33,212,635 acres; in 1895, 33,892,256 acres; and in 1900, 34,285,846, whilst for the same years the production of hay, in thousands of tons, was respectively 14,466; 12,238; and 13,742.

Ensilage is the name given to the practice of preserving green food for cattle in 'silos' or pits. The practice of 'caching' stores, etc., in such pits is very old, but it was not till comparatively recent years that the idea of using them for the preservation of fodder was carried out. M. Auguste Goffart, in 1877, published his *Manuel de la culture et de l'Ensilage des Maïs, et autres fourrages verts ;* this was translated into English, and successful experiments were carried out in England and the United States of America. The 'silos' used should be at least 15 ft. deep, and both air-tight and water-tight; an erection above the ground is sometimes used instead of a pit. Crops which are suitable for ensilage are grass, clover, vetch, oats, rye, maize, etc. They should be piled slowly, 1 ft. being added daily, to allow the mass to settle slowly and heat uniformly. When the pit is filled it is covered with straw, and afterwards with boards, to which a considerable pressure is applied. During the actual process the pressing is done by the application of the foot, as a rule. Ensilage forms a wholesome and nutritious food for cattle, and a very good substitute for root crops. One great advantage which it possesses over hay, for example, is that it can be obtained irrespective of the weather. Cows fed on ensilage give quite as good milk as when fed on any other variety of fodder, and it is calculated that a larger number

of cattle can be supported on a certain area by the use of ensilage than by the use of green crops.

Hayashi, Tadasu, Count (*b.* 1850), a Japanese statesman, born at Tokyo; sent to England by the Tokugawa government among the first batch of students. He had much to do with the modern rise of Japan, and figured in the revolutionary movement. He obtained office in 1871 and rapidly rose to the front rank, first serving as Vice-Minister for Foreign Affairs and then being appointed to represent his country, first in Peking then in St. Petersburg, and finally in London. He was created viscount for his services in negotiating the first Anglo-Japanese Alliance. Throughout the Russo-Japanese War he remained in London. In 1906 he returned to Tokyo and was created a count in 1907, for services performed during the war between Russia and his own country. He has translated many English works into Japanese, and is the author of *For His People*, 1903.

Haydn, Ferdinand Vandeveer, LL.D. (1829-88), an American geologist, born at Westfield, Massachusetts; graduated from Oberlin College and the Albany Medical College in 1850 and 1853, respectively. Through the influence of Professor James Hall, he joined a geological exploration of Nebraska. Was employed under the United States government in 1856 in a series of investigations of the Western Territories, the result of which was seen in his *Geological Report of the Exploration of the Yellowstone and Missouri Rivers in 1859-60.* He was employed as an army surgeon during the Civil War, and filled the chair of geology in Pennsylvania University in 1865-72, being subsequently connected with the United States Geological Survey. In 1877 he issued his *Geological and Geographical Atlas of Colorado*.

Haydn, Joseph (1732-1809), a composer, son of a village wheelwright at Rohrau, Austria. At the age of twelve he became a chorister at Vienna, receiving at the same time some instruction in the violin and pianoforte. After studying under Porpora, he produced with great success, when only twenty years old, his first opera, *The Devil on Two Sticks*, 1752; this was followed by a set of trios and his first important quartet, all of which earned the usual censure of pedantic critics for ' contrapuntal errors,' and ' daring innovations.' In 1758 he met Prince Antony Esterhazy, and two years later was appointed leader of his excellent orchestra. He remained

JOSEPH HAYDN

under the family's patronage for thirty years, during which time he composed a prodigious quantity of orchestral and chamber music, some operas, and also the music to the ' Seven Words on the Cross,' afterwards brought out as an oratorio in 1801. On the death of Prince Nicholas Esterhazy (1790), H. accepted Salomon's invitation to appear in London as conductor of his own compositions; and he remained until 1795, composing meanwhile, amongst others of his finest works, the *Twelve Grand Symphonies*, perhaps the best of the 120 or more that he wrote; also, the degree of Mus. Doc. was conferred on him by Oxford. On his return to Vienna (1795), he began work on the *Creation*, which he completed in 1798; a few weeks later its first performance caused an immense sensation in Vienna, and before long it had travelled round half Europe. Three years later he produced his last important work, a

splendid setting of a version of Thomson's *Seasons*. H. was a composer of amazing fecundity; in addition to the 120 symphonies, he left over twenty operas and eighty quartets, and a vast number of concertos, trios, and sonatas, wherein he developed with admirable symmetry the sonata-form of Emanuel Bach. He was the first to detach music from religious ceremonial and to give it a purely secular significance as an absolute art, and his music is the expression of a nature at once genial, devotional, warm, and vivacious.

Haydock, a tn. in Lancashire, England, 3½ m. E.N.E. of St. Helens. Has extensive collieries and iron foundries. Pop. (1911) 9649.

Haydon, Benjamin Robert (1786-1846), an English painter, born at Plymouth, England, chiefly noted for his historical paintings. He exhibited his first picture in 1807, after having been admitted a student of the Royal Academy for two years. His life was one of struggle and disappointment, because his talent was not properly appreciated, and he suffered a heavy blow in the rejection of his historical cartoons for the decoration of the new Houses of Parliament. Among his works are: ' Christ's Entry into Jerusalem ' (now at Philadelphia), the fruit of six years' labour; ' The Raising of Lazarus '; and ' The Judgment of Solomon ' (in the National Gallery). H.'s life-long struggle with debt so preyed upon his mind that he became unable to paint, and died by his own hand. *See* Paston's *B. R. Haydon and his Friends*, 1905.

Haydon Bridge, an eccles. par. in Northumberland, Hexham div., 6 m. N.W. of Hexham on the North-Eastern Railway. It has smelting works, iron and brass foundries, and coal and lead mines. Pop. 2500.

Haye, La, *see* HAGUE.

Hayes, Augustus Allen (1806-82), a chemist, born at Windsor, Vermont. Settled in Boston in 1828, and studied chemistry, carrying through numerous experiments. New processes for the manufacture of iron and copper were discovered by him, and he greatly improved boilers, furnaces, and copper-sheathing for vessels. He also studied the properties of alcohol, guano, sea-water, etc., and modified the methods of making chloroform and saltpetre. H. suggested the process of reducing pig to malleable iron without loss by the use of oxides of iron.

Hayes, Catharine, Mrs. (1690-1726), a murderess, *née* Hall, born near Birmingham. She married John H., a carpenter, at the early age of sixteen, and soon after they left Birmingham and set up a small shop in Tyburn, taking in lodgers. With the help of two of them—Wood and Billings—she murdered her husband in March 1726, and was arrested a few weeks later. At the trial she pleaded 'not guilty,' but was convicted and sentenced to be burnt, Wood and Billings being hanged. *See* Thackeray's 'Catharine' in *Fraser's Magazine*, 1839-40.

Hayes, Catherine (1825–61), an Irish operatic and ballad soprano, born at Limerick. She studied at Dublin, and frequently appeared at concerts there. In 1842 she went to Paris, where she studied under Manuel Garcia, and at his advice proceeded thence to Italy, where she was engaged at the Italian Opera House. In 1849 she came to England, and made her début at Covent Garden in *Linda di Chamouni*, where she was enthusiastically received. She then visited S. America and Australia, and after an absence of five years returned to England in 1856.

Hayes, Isaac Israel (1832-81), an American Arctic explorer, born in Chester co., Pennsylvania, where he graduated in medicine at the university, and in the Kane expedition sailed as surgeon. In 1860-61 he conducted a second Arctic expedition, and eight years later a third one still, fully described in his work, *The Land of Desolation*, 1871. He also published *An Arctic Boat Journey*, 1860, and *The Open Polar Sea*, 1867. H. firmly believed in the existence of an open polar sea up to the time of his death.

Hayes, Rutherford Birchard (1822-93), the nineteenth president of the U.S.A., born at Delaware; graduated at Kenyon College, Ohio, in 1842; practised law at Cincinnati from 1849 to 1861, where he won a considerable standing. At the outbreak of the Civil War in 1861, he was appointed major of a volunteer regiment, and saw active service at Western Virginia. Throughout the war he served with distinction and retired as a major-general. In 1865 he took his seat as a member of the National House of Representatives for Ohio, and held the governorship in 1867, 1869, and 1875. He was Republican candidate for the presidency in 1876, the candidate for the Democratic party being Samuel T. Tilden, and was duly elected. During his administration he devoted his efforts mainly to civil service reform, resumption of specie payments, and the pacification of the Southern states. *See* W. D. Howells, *Life of R. B. Hayes;* R. H. Conwell, *Life;* and J. Q. Howard, *Life, Public Services and Select Speeches.*

Hay-fever, a condition of discomfort, which occurs about the time of hay harvest. It is characterised by running of the nose and eyes, from irritation of the nose and air passages from the dust of plants; but this may also be induced by other forms of dust. In severe cases strict or absolute avoidance of the hay crop or other cause is necessary. As, however, the attack is either induced or aggravated by want of tone in the system, benefit always results from alteration of the mode of life and attention to minute details of hygiene. But the great thing is prevention more than cure. The nose and air passages are benefited by local applications, such as douches of boric acid, alum, common salt, sprays containing water or an oil. Good results follow vaccine treatment, when it is begun early. Having regard to the troublesome nature of the condition, it is advisable to have the nose examined for physical defects which may be amenable to treatment.

Hayingen, a tn. in Alsace-Lorraine, Germany, 16 m. N.N.W. of Metz. The seat of old iron-works. Pop. 11,482.

Hayle, a small seaport tn. of Cornwall, on St. Ives Bay, Great Western Railway. The harbour has a depth of about 11 to 20 ft. at high water. Tin mining and smelting are carried on. Pop. (1911) 1028.

Hayley, William (1745–1820), a friend and biographer of poet Cowper, born at Chichester; educated at Eton and Trinity College, Cambridge. Studied law for a short time, but abandoned it for a life of literary ease. Won fame by his political *Essays on Painting, History, and Epic Poetry*, and his poem, *The Triumph of Temper*. His most memorable work is *The Life of Cowper*, 1803. H. also wrote plays, a number of works in prose, a *Life of Milton* and a *Life of Romney*, and *Memoirs*, published in 1823.

Haym, Rudolf, a philosopher and writer, born at Grünberg, Silesia. Began to lecture on philosophy and German literature at Halle in 1851, and in 1868 was appointed professor of literature at that town. Previous to this, H. sat in the National Assembly at Frankfort. Chief publications: Biographies of Wilhelm von Humboldt, Hegel, Schopenhauer, and Herder.

Hayman, Francis (1708–76), an English painter, born at Exeter. Came to London at an early age and worked as a scene-painter at Drury Lane Theatre. Also became known as a designer by his illustrations to Sir T. Hanmer's edition of Shakespeare, and for Congreve's poems,

Smollett's *Don Quixote*, and the *Spectator*, 1747. H. is best known by the series of pictures ornamenting alcoves at Vauxhall. Regarded as first historical painter of the time and also a portrait painter. Occupies an important place in English art as one of the founders of the Royal Academy.

Haymarket Theatre, a London theatre standing in the Haymarket, opposite Charles Street, and, next to Drury Lane, the richest in theatrical tradition. During the patent monopoly it was a kind of chapel of ease or training-house to Drury Lane and Covent Garden. It was built in 1720, and leased to a company of French actors, who opened it with *La Fille à la Mode*. Fielding's is the first great name connected with the theatre. In 1730 he produced the *Tragedy of Tragedies, or Tom Thumb the Great*, and became manager in 1734. Ten years later, Charles Macklin opened the Haymarket with a company composed chiefly of his own pupils. In 1747 it was rebuilt and Samuel Foote assumed the management, and in 1766 he obtained a patent for the theatre during his lifetime. Foote sold the Haymarket to Colman the Elder in 1776, who continued to manage it till 1794; and in 1820 Harriss became manager and demolished the old house, whose site is now occupied by the Café de l'Europe. He erected a new theatre a little farther N., which was opened in July 1821 with *The Rivals*. A larger and finer building, under the same name was built in 1880, at which a large number of plays have been produced. Recently *Bunty Pulls the Strings* was produced there (July 1911), which achieved a great success and ran throughout the year. The approximate seating capacity of the H. T. is 1060, and it is one of the principal and best-situated theatres in London —just opposite Sir Beerbohm Tree's theatre, His Majesty's. The Haymarket is conspicuous also as being one of the few theatres in the West End of London where seats can be booked, if desired, for 2s. 6d. The present lessee of the Haymarket is Mr. Frederick Harrisson; business manager, Mr. H. Watson.

Haynau, see HAINAU.

Haynau, Julius Jakob, Baron von (1786-1853), an Austrian general, born at Cassel. Entered the Austrian army in 1801, and saw much service in the Napoleonic wars, being wounded at Wagram. Between 1815 and 1847 he rose to the rank of field-marshal lieutenant. He fought with distinction in the Italian campaigns of 1848-49, and was signalised by his ruthless severity at the capture of Brescia. In 1849 he was called to Vienna, and took supreme military command in Hungary where, as in Italy, he was accused of brutality. On the restoration of peace, he was appointed dictator of Hungary, but resigned in 1850 and travelled abroad. *See* Schönhal's *Life*.

Hayne, Robert Young (1791-1839), an American politician, and statesman, born in S. Carolina. He studied law in Charleston, S. Carolina, and was admitted to the bar in 1812. For a short time he served in the war against Great Britain. From 1814-18 he was Speaker of the state legislature, and from 1812-22, Attorney-General. He sat in the senate of U.S.A. from 1823-32, opposing Protection and supporting the doctrine of Nullification. In 1832 he was elected governor of S. Carolina. From 1837-39 he was president of the Louisville, Cincinnati, and Charlestown Railway. *See* Theodore D. Jervey, *Robert Y. Hayne and His Times* (New York), 1909.

Hayti, see HAITI.

Hayward, Abraham (1801-84), a miscellaneous author, was called to the bar in 1838, and though he never acquired a considerable practice, he was made Q.C. in 1845. He wrote in the *Edinburgh*, the *Quarterly*, and *Fraser's Magazine* on many subjects, and his *Essays* (of which there are three series, collected, 1858, 1873, 1874) are distinctly interesting. He wrote against the theory that Sir Philip Francis was Junius in *More about Junius*, 1868; and in 1861 he edited the autobiography of Mrs. Piozzi. His best-known book is on *The Art of Dining*, 1852, a subject on which he could discourse with knowledge. He was a figure in the society of his day, and had a vast acquaintance, numbering many distinguished men among his friends. His *Correspondence* was edited by H. E. Carlisle in 1886.

Hayward's Heath, a small market tn. in Sussex, England, on the London and Brighton Railway, at the junction of Lewes branch, 12 m. N. of Brighton. Pop. (1911) 4851.

Haywood, Mrs. Eliza (*née* Fowler), (1693-1756), an English authoress, born in London. She was associated for a time with the theatre, and made her first public appearance as an actress at Dublin in 1715, and subsequently wrote a comedy, *A Wife to be Lett*, playing the rôle of heroine. She soon abandoned the theatre, and became known as a voluminous writer of fiction, her books selling rapidly. Amongst her numerous works may be mentioned *Love in Excess, or The Fatal Enquiry; The Injur'd Husband, or Mistaken Resentment; The British Recluse; The Rash Resolve; The Surprise; The Fatal Secret*, etc., etc.

Hazara, the N.E. dist. of the Peshawar div. of the Punjab, British India. Its name is probably derived from the military colonies of 1000 (hazar) men each, left behind by Jenghiz Khan. Capital, Abbottábád. Pop. 560,000.

Hazaras, a race of Mongolian origin occupying the country between Kabul and Herat, and known in the western provinces as Taimanis. In other districts they are distinguished by the name of the territory they occupy. They speak a dialect of Persian ; are of middle size, stoutly made, with high cheek-bones, and smooth faces. They indulge in fierce intertribal disputes, and exercise great cruelty to the vanquished. They make good soldiers and excellent pioneers, and are uninfluenced by their surroundings. The H. are recruits of the Amir's companies of engineers and form an effective corps in his heterogeneous army.

Hazard (Old Fr. *hazard*), a game of dice, at one time very popular in England, and played at famous rooms in St. James' Street and Pall Mall for high stakes. There were many forms, the simplest being that in which two dice were used by two players only, one known as the ' caster,' and the other as the ' setter.' The former called ' a main,' *i.e.* any number from five to nine inclusive, and then threw. If he threw in or ' nicked,' he won the sum played for from the setter—a ' nick ' being 5, 6, 12, 7, 11, 8, and 9; whereas, if he threw out (the ace or deuce-ace) he lost to the setter. The best main for a caster to call is 7, as it can be thrown in six different ways, out of the thirty-six casts possible with dice. Any other number thrown by the setter was his ' chance,' and if this was thrown first, he won ; if the main, he lost.

Hazaribaugh, a town of Chota Nagpur, Bengal, India, on the new military road from Calcutta to Benares, picturesquely situated on the high central plateau of H. dist., which contains six coalfields, and several tea plantations. There are several hot-springs in the vicinity. The principal bazaar is regularly built and some of the houses are two stories high. H. was formerly a place of considerable importance. Pop. 16,000.

Haze (A.-S., *hasu, heasu,* grey, but origin of word uncertain, some suggest Ger. *hassen,* to hate, from the disagreeableness of such weather), a lack of transparency in the air; viz. obscurity, dimness. H. has the appearance of vapour or smoke with little or no dampness, and impedes the vision to a certain extent. It is often due to great heat. H. is really an obscuration of the atmosphere near the surface of the earth, caused by an infinite number of minute particles of vapour in the air. At one time, the word was applied to a thick fog or hoar-frost, but is now only used for that thin, misty appearance in the air which makes all objects look indistinct and uncertain. H. is less determinate than mist or fog.

Hazebrouck (Flemish, ' Marsh of the Hares '), an arron., com., canton, and tn. of France, dept. Nord, on the canal of the same name. It is well built, has an active trade in tobacco, grain, butter, soap, etc., and manufs. linen, cloth, and gingerbread. Pop. 12,800.

Hazel (A.-S. *Hœsel;* Fr. *noisetier, coudrier*), a British tree of the sub-order Coryleæ. The common H., of which the fruit is a nut, is distributed throughout Britain and all the temperate parts of Europe, Asia, and N. America. Commonly found in hedges and coppices, reaching a height of about 12 ft. The leaves are alternate, and the male flowers appear in cylindrical catkins, while the female ones are mere clusters of coloured styles at the extremity of the buds. A number of varieties are cultivated extensively in Kent around Maidstone.

Hazel Grove and Bramhall, a station in Cheshire, England, 2 m. S.E. by S. of Stockport on the London and North-Western Railway. Pop. (1911) 9634.

Hazleton, a city of Pennsylvania, U.S.A., 34 m. S.S.W. of Scranton in Luzerne co. Pop. (1910) 25,452.

Hazlitt, William (1778-1830), an author, was educated for the Unitarian ministry, but abandoned this profession for painting, in which art he showed some skill. Dissatisfied, however, with his progress as a painter, he determined to become a writer, and in 1805 published his first book, *Essays on the Principles of Human Nature.* He issued many books during the next years. ' The Round Table ' contributed to the *Examiner* (1815-17) attracted much attention, and the favourable impression created by these papers was increased by his *Characters of Shakespeare's Plays.* His lectures (afterwards printed) on the English Poets and the English Comic Writers placed him in the first rank of contemporary critics, and his reputation was enhanced with the publication of *The Spirit of the Age,* and *The Plain Speaker.* His *Life of Napoleon Buonaparte* was not a very satisfactory biography, but his *Conversations of James Northcote, R.A.*, were distinctly interesting. When unprejudiced—he often was prejudiced in the case of writers with whom he was acquainted —his judgment was usually sound, and generally well expressed. He wrote with sympathy, but declined, very rightly, to be influenced by the conditions under which a work was produced. He judged on its merits what was before him. His grandson, W. Carew Hazlitt, has written *Memoirs* (1867), and an appreciation by Augustine Birrell, 1902.

WILLIAM HAZLITT

Hazlitt, William Carew (b. 1834), a grandson of William H., essayist, born in London. He is above all things a bibliographer, his taste for rare books and ancient English poets being particularly marked. Also, a man of letters and a numismatist. He has issued many publications, among which may be mentioned his *Memoirs of William Hazlitt* (2 vols.), 1867; *History of the Venetian Republic* (3rd ed.), 1900; *Dodsley's Old Plays ; The Lambs ; Montaigne's Essays and Letters ; Shakespeare* (2nd ed.), 1903; *Our National Faiths and Customs ; Bibliographical Collections and Notes*, etc.

Hazor, the name of three towns in Palestine, viz.: 1. In Upper Galilee, also known under the name of Jebel Hadîreh, and mentioned on monuments, 1500-1300 B.C. 2. The ruin Hazûr, near Gibeon, the Hazor of Benjamin. 3. Probably identical with Hezron in the far S. of Palestine. On the plateau W. of Petra, the name is still in existence at Jebel Hadîreh.

Head. The human body is obviously separable into head, trunk, and limbs, of which the first is naturally divided into skull and face. Vertebrates possessing a head are termed *Craniata*, the higher types of which have the hard bony case of the skull containing the brain, which is con-

tinuous with the spinal cord, while the cavity of the face is almost entirely occupied by the mouth and pharynx, into the latter of which the upper end of the alimentary canal opens. It will be seen that the fundamental structure of the human body is that of a double tube, the dorsal and ventral, and in a comparison of the head with the trunk it will be found that in the former the dorsal tube is large relatively to the ventral. This condition is reversed in the trunk. The head is also remarkable on account of the large number of organs of special senses which it contains, such as those of smell (nose), taste (tongue), sound (ear), sight (eye) (*see* under these headings), hence there is no necessity to enlarge here on the vital character of this part of the human body.

Development.—In the embryo the distinction between the head and trunk by the formation of a cervical constriction is a change of comparatively late occurrence, though long before this constriction appears, the characteristic features of the parts have become apparent. At first the head may be said to consist wholly of the cranial part ; the face being developed later from a series of outgrowths or bars of the cranium.

Head, Barclay Vincent (b. 1844), a British numismatist, born at Ipswich, Suffolk, England. In 1893 he was appointed keeper of the medals and coins in the British Museum, when he began to issue catalogues of that department. He is joint-editor of the *Numismatic Chronicle*, and has written on the coinage of Syracuse, Persia, Bœotia, and Lydia. His most important publication is *Historia Numorum, a Manual of Greek Numismatics*, 1887.

Head, Sir Edmund Walker (1805-68), a governor-general of Canada, born near Maidstone, Kent. Educated at Winchester and Oriel College, Oxford, where he took first-class honours in classics. Made poor-law commissioner in 1841, and lieutenant-governor of New Brunswick in 1847. In 1854 he became governor-general of Canada, which position he retained till 1861, when he retired and was made a civil service commissioner and privy councillor in the course of a few years, Chief publications: *Handbook of Spanish Painting ; Ballads and other Poems*, etc.

Head, Sir Francis Bond (1793-1875), a soldier, traveller, author, and governor of Upper Canada, born at Hermitage, Kent. Entered corps of Royal Engineers and served at battles of Waterloo and Fleurus. In 1825 was placed in charge of an association formed to work the gold and silver mines of Rio de la Plata. In connection with this work, made several rapid journeys over the Andes and across the Pampas, described in his *Rough Notes*. Appointed governor of Upper Canada in 1835, but resigned office two years later, and in 1838 was created a baronet. The rest of his life was devoted to literary pursuits. Among his publications are: *Bubbles from the Brunnen of Nassau ; A Faggot of French Sticks ; The Royal Engineer*, etc.

Headache is present at the commencement of all fevers and many other diseases. When persistent, it may be due to tumour, or other changes in the brain. The term H. is often used to include neuralgia, or pain due to the nerves or nervous structure, as the eye, when it may be relieved by appropriate glasses to correct the otherwise fairly normal vision. The H. may also be caused by the fact that the glasses used are inappropriate, when measures should be taken to have them changed as soon as possible. H. may also be due to the general circulation, as in diseases of the kidney and heart. Ordinary Hs. often appear in the form of megrim or hemicrania, so called because only one part of the head is affected, or the pain is greater in one half than in the other. Broadly speaking, they are due to the alimentary canal, as is shown by the fact that they are frequently accompanied and relieved by vomiting. As the cause originates in connection with the food tract, the pain is prevented by modifying the diet or aiding its removal by laxatives or purgatives, or so treating the accompanying anæmia that the digestion is better able to put to a good use the food supplied to it. Apart from inducing vomiting, by tickling the back of the throat with the finger or a feather, plain hot water, or with salt or mustard, aids in unloading the stomach. In fact, the treatment of H. is that of gastric catarrh, dyspepsia, or whatever name is given to alimentary disturbance ; Hs., therefore, may be prevented by a plain diet at regular intervals. As the digestion is apt to be upset by worry, quarrels, vitiated air, railway journeys, and sea voyages, precautions should be taken when these risks are likely to be incurred. Particular search should be made for the dietetic or other cause of H., for there is no better example of the proverb that ' one man's food is another man's poison ' than H. Thus it may sometimes be relieved by strawberries or tomatoes, and sometimes they will produce it. And though usually starvation cures a H., food will sometimes relieve it.

Treatment.—This consists in local applications, of cold, by means of vinegar, or alcohol, in the form of spirit or scent ; counter-irritation, by means of menthol or capsicum. The soothing effects of quiet and a dim light are generally appreciated. The use of hypnotics and drugs derived from coal-tar are so very variable, and not unassociated with risk, that it is better not to take them, except under advice.

Hs. in early life often result in renal and other diseases ; or systemic troubles in later life, such as gout and rheumatism. Every effort, therefore, should be made to permanently remove the cause from which they originate.

Head-hunting, or Head-snapping, a custom once prevalent among all Malay races, but now rapidly dying out, of obtaining and treasuring the heads of their enemies. Even to-day it survives among the Dyaks of Borneo and other Eastern tribes. It is believed to have had its origin in religious motives, the worship of skulls among the Malays being universal, and is said to have existed in the Philippine Is., in 1577. The chief examples of head-hunters are the Was, a hill-tribe on the north-eastern frontier of India, and the Nagas and Kuhus of Assam. Severe repressive measures, however, have led to the decrease of the custom. *See* Bock, *Headhunters of Borneo;* T. C. Hodson, ' Headhunting in Assam,' in *Folklore*, xx. 2, 132.

Headington, a par. in Oxfordshire, England, 2 m. E.N.E. of Oxford, in the Woodstock div. Pop. (1911) 3400.

Headless Cross, an eccles. par., Warwickshire and Worcestershire, England, 5 m. S.E. of Bromsgrove. Pop. (1911) 3800.

Headmasters, Incorporated Association of, founded 1890, incorporated 1894. The association has exerted itself to place before the educational authorities and the public at large the issues raised by the organisation of secondary education under central and local authorities. To be qualified for membership it is necessary to be a headmaster of a boy's day-school, such school coming under the category of secondary schools recognised by the Board of Education, and controlled by a body of governors who have power to appoint and dismiss the headmaster, and to control the school's finances. Membership: 506 headmasters, 22 associates (ex-headmasters). Many of these members have seats on the educational committees of County Councils, and the association has established a scheme for the awarding of county council scholarships.

Headon Beds, one of the series of

British strata occurring in Hampshire, the Isle of Wight, and Devonshire, England. A variable series of clays, marls, sands, and limestones. The upper division is of fresh water, the middle partly marine partly fresh water, and the lower of fresh and brackish water origin. H. B., as well as Hampstead, Bembridge, and Osborne Beds, belong to the Oligocene system, and strata formed during the epoch between Eocene and Miocene times. During Oligocene times a wide land-surface seems to have extended over the whole of the British area. The climate of the period was uniformly genial, and the flora abundant.

Head Teachers' Associations, National Federation of, originated in a small meeting of headmasters at Uppingham in 1870, the object being the discussion of educational questions affecting schools in close connection with the older universities. The association admits of a further communication between head teachers throughout the country, and is a ready medium for ascertaining and giving voice to opinions and views generally.

Health, the condition of the body in which the various functions are performed normally. A district is said to be healthy when the prevailing conditions are accompanied by a scarcity of diseased individuals. In order that H. may be maintained in an individual or in a community, attention must be directed to the following among other considerations: (1) The duty of individuals in keeping their bodies clean and free from disease by attention to food, clothing, habits, and hereditary or occupational tendencies; (2) the duty of the community in relation to the drainage of houses and towns, the building of healthy houses, removal of waste matter, legislation against hurtful employments, and the prevention and stamping out of disease. The science of hygiene has done a great deal in both of these directions. By means of exhibitions, lectures, handbooks, and instruction in schools, the individual has been taught to look after and preserve his H. by attention to simple sanitary rules. To keep the body in H. the proper preparation of good food is essential, and girls and women are being encouraged and instructed in this art by means of lectures and classes in the city, and often by house visitation by the district visitor of H. in the country. The body must be kept clean by baths, and steps are being taken by town councils to ensure that the individual may be enabled to take a bath in comfort and at no great expense. Individuals then combine to make further progress for the good of the community by means of sanitation. Each town or district is now provided with a medical officer of H., whose duty it is to look after the H. of the town. He has control over the various sanitary inspectors, and one of the most important of his duties is the enforcement of the laws relating to compulsory notification of infectious diseases. By this means epidemics of a serious nature are averted or checked. He also enforces the law of compulsory vaccination for infants. Seaports are also watched by officers of H., and any suspicious case on board a vessel is carefully isolated, watched, and then dealt with if necessary. Bubonic plague, small-pox, cholera, all these contagious and devastating diseases are thereby held in check. Once they were the scourge of every European country, and now, in England at any rate, they are so carefully isolated that only solitary cases occur. Quarantine in foreign parts is also a great safeguard to public H.; its enforcement is particularly rigid in the United States.

Health, Bill of, see BILL OF HEALTH.

Health, Board of, an administrative body of the Privy Council; one of the many committees of that department constituted to deal with particular cases. The Board of Health was established early in the last century by the English government for the regulation of the sanitary conditions of life, prevention of infectious diseases, epidemics, etc., etc. Its jurisdiction may also extend to matters such as suppression of public nuisances, drainage of marshes, regulation of quarantine, control of asylums and hospitals and prevention of food adulteration. Similar boards exist all over the U.S.A.

Health Resorts, places frequented by the healthy in order to keep healthy, or by the diseased in order to regain health, or to check the progress of the disease. For the healthy such resorts may be roughly divided into seaside and country districts where the pure air and the generally more active outdoor life suffice to refresh mind and body. H. R. for the diseased are classified according to the conditions they are intended to cure. Consumptives frequent places at a high altitude, such as Davos Platz and Andermatt, or districts where the climate is mild and equable as at Bournemouth, Torquay, and the Isle of Wight in England, and the Riviera, Southern Italy, Algiers, Egypt, S. Africa, and Southern California. Many H. R. depend on the constitution of certain mineral waters, which are commonly regarded as of curative value in specific diseases.

Special organisations and physicians of specialised experience probably have more to do with such cures than the actual chemical constitution of the waters. *See* BALNEOLOGY.

Healy, Timothy Michael (*b.* 1855), a member of the Independent Nationalist party in the House of Commons, born at Bantry. He was called to the Irish bar in 1884, became a Q.C., 1899; in 1903 he was called to the English bar, and is a bencher of King's Inn and of Gray's Inn. Since 1880 he sat in the House representing Wexford, co. Monaghan, S. Londonderry, N. Longford, and N. Louth, in turn. Since 1911 he has been M.P. for N.E. Cork. He has always been a keen Nationalist, and in 1910 founded the Independent Nationalist Party with Mr. William O'Brien. He is the author of *A Word for Ireland ; Loyalty plus Murder ; Why Ireland is not Free.*

Heanor, an urban dist. in the Ilkeston parl. div. of Derbyshire, 10 m. N.W. of Nottingham. It has hosiery works and large collieries. Pop. (1911) 19,851.

Hearing, the result of the stimulus of the auditory neurons by impulses set up in the auditory nerves; hence the complete physiological apparatus will consist of (1) structures for the collection and conduction of the sound waves to the nerve of hearing; (2) the auditory centre in the brain. Sound waves are longitudinal waves produced by the action of vibrating bodies such as bells, etc. These sound waves are collected by the *pinna* of the ear and pass along the *auditory meatus* to the *tympanic membrane,* which vibrates. This vibrating membrane responds exactly to the number of vibrations (pitch), intensity of vibrations (intensity), and complexity of vibrations (quality or timbre). It conducts the sound from the external ear to the middle ear. This in its turn is separated from the internal ear by bone and two pieces of membrane. The middle cavity also contains a series of three small bones, the *ossicles,* which conduct the sound waves through it. The vibration of the ossicles is due to direct contact. The first bone, *malleus,* is affixed to the inner side of the tympani, it articulates with the second bone, the *incus,* and this in turn with the *stapes.* The base of this stirrup-shaped bone is united with the membrane (*fenestra ovalis*) which partitions off the internal ear. All structures are covered with mucous membrane. The changes of pressure in the middle ear are equalised by a channel, the *Eustachian tube,* which communicates with the pharynx. The internal ear has two well marked portions, an outer

(osseous) labyrinth, and an inner, the *membranous labyrinth,* the space between the two is partly filled with a fluid, the *perilymph.* The sound disturbance reaches the perilymph through the vibration of the fenestra ovalis. The membranous labyrinth in its turn is subdivided into (1) three *semicircular canals;* (2) a *vestibule ;* (3) a *cochlea.* The three semicircular canals are arranged in three different planes mutually at right angles. Each canal contains a fluid, the *endolymph,* and consists of a tube bulging out at each extremity so as to form the so-called *ampulla* in which, on a projecting ridge, there are cells bearing long auditory hairs which are the end organs of the vestibular branches of the eighth cranial or auditory nerve. The vestibule is formed by the dilated portions of the semicircular canals, and the cochlea is in direct communication with the cavity of the vestibula. It contains the remarkable *organ of Corti,* which constitutes the terminal organs of the cochlear division of the auditory nerve. It is by means of the cochlea that we discriminate pitch, hear beats, and are affected by quality of tone. This portion of the internal ear contains vibrators tuned to frequencies within the limits of hearing, say from 30 vibrations per second to 40,000 or 50,000 vibrations per second, though the sensibility of the ear is greatest for sounds produced by about 3000 vibrations per second. In the inner ear the vibrations which have been transmitted to the jelly-like endolymph affect the hair cells. The exact mechanism of these is unknown, as is also the means by which ' damping ' is produced, but the stimuli exciting the hair cells cause a nervous impulse to pass along the fibres of the auditory nerve to the auditory centre of the brain, where it is translated into a perception of sound and we hear.

Hearn, Lafcadio (1850-1904), an author, was the son of an English army doctor and a Greek mother, born in Leucadia, one of the Greek Ionian Is., whence he derived his name. He received a casual education, though he spent some time in Ushaw Roman Catholic College, Durham, and at the age of nineteen he went to the United States and became a journalist, first in Cincinnati, then in New Orleans. He was sent by the *Times Democrat* as correspondent to the W. Indies, and afterwards published his impressions in his book, *Two Years in the French West Indies.* In 1891 he went to Japan, and fell completely under the charm of that country; he married a Japanese wife, adopted the Buddhist religion, and became naturalised under the name of Yakumo Koizumi. For several years he held the post of English lecturer at the University of Tokio. He wrote several books on the history and lore of his adopted country, the best-known being *Glimpses of Unfamiliar Japan.* *See* Elizabeth Bisland, *Life and Letters of Lafcadio Hearn.*

Hearne, Samuel (1745-92), an English explorer, born in London. He entered the Hudson Bay Company and examined parts of the coast of the Hudson Bay, N. of Fort Churchill (then Fort Prince of Wales), in order to extend its trade area. In 1769 the company sent him on an expedition to discover some valuable copper mines which the Indians reported as existing, and to ascertain whether there was a sea upon the northern shores of America which would connect the two oceans. After two attempts in 1769 and early in 1770, he set out again in December of that year and accomplished both objects, besides learning the fate of James Knight (*q.v.*), the explorer, from Esquimaux. *See* Hearne's *Journal,* published posthumously in 1795.

Hearne, Thomas (1678-1735), an English antiquary, born at Littlefield Green, Berkshire. He graduated at St. Edmund Hall, Oxford, in 1699, whereupon he was appointed assistant keeper of the Bodleian Library, and in 1712 became second keeper. He was obliged to resign this office in 1716 on his refusal to take the oaths of allegiance to George I., which likewise prevented him from holding other academical positions. His chief works are: *Reliquiæ Bodleianæ,* 1703; *A Collection of Curious Discourses upon English Antiquities,* 1720; and edited Leland's *Itinerary* and *Collectanea,* Roper's *Life of More,* and numerous old chronicles.

Hearsay, *see* EVIDENCE.

Hearse (Lat. *hirpex,* harrow), a carriage for conveying the dead to the grave; originally a triangular framework for holding candles at a church service, especially at funerals. In the 15th and 16th centuries Hs. of great magnificence came into use, made of iron or brass, with a canopy and rich hangings, lighted by countless candles. They were erected in the churches over the bodies of distinguished persons.

Hearst, William Randolph (*b.* 1863), an American newspaper proprietor, born at San Francisco. On leaving Harvard University he became proprietor of the San Francisco *Journal* in 1895, with which he afterwards amalgamated the *Advertiser.* Since then he has acquired many papers, including the San Francisco *Examiner* (its evening issue being known as the New York *American*), the New York *Journal,* the *Morning American,* the *Chicago American,* etc. As a Democrat he was a representative in the Congress (1903-7), and unsuccessfully contested the New York mayoralty (1905).

Heart. In the various animals, this is the important propulsive structure concerned in the blood circulation. In some invertebrates there is no H., *e.g.* Acrania, while in others there is a dorsally situated rudimentary organ containing only pure blood. In the vertebrates it is situated ventrally and in the lower orders it is merely represented by the higher development of certain blood vessels. The comparative anatomy of the H. is a complicated subject, and only a brief reference can be given here. In fishes it resembles the $\curvearrowright$-shaped form of the human embryo, and, in most cases, it is concerned in the propulsion of impure blood through the gills, where the venous fluid becomes oxidised. In amphibia a development of the lungs has resulted in a three-chambered structure, having one ventricle and two auricles. In the reptiles a ventricular septum is commencing, and is almost complete in the crocodiles. In birds, the organ is four-chambered, but lacks development to the extent that the chordæ tendineæ (*see below*) are missing from the right auriculo-ventricular valve. In mammals, there is, in general, a close correspondence with the human form, though, in the lower orders, the structure is placed less obliquely. The ossification of certain of the fibro-cartilage tissue about the base of the great vessels of the H. is seen in the Ungulates, *e.g.* the *os chordis* of the ox.

The human H. is a hollow muscular organ, more or less conical in shape, situated in the thorax between the two lungs. It is found to be flattened in transverse section, and, in its natural condition, it is roughly equal in size to the closed fist of the individual, *i.e.* in the adult it appears to be about 5 in. long, $3\frac{1}{4}$ in. in its greatest width, and $2\frac{1}{4}$ in. thick, but it is subject to considerable variations in different persons, and even to variations at different times in the same subject. The ratio of H. weight to body weight, is normally about $\frac{1}{150}$ to $\frac{1}{175}$. Its capacity is 22 cubic centimetres, approximately, in the new-born infant, from 150 to 160 cubic centimetres in a youth of sixteen years of age, and increases rapidly for the next ten years, and more slowly later, reaching about 290 cubic centimetres capacity in a male aged fifty, while in the case of a female the capacity is some 25 cubic centimetres less. The H. is enclosed in a strong membranous sac (*the pericardium*), and is situated between the breast-bone and the costal cartilages. It has a very oblique position in the chest, the base being directed upwards, backwards, and to the right, and extending from the level of the fifth to that of the eighth dorsal vertebra. The stroke of the H. is most perceptible about 3 in. from the middle line of the sternum, and about 1½ in. below the left nipple. The organ contains a longitudinal partition, dividing it into a right and a left half, transverse constrictions further subdivide its interior into four chambers, viz. the right and left *auricles* and the right and left *ventricles*. The exterior is marked by a deep transverse groove, the *auriculo-ventricular furrow*, and by *two longitudinal furrows*, roughly corresponding to the interior septum and constrictions. In the furrows will be found the coronary arteries and veins which are concerned with the blood supply of the H's. component structures. Lymphatic vessels and nerves embedded in fatty tissue and covered by a layer of the pericardium also occur. This pericardium is a dense fibrous mantle of two layers which enclose the *pericardial cavity*. The outer and inner layers present smooth serous surfaces to one another and secrete a pericardial fluid which acts as a lubricant.

Cavities.—The *auricles* (so named from a fancied resemblance to an ear) which are situated at the broad upper base of the H., are thin-walled cavities acting as reservoirs for the blood. The posterior part of the right auricle receives the *venæ cavæ*, the *superior* being above and the *inferior* below, and the remains of the *Eustachian valve*, a relic of fœtal circulation, will be found attached to the right and lower margin of the orifice of the inferior vena cava. The right auricular appendage overlaps the root of the *aorta*, and lies in front of the superior vena cava. The *tricuspid valve* separates the right auricle from the right ventricle, which pyramidal chamber has much stouter walls than its corresponding auricle. The *pulmonary artery* is in communication with the ventricle, though a tricuspid valve closes the opening into this artery at certain stages of the *cardiac cycle*. Each cusp of the valve has a small knob (*Corpus Arantii*) in the middle of its curved edge, and the three flaps fit back into corresponding niches in the arterial tube. These hollows *Sinuses of Valsalva*) ensure that when the valve is fully relaxed, the blood shall have an uninterrupted passage into the efferent vessel. The left auricle receives the blood from the

pulmonary vein; it passes thence into the left ventricle, which in this direction is unobstructed by the *mitral valve*. The left ventricle is the stoutest walled of the four chambers, as its contractive force must propel the blood throughout the whole of the body.

Cardiac cycle and the circulation.— This cycle of activity comprises (*a*) the simultaneous contraction of the auricles followed by (*b*) a simultaneous contraction of the ventricles. The former occupies about one-third of the time of the latter, and the two contractions are termed *systole* of the H. They are followed by a pause, *diastole*, which occupies a period of time roughly equal to that of the complete systole. The whole cycle is repeated about seventy-five times per minute. During the contraction of the auricles the mass of blood contained in the large veins prevents regurgitation, and the total contents pass into the uncontracted ventricles. The valves which have been slowly closing during the filling of the lower chambers, are completely closed on the commencement of the ventricular systole. The valve sections are semilunar in shape, and are composed of endothelium, strengthened by enclosed fibrous tissue ; the two cusps of the mitral valve are unequal in size. Fleshy columns (*musculari papillares*) support strong tendinous cords (*chordæ tendineæ*), which are attached to the under surface of the valve flaps and prevent these from being forced into the interior of the auricle during the ventricular systole. From the left ventricle the purified and oxidised blood from the pulmonary vein is forced into the *aorta* with its three-cusped valve resembling that of the pulmonary artery. It is estimated that each ventricle propels forward 5¼ cubic in. of blood during each systole, and the total ' work ' of the H. in twenty-four hours is equivalent to 120 foot tons. The *fœtal circulation* is different from that described inasmuch as there is direct communication between the two auricles by means of a large opening (*foramen ovala*) in the interauricular septum ; the cycle in this case is: right auricle, left auricle, left ventricle to maternal placenta, and so on.

Sounds.—Heart complaints are frequently diagnosed by *auscultation*, or the listening to the H.'s sounds by means of a suitably applied stethoscope. These sounds in a healthy adult will consist of a longish dull sound followed by a short sharp sound, and resemble *loob-lub, loob-lub*, and so on. The former is probably caused by the contraction of the muscular fibres of the ventricle, and the tension of the auriculo-ventricular valves, the latter is due to the sudden closure of the semilunar valves on the completion of the ventricular systole. H. disease may be detected by irregularities in these sounds.

Detailed structure.—The main substance of the organ is composed of muscular tissue (*myocardium*), with a certain amount of interstitial areolar tissue containing numerous blood vessels and lymphatics, together with nerves and ganglia in certain areas. At the base of the H., beneath the pericardium, there is usually a considerable amount of fat. Fibrous tissue and fibrous cartilage occur at the large orifices at the base of the ventricles. A previous reference has been made to the ossification of this in certain animals. The inner surfaces of the H. cavities are lined by a smooth membrane termed the *endocardium*. The muscles are involuntary, but differ from the usual form of these in being striped. The exact arrangement of the fibres is very complicated, and but little understood (reference should be made to recent treatises, as Cunningham's *Anatomy*), but, in summary, there appear to be common superficial fibres for the two auricles and the two ventricles, and separate deeper fibres for each cavity. Recently, fibre bundles (*bundles of His*) have been traced connecting auricle to ventricle, the function of which is, presumably, to transmit the impulse of contraction.

Nervous system. — The nervous control of the organ is tripartite, and consists of cardiac nerves derived from the cervical ganglia of the sympathetic system, from ganglia in its own substance, and also from the pneumogastric or vagus direct from the brain ; this last system apparently exercises an arresting power on the H.'s action.

Diseases.—The H. or its investing membranes may be the seat of many different forms of disease.

Pericarditis is the inflammation of the pericardium, and is usually accompanied by an excessive effusion of fluid into the pericardial cavity; this may seriously affect the mechanical action of the H. *Endocarditis*, or the inflammation of the lining membranes of the H.'s cavities, may be caused by acute rheumatism, and may result in serious injury to the valves, usually those of the left side. Valvular damage usually causes *murmurs*, and these sounds are tested by auscultation, and in this manner a narrowing of the valve orifice (*stenois*) can be distinguished from an incompetence of the valves. An acute ulcerative endocarditis is due to micro-

organisms, and is usually fatal. *Myocarditis*, or inflammation of the muscle substance, may take one or more of several forms, and result in serious permanent trouble, *e.g. fatty degeneration*. All these complaints together with derangement of the cardiac nerves or disease of the coronary vessels, result in a demand for extra work on the part of the H. itself, and this usually results in *hypertropy* of the muscle until *compensation* is established. This, in its turn, may result in premature senility through malnutrition. Cardiac dilatation and other complaints may be consequents of influenza. Palpitation which may be due to digestive troubles, and is then caused by direct impulses from the stomach, must not be confounded with *tachycardia* in which the H.'s action is permanently accelerated as during exophthalmic goitre. *Bradycardia*, or the slowing of the rhythm, may be due to cerebral tumour, melancholia, jaundice, etc., in the form of *Stokes' Adam's Disease*, a senile degenerative change appears to lead to a weakening of the conductivity of the common deep-seated auriculo-ventricular muscle bundles. Congenital malformations of the H. are not unknown. The usual treatment for many forms of H. disease endeavours to ensure a maximum of rest for the patient, and a minimum of excitement, both mental and physical ; where necessary digitalis and strychnine are administered as cardiac tonics. *See* ANGINA PECTORIS.

Heart Burial, the burial of the heart in a separate place from the body. It appears to have been practised by the ancient Egyptians, and was not uncommon in Europe during the 12th and 13th centuries. The custom probably arose out of a veneration for the heart, which was regarded as the seat of a man's affections and conscience, and was associated with his soul. It was forbidden by Boniface VIII. (1294-1303), but his prohibition was withdrawn by Benedict XI. The heart of Richard I. was buried in Rouen Cathedral, and that of Edward I. at Jerusalem. Other notable instances of heart burial may be cited in the cases of Henry III. in Normandy, James II. in Paris, Robert Bruce at Melrose Abbey, the French kings, Louis IX., XIII., and XIV., Francis I. and II., Philip III., etc., and the Emperor Leopold of Austria. Shelley's heart, *cor cordium*, was sent home to Bournemouth, and Byron's was buried in the mausoleum at Missolonghi in Greece. The heart of the Marquess of Bute was buried in Jerusalem as late as 1900. Separate burial was sometimes given to other parts of the body. The viscera of the popes have been buried in the church of the Quirinal since the time of Sixtus V. (1590). Consult Pettigrew, *Chronicles of the Tombs*, 1857, and Hartshorne, *Enshrined Hearts*, 1861.

Heartburn, the common name for a burning sensation in the chest, often accompanied by a feeling of dis-comfort in the throat, and in the region of the heart. It is due to gastric disturbances, and is generally caused by irritation of the stomach wall by hyper-acidity of the gastric contents. The cardiac symptoms, when present, are generally due to an over-distended stomach interfering with the heart's action. The discomfort is rapidly relieved by a dose of bicarbonate of soda. The condition should be treated by ensuring a simple diet, regular exercise, and regular action of the bowels. Charcoal and bismuth are also very useful drugs.

Hearth-money, a tax of two shillings imposed in 1662 on every hearth in all houses except cottages. The principle was an old one, for in early English history an Anglo-Saxon king obtained part of his revenue from a *fumage*, a tax on the hearth smoke of all his subjects but the very poor. The tax of Charles II.'s reign was exceedingly unpopular, and was withdrawn in 1689, a window-tax being levied in its stead in 1695. The idea is also apparent in the hearth penny-tax paid annually to Rome as early as the 10th century.

Heart's Content, a seaport and town of Newfoundland, situated on the Avalon Peninsula, 40 m. N.W. of St. John's, on the E. coast of Trinity Bay. It is the terminus of three Atlantic cables from Valentia Is., Ireland. Pop. 1000.

Heart's-ease. *see* PANSY.

Hearts of Oak, a large friendly society founded in 1842, the objects of which are to provide relief for members during sickness, and for members' wives during confinement, to insure the tools and implements of trade of members against loss or damage by fire, and to provide sums at the death of a member and for funeral expenses. The society also defrays the expenses of residence of members in convalescent homes and sanatoria. It is an approved society within the meaning of the National Insurance Act. It is a purely centralised society, having no branches other than certain medical agencies; but is, nevertheless, one of the largest societies in the kingdom. Its membership is over 300,000, its income over £700,000 a year, while its reserve fund is close upon £4,000,000. It pays out in sick benefits annually over £400,000, and in funeral benefits about £70,000. Membership is re-stricted to persons over eighteen and under thirty years of age who are in receipt of 24s. a week, except that persons between eighteen and twenty-four years of age are not ineligible if the standard rate of wage in their particular calling is less than 24s. a week. No candidate for admission is accepted without a medical examination, the fee for which is 2s., and miners are ineligible. The total average contributions amount to about 10s. a quarter, and there is no entrance fee. At the end of a year membership is free. A free member during sickness is entitled to 18s. a week for twenty-six weeks; then half for the second period of twenty-six weeks, and if the illness still continues, a further reduced allowance and exemption from contributions. There are differential rates varying with the length of the period of membership. On death a free member's representatives get £20. The present secretary is Mr. C. W. Burnes, and the offices of the society are the Hearts of Oak Buildings, Euston Road, London, N.W.

Heat. The term H. is used in ordinary language in a number of different senses, of which the following are the most common : (*a*) sensation of H.; (*b*) temperature or degree of hotness; (*c*) quantity of H.; (*d*) radiant H.

(*a*) The sense of H. is distinct from that of touch, for the former sensation is experienced if we sit in front of a fire, or in the sun, or in the neighbour-hood of any hot body, and is, therefore, not dependent on actual contact with matter. It is from this sense of H. that we get our first ideas of H. as a physical entity, which is capable of passing from one body to another.

(*b*) If a hot iron is placed on a cold iron plate, we may observe by a sense of H. that the plate is heated and the iron cooled until they both attain the same degree of warmth. From the sense of H. we derive the idea of a continuous scale or order, which we express as summer H., blood H., red H., etc., and we speak of the temperature of a body as denoting its place in the scale as distinct from the quantity of H. it contains.

(*c*) The quantity of H. in a body must depend on its size (and also, it should be added, on its material). The temperature, on the other hand, does not depend on the size of the body, but on the quantity of H. per unit mass (other things being equal).

(*d*) It is well known that when the rays of the sun or of a fire fall on a body, they warm it; but it must not be supposed that H. has travelled across the intervening space from the sun or the fire to the body warmed. It is now known that the energy of radiation is not the same thing as H., though it is converted into H. when the rays strike an absorbing substance.

The question at once presents itself, ' What is heat? ' In this connection it will be well to follow briefly the development of the modern theory of H. It has long been known that H. can be developed by friction (e.g. between the wheels and axles of a carriage), or by percussion (e.g. by hammering a piece of iron on an anvil), or by compression (as in the case of a bicycle pump). This development of H. was accounted for by supposing that every body in a normal state possessed a certain capacity for H. and contained a certain quantity of caloric at a definite temperature. Percussion altered the condition of the substance and lessened its capacity for H. Some of the caloric was squeezed out of it, and being thus set free, manifested its presence by the rise of temperature. The weakness of this theory was shown by an experimental investigation carried out by Count Rumford in 1798. He mounted a gun-metal cylinder, so that it could be rotated by horse-power, while a blunt steel boring tool pressed against its bottom. The cylinder was covered with a layer of flannel to prevent loss of H., and its temperature was recorded by means of a thermometer placed in a hole drilled in the bottom. At the end of half an hour, when the cylinder had made 960 revolutions, the temperature had risen by 70° F. He found that the metallic dust rubbed off by the friction from the cylinder weighed only 837 grains troy (less than $\frac{1}{1000}$ of the weight of the cylinder). ' Is it possible,' he said, ' that the very considerable quantity of H. produced in this experiment could have been furnished by so inconsiderable a quantity of metallic dust, and this merely in consequence of a change in its capacity for heat? ' But Rumford went further and showed that the capacity for H. of the dust was the same as that of the solid metal. The H. had clearly been produced by the friction, and was equivalent to the work done in rotating the cylinder under the conditions of the experiment. The fatal blow to the caloric theory was delivered by Sir Humphry Davy, who first showed that two pieces of ice may be melted by simply rubbing them together. It is a well-known fact that the capacity of water for H. is much greater than that of ice, and ice must have an absolute quantity of H. added to it before it can be converted into water. Friction consequently does not diminish the capacity of bodies for H. The accurate investigation of the relation between the work done in driving an apparatus

and the H. developed was taken up by Dr. Joule of Manchester in the year 1840. The H. was produced by friction of a brass paddle revolving in water contained in a specially constructed brass vessel, so that the

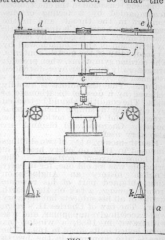

FIG. 1

water was heated by a kind of revolving churn process and the temperature was registered by a delicate mercurial thermometer. The paddles and the flywheel f were driven by two wheels d and e. If everything were free the friction between the brass

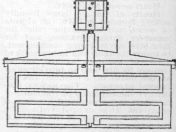

FIG. 2—BRASS VESSEL SHOWING PADDLES

vessel and the water would carry the vessel round with the paddles and the water could not be churned, and therefore it would not be heated. The vessel was prevented from rotating by two forces applied by two strings fastened in a groove round the vessel and passing over the pulleys j and j and weighted at k and k. From the number of revolutions made by the paddles, the work done was calculated. After all corrections were made, Joule decided that the work done in raising a weight of 1 lb. through 772 ft. (at Manchester) will, if spent in friction (between brass and water), raise the temperature of 1 lb. of water 1° F. Joule showed quite clearly that the amount of H. produced depended on the amount of work done and on nothing else. He found the same result for friction of water in a brass vessel with a brass paddle, for friction of mercury contained in an iron vessel with an iron paddle, and for friction of two iron rings rubbing against each other in mercury. Joule also proved that H. is absorbed when a gas does work in expansion; and measured directly the amount of H. liberated by the compression of a gas. The principle which these experiments have established is that 'when H. is transformed into any other kind of energy, or vice versâ, the quantity of H. which disappears is equivalent to the quantity of the other kind of energy produced, and vice versâ.' But we have not given satisfactory explanation of H. by saying that H. can be transformed into other forms of energy and vice versâ. The idea that H. is ultimately due to a motion of some sort has long been entertained. By friction and collision the sensible motion of bodies disappears and H. is generated. The supposition has been that the motion in such cases is not really lost, but is merely transferred from the body as a whole to its individual particles. Thus, when a moving body is brought to rest by friction or collision the energy of the original visible motion of the body is not annihilated, but passes over into the invisible molecules of the substances taking part in the friction or collision. This theory supposes that when a body is heated the rise in temperature is due to the increased energy of motion of the molecules of the body. But it goes further and explains the transmission of radiant energy from one body to another, as from the sun to an individual on the earth. There is evidence in favour of the supposition that light is due to wave motion in the ether, and we have exactly the same evidence in favour of the same supposition with regard to radiant energy. Radiant energy (for example the radiant energy emitted by hot water pipes or a blackened stove) and light behave in exactly the same way in a variety of experiments—in fact the only difference which can be detected is that light, as well as possessing

all the characteristic qualities of the radiant energy, is also able to affect the sense of sight. Radiant energy then, like light, is supposed to be due to wave motion in the ether. We say that the molecules of a hot body are in a state of very rapid vibration, or are the centres of rapid periodic disturbances of some sort, that they thus excite waves in the ether, that these waves travel through the ether between a receiving body and the hot body with the velocity of light, and that when they fall upon the receiving body they are more or less absorbed by the molecules of the receiving body, causing similar motions in these molecules. The sense of H. is thus excited in a human being, or an animal, by the waves of radiant energy which start from a hot body just as the sense of sight is excited by the waves of light which start from a luminous body. The fact that light waves possess heating properties if they are absorbed by a suitable substance suggests at once that there is no essential difference between waves of light and waves of radiant energy. Extensive spectroscopic experiments have shown that the two sets of waves differ only in degree and not in kind. The ordinary spectroscope cannot be used; as glass absorbs the waves of radiant energy. Lenses and prisms made of rock salt are used in the instrument, and the radiations are received on the blackened bulb of a thermometer, or on the blackened part of an electrical instrument for recording temperature. In this way the similarity between waves of radiant energy and waves of light has been established.

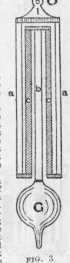

FIG. 3

The effects of H. may be summarised briefly as follows: (1) Change of dimensions or of volume, (2) change of internal stress, (3) change of state, (4) change of temperature, (5) electrical and chemical effects. Each of these will be considered in turn:—

(1) *Change of dimensions.*—Most bodies expand or increase in volume on being heated. In laying down the rails of a railway, an interval is left between consecutive rails to allow for

this. The expansion due to change of temperature must be taken into account in building steel bridges and in setting up pipes which are to carry hot water. The pendulums of clocks or the balance wheels of watches have to be compensated, so that the time of swing shall not be altered by changes of temperature.

In Fig. 3 is shown a ' compensated ' pendulum, where the bob G is supported by the rods a, a, b of one material and the rods c, c of another material. The lengths of the rods are so adjusted that, whatever the temperature, the centre of gravity of the bob G is always at the same distance from the point of support O. In Fig. 4 the downward expansion of the rod is 'compensated' by the upward expansion of the mercury. In Fig. 5 the rim of the wheel is made up of three segments, each of which consists of two metals securely fastened together, the more expansible being on the outside. When the temperature rises, the spokes increase in length, but this is ' compensated ' by the bending inwards of each of the segments of the rim. The expansion of liquids is, as a rule, much greater than that of solids, and is used in many forms of thermometers. The expansion of gases is very much greater than that of solids or of liquids, and is independent of the nature of the gas. That is to say, oxygen expands to the same extent as hydrogen, carbon dioxide, or any other gas for a given rise of temperature.

(2) *Changes of internal stress.*— Many of these changes in volumes are accompanied by changes in the internal forces or stresses between the molecules of the body. As a wheel tyre contracts it is subject to enor-

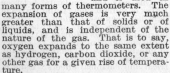

FIG. 4

mous force. If air or any gas is confined in a closed vessel, and its temperature is raised, the pressure exerted by the gas on the walls of the vessel is increased and may burst the vessel.

(3) *Change of state.*—Many substances can exist in three forms—solid, liquid, and gas—and the change from one form to another is accompanied by the evolution or absorption of H. Ice can be converted into water and water into steam by the application of H.

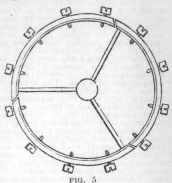

FIG. 5

(4) *Change of temperature.*—If a quantity of water be heated we can tell by means of our sense of H. that it is becoming hotter; and in scientific language we say that its temperature is rising. The measurement of change of temperature can be affected more accurately by means of thermometers where the expansion of a quantity of mercury or alcohol is observed. For scientific purposes all thermometers are compared with a thermometer filled with dry air, nitrogen or hydrogen, or helium.

(5) *Chemical and electrical effects.*— The chemical effects produced by H. are very varied. Thus when mercuric oxide (a red powder) is heated, mercury (a mobile, shining liquid) and oxygen (a colourless gas) are produced. Or, again, when coral is heated in air, it combines with the oxygen of the air and burns; this process, when once started, producing enough H. for its continuance. The electrical effects of H. are of two kinds: (*a*) That produced when a circuit is made up of wires of different materials, say copper and iron joined together at each end, and the temperature of the two junctions is different; then an electric current is produced in the circuit. Since a very small electric

current can be measured easily, this fact is made use of in several instruments for measuring small differences of temperature. (b) The change produced in the electrical resistance of bodies by H. This has been made the basis of a method of measuring high temperatures.

Modes of transference of heat.— There are three principal modes of transference of H. : (1) Convection, (2) conduction, and (3) radiation.

(1) In convection, H. is carried or conveyed by the motion of heated masses of matter. The most familiar instances of this method of transference of H. are the heating of buildings by circulation of hot water, or the equalisation of temperature which is produced by the movement of the hot water in a mass of water heated from below (as in the case of a kettle).

(2) In conduction, H. is transferred without visible relative motion of the parts of the body. Familiar examples of this are the transference of H. from one end of a poker, placed in a fire, to the other end, and the transference of H. from one end of a silver spoon, placed in hot tea or coffee, to the other end.

(3) In radiation, the heated body sends out waves through the ether, which are transmitted equally in all directions, travel with the velocity of light, and are converted into H. when they are absorbed by matter. This radiation takes place in the absence of matter and is the means by which H. is received from the sun.

In most cases H. is transferred by all three methods at once. It is sufficient to say that in a solid the effect is produced mainly by conduction, in a liquid mainly by convection, and in a gas mainly by radiation. It is very difficult to obtain so good a vacuum that H. is not transferred across it by convection as well as by radiation.

The chief sources of H. are : (1) The sun; (2) chemical action, as in the burning of wood, coal, etc.; (3) mechanical act, e.g. friction; (4) electric currents, e.g. as in electric lamps, and heaters; (5) change of physical state, e.g. steam condensing to water.

Heathfield, George Augustus Eliott, Baron (1717-90), a British general, a younger son of Sir Gilbert Eliott, born at Stobs, Roxburghshire. After having been educated at Leyden University and at Woolwich, he fought with the Prussian army in 1735-36, and as a grenadier guard in the War of Austrian Succession at Dettingen and Fontenoy. In 1775, at the outbreak of the American War, he was sent out as governor to Gibraltar. His heroic defence of that fortress against Spain, from June 1779 to Feb. 1783, is one of the finest achievements in British history. On his return to England in 1787 he was created Baron H. of Gibraltar.

Heating. A certain range of temperature is essential for the health and well-being of all warm-blooded animals. Naturally, when the external temperature rises, that of the body is regulated by perspiration, while a low external temperature is counteracted by increased bodily exercise. In the course of civilised life, however, man becomes more sedentary, and he needs some form of H. apparatus in addition to clothes and houses.

All systems of H. depend either upon convection or radiation (*see* HEAT), or upon a combination of both. The most obvious and common method of H. is, of course, by radiation, and is exemplified by the open fire. By this means the walls and furniture are heated and the air left cool. In good grates the sides are not at right angles to the back, but at an angle of at least 120°, the depth is equal to the back width, and the back of the grate should hang forward over the fire. Further, the grate should be bounded on both sides and at the back by firebrick, while the overhanging part should be made by the same substance. Such a method of H. is popular, because it is pleasant to see, provides ventilation, because of the draught up the chimney, and leaves the air cool. On the other hand, it must be remembered that a large amount of heat is wasted both up the chimney and by means of only partial combustion, and also objects in the room are warmed on one side only.

To economise the fuel, stoves are often used. By reason of the familiar long pipe in the room, it is evident that the gases continue to impart heat to the room long after they would be lost in the chimney of an open fire. There are several grave disadvantages connected with stoves, however, which render their use, particularly in schools, a matter of grave consideration. In the first place the iron in the stove and flue becomes spongy, and then, unless the fire is burning furiously, producing a large draught, the carbon monoxide percolates into the room. Because of the faulty fitting of the mouth of the stove after use for a while, the same thing happens, and this gas acts as a slow poison, producing anæmia and kindred states. Further, the air in the room becomes very dry, so producing very bad effects upon the throat and chest. This latter effect is overcome to a certain extent by means of pans of water placed upon the top of the stove. They certainly do tend to keep the air moist, but with a big fire the danger then occurs of getting the room supersaturated with moisture, with consequent bad effects upon the inhabitants of the room, and, incidentally, upon the furniture. Bad odours are also prevalent with stoves, owing to the burning of the dust in the air as it comes in contact with the hot metal. If the stove be made entirely of bricks, the first and last of these effects are, to some extent, obviated, but on hygienic grounds the open fire is the better of the two.

Gas stoves, which usually consist of asbestos, or some similar substance, heated by a row of Bunsen burners (q.v.), are used generally in those cases where fires are required only occasionally. They act, of course, more or less as open fires, but they have the grave defects of vitiating the atmosphere, and, unless they are of exceptionally good pattern, of pouring carbon dioxide into the room in such quantities as to make their use deleterious.

Schools, public buildings, offices, and to an increasing extent private houses, are frequently heated by means of hot-water apparatus. In these cases steam or hot water circulates through pipes, which by conductivity (see HEAT) become warm externally, and thence by convection the air is heated. The hot water may be made to circulate either at low or high pressure. In low pressure systems, the water is heated in a boiler in the basement. As it is heated, it, for well-known reasons, rises and circulates upwards through large pipes to an open tank at the top of the system, by means of which the pipes and boiler are kept full. Then, since the water is cooled, it sinks down a vertical pipe and so back into the boiler. Air cocks are placed at the tops of radiators, so that accumulating air which tends to impede circulation can be allowed to escape. In high pressure systems, the pipes are made much narrower and thicker of a special type of wrought iron. The water is heated in a ' boiler-coil,' and circulates in a manner similar to that of a low pressure system. The whole system is, however, closed, and is full of water except at the top, where there is a strong ' expansion-pipe,' containing air placed to provide for the expansion of the water on H. This type of apparatus can be heated to great pressures and temperatures. The pipes are tested to a pressure of between two and three thousand pounds per square inch, although the working pressure is seldom more than nine atmospheres, for at this pressure

a temperature of about 350° F. is obtained. Both systems have their own favourable and unfavourable features. Thus radiators can easily be attached to high pressure systems, although there is no reason to prevent their use in low pressure ones. Dirt, however, cannot enter the high pressure systems since the vessel at the top is closed, and therefore there is no danger of clogging the pipes. Further the smaller pipes look better than the large ones, but on the other hand the high temperatures attained in the high pressure system render them dangerous to touch, and cause charring of the dust in the air, and of surrounding wooden objects. Again, the air in the expansion pipe in the high pressure systems acts as a cushion preventing fracture, but such a system cools rapidly and a uniformity of temperature is difficult to obtain.

For H. by hot air see VENTILATION, since this concerns the heating of air before it is brought into a room. See Edwards, Ventilation and Heat ; Hood, Warming Buildings ; Dye, Hot Water Supply ; Jones, Heating by Hot Water. See also BOILERS, FURNACES, FUEL, VENTILATION.

Heat of Formation. Whenever a chemical reaction takes place, heat is either evolved (exothermic reaction) or absorbed (endothermic reaction) in the process. In the case of combustion, the quantity of heat evolved is large, in other cases smaller, and in some negative. The H. of F. of a compound is the amount of heat, measured in calories, which is evolved when the molecular weight in grams of the compound is formed from its elements. Thus, when 2 grams of hydrogen combine with 16 grams of oxygen to form 18 grams of water, 69,000 calories are evolved, which amount is said to be the H. of F. of water. The quantity is determined by carrying out the reaction in a calorimeter surrounded by water, the product of the mass of water and its rise of temperature giving the quantity of heat liberated. In cases where the H. of F. cannot be determined directly use is made of the fact, summed up in the law of Hess, that the quantity of heat evolved or absorbed in the formation of a compound is quite independent of its mode of formation. Thus the H. of F. of carbon monoxide may be arrived at from the following considerations : (1) On forming a gram molecular weight of carbon dioxide from carbon monoxide and oxygen, 67,000 calories are evolved. (2) On forming the same weight of carbon dioxide from its elements, 96,960 calories are evolved. Therefore, on forming one gram molecular weight of carbon monoxide from its elements, 96,960 minus 67,000, or 29,960 calories are evolved. This may be represented as follows :

$$C \xrightarrow{29,960} CO \xrightarrow{67,000} CO_2$$
$$96,960$$

Certain compounds, such as acetylene hydriodic acid, and nitric oxide are ' endothermic,' *i.e.* have heat ' stored up ' in them, which is liberated on their decomposition into their respective elements.

Heaton, Sir John Henniker (*b.* 1848), an English politician, born at Rochester, Kent, and educated at Kent House Grammar School and at King's College, London. He entered parliament, in 1885, as member for Canterbury, and successfully carried through many schemes for reforming the postal service, the chief being the reduction of postal rates to India and Australia (1890), the Imperial Penny Postage Scheme (1898), and the Anglo-American Penny Postage Scheme (1907). He is a keen chess-player, and inaugurated the parliamentary chess match between the United States and Great Britain, played by cable in 1897.

Heaton Norris, a tn. of Lancashire, England, situated on the Mersey, 4 m. S.E. of Manchester, and forming a suburb of Stockport; it is connected with the latter by a bridge and viaduct. It is a busy industrial town, with cotton and thread mills, bleachfields, rope factories, and saw mills; hats are manufactured. The Ashton, Manchester, and Oldham Canal ends here. Pop. (1911) 11,240.

Heat-stroke, *see* SUNSTROKE.

Heaven, in the popular use of the term, the extent of space which surrounds the world, and in more restricted terms that part of the atmosphere which we can ourselves see. This use was very common among the Jews, and in the O.T. the term denotes sometimes the region of the clouds, and sometimes the superior region of the stars In the mediæval scholastic philosophy (vide *Summa Theologiæ* of St. Thomas Aquinas) these two are grouped together as the ' firmament,' but it has been suggested that the Jews spoke of them as the first and second Hs., while the abode of God and the Saints, that is to say, H. in the theological sense, was spoken of as the third H. With this is connected St. Paul's reference to the ' third H.' in 2 Cor. xii. 2. Other classifications of the Hs. are found in Jewish and Latin theology, the most important being that of the Cabbala, representing the later Rabbinic conceptions. Here we find a sevenfold subdivision of the heavenly regions, of which the highest is the abode of God, the lowest, the region of the stars. This classification has passed into the Mohammedan theology, together with much of the Rabbinic angelology. As the abode of God, H. must be considered as some region of space in which God makes a special manifestation of Himself, and this conception is found running through the whole of the Biblical narratives and Patristic writings. Lastly, H. is often spoken of as a state, the condition of those souls who share the life of Christ. Thus, in Ephes. ii. 6 and in Phil. iii. 20 this conception, that even now the life and conversation of Christians are ' in H.' and ' in heavenly places,' is clearly present.

Heaves, or **Broken Wind,** *see* HORSE, DISEASES OF.

Heavitree, an eastern suburb of Exeter, Devonshire, England, included in the Exeter parl. bor. In the parish church is a marble monument to members of the Raleigh family, and several armorial shields. Pop. (1911) 10,950.

Hebbel, Christian Friedrich (1813-63), a German poet and dramatist, born in humble circumstances at Wesselburen in Ditmarschen, Schleswig-Holstein. After travelling on the Continent, he settled in Vienna (1846), where he died. His first tragedy, *Judith*, was performed at Hamburg in 1841, and made his reputation. His tragedies are very powerful, and show a fine sense of dramatic situations; but they depict for the most part the passionate struggles of hot and ugly natures, and his scenes are unrelieved by humour or by loveliness. His chief works are: *Maria Magdalene*, 1844; *Julia*, 1851; *Gyges und sein Ring*, 1856; and *Die Nibelungen*, 1862. His lyric poems are included in *Gedichte* (2 vols.), 1841-48, and *Mutter und Kind*, 1859. Consult Werner's critical edition of his works (12 vols.), 1901-3, and studies by Poppe, 1900; Scheunert, 1903; and Georgy, 1904.

Hebburn, a tn. of Durham, England, situated on the S. bank of the Tyne, in the Jarrow div., 4 m. N.E. of Gateshead. There are important chemical and engineering works, coal mines, lead smelting works, and manufactures of hemp, rope, etc. Shipbuilding is also carried on. Pop. (1911) 21,766.

Hebden Bridge, a tn. W. Riding of Yorkshire, England, on the R. Calder, in the Sowerby parl. div., 8 m. W. by N. of Halifax by the Lancashire and Yorkshire Railway. The town has cotton factories, dye-works, foundries, and manufactures of shuttles and ready-made clothing. The Hebden Bridge Fustian Manufacturing Society, founded in 1870, is a remarkable result of productive co-operation. Pop. (1911) 7170.

Hebdomadal Board, The, a governing body of the University of Oxford, instituted in 1631 by Charles I., probably at the suggestion of Archbishop Laud. It consisted of heads of houses and proctors, and its business was to discuss measures for the benefit of the University, which should afterwards be submitted to Convocation. In 1854 its right of initiative with regard to all matters concerning university legislation was transferred to a Hebdomadal Council, consisting of the chancellor, vice-chancellor, late vice-chancellor, two proctors, *ex officio*, and six heads of houses, six professors and six members of convocation, elected by congregation. The council holds its meetings weekly during term.

Hebe, a Greek divinity, goddess of youth, daughter of Zeus and Hera, and cup-bearer of the gods before the coming of Ganymede. She was the wife of the deified Hercules, with whom she was worshipped at Athens. In Rome she was worshipped as Juventas in a temple on the Capitoline Hill. She had the power of restoring the aged to youth. The most famous statue of H. is the masterpiece of Canova.

Hebel, Johann Peter (1760-1826), a German poet, born at Basel. He studied theology at Erlangen (1778-80), subsequently teaching at the Gymnasium at Karlsruhe. He wrote his poems in 'Alemanic' dialect; his *Allemannische Gedichte* was translated by Reinick into High German in 1891. His work was fresh, humorous, and full of vigour, and attained great popularity. The *Schatzkästlein des rheinischen Hausfreundes* (1811) contain first-rate stories. A complete edition of his works was published at Stuttgart (8 vols.), 1832-34. His life has been written by Schullheiss, 1831, and G. Längin, 1894.

Heber, Reginald (1783-1826), an English bishop, born at Malpas, Cheshire. After graduating at Brasenose College, Oxford, and touring in Europe, he entered holy orders (1807), and accepted a living at Hodnet, Shropshire. He was appointed Bampton lecturer, 1815; preacher of Lincoln's Inn, 1822; and bishop of Calcutta, 1823. He is chiefly remembered by the hymns he wrote, the best known being 'From Greenland's Icy Mountains,' 'The Son of God goes forth to War,' and 'Brightest and best of the Sons of the Morning.' Besides his *Hymns*

(new ed. 1878) his publications include: *A Journey through India*, 1828, and *Palestine: a Poem*, 1809. See Lives by his widow, 1838, and G. Smith, 1895.

Heberden, William, M.D. (1710-1801), an English physician, born in London. He was educated at St. John's, Cambridge, of which he became a fellow in 1730. He practised medicine at Cambridge (1739-48), and lectured on materia medica. In 1748 H. settled in London, where he soon worked up an extensive practice. He was elected a fellow of the Royal Society (1749), and an honorary member of the Paris Royal Society of Medicine (1778). He contributed to the *Phil. Trans.* of the Royal Society, and to the *Medical Transactions*, and published *Commentarii de Morborum historia et curatione in Latin*, 1802.

Hébert, Jacques René (1757-94), a French revolutionist called 'Père Duchesne,' born at Alençon, and went to Paris as a servant. At the outbreak of the Revolution he became an extreme Jacobin, propagating his views in *Le Père Duchesne* (which he edited, 1790-94), and in various pamphlets, such as *La Lanterne Magique*. He joined the Club of the Cordeliers (1791), became a member of the Commune (1792). He took part in the September massacres and sat on the commission which judged Marie Antoinette. He inaugurated a 'Worship of Reason,' the followers of which were called Hébertists or *Enragés*, but was arrested by his rival, Robespierre, and guillotined on March 24, 1794. *See* studies by Brunet, 1857; Mater, 1888, and Aulard, *Le Culte de la raison*, 1892.

Hebradendron (Gk. Ἑβραῖος, Heb. δένδρον, tree), a term which was formerly applied to several species of guttiferous trees in the genus *Garcinia*. They are indigenous to the Old World and yield the resin known as gamboge.

Hebrew Language, the language in which almost the whole of the O.T. was written, is a branch of the great Semitic family, so called from the name of Shem, one of the three sons of Noah (Gen. x.). The Semites probably first occupied the district of Arabia. The Semitic languages lend themselves to a fourfold division. The northern group includes Syriac, Western or Palestinian Aramaic and Samaritan. The middle group includes Phœnician, Hebrew, and various Palestinian dialects. In the southern group, Arabic and Ethiopic are the chief languages, while Babylonian and Assyrian form an eastern division. All these languages possess certain features in common, obscured, however, to a certain extent by the particular developments of each. The chief of these Semitic peculiarities are: (1) Stems consisting of only three consonants; (2) the writings of consonants only in the early texts, the vowels not being counted as stem-letters; (3) verbs composed of two tenses only, and nouns of only two genders; (4) system of writing from right to left; (5) similarity of roots of kindred meaning and general inability to form compound words. Of these Nos. 2 and 4 do not apply to the Assyro-Babylonian cuneiform script. The word Hebrew itself (עֵבֶר 'ibri) means 'belonging to the other side,' and is the term used when speaking of the nation and language in connection with other peoples. Otherwise it was seldom used by the Hebrews themselves, the general term for the language being 'the Jews' language,' or 'the language of Canaan (e.g. Isaiah xxxvi. 11 and 13; Isaiah xix. 18). There are but few monuments of Hebrew proper outside of the books of the O.T. The chief of these is known as the Siloam inscription, which forms the earliest example of written Hebrew, probably about 700 B.C. Aramaic and Moabite inscriptions are extant of a somewhat earlier date. The period of literary Hebrew covers about seven centuries, from the 9th to the 2nd B.C., but its most flourishing period ends some 400 years earlier. After the return from the Exile, the literary language gradually died out of popular use and was supplanted by Aramaic. In this language are written considerable portions of the books of Daniel and Ezra. We see even from 2 Kings xviii. 26, that by the time of Hezekiah, Aramaic was the international language of diplomacy between Judah and Assyria, and probably this was so with regard to most other nations of the East. Hebrew was still retained as the written language, but even here the later books of the N.T. are largely intermixed with Aramaic forms and coloured by Aramaic idioms. Hebrew, however, had now become the language not only of literature but also of religion, and scholars made continuous efforts to keep up the original standards. But this was impossible, for the old vocabulary was not adequate for the needs of a later generation, and thus a new form of the language, scholastic Hebrew, was developed. This contanied a large number of borrowings from the Greek and Latin languages, and shows the original Hebrew at a much later stage of development. The chief monument of this period is the Mishna. Hebrew was now extremely decadent, and the decline

continued till the 10th century A.D. This intermediate period shows a certain number of attempts at an elucidation of the sacred text, based partly on tradition, partly on analogy with kindred languages and partly on some ingenious but hopelessly erroneous etymological attempts. The Septuagint version of the sacred text shows the first of the early attempts at interpretation which were to culminate in the Targums, a series of Aramaic paraphrases of the sacred writings. In the 10th century and under Mohammedan influence a revival of Hebrew learning took place, and the school of the Massorites of Tiberias arose. To these scholars is due the introduction of vowel pointing, for in the older text all such pointing was scanty or entirely absent. The Massoretes were trustworthy scholars, and the good condition of the O.T. text at the present time is largely due to their labours. They treated their text with befitting reverence, and relegated their own hypotheses to the footnotes. At the present day there are no great Hebrew scholars among the Jewish people, and the ancient language has in many places become mixed with the common tongue of the people with whom they dwell, thus forming a kind of patois. The Yiddish spoken in London by Jews of the lower classes is a descendant of the ancient literary language.

Hebrews, Epistle to the, known also as the **Epistle of Paul the Apostle to the Hebrews,** bears in the oldest MSS. no further heading than the words, 'To the Hebrews,' and even this probably formed no part of the original letter, but was deduced from a reading of the contents. All other particulars with regard to the epistle are matter for conjecture, for there is no sign of any clear tradition with reference to authorship, date, or exact destination. It is morally certain, however, that the authorship is not Pauline, and this view is supported by the continuous tradition of the city of Rome where the epistle first appears (Clement, *Shepherd of Hermas*). But this city furnishes us with no positive tradition. In Africa an ancient tradition, which appears in Tertullian's *Di Pudicitia*, c. 20, ascribes the authorship to Barnabas, the companion of Paul, while the Alexandrian tradition seems continuously to have ascribed it to the Apostle of the Gentiles himself. Origen held that the epistle was the development by a disciple of some of Paul's oral instructions. It is impossible here to discuss in detail the objections to the Alexandrian theory, but they are quite overwhelming. Neither vocabulary nor style is Pauline, and the general character of the epistle shows that the writer was intimately acquainted with the circumstances of the congregation to which he wrote. There is nothing in this argument to indicate that Hebrews predominate in this congregation, and it is now generally held that Rome was probably its destination. The date is before 95 A.D., but the question of authorship is still quite unsolved. The names of Luke, Priscilla, Apollos, Clement, and Silas have all been suggested.

Hebrews, Gospel according to the, the most interesting of the apocryphal gospels of the first centuries. Origen and St. Jerome quote it occasionally, and the latter also made Greek and Latin translations of it, but these last have perished. All the quotations from it lead one to consider it as an expanded version of the First Gospel, though it is said to be somewhat smaller than the canonical book.

Hebrides, or **Western Islands,** are situated off the W. coast of Scotland, and are divided into the Outer H. and the Inner H. The Outer H. comprises Long Is. (Lewis-with-Harris), N. Uist, Benbecula, S. Uist, Barra, the Shiants, St. Kilda, and the Flannan Is. They are composed almost entirely of gneiss, and are therefore sometimes called Gneiss Is. The Inner H. are separated from the Outer group by the Minch and Little Minch. They are a scattered group, including Skye, Eigg, Muck, Coll, Tyree, Liamore, Mull, Staffa, Iona, Kerrera, Colonsay, Oronsay, Jura, Islay, and the Slate Is. The two groups contain more than 500 islands, of which about 100 are uninhabited. They are included politically among the counties of Ross, Argyll, Bute, and Inverness. The total area is 2812 sq. m. Only 200,000 acres are used as arable land, the islands for the most part being rocky or sandy. There are many small lochs and morasses. The climate is healthy and mild. The inhabitants are chiefly fisher folk, who still speak in the Gaelic tongue. The chief towns are Stornoway, on the E. side of Lewis; Rothesay in Bute, and Portree in Skye. The islands are very popular with tourists and sportsmen. The H. (ancient *Ebridæ*) were invaded by Scandinavians in the 6th century. The Celtic inhabitants accepted the Christian faith under the teaching of St. Columba. In the 9th century they were subdued by Harold Haarfager, King of Norway, and remained subject to the Norwegians till 1266. The islands were then governed by the Scottish race of Somerled until John Macdonald of Islay made himself ' Lord of the Isles ' (1346).

They were subsequently annexed to Scotland. Total pop. about 78,000. Consult Scott's *Lord of the Isles ;* Boswell's *Tour to the Hebrides with Samuel Johnson ;* Martin's *Description,* 1703 ; Macculloch's *Geological Account,* 1819, and Mackenzie's *History of the Outer Hebrides,* 1902.

Hebrides, New, *see* NEW HEBRIDES.

Hebron (mod. *el-Halil*), an ancient and important city of southern Judah. In Josh. xv. 13 we read of its capture by Caleb, but except for this incident little is known of its early history. It reaches great prominence, however, in the reign of David, for this king made it his royal city and his headquarters in the movement against Jerusalem. It was later seized by the Edomites, but was recovered by Judas Maccabæus. Finally, it fell before Vespasian.

Hecatæus of Miletus (c. 550-476 B.C.), a Greek historian and traveller, who vainly tried to dissuade his countrymen, the Ionians, from revolting against Persian rule, and after their defeat, was one of the ambassadors to the Persian satrap, Artaphernes. The only certain work of H. is the *Genealogies,* or *Investigations* (an account of Greek traditions and mythology); *Travels round the Earth* is sometimes attributed to him. *See* fragments in Müller's *Fragmenta historicorum Græcorum,* i.

Hecate, a Greek goddess, daughter of the Titan Perses and Asterie, retaining her mighty power under Zeus. She ruled in Heaven, Earth, and the Netherworld, being frequently identified with Selene (moon), Artemis, and Persephone, and sometimes represented with three bodies. As patroness of magic, she was mother of Circe and Medea. She also presided over birth and death. She was worshipped in the wilder parts of Greece, especially at cross-roads, where black victims were sacrificed to her.

Hecatomb, *see* SACRIFICE.

Hecker, Friedrich Karl Franz (1811-81), a German revolutionist, born at Eichtersheim, in Baden ; he abandoned the law for political life, joining the democratic and socialist party and becoming conspicuous as a revolutionary in the Baden Chamber of Deputies. After heading an unsuccessful revolution, he fled to Switzerland, where he founded a paper, *L'ami du Peuple.* Later he settled in America as a farmer near Belleville, in Illinois, and fought as a Federal in the Civil War. He died at St. Louis.

Hecker, Isaac Thomas (1819-88), an American Roman Catholic divine, born in New York City. In 1844 he joined the Roman Catholic Church, and in the following year was entered in the novitiate of the Redemptorists, Belgium. He returned to America in 1857 as a Redemptorist missionary, and asked permission at Rome to open a Redemptorist novitiate in America to meet its modern requirements. He was expelled from his order, and in 1858 founded the community of ' Paulist Fathers.' He founded the *Catholic World* and the Catholic Publication Society, and was the author of *Catholicity in the United States*, 1879; *The Church and the Age*, 1888, etc.

Hecker, Justus Friederich Karl (1795-1850), a German physician and historian of medicine, born at Erfurt, and became professor of medicine at Berlin. He wrote a famous *History of Medicine*, 1822-29 ; books on the Black Death, etc., and his great work, *Epidemics of the Middle Ages*, 1832 (translated for the Sydenham Society in 1846, and later in 1875).

Heckles, or Hackles, machines for separating the filaments of animal and vegetable fibres, especially of flax, and arranging them in parallel stricks or tresses. Hackling is the first operation in spinning and used to be done by hand, the tool being a metal comb, through which the fibre was drawn to equalise the threads and remove all knots. By this process ' tow ' is removed from ' line,' the long straight tresses. All modern heckling machines are fitted with metallic teeth, which do the work of the hand-comb.

Heckmondwike, a par. and market tn. of the W. Riding, Yorkshire, England, situated 2 m. from Dewsbury. It is noted for the carpet and blanket manuf., and there are coal mines, iron and chemical works, etc. Pop. (1911) 9017.

Hecla, *see* HEKLA.

Hectic Fever. This term literally means habitual fever, and was formerly applied to the regular and recurrent fever of pulmonary tuberculosis, that is, consumption. It is also found in other lung affections and diseases which have lasted for a considerable time. The fever and accompanying sweat are most marked at night, when the bodily resistance is at its lowest, but the sweating may occur at any time when the patient falls asleep. H. F. may be looked upon as an obsolete term in medicine, as it only indicates a condition of weakness.

Hector, a Trojan warrior, the son of King Priam and Hecuba, and the husband of Andromache, by whom he had Astyanax. During the Trojan war he slew Patroclus, the friend of Achilles. The latter, roused to anger, drove back the Trojans, but H. stood his ground, and, in spite of the tears and entreaties of his parents, awaited the approach of the enemy by the Scean gates. At the sight of Achilles he turned in flight and was pursued three times round the walls of Troy. At last Achilles pierced him with his spear, and, fastening the body to his chariot, dragged it through the dust of the city. At the bidding of Zeus, he gave up the body to Priam, who gave it an impressive burial in the citadel. *See* Homer's *Iliad*, vi. and xxii., and Virgil's *Æneid*, i.

Hecuba, the wife of Priam, king of Troy, to whom she bore Hector, Paris, Cassandra, and many others. On the fall of Troy she fell into the hands of Ulysses, and was carried away to Greece as a slave. At Thracian Chersonesus her daughter Polyxena was sacrificed by the Greeks, whereupon H. revenged the deaths of her many children by killing Polymestor, king of Thrace, who had murdered her son Polydorus. She was pursued, but was changed into a dog and leapt into the sea.

Heddle, one of the sets of parallel double threads which are arranged in sets, and, with their mounting, compose the harness employed to guide the warp threads to the lathe.

Hedemarken, a highly fertile ' amt ' (county) of Norway, forming a frontier to Sweden. The area is 10,600 sq. m. Pop. (1910) 134,555.

Hedesunda, a tn., 21½ m. S. of Gefle, in the prov. of Gefleborg, Sweden. Pop. less than 5250.

Hedge, *see* BOUNDARY and FENCE.

Hedgebote, an old term denoting the right of a tenant to cut wood on the land he holds for purposes of repairing hedges, etc.

Hedgehog, the name given to several species of insectivora, belonging to the family Erinaceidæ ; they are distinguished from their allies by their spines. *Erinaceus europœus,* the common European H., is generally about 9 in. long, and 4 or 5 in. high ; the spines reach a maximum length of 1 in., are sharply pointed and grooved along the sides, and controlled by the muscles of the back. The animal can roll itself into a ball, bristling with spines, and thus protected, will sometimes fall from a considerable height. The H. eats insects, slugs, mice, frogs, young birds, etc., and has been known to attack vipers ; it is sometimes domesticated as a protection against vermin.

Hedgehog Plant, the term sometimes applied to species of *Echinocactus,* a genus of spiny cacti, and hedgehog-grass is the name given to some species of *Cenchrus,* a genus of prickly grasses.

Hedgeley Moor, a tract of moorland

in Northumberland, England, situated in the Berwick div., and in the township of Beanley, 10 m. W.N.W. of Alnwick. It is noted as the scene of a battle in 1463 between the adherents of the houses of Lancaster and York, in which Sir Ralph Percy was killed.

Hedge-mustard, a genus of plants of the order Cruciferæ. Some species are natives of Britain, e.g. the common H., which in its wild state grows plentifully by the wayside, to a height of 1½ ft. This has a hairy stem and small pale yellow blossoms, with a pungent odour. It was formerly used in medicine for catarrh, etc., and is now cultivated for domestic purposes.

Hedge-nettle, the popular name of the species of *Stachys* (*q.v.*), a genus of labiate plants found in Europe, Asia, Africa, and America.

Hedge-sparrows, or *Accentor modularis*, a species of passeriform birds belonging to the family Turdidæ; it resembles a sparrow, having brown plumage streaked with black.

Hedin, Sir Sven Anders (*b.* 1865), a famous Swedish explorer, born at Stockholm. He is the son of Ludwig H., chief architect of Stockholm. He was educated at Stockholm, Upsala, Berlin, and Halle, and was a pupil of Von Richthofen. Whilst still a student (1885-86) he journeyed through Persia and Mesopotamia. In 1890 he was sent as a member of King Oscar's embassy to the Shah of Persia, and in 1890-91 he travelled through Khorasan and Turkestan to Kashgar. His real work as an Asiatic explorer began in 1893 when he began his journey across Asia from Orenburg to Pekin. He travelled *viâ* Lobnor and Tibet, and the journey took him four years. During these years he explored the glaciers of the Mustaghata, and the mountains around the sources of the Yarkand Daria, and he discovered the ruins of an ancient Buddhist city in the desert of Takla-Makan. In 1899 he made his second Asiatic journey. On this occasion he travelled down the Tarim R. to the Lake Lobnor. On the northern shore of the lake he found evidences of Chinese civilisation of the 3rd century. He then crossed Tibet, travelling S.E., and made two unsuccessful attempts to enter Lhassa. Publications : *Journey through Khorasan and Turkestan,* 1892 ; *Through Asia,* 1898 (published in nine languages) ; *Adventures in Tibet,* 1904 ; *Scientific Results of a Journey in Central Asia* (6 vols.), 1899-1902 ; *Trans-Himalaya,* 1909 ; *Overland to India,* 1910.

Hedjrah, see HEJIRA.

Hedley, William (1779-1843), an engineer, born at Newburn, near Newcastle. He is chiefly known as the improver of Trevithick's locomotives ; his invention 'Puffing Billy,' with smooth wheel, and rails, being patented by him in 1813.

Hedon, a municipal bor. of E. Riding, Yorkshire, England, in the Holderness parl. div., situated 8 m. E. of Hull, on the North-Eastern Railway. It stood formerly on a navigable creek, which communicated with the Humber; this is now dry, and the harbour is practically useless. The industries are chiefly agricultural and there are extensive brick-fields. Pop. (1911) 1171.

Hedonism, a word of Greek derivation signifying pleasure, hence, in ethical science, the theory that pleasure or happiness of one kind or another is the chief aim in life. Hedonistic theories have been held from the earliest times. According to one view, happiness is the chief good and moral end for each individual ; according to the other, the well-being and pleasure of the general community and of all sentient creatures is the main thing to be desired. The earliest and most extreme type is that of the Cyrenaic and Epicurean schools, who taught that the sentient pleasure of the moment is the only good for mankind. This view is known as Egoistic H. Opposed to this is Universalistic H., which owes its growth to modern writers, such as Hume, Bentham, and Mill, whose point of view is based on a wider conception of life, and who maintain that the only real happiness is that of the community—or, at any rate, the majority—the criterion is society, not the individual. Passing on to the theories of Utilitarianism and Social Ethics, one is confronted by the problem of reconciling and adjusting the claims of the individual with those of society. The chief recent exposition of the theory of Utilitarianism is contained in Sidgwick's *Methods of Ethics.* He associates the hedonistic theory of the moral standard with an intuitive theory of knowledge which utilitarians do not usually hold. *See also* J. S. Mackenzie, *Manual of Ethics,* 1897 ; J. H. Muirhead, *Elements of Ethics,* 1892 ; and J. Watson, *Hedonistic Theories,* 1895.

Hedysarum, a genus of leguminous plants, consists of herbs or under-shrubs growing in a mild climate. *H. coronarium,* the French honey-suckle, is a native of Spain and Italy, is used as food for mules and horses, and bears deep red or white flowers. *H. fruticosum* grows in sandy places of Siberia, is eaten by horses, and bears pale purple flowers.

Heem, Jan Davidsz (1604-84), the greatest Dutch painter of still life, born at Sandrant or, according to

Descamps, at Utrecht in 1600. He entered the Guild of Antwerp in 1635, and two years later became a burgher of the city. In 1667 he moved to Utrecht. His paintings chiefly consist of magnificent vases of flowers and fruit, rich garlands, etc., with a background of green.

Heemskerk, Maerten Jacobsz, often called Maerten van Veen (1498-1574), a Dutch painter, born at Heemskerk in Holland, and studied his art under Cornelisz Willemsz and John Schoreel, painters at Haarlem. In his early work he imitated Mabuse, but during a visit to Rome (1532-35) he came under the direct influence of the great masters. His pictures are well represented in the galleries of Europe, but in England he is best known by his drawings. His chief works are : a ' Crucifixion ' (in the Ghent Museum), ' Judgment of Momus ' (in the Berlin Museum), ' Triumphs of Silenus ' (in Vienna), and ' St. Luke Painting the Likeness of the Virgin and Child ' (at Haarlem).

Heemstede, a tn., 3 m. S. of Haarlem in N. Holland, Netherlands. Pop. 7074.

Heerde, a tn. 29½ m. N.E. of Arnhem in the prov. of Gelderland, Holland. Pop. 6557.

Heere, Lucas de (1534-84), a Flemish painter, inherited his artistic talent, as his mother painted miniatures and his father was a sculptor. There is a portrait of Queen Elizabeth at Hampton Court, where H. has flatteringly represented Aphrodite and the sister goddesses confounded and dismayed by the beauty of the earthly queen. One anecdote of H. tells how, when asked by the Earl of Lincoln to illustrate national costumes, he chose to represent the Englishman as naked but provided with shears and materials to fashion his own clothes, the suggestion being that he is never dressed two days alike. H. is also the author of the *Garden of Poetry* (' Boomgaard der Poësije ').

Heeren, Arnold Hermann Ludwig (1760-1842), a German historian, born at Arbergen, near Bremen. His *De Encomiis*, 1785, attracted attention, with the result that in 1787 he became a professor of philosophy, and in 1801 of history, at Göttingen. He is regarded as the pioneer of the modern method of historical study; he did not lay so much stress on political events as on the economic relations of states. His chief works are : *Iden über Politik, den Verkehr, und den Handel der vornehmsten Völker der alten Welt* (2 vols.), 1793-96 (Eng. trans. 1833); *Geschichte der Staaten des Alterthums*, 1799 (Eng. trans. 1840); and *Kleine historische*

Schriften (3 vols.), 1803-8. His *Historischen Werke* were published at Göttingen in 15 vols., 1821-30.

Heerlen, a tn. 12½ m. E.N.E. of Maastricht in the prov. of Limburg, Netherlands. Pop. 11,021.

Hefele, Karl Joseph von (1809-93), a German Catholic theologian, born at Unterkochen, Würtemberg, and educated at Tübingen. He became privat docent (1836) and professor-ordinary of church history and patristics in the Roman Catholic theological faculty of that university. He sat in the National Assembly of Würtemberg (1842-45), and in 1869 was consecrated Bishop of Rotten-burg. Of his contributions to theological study may be named : *Honorius und das sechste allgemeine Konzil*, 1870; *Causa Honorii papæ*, 1870; and *Konziliengeschichte*. He also published an edition of the Apostolic Fathers, 1839; a life of Cardinal Ximenes, 1844 (Eng. trans., 1860); and a history of the councils of the church in 7 vols., 1855-74.

Hegel, Georg Wilhelm Friedrich (1770-1831), born at Stuttgart, was the last of the four great German idealist-philosophers of that period, the others being Kant, Fichte, and Schelling (*q.v.*). He was educated at the University of Tübingen, where began his friendship with Schelling, who, although younger by five years, must rank as H.'s precursor by virtue of his extraordinary precocity —he had published several philosophical papers of importance even during his student days. In 1793 H. left Tübingen, and lived by teaching, principally in Frankfort. But whilst thus engaged, his mind, stimulated by his studies of Wolff, Fichte, and Plato, was slowly maturing, and in 1801 he published a brilliant comparative critique on the systems of Fichte and Schelling, somewhat to the latter's advantage. The same year he became a professor at the University of Jena; during the five years that he spent here, he became more intimate with Schelling, and, together they issued a philosophical journal. At this time, Napoleon was pressing against the Prussians, and the battle of Jena (1806) caused the university to be temporarily disbanded, with the result that H. had to accept the editorial duties of a small newspaper for a time. Before long, however, he had once more secured an appointment as teacher in Nuremberg, and it was during the nine years he spent in that position that he married (1811). Meanwhile, his first work of real significance had been published, *The Phenomenology of the Spirit*, 1807; and the *Science of Logic*, the first volume of his definitive philosophy, followed in 1812. In 1816 he left Nuremberg for a professorial chair at Heidelberg, where he produced his great *Encyclopædia of the Philosophical Sciences*, and two years later he succeeded Fichte in the chair of philosophy at the new University of Berlin, a post which he filled with distinction until his death, from cholera, thirteen years later. It was here that he wrote, amongst many other important works, the *Philosophy of Right*, 1821. During his later years he was esteemed the leading force in contemporary German philosophical thought. After his death many of his hitherto unpublished lectures and essays on religion, history, and æsthetics were collected and published by a circle of his chief students and friends. Hegelianism must be studied in relation primarily to that of Kant. Kant had contended that, whilst the value of an object was purely in the cognition thereof, and not in any degree intrinsic, a dualism existed between that object and the cognition, *i.e.* between the noumenon and the phenomenon. H., in his development of this idea, evolved the dualism out of consideration by identifying reality with rationalism. Agreeing with Kant that it is impossible to consider life philosophically as a purely material existence apart from essential idea, he urges that matter is non-existent except as a perception, that is to say, an expression to an individual mind of some essential idea. He therefore proceeds to examine, not the form, but the idea, of thought; since what is true of a perception is true of the object. Hegelianism is thus the outcome of the idealisms of Kant, Fichte, and Schelling, although less romantic and more absolute; it is divided into three headings : (*a*) logic, (*b*) natural philosophy, (*c*) philosophy of spirit. *Logic*, in which his whole system is traced out, both logically and metaphysically, has been described as the only production of modern thought worthy to rank with the *Metaphysic* of Aristotle; in it, H. analyses and systematises the fundamental conceptions that underlie external forms, by the method of ' dialectic,' for which he is largely indebted to Fichte. The *Natural Philosophy* is a concrete application of this analysis to science and to the social and spiritual individuality of man; but, on account of his lack of deep scientific knowledge, it is of very little value. *The Philosophy of Spirit* is a further application of *Logic*; in this, H. develops the moral and abstract element of the work in correlation with the idea of evolution.

Apart from the purely scientific significance of H.'s writings, they contain much of importance on religion and the æsthetics of art. In religion, he was influenced chiefly by Fichte's subjective idealism. His views on art are of great interest; to him, art is a thing apart from nature, for he holds that, since art should express idea in sympathetic form, nature is not intrinsically or necessarily beautiful, but is dependent for its beauty on individual perception. He classifies art, on this basis, into : (1) Symbolic, wherein the expression of indefinite ideas are attempted on a colossal scale (*e.g.* Oriental architecture); (2) Sensuous or Classical, which is best exemplified in Greek sculpture (the pagan æsthetic of idealised humanism); and (3) Christian Art, a return to the symbolic in style of idea, vague and indefinite in its concept of infinity and omnipotence, but more exquisitely expressed in the narrower limitations and more plastic media of painting, music, and poetry. H.'s teachings were subsequently developed in two directions, one of them on the lines of his own idealism, the other leading to arrant positivism. Of these the latter is more powerful, and tends to atheism and radicalism under Strauss, Feuerbach, and Bruno Baur, who claim their systems to be directly evolved from H., in spite of the orthodox and Conservative sympathies he professed.

Bibliography. — Complete works (18 vols.), 1832-45 ; Eng. trans., *Logic* and *Philosophy of Mind*, 1894. *Philosophy of History*, 1857; *Philosophy of Fine Art*, 1886; *Philosophy of Religion*, 1895; *Philosophy of Right*, 1896, etc. Lives and critiques: Rosenkrantz (1844), Erdmann (1853), Haym (1857), Kostlin (1870), Barth (1890), Ott (1904); (French) Michelet (1838); (English) Hutchison Stirling (1865), Caird (1883), Seth (1887), Macintosh (1903), McTaggart (1910),

Hegesias, the Cyreniac philosopher. lived in the reign of Ptolemy Philadelphus and was a disciple of Paræbetes. In the main he taught the doctrines of Aristippus, the founder of his school, but he so ingrained in his pupils an indifference to life and a contempt for death, and at the same time the belief that it is idle to look for happiness where the soul is for ever imprisoned in a suffering frame, that he drove many of them to suicide. This gloomy tendency of his teaching became so alarming that Ptolemy is said to have put a stop to his classes. H. further maintained the wisdom of complete egoism and the instability and unreality of such figments of the brain as kindness and friendship.

Hegesias (*fl. c.* 250 B.C.), a Greek historian of Magnesia who enjoyed great repute as an orator. Cicero refers to him and mentions how he spoilt the pure Attic Greek by the heedless adoption of Asiatic idioms.

Hegesippus (*c.* 350 B.C.), an Athenian statesman and orator, lived in the time of Demosthenes. He was a staunch supporter of the anti-Macedonian policy of Demosthenes, and became one of the ambassadors to Macedonia in 343 B.C., whose mission was principally to discuss the restoration of Halonnesus. In connection with this subject, H. delivered his famous oration ' De Halonneso.'

Hegesippus (*c.* 120-180 A.D.), an early Christian writer, of Palestinian origin, lived under the emperors Antoninus Pius, Marcus Aurelius, and Commodus. It is a disputed question whether he was a Judaistic Christian or not. He wrote a treatise, *Five Memorials of Ecclesiastical Affairs*, on Christian literature, unity of church doctrine, paganism, heresy, and Jewish Christianity, fragments of which are found in Eusebius. From Eusebius we learn that H. journeyed to Rome, visiting Corinth on the way. He compiled a list of the Roman bishops down to Anicetus (156-67 A.D.), and is looked upon as the father of church history. *See* Routh's *Reliquiæ Sacræ*, and Grabe's *Spicilegium*, ii.

Hegira, *see* HEJIRA.

Hegyalja, or **Hegyallya,** a range of hills which runs southward between the valleys of the Bodrog and Hernad Rivers, in N. Hungary. An extreme offshoot of a Carpathian spur, they are in the midst of the district where the Tokay wines are produced.

Heiberg, Johan Ludvig (1791-1860), a Danish dramatist, was the son of the celebrated novelist who afterwards became Baroness Gyllembourg-Ehrensvärd, and of the political writer Peter H., who was exiled in 1800. He attended Copenhagen University, and began publishing in 1814, when he brought out two romantic dramas. However, both in his satire, *The Prophecy of Tycho Brahé*, and later, when he edited the *Flyvende Post* (1827-30), etc., he persistently mocked at the excesses and sentimentalism of Ingemann and other popular Romanticists. A comedy entitled *A Soul after Death* (1841) is one of the best things he wrote, whilst a little play called *The Nut Crackers* (1845) contains his most pungent satire. H. also produced a number of successful vaudevilles, imitated from the French, but set in a truly Danish atmosphere.

Heiberg, Peter Andreas (1758-1841),

a Danish author and dramatist, was for two years (1798-99) official translator at Copenhagen, but was banished for expressing revolutionary ideas in his poems, and accordingly went to Paris, where he passed the remainder of his life. Whilst Napoleon was emperor he was employed by Tallyrand, who profited by his firsthand acquaintance with the northern languages and peoples, and when the emperor was exiled, H. was allowed to retain his pension. *The Voyager to China* and *The Solemn Entry* were his most successful operettas. His best comedy is *Heckingborn;* and his *Lettres d'un Norvégien* (1822) and *Three Years in Bergen* were once widely read.

Heide, a tn. near the North Sea, 34 m. N.N.W. of Glückstat, in the prov. of Schleswig-Holstein, Prussia. Pop. 9815.

Heidegger, Karl Wilhelm (1788-1861), a German general and painter, was a native of Saaralben in Lorraine. He served with conspicuous success in the wars against Austria, Prussia, and Tyrol. These campaigns emphasised his soldierly qualities, but his exceptionable gift for art remained almost undeveloped until he retired to Munich. Many of his pictures hang in the National Gallery of this city, and here too (in the Glyptothek) may be seen his fine fresco after Cornelius, inscribed ' The Horses of the Sun.'

Heidelberg, a tn. on the l. b. of the Neckar some distance from its confluence with the Rhine, 54 m. by rail from Frankfort-on-Main, and 12 m. E.S.E. of Mannheim in the grand-duchy of Baden, Germany. The chief glory of the picturesque old city, which is guarded by the forest- and vine-clad slopes of Heiligenberg and Königsstuhl, is the castle, which looks down on the river from a summit of over 300 ft. Begun in the 13th century, the castle was still being enlarged and beautified in the 17th century, when it was partially blown up by the French in 1689. In 1764 it was struck by lightning and was reduced to its present state of graceful ruin. The huge vat, known as the Great Tun of H., which has a storage capacity of 46,732 gallons, is entered from the castle courtyard. The famous university was founded in 1385. From here during the Reformation period Calvinist doctrines were disseminated far and wide, but for the thirty years of war (1618-48) its history is almost a blank. To-day there are some 1900 students and 150 professors, whilst the valuable library, which Otto Henry began to collect, and which has at different times been housed both in the Vatican and at Paris, now contains 4000 MSS. and

500,000 volumes. There is an excellent observatory on the Königsstuhl (built in 1894), and among the antiquities of interest are the Protestant Peterskirche, where Jerome of Prague pinned up his theses in 1460, and the fine Gothic Heilige Geist Kirche, which also dates from the 15th century. H. is of some commercial importance, more especially as trunk lines radiate to Karlsruhe, Würzburg, Mannheim, and Spires, besides to Frankfurt: Pop. (1910) 55,991.

Heidelberg, the name of a tn. (58 m. S. by E. of Pretoria) and dist. of the Transvaal, S. Africa. The town lies 5029 ft. above the sea on the slopes of the Rand, and was founded in 1865. Besides being a favourite health resort it is a gold-mining centre for the Witwatersrand fields, etc. The Vaal R. skirts the district southward. Pop. 3220.

Heiden, a small inland spa with mineral springs, 10 m. N.N.W. of Appenzell, in the highlands of Switzerland and connected by rail with Rorschach. Pop. 3800.

Heidenheim, a tn. with cotton, woollen, tobacco, and machinery manufactories, besides cattle markets, in the kingdom of Würtemberg, Germany. It is 31 m. N. by E. of Ulm by rail. Pop. (1910) 17,780.

Heidenstam, Werner von (b. 1859), a Swedish man of letters, was at first identified with the school of realists, but later developed a clearly-marked originality. Two of his early works of fiction are *Endymion* (1889) and *Hans Alienus* (1892), but his masterpiece is *Karolinerna* (1897), part of which was translated into English in 1902 as *A King and his Campaigners*. Other of his works are *Vallfart och Vandringsår* (1888) and *Den Hellige Birgittas Pilegrimsfärd* (1901). H. has made a name for himself as a stylist.

Height and Weight. For tables and information relating to the development of both height and weight of children, *see* CHILD.

Heights, Measurement of, *see* BAROMETER, LEVELLING, THERMOMETER, and TRIGONOMETRY.

Heijn, or Heyn, Piet (1578-1629), a Dutch admiral, born at Delfshaven. He was early captured by the Spaniards, and served in the galleys for four years. For some years he was a merchant skipper, and in 1623, becoming vice-admiral of the Dutch W. India Co.'s service, he captured treasure galleons from the Spaniards. Appointed lieutenant-admiral of Holland to clear the North Sea and Channel of the Dunkirkers, who acted for Spain in the Netherlands, he died fighting victoriously against them. He is the traditional Dutch ' sea-dog ' of the 17th century.

Heilbron, a tn. of S. Africa in the Orange Free State, situated on the main route to Pretoria, and about 90 m. S.S.W. of that place. The neighbourhood is rich in iron ore, and there are coal mines. Pop. 2500.

Heilbronn, a manufacturing tn. of Würtemberg, Germany, on the Neckar, 33 m. by rail N. of Stuttgart, having fine views of mountains, the Black Forest, and the Vosges. It is an ancient town of historical interest, containing many old buildings, such as the Gothic church of St. Kilian, a Rathaus, the Götzenthurm, and Schönthaler Hof, as well as fine modern buildings. It has reminiscences of the Emperor Charles V., Götz von Berlichingen, Gustavus Adolphus, and Schiller. The chief manufactures are chemicals, machinery, silver articles, paper, sugar, salt, cigars, coffee, etc., and it trades largely in groceries, agricultural products, wood, and coal. Pop. 42,709.

' Heil Dir im Siegerkranz,' the Prussian national anthem. The words are by Balthasar Gerhard Schumacher, and the music is that of ' God save the King.' John Bull's *Ayre*, 1619, is an early version of the same tune, but the music as it is now sung first appeared in 1745, the reputed composer being Henry Carey.

Heiligenstadt, a tn. which manufs. cigars, paper, and cotton goods, 31 m. W.S.W. of Nordhausen in Saxony Prussia. Pop. 8218.

Heilsberg, a tn. with dye works and tanneries, 39 m. S. of Königsberg in E. Prussia, Germany. It is situated at the confluence of the Alle and Simser. There is an old castle. Pop. 6070.

Heilsbronn (also **Kloster-Heilsbronn**), a vil. 16m. S.W. of Nuremberg by rail, in Bavaria, Middle Franconia, Germany. It is famous for the Cistercian monastery which Bishop Otto founded in 1132, and which flourished until 1555. High interest attaches itself to a series of sepulchral monuments to members of the Hohenzollern family, and also to the church, which is a basilica in the Romanesque style.

Heimskringla, a chronicle compiled by Snorri Sturluson (q.v.).

Heine, Heinrich (date of birth doubtful, 1797-1801 ; d. 1856), a German poet and journalist, born at Düsseldorf of Jewish descent. He was editor at the Lyceum in Düsseldorf, and began life at Hamburg in the banking business of his uncle, Solomon H., with whose daughter Amalie he incidentally fell in love. On account of his failure in business, his uncle sent him to study law at Bonn (1819), where he gave signs of literary talent—A. W. von Schlegel being one of his earliest admirers and advisers. In the following year he left Bonn for Göttingen, but before long became entangled in a duel, and found it advisable to leave there also. Arriving in Berlin, he was soon an eager student of Hegel; his new environments and friends, including Fouqué, Rahel, Chamisso, and the Humboldts, stimulated his genius, and the first volume of *Gedichte* appeared in 1821. Turning again to law for a while—for the poor success of his tragedies *Almansor* and *William Ratcliff* (1823) had discouraged him— he graduated in 1825. The same year he spent a holiday in the Black Forest, thereby gaining the material for the first volume of *Reisebilder* (1826), which attracted much atten-

HEINRICH HEINE

tion by its originality and brilliance of style. Meanwhile, he had become baptised in the Christian faith, purely, however, for social purposes. The next few years were spent visiting London, Munich, and Italy; the remaining three volumes of *Reisebilder* were published, and also the *Buch der Lieder*, 1827. After a return visit to Berlin (1829) and a brief sojourn in Hamburg (1829-31), H. made Paris his home, quite severing his ties with Germany; and he only revisited it for short periods in 1843 and 1847. In Paris—' the New Jerusalem '—he was welcomed by the brilliant romantic circle — Hugo, Georges Land, De Musset, Gautier, Sainte-Beuve, Chopin, Berlioz, and Delacroix; and he settled down to journalism and letters, *De l'Allemagne*, 1835, and *Die Romantische Schule*, 1836, being his chief works of this period. He first met ' Mathilde '

in 1834—Eugénie Mirat (*d.* 1883), a shop-assistant—first his mistress and subsequently (1841) his wife; and, although it is hard to understand the fascination of a badly-educated, shallow-minded grisette, for H.'s sensitive artistic soul, their mutual devotion was certainly unwavering. During H.'s early years in Paris, his uncle had allowed him 4000 francs a year, but his growing separation from the Hamburg family made it necessary to look elsewhere for support, and from 1837-48 he was in receipt of a pension of 4800 francs from the French government—ostensibly as a political refugee, although he was not associated with the young German party whose revolutionary ideas had exiled them to Paris. This was the last step in his absolute self-alienation from his compatriots; his writings had already been condemned by the Frankfort Confederation Parliament (1835). *Der Salon* (4 vols.) appeared between this time and 1840, including his famous essay, ' German Philosophy and Literature,' written for the *Revue des Deux Mondes*. *Deutschland*, a political satire in verse, was published in 1844, and *Atta Troll*, ' the Swan song of Romanticism,' in 1847. From 1848-56 H. was a victim to spinal disease; but through the agonies of this last long illness, during which Mathilde nursed him devotedly, he retained full control of his mental faculties, as his *Romanzero* (1851) and *Neuste Gedichte* (1853-54) bear witness. His Memoirs were probably destroyed; at any rate, they were withheld from publication for family reasons, when in 1847 his Hamburg pension was restored; doubtful fragments were published in 1884, but their importance is as slender as their interest.

H.'s genius was moulded by his German birth, Jewish descent, and Greek culture; Nietzsche wrote that H. and himself were the greatest literary artists Germany had ever produced. He was the *grand maître* of lyric expression; for his sense of the tragic and the beautiful was passionately intense. Gautier says that ' Heine combined the purest Greek form with the most exquisite modern inspiration; he was a true Euphorion, the child of Faust and lovely Helen.' His work is the emotional panorama of a soul almost neurotic in its exquisite sensitiveness, its keen appreciation both of beauty and ugliness, of joy and despair. And his style is equally nervous in his portrayal of them both: on the one hand, the lyric-idealist, sometimes sentimental to a degree bordering on the ridiculous; on the other, the bitterly ironical cynic, often malicious in his satire, merciless and irreverent to the most sacred feelings of others. But, confining attention to broader issues, he was the first and greatest of a type of which, unfortunately, a mediocre multitude has since arisen: a self-centred, narrow soul, of artistic and irritable temperament, aiming at hedonism, fretting at the rein of reality, a poet of happy illusions that bring but sadness. Whilst expressing disfavour of Romanticism, he was one of its leading exponents; and whilst often coarse and brutal in his attitude towards love, he was yet conscious of the supreme poetry of passion. Indeed, it is as the poetic psychologist of love that H. is pre-eminent; his *Lyrisches Intermezzo* (1823) and other poems have a wonderful fascination for translators, and have been set to music by nearly all the great song-writers—Schumann above all, Liszt, Rubinstein, Brahms, and Grieg. H.'s idealism towards life was a sanguine hope for the brilliant and glorious future of mankind—a future to be realised by fostering imagination and æsthetic culture.

Bibliography. — Works: Strodtmann (21 vols.), 1861-66; Elster (7 vols.), 1887-90; French edition, by Heine, De Nerval, and others (14 vols.), 1852-68; English edition (Leland), (13 vols.), 1892-1905. Critiques: Matthew Arnold, *Essays in Criticism;* J. Legras (1897); Prof. Lichtenberger (1905); and Brandes (Danish, 1890; Eng. trans., 1906). Lives: W. Stigand (1875) and W. Sharp (1888).

Heineccius, Johann Gottlieb (1681-1741), a German jurist, born at Eisenberg and educated in theology and law at Leipzig and Halle. He was made professor at Halle of philosophy (1713), and of law (1720). He then went as professor of law to Franeker and to Frankfort-on-the-Oder, but in 1733 returned to Halle, where he died. His works display great learning, especially in Roman and German law. The chief are: *Historia Juris Civilis Romani, Elementa Juris Germanici,* and *Elementa Juris Naturæ et Gentium,* the last translated into English, (1763).

Heinicke, Samuel (1727-90), the founder of a deaf and dumb school in Germany. He was born at Nautschütz, Germany, and fought in the Seven Years' War, being taken prisoner at Pirna. He had previously supported himself by teaching, and had one deaf and dumb pupil in 1754. In 1768 he taught a deaf and dumb boy to talk, and ten years later founded at Leipzig the first deaf and dumb institution in Germany. He adopted the methods laid down in Amman's *Surdus loquens. See* Stötzner's *Samuel Heinicke,* 1870.

Heinrich, Karl Friedrich (1774-1838), a learned German critic, born in the duchy of Saxe-Gotha. He was successively professor of Greek and of eloquence at the universities of Kiel and Bonn. He produced editions of Juvenal and Persius and of Cicero's *De Re Publica,* and wrote an essay on Epimenides and his works, entitled *Epimenides ans Creta.*

Heinrich von Meissen (1260-1318), a German lyric poet and wandering singer, born at Meissen. In 1278 he was in the army of Hapsburg, and in 1286 at Prague. It is said of him that he founded the first school of Meister singers at Mainz. He died at Mainz, and the women of the city bore him to his grave at the cathedral; a monument was erected to his memory.

Heinse, Johann Jakob Wilhelm (1749-1803), a German novelist, translator, and art critic, born at Langewiesen, Thuringia. He was a disciple of Wieland, and had some influence on Goethe. He studied art in Italy, where he also translated Tasso's *Gerusalemme Liberata* and the *Orlando.* His masterpiece, *Ardinghello,* contains remarkable digressions on the plastic arts, and another romance, *Hildegard von Hohenthal,* gives his ideas on music. He served the elector of Mainz, and became state librarian. *See* Schober, *Heinse, sein Leben und Werke.*

Heinsius, Anthony (1641-1720), a Dutch statesman and confidential agent of William, Prince of Orange, born at Delft, and studied law at Leyden. In 1688 he was grand pensionary of Holland and guided Dutch politics until his death. In his zeal for his prince and Protestantism, he incurred the enmity of France and was threatened with the bastile.

Heinsius, Daniel (1580-1655), a Dutch classical scholar, born at Ghent and educated at Franeker and Leyden, where he was a favourite pupil of Scaliger, and later became professor of politics and history, after some years as classical professor. He wrote good Latin and Dutch verses, and produced valuable editions of Theocritus, Bion, Moschus, Aristotle, Hesiod, and of Horace, Seneca, Terence, and Livy. He also produced Latin *Orationes* and other learned works, as well as a Dutch tragedy, *The Massacre of the Innocents,* and edited Scaliger's *Epistolæ.* He was a leading figure of the Dutch Renaissance.

Heinsius, Nikolaas (1620–81), a traveller, scholar, diplomat, and poet, son of Daniel, born and educated at Leyden. He obtained several valuable classical manuscripts from libraries of France and Italy, and published editions of Virgil, Ovid, Prudentius, Vellius Paterculus, and Valerius Flaccus. In 1650 he served Christina of Sweden; in 1854 became the Dutch minister at Stockholm, and in 1669 visited Russia.

Heir. The H. of English law is the person who takes by descent (q.v.) the lands, tenements, and hereditaments (q.v.) of another, the ancestor. There are also Hs. by custom, who are entitled by certain customary modes of descent to succeed to customary freeholds, a peculiar species of copyhold tenure prevailing in the N. of England, and within manors of the tenure of ancient demesne, or tenure by copy of court roll, but not expressed to be at the will of the lord of the manor. As noticed in the article DESCENT, the H. is an uncertain person till the death of the ancestor, on the principle that no one is the H. of a living person, and the maxim that Deus, non homo, facit hæredem (God, not man, chooseth the heir). Before the ancestor's death, a person can only be an heir-apparent, i.e. one whose right is certain and indefeasible, provided he outlives the ancestor and the latter dies without making a will at all, or dies intestate as to some part of the real property; or an heir-presumptive, i.e. one who, if the ancestor should die immediately, would succeed as H., but whose right to succeed may be defeated by the contingency of a nearer H. being born: e.g. an only daughter's presumptive right would be defeated by the birth of a son. (For the rules of descent in English law to real property, see under DESCENT.) By the Land Transfer Act, 1897, the ancestor's real estate, including legal and equitable estates in fee simple (q.v.), and estates held pur autre vie (i.e. for so long as another shall live), now vest after his death in his executors (q.v.) or administrators in the same way as chattels real or other personalty, and the personal representatives have the same power to dispose of such estates to pay debts, legacies, etc. (if necessary) as they have over personalty. After the expiry of one year from the death of the ancestor, the realty is conveyed either by the personal representatives or by order of court to the H. The Land Transfer Act does not apply to copyholds or customary freeholds, and therefore these vest directly in the H., and it is the better opinion that a feetail (see ENTAIL; ESTATE) is not affected by that Act.

Heirloom (A.-S. loom, limb or member). Hs. are those personal chattels which, by special custom,

descend on death with the freehold lands of inheritance with the occupation of which they are connected. Ordinary chattels devolve on the executor for distribution amongst the next of kin (see DISTRIBUTIONS, STATUTES OF), and the above-noted special devolution of Hs. is indicated by the name itself, which, according to Blackstone, is derived from Anglo-Saxon loom, a limb or member, and signifies a limb of the inheritance. Deer in a park, fish in a pond, doves in a dove-cot, accompany heritable lands, and, similarly, crown jewels are said to be Hs. Charters, court-rolls (evidences of title), and deeds, chests in which muniments of title are contained, also pass as Hs., and also things affixed to the freehold in such a way that they cannot be severed without damage, e.g. chimney pieces, benches, etc. Monuments or tombstones in a church, and coat-armour, pennons, and other insignia of honour of the ancestor, although hung up in a church, pass to his heir. Hs. may not be devised by will away from the heir, but under the Settled Land Acts, the court may sanction the sale (or purchase) of Hs. The court will not, however, sanction a sale merely to condone the extravagance of a tenant-for-life. On the principle that equity will construe an executory (q.v.) trust in such a way as to subordinate language to intent, it seems that a testator may effectually direct almost any chattels to be held as Hs., so that the first person taking under the gift will hold not absolutely but as trustee for himself and his successors.

Heissen, a vil. 3 m. W.S.W. of Essen in Rhineland, Prussia. Pop. 11,400.

Heister, Lorenz (1683-1758), a German surgeon, born at Frankfort-on-Main. For several years he was a professor at Amsterdam, and after serving with the Dutch army, was professor at Altorf and at Helmstadt, where he died. His works include Compendium institutionum sive fundamentorium medicinæ, 1736; Compendium medicinæ practicæ, 1754, etc.

Hejaz, or **Hedjaz** (' the land of pilgrimage '), a Turkish prov. and vilayet of Western Arabia. It extends along the N. coast of the Red Sea, from the Gulf of Akaba to the S. of Taif, and is bounded by Syria on the N., the Nefud Desert and Nejd on the E., and on the S. by Asir. Its length is 750 m., and its greatest width 200 m. It is stony and altogether desolate in character. The Tehama range traverses it, of which the chief summits are Jebel Shar (7000 ft.) and Jebel Radhwa (6000 ft.). The two sacred cities of Mecca and

Medina are contained in H., and also the ports of Yembo and Jedda. Pop. 300,000.

Hejira, Hejra, or Hegira (' flight,' from Arabic *hajara*, to go away), signifies the flight of Mohammed from Mecca on Sept. 13, 622 A.D. Since the institution of the new Moslem calendar by Caliph Omar (640), the Mohammedan era has dated from this event, being distinguished by the letter A.H. (*anno hegiræ*). The Mohammedan year is a lunar one, and therefore nearly eleven days shorter than ours. Consult Hughes' *Dictionary of Islam.*

Hekla, or Hecla, a volcanic mountain in Iceland, 68 m. E. of Reykjavik. Elevation, 5108 ft. There have been eighteen eruptions since the 9th century, the last being in 1878. By the outbreak of 1845, fine lava ashes and dust was scattered as far as the Orkney Islands, 500 m.away.

Hel, or Hela, in Scandinavian mythology, was the daughter of Loki and of the giantess Angevrboda. She was the goddess of the dead, and lived below the roots of the sacred ash Yggdrasil. She ruled over the nine worlds of Helheim, the abode of dead, and of the old and sick. After the introduction of Christianity, her dwelling-place became synonymous with hell, the abode of the wicked dead.

Helbra, a vil. of Prussia in Saxony, situated in the lake circle of Mansfeld and in the district of Asleben. Pop. 7000.

Helder, a seaport at the northern extremity of Holland, situated on the Marsdiep at the entrance of the Zuider Zee. There is an excellent harbour at Niewe Diep, the eastern side of the town, and there are fine embankments. It is an important naval and military station; the Dutch naval cadet school and Willemsoord, the stores of the Dutch navy, are near by, and there is a strong garrison. H. has also a meteorological observatory, lighthouse, zoological station, and town hall, etc. It was first fortified by Napoleon in 1811. The Dutch fleet, under De Ruyter and Tromp, defeated the English off the coast in 1673. Pop. (1910) 27,159.

Helderberg Formation, called after the Helderberg range in the E. of New York State. It is a division of the Silurian strata, and is on the horizon of the English Ludlow Beds. It consists of many characteristic fossils, such as Orthoceras, Pentamerus, Bronteus, and includes thick limestone, sandstones, and shales. It covers large areas in New York, Maine, and Nova Scotia.

Helen, or Helena, the heroine of the Trojan War and the most beauti-

ful of women. She was the daughter of Zeus and Leda, and the sister of Castor and Pollux. She was carried off by Theseus to Attica, but was rescued by her twin brothers. She chose Menelaus out of many suitors, but subsequently deserted her husband and fled with Paris to Troy. This led to the Trojan War, which lasted for ten years. After the death of Paris she married his brother Deiphobus, whom she later betrayed to the Greeks, and returned with Menelaus to Sparta. According to one tradition, on the death of her husband she married Achilles and lived with him in Leuce.

Helena: 1. The county seat of Phillips co., Arkansas, U.S.A., situated on the Mississippi at the foot of Crowly's Ridge. 50 m. S.W. of Memphis, Tennessee. It has a busy trade in cotton-seed products and lumber. Pop. (1910) 8772. 2. The county seat of Lewis and Clark co., Montana, U.S.A., situated at an elevation of 4000 ft. on the Rocky Mts., 50 m. N.E. of Butte. It is the seat of Montana Wesleyan College and of the Roman Catholic institutions of St. Aloysius and St. Vincent. It is a large commercial centre, with lumber and quartz mills, breweries, smelters, and numerous factories. Pop. (1910) 12,515.

Helena, St. (Flavia Julia Helena) (*c.* 247-*c.* 327), the wife of Constantius Chlorus,and the mother of Constantine the Great. She is supposed to have discovered the holy rood and sepulchre of our Lord at Jerusalem (326). Her festival is celebrated on Aug. 18. Several other saints of the Catholic Church have this name, among them being Olga, wife of Grand-Duke Igor, who changed her name to H. at her baptism (955).

Helena (*d.* 359 A.D.), the daughter of Constantine the Great and of Fausta. She married her cousin Julian, whom her brother Constantius II. made Cæsar at Milan (355). Her only son was supposed to have been killed at birth through the instigation of the Empress Eusebia.

Helensburgh, a police burgh and watering place on the Firth of Clyde, Scotland, in the co. of Dumbarton, at the mouth of the Gare Loch, opposite Greenock. It is the terminus of the Glasgow and Highland branch of the North British Railway, and the eastern terminus of the West Highland Railway. Pop. (1911) 8529.

Helenus, a soothsayer of Greek legend, the son of Priam and Hecuba. He foretold the fall of Troy to the enemy, and after the siege saved the life of Pyrrhus by warning him not to return home by sea. He accompanied Pyrrhus to Epirus, over part of which he ruled, and Pyrrhus gave him Andromache, the widow of Hector.

Helgoland, *see* HELIGOLAND.

Heliade-Radulescu, Joan (1802-72), a Roumanian author, born at Targo-vistea, and educated under Lazare at Saint Sava. He founded the first Roumanian literary journals : *Curierul Roman,* 1831-48, and *Curierul de Ambe Sexe,* 1840-44. He took a prominent part in the Revolution of 1848, after which he was for a time banished. Among his works are *Mihaida,* 1846, a national epic, and *Mircea,* 1844, a heroic drama.

Heliand, The (O.E. *Hœlend,* Saviour), a 9th - century old Saxon poem of the life of Christ. The best texts are the Cotton MS. in the British Museum, and the Munich MS., which are printed side by side in Siever's edition, 1877. From internal evidence modern scholars have concluded that it was written by the author of the fragments of the Genesis. Consult Siever's *Der Heliand und die angelsächsische,* 1875.

Helianthemum, a genus of Cistaceæ, is to be found in Europe, America, and round the Mediterranean; the species are often known popularly as rock-roses. *H. vulgare,* the common rock-rose, is a native of Europe, and is found in Britain in dry hilly pastures; the stamens, if touched in the sunshine, spread slowly, and lie down upon the petals. *H. canum,* the hoary sun-rose, has small yellow flowers, and occurs rarely in Britain.

Helianthus, *see* JERUSALEM ARTICHOKE and SUNFLOWER.

Helicidæ (Gk. ἕλιξ, a spiral), the name of a large family of pulmonate gasteropods, of which the typical genus is *Helix,* the Snail (*q.v.*).

Helicon, a mountain range in Bœotia, Greece, situated between the Gulf of Corinth and Lake Copais. It is celebrated in classical literature as the abode of the Muses; near by were the fountains, Aganippe and Hippocrene, which were said to give poetic inspiration. The western summit, Palæovoun, rises to 5000 ft.; the eastern summit is called Zagora.

Helictis, the name given to a genus of carnivorous mammals belonging to the family Mustelidæ, or badgers; they are natives of E. Asia, and all the species are arboreal. Their ears are small, and the nose is grooved; the palms are naked, but the soles of the feet are hairy. Many of them are brightly coloured, *H. subanrantiaca* being black and orange.

Helier, St., *see* JERSEY.

Heligoland, or Helgoland, an island of 'Germany, in the North Sea, lying 40 m. N.W. of the mouth of the Elbe, and 28 m. from the nearest point in the mainland. It was once a British possession (1807-90), and was ceded to Germany (1890) in return for concessions in E. Africa, being formally incorporated in the Prussian province of Schleswig-Holstein in 1892. The island is a mile long, its greatest breadth being less than a third of a mile. It is a rocky plateau, with a sand bank, the Dünsen-Insel, off the E. coast. It is a popular bathing resort. Area 130 acres. Pop. (1910) 3415.

Heliocentric (Gk. ἥλιος, sun), a term in astronomy, having regard to the sun as the centre of reference ; opposed to geocentric (Gk. γή, earth), referring to the earth as centre.

Heliodorus of Emesa in Syria, the earliest of Greek romance writers. He is known by his *Æthiopica,* the MS. of which was discovered in 1526 in the library of Matthias Corvinus, and was printed in 1534. It is in ten books, and narrates the story of the lovers Theagenes and Chariclea. Consult Hirschig, *Scriptores Erotici,* 1856, and an English translation in Bohn's Classical Library.

Heliogabalus (Emperor of Rome), *see* ELAGABALUS.

Heliograph, an instrument used for signalling swiftly between two distant points, by means of flashing the sun's rays from the face of a mirror. The flashes are made to follow each other in accordance with a pre-arranged signal code. The mirror, from which a part of the mercury back has been removed, is mounted on a tripod and two sights are provided in front with a screen. The sun ray is then directed through both sights, and the flash can be seen at a distance of many miles, the range of the H. flash depending upon the size of the mirror. If the mirror is directed at exactly the required spot, its flashes cannot be.read at a distance of more than 10 yds. on either side if the distance away is 1 m., or for more than 50 yds. at a distance of 2 m.

Heliometer, an astronomical instrument for measuring the diameter of celestial bodies or their distance one from another. It was invented by Fraunhofer in 1814 and, as its name indicates, was first used to obtain solar measurements. The H. is an equatorially mounted telescope with its object-glass divided into two movable halves (as shown in diagram). The largest H. is an 8½ in. at the Vienna Observatory (Küffer). Directions for use are thus given in the manual *Astronomy* by the present astronomer-royal, F. W. Dyson, F.R.S. ' If,' he says, ' two stars are looked at, and the glass is turned so that the direction in which the halves are separated is parallel to the line joining the stars, there will be seen, as in the diagram, four images in a straight line, viz. A and B, the images of the two stars formed by one half of the glass, and A¹ B¹, the images formed

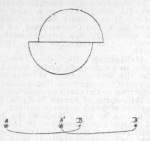

HELIOMETER

by the other half. The halves of the glass are separated by a distance AA¹ or BB¹. If they are now still further separated till A¹ coincides exactly with B, the distance between the stars is exactly equal to the amount by which the two halves of the glass are separated.'

Heliopolis (' city of the sun '): 1. an ancient city of Lower Egypt, called in the Bible On. It stood 5 m. E. of the Pelusiac branch of the Nile at the apex of the Delta. It was the chief seat of the Egyptian sunworship, and was famous for its schools of philosophy and astronomy. The site of the ancient temple is marked by a red granite obelisk. *See* Bædeker's *Egypt.* 2. The Greek name for Baalbek (*q.v.*).

Heliopora, the name of a genus of Cœlenterata belonging to the family Helioporidæ, and commonly called sun-corals. *H. cœrulea* is the only species among recent corals, but probably many more existed in earlier periods. They are found in the warm, shallow waters of the tropical Pacific and Indian Oceans, and usually from stony masses, 5 or 6 ft. in diameter, on the inside of the reef. These corals are distinguished by their bluish tinge.

Helios, the Greek god of the sun, known to the Romans as Sol. He was the son of Hyperion and Thea and the brother of Selene and Eos. In Homer (*Odyssey*, viii.) he is described as a god who rises from Oceanus in the east, traverses the heavens, seeing and hearing everything on his way, and descends to Oceanus on the west. Later writers tell of a magnificent palace in the east from which he comes forth in a fiery chariot drawn by four horses, and of another palace in the west. His horses grazed on the islands of the Blessed. The island on Thrinacia was sacred to him; there his daughters Phætusa and Lampeta tended his flocks. He was worshipped throughout Greece and in the island of Rhodes, where the mighty Colossus was erected to him.

Helioscope, a kind of telescope, particularly adapted, by means of blackened or smoked glasses which only partially reflect the light, for viewing the sun.

Heliotrope and **Turnsole** are popular names applied to several species of *Heliotropium* (*q.v.*). The H. plant most commonly cultivated in Britain is *H. Peruvianum*. Winter H. is a common name of *Petasites fragrans*, a sweet-smelling species of Compositæ.

Heliotrope, *see* BLOODSTONE.

Heliotropism. The direction of the rays of light affects the position of plant members, and it is these phenomena which are termed H. Stems and leaves grow towards the source of light, as may commonly be seen in window plants, and are said to be positively heliotropic and members, such as roots, which grow away from the light, are said to be negatively heliotropic. Young growing parts of plants respond more quickly to light than older parts.

Heliotropium, a genus of boraginaceous plants, contains numerous species which inhabit tropical lands and are often cultivated because of their fragrant blossoms. *H. Peruvianum*, the Peruvian heliotrope, turnsole, or cherry-pie, is a shrub growing one or two feet high and the scent of the flower greatly resembles that of the vanilla; it is a native of Peru. *H. villosum* is found in Greece, and *H. Europœum* in S. Europe and the Caucasus.

Heliozoa, the name given to a group of Protozoa commonly called the sun - animalcules. They are divided into Aphrothoraca, which have no skeleton, and are sometimes invested with a gelatinous membrane; Chlamydophora, which have always a gelatinous envelope ; Chalarothoraca, which have a skeleton of silicious spicules ; and Desmothoraca, which have a stalked or unstalked shell with numerous pores. H. are widely distributed, and are both fresh water and marine.

Helium (from Gk. ἥλιος, the sun), a rare gaseous element. Lockyer observed in 1868 a bright yellow line in the spectrum of the solar chromosphere close to but not identical in position with the D line of sodium. He ascribed it to a hypothetical element *helium.* Hillebrand had noticed that an inert gas was evolved when the mineral uraninite was treated with acid. Ramsay, repeating these experiments, found that the inert gas refused to combine with oxygen, and on submitting it to spectroscopic examination he saw that the spectrum was characterised by a bright yellow line coinciding with the new line discovered by Lockyer in the solar spectrum. The name helium was, therefore, adopted for the new gas. H. is abundant in many minerals, all of which contain uranium and bharium as important constituents. The richest known source is thorianite, which is mainly thorium oxide, and contains about 9·5 c.c. per grain. H. is also present in the gases which escape from the water of hot springs and in the atmosphere, of which it constitutes four parts in a million. To prepare H. from thorianite, the mineral is treated with nitric acid, when the H. is liberated together with hydrogen, oxides of carbon, and a trace of nitrogen. The hydrogen is removed by sparking the mixture with oxygen, and the remaining impurities are removed by Dewar's method of absorption with charcoal cooled in liquid air. The H. alone is unabsorbed by the charcoal, and it can be pumped off in a state of perfect purity.

Properties.—It is chemically inert. Its density is 1·98, referred to hydrogen as 1. The ratio of its specific heats is 1·66, so that its molecules are monatomic. The atomic weight is, therefore, double the density, *i.e.* almost 4. Its solubility in water is less than that of any known gas. It approximates more closely to the ideal gas than hydrogen. In 1908 Kamerlingh Onnes of Leyden University succeeded in liquefying it. Its boiling point is 4·3° abs., the density of the liquid is ·154, and its critical temperature is 5° abs. The α-particle expelled by radium, thorium, uranium, and actinium is identical with the atom of H. This conclusion is based on the following experimental evidence: (1) All α-particles have the same mass and differ only in their velocity of expulsion. This mass has been measured, and has been found to be the same as the mass of the H. atom; (2) The 'emanation' from radium which expels α-particles was stored in a thin-walled but perfectly gas-tight glass tube, enclosed within a wider vessel. After some days the gas in the outer vessel was found to contain H. It was proved that when H. was stored in the inner tube, none passed through the glass into

the outer vessel. In this experiment the velocity of expulsion of the α-particle was so great that the particle could get through thin glass. When it was brought to comparative rest in the space surrounding the thin glass vessel, its properties were identical with those of the atom of H. There is a good deal of evidence that one atom of a radio-active substance expels but one α-particle at each disintegration. Hence the change from radium to H. may be expressed quantitatively thus:

$$226 = 222 + 4$$
Radium = Emanation + Helium.

The numbers denote the atomic weights.

Helix, the snail, the typical genus of Helicidæ, and contains several thousand species ; *H. hortensis* is the common European snail, and *H. pomatia,* also found in England, is called the Roman snail.

Hell, popularly conceived of as the place in which the finally impenitent suffer eternal torment, is in the A.V. the English rendering of several Hebrew and Greek words with distinct connotations. Hence very considerable confusion has arisen. The various words represented thus are the Hebrew Sheōl (שְׁאוֹל), and the Greek words Hades (ᾅδης), Tartarus (τάρταρος), and Gehenna (γέεννα). It will be well first to trace slightly the development of the Hebrew conception of Sheōl, translated also in the A.V. sometimes as 'grave' and three times as 'pit.' The earlier view is well represented in passages of the Psalms xxxi. and lxxxviii., from which we see that Sheōl is conceived of as a region outside the jurisdiction of Yahweh, and as independent of His existence. Sometimes the dead are here regarded as cognisant of earthly affairs, sometimes as totally ignorant of them. According to the former of these views, which is also the earlier, the dead retain their self-consciousness, and the state of affairs in Sheōl is a shadowy reproduction of the earthly life. According to the later view, which is fully elucidated in the Book of Job (especially chaps.vii., xiv., and xxvi.),Sheōl is equivalent to utter destruction. It is the land of sleep, of utter forgetfulness, and silence. The dead are ignorant of what passes on earth, and are unable to affect its affairs. The same view is put forth in Eccles. ix., where vv. 5 and 10 insist on the fact that all knowledge has forsaken the dead. Considerable development of eschatological conceptions is seen, however, in the postexilic writings, and the doctrine of the resurrection comes into prominence, partly as a result of Persian influence. Two passages, in particular, are of importance as containing a clear enunciation of this doctrine, viz. Isa. xxvi. 1-19, and Dan. xii. By the 2nd century B.C. the general conception of the abodes of the departed has taken a more clearly-defined form, and Gehenna is the name given to the final abode of the wicked, where they suffer endless torments by fire, while Sheôl is an intermediate state for both righteous and wicked, divided into four parts, two for the wicked, two for the righteous. The Sadducees, however, still sustained the ancient denial of a resurrection. In the N.T., Hades is used for the place of departed spirits, Gehenna for that of endless (αἰώνιος) punishment for the wicked. Tartarus occurs once (2 Pet. ii. 4) as the abode of the fallen angels. Much controversy has gone on in recent years as to whether the Greek adjective αἰώνιος is equivalent to eternal in the modern sense of the term, that is to say, never-ending. The noun αἰων is frequently used for a long ' period of time,' and from the time of Origen onward, there have been those who held the opinion that ultimately the punishment of the most wicked and even of the devils, would have an end, and that thus all would be saved. This is not, however, the common conception of the Early or Mediæval Church, for here we find phrases which contain no ambiguity. Eternal punishment is never-ending, and there were not wanting some who could say that the joys of the blessed were enhanced by the sight of the sufferings of the damned. This view, found in the works of St. Thomas Aquinas, is also to be seen in the writings of Protestant divines. The pains of H. are conjectured to be both physical and spiritual, the latter consisting chiefly of the torments of despair and remorse. Writers and painters have shown a somewhat more becoming modesty than did those of the middle ages, and have not given their imagination so loose a rein in picturing these scenes.

Hell, Maximilien (1720-92), an astronomer, born at Chemnitz, in Hungary. After lecturing in mathematics at Klausenburg, he was appointed director of the observatory at Vienna in 1755. At the invitation of the King of Denmark, he visited Lapland (1768-69) to observe the transit of Venus and to study the direction of the magnetic pole. His chief publications are : *Ephemerides astronomicæ*, 1757-86 ; *De Satellite Veneris*, 1765 ; and *De Transitu Veneris ante discum solis*, 1770.

Hellanicus, or **Lesbos** (*c.* 495-411 B.C.), an early Greek historian, born at Mitylene in Lesbos. The

works attributed to him are : *The Priestess of Hera at Argos; Atthis; Carneonicæ*, etc., in all about thirty chronological and historical works. Consult Müller, *Fragmenta historicorum Grœcorum ;* and Bury, *Ancient Greek Historians*, 1909.

Hellas, a dist. of Southern Thessaly, often identified with Phthiotis. The Greeks, who called themselves Ἕλληνες (Hellenes), after their mythical founder Ἕλλην (Hellen), son of Deucalion and Pyrrha, came to use H. to denote all the lands on which they settled, but more particularly to the mainland of the Peloponnesus.

Hellebore, the popular name or species of the ranunculaceous genus *Helleborus*, found only in Europe. They are sometimes employed in medicine, and when used in moderation they possess stimulating properties; in large doses they act as a fatal poison. *H. viridis*, the green H., is indigenous to Britain; is herbaceous below, shrubby above, and bears pale green flowers. *H. niger*, the Christmas rose, has white flowers which turn green after fertilisation. A species of Liliaceæ, *Veratrum album*, is known as the white H. root.

Hellefors, a com. and tn. of Sweden in the prov. of Orebro. Pop. 5000.

Hellemmes-Lille, a com. of France in the dept. of Nord and in the arron. of, and 2¾ m. from the tn. of, Lille. There are manufs. of cotton and woollen goods, vannerie, and brasseries. The town has a fine 17th century church. Pop. 11,000.

Hellen, in Greek legend, was the son of Deucalion and Pyrrha. He ruled over Phthiotis and gave to his subjects the name of Hellenians. His three sons, Æolus, Dorus, and Xuthus, gave their names to the three nations, Æolians, Dorians, and Ionians.

Hellendoorn, a com. 18½ m. N.E. of Zutfen, in Overijssel, Netherlands. Pop. 9000.

Hellenism. The term was made popular in England by Matthew Arnold, who used it to denote the principle of classic purity in art, as opposed to Hebraism, which expresses itself as ' romantic ' exuberance in art. The word is more correctly applied by Droysen to the phase of Greek culture prevalent in the 2nd and 3rd centuries among certain Ἑλληνίσται of Alexandria, people, not Greek by birth, who had adopted the language and customs of ancient Greece. The Hellenistic language is a peculiar form of Greek, with many Hebrew and Aramaic words and idioms. *See* a very comprehensive article in the *Encyclopædia Britannica*, and Wendlanæ's *Hellenistischrömische*

Kultur in ihren Beziehungen zu Zudentum u. Christentum, 1907.

Hellenist (from Gk. ἑλληνίζειν, to imitate the Greeks), a term applied to a person who adopts the manners and customs of ancient Greece. It was first applied, during the 1st and 2nd centuries, to the Jews of Alexandria, who laid aside the language and customs of the Hebrews for all the usages of the Greeks. *See also* HELLENISM.

Heller, Stephen (1815 – 88), an Austrian musical composer, born at Pesth. At the age of nine he made some sensation as a boy pianist, and was sent to study under Czerny at Vienna. During his boyhood he made musical tours through Hungary and Germany, and in 1830 settled in Augsburg. Eight years later he went to study in Paris, and became one of the set of which Chopin, Liszt, and Hallé were prominent members. He wrote entirely for the pianoforte and still retains his popularity with amateur players. H. visited England in 1849 and 1862. Consult his *Life* by Barbedette, 1876.

Hellespont, *see* DARDANELLES.

Hellevoetsluis, *see* HELVOETSLUYS.

Hell Gate, or Hurl Gate, was named ' Helle Gat ' by the Dutch colonists because of the perils it offered to navigation. It is a pass which formerly blocked the N.E. entrance to the harbour of New York from Long Island in the East R. John Newton (1823-95) was the engineer, who, at the instance of the Federal government, conducted the blasting operations in 1885, which removed the dangerous reefs of H. G. and deepened the narrows at that point.

Hellin, a tn. of Spain in Albacete, situated near the R. Mundo in a rich wine- and oil-yielding country. There are sulphur mines and warm sulphurous springs, which were known to the Romans. The industries include potteries and manufs. of leather and coarse cloth. Pop. 13,000.

Hell's Glen, a narrow glen of Argyllshire, Scotland, which stretches from N.W. to S.E. between Loch Goil and Loch Fyne, and running parallel with Glencroe.

Helmbrechts, a tn. of Germany in Bavaria, situated in the gov. of Upper Franconia and the circle of Münchberg, 20 m. N.E. of Bayreuth. Pop. 5444.

Helmet, a protective covering for the head. At the time of the Norman Conquest a conical H. with nasal was worn with or without safeguards for the ears and nape of the neck. The casque was usually made of strong hide, strengthened with small iron plates. In the 11th century a mail hood was attached to the casque. A century or so later a *beaume* of heavy iron was frequently worn over a light basinet. The knights of the 14th century wore long pointed viziers, that could be moved up and down, while the chain mail was worn low over the shoulders. They bore their crests high on their Hs. The *salade* or *sallet* of the next century had a low, rounded crown and a long neck-guard. Other variations of the H. are the *armet, burgonet, morion*, and *cabasset*. *See* Demmin's *Arms and Armour*, and Hewitt's *Ancient Armour and Weapons in Europe*.

Helmet-shell, the name given to members of the genus *Cassis*, gasteropod molluscs belonging to the family Cassididæ, found in tropical seas in the Mediterranean. They resemble whelks in appearance, having thick heavy shells with prominent edges; some species attain considerable size, and, as they are composed of differently coloured layers, they are much used in the manufacture of cameos. *C. madagascarensis* is the largest of these, and *C. rufa* and *C. cornuta* are also commonly used.

Helmholtz, Hermann Ludvig Ferdinand von (1821-94), a German philosopher and man of science, born at Potsdam, near Berlin. His father was a teacher of philology and philosophy in the gymnasium; his mother, a Hanoverian lady, a lineal descendant of the great Quaker, William Penn. H. was delicate in early life and became a student by habit; he soon showed mathematical powers. In later years his attention was directed to higher mathematics by force of circumstances. He could not afford a purely scientific career, so he became surgeon in the Prussian army, In 1842 he wrote a thesis, in which he announced the discovery of nerve cells in ganglia; this was his first work, and from 1842-94, the year of his death, scarcely a year passed without several important papers on scientific subjects from his pen. In 1849 he became professor of physiology in Königsberg; in 1855 he removed to the chair of physiology in Bonn; in 1858 he became professor of physiology in Heidelberg, and in 1871 he was called to occupy the chair of physics in Berlin. To this professorship was added, in 1887, the post of director of the physico-technical institute at Charlottenburg, near Berlin, and he held the two positions together till his death.

Helminthology (Gk. ἕλμινς, worm, and λέγειν, speak), the science which treats of parasitic worms.

Helmond, a tn. of N. Brabant, Netherlands; on the Zuid Willems Canal, 23 m. N.W. of Venlo. It has manufs. of textiles, etc. Pop. 14,767.

Helmont, Johann Baptist van (1577-1644), a Belgian chemist, born at Brussels; educated at Louvain, where he became professor of surgery. For some years he devoted himself to the study of mysticism, but was turned to chemistry and natural philosophy by the works of Paracelsus. He spent some years in France, Switzerland, and England, but in 1609 settled near Vilvorde and devoted himself to chemical investigations. He made a special study of 'gases,' and established the present scientific sense of the word 'gas,' and investigated the chemical properties of the fluids of the human body. His chief work *Ortus Medicinæ* was published by his son in 1648.

Helmstedt, a tn. of Brunswick, Germany, 24 m. S.E. of Brunswick. It has manufactures of machinery, pottery, woollens, etc., and near it are valuable mineral springs. It grew up in the 9th century round the monastery of St. Ludger, and from 1575-1809 was famous for its university, founded by Duke Julius. Pop. 16,421.

Helmund, Helmand, or Helmend, a riv. of Afghanistan, rising in the Koh-i-Baba chain, S. of the Hindu Kush, and flowing S.W., W., and N.W. into the lake of Hamun, Seistan, or Savaran, near the Persian frontier, after a course of 680 m. Numerous tributaries flow into it from Southern Afghanistan. In its lower reaches it is wide and deep, but dries up at certain seasons. The water-power is largely used for mills.

Helm Wind, a wind which, under certain conditions, blows over the escarpment of the Pennines, near Cross Fell, from the eastward, when a helm (helmet) cloud covers the summit. The helm bar is a roll of cloud that forms in front of it to leeward.

Helobieæ (Gk. ἕλος, marsh, and βίος, life), the second cohort of monocotyledons in Eugler's classification of plants. Various orders are assigned to it by different botanists, but the chief are Naiadaceæ, Butomaceæ, Alismaceæ, and Juncaginaceæ.

Heloderma (Gk. ἥλος, nail, stud, and δέρμα, skin), the name given to the single genus of Helodermatidæ, a family of poisonous lizards found in N. America. They have fang-like teeth, and the poison-glands are situated in the base of the lower jaw. *H. horridum*, the Mexican caltetepan, is a squat, repulsive animal, dark brown and yellow in colour; *H. suspectum*, the Gila monster, inhabits New Mexico and Arizona, and is partial to dry localities.

Heloise, see ABELARD.

Helosciadium, a genus of umbelliferous plants, consists of a very few species found in brooks and ditches. It is now generally included in the genus *Apium* (*q.v.*).

Helotidæ, the name of a family of coleopterous insects consisting of a single genus; they are found in Japan, the Malay Peninsula, and E. Africa. They closely resemble the Nitidulidæ, but are distinguished by their coxal structure; their form is oblong and much sculptured on the metallic upper surface.

Helots (Gk. εἵλωτις or εἱλῶται), the serfs of the ancient Spartans. The word was derived in antiquity from the town of Helos in Laconia, but is more probably connected with ἕλος, a fen, or with the root of ἑλεῖν, to capture. Some scholars suppose them to be of the Achæan race, but they were more probably the aborigines of Laconia, who had been enslaved by the Achæans before the Dolian conquest. After the second Messenian War the conquered Messenians were reduced to the status of H., from which Epaminondas liberated them three centuries later, after the battle of Leuctra (371 B.C.). The H. were state slaves to the soil and assigned to individual Spartiates to till their holdings. Their masters could neither emancipate them nor sell them off the land, and they were under an oath not to raise the rent payable yearly in kind by the H. In time of war they served as light-armed troops or as rowers in the fleet. From the Peloponnesian War onwards, they were employed as heavy infantry, and distinguished bravery was rewarded by emancipation.

Helpmakaar, a tn. of Klip R. dist., Natal, S. Africa, 80 m. N. of Pietermaritzburg. Formerly a British military post, it had some importance during the Zulu War (1879) and the Boer War (1900-2).

Helps, Sir Arthur (1813-75), an English writer and clerk of the Privy Council, youngest son of Thomas H., a London merchant. Educated at Eton and at Trinity College, Cambridge, coming out thirty-first wrangler in the mathematical tripos in 1835. He was recognised by the ablest of his contemporaries there as a man of superior gifts. As a member of the Conversazione Society he was associated with such men as Alfred Tennyson, Arthur Hallam, and Monckton Milnes. Soon after leaving the university he became private secretary to Spring Rice (afterwards Lord Monteagle), then Chancellor of the Exchequer. In 1839 he went to Ireland as private secretary to Lord Morpeth (afterwards Earl of Carlisle), Chief Secretary for Ireland. His fitness for official life was unmistakable, and in 1860 he was appointed clerk of the Privy Council on the recommendation of Lord Granville. His appointment as clerk of the Council brought him into personal touch with the late Queen Victoria and the Prince Consort, both of whom respected him greatly. After the prince's death, H. was asked to write an appreciation of his life, and later he edited and wrote a preface to the *Queen's Leaves from a Journal of our Life in the Highlands*, 1868.

Helsingborg, a fortified seaport of Sweden, situated on the Sound, opposite Elsinore, 32 m. N.W. of Malmö. It has a good harbour, a fishing industry, and manufactures of sugar, chemicals, and machinery, while the export and import trade, especially with Denmark, is considerable. It figured largely in the Scandinavian wars, being almost destroyed in the reign of Charles XI. The Danes were defeated here in 1710. Pop. 30,294.

Helsingfors (Finnish *Helsinki*), a seaport and the cap. of Finland and of the prov. of Nyland. Centre of the administrative, scientific, educational, and industrial life of Finland. The fine harbour is divided into two parts by a promontory, and is protected at its entrance by a group of small islands, upon one of which stands the fortress of Sveaborg. A third harbour is situated on the W. side of the promontory, and all three have granite quays. The city, which in 1810 had only 4065 inhabitants, Åbo, the then capital, having 10,224, has increased with great rapidity, having 22,228 inhabitants in 1860, 61,530 in 1890, and 170,000 in 1910. It is the centre of an active shipping trade with the Baltic ports and with England, and of a railway system connecting it with all parts of the grand duchy; it possesses wide streets, parks, gardens, and monuments. The principal square contains the Cathedral of St. Nicholas, the Senate House, and the university, all striking buildings of considerable architectural distinction. The university has a teaching staff of 250, with 2500 students, of whom 328 are women. The university possesses 250,000 volumes in its library. The language of culture is Swedish. H. displays great manufacturing and commercial activity, the imports being coal, machinery, sugar, grain, and clothing. The manufactures of the city consist largely of tobacco, beer and spirits, carpets, machinery, and sugar.

Helsingor, or Elsinore, a seaport of Denmark, situated on the island of Zealand, in the prov. of Fredericksborg, and on the E. coast at the narrowest part of the Sound, 27 m. N. of Copenhagen, and exactly opposite to Helsingborg in Sweden. To the N.E.

is the fortress of Kronborg (1580). The harbour, enlarged in 1883-84, has 18-20 ft. of water, and is much used by ships for coaling and repairing. There is a patent slip and large shipbuilding yards, while good anchorage is afforded by the roadstead outside. The Sound dues were collected here till 1857. It is the birthplace of Saxo Grammaticus, and the scene of Shakespeare's *Hamlet*. Pop. 13,784.

Helst, Bartholomæus van der (1613-70), a Dutch painter. Probably born at Haarlem, and said to have been a pupil of Frans Hals. He also studied under Nicolaes Elias of Amsterdam. He was living in Amsterdam in 1636, and in 1654 was joint founder, with Nicholaes de Helt Stokade, of the Painters' Guild of St. Luke. His best work is in portraiture, and includes 'Muster of the Burgher Guard' (1648), in Amsterdam Museum, which is his finest production and contains twenty-four full-length portraits; 'A Protestant Dame' (1838), at the Hague; 'The Company of Captain Rogloff Bicker' (1639), and 'The Syndics of the Brotherhood of Saint Sebastian (1663), both in Amsterdam Museum.

Helston, a market tn. of Cornwall, England, 10 m. S.W. of Falmouth Noted for the 'Furry' or 'Flora' Dance held annually on May 8. It was made a borough by John in 1201; from the reign of Edward I. to 1832 returned two members to parliament, and one till 1883. Pop. (1911) 2938.

Helvella, a genus of fungi belonging to the Ascomycetes, characterised by their exposed hymenium, thick stipe, and cap-shaped pileus. They grow on the ground in woods in late autumn; the pale *H. crispa* is the best known.

Helvellyn, a mountain in the lake district. Cumberland, England, between Keswick and Ambleside. It is one of the highest peaks in England (3118 ft.), and is fairly easy of ascent, while magnificent views may be obtained from the summit.

Helvetia, a Swiss colony and tn. in Santa Fé prov., Gran Chaco, Argentine Republic, 50 m. N.E. of Santa Fé, founded in 1856. Pop. 2500.

Helvetic Republic, a system of government, consequent upon the occupation of Switzerland by the French, imposed by them in 1798, and abolished to allow of the re-organisation of the old cantonal system by Napoleon in 1803.

Helvetii, an ancient Celtic nation, which, according to Cæsar, inhabited a region roughly corresponding to the western part of modern Switzerland. Their chief town was Aventicum. They first appear in history as allies of the Cimbri during their invasion of Italy, but are best known in connection with their invasion of Southern Gaul in 58 B.C., when they were repulsed by Cæsar with great slaughter. They were again defeated by Cæcina, a general of Vitallius, after the death of Nero.

Helvétius, Claude Adrien (1715-71), a French philosopher and *litterateur*, descended from a family of physicians whose original name was Schweitzer (latinised as Helvetius). His grandfather introduced the use of ipecacuanha. His father was first physician to Queen Marie Leczinska of France. Claude Adrien was trained for a financial career, but occupied his spare time by writing verses. At the age of twenty-three, at the queen's request, he was appointed farmer-general, a post of responsibility and dignity, worth 100,000 crowns a year. Thus provided for, he proceeded to enjoy life to the uttermost. As soon as he had saved enough from his position as farmer-general, he retired to an estate in the country, and employed his large means for the relief of the poor. *De l'esprit* appeared in 1758, and this both attracted attention and roused formidable opposition. The author wrote three retractations, yet he had to give up his office at court, and the book was publicly burned by the hangman. Madame du Deffand said that he had written openly what every one thought secretly. His philosophy belongs to the utilitarian school. The keynote of his thoughts was that public ethics has a utilitarian basis, and he insisted on the importance of culture in national development.

Helvin, a translucent mineral of yellowish colour, occurring in regular tetrahedrons, which is found in Norway, Schwarzenburg in Saxony, and Virginia.

Helvoetsluys, or Hellevoetsluis, fortified seaport of S. Holland, Netherlands. William of Orange embarked here for England in 1688. Pop. 4517.

Helwan, tn. of Egypt, near R. Nile, 10 m. S.E. of Cairo. It is a favourite health resort for Europeans on account of its warm sulphur springs. Pop. 8000.

Hely - Hutchinson, Sir Walter Francis (*b.* 1849), an English colonial administrator, governor of Natal and Zululand, and special commissioner for Amatongaland since 1895, second son of Richard John, fourth Earl of Donoughmore. Educated at Cheam School, Surrey, Harrow, and Cambridge; B.A. Cambridge. Barrister of the Inner Temple, 1877. In 1895, when he was appointed special commissioner of Amatongaland, he completed the annexation of the Trans-Pongola territories, which are now an integral part of Zululand.

Hemans, Felicia Dorothea (1793-1835), an English poetess, born in Liverpool, the daughter of George Browne. She was a precocious child, and was encouraged in her taste for poetry. She published a volume of verse as early as 1808, and another entitled, *The Domestic Affections*, in 1812. In this year she married Captain H., an Irish officer who had served in Spain. In 1818 they separated, after the birth of five sons, Captain H. settling in Italy, and Mrs. H. living in N. Wales, Lancashire, and Dublin. Her work is not strong, but graceful and pleasing. She suffered from a fatal facility, but some of her pathetic and sentimental poems have become very popular. A complete edition of her works was published posthumously in 1839. They include : *The Forest Sanctuary ; Records of Women ; Songs of the Affections,* etc.

Hematin, or Hæmatin, the pigment radicle which, together with globin, constitutes the colouring matter of the blood.

Hematite, *see* HÆMATITE.

Hemel Hempstead, market tn. of Hertfordshire, England, 23 m. N.W. of London. It is a centre of the straw-plaiting industry, and also has boat-making, paper-making, iron-working, tanning, and brewing industries. A Roman villa has been discovered at Boxmore close by. There are fine public buildings, and the town is rapidly improving. Pop. (1911) 12,888.

Hemelingen, a vil. of Hanover, Prussia, 4 m. S.E. of Bremen, with a cigar-making industry. Pop. 7967.

Hemerobins, the name given to a genus of neuropterous insects belonging to the family Hemerobiidæ ; the larvæ devour plant lice, and some species conceal their bodies with the emptied skins of their prey, keeping this strange covering in position by means of elongate divergent hairs.

Hemerocallis, *see* DAY LILY.

Hemianopia, a peculiar and rare form of disease of the eye, usually due to disease within the brain, causing sight to be limited to one half of an object.

Hemichorda (Gk. ἡμι, half, αχορδή, cord), the name given by certain scientists to the group of worm-like marine animals generally known as Enteropneusta (*q.v.*).

Hemicidaris, the name of a genus of fossil sea-urchins belonging to the family Hemicidaridæ.

Hemicrania, *see* HEADACHE, and MIGRAINE.

Hemidesmus, *see* SARSAPARILLA.

Heming (or **Hemminge**), **John** (*d.* 1630), an English actor. He is known to have been one of the chief proprietors of the Globe Theatre during the reign of Elizabeth, and is connected with Shakespeare in several ways. He is said to have created the part of Falstaff, and also played in several of Ben Jonson's dramas. With Henry Condell (d. 1627), he was a co-editor of the first folio of Shakespeare, issued in 1623.

Hemingford (or Hemingburgh), Walter (d. 1347), an English chronicler. He was a sub-prior of St. Mary's, Gisborough, Yorkshire, and died there. His chronicle extends from 1066 to 1346, and was published by Gale in his *Veteres Scriptores*, and by Hearne (Oxford, 1731), and fully edited in 1848 by H. C. Hamilton.

Hemiplegia, the most usual form of paralysis, in which the leg, arm, and muscles of the mouth and tongue on one side of the body are affected. If the paralysis be on the right side, aphasia (q.v.), often accompanies H. Complete recovery is possible but not very frequent. Slight numbness, and not complete paralysis, of sensation, accompanies H., although if the fibres carrying sensory impulses to the surface of the brain are destroyed, there may be loss of sensation on the affected side. In certain cases they may be paralysed on the side opposite to the affected limbs. See PARALYSIS.

Hemipodius, an alternative name for the genus *Turnix*, which belongs to the family Turnicidæ, or quails (q.v.).

Hemiptera, the name given to a large order of insects which includes the bugs, plant-lice, scab-insects, etc., and is also called Rhynchota. All individuals belonging to this order are characterised by a mouth consisting of a proboscis or jointed beak, which is concealed by being bent back under the thorax ; wings, with rare exceptions, four in number, and the anterior pair more horny than the posterior pair. All H. are sucking insects, and the mouth of the individual, like that of Orthoptera, does not change during its lifetime, but they differ from all other orders of insects in respect of the structure of the mouth. The order is divided into Heteroptera, whose wings, partly horny and partly membranous, fold flat on the back ; and Homoptera, whose wings cover the body in a roof-like manner. The Anoplura, or Lice, are sometimes included in this group, or may be regarded as a separate order.

Hemitone, in ancient music, an interval of half a tone ; not exactly equivalent to the modern semitone, being a perfect fourth less two tones.

Hemling, Hans, see MEMLING.

Hemlock, a name given to several plants of different characteristics.

Two of these are umbelliferous species and occur in Britain. *Cicuta virosa,* the water H. or cowbane, is one well-known plant, and *Conium maculatum,* the common H., is another ; both contain a deadly poison. The latter has a mouselike smell, and is well-known as the plant from which the poison drunk by Socrates was obtained. The H. spruce is an evergreen coniferous tree found in N. America, and bears the botanical name of *Tsuga Canadensis.* It is a valuable plant on account of its bark, which is employed in tanning, the pitch it yields, and its strong timber

Hemmingsen, Niels (1513-1600), a Danish theologian, born in Laaland ; educated under Melanchthon at Wittenberg, becoming professor of Greek there in 1543 and of dialectics in 1544. In 1578 he returned to Denmark and became minister of the Church of the Holy Ghost at Copenhagen, and professor of Hebrew in Copenhagen University, which he made famous for its Protestantism. In 1577 he became professor of Divinity there, and in 1579 a canon in the Church of Roschild. He assisted in the first translation of the Bible into Danish.

Hemorrhage, see HÆMORRHAGE, and BLEEDING.

Hemp, a plant of the genus *Cannabis,* natural order Urticaceæ, of which *C. sativa* is the only known species. It is an annual, and is found wild in Western and Central Asia, Brazil, and tropical Africa, and has been cultivated in Russia and Turkey and in Europe. The H. plant is not unlike the hop family (to which it is botanically allied) in appearance, with erect stalk, growing from three to sixteen ft. high according to climate, square in shape, like the common stinging-nettle, five to seven-fingered leaves of lanceolate-acuminate form with serrated margins, and is diœcious. The seed is a valuable product, being used as bird-food, and, when crushed, as oil for soap and oil-cake. The H. plant secretes a resinous substance possessing narcotic and intoxicating qualities (see HASHISH), while Indian H. or Bhang has proved of value as an hypnotic in therapeutics. H. is, however, most valued for its fibre, which is obtained by rotting the stems under moisture in the same manner as flax-fibre is obtained (see FLAX). The fibre is tough and strong, and is used for sailcloth, ropes, and ship-caulking ; the largest supplies come from Russia, Italy, and France. English H. was esteemed for its strength in the 18th century, but its cultivation has largely died out. The cultivation of H., as well as the preparation of its fibre, is very similar to that of flax (q.v.).

Hemphill, Charles Hare, first Baron (1849-1908), an Irish barrister and politician, born at Cashel, co. Tipperary; educated at Dublin; called to the Irish bar in 1845. He contested unsuccessfully parliamentary elections at Cashel in 1857 and 1859. In 1863 he became chairman of a county (*i.e.* a county court judge), but retired in 1877. In 1882 he became a sergeant-at-law; in 1886 and 1892 fought two more unsuccessful elections at Liverpool and Hastings; was Irish solicitor-general during 1892-95, and in the latter year became M.P. for N. Tyrone. He was raised to the peerage in 1906.

Hemp-palm, or *Chamærops excelsa,* a species of palm found chiefly in Nepaul. It yields a useful fibre.

Hempstead, a vil. in Nassau co., New York, U.S.A., 20 m. E. of New York, of which it is a popular suburb. Farming and market-gardening are the chief industries. It was settled by New Englanders in 1643, and the Presbyterian Church was founded in 1644. Pop. (1910) 4964.

Hems, Hums, or **Homs** (Lat. *Emesa*), a city of Syria, near R. Orontes, 63 m. N.E. of Tripoli. The modern city, built of black basalt, is mean, dirty, and crowded, and is surrounded by half-ruined walls. The only ancient relics are columns, inscriptions, foundations, and fragments of pavements. There is considerable trade in silk, cotton, oil, gold ware, and sesame. In ancient times, as Emesa, it was famous for its Temple of the Sun, of which Heliogabalus, Emperor of Rome in 218, was a priest. In 272 the Emperor Aurelian defeated Zenobia here. It was taken by the Saracens in 636, and by the Crusaders in 1098. Ibrahim Pasha defeated the Turks here in 1832. Pop. 50,000.

Hemsley, William Botting (*b.* 1843), an English botanist, born in Sussex; educated privately, and entered Kew Gardens in 1860, ultimately becoming keeper of the Herbarium and Library. He is an F.R.S., a F.L.S., and a member of many learned societies at home and abroad. His published works include: *Handbook of Hardy Trees, Shrubs, and Herbaceous Plants,* 1873 and 1877; *Botany of the 'Challenger' Expedition; Botany of Salvin and Godman's Biologia Centrali-Americana; Flora of China; Flora of Thibet,* and numerous articles, reviews, translations, etc., dealing with geographical botany.

Hemsterhuis, Franz (1720-90), a Dutch philosopher, born at Groningen; educated at Leyden, and obtained a position in the Council of State of the United Provinces. His works deal with moral philosophy and æsthetics, and belong to the 'sentimental' school.

Hemsterhuis, Tiberius (1685-1766), a Dutch philologist, born and educated at Groningen. In 1704 he became professor of mathematics and philosophy at Amsterdam; in 1720 professor of Greek at Franeker, and in 1740 professor of Greek history at Leyden. He created a new school of Greek philology, which includes among its representatives Ruhnken and Valckenaer. He issued famous editions of works by Pollux, Lucian, and Aristophanes.

Hemsworth, a vil. of W. Riding of Yorkshire, England, 6½ m. N.E. of Barnsley, on the Great Northern Railway. Pop. (1911) 6300.

Hemy, Charles Napier (*b.* 1841), an English marine painter, born at Newcastle; educated in art there and at Antwerp. He made several voyages as a boy, and at one time joined the Dominicans at Lyons, but finally settled in England in 1870, living in London till 1881, when he removed to Churchfield, Falmouth. He became a member of the R.W.S. in 1897; of the A.R.A. in 1898; and of the R.A. in 1910. His works include: *Homeward; Oporto; Silent Adieu; Pilchards; Lost,* 1897; *Smugglers,* 1899; *Home Wind; Birds of Prey,* 1901; *The Crew,* 1902; *Youth,* 1903; *The Lifeboat; Haul Aft; London River; The Crab Merchant,* 1904; *Bound for London,* 1907; *Plymouth; Through Sea and Air,* 1910.

Hen, *see* POULTRY.

Henault, Charles Jean François, (1685-1770), a French historian. His father was a farmer-general of taxes, and a man of literary tastes. The son was educated at a Jesuit college. In his fifteenth year he entered the Oratory, with the view of becoming a preacher. His literary talent obtained his entrance to the Academy. The literary work upon which he bestowed his chief attention was the *Abrege Chronologique de l'histoire de France,* first published in 1744 without the author's name. In the compass of two volumes he comprised the whole history of France from the earliest times to the death of Louis XIV. This work was a prodigious success, and was translated into several languages, even into Chinese.

Henbane, or *Hyoscyamus niger,* is a species of Solanaceæ found in Britain. It is an herbaceous plant with large leaves and whitish-yellow flowers which are followed by an erect capsule dehiscing by means of its lid. The H. has an extremely disagreeable odour, hence its name, but in medicine it is sometimes used as a narcotic and sedative.

Henchera, a genus of plants included in the order Saxifrageæ. There are two dozen species, all of which are to be found in N. America, and the commonest is known as *H. Americana*. It contains tannin and because of its astringent properties has obtained the name of alum-root.

Henderson, cap. city of Henderson co., Kentucky, U.S.A., on R. Ohio, 10 m. S. of Evansville. The chief industry is the preparation of tobacco, but there are numerous other mills and factories, and the town is an important trade centre. Pop. 11,452.

Henderson, Alexander (1583-1646), a Scottish ecclesiastic, born in Criech, Fifeshire. Graduated at St. Andrews in 1603, and in 1610 was appointed professor of rhetoric and philosophy, and questor of the faculty of arts. Shortly after this he was presented to the living of Leuchars. As he was forced upon his parish by Archbishop George Gladstanes, and was known to sympathise with episcopacy, his settlement was at first unpopular, but he changed his views and became a Presbyterian in doctrine and in church government, and one of the most esteemed ministers in Scotland. H. is one of the greatest of men in the history of Scotland, and next to Knox is certainly the most famous Scottish divine. He was once called a ' Cabinet minister without office.' The existing Presbyterian churches of Scotland are indebted to him for the forms of their dogmas and their ecclesiastical organisation. He is justly considered the second founder of the reformed church of Scotland.

Henderson, David Bremner (1840-1906), an American politician, born in Scotland ; in 1846 he emigrated to Illinois and went to Iowa in 1849, where he was educated. He was called to the bar in 1865, having previously served in the army, and from then till 1869 was a collector of internal revenue. During 1869-71 he was an assistant district attorney ; in 1882 was elected to the Federal House of Representatives, and in 1899 became Speaker of the House.

Henderson, George Francis Robert (1854-1903), a British soldier and military writer, born in Jersey, educated at Leeds Grammar School, of which his father, after Dean of Carlisle, was headmaster. Went to Oxford, but soon left for Sandhurst, whence he obtained his first commission in 1878. He was the first man of his regiment to enter the enemies' works at Tel-el-Kebir. His conduct attracted the attention of the late Lord Wolseley, and he received the 5th class of the Medjidieh order. In the S. African war, Lieutenant-Colonel H. served with distinction on the staff of Lord Roberts, as director

of intelligence. Overwork and malaria broke his health, and he had to return home, being afterwards selected to write the official history of the war, but before he could complete it he died, and the War Office suppressed what he had written, and the work was begun afresh and carried on by Sir F. Maurice.

Henderson, John (*c.* 1747-85), an English actor, born in London. He made his début at Bath in 1772 as Hamlet, and came to be known as ' Bath Roscius.' In 1777 he appeared at the Haymarket, London; in 1778-79 with Sheridan at Drury Lane; and after 1779 at Covent Garden. He was a friend of Mrs. Siddons and Gainsborough. He was successful in many Shakespearean rôles.

Henderson, Thomas (1798-1844), a Scottish astronomer, who measured large displacements of a Centauri at the Cape in 1832-33, but delayed till 1839 to publish his result. Out of several hundred stars then examined, seventy or eighty have yielded fairly accurate, though very small, parallaxes.

Hending, Proverbs of, a series of Middle English verses, contained in the Harl. MS. 2253 (Brit. Mus.), consisting of six-lined stanzas, rhymed a a b a a b, each of which closes with an old folk proverb, many of which are still in common use. The proverbs seem to have been collected from older 13th century material.

Hendon, a tn. of Middlesex, England, on R. Brent, 8 m. N.W. of St. Paul's, London. A favourite residential suburb of London, and is also a popular holiday resort, the ' Welsh Harp' reservoir of Regent's Canal being much used for skating, fishing, etc. It is an aviation centre with aeroplane works and flying schools. There is a manuf. of mineral waters. Mill Hill, just to the N., has a large Nonconformist Grammar School (1807), and a Roman Catholic Missionary College (1871). Pop. (1911) 38,806.

Hendricks, Thomas Andrews (1819-85), an American political leader, vice-president of United States in 1885, born near Zanesville, Ohio. Graduated at Hanover College, Indiana, and in 1843 began a successful career at the bar. From 1868 till his death, he was put forward for nomination for the presidency at every democratic convention, save that of 1872.

Heneguen or **Sisal Hemp,** *see* FIBROUS SUBSTANCES.

Hengelo, tn. of Overijssel, Holland, 5 m. N.W. of Enschede, an industrial centre. There is a large cotton industry, also dyeing, brewing, and railway engineering. Pop. 20,073.

Hengist and Horsa, the brother

chieftains who led the first Saxon bands which settled in England. They were apparently called in by the British king, Vortigern, to defend him against the Picts. The place of their landing is said to be Ebbsfleet in Kent. The settlers of Kent are described by Bede as Jutes, and there are traces in Kentish custom of differences from the other Anglo-Saxon kingdoms. H. and H. were at first given the Isle of Thanet as a home, but soon quarrelled with their British allies, and gradually possessed themselves of what became the kingdom of Kent. In 455 there was a battle between the two brothers and Vortigern, and Horsa was slain. Thenceforward Hengist reigned in Kent together with his son.

Hengshan: 1. One of the sacred mountains of China, not identified with any particular mountain, but probably on the boundary of Chi-li, and Shan-si. 2. Another of the Wu-yo, or sacred mountains, in Hu-nan, to the N. of Heng-chow Fu, in lat. 27° N., long. 112° E. It is about 3000 ft. high.

Hengstenberg, Ernst Wilhelm (1802-69), a German Lutheran divine, and theologian, born at Fröndenberg. Educated by his father, who was a minister of the Reformed Church. Entered University of Bonn in 1819, and directed his energies principally to philosophy and philology, and his earliest publication was an edition of the Arabic *Moallakat* of Amru'l Qais, which gained for him the prize at his graduation in the philosophical faculty. In July 1827 appeared, under his editorship, *Evangelische Kirchenzeitung*. In 1828 he became professor ordinarius in theology, and in 1829 doctor of theology.

Henin-Liétard, a tn. of Pas-de-Calais, France, 7 m. N.W. of Douai, with a coal-mining industry. Pop. (commune) about 16,000.

Henle, Frederick Gustav Jakob (1809-85), a German pathologist and anatomist, born in Fraconia. Studied medicine at Heidelberg and Bonn, where he took his doctor's degree in 1832. Whilst at Heidelberg he published a zoological monograph on the sharks and rays, in conjunction with his master, Müller, and in 1846 his famous *Manual of Rational Pathology* began to appear. This marked a new era in pathological study. From 1852-73 he was publishing his great *Handbook of Systematic Human Anatomy*. During the latter part of his life, his researches were mainly histological in character.

Henley, John (1692-1756), ' Orator Henley,' born at Melton Mowbray, educated at Cambridge; became a teacher, and took holy orders, having charges in Melton Mowbray, London, and Chelmondiston, Suffolk. In 1726 he left the church and established in London his famous ' Oratory.' Here he preached primitive Christianity on Sundays, and taught ' universal knowledge ' on Wednesdays, attracting large numbers by the strangeness of his methods and doctrines. In 1730 he became a pensioner of Walpole and editor of the *High Doctor*. He wrote *Esther* in 1714.

Henley, William Ernest (1849-1903), a British poet, critic, and editor, born at Gloucester, and educated at Crypt Grammar School in that city. T. E. Brown, the poet, was headmaster there for some time. His appointment was a stroke of luck for H., to whom his coming meant the lad's first introduction to a man of genius. To the end, H. was no classical scholar, but his knowledge of and love for literature were vital. At the age of twenty-five he found himself ill; he was sent to a hospital in Edinburgh, and from there he sent poems, describing his experience in the ward, to Leslie Stephen, who was editing the *Cornhill*. The poems were full of poignant force, and Stephen visited his contributor in hospital, in company with Robert Louis Stevenson. The meeting between H. and Stevenson, and the friendship which arose between them, form one of the best known episodes in recent literature. In 1877 H. went to London and began his editorial career by editing *London*. At the end of 1886 he came before the public as a poet. Later he edited the *Scots Observer*, and had the knack of ' discovering ' literally men. It was that paper which gave to the world Kipling's *Barrack-room Ballads*. H. exercised by his originality an inspiring influence on the higher class of journalism, but his fame must rest on his poetry.

Henley-on-Thames, a tn. of Oxfordshire, England, on R. Thames, 35 m. W. of London. A favourite summer resort, and noted for the annual amateur regatta, founded in 1839. The town dates from Roman times. The fine five-arch bridge was built in 1786. Malting and brewing are the chief industries. Pop. (1911) 6456.

Henna, a substance made from the leaves of *Lawsonia inermis*, the Egyptian privet or henna-plant, and is much used in the East for staining nails, finger-tips, etc., and by men for dyeing their beards, the colour produced being a reddish-orange. The custom has prevailed from very early times.

Hennebont, a tn. of Morbihan, France; on R. Blavet, 6 m. N.E. of Lorient. Much of the town is very old. It is now a busy port, and has boat-building, tanning, and distilling industries. Pop. 9000.

Henner, Jean Jacques (1832-1905), a French painter, born at Bernwiller; educated under Drölling and Picot. In 1858 he obtained the Grand Prix de Rome. His most notable work is seen in his nude figure-studies. Among his pictures are: ' The Chaste Susanna ' (1865), in the Luxembourg; ' Biblis Changée en Source ' (1867), at Dijon; ' The Good Samaritan ' (1874), in the Luxembourg; ' Naïades ' (1875), in the Luxembourg; ' The Dead Christ ' (1876); ' St. John Baptist '; ' The Evening ' (1877); ' The Magdalene ' (1878); ' The Levite Ephraim ' (1898); ' The Dream ' (1900).

Henningsen, Charles Frederick (1815-77), a soldier and author, born in England, of Swedish parentage, served with the Carlists in Spain, with the Russians in Circassia, with Kossuth in Hungary, and with Walker in Nicaragua. In the American Civil War he commanded a Confederate brigade, and afterwards superintended the manufacture of Minie rifles. He wrote *The White Slave* in 1845, and the *Past and Future of Hungary* in 1852.

Henrietta Maria (1609-69), Queen of Charles I. of England, daughter of Henry IV. of France. When the first overtures were made for her hand on behalf of Charles, she was not much more than fourteen. Consent was given to the marriage on condition that the English Roman Catholics were relieved from the operation of the penal laws. She married by proxy and had already pledged her husband to a course of action which would bring unpopularity upon him as well as upon herself. The early years of the marriage were unhappy. Charles breaking his promise to relieve the English Catholics. After the assassination of Buckingham, the barrier between the married pair was broken, and the bond of affection that united them never loosened. In 1644 the queen left her husband, to see him no more, being exiled in France on account of religious and political difficulties in England. Her husband's execution in 1649 was a terrible blow to her. When, after the Restoration, she returned to England, she found no place for her in the new world, and in 1665 she went again to France, there to spend the remainder of her life.

Henry, the practical unit of electric self-inductance. It was defined by the International Congress of 1908 as ' the induction in a circuit when an electromotive force induced in this circuit is one international volt, while the inducing current varies at the rate of one ampere per second.' It derives its name from that of the discoverer of the property of inductance, Joseph Henry (1797-1878).

Henry I. (1100-35), King of England, the youngest son of William the Conqueror (b. 1068), and it is to be noted the only son born to William after he became king. This is of importance, since H. made this fact one of his chief claims to the throne of England against the claim of his eldest brother Robert. During the war between Rufus and Robert of Normandy, H. supported the claims of Robert, but in the treaty which followed, his claim to the English throne was utterly disregarded. On the death of Rufus, however, and whilst Robert was hastening back from the Holy Land, he seized the crown of England and was elected by the witan. The early part of his reign was taken up with struggles with Robert. These struggles ended in a compromise by which Robert was to receive an annual pension. Robert, however, again went to war and was overwhelmed at Tenchebrai (1105). This battle has been called the English revenge for Hastings. Robert remained a prisoner in the hands of H. until his death in 1133. The struggle in Normandy was continued by Robert's son, who found much support at the hands of the French king. Ultimately, Henry I. was entirely successful. H. had done much to commence the amalgamation of Norman and Saxon into a united English race, and although his marriage with the Saxon princess, Matilda, was scornfully regarded by the Norman nobles, it was an example which was followed later by many Normans. In England itself H. had issued a charter on the lines of the ancient charter of Edward the Confessor, and had restored *law* and order in the country. Many of the wisest reforms of Henry II. (*q.v.*) had their beginning in Henry I.'s reign. In 1119 his only son, William, was drowned in the wreck of the *White Ship*, and the remainder of H.'s reign was taken up in attempting to settle the succession. His daughter, Matilda, had married : (1) The Emperor Henry V., (2) Geoffrey of Anjou. Although H. compelled the barons to swear to recognise Matilda as queen on his death, the throne was ultimately obtained by Stephen. H. was a wise, just, and clever king, but he was cold, selfish, and at times brutal.

Henry II. (1154–1189), King of England. He was the eldest son of Matilda and Geoffrey of Anjou, and was born in 1133. On the death of his grandfather, Henry I., his mother was passed over in the English succession and Stephen succeeded.

Before H. had attained his majority, he had proved himself a great warrior, and was the possessor of wide dominions in France. He ruled Normandy, Maine, Anjou, and Tourraine, whilst by his marriage to Eleanor of Aquitaine, the divorced wife of the King of France, he succeeded to her dower as well. He landed in England in 1153, and by the treaty of Wallingford it was agreed that he should succeed Stephen as King of England. He was crowned in 1154, and immediately began to establish firmly the royal power. The ' nineteen long winters ' had left the nobility practically omnipotent in England, and H.'s first task was to crush the baronial power. This he did by turning the mercenaries out of the country, by disbandoning all castles erected with licence, and reverting to the crown all grants of land made during Stephen's reign. Having crushed the barons' power, he turned his attention to the church. The power of the church was admittedly great, but the church was by no means inclined to give up that power. He appointed his chancellor, Becket, Archbishop of Canterbury, but Becket proved as obstinate as archbishop as he had been subservient as chancellor. The constitutions of Clarendon placed the royal and the church courts on an equal basis, but Becket ultimately refused to acknowledge them, and in defiance of them appealed to the pope and fled the country. This ultimately led, after a pretended reconciliation, to his murder (1170). In 1174 H. did public penance at the tomb of Becket. H., however, cannot be regarded as essentially an English king. The greater part of his reign was spent in France in struggles with the King of France and with his own subjects. He probably regarded England as the least important of all his dominions. During his reign, also, attention had been turned to Ireland, where Strongbow had succeeded in establishing Norman power. H. went over to Ireland, reduced the Norman nobility to subjection to himself, and ultimately appointed his youngest son John, lord of Ireland. In France, in addition to struggling against the French king, he had also considerable trouble from his sons, Henry, Richard, and Geoffrey. Both Henry and Geoffrey died before their father, but the final struggle which broke H.'s power was against the King of France and Richard. H. was defeated, humiliated, and forced to agree to terms. He agreed that a general amnesty should be granted to his rebellious subjects. Weak and ill almost to death, he was

presented with a list of the rebels, the first name which he saw was that of his best loved son John, and with the words, ' shame on a conquered king ' he turned his face to the wall and died. His reign in England has been described as a reign of law and order, and certainly the system established by H. worked exceedingly well and was of vast importance in the building of the constitution of England. He was the greatest of the Plantagenets, and it is to be noticed that in order to successfully oppose and lessen the power of church and nobility, he enlisted by wise and enlightened measures of reform the people on his side, and by the Assize of Arms he raised a militia on which he could always depend. He was an able general, a wise, if unprincipled statesman, and a great legislator. *See* Stubb's *Constitutional History*, and Green's *Life of Henry II.*, English Statesmen Series.

Henry III. (1216-72), King of England, elder son of John, was born in 1207. At the age of nine he succeeded to his father's throne, at a period when the struggle for the maintenance of the Charter was at its height. So far indeed had the opposition to his father gone that Louis of France had been invited to accept the allegiance which many of the English barons had thrown off. By the judicious measures of the regent Pembroke, of Hubert de Burgh, and Stephen Langton, H. was generally received as king, and Louis was compelled to leave the country. On the death of Pembroke, Hubert de Burgh ruled for H., and adopted a distinctive and national policy. In 1227, however, H. declared himself of age. In 1232 he deprived Hubert de Burgh of all his offices, and finally began the period of personal government in 1234. His policy was weak and vacillating, and was influenced largely by the surrender of the kingdom to the papacy, a measure which his father was responsible for, but of which H. suffered the results. His numerous relations, or the foreign favourites as they were generally termed, were another cause of trouble to H., and caused much ill-feeling throughout the country. His early war with France, which was fought from a mistaken conception of the ideals of the English, ended in disaster, and would have had even more disastrous effects had it not been for the generosity of St. Louis. His continued misrule, his attempted extortions of money, the vast influence of the papacy over the kingdom, and his numerous grants to his favourites, finally united the English as a race against him. Matters came to a head when H. finally demanded a huge sum of money to purchase for his son Edmund support to obtain the kingdom of Sicily granted him by the pope. By the Provisions of Oxford his power was relegated to a committee of barons, led by Simon de Montfort, a former favourite and a brother-in-law, but now a much-hated rival. In 1263 the Provisions of Oxford were placed under the arbitration of Louis of France, who decided in favour of H., and war immediately broke out. The party of Simon de Montfort overwhelmed the king at Lewes, and for a time the government passed into their hands. In 1265 Simon summoned his famous parliament, the forerunner of our modern representative parliaments, but in the same year he was overcome and killed at Evesham by Prince Edward. The Montfortian party held power for a time, but finally terms were laid down by the Dictum of Kenilworth. Henceforth the troubles of the reign ceased, so much so that Edward was able to depart on crusade, and H. died peacefully at Westminster. It is important to notice that so thoroughly had affairs been settled that Edward succeeded peacefully to a kingdom which he did not return to until two years after his father's death.

Henry IV. (1399-1413), King of England, first of the Plantagenet house of Lancaster to ascend the throne. His accession was in reality the vital cause of the later Wars of the Roses. He was the son of John of Gaunt, the fourth son of Edward III. He was known in early life as Henry of Bolingbroke, the title being taken from the place of his birth. He supported Richard II. against Gloucester, but was, after being raised to the position of Duke of Hereford, exiled (1398). In the next year, whilst Richard was in Ireland, Bolingbroke landed at Ravenspur and marched down through England, proclaiming that he came but to claim his own. Finally, he forced Richard, deserted and betrayed, to abdicate, and was himself proclaimed king as Henry IV. He based his claim essentially upon its parliamentary character. Richard died at Pontefract four months later. His reign is characteristic chiefly for the lawlessness and rebellion which pervaded it, and for the impetus which his accession to the throne gave to parliament. The Welsh rebelled under Owen Glyndwr; the Scots were attacked, but the attack failed, and finally, when the Scots invaded England, they were beaten by the Percies at Homildon (1402). Irritated by the behaviour of the king, the Percies now rebelled, and attempted to form a junction with the Welsh under Owen Glyndwr: they were, however, defeated at Shrewsbury (1403). After this the power of the Welsh rebellion began to die out, but Wales can be said to have been practically independent of England's authority during the greater part of this reign. Prince James of Scotland was captured and kept a prisoner in England, and H. attempted some attacks in France. His religious policy was strongly in favour of the Church, and he commenced a rigorous persecution of the Lollards. Towards the end of his reign he was a chronic invalid and suffered from a particularly painful and, according to some authorities, loathsome disease. He died at Westminster. He was a capable and clever man, but towards the end of his reign degenerated into a suspicious and cruel tyrant.

Henry V. (1413-22), King of England, eldest son of Henry IV., was born in 1387, and created Prince of Wales in 1399. His youth was occupied in constant warfare, and many wild and probably exaggerated stories are told of him. That he disagreed with the policy of his father is obvious from his reversal thereof when he ascended the throne. He did all he could to popularise the Lancastrian dynasty on his accession. The Percies were restored to favour, Richard's body was interred in Westminster Abbey, but nevertheless he put down with a firm hand any attempts at rebellion. The year after his accession he claimed the throne of France by right of his great-grandfather, Edward III., and took an army across to France. Success attended his arms, and he was able to win the notable battle of Agincourt (1415) and to reduce Northern France. Finally came the treaty of Troyes (1420), by which H. married the French king's daughter and was acknowledged as heir to the French throne. Whilst he was in England attending the coronation of his queen, the English forces met with some reverses. H. thereupon returned to France, but died there in August. A just, pious, and conscientious ruler, he was without pity, and was a great persecutor of the Lollards.

Henry VI. (1422-71), King of England, the only son of Henry V. and Catherine of France. He was less than twelve months old when he succeeded to the realm of England, and shortly afterwards, by the death of his grandfather Charles VI. of France, he became king of France. His territories were administered for him by his uncles Bedford and Gloucester. At first the attempt of the French dauphin (Charles VII.) to obtain possession of his father's throne was in vain, but after the appearance of the Maid of France (Jeanne d'Arc), the English began gradually to lose their French possessions. The death of Bedford in 1435 was really the final blow to the English cause, and by 1453 Calais alone remained in English hands. In 1447 Gloucester, after having been arrested by the queen's party, was found dead a few days later. The queen (Margaret of Anjou) now became the real leader of the policy of the court; her husband, pious, learned, and amiable, was entirely under her influence, and unfortunately events were moving rapidly in England towards a climax. The loss of the French possessions, the return of the soldiers from France, and the resulting unemployment problem which followed, all conspired to make the Lancastrian dynasty unpopular. Nor did the influence of the queen have any better result. In 1454 H. became insane, and Richard, Duke of York, a nearer lineal descendant of Edward III. than H., became protector. H. recovered, York was deprived of his office, and it became obvious that war was at hand. The year 1455 saw the battle of St. Albans, and from that date until 1471 battles between Yorkists and Lancastrians were frequent. Wakefield (1460) delivered York into the hands of Margaret, by whom he was beheaded, but Towton (1461) placed Edward, Earl of March, son of Richard of York, securely on the throne. The power behind the throne was that of Warwick the king-maker, whom Edward, brave, clever, dissolute, and unscrupulous, now endeavoured to get rid of. Finally, he drove Warwick into the hands of Margaret of Anjou ; the alliance was at first successful, for Edward IV. was forced to flee the country, and for a short time H. was again king. But Edward returned, Warwick was slain at the battle of Barnet (1470), and the Lancastrian line defeated at Tewkesbury (1471). The night of the return of Edward from Tewkesbury to London saw the death of H.

Henry VII. (1485-1509), King of England, was born in 1457, being the son of Edmund Tudor and Margaret Beaufort. He was descended from that Owen Tudor who married the widow of Henry V., Catherine of France; he was thus connected with the royal line, and through his mother was descended from the Beauforts, the descendants of John of Gaunt and Catherine Swinford. He naturally supported the claims of the Lancastrians during the Wars of the Roses, and finally put a period to these wars at the battle of Bosworth (1485), where he overthrew Richard III. and

was acclaimed king on the battlefield. He was the founder of the Tudor dynasty, and practically established a system of absolute monarchy. By his marriage with Elizabeth of York he united the two houses of York and Lancaster, and by his overthrow of Simnel and Warbeck, the pretenders, he finally established his line firmly on the throne of England. His influence on the Continent was much greater than that of any previous English king, and his adoption of a national policy gave England a great position amongst the nations of Europe. The policy of royal marriages which he initiated was of vast importance when viewed by its later results. The marriage of his son Henry with Catherine of Aragon, after she had first wedded the elder son Arthur, was an immediate cause of the separation from Rome, whilst the marriage of his daughter with James IV. of Scotland led to the ultimate amalgamation of the crowns of England and Scotland. He adopted a policy of peace, he established sound commercial relations with the Continent, and he realised that whilst the nobility must be crushed, the people must be supported. This peace policy had wide effects upon the later history of England. When H. died he left a huge fortune (about £30,000,000) to his son Henry VIII. An austere, somewhat miserly king, but nevertheless a king who placed England on a securer and firmer basis than heretofore.

Henry VIII. (1509-47), King of England, born in 1491, being the second son of Henry VII. and Elizabeth of York. Until the death of his elder brother Arthur he was educated for the Church. He succeeded his father and married Catherine of Aragon in 1509. This marriage seems to have caused H. no scruples at the time. When he succeeded he was one of the most popular kings that England had ever had. He was young, handsome, tall, well built, of a jovial disposition, and free and easy with his subjects. No king ever had better prospects when he ascended the throne. His reign falls naturally into two parts, separated by the date 1528, which may be regarded as the critical year of the divorce. The early period was occupied in affairs at home, in promoting the commercial relations of the country, and in maintaining the balance of power in Europe. In all this he was ably supported by Cardinal Wolsey, but it must be remembered that H. was always the leading spirit. The aims of the king, of the cardinal, and of the nation conspired at this time to make the foreign policy popular and national. By 1524

H. had, however, grown tired of his wife, he began to have scruples as to the legality of the marriage. He had already, through Wolsey, incurred the displeasure of parliament by his increasing demands for money, now he finally determined upon the step which was to alienate Rome, to separate the churches, and in reality, though probably unconsciously, to complete the subjugation of the powers of the country to the crown. By 1528 the matter had advanced to an absolute demand for a divorce. From the point of view of H. there were many reasons for this step. He

HENRY VIII

wanted an heir to the throne—so far Mary alone of his children had survived; he desired to marry Anne Boleyn, and he alleged that his marriage had been without the sanction of God. The pope desired to help H., but his own position was unfortunate; he was, for the time being, in the hands of Charles V., the nephew of Catherine; Campeggio was sent to England, the trial ended without decision, and the immediate result was the overthrow of Wolsey. H.'s failure had, however, only increased the keenness of his desire. Since the papacy would not humour him, he would obtain a divorce in his own courts, and in his own way. In 1531 the clergy were outlawed, and, step by step, and by means of what is somewhat incorrectly termed the

Reformation Parliament, he proceeded until he was acknowledged as head of the Church, and the power of the bishop of Rome was declared at an end. But the way had been paved with blood, and Bishop Fisher and Sir Thomas More had paid the penalty of loyalty, not to Rome, but to principle. It must be definitely understood, however, that H. was strictly orthodox. His idea was not the reformation of a religion, but of a religious system; his motives may have been bad, but they were of vast importance to the nation at large. The Lutherans were far from encouraged, the Whip with Six Thongs (The Six Acts) imposed orthodoxy of the strictest type. The persecutions of Cromwell and the subservience of Cranmer made the path of H. fairly smooth. The monasteries, the last places that owned allegiance to the papacy, were abolished (1536 - 39), their lands confiscated and granted to a new nobility. The Pilgrimage of Grace was crushed with enormous severity, and the king became absolutely supreme. H. had, by this time, married Anne Boleyn and executed her; by her he had the Princess Elizabeth. His next wife, Jane Seymour, bore him Prince Edward and died. Anne of Cleves followed; H. was displeased with her, and the marriage was immediately dissolved; the immediate result was the execution of Cromwell. H. next married Catherine Howard, who was executed for infidelity, and finally Catherine Parr, who nursed him and managed to survive him. During the latter part of the reign the Reformed religion had made some progress with little or no encouragement from H. The later years of the reign were, however, marked by cruelties and bloodshed beyond measure, and H. died finally with the reputation of a bloody tyrant. He had accomplished the greatest work which any English monarch had yet done; the means employed were not above suspicion, but he was supported by, and accomplished the will of, the majority of the nation. He was popular, as were all the Tudors, and, to a certain point, he may have been sincere, but he outlived the promise of the earlier days; but he must be judged by the great results of his work, and only by the light of contemporary history.

Henry I. (1031-60), King of France, son of King Robert and grandson of Hugh Capet. The early years of his reign were spent in fighting the feudal nobles, who supported the claims of his younger brother Robert. When this dispute was settled he turned his attention to Normandy, where he attacked William the Bastard without success. His son was crowned the year before his death, and this was very necessary since H. was simply a feudal magnate and regarded only as *primus inter pares*.

Henry II. (1547-59), King of France, born in 1519, and in 1533 married Catherine de' Medici. He succeeded his father, Francis I. The influence of the family of Guise led to the interference of France in Scotland, and to war with England. This war resulted in the capture of Calais, which had for over two centuries been in the possession of England. This reign witnessed much oppression of the Protestants, but nevertheless he supported the reformers against the emperor with some degree of success, but was overthrown in the Spanish Netherlands by Alva. The treaty of Cateau-Cambrésis concluded the war with the empire and Spain. He was slain at a tournament by a Scottish nobleman.

Henry III. (1575-89), King of France, the last of the Valois, was the third son of Henry II. and Catherine de' Medici, and was born in 1551. He fought against the Protestants at Jarnac and Moncontour. He played a great part in the massacre of St. Bartholomew, and after being elected king of Poland, succeeded to the French throne on the death of his brother Charles IX. During his reign almost constant wars took place between the Catholics and the Protestants. Finally, he threw himself into the hands of the Huguenots, although he was at times violently anti-Protestant. He was assassinated on Aug. 1 by a friar named Clément. Before his death he nominated Henry of Navarre as his successor. His reign was one almost constant period of civil war.

Henry IV. (1589-1610), King of France and Navarre, the son of Antoine de Bourbon, and Jeanne D'Albret, the heiress of Navarre. He was educated as a Calvinist, and after 1569 was recognised as the Huguenot leader of France. He fought at Jarnac, and led the Protestants in the religious wars which were rife in France at this time. In 1572 he married Margaret de Valois, the sister of the King of France, but within a week followed the massacre of St. Bartholomew, after which H. remained practically a prisoner in the hands of the French court. He finally renounced his religion and later escaped to Alençon, where he repudiated that renunciation and again put himself at the head of the Protestants. Henry III. depended upon him for support, and on the death of that monarch, H. of Navarre became nominally the King of France. His Protestantism made him re-

pugnant to the majority of his subjects, and the Catholic League, strengthened by support from outside, especially from Spain, was strong enough to force him to the S. There he remained for some time until his renunciation of Protestantism, and his entrance into the Catholic Church secured for him the allegiance of the vast majority of his subjects. The peace of Vervins ended the war with Spain, and H. was at last free to turn to the internal affairs of the country. He, together with his minister, Sully, reformed the finances of the country, centralised the government, and above all reduced the power of the nobles. Commerce and trade received a great impetus, and the national debt was largely reduced.

HENRY OF NAVARRE

Just after the coronation of the second queen, and while he was on the point of setting out to war in Germany, he was assassinated by a Jesuit maniac. He was essentially a patriot king, and worked throughout for the good of his country. ' Paris,' he said, ' was worth a mass.' He had many mistresses, and his moral life was the worst side of his character.

Henry V. of France, *see* CHAMBORD, COMTE DE.

Henry II. (1333-79), King of Castile, surnamed ' El Bastardo,' was an illegitimate son of King Alphonso the Avenger. He led repeated rebellions against Pedro the Cruel, and was supported by the French leader Bertrand du Guesclin. In spite of the opposition of the English under the Black Prince, he was able to establish himself in 1369. He then led an army against Portugal. His reign was conducted more on lines of defence than aggressiveness.

Henry III. (1390-1406), King of Castile, surnamed ' The Sickly.' He succeeded his father at the age of eleven, and the period of the regency was somewhat disturbed. He was able, however, to assert his power, and under his personal rule the kingdom prospered. He married in 1393 Catherine of Lancaster. During his reign the Canary Islands were taken possession of by Castile.

Henry I. (919-936), King, but not Emperor, of Germany, the son of Otto, Duke of Saxony, and succeeded to these dominions on the death of his father. He was strong enough to resist the attacks of the emperor, and built up in Germany a strong and consolidated state, which contained Lorraine, and which held Hungary in check. He instituted new methods of attack in warfare, and built large cities throughout Saxony and Thuringia. He was on the point of claiming the imperial throne when he died. The value of his work towards the building up of Germany was very great indeed.

Henry II. (1002 - 24), German emperor, the son of the Duke of Bavaria and the grandson of Henry the Fowler. He was of considerable service to the Emperor, Otto III., whom, as the last representative of the Saxon house, he succeeded. He had many revolts to contend against, but he secured Lombardy for himself, defeated the Poles, obtained the promise of the incorporation of Burgundy with the empire, drove back the Greeks in Italy with the help of the Normans, and greatly increased the power of the Church. This latter side of his policy was of vast importance, since he raised up the power of the Church in order to balance the power of the nobility. He was one of the greatest patrons which the Church has ever had, and was by it canonised on his death.

Henry III. (1039-56), German emperor, son of Conrad II. Was successively King of the Germans, Duke of Bavaria, and Duke of Swabia, and finally became emperor in 1039. He restored and kept up the prerogatives of the empire, and encouraged the movement towards the reform of the Church. He deposed the three rival popes, and placed Clement II. on the papal throne. He forced Bohemia to acknowledge himself a vassal of the empire, and practically placed Hungary under the allegiance of the emperors. He encouraged art, architecture, and learning. One of his greatest achievements was the establishment of

supremacy over the Normans in Italy.

Henry IV. (1056-1106), German emperor, son of Henry III., born in the year 1050, and succeeded his father at the age of six. His mother, the Empress Agnes, at first acted as regent, but her rule was too weak, and at the age of twelve the emperor fell into the hands of Anno, Archbishop of Koln, by whom he was educated. The position of Anno was rivalled by that of Adalbert, the Archbishop of Bremen, who had great influence over H. The constant changing of his tutors, and the weakness of his training due to the constant rivalry of his regents, led to excesses on the part of the young emperor. He was not, however, without ability. He was declared of age in 1165, but his troubles began with the rebellion of Otto Duke of Bavaria, whom he was able to finally crush. The princes of the empire, however, gave him little or no support. The next great trouble of the reign was the quarrel with the papacy. Papal pretensions had increased enormously, and had been supported by previous emperors. Now, however, when H. demanded that Hildebrand (Gregory VII.) should excommunicate his enemies, the pope insisted on H. considering various charges brought against him by his subjects. H. called a council of prelates and announced Gregory deposed. Gregory issued sentence of excommunication again H. H.'s supporters quickly fell away, and he saw that his only hope of success lay in surrender to the papacy. He sought out the pope at Canossa, and there, after waiting for three days in the shirt of a penitent, amidst the snows of the Alps, he was admitted to the presence and forgiven. The power of the papacy had reached the limit of its success. The princes of the empire were still dissatisfied. Three anti-emperors were raised up in succession, and although H. won some successes, even his sons were induced to rebel against their father. The papacy also still continued its policy of opposition to the emperor, and although H. was successful in maintaining a pope of his own choice in Rome, he was forced finally to abdicate, and he fled from prison to Liege. Here he was preparing another attack on the German princes and the pope when he died. Pictured usually as a weak, struggling king, H. was, in reality, nothing of the kind. His work was of vast importance. He realised that the power of the papacy had increased, and must, for the safety of the empire, be diminished, and he sought also to crush the power of the secular nobles and centralise as far as possible the government.

Henry V. (1106-25), German emperor, was the second son of Henry IV. His elder brother, Conrad, was deprived of his rights of succession because of his rebellion against his father, but H. was guilty of the deepest treachery. When he succeeded it was held that, since he had supported the papacy previously, he would resign even such concessions as Henry his father had been able to win. After many struggles with the popes H. was able to obtain a settlement of the whole investiture question by the Concordat of Worms, which was concluded in 1122. By this the papacy kept the right of election and consecration, but the Church lands were invested by the emperor or his representative. He was the last of the Franconian dynasty.

Henry VI. (1190-97), German emperor, was the son of the Emperor Frederick Barbarossa. He was born in 1165, and was made king of Germany during his early childhood, and succeeded to the empire on the death of his father whilst leading the crusade. He aspired to definitely establish the power of his dynasty. He crushed the rebellions in Sicily, and overawed the whole empire. He even for a time forced the emperor of the eastern empire to do him homage. His Sicilian campaigns form the object of greatest interest in his reign, and he was able to raise a fine army from the ransom which he obtained from Richard I. of England. His attempts to establish his dynasty on the imperial throne failed principally because of his early death.

Henry VII. (1308-13), German emperor, was the son of Henry II., Count of Luxemburg, and was born in 1282. He owed his election as emperor to the fact that there was no strong opposition, and that he was regarded as being unimportant. He enriched his own family with the lands of Bohemia, and attempted to revive the old glories of the empire. He, however, made the error of supporting the princes against the growing power of the cities. He was crowned emperor at Rome in 1312, and died in the following year.

Henry, surnamed 'The Lion' (1129-95), the head of the Welf family. He was Duke of Saxony and Bavaria. His possessions in Europe were extensive, and he was restored to some of them by Frederick Barbarossa. He encouraged trade and commerce in Germany, built up ports on the Baltic, and founded the town of Munich. So great, however, did his power become in Germany that a

league of princes was formed against him, but this had so little effect that he was finally placed under the ban of the empire (1180). He was reconciled, however, to the Emperor Henry VI.

Henry the Navigator (1394-1460), the fourth son of King João I. of Portugal and the English princess, Philippa, daughter of John of Gaunt. He early distinguished himself by his bravery, but he is best remembered for the services which he rendered to geographical discovery. His ships sailed to places on the coast of Africa hitherto unknown. In 1418 the Madeira Islands were discovered. He and his sailors now explored many points of the coast of Africa. He established a school for navigation and an observatory. During his lifetime discoveries were pushed on apace, and his influence on the age which followed cannot be exaggerated.

Henry, Prince of Wales, *see* JAMES I.

Henry Frederick, Prince of Wales (1594-1612), the eldest son of James I. He was born at Stirling Castle some years before the accession of his father to the throne of England. On his birth he was created Duke of Rothesay, and in 1610 Prince of Wales. He died at the age of eighteen, when his career had already given great promise.

Henry, George, A.R.A., R.S.A., a Scottish painter, born in Ayrshire; educated at Glasgow School of Art and at Paris. Travelled in China, Japan, Egypt, and India (1893-94). He is a painter in pastel, water-colour, and oils. Works: ' Sundown,' ' A Galloway Landscape,' ' Springtime,' ' Harmony,' etc.

Henry, Joseph (1797 – 1878), an American scientist, born in Albany, New York. Educated at Albany Academy, he afterwards contemplated adopting the medical profession, but in 1825 he was unexpectedly appointed assistant engineer on the survey of a route for a state road from the Hudson R. to Lake Erie, and he at once embarked with zeal upon the new enterprise. He appears to have been the first to adopt insulated wire for the magnetic coil. He was the first to magnetise iron at a distance, and he was also the first to apply the telegraph to meteorological research. From 1868 he was chosen annually as president of the National Academy of Sciences, and he was also president of the Philosophical Society of Washington from the date of its organisation in 1871.

Henry, Matthew (1662-1714), an English Nonconformist divine, born on the borders of Flintshire and Shropshire, son of Philip H., who was ejected by the Act of Uniformity; he possessed private means, and educated his son well. The son relinquished legal studies for theology, and in 1687 he became minister of a Presbyterian church at Chester. His well-known exposition of the O.T. and N.T. is a commentary of a practical and devotional rather than critical kind. Its racy English style secured for it the foremost place among works of its kind.

Henry, Patrick (1736-99), an American statesman and orator, born at Studley in Virginia; the son of a well-educated Scotsman, his mother being of Welsh descent, musical, and a clever conversationalist. At the age of ten young H. was making slow progress in the three R's, when his father became his tutor, and taught him Latin, Greek, and mathematics for five years, with but limited success. Within seven years he failed—twice as storekeeper and once as farmer; but meantime he acquired a taste for reading, of history particularly, especially of Greece, Rome, and England, and of her American colonies. Then he decided to become a lawyer, and was admitted at the age of twenty-four to the bar. As a lawyer he was brilliantly successful, and from the time of his call onwards, his life was one unbroken line of success, both as statesman and orator.

Henry, Robert (1718-90), a British historian, the son of a farmer. He was educated at the Grammar School, Stirling; completed his course at Edinburgh University; and became master of the Grammar School at Annan. In 1746 he was licensed to preach. He received the degree of D.D. from Edinburgh University in 1771. In 1768 he began to work actively on his *History of Great Britain.* He received £3300 for the volumes published during his lifetime. In 1781 he received a pension of £100 per year from the British government. His *History* covers the years between the Roman invasion and the death of Henry VIII.

Henry, William (1775-1836), an English chemist; son of an apothecary and writer on chemistry. Born at Manchester, and began to study medicine in 1795, took his doctor's degree in 1807, but ill-health prevented him from practising, so he devoted his life to chemical research, especially in regard to gases. His *Elements of Experimental Chemistry* enjoyed considerable vogue, going through eleven editions in thirty years.

Henry of Huntingdon (c.1080-c.1150), an English chronicler. His father, by name Nicholas, was a clerk who became archdeacon of Cambridge, Hertford, and Huntingdon, in the time of Remigius, Bishop of Lincoln. The celibacy of the clergy was not strictly enforced in England till 1102, hence the chronicler makes no secret of his antecedents, nor did they interfere with his career. The only recorded fact of the chronicler's life is, that he went with Archbishop Theobald to Rome in 1139. On the way H. halted at Bec, and there met Robert de Toregni, who mentions their encounter in the preface to his chronicle.

Henry the Minstrel, *see* HARRY, BLIND.

Henryson, Robert (1425-1500), a Scottish poet. It is surmised that he was connected with the family of Henderson of Forfell. He is described as ' Scholemaister of Dunfermeling,' probably of the grammar school of the Benedictine abbey. There is no record of his ever having studied at St. Andrews, which was the only Scottish university in existence at that time; his studies were therefore probably completed abroad. His longest work is his *Morall Fabillis of Æsope;* he treated the subject with freshness. Efforts have been made, but in vain, to draw up a chronology of his poems.

Henschel, Georg (Isidor Gloig), (*b.* 1850), an English musician, naturalised 1890. Of German family, born at Breslau, and educated as a pianist; finally took up singing, having a fine baritone voice. In 1877 he began a successful career in England. He became prominent as a conductor, starting the London Symphony Concerts in 1886, and both in England and in America he took a leading part in advancing his art; he composed a number of instrumental works.

Henselt, Adolf von (1814-89), a German musical composer, born at Schwabach, Bavaria; educated under the patronage of King Ludwig I. at Weimar and Vienna. He made his début in 1837, and in 1838 went to St. Petersburg, where he obtained an appointment at court, and an inspectorship at the Imperial Educational Establishment. His work is small in quantity, but is distinguished by individuality. He himself was a most sympathetic and accomplished pianist. He wrote a pianoforte concerto in F. minor, *Poeme d'Amour,* op. 3; *Dallade,* op. 31, etc.

Henslow, Rev. George, M.A., F.L.S. (*b.* 1835), a professor of botany to the Royal Horticultural Society He was educated at Christ's College, Cambridge, and was ordained in 1858. He has lectured on botany at St. Bartholomew's Medical School and at Birkbeck and Queen's Colleges, and was examiner at Cambridge in 1867, and is still examiner to the College of Preceptors. His publications include : *Origin of Plant*

Structures; South African Flowering Plants; The Story of Wild Flowers; Poisonous Plants; Origin and History of our Garden Vegetables; Evolution and Religion; Christian Beliefs Reconsidered in the Light of Modern Thought; Plants of the Bible; The Vulgate, the source of False Doctrines.

Henslow, John Stevens (1796-1861), an English botanist and geologist, born at Rochester. Imbibed a love of natural history from his father. Educated at Cambridge, where he graduated as 16th wrangler in 1818, the year in which Sedgwick became Woodwardian professor of geology. He accompanied Sedgwick in 1819 during a tour in the Isle of Wight, and there he learned his first lessons in geology. He studied chemistry under Professor Cumming, and mineralogy under E. D. Clarke. On the death of Clarke he was appointed professor of mineralogy in the university at Cambridge. Two years after, he took holy orders. In 1837 he became rector of Hitcham in Suffolk. Some of his discoveries led to the establishment of the phosphate industry in Cambridge and Suffolk.

Henslowe, Philip (*d.* 1616), an English theatrical manager; started his connection with the stage when in 1584 he bought land, near what is now the southern end of Southwark Bridge on which stood the Little Rose Playhouse. Afterwards he acquired other theatres and it was in these that many famous Elizabethan dramatists first had their plays produced.

Henson, Very Rev. Herbert Hensley (*b.* 1863), born in London. He was educated at Oxford University, and was a fellow of All Souls' College from 1884 to 1891, being re-elected in 1896. He was vicar of Barking, Essex, 1888-95, incumbent of St. Mary's Hospital, Ilford, 1895-1900, and chaplain to the Bishop of St. Albans, 1897-1900. In 1900 he became rector of St. Margaret's, Westminster, and a canon of the Abbey. He was proctor in Convocation in 1903, and made a sub-dean of Westminster in 1911. In 1912 he succeeded Dr. Kitchin as dean of Durham. His publications include: *Light and Heaven*, 1897; *Apostolic Christianity*, 1898; *Cui bono*, 1899; *Ad Rem, Thoughts on the Crisis in the Church*, 1900; *Godly Union and Concord*, 1902; *The Education Act and After*, 1903; *English Religion in the 17th Century*, 1903; *The Value of the Bible*, etc., 1904; *Religion in the Schools*, 1906; *Christian Marriage*, 1907; *The National Church; Christ and the Nation*, 1908; *Westminster Sermons*, 1910; *Puritanism in England*, 1912.

Hentschel, Carl, C.C. (*b.* 1864), a member of the Corporation of the City of London, and founder and chairman of the firm of Carl Hentschel, Limited, of London, born in Lodz, Russian Poland. He has been a pioneer of newspaper illustrations and process works, and has invented the Hentschel Colour-type Process. He founded the O. P. Club, of which he was president (1902-3), and the Playgoers' Club (president, 1893-98). He was proprietor and editor of *The Playgoer* (1889), and has also published : *Papers on Process Engraving*, 1900; *The Discomforts of Playgoing*, 1903; *The Necessity of Trams across the Bridges*, 1904.

Henty, George Alfred (1832-1902), an English author, born near Cambridge. He was educated at Westminster School and Caius College, Cambridge, but left without taking a degree. On the outbreak of the Crimean War he volunteered for active service, and his letters describing the siege of Sebastopol were published in the *Morning Advertiser*. In 1865 he adopted the calling of a journalist, and wrote for the *Standard*, going upon many famous expeditions. His first boys' book appeared in 1868, *Out in the Pampas*, and was followed by *The Young Franc-Tireurs*, a tale of the Franco-Prussian war, 1872 (6th ed. 1910). He also tried his hand at novel writing, but without success, his great forte being tales of adventure for boys, of which he wrote about eighty.

Henzada, a tn. of Burma, India, cap. of the H. dist. It is 66 m. W.N.W. of Pegu on the Irawadi R. The district has an area of 2886 sq. m. and a pop. of 484,558. Pop. (town) 24,700.

Hepar (Gk. ἧπαρ, liver), the name given to various compounds of sulphur, because of their brown liverlike colour. *Hepatic* is used in reference to the artery, vein, etc., belonging to the liver; while *Hepatica* is a term for medicines affecting the liver, and *Hepatitis* means inflammation of the liver (*q.v.*).

Hepatica, sometimes considered to be a separate genus of ranunculaceous plants, is more usually included in the genus *Anemone*. The species are herbs and several occur in Britain. *A. Hepatica*, the common H., has a dense involucre of green bracts which resemble a calyx, and the blue flowers are visited by bees for the honey they secrete.

Hepatica, see HEPAR.

Hepatitis, see HEPAR.

Hepatus (Gk. ἥπατος, a fish, so named because of its being livercoloured), the name of a genus of malacostracan crustaceans belonging to the family Matutidæ; the species are found on the American coast, where they bury themselves in sand. They are characterised by a generally convex carapace, triangular frame, and claw-like endings to their legs.

⊢ **Hephæstion** ('Ηφαιστίων), the companion and friend of Alexander the Great, was the son of Amyntor. He appears to have served with distinction at the battle of Arbela, and was one of the seven select officers who were in close attendance upon the king's person. He was also commander of the horse guards (έταîροι) for a time, and was entrusted with many important commands during the campaigns in Bactria, etc., and the expedition to India. He died of a fever in 325 at Ecbatana.

Hephæstus ('Ηφαιστος), in Greek mythology, the god of fire, and of the arts which need fire in their execution. According to Homer he was the son of Zeus and Hera, and being a weakling from birth, was despised by his mother who dropped him from Olympus into the sea. But he was rescued by Thetis and Eurynome, with whom he dwelt for nine years, busying himself by making a variety of ornaments, and amongst them the golden chair which he sent to his mother by way of revenge. Having been brought back to Olympus by Dionysius he was a second time hurled from the mountain, and this time by Zeus for championing his mother's cause. He settled for a time in Lemnos, but finally returned to Olympus and acted as mediator between his parents. All the masterpieces of metal which appear in the stories of gods and heroes, the ægis of Zeus, the arms of Achilles, the sceptre of Agamemnon, the necklace of Harmonia, etc., were attributed to H., and his workshops were placed on Mount Olympus, and in various volcanic isles where he received the help of the Cyclopes.

Hepialidæ, the name of a family of lepidopterous insects which contain the ghost and swift-moths; there are about 150 species, which are widely distributed. Some individuals are small, insignificant moths and others are brilliantly coloured insects measuring 6 or 7 in. across the wings. *Hepialus* is the only British genus, and *H. humuli* the commonest species.

Heppenheim, a tn. in the grandduchy of Hesse - Darmstadt, Germany, 13 m. E. of Worms, is a health resort. It dates from the time of the Romans, and contains the ruins of Starkenburg Castle (1064), a former stronghold of the archbishops of Mainz. It has quarries, and manufs. tobacco and machinery. Pop. 7045.

Heppens, a com. in the grandduchy of Oldenburg, Germany, 2 m. W. of Wilhelmshaven. Pop. 15,336.

Heptagon, a figure with seven sides.

Heptarchy (from Gk. έπτά, seven, and άρχή, kingdom), the name given to the seven kingdoms, Kent, E. Anglia, Sussex, Wessex, Northumbria, Mercia, and Essex, comprising Saxon England. They were not contemporaneously distinct and independent kingdoms, but at some time between the 5th and 9th centuries they each had a separate existence. At the beginning of the 9th century, Wessex, under King Egbert, became the strongest, and absorbed the other kingdoms.

Heptateuch (from Gk. έπτά, seven, and τεûχος, book), a word applied to the first seven books of the Bible, is formed on the analogy of Pentateuch. It is specially used to designate an Anglo - Saxon translation of these books and the book of Job, made in the 10th century, copies of which are in the British Museum and the Bodleian Library.

Hera, in Greek mythology, the Queen of Heaven, daughter of Cronus and Rhea, and sister and wife of Zeus. She shared the power of her husband and had authority over the atmosphere, her handmaids being the Horæ, or goddesses of the seasons, and Iris, goddess of the rainbow. She is represented as being the most majestic of all the goddesses, and as the spotless and incorruptible wife of the King of Heaven. She was the mother of Hephæstus, Ares, Hebe, and Ilithyia, and was the only lawful wife in the Olympian court, hence she was regarded as the stern protectress of honourable marriage. She was worshipped throughout Greece, but the Peloponnesus was probably the earliest seat of her worship, and during the Homeric period, Argos, Mycenæ, and Sparta were her favourite seats. The cuckoo was sacred to her as the messenger of spring (the season in which she wedded Zeus), as well as the peacock and crow, and among fruits, the pomegranate, the symbol of wedded love and fruitfulness.

Heracleia, the name given to a number of ancient Greek towns : 1, An ancient place of Pisatis in Elis, distant about 45 stadia from Olympia, noted for its medicinal waters. 2. A city of Magna Græcia, between the rivers Aciris and Siris, on the Gulf of Tarentum. It was probably founded about 432 B.C., and was first established on the ancient site of Siris. It rapidly rose to prosperity, and was selected as the place of meeting of the General Assembly of the Italiot Greeks. During the war of Pyrrhus with the Romans, the consul Lævinus was defeated in 280 B.C. near this city. H. was still a flourishing and important town in Cicero's time, and was in existence much later still, but is now extinct. The ' Tabulæ Heracleenses,' bronze tablets containing the *Lex Julia Municipalis* of 45 B.C. for the regulation of the municipal institutions of the towns throughout Italy, were discovered on this site. 3. Surnamed Minoa, on the S. coast of Sicily, at the mouth of the R. Halycus, between Agrigentum and Selinus. It appears to have been a colony of Selinus, at first bearing the name of Minoa, but was seized by Euryleon, a Spartan, who gave it the name of H. It was occupied by the Carthaginian general, Hanno, in 260 B.C., and in 256 was the scene of the defeat of the Punic fleet, and appears to have been one of the principal naval stations of the Carthaginians in Sicily. It was still flourishing in Cicero's time, and is last mentioned by Ptolemy. 4. A tn. on the confines between Caria and Ionia at the foot of Mt. Latmus. In its neighbourhood was a cave containing the tomb of Endymion. 5. Surnamed Pontica, on the coast of Phrygia, situated a little to the N. of the R. Lycus. It had two excellent harbours, and was for a long time in a high degree of prosperity, maintaining a very prominent place among the Greek colonies in those parts. Its decline dated from about 54 B.C., when it was partly destroyed by Aurelius Cotta in the Roman wars against Mithridates. 6. A small tn. on the coast of Syria, to the N. of Laodicea-ad-Mare. Several graves cut in rock, and pieces of marble pillars, etc., have been found here. 7. A tn. on the coast of Æolis, opposite to Hecatonnesi. 8. A town in Gallia Narbonensis which is mentioned in the history of Pliny. 9. A name sometimes given to the town of Perinthus. 10. *H. Lyncestis*, chief tn. of the prov. of Upper Macedonia, situated at the foot of the Candavian Mts. 11. *H. Sintica*, the principal tn. of Sintice, a dist. on the r. b. of the Strymon, in Thracian Macedonia. Demetrius, son of Philip V. of Macedonia, was murdered here. 12. *H. Trachinia*, a tn. in the plain of Œta, a little W. of Thermopylæ, founded about 426 B.C. by the Spartans. It was besieged by the Roman consul, Glabrio, in 191 B.C., after the defeat of Antiochus at Thermopylæ.

Heracleitus, more generally **Heraclitus** (Gk. Ἡράκλειτος), of Ephesus, surnamed Φυσικός, son of Blyson, a Greek philosopher, who lived from about 535-475 B.C., during the time of the first Persian domination over his native city. He appears to have travelled in his youth, and on his return to Ephesus was offered the chief magistracy, which, however, he refused, likewise declining an invitation of Darius to visit his court, in order that he might live in retirement. His later years were devoted to the writing of his great philosophical work *On Nature*, in which he asserts that everything is in a state of eternal flux, so that nothing can escape final destruction, not even the gods, and that the ultimate principle into which all existence is resolvable is fire. That fire changes continually to water, and then into earth, and that the earth changes back again to water, and the water to fire. Thus, then, is the world evolved by a natural operation from fire which is also the human life and soul, and therefore a national intelligence which guides the whole universe.

Heracles, *see* HERCULES.

Heracleum, a genus of umbelliferous plants, is found in mild climates and on tropical mountains. There are seventy species in all, and *H. Sphondylium*, the cow-parsnip, is common in Britain in the meadows and hedges. It affords good food for cattle, and in Sussex, where it is known as hog-weed, it is used for fattening pigs. The seeds are diuretic and stomachic.

Heraclian, or **Heraclianus**, one of the officers of the Emperor Honorius, to whom he rendered good service during the invasion of Italy by Alaric, and the usurpation of Attalus. He revolted against Honorius in 412, and, proclaiming himself emperor, collected ships for the invasion of Italy. This he accomplished in 413 A.D., but was defeated and put to death. He is said to have murdered Stilicho in 408 A.D.

Heraclidæ (Ἡρακλεῖδαι), a patronymic from Heracles, and consequently given to all his descendants, but more especially to those who invaded and took possession of the Peloponnesus. It had been willed by Zeus that Heracles should rule over the empire of Perseus, but owing to a trick of Hera's, Eurystheus had taken first place, Heracles becoming his servant. After the death of the latter, however, his sons asserted their claims, and being led by Hyllus, the son of the hero by Deïanira, they invaded the Peloponnesus to take possession of the countries acquired by their ancestor. They were at first unsuccessful, but finally conquered Argos, Messenia, and Sparta, and established themselves there.

Heraclius (Ἡράκλειος), a Roman emperor of the East, reigned from A.D. 610-641. He was the son of Heraclius the Elder, governor-general of Africa, and was born in Cappadocia about 575. In 610 he was sent by his father against Phocas, who had usurped the throne of Constantinople, conquered him, and was elected emperor by the people. He found himself in a difficult position, for the Eastern empire was then in a miserable state, but he managed to get rid of the Avars in 619, and turned his attention against the Persians. The war which had broken out in 603 between Phocas and the Persian king was still raging, and in 616 Egypt fell into the hands of the Persians, so that Constantinople was deprived of its corn supply. Added to this Constantinople, too, fell into the hands of the Persians the same year. H. waited his opportunity, got ready an army, and commanding his troops in person, fought several battles against the Persians which resulted in the reconquering of Syria and Jerusalem, an achievement which seemed at the time impossible. But his glory was of short duration, and before he died Syria, Palestine, Jerusalem, Mesopotamia, and Egypt were annexed to the dominion of the caliphs, H. apparently doing nothing to prevent this.

Heræum, the temple of Hera, situated between Argos and Mycenæ, and, according to Strabo, the joint sanctuary for both these towns until the 5th century, when Argos vanquished the Mycenæans. In 423 B.C. the old temple was burnt down, and the Argives erected a new one built by Eupolemos, in which was placed the great gold and ivory statue of Hera, by the sculptor Polyclitus. Excavations have been made by the American Archæological Institute and School of Athens, 1892-95.

Herald, an officer who formerly superintended jousts, tournaments, and other public ceremonies, supervised the coat-armour, and acted as messenger between sovereigns. He was attended by 'pursuivants,' who were supposed to be learning the duties of the H. The chief of the Hs. acquired the title of 'King of Arms,' and in England in the reign of Edward III. there were two kings of arms, Norroy and Surroy, but in Henry V.'s reign a new king of arms was instituted called 'Garter King of Arms,' and he, together with the other kings of arms and Hs., was in receipt of certain fees connected with public ceremonials and creations of peers. In 1483 Richard III. incorporated the Hs. into a college known as the Heralds' College, or College of Arms, which still exists, and the business transacted by this institution is wholly connected with the tracing of genealogies and the granting of armorial bearings.

In ancient Greece the H. (κῆρυξ), whose person was inviolable, was of great importance. He summoned the assemblies of the people, at which he maintained order and silence, proclaimed war, and assisted at public banquets and sacrifices. So, too, in Rome the 'Apparitores,' whose duties were similar to those of the Greek κῆρυξ, and the 'Fetiales,' a special class chosen from the most distinguished families who managed the settlement of war and peace, were held in high esteem, only the 'Præcones,' who acted as 'criers' of public sales, etc., were despised.

Heraldry. The term originally denoted the knowledge and business of the herald, but it is now almost invariably applied to the science of armorial bearings. It has long borne this meaning, having supplanted the earlier name of armory. We find evidences of the use of some badge or sign to mark off a tribe, family, or individual, in the earliest days, and in all parts of the world, for it is a device that would naturally occur to primitive and half-civilised man. Many have held that the tribes of Israel took their standard from the figures to which they were likened in the prophecy of Jacob, and that these were placed before their tents. Homer and Æschylus describes the devices which the heroes bore on their shields, and antique vases of classical times show many such. Japan, China, Mexico, and India, might also be cited to show the widespread and early use of such devices. In spite of this, we must admit that H., in its restricted sense, was a much later development than was once thought. The Bayeux Tapestry, though it shows devices on the shields of the knights, proves also that these devices were not armorial bearings in the later sense, for, in different parts of the tapestry, the same knight is represented with different devices. We learn, moreover, from the description of Anna Comnena, of Constantinople, that in the first Crusade the shields of the French knights had plain polished metal faces. The mixture of nations caused by the Crusades must naturally have brought about a more regular system of insignia, and it is in the 12th century that we must place the establishment of H. At first it is probable that a knight might choose any symbol he wished, and it was not until later times that the possibility of confusion led to strict regulations. Early bearings were simple in character, and were generally chosen so that they might suggest the name of the bearer. The castle of Castile and the bear of Berne are well-known examples. The heraldic movement started in France and Germany, and English H. did not become systematised until the reign of Henry III. It developed rapidly during the 13th and 14th centuries, reaching its climax in the reign of Edward III.

by whom fresh grants of coat-armour are made. The Lyon King-of-arms performs these functions for Scotland, the Ulster King-of-arms for Ireland.

The shield and its parts.—At different periods the escutcheon or shield, on which in a coat-of-arms

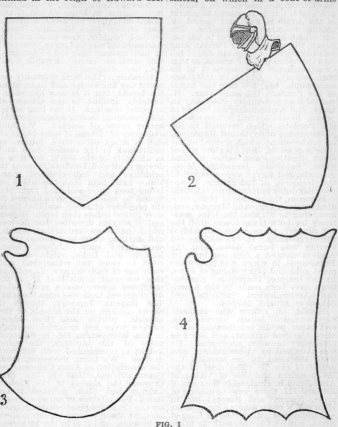

FIG. I

Then, like architecture, it started to decline, and during the 17th and 18th centuries became totally degraded. But H. is still a living science, and fresh coats of arms are still granted. The College of Heralds, founded in 1483, still continues its work. The Garter King-of-Arms is the head of the English kings-of-arms, by whom all heraldic questions are settled, and

the charges are placed, has varied considerably in shape. The simplest form, and that most commonly used, is shown in Fig. I. (No. 1). These shields were often placed at an angle, as in No. 2, when surmounted by a helmet or crest. This position is known as *couché*. In later times, more florid forms were used, such as are represented in Nos. 3 and 4.

These shields are of the late 14th and 15th centuries, and their somewhat square shape is noticeable. The notch on the dexter chief represents the lance rest. Shields in which these occur are said to be *à bouche*. A

FIG. II

widening of the base of the shield became necessary as quartering became more common. In order that coats-of-arms may be quickly and accurately described, or, as it is technically called, *blazoned*, different names have been given to the different parts of the escutcheon. The points thus named are as follows (Fig. II.): A is the dexter chief point; B the sinister chief ; C the middle chief ; D the dexter base ; E the sinister base ; F the middle base ; G the honour point ; H the fesse point. To these we may add I, the nombril or navel point; K, the dexter flank; and L, the sinister flank. The upper part

of the escutcheon is known as the chief, the lower as the base. It is to be noted that the dexter (right) and sinister (left) sides of the escutcheon are named in relation to the wearer of the shield, not from that of the spectator.

Tinctures.—The whole surface of the escutcheon on which a charge is placed is termed the *field*, and coats-of-arms are distinguished not only by their charges, but also by the colour of this field. This is technically termed the *tincture* of the field, and may represent a metal, a colour, or a fur. The names of these are derived from Norman French, as is most of the heraldic nomenclature. The metals are two in number *Or* (gold), and *Argent* (silver). They are represented in engravings, the one by dots, and the other by a plain field (*see* Fig. III. Nos. 1 and 2). There are five colours, viz., *Azure* (blue), represented in engraving by horizontal hatching ; *Gules* (red), represented by perpendicular hatching ; *Sable* (black), by perpendicular and horizontal hatchings crossing each other ; *Vert* (green), shown by diagonal lines drawn from dexter chief to sinister base ; *Purpure* (purple) represented by diagonal hatching from sinister chief to dexter base. These titles are also used to describe the charges. If the charge is represented in its natural colour, none of these conventional tinctures being used, it is said to be *proper*. Eight furs are also used as tinctures for fields. *Ermine* is represented by black marks resembling

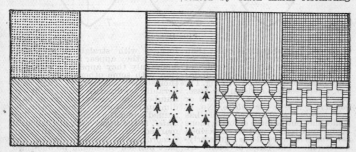

FIG. III

those of the fur itself on a white ground. *Vair* is said to be derived from the fur of a squirrel. It is represented by conventional bells arranged in horizontal rows, as shown in Fig. III. (No. 9). From these two are derived *ermines*, represented as ermine with the colours reversed, white on black ; *erminois*, consisting of black markings on a gold field, and *pean*, with gold markings on a black field. *Potent* is a crutch-shaped form of vair, and these two tinctures have also slightly varying forms, known as *counter-vair* and *counter-potent*. These four last are always argent and azure, unless otherwise specified in the blazon.

Divisions of fields. — Fields are divided in numerous ways, so that the different parts may have different tinctures and perhaps bear different charges. A shield divided as in Fig. IV. No. 1 is said to be divided *per pale*, and is described as *party*. A *pale* is a perpendicular strip (*see below*), and an escutcheon bearing three pales of one tincture upon a field of another tincture, making six pales in all, is blazoned as *paly*. Thus the Strelley arms were ' paly silver and azure.'

and indented. Hence, in early coats we often find a line sometimes of one type and sometimes of the other. During the 15th century there was, indeed, a tendency in bends, chevrons, and saltires towards the engrailed line. The distinction between indented and dancetty lines is modern, the former term being used by the old armorists to include both types. The invected and dovetailed lines are modern, the title invected being given by old writers to the engrailed line. These various forms are used not only for the lines of the ordinaries, but also for the crosses and similar charges and for the bordure.

Ordinaries.—The title *ordinaries* is given to certain of the earliest devices of H. They are marked by simplicity of form and are generally

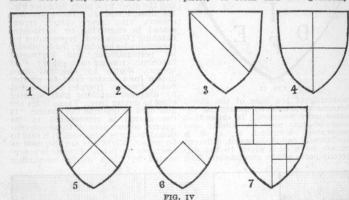

FIG. IV

If the number of pales is other than six, the number of pieces must be stated, as ' paly silver and gules of eight pieces.' Other methods of dividing a shield are also shown in Fig. IV. No. 2 represents a division *per fesse;* No. 3, *per bend;* No. 4, *per cross* or *quarterly;* No. 5, *per saltire;* No. 6, *per chevron.* A quartered shield has sometimes one or more of its divisions again quartered, and is described as counterquartered or quarterlyquartered. The large divisions are then known as the Grand Quarters. Thus in No. 7, the top right and bottom left are grand quarters, the other divisions being counterquartered. The lines which mark off the different partitions into which a shield is divided are not always straight, and Fig. V. shows the various lines used. The engrailed line is very common, and in early H. little distinction was made between engrailed

formed with straight lines. Occasionally they appear alone, but more commonly they appear in combination with some other figures, or are themselves charged. The chief heraldic ordinaries are eight in number, but many of them have diminutive forms which will be named under the main head. (1) The *Chief*, is the upper part of the shield marked off by a line of division. According to heraldic books, the part marked off should be one-third of the length of the shield, but in practice the width varies, being made larger if the chief is charged. A diminutive form of the chief is the *Fillet*, which should occupy onefourth of the shield. (2) The *Fesse* is a horizontal band across the centre of the shield occupying one-third of the depth, though it and the pale, which should also occupy a third of the whole space, actually vary, as does the chief. If there are two or more fesses they are generally blazoned as bars. Smaller bars, borne in pairs, are blazoned as *gemels*. A field divided by a number of bars alternating in colour is said to be barry; the normal number of pieces is six. Other diminutives of the fesse are the *closet* and the *barrulet*. (3) The *Pale* has already been explained as a vertical band in the centre of the field. It is not common, but still rarer are its two diminutives, the *pallet* and the *endorse*, which occupy respectively one-sixth and one-twelfth of the field. A pale placed between two endorses is said to be endorsed. (4) The *Cross* appears in numerous forms, of which the best known are those which appear in the Union Jack. The study of the cross in H. is complicated by the fact that many of the forms have themselves undergone much

FIG. V

adaptation in different times and under different hands. The cross should occupy one-fifth of the field unless charged, when it occupies one-third. All crosses are said to be *fitchy* when the lower limb terminates in a point. (5) The *Bend* is a band crossing the shield from the dexter chief to the sinister base. It occupies one-fifth of the field unless charged, when it fills one-third. Its diminutives are the *bendlet*, the *cotice*, and the *ribbon*. Sometimes a shield is coticed, that is to say, it has a cotice on each side of it. A shield divided by a number of bends of alternate colour is said to be *bendy*. The bend sometimes appears over other charges, and in a narrower form, sometimes called the *Baston*, it was commonly placed over the arms of a younger son. There seems to be no heraldic authority for the peculiar meaning which novelists have applied to the bar sinister, *i.e.* commencing at the sinister chief. The ribbon does not come to the edges of the shield but

is cut off square before reaching them. It is therefore described as couped. All charges placed on a bend are put bendwise, that is to say, they are slanted at the same angle as the bend. (6) The *Chevron* is formed from two bands starting respectively from dexter and sinister base and coming together about the honour point. It should occupy one-fifth of the field, and its diminutive is the *chevronel*, occupying one-half of this space. The angle at which the limbs meet varies considerably. (7) The *Pile* is a triangular wedge-shaped figure generally commencing at the middle chief and tapering downwards. When more than one pile is borne, the points are made to approach at the foot. (8) The *Quarter* is formed of the first quarter of the shield cut off by lines. It is now very uncommon, having been supplanted by the *canton*, which is smaller but of the same form. Other ordinaries are the *Scotcheon* or shield used as a charge, the *Tressure*, a narrow border with fleur-de-lys; the *Bordure*, a border marked of a different tincture from the shield itself; the *Flaunches*, formed by the two sides of the shield cut off by curved lines; the *Fret*, formed by diagonal lines crossing or interlacing. A field entirely covered by a fret is described as *fretty*. A *gyronny* field is one divided both per fesse and per saltire. The *Lozenge* has an elongated form termed the *fusil*. *Billets* are oblongs set vertically. *Roundels* may be considered together with the ordinaries. They consist of discs or balls of various colours; they have received different names according to the colours. Thus the *bezant* is or, the *plate* argent, the *hurte* azure, the *torteau* gules, the *pellet* sable, and the *homme* vert. The first two of these and the *fountain*, which is a roundel divided horizontally by wavy lines, are represented as flat, but the others are shaded to appear spherical. The ring or *annelet* is also a common charge.

Common charges. — Under this head are grouped representations of animals, birds, monsters, trees, plants, etc., and all common objects. They are distinguished from the ordinaries mentioned above, in that they can never themselves bear a charge, while most of the ordinaries can. The charged are described according to the position or condition of the charge represented. The lion, in particular, being the most popular beast in mediæval H., is found in many positions. Thus it is described as a lion rampant, rampant gardant, rampant regardant, passant gardant, salient, sejant, couchant, etc. We have also such forms as the demi-lion and the lion's head erased. Other common charges are the stag, leopard, eagle, dolphin, griffin, escallop, rose, fleur-de-lys, estoile (star), and various kinds of trees. The demi-lion, demi-man, demi-rose, etc., show the figure couped or cut off in the middle.

Differencing.—In early times the undifferenced arms, *i.e.* the whole coat, was borne only by one person, and was by him handed on to his heir. Until he succeeded to the undifferenced coat-of-arms, the heir frequently wore it with some difference, the commonest being the addition of a label. Younger sons also differenced the paternal arms, and this was done in various ways, sometimes by a change of tincture, or by the imposition of a bend, or by surrounding the arms with a bordure. Sometimes the ordinary was changed, and preference was given to those charges which came to be recognised as marks of cadency, such as the crescent, mullet (a five-pointed star), and martlet. The differencing of coats-of-arms has never been carried out in England with great care. The result is that marks of cadency have become very confused, and no order can easily be evolved. It is to be noticed, however, that what has been said on differencing, and the following section on marshalling, apply only to English heraldry. In Scotland, the question of differencing has received much more attention, and has remained in an earlier stage. Here a very common mark of cadency is the engrailing or investing of a partition-line.

Marshalling.—Marshalled arms are used chiefly to denote marriage or conquest. In the earliest times, the woman used the undifferenced arms of her father, and these were frequently placed on one shield by the side of her husband's arms on another shield. This custom gave way to 'dimidiation.' The shield was divided per pale, and the dexter side bore *half* the dexter half of the husband's arms, while the sinister side bore the sinister half of the wife's family arms. This practice never became common, for it is plain that some shields could not be halved in this way. Arms were then parts, *i.e.* the whole of the charge was placed on each side, the husband's occupying the dexter side, as the position of honour. Bordures, however, are still dimidiated, in order not to cramp the charge. In the case of a woman who married more than once, her paternal arms are often found in pale with the arms of her husbands on either side. English bishops part the arms of the see

with their own arms. The practice of quartering became common in the 14th century. It was used by the husband when he married an heiress (in the heraldic sense), though in later times in this case the wife's arms were placed on a shield in the centre of his own shield. This superimposed escutcheon is called a *scutcheon in pretence.* Kings may quarter with their own arms those of conquered countries, and in some cases quartering takes place for other reasons, a grant of this kind having been made in certain cases to noblemen by the king. In quartering, it is important to notice that the first quarter (dexter chief) bears the most important coat, the second (sinister chief) the next important, and so on.

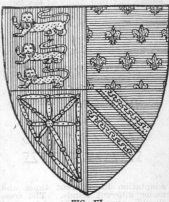

FIG. VI

If there are three coats, the most important occupies the first and fourth quarters, and the others the second and third. If it is necessary to quarter many arms, the shield is divided into more compartments by vertical lines, but the divisions are still called by the same name. Other quarters are themselves quartered, as explained above (*Division of Fields*). An early example of quartered arms are those of Isabella, wife of Edward II., who bore in the four quarters the arms of England, France, Navarre, and Champagne (*see* Fig. VI.). An achievement is a coat of arms conferred as recognition of some honourable deed.

Blazoning.—To blazon a coat of arms is to describe it accurately, so that it could be reproduced by any one having a knowledge of H. Besides the conventional terms of which the most important have been explained above, there are certain other conventions to be observed, chiefly as regards the order. First is named the field, in one word if it be of one tincture. If it be a quartered field, the tinctures are named in order, preceded by the manner of partition.

object, it is to be noted that two are always arranged in pale, and three in two rows—two above, and one below. In other cases it is necessary to specify the arrangement. Sometimes the ordinary is itself blazoned. Repetition is avoided, and the name of no colour is repeated if it can be avoided.

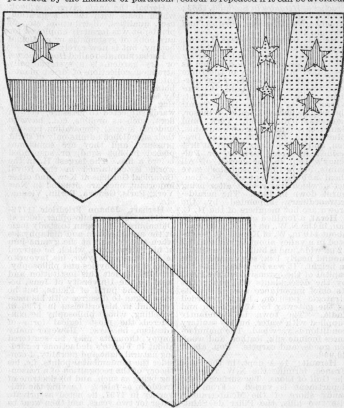

FIG. VII

Then follow the charges, the most important being named first. If a charge is in any position other than the centre of the field its position is described. Thus Odingseles bore the arms depicted in Fig. VII. No. 1, which are blazoned as 'argent a fesse gules with a molet gules in the quarter.' With reference to the arrangement of more than one charge of the same

Thus the arms of Robert de Chandos, differenced with mullets as a mark of cadency, are shown in No. 2 of Fig. VII. These are blazoned, 'or a pile gules charged with three mullets of six points gold between as many others of the second.' The ordinary, however, is named last if it surmounts another charge. When a bend or fesse crosses a field of two tinctures, it is often *counterchanged*, *i.e.* the colour of the bend, etc., is reversed as it crosses the field. This can be seen from the arms borne by the poet Chaucer (No. 3), ' per pale, argent and gules, a bend counterchanged.' *See* C. Boutell's *Heraldry, Historical and Popular*, 1864 ; Seton's *Law and Practice of Heraldry in Scotland*, 1863 ; Bouton's *Traité de blazon*, 1863 ; J. Woodward's *Heraldry, British and Foreign*, 1892.

Heralds' College, or College of Arms, a corporation founded by Richard III. in 1483. It is presided over by the Earl Marshal (whose office is hereditary in the family of the Duke of Norfolk), and consists of the Garter, Principal King of Arms ; Clarencieux, King of Arms S. of Trent; Norroy, King of Arms N. of Trent; the heralds named Chester, Windsor, Lancaster, Richmond, York, and Somerset; and four pursuivants, Bluemantle, Portcullis, Rouge Dragon, and Rouge Croix. They at first resided at Cold - harbour, or Pulteney's Inn, in the parish of All Saints, but in 1554 Queen Mary gave them a building opposite St. Bennet's, which was rebuilt after being burnt down in 1666. The heralds-extraordinary appointed by the crown are not members of the H. C.

Herat, a fortified city of Afghanistan, in the N.W., on the R. Heri Rud, about 410 m. W. of Kabul. It is situated in a valley about 120 m. long by 12 m. wide, and is built on an artificial mound nearly 1 m. square and 55 ft. in height. It was for a long time the capital of the extensive empire ruled by the descendants of Timur ; but its chief importance now lies in its strategic position, being regarded as the gateway to Afghanistan and India. The town is abundantly supplied with water, but its sanitary condition is very bad. The manufactures include silk, leather, and woollen goods, and carpets. Pop. about 20,000.

Hérault: 1. A dept. in the S. of France, forming the N.W. coast of the Gulf of Lions. The surface of the department is varied. From the sandy shore of the Mediterranean rise two hills, the Pilier de Saint-Clair and Saint-Loup, and behind this sandy tract lies a series of pools (*étangs*), and behind these again plains and hills. The rivers are the Aude, the Orb, and the Hérault. The department is especially famous for its wine, one-third of its surface being planted with vines, but wheat and oats are also grown. Fruit trees, too, flourish, but especially mulberries, olives, and chestnuts, and silkworms are reared. There is considerable mineral wealth, coal, iron, copper, and sea-salt being found in large quantities. The chief manufactures are coarse cloths, brandy, soap. Cap. Montpelier. Pop. 480,484. 2. A riv. of France which rises in the Cevennes and enters the Mediterranean near Agde. It has a length of 122 m.

Herbal, the name given to a book which deals with the classification, uses, qualities, distribution, etc., of plants; it was formerly employed for any book of systematic or medicinal botany, but is now rarely used.

Herbarium, also called *Hortus siccus*, or dry garden, is a systematically arranged collection of dried plants, intended to facilitate the study of botany. The specimens are prepared by being laid between sheets of blotting or botanical paper and afterwards subjected to pressure; certain flora, such as orchids, etc., have to undergo special preparation because their succulence admits only of slight pressure, and they are sometimes placed in hot sand, or suspended before a fire. The largest H. in the world is contained in the Royal Botanical Gardens at Kew, and other important ones are situated in New York, Paris, Geneva, Berlin, Vienna, etc.

Herbart, Johann Friedrich (1776-1841), a German philosopher, born at Oldenburg. He began to study logic at the age of eleven and metaphysics when twelve, and at the gymnasium of his native town, which he entered in his thirteenth year, his favourite studies were physics and philosophy. In 1794 he left this institution and went to the University of Jena, becoming the pupil of Fichte, but he soon began to disagree with his master, and in his criticism in 1796 of Schelling, whose philosophy he considered the most logical form of Idealism, he says: ' However many happy thoughts may be scattered about in Fichte's deductions regarding natural right and morality, I consider the fundamental points, *i.e.* his theory of the recognition of a reasoning being as such, and his doctrine of freedom, as false.' Leaving the university in 1797, he acted as private tutor for two years, and then went to Bremen to study philosophy, publishing his views on educational reform in 1801, *Ideen zu einem pädagogischen Lehrplan für höhere Studien*. This was followed in 1802 by his essay on Pestalozzi's work, *Wie Gertrud ihre Kinder lehrt*, as well as by a treatise on the same author's *Idee eines A B C der Anschauung*. The same year he went to Göttingen and published *A B C der Anschauung*, 1802; *Die aesthetische Darstellung der Welt als das Hauptgeschäft der Erziehung*,

1804; *Standpunkt der Beurtheilung der Pestalozzi schen Unterrichts-methode*, 1804; *Allgemeine Pädagogik* (his principal work on education), *Hauptpunkte der Metaphysik*, 1806; *Hauptpunkte der Logik*, 1806; and *Allgemeine praktische Philosophie*, 1808. In 1809 he accepted the chair of philosophy at Königsberg, and published in 1812 *Lehrbuch zur Einleitung in Philosophie*, his best known and most widely read book. His chief psychological work, *Psychologie als Wissenschaft neu gegründet auf Erfahrung, Metaphysik, und Mathematik*, appeared in two parts in 1824-25, and the system of metaphysics on which the fundamental principle of his psychology rested was published in 1828-29, *Allgemeine Metaphysik nebst deu Anfängen der philosophischen Naturlehre*. He also published, in 1831, *Encyclopädie der Philosophie*. In 1833 he returned to Göttingen, where he spent his last years, and wrote in 1835, as a supplement to *Allg. Pädagogik, Umriss pädagogischer Vorlesungen*. H. is important as being the only modern thinker who has not treated education casually in his works, indeed for him it was the starting-point and end of all his investigations. He says himself, ' I for my part have for twenty years called to my aid metaphysics and mathematics, besides self-observation, experience, and experiments, in order only to find the foundation of true psychologic knowledge.'

Herb Christopher, *see* BANEBERRY.

Herbede, a tn. in the district of Arnsberg, Westphalia, Prussia, on the Ruhr. It has stone quarries and coal mines. Pop. 12,081.

Herbelot de Molainville, Barthélemy d' (1625-95), a French Orientalist, born in Paris. He was educated at the University of Paris, and made a special study of Oriental languages. He visited Italy to continue his work, but returned to France and became secretary and interpreter of Eastern languages to the king. In 1692 he became professor of Syriac in the Collège de France. His *Bibliothèque orientale, ou Dictionnaire universel contenant tout ce qui regarde la connoissance des Peuples de l'Orient* is based on the Arabic dictionary of Hadji Khalfa.

Herbert, a dist. of Griqualand West, Cape Colony, between the Orange and Modder rivers; produces large quantities of salt. Pop. 9100.

Herbert, the name of a family (prominent in British history), who came over to England with the Conqueror (1066). H. Fitz-Herbert (H. of Winchester), a descendant, was chamberlain and treasurer to Henry I. (1100-35). The first Earl of Pem-broke (created 1468) was a member of this family, and the title was revived for Sir W. Herbert (c. 1501-70) in 1551. The fourth Earl became also Earl of Montgomery (1605). Some generations later the H. family diverged into several distinct branches, including the lines of Earls of Powis, of the Lords H. of Cherbury, of the H. of Muckross (Kerry, Ireland), and of several untitled branches in England, Wales, and Ireland. The Earls of Carnarvon are descended from the eighth Earl of Pembroke (1656-1733), who held office under Anne. For others of the family, *see* Luttrell, i.; *Powysland Club Coll.*, vii. and xi. ; *Dict. Nat. Biog.*, xxvi.; Burke's *Peerage*.

Herbert, Edward, first **Lord Herbert of Cherbury** (1583-1648), a philosopher, historian, and diplomatist, born at Eyton-on-Severn, near Wroxeter. He was educated at University College, Oxford, and while there taught himself French, Italian, and Spanish, besides gaining some proficiency in music, and becoming a good rider and fencer. In 1600 he presented himself at court, and was sheriff of Montgomeryshire in 1605. In 1608 he set out on a foreign tour, and became intimate with the grand constable of France, M. de Montmorency, and Casaubon. In 1614 he joined the army of the Prince of Orange as a volunteer, and stayed abroad two years, visiting the elector palatine and the Duke of Savoy. On his return he became intimate with Donne, Carew, Ben Jonson, and Selden, all of whom held him in high esteem and encouraged him to pursue his studies, but in 1619 he was again taking part in public affairs, and was made English ambassador at Paris. While holding this post he tried to bring about a permanent alliance between England and Holland, endeavoured to gain French support for the elector palatine on the outbreak of the Thirty Years' War, and suggested a marriage between Prince Charles and Henrietta Maria, but in 1621 he was recalled for quarrelling with De Luynes. He was created Lord Herbert of Cherbury in 1629, and in 1632 a member of the council of war, being reappointed in 1637. He aimed at neutrality during the Civil War, but was forced to admit the parliamentary force into Montgomery in 1644. H.'s philosophical work, *De Veritate*, is important as being the earliest purely metaphysical treatise written by an Englishman, and is interesting for its theory of perception. He makes the mind consist of faculties which are reducible to four classes, of which the chief is natural instinct (practically the Aristotelian νοῦς), the other three being conscience, sensation, and reason. He continued his theory in *De Causis Errorum* (1645), and completed his religious views in *De Religione Gentilium*, published in 1663 (Eng. trans. 1709). He makes all religions, Christian and pagan, resolvable into the five innate ideas, that there is a God, that He ought to be worshipped, that virtue and piety are essential to worship, that man ought to repent of his sins, and that there are rewards and punishments in a future life, thus pointing the way to the science of comparative religion. These works were criticised by Locke, Baxter, and others, but were praised by Gassendi and Descartes. H.'s *Poems* were published in 1665, and reprinted in 1881; his historical work, *The Life of Henry VIII.*, appeared in 1649.

Herbert, George (1593-1633), a divine and poet, younger brother of Lord Herbert of Cherbury, born at Montgomery Castle in Wales. He was educated at Westminster and Trinity College, Cambridge, and in 1618 was prelector in the rhetoric school at

GEORGE HERBERT

Cambridge, becoming in 1619 public orator. He was persuaded to adopt the religious life in 1626 by Ferrar, and was ordained priest in 1630 and received the living of Bemerton, Wiltshire. Here he wrote his sacred poems, afterwards published by Ferrar, *The Temple ; Sacred Poems and Private Ejaculations*, which were read by Charles I. in prison, and much praised by Henry Vaughan, Baxter, Coleridge, and Crashaw. His chief prose work, *A Priest to the Temple*, was first printed in his *Remains*, 1652. His style was influenced by that of Donne.

Herbert, Sir Michael Henry (1857-1903), an English ambassador, was the fourth son of the first Baron Herbert of Lea. He went to Paris as attaché in 1879, and was chargé d'affaires at Washington (1888-89). He was secretary to the British Legation at Washington (1892-93), at the Hague (1893-94), at Constantinople (1894-97), and at Rome (1897-98). He was in Paris from 1898-1902 as secretary to H.M. embassy, and in June 1902 was appointed British ambassador to the U.S.A. at Washington, in succession to Lord Pauncefote, but was compelled to return to Europe in 1903 owing to ill-health.

Herbert, Sir Robert George Wyndham (1831-1905), an English statesman, born at Brighton. He was educated at Eton, winning the Newcastle scholarship in 1850, and at Balliol College, Oxford, where he gained the Hertford scholarship in 1851, and the Ireland scholarship in 1852. In 1854 he was elected a fellow of All Souls, and in 1855 acted as private secretary to Mr. Gladstone. In 1858 he was called to the bar, and the next year went to Queensland as private secretary to the governor, Sir George Bowen. From 1860-65 he was member of the legislative council and first premier of the colony, but returned to England in 1867, becoming assistant secretary at the Board of Trade in 1868. In 1870 he went to the Colonial Office, and in 1871 became Under-Secretary of State for the Colonies, a post he held for twenty-one years. He also acted as agent-general for Tasmania (1893-96), and was for a time adviser to the Sultan of Johore.

Herbert, Sidney, first **Lord Herbert of Lea** (1810-61), an English statesman, born at Richmond. He was educated at Harrow and Oriel College, Oxford, where he distinguished himself as a speaker at the Union Debating Society. In 1832 he was Conservative member in the House of Commons for the southern division of Wiltshire, and made his first speech in 1834, when he seconded Estcourt's amendment to Wood's Bill for admitting dissenters to the universities. He held several appointments under Peel, and in 1845 was transferred to the office of Secretary for War, with a seat in the cabinet. In 1852 he again held this position under Lord Aberdeen, and became Colonial Secretary in 1855. He was responsible for the War Office during the Crimean War, and took a leading part in the movement for army reform after the war. He was also interested in the hospitals at Scutari, and it was he who sent out Florence Nightingale. In 1859 he was again Secretary for War under Lord Palmerston, and in

1860 was made Baron Herbert of Lea.

Herbert, Sir Thomas (1606-82), an English traveller and author, born at York. He studied both at Oxford, and at Trinity College, Cambridge, and in 1628 went to Persia with Sir Dodmore Cotton and Sir Robert Shirley, continuing his travels alone on the death of both his companions. He returned to England in 1629, and travelled in Europe (1630-31). On the outbreak of the Civil War he adhered to the side of the parliament, but was appointed to attend on the king in 1646, who bestowed upon him, amongst other things, the 1632 folio edition of *Shakespeare*. In 1660 he was made a baronet for his faithful services to Charles I. He published *Description of the Persian Monarchy*, 1634, reprinted as *Some Yeares Travels into divers parts of Asia and Afrique*, 1638 ; and *Threnodia Carolina* (reminiscences of the captivity of Charles I.), reprinted as *Memoirs of the Last Two Years of the Reign*, 1702 and 1813.

Herbert, William, third **Earl of Pembroke,** of the second creation (1580-1630), born at Wilton, Wiltshire. He was a patron of Ben Jonson, Philip Massinger, Inigo Jones, and William Browne, and to him and his brother Philip the first folio of Shakespeare's works was dedicated in 1623. He was also interested in the Virginia, N.W. Passage, Bermuda, and E. India companies. He was Lord Chamberlain in 1615 ; Commissioner of the Great Seal, 1621 ; Lord Steward, 1626 ; and Chancellor of Oxford University from 1617, Pembroke College being named after him.

Herberton, a tn. in Cardwell co., Queensland, Australia, is 50 m. S.W. of Cairns. It is an important mining centre ; tin, gold, silver, lead, and copper are found in the district. Pop. 2800.

Herbertshöhe, settlement on Blanche Bay, N.E. of Neu Pommern, the seat of government of the Bismarck Archipelago, the German Solomon Islands, and German New Guinea until 1909. The chief products are tobacco, cotton, coffee, cocoa. Pop. 1200.

Herb Gerard, *see* BISHOPWEED.

Herbivora, the name applied, because of their exclusively herbivorous diet, to the Marsupials, contained in the sub-order Diprotodontia ; kangaroos, wallabies, etc., are typical examples.

Herb Paris, *see* PARIS.

Herb-robert, *see* GERANIUM.

Herbs are those plants which contain no woody tissue above ground, and they are thus distinguished from shrubs and trees. They are further characterised by the usual habit of dying down every autumn, or after flowering. The term pot-herbs is applied to many plants, such as the carrot and turnip, which are largely used for culinary purposes on account of their roots.

Herculaneum, an ancient city of Italy, situated at the foot of the western slope of Mt. Vesuvius, close to the Portici Station, a short distance from Naples. The visible ruins are not so well known as Pompeii, being much smaller in extent and less visited. The city was probably founded by the Oscans, and it appears to have belonged to the Etruscans, and during the Samnite wars became Roman. According to Seneca, it suffered from a severe earthquake in 63 A.D., and Pliny the Younger describes how it was destroyed by the terrible eruption of Mt. Vesuvius in 79. The city was then entirely buried under showers of ashes, stones, and streams of lava ; few, if any, people could have escaped. Its very name was forgotten in the middle ages. In 1719, Prince Elbeuf discovered the ancient site by accident, in a search for marble for the villa he was building at Portici ; he learned from the peasants that there were pits quite close from which they obtained marble and had also extracted many statues. Excavations began on a small scale ; the theatre, many houses, the forum, and the basilica were discovered, with valuable and beautiful statues and paintings ; in the Villa Suburbana, a number of bronze and marble busts and statues, and especially a library of valuable papyri, containing works by Epicurus, Philodemus, etc. Among the most famous statues rescued from the ruins are the reposing Hermes, the drunken Silenus, and a pair of wrestlers or runners, and many more ; these were all in black bronze, and are now in the Naples Museum. Herculaneum, as we know, not only from the works of art discovered, but also from contemporary sources, was inhabited by a more cultured, refined, and intellectual class than the neighbouring town of Pompeii (*q.v.*). Nearly the whole site of the city is occupied by the town of Resina, and, therefore, it is difficult to excavate ; also, owing to financial trouble with the property owners, the proposals for systematic excavation, begun 1908, have been, at any rate, temporarily stopped. *See* C. Waldstein, and L. Shoobridge, *Herculaneum, Past, Present, and Future*, 1908.

Herculano de Carvalho y Avarijo, Alexandre (1810-77), a Portuguese poet and historian, born at Lisbon. He was educated for a commercial career, but had to leave Portugal in 1831, when the country was under the despotic ruler Dom Miguel. In 1832 he published *A Voz de Propheta*, and in 1834 *A Harpa do Crente*, in which he describes the bitterness of exile, etc., proving himself to be a poet of feeling. In 1837 he founded the *Panorama*, in imitation of the English *Penny Magazine*. This paper had a wide circulation, and H.'s articles were very popular with the middle class. In 1844 he started a new venture, and wrote historical novels in imitation of Sir Walter Scott, viz. *Eurico* and *Monge de Cister*, but his great work was his *History of Portugal from the Beginning of the Monarchy to the end of the Reign of Alfonso III.*, the first volume of which appeared in 1846. This book was regarded as an historical work of the first rank, and is still reckoned among the Portuguese classics.

Hercules, the son of Alexander the Great and Barsine, the widow of Memnon. He lived at Pergamus, and in 310 B.C. was brought forward by Polysperchon (a distinguished officer of Alexander the Great, who had been appointed in 319, on the death of Antipater, regent, and guardian of the king) as claimant to the Macedonian throne. He was, however, murdered by Polysperchon in 309, when the latter became reconciled to Cassander.

Hercules (Ἡρακλῆς), the most celebrated of all the heroes of antiquity, was the son of Zeus by Alcmene of Thebes in Bœotia. His step-father was Amphitryon, who was the son of Alcæus, the son of Perseus; and Alcmene was a grand-daughter of Perseus. Hence H. belonged to the family of Perseus. On the day destined for the birth of H. Zeus boasted that a son was going to be born to him who should rule over the house of Perseus, whereupon Hera, having exacted from him a promise that the descendant of Perseus born that day should be ruler, hastened to Argos, and caused the wife of Sthenelus (son of Perseus) to give birth to Eurystheus, and delayed the birth of H. by keeping away the Ilithyiæ, and so robbed H. of his empire. All the stories told of the hero point to the fact that he was strong from his birth, and under the protection of Zeus and Athena he escaped the dangers prepared for him by Hera, *e.g.* he strangled two serpents sent to destroy him in his cradle. As he grew up, he received instruction in music, wrestling, archery, etc., but happening one day to kill Linus who taught him the lyre, he was sent by his father Amphitryon to tend his cattle. While thus employed, he made further exhibition of his strength by killing a huge lion which haunted Mt. Cithæron, and did great damage both to his father's flocks and to those of the King of Thespiæ. His next adventure occurred on his way back to Thebes, when he met the envoys of Erginus to demand their annual tribute of 100 oxen from the Thebans. Cutting off the noses and ears of the envoys, he sent them back to Erginus, who immediately made war on Thebes; but H. defeated and killed Erginus, and was rewarded by the King of Thebes with the hand of his daughter Megara. Soon after this he is said to have paid a visit to Delphi to consult the oracle, and being told by the Pythian to serve Eurystheus for twelve years, went to Tiryns and carried out the injunctions laid upon him. He strangled the Nemean lion, fought the Lernean hydra, captured the Arcadian stag, hunted the Erymanthian boar, cleansed the stables of Augeas, King of Elis, destroyed the Stymphalian birds, captured the Cretan bull, captured and subdued the mares of the Thracian Diomedes, seized the girdle of the queen of the Amazons, captured the oxen of Geryon in Erythia, fetched the golden apples of the Hesperides, and brought Cerberus from the lower world. When he had performed these twelve labours, he returned to Thebes, where he sought Iole, the daughter of Eurytus, in marriage, but having in a fit of madness slain his friend Iphitus (the son of Eurytus), he was commanded by the oracle to serve three years for wages and give his earnings to Eurytus, and so entered the service of Omphale, Queen of Lydia. After this he sailed against Troy and killed Laomedon, defeated the Meropes and killed Eurypylus, and helped the gods in their fight against the giants. He also proceeded against Pylos and Lacedæmon, and then journeyed to Calydon, where he married Deianira, after fighting with Achelous for her. Subsequently he settled at Tractus and marched against Eurytus, whom he killed, and carried off Iole as prisoner. This caused Deianira to be jealous, so she sent a shirt to her husband steeped in the blood of Nessus, the centaur, hoping to restore his affection for herself. But the blood had been poisoned by the arrow with which H. had shot Nessus; and so as soon as H. put on the garment the poison entered his body and caused him extreme agony. He tried to tear off the shirt, but was unable to do so, and was brought to Tractus in a dying state. When Deianira saw what she had done, she hung herself; and H., seeing no remedy for his misfortune, placed himself on a funeral pyre on Mt. Œta, and ordered it to be set on fire. When it was burning, a cloud came from heaven, and carried him to Olympus, where he became a god and married Hebe. Sophocles's *Trachiniæ* gives some account of H. and Deianira.

Hercules, an ancient constellation, mentioned by Aratus and Ptolemy, situated in the northern celestial hemisphere between Draco, Boötes, Lyra, and Ophinchus. The constellation contains no star brighter than the third magnitude, the chief being a variable from 3·1 to 3·9 magnitude. ζ Herculis is a notable binary, with a period of thirty-five years, approaching the sun with a velocity of 45 m. per second. The fine cluster, Messier 13, is situated near β Herculis, a spectroscopic binary.

Hercules, Pillars of (*Herculis Columnæ,* αἱ Ἡρακλέους στῆλαι), the name given to the twin rocks which guard the entrance to the Mediterranean at the east extremity of the Straits of Gibraltar. According to Pliny and Strabo, Hercules tore asunder the rocks which had before entirely divided the Mediterranean Sea from the ocean. Another legend asserts that he forced the two rocks into temporary union to make a bridge for the safe conveyance of the herds of Geryon to Libya, and another that he narrowed the Strait so as to shut out the sea-monsters which had previously made their way in from the ocean and infested the Mediterranean.

Hercules-beetle, the popular name of *Dynastes hercules,* a species of lamellicorn Coleoptera, belonging to the family Scarabæidæ; they inhabit tropical America, and the male insect is remarkable for the possession of a pair of large unequal horns, resembling pincers. Some of the male beetles reach a size of 6 in.

Hercules' Club, or *Aralia spinosa,* a species of Araliaceæ, found in the W. Indies. The tree is closely allied to *A. Ginseng,* from which the drug ginseng is obtained.

Hercynian Forest, a name used in ancient times to signify the wooded mountain region N. of the lower and middle Danube, and sometimes to include the whole region from the Black Forest to the Sudetes. It is now a general designation for the entire wooded mountain ranges of middle Germany, from the Rhine to the Carpathian Mts.

Herd, David (1732-1810), a Scottish author, born in Marykirk, Kincardineshire. He spent most of his time in Edinburgh, and was president of the Cape Club, a literary association which had many distinguished members. He is praised both by Scott and

Archibald Constable, who acknowledges numerous obligations to him, but his fame rests on his publication of *Ancient and Modern Scottish Songs, Heroic Ballads, etc., collected from Memory, Tradition, and Ancient Authors* (2 vols.), 1776.

Herdecke, a tn. in the prov. of Westphalia, Prussia, 16 m. S.S.E. of Dortmund, on the Ruhr. It has considerable river trade and sandstone quarries. Pop. 5649.

Herder, Johann Gottfried von (1744-1803), a German critic and poet, born at Mohrungen in East Prussia. He was educated at the grammar school of his native town, and at the University of Königsberg, where he met Kant and Hamann. At an early age he began to write verses, and his first published works were occasional poems and reviews contributed to the *Königsbergische Zeitung.* In 1764 he became a teacher at the cathedral school at Riga, and a few years later assistant-pastor, and in 1767 published *Fragmente über die neuere deutsche Literatur,* in which he maintains that the truest poetry is the poetry of the people, and ridicules the ambition of German writers to be classic. In 1769 he went to Strassburg, where he met Goethe, and in 1771 became court preacher at Bückeburg. During this period he became one of the leaders of the new ' Sturm und Drang ' movement, and published a journal with others, including Goethe, to diffuse the new ideas. In 1776 he became court preacher at Weimar, and while in this city published *Stimmen der Völker in Liedern,* an admirable collection of folk-songs (1778-79) ; a celebrated work on Hebrew poetry, *Vom Geist der hebräischen Poesie,* 1782-83 (trans. 1833) ; and his masterpiece, *Ideen zur Philosophie der Geschichte der Menschheit,* 1784-91 (trans. 1880), which proves H. to be an evolutionist after the manner of Leibnitz. Other works of his are: *Kritische Wälder,* 1769; *Plastik,* 1778; and *Über den Ursprung der Sprache,* 1772; a work on language. His books have been edited by Suphan (1877-87).

Herderite (after Baron von Herder), a fluophosphate of beryllium and calcium, which is found in crystal in certain parts of Saxony and of the United States.

Herdman, Robert (1829-88), a Scottish painter, born at Rattray, Perthshire. He first studied art at the University of St. Andrews, but in 1847 went to Edinburgh, leaving that city in 1855 to go to Italy. He began to exhibit in 1850 in the Royal Scottish Academy, and was made an academician in 1863. He also sent pictures to the Royal Academy,

London, from 1861, as well as to the Glasgow Institute, etc. He produced many figure pictures, but he was most successful as a portrait painter, especially in his studies of females. Some of them are : ' Mrs. Shand,' ' The Countess of Strathmore,' ' Mrs. Simon Laurie,' but he also painted Thomas Carlyle, Tulloch, Sir Noel Paton, and Shairp. Of his other pictures, 'After the Battle, a Scene in Covenanting Times,' ' Interview between Jeanie and Effie Deans,' ' A Conventicle Preacher Arrested,' etc., are subjects from Scottish history, and he also published pictures from the life of Queen Mary, as well as illustrations for Campbell's *Poems*.

Herdman, William Abbot (*b.* 1858), a professor of natural history at Liverpool University, born in Edinburgh. He was educated at the university of his native town, and for a time was assistant to Sir Wyville Thomson in the *Challenger* expedition office. In 1880 he was demonstrator of zoology in Edinburgh University, becoming professor of natural history at Liverpool in 1881. He was largely responsible for the establishment of a marine biological station at Port Erin, Isle of Man, and a sea-fish hatchery at Piel, near Barrow, and in 1901-2 he was sent to Ceylon to investigate the pearl-oyster fisheries for the government. His publications include : *Report upon the Tunicata Collected during the Voyage of the ' Challenger';* The *Invertebrate Fauna of the Firth of Forth; Oysters and Disease*, 1896-99; *The Phylogenetic Classification of Animals; Fishes and Fisheries of the Irish Sea*, 1902; *Report to the Government on the Ceylon Pearl-Oyster Fisheries, Royal Society* (5 vols.), 1903-6.

Heredia, a tn. and cap. of the prov. of H., Costa Rica, 5 m. W. of San José. It is well situated (altitude 3786 ft.), and is the centre of an agricultural and coffee-growing district. Pop. 38,500.

Heredia, José Maria de (1842-1905), a French poet, born near Santiago de Cuba. He was educated at Senlis and Havana, but finally went to the Ecole des Chartes in Paris, and made France his home. He was a member of the new school known as Parnassiens, who regarded form as being of supreme importance, and his poems, *Les Trophées*, published in 1893, prove him to have been a powerful word artist, as well as a master of the art of verse. In 1894 he was elected to the Academy, and in 1901 became librarian of the Bibliothèque de l'Arsénal at Paris.

Hereditaments, a term in English law, meaning property which, unless devised by will or disposed of by the owner in his lifetime, must descend to his heir (*q.v.*). H. are practically synonymous with land, and are divided into *corporeal, i.e.* interests in land in possession, or which confer the present right to enjoy the land either personally or through tenants, and *incorporeal, i.e.* rights subsisting in or over lands in the possession of another, such as reversionary and contingent interests (*see* REMAINDER-MEN, REVERSIONERS), or rights of way, or other easements. The term also includes heirlooms, and such furniture or chattels as by custom descend to the heir and not as personalty. *See also* INHERITANCE, DESCENT.

Heredity, in biology, may be defined as the relation between parents or parents and offspring in respect to certain characters. It is one of the oldest of the sciences, the Greek philosopher, Hippocrates, having founded a theory of H. which possessed many points of value, but the real treatment of the subject as an exact science dates back to but recent times, in fact it is only during the 20th century that real definite progress has been made. On account of the fascination of the subject itself, together with its economic value in the improvement of plants and animals, it has attracted many investigators, and, in consequence, much material has accumulated which needs systematic classification and discussion. Before an attempt is made to trace out the tendency of ' like to beget like,' it is necessary to discuss briefly the mechanism by which an organism is produced by its parents. Amongst the higher animals and plants, sexual reproduction is almost universal, and in this, in animals, the male element or spermatozoon combines with the nucleus or the female ovum. The *sperm* is usually a free-swimming long-tailed body, in many cases less than $\frac{1}{1000}$ in. in breadth, though it varies in different animals. The ovum is usually microscopic, but in birds the yolk may reach a considerable size, as it acts as a reservoir of food for the young animal. Actual fertilisation comprises an attraction of sperms by the ovum, the forcible passage of the head of a sperm through the egg wall, and the fusion of the head of the sperm with the nuclear germinal vesicle of the ovum. In plants the pollen grains contain the male element, and the ovules the female. In either case fertilisation is normally followed at longer or shorter intervals by more or less complicated changes in the female germ-cell which results in the production of offspring.

Theories.—Various theories of the hereditary transmission of characteristics have been propounded, but in this place two only will be discussed. Darwin's great theory of evolution is based upon laws of H. and variation, and in connection with the former he devised an explanation which he termed the *Theory of Pangenesis* (1868). At the date of the issue of this theory, there was a widely-held opinion that acquired characters could be inherited. The controversy still rages and will be discussed later, but the majority of modern biologists deny such inheritance. Darwin decided that a most intimate relation must exist between the various parts of the body and the reproductive organs, and his ingenious theory demanded that every part and tissue of the body gave off minute particles, *pangenes* or *gemmules* which, *via* the blood current, finally collected in the reproductive organs, so that each ovum or sperm contained within itself the distinguishing features of bones, muscles, heart, brain, lungs, blood, kidneys, etc., throughout the complete list. Development of the germ-cell was the multiplication and elaboration of the gemmules, so that they yielded cells resembling those from which they were derived and were thus able to transmit the characteristics of one generation to the next. Darwin himself saw the weak points in his theory, to mention but one, if a gemmule must exist for each portion of the highly complex organism of, say, a mammal, and such an animal is known to produce countless millions of sperm-cells during its existence and each microscopic sperm contains the myriad of gemmules suggested, then the sheer weight of numbers must suggest the improbability of the theory. Nevertheless, it was the first definite attempt to account for all the varied aspects of H., and gathered within its scope, reproduction, variation, reversion, inheritance of inborn and acquired characters, etc. Although the theory gained but little acceptance, it had a stimulating effect on all later work. The second theory to be mentioned here was an outcome of the gradually accepted hypothesis that germ-cells were not epitomes of all parts of the animal structure, but, instead, had a definite continuity of their own. The development of this idea was due to the German biologist, A. Weismann, who, in 1885, brought forward his *Theory of the continuity of the germ-plasm.* Germ-plasm may be defined as 'the germinal substance which alone is able to give origin to new individuals ' (Doncaster). In Weismann's own words the theory is that

' part of this germ-plasm contained in the parent egg-cell is not used up in the construction of the body of the offspring but is reserved un-

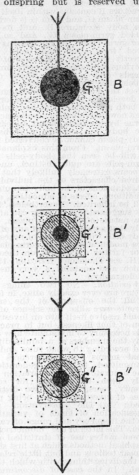

Fig. 1—Diagram to illustrate Weismann's theory of the continuity of the germ-plasm.

changed for the formation of the germ-cells of the following generation.' This may be illustrated in the following manner, though it is advisable to remark that graphical representation is difficult and this figure is strictly diagrammatic and very incomplete. A certain body structure B contains within itself the germ-plasm G, and from G is derived the body structure B' and its included germ-plasm G', and so on. The germ-plasm, in no case, is derived from the body-cells but directly from the germ-cells of the previous generation; the body simply guards and nourishes these cells which develop, as indicated, and affect the body-plasm development. A developing germ-cell gives origin to both germ-plasm and body-plasm for a new individual, hence characters borne by the germ-plasm appear in the body, but, on the other hand, body-plasm cannot be converted into germ-plasm. From this explanation it will be seen that body-cells and germ-cells are quite distinct, and it appears extremely unlikely that acquired characters of the individual, *e.g.* adaptions of the body to outside conditions, effects of education, etc., will be inherited. Nevertheless, it is not suggested that nothing can affect the nature of the germ-plasm, but only that a modification of any of the body-cells will not result of necessity in a modification of the germ-plasm. (For further discussions on theories of H. see Thomson's *Heredity*, 1908, which also contains a very useful bibliography.)

Variation. — No two things in nature are ever exactly alike, in fact, if all the offspring of the same parents *were* alike, the science of H. would resolve itself into an investigation of that likeness, but in practice it is necessary to investigate how and why the members of a family differ, and according to what rules and by what means these differences are transmitted to later generations. The accurate study of variation has only been in progress for some twenty years, though two distinct lines of investigation are being pursued : (a) The observation and classification of kinds of variation; (b) the frequency and range of variation. This latter or the ' biometrician' school makes use of statistical and graphical methods which at first sight appear tedious and but little related to the living things with which they deal. In the case of *discontinuous variation*, as in the classification of, say, horses into bays, blacks, greys, etc., the matter is fairly easy, but generally the variation is *continuous*, as *e.g.* in the stature of men, and in this case it is advisable to construct a *variability* curve. This is usually done by measuring a large number of individuals and drawing proportional perpendiculars indicative of the number of individuals having a definite height as expressed along a horizontal line. From such a curve many facts can be deduced. A low and wide curve would indicate a very variable character; a steep fall in any portion of it would show a rapid decrease in the numbers of individuals differing from some selected height, and so on ; in short, the shape of the curve would be a measure of the kind of variability. The length of the perpendicular to the highest point of the curve is technically termed the *mode* of that character, and the position of the mode relative to the general curve will distinguish between *normal* variations and the more common *skew* type in which the frequency of variation below the mode differs from that above it, so that the curve will be steeper on one side than on the other. This graphical method will sometimes result in two or more peaks showing on the curve which may thus suggest discontinuous variation. (For full discussions relative to graphical methods *Biometrika* should be consulted.) The classification of kinds of variation will demand a distinction between (i.) inborn variation, *i.e.* that which is inherent in the individual and not dependent on its mode of life, and (ii.) acquired characters which may result from the continued use or disuse of some organ or structure. In Weismann's theory it is suggested that the inborn characters alone are transmitted, as these alone are capable of affecting the germ-plasm. He regards acquired characters as capable of affecting the body-plasm only. Although a sharp distinction has been drawn between an inborn character and a modification, it should be remembered that in a certain sense every character is both inborn and acquired, for the former are expressed only under certain conditions of environment, and the latter can only appear when the individual possesses certain inborn tendencies to respond to outside conditions. Nevertheless, theoretically at least, the difference between what is ' inborn ' and what is ' acquired ' is made absolute.

Causes of variation. — This section of the subject is highly speculative, though considerable definite advance has been made recently. It is accepted that the action of environment on acquired characters is all important, but the special difficulty is that this action may be either direct or indirect. An example of direct variation due to environment occurs in the case of the variation in the size of an adult dependent on the supply of nourishment, etc., yet as this effects only the body it, by Weismann's theory, would not be transmitted to the offspring except by *indirect* action on the germ-cells. Nothing definite is known of such action; it may exist, and it may be effective immediately, or its effects may be cumulative and may demand several generations in which to accomplish themselves. On the other hand, it seems fairly certain that most of the inborn differences between parent and offspring are the direct result of the combination of previously existing characters, and in the case of sexual reproduction there is the possibility of a greatly extended range of such combinations, as the two elements may themselves be highly complex. Nor is the offspring of necessity a true sample of the two distinct parents, for in that case all offspring would resemble one another exactly. Many factors other than mere mixture are concerned.

Mutations and reversions. — The differences in type are sometimes due to the appearance of a *mutation*, *i.e.* a variety not connected with the first type by intermediates. A noted example of such a mutation is the appearance of the ancon or otter breed of sheep in 1791, as quoted by Huxley; but as far back as 1590 it was noticed that a ' sport ' arose unexpectedly amongst a growth of the greater celandine. This particular mutation which differed from the original plant in having its leaves divided into very narrow lobes, and its petals also lacinated was found to breed true to seed, and the modern garden plants are descendants of it. Within recent times de Vries of Amsterdam obtained ten distinct new types of Lamarck's evening primrose, all of which arose as mutations. The above seem to have appeared under natural conditions,

but Tower produced mutations artificially by subjecting the eggs of butterflies, beetles, etc., to extremes of heat and humidity. Mutations may either be progressive or retrogressive, *i.e.* a gain of a new character or the loss of a character gained previously. Closely connected with the latter are *reversions,* in which the variation leads to the recurrence of a characteristic of some remote ancestor, though it is quite possible that certain so-called reversions may be due to special cases of recombination. With regard to the actual causes of mutation practically nothing is known, though speculation has been rife. De Vries' *The Mutation Theory* (1910), and Loch's *Recent Progress in the Study of Variation*, etc. (1909), should be consulted for further work.

Mendelism.—In any explanation of H. extended reference must be made to the deductions of Gregor Mendel of Brünn, Bohemia, though it is impossible in this place to do more than touch the borders of Mendelism. Mendel in 1866 published the results of his now famous hybridisation experiments with common peas, but thirty-four years elapsed before the value of his discoveries was appreciated. Definite reasons guided his choice of a plant for experiment ; the common or garden pea is self-fertilised, which prevents any indiscriminate crossing, though different varieties be grown side by side. The plant is easily grown and is prolific, and many varieties exist with well-marked characters which vary and are inherited discontinuously. One of his most noted experiments was in connection with the character of ' tallness.' He crossed ' tall ' peas (which may reach 6 ft. in height) with short or ' dwarf ' peas (which seldom exceed 2 ft. in height) and the result is shown in the following table:

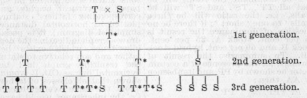

The first hybrid generation resulted in ' talls,' that is the character of tallness is *dominant* to the character of absence of tallness, in the same manner that on crossing a purple pea with a white one, the first hybrid generation is purple because the purple colouration is dominant to whiteness. The second generation

which resulted from the self-fertilisation of the first yielded three ' talls ' to one ' short,' clearly showing that ' shortness ' was *recessive* in the T* of the first hybrid generation. The experiments were continued, and it was found that in the third generation one set of tall (T) bred true to type, as also did the short (S), but two of the 'talls' indicated by T* produced offspring in the ratio of three 'talls' to one 'short', *i.e.* they acted as the T* of the first generation. This separating out in definite proportions in the second generation is termed *segregation*, and it is of the utmost importance, as many characters in animals and plants are inherited in accordance with this law. To specify but a few : in plants—flower colour, seed colour, hairiness or smoothness, resistance to 'rust' disease, long and short styles (primula) ; in animals— coloured coat, comb condition in fowls, horned or hornless condition in sheep and cattle ; in man—the presence or absence of brown pigment in the iris of the eye, some abnormal characters, as brachydactylous or short-fingered condition, etc.

At one time it was supposed that *dominance* was an essential factor of Mendelism, but apparently it was merely the result of coincidence that it existed in all cases studied by Mendel. If the Chinese primula (wavy petals with ragged margins) be crossed with the 'star' primula (flat petals with practically entire margins) the first generation product is intermediate in form. The second generation has ¼ chinese, ¼ star, and ½ hybrid, and of these the ¼ chinese and ¼ star breed true to type. This Mendelian ratio, which is obviously existent in the 'peas' experiment also, may be explained in their particular case somewhat as follows : the 'tall' possess some factor, call it T, by which they are tall, and the 'short' will lack this factor, call this condition S. Now both ovules and pollen grain of the former will possess T, which is absent in both ovules and pollen grains of the latter. The possible 'even chance' unions of pollen grains (T and S) and egg cells (T' and S') will be TT', TS', ST', SS' ; if T be dominant, the result will be that all TT', TS', and ST' will be 'talls,' *i.e.* the ratio will be three 'talls' to one 'short' ; if there be no question of dominance the result is 25 per cent. stock A, 25 per cent. stock B, and 50 per cent. hybrid stock AB. To summarise the result of matings, let the presence of a certain factor be shown by PP, and its absence by AA, then :

$$PP \times PP = PP$$
$$AA \times AA = AA$$
$$PP \times AA = PA$$
$$PA \times PA = \tfrac{1}{4} PP + \tfrac{1}{2} PA + \tfrac{1}{4} AA$$
$$PA \times PP = \tfrac{1}{2} PP + \tfrac{1}{2} PA$$
$$PA \times AA = \tfrac{1}{2} PA + \tfrac{1}{2} AA$$

In this necessarily brief account of Mendelism, the presence or absence of but one factor has been considered, while in practice it is frequently necessary to consider several factors, and this introduces a difficulty in the practical breeding of plants and animals, inasmuch as two breeds commonly differ in several pairs of characters, and if two characters are combined in an individual, only one in sixteen of its offspring will be 'pure' for one particular character; in the case of three characters, one in sixty-four, and so on. For further study Punnett's *Mendelism*, 1911, should be consulted, followed by Bateson's *Mendel's Principles of Heredity*, 1909.

Statistical study.—Not only is H. studied by the experimental method, but important branches of the subject also need special statistical treatment. Galton founded this biometrical study, and Pearson and Weldon have been its leading exponents. From the account given of Mendelism, it will be seen that there are only three possibilities with regard to any particular character, viz. two pure types and the hybrid, though attempts have been made from time to time, with but little success, to classify kinds of inheritance. Notwithstanding this, it is possible to determine *average* degrees of resemblance between parent and offspring. The usual elementary example of this is the relation between statures of sons and fathers, and in this a smoothed graph is drawn, which shows the mean statures of sons from fathers of varying but classified heights, *e.g.* Pearson and Lee after an investigation of some thousands of individuals discovered that the average height of sons from a group of 62-in. fathers was 65½-in.; from 65-in. fathers the sons' average was 67 in. ; 68-in. fathers, 69-in. sons ; 71-in. fathers, 70½-in. sons. Intermediate values were also determined. Now if the sons' statures be plotted on squared paper as vertical heights, and the corresponding fathers' statures be plotted as horizontal distances (*see* simplified diagram), it is possible to draw a graph indicating the degree of inheritance which exists between father and son relative to stature. If the resulting graph had been a horizontal line as CD, it would have shown that all classes of fathers had about the same average-height son, *i.e.* the inheritance would have been zero. If the graph were inclined at 45° to the horizontal, as in the case of AB, it would show that each class of father would tend to have sons of the same average size as themselves, *i.e.* the inheritance would have been complete or unity. In the example chosen, the graph lies between the horizontal and the 45° line as, say, EF, and the steepness of this line is a measure of correlation existing between the two statures. The actual *coefficient of correlation* is expressed as the tangent of the angle FOD, and in this particular example is about 0·51. This simple graphical method is not of absolutely general application, as it assumes that variation is normal and similar in parents and offspring, and it also assumes that the graph EOF is linear; any marked bend in it would demand complicated methods of treatment. Pearson has determined a large number of such coefficients between father and son, *e.g.* stature ·51, span ·46, forearm ·42, eye colour ·50; and has suggested ·48 as a mean value, *i.e.* on the average the off-

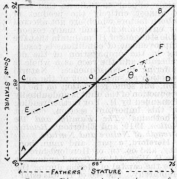

Fig. 2—Diagram showing degree of resemblance between statures of fathers and sons.

Tan θ = coefficient of correlation.

spring deviate from the mean about half as much as the parent does. If the second parent be also considered, the coefficient increases, though it does not equal unity. It should be remembered that statistical methods are supplementary to experimental methods, and they only apply to populations in the mass. The coefficient of H. does not enable the investigator to determine what will occur in any particular case as, for example, the son of a 6-ft. father may be anything within the whole range of statures, yet in those cases of H. too complex for Mendelian analysis, the statistical method has proved of great value. The ' Law of Ancestral Heredity,' formulated as a result of statistical methods, is of considerable interest. Galton calculated that, on the average, half of the H. of an individual may be taken as derived from the two parents, one

quarter from the four grandparents, and so on in the series ·50, ·25, ·125, etc. Pearson has more recently given ·6244, ·1988, ·0630 as the series, thus laying more stress on the parental bequest and less on the ancestral. (For more extended work in this section Yule's *Introduction to the Theory of Statistics*, 1911, is valuable.)

Points in dispute.—Consequent on the different lines of approach used by investigators and on a loose use of many terms, there are several questions in H. which are in a very unsettled state, and in some an active disagreement exists among biologists. One of the most stubbornly fought relates to the inheritance of acquired characters, a subject of the greatest importance to practical breeders. As the subject of this dispute has been referred to previously in this article, only a short summary will be given here. An acquired character may be defined as a feature developed during the life of the person possessing it in response to the action of use or environment (Doncaster). This presupposes something more or less abnormal in the environment, and this must also produce a change on the *body* of the organism. Numerous instances are reported of the apparent inheritance of these characters, but most of them are capable of other explanations, so that the majority of biologists deny this special form of inheritance, yet it is inadvisable to formulate a dogmatic denial of the *possibility* of such inheritance. The classical example quoted in support of the inheritance of acquired characters, in this case mutilations, is given by Dr. Brown - Séquard's experiments on guinea - pigs. In one set of animals the sciatic nerves had been cut, and in consequence sensation was lost in their hind limbs, with the result that many of them gnawed off their hind toes. A small proportion of the offspring from these animals also lacked hind toes. This example appears to support those who maintain that acquired characters can be inherited, but their opponents suggest that the limbs were perfect at birth but the dams mutilated their young. All rodents show a tendency to such acts and in these particular cases the habit had been unusually developed. So the controversy proceeds. The chief point in dispute with regard to Mendelian H. deals with segregation. One school maintains that complete segregation has not been established, and quotes as an instance the inheritance of skin colour in man, which has hitherto defied Mendelian analysis. The usual retort of the opposition camp is that Mendel's law of segregation does apply, but the number of involved characters is so great and their inter-relations are so complicated that the available statistics are not detailed enough for definite analysis. *Telegony*, which may be defined as the supposed influence of a former sire upon young born to a later sire by the same mother, also causes sharp differences of opinion. The belief in telegony is so widespread that many sheep breeders' societies do not consider that a ewe is pure bred after having been crossed with a ram of a different breed. Darwin's famous example is the case of Lord Morton's chestnut mare which bore a colt by a quagga, and afterwards when she was mated with a black Arab stallion, bore two colts in succession which were dun-coloured and bore stripes on the legs. Notwithstanding cases which have been reported and appear to favour the belief, careful experiments by Ewart (see *The Penicuik Experiments*, 1899) and others, and investigations by Pearson have yielded only negative results, and biologists are fairly well convinced that no definite evidence of telegony exists. Another popular opinion relates to maternal impressions, particularly in the case of mankind. There is a widespread belief that if a woman suffers injury or is frightened by horrible or grotesque objects, then the offspring will suffer deformity or bear some mark caused by the effect of the injury or impression on the mind of the mother. Though this tradition dates back as far as the time of Jacob's experiments with the peeled wands as chronicled in the O.T., yet carefully planned scientific investigations have not yielded positive evidence.

Practical breeding.—One of the most valuable applications of Mendelism is the fixing of pure types. A thorough systematic search for the best pure lines is one of the best methods of improving those economic plants which are self-fertilised, and Nilsson and his assistants have done valuable work in Sweden in isolating the best pure varieties from the mixtures of numerous types existing in that country. In the case of the maize experiments by Shull and East, a definite increase in vigour has followed systematic crossing. Professor Biffen has produced wheat which combines the valuable features of one race with the immunity to 'rust' of another otherwise less valuable type. Careful selection in sugar-beet has resulted in an increase of sugar percentage from 8 to 17. More difficulty is experienced with

regard to animal breeding, and theory at present does little else than give reasons for principles already discovered, such as careful selection and the 'balancing of defects.' 'In-breeding' to fix type has been a long-established practice and 'out-breeding' to secure vigour is its well-known companion rule. The matter becomes still more difficult when the principles have to be applied to mankind. *Eugenics*, described elsewhere, is the science which deals with the improvement of the inherent qualities of the human race, and although its principles are based on H. and are thoroughly sound, yet legislative schemes of positive eugenics seem almost impossible of enactment. As mentioned earlier, conclusions certainly appear to indicate that man is almost entirely the product of inborn factors which are not affected by environment, and many responsible students of H. maintain that the improvement of conditions is resulting in the propagation of the degenerate, and the race as a whole is suffering in consequence. Natural selection as such is out of the question, but some restriction on the re-production of the unfit is undoubtedly demanded by H. For further reading in this important section, consult Whethams' *The Family and the Nation*, 1910; and Elderton's *Relative Strength of Nature and Nurture*.

Hereford, a parl. and mun. bor., city, and co. tn. of Herefordshire on the R. Wye, 144 m. from London. It was the capital of Mercia during the Heptarchy. The see of H. was established in the 7th century, and in 1189 the town received its first charter from Richard I. The cathedral was built 1080–1150, and restored in 1863 from the designs of Sir Gilbert Scott. It is a very beautiful building and has a tower 160 ft. high. It also contains a map of the world dating from about 1316, which represents the world as surrounded by ocean, and is filled with grotesque figures of men, beasts, etc. Every third year the festival of the three choirs takes place here. The city is also interesting as being the birthplace of David Garrick, and contains the Coningsby Hospital (1614), the Cathedral School (1384) and the Blue Coat School (1710). The chief manufactures are encaustic tiles and leather, but cider-making and brewing are also carried on. Pop. (1911) 22,568.

Hereford, Earl of. This title dates from feudal times, the first holder of it probably being William Fitzosbern, who led the right wing of the Conqueror's army at Hastings. Then there was Henry de Bohun, who received the title in 1199, and his descendants, amongst whom may be mentioned Humphrey, fourth E. of H. (1276-1322), who was taken prisoner at Bannockburn. In 1380 the heiress of the earldoms of Hereford, Essex, and Northampton, May de Bohun, married Henry Bolingbroke, who was made Duke of Hereford in 1397. The first viscount was Walter Devereux (*d.* 1558), who received the title in 1550 for his services in the French wars; the second was the first Earl of Essex, the father of Elizabeth's favourite; the third, Robert, was the distinguished general in the Parliamentary army. The present holder of the title is the sixteenth viscount, the son of the fifteenth viscount, and was born in 1843. Viscount Hereford is the premier viscount of England.

Herefordshire, an inland co. on the S.E. border of Wales, bounded on the N. by Shropshire, and on the S. by Gloucestershire and Monmouthshire. Its area is 843 square miles, and its surface is undulating. The county is watered by the Wye and its tributaries, all of which abound in fish, the Wye being especially celebrated for its salmon. The soil is particularly suitable for the growth of timber, and the oak, ash, and larch abound, but the county is especially famous for its apple and pear trees. It is also noted for its cattle of bright red hue, with mottled or white faces, which produce very fine beef. There are no minerals of economic importance, and but few manufs. Pop. (1911) 113,088.

Herencia, a tn. in the prov. of Ciudad Real, Spain, 60 m. S.E. of Toledo. It manufs. soap and chocolate. Pop. 6000.

Herent, a tn. in the prov. of Brabant, Belgium, 2½ m. N.W. of Louvain; manufs. tobacco and lace. Pop. 5400.

Herenthals, a tn. in the prov. of Antwerp, Belgium, 12 m. S.S.W. of Turnhout. It manufs. lace, velvet, soap, and cloth. Pop. 7500.

Hereros, or **Ovahereros,** a Bantu tribe of Damaraland, German S.W. Africa, numbering about 80,000. They are nomadic, and employed wholly in cattle raising. They have a distinct language. The Hill Damaras, a lower type, speak Hottentot.

Heresy (Gk. αἵρεσις, choice), a term in theology, signifying ' a choice of doctrine.' In the N. T. it is used with various meanings, in the Acts of the Apostles it is applied to the Pharisees and Sadducees, in the Epistles of St. Paul it is used to denote the divisions in the Christian church, and in St. Peter's Epistle the modern meaning ' falsely chosen ' is first suggested in the words ' Among you also there shall be false

teachers, who shall privily bring in destructive heresies, denying even the master that bought them,' etc. Again, it was used by Ignatius to signify theological error, and as the doctrine became more important, it was restricted to views at variance with the recognised creed. Even in apostolic times, Hs. existed in the church, and before the council of Nice there existed many sects; but these earlier Hs. were chiefly concerned with the introduction of Jewish or pagan elements into the faith of the church, and were punishable by excommunication, etc., whereas the later Hs. were differences in interpretation of Christian truth, and were regarded as legal offences, and punished accordingly. Constantine enacted several severe laws for the repression of H., which appear under the title ' De Hæreticis ' in the Justinian code, and the penalty of death is even included among these, and in the English law the offender was tried by the archbishop and his council, and then handed over to the king for punishment. But the statute of Henry IV. (De hæretico comburendo) empowered the diocesan to hand over the criminal to the sheriff without waiting for the king's writ. This statute remained in force until Charles II.'s reign, after which time the punishment of heretics was left to the ecclesiastical courts.

Hereward the Wake (*fl.* 1070-71), an outlaw, received his title of ' the Wake ' from John of Peterborough. According to the Domesday Book he was the owner of lands in Lincolnshire, and he may have been identical with the owner of Marston Jabbet, Warwickshire, and Evenlode, Worcestershire. He headed the rising of the English at Ely in 1070, and plundered Peterborough with the help of the Danes. He was joined by Morkere, Siward Bain, and Æthelwine, Bishop of Durham, and held out against William until 1071, when Æthelwine and Morkere surrendered. H. escaped, and according to Gaimar, was pardoned by William, whom he accompanied to Maine, where he was murdered by the Normans.

Herford, a tn. on the Werre in the prov. of Westphalia, Prussia, 10 m. N.E. of Bielefeld. It is of ancient origin and contains many old buildings, including a 12th-century church. It carries on a considerable trade, and manufs. tobacco, cloth, and furniture. Pop. 32,540.

Hergenröther, Joseph von (1824-90), a German theologian, born at Würzburg in Bavaria. He studied at Würzburg and Rome, but in 1850 went to the University of Munich, and became professor of church history in 1855. In 1868 he was sent to Rome to arrange the proceedings of the Vatican Council, and in 1870 wrote *Anti-Janus* in which he defended the doctrine of papal infallibility. The work made a great sensation, and he was made a prelate of the papal household in 1877, becoming a cardinal in 1879, and curator of the Vatican archives. He also wrote *Katholische Kirche und Christlicher Staat* (a book on the relations of church and state); *Photius, Patriarch von Konstantinopel* (which occupied him twelve years); *Handbuch der allgemeinen Kirchengeschichte*, a universal church history; and *Der Kirchenstaat seit der französischen Revolution* (a history of the papal states since the Revolution).

Hergest, Red Book of, the name given to a manuscript of Welsh literature, which is now in the library of Jesus College, Oxford. It is a folio volume of 360 leaves written in double columns from the beginning of the 14th century to the middle of the 15th century, and contains eleven tales, the stories of which mostly relate to King Arthur and the early British kings. Lady Charlotte Guest printed these tales together with *Hanes Taliessin* under the title of *Mabinogion*, 1838-49. The manuscript is supposed to have been written at Hergest Court, a seat of the Vaughans, hence its name.

Heriades, the name given to a genus of hymenopterous insects belonging to the Apidæ; the species are British, and are known as the mason-bees. They build cells formed of a salivary secretion, mixed with earth, sand, and stones, and in these they store honey and pollen. *H. campanularum* and *H. carinatum* are well-known species.

Héricourt, a tn. in the dept. of Haute-Saône, France, is 7 m. S. W. of Belfort. Manufactures of cotton, hosiery, printing, and leather are carried on. Pop. 6600.

Heringsdorf, a tn. on the island of Usedom in the prov. of Pomerania, Prussia; is a popular watering-place on the Baltic. Pop. 1050.

Heriot, a curious archaic right incident to copyhold tenure, by which the lord of the manor is entitled, on the death of a tenant, to seize his best beast or other chattel. Bishop Stubbs traces the origin of Hs. generally to the reversionary right of the Germanic *princeps* in the horse and arms with which he supplied each of his comites or vassals, and considers that a H. came in Saxon times to be really a tribute of war-horses, weapons, or armour due to the king on the death of a thane. These ancient Hs. were subsequently rendered obsolete by the institution of reliefs, or sums paid by a vassal on taking up his estate. The copyhold H. had a different though analogous origin and related to socage lands as opposed to those held by knight service. The origin of the right is to be sought in the ancient custom of a freeholder furnishing his tenants in villienage with cattle and the implements of husbandry, which things properly reverted to the freeholder on the death of the tenant, but were usually allowed to be transferred to his successor, the lord satisfying his claims with the best beast, some other chattel, or a sum of money. The right of the lord to this kind of H. is restricted to such chattel as the manorial customary law allows, and that law varies in different manors. It is obvious that the lord has but little moral claim to such time-worn right, and popular feeling on the subject was strikingly illustrated in the case of a certain Norfolk lord of a manor who, having availed himself of his legal right by taking from his tenant's stables a valuable racehorse, incurred the odium of the whole countryside.

Heriot, George (1563-1624), a Scottish goldsmith, born in Edinburgh. He was brought up in the business of his father who was a goldsmith, and in 1601 became jeweller to James VI., having already been appointed in 1597 goldsmith to his queen, Anne of Denmark. In May 1603 he accompanied the king to London, and was one of the three persons appointed jewellers to James I. In 1620 a grant was made to him of the imposition on sugar for three years, and in 1622, having prospered in business, he conceived the idea of founding a charitable institution in Edinburgh to educate the sons of poor burgesses, and for this object bequeathed a sum of £23,625. Heriot's hospital was opened in 1659 with thirty boys, but by 1838 the funds had increased to such an extent that the governors were able to establish a number of free schools in different parts of the city. H. is the ' Jingling Geordie ' of Scott's *Fortunes of Nigel*,

Heriot-Watt College, Edinburgh, was subsidised from the funds left by George Heriot in 1624 to found and endow a hospital for the maintenance of the sons of poor burgesses. This school was completed in 1659, and in 1885 the funds had increased to such an extent that it was reconstituted as a middle-class school, and the H. W. C. was opened to provide a thorough scientific and technical instruction at moderate fees for older students. By 1905 there were about 4500 students in attendance.

Heri Rud, or **Hari Rud,** a river of Afghanistan, Asia, rises in the Koh-i-baba Mts. It flows W. for 300 m. to Herat, turns N. at Kuhsan, and is joined at Pul-i-Khatun by the Keshef Rud. At Sarakhs it is called Tejend. It enters Turkestan and is lost in the Kara-Kum desert. It contains quantities of fish. Length, 650 m.

Herisau, a tn. in the canton of Appenzell, Switzerland, cap. of the Ausser Roden dist., 5½ m. S.W. of St. Gall. It contains an old bell tower and town hall, and the sulphur baths of Heinrichsbad are quite near. It manufs. cotton goods and embroidery. Pop. 15,273.

Heristal, see HERSTAL.

Heritable and Moveable, in Scots law, a fundamental distinction between legal rights and things, more or less parallel to the Roman classification of things corporeal and incorporeal. The distinction is mainly of importance in respect of the rights of an heir as opposed to those of the executors or next of kin of a deceased person. The distinction does not necessarily correspond to the physical distinction between moveable and unmoveable property, although, generally speaking, all rights in or connected with land are *heritable,* and whatever can be moved without injury to itself or the property with which it is physically connected is *moveable* property. But, as in the English law of fixtures (*q.v.*), things which are physically moveable, may in Scots law, become heritable by accession (Lat. *accedo,* to add), and conversely, things in their nature heritable may be constructively converted into moveables by being made part of a moveable whole, as *e.g.* heritable things made part of the common property of a trading company. Lands, buildings, minerals, trees attached to the soil, natural and unsevered crops (*e.g.* grass), are heritable, but growing crops or *fructus industriales* (industrial fruits) are, as in the English law of personalty, moveables. Among heritable rights as opposed to heritable things, are titles of honour, superiorities, casualties (*q.v.*), ground-annuals (*q.v.*), teinds (analogous to tithe), servitudes (analogous to rights of way or other easements over or in connection with the lands of another), and leases (in English law leases are called chattels real (*q.v.*). In the class of moveables, besides physically moveable things, are copyrights, rights to trade marks and trade names, and simple personal debts, shares, bank and government stock, and arrears of heritable debts.

As in English equity so in Scots law. The owner may constructively convert things or rights of his with an opposite state by testamentary directions, or by some act done in his lifetime, *e.g.* moveable estate may be regarded as heritable so far as required to pay for the erection of buildings incompleted and not paid for at the date of the owner's death ; and a direction to sell lands may result in the notional conversion of the lands into money or moveable property. In bankruptcy the transfer to the trustee of heritable estate does not affect the rights of creditors who have claimed in the sequestration. *See* Erskine's *Principles of the Law of Scotland ;* Bell's *Commentarilus.*

Heritable Jurisdictions. In Scotland all jurisdictions were originally personal, *i.e.* granted in consideration of the fitness of the grantee, but when the feudal 'system was introduced, certain jurisdictions, such as sheriff-ships, were annexed to lands and became heritable or descendable to heirs, like the lands to which they were annexed. Later, when sheriff-ships ceased to be territorial, the crown made heritable grants of such jurisdictions to landowners. The Jurisdiction Act of 1746, in consequence of the Jacobite rebellion of 1745, abolished all H. J., compensated the persons who owned them, and made jurisdictions personal to the king's courts. *See* Erskine's *Principles of the Law of Scotland.*

Heritable Security, or **Securities on Heritable Estates,** in Scots law, include all bonds, heritable and of annuity, instruments entitling a creditor to appropriate the rents of land until debts are paid, and all deeds whatsoever capable of constituting a security for debt over lands or the rents and profits of land, and since 1874 also securities by way of ground-annual (*q.v.*). The form of a H. S. is either by (1) a direct conveyance of the lands either subject to the right of redemption or absolutely, or (2) by real or reserved burden containing no disposition of the lands. Any debtor possessed of heritable property and who has capacity to contract may grant a H. S. ; hence a pupil or minor cannot charge his lands, though his tutor or guardian may do so with the consent of the court, and a married woman must first obtain her husband's consent unless her husband has no right of administration over her lands. Different H. S. over the same lands rank not according to the date of their respective grants, but according to the date at which the disposition constituting the security or the notarial instrument upon it is recorded in the Register of Sasines.

An inhibition or writ under the signet preventing a person from incurring debts likely to become a burden on his heritable property, is fatal to all H. S. afterwards granted by the person inhibited, unless the lands, the subject of the inhibition, are acquired after the registration of the inhibition. A H. S. is extinguished by formal redemption. *See* Erskine's *Principles of the Law of Scotland.*

Heritor formerly denoted the owner in fee of a corporeal heritable subject or any parish landowner, but is a term now restricted to such landowners whose estates are subject to the burden of repairing the manse of an incumbent (*q.v.*), or of providing a church for newly erected parishes, or maintaining such parish churches as already exist. The term includes railway companies or other corporations and burgh councils, but not life-renters, tenants on long or short leases, or feu superiors. The question whether real-rent or valued-rent Hs. are to be assessed for repairs depends on the nature of the parish, whether landward or burghal. Hs. may, however, do the repairs voluntarily, and assess themselves at a meeting in the presbytery or in the sheriff court, and they are entitled to borrow money for the purpose. *See* Bell's *Comment.* ; Erskine's *Principles of the Law of Scotland.*

Herkimer, a tn. and cap. of H. co., New York, U.S.A., on the Mohawk R. It manufs. paper, furniture, and woollen goods, and is the centre of a district famous for its cheeses. Pop. (1910) 7520.

Herkless, Rev. John (*b.* 1855), a Scottish ecclesiastical historian, born in Glasgow. He was educated at the universities of Glasgow and Jena, and was for a time tutor in English literature at Queen Margaret College, Glasgow. He was minister of the parish of Tannadice from 1883 to 1894, when he was appointed professor of ecclesiastical history at St. Andrews University, a position he still holds. He was also provost of St. Andrews from 1911 to 1912. His publications include: *Cardinal Beaton,* 1891 ; *Richard Cameron,* 1896 ; *The Church of Scotland,* 1897 ; *Francis and Dominic,* 1901 ; *The Early Christian Martyrs,* 1904 ; *The College of St. Leonard,* 1905 ; *The Archbishops of St. Andrews,* vol. i., 1907 ; vol. ii., 1909; vol. iii., 1910.

Herkomer, Sir Hubert von (*b.* 1849), a British painter, born at Waal, in Bavaria. He first studied at the School of Art at Southampton, but in 1866 came to S. Kensington. He exhibited at the Royal Academy in 1869, but made his reputation in 1875, when his 'The Last Muster' was hung.

He was made A.R.A. in 1879, and R.A. in 1890, and from 1885-94 he was Slade professor of fine arts at Oxford. In 1883 he founded the Herkomer School of Art at Bushey, which he directed until 1904. In 1907 he was made Hon. D.C.L. Oxon. and knighted by the king, and is an associate of the Institute of France and of the Belgian Academy. His works include : 'The Herkomers,' 1910 ; 'Found,' 1885, and 'The Chapel of Charterhouse,' 1889 (both of which are in the National Gallery of British Art); 'Portrait of Miss Katherine Grant'; 'Portrait of the Lady in Black'; 'Hard Times'; 'On Strike'; 'The Guards' Cheer.'

Herkulesbad, or **Mehadia,** a tn. in the prov. of Croatia-Slavonia, Hungary, 20 m. N. of Orsova. It is a famous watering-place, containing hot springs. Hercules Baths, situated close by, and near the Iron Gates of the Danube, were frequented by the Romans. Pop. under 1000.

Hermæ Pillars, smaller at the base than at the top, which generally terminated in a head of Hermes. They were found in Attica in the streets of the towns, and after the time of Hipparchus, the son of Pisistratus, they were also erected along the country roads as mile-stones, Hermes being the god of traffic. They were particularly numerous in Athens, and in the market-place they formed a long colonnade reaching from the Hall of Paintings to the King's Hall.

Hermandad, The (Sp. 'brotherhood '), an association of the cities in Aragon and Castile, formed in the middle of the 13th century to defend their liberties. It was more firmly organised in 1295, when Sancho came to the throne with the express object of resisting the tyranny and exactions of the nobles, and received favour from Ferdinand and Isabella, who endowed it with large powers of summary jurisdiction. But as the power of the crown increased, so that of the H. decreased, and about the middle of the 16th century it ceased to exist. The name was, however, borne by a body of police in Castile, whose chief duty it was to protect the roads. See *Gil Blas,* passim.

Hermann, or **Herman** (Lat. *Arminius*), a German hero, chief of the Cherusci (*c.* 18 B.C. to 21 A.D.), liberated Germany from Roman dominion. He defeated Q. Varus in Teutoburg Forest, 9 A.D., but was himself subdued by Germanicus, 16 A.D. He continued to resist Rome till assassinated by a conspiracy of German chiefs. *See* Roth, *Hermann und Marbod,* 1817; Massmann, *Arminius Cheruscorum Dux et Decus,* 1839.

Hermann, Johann Gottfried Jakob

(1772-1848), a German classical scholar, born at Leipzig. He was educated at the university of his native city, and was made professor of philosophy there in 1798, becoming professor of eloquence and poetry in 1803. He made a special study of classical poetical metres, publishing his *Elementa doctrinæ metricæ* in 1816. He also wrote on Greek grammar, and published *De emendanda ratione Græcæ grammaticæ*, 1801. His other works include editions of Aristophanes, the *Clouds ;* of Aristotle, the *Poëtica ;* of Plautus, *Trinummus*, besides an edition of Æschylus, and the remainder of Erfurdt's *Sophocles*.

Hermannstadt, a tn. of Hungary, the Roman *Cibinium*, the former cap. of Transylvania, and one of the earliest Saxon colonies, lies on the R. Zibin about 370 m. S.E. of Budapest. It is now the capital of the county of the same name, and the seat of a Protestant Saxon bishop and of a Greek-Oriental archbishop. Its once very strong fortifications are represented by some fragments of the wall and by a few towers near the theatre. The Bruckenthal Palace, built by the governor of Transylvania (1777-87), contains a picture-gallery, a library of 100,000 vols., a collection of engravings, a cabinet of minerals, and an archæological collection. Then there is the Protestant church (14th to 16th centuries), the Rathaus, which contains the archives of the Saxon nation, and the Greek - Oriental cathedral, built 1906. The chief industries are the making of cloth, tanning, wax bleaching, and the manufacture of paper, candles, sugar, and hats. Pop. 33,200.

Hermanric, or **Ermanaric** (*d.* 376 A.D.), king of the E. Goths, founder of their kingdom, which probably included N. Hungary, Lithuania, and S. Russia. He was defeated by the Huns during the migrations of the peoples of N. Europe, and fell on his own sword. *See* Grimm, *Die deutsche Heldensage* (2nd ed.), 1867.

Hermaphrodite, so named from the mythical *Hermaphroditus* (*q.v.*), is a living organism containing in itself a combination of the essential male and female functions and structures. It is very doubtful if true hermaphroditism is present in the higher mammals, though it is common in many of the lower orders, as in the sluggish leech and snail, the fixed oyster, or the parasitic tapeworm. Many flowering plants are hermaphroditic, though of varying degrees of intimacy; in the case of the arum, the male organs are situated above and distinct from the female organs, but in the orchid the stamens and carpels are united; this is paralleled in the case of the leech, where the two elements are distinct and separate, though not so in the snail. Some animals may pass through embryonic hermaphroditism, though this condition is doubtful in man as sex appears to be predetermined in the fertilised ovum. Self-fertilisation is largely prevented by the two elements developing at different times in the organism. This ' want of time keeping ' is termed *dichogamy* in botany, and may be either *protandrous dichogamy*, in which the stamens reach maturity first, or *protogynous dichogamy*, in which the carpels first reach full development. The earlier maturing of the male element is the more common occurrence, the hag-fish yielding an example from the animal kingdom. Self-fertilisation among animals is rare, but it is found in the fish Serranus and in the tape-worm.

Casual or abnormal hermaphroditism is occasionally found in fish where an ovary is situated at one side and a testis at the other, in which case it is usual for only one organ to develop and one sex to predominate, with mere indications of the other. Sometimes in such insects as *e.g.* a butterfly, one pair of wings will be indicative of the male sex and the other pair will be female, or the under and upper surfaces may be of different sex appearance.

False hermaphroditism may occur in the higher mammals where malformation has resulted in a female animal possessing the exterior appearance of a male or *vice versâ*. Much discussion has taken place from time to time relative to hermaphroditism and primitive conditions, but the balance appears to favour the view that hermaphroditism is not a reversion to, nor a survival of, a primitive condition but rather a secondary acquisition.

Hermaphroditus (Ἑρμαφρόδιτος), a son of Hermes and Aphrodite, born on Mt. Ida. He was finally united into one person, having the characteristics of both sexes, with the nymph of the Carian fountain Salmacis. The representation of Polycles (4th century B.C.) is famous.

Hermas, probably author of *The Shepherd* (*Pastor Hermæ*), an early Christian allegorical and hortatory treatise divided into three parts: ' Visions,' ' Mandates,' and ' Similitudes.' H. is usually classed as one of the apostolic fathers, but there is much discussion as to his identity. The Muratorian canon makes him brother of Pius I., Bishop of Rome (c. 139-54). The work is prized as a relic of the primitive church, describing 2nd-century Christianity in Rome.

Some recent critics think it may originally have been a Jewish book, revised and enlarged later by a Christian writer. The date usually assigned to it is between 100 and 150 A.D. The shepherd or angel of repentance appears to H. in the fifth vision, and adds instructions (twelve mandates and ten similitudes) to the message he is to deliver to the people. The scene is laid in Rome and the neighbourhood. Irenæus, Clement of Alexandria, and Origen highly esteemed the work, and it was publicly read in churches at one time, but definitely outside the sacred canon by the 4th century. It aimed at rebuking worldliness and calling sinners to repentance. *See* Von Gebhardt and Harnack in Fasc. III. of *Patr. Apost. Opera*, 1877; edition of Funk, 1901; Taylor's Eng. trans. (S.P.C.K.), 1903-6; *Codex Sinaiticus* ; *Athos MS.* ; Hilgenfeld (Lat. text, 1873; Gk. 1888); Zahn, *Der Hirt des Hermas*, 1868; Cruttwell, *Early Christianity*, ii., 1893; Krüger, *Hist. of Early Christian Literature*, 1897; Lightfoot, *Apostolic Fathers* (ed. by Harmon, 1893); Donaldson, *Apostolic Fathers*, 1874; Neander, *Hist. of the Church* ; Bardenhewer, *Gesch. der altkirchl. Lit.*, i.; Harnack, *Chronologie der altchr. Lit.*, i.

Hermeneutics (Lat. *ars hermeneutica*, to interpret ; from Hermes, the messenger of the gods), the science or art of interpretation or explanation of the language of speakers or writers. More especially applied nowadays to the explanation of the Holy Scriptures, covering practically the same meaning as ' exegesis,' a term more often used at the present time. *See* EXEGESIS.

Hermes, one of the ancient gods of Greece, son of Zeus and Maia, identified by the Romans with Mercurius. The chief characteristics of his many-sided nature were inventiveness and versatility, and he is represented as possessed of fascination, trickery, and cunning. A legend tells of his invention of the lyre from the shell of a tortoise, and stealing of fifty head of cattle from his brother Apollo on the very day of his birth. His guilt was discovered through Apollo's gift of prophecy, but he was pardoned and granted his brother's friendship and various privileges in exchange for his wonderful musical instrument. His original functions and primitive character are quite uncertain. Mt. Cyllene in Arcadia was his reputed birthplace and the chief seat of his worship. He appears to have been closely connected with almost every phase of life. He was both the messenger of the gods and the guide of the dead to Hades (ψυχοπομπός).

As god of the roads and of wayfarers he was honoured by stone heaps and pillars or ' Hermæ,' often set up as milestones and terminating in a bust. H. was the god of exchange and barter, and even patron of thieves, hence regarded as the giver of gain—any unexpected windfall being called ἑρμεῖον. From this may have developed the conception of H. as a god

HERMES

of fertility. He was also the god of dreams, gymnastics, and eloquence. As herald he was mostly represented in art with winged feet, a flat broad-brimmed hat (πέτασος), and a wand (κηρυκεῖον or caduceus). *See* Homeric *Hymn. in Merc.;* Roscher, *Lexikon der Mythologie*, 1884-86 ; Frazer, *Golden Bough* (2nd ed.), iii.; Welcker, *Griech. Götterl.*, i., 1857-63 ; Lang, *Myth, Ritual, and Religion*, ʻi., 1887 ; Farnell, *Cults*, v., 1909.

Hermes, Georg (1775-1831), a German Roman Catholic theologian and philosopher. He taught at the gymnasium of Münster, 1798 - 1807 ; lectured on theology at the Academy, 1807-19, and was called to Bonn University, 1819. He was founder of the school of Hermesians, who were in high favour in Breslau and the lower Rhine provinces till the death of Spiegel, Archbishop of Cologne, 1836. H. encountered no opposition in his lifetime, but in 1838 Pope Gregory XVI. issued a brief condemning his teaching. The contest between the pope and the Hermesians lasted some three years, but by 1838 the school had practically vanished. His writings include : *Einleitung in die christkatholische Theologie*, 1819 and 1829; *Christkatholische Dogmatik*, 1834-36. *See* Niedner, *Philosophiæ Hermesii Explicatio*, 1838; Stupp, *Die letzten Hermesianer*,1844-45; Elvenich, *Der Hermesianismus und Johannes Perrone*, 1844; Esser, *Deukschrift auf G. Hermes*, 1832.

Hermes Trismegistus, *see* HERMETIC BOOKS and THOTH.

Hermetic Books, a form of encyclopædia, the sacred canon of the ancient Egyptians, fragments of which are all that survive. It originally consisted of forty-two books, divided into six sections, treating of religion, art, science, geometry, astronomy, medicine, liturgical rites and ceremonies, hymns, laws, the nature of the gods, etc. The word ' hermetic ' is derived from Hermes Trismegistus, the Greek designation of Thoth, the Egyptian god of intelligence. The books are evidently based on Egyptian mythology; but neither the time at which they were written, nor the author, can now be determined. Fragments of the Greek and Latin texts exist in the writings of Stobæus, Cyrillus, Lactantius, and Suidas, some of which were translated into French by Ménard in 1868. Traces of Neo-Platonist ideas can be traced in the books, as well as indications of the influence of the Jewish philosopher, Philo. *See* Kingsford's *The Hermetic Works*, 1885.

Hermione (mod. *Kastri*), an ancient coast-vil. of Greece, prov. Argolis and Corinthia. The rocky peninsula of Visti forms a double port N. and S. Ruins of a temple to Poseidon remain. It was founded by the Dryopes. *See* Pausanias, ii. 34 ; Herod., viii. Pop. about 3000.

Hermit (Gk. ἐρεμίτης, a solitary; from ἐρημία, a desert), the name given to one who retires into solitude in order to live a more holy life. The words ' hermit ' and ' eremite ' were apparently used indiscriminately until the middle of the 17th century, but ' hermit ' is the spelling now generally adopted, ' eremite ' appearing only in poetry, etc. Anchorite is another synonym. As early as the 3rd century Hs. began to appear in the Christian church, and the advocates of asceticism were the first to set the example by withdrawing from the cities and taking up their abode in rudely-formed huts in deserts or in forests. But these, as a rule, went in companies, whereas the H. went a step further and withdrew altogether from mankind, living alone. The first H. is said to have been Paul, a native of the Lower Thebaid, who, in the time of the Decian persecution (250), fled into the desert. His story is told by St. Jerome, who records that he was visited by St. Anthony, another anchorite, who was generally held to be the first great example and preacher of the H. life. But the Stylites, who spent their lives at the tops of pillars, and the Bosci, who lived on herbs, were not true Hs., nor were those who, in later times, separated themselves from their fellow-men to live in caves solely to avoid intercourse with society, and not from any religious motives. Hermitism was not so popular in the Western as in the Eastern church, probably owing to the unsuitability of the climate, and as monasteries developed, Hs. became more scarce.

Hermitage, a dry, red wine, resembling Burgundy in colour and body, obtained from the vineyards of the Rhone valley. It is not dissimilar to the best kind of claret.

Hermit-crab, the name given to the various species of Paguridæ, a family of unsymmetrical crustaceans grouped under Anomura. They are characterised by a hook-like attachment to the pleopods, by means of which the animal can secure itself within the shell ; so strong is this attachment that it is almost impossible to pull a H. out of the shell. The Paguridæ appropriate the empty shells of several species of gastropod molluscs, nearly always choosing those covered by some species of sea-anemone; it is held that the crab and the anemone mutually assist each other, the one by protecting the inmate of the shell, and the other by carrying round and feeding the outside occupant. *Eupagurus bernhardus*, the commonest British species, generally inhabits the shell of the whelk.

Hermocrates (c. 460-407 B.C.), a Syracusan statesman and general, who succeeded in uniting the Siceliots (424) so as to enable them to resist the Athenian expedition against Sicily (415). After the Athenian defeat (413) he helped Sparta against Athens, and held a high command at the naval battle of Cynossema (412). On his defeat at Cyzicus he was deprived of his command and exiled (409). H. fought later against Carthage, and was killed in attempting to return to Syracuse (407). He was one of the most energetic, patriotic, and incorruptible leaders of antiquity. *See* Thuc. iv.-viii.; Diod. xiii.; Grote, *Hist. of Greece*, x. 81 (1846-56).

Hermogenes (*fl.* 170 A.D.), a Greek rhetorician of Tarsus, Cilicia. At the age of fifteen his reputation as orator and lecturer won him the favour of Marcus Aurelius (161-80 A.D.), who soon made him public teacher of oratory. He published the famous Τέχνη ῥητορικὴ . . . at the age of eighteen, long regarded as a standard work, and elaborated by many commentaries. At twenty-five he lost his intellectual faculties. *See* Walz, *Rhetores Græci*, 1832-36 (new edition with commentaries by Rabe, 1882-83); Spengel's edition (1853-56); Aldus, *Rhetores*, i., ii.; Philostratus, *Vitæ Sophistarum*.

Hermogenes (*fl.* 168-200 A.D.), an heresiarch of the 2nd century, originally a painter and pagan philosopher of the school of Zeno. Converted to Christianity, he elaborated a system attempting to unite Stoic ideas and Christian dogmas. Tertullian accused him of heresy in *Adversus Hermogenem*. *See* Theodoret, *Fab. Hæret*, i. 19.

Hermon (modern *Jebel-esh-Sheikh*), a mountain-ridge and culminating point, forming S. extremity of the Anti-Libanus range, Syria, on the border of Palestine, 35 m. from Damascus. The crown has three peaks (*c.* 9160 ft. high) covered with snow for most of the year. The lower slopes have rich vegetation, and are planted with vines and fruit-trees. Ruins of ancient temples surround it, mostly consecrated to Baal. Hebrew poetry constantly mentions Mt. H.

Hermonthis (mod. *Erment*), a tn. of Kena prov., Upper Egypt, on R. Nile, 8 m. from Thebes. As the ancient Egyptian ' On of the South ' it was famous for its worship of the hawk-headed god Mont (Zeus) and Horus (Apollo). There are ruins of a temple of Cleopatra's time. The modern town has sugar refineries. *See* Plin. v.; Champollion, *L'Egypte*, i. Pop. about 7000.

Hermoplis Magna (mod. *Ashmunein*, or *Eshmunein*), a vil. of Upper Egypt, near l. b. of the Nile, close to Roda station. It is on the site of the ancient Khmunu, famous for the worship of Thoth, and faces the rock tombs of Beni-Hassan.

Hermosillo, or Pitic, cap. of Sonora State, Mexico, on Sonora R. and railway, about 80 m. from Guaymas. It has a cathedral, library, mint, distilleries, and flour-mills, and is an important trading centre. Sugar and silver are produced. Pop. about 18,000.

Hermoupolis, or **Syra** (Nea-Syros), a seaport and cap. of Syros Is., Greece, 78 m. from Athens. It is the seat of the nome of the Cyclades, of a Greek archbishop, and a Roman Catholic bishop. It is next important in commerce to Athens, the Piræus, and Patras, its position in the Ægean making it a centre of the Levant trade. There are manufs. of flour, leather, cotton, and ' Turkish delight.' H. has an arsenal, gymnasium, theatre, and custom-house. Shipbuilding is carried on. Pop. about 18,000.

Hermsdorf, Nieder, a tn. in Silesia, Prussia, is 2 m. W. of Waldenburg. It has coal and iron mines. Pop. 11,378.

Hermus, or **Gediz-Tchai**, a riv. of Asia Minor, rises on the E. of the Ak-Dagh and flows W. into the Gulf of Smyrna. Length 180 m.

Hernandiaceæ, an order of dicotyledonous plants, closely allied to the Lauraceæ (*q.v.*), but differing from that order in that the flowers are epigynous. It received its name from the Spanish naturalist Hernandez, who was sent out to Mexico by Philip II. There are four genera in all, and the chief of these is *Hernandia*.

Hernani, a tn. on the Urumea, prov. of Guipuzcoa, Spain, is 8 m. S.E. of San Sebastian. It played an important part in the Carlist wars (1835-40). It contains a modern palace, and has iron mines and cotton factories. Pop. 3700.

Herne, a tn. in Westphalia, Prussia, 11 m. N.E. of Essen. It has coal mines, powder mills, and manufs. machinery. Pop. 57,167.

Herne, James A. (James Aherne) (1840-1901), an American actor and playwright. After touring in travelling companies in U.S.A., and appearing in *Uncle Tom's Cabin*, 1859, he became actor-manager at San Francisco. One of the most noted figures of the American theatrical world of his day, he acted in many plays of his own, the first being *Hearts of Oak* (1878), *Drifting Apart* (1885), *The Minute Men* (1886), and *Margaret Fleming* (1890) followed, but his next great success was the rural comedy *Shore Acres*, performed as *The Hawthornes* at Chicago (1892), which ran for nearly six years. His latest production was *Sag Harbour* (1900). *See* Strang, *Famous Actors of the Day in America*, 1900.

Herne Bay, a tn. and watering-place, in the co. of Kent, England, on the estuary of the Thames, is 6 m. N.E. of Canterbury. It was founded in 1830. Quantities of canary grass, introduced by Flemish immigrants, is grown in the vicinity. Pop. 7000.

Herne Hill, a suburb of London in the co. of Surrey, 4 m. S. of St. Paul's. The name is supposed to be derived from the herons that frequented the Effra, a river formerly flowing through Herne Hill. Ruskin spent the early part of his life here. Pop. (1911) 32,585.

Herne the Hunter, a traditional figure of old English legend, popularly supposed to roam at midnight near an old oak, famed as ' Herne's Oak,' in Windsor Forest. The oak was thought to have been blasted by the hunter's evil spirit, and was blown down in 1863 (c. 650 years old).

Hernia (Lat. a rupture), a surgical term, signifying the protrusion of any part of the body from the cavity in which it should be contained. In popular language, a rupture means an extrusion of a portion of the contents of the abdominal cavity. A rupture may be present at birth, from the failure of closure of the cavity, as in the case of an umbilical H., when the navel is unclosed at birth. Again, ruptures may occur in early life, and are then known as infantile Hs. The opening of an infantile umbilical H. usually closes with age, the closure being generally firm and permanent. An umbilical H. may appear in fat individuals, particularly in females on account of pregnancy, and, if neglected, may attain an enormous size. Ruptures are generally due to weakness of the body wall, though they are more liable to occur in individuals who throw considerable strain on their abdominal walls, as, for example those who do heavy work. Persons who are subject to bronchitis are apt to suffer from H., the condition being brought about by the strain of coughing. The most common form of H. occurs in the groin, through the failure of closure of the canals, *i.e.* passages, in this region, or the reopening of these canals in later life. The first detectable sign of a H. is a swelling due to a bowel containing air or solid substance. Not unfrequently, however, the first symptom is obstruction of the bowel. The term ' a twist of the bowel ' may be due to this fact, because the twisting or blocking may occur at any moment and necessitate surgical interference. It is a common saying that a person with a rupture is in the condition of a man with a packet of gunpowder in his pocket, which may go off at any moment. The presence of a rupture prevents admission to all forms of government employment, and in the case of insurance a considerably increased premium is required. In early life ruptures may close with the aid of a suitably made and fitted truss. In healthy individuals, when a truss fails to cure, operation is desirable, and if the truss cannot close the aperture, so as to retain the bowel in the abdomen, operation is necessary. As in these circumstances the operation is performed under favourable conditions, it differs from one undertaken from emergency and urgency, when the bowel is obstructed (twisted). A rupture may cause obstruction of the bowel, or the bowel may be strangulated, when a portion of its wall is gripped so tight that death of the gripped part, and of the patient, results.

Hernici, an Italian people of Sabine origin, dwelling in ancient Latium in the Apennines between the Trerus and Lake Fucinus, about 40 m. from Rome. They made an equal alliance with the Romans in 486 B.C., remaining loyal till 362. They then rebelled, and though faithful during the Latin revolt in 340, later joined the Samnites against the Romans, by whom they were subdued in 306 B.C. In 241 they received the rights of Roman citizens. Anagnia was their capital, N. came the Æqui and Marsi, and S. the Volsci.

Hernösand, a seaport tn. of Sweden, cap. of the län of Vesternorland on the W. coast of the island of Hernö, in the Gulf of Bothnia. Pop. 10,000.

Hero and Leander, 'the Juliet and Romeo of the Dardanelles.' Hero was the priestess of Aphrodite at Sestos. Leander, a beautiful youth of Abydos, saw and fell in love with her at a festival of the goddess. Guided by a lamp, Leander swam across the Hellespont nightly to visit Hero, but one stormy night was drowned. In despair she cast herself from her tower and perished with him. The romantic poems of the Alexandrian period dealt with the tragedy.

Hero (Heron) of Alexandria : 1. A noted Greek mathematician and writer, probably of the latter half of the 1st century A.D. He was especially skilled in geometry, mechanics, and pneumatics, and famous for inventing various machines and contrivances, such as ' Hero's Fountain,' a steam-engine, a water-clock, and other automata. H. discovered the formula expressing the area of a triangle in terms of its sides—

$$\sqrt{s\,(s-a)\,(s-b)\,(s-c)}$$

(*a, b, c* being the lengths of the sides, *s* the semi-perimeter). 2. H. the Younger (*fl.* 7th or 10th century A.D.), probably a Byzantine land-surveyor, or a philosopher and writer on astronomy and warfare.

Herod, or Herodes : 1. *Herod the Great,* King of the Jews, so called from his great power and talents; became governor of Galilee in 47 B.C. After the death of Julius Cæsar, he was made King of Judæa by Antony (40 B.C.), but only made himself master of Jerusalem after a prolonged siege. He rebuilt the temple with great magnificence, and erected a theatre and amphitheatre in the city, where games in honour of Augustus were celebrated. In the last year of his reign (4 B.C.), the birth of Jesus Christ is said to have taken place, and the same year was signalised by the massacre of the Innocents at Bethlehem. 2. *Herod Antipas*, son of Herod the Great, and appointed Tetrarch of Galilee on his father's death. He put to death St. John the Baptist because he censured Herod's marriage with his brother Philip's wife, Herodias. In 38 A.D. he tried to obtain the title of king, stimulated by the ambition of Herodias, but his nephew, Agrippa, prejudiced the Emperor Caligula's mind against him, and he was stripped of his dominions and exiled. 3. *Herod Agrippa I.*, grandson of Salome, sister of Herod the Great. In 38 A.D. Caligula gave him the title of king and conferred on him the dominions of Herod the Great. This was that Herod who caused St. James to be put to death and St. Peter to be imprisoned. He died at Cæsarea in 44 A.D. 4. *Herod Agrippa II.*, son of the foregoing. He was reduced to a Roman province on his father's death, being too young to govern Judæa, and later was made superintendent of the temple at Jerusalem, and had the power of nominating the high priests. He lived a good deal in Jerusalem, but was driven from the city in the revolt which ended so fatally for the Jews. In the war (67 A.D.) he took the Roman side, joining Cestius, the Roman commander. He rendered great services to Titus during the siege of Jerusalem, and after its capture in 70 A.D., returned to Rome, where he is said to have died about 100 A.D. With him terminated the Herodian line.

Herodas, or Herondas, a Greek poet of the 3rd century B.C., belonging to the Alexandrian school. He was a writer of mimes, realistic dramatic scenes of everyday life, much in the style familiar from the celebrated idyll, *Gorgo and Praxinœ* of Theocritus, of whom he was a younger contemporary. They are written in racy Greek and in a curious limping metre, suitable to the talk of characters, as representing types of ordinary people, such as a schoolmaster, temple attendant, shoemaker, mistresses and their slaves, etc.

Though H.'s name had long been known, fragments only had survived till the discovery in 1891 of a papyrus MS. in the Fayum, Egypt. The mimes are vivid, clean-cut sketches in dialogue, some 100 lines each in length, frequently coarse but obviously drawn with unflinching realism from life. The parody of a scene in a Greek court of law, mime II., the little servant-maid's tactful wit, mime V., are good examples of H.'s powers. The MS. was edited by Sir F. G. Kenyon, 1891. *See also* editions by O. Crusius, 1905; by J. A. Nairn, 1904, the latter with notes, introduction, etc., and verse trans. by H. Sharpley in *A Realist of the Ægean*, 1906.

Herodes Atticus, *see* ATTICUS, HERODES.

Herodian, or Herodianus, a Greek historian of the 3rd century A.D., author of a history of the Roman empire from the death of Marcus Aurelius to Gordianus III., 180-238 A.D. Little is known of his life except that he held subordinate office in Rome, 203 A.D. His work is valuable as a contemporary continuation of the history of Dion Cassius, but his omissions, *e.g.* of the growth of Christianity, etc., are striking.

Herodians, a political party of Jews, who were adherents of the Idumæan dynasty and warm supporters of Herod the Great. In the N.T. they are mentioned with the Pharisees as being hostile to Jesus (Mark iii. 6; Matt. xxii. 6). They were also called Bœthusians by the rabbis because they were friendly to the family of Bœthus.

Herodotus (*c.* 484-*c.* 425 B.C.), a Greek historian, sometimes called the 'father of history,' born at Halicarnassus, a dependency of Persia in Asia Minor. He was the son of Lyxes and Rhæo (or Dryo), and the nephew of the epic poet Panyasis, who was put to death by the Persian tyrant, Lygdamis, on a charge of treason (*c.* 457). About the year 464 he left Halicarnassus and travelled in Greece and in foreign countries. He visited Athens, Corinth, and Thebes, and other great cities of Greece and the important islands of the archipelago. He also journeyed through Macedonia and Thrace to the shores of the Black Sea, and travelled inland to Susa, the capital of Persia, Babylon, and then southwards to the ancient city of Tyre through Palestine to Egypt. He also visited Southern Italy and Sicily, but the dates of his various journeys are quite uncertain. H. thus had a personal knowledge of the countries of which he wrote. On his travels he collected a great amount of geographical, ethnological, and archæological knowledge, of which he made such excellent use in his history. We know very little with certainty about the facts of his life. It is probable that he resided in the island of Samos about 457, thus putting himself under the protection of Athens. After six or seven years he returned to Halicarnassus, and, according to Suidas, took an active part in the expulsion of Lygdamis. He became a member of the Athenian confederacy, but about 447 went to Athens in the hope that his writings would be more appreciated there than they had been in his native place. In 445 he was voted a sum of

HERODOTUS

ten talents (£2400) as an acknowledgment of his genius. In 443 he assisted in the foundation of the Athenian colony of Thurii, of which he became a citizen, and where he probably died. The early books of his history describe the rise and growth of the two kingdoms of Greece and Persia. Books V. to IX. relate the history of the two great wars of the Persian invasion. His style is very discursive, and he expatiates with great charm on the climate and geographical features of the various countries he touches upon, as well as upon the manners and customs of the strange people who inhabit them. His history has always been praised for its style, which owes its attraction partly, no doubt, to the fact that it was written primarily for

recitation. Its veracity has not infrequently been questioned. With regard to ancient history he was no doubt very credulous, but his account of the two Persian wars is accepted as the great authoritative version by all modern historians. He was very diligent in collecting materials for the early part of his history, but lacked judgment. This history was first translated into English by Littlebury in 1737. Canon Rawlinson's translation (1858-60) has many valuable annotations. The best editions of the text are those of Stein (1869-71), Sayce (1883), and Macan, *Herodotus*, iv.-vi., 1895; vii.-ix., 1908. Consult Rennell, *Geography of Herodotus*, 1800, and J. B. Bury, *Ancient Greek Historians*, 1908.

Heroic, having the qualities of a hero. In classical mythology a hero was something between a god and a man, not quite equal to the former, but raised above the latter by his superior strength, courage, and intelligence. The qualities that go to make a hero may be divided into two classes, the physical and metaphysical. In ancient times the former alone were taken into account; a man who possessed great physical strength and courage coupled with daring and determination was H., whether in other respects he was good or bad, so that in olden times the majority of heroes were warriors. In later times it came to be understood that certain other qualities also went to the making of heroes, and moral courage and integrity were held to be the attributes of heroes equally with physical courage and daring. So that on one hand we have the heroes who have won the coveted title by their superior physical qualities, their courage, fortitude, and daring, and on the other, those who may be devoid of all the great physical qualities, but who possess moral courage, fortitude, and determination beyond their fellows, and who are equally, if not more, worthy of the title.

Heroic Play, The, a critical term, originating in Dryden, applied to the tragedy of the Restoration period. The chief characteristics of the heroic drama are strict observance of the unities, and careful adaptation of French models, largely from Corneille and Molière. It has a marked tendency to long rhetorical and declamatory speeches, and its vehicle is the heroic couplet. The link with the Elizabethan drama is Davenant, whose *Albovine* (1629) possesses all the characteristics of the heroic drama except the heroic couplet. In his preface to the *Conquest of Granada*, 1670, Dryden asserts that 'an heroic play ought to be an imitation in little of an heroic poem, and consequently that love and valour ought to be the subject of it.' Dryden was the chief exponent of the H. P., which had its vogue between 1660 and 1680. His chief plays of this sort are: *The Indian Queen*, 1667; *Tyrannic Love*, 1669; *The Conquest of Granada*, 1670; and *Aurungzebe*, 1675. In the last-mentioned play, Dryden confessed himself 'weary of his long-loved mistress, Rhyme,' and henceforth devoted himself to blank-verse tragedy. In 1671 the Duke of Buckingham and other wits had parodied the H. P. in a delightful burlesque, *The Rehearsal*. Heroics, however, still flourished, until the great craftsman, Dryden, deserted rhyme for blank verse. Nevertheless, the H. P. had not entirely disappeared by the end of the century. Consult Ker's *Essays of John Dryden*, 1900, and Maidment and Logan's *Dramatists of the Restoration* (4 vols.), 1873.

Heroic Verse, in prosody, is applied to rhymed iambic couplets, often called heroic couplets. It was first used by Chaucer in the *Legend of Good Women*. It attained its most polished form with Dryden and Pope, but has since been used with great freedom by Bryon, Keats, Swinburne, and others.

Hérold, Louis Joseph Ferdinand (1791-1833), a French musician and composer, born in Paris. He studied at the Paris Conservatoire, and in 1812 gained the Grand Prix de Rome with a cantata, *La Duchesse de la Vallière*. He then went to Italy and also visited Vienna. His first French opera was *La Rosières*, 1817, which was followed by numerous other works, of which the best known are: *Marie*, 1826; *Zampa*, 1831; and *Le Pré aux clercs*, 1832. See Jouvin's *Hérold, sa vie et ses Œuvres*, 1868.

Heron, the name given to the species of ciconiiform birds belonging to the family Ardeidæ; they are characterised by long necks and legs, slender bodies, and beautiful plumage. They frequent lakes, fens, and the mud-flats found on sandy shores, where they wade into the water and often stand ankle-deep for a considerable time, searching for prey; they capture fish, molluscs, worms, etc., by spearing them with their long bill and their appetite seems insatiable. Hs. nest on trees, bushes, ivy-covered rocks, or reeds, making a loose fabric of sticks lined with grass, leaves, etc.; they lay greenish or drab-coloured eggs, varying in number from two to seven with the different species. *Ardea* is the largest genus, and its distribution is world-wide; *A. cinerea*, the common European H., is found also in Africa, Asia, Japan, and Australia; white Hs., or egrets, are generally less than other species, *A. garzetta* being the smallest of all; this beautiful bird, which is called the little egret, has long filamentous plumes and two lengthened crest feathers, which are said to be temporarily lost after breeding; this species is occasionally found in Britain; *A. alba*, the great white H., ranges from Central Europe to Africa and Asia; *A. occidentalis*, the white H. of Florida, is an even larger bird; *A. goliath*, probably the largest of all species,

HERON

has a reddish head, neck, and undersurface. The genus *Nycticorax*, or night Hs., are remarkable for the long, occipital feathers, blackish or white in colour, which are lost for a time after breeding; the species vary greatly in colouring, *N. griseus*, which occasionally visits British shores, being greenish-black. *Botaurus*, the bitterns, and *Balæniceps*, the shoebills, belong to the same family as Hs.

Herondas, *see* HERODAS.

Herophilus (335-280 B.C.), a physician, who was founder of one of the earliest schools of medicine in Alexandria. He was a Greek of Chalcedon and a follower of Hippocrates, and was famous for his researches in anatomy, though he seems to have been equally skilled in the use of drugs. *See* Marx's *Herophilus*, 1838.

Herostratus, an Ephesian, who so hungered for notoriety that on the night of the birth of Alexander the

Great (356 B.C.) he set fire to the temple of Artemis at Ephesus.

Herpes, see SKIN DISEASES.

Herpetology (Gk. ἑρπετόν, a reptile, and λέγειν, speak), the science which treats of reptiles, their habits, structure, and distribution; it is sometimes extended to include certain amphibians, such as the Batrachia.

Herrenalb, a vil. on the Alb, Würtemberg, Germany, 16 m. S. of Karlsruhe. It is a health resort of the Black Forest. Near by was the Benedictine monastery of H., destroyed in 1642 by the Swedes. Pop. 1322.

Herrera, a vil. in the dist. of Estape and prov. of Seville, Spain. Pop. 5600.

Herrera, Fernando de (c. 1534-97), a Spanish lyrical poet, born at Seville. He had a profound admiration for the Italian poets and took a large share in introducing their metrical systems into Spain. His commentary on Garcilaso (1580) involved him in a series of literary polemics. His odes, especially those on the battle of Lepanto and Don John of Austria, and his elegies on King Sebastian of Portugal and Sir Thomas More, are marked by grandeur, melody, and profundity, and entitle him to rank as the greatest of Andalusian poets. His sonnets, addressed to the Countess of Gelves, have been condemned as insincere in sentiment, but their workmanship is admirable. All his works are printed in the *Biblioteca de autores españoles,* xxxii. *See* Angel Laso de Vega's *Historia de la Escuela Poetica Sevillana,* 1876, and A. Morel Fatio, *L'Hymne sur Lépante,* 1893.

Herrera, Francisco de (1576-1656), surnamed ' El Viego ' (the Elder), a Spanish historical and fresco painter, born in Seville. He was a man of such violent temper and coarse manners that neither his children nor pupils would remain with him, although both his son and Velasquez learnt from him his energy of design and bold, vigorous touch. His skill as a worker in bronze led to his being accused of coining false money, and he sought refuge in the Jesuits' College, Seville, which he adorned with his celebrated ' St. Hermengild in Glory,' and which won him the pardon of Philip IV.

Herrera, Francisco (1622-85), surnamed ' El Mozo ' (the Younger), to distinguish him from his father ' El Viego,' a Spanish painter, born at Seville, from which he fled to Rome on account of his father's cruelty. He became renowned for his pictures of still life, flowers, fruit, and fish. He also painted frescoes and, in later life,

portraits. On his return to Seville he became sub-director of its academy under Murillo (1660). His best picture is, perhaps, the ' San Francisco ' in Seville Cathedral. His ' Assumption of the Virgin ' in the Atocha Church in Madrid, won for him the title of painter to the king.

Herrera y Tordesillas, Antonio de (1549-1625), a Spanish historian, born at Cuellar, Segovia, Spain. He became secretary to Vespasian Gonzago, who commended him to Philip II. of Spain, by whom Herrera was appointed historiographer of the Indies and of Castile. His most valuable work is *Historia general de los hechos de los Castellanos en las islas y tierra firme del Mar Oceano* (Madrid), 1601-15 (translated into English, 1740). He also wrote *Historia general del Mundo del Tiempo del Senor Rey Don Felipe II.,* 1601-2. *See* Prescott, *Conquest of Mexico,* ii.

Herreshoff, Nathaniel Greene (b. 1848), an American yacht designer, born at Bristol, Rhode Island. He has designed numerous vessels, including some torpedo boats, and the *Vigilant, Defender, Columbia,* and *Reliance,* winners of the international yacht races for the America Cup.

Herrick, Robert (1591-1674), an English poet, born in Cheapside, London, was the son of a London goldsmith. In 1607 he was apprenticed to his uncle, one of the richest goldsmiths of the time, and during his apprenticeship joined the band of poets and wits who surrounded Ben Jonson. In 1614 he proceeded to Cambridge, and took his degree of Master of Arts in 1620. Some time before 1627 he must have taken holy orders. From 1629-48 he was vicar of Dean Prior, near Totnes, Devonshire, where he wrote his immortal lyrics of the countryside and rural customs. He was ejected by the Puritans, but returned to Dean Prior in 1662 and died there. Some poems of his were published in 1635, but it was not until 1648 that he published the *Hesperides, or the Works both Human and Divine of Robert Herrick.* His ' divine ' poems ring less true than the ' human ' ones, which, written partly under the influence of Ben Jonson, but chiefly modelled on the pagan poets, possess an exquisite lyric quality, and place him at the head of English pastoral lyrists. Complete works edited by W. C. Hazlitt (1869), collected poems edited by G. Saintsbury (1893), L. Magnus (1899), etc. *See* F. W. Moorman, *Robert Herrick,* 1910.

Herries, Sir John Maxwell, fourth **Lord** (c. 1512-83), a Scottish politician was the second son of Robert, fourth Lord Maxwell. In early life he was a supporter of the Reformed party and a friend of John Knox, but in 1566 he cast in his lot with Mary and joined her at Dunbar. He led her cavalry at Langside (*see* Sir Walter Scott's *Abbott*) and rode with her into England in 1568. On his return to Scotland he laboured in Mary's cause and was imprisoned by the Regent Murray. In 1578 he was concerned in the plot for depriving Morton of the regency, and after Morton's death in 1581, was closely allied with the Regent Lennox in his schemes for Mary's release. For his own version of his political conduct see his *Historical Memoirs* printed by the Abbotsford Club in 1836.

Herrin, a post tn., Williamson co., Illinois, U.S.A., 7 m. N.W. of Marion. It has coal mines, foundries, saw mills, and machine shops. Pop. (1910) 6861.

Herring (*Clupea harengus*), a fish which resembles the pilchard both in habits and in shape, but which is found further N. In size it is moderately small, and has thin, silvery scales which do not extend to the head, small teeth and open gills. It has only one dorsal fin and one short ventral, and there are no spines in the fins. It keeps close to the surface of the sea, swimming high in the water. The lower edge of the H. is flattened, and covered with bony plates and varyingly sharp or serrated. It feeds like the whale by straining the water through its long gill-rakers, which form a dovetailed screen capable of arresting the copepoda. It deposits its eggs on the bottom, which hatch out adhering in masses to stones and weeds. Its colour varies between a not very pronounced green and blue, and its scales easily detach when the fish is roughly handled. It is a cold-water fish, and develops to a larger size in more northern latitudes. In the Channel it averages 12 in.; in parts of the North Sea it reaches a length of 17 in. Those caught off the British Isles are smaller than those caught off Iceland, these latter being large and coarse. As regards the number of the sexes, the males are said to outnumber the females, a phenomenon which is rather unusual in the animal world. Hs. are usually caught by drift-nets, but the hook and line is sometimes used, and the ' jigger ' is often employed on the Scottish coast. The newly hatched Hs. measure about ¼ in., and are more developed than the young fishes hatched from floating eggs. They have no gill-covers, and the mouth is immediately beneath the eyes, and opens downwards. They take about two years to reach maturity, their silvery scales appearing when they have grown to a length of about 1½ in. The number of eggs deposited by the female varies from 20,000 to 50,000, and the eggs are opaque, and have a thick adhesive envelope. The larval Hs. live on the bottom; the post-larval forms at mid-water, and the H. becomes a surface swimmer when about ¼ in. long. This fish is found in large quantities off the shores of the British Isles, as well as along the E. border of N. America, up to the coast of Behring Strait, and is known in the White Sea of Russia and down the coasts of Norway and Denmark, and in the Sea of Japan, but it is not found in the Mediterranean. It is essentially a migratory fish, never remaining in any district for more than a few days, and is not influenced in this by latitude or climate, for often it is earliest in the further N., and in others the reverse. The spawn is shed twice in the year, of which that of the autumn is the most conspicuous; but the season of either of these is often extended or delayed beyond the regular time. Hence great vigilance, patience, and skill are needed in the capture of this fish. Hs. formed an important source of income in ancient times, and have been used as food from time immemorial. Blount's *History of Strange Tenures of Land* says the corporation of the town of Yarmouth (a town which has always been famous for its share in the H. fishery) had to send 100 Hs. baked in twenty-four pasties to the sheriffs of Norwich, who were to deliver them to the lord of the manor of East Carlton.

Herring, George (1833–1906), an English philanthropist. He was of obscure origin, but soon amassed a large fortune as a turf commission agent, and later as a financier. From 1899 until his death he contributed to the London Sunday Hospital Fund an additional 25 per cent. of the amount collected in the churches. He supported a ' Haven of Rest ' almshouses for aged people at Maidenhead, and the 20th Century Club at Notting Hill for working gentlewomen. He also assisted the Salvation Army in its social work and land schemes.

Herring-bone, a term used in architecture to describe an arrangement by which bricks, stones, wood-blocks, etc., are laid diagonally. Generally speaking, the members each make an angle of forty-five degrees with the general direction of the row, and are at right angles to the members of the row next to them.

Herrmann, Wilhelm (*b.* 1846), a German Protestant theologian, born at Melkow near Magdeburg. He lectured at Halle in 1874, and a few years later was appointed professor of dogmatics at Marburg in Hesse. H. is one of the most ardent and sincere advocates of non-metaphysical and independent Christian theology, and was largely influenced in his beliefs and theories by Ritschl. Amongst his most important publications are: *Der Verkehr des Christen mit Gott ; Faith and Morals ; Die Religion im Verhältniss zum Welterkennen und zur Sittlichkeit ; Christliche Ethik*, etc.

Herrnhut, a tn. in Saxony, Germany, 18 m. S.E. of Bautzen. It is chiefly noted as the headquarters of the 'Herrnhuter,' a branch of the Moravian Brethren, founded here in 1722. It has manufs. of linen, paper, and tobacco. Pop. (1910) 1364.

Herschel, a vil. and dist. in Cape Colony, the vil. lying 30 m. E.N.E. of Aliwal North. The district has an area of about 800 sq. m. and is bounded on the N. by the Orange R. Pop. 25,000.

Herschel, Caroline Lucretia (1750-1848), the sister of Sir William H., whom she assisted in his astronomical observations, born in Hanover. She lived with her brother at Bath from 1772, and acted as his assistant when he was appointed astronomer-royal. Between 1786-97 she discovered eight comets, five undoubtedly unobserved before, and many of the smaller nebulæ and star clusters included in her brother's catalogue were her discoveries. In 1798 she published for the Royal Society, *Catalogue of Five Hundred and Sixty-one Stars observed by Flamsteed.* In 1828 the Astronomical Society awarded her their gold medal, and elected her an honorary member in 1835. *See* Mrs. John Herschel, *Memoir and Correspondence of Caroline Herschel*, 1876.

Herschel, Sir John Frederick William (1792-1871), an English astronomer, son of Sir William H., born at Slough, Buckinghamshire, and educated at Eton and St. John's College, Cambridge, where he graduated as senior wrangler and Smith's prizeman in 1813. He entered his name at Lincoln's Inn in 1814, but took up astronomy in 1816, when he translated Lacroix's *Elementary Treatise on the Differential Calculus*, with an appendix on 'Finite Differences,' succeeded by two volumes of *Examples* in 1820. In 1821 he was appointed Copley medallist by the Royal Society. From 1825-33 he was engaged, with Sir James South, in reviewing the nebulæ and star clusters of his father's catalogues. In 1834 he established an observatory at Feldhausen, near Cape Town, where he spent four years in a review of the southern heavens, the results of which were published in 1847 as *Results of Astronomical Observations*

made at the Cape of Good Hope, etc., one of the most important astronomical works of the 19th century. He was appointed master of the Mint from 1850-55. He was the inventor of various astronomical instruments, sensitised paper, and the use of hyposulphite of soda for fixing in photography, and he made valuable researches on the undulatory theory of light. His miscellaneous *Essays* were published in 1857, and *Familiar Lectures on Scientific Subjects* in 1867.

Herschel, Sir William (1738-1822), an English astronomer, born in Hanover. He was educated as a professional musician, and when he came to England in 1757 taught music in Leeds, Halifax, and other northern towns. In 1766 he was appointed organist at the Octagon Chapel, Bath.

SIR WILLIAM HERSCHEL

At Bath he turned his attention to astronomy, and, with the aid of his sister and a new telescope which he constructed for himself, began his survey of the heavens. In 1781 he discovered a new planet, the Georgium Sidus (since called Uranus), and several of its satellites. In 1782 he was appointed private astronomer to George III., and went to live at Slough where he continued the observations, discovering two of the satellites of Saturn, the phenomenon of the motion of the double stars round one another, the periods of rotation of Saturn and Venus, the constitution of nebulæ, and much interesting matter about the Milky Way. In 1783 he published his *Motion of the Solar System in Space.* He received the Copley medal in 1781. In 1789 he erected his famous telescope of 40 ft. focal length, and 4 ft. aperture. *See* Holden's *Life and Work of Herschel*, 1881; Arago's *Analyse Historique*, 1842; Sime's *William Herschel and his Work*, 1900.

Herschell, Sir Farrer Herschell, Baron (1837-99), Lord High Chancellor of Great Britain, born at Brampton, Hampshire. In 1860 he was called to the bar and joined the northern circuit; in 1872 he was made Queen's Counsel. He was recorder of Carlisle (1873-80), member of parliament for Durham (1874-85), and Solicitor-General (1880-85). In 1886 he was Lord Chancellor for six months, falling with Gladstone's administration in that year, but returning to the Woolsack with the Liberal administration (1892-95). He was appointed a member of the Anglo-Venezuelan Arbitration Commission in 1898, but while at Washington met with an accident which proved fatal. *See* Atlay, *The Victorian Chancellors*, 1906-8.

Hersfeld, a tn., prov. of Hesse-Nassau, Prussia, on the R. Fulda, 24 m. N.N.E. of Fulda. It was famous for its Benedictine Abbey founded by Lullus, 769 A.D., and secularised in 1648. There are manufs. of cloth, leather, and machinery. Pop. (1910) 9613.

Hership, in old¹ Scots law, a name given to the crimes of carrying off cattle by force. Such forceful or 'masterful taking,' as opposed to simple theft, included any taking under circumstances of open force and alarm to the neighbourhood. Also known as *brigancy* and *stoutrief*. *See* Hume's *Commentaries on the Law of Scotland*.

Herstal, or **Heristal**, a tn. of Belgium and suburb of Liège, 2 m. to the S. It is the seat of the Belgian national small arms factory and cannon foundry, and has manufs. of iron and steel. It is the reputed birthplace of Pepin le Gros. It also claims to be the birthplace of Charlemagne. Pop. 20,114.

Herten, a vil., Westphalia, Prussia, 15 m. W.N.W. of Dortmund. It has manufs. of tiles, and coal is mined in the neighbourhood. Pop. (1910) 17,690.

Hertford ('ford of harts'), a municipal bor. and county tn. of Hertfordshire, is situated on the R. Lea about 24 m. N. of London and 2 m. from Ware. It is essentially an agricultural town, and is noted for its corn market, but it has no manufactures of importance. The 'harts-ford' is probably the origin of the name of this town, and in Saxon times it was a place of importance. It was re-

duced by the Danes several times, and the wall of the castle built by Edward the Elder still remains. Haileybury College, founded in 1806 by the East Indian Company as a training school for its civil service, and which is now a public school, is situated 2 m. from this town. Pop. (1911) 10,383.

Hertford College, Oxford, in its present form is a modern foundation. Between 1283-1300 Elias of Hertford acquired one of several halls which stood on the site and which became known as Hart Hall. In 1312 it was bought by Bishop Stapleton, the founder of Exeter College, on which college it was dependent until the second half of the 16th century. In 1760 Richard Newton became principal and, in spite of strenuous opposition, succeeded in obtaining a charter to establish Hertford as a college in 1740. It lapsed in 1805 and the buildings were acquired by Magdalen Hall, which was itself dissolved in 1874 when its principal and scholars were incorporated as part of the new Hertford College.

Hertfordshire, or **Herts**, an inland county of England, bounded on the N. by Cambridgeshire, and on the S. by Middlesex. The surface is hilly, but there are some fine pasture lands, and picturesque parks and woods. It belongs mainly to the Upper Cretaceous rocks which give place in the S. to the London clay. The principal rivers are the Lea, the Colne, and the Ivel, and the Grand Junction Canal passes through a part of the county. The chief industry is agriculture, and in addition to grain of a choice quality, hay, vegetables and numerous fruits are grown for the London market. There are a few manufactures, straw-plait, silk, and paper, together with brewing, tanning, parchment-making, brick, tile, and earthenware making, being the chief. The only mineral of importance is brick-earth. In 896 a battle took place in this county between Alfred and the Danes, and in the Wars of the Roses the battles of St. Albans and Barnet were fought here. It is divided into four parliamentary divisions, Northern or Hitchin, Eastern or Hertford, Mid or St. Albans, and Western or Watford. Pop. (1911) 311,284.

Hertha, or **Nerthus**, in Teutonic mythology was the goddess of fertility, 'Mother Earth.' Tacitus describes her worship, the chief seat of which was an island which has not been identified.

Hertogenbosch, *see* BOIS-LE-DUC.

Herts, *see* HERTFORDSHIRE.

Hertz, Heinrich Rudolf (1857-94), a German physicist, born at Hamburg.

He was intended for the profession of engineering, but deserted it to study experimental and mathematical physics under Von Helmholtz in Berlin. For the best solution of the problem of electric inertia he won the university prize, his paper, *Kinetic Energy of Electricity in Motion*, being published in 1880. In 1883 he was privat docent at Kiel, and from 1885-89 professor of physics in the Carlsruhe Polytechnic, where he made his remarkable experiments on electric waves based on Maxwell's theory of electricity and magnetism, for which the experimental proofs had been lacking hitherto. The result of his experiments was to prove beyond a doubt that ordinary light consists of electrical vibrations in an all-pervading ether which possesses the properties of an insulator and of a magnetic medium (Hertzian Electric-Magnetic Waves). The apparatus which he invented for the purpose might be called an 'electrege,' being sensitive to the passage of these Hertzian waves as the human eye is sensitive to the passage of waves of high resonance formed his guiding principle; his instrument was, in fact, an electric resonator which could pick out and make evident the oscillations of electric discharges which take place under certain conditions, as demonstrated by Kelvin. Having proved that these electric waves existed, he proceeded to show that they could be reflected, refracted, polarised, and diffracted just as light is, and he measured the velocity of propagation and found it to be of the same order as that of light and of radiant heat. The results of his observations have been employed for the practical purposes of signalling over considerable distances (*see* WIRELESS TELEGRAPHY). His papers have been translated into English by Professor D. E. Jones, and published as *Electric Waves*, 1893; *Miscellaneous Papers*, 1896, and *Principles of Mechanics*, 1899. *See* Oliver Lodge's *Hertz and his Work*, 1895.

Hertz, Henrik (1798-1870), a Danish poet, born of Jewish parents at Copenhagen. He passed his final examination in law in 1825, but the literary instinct in him was too strong and in 1826 he published his first play. His *Amor's Strokes of Genius* (1830) a comedy in rhymed verse was a complete novelty in Danish literature, and his *Gengangerbrevene* (Letters from a Ghost), is one of the best satires in Danish. His romantic national drama, *Svend Dyrings Hüs* (1837), is one of his finest works, while *Kong René's Datter* (1845) has been translated into almost every European language (Eng. trans. 1850 by

Sir Theodore Martin). His comedy, *Flyttedagen*, appeared in 1828, and his beautiful lyrics were collected in 1857-62. His *Dramatic Works* (18 vols.) were published 1854-73.

Heruli, a Teutonic tribe, first mentioned in the reign of Gallienus (260-68), when they joined the Goths in ravaging the Ægean coasts. In the 6th century they formed an alliance with Theodoric the Ostrogoth against Clovis, King of the Franks, but were overthrown by the Langobardi.

Hervé, Florimond Ronger (1825-92), a French musical composer, born at Houdain, near Arras. He became organist at several Parisian churches, but in 1848 first appeared on the operatic stage in his own composition, *Don Quixote et Sancho Pança*. He was manager at several Parisian theatres, a popular conductor of promenade concerts in England and Paris, and composer, librettist, conductor, and singer in operatic productions. He composed *L'Œil Crevé* 1867; *Chilpéric*, and *Le Petit Faust*, 1869.

Hervé, Gustave (*b.* 1871), sometime member of the Paris bar, is one of the foremost among French Socialist agitators. He was born at Brest on the first day of the year, and began life as a school teacher, and like many another teacher in the republic was early drawn into 'advanced' politics. After graduating as M.A. he was for a while professor of history in Rodez, in his spare time acting as editor of an anti-militarist and anti-patriotic journal, *Le Pioupiou de l'Yonne*. For the seditious nature of articles appearing therein, he was tried in 1900 but acquitted, the defending counsel being Aristide Briand, later Premier of France. In 1905 he was sentenced to five years' imprisonment for inciting conscripts to refuse service. After serving six months he was released, but since that date he has repeatedly been imprisoned for similar offences. He is now editor of the Paris weekly, *La Guerre Sociale* (founded 1905), though his contributions to it (often signed 'Un Sans-Patrie') are more frequently written within the walls of La Sante than in the editorial sanctum. Besides holding anti-national opinions he is an anti-parliamentarian, bitter in his denunciation of the *quinze-mille* (French deputies are paid 15,000 francs annually). He is virtually leader of the revolutionary trade unions forming the redoubtable G.C.T.; encourages 'direct action,' *i.e.* strikes, as a means of ameliorating the lot of the masses, and refuses to condemn *sabotage* (destruction of property). It is, however, for his anti-patriotism that he will be chiefly remembered, for no living person (with the possible exception of Carl Leibknecht, the Socialist deputy for Potsdam, Germany) has preached more consistently, fervently, and eloquently the anti-patriotic doctrine. His position is that national boundries should count for naught; that the working man has no Fatherland ; that the workers the world over have no quarrels ; and that defence of country is merely defence of the right to be exploited by one particular set of capitalists, patriotism being merely an invention of the governing classes.   Hence he advocates a military strike against war, and suggests that the proper billet for the proletarian's bullet is the back of his own officer. These subversive doctrines, preached with the eloquence of a Snowden and the pen of a Blatchford, will be found elaborated in H.'s book, *Leur Patrie* (English trans. *My Country, Right or Wrong* (Fifield), 1910).

Hervey, Arthur (*b.* 1855), a British musical composer and critic, born in Paris.   He was intended for the diplomatic service, but eventually devoted himself to music, studying under Berthold Tours. He became musical critic for *Vanity Fair*, and for the *Morning Post* (1892-1908). His orchestral compositions include the descriptive ballads, *The Gates of Night*, for voice and orchestra, written for the Gloucester Festival (Sept. 1901); *Youth*, a concert overture, composed for the Norwich Festival; *Two Tone Pictures*, for the Cardiff Festival, 1902; *In the East*, a tone poem, for the Cardiff Festival, 1904; *Prelude, Tone*, for the Philharmonic Society, 1907, and many songs and piano, violin, and violoncello music. He has published *Masters of French Music*, 1894; *French Music in the 19th Century*, 1903; *Franz Liszt and his Music*, 1911.

Hervey, James (1714-58), an English divine and writer, born at Hardingstone, near Northampton. At Oxford he came under the influence of John Wesley, but ultimately adopted a Calvinistic creed, and entered the Anglican Church succeeding to the family living of Weston Favell (1752). His popular *Meditations and Contemplations*, including, ' Meditations among the Tombs,' ' In a Flower Garden,' ' On Creation,' ' Contemplations on the Night—On the Starry Heavens,' and ' The Winter Piece,' appeared in 1745. His *Theron and Aspasio, or a Series of Letters upon the most important and interesting Subjects* (1755), provoked the adverse criticism of John Wesley

and led to the Sandemanian controversy as to the nature of ' saving faith.' *See* his *Letters*, with ' Life of Hervey,' profixed by Dr. Birch, 1782.

Hervieu, Paul Ernest (*b.* 1857), a French novelist and dramatist, born at Neuilly (Seine). He was called to the bar in 1877, and qualified for the diplomatic service, resigning on his appointment as secretary to the French Legation in Mexico in 1881. In 1882 he published his first novel, *Diogène-le-chien*, followed by *La Bêtise Parisienne*, 1884, a collection of newspaper ' chroniques '; *L'Inconnu*, 1887; *Flirt*, 1890; *Peints par eux-mêmes*, 1893, and *L'Armature*, 1895. His novels show a keen study of life blended with marked originality and delicate charm of style, but his more important work is found in a series of plays, including: *Point de Lendemain*, 1890; *Les Paroles Restent* (Vaudeville), 1892; *Les Tenailles* (Comédie Française), 1895; *La Course du Flambeau*, 1901; *L'Enigme*, 1901; *Théroigne de Méricourt*, 1902; *Le Dédale*, 1903; *Le Réveil*, 1905; *Connais-toi*, 1909. He was elected to the French Academy in 1900.

Herwarth von Bittenfeld, Karl Eberhard (1796-1884), a Prussian general, born at Grosswerther in Thuringia. He entered the Guard Infantry in 1811, and served through the War of Liberation (1813-15), distinguishing himself at Lützen and Paris.   In 1864 in the Schleswig-Holstein campaign he attained great fame through his daring capture of the Isle of Alsen. In 1866 he commanded the ' Army of the Elbe,' which overran Saxony and invaded Bohemia. He took a leading part in the brilliant victories over the Austrians at Hühnerwasser, Münchengrätz and Königgrätz. On the outbreak of the Franco-Prussian War in 1870 he was appointed to organise the reserve forces in the Rhine provinces, and in 1871 was promoted to the rank of field-marshal.

Herwegh, Georg (1817-75), a German lyric poet, born at Stuttgart. Originally intended for the church he went to the University of Tübingen, from which he was expelled in 1836, and he then took up journalism. During his term of military service insubordination resulted in his fleeing to Switzerland, where he published the book of political poems that, although they were confiscated, made him famous, *Gedichte eines Lebendigen* (1841). After a visit to Paris he returned to Germany, and his offence was pardoned, but in the S. German rising of 1848, he was once more involved, he raised a troop of German workmen in Paris and proceeded to Baden. He was quickly defeated and once more fled to Switzerland. He published a second volume of poems which like the first was confiscated, and translated Lamartine's works and several of Shakespeare's plays into German.

Herz, Heinrich (1806-88), a musical composer, known as Henri Herz, born at Vienna. He was of Jewish extraction and lived in Paris, where he became a professor at the Conservatoire and made a name as a teacher of the piano. He founded a concert hall in Paris, and also a piano manufactory. His works, which were very numerous, no longer command a sale.

Herz, Henriette (1764-1847), a Portuguese Jewess, born in Berlin. Her real name was Lemos, and she lived in Berlin, where her great beauty and learning attracted to her house many famous men. Schleiermacher was one of her greatest friends, and she held the same philosophical views as he did; others who frequented her salon were Börne, Fichte, and the Schlegels and Humboldts. In 1817 she embraced Christianity. See *Life*, in German, by Fürst (2nd ed. 1858).

Herzegovina, *see* BOSNIA AND HERZEGOVINA.

Herzen, Alexander (1812-70), a Russian author and publisher, born at Moscow. In 1835 while still a student he was tried and exiled to Viatka for a too free expression of his political views. In 1840 he returned to St. Petersburg and held an official post, but in consequence of too great frankness he was sent to Novgorod in 1842, and left Russia in 1847 to pass the remainder of his life between Paris, London, and Geneva. In London he established his *Free Russian Press* from which emanated a large number of works dealing with the cause of reform in Russia, and the periodicals *Bell* and *Polar Star*, which were smuggled into Russia and obtained an enormous influence. When the Polish insurrections of 1863 broke out, H. espoused the insurgents' cause, and lost his influence in Russia. He wrote *Mémoires de L'Impiratrice Cathérine II.*, 1869, and some novels, as well as his political works. His collected Russian works were published at Geneva in 1870.

Herzl, Theodor (1860-1904), the founder of modern political Zionism (*q.v.*), born at Budapest. Most of his life was passed at Vienna, where, in addition to his fame as a Jewish Nationalist, he also had a high reputation as a journalist and dramatist. His great ideal was to restore the Jewish nation to political autonomy. He treated the subject from an entirely secular standpoint, and did not at first bring Palestine into his calcula-

tions, though that was his ultimate aim, to establish the Jewish people as a nation in Palestine. He published his famous pamphlet, *Der Judenstaat*, in 1896, in which he set forth this ideal.

Herzog, Johan Jakob (1805-82), a German Protestant theologian, born at Basil. In 1847 he was appointed professor of theology at Halle, and from there went on to Erlangen as professor of church history (1854). His most famous work was the *Realencyklopädie für protestantische theologie und Kirche*, 1853-68 (22 vols.). In 1877, he commenced a second edition in conjunction with G. L. Plitt, and on the death of the latter in 1880, Albert Hauck took his place, and after the death of H. published a third edition (1896-1909). His other works include *Joh. Calvin*, 1843 ; *Leben Okolampads*, 1843 ; *Die romanischen Waldenser*, 1853, and *Abriss der gesamten Kirchengeschichte* (3 vols.), 1876-82 (2nd ed., G. Koffmane, Leipzig, 1890-92).

Hesdin, a tn. on the Canche, in the dept. of Pas de Calais, France, was formerly fortified. It has a 16th century town hall. The chief manufs. are brass and leather wares, and cotton. Pop. 3000.

Heshbon (Modern *Hesban*), the chief city of Sihon, king of the Amorites, captured by the Israelites, on their way to the Jordan (Num. xxi.). Its site is in a plateau in the N.E. corner of the Dead Sea.

Hesiod, or **Hesiodus** (*fl.* 8th century B.C.), the earliest didactic poet of ancient Greece. He was born at Ascra, a village at the foot of Mt. Helicon, and was the son of a shepherd. On the death of his father, he and his brother Perses had a law-suit over the patrimony, which the latter won by bribery, whereupon H. left his native place for Naupactus. His brother, who had wasted his substance, now applied to him for help. This incident is recorded in H.'s earliest poem, *Works and Days*, half of which contains good advice given to his erring brother, enforcing honest labour and laying down rules as to husbandry. The rest of the poem deals with lucky and unlucky days for rural work. The poem contains a beautiful description of winter and the earliest fable in Greek literature of which we have any knowledge, ' The Hawk and the Nightingale.' In this poem, too, H. relates how at some funeral games at Chalcis in Eubœa he won in a contest of song a tripod, which he dedicated to the Muses. The other poem attributed to H. is *Theogony*. It is a history of the creation of the world—the earth, hell, ocean, night, sun and moon, and a history and genealogy of the gods, originating in Zeus and Cronus. The authenticity of the poem was first doubted by Pausanias (200 A.D.); it is now generally accepted that it is the work of H., or of a disciple, and that it contains interpolations by a later hand. The *Shield of Heracles*, once thought to be H.'s, is probably spurious. It is a description of the expedition of Heracles and Iolaus against Cycnus, and obviously owes much to Homer's description of the shield of Achilles. H.'s poetry is mainly didactic, and his moral sayings were enforced on all Greek children. Consult the critical editions of Sittl (1889), Paley (1883), and Schömann (1869). The *Editio princeps* is the edition of 1493, published at Milan. Consult English translations by Elton (1815) and Mair (1908), and Adam's *Religious Teachers of Greece*, 1908.

Hesione, the name of the typical genus of Hesionidæ, a family of nereidiform annelids. They are small marine worms with few segments, and *H. sicula* is the commonest species.

Hesione, a daughter of Laomedon, king of Troy, who exposed her to a sea-monster, according to an annual custom, to appease the wrath of Apollo and Poseidon. Hercules rescued her from the rock to which she was chained, and slew the monster, claiming, as his reward, the horses given to Laomedon by Zeus. Laomedon refused to fulfil his promise and was slain by Hercules, who took Troy and gave H. to Telamon.

Hespeler, a vil. of Waterloo co., Ontario, Canada, 12 m. S.E. of Berlin. It has woollen and saw mills, and manufs. furniture and implements. Pop. 2500.

Hesperia, see HESPERUS.

Hesperides, in Greek mythology, the maidens who guarded the golden apples which Earth gave to Hera on her marriage with Zeus. Their numbers and genealogy vary in different accounts, but they are usually supposed to be three in number, and to be the daughters of Hesperus. According to Hesiod their dwelling-place was far away to the W. on the borders of Ocean, but Apollodorus places their garden near Mt. Atlas. For the account of how Heracles outwitted the H. with their fellow guardian, the dragon Ladon, and gathered the apples, see HERACLES. *See also* J. C. Lawson, *Modern Greek Folklore and Ancient Greek Religion*, 1910.

Hesperiidæ, the name given to a family of lepidopterous insects belonging to the Rhopalocera, or butterflies; they are called 'Skippers' because of their quick, jerky flight.

The body is short and thick, and the wings smaller than in other butterflies; the prevailing colour is brown. The skippers are widely distributed, and contain four British genera, *Hesperia* being the best known.

Hesperis, a genus of dicotyledonous polypetulous plants, which belong to the tribe Sisymbrieæ of the natural order Cruciferæ. The genus was classified by Linnæus.

Hesperornis (Gk. ἕσπερος, west, and ὄρνις, bird), the name of a genus of extinct birds belonging to the suborder Neomithes Odontolcæ, and found in the Upper Cretaceous strata of Kansas; they are marine diving birds of considerable size, with rudimentary wings, and a broad tail of moderate length; the sternum is broad and flat and without keel; the head small, with elongated jaws furnished with recurved teeth set in grooves. *H. regalis* stands about 3 ft. high, and *H. crassipes* is an even larger species.

Hesperus (Lat. *Vesper*), the Greek name for Venus as the evening star. Although originally they were regarded as two distinct personalities, H. was very early identified with Phosphorus (Lat. *Lucifer*), the morning star. The Greek poets called Italy 'Hesperia,' and later writers extended the name to Spain.

Hess, Peter von (1792–1871), a German painter, born at Düsseldorf. Having studied at Munich he took to painting battle scenes, and after serving with the Bavarians in the Napoleonic campaign from 1813-15, he painted a series of pictures illustrating incidents of the war. When Prince Otto became king of Greece, H. was commissioned by King Louis to go to Athens, where he painted an immense canvas depicting the entrance of King Otto into Nauplia, which is now in the Pinakothek at Munich, and did forty sketches of the War of Liberation, also in the Pinakothek, which were copied in wax by Nilsen in the Hofgarten at Munich. His painting was vivid, both in composition and colouring, and his style extremely finished, showing great attention to detail. He did horses especially well. Most of his pictures were on a large scale, and one of the finest is that of the battle of Waterloo in the Munich Gallery. He also painted a series of Napoleonic pictures for the Czar Nicholas.

Hesse, or **Hesse-Darmstadt** (Ger. *Hessen*, of doubtful etymology), a grand-duchy of W. Germany, and the sixth state of the German empire in size and population. Two separate parts comprise the duchy, on different sides of the R. Main. On the S. is the portion which is divided into the provinces of Starkenburg and Rhein-hessen, and on the N. the province of Oberhessen. Oberhessen and E. Starkenburg are mountainous in character, the former having the Vogelsgebirge (chief peak Taufstein 2530 ft.), and the latter, the Oden-wald (chief peak Melibocus 1700 ft.). Rheinhessen and W. Starkenburg are quite level, forming part of the Rhine plain. The Rhine is the principal river, all the others, save those rising to the N. and E. of the Vogelsgebirge, which flow into the Weser, being tributaries. There are no large lakes in the duchy, but mineral springs are found at Nanheim and elsewhere. As would be expected from the varied nature of the land, the climate varies from mild in the Rhine plain to severe on the heights of the Odenwald and Vogelsgebirge. Deer, foxes, and wild swine are among the fauna. The principal in-dustry of the duchy is agriculture; 60 per cent. of the land is tilled and 30 per cent. is wooded. Wine is one of the chief natural products, being produced in Rheinhessen, notably at Bingen, Oppenheim, and Mayence, and on the western slopes of the Oden-wald. The soil is eminently adapted for the cultivation of fruit and vegetables; among the crops grown are : potatoes, millet, hemp, flax, tobacco, poppies, buckwheat, etc. The mineral wealth is not great, in-cluding some salt, lignite, and iron ores, and a little copper, manganese, clay, etc. The principal manufactures are leather goods, tobacco, and cigars, machinery, matches, beer, chemical products, etc. There is a university at Giessen and a high school at Darmstadt. George I. (1567-96) founded the present reign-ing line. Hesse-Darmstadt was made a grand-duchy in 1806, and has belonged to the German empire since 1871. Area 2966 sq. m. Pop. 1,291,800.

Hesse-Cassel (Ger. *Kurhessen*), or **Electoral Hesse**, was until 1866 an electorate of Germany, but now forms the government district of Cassel in the Prussian province of Hesse-Nassau. (*See* article on the latter for particulars as to configura-tion, products, etc.) When Philip the Magnanimous died in 1567, he left half of Hesse, with Cassel as capital, to his eldest son, William IV., ' The Wise.' A large part of Schaumburg and other land was added after the Thirty Years' War. In 1803 (under Landgrave William IX.) H. was con-stituted an electorate, the sovereign bearing the title of Electoral Prince of Hesse. In 1807, however, nearly all the territories of H. were trans-ferred to Westphalia, but were re-

covered in 1813. As the Elector Frederick William had taken part with Austria in the war of 1866, a Prussian army entered his dominions, and they were annexed to Prussia in September of the same year.

Hesse-Homburg, a former land-graviate of Germany, composed of Homburg-vor-der-Höhe on the right and Meisenheim on the l. b. of the Rhine, with a total area of 106 sq. m. The former district is now part of Hesse-Cassel in Hesse-Nassau, and the latter of Coblentz. H. was con-stituted a landgraviate in 1596 by Francis I., son of George I. of Hesse-Darmstadt. It was incorporated with the latter duchy from 1806 to 1815, and again in 1866. Later in the same year it was annexed to Prussia.

Hesse-Nassau, a prov. of Prussia, situated between the rivers Rhine and Weser. The surface is very mountainous, the chief ranges being Taunus (highest point 2890 ft.), Westerwald, Rhöngebirge (highest point 3115 ft.), and the Hessian Mts. All its rivers are tributaries of the Rhine and Weser. Agriculture and cattle-rearing are extensively carried on, and timber is plentiful, the chief trees being beeches, oaks, and conifers. There is considerable mineral produce, iron ore occurring in large quantities, as well as man-ganese ore, coal, and copper. Mineral waters are found at various places, the brine springs of Wiesbaden and the soda-bicarbonate springs of Ems being famous, and excellent wines are produced in the Rheingau. The principal manufactures are machinery, pottery, leather goods, iron ware, chemicals, and textiles, which are carried on at Cassel (the capital), Diez, Eschwege, Frankfort, Fulda, Gross Almerode, Hanau, and Hers-feld. Other towns of importance are Wiesbaden, Homburg, and Marburg, which is the seat of a university. The province was formed in 1867-68 out of the territories of the duchy of Nassau, the landgraviate of Hesse-Homburg, the electorate of Hesse, and the territory of Frankfort, etc. Area 6060 sq. m. Pop. 2,220,956.

Hessenes, *see* ESSENES.

Hesse-Philippsthal, an offshoot of the house of Hesse-Cassel, was founded in 1685 by Philip (d. 1721), son of the Landgrave William VI. and Princess Sophia of Brandenburg. The Landgrave Ernest (b. 1846) is the present representative (1913). Hesse-Bardifeld is a branch of Hesse-Philippsthal, and was founded in 1721 by Philip, the son of William (d. 1761). The lands belonging to both houses are now mediatised.

Hesse-Rotenburg, a former land-graviate of Germany, which was founded in 1627 by Ernest, the younger son of the Landgrave Maurice of Hesse-Cassel. On his death in 1693, his two sons inherited it, but in 1700 they divided the territory and founded the families of Hesse-Rotenburg and Hesse-Wanfried. The latter died out, and the two were re-united in 1755. In 1801 part of the landgraviate was ceded to France, in 1813 some of the remainder to Prussia, and on the death of the Landgrave Victor Amadeus in 1834, what remained was re-united to Hesse-Cassel.

For the lineage, exploits, etc., of the houses of Hesse, *see* Hoffmeister, *Historisch genealogisches Handbuch über alle Linien des Regentenhausen Hesse*, 1874; Walker, *Literarische Handbuch für Geschichte und Landeskinde von Hesse*, 1841; C. von Rommel, *Geschichte von Hesse*, 1821 and 1858.

Hessian-fly, or *Cecidomyia destructor*, the name of a species of dipterous insects belonging to the family Cecidomyiidæ; they are minute fragile flies, having very few wing nervures; the elongated antennæ are furnished with rings of hairs. This fly does great injury to crops, and in some parts of the world causes considerable loss when it has once attacked cereals; the larvæ is lodged at a point in the stem of the wheat enfolded by a leaf; the stem consequently weakens and bends. When about to pupate, the larvæ of *C. destructor* exudes a substance from its skin and this forms a remarkable cocoon, which is called flax-seed.

Hessle, a tn. on the Humber in Yorkshire, 4 m. S.W. of Hull. It manufs. whiting. Pop. (1911) 5319.

Hestia (the ' fire goddess '), the daughter of Cronos and Rhea, one of the twelve chief deities in Greek mythology. She was the goddess of the hearth and home, the personification of family life, and, by extension of the idea of family life to the nation, she was the goddess of the state. In this character her sanctuary was in the prytaneum, where the central fire of every town and state was kept perpetually burning, and where the magistrates, as fathers of the state, held their meetings. If by any accident this fire was extinguished it might not be rekindled by ordinary fire, but only by the sun's rays or by friction. Apollo and Poseidon both sought her hand, but she took an oath of perpetual celibacy, and thereafter Zeus made her the presiding deity over all sacrifices. Intending colonists took some of the sacred fire with them to be kindled on the hearth of their new colony. H. is identified with the Roman Vesta

(*q.v.*). See *Homeric Hymns*, xxix. (ed. Allen and Sikes), 1904, and Farnell, *Cults, the Greek States*, v., 1909.

Heston and Isleworth, an urban dist. in the co. of Middlesex, England. It is a residential suburb of London, 12 m. S.W. of St. Paul's. Pop. (1911) 43,316.

Hesychasts, known also by the soubriquet of *omphalopsychoi*, were a sect of the Greek Church which arose during the 14th century. The sect was a mystic one, their practice being based on the theory that a divine light was hidden in the soul, which they believed to be situated in their stomach. By contemplation at stated times they endeavoured to draw out this light. They died out very quickly.

Hesychius, a Greek grammarian of Alexandria of the 5th century A.D. His lexicon of Greek words and phrases, with explanations of customs, usages, etc., is of the utmost value, especially in regard to rare words as used by writers like Æschylus. In the only MS., now in Venice, which survives, there are large interpolations of later Christian writers. H. based his work on that of Diogenianus. *See* M. Schmidt, 1868.

Hesychius of Miletus, the ' Illustrious,' a Greek chronicler of the 5th century A.D. His history of the reign of Justin I. and of Justinian is lost; of his universal history an extremely valuable fragment, giving the history of Byzantium (Constantinople) down to the reign of Constantine the Great, survives. His biographical dictionary remains in an epitome of Suidas. *See* Oralli (1820) and Flach (1882).

Hetæeræ, or **Hetairai,** the name usually applied in ancient Greece to the best class of courtesan. The education of Greek women was almost entirely neglected, but the H. were among the most beautiful, accomplished, and intellectual of Greek women. They were nearly all trained to play the cithera or the flute, and to dance; Lasthenia studied philosophy under Plato, Leontion was a pupil of Epicurus, while Aspasia, the mistress of Pericles, and perhaps the most famous of all the Greek courtesans, was one of the first advocates of woman's rights to education and culture, and the friend of Socrates. Other famous H. were Phyrne, the mistress and model of Phidias, Lais, Pythionice, and Theodote. Most of these lived in Athens, but Corinth was even more famous for the number, beauty, and refinement of its H. *See* Limburg-Brower, *Histoire de la Civilisation morale et religieuse des Grecs.*

Heterocercal, the term applied to that type of caudal fin in which the vertebral column is extended upwards and the ventral lobe is strongly developed, while the dorsal lobe is formed of the hind end of the tail with the dorso-caudal and part of the vento-caudal fins, thus presenting an enlarged and unsymmetrical appearance. The H. fin is found in Elasmobranchs, Chondrostean Ganoids, Ostracodermi, Acanthodei, Holocephali, and certain Teleostei; sharks and sturgeons are familiar examples of its possessors.

Heterocerus, the name of the single genus of coleopterous insects belonging to the family Heteroceridæ. They are small beetles which burrow in mud or sand in marshy places by means of their strong spiny legs, and produce a shrill noise by rubbing the posterior femora on the abdomen. Seven of the species are British.

Heterogangliata, the name proposed by Professor Owen for all mollusca whose nervous system is formed of scattered and unsymmetrical ganglia.

Heteromera, the name given to a sub-order of coleoptera, which comprises between 14,000 and 15,000 species, most of which are included in the large and widely distributed family Tenebrionidæ. Many of their beetles are terrestrial and live amongst fungi or timber.

Heteromys, the name of a genus of Rodentia belonging to the family Heteromudiæ, and found in N. and S. America; the species are about the size of a rat and inhabit warm regions. H. anomalus is common to Trinidad.

Heteropoda, the name given to a section of gastropod molluscs, and with the Platypoda constitutes the tribe Tænioglossa. The members of this section are free-swimming and pelagic, their chief characteristics are a large-sized head, furnished with two tentacles, transparent shell and tissues, and small visceral sac. In most families the foot is divided into the propodium, or anterior part, the mesopodium, on which is a small sucker, and the metapodium, which is elongated and forms the caudal appendage. The Heteropoda contain many families, the most important being Atlantidæ, Carinariidæ, and Pterotracheidæ.

Heteroptera, the name given to a sub-order of Hemiptera (q.v.); its members differ from those of the Homoptera in that their wings, when in repose, lie flat on the back. They are divided into Gymnocerata, in which the antennæ are conspicuous and easily moved, and Crytocerata, in which the antennæ are hidden under the head of each eye; the former series are terrestrial, and include the extensive and important family Pentatomidæ; the latter are aquatic bugs, containing six families, which are widely distributed.

Heteroscii ('other shadowed'), an astronomical and geographical term for those bodies which have their shadows falling only one day.

Hetman (Russian Ataman), a Polish word used as military title for the commander-in-chief of their army when the king was not present. It was adopted by Russia as a title for the head of the Cossacks (q.v.), and is now held by the Cesarevitch. It is also used for the elected elder of the Stanitsa in Cossack administration. See Cossack.

Hettner, Hermann Jules Theodor (1821-82), a German literary historian and writer, born at Leisersdorf in Silesia. He spent three years in Italy studying æsthetics, art, and literature, and in 1848 published a Vorschule zur bildenden kunst der Alten and an essay on Die neapolitanischen Mahrschulen. He became Privatdoyent for æsthetics and the history of art at Heidelberg, where he published Die romantische Schule in ihrem Lusammenhang mit Goethe und Schiller (1850). He was next appointed professor at Jena, and from there went to Dresden as director of the Museum of Antiquities. His chief work was his Literaturgeschichte des 18 ton Jahrhunderts in three parts, divided into English, French, and German literature between 1856 and 1870. See H. Spitzer, H. Hettner Kunstphilosophische anfänge und Literaturästhetik, 1903.

Hetton-le-Hole, a tn. in the co. of, and 5 m. N.E. of the city of, Durham, England. It is the centre of a coal-mining district. Pop. (1911) 15,678.

Hettstadt, a tn. in the prov. of Saxony, Prussia, 9 m. N.W. of Eisleben. It has important copper mines, and considerable manufactures of copper and brass ware, and pianos. Pop. 8500.

Heuglin, Theodor von (1824-76), a German traveller in Africa, born at Hirschlanden, in Würtemberg. Trained as a mining engineer, he became interested in scientific investigation. In 1850 he went to Egypt and learnt Arabic, and then went to Arabia Petraca. Two years later he went to Abyssinia with Dr. Reitz, Austrian consul at Khartum, and later became his successor. During his consulate he again went to Abyssinia and to Kordofan, bringing back a valuable collection of natural history specimens. His next expedition was to Somaliland, after which he went to Central Africa. In 1862 he joined the Tinne expedition, and in 1870 went to the polar regions. See Petermann's Mitteilungen for 1877, with list of his contributions.

Heumar, a vil. of Rhenish Prussia, in the dist. of Cologne, 5 m. S.E. of the town of Cologne. Pop. 9454.

Heustrichbad, a health resort, 8 m. S.E. of Thun in the canton of Bern, Switzerland; it has famous sulphur springs.

Hevelius (Hevel or **Howelcke), Johann** (1611-87), a German astronomer, born at Danzig. After travelling in France and England he settled as a brewer in his native town, and took a leading part in municipal affairs. Always interested in astronomy, in 1641 he built an observatory in his house and fitted it up with first-class instruments, including a tubeless telescope made by himself. He was the founder of lunar topography, the results of which he published in his *Selenographia* (1647). He discovered four comets in 1652, 1661, 1672, and 1677. In Sept. 1679 his observatory was burnt down, and the shock impaired his health. His works include: *Prodromus cometicus* (1665), *Cometographia* (1668), *Machina cœlestis* (1st part, 1673; 2nd part, 1679), and *Prodromus Astronomiœ* (1690).

Heverlé, a com. in Brabant, Belgium, 12 m. E. of Brussels. Pop. 6500.

Heves, a tn. in the co. of Heves, Hungary, 23 m. S.W. of Erlau. It is the centre of an agricultural and fruit-growing district. Pop. 7500.

Hevne, a tn. on the W. coast of Norway in the prov. of, and 40 m. S.W. of the town of, Trondhjem. Pop. 8000.

Hewins, William Albert Samuel (*b.* 1865), an English economist and politician, educated at Wolverhampton and Pembroke College, Oxford. He was professor of economics at King's College, London, 1897; director of the London School of Economics, 1895-1903, and a member of the Senate of London University till 1903, when the Tariff Reform movement of Mr. J. Chamberlain brought him prominently before the public as one of the chief economic supporters of the campaign and as secretary to the Tariff Reform Commission. In 1912 he was returned unopposed as a Unionist member for Hereford. His economic works include *English Trade and Finance of the 17th Century*, 1892, and *Imperialism*, 1901.

Hewlett, Maurice (*b.* 1861), an English novelist and poet, educated at Isleworth, and from 1896-1900 a civil servant in the Land Revenue department of the Woods and Forests. His first literary work was *Earthwork out of Tuscany*, sketch of Italy, 1895, and *The Masque of Dead Florentines*, in verse. His first popular success was gained by his brilliant, passionate romance, *The Forest Lovers* (1898), full of the colour of early mediæval

romance; this genre he followed with collections of short stories, English or Italian, *Little Novels in Italy*, 1899; *The New Canterbury Tales*, 1901; *Road in Tuscany*, 1909; his historical novels, *Richard Yea-and-Nay* (Richard Cœur de Lion), 1900, and *The Queen's Quair* (Mary, Queen of Scots), 1909, were essays in another field; in the *Fool Errant*, and *Renny's River*, he returned to his mediæval romances. *The Stooping Lady*, 1907, and other novels deal with more modern times. His poetry includes a dramatic pastoral, *Pan and the Young Shepherd*, 1898; *Artemision*, 1909; *Lore of Proserpine*, 1913.

Hexachord, a term used originally in Greek music for a diatonic series of six tones, or for the interval of a major sixth. It was also applied to an instrument having six strings. In mediæval music it referred to a diatonic series of six tones containing four whole steps and one half step.

Hexagon (Gk. ἕξ, six, and γωνία, angle), in mathematics a figure containing six angles and bounded by six sides. If these sides are equal the figure is known as a *regular* H. Hexagonal construction gives a body the greatest possible amount of strength and stability, and doubtless for this cause is the one adopted by bees for making their cells. Pascal's theorem with reference to the H. is important. It states that if a H. be inscribed in a conic section the points of intersection of the pairs of sides (*i.e.* 1 and 4, 2 and 5, 3 and 6), produced, lie on a straight line.

Hexahedron, a solid body having six faces, particularly a regular cube.

Hexameter, the form of verse used by the Greeks and Latins for epic and heroic poems, is perhaps the most important of classical metres. The *Odyssey* and the *Iliad* alone among Greek productions would have sufficed to make it famous, while the greatest example of its use in Latin is in the *Æneid*. Though both the Greek and Latin forms of the H. are based on the same plan, it is necessary to differentiate slightly between them. The normal line in both, however, consists of six dactylic feet, of which the last is catalectic. With a line of this type the *Odyssey* opens:

ἄνδρα μοι | ἔννεπε | Μοῦσα πολ | ύτροπον | ὅς μάλα | πολλά

Variations from this form are, of course, frequent. Spondees may occur in any or every foot, though a line composed entirely of spondees is rare in Greek, and in Latin still rarer and more barbarous. Thus it is only in an early poet such as Ennius that such a line could occur as:

ōllī | rĕspŏn|dĭt rēx [Ālbā|ī lŏn|
gāī

One or two cæsuras (breaks *in* a foot) occur in every line, in the third and fourth feet. In Greek a single weak cæsura (*i.e.* after the second syllable of the dactyl) is sufficient, but in Latin it is common to find a strong cæsura (*i.e.* after the first syllable of the dactyl) in the third foot, and a weak cæsura in the fourth, or *vice versâ*. Thus, for example, in the line from Ovid, ' āddēquŏd | ĭngĕnŭ|ās dĭdĭ|cĭssĕ fĭ|dēlĭtĕr | ārtīs,' the strong cæsura occurs in the third foot after *ingenuas*, the weak cæsura in the fourth foot after *didicisse*. Lines with only a weak cæsura are very rare except in the earlier poets.

Hexapla, an edition of the O.T. and version in parallel columns prepared in the 2nd century by the famous Alexandrian scholar, Origen. It consisted of the Hebrew, a transliteration of the Hebrew in Greek characters, an amended Septuagint version, and three other versions by the scholars Aquila, Symmachus, and Theodotion. The work has survived only in a few fragments (edited by D. and F. Field in *Origenis Hexaplorum quae supersunt*, but these are invaluable to critics and students of the O.T. It contains, indeed, almost all that remains of the Greek versions other than the Septuagint.

Hexateuch, a name now generally used to denote the first six books of the O.T., which modern criticism shows must be regarded as a literary entity. The name is coined on analogy with Pentateuch, which title was early used by Origen and Tertullian for the books of Genesis, Exodus, Leviticus, Numbers, and Deuteronomy. During the first eighteen centuries of the Christian era, the tradition of the Mosaic authorship of the Pentateuch was almost universally received, but such a tradition was bound to vanish before the first appearance of the light of criticism. In many places Moses is spoken of in the third person; and in Deut. xxxiv. 10, it is said that ' there arose not a prophet since in Israel like unto Moses,' while the account of Moses' death in which this occurs can hardly have been penned by the prophet himself. There are similar objections immediately apparent to the tradition that Joshua was the author of the book which bears his name. A more detailed examination of the Pentateuch led to the discovery of a great number of repetitions, discrepancies, and contradictions, and these led to the further conclusion that no one of these books was the work of a single hand. The most notable of the repetitions is in the accounts of the Creation. The account

given in Gen. ii. 4 f. differs irreconcileably from that which immediately precedes it. Similarly from the account of the Flood given in vii. 12, 17, and in viii. 6, 10, 12, it would appear that the Deluge lasted fifty-four days, while from vii. 24 and viii. 3, its duration must have been at least 150 days. Various different explanations of proper names are given, such as, for example, in the case of Leah. There is also uncertainty as to the position of the Israelites during their sojourn in Egypt. The story of the midwives and the account of the Passover with the necessity for marking the Hebrew houses, would lead one to suppose that the Israelites were living scattered among the Egyptians, whereas in Gen. xlvi. 34, and other passages, they are spoken of as forming a separate community in the land of Goshen, a district quite distinct from Egypt proper. These are but a few examples, but the statement of them shows the problem which faced the early critics of the Mosaic books. The first step in its solution was made by a French scientist, Jean Astruc, who published in 1753 his *Conjectures sur les mémoires originaux dont il paroit que Moyse s'est servi pour composer le livre de la Genèse*. The key to his solution was given him by the fact that in the first chapters of Genesis, two sections could be distinguished by two different names used for God. In the early narrative of the Creation, the name is Elōhīm, while in the second it is Yahweh. Guided by this fact, Astruc proceeded to divide the whole book into two main divisions or sources. In the hands of the German, Eichhorn, Astruc's theory was still further strengthened by linguistic evidence, which showed that a change of language accompanied the change of name. But as criticism moved on to the rest of the Pentateuch, results became far less positive. The clear guidance of the Divine names was no longer to be had, and at first it seemed that the rest of the Pentateuch was a mere disorderly collection of fragments with little or nothing in common. This Fragment Hypothesis owes its origin to the Scotsman, Geddes, and was supported by Vater. On it, also, De Wette took his stand when he commenced his historical study of the Pentateuch. This great critic in his *Dissertatio Critica* (1805) first propounded the now generally accepted theory that Deuteronomy, instead of being the oldest of the Pentateuchal books, is, in reality, the latest, probably being no earlier than the reign of King Josiah. Now, however, a new and more constructive school of criticism was arising under the leadership of Bleek, Ewald, and Hitzig, to whom we owe the Supplement Hypothesis, and to this school, which rapidly superseded the older one, De Wette himself later turned. Here the connection between the Elohist of Genesis and parts of the later books was first clearly seen, and this led to the conclusion that to the Elohist writer was due the *Grundschrift* or foundation which the Yahwist had used as the basis of the final redaction. This view was attacked by Hupfeld in 1853. Hupfeld distinguished two Elohistic sources, which he assumed were quite separate both from each other and the Yahwist source, the three having been wrought into one by a fourth writer. Nöldeke showed, however, that the second Elohist (*e.g.* Gen. xx.-xxii.) was preserved only in extracts used up by the Yahwist, and that there were thus two main layers still remaining. The same critic also showed in detail how the Elohist source was the *Grundschrift* of all the Hexateuchal books except Deuteronomy. These views, however, have all given way before the now generally received Graf-Wellhausen Hypothesis, which finds in the H. four main strata. These are known as : (1) P, the Priestly Document, or book of the four covenants (Wellhausen's Q), the work of the so-called older Elohist, which forms the framework; (2) E, the (second) Elohistic document; (3) J, the Yahwist source, and (4) D, the Deuteronomist. The chief feature of Graf's hypothesis is the alteration in the position of P. This had hitherto been considered the oldest of the documents, but Graf placed it after D, and later critics have endorsed his view. It is now realised that the legal and ritual religion which he seeks to codify came after and not before the prophetic and lyrical Yahwistic conceptions. J is the earliest of the four, but J and E have been wrought so skilfully into a single connected narrative, that it is almost impossible to consider them separately. The result of their union is known as JE. This combined narrative is remarkable for its life and vigour. The narratives are dramatic, and the actors in them are real persons. Everywhere there is freshness, natural poetry, patriotism, and local colour. For the rest it is impossible here to show the clear distinction between the E and J portions. D either is or contains the book of the law found in Josiah's reign, from a short period before which it is generally dated. Its characteristic feature is its uniform spirituality, and its pleading for re-

form. Its style is clearly marked, D was inserted into JE, and then the combined narrative was fitted into the framework provided by P. This last work, the Priestly Code, differs widely in spirit from the earlier works. It is historical and legislative, dealing with ceremonial regulations and the ordering of the feasts. It formed the framework in which the other three documents were united. *See* books on the various separate books of the Hexateuch, also Driver's *Literature of the Old Testament* (6th ed.), 1897; Wellhausen, *Die Comp. d. Hexateuchs und der historishen Bücher des A.T.*, 1889; Dillman's *Kurzes Exegetishes Handbuch. Gn.* (6th ed.), 1892, etc., and works by authors mentioned in the text.

Hexham, a market town, Northumberland, England, situated on the S. bank of the Tyne, about 21 m. by rail W. of Newcastle. It is an old town with narrow streets and a market square, and is famous for the ancient Abbey Church of St. Andrew, founded by Wilfrid, Archbishop of York in 673. The present building, which stands over the Saxon crypt, is a splendid specimen of Early English work. It contains a fine Perpendicular roodscreen of oak, and many interesting tombs, particularly one carved Roman slab. The Moot Hall and the Manor Office, two castellated towers of the 14th century, are also of interest. At a short distance S. of the town lies the battlefield where the Lancastrians suffered defeat in 1464, and in the neighbourhood are the remains of Dilston Castle where the last Earl of Derwent-water, was beheaded in 1716. Pop. 8417.

Heyden, Jan van der (1637-1712), a Dutch artist, born at Gorkum. His pictures were principally those of the exteriors of buildings, many of them parts of Amsterdam, where, as a rule, he lived, although he did visit other countries. His pictures are characterised by their warm colouring and their breadth of treatment, combined at the same time with a minute attention to detail. One of his best pictures is a view of Amsterdam town hall.

Heylin, Peter (1600-62), an English writer and divine, born at Burford in Oxfordshire. He graduated at Oxford and through the influence of Laud became chaplain to Charles I., 1629. He was deprived of all ecclesiastical offices during the Commonwealth, but at the Restoration was made subdean of Westminster. His works number more than fifty, chiefly theological and controversial. He belonged to the High Church party, and wrote a *Defence of the Church of England.*

Heyn, Piet (1578-1629), a Dutch admiral, born at Delfshaven. He was taken prisoner by the Spaniards, and afterwards gained victories over them in 1624, and in Brazil in 1626. In 1628 he was successful in capturing the Spanish fleet carrying silver, valued at a considerable amount. He met his death in a fight against the pirates of Dunkirk.

Heyne, Christian Gottlob (1729-1812), a German classical scholar, born at Chemnitz in Upper Saxony. Although very poor, he was a student at Leipzig University, and in 1753 obtained a post in the Brühl Library, Dresden. His edition of *Tibullus* which appeared in 1755, secured him the support of Ruhnken of Leyden, and although he suffered many vicissitudes during the Seven Years' War, the scholar was instrumental in obtaining for him, in 1763, an appointment as professor at Göttingen. His other works include editions of the *Enchiridion* of Epictetus; Virgil, 1767; Homer, Pindar, and Apollodorus, as well as many reviews of books. See *Life* by Ludwig Heeren, 1813.

Heyne, Moritz (b. 1837), a German philologist, born at Weissenfals. In 1869 he was appointed a professor of iterature at Halle, and in 1870 received an appointment at Basle as professor of German language and literature, finally occupying the same position at Göttingen in 1883. His works are chiefly those on German literature and language, among them being : *Deutsches Wörterbuch*, 1890-95, a continuation of Grimm's *Deutsches Wörterbuch ; Übungsstücke zur Laut- und Hexionslehre der alter germanischen Dialekte, Gotisch. Alto deutsch*, etc., 1881. He is also the editor of editions of *Beowulf*, 1910, and *Heliand* (3rd ed.), 1883.

Heyse, Paul (b. 1830), a German author was born at Berlin, and educated in that town and at Bonn. In 1854, on account of the fame of some of his works, he was one of the authors invited by Maximilian of Bavaria to take up his abode in Munich. He excels particularly as a writer of short stories, all of which are true pictures of life enhanced by humour, an immense power of rendering detail and a graceful style. He has also written some longer novels and a number of poems. Among his works are: *Das Buch der Freundschaft*, 1883, a collection of stories; *Die kinder der Welt*, 1873; *Thekla*, 1858, a poem; *Der Heilige*, 1902, and *Maria von Magdala*, 1899, both of which are dramas.

Heysham, a tn. and port in the co. of Lancashire, England. It is situated about 4 m. S.W. of Lancaster, and has since 1904 been used by the Midland Railway in connection with steamboat services to the Isle of Man and Ireland.

Heyst, a watering place in the prov. of W. Flanders, Belgium. It lies about 9 m. N.E. of Bruges with which it is connected by a steam tramway and by rail. Pop. about 4000.

Heyst-op-den-Berg, a tn. in the prov. of Antwerp, Belgium, situated about 17 m. S.E. of Antwerp. Pop. 6200.

Heywood, a bor. in the co. of Lancashire, England, situated 8 m. N.N.E. of Manchester. It is engaged chiefly in the manufacture of cotton, boilers, machinery, and chemicals. It has also brass and iron foundries, and coal mines. Pop. (1911) 26,698.

Heywood, John (c.1497-c.1580), an English author, born probably in London. He seems to have been introduced at court by Sir Thomas More, and to have been a favourite in the time of Henry VIII., Mary, and Edward VI. on account of his ready wit and skill in music. When Elizabeth ascended the throne, however, he retired to Malines. He is chiefly remembered as the writer of interludes, which differed from those of his predecessors in having real persons substituted for qualities personified, thus forming a link with the modern drama. He also excelled as a writer of epigrams. Among his works are: *A Mery Play between the Pardoner and the Frere*, 1533; *The Four P's*, 1545(?) ; *The Play of the Wether*, 1533.

Heywood, Thomas (c.1575-c.1650), an English dramatist, was a native of Lincolnshire, and a student at Cambridge. In 1596 he had begun his career as a playwright, and in 1598 was an actor in Henslowe's company. He was a prolific writer, for seventeen years before his death he claims to have written about 200 plays. His dramas deal with ordinary domestic life and with adventure, and in addition to these his works comprise pageants, elegies, and poems. Among his writings are : *A Woman killed with Kindness*, 1603; *The English Traveller*, 1633; *The Fair Maid of the West*, 1631; *The Wise Woman of Hoysden*, 1638; while among his other writings are: *Troia Britanica*, 1609; *An Apology for Actors*, 1612. See *Thomas Heywood*, with an introduction by J. A. Symonds, 1903.

Hezekiah (usual form חִזְקִיָּהוּ *Hizkijâhû*, ' Jehovah hath strengthened '), King of Judah, the son and successor of Ahaz, with whose reign his own provides a most favourable contrast. He was young when he ascended the throne (c. 715 or c. 720 B.C.), and the early part of his reign was doubtless spent under a regency.

The king was personally intimate with the great prophet Isaiah, and it may well have been to his influence that Hezekiah's reforming zeal was due. But the reign is memorable for great deeds without, as well as for reform within. The Assyrian overlordship was rejected, and in the second of the two expeditions sent to reinstate it, Israel won a conspicuous success.

Hiawatha, a legendary chief who flourished about 1450, belonging to a tribe of the N. American Indians. He is said to have formed the League of Six Nations, known as Iroquois, and to have been sent on earth to teach men the arts, agriculture, medicine, and navigation. He departed to the land of Ponemah (Hereafter) on the appearance of the white man.

Hibbert, Sir John Tomlinson (1824-1908), a politician, entered parliament as member for Oldham in 1862, which seat he retained till 1874. He was successful in regaining it in 1877, and was re-elected several times. He held appointments under Gladstone, being secretary to the Local Government Board, 1871; Under-Secretary to the Home Office, 1883; and afterwards Secretary to the Treasury, and Secretary to the Admiralty.

Hibbert Journal, a quarterly magazine dealing chiefly with religion, theology, and philosophy. The first volume appeared in October 1902, and the editor is Mr. L. P. Jacks. The publishing office is at 14 Henrietta Street, Covent Garden, London.

Hibbert Lectures are a course of lectures first begun in 1878. They were instituted by the trustees of a Jamaica merchant, Robert Hibbert (1770-1849), who left a certain amount of money for the founding of scholarships, particularly for Unitarians. Until the year 1878 the money was devoted to this purpose solely, but in that year the trustees decided to begin the lectures for the purpose of discussing, and if possible settling, doubtful points of religion, quite apart from any sect. The first series was given by Professor Max Müller, and since then the lecturers have included Renouf, Renan, Kuenen, Beard, Reville, Pfleiderer, Sayce, and Hatch.

Hibbing, a tn. in St. Louis co. Minnesota, U.S.A., situated 65 m. N.W. of Duluth. The chief industries are iron mining and lumbering. Pop. (1910) 8832.

Hibernation (Lat. *hibernum*, winter) is the term applied to the dormant condition of certain animals during the cold weather. The same process is to be seen in warm latitudes in the summer, and is then called æstivation (*q.v.*), from the Latin *œstivum*,

summer. The cause of the practice of H. is probably the failure of the food supply. By its means animals which do not migrate to warmer lands are enabled to survive the hardest period. Among the hibernating animals are the bat, the bear, the badger, the dormouse, the marmot, the hedgehog, many reptiles, and terrestrial molluscs. The animals take precautions against being exposed to the cold, and bury themselves in caves, hollow trees, under the snow, etc. Every stage between ordinary sleep and H. seems to exist; the squirrel, for example, is roused by a fine sunny day, but returns to his torpid condition if the weather again change. The animals which do not hibernate completely store up ' caches ' of food in the summer for the winter months. All such are vegetarians, save the Arctic fox, who hoards up dead hares, ermines, lemmings, etc. During H. death from starvation, and the wasting away of tissues is prevented by the absorption of fat which the animal has accumulated during the weeks of plenty preceding his retirement. In the case of cold-blooded reptiles, the temperature during H. is very little higher than that of the atmosphere; warm-blooded animals lose a little heat, but maintain a high temperature compared to that of the outside air. The distinguishing features of H. from a physiological point of view are: (1) The lowering of the temperature of the body; (2) the cessation of respiration to a very great extent, as proved by the fact that hibernating animals could be in a poisonous atmosphere for a long time with no ill effects; (3) the cessation of all activities connected with alimentation and excretion.

Hibernia, also **Ierne, Iverna,** or **Juverna,** was the old classical name for Ireland used by the Romans.

Hibernia, British battleship, was launched at Devonport in 1905. Its displacement is 16,350 tons, and it attains a speed of 18½ knots per hour.

Hibiscus, a genus of malvaceous plants, consisting of 150 tropical and sub-tropical species, most of which are herbaceous in habit. They abound in the hot parts of Asia, America, and Africa, while a few are to be found in Europe, and many are valued for their mucilage and the tenacity of the fibre of their bark. *H. esculentus* is a species which is cultivated on account of its unripe fruit, the abundance of mucilage which it contains rendering it a useful article of diet. *H. Rosa-sinensis* is well known as an ornamental plant.

Hiccough, or **Hiccup,** an abnormal form of respiration in which an inspiration is checked by the sudden closure of the glottis. The inspiration is due to a spasmodic contraction of the diaphragm, and this may be caused by an abnormal stimulus of any part of the phrenic nerve; it is, therefore, usually an involuntary reflex following irritation of the mucous membrane of the stomach. The characteristic sound is caused by the passage of the inward current of air through the narrowed aperture and its sudden arrest on the closure of the glottis. Temporary attacks may usually be cured by a draught of cold water, but in certain complaints the accompanying H. may last for days. Bismuth or potassium bromide is generally administered in such cases.

Hichens, Robert Smythe (b. 1864), an English novelist and journalist, born at Speldhurst in Kent. He was educated at Clifton College, and, deciding on a musical career, became a student of the Royal College of Music. However, he abandoned music for literature, and after studying for a year at the London School of Journalism, became connected with various newspapers. He is a very popular novelist, and a successful playwright. His first novel, *The Green Carnation*, met with great success, and his reputation increased with his subsequent publications. His chief novels are: *The Garden of Allah*, 1905; *The Call of the Blood*, 1906; *Bella Donna*, 1909; *The Dweller on the Threshold*, 1911; and *The Way of Ambition*, 1913. He collaborated in his two plays, *The Medicine Man* and *Becky Sharp*.

Hickes, George (1642-1715), an English divine and philologist, born at Newsham, near Thirsk, Yorkshire. He received many preferments at the beginning of his career, but at the Revolution, on refusing to take an oath of allegiance to William of Orange, was deprived of all his benefices. In 1694 he was consecrated suffragan Bishop of Thetford by a nonjuring prelate. His fame rests on *Thesaurus Grammatico-Criticus et Archæologicus Linguarum Veterum Septentrionalium*, 1705.

Hickey, William (b. 1749), an author, son of Joseph II. the attorney, who was a friend of Burke and Goldsmith. He was educated at Westminster School and served as a cadet in the East India Company; later on we find him serving the law in Jamaica. His memoirs give some light on 18th-century life. *See* his *Memoirs*, edited by Alfred Spencer, 1913.

Hickory, a native tree of N. America, belonging to the genus *Carya*. The word is contracted from the native Virginian pohickery. The husk which covers the shell of the H. nut separates with four valves, while the nut itself has four, or even more, blunt angles. The male flowers are borne in catkins, and the leaves are pinnate with serrate margins. The tree is fine and graceful with beautiful leaves. The wood is very valuable for fuel purposes. The best known species are : *C. alba* or shell-bark H., which produces very fine nuts ; *C. olivæformis*, which produces the popular pecan nuts ; *C. porcina*, which has pig-nuts; and *C. amara*, with very bitter nuts which are quite uneatable.

Hickory, a tn. of Catawba co., N. Carolina, U.S.A., on the Southern and the Carolina and North-Western railroads. Here are situated Lenoir College and Claremont Female College. It manufs. flour, lumber, carriages, and foundry products. Pop. (1910) 3716.

Hicks, Edward Seymour (b. 1871), an English actor and author, born at St. Heliers, Jersey. He first appeared on the stage in 1887, and became the chief light comedian of the Gaiety (1893-98). He became lessee of the Vaudeville Theatre (1902), at which he appeared in Barrie's *Quality Street*. He now chiefly acts with his wife, the well-known comedy actress, Miss Ellaline Terriss. In 1910 he published his autobiography, *Twenty-four Years of an Actor's Life*, and he has written many successful musical plays, including : *The New Sub; One of the Best; Bluebell; Catch of the Season; Earl and the Girl; Gay Gordons*, etc.

Hicks, Elias (1748-1830), an American minister, born at Hempstead, Long Island. He soon joined the Society of Friends, and spent his time as a travelling preacher, rendering untiring service to the society to which he belonged. He exercised his powers particularly with regard to the abolition of slavery. When, however, he preached against the divinity of Christ, and objected to an orthodox creed embodying this point, the society split into two portions—the ' Hicksites,' who followed him, and those who were willing to adopt the tenets above referred to. See *Journal of the Life and Religious Labours of Elias Hicks* (3rd ed.), 1832.

Hicks, William (1830-83), a British soldier. He entered the army in 1849, and served with distinction through the Indian mutiny. He took part in the Abyssinian War (1867-68), and retired with the rank of colonel in 1880. In 1882 he entered the Khedive's army, in which he was known as Hicks Pasha. As chief of the staff, he drilled the army into good order, and drove the dervishes out of the country between Sennar and Khartum. Although he objected that his troops were unfit to accomplish the task, he was despatched to recapture El Obeid, which had been taken by the Mahdi. At the battle of Kashgil on Nov. 1, between H. and the personally led forces of the Madhi, the majority of his men were slaughtered, and H.'s head was cut off. *See* J. Colborne's *With Hicks Pasha in the Soudan*, 1884.

Hicks-Beach, Sir Michael Edward, *see* ST. ALDWYN, VISCOUNT.

Hidalgo, a state of Mexico, bounded on the S. by Flaxcala and Mexico, Queretaro on the W., San Luis Potosi on the N., and Vera Cruz and Pueblo on the E. The N. and north-eastern part is mountainous and rugged, being traversed by spurs of the Sierra Madre range, while in the S. and W. the country is fertile. Mining is carried on to a large extent, silver, copper, lead, iron, quicksilver, zinc, and gold all being found. The capital is Pachuca. Area 8917 sq. m. Pop. about 610,000.

Hidalgo (from *hijo de algo*, son of something, or possibly *Italicus*), a Spanish title of the lower nobility. They had the right to use the title *don*, but when constitutional government was instituted their privileges were taken away.

Hidalgo del Parral, a city of Chihuahua, Mexico, situated about 120 m. S.E. of the town of Chihuahua. In the vicinity are gold and silver mines. Pop. about 14,800.

Hide of Land, a term applied in Anglo-Saxon times to a certain amount of land. Its exact size varied at different times, though it is usually considered to be about 120 acres, and seems to have been applied to the possessions of a man rather than to an actual measure.

Hides, *see* LEATHER.

Hiempsal, the name of two princes of Numidia: 1. Son of Micipsa, was murdered by Jugurtha, who had been given by Micipsa a share in the rule of the kingdom. 2. Probably grandson of Masinissa, and ruler of Numidia after the Jugurthine wars. He was afterwards driven from his kingdom by the followers of Marius, but in 81 B.C. the kingdom was restored to him by Pompey.

Hieracium, a genus of composite plants, belonging to the sub-order Cichoraceæ, and popularly known as Hawkweed. The most common species in Great Britain are *H. murorum,* which grows on walls and has small yellow flowers; and *H. Pilosella,* the mouse-ear hawkweed.

Hierapolis : 1. 'The Holy City,' so called by reason of its hot springs and cave, Plutonium, mentioned by Strabo, on account of which it was held sacred. St. Paul founded a Christian church here, and it was the birthplace of the philosopher, Epictetus. It was also a seat of worship of the goddess Cybele, and a centre of Phrygian nationality. *See* Ramsay's *Cities and Bishoprics of Phrygia,* 1895. 2. An ancient city of Syria (Gk. *Bambyce,* Arabic *Mumbij*) on the high road from Antioch to Mesopotamia. At one time an important centre of the cotton and silk trade, its decay dates from the Mongol invasion. Romanus Diogenes captured it in 1068, and it was stormed by Saladin in 1175. It was a seat of worship of Astarte, whose temple was ravaged by Crassus in 53 B.C.

Hierarchy (Lat. *hierarchia,* Gk. ἱεραρχία from ἱερός, sacred, and ἄρχος, leader), the governing body of the Church, consisting of the bishops and lower orders of clergy.

Hieres, *see* HYÈRES.

Hierochloe, a genus of Gramineæ, is found in cold and temperate lands, and contains only one British species. This is *H. borealis,* a grass met with but seldom.

Hierocles, the name of several Greeks, the chief of whom are : 1. (*fl. c.* 430 A.D.) A Neoplatonist writer of Alexandria. He studied under the Neoplatonist Plutarch at Athens, and for several years taught at Alexandria. He later removed to Constantinople, where his religious views caused such offence that he was cast into prison. To him is attributed a commentary on Pythagoras' *Carmina Aurea* (ed. Mullach, *Fragmenta philosophorum Græcorum,* 1860), and Φιλόγελως, a collection of over 250 jests (*ἀστεία*) (ed. Eberhard, 1869). 2. A Stoic, the author of *Elements of Ethics* (Ἠθικὴ στοιχείωσις), sometimes attributed to the above. *See* Prächter, *Hierokles der Stoiker,* 1901. 3. The author of Συνέκδημος, a list of provinces and towns in the Eastern empire (ed. Burckhardt, 1893). He flourished in the reign of Justinian. 4. (*fl. c.* 300 A.D.) A proconsul of Bithynia and Alexandria, supposed to be the instigator of the persecutions of the Christians (303), and the author of Λόγοι φιλαλήθεις πρὸς τοὺς χριστιανούς.

Hieroglyphics and Hieratic Writing (Gk. ἱερός, sacred, and γλυφή, carving), a general term denoting the pictorial symbols carved on Egyptian obelisks, temples, sarcophagi, and other monuments, or inscribed on paintings, and which, representing as they do certain syllabic or alphabetic values, were used by the ancient Egyptians as a sort of ideographic writing, *i.e.* writing which conveys the idea of a thing without actually expressing its name. Figs. 1 and 2 are illustrations of Egyptian hieroglyphics. The term is also applied to other symbolical, as opposed to conventional, systems of writing, like those used on Aztec monuments as a means of recording historical facts. The secondary meaning of the term, as denoting something mysteri-

FIG. I.—Figure in the British Museum, of the kind called altars. It is highly polished, and, like all 'compressed' and 'imprisoned' statues, answers to the description of a Canopus.

ous or emblematic, is easily accounted for by the fact that the Egyptian hieroglyphics for centuries defied all attempts on the part of antiquarians to decipher them, and it was not till 1799 that the finding among the ruins of Fort St. Julien, near the Rosetta branch of the Nile, of the celebrated Rosetta Stone (now in the British Museum), containing an inscription relating to the coronation of Ptolemy V., afforded some sort of key to the solution of these enigmatical characters. The discovery of this piece of

black basalt, which was secured for the British by Lord Hutchinson under the 16th article of the capitulation of Alexandria, excited the liveliest interest among archæologists. The stone contains three distinct inscriptions, the highest being in what is generally called hieroglyphics; the second, demotic or enchorial, *i.e.* the alphabet of the laity; and the third in Greek, which declares that the decree inscribed on the stone was cut in three different characters, the ' sacred ' (*i.e.* the language of the classical Egyptians, called sacred in contradistinction to the vulgar dialect of the era of the Ethiopian kings, 700 B.C.), ' those of the country,' and ' the Greek.' The fact that a large part of the hieroglyphic inscription is broken off, the beginning of the first fifteen lines of the demotic inscription wanting, and the end of the Greek mutilated, rendered the key a very difficult one to apply. But the labours of M. de Sacy, Dr. Young, who set himself the problem of determining what groups of enchorial characters corresponded to certain Greek words (Coptic and Greek being cognate), and above all, Champollion, paved the way for the subsequent work of Brugsch, M. de Rougé, and others, until at the present day much that is tolerably certain (among much that is only conjectural) can be postulated of the dialect of ancient Egypt.

Whether we take the Egyptian, the Aztec, or any other system of picture-writing, it seems probable that the development of symbolical or conventional hieroglyphics followed much the same course. It begins with crude pictures delineating objects such as those by which the Mexican scouts apprised Montezuma of the arrival of Cortez and his followers, *e.g.* representations of ships, horses, and fire-arms. Later, this method of communicating ideas becomes too slow and cumbersome, and more or less figurative objects are chosen to express compendiously a whole train of ideas by their essential relationship with that whole of which they form a salient part, *e.g.* flying arrows to indicate a battle. The transition from figurative imagery to symbols is a comparatively easy one, and it becomes clear that there may be no limit to eclectic ingenuity. For example, an eye with a sceptre beneath it denotes the king or kingly power; a hawk's head surmounted by a disc, the sun. Finally come combinations of such symbols to record events, which to any one who has the key to the whole system, will be readily decipherable without literal assistance. The developed hieroglyphics are indeed an abbreviated form of picture-writing, and are of two kinds: (*a*) ideographs proper, and (*b*) substitutes for syllables or letters. But notwithstanding the detailed grammars and histories of the Egyptian language, it is hazardous to assume over-much certainty in describing the different phases of that grammar. For one thing, the earlier and sacred language was constantly being bastardised by the introduction of vulgar forms and constructions; again, there was from time to time so considerable an importation of Semitic words as sometimes to have misled philologists into the assumption that the language was in its inception Semitic; while again, going back to the very key, Dr. Young early pointed

on papyrus of literary compositions. A fine example of hieratic writing is to be seen in the British Museum in the Great Harris Papyrus, reputed to have been written 1200 B.C. A page of this papyrus is reproduced in Fig. 3.

Now the merits of the controversies as to whether Champollion, Young, or even Zoëga (who conjectured that several of the hieroglyphics must represent sounds, and actually used the term phonetic in this context in his work on obelisks published at Rome, 1797) first hit upon the application of the phonetic idea to Egyptian hieroglyphics, it is unnecessary to enter, except perhaps to notice that it is beyond doubt that before 1822, when Champollion published

FIG. 2.—Specimen of Egyptian painting, with hieroglyphics, now in the British Museum.

out that the Greek is no infallible translation of the enchorial or sacred inscriptions on the Rosetta Stone. Still, the correspondence between the texts was such that the value of a great number of groups was accurately or proximately obtained. Dr. Young's was the first real attempt to determine the syllabic or alphabetic values represented by hieroglyphics, and his work is important because, in the opinion of archæologists, it gave the clue to Champollion's celebrated system of phonetic values as opposed to the then received theory that hieratic characters were signs of things and not of sounds. Hieratic, or priests' writing, was a simple modification of the hieroglyphic system, differing from it only in the form of the signs. It was a style of cursive writing employed in making copies

his *Lettre à M. Dacier* concerning 'l'alphabet des hiéroglyphes phonétiques employés par les Egyptiens,' he had Young's published discoveries in the Supplement to the *Encyclopædia Britannica*, 1819, to work upon as a basis, besides the ideas started by Zoëga about the same time. It was Champollion, however, who developed the theory. He commenced by applying phonetic hieroglyphics to the reading of the Greek and Roman proper names which occur on various monuments, *e.g.* on the Benevento obelisk. His principle was this: he established that the symbols were not syllabic but alphabetical; that the Egyptians transcribed proper names and foreign words by means of a real alphabet, of which each symbol was equivalent to a single vowel or consonant. Extending his views, he applied his alphabet to the reading of groups of hieroglyphics which represent common names, verbs, and other parts of speech, and to the establishing of his theory that the characters or groups of characters which in the tian characters, and then translated with the aid of an Egyptian dictionary and grammar. It seems, however, that the method employed was laborious in the extreme, and that quite obvious interpretations were

FIG. 3

hieroglyphic texts express genders, numbers, persons, tenses, etc., are only the phonetic signs of the letters or the words, which in the later Egyptian and Coptic languages perform the same function. This, however, means nothing more than that an hieroglyphic text is merely the given to certain pictorial representations, while other and less graphic symbols were ignored. Whether there is much reliability to be placed on the interpretation through the Greek language of hieroglyphical writing, may be inferred from the more or less established conclusions

FIG. 4

Egyptian language as known to moderns, written not in the ordinary Egyptian characters but in phonetic hieroglyphics. All then that remained to be done was to assign the value of each phonetic hieroglyphic, when the whole may be transcribed into Egyptian language as known to of Champollion, ' that there was no Egyptian writing altogether pictorial or representative, that the ancient Egyptians did not employ a mode of writing altogether phonetic, that there is no regular writing altogether ideographic existing on any Egyptian monuments, and that the hieroglyphic mode of writing is a complex system—a system figurative, symbolical, and phonetic in the same text, in the same phrase, I would almost say in the same word.' What makes Egyptian writing difficult to decipher, even by experts, is the fact that the original highly elaborated forms became successively modified first into what Champollion termed linear hieroglyphics, then into conventional characters called hieratic, and finally into apparently arbitrary forms called the demotic or enchorial writing. Letronne's table, showing the different modes of writing, is as follows:

Egyptian writing, divided by Herodotus, Diodorus, and the Rosetta Stone into two kinds of characters	Common	Demotic (δημοτιχά), Herodotus; δημώδη, Diodorus
		Enchorial (εγχώρια), on the Rosetta Stone
		Epistolographic (ἐπιστολογραφιχά), Clemens of Alexandria
	Sacred	a. Hieratic, or priest-writing, which may be called hierographic
		b. Hieroglyphics, according to Clemens, consisting of	1. Characters, *Kyriologic*, 'by the first *letters*'	
			2. Symbolic, comprising	1. *Kyriologic*, by imitation
				2. *Tropical*, or metaphorical
				3. *Enigmatic*

The above outline of Champollion's theories and system are, however, of mainly historical value at the present day, and for more accurate information on the subject reference must be made to more elaborate modern treatises, like those of philologists already mentioned.

Demotic writing, *i.e.* the people's writing, was a conventional system of signs constructed by the scribes as a simplification of hieratic writing. Practically all the chief characteristics of the hieroglyphics, or pictures, that had survived in the hieratic writing, disappeared. Early Egyptologists called demotic writing *enchorial* as denoting *native* writing, but modern Egyptologists prefer the former name as less ambiguous.

FIG. 5

Coptic, which was the ordinary language of Egypt, after the introduction of Christianity into that country, is written with the letters of the Greek

ꙍ, ꙋ, Ꚃ, ꙅ, ҳ, ꙍ, †

alphabet and seven signs derived from demotic characters, the phonetic values of which were not capable of expression by Greek characters.

Coptic long ago ceased to be a spoken language in Egypt, though the Scriptures and the services are still occasionally read in Coptic. It is chiefly through the translations of the Scriptures from Greek into Coptic that the language of ancient Egypt has come down to us.

The following précis of some of the salient features of the Egyptian grammar as evolved and explained in De Rougé's *Chrestomathie Egyptienne*,

Abrégé Grammatical, will give an idea of the uses and peculiar genius of Egyptian hieroglyphics. Hieroglyphics are written either horizontally or vertically (*see* Figs. 4 and 5), and are read generally from right to left, the heads of animals indicating the direction from which to read. Egyptian writing is composed of a mixture, according to conventional rules of signs of two classes: (1) Ideographic, each sign representing an idea; (2) Phonetic, either (i.) a simple articulation (alphabetic), or (ii.) a complete syllabic sound.

Ideographic signs.—The representative signs are an exact pictorial image of the idea intended. Tropical signs are a metaphorical or analogical expression of the idea intended, *e.g.* the sun is represented by a circle, the moon by a crescent.

Phonetic signs.—It is difficult to see how the alphabet originated. Assuming an alphabetic language to be merely ' a representation by signs of the elementary sounds which enter into words,' we are no nearer the method by which those sounds were analysed. Champollion's doctrine was that when the Egyptian had ascertained the possibility of representing indirectly or recalling the recollections of each sound of his language by the image of material objects, of which the oral sign or word which expressed them in the language *contained in the first line the sound it was intended to represent*, it became easy to represent such a sound by the image of a physical object to which the sound had a closer relation than to any other object in the language. Champollion's view was that a sound or articulation had as its sign the representation of a physical object, the name of which, in the spoken language, *began* with the sound or the articulation which it was intended to express, *e.g.* that the articulation R is represented in the names of Roman emperors written in hieroglyphics by a mouth (Fig. 1, p. 348) (Rô), which, reduced to its phonetic value, becomes ' r.' The difficulty in the way of this doctrine is that the articulation is often represented also by a tear (Rmeiê) and the flower of a pomegranate (Roman or Rman). Again, ' A ' ought to be represented by an ibis only (the Egyptians believing that Hermes invented the letters in Egypt, wrote the first of the letters an ibis), whereas it is represented also by a hawk and a duck. The whole difficulty is fundamental in the genesis of *kyriological* (or *kuriological*) signs; for *kyriological* may connote first *elements* and not first *letters*. However, once a sign had become stereotyped as representative of the

elementary principle in a thing, it is only a matter of time when that sign, simplified or not, can also come to signify the constituent parts of words or a letter of the alphabet.

Another difficulty is the determination of the number of articulations in the ancient Egyptian language, especially as comparisons with ancient Roman and Greek are misleading. According to De Rougé, there were fifteen principal articulations, while the different shades of sound point to an alphabet of twenty-one divisions. The Egyptian alphabetic characters or articulations with the corresponding Latin and Hebrew characters are as follows:

	A		H
	Ä		Ḥ
	Â		x (KH)
or \\	I		S
or Ǫ U or W			SH
	B		K
			Q
	P		Ḳ
	F		T
	M		TH (?)
			Ṭ
	N		ГCH or Ṣ (?)
	R and L		

These characters, as indicated, have all been arrived at by a process of comparison from the inferential values of symbols on different cartouches (*i.e.* the oval figure in which hieroglyphic writing is generally found). It is not surprising, therefore, that different Egyptologists assign somewhat different values and suggest other variants than those given above. For example, De Rougé gives as variants of *b* and *p*, Figs. 2 and 3 respectively; of K, Fig. 4; of *m*, Fig. 5; of *n*, Fig. 6; but does not give the form Fig. 7. Again, De Rougé gives no form for SH, using

▭ for Š, with a variant (Fig. 8). Finally, De Rougé makes no mention of an *l*.

The vowels are divided into soft, aspirate, and vague, the former occurring as aspirates or initials in the syllabic, the latter as finals or medials. The variants, or homophones, would appear to have been introduced at different periods in order to facilitate the filling in of spaces in sculptured inscriptions. There appears, however, to have been little or no rule in the use of the final ' vague' vowels, and one vague vowel often interchanges with another. The *initial* ' I' was generally a semi-vowel with the

monosyllabic. The former (*a*) are hardly to be distinguished from the letters of the alphabet, especially as they were often used at one time to give an idea of the sound of the vowels. A full list of syllabic signs is to be found in De Rougé's book, and they number over 300. It seems that all hieroglyphics were capable of being employed as syllabic signs. A syllabic proper is an ideograph which has lost its value qua ideograph and become a recognised symbol for use in many words. Ideographs which remain so are merely so many different words.

Determinatives.—Where ideographs

value *ia* or *iu;* while Fig. 9 is more often used for vague or final ' *i*.' The transcribed *ai* or *i*, ' to go,' was written with a vague initial *a* for the aspirate, and either Figs. 10 or 9 as final vowels, thus: Figs. 11, 9 over 12, 13, 10, 12, the striding legs conveying the notion of movement. The characters of the Coptic language are practically the demotic forms of the Eygptian hieroglyphics, but there is no resemblance between the above tabulated articulations and the Coptic characters. For example, Fig. 14 becomes 15, 16, or 17; 18 becomes 19, or sometimes 20 and 21.

Syllabic signs were either (*a*) an articulation and one or more vowels, or (*b*) two articulations with generally a medial helping vowel unexpressed. They were, of course, for the most part

or pictorial images were put after a phonetic word Champollion called such ideographs ' determinatives, because they fulfilled the function of determining the meaning of the word. Such use of hieroglyphics is not by way of inflection. But it is only the generic determinatives that have any grammatical value, the others belonging purely to a vocabulary. These latter are symbols attached to different radial words, *e.g.* Figs. 22 and 23 represent a man and a woman, but the determining ideas are the *human race*, its *divisions* and *classes.* Again, Fig. 24 represents a man with a long beard, the determining ideas of which are *gods, august persons,* and *kings;* again, *adoration, invocation,* and *prayer* are abstract ideas determined by the representative sign of a man with raised hands, and the ideas of *death, massacre, enemies,* and so forth, by the pictorial representation of the prone figure of a man.

Subjoined is a portion of the text on a coffin of the eleventh dynasty (2600 B.C.) at Cairo, for the reproduction of which the writer is indebted to the *British Museum Guide to Egyptian Collections,* 1909. The whole text is a prayer to the gods Râ, Tem, Seb, and Nut to grant that the ancestors and kinsfolk of one Sepa may gather together in the other world.

Grant ye this Sepâ,   he may traverse heaven,   he may

traverse earth,   he may traverse the waters,   he may meet

his ancestors,   he may meet his father,   he may meet his mother,

he may meet his children   and his brothers and sisters,   he may meet

his friends,   he may meet his uncles and aunts,   he may meet

his connexions,   he may meet his friends   who did things for

this Sepa upon earth,   he may meet his woman [whom]   he loved

and knew, etc.

Numbers.—The numbers 1 to 9 were expressed by short perpendicular strokes, as follows:

1 was	I	7 was	IIII III
2 ,,	II		
3 ,,	III	8 ,,	IIII IIII
4 ,,	IIII II		
5 ,,	IIII II	9 ,,	III III III
6 ,,	III III		

		Fig.
10 was represented by		25
100 ,,	,,	26
1000 ,,	,,	27
10,000 ,,	,,	28
100,000 ,,	,,	Fig. 29, a frog
1,000,000 ,,	,, ,,	30, a man

with upraised arms 10,000,000 was represented by Fig. 31; while tens, hundreds, thousands, up to 90, 900, 9000, and so on, by repeating the above signs.

The bibliography of the subject

hieroglyphics is enormous; but by far the best grammar is De Rougé's *Chrestomathie*. *See also* Birch's *Hieroglyphic Grammar;* and for first principles Champollion's *Grammaire Égyptienne*. The best dictionary is Brugsch's *Dictionnaire Géographique de l'Ancienne Egypte*, and the same author's *Grammaire Démotique*, and *Hieroglyphisch-Demotisches Wörterbuch*. For historical papyri, *see* Birch's *Select Papyri in the Hieratic Character*, and for texts the various works of Lepsius, Rougé, and Pierret.

Hieron, or Hiero I. (478-467 B.C.), a tyrant of Syracuse, the successor of his brother Gelon. He defeated the Etruscan fleet near Cumæ. On three occasions he won the crown at the Olympic games, and was a patron to Pindar, Æschylus, Simonides, and Epicharmus.

Hieron, or Hiero II. (270-216 B.C.), a tyrant of Syracuse, a descendant of Gelon born about 308 B.C. After his victory over the Mamertines (270 B.C.) he was unanimously elected king by all the states of Sicily. In the first Punic War he sided with the Carthaginians, but in 263 became a friend and ally of Rome, to whom he remained faithful till his death.

Hieronymites (' Brethren of Goodwill,' ' Gregorians '), the hermit order of Hieronymus (or St. Jerome), an offspring of the Franciscans, founded by Thomas of Siena (14th century). The community settled in Spain and later established branches in Portugal Italy, the Tyrol, and Bavaria.

Hierophant, a priest of the Temple of Eleusis whose duty it was to initiate in the ' Eleusinian mysteries.'

Hierro, or Ferro, one of the Canary Islands, occupying the most southwesterly position of the group. The meridian of Ferro was used in the 2nd century A.D. as the first meridian, the most westerly land then known—17° 39' 45" W. of Greenwich—and it was laid down by Louis XIII. of France as the first meridian. It is not, however, exactly true, as it runs 2 m. to the E. of the island. The chief town of the island is Valverde. Area about 106 sq. m. Pop. about 6000.

Hiesfeld, a vil. in the dist. of Düsseldorf, Rhenish Prussia, with tile works. Pop. 9918.

Higden, Ranulf (*d. c.*1364), an English chronicler, was a monk who belonged to St. Werburgh's monastery, Chester, and whose great work was a general history entitled *Polychronicon*. This work dealt with events down to his own time, and was printed by Caxton in 1482. It is now edited, with translations, for the Rolls Series (1865-86).

Higginbottom, Frederick James, a special parl. representative of the

Pall Mall Gazette and *Observer*, born in Accrington in 1859. He entered journalism in 1875, and was parliamentary correspondent for the *Pall Mall Gazette* from 1892-99; and for the *Daily Chronicle* in 1900. From 1900-9 he was managing editor of the *Pall Mall Gazette*, and manager of the *Pall Mall Magazine;* and from 1909-12 was editor of the *Pall Mall Gazette*. He is a reviewer and political writer, and has edited various handbooks.

Higgins, Matthew James (1810-68), an English essayist, born at Benown, Ireland, and was educated at Eton and Oxford. He was a strong supporter of Peel, and contributed articles to the *Morning Chronicle*. In 1846 his first article to be published—in the *New Monthly Magazine*—bore the *nom de plume* Jacob Omnium—by which he was known. Among other papers to which he contributed were the *Times*, in which he exposed abuses, the *Edinburgh Review*, the *Cornhill*, and the *Pall Mall Gazette*.

Higgins, Higins, or Higgons, John (*c.* 1545-*c.* 1602), a clergyman and schoolmaster; best known as the author of the popular work *Mirror for Magistrates*, of Holcot's *Dictionairie newlie corrected*, and a translation of the *Nomenclature of Adrian Junius*.

Higginson, John (1616-1708), an American divine, son of Francis H., was born in England and was taken to America by his father in 1629. From 1660-1708 he was pastor of the church in Salem. He corroborated Cotton Mather's *Magnalia* and published a number of theological treatises and sermons. Dr. R. W. Griswold speaks of him, viz.: ' John Higginson was one of the great men of New England, and incomparably the best writer, native or foreign, who lived in America during the first hundred years of her colonisation.'

Higginson, Thomas Wentworth (*b.* 1823), an American man of letters, born at Cambridge, Massachusetts. Graduating from Harvard (1841), he subsequently studied theology, and became pastor of a Unitarian Church at Newburyport (1847-50), and of the Free Church at Worcester (1852-58). He was an enthusiastic supporter of the anti-slavery agitation, and attempted to make Kansas a free state after the Kansas-Nebraska Bill passed in 1854. During the Civil War he was captain of the 51st Massachusetts Volunteers (1862-64), and of the 1st South Carolina Volunteers, a freed negro regiment. He has written voluminously, his works including *Army Life in a Black Regiment*, 1870; and *Part of a Man's Life*, 1905. See his *Collected Works* (7 vols.), 1900.

Higham Ferrers, a tn. in the co.

of Northampton, England, situated about 15 m. N.E. of Northampton. It is engaged in the manuf. of boots and shoes. Pop. (1911) 2726.

Highbridge, a tn. of W. Somerset, England. It is situated about 25 m. to the S.W. of Bristol, and has locomotive works. Pop. (1911) 2343.

High Commission Court, a judicial court established by Queen Elizabeth in 1559. It was composed of clerical and lay commissioners nominated by the crown, and its function was to investigate ecclesiastical cases. It attempted to extend its influence over cases which should have been dealt with in the common law courts, with the result that in the reign of James I. Coke tried to check its power by his ruling that it could only fine and imprison in cases of heresy and schism. In 1641 the court, with its lay counterpart, the Star Chamber, was abolished by the Long Parliament. It was revived by James II. in 1686, but finally abolished by the Bill of Rights (1689). A similar court existed in Scotland for thirty years (1608-38).

High Court of Justice, *see* APPEAL, CHANCERY, COMMON LAW, JUDICATURE ACTS, and SUPREME COURT.

Highgate, a suburb, N. of London, in the co. of Middlesex, about 4½ m. N.W. of St. Paul's. It is noteworthy as having been the place where Bacon and Coleridge died, and also for its cemetery containing the remains of Lyndhurst, Faraday, and George Eliot, among other celebrities. Whittington's stone is at the foot of H. Hill, and is said to indicate the place at which he turned again after hearing Bow Bells.

Highland Dress, the best illustration, which the British Isles offer, of a costume truly national. The 'garb of old Gaul' consisted of the 'Feilebreacan' or 'belted plaid.' A piece of tartan cloth, 4 yds. long and 2 yds. broad, was drawn in at the waist by a belt, which secured the careful folds of the lower part or skirt. The plaid, that is the upper portion, was usually fastened with a handsome brooch or buckle over the left shoulder, so that the right arm was quite free for use. This simple attire was admirably adapted to the wild, free life of a Highlander. For, if he were benighted or overtaken by a storm, he might wrap his warm plaid round both his shoulders, whilst his loose nether garment was no hindrance, whether he wished to scale heights or wade across streams. The tartan (from Fr. *tiretaine,* a linsey-woolsey cloth) was a device with chequered pattern, and one or more stripes relieved against a different-coloured background for describing the wearer's clan or district. Members of the same sept or clan wore tartans whose main characteristics were the same, and whose variations had a local meaning. Broadly-speaking, tartans are red and green: the badge of the Macleods, Graemes, and Forbes was a green tartan, whilst the Camerons, Stewarts, and Macgregors all wore red. In time the 'Feilebeag' or 'filibeg' superseded the 'Feile-breacan.' The lower part of the latter became the 'kilt,' which was carefully sewn and tucked, whilst the body part was separate and the shoulder-plaid became merely an ornament. The kilt stopped short of the knees, and over it in front was hung the 'sporran' or 'spleuchan,' that is a goat's skin purse. The Highland 'bonnet' was a cloth cap adorned with heather, or in the case of a chief with eagles' plumes. Through his belt a Highlander would thrust his dirk, knife, pistols, and fork, whilst on horseback he wore his 'truis,' or 'trews,' that is close-fitting tartan breeches and stockings made in one piece. The gentry were distinguished by silver ornaments and lace embroideries, whilst Highland regiments to-day are known by their plumed bonnets.

Highland Railway, The, the line running northward from Perth, feeding the Highlands of Scotland. The main line begins at Perth and reaches Inverness by way of Dunkeld, Pitlochry, Blair Atholl, and Kingussie. There are branches to Forres both by way of Grantown and Nairn, and thence to Keith and Portessie. From Inverness the line is carried up to Wick and Thurso through Beauly, Dingwall, Invergordon, and Helmsdale. An important branch connects Dingwall with the Kyle of Lochalsh, whence steamers daily cross to Skye and Stornoway, and the inland spa, Strathpeffer, and Dornoch, the golfers' resort, are also fed by branches. The H. R. was formed by the amalgamation of the Sutherland and Caithness, the Duke of Sutherland's, the Sutherland and the Inverness and Ross-shire Railways, the single company being first instituted in 1865. The main line is inferior in length only to that of the Great Western. The peculiarity of its passenger traffic is that in August, when the grouse-shooting is on, it is phenominally large, whilst in winter, and indeed for over half the year, it would probably not pay the company to run the daily express from King's Cross, were it not for the subsidy drawn from the Post Office for carrying the mails.

Highlands are to be distinguished in formation alike from table-lands and mountains. Generally speaking H. may be said to exist in the E. of the Old World, in the E. of Australia, and in the E. of N. America. They occur in broad, expansive masses, unlike high mountains, which are much more localised. Their structure, moreover, is peculiar. Both valleys and watersheds or divides radiate, and the river systems are like great branching trees; the distribution, as in mountainous countries, of parallel ranges separating valleys is only rarely visible—the Appalachians are an exception; as a rule the valleys branch like fingers in the inner H., thus collecting tributary streams, whilst they broaden and deepen as they pass outward. H. are formed by the denudations or washing out of valleys, as for example, the H. of Scotland, and by slow crustal movements and sometimes by volcanic activities. To make a broad generalisation, H. are primarily due to internal and lowlands to external forces acting on the earth's surface.

Highlands of the Hudson, a mountainous district, on both sides of the Hudson R., extends through the counties of Orange, Putnam, Rockland, Dutchess, and New York. The Highlands are from 1000 to 1500 ft. high. The chief peaks are, Breakneck (1635 ft.), Crow Nest (1405 ft.), Stony Point, and West Point.

Highmore, Joseph (1692-1780), an English painter, born in London. He abandoned a legal profession for art, beginning his studies under Sir Godfrey Kneller. His portrait-drawings for the 'Installation of Knights of the Bath' in 1725 were very popular, and he also executed portraits of the Prince and Princess of Wales, General Wolfe, Samuel Richardson, and other prominent people. His 'Hagar and Ishmael' may be seen in the Foundling Hospital. He also published a treatise *On the Practice of Perspective.*

Highness, a title of honour, used in referring to or addressing princes, minor crowned rulers, grand-dukes, and—until Henry VIII. substituted the title 'Majesty'—kings. The children of emperors are 'Your Imperial Highness;' of kings, 'Your Royal Highness;' and of princely families, 'Serene Highness' and 'Highness.' The Sultan of Turkey is 'Your Highness.'

High Peak, Derbyshire, England, is part of the Pennine Chain. Height 2 88 ft. It is 16 m. S.E. of Manchester, and contains the celebrated Castleton caverns. Also the name of a parl. div.

High Point, a tn. in Guilford co., N. Carolina, U.S.A., is 34 m. N.E. of Salisbury. It has a thriving trade, and manufactures bricks, cotton, machinery, and tobacco. Pop. 9525.

High Priest, the head of the Jewish priesthood. In the early days of the Jewish religion there is no trace of this office, which does not appear until the campaign against the local sanctuaries had concentrated worship at Jerusalem. The true prominence of the high priest dates from the Exile, after the return from which he becomes the head of a theocratic state. The regulations for the high priest are given by P. (*see* HEXATEUCH) in Leviticus with great detail, where his ancestry is traced from Aaron and his son Eleazar. The vestments of the high priest were extremely magnificent, and were worn in the exercise of his duties except on the Day of Atonement, when he alone, clad in white linen, entered the Holy of Holies to sprinkle the blood of sacrifice. The rules for his ritual cleanliness were also extremely stringent.

High Seas, a term of international law, denoting the whole extent of sea which is not under the sovereignty of any state. Every country adjacent to the sea owns ' territorial waters ' restricted to the area within three miles of its shores. The H. S. are free to all nations, subject to certain laws made for the common welfare.

High Steward of England, an office established prior to the reign of Edward the Confessor, and abolished by Simon de Montford in 1265. The office is revived, however, for special occasions. At the trial of a peer or peeress for felony or treason, the presiding peer is called Lord High Steward. The H. S. of the royal household has to make all the arrangements of precedence, etc., in connection with the procession at the coronation of a new sovereign. The H. S. at the coronation of King George V. was the Duke of Northumberland. There is a H. S. attached to both the universities of Oxford and Cambridge, whose duty it is to protect the rights of university courts.

High Treason, *see* TREASON.

Highwaymen, mounted robbers who frequented the highroads of England during the 17th and 18th centuries. They were good riders, and had the appearance of gentlemen, and by the nature of their calling became a popular feature in romantic novels. The most celebrated H. in history are: Dick Turpin (1705-39), to whom is attributed the famous ride to York; Swift Nick Levison (hanged at York, 1684), and Jack Sheppard (1702-24). The best known novels on the subject are Lytton's *Paul Clifford* and Ainsworth's *Rookwood.* Consult *Notes and Queries,* vol. viii. (5th series).

Highways. A ' highway,' which in common law (*q.v.*) is a term embracing carriage roads, horse or bridle roads, mere foot-paths, or any other public way, may be comprehensively defined as a way through or over lands of any ownership which is open to the public generally by virtue of an Act of parliament, a prescriptive right, or by express or implied dedication. The commonest mode by which a public right of way is created is by dedication, which may take the shape of a formal invitation by the owner in fee simple (*see* ESTATE) of the land in question to the public to use a new or existing road, but which more often than not is merely implied from the owner's conduct. Generally speaking, un-interrupted user for a substantial period of time acquiesced in by the owner creates a presumption of dedication which can only be rebutted by special circumstances. Uninter-rupted user for twenty-one years gives the public an absolute right of way by prescription. Dedication may confer only a limited right whether in respect of seasons, manner, or extent. For example, the circum-stances may show that the way was only intended to be used as a bridle-path, or drift-way for cattle, or foot-way, or, again, that the owner re-served the right periodically to dig up the soil of the way. A restriction to a limited number of the public is null and void; but where such limited user, as *e.g.* by the inhabitants of a particular parish, continues for over twenty years, it may well result in a prescriptive right in the public generally. So also a limitation in point of duration is void, for a dedica-tion is either in perpetuity or not a dedication at all. It is to be noted that the Highway Acts include in the statutory definition of H. bridges (not being county bridges, or bridges repairable by the inhabitants at large of a hundred), towing paths, and navigable rivers, but not railways. Indeed every way which is open to the public is a H., and in this con-nection it is immaterial on whom is cast the burden of repair and main-tenance. A street as defined by the Public Health Act, 1875, is usually, but not necessarily, a H.; a street under that Act being defined as ' any *highway* and any public bridge (not being a county bridge), and any road, lane, footway, square, court, alley, or passage, whether a thoroughfare or not.' A H. is also usually a *thorough-fare*, but may, of course, be a *cul-de-sac*. The public right over a H. is merely that of passing along it. There is no right to use it as a place for public meetings or assemblages, and there are several recorded cases show-ing that one's mere presence on a H. for ulterior purposes may well be illegal and actionable. For example, in the case of a man who repeatedly, and for the purpose of annoying, passed and repassed the plaintiff's window while the latter and his family were dining; and again in the now classic case of Harrison *v.* Duke of Rutland, where it was held that a man had no right to go on to a H. merely for the purpose of using it to interfere with another man's right of shooting by preventing the grouse from flying towards the butts occupied by the shooters. A public right of way is, as the very term implies, re-stricted to the surface of the land over which it goes, and the subsoil remains in the freeholder, or, if different freeholders' lands lie on either side of the H., then, generally speaking, the subsoil up to an imagin-ary line running down the middle of the road belongs to each adjoining landowner. Strictly speaking, the residuary rights in the surface also belong to the owner of the soil; but in the case of most Hs. such rights are not of any practical value. A mere occupation road laid out through an estate purely for the use and convenience of the inhabitants is not thereby dedicated to the public; such private right may, however, co-exist with a public right of way, and though in general the former would be merged in the latter right, it may well be inherently a larger, and there-fore independently subsisting right. A H. cannot at common law cease to be such by abandonment or non-user, for ' once a H. always a H.' But by Act of parliament, a H. may be de-stroyed, and such a course, *e.g.* in the case of Hs. running along dangerous cliffs, might well be advisable. Under the Highway Act, 1835, as amended by the Local Government Act, 1888 and 1894, two justices have power to grant a certificate to ' stop ' or ' divert ' a H. if both the district and parish councils (if any) concur in the proposal to stop or divert. The usual reason for diversion is that some proposed new way is more advantage-ous, and the only reason for stopping up a H. altogether is that the H. is no longer required. An appeal against the certificate of the justices lies to quarter sessions at the instance of any person aggrieved, who must give the District Council fourteen days' notice of appeal, and state the grounds of his appeal. The matter will then in due course be tried before a jury. The duty of repairing and maintaining a H. is theoretically still upon the in-habitants of the parish in which it is situated, and an indictment for nuisance lies against such inhabitants at the instance of any one aggrieved if a H. is allowed to fall into disrepair.

The Local Government Act, 1888, however, practically absolves inhabitants from all liability, so far as main roads are concerned, by instituting the county council the H. authority for such roads; and as both urban and rural district councils now have the powers and duties formerly exercisable by and imposed upon parish surveyors of Hs., and represent the inhabitants in vestry assembled of the parishes in their districts for the purposes of the Highway Acts, the theoretical liability of parish inhabitants is not often likely to materialise. Where a district council elects to retain control over main roads (the great arteries along which the principal traffic of the country flows and formerly called the ' King's Highways ') passing through its jurisdiction, the duty of repair and maintenance is on such district council, subject to a yearly payment towards the expenses by the county council. Where the county council is the H. authority it may either itself repair the main road or require the district councils concerned to effect the repairs and repay such councils their expenses. The Urban and Rural District Councils being the usual H. authorities for the whole of England and Wales are, apart from the special care of main roads, liable to repair all roads under their control. Under the Local Government Act, 1894, a parish council may undertake to repair a public footpath in a parish not being by the side of a public road, though such undertaking does not relieve the district council from liability in default of the parish council. By a curious rule of law a H. authority is not liable to be proceeded against on indictment for a mere non-repair or non-feasance, but only for misfeasance. The distinction is mainly academic, for a complaint of non-repair to the Local Government Board or the county council is equally effective. If the cost of repair of a H. is increased by extraordinary weight or traffic, the road authority may, under section 23 of the Highway and Locomotives (Amendment) Act, 1878, as amended by the Locomotives Act, 1898, recover the expenses certified by their surveyor to have been incurred by reason of such traffic from the persons by, or in consequence of, whose order such weight or traffic has been conducted. It is entirely a question of fact in each case what constitutes extraordinary traffic, e.g. military manœuvres, the erection of a mansion or factory in a remote rural district, excessive weight of a single waggon drawn by a locomotive, may each constitute or result in extraordinary traffic. It is

not easy to reconcile the cases on the subject, but apparently the true test for determining whether traffic is extraordinary depends on what is ordinary traffic on the particular road, not on what other and even similar roads in the neighbourhood have borne without injury; and the standard of 'ordinary' means ordinary *de facto*, not what the road may in its ordinary and fair use be reasonably subjected to. To obstruct a H. is a criminal offence, and any member of the public may remove the obstruction. The owner of any animals which stray upon a H. (not running over common or waste land) is liable for damage occasioned thereby to adjoining property, and to a small fine per animal, and the expenses of removing it, such fine and expenses not to exceed, in all, 30s. per animal. By the Lights on Vehicles Act, 1907, every vehicle except a bicycle, tricycle, motor car, locomotive (which are dealt with in other Acts), or vehicle drawn by hand must carry between one hour after sunset and one hour before sunrise a lamp or lamps displaying a visible white light or lights. If a single light only is used it must be affixed on the off-side of the vehicle. Rear lights must be red. The penalty for infringement is 40s. for a first offence, and for subsequent offences, £5. Harvesting carts and others may be specially exempted by by-laws for good reason shown. The regulations as to lights on motor cars are stricter (*see* Motor Cars), but the law as to lights on bicycles is substantially the same as in the case of carts. *See* Pratt, *On Highways*, 1911; Glen, *On Highways*, 1897; Wellbeloved, *The Law Relating to Highways*, 1829.

Highworth, a vil. in Wiltshire, England, is 6 m. N.E. of Swindon, near the Vale of the White Horse. It has an interesting old parish church. Pop. 2000.

High Wycombe, *see* Wycombe.

Higuera La Real, a tn. in the prov. of Estremadura, Spain, is 41 m. S.E. of Badajoz. It dates from the 14th century, and has famous mineral springs. Pop. 5500.

Hijar, a tn. in the prov. of Teruel, Spain, is 40 m. S.E. of Zaragoza. It manufactures silk, soap, and fabrics. Pop. 3400.

Hikone, a tn. in Hondo, Japan, on the E. shore of Lake Biwa, is 35 m. N.E. of Kyoto. It has an ancient feudal castle. Pop. 20,000.

Hilarion, St. (*c.* 290-372), an abbot, founder of the monastic system in Palestine. He was born at Tabatha, and while studying at Alexandria, became converted to Christianity. About 306, through the influence of

St. Anthony, he became a hermit, and lived in the deserts bordering on Egypt, and finally died in Cyprus. The chief authority for his life is St. Jerome.

Hilarius (or **Hilary**), **St.** (*c.*320-368), Bishop of Poitiers, born in Limonum (Poitiers) of pagan parents, and was converted to Christianity through his own studies. He was banished to Phrygia by Emperor Constantius for his vehement controversies with the Arians. He visited numerous churches in Asia Minor, and ultimately returned to Poitiers still undaunted. His most important work is *De Trinitate.* See Cazenove's *St. Hilary of Poitiers,* 1883.

Hilary, or Hilarius, surnamed **Diaconus,** a deacon of Rome, born in Sardinia. In 350 he was sent to Emperor Constantius by Pope Liberius on a special mission to uphold orthodoxy against the Arians at the council of Milan. His opponents scourged and exiled him, with the result that his views were strengthened. Two treatises imputed to him are usually incorporated the one with Augustine's, the other with Ambrose's works.

Hilary, a pope, successor of Leo I. (461), a native of Sardinia. He was created archdeacon by Leo I., and rigorously upheld the supremacy of Rome. When pope, he improved and enriched the monasteries and churches which had been damaged by the Vandals. He died greatly mourned (467).

Hilary, St., of Arles (401-449), born in a town between Lorraine and Champagne, brought up in the monastery of Lérins. He became Bishop of Arles, and later deposed the Bishop of Besançon, which seriously embroiled him for some time with Leo I.

Hilda, or Hild (614-680), a patroness of Whitby. She was abbess of Hartlepool or Heorta (*c.* 650). She ruled for twenty-two years the monastery for monks and nuns at Whitby (Streoneshalh), which she had founded in 658.

Hildburghausen, a tn. of Saxe-Meiningen on the Werra, 19 m. S.E. of Meiningen. It manufactures linen fabrics, cloth, cutlery, condensed milk and soup, toys, and fancy goods. There are interesting ancient and modern buildings. It was formerly (1683-1826) capital of the duchy of Saxe-Hildburghausen. Pop. 7710.

Hildebrand, see GREGORY VII.

Hildebrande, Emil (*b.* 1848), a Swedish historian, born and educated at Stockholm. In 1880 he was appointed to the post of historical lecturer at the Stockholm high school, and in 1901 he became director of the Swedish archives. Since its foundation, in 1881, he has edited the organ of the Swedish Historical Society. In conjunction with O. Alin he has published *Svenska Riksdagsakter,* 1521-1718, and amongst his own publications may be mentioned : *Svenska Skriftprof från Erik den Heliges Tid till Gustaf III.'s; Svenska Statsförfattningens Historiska Utveckling; Wallenstein und seine Verbindungen mit den Schweden,* etc. H. is also the editor of the illustrated *Sveriges Historia intill 20de Seklet,* 1902.

Hildegarde, St. (*c.* 1098-*c.* 1179), a visionary, seer, and an appreciated writer, born at Böckelheim, Germany. She is called the Sibyl of the Rhine, and was abbess of the nunnery of Disibodenberg, Lorraine, at which she was brought up. She founded the abbey of St. Rupert, near Bingen. See Schmelzeis's *Leben,* 1879.

Hilden, a prospering tn. of the Prussian Rhine Province, 8 m. S.E. of Düsseldorf. It manufs. velvet, silk goods, carpets, machinery, etc. Pop. 16,902.

Hildenborough, a very picturesque vil., Kent, England, 2 m. W.N.W. of Tonbridge, celebrated for its village plays which are performed yearly.

Hilderthorpe, a par. and vil. S. of Bridlington, E. Riding, Yorkshire, England. It is a popular seaside resort. Pop. 2500.

Hildesheim, a tn. and episcopal see of Germany, in the Prussian prov. of Hanover, situated at the foot of the Harz Mts., on the R. Innerste. There is an old and new part to the town, and the streets for the most part are narrow and irregular. There are some very interesting buildings, the Roman Catholic Cathedral, which dates back to the 11th century, noted for the beautiful bronze doors executed by Bishop Bernward, its brazen font (13th century), the sarcophagus of St. Godehard, the tomb of St. Epiphanius, and a bronze column 15ft. high dating back to 1022. Then there is the Romanesque church of St. Godehard, built in the 12th century, and the church of St. Michael, founded in the 11th century by Bishop Bernward, of whom it contains a monument. Besides these, there is the Rathaus town hall, which dates back to the 15th century; the Wedekindhaus (1598), now a savings bank; the gild-house of the butchers (1529), a fine example of a wooden building; the St. Michael Monastery, now a lunatic asylum; and the Römer Museum. The chief productions are sugar, tobacco, stoves, machinery, vehicles, and bricks; brewing, gardening, fruit-growing, and tanning are also carried on. H. has been the seat of a bishopric since 822; and was one of the original members of the Hanseatic League. A unique collection of Roman silver plate of the time of Augustus was found on the Galgenberg, E. of the town, in 1868. Pop. 50,246.

Hildyard, Sir Henry John Thoroton (b. 1846), a British general, born near Newark, and educated at the Royal Naval Academy, Gosport. He entered the army in 1867, having first served in the navy (1859-64), and rose to the rank of major in 1882, after fighting in the Egyptian campaign. He was present at the battles of Kassassin and Tel-el-Kebir. In 1899 he was despatched to S. Africa, at the outbreak of the Boer War, in command of the 2nd Infantry Brigade, and subsequently, succeeding Sir Charles Warren, was put in command of the 5th Division (1900-1). H. distinguished himself at the relief of Ladysmith, and as a reward for his services was created K.C.B. On his return to England he was appointed Director-General of Military Education (1903-4). In 1904 he went back to S. Africa as lieutenant-general in command of the troops, and in the following year was appointed general officer commanding-in-chief (1905-8). He retired in 1911, when he was created G.C.B.

Hilgenfeld, Adolf Bernhard Christoph (1823-1907), a German theologian, born at Stappenbeck in Prussian Saxony, and educated in Berlin and Halle. In 1850 he became a theological professor at Jena, and in 1858 was appointed editor of Zeitschrift für wissenschaftliche Theologie. He was an adherent of the Liberal school of theology. His chief writings are : Das Markusevangelium, 1850; Der Galaterbrief, 1850 ; Das Urchristenthum,1855; Die jüdische Apokalyptik, 1857; Hermas, 1873; Ketzergeschichte des Urchristenthums, 1884; and Ignatii et Polycarpi epistolæ, 1902.

Hill, Aaron (1685-1750), an English writer, born in London. On leaving Westminster School he travelled in Turkey, on the state of which he published A Full and Just Account, 1709. His contributions to the drama include : Elfrid (produced at Drury Lane in 1709), Zara (1735), and Merope (1749). He was included in Pope's Dunciad, and retorted in The Progress of Wit, being a Caveat for he use of an Eminent Writer, 1730. His Works, including poems and letters, were published in 1753, and his Dramatic Works in 1760. Consult Life in Cibber's Lives of the Poets (vol. v.).

Hill, Emmanuel (1834-99), a Flemish poet, born near Dender-

monde. After holding a government post he became a professor at Brussels Conservatory. His lyric poetry ranks among the best in Flemish literature, and some of his poems have been set to music. Among his best known works are : Nieuwe Liedekens, 1861; Gedichten, 1863; Liederen voor Groote en Kleine Kinderen, 1875; Bloemardinne, 1877; and his great poems Lucifer and De Schelde. Volledige Dichtwerken was a collection of his works published in 1885.

Hill, George Birkbeck (1835-1903), an English literary critic, educated at Bruce Castle School and Pembroke College, Oxford. In 1868 he succeeded his father as headmaster of his old school, and, like him, proved averse from exercising any kind of coercion with his pupils. A contributor to the Saturday Review (1869-84), he published, after his retirement from teaching (1877), a series of scholarly editions of Johnsonian literature, including Boswell's Life of Johnson, 1887. His Dr. Johnson, his Friends and Critics, appeared in 1878.

Hill, Sir John (c. 1716-75), an English author, born at Peterborough. He set up an apothecary's shop in St. Martin's Lane, London, became editor of the British Magazine (1746-50), and contributed to the London Advertiser and Literary Gazette. He also published a translation of Theophrastus's History of Stones (1746), and wrote many botanical works, including The Vegetable System (26 vols.), 1759-75. He had many literary quarrels with Fielding, John Rich, Garrick, and others. Christopher Smart satirised him in his mock-epic, The Hilliad.

Hill, Octavia (1838-1912), an English social reformer, was educated at home. Encouraged by Mr. Ruskin she bought three cottages in Marylebone (1864), and was so successful in increasing the self-respect and improving the material welfare of her tenants that the Countess Ducie gave into her charge a property in Drury Lane. Appalled by the misery of life in the slums, she devoted all her energy, tact, and practical ability to its amelioration. Latterly, she was at the head of a staff of assistants who, between them, collected the rents of 6000 dwellings and tenements in the metropolis. At different periods she was identified with many philanthropic associations, including the Charity Organisation Society and the Women's University Settlement. The results of her intimate experience were published in Homes of the London Poor, 1875; Our Common Land, 1878, etc.

Hill, Rowland (1744–1833), a preacher, the sixth son of Sir Rowland H., first baronet, born at his father's seat, Hawkstone Park, Shropshire, on Aug. 23. Educated at Shrewsbury and Eton, and whilst still young received deep religious impressions from his eldest brother Richard. Entered St. John's College, Cambridge, in 1764, and whilst there visited the sick and prisoners and preached wherever he could. In 1769 he graduated B.A. with honours, and endeavoured to obtain orders. Ordained June 1773 to the curacy of Kingston, Somersetshire, but refused priest's orders on account of his unconventional style. He continued to preach to immense congregations. In 1783 Surrey Chapel was built for him, which remained the ordinary scene of his labours till the end of his life, and under its pulpit he was buried. H. was deeply interested in Sunday-schools, and there were thirteen attached to Surrey Chapel with over 3000 scholars. He took a prominent part in all philanthropic and religious movements, and his earnest, eloquent, and eccentric preaching attracted large congregations. See *Life* by Rev. Edwin Sidney (4th ed.), 1861.

Hill, Rowland, Viscount (1772–1842), a British general, nephew of the preacher Rowland Hill, was born at Prees Hall, near Hawkstone. He commanded the 90th regiment in Abercromby's Egyptian Expedition (1801), and served throughout the Peninsular War as Sir Arthur Wellesley's ablest coadjutor. He captured the forts of Almarez, for which he was created Baron (1814). He distinguished himself by his brigade charge at Waterloo, and succeeded Wellington in 1828 as commander-in-chief. See *Life* by Rev. Edwin Sidney (1845).

Hill, Sir Rowland, K.C.B., (1795–1879), the originator of the penny postal system, born at Kidderminster. As a boy he was interested in mathematics, and later in life became engaged in mechanical inventions. His ideas on a uniform rate of postage, regardless of distance, were published in pamphlet form, *Post Office Reform*, 1837. In 1839 he was attached to the Treasury, and his schemes were realised in the following year. He was dismissed from office when the Conservatives came into power (1841), but on the return of the Whigs, was appointed secretary to the Postmaster-General (1846). In the same year he was presented with £13,360 as a public appreciation of his services. Consult *Sir Rowland Hill, the Story of a Great Reform*, by his daughter, 1907.

Hillah, Hilla, or **Hellah,** a tn. and vilayet, built of materials from the ruins of Babylon near by. It is on the Euphrates, 60 m. S. of Bagdad, Asiatic Turkey. H. is a resting-place for pilgrims to Meshhed Ali and Meshhed-Hussein. It manufs. cotton, silk, and woollen goods. Pop. 30,000.

Hille, a tn., Sweden, in Gefleborg gov., 4 m. N.N.E. of Gefle. Pop. 4000.

Hillegersberg, a com. of S. Holland, 2 m. N. of Rotterdam. Pop. 3296.

Hillegom, a com. of S. Holland, 2½ m. N. of Rotterdam. Pop. 7976.

Hillel, called **Hazaken** (' the Elder ') and **Hababli** (' the Babylonian ') (*c.* 75 B.C.-10 A.D.), a Jewish rabbi, was a native of Babylon. When he was already verging towards old age, he began to study law under Shemaieh and Abtalion in Jerusalem, and soon grew famous for his profound lore, whereby, according to the Talmud, he comprehended all tongues, even those of trees and beasts. Being well-nigh penniless, his learning was only acquired by exceptional zeal and self-denial. It is unlikely that he was ever president of the Sanhedrin, yet his humility and loving-kindness, and what has been described as the 'sweetness and light' of his personality, ensured the popularity of his teaching, which, like that of Jesus, was ever averse from ' sacerdotal traditionalism ' and blind adherence to legal ordinance.

Hiller, Ferdinand (1811–85), a musical composer, played a concerto of Mozart at the age of ten, and in 1827 was present at the deathbed of Beethoven. Born at Frankfort-on-Main, he visited Weimar, Vienna (with Hummel, his master), Paris (where he lived from 1828-35), Italy, St. Petersburg, and England, etc. From 1850 till his death, he was municipal capellmeister at Cologne, where, besides organising the Conservatoire, he composed, conducted, wrote, and taught, Max Bruch being his most famous pupil. Among his wide circle of friends were Berlioz, Mendelssohn, Cherubini, the Schumanns, Spohr, Liszt, and Chopin. His numerous compositions include chamber, orchestral, and vocal music: these display conspicuous inequalities, but since its first publication, his oratorio entitled *Die Zerstörung Jerusalems,* 1839, has been recognised as a masterpiece. In Paris he was celebrated for his fine interpretation of Bach and Beethoven.

Hilleröd, a tn. on the Island Zeeland, 20 m. N.N.W. of Copenhagen. Close by is the royal palace of Frederiksborg. Pop. 4600.

Hill-forts are, as their name implies, fortifications erected on the top of a steep cliff or mountainous crag. The summits of hills, like islands and fens, were peculiarly adapted to serve as the last refuge of a native race in a country invaded by a stronger people. So H. are found of great antiquity, constructed by uncivilised peoples; as Mr. D. Wilson says, 'the simple circular H. wherein we have the mere rudimentary efforts of a people in the infancy of the arts.' To this category belong the rude earthworks found on the top of many peaks in the British Isles. Scotland is especially rich in H., many of which are of a somewhat more advanced type. Two or three concentric circular ramparts defend the summit of the hill, so that as the invading party stormed one line of defence the defenders might retire gradually into their innermost stronghold. The H. which is at the summit of White Caterthun in Forfarshire, may be described in some detail as being typical of many others. The hill in question is 976 ft. high. The first resistance to an attacking force is offered by a double entrenchment 200 ft. below the summit; the formation of the cliff then precludes further advance, save on one side. The end of this path leads to an oval rampart of stones 436 ft. by 200 ft.; the width of the walls, in which are found chambers, as in the Irish cashels (q.v.) is 26 ft. Among other H. in the British Isles may be mentioned Arbory Fort in Lanarkshire, Dun Murray in Argyllshire, and Dun Aengus in the Aran Isles. In many cases, of course, a H. was the residence and headquarters of a warrior chief, or a robber-baron, as in the mediæval ages. In this class come the H. of the wild tribesmen of Afghanistan, and the N.W. frontier of India. For the vitrification of the stones of H., see under VITRIFIED FORTS. See Dr. Christison, Early Fortification in Scotland, 1818.

Hillgrove, a gold and antimony mining tn. on Baker's Creek, Sandon co., 20 m. E. of Armidale, New South Wales. Pop. 3000.

Hillhead, Scotland, a suburb to the N.W. of Glasgow.

Hillhouse, James (1754-1832), a politician and poet, born in Montville, Connecticut, U.S.A. He graduated at Yale College (1773), was a member in the U.S. House of Representatives (1791-94), and the U.S. Senate (1794-1810). From 1782-1832 he was treasurer of his college. His best known poems are The Judgment and Hadad. See Life by Bacon.

Hilliard, Henry Washington (1808-92), a United States lawyer, entered the state parliament of Alabama in 1838, and from 1845 sat in Congress. For some time he was employed in Belgium in the diplomatic service, and later represented his country in Brazil. His Politics and Pen Pictures

1892, contains many autobiographical details of interest.

Hilliard, Nicholas, a miniature-painter and goldsmith, painted Queen Elizabeth and Mary Queen of Scots, and for twelve years enjoyed the exclusive privilege of executing portraits of James I. and other members of the royal family. Charles I. counted among his art treasures a jewel of his workmanship with an enamelled picture of the field of Bosworth, and the likenesses of four sovereigns.

Hillsborough, or **Hillsboro,** cap. of Hill co., Texas, U.S.A., 50 m. S.S.W. of Fort Worth. It manufs. cotton, hosiery, leather, flour, and carries on lumbering. Pop. (1910) 6115.

Hillsborough: 1. A tn., Alberta co., New Brunswick, Canada; on Petitcodiac R. There are valuable granite-gypsum quarries and coal mines near. Pop. 1000. 2. A par. and market tn., N. of co. Down, Ireland, 12 m. S.S.W. of Belfast. Its chief industry is linen manuf. Pop. 2500. 3. The chief tn. on the coast of Carriacou, an island N. of Granada, British W. Indies.

Hillsdale, cap. of H. co., Michigan, U.S.A., on the Riv. St. Joseph, 90 m. S.W. of Detroit. It manufs. shoes, waggons, gas engines, and furniture, and is an agricultural centre. Pop (1910) 5001.

Hill States, a general name for the small native states on the S. slope of the Himalayas in the vicinity of Simla, India.

Hill Tipperah, an Indian native state of about 4000 sq. m., at the extreme E. of Bengal, and adjoining the British dist. of Tipperah. It is for the most part thick forest land, and produces cotton, chillies, and rice. The inhabitants are hill tribes. Argartala, the cap., is 70 m. N.E. of Dacca.

Hilo, a seaport, and the tn. second in importance of the Sandwich Is., picturesquely situated on the E. coast of the island of Hawaii. It exports sugar, molasses, arrowroot, and rice. Pop. 6745.

Hilongos, a pueblo on the W. coast of Leyte Is., Philippines, 60 m. S.W. of Tacloban. Pop. 13,500.

Hilton, John (1804-78), an English surgeon, attended Guy's Hospital at first as a student and afterwards as demonstrator of anatomy (1828), assistant-surgeon (1845), and surgeon (1849). As president of the Royal College of Surgeons, he gave the Hunterian address in 1867. 'Anatomical John,' as he was called, was joint-founder with Towne of the excellent museum of models at Guy's, and was the foremost anatomist of his day. His Rest and Pain (1863) is a valued addition to medical literature.

Hilton, William (1786-1839), an

English painter, studied at the Academy schools (London), and afterwards visited Italy with Thomas Phillips, the portrait-painter. In 1820 he was elected to the Royal Academy, which to-day possesses his masterpiece, a representation of ' Christ crowned with Thorns ' (1823). This picture, like his others, as, for example, ' Rebecca and Abraham's Servant,' 1829, and ' Edith finding the Body of Harold,' 1834, is characterised by thoroughness and a judicious taste in colour and design rather than by a display of superlative talent.

Hilversum, a prosperous tn., prov., N. Holland, 18 m. S.E. of Amsterdam. It manufs. horse-blankets and floor-cloths. It is a popular summer resort, and its neighbourhood is attractive. Pop. 31,458.

Himalaya Mountains, the most elevated highland system in the world. The word Himalaya is Sanskrit, and means ' Abode of Snow,' the same Aryan root being preserved in the Greek χεῖμα, snow, and the Latin *hiems*, winter. They stretch from the seventy-second to the ninety-sixth meridian E. of Greenwich, and with a breadth varying from 180 to 220 m. form a broad, sweeping barrier between Tibet and British India from the western confines of Kashmir to the eastern limits of Assam. Undoubtedly they belong structurally to the great plateau of Central Asia, of which they may be regarded as forming the southern scarp. On the Indian side the slopes of the main ridge are precipitous right down to the marshy ' Tarai ' or ' Tariyáni.' This is a belt of grassy lands, about 12 m. wide, traversed by many sluggish streams, along whose banks are treacherous morasses covered with tall reeds; it fringes the British and Nepal frontiers for almost 500 m. from W. to E. Towards C. Asia the fall of the Himalayas is gentle. Broadly speaking, their direction W. of Mt. Everest, the highest known peak on the globe (29,002 ft.), is N.W. and S.E., but from this height to the boundaries of China the lie is almost due E. It is a mistake to regard the Himalayas as a single unbroken chain ; they are rather a series of ridges roughly parallel, whose symmetry is confused by a multitude of subsidiary spurs, which strike out from them in all directions. What is sometimes called the Indian watershed separates the rivers which pass out to the Indian Ocean into two classes: those which cut a direct way through the mountains on to the plains of India, and those which, after being gathered on the top of the table-land, reach the sea by two

streams which set out at distant points towards opposite limits of the chain. But the great divide, sometimes referred to as the Turkish watershed, is the summit of the northern range, which is the natural cleavage line between the rivers which disappear somewhere in the level stretches of Mongolia and Turkestan, and those which eventually join the Indian Ocean. The Indian watershed is remarkable for its height, which reaches an average of 18,000 ft. between the Brahmaputra and the Indus. The valleys traversing the highlands from the watershed to the Indian plains, are gigantic gorges, and offer small encouragement to human habitation. Yet some few, with an elevation of from 6000 to 7000 ft., are fast becoming favourite situations for summer retreats of Europeans eager to escape the sweltering heats of Bengal. Other valleys reach right up into the line of highest summits without rising to a higher elevation than 3000 ft., and thus harbour tropical heat and vegetation at the foot of snow-capped heights. For the most part the valleys slope gradually till within 10 m. or so of the line of greatest elevation, and afterwards often shoot upward from 5000 to 10,000 ft. within an incredibly small distance.

It is convenient to divide the Himalayas into three sections. The western begins from that point where the Indus turns southward between Gilgit and Kashmir, a point which is marked by Mt. Nanga-Parbat (26,629 ft.). This section, which also contains Nanda-Devi (25,661 ft.), is not conspicuous in well-marked ranges, but it is crossed longitudinally by several valleys which confine the Indus and other rivers for hundreds of miles before giving them an opening southward. The Central Himalayas contain the highest summits in the world, and comprise the regions of Hundes, Garhwal, and Kumaon, which were scientifically surveyed in 1892. They are sometimes called the Nepal Highlands and extend from the source of the Indus to the Tista—an affluent of the Jumna. Other outstanding crests besides Everest are Monut Godwin-Austen (28,265 ft.), Kunchinjinga (28,156 ft.) on the Sikkim frontier, N. of Darjeeling, and Dhawlagiri (26,286 ft.) in the W. Some conception may be conveyed of the stupendous scale upon which these mountains are built, if the peaks which lie between the seventy-eighth and the eighty-first meridians—a distance under 150 m. in length—or rather their main groups, are enumerated : (1) Between the Alaknanda and

Bhagirathi, tributaries of the Ganges, are the heights of Badrinath, Kedarnath, and Gangotri; (2) the peaks between the Dhaoli and Vishnuganga; (3) Nanda-Devi, Nanda-kot, and Dunagiri between the Gori and the Dhaoli; (4) the Pánch-chuli cluster between the Gori and the Darma; (5) Yirnajang between the Kali and the Darma; (6) the Api cluster in Nepal. In altitude these summits range one and all from 22,000 to 22,900 ft., and it is likely that a more thorough survey will reveal peaks exceeding 30,000 ft. in height. Before the highlands of this division roll down to the plains, there rises a sandy, waterless ridge, known as the Bhabar, whose average elevation is some 4500 ft. This tract is densely forested, and absorbs all the streams which flow down from the outer highlands, but as it undulates down to the Tarai, the waters are collected together, and once more reappear above the surface. The easternmost section covers a great part of Sikkim, Bhutan, and Northern Assam. Its loftiest peak is Chumolhari (23,933 ft.), but 16,000 ft. probably represents the mean altitude. There is still a wide field open to ambitious surveyors in this part of the mountains, for the lower reaches of the Sanpo have never been traced, and little is known of the eastern uplands.

There are naturally great variations of climate at different heights and in different regions of the Himalayas. A comparison between ranges in the W. and E. shows that the latter enjoy a warmer and more equable but also a wetter climate. Moreover, the forest tracts are more widely dispersed in the E., and the area of lands under cultivation is probably less. Both the meteorological conditions and the scenery in the W. are similar to those of Southern Europe, provided, that is, that the Himalayan altitude be over 5000 ft. The snow line is much higher on the Tibetan than on the Indian side, because the latter has the greater snowfall. On the southern exposures of the Himalayas there are perpetual snows to within some 15,500 ft. of the sea-level, whilst at the top of the northern table-land of Tibet the snow line is actually as high as 20,000 ft. Precipitation is naturally greatest on the slopes of the outermost spurs, and by the time the limits of Tibet are reached, beyond the line of highest peaks, it is so small as almost to elude measurement. Rain falls between May and October, and the season is known as the S.W. monsoon, which is accompanied by moisture-laden winds from the S.W. As regards temperature, both the annual and diurnal range diminish with increase in elevation, whilst the variation of temperature according to altitude is greatest in summer. The rivers hardly ever freeze, probably because they are too rapid. Glaciers descend much lower on the outer than on the Tibetan slopes. On the valleys of the latter they come down to within 15,000 ft. of the sea-level, but on the southern faces 11,500 ft. is a normal limit. In different parts Alpine, European, and tropical flora abound; the Sal, Toon, Sissoo, and Deodar supply the only timber of commercial value; cereals, fruit, and tea are grown with success up to a height of 7000 ft.

The Himalayas afford the supreme illustration of the sublimity and incomparable grandeur of mountain scenery. The reader has only to remember that the mean elevation is some 18,000 ft., and that at least forty heights exceed 24,000 ft., to grant the truth of the assertion that ' the great mountain solitudes of the Himalayas, . . . the apparently endless succession of range after range, of ascent and descent, of valley and mountain top, of river, torrent, and brook, of precipitous rock and grassy slope, of forest and cultivated land, cannot fail to produce impressions of wonder ' and awe of such intensity as can be conjured up by no other range in any quarter of the globe.

Himantopus, the name of a genus of charadiiform birds belonging to the family Charadiidæ; they are plover-like in their habits, and are commonly called stilts. *H. candidus* is an occasional visitor to Britain.

Himeji, a tn., Hiogo prefecture, Hondo, Japan, 60 m. W. of Osaka. Cotton and stamped leather goods are manufactured. It posseses an ancient castle. Pop. 42,000.

Himera, a famous ancient Greek city of the northern coast of Sicily, Italy. In 409 B.C. it was razed to the ground by Hannibal. H. was never rebuilt, but the Carthaginians built Thermæ, a town on the opposite bank of the R. Himera.

Himmel, Friedrich Heinrich (1765-1814), a German composer, profited much by the patronage of Frederick William II., who, besides giving him a three years' musical education and sending him to Italy for two years of further study, gave him, on Reichardt's dismissal, the court-capellmeistership of Berlin. H.'s *Trauer-cantate* was especially written for the king's funeral in 1797, and his opera *Alessandro* was the result of a commission from the Czar. But his finest operatic work was *Fanchon, das Leiermädchen* (1804), for which Kotzebue wrote the libretto. Despite their melodic charm, his songs and pianoforte sonatas are rarely performed.

Himyaritic is descriptive of the language in which the primitive Sabæan inscriptions of south-western Arabia are written, but the word has grown obsolete. *See* SABÆANS.

Himyars, or Sabæans, The, once dwelt in Yemen, Arabia, and are identical with the Homerites of Ptolemy. *See* SABÆANS.

Hinayâna, or the ' Little Vehicle,' is, in Buddhistic literature, opposed to the *Mahayana*, or ' Great Vehicle.' At the council summoned to Patna by King Asoka about 260 B.C., disputes arose as to which were the sacred and canonical books of Buddha. The names *Hinayâna* and *Mahayana* were clearly defined at another great council called together by Kanishka, ruler of Kashmir, about 4 B.C. The books of the H., which are written in Pali and are fewer in number than those of the ' Great Vehicle,' are recognised by the southern Buddhists, and are probably the earlier and more venerable. But it was the *Mahayana* which led to the wide proselytism in China and Tibet.

Hinckley, a market tn., 13 m. S.W. of Leicester, England. It is an ancient town on Watling Street, and has mineral springs. The chief trade is in boots, shoes, hosiery, and coarse pottery. Pop. (1911) 12,838.

Hincmar (*c.* 806-882), Archbishop of Rheims from 845; was educated in the abbey of St. Denis and held the abbacies of Compiègne and St. Germain before he attained to his archbishopric. He was a bitter opponent of Gottschalk, the refractory monk and champion of predestinarianism, and exposed his ' heresies ' in a series of theological polemics. As metropolitan, he had excommunicated his suffragan bishop, Rothad ; by eventually reinstating the offender, he undoubtedly encouraged papal autocracy. Yet in the matter of the sovereignty of Lorraine he boldly refused to countenance Pope Adrian's interference.

Hind, the name given to the female of *Cervus elaphus*, the red-deer, a ruminant ungulate mammal belonging to the Cervidæ; *hart* is the correlative term for the male.

Hind, John Russell (1823-95), an astronomer, displayed from boyhood a strong bent for that science with which his life-work was connected. After working for four years in the Royal Observatory at Greenwich (1840-44), he was given the direction of Bishop's observatory in Regent's Park. Here he discovered ten planetoids and two comets, and worked out the orbits and declination of over seventy constellations. In 1851 he observed the total eclipse in Sweden, and two years later accepted the editorship of the *Nautical Almanac.* Among his works are : *The Solar System*, 1852, and *Descriptive Treatise on Comets,* 1857.

Hindaun, a tn., Rajputana, India, 50 m. S.E. of Bhartpur. Pop. 13,000.

Hinderwell, a par. and fishing vil., N. Riding, Yorkshire, England, 9 m. N.W. of Whitby. There are iron mines. Pop. (1911) 2491.

Hindhead, an extensive hill ridge and common, rising 2 m. N.W. of Haslemere, Surrey, England. Gibbett Hill, the highest point, is 895 ft.

Hindley, a township, 2 m. E.S.E. of Wigan, Lancs., England, celebrated for cannel coal. There are iron works and cotton mills. Pop. (1911) 28,000.

Hindmarsh, a suburban post tn. on Torrens R., 2 m. N.W. of Adelaide, S. Australia. Pop. 10,000.

Hindö, the largest isl. of the Lofoten group off the coast of Norway, within the Arctic circle. It is mountainous and somewhat wooded. Digermulen to the S.W. is a port of the Vesteraalen steamers. Area 864 sq. m. Pop. 10,000.

Hindol, a small trib. state, Bihar and Orissa, Bengal, India, 50 m. W.N.W. of Cuttack. Area 312 sq. m. Pop. 380,000.

Hinduism, a comprehensive term which is used to designate not only the social customs, but the religious beliefs of the majority of the peoples of India. The actual proportion of the total population which comes under the heading ' Hindu ' is over 70 per cent., and the number of ' Hindus ' exceeds 207,000,000. The creeds and practices of H. differ no less than the organically connected social principles, rendering it very difficult of definition. The close alliance and interaction between Brahmanism (*q.v.*) and H. make it impossible for a strict line of demarcation to be drawn from a chronological or a sectarian point of view. H. may be said to date roughly from about the 6th century, when the local revolts of the laity against Brahmanic supremacy culminated in Buddhism and Jainism. Until then the authoritative doctrine of pantheistic belief formulated by speculative theologians during the centuries succeeding the Vedic period had held sway; these revolts had the effect of rendering Brahmanism still more tolerant, although its erstwhile severely metaphysical and ritualistic rigour had previously been modified by the currents of Sivaite and Vishnuite thought. The doctrine of the Trimurti, or Trinity, was often put forward under the influence of Upanishad monism. Brahma, the creative principle of the universe; Vishnu, the conservative principle; and Siva, the destroying, but also the generative, principle, are represented as a Trinity of equal and identical deities. But to the vast majority of Hindus some form of either Vishnu or Siva is the highest source of all existence, and the object of supreme adoration. The subdivisions of the Vishnuite sects range from the broadest pantheism to extreme sectarianism. The cult of Siva affects the two extremes of society; he is favoured by many high-class Brahmans and metaphysical ascetics, and also by the lowest classes. The reason for this is that he is regarded not only as a mystic miracle-working deity, but as a blood-loving, awe-inspiring god. The Sakla movement, the worship of Siva's wife, under various names, as the cosmic energy of the universe, is closely allied to Siva-worship. The whole ground of Hindu sectarianism is by no means covered by these broad outlines; many miscellaneous cults exist which are still included under the general term H. The pantheon of the latter finds room for hosts of minor deities, which are in the main accepted both by Vishnuites and Sivaites. Closely allied and interwoven with all the sects of H. is the system of caste. The infinite variety of caste-divisions, each with a social and religious organisation of its own, was evolved from its beginnings in the Vedic age by the Brahmans. For details, see INDIA. Although H. has preserved numberless myths, and has incorporated much that is gross and unworthy, it has also gathered many spiritual truths from nature and the universe. Its main planks, the doctrines of 'Karma' (works), 'Samsāra' ('wandering,' *i.e.* metempsychosis), and 'Moksha' (release and absorption, or union, with the Infinite), may seem fantastic to the European mind; but the Hindu mind is essentially mystic and transcendental, regarding all finite phenomena as evanescent and illusory, and, if this is remembered, due honour and praise will not be withheld from its vast and beautiful religious literature. In such works as the *Upanishads*, the *Bhagavad-gita*, the *Tamil-Sivaite* poems, the *Ramāyana*, and many others, the truth that the pure in heart, of whatever creed or race, shall see God is manifested. Despite their faults they represent a notable progress of the human mind in spiritual and religious evolution; 'They are but broken lights of Thee, and Thou, O Lord, art more than they,' and more than any other religious system. See J. Murray Mitchell, *Hinduism,*

Past and Present, 1897; J. Robson, *Hinduism and Christianity,* 1883; Monier Williams, *Hinduism,* 1877, and *Religious Thought and Life in India,* 1883; L. D. Barnett, *Hinduism,* 1906, etc., etc. *See also* INDIA, BRAHMANISM, VISHNU, SIVA, ARYA SAMAJ, etc.

Hindu-Kush, the name of a mountain chain of Central Asia which, for 200 m. from its eastern extremity, forms the southern frontier of Afghanistan. It is the great watershed between the Kabul and the Oxus basins, and its general direction is from W.S.W. to E.N.E. As the range turns away from Ab-i-Panja, an affluent of the Oxus, it attains greater elevation, rising sometimes as much as 24,000 ft. above the sea. One of its loftiest summits is Tirach Mir, 25,400 ft. which towers above the fort and Chitral. The passes of Barogil, village of Agram, and Khartaza, etc., link the Oxus with the Chitral, whilst westwards the chief passes are the Khawak, the Kaoshan (14,340 ft.), the most frequented of them all, the Chahardar, and the much lower Shibar (9800 ft.), after which the range is merged into the Koh-i-baba.

Hindu Law is theoretically of divine origin, and cannot be changed by human agency. The books which lay down the law, the Shastras, are of very ancient origin, and the state of society in the time in which they were written was quite unlike that of the present time. Consequently, they enact rules which no Hindu follows, and do not give any pronouncement on many things which need regulation. The chief agents in changing the operation and scope of the law are custom, and different interpretations, as laid down in commentaries. Legislation has not been employed, although the British parliament and the Hindu legislatures have power to legislate on all matters. In the *Laws of Manu* it is said that ' the king who knows the sacred law must inquire into the laws of castes of districts, of gilds, and of families, and thus settle the peculiar law of each.' Formerly the only persons whose interpretations of the law were binding were the writers of commentaries, but the Indian courts will not accept the opinions of modern commentators, although their own rulings are binding. Thus different schools of H. L. have arisen, which may be divided into two main branches, that of Benares (including those of Bombay, Dravida, and Mithila, for Western India, Southern India, and Nepaul, respectively), and that of Bengal, or Gawinja. The most important books laying down the law are: the *Laws of Manu,* the *Smitri of Yaghavalkya,* and the *Smriti of Narada*. More important still are the commentaries which are not sacred: the *Mitacshara of Vijnaneswara*, on the *Smriti of Yaghavalkya*, is the commentary which exercises the most influence, though in the valley of the Ganges the *Dayabhaga of Jimutavahana*, in Southern India the *Smriti Chandrika*, in Western India the *Vigavahara Mayukha*, and in Mithila the *Vivada Chintamani* are respectively of importance. See J. D. Mayne's *Hindu Law*, 1892; Jogendra Chundar, *Principles of Hindu Law*, 1906; Stokes's *Hindu Law Books*, 1865; Jogendra Nath Bhattacharya, *A Commentary on Hindu Law*, 1894; etc.

Hindur, a hill state, Punjab, some 50 m. N. of Ambala, India. Chief products, opium and grain. Area 250 sq. m. Pop. 50,000.

Hindustan, or Hindostan, means the ' country of the Hindus.' The Persians used to call the R. Sindhu ' Hindhu,' and that part of the district was therefore called H. The region denoted was gradually extended, until the whole tract of country between the Himalaya Mts. and the Vindhya Mts., W. of Bengal, was so designated. In many instances even H. was used as a synonym for India, but in this sense it is not now used, and in a more restricted sense is less often employed.

Hindustan, a British battleship of the *King Edward VII.* class; displacement 16,350; speed 18·5 knots. It was launched at Clydebank by the Duchess of Connaught, Dec. 21, 1903.

Hinganghat (ancient *Innycotta*), a tn., Wardha dist., Central Provinces, India, 48 m. S.S.W. of Nagpur. It is the centre of the trade in Wardha valley, which is famous for raw cotton. Pop. 12,000.

Hinge (Middle Eng. *henge*, a hook, hinge, etc.), the name given to the articulation of a door, etc., to its support, or of two movable parts to each other, as in a screen. The ordinary metallic H. consists of the two ' leaves,' the ' knuckle,' formed by the union of the alternate rounded projections and perforations at the inner end of the leaves, and the ' pin,' or ' pintle,' which passes through the knuckle, and on which the H. turns.

Hingham, a tn., Plymouth co., Massachusetts, U.S.A., on Massachusetts Bay, 12 m. S.E. of Boston. It is a popular summer resort. Here is the Derby Academy. Pop. (1910) 4965.

Hinkson, Mrs., *see* TYNAN, KATHARINE.

Hinnites, the name of a genus of pseudolamellibranchiate molluscs belonging to the family Pectinidæ; they have ribbed shells and emerald green pallial eyes.

Hinny, the hybrid offspring of a stallion and a female ass. Compared with the mule, which is the cross between a male ass and a mare, it is more tractable and less obstinate: at the same time it is not so sturdy and is smaller in size. It is less common than a mule, because less useful.

Hinojosa del Duque, a tn. 48 m. N.N.W. of Cordova, Spain. There are valuable copper mines, and linen and woollen goods are manufactured. Pop. 11,000.

Hinterland, a German word expressing the country which lies at the back of colonies which, in an unexplored continent, naturally grow up near the coast. It is connected with a theory of colonial expansion. Most early settlers, like those in N. America and in Africa, assume rights over a much wider area than that which they have so far developed or explored. Thus those English colonists who had peopled a mere coastal strip arrogantly claimed jurisdiction over vast regions W. of the Mississippi, and were not slow to show their resentment at what they regarded as the iniquitous appropriations of French explorers along that river's course. The theory about the ' hinterland ' made a very strong appeal to the German emigrants of Bismarck's day.

Hinton, James (1822-75), an aural surgeon and writer, was the son of a Baptist minister. Before he was sent to St. Bartholomew's Hospital he had already served a woollen draper in Whitechapel, and been a clerk in an insurance office. In 1847 he took his medical degree, and after a year in Jamaica, settled down to surgery in London, being appointed aural surgeon to Guy's Hospital in 1863. From this time his reputation as an ear specialist steadily rose, and his *Atlas of Diseases of the Membrane Tympani* and *Questions of Aural Surgery* have established him as an authority on that organ. His was a morbidly excitable temperament, which aggravated the unrest produced by those moral questionings to which he was continually a prey. Among his ethical or metaphysical writings may be mentioned : *The Mystery of Pain*, 1865; *Philosophy and Religion*, 1881, and his early publication, *Man and his Dwelling Place*, 1858.

Hip-joint, a ball and socket joint (*enarthrosis*), somewhat resembling that of the shoulder but with considerably less extent of movement. The pelvis socket (*acetabulum*) is considerably deeper than is the case in the glenoid cavity of the shoulder joint. The investing membranes and tissues are also much less lax than those of the upper limb, and in consequence the whole is considerably stronger. The capsule has three well-marked investing bands : (1) The *ligament of Bigelow*, which is mainly concerned in the maintenance of the erect position of the body, is particularly strong and seldom ruptures, even in cases of the dislocation of the joint. It is in the form of an inverted Y, in which the upper part is attached to the *ilium* and the limbs of the Y are fastened to two distinct portions of the head of the *femur*. The other ligaments connect the femur with the *pubis* and the *ischium* respectively.

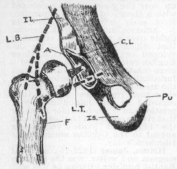

RIGHT HIP-JOINT

Head of femur (F.) removed from acetabulum (A.); ▪ ▪ ▪ ▪ diagrammatic representation of ligaments; L.B., ligament of Bigelow; C.L., cotyloid ligament ; L.T., ligamentum teres ; Is., ischium ; Pu., pubis; Il., ilium.

The *ligamentum teres* or round ligament passes from a slight fossa in the spheroidal head of the femur to the interior of the acetabulum. This ligament on account of its situation, has been made the subject of much discussion. It is absent in some mammals. Gripping the head of the femur is the *cotyloid ligament*, which lies inside the capsule and deepens the margin of the socket; it is continued as the *transverse ligament*. The *synovial cavity* extends along the neck of the femur beyond the limits of the *auricular cartilages*.

Diseases.—The H. is peculiarly subject to many of the diseases which attack joints. *Hip disease* has been definitely associated with scrofula, and the symptoms of it usually appear before puberty. Failing satisfactory treatment the disease passes through well-marked stages, and finally dis-

location may result from the breaking down of the surrounding tissues, which is frequently accompanied by a fungoid growth from the base of the acetabulum, which growth pushes the head of the femur from the socket; the whole may be rendered immovable (*anchylosed*), and although cases occur in which a permanent lateral displacement and shortening of the limb are the most serious consequents, yet more frequently the characteristic tubercular infection of the synovial membrane supervenes with dire results. *Accidental dislocation* is not frequent, largely due to the depth of the cavity and the general strength of the joints. In adults such dislocation is often accompanied by a fracture of the head of the femur ; its rarity of occurrence is partly neutralised by the much greater difficulty which is experienced in reducing this dislocation. *Congenital dislocation* which may be double, may be caused by the position of the child during intra-uterine life. The dislocation may not be discovered until walking commences, when the peculiar rolling gait will hint at it. X-rays examination is necessary in order to discover whether a hollow exists in which the head of the femur may be placed, otherwise the treatment is much more difficult and may even demand the artificial construction of a socket. *Rheumatoid arthritis* often makes its appearance at the H. which, in certain cases, it renders totally inoperative.

Hippa, the generic name of several species of sand-crabs, decapod crustaceans belonging to the tribe and family Hippidea, and common in tropical or sub-tropical seas. The mandibles are functionless and fused with the shell, which is subcylindrical, and the second antennæ have long curved flagella. *H. eremita*, the best-known species, is found in great numbers on the E. coast of the United States, where it burrows in the sand, on which it also feeds.

Hippalimus, the name of a genus of Cœlenterata belonging to the sub-order Actiniaria ; the species are found in the blue marls of Calvados.

Hipparchus, *see* HARMODIUS.

Hipparchus (*c.* 160-120 B.C.), the founder of scientific astronomy, born at Nicæa (in Bithynia), and lived in Rhodes and Alexandria. His greatest discovery was that of the precession of the equinoxes, but he also investigated the true periods of the revolution of the moon and of the solar year, and showed how places might be more accurately located on the globe with reference to the latitude and longitude of stars. To H. also are traceable the beginnings of trigonometry both plane and spherical. It is only recently that the true greatness of H. has been appreciated, as Ptolemy had for centuries the credit of his predecessor's observations.

Hipparion (Gk. ἱππάριον, a pony), the name of a genus of extinct fossil ungulate mammals belonging to the sub-order Perissodactyla and the family Equidæ, and found in the Upper Miocene and Pliocene strata of Europe, N. America, and Asia. This animal is usually regarded as one of the ancestors of the horse, though differing considerably in structure and size. The H. has three toes, the outer digits not reaching the ground, the ulna being better developed than in the horse, and its size is rather less than that of a donkey.

Hipperholme, a par. and tn., W. Riding, Yorkshire, England, 2 m. N.E. of Halifax. Quarries and tanneries. Pop. (1911) 4438.

Hippias of Elis, a Greek sophist, contemporary with Socrates, who taught in Athens and figures in the *Hippias Major* of Plato as a man puffed up with his own conceit. In learning he was a pedant; in literature a dilettante who tried his hand at every form of composition. Once at the Olympic games he boasted he had made all his apparel and was master of every mechanical as well as liberal art.

Hippocampus, the name of a genus of teleostean fishes belonging to the family Syngnathidæ and commonly called sea-horses. They are widely distributed, and *H. antiquorum* is occasionally seen on the British coast. The name indicates the remarkable resemblance between the head and neck of H. and those of the horse. These fishes swim in an upright position, and are characterised by the finless, prehensile tail, with which they cling to the stems of sea-weeds, corals, etc. In most species the males carry the eggs in a pouch under the tail. *H. brevirostris* utters a monotonous musical sound. Fossil remains are found in the Upper Eocene and Miocene strata of Europe.

Hippocras, or *Vinum Hippocraticum*, an old aromatic medicinal wine, prepared from spices, such as cinnamon, ginger, lemon peel, and almonds mixed with white wine and sweetened with sugar or honey.

Hippocratea, the chief genus of the order Hippocrateaceæ, and was named after Hippocrates, despite the fact that the species have no medical value. The species are twining shrubs indigenous to the tropics.

Hippocrateaceæ, a small natural order of dicotyledons which inhabit Africa, tropical America, and the Mauritius. The species are woody and often climbers; they are of little economic importance. The inflorescence is a cyme of hermaphrodite flowers consisting of five free sepals and petals, two to five free stamens, and a superior ovary formed from three united carpels with from two to ten ovules in each loculus, the fruit is a berry or a shizocarp. The chief genera are *Hippocratea* and *Campylostemon*.

Hippocrates (*c.* 460- *c.* 357 B.C.), the celebrated Greek physician, a native of the island of Cos. As a youth he is said to have studied the tablets in the temples of the gods, where each person had inscribed the ailments from which he suffered and the means by which he had recovered. At the beginning of the Peloponnesian war he is said to have saved Athens from a dreadful pestilence. Subsequently, on being invited to the court of Artaxerxes, he patriotically refused and said that he must serve his own country. He was given the civic privileges of Athens, and rewarded with the golden crown. He travelled widely throughout Greece, and died at Larissa in Thessaly. His two sons, Thessalus and Dracon, and his son-in-law, Polybus, all followed the same profession. He was a careful and observant physician, and a strong believer in surgery. The presence of disease, he believed, was due to a wrong proportion in the body of the humours, which he classified as phlegm, blood, and black and yellow bile. The chief works attributed to him are: *Aphorisms, Prognostics,* and *About Air, Water, and Places.* The best known editions are: Fœsius (Geneva, folio), 1657; Littré (10 vols.), 1839-61, with French translation; Ermerius, 1859-63 (with Latin translation), and the English translation of Adams, 1849.

Hippocrene, *see* HELICON.

Hippocrepis, a genus of leguminous plants, contains a dozen plants which flourish round the Mediterranean, and are known popularly as the horse-shoe vetch. *H. comosa*, the common horse-shoe vetch, is a bee-fertilised plant found in dry chalky banks of Britain; *H. Balearica* is a native of Minorca.

Hippodamia, wife of Pelops (*q.v.*).

Hippodrome (Gk. ἱπποδρομος, from ἱππος, horse, and δρομος, race-course), the course used by the ancient Greeks for chariot or horse racing. It was much wider than the Roman circus, and was usually made on the slope of a hill. Its length varied from 650 to 750 ft., and it was about 450 ft. wide. In shape it was oblong with one semicircular end, and the right side was somewhat longer than the left. Homer gives a fine description of a chariot-race, and shows that the critical point of the race was to turn the goal as sharply as possible, with the nave of the near wheel almost grazing it, and to do this safely.

Hippodrome, London, a place of amusement which was opened at the beginning of 1900. It affords a good entertainment, which is a combination of that given at a music hall, circus, and hippodrome; but the chief feature of the performance is the aquatic display, which generally comes last, and for which the building is specially adapted. The arena can be filled with water to a depth of 8 ft., and has a capacity of about 98,000 gallons.

Hippogriff, or **Hippogryph** (Gk. ἵππος, horse, and γρύψ, griffin), a fabulous animal, unknown to ancient writers, represented in comparatively modern literature as a winged horse with the head of a griffin, and described as the horse of the muses. It was used by Ariosto in his *Orlando Furioso*, and by many writers of the Renaissance.

Hippolyte, in ancient Greek legend, the queen of the Amazons. She was the daughter of Ares and Otrera, and the sister of Antiope and Melanippe. She headed a troop of Amazons in pursuit of Antiope, but was defeated and fled to Megara, where she died of shame and grief. According to another version, after her defeat she became the wife of Theseus. Still another tradition recounts that Theseus slew her in order to become possessed of her girdle, the gift of Ares.

Hippolytus, in ancient mythology, the son of Theseus, by Hippolyte or Antiope. His step-mother, Phædra, fell in love with him, and, on his refusing to gratify her desires, complained to Theseus that he had made attempts on her honour. His father thereupon cursed him and besought Poseidon's aid to bring about his destruction. While H. was riding in his chariot by the sea-shore, Poseidon sent from the water a sea-bull which frightened the horses, so that the chariot was overturned and H.'s body dragged along the ground till he died. According to Virgil, Artemis persuaded Æsculapius to restore him to life, and placed him under the care of Egeria in the grove of Aricia in Latium. He is the hero of Euripides' play of that name.

Hippolytus (c. 160 - c. 236 A.D.), an early Christian writer, supposed to have been born in the East and to have become a disciple of Irenæus. Very little is known about his life. He became a presbyter of the church at Rome in the time of Bishop Zephyrinus (199-217). He disagreed with the succeeding bishop, Calixtus I., with the result that there was a schism, when apparently H. became the head of a separate church and styled himself Bishop of Rome. In 235, during the persecutions of Maximinus, the Thracian, he was exiled to Sardinia, where he died in the following year. Origen ascribed to him the *Philosophumena*, with which has been identified a 14th century MS., found in 1842 and published in 1851. His works have been collected by Fabricius (1716-18) and Lagarde (1858). *See* studies by Bunsen (1852), Christopher Wordsworth (1853), Döllinger (1853), and Adhemar d'Ales (1906).

Hippomane Mançanilla, the manchineel-tree, a genus and species of Euphorbiaceæ which frequents Central America, Columbia, and the W. Indies. It is a tall, handsome tree, containing a most venomous milky latex, and is among the most poisonous of all known vegetable productions. The juice, dropped on the skin, produces a sensation of severe burning, and is followed by a blister; the fruit, which resembles a yellowish-green crab-apple, causes dangerous inflammation of the mouth when bitten; the wood is of fine quality and well suited for cabinet-makers' purposes.

Hippomenes, the son of Megareus, won the Bœotian Atalanta by fraud. The swift-footed maiden promised to marry the suitor who should outrun her. H. had three golden apples dropped in her path, which she stopped to pick up, thus losing the race. *See* ATALANTA.

Hipponax (*fl.* 6th century B.C.), a Greek iambic poet of Ephesus. He was banished from his native city by the tyrant Athenagoras in 546, and spent his exile in Clazomenæ. He was regarded as the inventor of a limping metre, called the *choliambus* or *scazon*, in which a spondee is substituted for the final iamb of an iambic senarius. His poems are satirical and not infrequently coarse. *See* fragments collected in Bergk's *Poetæ lyrici Græci.*

Hippophaë, a genus of Elæagnaceæ, containing only two species. One of these is found on the Himalayas while the other, *H. rhamnoides,* the sea buck-thorn, occurs in Britain, and in other parts of Europe. The plant yields a yellow colouring matter, and in Britain and France the acid berries are often eaten as a salad.

Hippophagy. The Greeks described a certain Scythian tribe, who dwelt to the N.E. of the Caspian, as Hippo-phagi (Gk. for horse-eaters), and seem also to have applied the name to a Sarmatian people living N. of the Euxine. The Scythians are amusingly described by Herodotus in an elaborate digression at the beginning of his fourth book. Geoffroy St. Hilaire founded a society of 'hippo-phagists' in France, and to-day horse-flesh is consumed in great quantities by the poorer classes of both Germany and France.

Hippopotamus (Gk. for river-horse), the sole member of a family of artiodactyle ungulate mammals. To-day it is found only in Africa, but fossils of a larger breed of hippopotami have been found in England, the rest of Europe, and in India, etc. The common species, *H. amphibius*, inhabits rivers in all parts of Africa, but the smaller, *H. liberiensis*, is restricted to the W. of that continent. In size a H. is only a little inferior to the elephant; its legs are very stunted, so that its belly touches the ground when it walks on mud or other yielding surfaces; there is often as much

HIPPOPOTAMUS

as 2 in. of skin on the back and flanks, but no hair covers its dark brown hide; its small eyes are set high in the huge, ungainly head with its great snout and enormous rounded muzzle; the tail is quite short, and on each foot there are four even and hoofed toes. The animal is aquatic, nocturnal, and voracious. It is a good swimmer and diver, and as its respiration is slow, it can stay a long while under water. By day it is sleepy and languid, but by night it often comes out of the water to graze on the banks, or if it lives in a cultivated region, it will make substantial inroads into crops and cause terrible destruction. It is this bad habit which accounts for its disappearance from the fertile plains of the lower Nile. It is gregarious by nature and usually playful and good-tempered, but persistent pursuit often provokes a dangerous passion. When angered it emits a loud and piercing noise, which has been likened to the grating sound of a creaking door. Hunters chase it in a variety of ways, sometimes it is en-

snared in pits, sometimes it is shot, harpooned, or pierced with spears from a canoe. The teeth are valuable as ivory, the tongue, the fat, and the jelly from the feet are favourite articles of diet, whilst the hides find many markets.

Hippo Regius, The Ruins of, on the coast of Algeria (anc. *Numidia*). It was once a royal residence, and afterwards noted as the bishopric of St. Augustine, who died here in 430 A.D.

Hippuric Acid, or Benzoyl-glyco-coll ($C_6H_5.CO.NH.CH_2.COOH$), a colourless crystalline substance, melting at 187° C.; it is soluble in hot, but scarcely soluble in cold, water. It occurs in the urine of herbivorous animals, from which it may be obtained by evaporation. It is best prepared by the action of benzoyl chloride on glycocoll, or of chloracetic acid on benzamide. On boiling with dilute acids H. A. is hydrolysed to benzoic acid and glycocoll.

Hippuris vulgaris, the mare's tail, a single species forming a genus in itself, belongs to the order Haloragidaceæ. It is a water-plant, cosmopolitan in distribution but for Africa, and its favourite habitat is stagnant water or a slow stream.

Hippurites, the name of the single genus of lamellibranchiate molluscs belonging to the family Hippuritidæ; all the species are extinct, and found only in the Cretaceous strata, *H. dilatatus* being one of the best known.

Hippuritidæ, the name of a family of extinct lamellibranchiate molluscs containing the single genus *Hippurites*; these fossils are found only in the Cretaceous strata, and are characterised by an inequivalve shell, with strong hinge teeth and grooves on the left valve, and no ligament proper.

Hipurinas, a race of S. American aborigines, found chiefly in Western Brazil, who are fast dying out, so much so that there are only about 3000 left. They are cannibals, and armed with poisoned shafts will travel far in bark canoes to seek their foes. Their language is poly-synthetic, and in the *Anthropological Journal* for 1894 will be found a grammar compiled by missionaries who took the trouble to write down their speech.

Hirado, or Firando, an island of Japan in the Strait of Korea, lying to the W. of Kiushiu, from which it is parted by the Spex Straits. It is noted for its beautiful blue and white porcelains (*Hiradoyaki*), and also because the missionary, Francis Xavier, worked here, and the Dutch once used it as a trading centre (1609-40). It is 19½ m. long and 6 m. broad.

Hiranyagarbha, a name for the Creator or First-Born, and may be rendered into English as ' Golden Embryo ' or ' Golden Child.' To him is addressed an exquisite hymn of the *Rig-Veda-Samhitâ*, which is an anthology of sacred songs composed by the Aryas of India from 1500 to 1000 B.C. The hymn referred to, which, as poetry, ranks with the Book of Job, shows how the Vedic philosopher was groping his way towards the Oneness of Deity. H. was Brahma, who came forth from a golden egg.

Hircic Acid, a mixture of certain homologous fatty acids present in mutton suet and other animal fats. It was once thought that mutton suet derived its smell from this constituent.

Hircin, a peculiar substance found in the fat of goats and sheep, which is believed to give them their characteristic smell.

Hiring Agreement, an agreement under what is called the *hire system*, is a document whereby goods, generally furniture, are delivered to a person by the vendor to be paid for by instalments of rent, the goods to become the property of the hirer if he pays the whole of the instalments. By the terms of some agreements the so-called ' hirer ' is bound to pay for and purchase the furniture, which is therefore his property *ab initio*, subject to the obligation to pay on easy terms. But usually H. As. are so drawn as to reserve the property in the goods in the vendor until all the instalments have been paid, the hirer, properly so called, being under no obligation to purchase. The disadvantage to the hirer in this latter form of H. A. is that if he does not keep up his instalments, or exercise his option to purchase, the vendor is entitled to seize the goods and keep the whole of the payments already made to him. Most firms who sell goods like pianos, bicycles, and sewing machines on ' easy terms ' have printed forms of H. As., and it is essential thoroughly to master the details of the agreement before signing it, so as to avoid liability in the event of inability to keep up instalments. Knowingly selling or pledging goods not completely paid for under a H. A. which does not vest the property in the hirer *ab initio*, may render the hirer liable to prosecution for larceny as a bailee. A purchaser from the hirer of goods let on a H.A. only acquires a good title against the vendor where the agreement between him and the hirer operates as a contract to buy as well as sell. A H. A. under which the goods remain the property of the vendor till full pay-

ment, is not a bill of sale within the meaning of the Bills of Sale Acts, and therefore the goods, not being within the hirers ' apparent possession,' may not be seized in execution (*q.v.*) by the hirer's creditors, and now by the Law of Distress Amendment Act, 1907, they cannot, generally speaking, be distrained upon for rent owing in respect of the premises in which they may happen to be. The licence to seize frequently inserted in such H. As. merely enables the vendor to retake what is his own property in the event of non-payment. The goods of a bankrupt trader delivered under a true H. A. or hire-purchase agreement, vest in his trustee in bankruptcy and form part of the assets available for his creditors generally, unless there is a well-recognised custom in the bankrupt's trade to hire goods of the kind comprised in the H. A. A H. A. requires a 6*d.* stamp, and if under seal (*see* DEED), a 10*s.* stamp.

Hirosaka, a tn. in the N. of Hondo, Japan; famous for its apples and lacquered ware. Valuable manganese mines in the vicinity (Fukaura). Pop. 37,000.

Hiroshima, the cap. of the gov. of Hiroshima (3000 sq. m.), in Honshiu, Japan. It is an important seaport, and the centre of a thriving commerce, but with every Japanese and traveller its name is inseparably associated with the ' Island of Light,' Miyajima which rises from the picturesque bay opposite. This island of woods and crags is famous for the great temple of the goddess Bentin (begun in 587), which is accounted one of the three wonders of Japan, and is yearly thronged by a multitude of pilgrims. Pop. (1908) 142,763.

Hirpine, one of the hardy tribes belonging to the country of Samnium, E. of Naples, Italy. In 4 B.C. they joined the Samnite alliance; their chief town was Æculanum.

Hirsch, Maurice, Baron de (1831-96), a Jewish philanthropist, was by birth a German. As partner in the banking house of Bischoffsheim and Goldschmidt, of Brussels, London, and Paris, he amassed a huge fortune, which was further augmented by fortunate speculations in copper, etc., and on the turf. He founded the Jewish Colonisation Association, and endowed it with a capital of £9,000,000, the object of which was to give his persecuted co-religionists of Russia facilities of emigration. Thus agricultural colonies were established in S. America and Canada, and numerous agenices and loan banks, etc., were set up to aid the would-be colonists in their passage abroad. In 1889 he presented the Alliance

Israélite Universelle of Paris with securities which were worth £16,000 a year, and in 1891 gave £493,000 for the establishment in America of a charitable trust for Jewish aliens.

Hirschberg, a tn. 1120 ft. above the sea-level, 48 m. S.E. of Görlitz, and connected by rail with Glatz, Schmiedeberg and Grünthal, in Silesia, Prussia. Situated at the meeting of the Bober and Zacken rivers, it is especially noted for its beautiful surroundings, but its commerce is both varied and considerable Pop. 20,560.

Hirson, a tn. on R. Oise, dept. Aisne, France. There are nail and glass works and foundries; basket making is carried on. Pop. 8600.

Hirt, Aloysius (1759-1837), a German archæologist, studied classical architecture and sculpture in Italy, and on his return home became lecturer on architecture and archæology first at the Academy and then at the University of Berlin. In his *Geschichte der Baukunst bei den Alten* (1821-27), he traces with minute care the history of Egyptian, Greek, and Roman architecture down to the days of Constantine. His other *magnum opus* is his *Baukunst nach den Grundsätzen der Alten,* 1809.

Hirtius, Aulus (*c.* 90-43 B.C.), a Roman historian, was a friend of Cicero and Cæsar, and the reputed author of the eighth book of the Gallic wars. The narrative also of both the Alexandrian and Spanish campaigns is usually attributed to him. The colleague of Pansa in the consulate of 43, he was slain in the battle of Mutina, though it was Antony, his enemy, who encountered defeat.

His Majesty's Theatre, has only been in existence a comparatively short period, but ever since 1705 the site has been occupied by buildings for dramatic representations. The original theatre was designed by Sir John Vanbrugh, and was opened as 'the Queen's' in 1705. In 1789 it was burnt down, and a second theatre erected which lasted from 1791 to 1867, when it, too, was utterly demolished by fire. It was in this building, which became known as the 'Italian Opera House,' that Madame Rachel appeared in 1841, and here Jenny Lind made her début six years later. In 1859 there were gala performances on the occasion of the marriage of the Princess Royal, and from 1862-67 Mr. Mapleson held his first season of Italian opera (again in 1877 and 1889). The third theatre dates from 1872 to 1892. It was put to various uses; for Moody and Sankey hired it for revival meetings, and it was also the scene of prome-

nade concerts, Wagner's operas performed by the Carl Rosa Company, and French plays with Madame Sarah Bernhardt in the caste. The fourth theatre was opened in 1897 when, as now, Sir H. Beerbohm Tree, was both proprietor and manager. Under his skilful direction many remarkable productions of Shakespeare's plays have been staged, and there have been excellent performances of other dramatic works, including Stephen Phillips' *Herod* and *Ulysses,* and the Japanese play entitled *The Darling of the Gods.* Madame Sarah Bernhardt has reappeared, and Coquelin ainé here played Cyrano de Bergerac in Rostand's play of that name.

Hispaniola, *see* HAITI.

Hispar, a pass (17,650 ft.), and glacier (40 m. long), explored by Sir William Martin Conway in 1892. It is situated in the Karakoram Himalayas, India.

Hissar, the cap. of the dist. of H. in Russian Bokhara, Central Asia. It guards the approach to the fertile valleys of the Kafirnihan and Surkhan, and is noted for its silk goods and its cutlery. The pop. exceeds 10,000.

Hissar, the name of a dist. and tn. in the Delhi div. of the Punjab, British India. The district (5217 sq. m.), which is fed by three railways, is partly irrigated by the Western Jumna Canal, but the inhabitants of its sandy stretches are constant victims of famine. Ginning and cotton-weaving are carried on in Hansi and Sirsa, besides H. Founded in 1356 by the Emperor Feroz Shah, the city of H. suffered terribly from the inroads of the Sikhs, etc. Pop. (1901) 17,647.

Hissar, Afiorim Kara, *see* AFIUM KARA HISSAR.

Hissarlik, in N.W. corner of Asia Minor, 4 m. S.E. of the Dardanelles. The supposed legend that this site was that of ancient Troy is considered by Schliemann to be an historical fact.

Histology, that branch of microscopic anatomy which deals with the intimate structure of the textures. A differentiation of functions in the higher animals has led to the development of a large number of organs, each composed of various tissues and textures. The result of minute dissociations and microscopic analyses proves that the actual number of elementary tissues, which are distinct in origin and structure, is small though transition forms are encountered. The general enumeration is as follows: epithelium, or epithelial tissue; connective tissue (many varieties, including adipose tissue); cartilage and its varieties; bone or osseous tissue; muscular tissue, and nervous tissue, to which it is usual to add the elements suspended in the fluids of the body, viz. blood and lymph corpuscles. Many of the organs are formed wholly of one form of tissue, or showing but slight admixture, other parts are much more complex in composition, yet in some cases their uniformity of structure leads to their being described along with the elementary tissues. Examples of these are: blood and lymphatic vessels ; lymphatic and secreting glands ; serous, synovial, and mucous membranes ; and integument, all of which are described in detail elsewhere.

Historical Manuscripts Commission, The, a royal commission which began to sit in 1869. Sir Thomas Duffus Hardy (1804-78) was influential in obtaining its appointment, as he felt keenly the desirability of some systematic investigation into the collections of valuable MSS. which at present are dispersed up and down the country in the libraries of colleges, corporations, and private individuals. Under the auspices of this commission some twenty records and over a hundred volumes of appendices have been issued, twelve of which deal with the 16th century MSS. in the possession of Lord Salisbury at Hatfield House.

History. Defined shortly this is the record of what is known to have occurred. A definite statement which contains what as nearly as possible in the judgment of the historian is the truth. Usually—and this forms an essentially important side of H.— such narrative is accompanied by an account of the causes and effects which have governed the events narrated, and also contains the personal judgments of the historian himself, which are not always even as infallible as the facts which he records. The great distinctions which must be made are between H. and fiction and myth. Tradition may often be and often is historical fact, but it is not of necessity so. One may apply the proverb that ' there is never smoke without fire ' here, and say almost definitely that the weirdest, most impossible traditional myth which has come down to us has its foundations far away back in some actual fact, some real occurrence. But here it is necessary to guard against error. Often a tradition contains only that which a nation desired to have happened, which it regarded as being the only thing that should have happened, but which is often diametrically opposed to what did actually happen. The H. of every nation is in its beginning hidden away in the mists of tradition, some of which has the basis of truth, other of desire. Again, often in the

records of the ancient nations we come across some isolated fact, some event which stands out fully authenticated from the midst of tradition and myth. Often it is interesting, often of importance, but never of a necessity sufficient by itself to constitute H. The date of the birth or death of a king, the overthrow of a rebel, cannot, apart from a multitude of other events, constitute an important part of the H. of a nation. H., to be of value, must reflect the great movements of the time, and relate the effect of those movements on the social fabric, it must narrate the cause of all movements and the effects of these same movements, and as far as it is humanly possible it should make judgments without bias. Contemporary H. usually suffers in this latter respect, but that does not of itself make the record useless. The later historian, however, must himself act the part of judge, and in examining the evidence on which his own work is to be based, must decide whether the records which he peruses are correct and unbiassed, or merely the statements of political partisans. Often the biassed H. is far less colourless than the authentic record, and is of vast importance in allowing the historian to see from down the ages a glimpse of the point of view of the contemporary writer. Bias is essentially human, all historians have fallen into the errors of its ways. The true H. theoretically has yet to be written, but the violent partisanship of bygone ages has departed, and we approach nearer the ideal every day.

The written, recorded H. may be said to have begun with the historical books of the O.T. These records of the Jews are, as far as we know, the first attempt of mankind to record events as they actually happened. We have other and earlier records amongst the other ancient nations, but these must be treated more in the light of historical evidence than as H. itself. H., not unnaturally sprang up in the centre of the civilisation of the world. Since the records were begun by the Jews there has never been a time when these records failed. The Greeks continued the work begun by the Jews, the Romans continued that work, and so H. was recorded until at the present time records of the H. of every side and department of life are kept. It is impossible here to narrate in detail the many steps which have been made in what may be aptly termed the history of H. It is possible, however, to divide H. into three very definite sections or types. H. from the beginning down to the middle of the 17th century is the narrative, personal, artistic type. Between that period and the 19th century H. decays; it is despised, and although the age was prolific in the output of literature of all kinds, it fails to produce a H. worthy of the name. With the beginning of the 19th century, however, comes a great change. The whole field is widened and, if one may so speak, narrowed at the same time. Research is made into the details of the past, a real attempt is made to conjure up a living picture of the times gone by. It becomes obvious that H. is the record of the failures and successes of peoples, not of individuals; it is necessary to inquire into the well-being of the people themselves, to discover how they lived, and why success or failure attended them. Above all, the false economic notions of past time were swept away. In the comprehensions of the essential facts of H. the latter fact has perhaps played the greatest part. We must notice also that the type of H. changes, practically up to the 18th century the Hs. which existed were practically contemporary Hs. No great work had endeavoured to portray the H. of the past ages from some far distant point and trace if possible the principle, elucidate the theories of the problems which constantly recur in the H. of the nations. The great historical writers of mediæval times and of antiquity had only written from the contemporary or little after the contemporary period. If we bear in mind this one fact alone, that since the beginning of the 19th century the H. of the world has been rewritten and has superseded all past attempts, we shall understand at least one important change which has come over this department of science or art. Science perhaps at the present day, but art of the past. As has been already remarked, there are three distinct types of H., and we can perhaps now proceed to an examination of these three types. The history of the ancients and of the middle ages were what may perhaps be termed here literary Hs. They aimed at giving a portrait of the time in carefully chosen, well-balanced periods. They made little or no attempt to verify the statements which they made. They overlooked entirely the value of research, in fact it probably did not occur to them; but they give us real and vivid pictures of the past. The figures they portray for us are clear and definite. The outline is firm, clear, and steady; they draw a picture the details of which can at once be comprehended: there is no hesitation, no doubt, every line which they have drawn is of importance. The one criticism which can be levied against them seems heavy, and is sweeping, but nevertheless a little examination will show that it is neither as heavy or as sweeping as it appears. Often the portrait bears little or no resemblance to the original. It was but the ideal of the writer, the creature of his imagination, just as the picture is the creature of the mind of the painter. But equally as often the main characteristics were portrayed with a skill which we can only envy at the present time. The details of the history-picture may have been all wrong, but the main outline was pencilled in with a clearness of thought, of sympathy and understanding, which makes the period or the man real to us at the present day. It is customary at the present time to sneer at their efforts, and to deride their work as something which does not even approach H. It is true that their imaginations played a great part, but modern historical research has proved that the wide sweeping lines portrayed by the ancient writer has in reality given the true outline with a clearness which we cannot attain at the present time. It was also customary in those days to put into the mouths of the heroes or the villains of H. speeches invented by the historian. This, from the point of view of the modern historian, cannot be defended, but from the point of view of the writer of antiquity or of the middle ages, the defence is obvious, and carries some weight even now. It is possible by means of an imaginary speech to delineate character easily and well. The imaginary speech was never to the author anything but an imaginary speech, but at the same time, by means of it he was able to add yet another line to a portrait and to make the portrait approach still nearer the truth. The literary historians also paid no attention to research; they had no reasonable opportunity for deep research. But here again we must bear in mind the fact that they wrote for a public which did not have the privileges of the present day, and which was not an age of specialists.

H. has but within recent days become an exact science. During the period which preceded it was an art, and as an art it more nearly attained perfection than now. The historical models of Thucydides and Tacitus are unparalleled, and have only since been feebly imitated. Almost the last of the old school of historians, Gibbon, modelled himself closely upon the examples of the ancients, and Freeman remarks that Gibbon is the only historian whose work has not been superseded by the writings of the 19th century. It must ever come as more or less of a great surprise that the historical writings of the later 17th century and of the 18th century fall so far below those which precede and those which follow. But there are many and good reasons for this. In the first place, although obviously it could not be widely comprehended at the time, that age was an age of transition, the beginning of a modern age, when the trend of thought and the tendencies of the time did not allow men to realise exactly their position. In literature it was one of the greatest of all ages, and is usually dignified with the title the Augustan Age. Why then did it fail so signally on one of the most important sides of literature ? One reason has already been given; others are that the wideness of the field to be covered made men hesitate before they attempted to write the H. of so large a period. Secondly, the historians of the time were often men of little or no learning, who made H. hack-work, and simply gave their readers the dry-as-dust bones of the subject. But the important point to notice is that the spirit of the age was very much against the writing of H. H. has always reflected the spirit of the age, in fact we may almost regard the spirit of the age as the genius of H. The trials and tribulations of Greece spurred on the achievements of Thucydides ; the rise and the glorious days of Rome gave subject and inspiration to the host of Roman historians; but the 18th century had no inspiration to give to its historians at all. They were unable to comprehend a state of affairs which differed from their own. They regarded the Greeks as barbarians, themselves as the men who had mastered the earth. The age of scepticism and of stagnation, to them the ideal kingship was of the type of the Grand Monarque, and when they did attempt to write H., they clothed the figures of the past in the paraphernalia of their own type. In many respects there were giants in the land in those days, but the grotesqueness of their figures made them lose all sense of proportion. They could not understand, they did nothing, and they not unnaturally despised that which they felt to be beneath them.

There were many other difficulties which the historian of the 18th century had to contend with, although we must own that the century was eventful enough to have given rise to some really great historian. The men of the 18th century stood in a difficult position; they looked back into a long distant past and found nothing to inspire them, really nothing that they could imitate. Historians of the

present day treat their subject from the scientific point of view ; there is no fact, no tradition, no rumour, which they do not examine, probe, and attempt to put in its right place, and to give to it the proper amount of credence. But the 18th century lacked the scientific spirit; unconsciously it was on the verge of a great change, but it could *not* be expected to know that, and it had only the ' artistic ' example of H. writing to imitate. They also seemed physically incapable of understanding a state of society which differed from theirs ; they were a self-satisfied generation of people, one might almost add an easily satisfied generation. They were filled with a spirit of criticism, but they failed to apply that criticism properly. They clothed the ancients and the ages of chivalry in the same garments as themselves ; they gave them the same manners and customs; they were incapable of comprehending differences. But they must not be absolutely and entirely blamed, much of their apparent incapability was due *not* to themselves, but to the fact that they were working along the wrong lines. The theory of economics, shortly to be changed, was at this time hopeless. Wealth was to them accumulation of huge reserves of gold. A nation was poverty-stricken only because she had lost her ready-money supplies. Gold was not to be used, but to be stored up in lockers and kept as a reserve. The essential causes of events were misunderstood; the cause of the fate of Rome was ascribed variously by one historian as because the gold reserves of that city were removed; by another, as because the Roman soldiers ceased to wear defensive armour. From the modern point of view it is pitiable, but they were working on the only lines they knew. They could not understand the inner workings of a people; to them H. was but the thin veneer that glossed the reign of a king; the importance of the reign lay with the monarch; the people upon whom the history of the country depended entirely were passed over unobserved. H., then, in the 18th century, was poor and neglected, principally because of the fact that it was not understood, and because the spirit of the age was against it.

As has been already pointed out, the historians of the 18th century were labouring on the verge of a great change. a change both in feeling and in method. Towards the end of the 18th century a new movement, which we usually term the Romantic movement, developed. It had developed slowly, but it was in greatest contrast to the movement which had preceded it. The lines of thought were changed altogether; it was, in fact, the main principle of the new school to overthrow the work of the old school, to view with contempt the ideals of that age, to shatter the idols which that age had made for itself. It was not a literary movement alone, it was a movement which was found everywhere and in everything. It raised up idols and ideals for itself, and not unnaturally, following on the lines of its own developments, it idealised those subjects which had been derided by its contemporaries. The romancer of the age of chivalry appealed to it; it developed the story of the middle ages; its literature abounded in reference to war, and to knights and tournaments. It was a realistic school; it tried to understand the age it wrote of; it was not content to clothe it in the garments of the present and speak simply of it as the past. The whole movement was a drastic change in thought of importance to us since it led to an examination in an historical spirit of the middle ages, and when this had been examined historical research went further back and examined the ages of antiquity. But this was but part of the change, and the least important part also. The other change was due to the development of the world, that development which was the stumbling-block of previous historians. The 18th century had seen vast changes in almost every aspect of life; the explorations of the time, the commercial developments with the Americans, gave men a wider and a deeper outlook upon the things of this world. Industry and wealth were growing rapidly. To take alone the example of England : at the beginning of the 18th century she had been an agricultural country, which was just beginning to awaken to the fact that even if her agriculture was to be successful, she must awaken and develop. Then gradually through the century crept on that change which we call the Industrial Revolution, supported by many other changes. Growth of colonies, expansion of trade, all helped until, by the end of the century, England was an industrial country altogether. What had brought about the change, and what was the effect of the problems of industry and wealth on the H. of society? The answer to that question shed such a light on the H. of the world as changed the whole aspect of H. itself. It is well nigh impossible to do more than sketch here the main outlines of the changes wrought by the last century in the 'history of History.' We may consider this the third of our periods as

almost a complete contrast to the first period, and as differing essentially from the second period. We desire nowadays to make a full and complete picture of the whole H. of the world. We go back to any art or science which can help us to reconstruct the life of the past. The great upheaval at the end of the 18th century taught us that the H. of the world is the H. of mankind, that in order to reconstruct the past we must realise to the best of our ability the life and work of the people of the past. That H. is not the interminable story of king and court and court intrigue, that beneath that which gilds the whole, we have a leaven working which has produced the nations and the people. It is being borne on our minds that court life and palaces intrigue did not mould the life of the people, and that when the people spoke they decided the lines on which development should run. No longer do we try to clothe the figures of the past in the panoply of the present, but we try to see beyond the thin veneer and penetrate the thought and purpose behind it all. H. can never be an exact science, but we can attempt to get nearer the truth than previously, and try our best to penetrate the veil which hides the past. Until the beginning of the last century we cannot truthfully say that ' the people ' played consciously an active part in the H. of the world, but the force of what for want of a better term we can call ' democracy ' has revolutionised the set forms of H. We desire to know how the people ' lived and moved and had their being, what forces influenced, how they lived, under what conditions they lived, and where and how and why. Above all we strive to discover what influence they had on the people of the present day. This is largely the theory, in practise we have many advantages. The output of historical literature to-day is vast. A history of history has never yet been written, but the amount of historic evidence grows larger every day and increases the difficulty of the task. We have almost everything that we desire to enable us to look closely into the lives of the past. The work of the past century has opened up channels unheard of and unthought of before. We have the chronicles of the past edited and published by the government. All documentary evidence of present day H. is carefully preserved ; the newspapers give us a daily H.; the biographies and the memoirs of the present day throw light on every side and every source. We live in an age of enlightenment, and we no longer despise a past which we cannot understand, because we try to understand it. We have taken almost every period, and have examined it with care and detail. Many of our theories, political and economic, are found to be but idols of clay, but they stimulate to further research, to greater results. We attempt to draw the whole figure in detail and with care, to give the body politic a soul. The faults of the past are not all remedied, and we have created many new faults, but the picture goes on increasing in detail and clearness every day. To the first period we have described we can ascribe the characteristic of bold outline, to the second stagnation and contempt, to the third a striving after truth and the drawing of a detailed picture.

Hit (ancient *Is*), a tn., Asiatic Turkey, on the r. b. of the Euphrates, 100 m. W.N.W. of Bagdad. Camel posts start from here for Damascus, and the Euphrates is navigable up to this point. There are famous ancient bitumen and naphtha pits. Pop. 5000.

Hitchcock, Edward (1793-1864), an American geologist, began life as a congregational minister in Conway, Massachusetts, but in 1825 accepted the chair of chemistry in Amherst College—a post which had been offered him largely because of his *Geology of the Connecticut Valley*, 1824. In 1830 he gave up his professorial duties, as his native state had appointed him head of a geological survey. Eleven years later he published the third and final report of his indefatigable researches into the geology and mineralogy of Massachusetts. In 1844 he became president of his old college, where he taught natural theology, besides his chosen science. His valuable *Report on the Agricultural Schools of Europe*, 1851, was the result of a second state commission. An assiduous contributor to scientific journals, H. strove to popularise his subject, and also published in 1851 the *Religion of Geology*.

Hitchin, a market tn. 32 m. N.W. of London, England. The chief trade is in corn, malt, and flour, while lavender and peppermint are grown, and their oils distilled. Girton College (Cambridge) was originally established here; there is a beautiful old parish church. Pop. (1911) 11,905.

Hitopadesa, or ' Friendly Instruction,' a free adaptation of the *Fables of Bidpai* (or Pilpay), which was itself a collection of old Hindu stories, derived eventually from the *Pancha Tantra*, or the legends and apologues of the Brahma Vishnu Sarman (2nd century B.C.). Though the *Fables of Bidpai* were translated in the 6th century A.D. into Pahlavi (ancient Persian), and afterwards into Arabic,

Greek, Latin, and so into the tongues of modern Europe, they are best known to Western peoples by their modernised version, the H. This latter anthology, of which there are at least three English translations, contains a number of loosely-interwoven animal tales, etc., which are strewn with moral apothegms and quaintly recounted after the manner of Æsop, or La Fontaine.

Hitteren, a craggy island (area 10×30 m.), situated at the entrance of Trondhjem Fjord, off W. coast of Norway. It has a harbour, Havnen. Pop. 2500.

Hittites, an ancient people, or group of peoples, whose origin is still a matter of dispute. Their settlements and rule extended at various periods from Armenia to Western Asia Minor, and as far S. as Palestine. It is possible that they were the White Syrians, or Syro - Cappadocians, known to Herodotus, if so, their descendants may still be seen in the villages of Cappadocia, appearing to be closely related to the modern Armenians. Many monuments and tablets have been discovered in different parts of Asia Minor, particularly on the site of one ancient city, now known as Boghaz Keui, formerly Pteria, the ancient capital of Cappadocia, which appears to have been occupied by the H. at a very early date. Pteria lies E. of the Halys, from which point roads radiated to harbours on the Ægean, to Northern Syria, and the plain of Cilicia. In the O.T. they are spoken of in Gen. xxiii. 10 as the children of Heth, dwelling in Kiriatharba (Hebron). In this reference Abraham appears dwelling among them as a stranger, and wishing to purchase a place to bury his dead wife in. This he accomplished through Ephron the H., who sold him the cave and the fields of Machpelah. Previous to this, Gen. xiv. 9 refers to the battle of ' the five kings against four,' one of whom, ' Tidal, Lord of Nations ' (Goiim), or of the north, appears to bear the same name as a king of the people of Boghaz Keui. In the book of Ezekiel (xvi. 3), Jerusalem is described thus: ' The Amorite was thy father, and thy mother was a Hittite; ' there are several other general references in the O.T., and they are also mentioned as individuals, *e.g.* Uriah the Hittite. One reference (1 Kings x. 28, 29) mentions the kings of the H. buying horses and chariots from Egypt. This is interesting, because until the coming of the Hyksos to Egypt, the horse appears practically unknown or little used, and the H. people came from a country where horses had probably been bred and used for a considerable time. To the Egyptians the H. were known as the Kheta, and they appear to have borne them an extraordinary hate; there is a probability that the Hyksos who conquered the Egyptians were the same as the Kheta, but at present it cannot be proved, and so far the extreme difficulty of correct dates makes it impossible to do more than theorise. Thothmes I. led his triumphant armies over Northern Syria, and took the town of Kadesh, or Qedesh, the stronghold of the Kheta; this was not long after the expulsion of the Hyksos from Egypt. Thothmes III. waged terrible war against the Kheta, who were by this time evidently strong enough to be regarded as serious foes. They rose in revolt against Egypt, and Thothmes III. marched over Northern Syria and reduced the tribes who had banded together with the H. to utter submission. Kadesh and Carchemish on the Euphrates fell into the hands of Thothmes, who marched back to Egypt, laden with plunder and captives; the king of Kadesh, however, escaped. In the reign of Amenhotep IV. (Akhnaton) the H. appear to have gathered great strength, and, throwing off the yoke of Egypt, began to press steadily down on to the frontiers of her empire, taking forcibly one by one the towns of Syria. The Tel-el-Amarna letters contain reports from various governors in the Syrian districts, asking for help against the H. Some of these letters are pathetic, coming from petty kings and princes who had long been loyal tributary states to Egypt. All of them implore help from ' their Lord the King ' against the terrible H. They cried to deaf ears, for the king (Akhnaton) was busy in his sacred city, dreaming of universal peace and brotherhood, and the H. took for themselves all that the fierce Thothmes III. had won. Among the kingdoms that were thus conquered was Mitanni, a country that had acted as a buffer between Egypt and the Kheta for a considerable period and enjoyed the friendship and protection of Egypt. Amenhotep IV. took no notice of their perilous position, and Mitanni was overcome by the H. king, Subiluliuma, who now overran the country as far as the Tigris. Seti I. led two campaigns against the H., now spoken of in Egypt as ' the abominable Kheta.' He appears to have won some victories over them, but by no means to have broken their strength, for his son Rameses II. was unable to conquer them. The H. king, Mauth-nuro, collected a vast army, and prepared for a final struggle with Egypt for the possession of N. Syria. He allied himself to many of Egypt's ancient enemies, among them the king of Aleppo and the men of Naharina and of Arvad. Rameses marched northwards with his army, expecting an easy conquest, but ' the abominable Prince of Kheta ' was an exceedingly able general. A great battle was fought in the fields of Kadesh, which ended in the victory of neither. After this a treaty was arranged, and the two kings formed an alliance, which apparently seems to have been very necessary, against some other unnamed enemy, probably Assyria, who appears at this time as a growing danger. Trouble was also threatening from the Mediterranean—' the islands were restless ' —so these two great empires allied themselves for mutual protection. The treaty was drawn up, but the H. king died, and his successor, Hattusil II., concluded and ratified it. It was engraved on a silver tablet, and held stipulations about boundaries that were not to be invaded, while in the case of war upon their frontiers, both kings were to act together. There were also special conditions about subjects deserting from one kingdom to another. This is a very early example of an international agreement. Some years later this newly-formed friendship was cemented by Rameses marrying a H. princess. The king of the H. apparently travelled to Egypt with his eldest daughter and a large train of attendants. It must have appeared curious to the Egyptians to see the ' abominable Kheta,' their loathed enemy for generations, being entertained and feted. In Assyrian references, the H. (whom they call Khatti) appear as a powerful people, occupying Carchemish on the Euphrates. The Assyrian kings raided the Khatti year after year. In the inscriptions of Assur-Nazir-pal, 9th century B.C., the Khatti power extended over N. Syria, and into Mesopotamia. Sargon III., in 717 B.C., leaves records of how he finally overthrew the Khatti of Carchemish, and captured their king, Pisiris. From all these records, and from the discoveries of archæologists, we gather a brief history of the H. First that they were probably north-western Asiatic people, non-Semitic, and that they were a political force before 2000 B.C., occupying Cappadocia, and parts of Northern Syria. One of their early kings was called Hattusil, and one great king was Subiluliuma. The H., or Hatti, certainly treated on terms of equality with Babylon, and waged war on several Syrian tribes. Hattusil II., who formed the Kheta-Egyptian alliance, is one of the last kings we know anything about; it is possible that they moved their capital to Carchemish (Jerablus), and among those ruins more of their history may be discovered. White Syrians, or Hatti, were found in Cappadocia, after the Cimmerians had destroyed Phrygia. Crœsus, King of Lydia, defeated what remained of them. Boghaz Keui, formerly Pteria, is the only H. city that has been really thoroughly examined at present. It was evidently a city of immense size. The acropolis was strongly fortified, and a wall 14 ft. thick surrounded the whole city. Many inscriptions and sculptured reliefs were found, and a number of tablets in Babylonian and in the H. language, among them a cuneiform copy of the treaty with Rameses II. Other cuneiform documents were discovered, relating to Babylonian merchants, proving that it was a sufficiently important community at the time of the first Babylonian dynasty for the wealthy merchants of that city to trade with Boghaz Keui. Near the city were found the rock reliefs of Yasili Kaya, composed of two processions of over sixty figures. Euyuk possesses remains of a large palace entered between sphinxes, on one of which is sculptured a relief of a double-headed eagle; this device is said, without definite proof, to have been adopted by the Seljuk Sultans of Konia, and to have been brought by the crusaders to Europe, where it was taken by the German emperors as their arms. In various places, widely distributed, fragments of pottery, sculptured lions, reliefs, and buildings have been discovered; in some of the buildings, columns rested on bases carved with winged lions. The style of all their sculptures is quite individual and easily distinguished from the Assyrian and Babylonian art. The facial type is very markedly non-Semitic, the figures are usually depicted short and heavily built, with prominent bones, broad-shaped heads, receding foreheads, long noses, thick lips, and short chins. The hair of the men is frequently worn in a pig-tail. The dress usually represented consists of a long robe worn over a tunic, a high conical cap, and long boots turned up at the toes. The outer robe was bordered with a fringe. The females wore a long veil or shawl covering the head and forehead and falling to the feet; one relief pictures two H. women sitting together with this veil or mantle draped over a head-dress resembling a modern brimless top hat. Very little can be said with certainty of their social conditions; one thing is clear, that their women enjoyed the same high status and freedom as in Babylonia. They appear to have adopted the Babylonian

cult of the goddess Istar (Ashtoreth); she is depicted in the sculptures of Boghaz Keui with a mural crown; the H. may have introduced her worship to Lydia where she became known as Cybele, ' the Great Mother of the Gods.' The bee was sacred to her, and a H. gem, found at Aleppo, represents her standing on a bee. Her priestesses who served her in Lydia are represented bearing a double axe, a symbol found frequently at Knossus in Crete. The Lydians who were among the first to use coined money, employed the silver ' Mina ' of Carchemish, i.e. a H. silver coin. There are now some sixty inscriptions all in pictographic character, most of them are in relief. Long, patient, and persistent efforts have been made to decipher this script by Professor A. H. Sayce and others, but at present they remain undecipherable, See A. H. Sayce, The Hittites, 1892; L. Messerschmidt, The Hittites, 1903; D. G. Hogarth, Ionia and East, 1909, and his article in Ency. Brit., vol. xiii. (11th ed.); Garstang, Land of the Hittites.

Hitzacker, a hydro. with iron springs, prov. of Hanover, 33 m. N.E. of Lüneburg, Prussia, Germany. Pop. (1910) 976.

Hitzig, Ferdinand (1807-75), a German biblical critic, studied theology at Heidelberg, Halle, and Göttingen. In 1833 he became professor of theology in Zürich, and in 1861 succeeded Umbreit in the same chair at Heidelberg. A formidable list of exegetical works bears his name, including a monograph on the author of the second gospel (1843), Geschichte des Volkes Israel, 1870; Zur Kritik Paulinischer Briefe, 1870; and various commentaries on the Psalms, Jeremiah, Ecclesiastes, etc. H. was a somewhat speculative historian, a critic of penetration, and a Hebrew scholar of no mean attainments.

Hivites, an aboriginal people of Palestine who were scattered before the intruding Israelites. Their name is variously explained as ' dwellers in encampments,' or as ' snake clan.'

Hjelmar, a lake lying westward of Stockholm, and confined between the provinces of Södermanland, and Örebro, Sweden. A canal connects it with the Arboga, and on the E. it opens out into Lake Mælar. The area is 198 sq. m.

Hjörring, an ancient city of Denmark in the N. of Jutland, 7 m. from Jammer Bay. It is the cap. of H. co. (' amt '), and is on the Jutland Railway. Pop. 8000.

Hkamti Long, a collection of seven Shan states controlled by Burma, and bounded northward by the Mishmi region, E. and S. by various Ching-paw (or Kachin) communities, and westward by the Hukawng valley. The estimated area and population of this little-known country are 900 sq. m. and 11,000 respectively.

Hlassa, *see* LHASSA.

Hoadly, Benjamin (1676-1761), an English divine, graduated as M.A. from Catherine Hall, Cambridge, and after holding several minor livings, became in turn Bishop of Bangor (1715), Hereford, Salisbury, and Winchester (1734). An eminent theological controversialist, he stoutly upheld the doctrines that the church is subject to the jurisdiction of the civil magistrate, and that its authority does not extend to the individual conscience. The first is expounded in his *Measures of Submission to the Civil Magistrate,* etc., and the second his celebrated sermon on the ' Kingdom of Christ,' which gave rise to the Bangorian dispute, and so exasperated and disorganised the lower house of convocation, that to this day it has never been allowed to despatch any but formal business. H. anticipated many of the modern Unitarian views, and in his own day was both praised and blamed as a latitudinarian and as a rationalist.

Hoadly, Benjamin (1705-57), a physician and dramatist, was the son of Bishop H. He lives to-day as the author of a rollicking comedy entitled *The Suspicious Husband,* 1747, in which Garrick played the part of Ranger, but in his own time he was equally in high repute as physician to Frederick, the Prince of Wales, and to the king. Among his little-read medical treatises are *Three Letters on the Organs of Respiration,* which were lectures addressed to the Royal College of Physicians (1737).

Hoang-Ho, or **Hwang-Ho,** *see* YELLOW RIVER.

Hoare, Prince (1755-1834), an author and painter, son of William H. He studied painting in London and Rome. Became honorary foreign secretary to the Royal Academy in 1799. Some of his publications are: *Academic Correspondence, Academic Annals of Painting;* a play (acted at Drury Lane), *No Song, No Supper;* and the well-known poem entitled *The Arethusa.*

Hoare, Sir Richard Colt (1758-1838), an English antiquary, entered a banking house, but having inherited landed property from his grandfather, was able to devote his life to travel and the study of antiquities. His *Classical Tour through Italy and Sicily,* 1819, contained the records of over four years of travel, but his most meritorious contribution to topography is his *Ancient History of North and South Wiltshire,* 1812-19, which includes the period of Roman occupation. H. also translated and annotated the *Itinerarium Cambriæ,* etc., of Giraldus, and his portfolios proved him to be a skilful and assiduous draughtsman.

Hoare, William (1706-92), an English artist, was for nine years in the studio of Fernandi in Rome, and then returned to his native Bath, where he soon grew famous as a portrait painter, so much so that in 1768 he was elected as one of the original members of the Royal Academy. Two of his pictures—one an altarpiece which depicts ' Christ bearing the Cross '—may be seen in St. Michael's Church, Bath.

Hoar-frost adorns trees, grass, and twigs in winter, because they freely radiate their heat. The cause of its formation is as follows: On a clear night dew is deposited because after sunset the earth cools and lowers the temperature of the atmosphere in contact, until its moisture begins to condense. This it will do as soon as the temperature has fallen below that point at which the air would just be saturated by the amount of aqueous vapour, which happens to be present. Now H., instead of dew, is precipitated when at the time of its formation the temperature is already below freezing-point (32° F. or 0° C). It is therefore not frozen dew, as such an expression would imply that the vapour was first of all deposited as dew, but rather water directly deposited in a solid form. If the dew-point is below 32° F., gardeners should screen young or delicate plants from the atmosphere, as there is every likelihood of a hoar-frost.

Hoarseness, a condition of the voice in which the sound is diminished in intensity and purity; it is usually accompanied by a feeling of pain or undue effort in producing sounds. H. is caused by the swelling or roughness of the vocal chords, the vibration of which causes the sound which we know as voice. It is possible that the roughness of these ligaments is sometimes due to fatigue or lack of tone in the muscles and nerves controlling them, but in the majority of cases there is definite inflammation of the mucous membrane of the larynx. H. is therefore usually indicative of some form of laryngitis, and should never be neglected. Inflammation may be set up as the effect of irritating vapours or dust, or as the result of a cold; it may be induced by fatigue through excessive use of the voice, or may accompany some other disease such as influenza. The swelling of the parts which interferes with normal voice-production may progress so as to constitute a danger to respiration. An attack of H. should therefore be construed as a symptom of laryngitis, and examination should be made by means of the laryngoscope. At any rate the question of resting the voice completely should be seriously considered. Neglected H., particularly if associated with excessive use of the voice, may lead to a chronic condition in which a certain amount of inflammation is always present, and a more or less permanent change in the constitution of the pharyngeal membrane may take place. The treatment consists primarily of rest; gargling with plain water or mild astringents, and the avoidance of changes of temperature should bring about improvement.

Hoar-stones, called Hare Stanes in Scotland. They are single blocks of unhewn stone, which now serve the purpose of boundaries, but which must at one time have been commemorative. Usually they stand alone, though rarely a ring is indicated by pieces of rock clearly arranged by human agency.

Hoatzin, or Hoazin, the name given to the galliform birds belonging to the family Opisthocomidæ, which consists of the single genus and species, *Opisthocomus cristatus*. They are fowl-like in appearance and about the size of a pigeon; the plumage is olive with white markings, and reddish underneath; the sternum has a large patch of thick, naked skin, on which the bird generally rests. They are chiefly arboreal, nesting on low trees or shrubs, but are also able to swim and dive. The H., which ranges from Guiana to Venezuela, is also called the stink-bird, or stinking-pheasant, because of its strong, musky odour.

Hobart, the cap. of Tasmania in the co. of Buckingham, 100 m. S. of Launceston on the southern shore of the island. Situated at the foot of Mt. Wellington (4166 ft.) amid delightful scenery, of which the bay of Sullivan's Cove is a picturesque feature, it draws many visitors from New South Wales and Victoria, especially at the season of the Derwent regatta. Its deep and sheltered harbour can receive vessels of the largest tonnage. There are numerous saw and flour mills, iron foundries, and potteries, etc., and it is from H. that the fruits of the country districts are shipped to Sydney and to London. H. is the see of an Anglican bishop and a Roman Catholic archbishop, and possesses many fine squares, parks, and buildings, among which the university, town hall, and St.

Mary's Cathedral deserve especial note, and also a statue of the explorer, Franklin, who was governor here from 1837 to 1843. Pop. (1911) 27,719.

Hobart, Pasha Augustus Charles Hobart-Hampden (1822-86), an admiral of the Turkish fleet, the son of the Earl of Buckinghamshire. Having won his captaincy in the English navy, he retired in 1862. As blockade-runner during the American Civil War, he gained considerable distinction, but his daring and strategic ability were most in evidence during his blockade of Crete at the time of the insurrection, and during the Russo-Turkish War (1878), when he cleared the Black Sea of the enemy. H. had entered the Turkish navy in 1867.

Hobbema, Meindert (1638-1709), a Dutch landscape painter, was a contemporary of Berchem, Van de Velde, and Wouverman, who sometimes inserted animals and figures in his pictures. Save that he married, died in poverty like Rembrandt, Hals, and Jacob Ruysdael, and was buried in the pauper section of an Amsterdam cemetery, little has survived either about his personality or life. In this country he is honoured chiefly for his 'Avenue at Middleharnis' (National Gallery), but his masterpieces are scattered over the museums of Antwerp, Brussels, St. Petersburg, Rotterdam, etc. H. was content to paint his native woods and mills, hedgerows and pools, winding tracks and leafy cottages, but his manipulation of cloud and light, the truth and finish of his varied foliage, and the sympathy with which he expresses nature in her moods of tender melancholy and puritanic calm, proves him the equal of Ruysdael in all except the broadness of his range.

Hobbes, John Oliver (pen-name of Mrs. Pearl Mary Theresa Craigie, *née* Richards) (1867-1906), an American novelist, made an unhappy marriage (1886), which was dissolved on her petition in 1891. Reared in an atmosphere of Nonconformity, she entered the Roman Catholic Church in 1892, and that mystical philosophy, which so pervades *The School for Saints* (1897) and its sequel, *Robert Orange* (1900), was assuredly the cause or effect of this conversion. Her positive genius for epigram is conspicuous in her first publication, *Some Emotions and a Moral* (1891), and likewise in her *Love and the Soul Hunters* (1902). As a dramatist she was most successful with *The Ambassador* (1898), though as joint-author she shared in the success of *The Bishop's Move* (1902). A follower of Meredith in her earlier fiction, she imparted an original flavour to her simple romance, *The Herb Moon* (1896), but her strength lies in the grace and finish of her style and the sprightly sallies of her wit.

Hobbes, Thomas (1588-1679), an English philosopher, the son of a clergyman. He graduated at Magdalen College, Oxford, and between 1610 and 1637 thrice went abroad as private tutor, visiting France and Italy, where he made the acquaintance of the Cartesian Father Mersenne, and of Galileo. Many other illustrious men, including Ben Jon-

THOMAS HOBBES

son, Bacon, Lord Herbert of Cherbury, and among foreigners, Descartes and Cosmo de' Medici were counted among his friends. For some time he was mathematical tutor to the Prince of Wales (afterwards Charles II.), and though, after the issue of the *Leviathan* (1651), his pupil forbade him his presence, yet the pension he freely gave to H. on his accession (1660), showed that he knew no other feelings than gratitude and respect for his former teacher. The Homeric and Thucydidean translations, and likewise the many controversial writings of the philosopher, which at the time loomed so important, have long been condemned to the dust of oblivion; his *Behemoth*, or narrative of the Civil War (1640-60), is now a curiosity in literature. But his *De Cive* (1642 and 1647), and his *magnum opus*, the *Leviathan*, both of which were censured by parliament in 1666,

gave 'an extraordinary impulse to the spirit of free inquiry in Europe,' and have won for their author the title of founder of political science, as other of his works make him the true father of English psychology. H., who was besides a great stylist and one of the first to deem his native language worthy of expressing abstruse thought, taught that the end of philosophy was social, and that theology and transcendentalism did not come within its sphere; that the basis of all government is force and that, whereas to be effectual every government must be supreme, the spiritual must ever give way to the temporal, and the people must implicitly accept not merely the laws but the mode of faith, which the king or his ministers have seen fit to ordain. See *Life* by Leslie Stephen.

Hobby, or *Falco subbuteo*, a long-winged, short-tailed falcon, dull grey above and mottled underneath, which visits Britain in the summer, especially the south-eastern counties. In length the female bird, which is somewhat larger than the male, is 14 in. Larks are its favourite prey, but it has been known to feed on insects. Falconers once trained hobbies for the hunt.

Hobhouse, John Cam, Baron Broughton (1786-1869), an English statesman, was educated at Westminster School and Trinity College, Cambridge. His intimacy with Byron began in his undergraduate days and extended till the latter's death. Thus he was 'best man' at the poet's wedding, wrote the historical notes to the fourth canto of *Childe Harold*, and in his company visited Portugal, Spain, Italy, and Switzerland. He began his political career as Radical M.P. for Westminster, having been already in Newgate for a satirical pamphlet published anonymously. But when in 1846 he sat in Russell's cabinet as president of the (Indian) Board of Control he was regarded as a reactionary by the younger Radicals. The activities of the Greek committee in London (1823) were largely the result of his enthusiasm.

Hoboken, a seaport on the Hudson R., in the Hudson co. of New Jersey, U.S.A. To the S. and W. lies Jersey city, and across the river is New York. It has important stations on the Delaware, Lackawanna and Western and the West Shore Railways, and is served by four large steamship companies. Pencils, silk and leather goods, etc., are manufactured, and the coal industry thrives. Two important buildings are Stevens Institute of Technology (1871) and the

Hoboken Academy, founded in 1860 by the Germans, who to-day make up one-fifth of the entire population (70,324 in 1910).

Hoboken, a suburb of Antwerp, Belgium. It is situated on the Scheldt, 3 m. S.W. of the city, and has important shipbuilding and lace industries. Pop. 12,816.

Hobson, Richmond Pearson (b. 1870), an American naval officer, a native of Greensboro, Alabama. In the war between the United States and Spain he was fighting as lieutenant on a flagship. At one time a squadron of Spanish vessels was trying to escape from Santiago, H. tried to prevent this, and notwithstanding he was all the time exposed to the enemy's fire, managed to sink one of their ships at the harbour entrance. Although he was subsequently taken prisoner with his crew he was released at the conclusion of hostilities. He retired from active service in 1903.

Hobson, Thomas (1544?-1631), the Cambridge carrier, inherited from his father ' the team ware that he now goeth with,' and from 1568 till 1630, when the plague put a stop to his journeys, continued to drive his cart to and fro from Cambridge to London. He is immortalised in the saying, ' Hobson's choice.'

Hobson - Jobson, a corruption of ' Ya Hasan! Ya Hosain,' the cry of the Shiites during the procession of Mohurram, which is part of one of the great Mohammedan festivals. It originated from British soldiers in India, who thus colloquially described the celebration. Yule and Burnell used it as the title of their Anglo-Indian glossary (1886).

Hoccleve, or Occleve, Thomas (c. 1370-c. 1450), an Early English poet and lawyer, a clerk in the Privy Seal Office, London, for over twenty years. He knew Chaucer, the ' floure of eloquence,' and his ' maister dere,' drawing in colours the well-known portrait on the margin of one of the MSS. of his chief poem, De Regimine Principum (c. 1411), a work largely compiled from the Latin of Ægidius Colonna (c. 1280). Other poems were: The Story of Jonathan, and Moder God. . . . See Furnivall's edition of Works (Early English Text Society), 1892; De Regimine, 1897; Mason's edition of six poems, 1796; Wright's edition, 1860 (Roxburghe Club); Phillipp's MS., 8151 (Cheltenham); Morley, English Writers, vi.

Hoche, Louis Lazare (1768-97), a general of the French Revolution, enlisted, 1784, joining the National Guard, 1792. Having repulsed the Duke of York, he commanded the forces on the Moselle and drove the Austrians from Alsace, 1793. He helped to suppress the Vendean revolt, 1795-96, and then headed the expedition to Ireland, which failed owing to storms, 1796. H. won several victories over the Austrians again in 1797, but the armistice at Leoben checked his successes, and he died suddenly at Wetzlar soon afterwards. See Lives by Privat, 1798 ; Desprez, 1858; Dutemple, 1879; Font-Réaulx, 1890 ; Chuquet, 1888 · Daunon, Eloge, 1798; Escaude, Hoche en Irlande, 1888; Griffith's French Revolutionary Generals, 1891.

Hochelaga, a co. and vil. of Quebec, Canada. The village on the St. Lawrence R. forms a suburb of Montreal, 2 m. distant. Pop. about 16,000.

Hochheim, a vil. of Hesse-Nassau, Prussia, near R. Main, 4 m. E. of Mainz. The vineyards of its slopes produce the true hock. Pop. c. 4000.

Hochkirch, or Hockirchen, a vil. of Saxony, 5 m. E. of Bautzen. The Austrians defeated Frederick the Great here in Oct. 1758, field-marshal Keith being killed in action.

Höchst, a tn. of Hesse-Nassau, Prussia, on R. Main, 10 m. W. of Frankfurt. Tilly defeated Christian of Brunswick here, 1622. There are dye works, manufactures of gelatine, aniline, oilcloth, tobacco, beer, machinery and furniture. Pop. 17,224.

Höchstadt, a tn. of Swabia gov., Bavaria, Germany, on R. Dunube, 30 m. N. E. of Ulm. Here Frederick the Staufen was defeated by Hermann of Luxemburg, 1081, and the Austrians by Marshal Villars, 1703. The victory won by Marlborough and Prince Eugene over the Franco-Bavarian forces in 1704, fought near by, is better known as the battle of Blenheim. Pop. about 2301.

Hock, strictly the white wine (sparkling or still), called in Germany ' Hochheimer,' produced at Hochheim The English name ' hock ' has been in use since before 1625, and is commercially extended almost indiscriminately to light white German wines, especially Rhenish wines. H. is usually dry, but some brands are sweet. It has a distinctive flavour and bouquet, and the alcoholic strength is from 9 to 13 per cent. Important brands are, Erbach, Nierstein, Rudesheim, Marcobrunn (still); Johannisberg, Liebfraumilch, Rauenthal (sparkling). Good vintages were those of 1880, 1883, 1884, 1886, 1889, 1892, 1893, 1895, and 1897. The natural dry white wines of the Californian ' Riesling ' or hock-grape slightly resemble the German varieties, but generally have more ' body ' and are less acid.

Hockenheim, a com. and tn. of Baden, Germany, circle of Mannheim,

10 m. from Heidelberg, with tobacco factories. Pop. about 7100.

Hockey (possibly derived from the ' hooked stick ' with which the game is played; *cf. hoquet*, Old Fr. for shepherd's crook), a game played with a ball or some similar object between two opposing sides; the stick used to propel the ball is of a curved shape, and the object is the same as in football—to score goals. The Romans had a game very similar to H., which was played on frozen ground or on the ice. In some form H. has been known to most of the northern peoples of Europe and Asia. In Scotland the game was known as ' shinty,' and in Ireland a game called ' hurley' was played on the sea-shore; the rules were simple, and the play usually very rough in character. Modern H. is played on turf during the same time as football—from September to April; it owes much of its present vogue to the formation of the Men's Hockey Association in England in 1875. The rules drawn up by the Wimbledon Club in 1883 still obtain in essentials. As regards the equipment and tools of a H. player the following are the more important points. A H. stick shall have a flat face on its left-hand side only; there are no regulations as to length, but every stick must be of such size that it can be passed through a two-inch ring. The head of a stick shall not be edged with or have insets or fittings of hard wood or of any other substance, nor shall there be any sharp edges or dangerous splinters; the extremity of the stick must not be cut square or pointed, but must have rounded edges. An india-rubber ring of four inches external diameter may be used as a guard, but the total weight of the stick and guard and binding, if any, must not exceed 28 oz. The ball is a leather cricket ball, either painted white or made of white leather. Boots very similar to football boots are usually worn; no dangerous materials, such as spikes or nails, etc., must be worn. The rubber ring is not now much used, padded gloves being worn instead. Shin-guards are, from the nature of the game, almost a necessity. The ground for H. is of a rectangular shape, 100 yds. long and not more than 60 yds. nor less than 55 yds. wide. The ground is marked out with white lines, of which the longer are called the side-lines and the shorter the goal-lines. Flag-posts are placed at each corner, and at the centre of each side-line, one yard outside the line. The goals are in the centre of the goal-line; their dimensions are 12 ft. wide by 7 ft. high. The posts are 2 in. broad and not more than 3 in. in depth. Nets are attached to the posts, cross-bars, and to the ground behind the goals. No shooting at goal can take place except in the striking circle, which is thus defined. In front of each goal shall be drawn a white line 4 yds. long, parallel to and 15 yds. from the goal-line. This line shall be continued each way to meet the goal-line by quarter circles having the goal-posts as centres. The space enclosed by these lines and the goal-lines is the striking circle. The game is started by one player of each team bullying the ball in the centre of the ground. To bully the ball, each player strikes the ground on his own side of the ball, and his opponent's stick over the ball, three times alternately; after which one of them must strike the ball before it is in play. In all bullies the two players who are bullying shall stand squarely facing the side-lines. A player is off-side if he is nearer to his opponent's goal-line than the person who last struck or rolled the ball in, unless there be at least three of his opponents nearer to their own goal-line than he is. No player can be offside in his own half of the ground, nor if the ball was last touched or hit by one of his opponents. The penalty for offside is a free hit. When a player strikes at the ball no part of his stick must in any event rise above his shoulders at either the beginning or the end of the stroke; the penalty for ' sticks,' as it is called, is a bully. In the case of breaches of the rules inside the circles a ' penalty bully,' or a ' penalty corner,' is awarded. When a penalty bully is played, all players, save the two taking the bully, shall remain beyond the nearer 25 yds. line in the field of play until the bully is completed. When a penalty corner is awarded, the player taking it shall have a hit from any part of the goal-line he may choose, at least 10 yds. from the nearest goal-post. At the moment of such hit all the defending team must be behind their own goal-line, and all the attacking team must be outside the striking circle in the field of play. A corner differs from a penalty corner only in that the hit is taken from a point within 3 yds. of the nearest corner flag. The game is in charge of two umpires, who each have charge of half of the field of play; if two umpires are not available one umpire and two linesmen take their place. Since 1895 International Matches between England, Scotland, Ireland, and Wales have been played, and Belgium and France now play England. County matches are also played, and Divisional Association matches. In the season of 1911-12, England beat Wales 6-3, Ireland 10-3, Belgium 19-1, France 9-1, and was beaten by Scotland 1-2; Ireland beat Scotland 1-0, and Wales 2-1; Scotland drew with Wales 2-2; Oxford beat Cambridge 3-1, and the army beat the navy 4-2. For English ice H. *see* the article on BANDY. In America ice H. is so popular that the term ' hockey ' is used for that variety, and the other game is called field H. The game differs from English ice H. in several respects. A ' puck ' which is a flat vulcanised disc, 1 in. thick and 3 in. in diameter, is used instead of a ball. The stick used is all in one piece and must not exceed 3 in. in width. The size of the rink is 112 ft. long by 58 ft. wide, at least; the goals are 6 ft. long by 4 ft. wide. There are only seven players on each side. The stick can be raised above the shoulder when the player is actually striking the puck. Ice polo is a game very similar to ice H., played almost exclusively in the New England states. It is played with a rubber-covered ball and a heavier stick. Five men only play on a side, and there is no offside rule. The rink is 150 ft. in length. Ring H. is a variety of H. which can be played on the floor of any gymnasium or large room. The goals are 3 ft. high and 4 ft. in width; six men are on a side, a goal keeper, a quarter, three forwards and a centre. A ring is used as the ball, of 5 in. diameter, with a 3 in. hole in the middle, weighing from 12 to 16 oz. The stick is a light but tough wand, from 36 to 40 in. in length, ¾ in. in diameter, and with a 5 in. guard at a distance of 20 in. from the lower end. The end of the stick is inserted into the hole in the ring; a goal from the field counts 1 point, and from a foul, ½ point. Roller polo is an adaptation of ice polo to roller skating rinks, and is very popular in the U.S.A. Five players form a side. *See* Smith and Robson, *Hockey*, 1899; F. S. Creswell, *Hockey*, 1906; E. Thompson, *Hockey for Women*, 1904; E. E. White, *The Hockey Player*, 1909; E. H. Green and E. E. White, *Hockey*, 1912.

Hocking, Joseph (*b.* 1855), an English novelist, born in Cornwall, younger brother of Silas Kitto H. He was educated at Owen's College, Manchester, and became a land-surveyor in 1878, but left this profession in 1884 and entered the Non-conformist ministry, for the next few years, travelling in Egypt, Palestine, Greece, Turkey, and Syria. He has written widely, his chief publications being: *Jabez Easterbrook; Ishmael Pengelly; All Men are Liars; Zillah; The Monk of Mar Saba; Fields of Fair Renown; The Birthright; The Scarlet Woman; The Purple Robe; The Madness of David Baring; Lest We Forget; O'er Moor and Fen;* *Greater Love; A Flame of Fire; The Woman of Babylon,* etc., etc.

Hocking, Silas Kitto (*b.* 1850), an English novelist, born in Cornwall, brother of Joseph H.; educated at the Grammar School of St. Stephen's, Cornwall, and privately. In 1870 he was ordained and held various pastorates, resigning in 1896, and seeking to enter parliament, contested (unsuccessfully) Mid-Bucks 1906 and Coventry 1910. Among his numerous publications may be mentioned: *Alec Green; Her Benny; His Father; Caleb Carthew; One in Charity; In Spite of Fate; The Awakening of Anthony Weir; The Wizard's Light; A Bonny Saxon; Meadowsweet and Rue; Pioneers; The Silent Man; Who shall Judge; The Third Man,* etc.

Hocktide, formerly a popular festival in England, kept on the second Monday and Tuesday after Easter. Hock Tuesday and Michael-mas were the rent-days in rural England. The derivation is un-certain; the term hock-day was in use by the 12th century. The chief pastime was that of ' binding ' members of the opposite sex (men on Monday, women on Tuesday), till a small payment was made for release. The money was used for church or parish purposes. ' The Old Coventry Play of Hock-Tuesday,' was revived on Elizabeth's visit to Kenilworth (1575). *See* Hone, *Every-day Book,* i., 1826; Brand, . . . *Pop. Antiq.,* 1777; *Chambers's Journal,* 1888.

Hoddeson, a par. and vil. of Hert-fordshire, England, 4 m. S.E. of Hert-ford, 1½ m. from Broxbourne Junc-tion. Izaak Walton used to fish there. It was a coaching station on the Old North Road. Pop. (1911) 5196.

Hodeida, Hodaida, or Hodidah, a fort and seaport of Yemen, Arabia, on the E. coast of the Red Sea, 100 m. from Mocha. A harbour is to be built at Ras-el-Ketib, 10 m. away. A railway connecting Hodeida, Ras-el-Ketib, Sana'a, and Amran is under construction. The chief exports are: Coffee, skins, cotton, and some pearls, senna, myrrh, sesame, and jowari (a kind of millet). Other grains are imported. Pop. about 42,000.

Hodge, Charles (1797-1878), an American Presbyterian theologian, born at Philadelphia. In 1819 he became professor of Oriental and Biblical literature at Princeton Theo-logical Seminary. In 1825 he founded the *Princeton Review,* and wrote several commentaries on Romans, Corinthians, and Ephesians, besides a history of the Presbyterian church in America, and his well-known *Systematic Theology* (1871-72) one of the most important theological works ever written in America, and now a standard work of the Calvinistic churches. A professorship bearing H.'s name was founded in his honour in 1872. *See* Lives by Patton and A. A. Hodge.

Hodges, William, R.A. (1744-97), an English landscape painter, born in London. On leaving school he was engaged to accompany Captain Cook in his second voyage round the world as draughtsman, and the outcome of this was a number of interesting views of the countries discovered or visited by the navigator. A few years after his return he went to India and lived there till 1784. He exhibited at the Royal Academy in 1776, became an associate in 1786, and an academician in 1787.

Hodgkin, Thomas (*b.* 1831), a British historian, born in London, of a Quaker family. After graduating at the London University, he entered business as a banker, at the same time applying himself to historical study, and soon becoming a leading authority on the history of the early middle ages. His chief works are: *Italy and Her Invaders* (8 vols.), 1880-99; *The Dynasty of Theodosius,* 1889; *Theodoric the Goth,* 1891; *Life of Charles the Great,* 1897; and vol. i. of Longman's *Political History of England,* 1906.

Hodgkinson, Eaton (1789-1861), an English engineer, born at Anderton, Cheshire. On his father's death, he persuaded his mother to move to Manchester, where he made the acquaintance of John Dalton (1811), and after researches on the strength of materials, became the great authority on iron beams. In 1847 he became professor of engineering in University College, London, and in 1851 was elected an honorary member of the Institution of Civil Engineers.

Hodgson, Brian Houghton, F.R.S. (1800-94), an English Orientalist, entered the East India Company's College at Haileybury, 1816, becoming a servant of the company, 1818. He was resident in Nepaul, 1820-43, returning to England, 1858. H. wrote valuable papers on the ethnology, languages, and zoology of Nepaul and Tibet, including *Miscellaneous Essays on Indian Subjects,* 1880. The libraries of London, Paris, and Calcutta have his collections of Oriental MSS. *See* Hunter's *Life,* 1896; *Dict. Nat. Biog.* (Suppl. vol. ii.).

Hodgson, Shadworth Hollway (*b.* 1832), educated at Rugby and Oxford. He became president of the Aristotelian Society for the Systematic Study of Philosophy, 1880. In some ways H.'s views resemble Kant's, and he aims at continuing the latter's critical work, but his philosophy, as a whole, is strongly opposed to the idealism into which Kant's system often develops, and he protests against the ' Noümenon ' theory. His works include: *Time and Space,* 1865; *Principles of Reform in the Suffrage,* 1866; *The Theory of Practice* . . ., 1870; *The Philosophy of Reflection,* 1878; and *The Metaphysic of Experience,* 1898, the most valuable of all. He also wrote *Outcast Essays and Verse Translations,* 1881; addresses such as *The Relation of Philosophy to Science* . . ., 1884, and *The Unseen World,* 1887; and *Century of Kant's Death,* 1905. See *Sat. Rev.,* xxx., xlvi.

Hód - Mezö - Vásárhely (' marketplace of the beaver's meadow '), a tn. of Czongrád co., Hungary, on Lake Hodos, about 14 m. N.E. of Szegedin. It has fairs, a brewery, oil manufactures, produces tobacco, fruit, wine, and wheat, and rears cattle. Pop. about 60,000.

Hodograph. If a point P be moving in any path, and from any fixed point O a vector OP¹ be drawn parallel and proportional to the velocity of P, then the locus of P¹ is called the hodograph of the path of P. Let P_1 and P_2 be two consecutive positions of P₁, the time from P_1 to P_2 being very small.

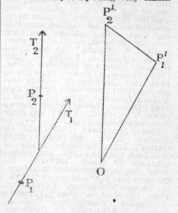

Then the tangents P_1T_1 and P_2T_2 at P_1 and P_2 to the path of P are the directions of motion at P_1 and P_2. Draw OP₁¹ and OP₂¹ parallel to P_1T_1 and P_2T_2 and proportional to the velocities at P_1 and P_2 respectively. Then by the triangle of velocities, $P_1^1P_2^1$ represents, in magnitude and direction, the change of velocity of P during the small time, *i.e.* $P_1{}^1P_2{}^1$ is proportional to the acceleration of P. As P traces out its path, so P^1 traces out the hodograph, and the velocity of P^1 in the hodograph represents, in magnitude and direction, the acceleration of P in the original curve. In particular, if P moves with a uniform velocity in a circle, P^1 describes a circle with a uniform velocity. Hence P has a constant acceleration, which will be seen from a figure to be always directed towards the centre of the circle.

Hodometer, see PEDOMETER.

Hodson, Major William Stephen Raikes (1821-58), an Anglo-Indian soldier, leader of light cavalry in the Indian Mutiny, usually known as ' Hodson of Hodson's Horse.' Educated at Rugby and Cambridge, he joined the Indian army in 1845, fighting in the first Sikh War. Rising to be commander of the Punjab Corps of Guides, 1852, he was dismissed in 1855 for harsh administration and alleged errors in the regimental accounts. On the outbreak of the Mutiny he rode with despatches from Karnal to Meerut and back, and was allowed to raise his famous regiment of horse and become head of the Intelligence Department. H. helped in the reduction of Delhi, and afterwards brought in Bahadur Shah, the last of the Moguls, as prisoner, but shot the three princes down to overawe the mob. His conduct over this and over money matters has been severely censured, and he was even accused of ' looting.' He was killed in an attack on Lucknow. *See* Hodson, *Hodson of Hodson's Horse*, 1883 ; Trotter, *A Leader of Light Horse*, 1901, and Chamberlain on this biography (1901); Bosworth Smith, *Life of Lord Lawrence* (App. to 6th ed.), 1885 ; Holmes, *Hist. of Indian Mutiny* (App. N to 5th ed.), 1898 ; and *Four Famous Soldiers*, 1889.

Hody, Humphrey (1659-1707), an English divine, graduated from Oxford, 1679, becoming fellow of Wadham College, 1685, and regius professor of Greek, 1697-98. He sided with the government in the controversy over the ' non-jurors ' (1689). H. became archdeacon of Oxford in 1704. His chief works are : *A History of English ' Councils and Convocations* . . ., 1701, and *De Bibliorum Textibus Originalibus*, 1703 (containing a reply to Vossius' attack on H.'s earlier work concerning the Septuagint). He also wrote the *Prolegomena* to the Greek chronicle of Malalas (1691), and his MS. of *De Græcis Illustribus* was edited by Jebb (1742) with a *Life*.

Hoe (Fr. *houe*, modern Ger. *Haue*), an implement used in gardening and

agriculture for extirpating weeds, singling out root crops, stirring the surface-soil, and such-like purposes. The ordinary garden H. has a flat blade set transversely in a long wooden handle, and the best one for agricultural purposes is the swan-neck H., having a long curved neck joining the blade to the handle. There is also the Dutch or thrust H., with the blade fixed into the handle as in a spade. Besides these there are several types of horse-drawn H. used among root and grain crops, and capable of working one or several rows at a time.

Hoe, Richard Marsh (1812-86), an American inventor, born in New York City, son of Robert H., a mechanic. He established a manufactory of printing-presses, using steam to run the machinery, in New York City in conjunction with two brothers-in-law, and became head of his father's firm soon after. His principal invention was the printing-machine known as the H. rotary or ' lightning ' press, patented in 1846.

Hoek van Holland, see HOOK OF HOLLAND.

Hoerberg, Pehr (1746 – 1816), an eminent Swedish painter, born in Småland, Sweden. Attended studios at Gothenburg and other towns, and went to the academy at Stockholm in 1784. In 1797 he was made a member of the Academy and court-painter to King Charles XIV. He painted chiefly religious subjects, one of his best-known works being a large altar-piece of the Ascension in the church of Ostra-Husby. *See* C. Molbech, *Leben und Kunst des Malers P. Hoerberg*, 1819.

Hoest, Jeus Kragh, see HÖST.

Hoeven, Jan van der (1801-68), a Dutch physician, and zoological professor, born at Rotterdam. He gained world-wide distinction by his handbook of zoology, the second edition of which was translated into English (1856-58). His other works consist chiefly of memoirs. He was professor of zoology at Leyden, and his brother Cornelis was professor of medicine at the same university.

Hof : 1. A tn. in N.E. of Bavaria, Upper Franconia, 30 m. N.E. of Bayreuth, on the Saale. It was destroyed by fire in 1823, since when it has been almost entirely rebuilt. H. is a great seat of the textile industry, and manufs. calico, cloth, and hosiery. It has a hospital founded in 1262, and some interesting churches. Jean Paul's earlier years are closely associated with the town. Pop. 41,121. **2.** A tn. in Norway, 50 m. N. of Christiania. Pop. 5000.

Hofer, Andreas (1767 – 1810), a Tyrolese patriot peasant-leader, born at St. Leonard in the Passieir valley, where his father was an innkeeper, which trade H. inherited, and in addition dealt in wine and horses with the N. of Italy. In 1809 he called the Tyrolese to arms to expel the French and Bavarians, and they responded with ardour, and swept the latter out in seven weeks, overwhelming them at Sterzing. By this victory the Austrians temporarily occupied Innsbruch and H. was conspicuous amongst the insurgent leaders. By the treaty of Schönbrunn, the Tyrol was again ceded to Bavaria, and although H. again took up arms, he had to disband his followers and seek refuge in the mountains, where he was betrayed, captured, and shot. *See* Lives by Weidinger, Stampfer, and Heigel.

Hoffman, Friedrich (1660-1742), a German physician, born at Halle, where he subsequently became professor of medicine, and physician to Frederick I. of Prussia. He studied medicine at Jena, and afterwards taught there. Later he journeyed to Holland and England, becoming acquainted with many illustrious chemists and physicians. In 1688 he removed to Halberstadt, where he was appointed physician to the principality, and on the founding of Halle University in 1693 filled the chairs of medicine and natural philosophy. His chief work is *Medicina Rationalis Systematica*, 1718-40.

Hoffmann, August Heinrich, known as **Hoffmann von Fallersleben** (1798-1874), a German poet and philologist, born at Fallersleben in Lüneberg, his father being the mayor of the town. He was educated at Göttingen and Bonn, his original intention being to study theology. He soon abandoned this for literature, and in 1823 became custodian of the university library at Breslau, and later on professor of German there. In consequence of his publication. *Unpolitische Lieder*, 1840-41), he was obliged to resign his chair, and then travelled for three years, returning to Prussia after the revolution of 1848. He wrote, *Horæ Belgicæ, Geschichte des Deutschen Kirchenlieds, Soldatenlieder*, etc. *See* J. M. Wagner, *Hoffmann von Fallersleben*.

Hoffmann, Christian Gottfried (1692-1735), a German juris-consult, born at Lauban. In 1718 became professor of law at Leipzig, and later at Frankfort-on-the-Oder. He wrote a *History of the Roman Law of Justinian*, and *Library of German Public Law*.

Hoffmann, Ernst Theodor Wilhelm (1776-1822), a German writer and composer, was born at Königsberg. He assumed the name Amadeus in place of Wilhelm in homage to Mozart.

In 1792 he entered the university of his native city to prepare for a legal career, and in 1795 began to practise as a jurist at Königsberg, subsequently going to Berlin; but music interested him more than his legal duties. In 1796 he was appointed assessor at Posen; unfortunately, however, his brilliant powers of caricature got him into trouble, and he was obliged to leave Posen. In 1804 he was transferred to Warsaw, where he made the acquaintance of Werner, but was forced to quit office in 1806, when Warsaw was occupied by the French. For the next ten years he led a precarious existence, supporting himself by composing and giving music lessons, and was, for a time, director of a new theatre in Bamberg, but in 1814 he resumed his legal profession in Berlin, and in 1816 was appointed councillor of the Court of Appeal. Some of his shorter tales appeared in the collection *Phantasiestücke*, 1814, and were followed by the gruesome novel, *Die Elixiere des Teufels*, 1816. Two other collections are *Nachtstücke,* and *Die Serapionsbrüder*, the latter of which includes pictures of German life, and incidents from Italian and French history, as well as gruesome tales; indeed it contains *Das Fräulein von Scudéri*, generally considered his best work. Other books of his are *Seltsame Leïden eines Theaterdirektors, Klein Kaches,* and *Lebensansichten des Katers Murr*. His fairy tales, *Der Goldene Topf*, have been translated by Carlyle. He also wrote an essay on Mozart's *Don Juan*, and composed an opera on Fouque's *Undine*. H. was one of the master novelists of German Romanticism, and his works are remarkable for their humour and realism.

Hofgeismar, a tn. in Prussia, prov. Hesse-Nassau, 15 m. N.W. of Cassel. Pop. 4765.

Hofhuf, or **El Hofhuf,** the chief tn. in the dist. of El Haza, Arabia, about 40 m. from the Persian Gulf. Pop. estimated at about 41,000.

Hofman, Johann Christian Karl von (1810-77), a German theologian and historian, born at Nuremberg. He studied first at Erlangen and then went to Berlin, Schleiermacher and Raumer being amongst his teachers there. In 1833 he became professor of theology at Erlangen, and in 1842 at Rostock, whence he returned to Erlangen in 1857. In theology, H. was a Conservative, but in politics an adherent of the Progressive party. In his works he maintained unswerving Lutheranism, the chief being his book on prophecy, and the defence of Christianity from its records, *Der Schriftbeweis*, 1857-60 (2nd ed.).

Hofmann,AugustWilhelm(1818-92), a German chemist, born at Giessen. He first studied law and philology at Göttingen, but later turned his attention to chemistry, and in 1845 was appointed director of the Royal College of Chemistry in London. From 1856-65 he was chemist to the Royal Mint, when he returned to Berlin as professor of chemistry, and spent the rest of his life in that city. His work covered a wide range of organic chemistry—his contributions to the scientific journals were mainly on this subject. He also devoted much labour to the theory of chemical types. His chief works are : *Introduction to Modern Chemistry, The Life-Work of Liebig*, and *Chemische Erinnerungen.* See *Memorial Lectures delivered before the Chemical Society, 1893-1900* (London).

Hofmann, Josef (*b.* 1877), a Polish pianist, born at Cracow. Pupil of his father (professor at Warsaw Conservatory). Made his appearance before the public at the age of six, and three years later made a tour of Germany,Denmark,Norway,andSweden. Also played in Vienna, Paris, and London, becoming known as a celebrated musical prodigy. Visited the United States in 1887-88, and, after studying two years under Rubinstein, made his début at Dresden in 1894. Subsequently played in London, Vienna, and New York. Has published pianoforte compositions, and is one of the leading modern pianists.

Hofmeister, Wilhelm Friedrich Benedict (1824-77),a German botanist, born at Leipzig, where he was educated and entered business as a musicdealer, studying botany in his spare time. In 1863 he was appointed to a professorship in Heidelberg, and nine years later was transferred to Tübingen. In 1851 he published his principal work, *Vergleichende Untersuchungen der Kennung, Entfaltung und Fruchtbildung höherer Kryptogamen und der Samenbildung der Coniferen*, which stands in the first rank of botanical books, and is a typical work on plant-morphology. H. also contributed two notable parts to a handbook of physiological botany never completed, under the titles of *Die Lehre von der Pflanzenzelle* and *Allgemeine Morphologie der gewächse.*

Hofmeyr, Jan Hendrik (1845-1909), a S. African politician, born at Cape Town, where he was educated, leaving school at the age of sixteen and becoming a journalist. He joined the staff of the *Volksvriend*, which he bought in 1861 and amalgamated with the *Zuid Afrikaan*, under the title of *Ons Land.* In 1879 H. entered parliament where he remained for sixteen years, becoming

leader and spokesman of the Dutch party in the colony. In 1887 he was one of the Cape delegates to the first colonial conference held in London. Until the Jameson Raid of 1895, he was a supporter of Cecil Rhodes, and during the earlier part of the S. African War, he was chairman on the committee of the relief fund for Boer widows and orphans.

Hofwyl, an estate some 6 m. to the N. of Bern in Switzerland, which was purchased by Fellenberg to start his educational institution. *See* FELLENBERG, P. E.

Hog. A sheep still retaining its first fleece is known as a H. in Scotland, and a hogget is a two-year-old sheep. *See* PIG.

Hogan, James Francis (*b.* 1855), a British journalist and author, born at Tipperary. Educated at St. Patrick's College, Melbourne, his parents having emigrated to Australia. He entered the Education Department, Victoria, in 1873, and eight years later joined the literary staff of *Melbourne Argus.* In 1887 he settled in London and was M.P. for Mid-Tipperary, 1893-1900. His chief publications are : *The Irish in Australia; The Australian in London; The Lost Explorer; The Convict King; Robert Lowe, Viscount Sherbrooke ; The Sister Dominions; The Gladstone Colony*, etc.

Hogarth, David George (*b.* 1862), an archæological explorer, geographer, and author, born at Barton-on-Humber. He was educated at Winchester and Magdalen College, Oxford, and was a tutor at Magdalen from 1886-93. He explored Asia Minor in 1887, 1890, 1891, and 1894, and excavated at Paphos (1888), Der-el-Bahari (1894), Alexandria (1895), in Fayûm (1896), Naukratis, (1899 and 1903), Ephesus (1904-5), Assuit (1906-7), and Jerablus (1911). He was director of the British school at Athens (1897-1900), and conducted excavations at Knossos and the Dictacan Cave (1900). In 1909 he became keeper of the Ashmolean Museum, a post he still holds. His publications include : *Devia Cypria*, 1890; *Modern and Ancient Roads in Asia Minor*, 1892 ; *Philip and Alexander of Macedon*, 1897; *The Nearer East*, 1902; *The Penetration of Arabia*, 1904; *The Archaic Artemisia of Ephesus*, 1908; *Ionia and the East*, 1909; *Accidents of an Antiquary's Life*, 1910.

Hogarth, William (1697-1764), a painter and engraver, and founder of the British School of Painting, born in London. He began to draw at an early age, and was apprenticed to a silver-plate engraver, finishing his time at the age of twenty when he started engraving on copper. In 1724 he published on his own account his plate ' Masquerades and Operas, Burlington Gate,' but he first became known as an engraver by his plates for Butler's *Hudibras*, of which the last two, representing the ' Burning of Rumps at Temple Bar ' and the ' Procession of the Skimmington,' are the best. He next turned his attention to oil-painting, executing ' small conversation pieces, from twelve to fifteen inches high,' and in 1731 won reputation by ' A Harlot's Progress,' a series of pictures in which he portrays the enticement of his heroine

WILLIAM HOGARTH

into the paths of evil, her passage through a ' Martin's summer ' as the mistress of a rich Jew, to ' Captain Macheath ' and Drury Lane, to Bridewell and beating hemp, to disease and death, to a shameful funeral, and a forgotten grave. This was speedily followed by ' A Rake's Progress,' which did not meet with such success as ' A Harlot's Progress,' owing to the fact that it attacked the vices of the man instead of those of the woman, and ' The Fair,' or ' Southwark Fair,' which depicts the carnival suppressed in 1762. In 1736 he attempted ' the great style of history-painting,' and produced on a staircase of St. Bartholomew's Hospital two Scripture stories, ' The

Pool of Bethesda ' and ' The Good Samaritan,' but these did not meet with the encouragement he expected, so he again turned his attention to his former work and painted the ' Strolling Actresses dressing in a Barn, ' The Enraged Musician,' ' The Distrest Poet,' etc. In 1745 H. had a sale by auction of his pictures, and the ticket of admission was the etching known as the ' Battle of the Pictures.' The same year his masterpiece, the ' Marriage à la Mode ' (now in the National Gallery), appeared, which represents a variety of ' Modern occurrences in high life,' and in 1746 his portrait of ' Garrick as Richard III.,' for which he received £200, as well as that of ' Simon, Lord Lovat.' In 1747 he produced ' The Stage Coach,' and the series ' Industry and Idleness,' in 1756 ' The Invasion,' and in 1764 ' The Bathos,' his last work. He also painted a portrait of himself which resulted in the publication of *The Analysis of Beauty*, 1753. H. is famous most especially as a satirist on canvas, and as such has never been surpassed; he represented the foibles of his time in a series of engravings which exhibit character, humour, and power. *See* Austin Dobson, *William Hogarth.*

Hogg, Professor Hope W., M.A. (1863-1912), a professor of Semitic languages and literatures in the University of Manchester (1903-12), born in Cairo. He contributed to the *Encyclopædia Biblica*, and was a member of the editorial staff (1895-1903). He also published, with his wife, an English translation of the Arabic version of the *Diatessaron* of Tatian, with introduction and critical notes; various articles on Semitic subjects in the *Jewish Quarterly Review*, and elsewhere, and a *Survey of Recent Assyriology*, 1908 and 1910.

Hogg, James (1770-1835), called ' The Ettrick Shepherd,' a poet, born at Ettrick, Selkirkshire, was the son of a small farmer. He was entirely self-educated, but at an early age began to compose verses, though the setting of these to paper was at first a task of great difficulty. He first appeared in print in 1800 with the patriotic song, *Donald M'Donald,* which became popular at once. Encouraged by his success, he, in the following year, published his *Scottish Pastorals, Poems, and Songs.* In 1802 he met Scott, and not long after became friendly with Allan Cunningham. His next publication was *The Mountain Bard* (1807), and in 1810 issued *The Forest Minstrel,* which was not a financial success. Three years later appeared the admirable work,

The Queen's Wake, and in 1816 *Madoc of the Moor*. In that year he also brought out *The Poetic Mirror, or The Living Bards of Great Britain*, a volume of clever parodies of the leading poets of the day, including Scott, Coleridge, Southey, Bryon, and Wordsworth. Among his subsequent books are : *The Brownie of Bodsbeck, and other Tales*, 1817 ; *Jacobite Relics of Scotland*, 1819 ; *Winter Evening Tales*, 1820 ; and *Queen Hynde*, 1826. He contributed to *Blackwood's Magazine* many articles, some of which he collected in 1829 under the title of the *Shepherd's Calendar* ; and in 1834, to the great annoyance of Lockhart, he printed *The Domestic Manners and Private Life of Sir Walter Scott*, a book that is now too seldom read. H. has been described as the greatest poet, after Burns, that has ever sprung from the common people, and it is certain that he attained to very great heights when dealing with local or legendary stories, while his gift of imagination was so great as rightly to be entitled genius. He had in a great degree the lyrical gift, and some of his poems, such as *When the Kye come Hame* and *Flora Macdonald's Farewell* are exquisite. H. wrote his *Autobiography*, and his *Memorials* were published by Mrs. Garden.

Hogg, Quintin (1845 – 1903), an English philanthropist, seventh son of Sir James Weir H., born in London. He was educated at preparatory schools and Eton, which he left in 1863 and entered business, being first with a firm of tea merchants and later with sugar merchants. Philanthropy, however, was the main concern of H.'s life, and in 1864 he started a ragged school for boys. In 1881 he purchased the Royal Polytechnic Institution in Regent Street for providing young men and women of the lower middle classes with instruction, recreation, and social intercourse, and by this successful inauguration, initiated the polytechnic movement in London.

Hogland, a small island situated in the Gulf of Finland, 110 m. W. of St. Petersburg. In 1788 a battle took place here between the Russians and the Swedes. There are extensive quarries of granite and porphyry. It has an area of about 11 sq. m. Pop. 800.

Hogmanay, the name applied, in Scotland and a few parts of England, to the last day of the year, viz. New Year's Eve, Dec. 31. It is also used for the cake given to the children who beg for gifts and alms on the morning of that day. In former times, H. marked the beginning of holiday festivities in Scotland, when the New Year was ushered in with various quaint ceremonies. The derivation of the term has been much disputed and remains in obscurity.

Hogolen, Hogolu, or Rug, a group of small volcanic islands in the centre of the Carolines, Pacific Ocean. They are mountainous and wooded. Area, 50 sq. m. Pop. 15,000.

Hog-plum, the name given to the fruit of the species of *Spondias*, a genus of Anacardiaceæ. The fruit is edible and is a drupe containing from one to five seeds. It grows in the tropics, but may be cultivated in Britain.

Hog-rat, the name given to the species of *Capromys*, a genus of rodents belonging to the family Octocontidæ. It is found only in the islands of Cuba and Jamaica, and the native name for the animal is ' hutia.' *C. melanurus* is a dark brown-coloured animal, about the size of a rabbit.

Hogshead, a liquid measure of capacity, varying with the nature of the contents, but equivalent for wine to sixty-three gallons, and for ale and beer to fifty-four gallons. In England it has now fallen into disuse, but the measure still obtains in the United States, and is equivalent to sixty-three American gallons. The etymology of the word has been much discussed, and its origin is uncertain.

Hogue, a British cruiser, completed in 1902. Displacement, 12,000 tons ; speed, 21 knots.

Hogue, or Hougue, La, a roadstead on the E. side of the northern part of Cotentin Peninsula, France, dept. Manche, off a rocky and dangerous coast. Gives its name to the naval victory of the English and Dutch over the French in 1692.

Hohenelbe, a tn. in Bohemia on the Elbe, 16 m. N.E. of Gitschin. It is engaged in various branches of manuf., principally the textile industry. Pop. 7074.

Hohen Ems, a vil. in Austria-Hungary, in Vorarlberg, 10 m. N.E. of Feldkirch and 10 m. S.S.W. of Bregenz. It has cotton and other textile manufs., and sulphur baths. Pop. 6452.

Hohenfriedeberg, a tn. in Silesia, 35 m. W.S.W. of Breslau. Noted for Frederick the Great's victory over the Austrians and Saxons in 1745. Pop. about 2000.

Hohenheim, a village in Würtemberg, Germany, 7 m. S. of Stuttgart. A royal castle is situated in the neighbourhood, and there is a famous school of agriculture.

Hohenlimburg, a tn. in Prussia, prov. of Westphalia, on the R. Lenne, 5 m. E. of Hagen ; the seat of an iron industry and textile manufs. Pop. 13,878.

Hohenlinden, a vil. in Upper Bavaria, 20 m. E. of Munich, celebrated for the victory gained there over the Austrians, by the French and Bavarians under Moreau in 1800. The battle is described in Campbell's lyric of the name.

Hohenlohe, a former principality of Germany in Franconia, now comprised chiefly in Würtemberg and Bavaria.

Hohenlohe-Schillingsfürst, Chlodwig Karl Viktor, Prince of (1819-1901), a German statesman, born at Schillingsfürst, Bavaria. Entered the Russian diplomatic service and acquired a taste for jurisprudence in the courts of Coblenz. In 1843 he travelled for some months in France, Italy, and Switzerland, and in 1844 went to Potsdam as a civil servant. He was early known for his Prussian sympathies, and in 1846 became a member of the Bavarian Reichsrath, receiving his formal discharge from the Prussian service the same year. Was appointed chief minister of Bavaria in 1866, and endeavoured to bring about the union of Southern and Northern Germany, but was forced to resign. During the Franco-German War he advocated the alliance between Bavaria and Prussia. In 1873 he was appointed, by Bismarck, German ambassador in Paris, and in 1885 became governor of Alsace-Lorraine; imperial chancellor in 1894, but resigned in 1900. See *Geschichte des Hauses Hohenlohe*, 1904.

Hohenmauth, a tn. in Bohemia, Austria, 16 m. E. of Chrudim. Manufs. musical instruments. Pop. 10,858.

Hohensalza, a tn. in the prov. of Posen, Prussia, 66 m. E.N.E. of Posen. Until 1905 known as Inowrazlaw or Jung-Breslau. Salt works and saline springs are in the vicinity. Pop. 25,695.

Hohenschwangau, a royal castle in Bavaria, Germany, near Füssen, standing 2933 ft. above sea-level in a picturesque district. It belonged originally to the house of Guelph, and in 1832 was purchased by Maximilian II. of Bavaria, who restored it in the style of a mediæval feudal castle and made it into a royal residence.

Hohenstaufen, a German princely house, members of which were emperors or German kings from 1138 to 1254. The earliest known member of the family was Frederick von Buren, who died at the end of the 11th century. His son, Frederick, built a castle at Staufen or H., and called himself by this name. He was a supporter of the Emperor Henry IV., who gave him the duchy of Swabia,

and when Henry was absent in Italy acted as vicegerent. In 1105 he was succeeded by his son Frederick II., the one-eyed, who, together with his brother Conrad, held S.W. Germany for their uncle, the Emperor Henry V. On the death of Henry in 1125, his estates fell to Frederick, but Lothair, the Saxon, being chosen emperor, a furious war broke out which ended in the submission of Frederick. In 1138 Conrad was elected Emperor of Germany as Conrad III., and was succeeded by his nephew, Frederick Barbarossa, in 1152. Other emperors of this family were Henry VI. (1190-97), Philip I. (1198-1208), Frederick II. (1212-50), and Conrad IV. (1250-54), the male line becoming extinct in 1268, when Conradin was put to death in Italy by Charles of Anjou. *See* HOLY ROMAN EMPIRE.

Hohenstein-Ernstthal, a tn. in the kingdom of Saxony, Germany, 12 m. N.E. of Zwickau. Textile manufs. and knitting are the chief industries. Pop. 15,632.

Hohenzollern, a German imperial dynasty, which traces its origin back to the 9th century to one Count Tassilo, who built the castle of H. at Zollern in Swabia. A descendant of his, Frederick III., married Sophia, daughter of Conrad, Burgrave of Nuremberg succeeding his father-in-law as Burgrave about 1192. When he died about 1202 his sons Conrad and Frederick succeeded him, Conrad becoming Burgrave of Nuremberg and founding the Franconian branch of the family, while Frederick received the county of Zollern, and became the ancestor of the Swabian branch. On the death of Conrad, his son Burgrave Frederick III. was the representative of the Franconian branch, and he took a prominent part in German affairs, securing the election of Rudolph of Hapsburg as German king in 1273. In 1415 Burgrave Frederick, the son of Frederick V., received Brandenburg from King Sigismund, becoming Margrave of Brandenburg as Frederick I., and in 1701 the elector of Brandenburg, Frederick III. became king of Prussia. In 1871 William, the seventh king, took the title of German emperor. The Swabian line was divided in 1576 into the branches of Hechingen and Sigmaringen. These continued unbroken until 1849, when they fell into the hands of Prussia. The proposal to raise Prince Leopold of Hohenzollern-Sigmaringen (1835-1905) to the Spanish throne in 1870 was the immediate cause of the war between Germany and France. Prince Charles of Hohenzollern-Sigmaringen became king of Roumania in 1881.

Hohenzollern, two united principalities of S. Germany. The modern Prussian province was formed in 1850, when Hohenzollern - Sigmaringen and Hohenzollern-Hechingen were united. It consists of a narrow strip of land bounded on the S.W. by Baden and on all other sides by Würtemberg. Its area is 441 sq. m., and population of 71,009. The surface is mountainous, and the chief industries are agriculture and cattle-rearing. Iron, coal, gypsum, and salt are found, and there are also some mineral springs. The castle of H. was destroyed in 1423, but* has been restored several times, the present one being built by King Frederick William IV. The seat of government is Sigmaringen.

Hohkönigsburg, the second largest castle in Alsace, was presented by the town of Schlettstadt to Emperor William II. in 1899. In 1147 it belonged to the Hohenstaufen family, and subsequently to the Sickingen until 1770. It has twice been destroyed, the first time by the confederation of the Rhenish towns in 1462, and the second by the Swedes in 1633.

Hohndorf, a village in Prussian Saxony, 8 m. E.N.E. of Zwickau. Pop. 5787.

Höhscheid, a tn. in the Rhine prov. of Prussia, about 9 m. from Elberfeld. It has iron and lead foundries, and manufactures whetstones. Pop. of com. 16,083.

Hoi-Hau, a port, 3 m. N.W. of Kiung-chau-fu, the chief town in Hainan Is., China.

Höijer, Benjamin Carl Henrik (1767-1812), a Swedish philosopher, born at Klingsbo in Dalecarlia. He was educated at the University of Upsala, and obtained the chair of philosophy there in 1808. He wrote chiefly on metaphysics and æsthetics, his works on the latter being the most important. Among them may be mentioned, *Outline of a History of the Fine Arts* and *The Eloquence of the Ancients and Moderns compared.* Although his style was of the classic order, correct and elegant, his sympathies were with the romantic, rather than with the classic school.

Hoists, *see* LIFTS.

Hokitika, a tn. in New Zealand, South Is., cap. of Westland co., on the N.W. coast, about 24 m. S. of Greymouth. It is noted for its goldfields, but brewing and tanning are also carried on, and there are sawmills and door factories. Greymouth is the port for the goldfields. Earthquakes are frequent. Pop. about 2200.

Hokkaido (*Hoku*, north, *kai*, sea, and *do*, road), a term used by the Japanese for the northern div. of the

Empire, including Yezo, the Kuriles, and the S. half of Sakhalin.

Holacanthus, the name of a genus of teleostean fishes belonging to the family Chætodontidæ. The species are marine and carnivorous, and are particularly abundant near volcanic rocks and coral islands. They are remarkable for their beautiful colouring, *H. imperator*, a native of the E. Indies, being deep blue, with bands of orange. The flesh is highly esteemed as diet.

Holaster, the name given to a genus of fossil echinoderms belonging to the sub-order Spatangoidæ, or heart-urchins, and to the family Anan-chytidæ. *H. subordicularis* is the best known species.

Holbach, Paul Henri Thyry, Baron d' (1723-89), a French philosopher, born at Heidelsheim in the Palatinate. He spent most of his time in Paris, and having great wealth and being of hospitable disposition, entertained and was intimate with the most distinguished men of his day, viz. Diderot, Grimm, Hume, Garrick, Wilkes, Sterne, Rousseau, etc. He wrote a large number of articles on chemistry and mineralogy for the *Encyclopédie*, and in 1767 published his *Christianisme dévoilé*, in which he attacks Christianity and religion. In 1770 his famous book, *Le Système de la Nature*, appeared, and in it he denied the existence of the deity and asserted that happiness is the end of mankind. The book evoked much criticism, and was answered by Frederick the Great and Voltaire. In philosophy H. was a follower of Diderot, and his portrait appears in the character of the virtuous atheist, Wolmar of the *Nouvelle Héloïse* of Rousseau.

Holbäk, a seaport, island of Seeland, Denmark, 35 m. W. of Copenhagen. Manufactures arms, exports grain. Pop. 4600.

Holbeach, a very ancient market tn., Lincolnshire, England, 8 m. E. of Spalding. It was once on the shore of the Wash, but is now 6 m. inland. H. is the birthplace of the antiquary, William Stukeley. Pop. (1911) 5259.

Holbein, Hans (*c.* 1460-1524), the Elder, a German painter, was a native of Augsburg. His early works bear the impress of the schools of Van der Weyden and Memlinc, while his later pieces, *e.g.* the basilica of St. Paul (1502) in the gallery of Augsburg, show Flemish influence. He was a prolific artist, and devoted his energy mainly to religious subjects, his crowning work being the altar-piece of St. Sebastian in Munich with the picture of the Annunciation, and the graceful figures of St. Barbara and St. Elizabeth on the wings.

Holbein, Hans (1497 - 1543), the Younger, a great German painter, born at Augsburg. Little is known of his early years, but in 1515 he went to Basel with his brother Ambrosius, and while there drew illustrations for Erasmus's *Praise of Folly*, which were as popular as the work itself. Besides this he painted the portraits of the burgomaster, Jacob Meyer, and his wife, and the exquisite skill of the artist is shown in the elaboration of every detail in the rich embroidery of the latter's attire. In 1517 he was in Lucerne, and was employed by the mayor of Lucerne to decorate his house with wall-paintings, but he soon returned to Basel, and executed in 1519 the portrait of Bonifacius Amerbach, which is one of the most perfect of his works. Here, too, he was greatly occupied with mural decoration, his celebrated ' Peasants' Dance ' being a wall-painting on a house at the corner of the Eisengusse. He also decorated the town hall, and executed many original designs for glass paintings, as well as for woodcuts, among which his book entitled the *Dance of Death* is the most famous. This series is most original, and represents every class of humanity terrified by Death. The king at a well-spread board is served by Death, who fills his bowl. The queen walking with her ladies is seized by Death dressed as a woman. In a landscape with flocks of sheep, Death terrifies an aged bishop. The miser with his money, the knight in his armour, the pedlar with his basket are alike surprised by Death, only one, a parish priest administering to the sick, escapes. He also designed a title page for More's *Utopia*, as well as for Luther's German translation of the N.T., besides illustrations for other well-known books, and a series of woodcuts from the O.T. history. But of his sacred pictures the most celebrated, perhaps, are the ' Solothurn Madonna ' and the ' Meyer Madonna.' The former was only discovered in the middle of the 19th century, and represents the Madonna with the Holy Infant in her lap, St. Ursus, patron saint of Solothurn, on her left, and Martin, Bishop of Tours, on her right. In the world - renowned ' Meyer Madonna ' at Darmstadt, the Virgin again occupies the central position, and holds the infant in her arms in a caressing manner, while around her are grouped in rapt adoration the Burgomaster Meyer of Wasen and his family. But marvellous as H.'s paintings were, his fame in his own day rested on his portraits, and among these his portrait of Erasmus at Longford Castle is worthy of

mention, as well as his portrait of himself, both of which were executed before his visit to England. In 1527 he came to London, and was introduced to Sir Thomas More whose portrait he painted as well as that of Warham, Archbishop of Canterbury, and Bishop Fisher, besides eighty-seven portraits on tinted paper in Windsor Castle. In 1528 he produced ' The Family of Sir Thomas More,' a magnificent group of portraits which has unfortunately been lost, and on his return to Basel painted a life-like picture of his own family, which is now in the Museum of that town. In 1531 he was again in London, and executed portraits of the German merchants of the Steelyard, the most valuable of which is that of Jörg Gyze (Berlin), much praised by Mr. Ruskin. In 1533 he painted ' The Ambassadors,' a panel representing two life-size male figures, which has very beautiful colouring, and is considered one of his finest productions. Soon after this he came under the notice of Henry VIII., and painted for him the picture containing Henry VII., Henry VIII., Jane Seymour, and Elizabeth of York. This master-piece, noticed by Van Mander, and mentioned in the account of the Duke of Saxony's visit to England in 1613, was destroyed by fire in 1698. Besides this he painted a portrait of Jane Seymour, now in Vienna, and one of Morett in the Dresden Gallery. H. also executed designs for ornament, his drawing for the ' Jane Seymour Cup,' in the Bodleian Library at Oxford being perhaps the most beautiful example of this class of art in the world. In 1537, on the death of Jane Seymour, he went to Brussels to paint the young Duchess of Milan, a proposed candidate for the king's hand (National Gallery), and in 1539 to Cleves to paint the Princess Anna (Louvre). Among other portraits of this period may be mentioned that of the Duke of Norfolk, Martin Luther, Prince Edward, and another portrait of himself. The importance of Hans Holbein's work cannot be over-estimated ; before his time portrait painting was scarcely known, and it was he who first raised the art of painting to perfection in England; indeed, it may be questioned whether in many of the finest requirements of portraiture his work has ever been surpassed. *See* Woltmann, *Holbein und seine Zeit ;* Cundall, *Hans Holbein ;* R. N. Wornum, *Some Account of the Life and Works of Hans Holbein.*

Holberg, Ludwig, Baron (1684-1754), a creator of modern Danish literature, born at Bergen in Norway. He was educated at Bergen and at the University of Copenhagen. In 1704 he came to England and spent two years amongst the libraries at Oxford, and in 1711 printed his first work, *An Introduction to the History of the Nations of Europe.* Soon after this he received the Rosenkrantz grant, the holder of which was expected to travel and spent the years 1714, 1715, and 1716, visiting the various countries of Europe. On his return to Denmark he published his *Introduction to Natural and Popular Law,* and in 1718 became professor of metaphysics at Copenhagen. In 1720 he was promoted to the chair of public eloquence, and in 1730 to that of history, becoming quæstor of the University in 1737, and a baron in 1747. Up to about 1716 his writings had been concerned with law and history, but after that date he began a new class of humorous literature, and his *Peder Paars,* 1719, the earliest of the great classics of the Danish language, is a satire on the pedantic stiffness and stupidity of contemporary life and thought. In 1721 the first Danish theatre was opened at Copenhagen, and Holberg produced in 1722 a Danish translation of *L'Avare* (before this no plays had been acted in Denmark except in French and German). This was followed by numerous original comedies, amongst which may be mentioned *Den .Vægelsindede; Jean de France; Jeppe paa Bjerget; Gert the Westphalian; Den politiske Kandestöber;* and *Henrik and Pernille,* his most famous piece, produced in 1724. After the closing of the theatre he turned his attention to historical and philosophical writings, and produced in 1726 *Metamorphosis,* a poetical satire; *Epistolæ ad virum perillustiem,* 1727 ; *Description of Denmark and Norway,* 1729 ; *History of Denmark ; Universal Church History ; Biographies of Famous Men ; Moral Reflections ; Description of Bergen,* 1737; *A History of the Jews,* etc. In 1741 there appeared another classic in his famous poem, *Niels Klim's Subterranean Journey,* and from 1748-54 *Epistles,* his last published work. He also wrote his *Autobiography,* which, together with *Peder Paars* and the *Subterranean Journey,* has been translated into English. The importance of H. cannot be over-estimated. He was the first writer in Europe of his time (omitting Voltaire), surpassing both Pope and Swift in genius, and created a literature for a country up to his time without books; indeed it is said that before H. went to Denmark the Danish language was seldom heard in polite society.

Holborn, a metropolitan bor. of London, bounded on the N. by St. Pancras and Finsbury, on the S.E. by the city of London, and on the S. and W. by the city of Westminster. 'Holebourne' means the stream in the hollow, and alludes to the river Fleet, over which a bridge was built in early times, now replaced by the viaduct built in 1869. H. contains some interesting buildings, among which may be mentioned the chapel of St. Etheldreda in Ely Place (so called from the bishops of Ely who held land here as early as the 13th century); the parish church of St. Giles in the Fields, dating from 1734, originally the site of a leper's hospital founded by Matilda in 1101; the church of St. Andrew, which numbers Sacheverell among its rectors; Lincoln's Inn, with its Tudor gateway, upon which Ben Jonson is said to have worked as a bricklayer ; Gray's Inn, with its 14th-century chapel ; the half-timbered houses of Staple Inn ; and the British Museum. H. has an area of 405 acres, and a population of (1911) 49,357.

Holcombe, eccles. dist. and vil., 4 m. N.N.W. of Bury, S.E. Lancashire, England. There are cotton mills. Pop. (1911) 100.

Holcroft, Thomas (1745-1809), a dramatist and author, born in London. He was successively stable-boy, shoemaker, tutor, and actor. In 1780 he published his first novel, *Alwyn, or the Gentleman Comedian,* in which he describes his own experience as a strolling actor. In 1781 his first comedy, *Duplicity,* appeared, and in 1783 he visited Paris as correspondent of the *Morning Herald.* He translated *Mariage de Figaro* from memory, and produced it at Covent Garden in 1784, himself playing the title-rôle. In 1792 *The Road to Ruin,* his best and most successful play, appeared, and in 1802 his musical adaptation *A Tale of Mystery* was acted at Covent Garden. H. published numerous comedies and comic operas, besides novels and translations, also *Human Happiness* (a poem). He is praised by Lamb, and was intimate with William Godwin and Hazlitt, who edited his *Memoirs.*

Holcus, a genus of Gramineæ closely allied to *Sorghum.* There are eight species, natives of Europe and Africa, and in Britain are to be found *H. lanatus,* a meadow-plant, and *H. mollis,* which grows in thickets.

Holden, Hubert Ashton (1822-96), an English classical scholar, a native of Staffordshire. He was educated at King Edward's College, Birmingham, and Trinity College, Cambridge, and was elected a fellow in 1847. He was ordained in 1848, and in 1853 was appointed vice-principal of Cheltenham College. From 1858-83 he was headmaster of Queen Elizabeth's School, Ipswich, and in 1890 became a fellow of London University. He edited a number of classical works for students, his best known being *Foliorum Silvula* and *Foliorum Canturicæ*, both of which are collections of pieces for translation into Latin and Greek. Other works of his are· Cicero's *De Officiis;* Thucydides, book vii.; the comedies of Aristophanes; and Plutarch's *Lives* of Pericles, Themistocles, Demosthenes, Sulla, and the Gracchi.

Holden, Sir Isaac (1807-97), an inventor, born at Hurlet, near Paisley. In his early years he worked in a cotton mill, and also had a year's experience at shawl weaving, but this proving too much for his strength, he, in 1823, joined the school of James Kennedy at Paisley, where he soon became assistant teacher. He subsequently became mathematical teacher at Leeds, Huddersfield, and Reading, and it was then that the idea occurred to him of applying sulphur to the explosive material that was necessary to produce instantaneous light. In 1830 he left Reading and became book-keeper in the firm of Townend Brothers, worsted manufacturers, but he soon left the counting-house for the mill, and conceived the application of machine power to the various operations of the wool-combing. In 1846 he became associated with Lister, and with him brought out a patent for a new method of carding and combing and preparing genappe yarns. In 1848 he opened a large fabrique at St. Denis, and in 1864 concentrated his business at Bradford, which rapidly became the largest wool-combing concern in the world.

Hölderlin, Johann Christian Friedrich (1770-1843), a German poet, born at Lauffen on the Neckar. He studied theology at the University of Tübingen, but in 1793-94 he became acquainted with Schiller and Fichte, who encouraged him to take up literary work. His writings are the productions of a sensitive mind, and are somewhat lacking in strength. His chief work is *Hyperion*, a novel which is conspicuous not for its story but rather for its language. He also wrote poetry and translated Greek plays, *e.g.* the *Antigone* and *Œdipus Rex* of 1804.

Holderness, a flat and fertile dist. of Yorkshire, England, between the North Sea and the estuary of the Humber.

Holding, in Scots feudal law, denotes the tenure subsisting between the feu superior and his vassal. A ward-holding was one granted for military service, but has now been abolished. A feu-farm H. is one by the terms of which the vassal had to pay the superior a yearly rent in money or in corn, or render appropriate agricultural services like ploughing and reaping. A blench H. is one under which the vassal pays an elusory or nominal yearly duty, *e.g.* a rose, a pair of gilt spurs, the object being merely to acknowledge the superiority. But the duty must be enacted within the year, provided it be a thing of annual growth, otherwise it can never be demanded thereafter. A burgage H. is that by which burghs-royal hold lands of the sovereign specified in their charters of erection (*see* BURGH). A H. by a church, monastery, or other religious or charitable society is called a mortification (*cf.* English Mortmain or H. 'in the dead hand'). *See* Erskine's *Principles of the Law of Scotland.*

Hole, William (*b.* 1846), a painter and etcher, born at Salisbury, Wiltshire. He was educated at the Edinburgh Academy, and served an apprenticeship as a civil engineer, but having travelled to Italy, and being commended by the artists in Rome, he adopted art as a profession in 1870. He practised both etching and painting, but his more recent work has been mural decoration. He became A.R.S.A. in 1878, and R.S.A. in 1889. His chief paintings are: ' End of the '45,' 1879; 'Prince Charlie's Parliament,' 1882; 'If thou hadst known,' 1887; 'The Canterbury Pilgrims,' 1889; 'The Ascension;' ' The Life of Jesus of Nazareth,' a series of eighty water-colour pictures completed in 1906. His etchings include: ' Illustrations of Burns' Poems,' 1896; ' The Mill' (after Crome), 1888; ' The Sawyers' (after Millet), 1890; ' Jumping Horse' (after Constable), 1890; ' Admiral Pulido Pareja' (after Velasquez), 1893. Mural paintings: The chancel of St. James's Church, Edinburgh, 1896; A series of historical paintings in the National Portrait Gallery of Scotland, 1900, and another series in the Municipal Buildings, Edinburgh, 1903.

Holguin, a city, Cuba; a healthy hilly region of the prov. of, and 65 m. N.N.W. of, Santiago de Cuba, in the midst of sugar and tobacco plantations. Pop. 8000.

Holics, a market tn. in Neutra prov., 45 m. N. of Pressburg, Hungary. It manufs. earthenware, and carries on sheep-breeding. Pop. 5800.

Holidays, *see* BANK HOLIDAYS.

Holinshed (or **Hollingshead**), **Raphael** (*c.* 1520-80), a chronicler, is said to have been a native of Cheshire. He came to London early in Elizabeth's reign, and was employed as translator in William Wolfe's printing-office, rendering great assistance to Wolfe in the compilation of his *Universal History;* indeed H. wrote most of the descriptions of the British Isles. Wolfe, however, died before the work was completed, and it was consequently abridged, and appeared in 1578 as the *Chronicles of England, Scotland, and Ireland.* A second enlarged edition was published in 1587, but did not meet with the approval of Queen Elizabeth, and in 1808 a reprint of the original was published in six volumes. The *Chronicles* are valuable for their historical information, and are interesting as being the source from which the Elizabethan dramatists drew their plots. Indeed, nearly all Shakespeare's historical plays, as well as *Macbeth, King Lear,* and *Cymbeline* are based on H.'s work.

Holitz, a boot manufacturing tn., 70 m. E. of Prague, Bohemia. Pop. 5929.

Holkar, Mulhar Rao (1693-1766), a Mahratta soldier, born in the Deccan. He was the founder of the family of H., the members of which have always shown themselves hostile to the British rule in India. Before his death he obtained the western half of Malwa, with Indore for its capital. At the end of the century the state was in the hands of Tukoji H., whose son, Jaswant Rao, took an important part in the contest for predominance in the Mahratta confederation. In 1899 a British resident was appointed for Indore, and the government from that time was carried on by a council. *See* INDORE.

Holl, Elias (1573-1636), a German architect, born at Augsburg. After spending some time at Venice he returned to his native town, where he built (1615-18) a town hall, the largest and finest of its kind in Germany. At the time of the Catholic reaction in Augsburg in 1630, H. was destitute, but was reinstated when the town was taken by the Swedes.

Holl, Francis Montague (1845-88), an English portrait painter, born in London. He became a student at the Royal Academy schools in 1861, and first exhibited in 1864. After this date he was a regular contributor to the Royal Academy, but he did not begin portrait-painting until 1876, when he undertook a portrait of Mr. G. C. Richardson. This picture was exhibited in 1878, and H. was elected A.R.A. After this, though not abandoning subject - painting, he devoted himself chiefly to portrait work, and executed in all about 200, some of his best being the Prince of Wales, the Duke of Cambridge, Sir George Stephen, and Mr. W. E. Gladstone. H. was elected R.A. in 1883.

Holland, or **The Netherlands,** a kingdom with a long coast-line lying between 50° 43' and 53° 36' N. lat., and 3° 22' and 7° 16' E. long. It is bounded on the N. and W. by the North Sea, on the S. by Belgium, and on the E. by Prussia. Its greatest length from N. to S. is 195 m., and greatest breadth, 110 m. Its area is 12,648 sq. m. Pop. 5,945,155. The principal towns are Amsterdam (the capital), Rotterdam, The Hague, Utrecht, Groningen, Haarlem, Arnhem, Leyden, Nimeguen, and Tilburg, with populations varying between (Tilburg) 51,600 and (Amsterdam) 573,983. In a small space it is difficult to give an adequate idea of the history, so rich in events that strike the imagination, as that of the people of the Hollow-land, for that is the significance of the name, Holland. ' Here, within a half-submerged territory, a race of wretched ichthyophagi dwelt upon terpen or mounds which they had raised, like beavers, above the almost fluid soil. Here at a later day, the same race chained the tyrant ocean and his mighty streams into subserviency, forcing them to fertilise, to render commodious, to cover with a beneficent network of veins and arteries, and to bind by watery highways with the furthest ends of the world, a country by nature disinherited of its rights. A region, outcast of ocean and earth, wrested at last from both domains their richest treasures. A race, engaged for generations in stubborn conflict with the angry elements, was unconsciously educating itself for its great struggle with the still more savage despotism of man.' In these words Motley sketches the cosmo- and techno-drama of the Dutch folk. The features of the low-lying Dutch landscape are too well known to need description ; but the placid aspect of the waterways studded with the peculiar windmill-pumps for regulating the supply of water, gives no indication of the unmitigated toil that is represented by the dykes and embankments which hold the sea in check and keep canals and rivers from overflowing their banks. The people have a saying that ' God made the sea, but the Hollander made the land,' and, as far as their own land is concerned, that is perfectly true. They have turned the marshes formed by the delta of the Maas, the Rhine, and the Scheldt, into arable land and have reclaimed vast tracts from the sea. The lands thus reclaimed are called polders, and are highly valued. The maintenance of the canals which run like a network all over the country, linking up river and lake, and the reclamation and drainage of the land, are the work of a special public department called the Waterstaat, and involve the country in an expenditure of considerably more than £500,000 a year. Locks were in use on canals early in the 14th century. The climate is not unlike that of England, though the temperature is lower in winter and higher in summer.

The inhabitants of the Netherlands are descendants of a people called by the Romans the Batavi, who lived on an island between the two branches of the Rhine, and the Frisians who dwelt further N. They are described as a hardy, hospitable, faithful folk, who hunted, fished, or led a pastoral life. Their religion was simple, and they were chaste and honourable. The Roman rule lasted until the 4th century, when the Franks overran the country. Charlemagne's dominion in the 8th century extended to the Netherlands, and he built a palace at Nimeguen on the Waal. Upon the establishment of the feudal system the country was divided into small sovereignties. In the year 922 Dirk became Count of Holland and the other Netherland provinces, such as Namur, Hainault, Limburg, and Zutphen, were divided between various barons and counts, autocratic rulers, owning allegiance to the dukes or earls of Lorraine, Brabant, and Flanders. Holland, Zealand, Utrecht, Overijssel, Groningen, Drenthe, and Friesland, which were afterwards to form the United States of the Netherlands, were chiefly under the rule of the counts of Holland and the bishop of Utrecht. It was during the ' five dismal centuries of feudalism ' that cities began to spring into importance and the rise of a world-wide commerce began. In 1384 the Netherlands became the property of the Duke of Burgundy, and a little more than a century later was united to Spain under Charles V. The struggle for freedom and for civic and religious independence that was to last so long, had already begun and came to a crisis in the reign of Philip II. of Spain in the middle of the 16th century, the immediate causes being the imposition of the Inquisition with all its horrors upon the people, and the maintenance of a standing army. William, Prince of Orange, known as William the Silent, was the king's lieutenant in Holland, Zealand, and Utrecht, and to his devotion to the cause of the rights and liberties of the people, the republic ultimately owed its existence. It would cover too much space to give even an outline of the story of the war waged by the burghers against political and religious tyranny. By the capture of Briel in 1572 Spain received the first

reverse, and the people who had been ground into dust began to hope. In 1579 the union of Utrecht was formed, by which the northern provinces banded themselves together to resist Spain, and in 1581 the Netherlands declared their freedom. William's assassination in 1584 did not prevent the continued success of the people against the efforts of Philip to regain the lost provinces. He was beaten again and again at sea, and his successor was obliged to sue for a cessation of arms for twelve years. These years enabled the Dutch to recoup themselves for losses by attention to trade, but their dearly won freedom from outside religious persecution did not prevent them from internal religious strife and persecution. The war, renewed after the armistice, was continued until 1648, when by the treaty of Munster Spain recognised the independence of the Netherlands. While this protracted struggle was in progress, the Dutch were making themselves masters of the sea. Their ships were in every ocean. The East India Company, which led to the foundation of their Indian empire, was started in 1602. Amsterdam, which instituted the first Stock Exchange or Bourse, in 1532, had become one of the richest cities in the world. Trade brought rivals, and two great naval wars were fought against England in 1652-54, and again in 1664-67 in which the English admirals found themselves about equally matched by De Ruyter, Van Tromp, and others —the former, inflicting upon England the indignity of sailing up the Medway and the Thames, destroying ships, in 1667. Then followed the war in which France and England were united against the republic ; and which, but for the Dutch prowess at sea, might have ended disastrously for the Netherlands. The political struggle between the De Witt faction and that of the Prince of Orange, ended by the terrible death of the brothers De Witt and the triumph of William of Orange who secured the friendliness of England by his marriage with Mary of York. This led to his subsequent elevation to the throne of England, under the title of William III. English and Dutch then fought side by side in inflicting defeat upon Louis XIV. of France. The treaty of Utrecht in 1713 concluded the war, and also the period of Holland's greatness as a world power. The close of the 18th century saw the Netherlands overrun by Napoleon's troops and paying tribute to France. Louis Bonaparte was made king of Holland in 1806, but resigned four years later and the country was attached to the French empire. During these changes the Orange family had been obliged to make their escape, but on the fall of Napoleon they were recalled, and the northern and southern provinces were formed into the kingdom of the Netherlands. This union was not satisfactory ; there were temperamental and religious differences between the people that were not easy to harmonise. In 1830, therefore, the southern provinces seceded and Belgium was formed into a separate kingdom. The principal events in the history of the kingdom since then are, briefly, the following : In 1840 William, for political reasons, abdicated in favour of his son who, in 1848, granted a new constitution to the people. In 1862 the slaves in the Dutch West Indian colonies were set free. The question of the Duchy of Luxemburg (from 1815 a title of the king of Holland) was settled in 1868 by making it an independent state. In 1872 a treaty was signed with Great Britain in respect to the sphere of influence of the two countries in the Indian Archipelago. In 1887 the Dutch obtained from their sovereign a new constitution by which the electorate was largely increased. In 1890 the present Queen Wilhelmina, then only a child, came to the throne. Her husband is Prince Henry, Duke of Mecklenburg-Schwerin, and the present heiress to the throne is a princess born in 1909. The first Peace Conference, held at The Hague in 1898, marks an important stage in the development of the idea of inter- national peace. The government of Holland is a limited monarchy under a constitution. The king selects ministers who sign with him all decrees. Legislation is in the hands of the States-general, a two-chambered parliament. The Second Chamber of 100 members is elected for four years by direct suffrage; the First Chamber is elected by provincial councils every nine years. Members are paid £166 a year, with travelling and incidental expences. During the years of her greatness, and while she was fighting against enormous odds for political and religious liberty, Holland added many names to the roll of the world's illustrious men. To mention a few, among explorers we find the names of Hudson Heemskerck, Schouten, Lemaire, and Tasman ; in science, Van Helmont, Huyghens, and Boer- have ; in literature, Erasmus, Grotius, Vossius, Burmann, Gronovius; in art, Rubens, Rembrandt, Van Dyck, Hobbema Potter. The liberty of the press brought much foreign printing to Holland, and the *Gazette de Leyde*, which distributed news to all parts of the world, was in existence from 1680- 1814. The language of Holland,

though akin to both English and German, has yet a separate identity. In the 11th century the language, which was afterwards modified into modern Dutch, was spoken in a far wider area than that now occupied by Holland and Belgium, and old Dutch is still to be heard among villagers in the N. of France. Early in the 15th century literary clubs were founded by the Rederijkers, or lovers of letters, who met together to study literature and plays. To these clubs modern Dutch owes its origin. Grammars began to be written, and efforts were made to clear the language of foreign importations. In this connection the club formed at Muiden by Hooft had great influence. The 17th century, as in so much else, saw Holland's greatest literary output. Vondel's plays (1587- 1679) are still staged. Cats was another popular poet. Erasmus and other learned disputants wrote in Latin, the medium of international intellectual intercourse. In the 18th century the names of Leith, the poet, Bilderdijk, the historian, and Helmers stand out. Pictures of 18th century Dutch life have been preserved in the novels of two women, Mesdames Deken and Bekker. Some 19th cen- tury writers are Tollens, Van Beers, Beets, Da Costa, Schimmel, Hofdijk, and Van Lennep ; and among poets are Potgieter, Ter Haar, Heige, Ten Kate, and others have produced admirable work. H. Conscience, Miss Wallis, Mrs. B. Toussaint, and Douwes Dekker are among well- known novelists, but of present-day writers perhaps the best known in England are Maarten Maartens and Maeterlinck. Dutch is written and spoken in parts of Belgium as well as in Holland. Since 1900 education has been compulsory. The ancient uni- versities of Leyden, Utrecht, and Groningen have recently been supple- mented by a municipal university at Amsterdam. There are naval and military colleges at Breda, and technical colleges at Delft—noted in the 16th century for its pottery. The people of Holland have many charac- teristics in common with the British. They are a freedom-loving people, and have proved themselves as a nation and as colonists willing to make great sacrifices to gain or retain liberty. Their colonial possessions, like those of Great Britain, are vastly out of proportion to the size of the mother country. Their E. Indian pos- sessions include Java and Madura, Sumatra, the Moluccas, Celebes, Timor, parts of Borneo, and New Guinea ; in the W. Indies, Surinam, and Curaçao are their principal pos- sessions. The Boer nation are de- scendants of 16th-century Dutch colonists in S. Africa. The Dutch have all the courageous qualities of sea-faring folk, and are inventive and industrious, though the conservatism of their dairy farmers at one time cost their country the title of the ' dairy of Europe,' which has now passed to Denmark, and at the present time Holland, once the greatest market for butter, exports the largest quantities of its substitute——margarine. Agriculture is the most important industry. The bulk of the land is farmed by peasant proprietors, and about two-thirds of the holdings are under 25 acres, and a great trade is done in sheep, cattle, and horses. Cheese is a staple export—the round red balls being known all over the world. Horticulture is largely carried on at Haarlem. In the middle ages the Netherlands were famous for their great silk manufactures, and silken fabrics, as well as linen, cotton, and woollen goods, are exported; other manufactures are paper, leather, and glass. The large supply of potters' clay in the country was responsible for the renown of Dutch pottery which is once more on the up grade. The many breweries and distilleries of Holland produce beer, gin (Hollands), and liqueurs in large quantities; and sugar refining, as well as the manufacture of beetroot sugar and salt, give employment to numbers of people. Great Britain imports immense quantities of margarine as well as butter, cheese, and sugar. Cocoa is manufactured in enormous quantities in Rotterdam, Amsterdam, and other towns. The diamond-cutting trade was once almost the monopoly of Amsterdam, and had at least 10,000 people engaged in it; it is, however, a diminishing industry. The fisheries give occupation to many thousands and are estimated to yield at least £3,000,000 a year. Herring-fishing is carried on in the North Sea extensively, and salt herrings are largely exported. Oysters are also taken in large quantities and from five to six million are exported annually to England.

The army is composed partly of volunteers and partly of men drawn by lot for five years' service, and is kept on a peace footing of 34,000, and a war footing of 175,000. The colonial army numbers nearly 40,000, of whom about 14,000 are Europeans. The Schutterij are a kind of soldier-policeman who, in times of war can be mobilised. The building of Dreadnoughts for the increase of the navy is now under consideration. The railways belong to the state, but are worked by a company which pays a certain proportion of profits to the treasury. The national debt is nearly

£97,000,000. Holland and Belgium are always classed together in the popular mind, and at one time the term Netherlands applied to both. The following short quotation from the historian Motley may throw some light on the fact that the inhabitants of the British Isles, though composed of varying races, because they possessed in a peculiar degree the faculty of adaptation, have known no looking back either in prosperity or culture; while the Netherlands, in no way behind the British in the 17th century, ceased, later, to count as a world power : ' The population of the country was partly Celtic, partly German. Of these two elements, dissimilar in their tendencies and always difficult to blend, the Netherland people has ever been compounded. A certain fatality of history has perpetually helped to separate still more widely these constituents, instead of detecting and stimulating the elective affinities which existed. Religion, too, upon all great historical occasions, has acted as the most powerful of dissolvents. Otherwise, had so many valuable and contrasted characteristics been early fused into a whole, it would be difficult to show a race more richly endowed by nature for dominion and progress than the Belgo-Germanic people.'

Consult the annual reports of British consuls in the Netherlands ; the works of Montégut, Esquiros, Henri Havard, D'Amicis, Meldrum (Holland and the Hollanders, 1899), and Beatrix Jungmann (1904); also the historical writings of Prescott, Motley (Rise of the Dutch Republic), Thorold Rogers, and of the Dutch historians, Th. Juste, Bilderdijk, Fruin, Arend, Nuijens, Hofdijk, and P. J. Blok ; for literature, J. Ten Brink (1877), Jouckbloet, (1873) and Van Vloten (1879); and for the Dutch school of painting, see Kugler's handbook of The German, Flemish, and Dutch Schools, 1898; Martin Conway's Early Flemish Artists, and Van Dyke's Old Dutch and Flemish Masters, 1896.

Holland, a city in Ottawa co., Michigan, on the S. bank of the Black R., 25 m. S.W. of Grand Rapids. It is the seat of Hope College (1865), and of the Western Theological Seminary. It has large tanneries, beet-sugar, basket, and pickle factories, and carries on an extensive trade in grain. The town was founded by Dutch settlers in 1847, and received its charter in 1867. The population, in which the Dutch element predominates, in 1910 was 10,490.

Holland, a coarse variety of linen, unbleached, and often dyed brown. Its texture is strong, and it washes very well. H. was formerly fine linen manufactured in the Netherlands; hence its name.

Holland, Baron, see FOX, HENRY RICHARD VASSALL.

Holland, Henry (1746–1806), an English architect, is likely soon to be forgotten, as neither details of his life nor illustration of his best work have survived even to our time. He designed the portico of Carlton House in the massive and ornate Roman-Corinthian style, the Pavilion at Brighton, and the old Drury Lane Theatre, none of which to-day are standing. The India House, Leadenhall Street, is another example of his florid and pseudo-classical style.

Holland, Sir Henry Scott (1788–1873), an English physician and writer, born at Knutsford, Cheshire. After graduating at Edinburgh University (1811) he travelled on the Continent, and settled down to practise in London in 1816, in which year he was elected F.R.S. He was appointed physician-in-ordinary to the Prince Consort in 1840, and to Queen Victoria in 1852. His publications include: *Travels in Albania*, 1815; *Medical Notes and Reflections*, 1839; *Chapters on Mental Physiology*, 1852; and *Recollections of Past Life*, 1871.

Holland, Henry Scott (b. 1848), a clergyman of the Church of England. He was educated at Eton and Balliol College, Oxford. He entered holy orders in 1872, and became canon of Truro (1882-84) and of St. Paul's (1884-1910). He is now regius professor of divinity at Oxford and editor of the *Commonwealth*. His publications include : *Logic and Life*, 1882 ; *Creed and Character*, 1887 ; *Personal Studies*, 1905 ; *Vital Values*, 1906 ; and *Fibres of Faith*, 1910.

Holland, Josiah Gilbert (1819-81), an American man of letters, born at Belchertown, Massachusetts. In early life he studied medicine, but in 1848 was appointed superintendent of schools in Richmond, Virginia. In the following year he joined the staff of the Springfield *Republican*, and in 1870 he became editor and part-proprietor of *Scribner's Monthly*, to which he contributed serially *Arthur Bonnicastle* (1873) and other novels. He also wrote a *Life of Lincoln*, 1865. *See* Mrs. Plunkett's *Josiah Gilbert Holland*, 1894.

Holland, Sir Nathaniel Dance- (1743-1811), an English painter, a son of George Dance, who designed the Mansion House, London. After working in Hayman's studio, he spent some months in Rome. His name in art was soon made, for at twenty-five he was elected a member of the Royal Academy, which had just come into existence. A few of his portraits,

landscapes, and historical pictures are scattered among private collections.

Holland, Philemon (1552 – 1637), called ' the translator-general of his age,' born at Chelmsford, Essex. Having obtained his M.D. degree at Cambridge (1591), he practised medicine at Coventry, and became headmaster of the Free School there (1628). His fame rests on his translations of Pliny's *Natural History* (1601), Plutarch's *Morals*, Xenophon's *Cyropædia*, and other classical works. He also published an English version of Camden's *Britannia*, 1610.

Holland, Thomas Erskine (b. 1835), an English jurist, born at Brighton, and educated at Balliol and Magdalen colleges, Oxford. In 1874 he was appointed Vinerian reader in English law, and professor of international law and diplomacy at Oxford. He sat on the Royal Commission of 1903-5 to inquire into the supply of food in time of war, and was sent as plenipotentiary to the Geneva Conference of 1906. He belongs to many learned societies, and has written weighty volumes on jurisprudence. His publications include : *Elements of Jurisprudence*, 1880 (11th ed. 1910); *Institutes of Justinian*, 1873-81 ; *Studies in International Law*, 1898 ; *Laws of War on Land*, 1908 ; *Proposed Changes in the Law of Prize*, 1911 ; and *Zouche's Jus Feciale*, 1911.

Holland, New, a seaport in the estuary of the Humber, Lincolnshire, England. There are docks, and a steam ferry to Hull, which is opposite.

Holland, North, a prov. of the Netherlands, comprising the peninsula between the Zuyder Zee and the North Sea and the islands on the N. side, and bounded on the S. by the provinces of South H. and Utrecht. Area 1070 sq. m. The inhabitants are chiefly engaged in cattle-raising, agriculture, and gardening. There is considerable trade in dairy produce, and linen is manufactured in the towns. Much of the land is below sea-level, and there are several canals, notably the North Holland Canal and the North Sea Canal. The chief towns are Haarlem (capital) and Amsterdam. Pop. 1,107,693.

Holland, Parts of, an administrative division of Lincolnshire, which includes most of the fens in the S.E. Area 268,992 acres. Pop. (1911) 82,849.

Holland, Prussian, a tn. of E. Prussia, Germany, 13 m. S.E. of Elbing. There are tanneries, and woollen and linen goods are manufactured. Pop. 4750.

Holland, South, a prov. of the Netherlands, bounded on the N. by North Holland, on the E. by Utrecht and North Brabant, on the S. by

Zealand, and on the W. by the North Sea. Area 1166 sq. m. The chief industry is agriculture, and there is considerable shipping trade. The chief towns are Rotterdam (capital), The Hague, Dordrecht, and Leyden. Pop. 1,390,744.

Holland-American Line was established at Rotterdam in 1872. It possesses thirteen steamers, with a total tonnage of 126,000. Of its boats the *Potsdam* (1900) and the *Noordam* (1902) have a speed of 15 knots, the *Nieuw Amsterdam* (1906) a tonnage of 17,149 and a speed of 16 knots, while the *Rotterdam* (1908) has a speed of 17 knots and a tonnage of 24,149.

Hollands, *see* GIN.

Hollandsch Diep, a sheet of water at the mouths of the rivers Waal (Rhine) and Maas, between the provinces of N. Brabant, S. Holland, and the island of Overflakkee. It was formed by the great inundation in 1421. To the W. it is named Haringvliet.

Hollar, Wenceslaus, or **Wenzel** (1607-77), a Bohemian etcher, born at Prague and died in London. He studied at Frankfort, Strassburg, and Cologne, and in the last-named city attracted the notice of the Earl of Arundel, who brought him to England (1637). During the Civil War he took refuge for eight years in Antwerp, but afterwards returned to London. He worked with unceasing industry for his publishers, who took advantage of his poverty and his ignorance of the country to underpay him disgracefully. He illustrated Ogilvy's *Homer* and *Vergil*, made etchings of the works of Holbein, Titian, and Van Dyck, and executed some beautiful ' Views of London.' *See* study by Parthey (1853-58), with catalogue of his plates.

Holles, Denzil, Lord (1599-1680), an English statesman, is conspicuous among a host of good and true men, and at a time which was politically a period of *Sturm und Drang*, for his public spirit and his single and high-minded aims. An aristocrat by birth, he was always a staunch Whig in principle, and accordingly averse from Cromwell and his rough-riding over time-hallowed institutions. As member of parliament he supported the impeachment of Buckingham (1627), forcibly held the speaker in his chair till Sir John Eliot's protestations were passed (1629) assisted in the impeachment of Laud (1641), endeavoured to impeach Cromwell as an incendiary (1644), and tried to compass the dissolution of the parliamentary troops (1647). Thus, as a Presbyterian and a moderate, he bravely spoke for

freedom; in 1629 he suffered a year's imprisonment, and in 1649 only escaped formal expulsion by Colonel Pride by fleeing to France. After the Restoration he served King Charles.

Holleschau, a tn., 40 m. E.N.E. of Brün, Moravia, Austria. The chief industry is in cloth and linen. Pop. 5954.

Hollingshead, John (1827-1904), a theatrical manager, was for many years a journalist and a contributor to *Household Words* and the *Cornhill*. He became a theatrical manager in 1865, and three years later opened the Gaiety Theatre, London, which he controlled until his retirement in 1888. During this period he devoted himself mainly to the production of what he called ' the sacred lamp of burlesque,' and in his productions appeared such ' stars ' as Toole, Edward Terry, Fred Leslie, and Nellie Farren. He acquired a large fortune, but lost it in later days by unfortunate investments. He published : *My Lifetime*, 1895, and *Gaiety Chronicles*, 1898.

Hollingworth, a par. and vil., Cheshire, England, 3½ m. S.E. of Stalybridge. The spinning and printing of cotton fabrics is carried on. There are iron foundries. Pop. (1911) 2581.

Hollinwood, an eccles. dist., par. of Prestwich, and vil., 1½ m. S.W. of Oldham, Lancashire, England. Pop. (1911) 9915.

Holloway, a dist., par. of Islington, N. London, England. The old Copenhagen Fields have been occupied by the cattle market since 1855. At the N. end of Camden Road is the City Prison (for women), a castellated edifice of 1850.

Holloway College, The Royal, situated at Mt. Lee, Egham, Surrey, England. It was founded in 1883 by the late Thomas Holloway, the proprietor of the noted pills and ointment. Its object is to supply a suitable education for women of the middle class. The students are prepared for university degrees, and must read for honours. The building, which is constructed in the style of the French Renaissance, was opened by Queen Victoria in 1886, and contains a fine collection of paintings by Constable, Landseer, Millais, Frith, and other famous artists.

Holly, or *Ilex aquifolium*, a species of Aquifoliaceæ, found very commonly in Britain. It is cultivated both as an ornamental evergreen tree and as a hedge-plant on account of its dense and prickly foliage. The timber is fine-grained, heavy, and compact, and is valued by both the turner and the mathematical instrument maker ; the flowers are small and white; the berries are scarlet and glossy, giving the plant a brilliant appearance in late autumn. They are very poisonous, producing purgative and violent emetic effects.

Hollyhock, the popular name for the species of Malvaceæ, known botanically as *Althœa rosea,* a near ally of the marsh-mallow. It is a hardy perennial, herbaceous in habit, and is frequently cultivated in Britain, especially in the gardens of country cottages.

Holm, Peter Edvard (*b.* 1833), a Danish historian, born at Copenhagen. He was tutor at the university there (1865), professor of history (1868), and president of the Danish Historical Union (1882-96). His chief works are : *De græske Undersaatters Stilung under de romerske Kejsere indtil Caracalla,* 1860; *Danmarks Politik under den svensk-russiske Krig,* 1788-90, 1868 ; *Danmarks Politiske Stillung under den Franske Revolution,* 1869 ; *Danmark-Norges Udenrigske Histoire,* 1791-1807, 1875 ; *Danmark-Norges Indre Historie under Enevælden fra* 1660-1814 (4 vols.), 1885-93 ; and important contributions to Steenstrupp's *Danmarks Riges Historie.*

Holman, James (1786-1857), 'The Blind Traveller,' a native of Exeter. Being compelled through total loss of sight to quit the navy, he travelled alone through the greater portion of Europe (1819-24) and round the world (1827-32). He published interesting journals of his travels.

Holmby House, more correctly **Holdenby House,** 6½ m. N.W. of Northampton, a Tudor mansion of which Sir Christopher Hatton was the architect. It was bought by James I., and Charles I. was imprisoned here for four months (1647). In 1652 it was dismantled.

Holm Cultrum, Abbey Holme, or **Abbey Town,** on the Solway Firth, Cumberland, England. It manufs. agricultural implements. A Cistercian monastery was established here (*c.* 1150). Pop. (1911) 4494.

Holmes, Oliver Wendell (1809-94), an American writer, graduated at Harvard University in 1829, studied medicine for two years in Paris, and took his M.D. degree in Cambridge, Massachusetts (1836). He continued to practise as a doctor till 1849, and from 1847 till 1882 delighted the medical students of Harvard with his anatomical lectures, which were conspicuous, no less than his essays on homœopathy, etc., for their vivacity, unfailing freshness, and humanity. At the invitation of James Russell Lowell, Dr. Holmes collaborated with him in the issue of a new magazine, *The Atlantic Monthly,* 1875. To

this he contributed his *Autocrat* papers (1858), whose sweet and guileless merriment and informing spirit of New England fascinated and cheered even the most harassed Americans, achieving in truth just that result which the *Spectator* papers had in England a century and a half before. There followed *The Professor* (1860) and *The Poet* (1872). His novels, the best of which are *Elsie Venner,* 1861, and *The Guardian Angel,* though they have been described as merely monologues of H. himself, illustrate in the most intimate and charming manner the New England life of the day, and likewise

OLIVER WENDELL HOLMES

the author's gift for picturesque description and the elasticity and force of his temperament. One critic has written that in his many songs and occasional verse he distills ' the quintessence of Yankee humour,' whilst such lyrics as *The Last Leaf* exhibit ' that atmospheric quality of humour ' which is blended with pathos like the sun and shower of an April morning. His *Life of Emerson* appeared in 1885. From boyhood H. enjoyed all the blessings of good fellowship and fortune, and among such distinguished companions as Emerson, Lowell, Whittier, and Longfellow was esteemed a most brilliant and entertaining talker, besides a master in mockery and happy illustration.

Holmes, Sir Richard Rivington (1835-1911), an author and artist, worked as an assistant in the British Museum from 1854, and in 1868 joined the expedition to Abyssinia as archæologist. Librarian at Windsor

Castle from 1870 to 1903, he was sergeant-at-arms to Queen Victoria and King Edward VII. His water-colours were hung in London galleries, and his illustrations embellished Mrs. Oliphant's *Makers of Venice*. In 1893 he published his book on artistic book-binding. Four years later his *Queen Victoria* appeared.

Holmes, Sir Robert (1622-92), an English admiral, became governor of Sandown Castle in the Isle of Wight (1660), and seems to have owed his naval preferments chiefly to the patronage of the Duke of York. In 1663 he captured a number of Dutch factories in Africa, and in the follow-ing year crossed the Atlantic and seized their settlement of New Am-sterdam (renamed New York). His destruction of over 100 richly-laden East Indiamen (1666) was his most conspicuous service in the second Dutch War, whilst in the third (1672) he made a gallant effort against great odds to stop the progress of the Dutch fleet up the Channel, and took a prominent part in the battle of Solebay. H. once seconded Bucking-ham in a duel, and was disliked by Pepys as ' a rash, proud coxcomb.'

Holmes, Thomas (*b.* 1846), late police court missionary, North London Police Court, born in Walsall. He was an ironworker for many years, but having to give up his trade in consequence of an accident, taught for a time in various schools. In 1885 he was police court missionary at Lambeth Police Court, but was trans-ferred to the North London court in 1889. He has done much to improve the conditions under which home workers live, and has established a Home of Rest for women engaged in the home industries as well as the Home Workers' Aid Association. He has published : *Pictures and Problems from London Police Courts ; Known to the Police ; London's Underworld ; The Psycology and Crime.*

Holmfirth, a tn., 6 m. S. of Hudders-field, W. Riding, Yorkshire, England. There are cloth and wool mills and stone quarries. The Bilberry reser-voir here burst in 1852 ; eighty-one people were drowned and much damage to property was done Pop. (1911) 9248.

Holocaine, a local anæsthetic. It is prepared by condensation from phe-nacetin and paraphenetidin, and has an action somewhat similar to that of cocaine. While useful for operations on the nose and eye, it has properties which make it unsuitable for inhala-tion or injection under the skin.

Holofernes, called in Judith ii. 4, ' the chief captain of the army of Nebuchadnezzar.' The book of Judith (apocryphal) tells the story of how the Jewish maiden saved her nation by assassinating H. before the walls of Bethulia, *i.e.* Jerusalem. The story is extremely legendary, and it is quite clear that H. cannot be connected with the historical accounts of Nebu-chadnezzar's reign. His identification is extremely difficult, a large number of suggestions having been made. Many would connect him with Oro-fernes, who in 158 B.C. was king of the Cappadocians.

Holograph, in Scottish law, a H. deed or will is one written wholly in the granter's own hand. Such an instrument is admissible in evidence without proof of attestation, because it is unquestionably the strongest proof and a document least capable of imitation. But the presumption of authenticity may, of course, be re-butted by proof to the contrary. H. deeds bind the granter as effectually as if executed with the statutory solemnities essential to other deeds ; but such effect endures only for twenty years. Deeds in which all the material parts are in the granter's handwriting, or in which what is not in his handwriting is by the deed formally adopted by the granter, have the same effect as H. deeds. H. wills, even if unattested, are pre-sumed to have been executed at the date upon which they are expressed to have been made, but it is otherwise with H. deeds. *See* Erskine's *Prin-ciples of the Law of Scotland.*

Holoptychius, the name of a genus of fossil ganoid fishes belonging to the order Crossopterygii, family Holop-tychidæ, and found in the Devonian strata.

Holosteum, a genus of caryophyl-laceous plants, occurs in N. lands. *H. umbellatum* is the only one of the half-dozen species which is British.

Holothurian (Gk. ὅλος, whole, and θυροειδής, like a door), the name given to any individual of Holo-thuroidea, a class of Echinodermata commonly called the sea-cucumbers. It is an elongated, worm-like animal with a ring of about twenty large retractile tentacles surrounding the mouth; these tentacles are modified tube-feet, and contain an extension of the water-vascular system. The ambulacral feet are furnished with a suctorial disc, and the ambulatory papillæ are pointed at the ends, with elementary or no calcareous plates. The water-vascular system consists of a circular vessel with two append-ages, the polian vesicle and the stone canal, and five radial vessels. Holo-thuroidea are divided into two orders, Actinopoda, in which tentacles are always present but feet and papillæ may be absent, and Paractinopoda, in which tube-feet, ambulacral papillæ, respiratory trees and cuvierian organs are absent. The former contains the family Holothuriidæ, with the British genus *Holothuria* ; Synallactidæ, whose species have a flattened body ; Elaspodidæ, with a more or less ventral mouth and elongated body ; Pelagothuriidæ, pelagic forms with a cylindrical body ; Molpadiidæ, burrowers in mud or clay ; Cucumariidæ, with the familiar British genera, *Cucumaria*, *Thyone*, *Psolus*, and *Phyllophorus*. The order Paractinopoda contains the single family Synaptidæ, whose typical genus *Synapta* is known on British coasts, *S. inhærens* and *S. digitata* being the commonest species.

Holst, Hermann Eduard von (1841-1904), a German historical writer, born in Fellin, Livonia. He studied at Dorpat and Heidelberg. In 1867 he emigrated to New York and became assistant editor of the *Deutsch-Amerik. Konversations-Lexikon*. He returned to Germany and became professor of history at the University of Strassburg and later of Freiburg. From 1892-99 he was professor of history at Chicago University. His books include *Constitutional and Political History of the U.S.A.* and *French Revolution Tested by Mirabeau's Career*.

Holstein, *see* SCHLESWIG-HOLSTEIN.

Holsten, Karl Christian Johann (1825-98), a German theologian, studied at Leipzig, Berlin, and Rostock, became teacher of religion in Rostock Gymnasium (1852), and later lectured as professor of N.T. studies at Bern (1870) and Heidelberg (1876). A member of the Tübingen school, he adopted the attitude of Baur towards the supposed divergence between the teaching of Peter and Paul. *Zum Evangelium des Paulus und Petrus* (1867) and a treatise on the synoptic gospels (1886) show him an authority on biblical exegesis.

Holstenius (or Holste), Luc (1596-1661), a German scholar, made the acquaintance of Peiresc in Paris, and was by him introduced to Cardinal Barberini, the pope's nuncio. The cardinal became his life-long patron, made him his librarian, and probably was the means of his obtaining a similar post in the Vatican. A convert to Roman Catholicism himself, Holste was despatched with others to receive Queen Christiana's abjuration of Protestantism at Innspruck. His writings were chiefly commentaries on obscure classical authors.

Holsterhausen, a former com. of Prussia in Westphalia, now incorporated with Eickel. There are coal mines. Pop. of Eickel (1910) 33,524.

Holston, a river of the United States. Rising with two branches in south-western Virginia, it flows with a south-westerly course into the N.E. of Tennessee, where the forks unite at Kingston. At a spot some 4 m. E. of Knoxville is the confluence of this river with the French Broad, after which their united streams are called the Tennessee. Length 350 m.

Holsworthy, a par. and market tn., Devonshire, England, 17 m. W.N.W. of Okehampton. It trades in agricultural produce, and has an important cattle market. Pop. (1911) 1499.

Holt : 1. A clean and prettily-situated market tn., 9 m. W. by S. of Cromer, on the Midland and Great Northern Railway, in Norfolk, England. Pop. (1911) 2104. 2. A vil. on the Dee, 5 m. E.N.E. of Wrexham in Denbighshire, Wales. Pop. (1911) 1144.

Holt, Sir John (1642-1710), a lord chief justice of England, seems to have sown his wild oats at Oriel College, Oxford. Called to the bar in 1663, he appeared as counsel for the defence in a series of state trials, and William III. rewarded his ability and zeal by making him lord chief justice (1689). H. was noted in court for his courtesy towards prisoners, his aloofness from all party prejudice, and his exceptional moral courage.

Holtei, Karl Eduard von (1798-1880), a German actor and author, was a man of versatile talent and varied experience. Having volunteered in the Prussian army and studied law in Breslau, he became an actor, and appeared as Mortimer in Schiller's *Maria Stuart*. His popular vaudeville *Die Wiener in Berlin* was produced in 1824, and his successful play *Lenore* in 1829. Meanwhile, he toured with theatrical companies at home and abroad, conducted theatres at Vienna and Riga, and won golden opinions by truly dramatic recitals from Shakespeare and his own poems. These latter reveal his natural gift for lyrical outpouring; his *Schlesische Gedichte* (1830) had reached their twentieth edition in 1893. Finally, H. has left behind him three novels and eight volumes of fascinating autobiography (1843-50).

Holtzendorff, Joachim Wilhelm Franz Philipp von (1829-89), a German criminologist, attended the universities of Bonn and Heidelberg, and finally graduated in law at Berlin (1852). Privat docent in 1857, he was three years later appointed professor extraordinary, but his advanced and enlightened political opinions long hindered his preferment. In 1873, however, he became head of the faculty of jurisprudence at Munich University and held his chair until his death. An authority on criminal law, he is esteemed also as the editor of many invaluable legal compendia, to wit *Handbuch des deutschen Strafrechts* (1871-77) and *Handbuch des Völkerrechts auf Grundlage europäischer Staatspraxis* (1885-90), and as the author of a series of independent treatises, such as *Die Principien der Politik*, 1869.

Holtzmann, Adolf (1810 – 70), a celebrated Germanist and philologist, born at Carlsruhe. He studied theology in Berlin, Old German philology in Munich, and Sanskrit in Paris. In 1852 he was appointed to the chair of German literature and language, and of Sanskrit at Heidelberg University. His publications include : *Kelten und Germanen*, 1855; *Untersuchungen über das Nibelungen-lied*, 1854; *Deutsche Mythologie* (ed. by Holder), 1874.

Holtzmann, Heinrich Julius (1832-1910), a German theologian, a son of the eminent philologist, Adolf H., Professor of theology at Heidelberg from 1861 to 1874, he afterwards accepted the same chair at the University of Strassburg. His reputation as a critic and scholar rests on his exegetical works anent the N.T., and especially on the Johannine books (1890), the synoptic gospels (1889), and the Acts of the Apostles (1901). He upheld that both Matthew and Luke based their narratives on that of Mark. At first somewhat conservative of older theories, he later became a leading representative of the advanced and modern school. Another of his critical publications was the *Lehrbuch der neutestamentlichen Theologie*, 1897.

Holub, Emil (1847 – 1902), a Bohemian traveller, born at Holitz, Bohemia. He took his M.D. degree at Prague University, and went out to S. Africa in 1872. He travelled over various parts of the country, collecting valuable natural history specimens. His books are : *Die Kolonisation Afrikas*, 1881-82; *Sieben Jahre in Südafrica*, 1872-79, 1881 (Eng. trans. 1881); and *Von der Kapstadt ins Land der Maschukulumbo*, 1888-90.

Holy Alliance, a league ratified at Paris in 1816 after the downfall of Napoleon. Alexander I. of Russia and the sovereigns of Austria and Prussia made a solemn covenant that in all matters, both of domestic and foreign policy, they would be guided by the principles of Christian ethics. The main issue of the alliance, one of whose first aims was the preservation of peace, was, ironically enough, the suppression of the popular movement for freedom and equality, which was at that time a growing menace to royal prerogative and despotism in

every western nation. The league, which was discountenanced in this country as an insidious check on true liberty, soon died a natural death. At the time of its formation, Alexander was under the sway of Madame de Krüdener, the mystic.

Holy Coat of Trèves, a famous relic of the 11th century cathedral of SS. Peter and Helena in Trèves, Rhenish Prussia. Legend says that it was brought by the Empress Helena from Palestine, but the first reference to it is in a monkish manuscript of 1106. It is reputed to be the ' seamless coat ' of Christ, but is now little more than ' connected fragmentary particles ' of cloth. In 1512 the Pope sanctioned its exhibition once in seven years, and ever since it has been a source of income to the Church. This relic, like others, is believed to cause miracles and wonder-cures, and in 1891, when it was on view for the first time since 1844, was the object of pilgrimage for almost two million people.

Holycross, a par. and vil., co. Tipperary, Ireland, 20 m. N.W. of Tipperary ; much visited for its magnificent ruins of a Cistercian abbey. The district is very fertile, and there are good pastures. Pop. 1000.

Holy Cross Mountain, a peak, 14,000 ft. in height, of the Saguache range and branch of the Rockies, Colorado, U.S.A., in Eagle co., 15 m. N.W. of Leadville. Its name is taken from two huge snow - filled ravines which have the appearance of a cross.

Holy Grail, The, *see* GRAIL and IDYLLS OF THE KING.

Holy-grass, a term applied to several species of *Hierochloë*, a genus of scented graminaceous plants; it is given particularly to *H. borealis*, and *H. odorata*. The name arose from an old custom, prevailing in some parts of Europe, of strewing these grasses before church-doors on feast-days.

Holyhead, a seaport and market tn. on H. Bay, Anglesey, N. Wales. It is the most important mail-packet station for Ireland. It possesses a fine harbour, with an area of 267 acres, begun in 1846 and finished in 1873, and a breakwater 1½ m. long. This refuge is extended by 400 acres of roadstead. There is a wireless station and a fine old embattled church (St. Cybi). Pop. (1911) 10,638.

Holyhead Island, or Holy Isle (8 m. long by 3½ m. broad), a rocky and barren island, W. of Anglesey, N. Wales, separated from it by a sandy causeway. Tre Arddur on Penrhos Bay is a seaside resort.

Holy Island (ancient *Lindisfarne*), an island off E. coast of Northumberland, England, connected with the mainland at low tide. It is chiefly noted for its ruins of sacred edifices. St. Aidan founded here a priory in 634 with which later St. Cuthbert was connected. This was destroyed in 893 and in 1093 its remaining materials were used to build a Benedictine priory. The island was several times ravaged by the Danes, and this, added to the increasing importance of the see of Durham, caused it to be ultimately abandoned. To the S.W. is a small fishing village with harbour. Area 1050 ac. Pop. 650.

Holy Land, see PALESTINE.

Holyoake, George Jacob (1817-1906), an agitator, the son of a Birmingham engineer, was very early in life inspired with notions of reform, and at the age of fifteen became a Chartist. He was a workman until 1840, when he became a teacher of the Owenite movement at Worcester. Later he went about the country lecturing, and having decided that the evidences of Christianity were insufficient, he made remarks in public for which he was charged with blasphemy and imprisoned for six months. Subsequently his energies were mainly devoted to social reform and the persistent advocacy of co-operation. He wrote a *History of Co-operation in England* (1875), and biographies of Tom Paine, Richard Carlisle, Robert Owen, and John Stuart Mill, as well as many pamphlets on controversial subjects. His autobiography is entitled *Sixty Years of an Agitator's Life* (1892). There is a biography by MacCabe (1908).

Holyoke, a city on the r. b. of the Connecticut, 8 m. N. of Springfield in Hampden co., Massachusetts, U.S.A. An insignificant village till 1849, it rapidly became a thriving industrial centre when a huge dam was constructed so as to utilise the power of Hadley Falls on the Connecticut R.; a second and larger dam was built in 1900. The first town in America to manufacture paper, H. is noted also for its cotton goods. Pop. (1910) 57,730.

Holy Orders, see ORDINATION.

Holy Roman Empire. This name is usually applied to the empire founded by Charles the Great in the year 800, and which was regarded as the revival of the West Roman empire. It did not include all the territory of the latter organisation, but nevertheless it typified the ideal. The Western Roman empire had come to an end in 476, when Odoacer had finally taken possession of Italy, and had signified to Zeno, the ruler of the Eastern empire, that henceforth he alone should rule as emperor of a Roman empire, and he, Odoacer, should rule as patrician and, in all but name, king

of Italy. Since those days the face of Europe had changed considerably. Odoacer had been deposed, executed, and succeeded by Theodoric, the leader of the Ostrogoths; and the death of the latter (526) had witnessed the break up of the power of the Ostrogoths, and for a time Italy became the scene of constant wars. Justinian and his great general, Belisarius, had conquered much of Italy, but had finally been held in check, and then the northern part of the peninsula passed into the hands of the Longobardi (Lombards). In another part of Western Europe the power of the Franks had been constantly on the increase. The line of Clovis had passed away with the last of the *rois fainéants,* the Mayors of the Palace had usurped the kingly powers, and finally, in 732, the greatest of the Mayors of the Palace, Charles Martel, had held in check the inroad of the Saracens, and had, according to one great authority, saved Western Europe for Christianity. The victory at Poitiers, according to Gibbon, prevented the Moslem from establishing his faith to the uttermost isles of the West. Charles Martel also helped the papacy in the struggle against the Lombards, and commenced the long alliance of Carolings and papacy. In the meantime the growth of the power of the bishops of Rome had been equally great. By the beginning of the 8th century the papacy had based its claims on the forged donation of Constantine, had declared itself the spiritual head of the world, and had prepared the way for that union of the spiritual and temporal power which was to rule the world, acknowledged by all.

The idea of a universal empire has remained as an ideal in the minds of men since the downfall of the Western Roman empire. Barbarians such as Clovis had been honoured by the title of patrician, and had been more than pleased to receive such indirect recognition from the emperors of the East. The Carolingian house had been in close touch with the East, but, as has been pointed out, in closer touch with the West. A new factor had also appeared. In the days of the Roman empire the emperor had been recognised as a divinity; he was the recognised 'head' of the Roman religion. Now, however, the papacy, claiming special powers and privileges from the forged donation of Constantine, claimed that position for itself. The new Roman empire was to be dual: the sword of temporalities was to be wielded by the Carolingians, the spiritual sword by the papacy. The accession of Charles the Great in 768 marks the beginning of the closer unity of papacy and empire. Twice Charles the Great crossed the Alps to rescue the papacy from the clutches of the Lombard. Finally, during his second expedition, he wrested for himself the iron crown of Lombardy. Henceforth the papacy was to be protected by its most helpful ally. The gratitude of the pope was speedily seen: as Charles knelt in prayer in the great church of St. Peter's on Christmas Day in the year 800, he was saluted and crowned by the pope as emperor. Whether this was the surprise to Charles that it appeared to be or not, we are not able to judge, but it involved the mistake which caused the Middle Ages to be practically one long quarrel between the nominal heads of christendom. Could Charles but have foreseen the results of his coronation by the pope, and the claims which the later successors to the chair of St. Peter founded on it, he probably would have, as in later days Napoleon did, crowned himself. The arrogant pretensions of the later papacy were based on the fact that the pope had raised a mere king to the empire.

It must be borne in mind particularly that, as H. W. C. Davis points out in his *Mediæval Europe*, the Carolingian empire was based upon the model not of Augustus but of Constantine, and an empire which, in unity with the Christian Church, was to establish that faith and extirpate the heretic. The empire did not, save as an ideal, outlive its founder. The reign of his son witnessed the beginning of the end, and the Treaty of Verdun (843) established a potential France, Germany, and Italy. Of these France was the only nation which immediately developed, but the long connection of Italy and the states which we now call Germany with the empire, prevented a development on similar lines. Only once again, under Charles the Fat (884-887), were the three portions of the empire of Charles the Great again united. The later Carolings were as weak as the *rois fainéants*, and the invasions of the Norsemen gave greater power to the local nobility, and this was aided by the rise of feudalism. In Germany the power concentrated in five great duchies, Saxony, Swabia, Franconia, Bavaria, and Lotharingia. In 918 the dukes refused to recognise the Caroling line, and elected Henry the Fowler of Saxony as king. The Carolings continued in France until 987, when they were superseded by the Capetian line. The year 918, although it does not seem to have affected contemporary historians to any great extent, makes the final separation of France from

the empire. Henry the Fowler concentrated his attention upon extending towards the East, conciliating the other duchies, and preparing the way for his son Otto. His position throughout the whole of his reign was merely that of a *primus inter pares*, and his power was therefore not as great as that of an independent ruler. The value of his work is seen best in the reign of his son Otto the Great (936 973). In Germany he put down two civil wars in the duchies, first giving them into the hands of his relatives, then seeking active alliance with the Church to produce unity. His greatest success was the victory over the Huns on the Lechfield (954) and his policy of ' Marks ' (Marches) along the eastern borders. The alliance with the papacy led to the request to interfere in Italian politics, which he did in 951 and 962. The second intervention led to his coronation as emperor of the West.

Otto regarded himself as the successor of Charles the Great, but notice that his territories differed, though probably his effectiveness was much the same. He appointed and deposed popes from 963 till his death. Otto II. (973-983) began to split the great duchies, but still extended towards the East. Otto III. (983-1002) was educated by his mother, a Byzantine princess, and by the bishops. Therefore his ideals were more universal, and he wished to make Rome and not Aachen his centre. In Germany he departed from the Saxon policy of unity by establishing separate archbishoprics for Hungary. Rome revolted; he obtained no support in Germany, and died a fugitive. Henry II. (1002-25), the last of the Saxon house, only succeeded in making himself emperor in 1014, and was generally less important than his predecessors. The empire now passed to the Salian house, the first emperor of which was Conrad (1025-37). His energies were concentrated upon insuring the hereditary succession of his house. To this end he made feudal benefices hereditary in Germany and Italy. His time was spent in preparing his son, Henry III., for the position of emperor. As a result the reign of Henry III. (1037-50) is usually regarded as the most glorious period of the mediæval empire. Hungary, Poland, and Bohemia became fiefs of the empire. There was comparative peace, and the development of almost a national feeling in Germany. More interesting to the time was the relation of empire and papacy. During this period the papacy had been gradually developing its resources. In 918 there had been established the monastery of Cluny.

During the 10th and 11th centuries the Cluniacs had been proceeding with a movement which was to bring a revolution in the papal power. Their aims were the purification of the Church and the release of the Church from any lay interference, and the exaltation of the papacy. Henry III. showed deep interest in their work, but in his actual relations with the papacy appointed and deposed popes. His power may be best gauged from the fact that his son, although an infant, succeeded and kept his throne through a long struggle with the papacy. Henry IV. (1056-1106) was faced with the ' noblest figure ' in history, Gregory VII. (Hildebrande). The pope had already guided his predecessors, and was the embodiment of the Cluniac ideals. The papacy was exceptionally powerful, having for its support the Cluniacs, the Normans of Southern Italy, Matilda, Countess of Tuscany, and all discontented nobles in Germany. In 1075 Hildebrande at a synod formulated the claims of the papacy by stating that no lay prince must interfere with the election and investiture of clerics. Henry defied the pope, principally because a bishop, for instance, was a temporal as well as a spiritual prince. The pope excommunicated the emperor, who at once found himself in great difficulties, because his nobles refused to recognise an excommunicated king. He was forced to cross the Alps, and in 1077 to undergo the dramatic humiliation at Canossa. But Hildebrande's severity defeated his own ends by alienating the German princes, who appointed Rudolf of Swabia as king, in disgust at Henry's cowardice. But Henry defeated the rebels at the battle of the Elster (1080), and then invaded Italy. In 1085 Hildebrande was driven from Rome, and found a refuge in Apulia with the Normans. In the same year he died. Henry IV. was deposed by his son (1106), and also died in the same year. Henry V. (1106-1125) concluded his phase of the struggle by the Concordat of Worms (1122). By this concordat the spiritualities were to be conferred by the papacy, whilst for the temporalities of the bishopric homage was to be done to the reigning prince (compare Anselm and Henry I., 1106). After Lothair another dynastic change took place with the election of the Hohenstaufen candidate, Frederick I. (1152-90), who combined the claims of Salia and Saxon. He and all his house had to face the greatest power of feudalism. Frederick I. was an essentially German king, and was most successful in his German policy, yet he had to contend with many revolts. He again

was drawn into a long struggle with the papacy, whose ally now was a new organisation, the Lombard League, formed by the towns of N. Italy. Notice, however, that the cause of quarrel remains almost identically the same, while the phases of excommunication again do not vary. Frederick I., however, was defeated at Legnano (1176), and again an emperor made submission to a pope in 1177. But Frederick had succeeded in establishing a conditional supremacy over the important towns of N. Italy. By the marriage of his son to Constance, heiress of the Norman dominions, it seemed that the dream of an empire from Sicily to the Baltic would be realised. Frederick I. was drowned in a river of Asia Minor on the way to the third Crusade.

Henry VI. (1190-98) had greater promise than any previous emperor. The brevity of his reign, however, prevented any great developments, and his death left the throne to a child. The power of the papacy is well illustrated by the events of the next few years. Innocent III. took Constance and her son under the protection of the papacy, giving them the two Sicilies. The empire was granted to Otto IV. on condition of alliance with the papacy. Otto proved recalcitrant, and in 1214 the papacy offered the empire to the young Frederick. John of England allied with Otto, who was his nephew. Frederick found support in Philip Augustus, and defeated the allied forces of John and Otto at Bouvines, a battle which influenced England in that it led to the granting of Magna Charta; France in that it removed fear of English interference and helped the Capetian monarchy. Frederick II. had been educated in an Oriental atmosphere and had lived under Mohammedan influences. As a result his attitude towards the papacy was novel. For political reasons he persecuted heretics, but over his conduct of the fifth Crusade he found himself plunged into a new quarrel with the papacy. In this case, the last phase of the great mediæval struggle, the cause of papal enmity seems to have lain chiefly in the fear of the position of the emperor, who now held both Sicily and Northern Italy. The northern towns were again persuaded to revolt, but were definitely defeated at Corte Nuova (1237). Frederick II. was most successful in Sicily, where his policy included a system of representative government which was far ahead of his time, and which therefore proved only temporary. His most practical work was his plan for checking the Tartars, who threatened to overrun Western Europe, and who actually dominated Russia until the time of Peter the Great (*see* RUSSIA). With the death of Frederick the papacy gathered itself together for a final attack on the Hohenstaufen. His direct successor was ' the little Conradin,' but he did not gain election in Germany. Various candidates appeared, among whom were Alfonso of Castile, Richard of Cornwall, and William of Holland. But none were actually recognised as emperor. Therefore the period from 1250-73 is known as the Great Interregnum, so that the death of Frederick II. marks the end of the great period of the mediæval empire. In 1273 Rudolf of Hapsburg was elected emperor, but he never ruled over Italy. Henceforth the H. R. E. does not include Italy, and may to a very great extent be regarded as the personal and private possession of the house of Hapsburg.

After the Great Interregnum, the hold of the empire on Italy became ineffectual. In fact, after the death of Frederick II., his successors, although they were called kings and emperors of the Romans, were little more than kings of Germany. Most of the later emperors were chosen from the House of Hapsburg, whose chief possessions were in Austria, acquiring Bohemia by marriage. In 1364 the granting of the Golden Bull by Charles IV., which settled the method of choosing the emperor, restricting the number of electors to seven, and naming them, lessened the power of the emperor in favour of the princes. During the 14th and 15th centuries, the elected emperor often paid more attention to his hereditary domains than to his imperial claims, because the empire was becoming so weak and poor. Therefore the emperor was chosen from the most powerful House, Austria, so that his private possessions would lend dignity to his position. During the 16th century, Maximilian added Burgundy to the possessions of Austria; his son, Charles V., held Spain, the Netherlands, Burgundy, Milan, the Two Sicilies, Austria, Hungary, the Spanish dominions in S. America, and the empire. But the empire itself was purely German, and had little to do with affairs outside. The Reformation and the Counter Reformation, however, affected it greatly. There is no clear line of demarcation, and by the settlement of the Peace of Augsburg, 1555, the two religions were placed on an equality, each state setting up its own religion (*cuius regis, eius religio*). This was most unsatisfactory, and led to the Thirty Years' War which raged between the powers of Europe, with the empire as a battle-ground. In 1648 the Peace of Westphalia was concluded, Protestantism and Catholicism were put on a level again, but the empire was ruined by the war. From this time Germany was a mere lax confederation of petty despotisms and oligarchies; Switzerland received its independence, as did also the Netherlands. Sweden and France received territories within the empire. There could be no national feeling in such circumstances; the power of the emperor had departed, and interest must centre in the rising power of Prussia and its rivalry with Austria, shown especially in the wars from 1740-63, in which Frederick of Prussia opposed Maria Theresa of Austria. But with the world schemes of Napoleon Bonaparte the empire found itself in grave difficulties. First the Austrian Netherlands and all Germany W. of the Rhine were added to France. When Bonaparte in 1804 crowned himself emperor of the French, Francis II., who was Emperor Elect of the Romans and King of Germany, changed his title to Hereditary Emperor of Austria. In 1805, at the Treaty of Pressburg, he again changed it to Emperor of Germany and Austria. Many of the German princes now seceded from the empire, and formed themselves into a Confederation of the Rhine under the protection of Napoleon Bonaparte. In the same year, 1806, Francis resigned the empire; since then, no other emperor of the Roman empire has been chosen. Thus we see that Italy passed from the empire after the long struggle with the Hohenstauffen; Burgundy was gradually annexed by France, and Germany by its lack of national feeling had ceased to be a unity; so that long before the actual resignation of Francis the H. R. E. of the West had ceased to be a political force.

Holyrood, the name of the royal palace of the Scottish kings. David I. founded an abbey in Edinburgh (1128), and dedicated it to the Holy Rood or Cross with reference to the shape of a beautifully-wrought casket which Margaret, wife of Malcolm, the king, brought to Scotland in 1070. The monastery, which was built in the Norman and early Gothic styles, was dissolved in Henry VIII.'s reign, when the chapel became a parish church, until James II. (of England) made it a chapel royal (1687). Since 1768 it has been left a ruin. Begun by James IV. in 1501, the palace was a royal residence till the Union, and is now thrown open to the public, who are shown where Mary slept and Rizzio was murdered. Bonnie Prince Charlie danced in the picture gallery (1745);

Robert Bruce convoked a parliament within the abbey precincts, and De Quincey once took refuge in the debtors' sanctuary.

Holy Sepulchre, Knights of the, were an order first sanctioned, it seems, by Pope Alexander VI. Their purpose was to protect the burial-place of Christ and to befriend pilgrims. When the Ottomans regained possession of Jerusalem the knights left Palestine and settled in Perugia (Italy).

Holy Spirit, The, or Holy Ghost, or **Paraclete,** in orthodox Christian theology, the Third Person in the Blessed Trinity. Foreshadowings of the Christian doctrine are found in certain parts of the O.T. writings, as, for instance, in Gen. i. 2, 1 Sam. xvi. 13, and Joel ii. 28 ff., quoted as a prophecy of the descent of the Holy Spirit at Pentecost in Acts ii. 17 ff. It becomes much clearer, however, in the N.T., where the Holy Spirit is spoken of in a way that makes His Divinity distinct in such passages as 2 Cor. iii. 16 ff., 2 Tim. iii. 16., Gal. v. 22, etc. From other passages still more may be gathered. Matthew xxviii. 19, 1 Pet. i. 1-14, speak of the Holy Spirit as distinct from the Father and the Son, while His Personality is insisted on in the important passage beginning John xiv. 16, as also in John xv. 26, ' But when the Comforter is come whom I will send unto you from the Father, even the Spirit of truth, which proceedeth from the Father. He shall testify of me.' In this text we have also a reference to the question of the Procession of the Holy Ghost, which caused such serious misunderstandings between the Eastern and Western churches in later centuries. The Easterns condemned the churches of the West for the addition of the Filioque clause in the Nicene Creed, and they further denied that the procession of the Holy Spirit was ' from the Father and the Son.' It must be pointed out, however, that there is probably no real doctrinal difference involved, as the West has never held that this rather unfortunate addition to the Œcumenical Creed teaches a Dual Procession, but rather a procession *from* the Father *through* the Son. This doctrine Eastern theologians would endorse. Many questions relating to the Holy Spirit are bound up with the controversies as to the Holy Trinity which occupied the mind of the Church in post-Nicene times. The most important results, embodied in the Athanasian Creed and the additions to the Nicene Creed, lay stress on the *personality* of the Holy Spirit. *See* Swete's article in the *Dict. of Christ.*

Biog., and the same writer's *Holy Spirit in the New Testament,* and *Holy Spirit in the Ancient Church* (1912), also any systematic works on Christian theology.

Holytown, a tn., Lanarkshire, Scotland, 14 m. N.N.E. of Lanark. Situated in the most productive region of the Lanarkshire mineral deposits, its coal mines and steel works are valuable. Pop. (1911) 4500.

Holy Water, the water blessed by the bishop or priest for ceremonial purposes. Water is naturally used as a symbol of spiritual cleansing, and that the habit of using holy water was common very early in the Christian church we are told by Tertullian. In the Roman Catholic Church there is a solemn blessing of Holy Water on Saturday in Holy Week, but the rite may be performed by the priest at any time. Stoups with Holy Water stand at the entrance to Roman Catholic churches, and before High Mass the priest sprinkles the congregation with blessed water. It is also used at funerals, in blessings, etc. Salt is mixed with the water at the benediction.

Holy Week, the week immediately preceding Easter in which the events of the last week of our Lord's life on earth are commemorated. It is observed by all Catholics with strictness and penitence, all the offices and devotions bearing this note. It begins with Palm Sunday, on which the palms are blessed in commemoration of Christ's entry into Jerusalem. On Maundy Thursday white is used at the Mass, because on that day Christ instituted the Blessed Sacrament, but immediately afterwards the altars are stripped and washed. No Mass is celebrated on Good Friday. During the last three days of Holy Week, the offices of Matins and Lauds (Tenebræ) are sung with impressive ceremonial, generally on the previous evening.

Holywell: 1. A market tn., 4½ m. W.N.W. of Flint in Flintshire, North Wales. It is served by the London and North-Western Railway, and besides lime quarries has zinc, lead, and copper ores and a growing metal industry. Close by are the ruins of the Basingwerk Cistercian abbey, which dates back to the 12th century, but H. is named after St. Winifred's Well, long a Mecca for pilgrims and invalids in search of a miraculous cure. A Gothic structure, believed to be the work of Henry VII.'s mother, Margaret, the Countess of Richmond, now covers the spring. Crutches adorn the sheltering walls. Pop. (1911) 2700. **2.** A vil., 4½ m. N.W. by N. of North Shields in the Wansbeck division of Northumberland, England. Pop. (1911) 2549.

Holywell Street, part of old London, since done away with to widen the Strand between St. Mary's and St. Clement's churches. It was named after a holy well near by. In early times the residence of silk merchants, it was latterly notorious for the number of booksellers who made a livelihood by selling coarse and obscene literature.

Holywood, a picturesquely situated seaport, co. Down, Ireland, 4½ m. N.E. of Belfast. Here took place (1644) the signing of a solemn league and covenant for the defence of the kingdom. The church dates from the 12th century.

Holzer, Johann Evangelist (1709-40), a German fresco-painter, the son of a Tyrolese miller. His precocity as an artist was such that he was famous at eighteen and was soon engaged, at the instance of Merz, the painter, to assist him in some frescoes for a convent church in Straubing (Bavaria). The popular paintings he executed on the outside of houses in Augsburg can now only be studied from prints, and time, unfortunately, has treated his best work, namely the mural designs in the Benedictine church of Schwarzach, so badly that they no longer convey adequately the high merit of their painter.

Holzminden, a tn. on the r. b. of the Weser, 29 m. N.W. of Göttingen, at the base of the Sollinger Mts. in the duchy of Brunswick, Germany. It is an agricultural centre, and has iron and steel and weaving industries. Pop. (1905) 10,246.

Homage, in feudal times, the formal expression (*homo vester devenio,* I become your *man*) of allegiance of a vassal to his lord. Noblemen at a coronation and bishops on appointment do H. to the sovereign.

Homalium, a genus of Flacourtiaceæ, occurs in tropical countries and consists of about forty species. These are shrubby plants with small starry flowers of no known utility.

Homalonotus, the generic name of several species of trilobites belonging to the family Calymenidæ, and found from the Ordovician to Devonian strata. *H. delphinocephalus* is the best-known species.

Homberg, a tn. of Rhenish Prussia, 8 m. W.N.W. of Mulheim, Germany. There are collieries and engineering works. Pop. 24,804.

Homburg, Pfalz, a tn. of the Palatinate, Bavaria, 5 m. W.N.W. of Zweibrücken. There are iron foundries. It possesses a fine church. Pop. 7196.

Homburg vor der Höhe, a tn. and watering-place in Prussian prov. of Hesse-Nassau, situated on a spur S.E. of the Taunus Mts., 8 m. N.N.W.

of Frankfort-on-Main. It is one of the most fashionable spas in Europe, and is yearly visited for its saline and chalybeate springs by some 12,000 people. Machines, hats, and whitelead are manufactured. Pop. (1910) 14,315.

Home, Earls of, belong to an historic Scottish border family. Sir Alexander Home (*d.* 1491) was created a peer by James III., but afterwards joined the nobles against the king and was present on the field of Sauchieburn (1488), where the latter died. His great-grandson, Alexander, the third Lord Home (*d.* 1516), was chamberlain to James IV., actually escaped with his life from Flodden, and was finally enticed to Holyrood by specious offers from Albany, the regent, and summarily executed for treason. Alexander, the sixth Lord Home and the first earl (created 1605), carried on endless feuds with the Hepburns when he was warden of the marches. His father, Alexander, the fifth Lord Home (*d.* 1575), had fought against the queen at Carberry Hill and Langside, probably because Bothwell was the head of the Hepburns, his hereditary foes. The ninth earl (*d.* 1786), from whom the present earl traces his descent, succeeded his brother, who fought against the Pretender at Prestonpans.

Home, Daniel Douglas (1833-86), a Scottish spiritualist, was brought up by an aunt in America, where, in 1850, he was already known as a spiritualistic medium. His life was spent in giving seances in England and on the Continent, especially in Russia, where he had an audience with the Czar. Browning, who was present at his meetings, records his unfavourable impressions in *Sludge, the Medium,* 1864. It was his table-turnings and traffic with ghosts which led to his expulsion from the Roman Catholic Church.

Home, Gordon Cochrane (*b.* 1878), an author and artist, born in London. He has exhibited pictures at the Royal Academy, and in addition to his contributions to several magazines, has written the following works : *What to See in England,* 1903; *The Evolution of an English Town,* 1905; *Yorkshire Coast and Moorland Scenes,* 1904; *Along the Rivieras of France and Italy,* 1908, all illustrated by the author. Other works are : *The Motor Routes of England,* 1909; *The Motor Routes of France,* 1910; *The Romance of London,* 1910.

Home, Henry, *see* KAMES, LORD.

Home, John (1722-1808), a dramatist, served as a volunteer in the rising of '45, and two years later became minister of Athelstaneford, but in 1757 he retired from his charge. He made many acquaintances with literary folk, and was introduced to Lord Bute soon after he resigned his clerical duties, and for some years served as his private secretary. In 1802 he published a *History of the Rebellion of 1745*, but it is as a dramatist he is best known. His principal plays were : *Agis*, 1758; *The Siege of Aquileia*, 1760; *Alonzo*, 1773; and *Alfred*, 1778. His first drama, *Douglas*, produced at Covent Garden in 1757, with Barry and Peg Woffington in the cast, was his greatest success, and it is still remembered for the speech beginning ' My name is Norval,' which was long a favourite recitation. Then hailed as a second Shakespeare, he has since taken his place as a very mediocre writer, and his works no longer hold the stage.

Home and Colonial School Society, came into existence in 1836. John Stuckley Reynolds (1791-1874), who had a great deal to do with its inauguration, was eager to introduce into this country the methods of Pestalozzi, the great Swiss educationalist (1746-1827). At first the association concentrated on sending out teachers properly equipped to teach young children. It still has a school at Wood Green, and until quite recently controlled a school and training college on Highbury Hill (N. London), which is now under the London County Council.

Home Arts and Industries Association was founded in 1884 for the purpose of spreading a knowledge of the handicrafts among the people. Central studios have been established for training teachers, who afterwards give gratuitous instruction both to adults and children of the working classes.

Homecourt, a com., Meurthe-et-Moselle dept., France, 38 m. N.N.W. of Nancy. Pop. 5000.

Homel, *see* GOMEL.

Home Office. The Home Secretary is, as regards home affairs, the constitutional channel of communication between the king and his subjects, and all petitions or addresses to the king must be addressed to him through the Home Secretary. The powers and duties of the H. O. are of the widest and most varied kind, but perhaps the most important relate to the control of the Metropolitan Police, the exercise of the prerogative of mercy, the administration of the Factory Acts (*see* FACTORY AND WORKSHOP ACTS), extradition proceedings, the carrying out of the provisions of the Aliens Act and the Naturalisation Acts, and the general superintendence and control over prisons, criminal lunatic asylums, reformatories, and industrial schools. The Home Secretary appoints recorders, stipendiary magistrates, factory inspectors, and inspectors under the Explosives Acts, and the Anatomy Acts, and the Cruelty to Animals Act (or Vivisection Act). He sanctions by-laws of municipal boroughs so far as they relate to ' order and good governance.' He advises the crown (*q.v.*) as to pardoning convicted persons or commuting or otherwise reducing their sentences, and he can license prisoners under sentence of penal servitude either conditionally or unconditionally. He inspects the country police forces and can advise the Treasury to withdraw exchequer contributions if he finds such forces inefficient. All extradition proceedings pass through the hands of the Home Secretary, who makes the final order for extradition. He may refuse a certificate of naturalisation to an alien, and need give no reasons for so doing. He grants licences to scientific bodies to experiment on animals. He has power to authorise the exhumation and removal of bodies. He performs the routine work in respect of the licensing, the making of a canon law, and its subsequent promulgation. He prepares patents of nobility for peers, and formal proceedings for the bestowal of honours also pass through the H. O. The Home Secretary is assisted in his duties by a parliamentary under-secretary, a permanent under-secretary, three assistant under-secretaries, and a large clerical staff.

Homer, the great epic poet of Greece. The works attributed to him are the *Iliad* and the *Odyssey*, the *Batrachomyomachia* or ' The Battle of the Frogs and Mice,' the so-called *Epigrams*, and the *Margites*, a poem which is lost. The date of his birth is quite uncertain. Herodotus declared that Hesiod and H. were contemporaries, and lived 400 years before his own time, but later authorities place his life about the 11th century B.C. His poems were regarded as the basis of Greek literature, and every educated Greek had learnt them by heart in his schooldays. Many towns claimed the privilege of being his birthplace—Smyrna, Chios, Argos, Athens, Salamis. No real records of his life existed, but many legends grew up around his name. There are extant eight lives of H., included in Westermann's *Vitarum Scriptores Græci minores*. One of these, which is probably a literary forgery belonging to the 2nd century A.D., was formerly ascribed to Herodotus, and contains the most popular legend with regard to his life. The biographer declares that H. was the illegitimate son of Crithers, and that he was born near Smyrna on the banks of the Meles. He was subsequently adopted by his mother's husband, Phemius, and travelled extensively in Egypt, Italy, and the islands of the Mediterranean, collecting materials for his epics, which he wrote on his return to Smyrna. During the course of his travels he had become blind, and spent the rest of his life as a wandering minstrel, singing his songs in the towns of Asia Minor and the islands of the Archipelago.

The tradition that the poet was blind probably arose out of two references to blind bards in the *Odyssey*, in which a personal allusion was traced. Demodocus, the blind harper who sang his lays in the halls of King Alcinous, is spoken of with great sympathy. He was beloved of the Muses, who, having deprived his eyes of light, endowed him with the divine gift of song. Phemius, who sang to divert Penelope's suitors, was also blind. *Epigram IV.* in which there is a blind poet, ' Melesigenes,' born near Smyrna by the sacred waters of the Meles, was regarded as a clear reference to H. It is quite possible that the Herodotean *Life* mentioned above owed some of its information to this source, but it is now generally accepted that these epigrams only embodied the legendary anecdotes which were told about the poet. If his blindness is accepted, it must be assumed that he became blind in later life, for the two epics show a keen perception of and exuberant delight in line and form and motion. The claims of Smyrna as his birthplace were supported by Pindar, Scylax, and Stesimbrotus. But Chios had equally strong, if not stronger, claims. In that island there was worship of an ancient hero, Homeros, and an existing tradition of a family of Homerids. Its claims were also supported by Thucydides, Simonides, Acusilaus, and Hellanicus.

The only certain testimony of the period in which H. lived is the internal evidence to be found in the acknowledged Homeric poems of the *Iliad* and the *Odyssey*. From these it is clear that their author lived prior to the earliest recorded history of Greece, that is to say, before the Dorian conquest. The chief reasons brought forward as a proof are as follows : H. speaks of the Greeks as Achæans, Argives, and Danai, whereas their own national name in the post-Doric period was Hellenes, subdivided into Dorians, Ionians, and Æolians. The Achæan name probably became insignificant at the time of the Dorian conquest. The Dorian invasion was, apparently, unknown to H.; there is a slight reference to Dorians in *Odyssey*, xix., where they are placed in Crete. The civilisation with which the poet was familiar was that of Mycenæ. Athens takes a very secondary place in the action of the *Iliad*. There is no evidence that he knew of the brilliant civilisation which, according to early historical records, flourished along the eastern coast of the Ægean Sea, nor of the Greek settlements in Asia which were made during the 11th century B.C.

HOMER

The armour and military tactics as described in the epics are of a primitive nature. The chariot was the chief instrument of war. The chief defensive weapons were the helmet, breastplate, and greaves, and circular or oblong shields. The back and the calf were left unprotected. The offensive weapons were the half-axe, or axe with one edge, the javelin, spear, and sword, and large boulders, which were hurled only by the strongest. The trumpet was apparently not used, as later, as a signal for the charge, and there was no cavalry. Art, as described by H., is decoration of weapons (as, for example, the shield of Achilles) and of articles in common use. There is no mention of sculpture or of any art-work in stone. The decoration described is skilled workmanship in metal. The manners and customs of the heroes of the *Iliad* and *Odyssey* belong to a very early age. The heroes themselves are drawn on a stupendous scale, and leave the impression of being demi-gods. All this goes to prove that the *Iliad* and the *Odyssey* must have been composed before the 11th century B.C., as the author is ignorant of the events, manners, and institutions subsequent to that date. An internal examination of the language, which is a primitive dialect form known as that of Attica, substantiates the statement.

The works of H. were studied critically in very early times. Theagenes of Rhegium (*c.* 530 B.C.) regarded the epics as allegories, so that he might reconcile its principles with the morality of his own time. His theory was accepted by Anaxagoras and Metrodorus. Xenophon, Plato, and Aristotle carefully studied the structure and meaning of the poems, while Antimachus paid attention to the text. The great textual critic of ancient times was Aristarchus, who studied the Homeric language and divided the *Iliad* and the *Odyssey* into twenty-four books each. Other Alexandrian critics of importance in this connection were Zenodotus and Aristophanes. The critical emendations and suggestions of Aristarchus are preserved in the *Codex Venetus* in the library of St. Mark, Venice (published by Villoison, 1788). The view of antiquity that the two great epics of Greece were written by a man called H. was unquestioned down to the 18th century. By his publication of the *Prolegomena ad Homerum* in 1795, F. A. Wolfe opened the controversy which is known as the ' Homeric question.' Wolfe held that the *Iliad* and the *Odyssey* consisted of a series of songs which were not put together until about 500 years after they were composed. He argued that writing must have been unknown to Homer; that therefore the songs were passed on from one generation to another orally by the Rhapsodists ; that since poems of such length could not be transmitted through centuries without any recourse to writings, the present form of the poems could not be the original form, and that, according to the ' voice of antiquity,' Peisistratus ' first committed the poems of H. to writing and reduced them to the order in which we now read them.' It is now generally admitted that the poems were certainly unwritten, whereas it is also agreed that it is possible for poems, even of such

length, to have been memorised by the professional trained singers and minstrels of the Grecian courts. There may, at the same time, exist in the text many interpolations or deviations from the original form of the poems. Wolfe's statement about Peisistratus's collection of the poems has no earlier authority than Cicero (*De Oratione*, iii. 34). The controversy raised by Wolfe was hottest during the first half of the 19th century. Gottfried Hermann, in *De interpolationibus Homeri* (1832) and *De iteratis Homeri* (1840), maintained that he was able to distinguish three elements in the *Iliad*, a pre-Homeric element, a Homeric, and a post-Homeric. Lachmann went so far as to divide the *Iliad* into twenty-two lays, and declared that the original lays had been broken up by interpolations and finally put into shape by Peisistratus. The Wolfian theories were strongly opposed by Nitzsch in his *Meletemata* (1830) and *Die Sagenpoesie der Griechen* (1852). Welcker, in *The Epic Cycle*, showed the early cyclic writers had been influenced in the structure and substance of their epic poems by the *Iliad* and the *Odyssey* ; and that the latter in their present unity of form must be dated before the cyclic writers.

The question as to whether the *Iliad* and the *Odyssey* were written by the same author was first raised by Xeno and Hellanicus called οἱ χωρίζοντες, the Chorizontes or Separators. The chief arguments which have been raised in favour of a sole authorship of the two poems are as follows: It is difficult to believe that in an age of no hereditary literature there should have arisen one supreme genius near whom none can be placed in the world's literature save Dante and Shakespeare; but that two poets of such equal and solitary greatness should have lived then is incredible. It is also argued that though there must be some difference in style between the *Iliad*, a poem of war, and the *Odyssey*, a poem of peace, the great outlines and essential styles of the two poems are similar, whereas each is wholly different from anything else produced by the writers of ancient Greece. The early Chorizontes argued in favour of two authors, by pointing out certain discrepancies between the two poems, such as the fact that the wife of Hephæstus in the *Iliad* is Charis, while she is Aphrodite in the *Odyssey*. Modern scholars have based their arguments in favour of a later date for the *Odyssey* (and, therefore, a different author) on differences between the two poems of vocabulary, grammatical forms, of treatment of the heroic legends, of institutions, political and social, and of religious or moral outlook. For the literature of the 'Homeric question' consult Wolf's *Prolegomena*, 1795; Müller's *Homerische Vorschule*, 1836; Hermann's *De iteratis apud Homerum*, 1840; Welcker's *Der epische Cyclus oder die homerischen Dichter*, 1835-49; Nutzhorn's *Die Entstehungsweise der homerischen Gedichte*, 1869; Kirchhoff's *Die Composition der Odysse*, 1869; Wilamowitz - Möllendorf's *Homerische Untersuchungen*, 1884; Andrew Lang's *Homer and his Age*, 1907. The best modern editions of the text are: *Iliad* of La Roche, 1873-76; Leaf, 1886-88; and Monro, 1896; *Odyssey* of La Roche, 1867-68; Merry and Ridell (2nd ed. 1886); Monro, 1901; and Allen, 1908. Consult *Scholia Græca in Homeri Iliadem* (Oxford Press ed., 6 vols.), 1875-88; A. Lang's *Homer and the Epic*, 1893; Gilbert Murray, *Rise of the Greek Epic*, 1907; Jebb, *Introduction to Homer*; Ridgeway, *The Early Age of Greece*; Schulze, *Quæstiones epicæ*, 1892; Hartel, *Homerische Studien*; and C. Robert, *Studien zur Iliad*, 1901. Also, for grammar, etc., see Seber's *Index Homericus*, 1780; Monro's *A Grammar of the Homeric Dialect*, 1891; Prendergast's *Concordance to the Iliad*, 1875, and Autenrieth's *Homeric Dictionary* (Eng. trans.), 1877.

Home Rule. The demand of Ireland for H. R., which is defined by Mr. John Redmond, the leader of the movement, as the rule of a local Irish parliament created specially to deal with Irish affairs, may be said to be the stumbling block of British politics. It is by no means easy to adjudicate on the merits of the controversy. Out of all the tumult of political rhetoric rises on the one hand a clear call for long-delayed justice to a gifted and down-trodden race, and for an opportunity to fulfil a national destiny; on the other a denial that one integral part of a kingdom can have an absolute right to autonomy regardless of the security of the rest of the kingdom. The demand was first put forward as a definite policy in 1871, but it was not till 1885, after the extension of the franchise, that Ireland returned a majority for H. R., when 85 members out of 103 were pledged to support H. R. From that time down to 1893 the Liberal party's adherence to the policy of self-government for Ireland was associated with the name of Mr. Gladstone, and the Bill he introduced in 1893 was carried in the House of Commons by a narrow majority, and promptly thrown out by the House of Lords. That Bill set up a legislation and executive in Ireland to control Irish affairs, subject

to the supremacy of the Imperial Parliament; and there were further safeguards to that supremacy in the shape of provisions analogous to those of the Colonial Laws Validity Act (*q.v.*), an express prohibition from dealing with the land question for three years, and a reservation of some thirteen important topics of legislation to the exclusive consideration of the Imperial Parliament. The depression in the fortunes of the Liberal party which endured thereafter for a period of seventeen years left the question dormant until after they were returned to power in 1906. The election of 1906 was generally understood to have been contested on the fiscal issue, the nominees of the Liberal party expressly undertaking not to introduce a H. R. Bill. At the two later elections they made no such declarations of intention, and in April 1912, Mr. Asquith introduced the second H. R. Bill. This Bill, which passed its second reading by a majority of over 100, is based on the model of the first Bill; but the financial provisions are more explicit. The Bill establishes an Irish Exchequer and an Irish Consolidated Fund, and provides that the whole of the present and future cost of Irish government, with the exception of the expenditure on the reserved services (chiefly the army and navy, Irish Land Purchase Acts, Old Age Pensions Acts, and the Insurance Act, Royal Irish Constabulary, Post-Office Savings Bank, public loans so far as respects loans made in Ireland before the passing of the Act, and the collection of taxes other than duties and excise), shall be borne by the Irish Exchequer. That Exchequer will for a period consist of a sum made up of (1) a sum equal to the present cost to the Exchequer of the Irish services; (2) £500,000 annually for three years, diminishing by £50,000 a year for six years until it reaches £200,000; (3) a sum equal to the proceeds of Irish taxes imposed under the Bill, the amount to be determinable by the Joint Exchequer Board, consisting of two Irish Treasury and two British Treasury members, and a chairman appointed by the crown. Exactly what the present state of feeling of the British electorate towards this Bill may be, is difficult to gauge, not only because a reforming party goes to the polls on many issues, but because the public interest in other measures, notably the Insurance Act, so dominated all other questions as even to give the appearance of general apathy. Probably the electorate is as nearly as possible equally divided, the majority for the Bill being almost accounted for by the Irish vote. Among a section of politicians and their supporters, however, the controversy excited by the Bill rose in Ulster almost to the pitch of actual rebellion. That campaign, which was permeated with the trenchant personality of Sir Edward Carson and the adventurous Mr. F. E. Smith, suddenly died down, and in all probability will only be resuscitated if after two years the Bill, by virtue of the Parliament Act, has been sent up the requisite number of times to entitle it to be placed on the Statute Book. That the Irish 'loyalists,' as they are called, are in their own minds genuinely aggrieved hardly any will doubt who realise and appreciate the sincerity and passion of the Irish temperament. By the Ulstermen it is unequivocally assumed that the Bill is a reversion to Papacy, and a base betrayal of their whole interests into the hands of the Irish Roman Catholic priests and the Catholics generally, who will, it is feared, absorb all the patronage, municipal and otherwise. Hitherto among English anti-Home Rulers the principal objection has been not upon religious grounds, but firstly, that the formulated bills are mere steps towards a total separation, and secondly, that the Irish question is purely economic and non-political, and therefore incurable by political measures. The demands of the Ulster Protestants for differential treatment, in so far as that demand is motived by religious antipathies, has not, however, passed altogether unnoticed, for the Bill contains special provisions for the protection and preservation of religious equality, and a further provision that the head of the Executive, the Lord-Lieutenant, will be chosen regardless of any question of religious disability. Whether the Nationalist party actually desire a total separation is not certain. The unhappy fate of Mr. Birrell's Irish Councils Bill, which was the last word on devolution or local government as opposed to the autonomy of a self-governing colony, hardly indicates any possibility of a solution in the direction of merely delegated governmental powers. Mr. Redmond has often in the House of Commons declared that he desires an Irish parliament subject to the supremacy of the Imperial Parliament; but at a public meeting in Kanturk in 1895 he said that the consummation of their hopes was to drive English rule bag and baggage from their country, and later, in 1909, he is reported in the *Freeman's Journal* to have spoken of 'tearing up and trampling under foot that infamous Act of Union.' It is obvious that on merely tactical grounds a politician may have to frame his utterances in parliament in very different terms from those he makes use of to the world outside. But as to the question of separation generally, it is certainly a matter of grave doubt whether Ireland could benefit in the long run by total severance. This question indeed leads to the wider one of the whole principle of federation, which is to weld communities together in a union which is not actual unity by a 'political contrivance intended to reconcile national unity and power with the maintenance of "state rights."' (*See* on this Professor Dicey's *Law of the Constitution*.) Some assert that Ireland forms no parallel to S. Africa—the latest part of the empire to acquire self-government—nor to any existing member of a federal union or confederation of states, and that H. R. is essentially a disintegrating and not a consolidating measure. It is argued by those opposed to H. R. for Ireland that the colonies stand in a totally different relation to England, racially, socially, and politically, from that subsisting between England and Ireland, an argument which loses some of its force in the modern, as yet hardly articulated, cry for 'H. R. all round,' or, in other words, the policy of general decentralisation. Mr. Samuel, speaking before the Economics Section of the British Association in Sept. 1912, supported decentralisation on the ground that our legislature is a hybrid of unitary and federal principles, and that our executive and judiciary were practically federal in character throughout, and that such want of harmony necessarily resulted in congestion of business in the Imperial Parliament. Mr. Churchill at Dundee went still further, and spoke of self-governing areas in England itself, and the question of H. R. for Scotland is not without its supporters, a Bill having been brought in on Aug. 16, 1911, by Sir Henry Dalziel and others, to provide for a Scots' parliament. *See* W. F. Monypenny's *The Two Irish Nations*.

Homestead, a bor. in Allegheny co. Pennsylvania, U.S.A., on the R. Monongahela, 6 m. S.E. of Pittsburg. It was founded in 1871, and was incorporated in 1880. Here are the famous iron and steel works of the Carnegie Co., which rank with the largest in the world. At these works in 1892 occurred a tremendous strike, the rioting in connection with which had to be quelled by state troops. Pop. (1910) 18,713.

Homicide, see MANSLAUGHTER and INSANITY.

Homildon Hill, one of the Cheviot peaks, near the village of Homildon or Humbleton, 20 m. S. of Berwick,

Northumberland, England. It was the scene of the battle (1402) in which Hotspur and the Earl of March defeated the Scots under Earl Douglas.

Homily, a discourse addressed to the congregation in a church. It was customary in the Jewish synagogues after the reading of the law for an explanatory discourse to be given, and this practice was early adopted by the Christian Church. The Alexandrian school was particularly rich in such exegetical expositions, the most famous ancient collection of Hs. being that of Origen in the 3rd century. The Hs. of the Church of England are a collection of sermons (*see* Article xxxv.) for the use of unlearned preachers. The first part was published in 1547, the second in 1563.

Homocercal, *see* HETEROCERCAL.

Homœopathy (Gk. ὅμοις, like, πάθος, disease), the name given to a system of medicine introduced by a German physician, Samuel Hahnemann, who was born at Leipzig in 1755 and died in 1843. In his *Organon of Medicine,* Hahnemann set forth the principles on which his system was based. These were : (1) That morbid conditions are cured by the same medicines which would produce the disease in healthy bodies, in accordance with the old belief expressed by the Latin phrase ' similia similibus curantur ' (like is cured by like). (2) That drugs administered should be simple and not compounded. (3) That in most cases only very small quantities of the drug should be given, on the theory of dynamisation, or increase of force with diminution of matter, such dynamisation, it is alleged, being produced by trituration. In contradistinction to H., the ordinary method of treating disease is described as *heteropathy* or *allopathy. See also* HAHNEMANN and MEDICINE.

Homogeneous and **Heterogeneous** are two mathematical terms. The former is applied to magnitudes which are commensurable, and in algebra to all terms of the same degree, as for instance x^5 and y^5. The word is Greek for ' of the same kind.' ' Heterogeneous,' which is Greek for ' of a different kind,' is the opposite of ' homogeneous,' and therefore describes spheres and plane circles, for example, which are incommensurable.

Homologation, in Scots law, denotes an act by which a person signifies his approval of a deed so as to make it obligatory upon him in spite of any defects in it. A common instance of H. occurs where a person capable of consenting approves a deed granted by him at a time when he was legally incapable of giving his assent to its terms, as *e.g.* by a minor on his attaining majority in respect of a grant

made during minority without the consent of his curator. But to be valid H. must be an act from which it may be clearly inferred that the person homologating both knew and approved the contents of the instrument. *See* Bell's *Com.* ; Erskine, *Principles of the Scotch Law.*

Homologous Series, in chemistry, a group of organic compounds whose molecular weights form an arithmetical progression. There are several such series, and owing to a certain amount of similarity of constitution the substances forming them are conveniently studied by reference to their particular series. For example, the paraffins comprise the following bodies: methane, CH_4; ethane, C_2H_6; propane, C_3H_8; butane, C_4H_{10}; pentane, C_5H_{12}, etc. It is seen that each member contains one atom of carbon and two atoms of hydrogen more than a molecule of the preceding member, and this is expressed by saying that the general formula for the series is C_nH_{2n+2}. The homologues, or members of a H. S. may usually be obtained by similar methods, and they are alike in their general properties. Other H. S. are the olefines, general formula C_nH_{2n}; the acetylenes, general formula C_nH_{2n-2}; the monohydric alcohols, general formula $C_nH_{2n+1}.OH$; the aldehydes ; fatty acids, etc.

Homology, a conformity of type which is suggestive of development or inheritance from a common ancestor, and is used as one of the morphological arguments which support the Darwinian theory. H. may be indicated by members of the same class, resembling one another in their general plan of organisation, as in the case of the mouths of insects, though these show innumerable varieties of form and use, or as in the case of the general structural resemblance of the arm of man, foreleg of horse, wing of bird, flapper of seal. *Serial homology* is that unity of type found on comparing the different parts or organs in the same individual *e.g.* the segments or rings and their appendages which comprise the body of a worm.

Homoousion (Gk. ὁμοουσιων), a theological term, which became a party word at the time of the Arian controversy. It is derived from the words ὁμός, ' same,' and οὐσία, ' substance,' and denotes the consubstantiality of the Father and the Son in the Blessed Trinity. The more moderate Arians, unwilling to say that the Son was of a different substance from the Father, wished to use the phrase ὁμοιούσιον, ' of like substance.' *See* ARIUS ; ATHANASIUS.

Homoptera, the name given to one of the two sub-orders of Hemiptera (*q.v.*), whose members differ from those of the Heteroptera in that their wings cover the abdomen in a roof-like manner. The basal and apical parts of the wings are generally of the same consistency, and sometimes all four wings are transparent; the head is furnished with three ocelli, placed triangularly on the summit, and the front of the head is bent over, touching the coxæ. This sub-order includes the Cicadidæ, Fulgoridæ, Membracidæ, Cercopidæ, Jassidæ, Psyllidæ, Aphidæ, Aleurodidæ, and Coccidæ.

Homotaxial, a term by which Professor Huxley proposed to describe geological deposits which contain the same suite of fossils. He pointed out that different regions of the globe are inhabited by very different plant and animal assemblages, and some of the existing faunas (that of Australia, for example) resemble more closely that of Europe in the early Tertiary epochs than in the present day; hence the fact that two series of rocks in different regions contain similar fossil remains does not prove that they were simultaneously deposited. The truth of this is disputed by many authorities.

Homs, *see* HEMS.

Ho-nan, one of the Central Provinces of China, bounded on the N. by the Hwang-ho, on the S. by Hu-peh, on the E. by Ngan-hui, and on the W. by Shen-si. The country is traversed by the Fu-niu Shan Mts., running E. and W. It is very densely populated, largely owing to the fertility of the soil. The chief products of the province are cotton, wild silk, cereals, and fruit. Coal is found near Ho-nan-fu, Ju-chow, and Lu-shan. To the N. of the Hwang-ho, there is a beautiful fertile plain, with bamboo plantations and groves of cypress. There are good roads and the Peking-Hankow Railway traverses the province, having branch lines to Ho-nan-fu and Kai-feng-fu (the capital). Area, 67,940 sq. m. Pop. 35,316,800.

Ho-nan-fu, a city in Ho-nan, China, situated on Lo R., a tributary of the Yellow R. Under the Chou and following dynasties, it was the cap. of China, and was called Lo-Yang. Coal mines are in the vicinity.

Honawar, or **Honore,** a seaport on W. coast of India. N. Kanara dist., in Presidency of Bombay. It was visited by Ibn Batatu (1342). Pop. 7000.

Honda, a tn. (alt. 690 ft.), Colombia, S. America, on the Lower Magdalena R., 60 m. N.W. of Bogota. The river is navigable up to this point. Pop. 7000.

Hondecoeter, Melchior d' (1636-95), a Dutch painter, born in Utrecht, Holland, a pupil of his father and uncle. He was a skilful painter of poultry, depicting the feathered families with great sympathy. His most famous painting ' The Floating Feather ' hangs in the Amsterdam gallery. Hondecoeter's paintings may be seen in the National Gallery, London, and in the Liverpool, Berlin, Dresden, Hague, Paris, Petersburg, Florence, Venice, and Vienna galleries.

Hondo, *see* JAPAN.

Honduras, a republic of Central America, lying between the Caribbean Sea on the N., Nicaragua on the S. and E., and Guatemala on the W. Area about 46,250 sq. m. The country is mountainous, forming an elevated table-land of an average height of 8000 ft., rising to 10,120 ft. in the case of Montana de Selaque. The Cordilleras are continued from Nicaragua into the southern portion of the country. The chief valleys are the plain of Comayagua, and those formed by the rivers Humuya and Goascoran. The former is a tributary of the Ulua, the largest river in the country, which flows N. into the Gulf of H. Other important rivers are the Segovia, forming the boundary with Nicaragua, the longest river in Central America, the Nacaome, Aguan, Rio Negro, and Choluteca. The chief islands belonging to H. are the Bay Islands, and Tigre, Sacate Grande, and Gueguensi in the Bay of Fonseca. The climate along the Atlantic coast is oppressively hot, but on the highlands the temperature is mild. Cattle-rearing is the chief industry of the inhabitants. The woods yield valuable timber ; and bananas cocoa-nuts, oranges, lemons, maize, tobacco, cocoa, and indigo are cultivated. The mineral resources of the country—which comprise gold, silver, platinum, copper, antimony, zinc, etc. —have not been developed on a large scale. Cape H. was discovered by Columbus in 1502, and became a Spanish colony. In 1821 it threw off the Spanish yoke and joined the Federation of Central America. In 1839 it became an independent state, and was subsequently involved in frequent wars with Guatemala. It has suffered from internal strife, particularly during the civil wars of 1883 and 1903. In 1907 war was declared against Nicaragua in which Bonilla, the Honduran president, was defeated. In 1911 that general was re-elected president. The legislative power is vested in a national assembly and a council of state. The capital is Tegucigalpa (pop. 34,692); the chief ports are Roatan, La Ceiba, Puerto Cortez, and Truxillo. Total pop. (1910) 553,446.

Honduras, British, *see* BALIZE and BRITISH HONDURAS.

Honduras, Gulf or Bay of, the broad

basin of the Caribbean Sea, skirting Honduras, Guatemala, and British Honduras in Central America.

Hone, William (1780-1842), a pamphleteer, set up in 1817 as a bookseller, and soon became notorious as a publisher of political lampoons, for the issue of one of which he was unsuccessfully prosecuted. He became yet better known when he issued several satires written by himself, with illustrations by George Cruikshank. The best of these are the *Political House that Jack built*, 1819, and *The Man in the Moon*, 1820. Perhaps he is to-day best remembered by his *Every Day Book*, 1827, and his *Table Book*, 1819, which are still obtainable in modern editions.

Hones, the same as whetstones or oilstones. They are made of fine-grained siliceous rock, and are used for giving a fine edge to cutting implements like knives and razors.

Honesty, or *Lunaria biennis*, a species of Cruciferæ, grown in British gardens, and is a native of Europe. It is a hardy plant bearing racemes of lilac-coloured flowers which have no scent, and the fruit which follows them is a silicula.

Honey, a thick syrup collected by bees and also by a few species of wasp and by honey- or pouched-ants. The bees suck nectar from flowers and empty it from their crops into the cells of their hives. H. is most plentiful where flowers luxuriate and when the weather is dry and warm. The ancients vaunted the H. of Mt. Hybla in Sicily, and the aromatic, highly-granulated H. of Narbonne is famous to this day. Virgin-honey, gathered by young bees before they have swarmed, is finer than the H. of old hives. The colour varies with the source: heather-honey is a deep golden-yellow, and the H. from white clover a greenish-white. The Koran refers to H. as a liquor ' wherein is a medicine for men,' and in India and elsewhere its value as a gentle laxative has long been recognised. It was a favourite article of food among the ancient Greeks, and was an ingredient in such popular beverages as mead, the ' clarre ' of Chaucer's day, and the Roman ' mulsum.' Chemically, H. is composed of læ vulose (36·45 per cent.), dextrose (36·57), water, mineral matter, pollen, and wax. Starch, water, glucose, gelatin, and gypsum are common adulterations.

Honey-buzzard, the popular name of *Pernis apivorus*, a species of falconiform bird belonging to the family Buteoninæ. It is occasionally found in England and is common in the wooded districts of W. Europe, from whence it migrates in winter to Africa. Its food consists of insects,

small mammals, birds, etc., which it devours upon the ground; it derives its name from the habit it has of plundering the nests of bees and wasps for the sake of the honey. The plumage is variously coloured and is often indistinguishable from the dense foliage in which the H. prefers to nest.

Honeycomb - moth, the popular name given to members of *Galleria*, a genus of lepidopterous insects belonging to the family Pyralidæ. Certain of the species infest beehives, where they deposit their eggs; the larvæ feed on the comb, through which they make tunnels. There are two broods in the year, the first appearing in May and the second in full summer. *G. mellonella* is the largest and best-known species.

Honey-dew, a sweet and sticky exudation found, especially in warm, dry weather, on the leaves and stems of many trees and plants. Some hold that it is invariably associated with Aphides, Cocci, as, for instance, *Coccus mannifera*, and other insects. For it is known that Aphides excrete from the abdomen a fluid indistinguishable from H., the theory being that they prick a hole in the leaf or stalk and so suck the excess of sugar from the flowing sap. Others believe that without these insects H. would still form whenever the tissues of the plant are broken. H., which is also called manna, has been known to fall in showers. As it closes the pores when it dries, and thus hinders the natural growth of a plant, gardeners use a syringe to wash it away.

Honey-eaters, the name given to the species of Meliphagidæ, a large family of passeriform birds found in the Australian region. They are small birds with beautifully coloured plumage, long curved beaks, and long tails; their habits are active and pugnacious, and they are constantly hopping from tree to tree in search of honey and insects, which constitute their food. The species of *Meliphaga* are among the most brilliantly plumaged of all birds, *M. auricomis* being one of the best known. *Anthomis*, the New Zealand bell-birds, and *Manorhina melanophrys*, the bell-bird of Australia, are remarkable for their clear, tinkling voice.

Honey-guide, the name given to the species of *Indicator* and *Protodiscus*, two genera of coraciiform birds which constitute a sub-family Indicatorinæ. They were formerly placed among the cuckoos, but are more nearly related to the woodpeckers and barbets; most of the species are found in Africa, but *I. archipelagus* and *I. minor* inhabit the

Malay Peninsula and Borneo. Their name is derived from their curious habit of conducting travellers in the direction of bees' nests by means of a shrill cry or hiss, and they will flutter round until they are sure that they are being followed. *P. regulus* is a native of Natal, and *P. insignis* of E. Equatorial Africa.

Honey-locust Tree, or Three-horned Acacia, the popular name of the leguminous plant *Gleditschia triacanthos,* a native of the Carolinas and Virginia. The trunk and branches of the young tree are covered with prickles, the foliage is of a light shining green, and the seeds are covered with a sweet pulp.

Honeystone, or Mellite, a mineral found in the beds of coal and bituminous lignites in Bohemia and Moravia and in Germany. It is a mellate of alumina, and is a compound, therefore, of mellitic acid and alumina, with which water also is associated. It has the appearance of a honey-yellow resin, can be cut with a knife, and crystallises into small, honey-yellow, pyramidal shapes of the tetragonal system.

Honeysuckle, or *Lonicera Periclymenum,* a species of Caprifoliaceæ found in hedgerows of Britain, often known by the name of woodbine. It is a shrub of climbing habit, bearing heads of white flowers which yield a sweet fragrance; at night hawk-moths are attracted to the plants by their scent, fertilisation takes place, and the flowers change to a yellow colour. The fruit of the H. is a bright red berry. The term French honeysuckle is applied to the leguminous herb *Hedysarum coronarium,* which grows in Spain and Italy. It is a hardy perennial which bears deep red or white flowers, and in Calabria is given to horses and mules as food.

Honfleur, a seaport on the S. bank of the Seine estuary, 8 m. S.E. of Havre, in the department of Calvados, France. It is a railway terminus, controls a brisk fishing-trade, and exports agricultural produce to England. There are antiquities of interest. Pop. 9600.

Hongai, or Port Courbet, a coal-mining centre on the N.E. coast of Tongking in French Indo-China. It is situated in a bay of the same name, which a canal connects with the Bay of Along.

Hong-kong (from *Hiang-kiang,* fragrant streams), an island in the China Sea, separated from the coast of China by the Laimun Pass, a strait about 1 m. in width. It was ceded to Britain in 1842, and with Kowloon forms a crown colony. It has an area of 30 sq. m. with a length of 9 m., and a breadth varying from 3 to 6 m. The surface is mountainous and rocky, but bare and almost destitute of vegetation; the highest point is Victoria Peak (1824 ft.). The climate is unfavourable to Europeans owing to the rapid alternations of heat and cold, and the chief town retains the violent heat of the sun long after sunset, being hedged in by rocks which keep off the cool evening breezes. The chief town is Victoria, the seat of government and of trade, which stretches for 5 m. along the N. coast. It is built in three layers, the Praya or esplanade, which is given up to shipping, the Chinese quarters being beyond the commercial portion; the second layer which contains government house and other public buildings; and the Peak, or third layer, which is reached by a cable tramway. The chief industries are sugar-refining, the manufacture of cement, paper, bamboo, carving in wood and ivory, working in copper and iron, gold, silver, and sandal wood ware; the manufacture of cotton has also been introduced and granite is quarried. H. is very important as a free port and the value of its exports and imports is estimated at about £52,000,000 a year, the chief trade being in tea, silk, and opium. Regular steam communication is kept up with England, India, Manilla, Canton, Macao, Shanghai, and all the important ports. A university was opened in H. in 1912, and there is a secondary school for boys, Queen's College, and a few government schools. H. also has a police force and a strong military garrison. Pop. 456,739, most of whom are Chinese.

Honiton, a market tn. on the Otter, 16½ m. E.N.E. of Exeter by rail, in Devonshire, England. It is famous for its lace-making, an industry introduced by the Flemish in Queen Elizabeth's reign. Pop. (1911) 3191.

Honley, a small tn. engaged in the woollen industry, 3 m. S. of Huddersfield in the W. Riding of Yorkshire, England. Pop. (1911) 5100.

Honnef, a health resort, with a mineral spring, beautifully situated on the Rhine, 8 m. S.E. of Bonn in Rhenish Prussia. Pop. 6766.

Honolulu, a city, port, and cap. of Hawaii, Pacific Ocean (belonging to U.S.A.), situated on the S. coast of the island of Oahu. In 1907 an Act was passed by which the island and county of Oahu, and the small islands adjacent, became the 'city and county of H.' The chief industries are the manufacture of machinery and carriages, rice-milling, and ship-building. The city, too, has a plentiful water supply, and hence the vegetation is luxuriant. There is a natural harbour which is formed by a lagoon within the coral reef which has 22 ft. of water at the entrance at high tides, and can hold a large number of ships. This and Pearl Harbour are the only safe ports in the archipelago. From 1820 to 1893 the city was the residence of the sovereign, and is now the seat of government and the foreign consuls. It is an entrepôt for European and Indian goods, and has communication by steamship with San Francisco, Seattle, Vancouver, Victoria, Sydney, and Chinese and Japanese ports. Pop. 52,183. See HAWAII.

Honorarium, a Latin word which originally meant a gift made to an individual after attaining some office of distinction. To-day it is an honorary reward bestowed in recognition of services rendered by conductors of orchestras, lawyers, and other professional people.

Honorius (reigned 395-423 A.D.), an Emperor of Rome, born in 395. Three things characterise his reign, namely, the inroads of barbarians, the energy of Stilicho, and the pusillanimity of the emperor. Stilicho was appointed H.'s guardian during his minority, and it was he who quelled the revolt of Gildo in Africa (397) and thrice drove the Goths and Huns from Italy. In 400 he defeated the combined forces of Alaric and Radagaisus; in 402 he defeated Alaric alone at Pollentia, and a year later he put Radagaisus to death near Fœsulæ. H. executed Stilicho in 408, and so was powerless to repulse Alaric, when he captured Rome a second time in 410. Ataulphus, Alaric's son, married Placidia, H.'s sister, but neither he nor H., nor any of the host of usurpers could maintain even a semblance of imperial power.

Honorius I. (625-37), a pope, succeeded Boniface V. He wrote a letter to Edwin, king of Northumbria, urging him to be true to the new faith, and at his request conferred the pallium on the bishops of York and Canterbury. The Celtic Church was a source of continual anxiety to him, as it failed first of all to acknowledge his supremacy, and secondly continued to observe Easter according to a rule for fixing the time that Rome had discarded, and in its own way. H. also corresponded with Sergius, patriarch of Constantinople, who maintained that the twofold nature of our Lord was animated by a single will. This heresy, which was called Monothelism, was wrongly, it seems, laid to the emperor's charge after his death.

Honorius II. (1124-30), a pope, was Cardinal Lambert Scannabecchi, Bishop of Ostia, before his election to the papal chair. Besieged by Roger, Count of Sicily, in Benevento, H. afterwards countenanced his investiture as Duke of Apulia and Calabria. He excommunicated Conrad, Lothair's rival for the throne of Italy.

Honorius III. (1216-27), a pope, was Cardinal Cencio Savelli before he succeeded Innocent III. A zealous supporter of St. Dominic, he failed to induce Frederick II. to lead a crusade against the Mussulmans, and was so unpopular at Rome that he was repeatedly driven beyond that city's gates.

Honorius IV. (1285-87), a pope, was Cardinal Gigacomo Savelli. He favoured Charles of Anjou, and actually proclaimed his expedition against the men of Aragon as a ' holy war.'

Honour, a legal description of a seigniory of two or more manors under the control of one baron and subject to a single jurisdiction. See MANOR.

Honour, Maids of, see HOUSEHOLD, ROYAL.

Honourable (from Fr. honorable. and Lat. honorabilis, deserving honour), a title of honour prevalent in the United Kingdom and her colonies and also in the United States. In the United Kingdom marquesses should be addressed as ' most honourable '; earls, viscounts, barons, and privy councillors, as ' right H.'; whilst the title of H. is reserved for maids of honour, judges of the high court, and the sons and daughters of peers. Formerly the style was loosely applied. Major-General Lowther, whose father was a merchant, is described on his tomb in the abbey as ' The Hon.' (1746). In America and the colonies judges and members of state legislatures or the executive councils have a right to the distinction.

Honshiu, see JAPAN.

Hontheim, Johann Nicholaus von (1701-90), a German historian and theologian, educated by the Jesuits. From 1732-79 he was dean of St. Simeon's in Trier, his native place, and from 1738-47 represented the interests of the archbishop-elector at Coblenz. From 1748 he was suffragan bishop of Trier, and he was also pro-chancellor of the university. Under the penname of ' Febronius,' he discussed the limits of papal authority in what became a famous treatise. His three histories of Trier are in the highest degree erudite.

Honthorst, Gerard van (1590-1656), a Dutch painter, has left many pictures behind him, which are now scattered over the galleries of Europe. Born in Utrecht, he studied under Abraham Bloemaert, migrated to Rome, where he executed his masterpiece, ' Christ before Caiaphas ' (till recently in Stafford House). In White-hall, as in the Palace of the Hague, etc., he painted allegorical subjects, and there are still in existence many excellent portraits from his hand, as, for example, the 'Countess of Bedford' in Woburn Abbey.

Höntrop, a coal mining vil. of Prussia in Westphalia, dist. of Arns-berg. Pop. (1910), 5465.

Honvéd ('Land-defenders'), a term first used under the early monarchy of Hungary to describe the national champions. During the revolution of 1848 it was used of the patriotic party, and after independence was established (1868) was applied to the Landwehr.

Hooch, Pieter de (1632?-81, or later), a Dutch painter, born near Rotterdam, worked at Delft, and died, some say, at Haarlem. Like Hobbema and Cuyp he was held in small esteem by his contemporaries. A pupil, perhaps, of Rembrandt, whose style has left an impress on his (H.'s) work, this artist has left a few, but, in their way, ex-quisite pictures of native interiors. His clean and cheerful scenes inti-mate an earnest appreciation of the joys of domestic life and a warm love for sun and light.

Hood, part of academic dress. It is a development of the monk's cowl, and indicates by its colour, material, and shape, the faculty in which the owner has graduated, the status to which he has attained, and the uni-versity to which he belongs.

Hood, Alexander (1758-98), a naval captain, was an elder brother of Sir Samuel H. (1762-1814). As flag-captain to the *Barfleur*, he took part in a series of actions fought in W. Indian waters under Sir George Rodney (1781-82). He died at sea, having received a mortal wound during the encounter between his vessel, the *Mars*, and the French war-ship, *Hercule*. The latter was worsted.

Hood, Alexander, Viscount Bridport (1727-1814), an English admiral, younger brother of Samuel, Viscount H. (*q.v.*), entered the navy in 1741. After proving his mettle in various subordinate posts, he sailed with Lord Howe, as second in command, in the squadron sent to the relief of Gib-raltar (1782). Once more, under the same commander, he sailed with the Channel fleet, and established a high reputation for gallantry by the part he took in the actions culminating in the victory of June 1, 1794. His de-feat of a French squadron off L'Orient (1795) was hailed at home as a splendid achievement, but he had it in his power, it seems, to have annihi-lated the enemy, which he did not do.

Hood, Sir Alexander Fuller Acland (now first **Baron St. Audries**, created

1911) (*b.* 1853), fourth baronet, was educated at Eton, and later graduated from Baliol College, Oxford. In 1875 he entered the Grenadier Guards, and as adjutant (1881-86) served in the Egyptian campaign of 1882. For two years (1889-91) he was governor of Victoria. After retiring from the army (1892) he was for many years a Conservative member of the House of Commons, and for four years (1902-6) was parliamentary secretary to the Treasury.

Hood, Basil (*b.* 1864), a dramatist, passed through Sandhurst, and in 1883 joined the Princess of Wales' Own (Yorkshire) regiment as lieu-tenant. In 1893 he received his cap-taincy, and five years later retired. His English versions of the *Merry Widow* and *The Dollar Princess* were very well received, whilst of his original plays, most of which are light comedies, *A Princess of Ken-sington* and *Merrie England* have been most successful.

Hood, John Bell (1831-79), an American soldier, graduated from the military academy at West Point in 1853. On the declaration of Civil War he joined the Confederates, and after the battle of Gaine's Mill (1861) was promoted to major-general. At Get-tysburg (1862) he was wounded and, after the battle of Chickamauga (1863) lost one of his legs by amputation. Disaster attended him on winning the temporary command of the Ten-nessee army, and at the battle of Nashville his forces were utterly overwhelmed (1865).

Hood, Robin, *see* ROBIN HOOD.

Hood, Samuel, Viscount Hood of Whitley (1724-1816), a British ad-miral, entered the navy in 1741. From 1780 to 1783 he was fighting in the West Indies, at first under Rodney, but afterwards as com-mander-in-chief. In 1781 he made an unsuccessful attempt to prevent the French admiral, De Grasse, from blockading Chesapeake Bay, and the following year failed likewise, in spite of adroit manœuvres, to dislodge the French, again under De Grasse, from the island of St. Christopher. The tactics he adopted in extricating himself from this engagement have again and again been commended by naval experts. Finally, he assisted at the discomfiture of his old enemy in the action off Dominica (1783). In 1784 he was returned to parliament, the unsuccessful candidate being none other than Fox. During the Napoleonic wars he succeeded in occupying Corsica (1794).

Hood, Sir Samuel (1762-1814), an English vice-admiral, joined the navy in 1776, and from that year till his death was in active service almost without remission. He took part in the action off Ushant (1778). For the next two years he was fighting in the West Indies, and in 1791 effected a brave rescue of some shipwrecked sailors outside the harbour of Jamaica. As commander of the *Zealous* he distinguished himself for his intrepidity and promptitude at the battle of the Nile (1797). In 1802, being promoted to commodore, he almost drove the French out of the West Indies, and in 1805 seized four French frigates near Rochefort, but this action unfortunately cost him an arm. Commander of the *Centaur* in 1808, he was publicly decorated by the King of Sweden for his brilliant seizure of Russian gun-ship *Sewolod*. Useful reforms followed his promotion to commander-in-chief of the East Indies (1812).

Hood, Thomas (1799-1845), a poet, began his literary life by contributing to the *London Magazine* at the age of twenty-two, and through this connection he made acquaintance with many of the leading writers of the day. He published *Whims and Oddities* in 1826, and began to publish his *Comic Annual* four years later. He was abroad from 1835, but returned to England in 1840, and in the following year took up the editorship of Colburn's *New Monthly Magazine.* In the year before his death he started *Hood's Magazine,* and issued *Whimsicalities.* His works were collected by his son and daughter (1882-84). H. is best known as a humorist, and as a humorist he occupies a very high place in English letters. He was unduly addicted to the use of the pun, a now discredited form of wit, but he had a happy way of playing upon words that redeems his jokes from the charge of silliness. Though primarily a humorist, he could write in other veins. *The Dream of Eugene Aram* (1839) is one of his most famous poems, second only to the pathetic and beautiful *Bridge of Sighs.* *The Song of the Shirt,* published anonymously in *Punch* in 1843, attracted as much attention to the lot of the worker as *Oliver Twist* did to the abuses of the workhouse system. The *Memorials of Thomas Hood,* by his daughter, appeared in 1860, and there is a biography by Walter Jerrold (1907).

Hood, Mount, an extinct volcano, 11,225 ft. high, belonging to the Cascade Range, in the N.E. of the Clackamas county of Oregon, United States. Pines and firs cover its lower slopes. On one side is a sheer descent of 7000 ft. Its summit is glaciated.

Hood of Avalon, Arthur William Acland, Baron (1824-1901), an English admiral, entered the navy in 1836. During the Crimean War he was with the naval brigade before Sebastopol, and in the China War participated in the action of Fatshan Creek (1857) and in the seizure of Canton (1858). Director of Naval Ordnance (1869-73), he finally rose to the rank of First Sea Lord of the Admiralty (1885), when his conservatism proved a formidable obstacle to crying reforms.

Hoofs are horny boxes which protect the sensitive parts of the foot. The possession of H. is a distinction on which the large order, Ungulata, is based. They are equivalent to the claws and nails of other mammals, and are renewed from the superior to the inferior border like the human nail. The flexibility of the H. is promoted by a fluid secreted by the keratogenous (horn-producing) membrane. The so-called cloven H. has been evolved for walking and climbing on irregular surfaces by the formation of separate digits on the foot, each bearing its own distinct H. The horse's H. is too brittle for road wear, and the art of shoeing was practised as early as 333 B.C.

Hooft, Pieter Corneliszoon (1581-1647), a Dutch dramatist and historian, is, perhaps, after Vondel, the greatest literary genius Holland has so far produced. Born in easy circumstances—his father was for some time burgomaster of Amsterdam—H. spent over three years travelling in Italy and Germany, and after studying law and history at Leyden University (1606-9), received a highly remunerative appointment from the Prince of Orange. The value of his European culture is manifest in his fine pastoral *Granida* (1605), his tragedy *Geerœrdt van Velzen* (1612), and his monumental *Dutch History,* 1555-85.

Hooge, Pieter de (*c.* 1643-1708), a Dutch painter of interiors and of groups of conversing people dressed according to the fashions of his own period. He produced a wonderful effect by means of sunlight falling through a window upon objects in a room.

Hoogeveen, a tn., prov. Drenthe, Holland, 32 m. S.W. of Groningen. The Protestants here are summoned to church by the beat of a drum. There are shipyards, spacious peat deposits, and works. Pop 12,652.

Hoogeveen, Hendrik (1712-91), a Dutch classical scholar, attended Leyden gymnasium, and in after life was rector of many schools at Wœrden, Breda, and Delft, etc. His *Dictionarium Analogicum Linguœ Grœciœ* (1800) has been of use to etymologists, as the words are arranged according to their terminations instead of their first letters. His treatise on Greek particles appeared in 1769.

Hoogeveld, a plateau, 4000 to 5000 ft. in height, situated in Southern Transvaal, S. Africa. Here the and at Witwatersrand are some of the most valuable goldfields of Africa.

Hoogezand, a com. of Netherlands, and prov. of, and 18 m. E.S.E. of Groningen. Up to 1650 the district in which this town is situated was a waste, but by incessant toil it has been transformed into fertile fields. Pop. 10,666.

Hooglede, a tn. of Belgium, in W. Flanders, about 12 m. N.E. of Ypres. Pop. 5000.

Hoogly, or Hooghly, *see* HUGLI.

Hook, James Clark (1819-1907), an English painter, studied at the Royal Academy, and in 1846 set out on his foreign tour, as the Academy had awarded him the travelling student-ship for his ' Rizpah watching the Dead Sons of Saul,' 1846. So far he had mostly chosen romantic or his-torical subjects, like ' The Finding the Body of Harold,' 1845. But after his return from Italy and Paris, he embarked on his splendid series of English sea and land scapes, among them being: ' A Rest by the Wayside,' 1854; ' Luff, Boy,' 1859, which Ruskin so much admired; and ' Sea Urchins.'

Hook, Theodore Edward (1788-1841), a humorist, at an early age acquired fame as a wit, an im-provisatore, and a practical joker, and became a popular figure in London society. In 1813 he was appointed accountant - general of Mauritius, without having any ex-perience to qualify him for the post. When he retired four years later, large sums were missing from the treasury, and, though he was clearly innocent of malversation, he was on his return held liable for the deficit, and was imprisoned for debt from 1822 until 1825. In 1820 he edited in the court interest, the scandalous *John Bull*, in which disgraceful attacks were made on Queen Caroline and her party. He published : *Sayings and Doings*, 1826-29; *Maxwell*, 1830; *Gilbert Gurney*, 1836, and other novels, now little read. He was editor of *The New Monthly Magazine* from 1836 until his death, and had the honour of being satirised by Disraeli and Thackeray. There is a biography by Barham (1849).

Hook, WalterFarquhar (1798-1875), an English divine, was educated at Winchester and Christ Church, Oxford. In 1827 he was appointed chaplain-in-ordinary to George IV., an office which he held also under William IV. and Queen Victoria. From 1837 to 1859, when he accepted the deanery of Chichester, he had charge of a parish in Leeds. Here he was instrumental in the erection of many new churches and schools, and despite his High Church tenets, won the respect and esteem of all the working classes. Moreover, he was an earnest advocate of state-provided secular education and wrote a number of ecclesiastical histories, including *An Ecclesiastical Biography*, 1845-52, and *Lives of the Archbishops of Canterbury*, 1860-76.

Hookah (from Arabic *huqqa*) or **Nargileh,** the water tobacco-pipe so popular in India, Persia, Turkey, and other countries of the East. The tobacco bowl is connected by a wooden tube with a water vessel so that the smoke is cooled in the liquid before passing through a flexible tube up to the smoker's mouth.

Hooke, Nathaniel (c. 1690-1763, or 1764), an English author, was inti-mate with Pope and his literary coterie. He translated Ramsay's *Life of Fénelon*, 1723, and his *Travels of Cyrus*, 1739, but his claim to remembrance rests on his *History of Rome*, 1733-71 (4 vols.), notwith-standing it has long been eclipsed by later works and is spoilt, moreover, by an excessive bias for the plebeian cause.

Hooke, Robert (1635-1703), an Eng-lish experimental philosopher, was a pupil of Dr. Busby at Westminster, and at Christ Church, Oxford, worked in the laboratory of Robert Boyle. In 1664 he began to teach geometry at Gresham College, and in 1677, after being surveyor to the City of London, became secretary to the Royal Society. The range of his invention was pheno-menal. Among his contrivances were a double - barrelled air - pump, the spirit-level, areometer, marine baro-meter, and a sea-gauge. His regret-table quarrel with Newton arose out of the fact that he believed, rightly it seems, that he had already discovered certain of his rival's principles, especially as to gravity and the laws which rule celestial motions.

Hooker, Joseph (1814 - 79), an American general, graduated at the military academy of West Point (1837) and was promoted to the rank of lieutenant - colonel for his gal-lantry in the Mexican War (1846-48). On the outbreak of civil war (1861) he joined the Federals and was soon commissioned major-general (1862). His sobriquet of ' Fighting Joe ' was won during the Peninsular campaign. He fought at ' Fair Oaks ' and Man-assas, and won the new brevet of brigadier-general for his services in the battle of Antietam when Jackson was repulsed. In 1863, as com-mander of the army of the Potomac, he suffered a somewhat inglorious defeat at the hands of Lee, the Confederate general, and in spite of his brilliant occupation of Lookout Mt. after the ' Battle above the Clouds,' which was his victory, was never again entrusted with the single command. In 1868 he retired from the army as he was not given the preferment to which he felt himself entitled.

Hooker, Sir Joseph Dalton (*b.* 1817), an English botanist, took his M.D. degree at Glasgow (1839), and as assistant-surgeon accompanied Sir James Ross to the Antarctic in the *Erebus*. From 1847-51 he was with a party exploring the northern confines of India and at later periods visited Palestine, Morocco, and the United States (1877). His foreign tours were all fruitful in scientific and especially botanical discoveries, which were fully described in his *Flora Antarctica, Flora of British India*, etc. In 1865 he succeeded his father, also an eminent botanist, as director of Kew Gardens. A friend of Darwin, he boldly championed his theories in his presidential address to the British Association (1868). His presidency of the Royal Society extended from 1872-77. Other publications of his were a *Himalayan Journal*, and *Genera Plantarum*.

Hooker, Richard (1554-1600), an English theologian, was, through the patronage of two bishops, able to take his M.A. degree at Corpus Christi, Oxford, in 1577. For some time he was tutor to George Cranmer, grandnephew of the archbishop, and Edwin Sandys, son of the Bishop of London, and later became master of the Temple, whence his more popular rival, Travers, the Puritan, was eventually expelled. The eight books of the *Laws of Ecclesiastical Polity* were composed within the quiet of a country vicarage. Five books only were published in his lifetime, and considerable mystery attended the publication of the last three during the half century following his death. The standard edition is that of Keble (1836), to which Walton's inimitable *Life* (1666) is fitly appended. In spite of its quaint and somewhat archaic flavour II's. work, by reason of its stateliness and charm, its lucidity, even where the thought is most profound, and its noble expression of a lofty intellect and unswerving religious enthusiasm, is justly deemed the fountain-head of modern literature in prose. His theory, which he gradually unfolds from book to book, is based first on the unity and omnipotence of law, ' whose seat is the bosom of God,' and secondly on the supremacy of calm and temperate reason to which all things, even divine revelation, are finally referred.

Hooker, Thomas (*c.* 1586-1647), an American divine, born in Marfield, Leicestershire, England. He was educated at Emanuel College, Cambridge, and later became fellow of his college. After being ordained priest, he preached in London and Chelmsford (1629); it was at the latter town that Laud, Bishop of London, dismissed him for Nonconformity. He went to Holland (1630), and lived in Delft, Amsterdam, and Rotterdam. In 1633 he emigrated with John Cotton and Samuel Stone to Boston, U.S.A.; appointed pastor at Newtown (now Cambridge, Massachusetts); and in 1636 he founded Hartford, which he named after the birthplace of his assistant, Samuel Stone. Some of his works include: *A Survey of the Sum of Church Discipline, The Soul's Implantation, The Application of Redemption. See* Life in Mather's *Magnalia*, and Tyler's *American Literature*, vol. i.

Hooker, Sir William Jackson (1785-1865), an English botanist, published his *Tour in Iceland*, 1811. It was written from memory, as all his notes and drawings were accidentally burned on his way home. Other of his scientific works were *British Jungermanniæ*, 1816 ; *Muscologia Britannica*, 1818, in which Dr. Taylor collaborated, and *Flora Scotica*, 1821. From 1820 he held the chair of botany in Glasgow University, and from 1841 till his death was director of Kew Gardens. He collected an invaluable herbarium, and edited three botanical journals besides numerous treatises on botany.

Hooker, Mount, a peak of the Rocky Mts., between British Columbia and Alberta, Canada, S.E. of Mt. Brown, about 52° 27′ N. Its altitude is computed at 10,500 ft.

Hook of Holland(*Hoek van Holland*), a little village at mouth of the Nieuwe Waterweg on a small peninsula in S. Holland. Here is an important landing stage for passengers and mail steamers from England.

Hooks and Eyes, a form of dressfastener, frequently employed about the middle of the 19th century, but nowadays more or less superseded by buttons of various forms and designs, and by patent fasteners—the latter a far more efficient article for the safe fastening of dresses, blouses, etc. At one time H. and E. were made by hand by means of pliers, which bent the wire into the desired shape, but for many years past various machines of more or less complex design have been in use.

Hoole, John (1727-1803), an English poet and translator, born in London. Was a friend of Dr. Johnson, and for forty years was a clerk in the East India House. He is chiefly remembered as the translator of Tasso's *Jerusalem Delivered*, Ariosto's *Orlando Furioso*, and other Italian poems, and he also wrote several tragedies, none of which are of any particular note.

Hoop Ash, *see* NETTLE TREE.

Hooper, John (*c.* 1495 - 1555), an English divine, was born in Somerset. He was educated at Oxford, but on leaving the university entered the Cistercian monastery at Gloucester, where he was ordained. He became an ardent reformer, and after a dispute with Gardiner had to flee from England in 1539 to avoid persecution. On his return he was made Bishop of Gloucester in 1550, suffering imprisonment for some weeks because he refused to wear vestments. In 1552 he received the bishopric of Worcester *in commendam*, but in 1553 he was deprived of his office by Queen Mary, and burnt for heresy at Gloucester. A collected edition of his works was issued in 1855.

Hooping Cough, *see* WHOOPING COUGH.

Hoopoe (Fr. *huppe;* Lat. *upupa;* Gk. ἔποψ, all names bestowed apparently from its cry), a bird long celebrated in literature, and conspicuous by its variegated plumage, and its large erectile crest. The common H. (*Upupa epops*) is about

HOOPOE

the size of a thrush, with a long, pointed, and slightly arched bill. Its head and neck are of a golden buff, the former being adorned by the crest which begins to rise from the forehead and consists of broad feathers, gradually increasing in length, tipped with black, and having a subterminal bar of yellowish-white. The upper part of the back is of a vinous-grey, and the flight-feathers and tail are black, broadly barred with white. This bird visits Britain during the spring and autumn migration, but seldom breeds

in any part of the island. Besides the *U. epops* there are *U. indica*, which frequents India and Ceylon; *U. longirostris*, common in the Indo-Chinese countries, *U. africana*, which inhabits S. Africa, and *U. marginata*, found in Madagascar.

Hoopstad, a div. and tn. on the R. Vet, Orange River Colony, S. Africa, 80 m. N. of Bloemfontein. Pop. (town) 450.

Hoorn, a tn. and seaport, Holland, prov. N. Holland, W. coast Zuider Zee, 25½ m. N.N.E. of Amsterdam. It is a picturesque town with most interesting old buildings. There are noted cheese and cattle markets, besides shipbuilding and saw-milling yards. Willem Schouten, who doubled Cape Horn and named it after his birthplace, was born here. Pop. 11,016.

Hoosac Mts., a mountain range in Berkshire co., Massachusetts, a portion of Green Mts. H. tunnel, 4¾ m. long, is pierced through this range, and is the longest railway tunnel in U.S.A.

Hoosick Falls, a vil. of Rensselaer co., New York, U.S.A., 24 m. N.E. of Troy. It manufs. paper - making, reaping and mowing machines, woollen and cotton goods, and flour. Pop. (1910) 5532.

Hoove, Hoven, or **Tympanites**, a common derangement in ruminants due to the accumulation of gases in the rumen or first stomach. Is most frequent when animals are allowed to eat immoderately of clover. Before turning for the first time into luxuriant pasture, they should be well fed on dry stuffs. Too much wet grass or frosted turnips or too many potatoes are other causes. The usual treatment is one wineglassful of turpentine in one pint of raw linseed oil. Failing this, the stomach is punctured with a trocar and cannula, or even a pocket knife, to liberate the gas. Stoppages due to foreign bodies, or to rupture or stricture also cause H., and are very rarely cured. Small doses of chloride of lime sometimes give relief.

Hope, Queen's Hope, or **Estyn**, a par. and vil. on R. Alyn, Flintshire, Wales, 7 m. N.N.E. of Wrexham. Pop. (1911) 5116.

Hope, Alexander James Beresford (1820-87), an English politician and writer, born in London. He entered parliament in 1841 on the Conservative side, and up to the time of his death, took an active part in all the debates. In 1855 he founded the *Saturday Review* in conjunction with John Douglas Cook. H. always had at heart the interests of the Church of England, and to this end wrote *Worship in the Church of England* and various other works on church affairs.

Besides these he wrote *The English Cathedrals of the 19th Century, A Popular View of the American Civil War*, etc.

Hope, Anthony, *see* HAWKINS, ANTHONY HOPE.

Hope, Sir James (1808 - 81), a British admiral. Entered Royal Naval College in 1820, and rose to rank of captain in 1838. From 1859-62 was commander-in-chief in the E. Indies, and brought about capture of Peking. Made admiral in 1870, and retired two years later. Decorated with the grand cross of the Legion of Honour in 1861.

Hope, Thomas (*c.* 1770-1831), an English novelist and antiquarian, born in London. A great lover of architecture, paintings, and statues, he formed a fine collection of works of art, and in 1807 published a work on *Household Furniture* which produced a marked improvement in public taste. He also wrote *Costume of the Ancients, Modern Costumes, Anastatius* (a novel), and an *Historical Essay on Architecture*.

Hopedale, a missionary station of the Moravians, on the E. coast of Labrador, Canada, in 55° 30' N.

Hopefield, a sub-dist. of the Malmesbury div. of Cape Colony, 40 m. N.N.W. of Malmesbury, S. Africa.

Hope Islands, a cluster in Van Diemen's Gulf, Northern Territory, Australia.

Hope-Scott, James Robert (1812-73), an English barrister and parliamentarian, third son of General the hon. Sir Alexander H., born at Great Marlow, Bucks. Educated at Eton and Christ Church, Oxford, and called to the bar in 1838. Was made a Q.C. in 1849. Was a friend of W. E. Gladstone, with whom he corresponded on 'The State in its Relation with the Church.' In 1853 he married a grand-daughter of Sir Walter Scott, hence his assumed name. He is the author of *The Bishopric of the United Church of England and Ireland at Jerusalem. See* R. Ormsby, *Memoirs of J. R. Hope-Scott.*

Hopetoun, Earl of, *see* LINLITHGOW, MARQUIS OF.

Hopetoun, John Hope, fourth Earl of (1765-1823), a British general, born in Linlithgowshire, served with distinction in the W. Indies, Holland, Egypt, and Spain. Also saw service in the Walcheren expedition, and in the Peninsular campaign, where he was wounded and taken prisoner.

Hopetown, a div. of Cape Colony. (Pop. 6000.) The town of this name near the Orange R. is 70 m. S.S.W. of Kimberley. There are diamond fields and ostrich farms in the vicinity. Pop. 1500.

Hop-flea, or *Haltica concinna,* a species of small coleopterous insects, belonging to the sub-order Heteromera, and the family Chrysomelidæ ; it is closely allied to *Haltica memorum,* the turnip-flea, and does great damage to the young shoots of hop-plants. The H. is generally about one-tenth of an inch long, and of a bright metallic colour.

Hop-fly, or *Aphis humuli,* the name of a species of hemiptera-homopterousinsects belonging to the family Aphidæ. They are pale green in colour, and do great harm to hops and other plants.

Hôpital, Guillaume François Antoine l', *see* L'HÔPITAL, GUILLAUME FRANÇOIS ANTOINE.

Hôpital, Michel de l', *see* L'HÔPITAL.

Hopkins, a riv. of Western Victoria, Australia. It rises in the Pyrenees Mts. and flows in a generally southern direction to the Indian Ocean at Warrnambool. Only about 5 m. are navigable. Length, 110 m.

Hopkins, Edward John (1818-1901), an English organist, born at Westminster. From 1826-34 he was a chorister at the Chapel Royal, St. James's, and on leaving, became organist at Mitcham Church, Surrey, eventually becoming organist at the Temple Church, London. While there he issued a *Book of Responses,* and a collection of chants, which appear in the *Temple Church Choral Service Book,* and the *Temple Psalter.* He was regarded as an authority on organ construction, and published *The Organ, its History and Construction,* with Dr. Rimbault in 1855 (4th ed., 1898).

Hopkins, John (*d.* 1570), an English hymn writer, was part translator with Thomas Sternhold of the famous metrical version of the Psalms. Of the complete edition which appeared in 1562, sixty psalms bore the name of H., and forty that of Sternhold. H. also contributed some commendatory verses to Foxe's *Acts and Monuments,* and is often credited with the authorship of the ' Old Hundredth.' He was rector of Great Waldingfield, Suffolk (1561-70).

Hopkins, Sir John Ommanney (*b.* 1834), an English admiral, born at Nuffield, Oxfordshire, and educated at Marlborough College. He served during the Crimean War before Sebastopol (1854-55) ; was secretary to the First Lord of the Admiralty (1881-83); director of Naval Ordnance (1883-86); superintendent of Portsmouth dockyard (1886-88) ; naval Lord of the Admiralty and controller of the navy (1888-92), and commander-in-chief on the Mediterranean station (1896-99).

Hopkins, Johns (1795-1873), an American philanthropist, born in

Anne Arundel co., Maryland. His Quaker parents educated him for a farmer, but at the age of seventeen he went to Baltimore and became a grocer, eventually founding the house of Hopkins & Brothers, and amassing a large fortune. This he devoted to various philanthropic purposes; he presented Baltimore with a public park, founded the Johns Hopkins University, and gave money towards a free hospital.

Hopkins, Lemuel, M.D. (1750-1801), a doctor and poet, descendant of Governor H., born in Waterbury, Connecticut, U.S.A. He practised at Litchfield (1776-84) and Hartford (1784-1801), and gained a high reputation. His best known works are *The Hypocrite's Hope* and *Elegy on the Victim of a Cancer Quack*. He helped Barlow, Alsop, Trumbull, and others in the compilation of *The Anarchiad*. See Thacker's *Medical Biography* and Kettell's *Speculations of American Poetry*, vol. i.

Hopkins, Mark (1802-87), an American educationist, born at Stockbridge, Massachusetts. He graduated at Williams College in 1824, and was appointed professor of moral philosophy there in 1830, becoming president of the college in 1836, a position he held until 1872. He also lectured before the Lowell and Smithsonian Institutes, and took an active part in the deliberations of the American board of commissioners for foreign missions. His publications include: *Lectures on the Evidences of Christianity*, 1846; *Lectures on Moral Science*, 1862; *Outline Study of Man*, 1873; *Teachings and Counsels*, 1884.

Hopkins, Matthew (c. 1596-1647), a witch-finder, was a native of Suffolk. He is said to have been a lawyer at Ipswich and at Manningtree, but in 1644 he began his career as witch-seeker, 'a trade never taken up in this country till then.' He made journeys through Essex, Suffolk, Norfolk, and Huntingdonshire, searching and torturing all suspected persons, but in 1647 he himself was accused of witchcraft and subjected to his own method of trial; his thumbs and toes were tied, and he was thrown into a pool; he swam, and was hanged. He published *The Discovery of Witches*, 1647. See WITCHCRAFT.

Hopkins, Samuel (1721-1803), an American theologian, born at Waterbury, Connecticut. He studied under Jonathan Edwards, and in 1743 was ordained at Housatonic, now Great Barrington, Mass., where he continued until 1769 when he became minister of Newport, Rhode I. He was an opponent of slavery, and in 1776 published *Dialogue showing it*

to be the Duty and Interest of the American States to Emancipate all their African Slaves. His *System of Doctrines contained in Divine Revelation, Explained and Defended*, 1793, sets forth his theological opinions, which differ from orthodox Calvinism in their opposition to the doctrines of original sin and of the Atonement. The publication of his views was the cause of the famous 'Hopkinsian controversy.' H. is the central figure in Mrs. Stowe's novel, *The Minister's Wooing*.

Hopkins, William (1793-1866), a mathematician and geologist, born at Kingston in Derbyshire. He entered Peterhouse, Cambridge, in 1822, and became seventh wrangler in 1827. He settled at Cambridge as a tutor, and was so successful in his work that he was called 'the senior wrangler maker'; indeed in 1849 he had nearly 200 wranglers among his pupils, amongst whom may be mentioned such distinguished men as Todhunter, Tait, Fawcett, Stokes, and Clerk-Maxwell. About 1833 he began to study geology, and in 1850 received the Wollaston medal for his researches in the application of mathematics to physics and geology. In 1851 he was elected president of the Geological Society, and in 1853 became president of the British Association. His publications include *Elements of Trigonometry*, 1833, and *Theoretical Investigations on Motion of Glaciers*, 1842.

Hopkinson, Francis (1737-91), an American author, born in Philadelphia, U.S.A. He was educated at the University of Philadelphia, and then studied law. In 1776 he was elected representative of New Jersey in the American Congress, and was a signer of the Declaration of Independence. He was appointed judge of the Admiralty in Pennsylvania (1779), and judge of the District Court of the United States. H. was a very versatile writer, and was very popular during the revolution, when he wrote his famous ballad *Battle of the Kegs*. His writings include: *The Treaty, An Evening Hymn, Science, A Camp Ballad, The Typographical Mode of Conducting a Quarrel, Essay on White-washing and Modern Learning, The Prophecy, The Pretty Story, The Political Catechism.* See Allen's *American Biog. Dict.*

Hopkinson, John (1849-98), an English electrician, born at Manchester and educated at Trinity College, Cambridge, where he graduated as senior wrangler. He then took up electrical engineering, and made many important investigations; in 1890 being awarded a royal medal for researches in electricity and magnetism. He was professor of electrical engineering at King's College, London, at the time of his death. He published: *Dynamic Electricity, Original Papers on Dynamo Machinery and Allied Subjects,* and other papers on similar themes. He was killed with a son and two daughters ascending the Dent de Veisivi in the Alps.

Hopkinson, Joseph (1770-1842), son of Francis H., born at Philadelphia and educated at the University there. He studied law and practised at Easton and Philadelphia. H. was a member of the national House of Representatives from 1815-19, and judge of the District Court of the U.S.A. in 1828; he was also vice-president of the American Philosophical Society and president of the Philadelphia Academy of Fine Arts. He published some of his addresses which he delivered before various societies, but he will be chiefly remembered for his song, *Hail, Columbia.* See *Life* by Francis Wharton, and Griswold's *Poets and Poetry of America.*

Hopkinsville, a city of Kentucky, U.S.A., co. seat of Christian co., 74 m. S. of Henderson. It is important, principally for its tobacco; it trades also in agricultural produce, live stock, and coal. Pop. (1910) 9419.

Hoppner, John (1758 - 1810), a portrait painter, born in Whitechapel, London. He was admitted as a student to the Royal Academy in 1775, and in 1782 gained the gold medal for an original painting of a scene from King Lear. In 1785 he exhibited portraits of the youngest three princesses, Sophia, Amelia, and Mary, and in 1789 was appointed portrait painter to the Prince of Wales. In 1795 he was elected R.A. H. acquired some reputation in his own day, especially for his portraits of women and children. His figures were graceful and natural, and his colouring brilliant and mellow. Some of his best pictures are the group of 'Lady Culling Smith and Children' (belonging to the Duke of Wellington), the fine portrait of 'Mrs. Lascelles' (the property of Lord Harewood), both of which were exhibited at the Royal Academy in 1876, 'The Countess of Oxford' (National Gallery); 'William Pitt,' and 'Lord Grenville' (National Portrait Gallery).

Hops (*Humulus lupulus*), a perennial herbaceous plant belonging to the order Cannabinaceæ which has long twining stems which climb freely over hedges and bushes. Its leaves are stalked and three to five lobed and very rough to the touch, the plant being of luxuriant growth and abundant foliage. The male flowers consist of a small five-parted perianth enclosing five stamens, and grow in loose axillary panicles. The female flowers are in 'strobiles,' or cones, and it is these ripened cones which are sold under the name of H., so that female plants are most generally planted, a few male only being necessary to fertilise the female flowers. The H. is first mentioned by Pliny as being a garden plant of the Romans who were in the habit of eating the young shoots as we eat asparagus (indeed in Belgium the young tender tops are even now cut off in spring and used as food, the plant being forced from December to February for that purpose), and as early as the 8th and 9th centuries H. gardens (*humularia*) were cultivated in France and Germany for the manufacture of beer, but up to the 16th century the plant seems only to have been grown in a fitful manner. It was introduced into England from Flanders in 1525, but did not become sufficient for the supply of the kingdom till the end of the 17th century. The chief counties concerned with H. production in England are Kent, Hereford, Sussex, Worcester, Hants, and Surrey, and of these Kent has always taken the lead, and includes about two-thirds of the H. acreage of the British Isles; indeed out of 413 parishes in the county, about 335 have H. plantations. These are prepared in October and November; the earth is ploughed, dug, and manured (for a rich soil is required) and the plants put in in rows 6 ft. apart. Later they are poled and dressed, the former being done in various ways, and at various times. Some owners pole their plants the first year to produce H. in the first season, but as a rule planters nurse their young plants for twelve months as they make very little growth the first year. When the cones are ripe, *i.e.* have become amber coloured and firm, they are picked and conveyed to the kiln to be dried, and great care is required to prevent over-heating, by which the essential oil would be volatilised. The cultivation of H. is very precarious, as the plant suffers from various pests, both insect and fungoid parasites; of the former the red spider, *Tetramyelius telarius*, is most destructive in very hot summers, and of the latter the fungus *Podasphæra costagnei* does much mischief to the cones.

Hopson, Sir Thomas (1642-1717), an English vice-admiral, born in the Isle of Wight. Was present at the battle of Solebay in 1672, and commanded the *York* in the battle off Beachy Head in 1690. In 1692 he commanded the *St. Michael* in the battle of Barfleur. Ten years later he was second in command under Rooke in the expedition against Cadiz, and, at the battle of Vigo Bay, led the attack. On his return to England, he was rewarded with knighthood and pensioned.

Hop Substitutes, bitter substances which are used as a substitute for hops. The fruit of an American shrub of the rue family (*Rutaceæ*), which is intensely bitter, is sometimes used.

Hoquiam, a tn., Washington, U.S.A., co. seat of Chehalis co., 18 m. W. of Montesano. Lumber, fish, and fur trade; shipyards. Pop. (1910) 8171.

Hor, a mountain of Arabia which cannot for certain be identified, but it is reputed to be Jebel Harun (' Aaron's Mount '); ' by the border of the land of Edom ' (Num. xx. 22; xxxiii. 37). At the summit is a whitewashed sanctuary which is supposed to be Aaron's tomb.

Horace, Q. Horatius Flaccus (65-8 B.C.), a Roman poet, born at Venusia in Apulia. He was of servile descent, but his father had acquired the status of freedman, and from his profits as auctioneer's collector had been able to purchase a small farm at Venusia. One of the most endearing traits in the character of H. is his reverence for his father and his pride in his descent. H.'s father recognised the genius of his son and, comparatively poor though he was, he contrived to give him the best education obtainable by a Roman youth. He therefore declined to send the boy to a provincial school, and had him educated in Rome at the school of Orbilius, where the sons of knights and senators were trained. The father himself acted as attendant on the boy, accompanying him to school, and carrying his slate and books. In H.'s time Roman youths received their university training at Athens, and thither H. repaired at the age of eighteen. When Brutus went to Athens to levy forces against Octavius, H. enlisted in his service and was given the rank of military tribune in command of a legion. He was on the field at Philippi, and his depreciation of his own valour must be regarded as an imitation of Archilochus and Alcæus, and not as serious information (*Odes*, II. vii. 9; *Epodes*, II. ii. 46-50). In the land settlements after the war, the property of H.'s father at Venusia was confiscated and H. became a scribe in the quæstor's office at Rome. Varius introduced the young poet to Mæcenas, who became his life-long guide, philosopher, and friend. Mæcenas introduced the young poet to Augustus, who soon, to the glory of Rome and the fame of his protégé, enlisted his services to voice the ideals of his new empire.

From this time H. became a court poet, but his genius was strengthened rather than cramped by the guiding influence of his patrons. In the year 33 B.C. Mæcenas presented to the poet the Sabine farm, which throughout the remainder of his life satisfied his deep-seated love of country life and scenery. Though towards the closing years of his life, H. was drawn into the inmost bosom of the court, he never forgot his former patron. To his fervent love of Mæcenas the seventeenth ode of the second book and the eleventh ode of the fourth book bear speaking testimony. Mæcenas himself, on his deathbed, thus commended the poet to the emperor, 'Horati Flacci ut mei esto memor ' (*Suet. vit.*), but H. only survived his patron a few weeks. H. died suddenly and without making a will, and to Augustus he left the entire control of his affairs. H.'s earliest publication was the first book of the *Satires*. These follow the didactic aims and semi-dramatic setting of the early *Satura* of Lucilius, but they are not personal like the work of the early master. Unlike the fierce invective of Juvenal, the satiric vein in H. is kindly and sympathetic in tone. The *Epodes* appear to have been written about the same time as the second book of the *Satires*. They are based on the works of Archilochus, but are coarse in sentiment and immature in expression. The *Epistles* are also didactic in theme, but the sentiment is mellow, and the workmanship perfect. In subject and style the *Ars Poetica*, a metrical treatise on the art of poetry, is closely allied to the second book of the *Epistles*. This work is somewhat desultory in treatment and capricious in judgment; its standpoint is uncompromisingly mechanical, yet it throws valuable light on H.'s own poetic methods, and the state of literary criticism at Rome. But H.'s great work was the composition of the *Odes*. These do not stand high on account of any startling originality of thought or depth of feeling, but in finish and technique they are perfect. The finest odes are, perhaps, those which deal with Rome's expansion and conquests; the love lyrics, although charming and graceful, are insincere and insipid, and are much inferior to the flaming lyrics of Catullus. The philosophy of H. is eclectic, but if he inclines to any sect, he is epicurean and *carpe diem* is his guiding precept. As a Roman poet he is generally held to rank second only to Virgil. *See* the editions of Palmer, Wickham, and Page; the translation by Wickham, and Sellar's appreciation entitled *Horace and the Elegiac Poets.*

Horæ (Lat. *hora*, hour), in Greek mythology, the personification of the seasons. They are weather-goddesses; the children of Zeus and Themis, whose function it is to regulate the order of nature, superintend agriculture, etc. They are companions of the nymphs and graces, and are represented as goddesses of youthful bloom and grace, typical of the springtime. They are sometimes indicated as being three in number, with parents as above mentioned; but under Alexandrian influence, they became the four daughters of Helios and Selene. *See* J. H. Krause, *Die Musen, Grazien, Horen und Nymphen,* 1871.

Horapollo, or Horus Apollo, a Greek grammarian who taught at Alexandria and Constantinople in the reign of Theodosius. He is often confounded with the Egyptian Horapollo, who lived in the time of Zeno. There is still extant a work by him on hieroglyphics.

Horary (Lat. *horarius,* from *hora,* hour), pertaining to an hour, noting the hours. In astronomy H. circles are great circles of the heavens passing through the poles.

Horatii, the three Roman brothers, chosen by the king, Tullus Hostilius, to fight against the Curiatii (three Alban brothers) in order to decide the contest between Alba Longa and Rome. Two of the Romans quickly fell in the combat, but the surviving Horatius was victorious and was led back in triumph to Rome.

Horatius Cocles, a descendant of the survivor of the three Horatii, who, according to tradition, along with Titus Herminius and Spurius Lartius, held the bridge over the Tiber against Lars Porsena, king of Latium, in 507 B.C. H. sent back his two companions when the fight was almost finished and defended the bridge single-handed. He then escaped by swimming the Tiber, though enfeebled by wounds, and was overwhelmed with honours by his compatriots. *See* Macaulay's *Lays of Ancient Rome,* ' Horatius.'

Horbury, a tn., eccles. par., 3 m. S.W. of Wakefield, Yorkshire, England. The chief industries are connected with the manuf. of woollen and cloth goods, railway waggons, and with stone quarries. Pop. (1911) 7509.

Hörde, a tn., Prussian prov. of Westphalia, in gov. of Arnsberg, 3 m. S.E. (rail) of Dortmund. There are iron works and coal mines. Pop. 32,785.

Hordein (Lat. *hordeum,* barley), the name applied to a substance extracted from barley, which is a mixture of nitrogenous matter, starch, and cellulose left as a residue when barley meal is digested with acidu-lated water. It is not a definite chemical compound.

Hordel, a coal mining vil. in Westphalia, Prussia. Pop. 7856.

Hordeum, the genus of Gramineæ, to which the barley belongs. There are sixteen species in all which inhabit temperate parts of Europe, Asia, Africa, and America, and four are to be found in Britain. The cultivated barley is known as *H. vulgare,* but the varieties *distichum* and *hexastichum* are more generally grown. The former variety is the two-rowed barley found in Britain during the summer months; the latter is the six-rowed barley of winter and is very hardy. *See* BARLEY.

Horeb (Arabic, *Jebel Musa,* Mountain of Moses), a mountain in the northern part of Arabia, traditionally known as the sacred mountain of the Hebrew law-giving, on the same ridge as Mt. Sinai. The monastery of St. Catherine lies at its foot, in a ravine, and near by is the chapel of St. Elias (Elijah). The rock on H. from which water is said to have issued at Moses' blow is pointed out by the monks to sightseers.

Horehound (Old Eng. *harhune,* Ger. *Andorn,* Fr. *marrube*), a species of perennial herb, belonging to the natural order Labiatæ, growing about 1 ft. high, with thick stems and a short rootstock. Most of the species are herbaceous plants occurring in Europe, N. Africa, and W. Asia. Common or white H. is found throughout Europe, and occurs in Britain, on sandy or chalky ground, but is not at all common. Black H., a perennial herb of the same genus, is also a native of Britain, S. of the Forth and Clyde, and occurs also in Europe and N. Africa. H. has likewise been naturalised in parts of America.

Horgen, a tn. of Switzerland on Lake Zurich in canton of and 10 m. E.S.E. of Zurich; amidst vineyards, orchards, and fine walks. Manufs. cotton, silk, and chemicals. Pop. 8006.

Horitz : 1. A tn. in Bohemia, 14 m. N.W. of Königgrätz, noted for its cherries. It has a training school for sculptors, and sandstone quarries, and manufs. textiles. Pop. 8969. 2. A small vil. in the dist. of Krumau, Austria, noted for the frequent performance of the Passion play by the natives of the village and environs.

Horizon (from Gk. ὁρίζων, dividing or bounding), the circular line round which the earth and sky seem to meet, most clearly defined at sea, where it is called the sea H. This is known in astronomy as the *sensible* H., while the name *rational* H. is given to the circle whose plane passes through the centre of the earth. The sea H. is depressed by a *dip* which varies according to the height of the observer's eye from the water, this being due to the roundness of the earth. *See* treatises on *Spherical Astronomy*.

Horley, a par. and residential vil. in Surrey, England, 5 m. S.S.E. of Reigate. It possesses an Early English church (St. Bartholomew). Pop. (1911) 4916.

Hormayr, Joseph, Baron von (1782-1848), a German historian, born at Innsbrück. In 1815 he was appointed historiographer of Austria, and in 1828 became councillor for the foreign department of Bavaria, holding the position of Bavarian minister to Hanover in 1832. He wrote widely, among his works being : *History of Tyrol; Lives of the Austrian Princes; General History of Modern Times; Vienna, Its History and Curiosities,* etc. *See* Hirn, *Tiroler Aufstand,* 1909, and Brockhaus, *Conversations-Lexikon.*

Hormones, term applied by E. Starling to those juices prepared by organs, not for secretion nor even for partial excretion, but for the maintenance of certain physiological activities. They pass into the blood from every organ and tissue, and act and react until each part of the human system affects every other part. The most highly complex inter-relations appear to exist between the glands, so that the effect of a drug on one of them is very far-reaching. W. Bayliss and E. Starling prepared an extract, *secretin,* by digesting duodenal mucous membrane with hydrochloric acid. The product is soluble in alcohol, and is not destroyed by boiling. If secretin be injected into the blood, it leads to active stimulation of the pancreas. This H. is apparently naturally formed by the action of the acid chyme on some prosecretin in the intestine. It passes to the pancreas, which it stimulates, and then possibly a pancreatic H. actuates a ferment in the muscles, and hence physiological equilibrium is maintained. The discovery of H. appears to suggest that glands may have a double or even triple function, and their external secretion may not be as important as their internal; this is supported by the fact that profuse perspiration which eliminates but few substances directly, and these not strikingly toxic, has frequently a most beneficial action on the whole system.

Hormuz, or **Ormuz,** an ancient city on the Persian Gulf on the northeastern extremity of the island of Ormuz. It sprang up in the latter part of the middle ages, and became a great emporium of the trade between Persia and India. In 1594 the Portuguese captured it and held it till 1622, during which time it served as a great depôt for the products of India and China. In little more than a century, on the rise of Shah Abbas, its trade was transferred to the new town of Bender Abbas. The ruins of the Portuguese fort still remain at the village of H.

Horn, Cape, generally considered the southernmost point of S. America, at the S. of a small island to the S. of Tierra del Fuego. Discovered in 1616 by the Dutch navigators, Lemaire and Schouten, and named after the Dutch town, Hoorn, the birthplace of the latter.

Horn, French (Fr. *cor, cor de chasse,* Ger. *horn, waldhorn*), a brass wind instrument, used in orchestral music, with a particularly soft tone, due chiefly to the funnel-like bore of the mouthpiece, but also to the length of tube and shape of bell. Originally it was employed in hunting from a very early period, but was introduced into the orchestra at the beginning of the 18th century, and now holds one of the most important positions, as it is the softest toned brass instrument used, and forms a fine contrast to the others. It is seldom used singly, two or four being the usual number in the orchestra. It consists of several spiral coils, with a funnel-shaped mouthpiece at the upper and a bell at the lower end of the tube, the length of which is varied by the introduction of crooks of different lengths. There are also supplementary tuning crooks and a tuning slide. Music for the horn is always written in the G or treble clef, the notes actually sounded depending on the crooks used. In 1770, Hampl, at Dresden, discovered the method of forming intermediate notes by hand-stopping, viz. introducing the open hand with fingers close together into the bell, and thus lowering the pitch by a semitone. Nowadays, the horn is provided with valves which bridge over the intervals and render the hand-stopping unnecessary. The horn is a difficult instrument to play by reason of the number of open notes and frequent changes of pitch.

Horn, Arvid Bernhard, Count (1664-1742), a Swedish statesman, born at Vuorentaka, Finland. He served in the Swedish army against France and gained rapid promotion, being sent, in 1704, as Swedish ambassador to Warsaw, and assisting in the deposition of King Augustus of Poland. In 1705 he became councillor to the new King Stanislaus, and as head of the party of ' Bonnets ' practically ruled Sweden, converting it into a limited monarchy. His party remained in power till 1738, when it was ousted by the 'Hats.' Under his leadership the country prospered, and the years when he was marshal came to be spoken of as the 'time of Arvid Horn.' *See* Gustav Horn, *A. B. Horn.*

Horn, Gustav, Count (1592-1657), a Swedish general, born at Orbyhus, Upland, Sweden. In 1631 he saw action at the battle of Leipzig, and accompanied Gustavus Adolphus to Germany in the Thirty Years' War, taking part in the battle of Lützen in which the king fell. He was taken prisoner at Nördlingen in 1634, and on being liberated eight years later was made commander-in-chief of the Swedish army in the war with Denmark. *See* Emporagrius, *Likpredikan öfver G. C. Horn,* 1660.

Hornbeam, or *Carpinus betulus,* a species of Petulaceæ, found in N. climates and a native of Britain. It greatly resembles the beech in habit, but its leaves are rough and elm-like. The timber is extremely tough, but is not very often used. In April it bears male and female catkins, and the latter precede a number of one-seeded nuts with a three-lobed wing on one side.

Hornberg, a picturesquely situated tn. in the Black Forest, grandduchy of Baden, Germany, 32 m. S.E. of Strassburg. The peasantry here wear interesting costumes. It is a summer resort, and has industries in earthenware and woollen goods. Pop. 2769.

Hornbill, the name given to the many species of coraciiform birds belonging to the family Buccerotidæ. They are of considerable size, and derive their name from their immense dentated, downward-curved beak, with the horn-like casque at the base. The species range from Africa, India, to the Malayan region, and are remarkable for their slow and heavy flight, which, however, is counterbalanced by the pneumatic nature of their bones. The members of *Bucorvus* are omnivorous, and feed chiefly on the ground, their food consisting of roots, insects, tortoises, etc. During breeding the female is imprisoned by the male in the hollow of a tree which he plasters up, leaving only a small slit for the admission of food. *B. abyssinicus* is the best-known species, other genera being *Rhinoplax, Aceros, Lophoceros,* and *Anorhinus.*

Hornblende, the commonest member of the amphibole group of rock-forming minerals. It is of all colours, but the name is generally restricted to the black or very dark green varieties.

It is similar to augite, from which it can only be distinguished by its cleavage angle (*q.v.*). The monoclinic crystals are prismatic in habit with a six-sided cross-section; the angle between the prism-faces, parallel to which there are perfect cleavages, is 55° 49'. In metamorphic rocks it generally forms irregular masses without definite crystalline form. The dichroism is always marked. H. occurs as an essential constituent of many kinds of igneous rocks, and many crystalline schists are almost entirely formed of it.

Hornblende Schist, a mineral commonly associated with gneiss and, less frequently, with mica schist. It follows the contortions of gneiss, and is traversed like it by granitic veins.

Hornbook, a primer, formerly used by children in England to learn the elements of reading, prior to the days of printing. It consisted of a piece of paper or parchment on a tablet of wood, with a slice of transparent horn in front, hence the name. It contained the alphabet, large and small, the Lord's Prayer, and the Roman numerals, and was prefaced with figures of the Cross. There was a handle attached to it with a hole bored for a string, by means of which the book was fastened to the scholar's girdle. At one time Hs. were quite common, but they have now become very scarce.

Horncastle, a market tn. of Lincolnshire, England, 130 m. N. of London. The church of St. Mary is, in part, Early English, and Queen Elizabeth's Grammar School dates from 1562. The great horse fair, described by George Borrow in *Romany Rye,* is still held annually in the second week of August. The chief industries are brewing and matting. Pop. (1911) 3900. *See* Walter's *History of Horncastle,* 1908.

Hornchurch, a vil. and par. in Essex, England, 2 m. S.E. of Romford. It has manufs. of agricultural implements, cycles, tiles, and bricks, and there are iron foundries. Pop. (1911) 9461.

Horne, George, D.D. (1730-92), an English divine, born at Otham, near Maidstone, and educated at Maidstone School and University College, Oxford. He became a fellow of Magdalen in 1749 and president in 1768. He was made vice-chancellor of the university in 1776, dean of Canterbury in 1781, and Bishop of Norwich in 1790. He published a satirical pamphlet, *The Theology and Philosophy of Cicero's Somnium Scipionis* (1751), and other pamphlets, and a *Commentary on the Psalms,* 1771.

Horne, Richard Henry, or **Hengist** (1803-84), an author, born in London.

He became a midshipman in the Mexican navy, and served in the war against Spain. His literary career began in 1828 when he contributed a poem, *Hecatompylos*, to the *Athenæum*. He was a talented and versatile writer, but is chiefly known by his epic poem *Orion*, which appeared in 1843. He was a correspondent of Miss Barrett (afterwards Mrs. Browning) from 1839 to 1846.

Horne, Thomas Hartwell (1780-1862), an English theologian and biblical critic, born in Chancery Lane, London. In 1818 he published *Introduction to the Critical Study of the Holy Scriptures*, at which he had laboured for seventeen years. In 1814 he had been appointed librarian of the Surrey Institution, and on its breaking up in 1823 he became senior assistant librarian at the British Museum, a post which he retained till 1860, taking part in the compilation of the alphabetical catalogue. See *Reminiscences* by his daughter, Mrs. Cheyne, 1862.

Horne Tooke, *see* TOOKE, JOHN HORNE.

Horned Screamer, the popular name of *Palamedea cornuta*, a species of anseriform birds belonging to the family Palamedeidæ. It is found in certain parts of S. America, and has glossy black plumage with a white abdomen; its most remarkable feature is the long, slender, yellowish horn which adorns the head.

Horned Toad, the popular name given to the species of *Ceratophrys*, a genus of amphibians, belonging to the order Anura and the family Cystignathidæ. The name is derived from the triangular, upright, horny appendage above each eye. The head and mouth are huge, and the general appearance is toad-like. *C. cornuta* of N. Brazil is beautifully coloured, as also is *C. ornata*, a species found in Uruguay, Paraguay, and N. Argentina.

Horned Viper, the popular name of *Cerastes cornuta*, a species of reptiles belonging to the family Viperidæ. It is found in N.E. Africa, and is remarkable for the possession of a large spiky scale above each eye. *See* CERASTES.

Hornel, Edward Atkinson (b. 1864), a Scottish painter, born in Victoria, Australia. In 1880 he entered the Edinburgh Art Schools, proceeding to Antwerp in 1883 to study under Professor Verlat. On his return to Scotland he associated himself with the Glasgow School of Artists, and was an influential member of the Kirkcudbright group of painters. His early paintings were of field workers, etc., but a visit to Japan and the East (1893-94) determined his adoption of the peculiar beauty of colour and decorative design which marks his later works, of which ' Summer,' in the Liverpool Gallery, is a noted example. Examples of his art have been purchased by many public galleries in the British Isles, in Canada, and the U.S.A.

Hornell, formerly **Hornellsville,** a city of Steuben co., New York, U.S.A., 70 m. S.E. of Buffalo. It has large car shops of the Erie Railway, and manufs. silk goods, furniture, shoes, electric motors, and bricks and tiles. Pop. (1910) 13,617.

Hornemann, Friedrich Konrad (1772- c. 1801), a German explorer in Africa, born at Hildesheim. In 1796 he was engaged by the African Association in London as an explorer, and in 1797-98 penetrated from Cairo through Fezzan to Murzuk, whence he returned, across the Libyan Desert, to Tripoli. From Tripoli he forwarded his journals to London where they were published as *Travels from Cairo to Mourzouk*, 1802. From Tripoli he returned to Murzuk with the intention of penetrating to the Hausa country, but nothing further is known of him.

Horner, Francis (1778-1817), a statesman, born at Edinburgh, and educated at the University of that city. After studying law he was called to the Scottish bar in 1800, and two years later became a student at Lincoln's Inn, being called to the English bar in 1807. In 1806 he had become a Whig member of parliament, and among the various reforms which were influenced by him may be mentioned that of the ' bullion question,' restricting the issue of paper money. H. is also remembered as a contributor to the *Edinburgh Review*.

Hornet, or *Vespa crabro*, a hymenopterous insect belonging to the suborder Petiolata and the family Vespidæ. It is the largest of all British wasps, measuring about 1 in. in length, and is not found N. of the Midlands; the predominant colour is red, with some yellow on head, abdomen, and wings. The colonies include not more than 200 individuals, and nest in hollow trees or other sheltered places. The H. is common all over Europe.

Horniman Museum is situated in London Road, Forest Hill, S.E., and is under the control of the London County Council. It is open free to the public every week-day, and also on Sundays in the afternoon and evening. It deals principally with botany, zoology, and ethnology, and has a library which is also open to the public.

Horning, Letters of, a term used in

Scots law to signify a writ issued to compel a debtor to pay under the penalty of being considered a rebel. Originally, these writs were very common and the only means of securing the desired end, but they have now practically fallen into disuse. Their name was derived from the practice of making three blasts with a horn to declare the man a rebel if he neglected to pay.

Hornpipe, a musical instrument originally used in parts of England. The name is now applied to a lively kind of dance which was used to accompany the music and which was, as a general rule, written in common time, though this was occasionally departed from. The best known dance of the kind at the present day is the college H.

Horns, the weapons that occur on the heads of various animals. They differ in substance; the H. of the deer are made of bone, and are processes of the frontal bone, while those of the giraffe are bony prominences covered with hair, and are entirely separate from the bones of the skull at first, but afterwards join on to them. Those of sheep, oxen, and antelopes are developed from the frontal bones of the skull, and are covered by a corium and by a horny sheath; but the prong-horned antelope has H. which consist at their basis of bony processes covered by hairy skin, and are covered by horny sheaths elsewhere. The H. of the rhinoceros alone are made of horn, and this occurs in fibres, growing from the skin like a mass of coarse bristles. H. are weapons of defence, and occur in both male and female animals, except in the case of antelopes, when they are generally confined to the male sex.

Hornsea, a seaside tn. of the E. Riding of Yorkshire, England, about 15 m. N.E. of Hull. It is now popular on account of its bathing facilities. Pop. (1911) 3026.

Hornsey, a mun. bor. and suburb of N. London, situated in the co. of Middlesex, 5 m. N.W. of St. Paul's. Pop. (1911) 84,592.

Horn Silver, the name applied to cerargyrite or chloride of silver because of its horny appearance. It occurs as a native mineral chiefly in Chili and Peru, and on being exposed to the light becomes dark in colour.

Hornstone, a variety of stone which resembles flint very closely. It is exceedingly brittle and splintery, and is sometimes identified with chert, these two being practically un-distinguishable from flint.

Hornu, a coal-mining vil. in Hainault, Belgium, 6 m. W. of Mons. Pop. about 10,600.

Horn Work, a term used in the science of fortification to denote an outwork of the fortifications which is formed by two semi-bastions. This form of outwork is much used for gateways and similar fortifications. Two long wings connect it usually with the works enclosed by the fortifications.

Horodenka, a tn. in the prov. of Galicia, Austria, situated about 34 m. N.N.W. of Czernowitz. Pop. 11,250.

Horologium (the Clock), the name of a southern constellation introduced about the middle of the 18th century by Lacaille.

Horology, the science which deals with the construction of contrivances for telling the time. It is well to point out in the first place that exact measurement of either space or time is impossible, as no distance can be shown as a multiple or sub-multiple of any particular unit, nor can any period of time be said to contain another period or definite number of times. The problem of measuring time, therefore, resolves itself into an attempt to attain a near approximation to the definition of a unit and the nearest possible measure of a given period in terms of that unit. Time can only be made appreciable by the regular recurrence of certain phenomena. The particular phenomena which have been recognised as dividing time into regular periods are those associated with the revolution of the earth about the sun, and its rotation about its own axis. The recurrence of seasons due to the earth's revolution has given us the conception of the year, and the problem of calendar-making has involved the measurement of the year in terms of the period of the diurnal rotation of the earth. Machines for telling the time are, however, only concerned with the latter unit. The rotation of the earth about its axis is uniform, and occupies the same period every day. This statement is probably not perfectly true; there are evidences that point to the fact that the rotation of the earth tends to be retarded, but we have no means of discovering gradual small changes other than those which are ultimately based on that rotation. The period of rotation is measured by observing the successive returns of a ' fixed ' star to the meridian. Such a period constitutes the sidereal day, and is used only by astronomers. The sidereal day is divided by universal consent into twenty-four hours, and the day is said to begin at noon. For most practical purposes, however, the time between two successive passages of the sun over the meridian is taken as the unit, and the day is divided into twenty-four hours, commencing at midnight. The solar day is not a uniform quantity owing to variations in the velocity of the sun, and to the inclination of the equator to the plane of the ecliptic. It is, therefore, necessary to imagine the sun moving at an average rate every day, thus giving us the measure of a ' mean ' solar day. It is possible, therefore, to assign three different times to any given instant : sidereal time, mean solar time, and true, or apparent, solar time. The sidereal day is shorter than the mean solar day by about four minutes on the average, or, to be more exact, twenty-four hours of mean solar time = 24 hours 3 minutes 56·5554 seconds of sidereal time. The division of the day into twenty-four hours is a relic of the sexagesimal system of notation, as also are the division of the hour into sixty minutes and that of the minute into sixty seconds. The Greeks counted the period between sunrise and sunset as the day, and that between sunset and sunrise as the night. Both day and night were divided into twelve hours each, so that the length of an hour varied with the season. The Egyptians divided the day from midnight to midnight into twenty-four hours, and appear to have reckoned sidereal time.

Early methods of time measurement. —The division of the day into recognised periods is a natural consequence of any attempt at the proper conduct of affairs. For ordinary purposes an approximate arrangement is sufficient, but amongst certain nations we find attempts at accuracy dictated by regard for the regular performance of religious duties. Thus the Egyptians used a horoscopus consisting of a tapering palm-branch with a sight-slit in the broader end, and provided with a handle from which hung a plummet. The apparatus was evidently held by the handle at arm's length, and supported by the other hand with the sight-slit at the eye. In this way the transit of a star over the meridian could be observed, and the hour fixed. Later on, we find the use of the clepsydra, or water clock, and the sand clock fairly universal in Greece and Rome and Hellenised and Romanised countries. The water-clock consisted of a vessel of known capacity, whose base was perforated in such a way that the water leaked away slowly, and at a fairly uniform rate. Some instruments were provided with floats pointing to the hours inscribed on a vertical scale. The water clock and the sand clock (which was constructed on the same principle) were used to assign a limit to the duration of speeches in courts of justice, a use which has persisted in the form of the hour-glass established in certain churches to this day. The rate at which the water or sand flowed away varied according to the pressure and amount of the material, so that the indications could not be very exact. Among other methods of computing time may be mentioned King Alfred's device of burning candles marked in sections, and supplied with a uniform current of air.

Sun-dials.—The most exact instrument known to the ancients was the sun-dial. Mention is made of a sun-dial in Isaiah xxxviii. 8, which would refer to about 700 B.C. The hemisphere of the Chaldæan Berossus (c. 300 B.C.) was half a hollow sphere with its rim horizontal, and a small sphere fixed at the centre. The shadow cast by this object on the inner surface of the hemisphere, traced out a circular arc during the time the sun was above the horizon. The Greeks adopted the use of the sun-dial from the Babylonians, and mention is made of one placed in Rome in 290 B.C. The Romans themselves did not develop the theory of sun-dials, and appear to have relied mainly on foreign mathematicians. The science pertaining to the construction was called *gnomonics ;* the Arabians were chiefly responsible for its development, though several capable writers appeared in Europe in the 17th century. The essential parts of a sun-dial are the dial itself and the style, a piece of rigid metal which casts its shadow on the dial. The dial may be fixed horizontally, vertically, or inclined to the horizon. In the horizontal dial, which is the commonest type, the plane of the style must lie along the meridian, which may be found by observing the successive shadows cast by a vertical rod and plummet and bisecting the angle formed by shadows of equal length. This gives the direction of the shortest shadow, and consequently indicates twelve o'clock noon on the dial. The other hours are obtained by calculating the angles on either side of the twelve o'clock shadow. It is obvious that sun-dials only tell the time during the day, and then only when the sun casts a distinct shadow. The time, moreover, is true solar time, which has to be corrected by the ' equation of time ' to give mean solar time. Portable dials were made and were commonly set in the meridian by the aid of a compass. Ornamental dials formed a feature of many country houses, but the growing perfection of clocks and watches rendered their employment unnecessary after the 17th century.

Clocks.—A clock is said to have

been constructed by Pope Sylvester VII. in A.D. 996, with weights as motive power. Many of the early church clocks were simply striking instruments, with no dial to show the time. In 1288 a clock supplied with bells was put up in Westminster Abbey, and many cathedrals possessed clocks as early as the 14th century. The famous clock at Strasburg Cathedral was constructed in its original form between 1352 and 1370. Another famous clock of the 14th century was that constructed by Henry de Vick for Charles V. in 1379. The regulating mechanism of these clocks consisted of a verge escapement with a balance. The escapement was applied to a crown wheel, that is, a wheel with serrations cut parallel to its axis. Two pallets engaged with the crown wheel in such a way that when one was pushed past a tooth, the other was applied to a tooth on the other side. The resistance of the pallets to the motion of the wheel was adjusted by weights fixed on two arms pivoted with the pallets. As the first pallet was pushed clear, the motion was communicated to the arms of the balance which swung round, thus increasing the resistance of the other pallet, which could only be overcome by bringing the balance to rest and reversing its motion. The weights of the balance could be moved along the arm, thus making it possible to regulate the resistance of the escapement, and so determine the period of revolution of the crown wheel. The pendulum was adapted to clock mechanism in the 17th century, and corrections for temperature were introduced by John Harrison (1693-1776), and Matteo Campani-Alimenis ; the latter also invented the illuminated dial plate. Many modifications of the general structure of clocks have been introduced from time to time. Clocks which do not strike the hours are usually differentiated as timepieces ; many play chimes or tunes in addition to striking the hours, and ' alarm ' clocks have a special bell-ringing arrangement which is put into operation by previously adjusting the time on a separate hour indicator.

General construction of clocks.—All clocks made on the usual principles contain their own motive power, which may be a coiled steel spring or a weight suspended by a chain or wire ; a train of wheels, by which the motion is communicated to the hands on the dial ; a pendulum or other device for regulating the motion of the wheels; an escapement by which the motion of the pendulum is applied to the wheels; there is often a striking mechanism. In the case of a clock

actuated by a suspended weight, the motion is first of all communicated to a barrel around which the cord holding the weight is coiled. The axis of the barrel and the arbors of the other wheels are socketed in two parallel plates kept at a constant distance by rigid pillars. Having the same axis as the barrel is the great wheel of the clock which drives the centre pinion on the arbor of the centre wheel. The arbor of the centre wheel is produced through the front plate to the dial and to it is attached the minute hand. The centre wheel engages with the pinion of the second wheel, and the second wheel with the pinion of the escapement wheel. The pallets of the escapement oscillate on an arbor which joins a lever or crutch at right angles, having at its other end a fork by which the motion of the pendulum is communicated to the escapement. In front of the front-plate of the clock, the prolonged arbor of the centre wheel is socketed into a spring pressing against a wheel communicating with the minute hand. The contact is sufficient to ensure the proper motion of the minute hand, but is not strong enough to prevent the adjustment of the hands from the front. Engaged with this wheel is another wheel with the same number of teeth, but bearing on its arbor a pinion which engages with the hour-hand wheel, which has twelve times the number of teeth of the pinion, and is concentric with the minute-hand wheel, though it is mounted on a hollow tube surrounding the arbor of the minute-hand wheel.

Pendulum.—The biggest advance in H. is that due to the introduction of the pendulum. The mechanics of a suspended body had been investigated to some extent by Galileo, but there is some doubt as to the horologist responsible for its adaptation to clock mechanism, though the honour is usually ascribed to the Dutch physicist, Christiaan Huygens. In theory, a pendulum consists of a small heavy mass concentrated at the end of a light string or rod which is free to move about a fixed point. When the arc of oscillation is large, the period of the oscillation depends upon the amplitude of the swing, but this is not so when the arc of oscillation is small. The forces acting upon the bob of the pendulum are its weight acting vertically downwards, and the tension of the string acting in the direction of the swing. At a given moment the motion of the bob is along the tangent to the arc, and as this is at right angles to the direction of the string, the tension of the string cannot be resolved along the tangent. Let $mg =$ weight of the bob, m being the mass and g the acceleration due to gravity. Then the part of the weight resolved along the tangent=mg cos a, .where a=the angle between the tangent and the vertical line through the point of suspension. It therefore equals mg cos θ, where θ is the angle of single oscillation. Now if the angle be small, the arc of oscillation, the length of the tangent cut off by the vertical line, and that of the chord cut off by the vertical line may all be reckoned as equal. Therefore, the resolved force along the arc=mg × arc ÷ length of string. This means that the bob is acted on by a force along the arc which varies with the amplitude. The motion of the bob, therefore, constitutes simple harmonic motion, so that the vibration is isochronous; that is, whatever the amplitude of the vibration the periodic time is the same. This result is of the utmost importance in considering the pendulum as a time regulator. It means that whatever the power of the driving mechanism, whether the pendulum is moving strongly or feebly, as long as the angle is small, the time taken for it to complete each double oscillation is the same. It can be shown that the period of a single vibration=$\pi\sqrt{l/g}$ seconds. Therefore, if the period is required to be a single second, $l=g/\pi^2$. At Greenwich the value of g is 32·1912 .., and the seconds pendulum needs to be, therefore, 39·13983 inches long. In clocks, the pendulum is a bob fixed to the end of a rigid bar ; the bar itself has weight, so that the centre of oscillation is somewhat above the centre of gravity of the bob. The great desideratum is that the length of the pendulum from point of suspension to centre of oscillation should remain constant.

Compensation.—As metals expand on increase of temperature, the length of a pendulum tends to increase in hot weather, with the result that the period of oscillation is increased and the clock loses. Steel, though otherwise a good material for pendulum rods, expands ·0000107 of its length for each degree centigrade rise in temperature. It is, therefore, necessary to make some contrivance so that the centre of gravity of the whole pendulum shall be moved upwards to the same extent as the expansion due to heat moves it downwards. One of the earliest devices for this purpose is demonstrated in Graham's mercurial pendulum. The bob consists of two glass cylinders containing mercury. Now the co-efficient of expansion of mercury is comparatively large, and that of glass small; so that, when heated, the glass does not expand laterally to a suffi-

cient extent to maintain the level of the mercury, and the mercury rises upwards in the vessels, thus raising the centre of gravity. By adjusting the quantity of mercury in the glass vessels, the moving upwards of the centre of gravity of the mercury can be made to compensate for the lowering of the centre of gravity due to the increased length of the rod. Another compensation device is that invented by John Harrison in 1726, and commonly known as the gridiron pendulum. It consists of a framework of metal rods of two different metals, iron and brass being generally used. The rods are so arranged that the steel bars lengthen downwards in expanding, while the brass rods are fixed at the bottom and lengthen upwards. By adjusting the lengths of the respective metals in the inverse ratio of their co-efficients of expansion, the expansion upwards can be made to counteract exactly the expansion downwards. An improvement in these methods of compensation has now been effected by the use of ' invar,' an alloy of nickel and steel with a coefficient of expansion of ·000001 for each centigrade degree. This can easily be compensated for by quite a small length of steel expanding upwards.

Escapements.—The function of an escapement is to apply an impulse to the pendulum to cause it to vibrate and to lock the escapement wheel until the pendulum has completed a vibration. In this way the clock mechanism proceeds in jerks, one tooth of the escapement wheel being advanced for each single vibration of the pendulum. Soon after the introduction of the pendulum, the anchor escapement was invented by R. Hooke. It consists of two pallets mounted on two limbs oscillating about an axis at the junction of the limbs. The pallets are claw-shaped, but are so cut that the acting surface in each is convex, in order that the sharp teeth may not wear holes in them. Each pallet is driven in turn into a notch between two teeth, and as it is being withdrawn, it receives an impulse from the turning wheel which serves to keep the pendulum oscillating. The pendulum is, therefore, never free, and a recoil is occasioned at the end of the vibration. This disadvantage is obviated in the deadbeat escapement. In this the serrations of the wheel point in the opposite direction. The pallets have two faces each, a live face, which is acted upon by the escapement wheel, and a dead face. The dead faces are arcs of the circle having its centre at the axis of the pallets. The advantage of the escapement is that there is no recoil, so that it is well adapted for clocks in which great accuracy is required. The action is more of a gentle push than a blow, for the dead faces are in contact with the points of the teeth during each oscillation. Hence there is some retardation through friction, but this is rather an advantage than otherwise; for if the driving force of the clock be greater than normal, the friction is also greater, and thus the velocity of the pendulum tends to be brought to its average. Many escapements are constructed on the 'remontoire' system, in which the escapement has a driving power of its own, supplied either by separate winding by the clock-train, or by allowing the pallets to drop on to the pendulum by the action of gravity.

The wheels of a clock are usually made of hard brass, and are cut by a wheel-cutting machine adapted to the pitch of the wheel. By pitch is meant the number of teeth to each inch of circumference (circumferential pitch) or to each inch of diameter (diametral pitch). Pinions are sometimes made in lantern form, and with specially-shaped cogs give satisfactory results. It is necessary to have some arrangement in a clock by which the motion of the clock-train is not interfered with by the action of winding. This is effected by such a contrivance as Harrison's going ratchet. The great wheel has on its face a ratchet wheel with a click set in the clock frame. Upon this ratchet wheel is set another with its teeth pointing in the opposite direction, and its click set upon the larger ratchet wheel. The winding of the clock, therefore, does not cause the revolution of the larger ratchet, as that is prevented by the click set in the clock frame. At the same time the great wheel is impelled in its customary direction by the action of a spring pressing against pins in the great wheel and the larger ratchet with a tension which is temporarily equivalent to the weight. As the winding takes but a short time, the tension of this spring is sufficient to keep the clock going, until the weight comes into operation again. Striking is effected by a somewhat complicated mechanism at the front of the clock. The essential part is a snail wound round the hour wheel. The snail has a step for each hour, so that a lifting piece is allowed to fall into a position along a rack from which the number of notches to the end determine the hour to be struck. A pin on the minute wheel sets the striking mechanism in readiness for going a few minutes before the hour. Other additional mechanisms are 'alarm' arrangements, 'tell-tale' contrivances, etc. The alarm is set by turn-

ing an indicator upon a small dial; the indicator is attached to a wheel set upon the hour-hand wheel by means of a friction spring. This wheel carries a pin which raises the lifting piece connected with the alarm train, which is, therefore, discharged at the appropriate hour. The alarm train is actuated by a separate coiled spring, and the motion is communicated to two pallets which have a short hammer attached to the axis instead of a pendulum, so that a quick to and fro movement sufficient to ring a bell with some force is set up. A form of watchman's clock is that in which a set of spikes project round the dial in such a way that when a handle is pulled, the spike which happens to be opposite is pulled in. In the morning the spikes pushed in indicate at what hours the watchman operated the clock. Electric clocks are of several different types. In some, the pendulum is driven by electricity, and the clock-train is set in motion by the pendulum. Other so-called electrical clocks are dials connected up with a master clock, the movement of whose hands is communicated by the electric current to the several dials situated in different parts of a building or ship. Clocks are made in enormous quantities in the United States, particularly in Connecticut and New York. In England the chief centres of the industry are London and Handsworth near Birmingham. Many cheap but excellent clocks are made in the Black Forest region in Germany, while the industry also flourishes in France, Italy, and Switzerland.

Watches. — Early watches were really portable clocks. They were driven by a mainspring, and the motion was regulated by a small balance escapement as in the clocks of the same period. Such instruments were often too large to be carried in the pocket, and were suspended from the girdle by a chain or cord. Frequently they were globular in form, and gained the name of 'Nuremberg eggs' on that account. Early in the 16th century an arrangement called the fusee was adopted. This consists of a mainspring enclosed in a barrel on which is wound a piece of catgut or a chain which is also wound upon a spiral drum in such a manner that when the mainspring weakens as it relaxes, the leverage on the spiral increases, so that the force remains fairly uniform. The form of the watch lent itself to a high degree of ornamentation, and the watches of Tudor times are remarkable for the delicacy of the engraving on their cases. Many of them contained a striking mechanism, and when this was dispensed with, a decrease in size and weight became possible. Thomas Tompion (1639-1713) invented a dead-beat escapement for watches, which was afterwards improved upon by George Graham (1673-1751). The next great development was the invention of the curb-compensation for the hairspring by John Harrison (1693-1776), who himself constructed chronometers of marvellous efficiency. In 1713 the British government offered rewards of £10,000, £15,000, and £20,000 for chronometers which would determine longitude within an error of 60, 40, and 30 geographical miles respectively. In 1761 John Harrison sent his son on a voyage to Jamaica with a watch of his own construction. It lost one minute fifty-four and a half seconds on the double journey, which was equivalent to a determination of longitude within an error of 18 m., according to the terms of the government's offer. On a subsequent voyage of four months' duration to Barbadoes, one of Harrison's chronometers showed an error equivalent to only ten geographical miles. The reward offered was tardily paid by the government, who did not sympathise with the principles upon which Harrison constructed his watches. A modern watch possesses a case for containing the mechanism, a mainspring and winding-up mechanism, a balance wheel and hairspring, and an escapement. The mainspring is a thin strip of tempered steel, and in most modern watches tapers very gradually from one end to the other. The fusee is now little used, and inequality in the driving force is compensated for in other ways. The mainspring was formerly wound up by a separate key, but this is now avoided by connecting the mainspring barrel with the pendant. A push button is also provided by which the wheels connected with the pendant can be thrown out of gear with the barrel wheel and connected up with the hand wheels to set the hands when required. The driving power of the mainspring is communicated to the train of wheels as in ordinary clock mechanism. The function of the pendulum in regulating the speed of the train of wheels is taken up by the balance wheel. This consists of a small brass wheel to which is attached the hairspring, a fine spiral spring whose centre of gravity is on the axis of the balance wheel. The elasticity of the spring causes the wheel, when impelled from its normal position in either direction, to return beyond its normal position, and the time of oscillation is the same for different impulses within certain limits. Isochronism is more disturbed by changes in the elasticity of the spring due

to changes in temperature than by slight variations in the driving force, and as a watch mainspring is wound up so as to use only a portion of the power derived from its elasticity, the balance wheel and hairspring form a convenient substitute for the pendulum. The impulse is supplied to the balance wheel by the escapement, which also communicates the rate of oscillation to the train of wheels. The commonest escapement in English-made watches is the lever escapement. This device, invented by Thomas Mudge in the latter part of the 18th century, is an adaptation of the dead-beat escapement applied to clocks. The pallets are fixed to a lever pivoted at a point midway between the pallets, and furnished with a notch which engages with a small pin on the balance wheel near its axis. The motion is so adjusted that when a tooth of the escape wheel escapes from one of the pallets the pin slips out of the notch and enters it again on the return of the balance wheel, moving the lever sufficiently for the next tooth to escape. The pallets of the level and the pivots of lever and escape wheel are usually jewelled, and undue motion of the lever is prevented by safety pins. What is called the chronometer or spring-detent escapement possesses a cam or tooth on the verge of the balance which unlocks a detent which is applied to a tooth of the escape wheel by means of a spring, and the impulse is immediately applied to the escape wheel by a jewelled tooth in the balance wheel. When the balance returns, the unlocking cam has to get to the other side of the detent without moving it as a whole. This is effected by furnishing the end of the detent with a section which bends in one direction only, so that the unlocking cam only moves the detent when it moves in the direction in which the balance wheel receives the impulse. This escapement is sometimes called the 'detached' escapement, because it provides for one impulse only in a double oscillation, and the unlocking occurs every other vibration. It is too delicate for use in ordinary portable watches, and is specially adapted for chronometers which are maintained in a horizontal position by gimbals. Compensation for changes due to difference of temperature is necessary for two reasons. The expansion of the balance wheel increases the moment of inertia of the wheel, so that it requires a greater force to turn it in a given direction. The ordinary compensated balance-wheel has a circumference consisting of two or more sections, each of which is composed of an inner bar of steel melted upon an outer bar of brass, this compound bar carrying a small weight. The inequality of the expansion of the two metals results in a bending of the bar inwards, thus carrying the weight towards the centre of the wheel. Such a contrivance requires careful adjustment. Secondary compensation is necessary on account of the weakening of the elasticity of the hairspring 'through rise of temperature. In Dent's compensation-balance a compound bar carries at either end weights set vertically upon horse-shoe-shaped compound pieces. On a rise in temperature, the horizontal bar bends upwards, thus throwing the weights towards the centre. This is not sufficient for secondary compensation in itself, so the horse-shoe pieces are made to bend upwards, thus throwing the weights still further towards the centre. Apparatus designed to record very small divisions of time with great accuracy are called *chronoscopes* (*q.v.*), and when they are arranged so as to preserve a more or less permanent record, they are called *chronographs* (*q.v.*). Such mechanisms are often dependent upon the breaking and establishing of electrical contacts, and are brought to a high pitch of perfection. Greater and greater degrees of accuracy are constantly being achieved, but it must be remembered that absolute accuracy is not only impossible by the nature of time, but also through the fact that no physical process can be said to be ultimately instantaneous. For instance, if two clocks are supposed to be exactly synchronous, they are not so when viewed from each other; their difference being a function of the velocity of light. *See* Wood's *Curiosities of Clocks and Watches*, 1866 ; Reid's *Treatise on Clock and Watch-making*, 1849; Grimthorpe's *Rudimentary Treatise on Clocks, Watches, and Bells*, 1903.

Horoscope, a term used in the phrase ' casting the horoscope ' in astrology (*q.v.*).

Horowitz, a tn. of Bohemia, Austria, 29 m. S.W. of Prague. In the vicinity are coal and iron mines, and iron goods are manufactured. Pop. 4009.

Horrebow, Peter (1679-1764), a Danish astronomer; was the pupil of Claus Rœmer, himself an astronomer and mathematician. Early in the 18th century he succeeded Rœmer as professor of mathematics in Copenhagen University, and during the time that he occupied this post was the author of several scientific works. His son Christian (*d.* 1776) succeeded him, and devoted some of his time also to scientific writing.

Horrocks, Jeremiah (*c.* 1617-41), an astronomer, born at Toxteth Park,

near Liverpool. After studying at Cambridge, he returned to his native place and there began his astronomical observations. In 1639, however, he was ordained curate at Hoole in Lancashire, and there made his observation of the transit of Venus. Among his writings may be mentioned *Venus in Sole visa*, printed by Hevelius in 1662, and portions of his writings published by the Royal Society under the title *Jeremiœ Horroccii Opera Posthuma.*

Horse: *History.*—When Cæsar invaded Britain, he found in the south-eastern part of the island that the Belgic tribes employed not only cavalry, like the Gauls, but Hs. to pull the scythe-wheeled chariots. At the same time there is abundant evidence of the existence of British or Celtic ponies throughout the greater part of the British Isles. Some of these breeds, notably the Shetland, have very little altered in the intervening period, and except as a result of the introduction of Arabian or thoroughbred blood, show no tendency to increase their size. The large H. was probably unknown until the Norman invasion. Then animals of the Andalusian or Chestnut type were introduced, and from these and the large Belgian or Flemish H. the war H. ridden by knights in armour, and later the modern heavy cart H. were evolved. Although the evidence of the oldest writings, sculptures, and frescoes goes to show that Hs. were driven long before they were ridden, the H. was probably employed and bred almost solely for war purposes for a long period. As far back, however, as the time of Henry II., the tournament was introduced and H. racing first captivated the English people. But wars, civil and foreign, seriously depleted the H. supply, and in 1495, Henry VII. forbade the export of any H. without royal permission, and of any mare whose value exceeded 6s. 8d. It was Henry VIII. who made H. stealing a capital offence. During his reign, the weight of armour reached its maximum, and in consequence, large and strong Hs. were in heavy demand. By this time the value of the H. in agriculture had been realised, and the pack H. was in extensive use for transporting goods. The Devonshire pack H. still survives. The use of state chariots by noblemen virtually originated the present road system and modern methods of travel. Coaches were introduced in the reign of Queen Elizabeth, and the importation of Arabs and other foreign stock laid the foundations of the modern race H. or English thoroughbred. With the improvement of the roads, and the use of coaches, carriages, and lighter vehicles, great attention was paid to the development of the harness H., and the Hackney or Norfolk Trotter was evolved from a foundation stock of Scandinavian Hs., and the Cleveland Bay and the Yorkshire coach H. were developed to their modern excellence.

BREEDS.—The majority of Hs. in use in Great Britain belong to no distinct breed, being of a general utility character, such as those used in tradesmen's carts and to a diminishing extent in cabs and omnibuses. With the development of motor traction, however, the number of these is declining rapidly, and the percentage of pure bred animals increasing. The following are the distinct breeds : The Racehorse or Thoroughbred, and the Hunter, the Hackney, the Yorkshire Coach H. and Cleveland Bay, the Shire H., the Clydesdale, and the Suffolk Punch ; while among ponies, the Polo pony, the Hackney pony, the Welsh, the New Forest, the Highland, the Shetland, the Dartmoor, the Exmoor, the Fell, and Connemara are the most important.

The *Thoroughbred* is said to have developed an inch in height in every twenty-five years since 1700, and for considerably more than a hundred years has been kept absolutely pure. While it owes much to the Arab, all authorities agree that it would not benefit by further introduction of Arab blood. The majority of thoroughbreds are bay in colour, and their number appears on the increase. Chestnut is a fairly frequent colour, blacks and browns are rare, and grey thoroughbreds are practically extinct. Some 5000 or 6000 race Hs. are bred in the British Isles yearly, and for the past century there has been a steady demand for them from foreign countries.

Hunters are bred from at least one thoroughbred parent, excellent animals for the purpose being produced by crosses with small Clydesdale or Suffolk mares. Irish hunters have long been considered the best, a fact partly due to the suitability of the climate and to the limestone soil, and partly to the greater attention paid to the subject in Ireland than elsewhere. A mahogany - brown colour is preferred, black, bay, or dark chestnut coming next in favour. Greys, roans, and light chestnuts are not fashionable. A hunter should be thick and strong on the back and loin, with long powerful quarters, and muscular thighs and neatly-shaped and clean hocks. Size, stamina, action, and reliability at fences are essentials in a good hunter. The number of

hunters in the British Isles is greater than it ever was, and continues to increase. It is computed to exceed 250,000.

The *Hackney H.* is the beautiful harness H. of high action, arched neck, and fast pace. This more than any breed has had its existence threatened by the motor, but popularity of harness classes at H. shows is so remarkable, and the charm of driving a good Hackney so undeniable, that it promises always to remain the pet of wealthy breeders. It has been developed so much for harness purposes that it seems out of place under the saddle, but some strains make fair saddle Hs., and many breeders are paying greater attention to the saddle Hackney. A Hackney must be over 14 hands high, *i.e.* exceeding 56 in., but the average height is about 15·3 hands. Hackney-bred carriage Hs. of 17 hands high can be obtained. The distinguishing feature of the breed is its very high and free action. It is a powerfully built, short-legged, big, broad H., with an intelligent head, neat neck, strong level back, powerful loins, flat-boned legs and good feet.

The *Cleveland Bay* with its offshoot, the Yorkshire Coach H., which tends again to amalgamate with the parent stock, is the general utility H., combining all the most useful and ornamental equine qualities. There is no better base or foundation for crossing to obtain hunters, cavalry Hs., and harness H. Unfortunately, good representatives of the breed are none too numerous. It has been bred pure longer even than the Thoroughbred, and the bay colour is extraordinarily prepotent. The Cleveland Bay is about 16 hands 2 in. in height, has a short back, powerful loins, and long quarters. Black zebra-like stripes above the hock, which occasionally occur, are supposed to denote special purity of breeding. The colour of the Yorkshire Coach H. is usually dark bay or brown. The mane and tail are abundant and black in colour. A fine head, sloping shoulders, strong loins, lengthy quarters, high stepping action, and abundance of bone and muscle characterise the breed which undoubtedly owes something to the Thoroughbred.

The *Shire* is the largest draught H. in the world, commonly attaining a height of 17 hands weighing as much as 2000 lbs. Though immensely strong, it is very docile and intelligent, and has a good free action. The prevailing colours are black, bay, and brown. The short stout legs have a plentiful covering of long hair known as 'feathering,' from the back of the knees and hocks to the pasterns. The neck is well arched, chest wide and full, back short and straight, ribs round and deep, and the quarters long, level, and well down to muscular thighs. The breed is directly descended from the great war H. of mediæval times.

The *Clydesdale* is the agricultural H. of Scotland. It is somewhat smaller than the Shire, but is claimed to be of finer finish. Bay and brown are the commonest colours, black and grey coming next and more rarely, chestnut and roan. The breed is believed to have originated by crossing the big war H. with the native 'garrons.' The shoulder is more oblique than in the Shire, but the 'feathering ' on the backs of the legs approaches the style of the latter. The breed is remarkably active in work, and is possessed of great strength and endurance. It is in active demand for export, over a thousand export certificates having been issued annually by the breed society in recent years.

The *Suffolk Punch* is quite distinct from the other native draught Hs., and its clean legs, or freedom from ' feathering,' make it specially well adapted for working on the land. The Suffolk is always a chestnut, varying from light sorrel to dark mahogany. It has long been kept pure, and always breeds true to colour. It averages 16 hands in height, and sometimes weighs as much as 2000 lbs. The Suffolk is famous for its willingness to pull at a dead weight, and is an exceedingly active animal. It has a very finely arched neck, low shoulders, thick withers, and a deep round barrel-like build.

Ponies.—With the exception of the Shetland, British ponies owe much to Arabian and Thoroughbred blood, introduced by turning old stallions loose among the droves. The pony breeders' object is to compress the most valuable qualities into the least compass, the aim being an animal with a small head, perfect shoulders, true action, and good manners. Yet a pony must be not only a diminutive H.; it must have true pony character. The various breeds range in height from 14 hands, or even a little higher, down to 8 hands. The Shetland has been known sometimes to be no more than 26 in. high. It is one of the oldest breeds of ponies in existence, and resembles a well-shaped miniature Clydesdale, and has been described as the strongest H. inch for inch existing. Black, bay, and brown are the favourite colours. The Shetlands' sure-footedness, intelligence, and good nature make them ideal companions for children. The High-

land pony is the largest and strongest of native ponies, and is unequalled for hardiness and staying power. The commonest type is the Garron (an Irish word meaning a stout H. or hack). This breed is said to owe some of its features to the Percheron. Allied are the Barra, the Uist, the Rum, and the Skye ponies. The Welsh pony is somewhat similar to the Highland pony, but a good many types exist. It is a faster animal, and is extremely sound in limbs and feet, in colour bays and browns are the usual shades. The New Forest pony is most commonly a fleabitten grey. Its height ranges from 12·2 to 13·2 hands, and though a very good-tempered animal when thoroughly broken, it is very wild before. The Dartmoor and Exmoor ponies are other perfectly hardy breeds. The original type has extremely fine, hard bone, excellent feet, powerful loins, short back, and well ribbed up middle. Black, brown, and bay are the commoner colours of the Dartmoor, and dark grey or brown with black points those of the Exmoor. The Fell pony is a native of Cumberland and Westmoreland, used by the farmers for all sorts of work. In colour it is usually black, brown, and bay. The withers are fine, and the chest deep, and the shoulders of good slope, making an excellent riding pony of the weight-carrying class. The Connemara pony, an Irish breed, supposed to be derived from Spanish crosses with native mares, is a big pony, and is much sought after for polo. The body is rather long and the limbs short and muscular; chestnut grey or bay are the usual colours. The Polo pony : The rapid growth in the popularity of polo since about 1880 has created a demand for a polo pony. A pony suitable for polo must have powerful riding shoulders, with strength across the loins, and muscular hind quarters. It has to carry at top-speed weights considered ample for hunters of 15 hands and upwards. All descriptions of native breeds have been drawn on in creating the Polo pony, which should measure from 14 hands to 14 hands 2 in. The Hackney pony is another very recent product. It is the Hackney in miniature, and has attracted much attention. The most frequent colours are chestnut and grey.

Foreign horses.—The Arab is the most distinguished non-British H. The earliest traces of it go back to the 6th century A.D., and since the breed has been consistently improved by rigorous selection. It has enormous powers of endurance, fine intelligence, and rare courage, as well as perfect shoulder action and a light mouth. It is the ideal cavalry horse, and is in request by the Remount Department of every war office in the world. There are several Arab studs in Great Britain. Amongst other foreign breeds, the Percheron, the famous cart-horse breed of France, the Brabant of Belgium, the Russian Orloff, the Prussian Trakehner, the Jutland, and the beautiful American Trotter should be mentioned.

DISEASES.—The various diseases of the H. may be dealt with in alphabetical order. *Abortion* is not very common in the mare, and though infectious, is generally in her case the result of an accident. Aborting animals should always be isolated and the premises disinfected. *Amaurosis*, or *Glass Eye*, is a derangement of the optic nerve. The H. carries its head well up, and steps very high. It is incurable, and its detection is very important in buying Hs. *Anthrax (q.v.)* is a very contagious disease, and must be at once reported to the police. *Asthma, Broken Wind*, or *Heaves*, is sometimes due to influenza, bronchitis, or pneumonia, but more frequently to bad food, such as musty hay or corn, or to too much exertion after feeding. Two or three grain doses of arsenic once a day in a mash may give relief. *Azoturia* occurs when animals are too well fed, and have too little exercise. After a little work, the H. sweats profusely and ejects large quantities of blood-coloured urine. Bleeding gives great relief. Exercise and feeding must be attended to. *Bog Spavin* is a distention of the capsular ligament of the hock joint, and is commonest in cart Hs., especially young Clydesdales. It sometimes disappears without treatment. But a dressing of green tar and turning out to grass has a good effect. *Bone Spavin* is a bony enlargement on the lower part of the hock joint brought on by injury or over-exertion, and often causing great pain and unsoundness. Rest, blisters, and firing are recommended. *Bots* are the grubs of a gadfly. The eggs are laid in summer on the shoulders and forelegs, and are licked off and swallowed. In the gullet they attach themselves to the lining and cause a morbid appetite and loss of flesh. There is no satisfactory remedy, but a H. singeing lamp should be used to destroy the little yellow eggs. *Broken Knees* are of frequent occurrence. After washing and dressing with antiseptics, cold water bandages are applied. *Bronchitis* causes great debility. The H. should be placed in a well-ventilated box, the legs bandaged and warm sheets put on the body and a pail of cold water containing a tablespoonful of nitrate of potash given it to drink. Drenches are danger-

ous in all chest troubles. *Calculi* are stony accumulations, occurring in the large intestine, and commonest in millers' Hs. They are often passed naturally, but strong purgatives must be avoided. *Canker* in the foot is a growth of horn on the sole, produced by injuries or by dirty wet litter. The H. must be kept dry and the foot dressed with powdered alum and dried tow. *Capped Hock, Knee*, or *Elbow* is a swelling due to a collection of fluid under the skin. Apply hot or cold applications and stimulating lotions. *Cataract* is a pearly-white appearance of the crystalline lens of the eye, which must be carefully looked for in a possible purchase. There is no treatment. *Catarrh*, or cold in the head, bowels, or bladder, causes irritation of the mucous membranes with watery discharge. This is often neglected, but should have prompt attention. Warm clothing, bandaging the legs, a tablespoonful of nitrate of potash, and good varied feeding should restore health. *Colic*, or *Gripes*, is a spasm of the bowels, due to improper food or over-exhaustion. Two to four ounces of laudanum, with two ounces of turpentine, in a pint of linseed oil helps the attack to pass off. *Conjunctivitis* is an inflammation of the outer covering of the eye often due to dust, hay seed, or chaff. Bathe with tepid water to remove the irritant, and apply a boracic acid lotion. *Corns* generally occur in the fore-feet. The shoes should be removed and the feet examined. A poultice of cold water and bran will reduce the inflammation, and an indiarubber bar pad is advisable in bad cases. *Cough* is a symptom of various troubles. *Crib biting and wind sucking* is often a bad habit, though it may be a form of dyspepsia. Feeding on the ground, providing a muzzle, or substituting iron for wooden stable fittings may effect a cure, but the habit is a characteristic of unsoundness. *Curb* is an enlargement of the back and lower part of the hock joint. Rest, cold water bandages to reduce the inflammation followed by blistering and firing are beneficial. *Diabetes* is characterised by the passing of enormous quantities of urine due to bad food and impure water. Rest, good food, dram doses of iodine in a ball, and twenty-five drops of hydrochloric acid in the drinking water are advisable. *Diarrhœa* is sometimes constitutional, but improper feeding is a common cause. Small doses of linseed oil and laudanum will check an attack. *Eczema* is very contagious. Treat the affected parts with a disinfectant fluid. *Enteritis*, or *Inflammation of the bowels* is a very fatal disease, the pain being continuous, and death often occurs in five or six hours. Hypodermic injections of morphia and atropine are the safest treatment. *Farcy* and *Glanders* are allied forms of a highly dangerous and contagious disease which is compulsorily notifiable to the police. As a result of the mallein test—an injection under the skin—the disease is rapidly being stamped out. With chronic glanders, a H. may go on working and feeding for months with a ragged unhealthy coat and a leaden hue to the membrane of the nostril as the only signs, but such an animal may be a general source of infection both to man and beast. All Hs. and ponies have to be inoculated with mallein before being put down into a coal mine. *Founder*, or *Laminitis*, is an inflammation of the feet due to many causes. The patient's shoes should be removed and the feet put into cold water bran poultices, and kept constantly wet. Bleeding often gives relief, and an injection under the skin of a solution of adrenalin has been used with success. *Fractures* are of six kinds: one, simple; two, compound; three, compound comminuted; four, complicated; five, green stick; six, impacted. In the second and third cases treatment is practically useless, and the H. is best destroyed. All the bones of the H.'s body are subject to fracture. They must be put in position and splints and bandages applied. *Gastritis*, or *Inflammation of the stomach*, usually proves fatal. Four ounces of laudanum in a pint of linseed oil will relieve the pain. Injections of sixty to eighty drop doses of morphia and atropine are very beneficial. *Grease* is an inflammation of the skin, the hind legs of cart Hs. being most subject. The hair stands on end, and a fœtid irritating discharge oozes through the skin. Wash with disinfectants, and dust with boracic acid, iodoform, and charcoal. *Hernia* is a displacement of the bowel. A bandage should be sewn tightly round the body until the rupture is reduced. *Influenza* is a very infectious and common disease in Hs. It manifests itself in different forms. The patient must be isolated and kept warm. *Laryngitis* needs careful attention, as if acute the H. may become a roarer. Mustard mixed with cold water rubbed on the throat generally effects a cure. Steaming the nostrils with eucalyptus oil three or four times a day has a soothing effect. *Lockjaw*, or *Tetanus*, is a highly fatal disease communicable to man. Anti-tetanus serum injected at the lower portion of the neck has been successful in some cases. *Lymphangitis* generally appears on Monday mornings after

Sunday's rest, affecting the hind legs of heavy Hs. Cold water bandages should be applied to the leg and linseed oil followed by nitrate of potash given in the drinking water. Reduce Sunday's food allowance. *Mange* is a parasitic disease due to the presence of small mites which cause great irritation. The mites are highly prolific, and the mange is readily spread. Any parasiticide except those containing arsenic can be applied, but as the disease may be deep-seated or superficial, treatment varies greatly in effectiveness. The disease has been compulsorily notifiable since January 1912, and in that year 6066 animals were attacked in Great Britain. *Nephritis*, or *Inflammation of the kidneys*, requires perfect rest, hot clothes, and small doses of linseed oil and laudanum. *Pneumonia* is much relieved by bleeding, accompanied by a dose of from ten to twenty ounces of linseed oil mixed with one or two ounces of spirits of nitre, and ten to fifteen drops of aconite tincture. *Quittor*, a fistulous sore in the coronet of the foot is commonest among railway horses. Wash with antiseptics, and apply blisters, caustic dressings, and a hot iron. *Roaring* is a peculiar noise made in the act of inspiration, and is a characteristic of unsoundness. Operations sometimes effect a cure. *Saddle galls* are the result of badly-fitting harness. Wash with antiseptics, and dress with zinc and lead lotion. *Sandcrack* is a fissure in the hoof commonest in towns. After dressing and nicking with a hot fire-iron, the hoof is bound with a leather strap. *Sidebone*, the ossification of one or both of the lateral cartilages at the sides and top of the hoof, is commonest in cart Hs., and is often caused by high-heeled shoes. Hs. with sidebone are unsound. An operation, the use of the bar shoe, and blistering may restore soundness. *Strangles* is an infectious disease commonest in young Hs. and most seen during the spring months. Abscesses are formed under the jaw, round the throat, and beneath the ears. With good nursing, it often passes off mildly. If necessary, small doses of linseed oil or of Epsom Salts may be given. A preventive serum is recommended. Strangles frequently terminates in roaring. *Thoroughpin*, a distention of the sides of the hock, which, though seldom causing lameness, is unsightly. Apply an indiarubber bandage to cause compression and absorption.

A large vocabulary has attached itself to the breeding and management of Hs. The following is a glossary of terms in more general use: *Arm* or *shoulder*.—The upper part of a foreleg from just below the withers, to just above the elbow. *Bars of the mouth.*—The spaces between the canine teeth and the grinders; they occur at the angle of the lips and in them the bit is placed. *Bay.*—A reddish nut-brown colour with black points. *Blaze.*—A stripe of white down a horse's face. *Calf knee.*—A knee that bends sideways towards its fellow, knock-kneed. *Castors, chestnuts,* or *ergots.*—Horny excrescences on the inside of each leg above the knees and below the hocks. *Chestnut.*—Reddish brown lighter than bay, but without black points, and frequently with one or more white stockings. *Clicking,* or *forging.*—A defect in a H's. paces when it knocks the feet against one another. *Cob.*—A compact short-legged H. *Coffin bone.*—The bone in the centre of the hoof. *Coronet.*—The bony fringe round the top of the hoof. *Dappled.*—Coat sprinkled with rings or spots of a darker colour. *Docking.*—Shortening the tail. *Dun.*—A dull dark brown generally with black extremities and a black line down the back. *Elbow.*—The bony projection just below the junction of a H.'s foreleg and body. *Fetlock.*—A lock of short hair hanging from the back of the fetlock joint—the junction of the pastern and the shank or cannon bone. *Flank.*—The part of the H.'s side between the ribs and the hip. *Fleabitten.*—Small red or dark spots on a white or grey coat, also used of a H. with white spots on a dark ground. *Forearm.* The part of the foreleg between the knee and the junction of the leg with the body. *Frog.*—The protuberance in the centre of the bottom of the H.'s foot. *Gaskin.*—The part of a hind leg between the hock and the junction of the leg with the body. *Grey.*—The colour composed by a mixture of black and white hairs. *Hand.*—A measurement of four inches. *Haunches.*—The fleshy part at the junction of body and hips. *Hock.*—The backward bending joint on the hind leg. *Knee.*—The foreward bending joint of the foreleg. *Mark (infundibulum).*—The hollow upon the top of a young H.'s teeth which by gradually wearing down serves as an indication of age. *Pastern.*—The bone joining hoof and fetlock joint. *Piebald.*—The colour which consists of patches of white and black. *Points.*—The extremities of the limbs. *Roan.*—A red or blue coat closely flecked with grey hairs. *Shoulder.*—The upper part of the foreleg from its junction with the body to the shoulder joint. *Skewbald.*—The colour consisting of patches of any two colours except white and black. *Snip.*—A small patch of white upon the nose. *Sorrel.*—The colour

formed by yellowish or reddish brown hairs. *Splint bones.*—Small bones running from hock or knee to fetlock. *Star.*—A square white patch upon the forehead. *Stifle.*—The joint at the junction of the hind leg with the body. *Thigh.*—The upper part of the hind leg. *White stocking.*—The white colouring of one or more legs of a dark or brightly coloured H. *Withers.*—The highest point of the back just behind the neck.

Horse-chestnut, or *Æsculus Hippocastanum,* a well-known species of Hippocastanaceæ, commonly grown in Britain as an ornamental plant. It has large leaves divided into five or seven long, distinct leaflets, and the white flowers are arranged in tall spikes; the fruit is a prickly capsule. *See* CHESTNUT.

Horse-fly, or **Forest-fly,** the popular name of *Hippobosca equina,* a species of dipterous insects, belonging to the family Tabanidæ. These flies are found all over England, but are commonest in the New Forest; they attack horses, generally on the under surface of the body, and suck the blood. They are distinguished by their loud humming, and by the two small head cavities in which the antennæ are concealed ; the general colour is yellowish-brown.

Horse Guards, the name of a building in Whitehall, London, where the offices of the departments under the commander-in-chief of the army are situated. It is also the term applied to distinguish the military jurisdiction of the officers of the war department from the civil, as exercised by the Secretary of State for War.

Horse Latitudes, the belt of calms and light, variable winds on the polar edges of the N.E. and S.E. trades, commonly applied to the ill-defined tropical belts of high barometric pressure which encircle the globe at 30° N. and S. There are two explanations of the name, one, that the calm kills horses on a sailing ship, the other that the name distinguishes the boisterous winds here from the pleasant trades.

Horse-mackerel, the popular name of *Caranx,* a genus of teleostean fishes belonging to the sub-order Acanthopterygii and the family Carangidæ. *C. trachurus,* the British H., is common on our coasts, where the young are often found in large colonies, sheltering under medusæ. They have a compressed oblong body covered with small scales.

Horse, Master of the, the officer of the court who has charge of the royal stables and of all the horses of the king. His authority extends to all the people employed in the stables, and he has the privilege of using the horses—the servants also being at his command. In state processions his place is next to the sovereign. The office, which dates from very early times, is tenable during the time that a particular political party is in power, and the Master of the Horse is appointed by letters patent.

Horsens, a seaport in the prov. of Aarhus, Denmark, situated 25 m. S.W. of Aarhus, on the fjord of H. The old church is noteworthy on account of its carvings. The chief industries are shipbuilding, weaving, and iron-working, and the exports dairy produce and pork. Pop. about 22,000.

Horse-power, the unit used to denote the power of steam and other engines. James Watt was the man who worked out the value of a H., after experiments with strong dray horses. In consequence of the exceptional power of the animals employed, Watt's result is in excess of the amount of work an average horse can compass. It represents the amount of work done when 33,000 lbs. is raised 1 ft. in one minute, and equals 746 watts. The French cheval-vapeur is equal to 4500 kilogrammetres a minute (32,549 foot-pounds), or 736 watts, slightly less than the English H. The nominal H. of an engine is a term which is quite arbitrary, and is rapidly falling into disuse. The formula for obtaining it is $\dfrac{D^2 \sqrt[3]{S}}{15 \cdot 6}$ for high-pressure, and $\dfrac{D^2 \cdot \sqrt[3]{S}}{47}$ for condensing engines, where D = the diameter of the piston in inches, S = the length of the stroke in feet. The indicated horse-power (I.H.P.) of a reciprocating engine is given by the formula $\dfrac{2\,APRS}{33,000}$, where A = the area of the piston in sq. in., S = the length of the stroke in feet, P = the mean pressure on the piston in lbs. per sq. in. (ascertained from the indicator), and R = the number of effective strokes per minute, one for each revolution of the crank-shaft if the engine is single-acting, or two if double-acting. This formula will not apply in the case of steam turbines, as a statement of the I.H.P. supplies the measure of force acting on the cylinder of an engine, but before the power available for doing external work off the crank-shaft can be obtained, that required for driving the engine itself must be subtracted. The result, when this has been done, is known as the actual, effective, or brake horse-power (B.H.P.) of the engine. For high-class condensing engines 80 per cent. of the I.H.P., as shown by the dynamometer, or 85 per cent. for non-condensing engines,

may be taken as the B.H.P., or a little more in each case if the turbines are very large. If the turbines are directly coupled to electrical generators, as is often the case on land, the H. can be deduced from the electrical output. Similarly, in an electric motor, if the electrical horse-power (E.H.P.), which is found by the formula *amps* ×*volts* = 10, and the efficiency of the motor is 86 per cent., 8·6 will be the B.H.P. of the motor. The power required to operate machinery can be exactly measured by connecting it to an electric motor, either as single units, or in groups driven from shafting. The H. of a boiler is an expression for the pressure and volume of steam required to supply an engine of the same H. It is a question of the grate area and heating surface, or, in other words, the evaporative capacity to produce the required amount of steam. For convenience, boilers are often so classed, their H. under given conditions being stated by the manufacturers.

Horse-racing. The qualities of speed and endurance for which the horse has always been notable, irrespective of any conscious or artificial process of selection, would naturally suggest the inference that H. is a sport of some antiquity. Such is indeed the case, for classic writers record systematic H. at the Grecian Olympiads in 600 B.C., while Grote (*History of Greece*) speaks of races for one year old colts. A tolerably full historical account of turf matters up to the middle of the 19th century will be found in Whyte's *History of the British Turf*, from which it seems that the earliest mention of race-horses (or ' running horses,' as they were called) in British national annals is not till the 9th century, when, we are told by Malmesbury, that Hugh Capet in soliciting the hand of Ethelswitha, King Athelstan's sister, in marriage, sent over a present of German ' ronning-horses.' It was not, however, till the reign of Henry II. that horse-races began to be frequent. They were generally held at Smithfield, which at that time was the principal horse-market of England. But in the public favour tournaments and jousts held the first esteem, and by the Tudor period, H. had ceased to be a great public amusement. The sport revived under James I., at which time, Garterly in Yorkshire, Croydon, and Enfield Chase were the customary places for the best races. It was not till about 1640 that races took place at Newmarket, although James I. built stables there near his palace. The most ' respectable races throughout the kingdom ' were, it is recorded, called ' Bell

Courses,' from the fact that the winning horse won a bell. But at the Chester meeting, which is probably the most ancient of all, the customary prize of one silver bell would appear to have been changed in 1610 into three cups, the race then being known as 'St. George's Race.' Generally speaking, it may be said that H. owes its position as pre-eminently the national pastime to the royal favour of the Stuart monarchs, Charles II. being a particularly devoted patron of the sport, and a constant spectator at the races, especially at Newmarket and at Datchet Mead, near Windsor. It was during this period, too, that the English breeds of horses became famous, a fact due partly to importations and partly to the various old ordinances and statutes regulating horse-breeding generally. Royal patronage continued to be extended to H. up to the accession of the Georges, both Anne and William III. adding several plates to the existing number for competition, and the former also keeping running horses in her own name. The earlier Hanoverian monarchs do not appear to have taken so kindly to the national sport; but if during that period H. was not the sport of kings, it certainly became that of the Princes of Wales. Prince George, afterwards George IV., owned race-horses in 1784, and though his stud was sold as a result of his pecuniary embarrassments, parliament increased his income and thereby enabled him to return to the sport. The memory of the late King Edward VII., especially when Prince of Wales, will long be cherished as a patron of H. and his winning the Derby on more than one occasion has permanently enshrined him in the hearts of every follower of the turf. Epsom, which from the fact of the 'Derby' being habitually run there, is probably the most popular race-course in England, does not appear to have been the scene of H. till 1648 (see Pepys' Diary). The Derby Stakes were inaugurated in 1780, but although that race continues to be regarded as the 'blue riband' of the turf, the number of entrants has at times compared unfavourably with that in other less classic races where the stakes have often been pecuniarily much more valuable. The St. Leger sweepstakes were instituted by a Colonel St. Leger in 1776, who lived near Doncaster Town Moor. The 'Ladies' Race' of the Oaks first took place in 1779. Ascot as a popular H. place can trace its history from 1711. But practically all the great annual steeplechases, like the Grand National, the Liverpool, and the Sandown Park Eclipse, began long after the establishment of the great classic flat-race meetings.

Occasional steeplechasing across country is traceable, according to the Badminton Racing-book, as far back as 1752, Ireland apparently being the home of its early popularity. They would appear to have been of frequent enough occurrence after that, generally taking the form of matches between two or three of the county gentry for a more or less nominal stake, the primary object being the healthy sporting one of testing the prowess of the rival animals. The term 'steeplechasing' itself merely denotes the fact that some convenient goal like a neighbouring church steeple was selected as a point in the race for the horses to mark on in their cross-country run over ditches and hedges, and it is at the present day without other than historical significance as the course is now marked out with flags. Steeplechasing as a regulated sport is not recorded much earlier than about 1825, when the younger devotees of fox-hunting took it up, plates being put up for prizes, and restrictions placed on the weights of the riders. From all accounts the conditions of these early steeplechases point to the sport as having been an extremely dangerous one, both to the rider and to the horse, the courses being too long and the obstacles more or less impracticable. The sport became increasingly popular some ten years later, when the first Liverpool steeplechase was run round a two-mile course near Aintree, the merit of this, the oldest annual steeplechase meeting, being that for the first time the conditions of the race were so regulated as to not only secure for the spectators an uninterrupted view of the race, but to ensure fair play for all the competitors. After this, meetings were instituted at St. Albans, Aylesbury, and other places, but the contest originated at Liverpool, especially after the selling race became superseded by the Grand National, has continued down to the present day to be the principal annual steeplechasing event. It is now run over different courses each year, and there are always two races annually. In 1866, as a result of the efforts of Lord Suffolk, Lord Coventry, the Duke of Beaufort, and others in the interests of fair play, the Grand National Hunt Committee was formed as the authoritative governing body over steeplechasing, the Jockey Club refusing to assume control over disputes unconnected with flat-racing. The recognised rules and regulations of steeplechasing are to be found in Weatherby's *Steeplechase Calendar* a publication which has been annually issued ever since 1866, and which records all the big annual races from that time. The above-named committee was dissolved in 1883 as a preliminary to re-organisation on lines which should bring it into closer touch with the Jockey Club, though it seems that most of the old committee men found places on the new committee. New members are now elected by the committee.

The Jockey Club is the governing body over all matters appertaining to flat-racing. Its first existence is variously assigned to the years 1750 and 1758. The first express mention of it, according to Dey's book on H., occurs in Heber's *Racing Calendar* for 1758, in connection with a regulation passed in that year directing all riders to pass the scales when they came in, under pain of dismissal. This, however, would seem to indicate that the club had by that time got into full working order, and the tradition of 1750, as the year of its foundation, is further confirmed by the fact that in 1752 a room on the site of the present club buildings was erected and leased to the Duke of Ancaster and the Marquis of Hastings in trust for fifty years as the place for general meetings of the aristocracy of the racing world during the Newmarket meetings. (*See also* the Badminton Racing-book.) The Jockey Club promulgates the rules of racing, and amends them according to the dictates of the racing world; it also regularly appoints stewards and defines their powers. The rules prescribe that the full programme of every meeting must be published in the *Racing Calendar*, with a statement of the names of two or more persons as stewards, and of the various other racing officials—the judge, clerk of the course, handicapper, stakeholder, clerk of the scales, and starter. The clerk of the course is solely responsible to the stewards for all general arrangements. All the above - mentioned officials require as a qualification of office, an annual licence from the stewards of the Jockey Club, though in an emergency, the stewards may employ an unlicensed deputy. The principal, or, at all events, most essential, function of the clerk of the course is to canvass, months before the meeting, for entries for the races.

For upon the number of entrants depends no less the success of the meeting than the amount of the annual revenue of the racing executives. It is the opinion of the true lovers of the steeplechase that none but chasers with catch weights should compete. The race in its origin was essentially a competition between hunters, and it is truly said that hunters are bought to carry their riders, whatever the weights of the latter may be. Hence it is that the conditions are sometimes that only horses that have regularly hunted with certain hounds during a certain season shall be entered, a condition which excludes that class of animal for which the ' hunt ' was never intended.

Hurdle-racing is also a popular form of race; possibly because the fact that a favourite may so easily fall in jumping, adds to the zest in gambling on the result. In the early days of this kind of H. the hurdles were customarily about 5 ft. in height and fixed very tightly in the ground; but the modern hurdle is not above 4 ft. high, and is put so loosely in the ground that a horse failing to clear it may easily carry it along with him to its own great danger. The whole art of hurdle-racing is to take the hurdles smoothly and easily without a perceptible pause either at making the spring or at landing.

There can be no two words about the continued popularity of H. A peaceful provincial town or village that has slumbered in tranquillity during the months that intervene between its race-meetings will, on race-day, often resemble, as to its roads, the line of march of an army of soldiers, and sleepy country stations bustle with an altogether unwonted activity. For whatever the race and wherever it may be held the sporting fraternity comprising all sorts and conditions of men, some perhaps with hardly a shilling to their credit, will contrive to be present. The love of the average Englishman for the turf may be gauged if by no other method than by the amount of money annually spent in and about the hundred and twenty odd first-rank meetings of the year. An interesting table compiled by Mr. T. H. Dey in his booklet on H. gives the total annual cost of H. as about £10,818,000, made up as follows:

1. Race-courses, rent and expenses of management	£50,000
2. Stakes	318,000
3. Horses, racing and training (including cost of the horses themselves, food, attendance, rent on stables and training grounds, jockeys' fees, and travelling expenses), at about £300 a horse for some 16,000 horses in training	4,770,000
4. Breeding establishments	3,180,000
5. Expenses of spectators	1,000,000
6. Small country meetings and hunt club steeplechases	1,500,000

The principal events of the modern (1913) racing year are the Derby Stakes (£6450 in 1912), Oaks Stakes (£4950), Grand National Steeplechase, Two Thousand Guineas (Newmarket), One Thousand Guineas (Newmarket), St. Leger (Doncaster), Lincolnshire Handicap, Cesarewitch, Liverpool Spring Cup, Goodwood Cup, Eclipse Stakes, Great Metropolitan Stakes, Chester Cup, City and Suburban, Royal Hunt Cup, Manchester Cup, Great Jubilee Handicap, Prince of Wales Stakes, Princess of Wales Stakes, Ascot Gold Cup, Coronation Stakes, and Ebor Handicap.

The season for H. in England is between March 24 and Nov. 22, or thereabouts. The rules provide for two races of 1 mile or upwards—not being selling races—for each day's racing, and that no race shall be run over a less distance than five furlongs, colloquially known by those who do not favour such races, 'five-furlong scrambles.' It is not often, however, that a 2-mile race is run, though at Ascot the Gold Cup course is 2½ miles, the Alexandra Plate 3 miles, while the Cesarewitch course is 2¼ miles. The Derby course is 1½ miles, while the Grand National is run over a 4½ mile course. The Derby and St. Leger are restricted to horses three years old, both fillies and colts being eligible, and except that fillies have a sex allowance of 3 lbs., all the horses carry the same weight. The Oaks is for fillies only. 'Weight-for-age' races are open to horses of varying ages, horses of equal age carrying equal weights, the younger less than the older. Horses of six years and upwards give weight, according to a prescribed scale, to younger competitors. (A scale of Weights for Ages will be found in the Badminton Race-book). The scale is published under the sanction of the stewards of the Jockey Club as a guide to race-meeting managers, but is not intended to be imperative. The third kind of race is the handicap, which did not become a regular feature much before 1820. In handicaps the idea is to equalise the chances by apportioning to each horse the weight which, in the opinion of the official handicapper, will bring them together in a dead-heat. The rules provide for the due publication of the conditions of any handicap and the date at which the entries close. The weights assigned are published in the *Racing Calendar*, and owners who do not agree with this handicap can cut their further loss by declining to accept, in other words by becoming non-starters.

Betting.—All contracts or agreements by way of gaming or wagering

are null and void by the Gaming Act of 1845, and securities like cheques or bills of exchange given for money lost on wagers are void under an Act of 1711. (In the case of *Woolf* v. *Hamilton*, decided as late as 1898, it was held that H. had always come under the wagers contemplated by the Act of 1711). Money lent with the knowledge that it is to be used to make bets on horse-races cannot be recovered (Gaming Act, 1892), nor can a promise to pay commission for making or paying such bets be sued upon. Contributions or subscriptions or agreements to subscribe or contribute towards any plate prize or sum of money to be awarded to the winner of any lawful sport (including, of course, H.) are expressly excepted from the operation of the Gaming Act, 1845 (*see also* BETTING, CONTRACTS, GAMING, and GAMBLING). The business of bookmaking is only illegal if carried on in contravention of the Betting Act, 1853, which Act prohibits 'the keeping or using a house or other place for the purpose of the owner, occupier, or any person using the same . . . betting with persons resorting thereto; or for the purpose of any money being received by or on behalf of any such person (as above) as consideration for any promise to pay any money or valuable thing on any contingency relating to any horse-race.' So that a man may safely make bets and habitually bet on horse-races and carry on a betting business, provided his business does not fall within the prohibition of the Act of 1853. The whole question turns on the judicial construction of a *place* within the meaning of the Act, and it has been held that Tattersall's enclosure is not such a place, that word apparently being construed *ejusdem generis* with *house, office*, or *room*.

H. is gradually becoming popular all over Europe and America. The Auteuil and Longchamps races of France are already as notable as many English race-meetings, the chief races run there being the Derby, Oaks, and Grand Prix. In Germany many great meetings are annually held, and in Austria and Italy the sport is also developing. In Belgium there is a Jockey Club with headquarters at Boisfort, while race-meetings are held at Antwerp, Ostend, Bruges, and Spa. Foreign-owned horses are allowed to compete in English races, but so far a similar privilege has not been extended to the horses of English owners on foreign courses. See *Racing* (Badminton Series), 1907; Dey, *Opinions of a Betting Man ; Horses and Horse Racing.*

Horse-radish (*Cochlearia Armoracia*), a cultivated plant belonging to the natural order Cruciferæ. The root has a strong pungent taste which closely resembles mustard, and is used either grated or made into a sauce, as a condiment with beef. It is also used medicinally as a stimulant.

Horse-shoeing, see FARRIERY.

Horse-tails, see EQUISETUM.

Horsforth, a tn. situated in the co. of Yorkshire, England, 5 m. to the N.W. of Leeds. It manufs. woollen goods. Pop. (1911) 9145.

Horsham: 1. A market tn. in the co. of Sussex, England, lying 18 m. N.W. of Brighton, and about 36 m. S.S.W. of London. Among its buildings of interest are the old church, which has been restored, the grammar school, and corn exchange. The chief industries are tanning, brewing, ironfounding, and coachbuilding. Here also is situated Christ's Hospital, which was moved from London. Pop. (1911) 11,314. 2. A tn. of Australia, situated about 200 m. N.W. of Melbourne, in Borung co. Pop. about 2800.

Horsley, John Calcott (1817-1903), an English artist, born at Brompton, London. After completing his studies at the Royal Academy he was appointed one of the head masters in the National School of Design, Somerset House. In 1856 he was elected an R.A. and from 1882-97 he was treasurer of the Academy. Although in 1844 and 1847 he painted some of the decorations for the Houses of Parliament, and also executed one or two other pictures of that kind, his best works are those dealing with everyday life. Among his works are ' Rent Day at Haddon Hall,' ' Caught Napping,' ' L'Allegro, Il Penseroso,' and ' The Healing Mercies of Christ '— the altarpiece in St. Thomas's Hospital Chapel.

Horsley, Samuel (1733-1806), an English prelate, born in London, and educated at Westminster School and Cambridge. In 1759 he became rector of Newington, a living which he held till 1793. He devoted a great part of his time, however, to a controversy with Dr. Priestley on the doctrine of the divinity of Christ. Among his other preferments may be mentioned that of bishop of St. Davids in 1788, Rochester in 1793, and St. Asaphs in 1802. He also devoted some of his time to science and edited the works of Sir Isaac Newton (1785).

Horsley Sir Victor Alexander Haden (*b.* 1857), a British surgeon and neurologist, born at Kensington, London. He was appointed professor-superintendent of Brown Institution (1884-90); secretary to the Royal Commission on Hydrophobia (1885);

surgeon to the National Hospital for Paralysis and Epilepsy (1886); Fullerian professor at the Royal Institution (1891-93); president of the Pathological Section of the British Medical Association (1892-93); professor of pathology, University College (1893-96). Since 1906 he has been Emeritus professor of clinical surgery and consulting surgeon at University College Hospital. He has been one of the leaders of the medical crusade against alcoholism, and is the author, in collaboration with Dr. Mary Sturge, of *Alcohol and the Human Body.* Among his other works are: *Brain Surgery*, 1887; *Hydrophobia and its Treatment*, 1888; and *Experiments upon the Functions of the Cerebral Cortex*, 1885.

Horst: 1. A vil. in the prov. of Westphalia, Prussia. It is situated about 5 m. N. of Essen, and is engaged in coal mining. Pop. 20,990. 2. A vil. in the prov. of Limburg, Netherlands. Pop. 5445. 3. A vil. in the dist. of Arnsberg, prov. of Westphalia, Prussia. Pop. 4930.

Hort, Fenton John Anthony (1828-92), a scholar and ecclesiastic, was a native of Dublin, and a student at Cambridge, being a fellow of Trinity College from 1852-57, and Hulsean professor of divinity at Cambridge in 1878. His chief work was his edition of the Greek text of the N.T. in which he was aided by his friend Dr. Westcott. See his *Life and Letters* by Sir A. F. Hort, 1896.

Horta, the cap. of the island of Fayal, belonging to the Azores group. It is situated on the S.E. coast of the island, and is also the cap. of the dist. of H. Pop. about 6730.

Horten, a tn. situated on Christiana Fiord, Norway, about 30 m. S.W. of the town of Christiania. It is a naval port, and has an arsenal and an observatory. Pop. 9823.

Hortense, Eugénie Beauharnais (1783-1837), Queen of Holland, the daughter of the Empress Josephine by her first husband, was born in Paris. In 1802 she married Napoleon's brother, Louis Bonaparte, king of Holland. On the fall of Napoleon and his family in 1815, she fled to Switzerland. The youngest of her sons afterwards became Napoleon III. See Fourmestraux's *La Reine Hortense*, 1864; and Taylor's *Queen Hortense and her Friends*, 1907.

Hortensius, Quintus (114-50 B.C.), surnamed Hortalus, was, after Cicero, the most famous of the Roman orators. He was the son of Q. Lutatius Catulus, and so belonged to the aristocratic party. He supported Sulla in the civil wars; fought during two campaigns (90-89) in the Social War.

and became consul in 69 B.C. In 63 B.C. he came into conflict with Cicero and, on Pompey's return from the East in 61 B.C. retired into private life. His speeches are not extant, but are described by Cicero as Asiatic and florid in style.

Horticultural Colleges. Almost every English county now provides special facilities for the study of horticulture and gardening; Kent, Staffordshire, and Norfolk, offering county council scholarships. The chief colleges which make a speciality of horticultural education are the Horticultural College, Swanley, Kent (founded 1889); Studley Agricultural and Horticultural College for Women, Warwickshire; the Agricultural and Horticultural College, Wellfield; and a School of Gardening for Women at Edinburgh. The Royal Horticultural Society holds annual examinations in April.

Horticulture, see GARDENING.

Horton, Robert Forman (b. 1855), an English congregational minister, born in London, and educated at Shrewsbury and New College, Oxford. In 1877 he was president of the Oxford Union, and in 1879 he became fellow of New College and lecturer on history. Since 1880 he has been pastor of the Lyndhurst Road Church, Hampstead. In 1893 he delivered the Lyman Beecher lectures at Yale, U.S.A., in 1898 he was chairman of the London Congregational Union, and in 1903 of the Congregational Union of England and Wales. His publications include *Inspiration and the Bible,* 1888; *The Book of Proverbs,* 1891; *The Apostle's Creed,* and *The Teaching of Jesus,* 1895; *The Trinity,* and *Pastoral Epistles,* 1901; *The Holy Spirit,* 1907; *The Early Church,* 1908; *Great Issues,* 1910.

Hortus Siccus, see HERBARIUM.

Horus (Egyptian *Hōr*), in ancient Egyptian mythology, was the sun-god and equivalent to the Greek ' Apollo.' He is sometimes identified with Harpokhrates, *i.e.* ' Hōr the child,' when he is represented as seated on a lotus-flower with his finger in his mouth, perhaps as a symbol of secrecy and silence. The name Hōr was also probably applied to lesser divinities, but to all forms the falcon was held sacred, and the name Hōr was the commonest title of the king in the earliest dynasties. The Northern Kingdom in particular was under the patronage of H.

Horvath, Michael (1809–78), a Hungarian historian and statesman, born at Szentes (county Csongrad). In 1844 he became professor of Hungarian in Vienna, and in 1848 bishop of Csanad. He took an active part in the revolutionary war and was minis-

ter of public worship and instruction under Kossuth. The defeat of the Nationalist movement drove him into exile, and he did not return until the amnesty of 1867. He published *History of Hungary until* 1823 (1842-46); *Twenty-Five Years of Hungarian History,* 1823-48 (1863) (2nd ed. 1868) ; and *History of the Hungarian Revolution of* 1848-49 (1865) (3rd ed. 1898).

Horwich, a tn. and urban dist. in Lancashire, England, 6 m. W.N.W. of Bolton. It has extensive locomotive works, and stone is quarried in the neighbourhood ; other industries are bleaching, cotton-spinning, and the manuf. of bricks and tiles. Pop. (1911) 16,286.

Hosanna, the shout of praise and adoration used by the multitude at the triumphal entry of Jesus into Jerusalem (Matt. xxi. 9).

Hosea, the first of the twelve minor prophets according to the Biblical order. Nothing is known of him beyond what is told us in the Book of H. From this we learn that he was a native of the northern kingdom of Israel, and that his father's name was Beeri. The period of his prophecies is given in the first verse: ' In the days of Uzziah, Jotham, Ahaz, and Hezekiah, kings of Judah, and in the days of Jeroboam the son of Joash, king of Israel.' Since the last-named king died during the life of Uzziah, these dates are not in full agreement. The prophecies fall into two parts : (1) Chaps. 1-3, which tell the story of the prophet's marriage with Gomer the daughter of Diblain, a profligate woman, and of the birth of his three children to whom allegorical names are given (i. 4, 6, and 9). The application of this story is then made to the relations between Yahweh (Jehovah) and his people. (2) Chaps. 4-14, wherein he denounces more fully the particular sins of unfaithfulness committed by the Israelites against Yahweh, such as their introduction of idolatrous ceremonies and their alliance with and trust in foreign nations. The question as to whether the account of the prophet's marriage is truly biographical, or is merely introduced to give point to the later accusations, has been much discussed. There seems to be no sufficient reason why it should not be biographical. There are some interpolations such as (1) those passages which extend the application of the prophecies to the southern kingdom of Judah; (2) those which interrupt the denunciation to speak of a period of final happiness. *See* Smith's *Twelve Minor Prophets,* 1876; Cheyne Cambridge Bible, etc., 1889; and works by Simson, Nowack, Sayce, and Duhm.

Hoshangabad, a tn. and dist. of India in the Nerbudda div. of the Central Provinces, on the l. b. of the R. Nerbudda, 40 m. S.S.E. of Bhopal. The chief industry of the town is brass-working. Pop. 14,940. The principal crops grown in the district are wheat, millet, and oil-seeds. Area 4500 sq. m. Pop. 449,165.

Hoshiarpur, a cap. of a dist. of the same name in the Jullundur div. of the Punjab, India, 62 m. E. of Amritsar. It has manufactures of cotton goods, inlaid woodwork, laquer, shoes, and upper-work. Pop. 17,549. The district exports sugar, rice, and other grains, tobacco, and indigo. Area 2244 sq. m. Pop. 989,782.

Hosiery, the term used to designate all textile fabrics which are manufactured on the looped-web principle. It may be done by hand or on a frame.

1. *Hand knitting* requires very few and simple implements, consisting of two or more straight needles or wires. On to these an indefinite number of loops are ' cast,' made of one continuous thread of yarn, which is passed through the previously made loops to make a fresh series, and left hanging free. The needles may be of steel, bone, or wood, and of any length; if two only are used the fabric will have a selvedge on both sides; if three or more are employed, a circular web will be formed as in stockings.

2. *Frame-work knitting* in its simplest form consists of rows of loops supporting each other, formed of a continuous thread running from one side of the fabric to the other and back again; it is the form of stitch most widely used in H. The frame was introduced about 1589 by the Rev. William Lee, of Nottingham, and, with a few trifling additions and alterations, has formed the basis of all H. and lace machines down to the present time. Lee's ' hand stocking frame ' differed from the principles of hand knitting in having a separate needle for each loop, instead of ' casting ' all the loops on to one needle, which increased the speed 500 per cent. on the rate of hand knitting. Lee's frame has only sixteen needles for 3 in. (many modern machines have as many as 135 needles for 3 in.). Each needle consists of a shank with a terminal, spring-pointed hook, termed a ' beard,' which can be pressed into a socket or eye in the shank. Between each needle is a ' jack sinker ' which falls, carrying down the yarn and so forming a new loop, regulated in size by the distance to which the sinker is allowed to fall. Then the loops are brought forward under the beards and a horizontal bar, called a ' presser,' is brought down to close all the points of the needle beards into the eye in the shank. The last row of loops is brought over the needle beards and off the needle altogether, being left hanging until the beards are released, and they are drawn back along the shanks for the next course of loops. In later machines, when the number of needles was increased and they were placed closer together, a second set of sinkers, called ' lead sinkers,' was placed alternately with the ' jack sinkers,' and two ' lead sinkers ' working alternately with a ' jack sinker,' which drew a loop over three needles, produced a very fine stitch. The first fabric made by Lee was a flat piece with selvedge on both sides from which the garment had to be cut to shape and sewn at the seams, but he soon learned to ' fashion ' the garment by transferring loops at the edges, inwards to narrow and outwards to widen. In Lee's machine the thread had to be placed over the needle by hand, and it was not until 1857 that Luke Barton invented the first successful machine fitted with self-acting mechanism for fashioning, known as the ' straight bar rotary frame.'

3. *Warp knitting* varies from frame-work knitting in having a separate thread for each needle instead of the same thread for the whole row. The warp threads are laid on the needles to right and left, thus forming a series of loops without the employment of sinkers, the threads running lengthwise. By the invention of the Dawson wheel (1791) the threads can be laid in any direction and thus give greater scope for variety of design in openwork and colour, which makes this form of knitting specially suitable for shawls and fancy stockings.

4. *Mechanical frames,* driven by steam-power, have been in general use since their introduction in 1828; one of the best known being the ' Cotton patent rotary frame,' invented by William Cotton of Loughborough in 1864. Hand-frames are still in use for special work, such as gloves and fancy shawls.

5. *Circular knitting* was first rendered possible by a machine patented by Sir Marc I. Brunel in 1816, and improved upon by Peter Claussen of Brussels who exhibited it in Nottingham in 1845. This frame had horizontal bearded needles fixed on a rotating ring and produced seamless garments. The position of the needles was altered to perpendicular a few

years later, and is known as the English loop-wheel circular frame. The adoption in 1858 of the self-acting or 'latch' needle rendered the making of circular fabrics much easier and cheaper. The circular knitting machine in most general use is an American invention, and will make plain or ribbed seamless fabrics.

6. *Rib-work* was the first variation of the plain fabric produced in Lee's machine, and was produced by an invention of Jedediah Strutt in 1758, by which a second set of needles, placed at right angles to the first, drew their loops to one side, while the first set of needles drew theirs to the other side of the frame. Open-work and lace in which certain loops are removed from one needle and added to another, the empty needle making a small hole in the fabric, is an off-shoot of rib work and dates from about 1763. H. can be made of silk, wool, and cotton threads, and the chief centres of its manufacture in England are Leicester and Nottingham.

Hoskins, Sir Anthony Hiley (1828-1901), a British admiral. He entered the navy in 1842 and saw service at Tamatave (1845), at Anjoxa in the Mosambique Channel (1847), in the Kaffir War (1852-53), and in China at the capture of Canton and Taku forts (1857), Egypt (1882). He became commander-in-chief of the Mediterranean (1889-91), and was three times a lord of the Admiralty.

Hosmer, Harriet (1830-1908), an American sculptor, native of Waterton, Massachusetts, U.S.A. She studied under Gibson in Rome. Her animated and original statue of 'Puck' was a great success. Her other best works are : 'Zenobia in Chains,' 'Beatrice Cenci,' 'A Sleeping Fawn,' and 'A Waking Fawn.' Certain technical processes of the art of sculpture are of her invention.

Hospice (Lat. *hospitium*, entertainment), the name given to the homes of rest provided as a shelter for travellers passing over the Alps, by the various monastic orders. The most famous Hs. are those on the Great St. Bernard, founded 962, on the St. Gothard, dating from the 13th century, on the Mt. Cenis, the Simplon, and the Little St. Bernard.

Hospitalet, a com. in Barcelona, Spain, 4 m. S.W. of the tn. of Barcelona. Pop. 5000.

Hospital Fund, King Edward's, founded in 1897 by the late king when he was Prince of Wales, to commemorate the sixtieth anniversary of his mother's reign. Its object is to secure adequate support of the hospitals of London. In 1911 the sum of

£189,000 was distributed among 145 institutions, and the total amount received by the charity up to the end of that year was £3,229,290.

Hospitallers, Knights (Old Fr. *hospitalier*, Lat. *hospitalis*, from *hospes*, a guest), the name applied to charitable brotherhoods founded at different periods, and in different countries, for the care of the sick in hospitals. The Knights of the Holy Sepulchre or of St. John of Jerusalem were a body of monks under whose auspices had been founded a church in Jerusalem. They had their origin in Palestine in the 11th century, their object being to take Christian pilgrims visiting the Holy Sepulchre under their care and protection. Their military organisation was perfected in the 12th century, when they unsuccessfully defended Acre after the taking of Jerusalem by the Moslems. In the 14th century they captured and occupied the island of Rhodes and continued to hold it till 1523, when it was seized by the Turks. After this their influence materially declined. In 1530 they found a shelter in Malta, and administered the government of that island until it was occupied by Napoleon in 1798. On account of their wealth and power, they were envied by most of the sovereigns of W. Europe, and in 1530 Henry VIII. confiscated their property in England. The vow to devote oneself to the work of a hospitaller is generally added to the ordinary vows of poverty, chastity, and obedience commanded by Saint Augustine. The mark of the order was the black robe and cowl, with the cross of eight points on the left breast, consisting of four barbed arrow-heads meeting at their points—the well-known Maltese cross. In modern times this has been slightly altered and modified in the many institutes or congregations under various names and various rules. At different periods this order has been termed Knights of Rhodes and Knights of Malta. In 1879 the headquarters were fixed at Rome and governed by a council under a grand master. The Hospitallers owned many strong castles in Syria, like their contemporaries, the Templars, and on the suppression of the latter in 1312 the pope transferred most of their possessions to the Hospitallers. Besides the Knights of St. John of Jerusalem there have been twelve or more monastic congregations, whose members were popularly termed Hospitallers. The two modern associations ascribing their origin to this order are the Brandenburg ' Johanniteroden ' and the English order of the Knights of St. John. The former was reorganised in 1853 and the latter in

1827. This society has its head-quarters in Clerkenwell, London, and has founded the street ambulance systems and originated the Red Cross Society. It is a purely philanthropic institution, distributing charity to convalescents, etc. *See* Le Roulx, *Hospitaliers,* 1904; Larking and Kemble, *Knights Hospitallers in England;* Bedford's *Malta and the Knights Hospitallers;* Vertol's *Historie des Chevaliers Hospitaliers de S. Jean de Jerusalem;* Woodhouse's *Military Religious Orders of the Middle Ages;* Delaville de Roux, *Les Archives, la Bibliotheque et le Trésor de l'Ordre de St. Jean à Malte,* etc.

Hospitals are institutions for the temporary reception of the sick. The word H. is derived from the Latin adjective *hospitalis,* which belongs to the noun *hospes* (genitive *hospitis*) meaning host or guest. Hotel and hostel have a similar derivation, but like H. these terms have become limited and specialised in their application.

*Classification.—*H. are clinical or non-clinical, according to whether or not they have attached to them medical schools where students receive technical instruction by properly qualified lecturers and demonstrators. According to another classification they are divided into general and special H. A general H., as its name implies, is designed to treat all kinds of patients and should therefore be equipped with every appliance, both for medicine and surgery. Particular classes of patients or patients suffering from infectious diseases, such as fever or small-pox, or from diseases of a particular organ, such as eye, ear, nose, and throat, or from maladies like cancer, are treated in special H. The following is a list of the main classes of H. with examples from London and elsewhere :

I. GENERAL HOSPITALS.—(*a*) *Clinical :* Charing Cross H. (founded 1818), Guy's H. (1724), University College H. (1833), Royal Free H. (1828), St. Bartholomew's H. (1123), St. George's H. (1733), St. Thomas's H. (1200), Westminister H. (1719). (*b*) *Non-clinical :* Great Northern Central H. (1856), London Homœopathic H. (1849), Metropolitan H. (1836).

II. SPECIAL HOSPITALS.—1. *For special classes of persons :* (*a*) *Children's hospitals :* Alexandra H. for Children with Hip Disease (1867), Victoria H. for Children (1866). (*b*) *Hospitals for women and children :* Royal Waterloo H. for Children and Women (1816). (*c*) *Maternity and lying-in hospitals :* City of London Lying-in H. (1750), Queen Charlotte's Lying-in H. (1752).

(*d*) *Hospitals for foreigners :* French H. (1867), German H. (1845). 2. *For infectious diseases :* (*a*) *Hospitals for fever and diphtheria :* London Fever H. (1801), Gore Farm H., Kent (1890). (*b*) *Small-pox hospitals :* Joyce Green H., Kent (1903). (*c*) *Hospitals for consumption and diseases of the chest :* Brompton H. (1841), Mount Vernon H. (1860), Royal National H., Isle of Wight (1867). 3. *For diseases of particular organs :* (*a*) *Dental hospitals :* Royal Dental H. of London (1858). (*b*) *Ophthalmic hospitals :* Royal London Ophthalmic H. (1804). (*c*) *Throat, Nose, and Ear Hospitals :* H. for Diseases of the Throat, Ear, and Nose (1863). 4. *For special maladies :* (*a*) *Cancer :* Cancer H. (Free), (1851). (*b*) *Paralysis and epilepsy :* National H. for the Paralysed and Epileptic (Albany Memorial) (1859). (*c*) *Skin diseases :* St. John's H. (1863). (*d*) *Deformities :* Royal National Orthopædic H.(1904). *N.B.—*The above hospitals are in London unless otherwise stated.

*Administration.—*In the British Isles H. are largely supported by voluntary contributions, whilst on the Continent and in the United States these institutions are, for the most part, supported and controlled by municipalities. The rate-supported H. in England are almost confined to fever and small-pox H., a few ambulance stations, and some homes for sick and convalescent children both in the country and at the seaside. Under the Insurance Act, 1911, however, the state has promised to provide sanitoria for the accommodation of tuberculous patients. There is a good deal to be said for the voluntary, as opposed to the municipal institution. Firstly, the principal medical and nursing schools are mostly attached to voluntary H., and this ensures each patient having the benefit of expert knowledge and the most scientific and up-to-date methods and appliances. Moreover, the number of doctors, whose advice may be sought, minimises the danger of wrong diagnosis. Secondly, these institutions can only rely on maintenance so long as they carry out their work efficiently. Competition constantly leads to improvement in construction, organisation, and provision for the comfort of the individual patient. Thirdly, they are freely open to the public for inspection, and the fact that thousands of visitors annually visit them probably helps the officials to perform their duties better, and leads to the speedy remedy of defects and shortcomings. Fourthly, they undoubtedly exercise a humanitarian influence and serve as a continual reminder of the need of charity and social work. The following are the drawbacks of state or rate-supported institutions. Firstly, they are under the management of permanent doctors and officials who, however worthy their intentions, are likely to grow somewhat slack in the discharge of their duties and to feel in time the monotony of routine. Thus the absence of competition may retard the influx of healthy innovations, experiments, and improvements. Secondly, there is a likelihood of all these institutions being built and superintended on the same lines, with the result of a dead level of comparative inefficiency. Such drawbacks, at least, are remarked in certain countries where these H. exist. Yet it is likely that in the future the erection and supervision of H. will be one of the duties of municipalities, and there are many benefits which should accrue from such a system. For instance, there would be a central controlling body to effect an economic administration; to see that the H. were disposed over any given district so as to meet the needs of the community; to prevent waste and overlapping; and to encourage co-operation wherever possible. Even under our present system co-operation might be much more practised than it is. If managers would only agree to a central office, it would be easy to distribute the sick according to the vacancies in different H. and to prevent the wards of one being overcrowded, whilst those of another are only half-full. Those who urge that district councils and other public bodies should undertake the care of the sick, look forward to the growth of H. villages in pleasant and salubrious situations some distance away from the towns, for whose inhabitants they are intended, and some of them have even conceived a great H. city. As things are there is no doubt that the convalescence of a patient in a metropolis like Manchester, Glasgow, or New York is appreciably delayed by the city atmosphere.

Sir William Fergusson's Commission on Hospital Abuse (1871), made the following recommendations which are here quoted as indicating other deficiencies in our present system: (1) To improve the administration of poor-law medical relief; (2) to give the poor-law authorities control of all free dispensaries; (3) to check the unrestricted system of free relief; and (4) to pay the medical staff. It is a well-known fact that at present hundreds of people, who can afford payment, avail themselves of free treatment, which is only intended for the poor. It is suggested that pay wards should be attached to all large

H., and that the patients admitted to them should give fees according to their social status. Since 1909 almoners have been appointed in certain H. to decide whether or not applicants for medical assistance are in a position to contribute towards its expense, and it is to be hoped that other steps in the same direction will soon be taken.

History.—It is no exaggeration to say that until the 18th century the sick could only be cared for at home or at least in private houses. As late as 1710 St. Thomas's and St. Bartholomew's H. were the only asylums for the sick in London, and in the provinces such institutions were unheard of. But since that day, and especially in the last century, rapid strides have been made, especially in England and Germany, and the H. is regarded as an indispensable factor in all towns of any size, whilst cottage H. are springing up all over the country. Popular education and the realisation of the importance of observing the laws of health wherever people congregate together are responsible for this extraordinary advance. The truth that the welfare of the community depends on the isolation of the sick is more appreciated every year, and an attempt is now to be made to stamp out tuberculosis by confinement of the infected in sanitoria, the expectation being that in time this scourge will lose its virulence as surely as plague, small-pox, and typhoid fever have already done.

It is a mistaken belief that H. were primarily Christian institutions. Egyptian invalids slept in the shadow of their temples of Saturn 4000 B.C. in the hope that the god would make them well. The temple of Æsculapius at Cos was frequented by Greek sufferers, and to turn to the East, it is known that the Indian emperor, Asoka, founded a H. at Surat (c. 260 B.C.), and that Haroun al-Raschid (d. 809 A.D.) built many asylums at Bagdad.

Hospodar (Russian *Gospodar*), a Slavonic term meaning ' lord,' ' master,' is the title which is specially applied to the head of a family or the master of a house. It was a title of the rulers of Walachia and Moldavia from the 15th century to 1866, when Roumania became independent. The title was also used by the grand-dukes of Lithuania and the kings of Poland down to John Sobieski.

Host (Lat. *hostis*, a victim), the sacrifice of Christ's body and blood in the Holy Eucharist, applied more particularly to the consecrated wafer used in the service of the Mass in the

Roman Catholic Church, when it is regarded literally as a propitiatory sacrifice. It is a thin, unleavened, flat wafer of circular form with certain mystic signs impressed upon it, such as the Crucifixion or the Lamb; when used in the Anglican Church it is usually quite plain. In the Roman Church the H., after being blessed, is supposed to be no longer bread but the real body of Christ, as the wine is His blood (*see* TRANSUBSTANTIATION). The celebrant breaks the wafer into two pieces, keeping one himself and breaking the other over the chalice. In the Greek Church the H. is dipped in the wine before being handed to the celebrant. The ceremony of the ' Elevation of the Host ' dates from the 12th century.

Höst, Jens Kragh (1772-1844), a Danish historian, born at St. Thomas, West Indies. He wrote several important works illustrative of the modern history of Denmark, and was one of the founders of the Scandinavian Literary Society for the encouragement of historical research. He also published *Grev Struensee*, 1824 ; *Märkvärdigheder i Kong Frederik V.'s Levnet*, 1820; and *Clio* (4 vols.), 1813-21.

Hostage, either a person seized by one of two belligerent parties during a war as a preventive measure against certain acts of aggression, or one handed over by one government to another as a security for the carrying out of an agreement. The practice dates from very ancient times, and is still occasionally employed.

Hoste, Sir William (1780-1828), an English naval officer, born in Ingoldisthorpe, Norfolk. He saw service in all parts of the Mediterranean, and in 1811 he defeated Dubourdieu in a fight of Lissa, ultimately he took Cattaro and Ragusa. He was a brilliant commander, and was a favourite of Nelson.

Hostilius, Tullus (*d.* 640 B.C.), according to tradition third King of Rome and grandson of Hostius H. He is supposed to have succeeded Numa in 670, and to have waged successful wars against Albans, Fidenæ, and the Sabines. Jupiter is supposed to have smitten him with fire. *See* Mommsen's *Rome*.

Hostrup, Jens Christian (1818-92), a Danish dramatist, born at Copenhagen. He studied theology for some time, but encouraged by the success of some of his poems and comedies he soon turned his attention to the theatre and wrote numerous comedies and sketches for the Theatre Royal, Copenhagen, among which the best known are: *Some Neighbours* (comedy), 1846 ; *A Sparrow at the Ball of the Cranes*, 1846, a satire on

snobbery ; *Master and Apprentice*, 1852. Returning to theology in 1855, he became pastor at Silkeborg and later at Frederiksborg (1862-81). Between 1880 and 1888 he furnished three pieces for the Theatre Royal, including the realistic drama *Eva*, 1880. *See* his *Memoirs*, published and completed by his wife (1891).

Hotbed is prepared with stable manure, tree leaves, half-spent tan, lawn mowings, and general garden refuse. The stable manure must be not less than three weeks old. When quite fresh it gives off a violent heat and consequently is unsafe for use, but if thoroughly turned and shaken three or four times a week and well mixed with the other material it will then generate a moist, gentle, and lasting heat. If dry, the material must be damped, and when it ceases to generate a disagreeable odour will be fit to form the H. A dry sunny site should be chosen and the material spread over a space 18 in. to 2 ft. on all sides larger than the frame. The material is put on in layers, each well beaten and trodden, until the whole is about 4 ft. high. The frame is then placed in the centre of the heap and a stick 3 ft. long pushed down into the bed. The ' light ' is put on the frame but raised a little to allow gases and steam to escape. The stick is withdrawn each day and tested with the hand, and until the bottom end can be held without inconvenience the frame should not be used. A H. retains its heat for eight to ten weeks, and is invaluable for forcing early crops of salad plants, carrots, asparagus, potatoes, and much else, for raising annuals and other seedlings, and for striking cuttings. A layer of soil may be put into the frame and seeds raised or cuttings struck in it, or if pots and pans of soil are used, cocoa-nut fibre refuse may be spread over the bed to stand pots on or plunge in. As the atmosphere in a H. frame is moist, special attention must be given to ventilation when it contains seedlings or they will damp off. When the heat begins to decline, additional warmth can be provided by banking up more fermenting material round the sides of the frame. This material can be almost fresh, having been turned and shaken but once. When this has cooled and extra heat is still required, the added material can be removed and fresh put in its place. When properly managed, the H. is one of the most useful aids to gardening, and enables many successful gardeners with limited means and accommodation to dispense with the hothouse.

Hotchpot. The object of the H.

clause, which is inserted by conveyancers in all marriage settlements, is to ensure that none of the younger children of the marriage who have been advanced a sum out of the portions' fund during their father's lifetime shall be able to claim a further share at his death in the sum remaining for division among all the younger children without first bringing into account the sum or sums so advanced. Power is usually expressly given in the settlement to the tenant for life under the Settled Land Acts to declare on making an advance, or ' appointment ' as it is termed, that the share appointed shall not be brought into H., which power is of use where it is the wish of the tenant for life to divide the fund equally subject to a first charge in favour of a particular child. Where residuary estates is by the terms of a will to be divided between the children of the testator and a stranger, advancements do not have to be brought into H. so as to benefit the stranger.

Hotch-potch, or **Hotch Pot,** the name of a Scottish dish dating from the 15th century, and consisting of a sort of broth with many ingredients, whence the term has come to be used for any heterogeneous mixture.

Hotel (Fr. *hôtel*, Old Fr. *hostel*, Lat. *hospitale*), a superior kind of inn. It provides lodging and refreshment for travellers generally, and may be set up without a licence, unless the proprietor sells excisable liquors; in that case a licence must be sought. A proprietor is bound to provide for any one who applies to him, and may not refuse either lodging or refreshment, unless the applicant is tainted by disease or drunk; but, on the other hand, a traveller cannot select what rooms he chooses, and if he will not accept the accommodation offered him, the proprietor need not oblige him at all. Then, again, a proprietor can retain any of the property of his guest if he fails to pay his account. But the hotel-keeper is liable for the loss of his visitors' property within the H. to the value of £30, unless it can be proved that his guest was at fault. The word H. has different meanings. In France it originally meant the mansion of a distinguished person, then the residence of a maire, and later a place where people were lodged and fed at a fixed price. The modern French word is still used for the house of a rich man, or for a public building, *e.g.* Hôtel de Ville is the town hall, and Hôtel de Dieu is the name given to the principal hospital in any French town; the Hôtel des Invalides in Paris is a famous military hospital and soldiers'

home, founded in 1670, which contains the tomb of Napoleon. The modern H. practically dates from the formation of railways, and is a palatial dwelling in comparison with the old-fashioned inn which it has superseded. At present travellers can have everything they require, and that, too at a moderate charge, viz. from about 10s. 6d. to 16s. per diem, the modern Hs. containing telegraph, post, and telephone offices, as well as reception, reading, smoking, and writing-rooms, drawing-rooms, comfortable bedrooms, and sitting-rooms. In America a fixed charge is made for board and lodging, but in Europe H. proprietors generally make a charge for the accommodation and an additional one for each meal taken in the H.

Hötensleben, a vil. of Prussian Saxony, 26 m. W. of Magdeburg; has manufs. of iron goods and copper and sugar refineries. Pop. (1910) 5235.

Hotham, William, first **Lord** (1736-1813), an English naval officer. He entered the navy in 1748, in 1751 sailed to N. America, and ultimately served in the West Indies. He took part in the defence of Sandy Hook and Rhode Is. under Lord Howe. H.'s actions against the French off Genoa and off Hyères (1795) were adversely criticised by Nelson in his letters.

Hotham, Mount (alt. 6100 ft.), one of the highest peaks in the Barry range, Victoria, S. Australia, about 135 m. E.N.E. of Melbourne.

Hothouse, a structure largely built of glass and permitting close control over conditions of temperature, lighting, and air. Hs. are built in three common forms : A span roof admits the maximum amount of sunlight if erected with its ridge running N. and S. and its sides facing E. and W.; the three-quarter span is built against a wall, preferably facing S.W. but admits light from all sides; the commonest and cheapest form is the lean-to. For all but the smallest Hs., hot water circulating in pipes is generally the most suitable form of heating. Much fuel may be wasted in heating, but with modern stoves and with good management, the cost is very low. Glass structures are classified according to the minimum winter temperatures, the greenhouse or cool house requiring not less than 40° F., the intermediate house 50° F., and the stove house 60° F. Red spider, mealy bug, aphis, thrips, and scale are among the worst pests of plants. Fumigation with nicotine preparations or cyanide of potassium is an effective though dangerous remedy. Mildew, the worst of the diseases, usually indicates a too close and damp atmosphere. Sulphur applied with powder bellows, removes it. Tenants erecting a H. on landlord's property should, failing a satisfactory arrangement with the landlord, build the house so that it can be legally moved when necessary. It must not be connected by nails, mortar, or cement with the wall and must not be attached to piles or stakes in the ground, but must rest on a brick foundation.

Hot Lakes, a dist. in the N. island of New Zealand, stretching S.W. from the Bay of Plenty, and containing hot springs, geysers, and active volcanoes.

Hotman, François (1524 – 90), a French publicist, of Silesian origin, born at Paris. In 1546 he was appointed lecturer in Roman law at the University of Paris. Having embraced Calvinism he went to Geneva and became professor of Bible letters there. He suffered greatly during the Huguenot persecutions, but his principal work, *Franco Gallice* (1573), was unpopular with his fellow-religionists. He published also many works on law, politics, and the classics.

Hot Springs, a city and the co. seat of Garland co., Arkansas, U.S.A., in the Ozark Hills, 45 m. W.S.W. of Little Rock. It is situated in a narrow valley and contains about forty-four mineral springs which are famous as cures for chronic diseases, such as rheumatism, gout, and neuralgia. Their temperature ranges from 76° to 160° F., and the daily output is about 1,000,000 gallons. They are all contained in a reservation which has been held, since 1903, by the United States government, which maintains here a naval and military hospital and a free bath-house. Pop. (1910) 14,434.

Hotspur, a name applied to Henry Percy, son of the first Earl of Northumberland. In the reign of Henry IV., H. and his father gained the great victory of Homildon Hill (1402). He joined with Owen Glendower against the king, but was killed in the battle of Shrewsbury (1403).

Hottentot, a native race of S. Africa, so called probably from their jabbering or unintelligible chatter. This race includes the Khoi - Khoi, or full-blood Hs., and the Bushmen. Of the former the Namas proper are the most typical branch of the H. race, and can be distinguished by their yellowish-brown complexion, oblique brown eyes, prominent cheekbones, pointed chin, broad flat nose, and black woolly hair. They are essentially a pastoral people, whereas the Bushmen live exclusively by the chase, and their national garb is the ' kaross,' or sheepskin. worn with the woolly side out in summer and reversed in winter. Their huts are frail structures of matting which can be carried from one camping ground to another. They are a sluggish, indolent people, and the majority of them lead a nomadic life. Most of the tribes have been converted by Protestant missionaries, but under the outward form of Christianity many old superstitions survive, and the ' Heitzi-Eibib,' or great spirit, is still alternately rewarded with offerings or overwhelmed with maledictions, according as he shows himself propitious or hostile to the community. Their speech is highly developed, possessing very delicately graduated series of vowels and diphthongs, and like the Indo-Chinese has tones by which different meanings are imparted to the same word. There is also an accusative case indicated by endings in the singular, dual, and plural, and gender is marked by distinct terminations for the masculine, feminine, and neuter of all three numbers.

Hottentots Bread, *see* DIOSCOREACEÆ.

Hottentots Holland, a mountainous district of Cape Colony, which is famous for its scenery. Jonkershoek among the mountains is noted for its old picturesque farm where the government trout hatchery is.

Hottinger, Johann Heinrich (1620-67), Swiss reformer and Orientalist, born at Zurich. In 1655 he was appointed professor of Oriental languages and biblical criticism at Heidelberg, and in 1662 was chosen principal of the University at Zurich, having previously held many professorships. His chief works are: *Historia ecclesiastica Nov. Test.*, 1651-67 ; *Thesaurus philologicus seu clavis scripturæ*, 1649 ; *Etymologicon orientale, sive lexicon harmonicum heptaglottan*, 1661. His son, Johann Jakob H. (1652-1735), was the author of *Helvetische Kirchengeschichte*, a book written against Roman Catholicism.

Hot-wall, a wall with included flues, built in cold countries to give warmth to trees trained against it, and counteract the effects of frosts in autumn and spring. Sometimes attempts are made by this means to assist in ripening fruits that do not readily mature in the natural temperature of the latitude, such as peaches, nectarines, or apricots in England. One furnace is sufficient to heat about 40 ft. of wall.

Hotze, Friedrich, Baron von, or Johann Konrad Hotz (1739-99), Austrian general, born at Richtersweil, Zurich. He gained experience in military affairs in the Würtemberg and Russian armies, and afterwards entered the Austrian service and rose to the rank of field-marshal. He distinguished himself in the Rhine campaign, 1793-95, commanded the Austrian force in S. Germany in 1796, and in 1797, as commander-in-chief, led the invading army into Switzerland.

Houbigant, Charles François (1686-1783), a French Orientalist, born in Paris. He published in 1753-54 an excellent edition of the Hebrew Bible, with a Latin version and notes in 4 vols. For this he was honoured by Benedict XIV. with a brief and a medal, while the French clergy awarded him a pension.

Houbraken, Arnold (1660 – 1719), painter and biographer of the Dutch artists, born at Dordrecht. He painted portraits and historical subjects, but is best known by his work, published in Dutch in 1817, entitled *The Great Theatre of the Dutch Painters*, with their portraits, in three volumes. There are also some etchings by him, among which are, ' Jupiter and Semele '; ' Heraclitus and Democritus '; ' Vertumnus and Pomona,' 1699; and ' Christ with the Disciples at Emmaus.'

Houbraken, Jacob (1698-1780), a Dutch engraver, son of Arnold, born at Dordrecht. He particularly excelled in portraits, and it has been said that no one has ever equalled him in the manner of imitating the flesh and hair by means of the graver. He published in London, 1743-52, *Heads of Illustrious Persons of Great Britain*, with Lives by Dr. Birch.

Houdeng-Goegnies and **Houdeng-Aimeries**, two adjoining villages in Hainault, 10 m. W. of Mons, Belgium. There are iron works. Pop. of each, 8000.

Houdin, Robert (1805-71), *see* CONJURING.

Houdon, Jean Antoine (1741-1828), a French sculptor, born at Versailles. When only twelve years of age he entered the Ecole Royale de Sculpture, and in 1751 carried off the Prix de Rome, and went to Italy. Here he remained ten years, and executed the colossal figure of ' St. Bruno,' of which Pope Clement XIV. said that it would speak did not the rules of its order enforce silence. On his return to France he was received into the Academy, becoming a member in 1796. In 1785 he visited America to execute a monument of ' Washington '; indeed it was in portraiture that he was especially successful. Some of his most famous busts are ' Turgot,' ' Rousseau,' ' Lafayette,' ' Mirabeau,' ' Napoleon,' ' Mdlle. Arnauld,' and ' Molière.'

Houghton, a tn. in Houghton co., Michigan, U.S.A., on the S. side of Portage Lake, about 68 m. N.W. of Marquette. It is the centre of the great copper-producing district of Keweenaw. The largest mine is Calumet and Hecla, where about 4000 men are employed, and an annual profit of $4,000,000 is made, the total product of the district being about £150,000,000 per annum. Pop. (1910) 5113.

Houghton, Marquis of, *see* CREWE, EARL OF.

Houghton, Richard Monckton Milnes, first **Baron** (1809-85), was an example of the best type of man about town. At Cambridge he moved in the literary set, and became intimate with Thackeray, Tennyson, and Brookfield, which friendships endured through life. Later in life he founded the Philobiblon Society, and was always in the van of such movements as mechanics' institutes, franchise, and the reform of the copyright law. A minor poet of some distinction, an excellent after-dinner speaker, gifted with an incisive wit, he was very popular in society, and he entertained largely both at Fryston and at his London house. He edited Keat's *Life and Letters* (1848), and collected his poems in 1863, and again in 1876. He published an interesting volume of essays, *Monographs*, in 1873. His biography, *The Life, Letters, and Friendships of Lord Houghton*, by Sir T. Wemyss Reid, appeared in 1890.

Houghton-le-Spring, a tn. 6 m. N.E. of Durham, England. There are colleries and iron works. The ancient church here contains the tomb of Bernard Gilpin, the ' Apostle of the North,' who was rector here, and also founded the grammar school. Pop. (1911) 9753.

Houlder Steamship Line was established in 1849 by Houlder Brothers in London, and carries on an important cargo service between England and Australia, S. Africa, and N. America. It owns some of the largest steamers fitted with refrigerating appliances, and thus has an extensive trade in frozen meat. The *Sutherland Grange*, built in 1907, with a gross tonnage of 6852, contains eleven insulated cargo chambers with a capacity of 397,134 cubic ft. Houlder Bros. & Co., Ltd., now possess sixteen vessels, with a gross tonnage of about 80,000.

Houlton, a tn. in Maine, U.S.A., in the co. of Aroostook, about 98 m. from Bangor. The Aroostook region has been opened up by the Bangor and Aroostook Railway, which is connected at H. with the Canadian Pacific. Pop. (1910) 5845.

Houma, a co. seat of Terrebonne par., Louisiana, U.S.A., about 50 m. S.W. of New Orleans. There are sugar, rice, and cotton plantations. Pop. (1910) 5024,

Hound, a term applied to dogs of the chase which hunt by scent alone, such as bloodhounds, foxhounds, staghounds, bassethounds, beagles, and harriers. Deerhounds and greyhounds, which run by sight alone, are not, strictly speaking, hounds.

Hound, a par. and vil., Hampshire, England, on Southampton Water, ½ m. from Netley station. It contains an Early English church and the Royal Military Hospital. Pop. 4000.

Hound's-tongue, the name given to various species of the boraginaceous genus *Cynoglossum.* The plants grow in tropical and temperate lands, and two grow wild in Britain. Of these the better-known is *C. officinale,* the common H., which grows on waste ground, and was formerly used in medicine. It grows to a height of 2 ft., has downy leaves and bears red flowers.

Hounslow, a tn. in Middlesex, which stands at the junction of the two great W. of England roads from Bath and Exeter, and is about 14 m. from London and 2½ m. from Brentford. Hounslow Heath, W. of the town, was the site of Roman and British camps, and was also a favourite resort of highwaymen. The large cavalry barracks built in 1793 is the chief military depôt for Middlesex. The manufacture of gunpowder is carried on, and the local gardens send supplies to the London market. A priory of friars of the Holy Trinity was founded at H. in 1296, and the chapel was used as a church until 1830, after which the present church of the Holy Trinity was built. Pop. (1911) 21,383.

Houplines, a com., Nord dept., France, 7 m. W.N.W. of Lille. There are important textile works, flour mills, distilleries, and breweries. Pop. 7600.

Hour, the twenty-fourth part of a day. In most countries the Hs. are counted from midnight, and two twelves are reckoned, but in some parts of Italy twenty-four Hs. are counted, beginning with sunset, so that noon and midnight occur at different times each day. Each H. is divided into 60 minutes, and each minute into 60 seconds. Many nations, *i.e.* Greeks, Jews, and Babylonians, were not accustomed to divide their day and night into equal parts, but into unequal or planetary Hs., and double Hs. of 120 min. were employed by the Japanese and Chinese.

Hour-angle, the angle made by any hour-circle with the meridian of the observer. For example, when the sundial at a certain spot registers ten o'clock in the morning, and the sun is therefore two hours distant from the meridian, the hour-circle makes an angle of 30° with the meridian.

Hour-circle, in astronomy, any great circle drawn through the poles. The fixed stars complete their apparent revolution round the earth in twenty-four hours of sidereal time, passing through 360° in twenty-four hours, *i.e.* 15° in one hour. If, therefore, two observers are 15° of longitude from each other, one has any fixed star one hour of sidereal time later in his meridian than the other. Meridians in dialing are known as Hs.

Hour-glass, an instrument for measuring intervals of time, which consists of two glass bulbs joined by a narrow neck. One of the bulbs is almost filled with sand or mercury which passes through the narrow aperture to the other bulb in the space of an hour if an H., or of a minute if a minute-glass. This device was frequently employed in churches during the 16th and 17th centuries, and in the English House of Commons, as a preliminary to a division, a two-minute sand-glass is still turned.

Houri, the name for a beautiful damsel endowed with perpetual youth, whose companionship in Paradise is the reward of devout Mohammedans after death. The word comes from the Persian *hûrî ;* Arabian *hawrā,* a black-eyed virgin.

Housatonic, a river (length 150 m.), New England, U.S.A., rises in Berkshire co., Massachusetts, and flows generally S. through Connecticut, enters Long Island Sound 4 m. E. of Bridgeport.

House, the term used for a building erected for habitation as distinguished from one built for ecclesiastical or secular purposes. It, therefore, includes dwellings of any size from a single-room building to a palace. The earliest Hs. of which remains have been found are those of the village of Kahun in Egypt. These varied in size, some only consisting of a single room, and were built of unburnt brick. In Greece and Rome, too, the Hs. were built of unburnt brick, and often coated inside and outside with stucco; besides this, there is evidence that the Hs. consisted of two or three stories, and had a wooden or stone staircase which led to the upper part of the dwelling. The H. of Livia on the Palatine Hill was in two stories, and remains of similar dwellings have also been found in Crete, Delos, and the Peiræus. In England and in Europe generally, in the dark ages, the Hs. were built mainly of wood, even in large towns like London ; but in the 12th and 13th centuries, stone was used, as can be gathered from some interesting relics : *e.g.* The Jew's House at Lincoln (12th century), the Rectory House at West Dean, Sussex (13th century), and the Musicians'

House at Rheims. In the 15th and 16th centuries half-timber Hs. were built, e.g. Speke Hall, near Liverpool; other examples being found at Bacharach and Hildesheim. The character of the English H. has varied with time, but perhaps the greatest change made has been the adoption of flats; and the demand for these has steadily increased, since their institution about the middle of the 19th century.

Houseboat, a river boat which is fitted with every convenience for habitation, *i.e.* has living, sleeping, and cooking apartments. In England these boats are found mainly on the R. Thames, and are only used as temporary houses by people making river excursions; but in the Eastern countries Hs., which very much resemble floating huts, are common on all the large rivers, and are used as permanent residences, indeed many of the Chinese, Burmese, etc., spend their whole lives on these floating crafts.

Housebreaking, see BURGLARY.

House-duty, a tax imposed on inhabited dwelling-houses of the annual value of upwards of £20, and limited to England and Wales and Scotland. It falls not upon the owner, but upon the legal occupier. Houses belonging to the royal family, hospitals, charity schools, almshouses, school buildings, and exclusively for education, worship, or exercise, trade and business houses occupied exclusively for any trade or business, dwelling-houses of a less annual value than £20, and dwelling-houses which are unoccupied or unfurnished and occupied by caretakers who do not pay poor rate, are exempt. The duty on inhabited houses and upon houses solely let in flats or tenements not exceeding £40 annual value, is 3*d.* in the £; exceeding £40 and not exceeding £60, 6*d.*; exceeding £60, 9*d.* On houses occupied as farm-houses, public-houses, shops, warehouses, or lodging-houses, 2*d.*, 4*d.*, and 6*d.* respectively, according to the above scale of annual values.

House-fly, Flesh-fly, or *Musca domestica,* the name given to a species of dipterous insects belonging to the family Muscidæ. These flies are widely distributed and very numerous, especially in summer. The eggs are deposited on dung-heaps, or similar places, and the larvæ feed on their surroundings until pupation, which takes place in a few days' time; at the end of a fortnight they are fully-developed winged insects. The chief characteristics are the sucking proboscis, and the bristle-feathered antennæ. Hs. are considered frequently to be agents in the spreading of disease; they pass the winter chiefly in the pupal state.

Household, Royal. The R. H. probably had its origin in the *comitatus* described by Tacitus which consisted of *comites* or companions who were the personal attendants of the Teutonic chieftain. In England before the Conquest the *comites* had been replaced by thegns, the chief of whom were the staller or horse-thegn, and the bowerthegn, while in Normandy a similar arrangement had been established and each duke had his seneshal or steward, his chamberlain, and his constable. After the Conquest this ducal household was reproduced in the R. H. of England. The history of the R. H., however, is difficult to trace, as very few records concerning it are forthcoming. The *Black Book of the Exchequer* enumerates its offices in Henry II.'s reign, but gives no account of their functions, and the *Collection of Ordinances and Regulations for the Government of the Royal Household, made in Divers Reigns from Edward III. to King William and Queen Mary* (printed 1790) contains very scanty information. The *Black Book of the Household* and the *Statutes of Eltham* do, indeed, give some details about the court arrangements during the 15th and 16th centuries, and Chamberlayne's *Present State of England* contains a catalogue of the officials at the court of Queen Anne, but no connected history is forthcoming. Be this as it may the existing R. H. is essentially the same as that under the Tudors or Plantagenets and consists of three main departments, the Lord Steward's Department (Board of Green Cloth), the Lord Chamberlain's Department, and the Master of the Horse's Department. At the head of the first is the Lord Steward (at present the Earl of Chesterfield), who must always be a member of the government and a peer, and it is interesting to note that he still possesses a criminal jurisdiction such as was originally inherent in every head of a department: indeed, all jurisdiction relating to homicide in respect of the R. H. resides in him, and under his mandate alone can inquests be held or criminals be indicted and tried. Under him are the Treasurer (Capt. the Hon. Fred E. Guest), the Comptroller (the Lord Saye and Sele), the Master of the Household (Sir Derek Keppel), the offices of the Almonry, and the Paymaster of the Household (Hon. Sir Sydney Robert Greville). At the head of the second is the Lord Chamberlain (the Lord Sandhurst) who also must be a member of government and a peer, and under him are the Vice-Chamberlain, the Master of the Ceremonies, whose duty it is to enforce the observance of the etiquette of the court, the Gentleman Usher of the Black Rod, the principal usher of the kingdom, the Lords- and Grooms-in-Waiting, who attend on the king in turn for about three weeks at a time, the Captain of the Corps of Gentlemen-at-Arms, the Captain of the King's Bodyguard of the Yeomen of the Guard, the Comptroller and Examiner of Accounts, the Paymaster of the Household, the Dean and Subdean of the Chapels Royal, the Pages, the Poet Laureate, the Royal Physicians and Surgeons, Chaplains, Painters, Librarians, and Musicians.

The Queen Consort's Household is also in this department and comprises a Lord Chamberlain (the Earl of Shaftesbury), a Vice-Chamberlain, a Treasurer, Equerry, and various ladies. These include the Mistress of the Robes, (at present the Duchess of Devonshire), who attends the queen at all state functions, and is the only lady of the court who comes into office with the government, the ladies of the bedchamber, the women of the bedchamber, and the maids-of-honour. The ladies of the bed-chamber, who must be peeresses, are eight in number and attend the queen throughout the year for about three weeks at a time, but the women of the bedchamber, also eight in number, only appear at court functions. The eight maids-of-honour are as a rule the daughters or grand-daughters of peers and have the right of prefixing ' honourable ' to their names when not entitled to it by birth. They are immediate attend-ants on the queen like the ladies of the bedchamber. The third depart-ment has at its head the Master of the Horse (at present the Earl of Granard), who also is a member of the government. He has charge of all matters connected with the horses and hounds of the king, and under him are the crown equerry who prac-tically manages the royal stables and stud, the equerries who are always officers of the army and attend the king in turn like the lords-and grooms-in-waiting, and the pages-of-honour, youths who wait on the king at state ceremonies. Besides the three depart-ments mentioned, there is also the Privy Purse Department which con-sists of the king's ' personal ' staff and includes the keeper of the privy purse (Rt. Hon. Sir William Caring-ton), and the Private Secretary (Lord Stamfordham). The civil list provides for the maintenance of the R. H., £125,800 being granted for salaries and £193,000 for expenses, besides grants of £110,000 for their majesties' privy purse, £20,000 for works,

£13,200 for royal bounty, and £8000 unappropriated.

Household Troops are those whose special duty it is to guard the reign-ing monarch and the metropolis. There are three regiments of cavalry and four of infantry, the cavalry being the Royal Horse Guards and the first and second Life Guards, and the infantry the Grenadier Guards, the Coldstream, Scots, and Irish Guards.

House-leek, the popular name given to various species of *Semper-vivum*, a genus of Crassulaceæ. The plants are succulent, have star-shaped flowers, and flourish on the moun-tains of Europe, Asia, and Africa. Several species occur in Britain as hardy plants, and their cultivation requires little trouble, as they thrive in the poorest soil. *S. tectorum,* the common H., is frequently planted on the roofs and walls of cottages to keep the slates together. The leaves are arranged in rosettes, are fleshy, and in colour are a greyish-green ; the flowers are purplish ; and vegetative multi-plication takes place by offsets.

Housemaid's Knee, *see* KNEE.

House of Commons and **House of Lords,** *see* PARLIAMENT.

Housing of the Working Classes. It seems almost incredible that less than thirty years ago the Statute Book contained no legislative enactment (beyond one or two ineffective Acts to enable local authorities to acquire labourers' lodging-houses or artisans' dwellings) even purporting to deal at all comprehensively with the hous-ing problem. That problem is nothing more than a corollary of the intense industrialism of England consequent on the development of machinery. Practically all the great manufactur-ing towns, each with its squalid alleys and festering slums, sprang up in the course of the last century. The Factory Acts (*see* FACTORY AND WORKSHOP ACTS), the first encroach-ment on the unfettered activities of capitalist employers, interfered with a one-sided freedom of contract by imposing on the employer the necessity of making the environment of factory work less dangerous and less insanitary. The Housing of the Working Classes Acts, the first of which under that title was passed in in 1890, have practically included in that environment the home itself. That Act and the various amending Acts up to Mr. Burns' Act of 1909, have done something to abate the slum evil, but the housing problem is yet far from solution. That pro-blem differs in rural and urban areas. In the latter the rural exodus of a fast-multiplying population seeking work and getting it at a starvation wage soon resulted in numerous slum areas and the various diseases, moral and physical, consequent on overcrowding; in the former, in spite of emigration and the townward rush, there is even now not a spare cottage in the country, while a high proportion of the existing cottage dwellings are insanitary to a degree and a picturesque relic of the days of villeinage.

The Act of 1890 was passed, after the report of the Royal Commission on the Housing of the Working Classes of 1884, to consolidate Cross's Acts, the Artisans' and Labourers' Dwellings Improvement Acts, 1875 to 1885. The object of these latter Acts was to pull down and reconstruct crowded areas, or areas which, in the words of the preamble to the Act, were injurious to moral and physical welfare, from the great number of their houses, courts, and alleys, which latter, by reason of the want of light, air, and ventilation, or of proper conveniences or other causes, were unfit for human habitation, and generated fever and disease, which spread from the areas to the whole city or town. The principle was novel, for hitherto the legislature had not recognised the impossibility of mitigating the whole evil by proceedings against individual owners; or, conversely, the fact that there being a number of owners in respect of any particular area, no one of whom was responsible for the slum as a slum, municipal action by compulsory reconstruction of the whole area, with compensation to the owners, was the only feasible and equitable solution. Compared with its predecessors, the Act of 1890 was an ambitious piece of legislation. It contains three principal parts, which though amended by the Act of 1909, remain the basis of the purely Housing Acts (as to town planning, *see below* and under TOWN PLANNING). The first part deals with 'Unhealthy Areas' and the making of 'Improvement Schemes.' The Act requires the medical officer of health to inspect unhealthy areas and state his opinion thereon. He may act either on his own initiative, or when two or more justices or twelve or more ratepayers make complaint to him of the unhealthiness of any particular area in his district. If he comes to the conclusion that any houses or alleys are unfit for human habitation, or that the narrowness, closeness, and bad arrangement, or the bad condition of the streets and houses within such area, or the want of light, air, or proper conveniences are inimical to the health of the inhabitants of the area or of neighbouring buildings,

and that the most satisfactory method of dealing with those evils is by a scheme for rearranging and reconstructing the streets and houses, or some of them, in the area in question by the local authority, he should make a representation to that effect to the local authority, which body, if satisfied of the truth of the representation and the sufficiency of their resources, shall proceed to make a scheme for the improvement of that area. Power is also given to the local authority to acquire land compulsorily, subject to compensation, for the purposes of a scheme, and to borrow money on the security of the rates as under the Public Health Acts. Part II. relates specifically to unhealthy dwelling-houses, and consolidates with many amendments and additions various provisions of the Artisans' Dwellings Acts, 1868 to 1885 (Torrens' Acts), Acts which were designed to enable local authorities not only to improve or demolish houses unfit for habitation, but also to deal with 'obstructive buildings,' *i.e.* buildings, which though not in themselves unfit, are so close to other buildings, as to stop ventilation or to be otherwise conducive to the unfit condition of such other buildings. Part II. of the Act of 1890 makes provision for the compulsory closing and demolition of unhealthy dwelling-houses, but these provisions have been entirely superseded by the much more stringent provisions of the Act of 1909, and empowers a local authority to make 'reconstruction schemes' for areas comprising houses closed by closing orders. A reconstruction scheme is virtually an improvement scheme on a small scale, but involves less expense and a less elaborate means of procedure. With the object of counteracting the delinquencies of a district authority under this part of the Act, power is given to the county council to exercise the necessary duties and to recover the incidental expenditure as a simple contract debt from the district authority. Part III. gives ample powers to local authorities to provide and let lodging-houses for the working classes. Lodging-houses in this context includes separate houses or cottages for the labouring classes, whether consisting of one or several tenements. The local authorities may purchase or rent land and erect thereon suitable dwellings, or convert existing buildings thereon into lodging-houses, or alter, enlarge, repair, and improve such buildings and fit them up with the requisite furniture, fixtures, and conveniences. As in the other parts of the Act power is given to the local authority to borrow from the Public Works Loan Commissioners. Acts were passed in 1900 to enable local authorities to lease land acquired by them for the purpose of providing lodging-houses, and in 1903 to extend the term for repayment of loans, and to enable the Local Government Board, after a local inquiry, to compel the local authority by mandamus to make and carry out necessary schemes. These Acts and the principal Act of 1890 undoubtedly effected some improvement and awakened the public conscience to the necessity of ameliorating housing conditions. Overcrowding decreased, less people were found in one-room dwellings, and the number of persons per house diminished slowly but surely, while the transit facilities afforded by cheap trams and electric trains relieved the congested centres of towns by encouraging the inhabitants to radiate outwards. But there was prior to 1909, and is still, ample room for improvement. Besides the confirmed dearth of cottage accommodation in rural districts, there is still a tendency for new slums to break out in place of the old ones. Alderman W. Thompson, chairman of the National Housing Reform Council in his *Housing Up-to-Date* (1907) records that between 1891 and 1901 no less than 500,763 persons migrated from rural to urban districts; that in urban districts over 500,000 persons were living in 250,000 one-room dwellings, and 2,158,000 in 658,000 dwellings of only two rooms. The census returns of 1901 showed that over 2,500,000 or 8·2 per cent. of the population were living in overcrowded dwellings, of which 726,096 were in London, 53,000 in Birmingham, 43,000 in Leeds, 54,000 in Liverpool, 34,000 in Manchester, and 36,000 in Sheffield. The evils of overcrowding need no detailed description. Bad housing and overcrowding are among the primary conducing factors to such diseases as tuberculosis, diphtheria, and purulent ophthalmia (*see under* BLIND). Infant mortality, intemperance, and lunacy are concomitant evils. Mr. Thompson points out, *e.g.* that the infant mortality in 1904 in St. Mary's, Birmingham, was 331 per 1000 births, as against 65 in the model village of Bournville. Every housing reformer realises the truth of Professor Koch's dictum, that it is not poverty or heredity that favours corruption, but the bad domestic conditions in which the poor live; that the slum breeds the unemployable, physical and moral degenerates, and hooliganism, and that the financial cost of these evils to the community is far heavier in the long run than that involved in a heavy initial outlay on improved housing conditions.

Broadly speaking, the Acts of 1890 to 1903 were a failure, and that failure was due to the inaction of local authorities, which inaction was itself due partly to the want of coercive provisions in the Acts themselves, partly to the defective nature of the administrative provisions, but chiefly to the obstructive tactics of such members of municipalities who were 'interested in preventing a large number of cheap and healthy dwellings being provided to compete with their own unhealthy hovels or highly rented dwellings, or those of their friends.' Numerous instances of obstructive tactics and dilatoriness in respect of rural districts are recorded in Mr. W. Walter Crotch's *The Cottage Homes of England* (1908), from which it will be seen that even where parish councils have realised the necessity for action, the reports to the Local Government Board by county councils after local inquiries have effectually paralysed all further action. In one typical instance the chairman of a county council shelved his responsibilities by stating that it could never be prudent for a district council to adopt Part III. of the Act of 1890, because suitable cottages could not be built and let at a rent which would save *the rates* from liability. On the purely economical side of the question it was clear that the one-sided system of valuation of land and the cumbersome procedure adopted from the Lands Clauses Acts for the compulsory acquisition of land, made land far too expensive, while the cost of building was enhanced by a needlessly restrictive by-law system, the most burdensome regulations of which were that too great a width was prescribed for new streets, regardless of the class of dwellings to which they formed approaches, the materials of road-construction were unnecessarily expensive, and no allowance was made for cheaper and yet no less hygienic methods of house construction. Finally, the borrowing powers of local authorities were inadequate, the annual charges on capital account being excessive as compared with the market rate of interest, and the period too short for which loans might remain outstanding. In short, the policy of *laissez-faire*, which in this connection favours the jerry builder and slum speculator, has had its day, and the struggle between the advocates of private enterprise and those of municipal action has necessarily eventuated in legislation of a socialistic character. The Housing and Town Planning Act, 1909, emasculated as it was in committee, marked a real advance. It embodies many of the proposals of the Royal Commission of 1885.

The object of this Act on its housing side was expressed by Mr. Burns to be ' to do something to efface the ghettos of meanness and the Alsatius of squalor that can be found in many parts of the United Kingdom . . . to diminish what have been called byelaw streets with little law and much monotony . . . to improve the health of the people by raising the character of the house and the home, and by extended inspection, supervision, direction, and guidance of central control to help local authorities to do more than they do now.' The Act by no means accomplishes this ambitious object, but it does as much as could be expected in the face of party opposition. The most important sections of the Act are those which provide a drastic procedure for the issuing of closing and demolition orders in respect of dwelling-houses represented, whether by any officer of the local authority or by any other person, to be unfit for human habitation; and as incidental thereto, imposes on every local authority the duty of making periodical inspections of their districts. A tour of slum-districts will convince any one that full advantage is everywhere being taken of the simplified procedure prescribed by the Act. In 1908-9, prior to the Act coming into operation, orders were made in respect of 587 houses. In 1909-10, 1511; in 1910-11 no less than 2678; while the obligation on landlords under section 15 to keep houses let to the working classes in repair by an extension of the principle in section 75 of the Act of 1890 as to implied covenants of repair has been enforced in the case of 13,000 houses up to 1911. In regard to the provision of dwellings under Part III. of the Act of 1890, the Act of 1909 provides increased facilities for the compulsory acquisition of land by authorising a local authority to acquire land by means of an order submitted to and confirmed by the Local Government Board. Furthermore, Part III. of the Act of 1890 now takes effect everywhere without formal adoption. Loans by the Public Works Loan Commissioners may now be made at the minimum rate allowed for the time being for loans out of the Local Loans Fund, which rate under the Treasury Minute of March 21, 1904, was fixed at $3\frac{1}{2}$ per cent., and the period for which loans may be outstanding is now eighty years. Encouragement is now given to public utility societies (societies registered under the Industrial and Provident Societies Act, 1893) by enabling them to get loans up to two-thirds instead of as theretofore only one-half of their securities. The Act also attempts to keep the various local authorities up to their duties by providing that parish councils or meetings, as well as inhabitant householders, may make complaints against rural district councils, and county councils and inhabitant householders may make complaints against urban district councils to the central authority, the Local Government Board, that the bodies complained of have failed to exercise their powers in a proper case. Upon such complaint the Board may hold a local inquiry and make an order enforceable by mandamus of the High Court. County councils may also exercise the powers of a rural district council in default of the latter doing so, and recover the expenses from them. The tendency of the Act in all respects to increase the powers of the central authority is seen in the provision by which the Local Government Board may now appoint an inspector or other officer to make inspection or inquiry as to unhealthy areas instead of leaving the duty solely to medical practitioners employed by the local authority.

There is a useful prohibition of the erection of back to back houses, an expression which denotes these undesirable arrangements where houses are constructed without any space in the rear or any windows except in the front walls, so that there is no possibility of any through ventilation from front to rear. But where there are no by-laws requiring open space in front as well as in the rear, the erection is not prohibited of houses one room in depth with no backyard and no rear-wall windows, provided they do not back on to similar houses. A most useful power is also given to the Local Government Board to revoke unreasonable by-laws with respect to new streets or buildings, and this power has been exercised recently in a paper issued by the Board in 1911 allowing thinner walls where made of more modern and equally efficacious materials, the result being that a considerable reduction can be effected in the cost of estate development, a result of especial value in agricultural districts where wages and rents run very low. In April 1913 a Unionist member moved the Second Reading of a bill which embodied some of the aims of the Rural League. Its objects were the provision of three-bedroom cottages with an eighth of an acre of garden land attached, by rural district councils, societies, or private owners; the idea being that an owner providing the cottages should provide the land free in return for a loan payable in sixty-eight and a half years, the rent chargeable not to exceed 2s. a week; but that where the council had to buy land a rent of 2s. 6d. a week might be charged them. No profits were to be made out of the tenants, and no liability might fall on the rates where owners were supplying the cottages. Mr. Burns, who invariably, and not without justification, resents intrusions on the domain of housing legislation, characterised the bill as a mere vehicle for extracting money out of the Treasury, while other Liberal members criticised it as a bill designed to pledge the credit of the state for the purpose of placing rural landowners in a privileged position in regard to the fulfilment of their obligations to those whom they employed. The bill was eventually talked out, meeting thereby no better fate than a bill promoted by Sir Arthur Griffiths Boscawen in 1911 to grapple with the housing problem through the medium of state grants in aid; Mr. Burns has recently (April 1913) suggested a new plan to local governing bodies and builders in the matter of the style of erection of cottages for workmen. The idea is to reverse the existing style by relegating the public roads to the backs of every two rows of cottages, and occupying the space intervening between the rows with front-to-front garden plots separated only by a narrow pathway. The cost of development would by this means be reduced as the drains could be laid directly from the back of the house instead of from the whole space underneath; and the roadway could be made narrower by reducing the width of footways. The chief advantage would be to the tenant himself, as his children would have no need to resort to the public roadway for a playground, and the fronts of the houses would be immune from the dust and din of the roads. Such house-planning ideas are, of course, suggestions in the direction of the larger idea of town-planning, powers in regard to which have been conferred by the Act of 1909 on local authorities in accordance with the recommendation of the Royal Commission of 1885. Town-planning is a wider subject than that of the Housing of the Working Classes, for all alike would benefit from its universal adoption. Briefly it aims at regulating and controlling the unconscious and chaotic growth of buildings on the outskirts of towns, by considerations both of hygiene and amenity. Hitherto it had never been thought necessary for any one owner to concern himself with the operations of his neighbour. The result has been the hideous ugliness of most of our modern towns, in parts of which the villas or houses of the well-to-do, factories, shops, railway embankments, warehouses, hospitals, slum dwellings, municipal tenements, gasometers, sewage disposal works, etc., are herded together in a heterogeneous mass. Whether, however, anything tangible will be accomplished, must depend eventually on the extent to which landowners and local authorities show themselves disposed to co-operate with one another. In a manner town-planning is a somewhat visionary ideal judged in the light of a business proposition. The enthusiast regards the provisions of the existing housing Acts as of a meticulous and tinkering kind, effecting nothing towards the accomplishment of his comprehensive schemes for the correlation along hygienic and agreeable lines, of all the different parts of a developing town. A great number of local governing bodies have adopted or applied for leave under the Act to adopt town-planning schemes, generally for very small areas and falling far short of the town-planners ideal (see further under TOWN PLANNING). Garden cities are a familiar instance of schemes that make a very praiseworthy and apparently economically sound experiment in the way of imparting to town-extensions or model villages something of the æsthetic. Housing reformers have for years agitated against the monotony and ugliness of the average by-law road and the houses in them. It has sometimes been said that the garden city, with the effect of brightness, colour, lightness, and warmth, lent to its small dwellings by the use of red tiles, steep-pitched roofs and gables, green-painted woodwork, and rough-cast walls, has succumbed to the craze for mediævalism and sacrificed comfort and convenience to artistic effects and hygienic fads. It is admitted, says Mr. Thompson, that this criticism may in some cases be just, but for the most part it is one based upon prejudice. There are a number of excellent model villages like Port Sunlight, Bournville, and Earswick, but these are largely the outcome of private munificence and benefiting a narrow class of employees. There are now certain co-operative societies, e.g. the Hampstead Garden Suburb Trust, but such co-partnerships, excellent in their way, effect but little towards the solution of the great problem of the Housing of the Working Classes.

Bibliography. — Thompson, *The Housing Handbook*, and *Housing Up-to-Date*, 1907 ; J. S. Nettlefold, *Practical Housing*, 1910 ; Casson and Ridgway, *Housing and Town-Planning Act*, 1909, 1912 ; Thompson, *Municipal Year Book*—Housing Section.

Houssain, or **Hussein**, sons of Ali and Fatima, *see* HASSAN.

Houssas, *see* HAUSAS.

Houssaye (or Housset), **Arsene** (1815-96), a French littérateur and poet, famous by 1836 for his novels, *La Couronne de Bluets*, and *La Pécheresse*. He was director of the Théâtre Français (c. 1849-56), and then became inspector-general of the Musées. His works include criticisms of art and literature, poetry (*Poésies Complètes*, 1849), and many novels. His *Confessions* appeared in 1885-91. *See* Lemaître, *A. Houssaye*, 1897.

Houssaye, Henry (b. 1848), a French historian, son of Arsène. His early works, such as *Histoire d'Apelles* (1867), *Histoire d'Alcibiade* . . . (1873), dealt with classical antiquities. His best writings are those treating of the Napoleonic period, '1814' (1888), followed by '1815' in three parts (1893 - 1905), the second dealing with *Waterloo*, the third with *La seconde restauration, la terreur blanche. Napoléon, homme de guerre*, appeared in 1904. H. became a member of the French Academy, 1894. He has edited and contributed to various papers, sometimes under the pseudonym ' Georges Werner.'

Houston, cap. of Harris co., Texas, U.S.A., on Buffalo Bayou, 48 m. N.W. of Galveston. It is a very important railway centre, situated on various different lines, and has water communication with the Gulf of Mexico and the Atlantic. Manufactures include engines, machinery, railway-cars. Sugar, cotton, and oil are produced, and lumber trade flourishes. Settled in 1836, it was named after Sam Houston, and has fine public buildings. Pop. (1910) 78,800.

Houston, Samuel (Sam) (1793-1863), an American soldier and politician, first president of Texas (1836). In early life he lived among the Cherokee Indians in Tennessee. He enlisted, 1813, serving in the army till 1818 notably in Jackson's campaign against the Creeks. H. then left to study law, and became governor of Tennessee, 1827. In 1829 he again went to live among the Cherokees who were now settling in Arkansas. In championing the cause of these friends he came into conflict with Stanbery (Stanbury) of Ohio (1832). On the outbreak of the Texan War H. became leader of the American colonists. After some losses he de-

feated the Mexicans under Santa-Anna on the San Jacinto (1836), thus winning independence for Texas. He was elected president, and served again from 1841-44. On the annexation of Texas (1845), he represented it in the United States Senate, 1846-59. Again governor of Texas in 1859, he was dismissed (1861) for opposing his state's secession. *See Life* by Williams, 1893 ; Crane, 1884 ; Bruce, 1891.

Houston Heights, a post tn. of Harris co., Texas, U.S.A., 4 m. N.W. of Houston, with manufactures of furniture and cotton-seed oil. Pop. (1910) 6984.

Houston Steamship Line, formed at Liverpool, 1883. R. P. Houston and Co. possess twenty-three vessels for carrying on cargo service between London, Liverpool, New York, R. Plate and S. Africa. Steamers also run from Australia to the Continent and the British Isles. The offices are at 16 Leadenhall St., London, E.C., and at 10 Dale St., Liverpool.

Hova, a race of people inhabiting the central prov. of Imerina, *see* MADAGASCAR.

Hove, or **West Brighton**, a municipal bor. and the most fashionable quarter of Brighton, on the coast of Sussex, England. Pop. (1911) 43,173.

Hoveden, or **Howden, Roger of** (c. 1117-1201), a chronicler, was probably a native of Yorkshire. He was one of the clerks of Henry II., and in 1189 served as an itinerant justice for the forests in Northumberland, Cumberland, and Yorkshire. After Henry's death he devoted himself to the writing of his *Chronicle* which opens with the year 732 and ends in 1201. From 732-1148 H. copies the *Historia Saxonum vel Anglorum post obitum Bedæ*, and from 1162-92 he relies on the *Gesta Henrici*, the other parts of his work are original, the latter part 1192-1201 being of great value. It was first printed by Sir Henry Savile in his *Scriptores post Bedam*, 1596, and has been edited for the Rolls Series by Bishop Stubbs, 1868-71.

How, William Walsham (1823-97), an English prelate, educated at Shrewsbury and Oxford. Ordained in 1846, he worked for many years at Whittington (Shropshire), and Oswestry. In 1879 he became suffragan bishop of London (East End), as Bishop of Bedford. He founded the E. London Church Fund, inspired fresh interest in church work, and became popular with all classes. For his love of children he was sometimes known as ' the children's bishop.' In 1888 he became first Bishop of Wakefield. His works include, *Commentary on the Four Gospels*, 1863-68; *Manual* for the Holy Communion, 1868; Poems, and Hymns, 1886. See Life by his son, 1898.

Howard, an illustrious English family, dukes of Norfolk since the 15th century, at the head of the nobility, perhaps descended from the Hereward of Edgar's reign (957-75). The first noted member of the house was Sir William H., or Haward, chief justice of the Common Pleas under Edward I. and Edward II. (1297-1308). His grandson, Sir John, was admiral and captain of Edward III.'s navy in the N., and sheriff of Norfolk. The admiral's great-grandson, Sir John, was a prominent Yorkist, created first Duke of Norfolk and Earl-Marshal of England (1483). He fell at Bosworth Field (1485) fighting for Richard. His son, Thomas, Earl of Surrey, was imprisoned for three years, but then regained his rights and titles, commanding the English at Flodden (1513). His son, Thomas, third Duke of Norfolk, was attainted by Henry VIII., and only escaped a death similar to that of his son, Surrey, the poet, by Henry's own death. Thomas, the fourth duke, was beheaded for communicating with Mary Queen of Scots (1592). His son, Philip, Earl of Arundel, died in the Tower (1595). The family honours were restored by the Stuarts to his descendants. Thomas became Earl of Arundel and Surrey (1604), and Earl Marshal (1621). Bernard Edward H. (Duke of Norfolk, 1815) was grandfather of the present (15th) duke, Henry Fitz-Alan H. (b. 1847). The numerous branches of the family are represented by the dukedoms or earldoms of Carlisle, Suffolk, Berkshire, Northampton, Arundel, Wicklow, Norwich, Effingham, and the baronies of Bindon, Howard de Walden, Howard of Castle Rising, Howard of Effingham, and Howard of Glossop. See Tierney, Hist. of Arundel, 1834; Causton, The Howard Papers, 1863; Howard, Hist. Anecdotes of the Howard Family, 1769; Howard of Corby, Memorials of the Howard Family, 1834; Collins, Peerage of England, 1779; Dugdale, Baronetage of England, 1675-76; Blomefield's Norfolk; Gatty, The Noble Family of Howard, 1879.

Howard, Bronson (1842-1908), an American dramatist who married a sister of Sir Charles Wyndham. As a journalist in New York (1867-72), he contributed to various newspapers, including the Tribune and Evening Mail. Some of his plays have been acted in London. They include Saratoga, 1870; The Banker's Daughter, Old Love-Letters, 1878; Young Mrs. Winthrop, 1882; One of Our Girls, 1885; The Henrietta, 1887;

Shenandoah, 1889; Aristocracy, 1892. Peter Stuyvesant was written with Brander Matthews (1899).

Howard, Catherine (c. 1520-42), a grand-daughter of the second Duke of Norfolk (d. 1524), brought up by his widow, she became fifth wife of Henry VIII. soon after the divorce of Anne of Cleves (1540). This marriage pleased the Roman Catholic party, but Catherine was soon accused of immorality with Culpepper and Dereham. She protested that she had been faithful to the king since her marriage, but was beheaded with all the partners of her intrigues, including Lady Rochfort (1542). See Froude, Hist. of England, iv., 1858; Strickland, Lives of the Queens of England, iii., 1877.

Howard, Charles, second **Lord Howard of Effingham** (1536-1624), an English admiral, grandson of the second Duke of Norfolk. He held various civil and military posts under Elizabeth, becoming Lord High Admiral (1585). As commander-in-chief against the Spaniards of the Armada (1588), he had Drake as his second-in-command. H. was associated with Essex (1596) in the successful expedition against Cadiz, and made Earl of Nottingham in reward for his services. When fresh Spanish invasions were feared, between 1597-99, Nottingham was appointed lord-lieutenant of England. He continued to hold high office under James I. See Campbell, Lives of British Admirals, i.; Barrow, Memoirs of Naval Worthies of Elizabeth's Reign, 1845; Collins' Peerage, v., 1768.

Howard, Henrietta, Countess of Suffolk (1681-1767), the eldest daughter of Sir Henry Hobart, Bart., married at an early age Charles H., afterwards (1731) ninth Earl of Suffolk. Appointed on the accession of George I. to a post in the household of the Princess of Wales, she attracted the attention of the Prince of Wales, whose mistress she became for some years. After the death of the earl in 1735, she married the Hon. George Berkeley (d. 1847). She lived at Marble Hill, Twickenham, and was intimate with her neighbour Horace Walpole. Her correspondence was edited by Croker (1824).

Howard, Henry (1769-1847), an English painter, studied under Reinagle. In 1790 he won the R.A. gold medal for historical painting (' A scene from Mason's " Caractacus " '), and silver medal for drawing from life. H. visited Rome, working with Flaxman and Deare. He became R.A. in 1808, secretary in 1811, and professor of painting in 1833. Among his best works are ' The Birth of Venus . . .,' ' The Solar System,' ' The

Story of Pandora ' (Soane Museum), ' Hylas carried away by the Nymphs,' ' Christ blessing Little Children,' 1808; ' The Flower Girl ' (National Gallery). He also made designs for Wedgwood's pottery. His lectures were published by his son Frank in 1848.

Howard, John (1726-90), an English philanthropist, especially famous for his labours to secure prison reforms. While attempting to go to the relief of the survivors of the Lisbon earthquake (1755), he was captured by the French, but soon managed to effect an exchange for himself and his fellow-prisoners. H. became high sheriff of Bedfordshire (1773), and in this capacity had his interest in the condition of prisoners roused. He travelled widely, visiting gaols throughout England and Europe. His *State of Prisons in England and Wales* . . ., 1777, resulted in the adoption of the hard-labour system. An Appendix was added in 1780. His *Account of the Principal Lazarettos in Europe* appeared in 1789. He died of camp-fever at Dophinovka, now Stepanovka, near Kherson in Russia *See* Lives by Brown (1818), Taylor (1836), Dixon (1849), Stoughton (new ed., 1884), Aikin (1792), Field (1850), and his *Correspondence of J. Howard*, 1855 ; *Anecdotes of J. Howard by a Gentleman*, 1790.

Howard, Oliver Otis (1830-1909), an American general, educated at Bowdoin and West Point, where he was assistant-professor (1857-61). He then became a colonel of volunteers, and fought with distinction at Bull Run, Fair Oaks (1862), Antietam, Chancellorsville (against ' Stonewall ' Jackson), Gettysburg, and Chattanooga. He served under Sherman throughout the Atlanta campaign, and was breveted major-general, U.S.A. (1865). H. then became commissioner of the Freedmen's Bureau (1865-74). He commanded the Departments of the Columbia, the Platte, California, and the East successively till his retirement (1894). He was one of the founders of the Howard University at Washington (1867), and founded the Lincoln Memorial University at Cumberland Gap (1895). His works include : *Chief Joseph* . . ., 1881 ; *General Z. Taylor*, 1892 ; *Fighting for Humanity*, 1898 ; *Autobiography*, 1907. *See* Stowe, *Men of Our Times*, 1868.

Howden, a par. and market tn. of E. Riding, Yorkshire, England, on the Ouse, 3 m. N.N.E. of Goole. It has a 13th century church and a famous horse fair. Coal is mined. Pop. (1911) 2007.

Howe, Elias (1819-67), an American inventor of Massachusetts. While employed as a machinist he conceived the idea of inventing a sewing-machine, entered into partnership with Fisher (1844), and completed his lock-stitch machine, 1845. H. was granted a patent (1846), but success was long in coming to him. Singer's imitations and improvements infringed his patent, but H.'s rights were finally established after a law suit (1854). *See* Parton, ' Hist. of the Sewing-Machine,' in the *Atlantic Monthly* (May 1867) ; Hubert, *Inventors*, 1893.

Howe, George Augustus, third Viscount (c. 1725-58), an English soldier, fought in Flanders under the Duke of Cumberland (1746-47). Pitt made him second to Abercromby during the campaign in America and attempt to capture Ticonderoga from the French as a preparation for the invasion of Canada. H. was killed in a skirmish with the French. See *Gent. Mag.*, 1747 and 1758 ; *Newcastle Weekly Chron.* (Suppl. Jan. 2, 1892) ; Mante, *Hist. of the Late War in America*, 1772.

Howe, Henry (1812-96), an English actor, his full name being H. H. Hutchinson. He made his début as ' Rashleigh Osbaldistone ' (1834), and acted at Covent Garden with Macready (1837), taking part in *The Lady of Lyons*, 1838. He joined the Haymarket under Webster, remaining for forty years. H. went to the Lyceum (1881), later accompanying Sir H. Irving to America. See *The Player* (May 12, 1860) ; Pascoe's *Dramatic List, Theatrical Notes*, 1893.

Howe, John (1630-1705), an English dissenting minister, known as the ' Platonic Puritan.' He was domestic chaplain to Cromwell the Protector and his son, Richard (1656-59). The Act of Uniformity (1662) ejected him from Great Torrington, and in 1668 he became chaplain to Lord Massereene of Antrim Castle, Ireland. H. returned to London as minister of a Puritan congregation (1675). He travelled abroad with Lord Wharton (1685), but returned on James's ' Declaration for Liberty of Conscience' (1687). His works include: *The Blessedness of the Righteous*, 1668; *The Redeemer's Tears* . . ., 1684; and his fine production *The Living Temple*, 1674-1702. See *Works* with memoir, published 1822, 1838, and 1862-63. Consult Life by Calamy (1724), Rogers (1836), Horton (1896), Taylor (1835), Dunn (1836); Southey in the *Quarterly Review*, x. (Oct. 1813); Macaulay, *Hist. of Eng.*, ii.

Howe, Julia (*née* Ward) (1819-1910), an American poetess and philanthropist, married in 1843 to Dr. Howe. With him she edited the *Boston Commonwealth* (1851-53). She lectured on social subjects, and was active in championing the cause of women, and urging prison and other reforms. She helped to organise the American Woman Suffrage Association (1869), and in 1872 was president of the New England Women's Club. Her works include: *Passion Flowers*, 1854; 'Battle-Hymn of the Republic' and other poems, all collected in *From Sunset Ridge*, 1898; two dramas (1855, 1858); the prose works *Sex and Education*, 1874 ; *Modern Society*, 1881 ; *Reminiscences*, 1819-99, 1900; *Sketches of Representative Women of New England*, 1905.

Howe, Richard, first **Earl** (1726-99), an English admiral, brother of George Augustus. He served with distinction in the Seven Years' War against the French (1756 - 63), accompanying Boscawen to N. America, helping to capture the *Alcide* and the *Lys*, and being present at Quiberon Bay (1759). H. became treasurer of the navy (1765-70). In 1776 he returned to N. America as commander-in-chief, and forced the passage of the Delaware, successfully resisting the French under D'Estaing. He next won fame by his relief of Gibraltar (1782), and returning to England became First Lord of the Admiralty (1783-88). His most famous achievement was the victory of ' the glorious first of June ' (1794) over the French off Ushant. See *Life* by Barrow (1838), Mason (1803); Charnock, *Biographia Navalis*, v.; Ralf, *Naval Biographies*, i.; Campbell, *Lives of British Admirals*.

Howe, Dr. Samuel Gridley (1801-76), a noted American philanthropist, known as ' the Lafayette of the Greek Revolution ' for his services in the War of Independence from 1824-30. Returning to Boston he worked to establish there a school for the blind, becoming director of the Perkins Institute (1832) after travelling in Europe to study existing methods for the education of the blind. He was especially successful over the case of Laura Bridgman (1829-89). In 1846 Dr. Howe concerned himself over the education of idiots and the feeble-minded. He founded the *Daily Commonwealth* (1851), championing the anti-slavery cause. Howe wrote *Historical Sketches of the Greek Revolution*, 1828, and a *Reader for the Blind. See* Whittier's poem *The Hero ; Memoir* by his wife, J. H. Howe, 1876; Sanborn, *Life*, 1891 : *Letters and Journals* (Richards' edition), 1910.

Howe, Sir William, fifth **Viscount** (1729-1814), a British soldier of the American Revolution, succeeded his brother Richard as Viscount H. (1799), this Irish peerage becoming extinct on his death. Going to America (1758), he helped in the capture of Louisburg, and accompanied Wolfe to Quebec. H. returned to Europe (1760), and after holding various commands became major-general (1772). He was again sent to America, commanding the British at Bunker's Hill (1775). Driven from Boston by Washington (1776), he won the battle of Long Island, and entered New York. He later defeated Washington at the Brandywine (1777), and occupied Philadelphia, resigning soon afterwards. See *Narrative of Sir W. Howe . . .*, 1780; Bancroft, *Hist. of U.S.A.*, ix.; Beatson, *Naval and Military Memoirs*, iii.-vi.

Howell, James (*c.* 1594-1666), a British author, graduated from Oxford (1613). He travelled abroad (1616-22), and then engaged for a time in diplomatic work. He was imprisoned from 1643-51, but released on the Restoration (1660), and appointed historiographer-royal of England. His works include: Δενδρολογία; *Dodona's Grove . . .*, 1640 (a poem); *Instructions for Foreign Travel*, 1642; *Lexicon Tetraglotton*, 1660; and the *Epistolæ Ho-Elianæ . . .*, 1645-55 (of which see Jacobs' reprint of 10th ed., (1890-91), Repplier's edition (1907), (Temple Classics series). Consult *Biog. Britannica;* Bliss's edition of Wood's *Athenæ Oxon.*, iii.

Howells, William Dean (*b.* 1837), a noted American novelist, critic, and poet. He early became a journalist in Ohio, was United States consul at Venice (1861-65), and on his return was connected with several New York newspapers, and with the Boston *Atlantic Monthly* (1866-81), becoming editor about 1871. H. is the recognised leader of the realistic school, and his works describing familiar incidents and details of ordinary everyday life in America have been both popular and influential. He published a campaign *Life of Lincoln*, 1860; and *Poems by Two Friends* (H. and Piatt). Other works are: *Venetian Life*, 1866; *Their Wedding Journey*, 1872; *The Lady of the Aroostook*, 1879; *A Modern Instance* 1882; *A Woman's Reason*, 1884; *The Rise of Silas Lapham*, 1885 ; *The Minister's Charge*, 1886 ; *A Hazard of New Fortunes*, 1889 ; *The Landlord of Lion's Head*, 1897 ; *Certain Delightful English Towns*, 1906 ; the farces *Out of the Question* and *The Mouse-trap ; Poems*, 1873, 1886, 1895 ; *Literary Friends and Acquaintance*, 1901 ; *Heroines in Fiction*, 1901; *Literature and Life*, 1902; *London Films*, 1905; *Between the Dark and the Daylight; Fennel and Rue*, 1908 ; *Imaginary Interviews*, 1910. *See* Robertson, *Essays towards a Critical Method*, 1889 ; Vedder, *American Writers*, 1894.

Howell's State Trials. The true originator of this series of ' State

Trials' was Cobbett (1762-1835), in 1809, but they received their present title as T. B. Howell (1768-1815) edited vols. i.-xxi. (1809-15), and his son, T. J. Howell (d. 1858), vols. xxii.-xxxiii.

Howitt, Mary (1799 – 1888), an author, wife of William H., wrote much in collaboration with her husband. She wrote numerous children's books, which were very popular in their day; and she rendered a distinct service to literature by translating the novels of Frederika Bremer and many of the tales of Hans Andersen. In 1886 she published her ' Reminiscences of my Later Life ' (in *Good Words*). Her work was healthy, but, apart from the translations, ephemeral. There is a biography by her daughter, Margaret H. (1889).

Howitt, William (1792–1879), an author, began to write at an early age, and when he was thirteen, one of his poems appeared in the *Monthly Magazine*. In 1821 he married Mary Botham, and husband and wife wrote many books in collaboration. He had no special call to authorship, and became a very miscellaneous writer. *The Book of the Seasons*, 1831; a *Popular History of Priestcraft*, 1833; *Pantilla, or Traditions of the Most Ancient Times*, 1835; and the *Rural Life of England*, 1838, give some idea of his scope. In 1852 he visited Tasmania and Australia, and on his return wrote several books on these places, but none of them have any particular value. His most successful work was a *Popular History of England*, 1856-62.

Howitzer, the name applied to a particular piece of ordnance which is under present conditions of the greatest value in sieges. The word is derived from a Bohemian word meaning a catapult. This particular form of gun has been in fairly general use since the 16th century. It is a small, light gun which fires a shell at a small velocity but at a steep angle of descent. It has therefore proved invaluable as a means of bombarding trenches and searching low-lying and hidden defences. In modern artillery it is the ' arm ' which is of greatest use in sieges.

Howling Monkeys, the name given to the species of *Mycetes*, a genus of mammals belonging to the order Primates and the family Cebidæ. They are hideous in appearance, having a prominent face and deep jaw, while the tail is long and prehensile. The howling is produced by the unusually developed saccular diverticula of the larynx. These monkeys are common to Central and S. America.

Howorth, Sir Henry Hoyle (b. 1842), an English author, born at Lisbon,

educated at Rossall; became a barrister of the Inner Temple, 1867. He was for many years an active participant in politics and public life in Lancashire, being Conservative M.P. for S. Salford (1886-1900). He was created K.C.I.E. in 1892, D.C.L. and F.R.S. in 1893, and became a trustee of the British Museum in 1899. He has written numerous contributions to the *Times*, the *Quarterly Review*, and the *Edinburgh Review*, a large number of scientific memoirs and several works on historical and archæological subjects.

Howrah, a tn. of Bengal, India, on the R. Hugli, opposite Calcutta, of which it forms a suburb. A railway terminus, and has dockyards and manufs. of jute and cotton. Pop. 157,847.

Howson, John Saul (1816–85), a dean of Chester, born at Giggleswick-in-Craven, Yorkshire, was appointed, in 1849, principal of Liverpool College, which post he held until 1866, when he became vicar of Wisbech. In 1867 he was preferred to the deanery of Chester Cathedral, which underwent a thorough renovation under his auspices. He, with Rev. W. J. Conybeare, published the *Life and Epistles of St. Paul* (1852); his other writings deal chiefly with this apostle.

Howth, a tn., situated on a rocky peninsula (563 ft. high) of the same name, N. side of Dublin Bay, Ireland. It is an important fishing depôt and a summer resort. There are ruins of an abbey of the 13th century. Pop. (1911) 1147.

Höxter, a tn. on the Weser, Prussian prov. of Westphalia, 37 m. N.E. of Paderborn. Here are Renaissance timber buildings. It manufs. linen and cotton. Near by at Corvey is the famous castellated Benedictine abbey, suppressed in 1803. Pop. 7891.

Hoxton (the ' Hochester ' of the Domesday Book), a dist. of London, metropolitan bor. of Shoreditch, 2 m. N.E. of St. Paul's. In the Elizabethan era it was a pleasure resort. Cabinet-making and upholstery are carried on. Pop. 16,396.

Hoy (Scandinavian *Hoey*, high island), one of the Orkney Is., Scotland, 4 m. S. of Stromness, and separated from the mainland by the Sound of H. Area 53 sq. m., length 13¼ m., breadth 3 furlongs to 6¼ m. It rises abruptly from the sea and has magnificent cliff scenery. The chief heights are Bracbrough Head (1140 ft.), Ward Hill (1564 ft.), and Cuilage Hill (1420 ft.). The ' Old Man of Hoy ' is a detached sandstone rock, 450 ft. high, 1 m. from

Roray Head. There is a good harbour at Longhope, and weekly steamship communication with Leith. Pop. 1320.

Hoy, a term of Low-Country origin, formerly applied to small sloop-rigged river and coasting vessels and now to heavily built barges.

Hoyerswerda, a tn. of Prussia in Silesia, 40 m. N.W. of Görlitz. Industries are in shoes, glass-ware, weaving, and bell-casting. Pop. 5955.

Hoylake, a tn. and eccles. par. on the Wirral Peninsula, 8 m. W. of Liverpool, Cheshire, England. There is fine sea-bathing, and many Liverpool business men have residences here. Pop. with W. Kirby (1911) 14,029.

Hoyland Nether, a tn. in W. Riding, Yorkshire, England, 5½ m. S.E. of Barnsley. There are coal mines, rolling mills, brick works. Pop. 14,969.

Hoyle, Edmund (1672–1769), a writer on whist and other games. Of his early life nothing is definitely known, but is supposed to have read for the law. He lived in London, giving instruction in and writing on whist; both Fielding and Byron have alluded to him. His books include: *Short Treatise on Whist,* 1742; *Quadrille, Piquet, Backgammon, and Chess.*

Hroswitha, Hrotwitha, Roswita, Roswitha, or **Hrotsuit** (c. 935-c. 1000), a German poetess and chronicler. Little is known of her life, but she appears to have been a Benedictine nun of Gandersheim, near Göttingen, entering the nunnery previous to 959. Here she studied the scriptures and the classics. Her works, written in Latin, have considerable merit, but great coarseness. They include Latin legendary poems, six prose Terentian comedies for the entertainment of the sisterhood, of which *Callimachus,* written in praise of chastity, is the best, and a poetical panegyrical chronicle of Otto I. Her works were edited by Konrad Celtes at Nuremberg in 1501, by Schwizfleisch at Wittemberg in 1717, and by Barack at Nuremberg in 1858. *See* W. M. Hudson, *English Historical,* 1888.

Hsi-an-fu, or **Si-ngan-fu,** cap. of Shen-si, China, on the r. b. of the Wei-ho, 75 m. above its confluence with the Hwang-ho.

Hsiang, River, a trib. of the Yang-tse-kiang, in Hu-nan, China; very important as connecting Kwang-tung with Central China. Its W. branch is connected by canal with the Kweikiang in Kwang-si.

Hsiang-tau, an important dist. and tn. of Hu-nan, China, where produce for Canton (300 m. to the N.) and coal for Yang-tse-kiang are transhipped. The Hsiang R. is navigable

for junks up to this town. Pop. upwards of 600,000.

Huai-an, or **Hwai-an-fu,** a city of Kiang-su, China, on the Grand Canal, 100 m. N.N.E. of Nanking; a great centre of the salt industry.

Huallaga, a river of Peru, rising in the Andes, about 10° 40′ S. It flows generally northward for some 700 m. and joins the Amazon (Marañon) about lat. 5° S., 73° W.

Huambisas, a race of S. American half-breeds, belonging to the Jivaroan stock, and dwelling on the borders of Peru and Ecuador on the Upper Santiago and Marañon-Amazon rivers. The Spanish blood in them, shown by their light complexions and beards, dates from the sack of Sevilla del Oro in 1599 when 7000 Spanish women were carried off.

Huancavelica, or **Guancabelica :** 1. A dept. of Peru. Area 9300 sq. m. The surface is mountainous and mineral wealth abundant. Pop. 223,796. 2. Cap. of dept. of same name, and of a prov. of Peru in the Andes, 150 m. S.E. of Lima. The chief industry is the mining and smelting of gold, silver, and mercury. Elevation 11,850 ft. Pop. 4000.

Huanchaca, a tn. and dist. of Bolivia, 85 m. S.W. of Potosi, with important silver mines. Elevation 13,000 ft.

Huang-ho, *see* YELLOW RIVER.

Huanuco, or **Guanuco :** 1. A dept. of Peru. Traversed by the Cordillera Oriental, and watered by the R. Huallaga. There is much mineral wealth. Area 14,020 sq. m. Pop. 394,393. 2. Cap. of the above dept., Peru, on R. Huallaga, 170 m. N.E. of Lima. It stands in a lovely and fertile valley. A bishop's see. Pop. 7000.

Huaraz, the cap. of Ancachs dept., Peru, on the R. Huaraz, 185 m. N.W. of Lima. Elevation 10,000 ft. Pop. 8000.

Huascar, a Peruvian ironclad (1870 tons), which in 1877 was captured in the harbour of Callao by revolutionists, who sailed for Cobija, where Nicolas de Pierola, the insurgent leader, was picked up and assumed command. After it had committed outrages against British subjects and British property, the Peruvian government offered a reward for its capture. Two British warships endeavoured to seize it, but were unsuccessful; the ship ultimately surrendered to the Peruvian government. In the war with Chile (1879), it was captured off Angamos.

Huasco, or **Guasco,** a seaport tn. in the prov. of Atacama, Chile, is at the mouth of the Huasco R. It is the centre of a fine fruit-growing district, is noted for its grapes and raisins, and has considerable coasting trade. Pop. 8000.

Huber, François (1750 – 1831), a Swiss naturalist, native of Geneva. Early in life he lost his eyesight, but with the help of his wife and secretary, F. Burneus, he made a study of bees and their habits. The results of this study were published under the title *Nouvelles Observations sur les Abeilles* in 1792 (English translation 1821). His son, Jean Pierre (1777-1841), published a standard book on ants, *Recherches sur les Mœurs des Fourmis-indigènes*, in 1810 (Eng. trans. 1820).

Huber, Johann Nepomuk (1830-79), a German theologian and philosophical writer, born in Munich, where he ultimately became university professor. He was leader of the Old Catholics and a bold opponent of the Ultramontanes. His work, *Die Philosophie der Kirchenväter*, 1859, and *Der Jesuitorden*, 1873, were placed upon the Index Expurgatorius. He collaborated with Döllinger in writing the celebrated *Der Papist und das Konzil von Janus*, 1869.

Hubert, St. (656-727), the patron saint of hunters (Day, Nov. 3). Hunting on Good Friday, although a holy day, he saw a cross growing out of the forehead of a stag. This he took as a sign from Heaven ; became a monk, and founded an abbey. He was son of a Duke of Guienne, and became bishop of Liège (Maestricht).

Hubertusburg, once a royal hunting seat, Saxony, 25 m. S.S.E. of Leipzig, built by Prince Frederick Augustus, afterwards Augustus III., King of Poland. In 1763 the treaty was signed here which ended the Seven Years' War. From 1840 it has been used as a prison, hospital, and asylum.

Hubli, a tn. in the dist. and 15 m. S.E. of Dhariwar, Bombay, British India, has important cotton manufs. and considerable trade. Pop. 55,000.

Hübner, Emil (1834-1901), an eminent German philologist and archæologist, born in Düsseldorf. He became professor of classical philology at the University of Berlin (1870). His close study of Latin epigraphy and his archæological researches during his travels in Europe resulted in some valuable books, amongst which are *Inscriptiones Hispaniæ Latinæ*, 1869 (supplementary, 1892); *Inscriptiones Britanniæ Latinæ*, 1873; *Grundriss zu Vorlesungen über die römische Litteraturgeschichte* (4th edition),1878; *Grundriss zu Vorlesungen über lateinische Grammatik* (2nd edition), 1880.

Hübner, Joseph Alexander, Count (1811-92), an Austrian diplomat and author, born in Vienna. He was minister plenipotentiary at Paris (1849-59), ambassador at Rome (1865-67), then toured the world, writing his observations in *Ein Spaziergang um die Welt*, 1872. His other works are *Sixtus V.*, 1872; *Durch das britische Reich*, 1883-84 (1886), *Ein Jahr meines Lebens*, 1848-49 (1891). His works, which are very interesting, show considerable insight. See *An Austrian Diplomatist in the 'Fifties*, Sir E. Satow, 1908.

Hübner, Rudolf Julius Benno (1806-83), a German painter, born at Oels in Silesia. He studied art at Düsseldorf, and was appointed professor of painting at the Dresden Academy (1841). He was director of the gallery at Dresden from 1871-82. H. belonged to the romantic school and painted sacred and historical subjects. His most famous pictures are ' Samson overthrowing the Pillars,' ' The dispute between Luther and Dr. Eck,' ' Job and his Friends,' ' Charles V. at San Yuste,' ' Frederick the Great in Sansouci.'

Huc, Evariste Régis (1813-60), a Roman Catholic missionary, born at Toulouse, educated under the Lazarists in Paris. In 1839 he was ordained and joined the Lazarist Mission to China at Si-Wang. In 1844 he and M. Gabet were sent into Tibet to determine the extent of the new apostolic vicariat of Mongolia. They spent some time in a Lama monastery, learning the language, and in 1846 reached Lhasa after much danger and difficulty. They were, however, expelled and forced to return to China. H. returned to France in 1852 and published several books on his journey.

Huchieson, or **Huchown** (*d.* 1376), of the Awle Ryale ' (Hall Royal), author of the *Morte Arthure* and other Scottish romances. He is identified with ' gude Sir Hew of Eglintoun ' in Dunbar's *Lament*. Wyntoun mentions him. *See* G. Neilson's *Huchown*, 1902.

Huchtenburg, Jan van (1646-1733), a Dutch battle painter and engraver, born in Haarlem ; pupil of Thomas Wyck and later of Van der Meulen in Paris. *See* National Gallery, ' A Battle.'

Huckaback, a coarse and durable cloth of linen, or linen and cotton, woven with alternate elevations and depressions, thus presenting a rough surface ; it is used for towels, table-cloths, etc.

Huckarde, a vil. in the prov. of Westphalia, Prussia, is 2¼ m. N.W. of Dortmund. It has coal mines. Pop. 7312.

Huckingen, a tn. in the Rhenish prov. of Prussia, and dist. Düsseldorf, with manufs. of cotton, hosiery, etc., Pop. 8262.

Huckleberry, *see* WHORTLEBERRY.

Hucknall, formerly **Hucknall Tor-**

kard, a tn. in Nottinghamshire, 8 m. N.W. of Nottingham. The body of Lord Byron was brought from Greece and buried in H. parish church, restored in 1873. It has extensive collieries. Pop. (1911) 15,870.

Hucknall-under-Huthwaite, a tn., 5 m. S.W. of Mansfield, in Nottinghamshire, has extensive coal mines. Pop. 5000.

Huddersfield, a tn. in West Riding of Yorkshire, England, at confluence of R. Colne and R. Holme, 14 m. S.W. of Leeds. It has numerous railway connections and stands on the Huddersfield Canal (23½ m. long). The surrounding district is rich in coal and stone. The town is entirely modern and well built. Among the chief buildings is the circular Cloth Hall 880 yds. in circumference (1765). It is the chief seat of the N. of England 'fancy trade,' all varieties of mixed and plain woollen goods being produced, including worsted, silk, and cotton mixtures, broadcloths, and trouserings. There are two parks. Pop. (1911) 107,825.

Hudiksvall, a seaport tn. on the E. coast of Sweden, in the prov. Gefleborg, is 45 m. S.W. of Sundsvall. It has a good harbour and public quays. Pop. 6000.

Hudson, the cap. of Columbia co., New York, U.S.A., on Hudson R., 28 m. S. of Albany. It has a large river trade and numerous manufs. of engines, paper, leather, flour, clothing, knit goods, tobacco. Founded in 1783, and formerly a whaling port. Pop. (1910) 11,417.

Hudson, a tn. of Middesex co., Massachusetts, U.S.A., on Assabet R. 15 m. N.E. of Worcester. It has manufs. of leather, rubber shoes webbing, gossamers, paper boxes, lasts, etc. Pop. (1910) 6743.

Hudson, a riv. of New York, U.S.A. Rises in the Adirondack Mts., and flows about 350 m., roughly, in a southerly direction, into New York Bay. Its estuary, known as North R., forms part of New York Harbour. It is navigable for small boats up to Glen Falls (200 m.) for small steamers to Troy (151 m.), and for large steamers to H. (117 m.). Much of the scenery on its banks is very fine, especially in the highlands of the H., part of the Appalachian Range, below Newburgh. Chief tributaries, the Mohawk, Wallkill, Hoosic, and Sacondaga. It was first explored by Henry Hudson in 1609, and the first successful American attempt at steam navigation was made upon it in 1807.

Hudson, George (1800-71), an English railway promoter, ' the Railway King,' born at Howsham, Yorkshire. He started life as a linen draper, but in 1828 inherited a fortune of £30,000.

This allowed him to interest himself in railway promoting with very successful results, and he became the dictator of railway speculation. But the railway crisis of 1847-48 proved his ruin, for he was accused of fraud. Carlyle alluded to him as 'the big swollen gambler.' He died in straitened circumstances.

Hudson, Henry (d. 1611), a distinguished English navigator. He was employed by the Muscovy Company, and later by the Dutch East India Company, to discover the N.E. and N.W. passages in 1607-10. In 1609 he explored the Hudson R. On his last voyage in 1610 he discovered the Bay and Strait which are named after him. Early in 1611 his crew mutinied, and set him and his son with seven others adrift in a small boat, and nothing further was heard of him. See *Henry Hudson, the Navigator,* edited by the Hakluyt Society, 1860.

Hudson, John (1662-1719), a great classical scholar, who edited ancient writings. He graduated at University College, Oxford (1681), became fellow (1868), and in 1701 was appointed keeper of the Bodleian Library. He was also principal of St. Mary Hall, Oxford.

Hudson, Thomas (1701–79), a portrait painter, who succeeded to the connection of his father-in-law, Richardson. When Reynolds, his former pupil, returned from Italy, H.'s place was taken by him as the superior artist. His masterpiece is a painting of the Marlborough family, and hangs at Blenheim Palace.

Hudson Bay, or Canadian Sea, an inland sea of the N.W. of N. America, communicating with the Atlantic Ocean by Hudson Strait and with the Arctic Ocean by Fox Channel, Fury and Hecla Strait, and the Gulf of Boothia. It lies entirely in British territory, having Manitoba on the W., Ontario on the S., and Southampton Is. on the N. A long narrow arm in the S. is known as James Bay. Area about 500,000 sq. m., length 850 m. to 13,000 m., greatest width, 600 m. It occupies a basin in the old Laurentian area, and is mostly shallow, with low shore-lines especially in the S. and W. The average depth is 70 to 100 fathoms. The eastern shores are rocky, and steep bluffs occur here and occasionally in the W. A chain of small islands lies off the E. shore. There are few submerged rocks or shoals, but ice renders navigation impossible for three-fourths of the year. The climate is very rigorous in winter, but mild and pleasant during the short summer. The Bay is the great drainage area of the Canadian N.W. Territories, and is fed by the Rs. Churchill, Nelson.

Albany, Main, Rupert, Severn, and Moose. There are fisheries of salmon, seal, whale, and walrus, and the surrounding country is rich in minerals and fur-bearing animals. York Factory is the chief port. The Bay was discovered by Henry Hudson in 1610. He wintered in James Bay, and the next year was abandoned by his mutinous crew.

Hudson Bay Company, an English chartered company incorporated by Charles II. in 1670. It was founded by Prince Rupert and other adventurers for the purpose of trading with the N. American Indians on the shores of Hudson Bay. It started with a capital of about £110,000, and its progress was slow but steady. Continual fighting about the Company's forts went on with the French, who laid claim to the territory, but these claims were finally resigned at the Treaty of Utrecht in 1713. The prosperity of the Company increased enormously when Canada became British and the territory became accessible from the S., but the magnificent opportunities brought many competitors, notably the N.W. Fur Company, which joined hands with the Hudson Bay Company in 1821. The trade monopoly was abolished in 1859, and the property rights settled in 1869.

Hudson Bay Territory, *see* NORTH-WEST TERRITORIES.

Hué, a fortified tn., is the cap. of Annam, French Indo - China. It is on the Hué R., 10 m. from its mouth, and carries on considerable trade through Thuanan. It is surrounded by a wall and moat, and contains an old palace. Pop. 40,000.

Hue and Cry, an old phrase derived from the method of pursuit of felons by the general public, as provided for in common law. Also the title of a gazette containing the names of deserters, persons charged with crimes, etc., published in 1710.

Hueffer, Ford Madox (*b.* 1873), an English author, son of late Dr. H. His works include: *The Brown Owl ; The Face of the Night,* 1904; *The Soul of London,* 1905; *The Heart of the Country ; The Fifth Queen,* 1906; *Privy Seal; From Inland; The Spirit of the People ; An English Girl,* 1907; *The Fifth Queen Crowned ; Mr. Apollo,* 1908; *The Half-Moon,* 1909; *Songs from London ; A Call,* 1910; *Ancient Lights ; The Critical Attitude,* 1911.

Hueffer, Francis (1845 – 89), a musical critic, born at Münster, Westphalia; educated at Göttingen. In 1869 he came to London, and was naturalised as a British subject in 1882. In 1871 he became assistant editor of the *Academy,* was editor of the *New Quarterly Magazine,* and *The Musical World* (1886), and musical critic to the *Times* (1879). He was the apostle of Wagner in England, and published *Richard Wagner and the Music of the Future,* 1874; *The Troubadours,* 1878, etc. In 1888 he issued a translation of the *Correspondence of Wagner and Liszt.*

Huehuetenango, a tn. in the dept. of Guatemala, Central America, is the cap. of H. dept., 106 m. N.W. of Guatemala. It is the centre of a leadmining district, and quite near are the ruins of an old Indian city. Pop. 12,000.

Huejutla, a tn. in Mexico, in the state of Hidalgo, 69 m. distant from Pachuca. Pop. about 20,000.

Huelva: 1. A prov. of Andalusia, Spain, bordering on Portugal and the Atlantic Ocean. Area 3913 sq. m. Much of the surface is occupied by the Sierra Morena, and it is watered by the Lepe, Odiel, and Tinto Rs., and tributaries of the Guadiana and Guadalquivir. There are rich deposits of iron and copper pyrites, and valuable mineral waters, while some districts are very fertile. Pop. 309,744. 2. Cap. of above prov., on the estuary of the Odiel and Tinto Rs., 49 m. S.W. of Seville. The harbour is large and safe, but the entrance is partially blocked by a bar. There is a large export trade of metallic ores and agricultural produce. Pop. 20,927.

Huercal Overa, or **Huercal Obera,** a tn. in Spain in the prov. of, and 40 m. N.E. of the tn. of, Almeria, is near an important mining district and has considerable trade in agricultural produce. Pop. 16,500.

Huerta, Vicente Garcia de la (1730-87), a Spanish poet and critic, born at Zafra; educated at Salamanca. He obtained a post in the Royal Library at Madrid, and later in the office of the Secretary of State. He got into trouble, was imprisoned, and on his release joined the household of the Duke of Alva. He attempted to revive the old national comedy in opposition to the new French school of drama. His best tragedy was *Raquel* (1778). He also published a dramatic collection *Teatro Español* (16 vols.), 1785, and *Obras Poeticas.*

Hues (or **Husins**), **Robert** (1553-1632), an English geographer, born in Hertfordshire ; graduated at Magdalen Hall, Oxford, 1578. It is probable that he accompanied Thomas Cavendish and Sir Richard Grenville to Virginia, and he is known to have sailed round the world with the former. He was a friend of Chapman's. His works include : *Tractatus de Globis et eorum Usu* (1594), and *Breviarium Oribis Terrarum* (pub.

1667). The former was edited by Sir Clements Markham in 1889 for the Hakluyt Society.

Huesca : 1. A prov. of Aragon, N. Spain, bounded on the N. by France and on the E. by the prov. of Lerida. Area 5848 sq. m. Pop. 247,027. 2. A cap. of the above prov. on R. Isuela, 45 m. N.E. of Saragossa. It is picturesquely built on a height above a fertile valley. The Romans knew it as Osca, and Sertorius was murdered here in 72 B.C. The town was important under the Arabs and the kings of Aragon, and part of its old walls still remain. Among the notable buildings are the Gothic cathedral (1300-1515), the university (1354), and the ancient palace of the kings of Aragon, where the ' Massacre of the Bell ' occurred in 1136. Pop. 11,976.

Huescar, a city in Spain, 68 m. N.E. of Granada. Manufs. woollen fabrics. Pop. 7917.

Huet, Pierre Daniel (1630-1721), a French scholar and churchman, born at Caen. In 1652 he visited the Swedish court in company with Bochart, and discovered at Stockholm the famous Origen MS., which he edited in 1668. In 1670 he and Bossuet were appointed tutors of the Dauphin, and prepared an edition of the classics for their pupil's use. He took orders in 1676; became Abbot of Aunay (1678), Bishop of Soissons (1685), Bishop of Avranches (1692), and Abbot of Fontenay (1699). In 1701 he settled in the Jesuit College in Paris. His works include: *De Interpretatione,* 1661; a collection of poems, 1664; *Demonstratio Evangelica,* 1679 ; *Traité de la Faiblesse de l'Esprit Humaine,* etc.

Hufeland, Christoph Wilhelm (1762-1836), a German physician, born at Langensalza in Thuringia. He was educated at Jena and Göttingen; took his medical degree and succeeded his father as court physician at Weimar. In 1793 he was professor at Jena, and in 1798 he became president of the medical college and hospital, Berlin. He published several scientific works, the best known being *Makrobiotek, or The Art of Prolonging Life.*

Hug, Johann Leonard (1765-1846), a Roman Catholic theologian, born at Constance. In 1783 he entered Freiburg University and attained distinction in Oriental philology and Biblical criticism. He taught in the seminary there till 1790, when it was closed. He was then appointed to the chair of Oriental languages and O.T. exegesis, and held it till his death. His literary work included contributions to ecclesiastical periodicals; his most important work is *Einleitung in die*

Schriften des Neuen Testaments, published in 1808, and translated into French and English.

Huggins, Sir William (1824-1910), an English astronomer, born in London. In 1852 he joined the Royal Microscopical Society and devoted himself to science. He joined the Royal Astronomical Society in 1854, and in 1856 built himself an observatory at Tulse Hill. During 1858-60 he made observations of the belts and spots of Jupiter ; in 1862 of Saturn's rings ; and by 1864, together with Miller, had invented the star spectroscope, with which valuable discoveries were made. The society's gold medal was presented to H. and Miller in 1867. H. proceeded to make valuable observations of nebulæ, and later studied the spectroscopic measurement of the motions of stars and the application of photography to stellar spectroscopy.

Hugglescote, a par. in Coalville urban dist., 6 m. S.E. of Ashby-de-la-Zouch, Leicestershire. It has collieries. Pop. (1911) 4500.

Hughenden, or **Hitchendon,** a par. in Buckinghamshire, 1 m. N. of Wycombe. H. Manor was the residence of Disraeli. He was buried in the parish church, which contains a monument to him erected by Queen Victoria. Pop. (1911) 2134.

Hughes Capet, *see* CAPET, HUGHES.

Hughes, David Edward (1831-1900), an Anglo-American inventor, born in London; went to Virginia in 1837; in 1850 became professor of music at Bardstown College, Kentucky. His inventions include an improved telegraph type-printer (1854-55), and the microphone (1878), which was produced almost simultaneously by Lüdtge. He was made F.R.S. in 1880, gold medallist of the Royal Society in 1885, vice-president of the Royal Institution in 1891, and Albert medallist of the Society of Arts in 1898.

Hughes, Sir Edward (c.1720-94), born at Hertford, and entered the navy, 1735. He assisted in the attacks on Cartagena and at the taking of Louisburg and Quebec. He became commander-in-chief in the East Indies, 1773, and was created a Knight of the Bath, 1778. During 1782-83 he had five encounters with the French, and on the conclusion of peace he returned to England and was made admiral in 1793. He died at Luxborough, Essex.

Hughes, Hugh Price (1847-1902), a Welsh Wesleyan minister, born at Carmarthen; educated for Wesleyan Methodist ministry at Richmond College. He began work at Dover in 1869, and on the ' itinerating ' plan moved successively to Brighton,

Tottenham, Dulwich, and Oxford. In 1884 he became prominent in London at Brixton Hill as a leader of the ' Forward party,' and in 1886 started the W. London Mission. In 1885 he became editor of the *Methodist Times*. In 1896 he became first president of the National Council of the Evangelical Free Churches, and in 1898 president of the Wesleyan Methodist Conference.

Hughes, John (1677-1720), a poet, born at Marlborough, Wiltshire, and educated in London. He became a clerk in the ordnance office. He was delicate and suffered much from poverty till his appointment as secretary in the Court of Chancery. His best work, *The Siege of Damascus*, was produced at Drury Lane Theatre, but he died the same evening from consumption. Besides his poems, he wrote a *History of England*, *The Works of Mr. Edmund Spenser*, and contributed to several periodicals.

Hughes, Thomas (1822-96), an author, began life as a barrister and a follower of Frederick Denison Maurice and other leaders of the Christian Social School. He was a founder of the Working Men's College, and principal of that institution from 1872 to 1883. He was in parliament from 1865 to 1874, and a county court judge from 1882. The author of several books, his fame rests entirely upon *Tom Brown's School Days*, published anonymously in 1857. It is a simple story of public-school life, admirably presented, and underlying it a strong, sound religious sense, that had the greater influence for not being unduly obtruded.

Hughes-Gass, Annie (*b.* 1869), an English actress, born at Southampton; educated for the stage by John Maclean. She first appeared as Zamora in *The Honeymoon* in 1883; in 1885 began a provincial tour as Eva Webster in *The Private Secretary*, and first appeared in London in the same part at the Globe Theatre at the end of that year. In 1886 she appeared at the Criterion with Charles Wyndham; in 1889 toured with the Kendals; in 1894 was engaged by Henry Irving; in 1906 visited America, and on returning to England toured with her own company.

Hugh of Avalon, St. (*c.* 1135-1200), Bishop of Lincoln, born at Avalon, Burgundy, of noble parentage: entered the Grande Chartreuse about 1160, and became bursar there. About 1175 he was invited to England by Henry II., who made him head of a Carthusian monastery at Witham, Somerset. In 1186 he became Bishop of Lincoln; in 1189 went on an embassy to France; in

1194 excommunicated King John, and in 1198 led the first refusal of a money grant. He was canonised in 1220. See *Life* by Marson, 1901.

Hugh of Lincoln, St. (*c.* 1246-55), an English Christian child who is traditionally alleged to have been at the age of eleven crucified by a Jew of Lincoln, named Copin, after having been tortured and starved on account of his faith. His body was buried near that of Grosseteste in Lincoln Cathedral. The story of his martyrdom was a favourite one with English ballad-makers and chroniclers. It is the theme of the ' Prioress's Tale ' in Chaucer's *Canterbury Tales*, and is also referred to by Marlowe. *See* Professor Child's *Ballads*, Pt. v., 1888, and the monograph on the subject by Joseph Jacobs, 1894.

Hugh Town, a tn. and cap. of the Scilly Is., Cornwall, on St. Mary's Island.

Hugli, or **Hoogly:** 1. The most westerly and most important of the mouths of the Ganges, India, formed by the confluence of the Bhágirathi, the Jalangí, and the Churné streams. Its length is about 200 m., and it is about 10 m. wide at the mouth. It is the only mouth of the Ganges navigable by large vessels, which can safely go up to Calcutta. Navigation is, however, much hindered by silting, and the formation of sandbanks. The ' bore ' is often of great height and velocity. The Hugli is held sacred by the Hindoos. 2. The cap. of dist. of same name, Bengal, India, on R. Hugli, 23 m. N. of Calcutta. The chief building is the Inambana, a Mohammedan institution. The town was founded about 1537 by the Portuguese, who were diven out a century later by the Mohammedans. Pop., with Chinsurah, 29,383.

Hugo, Victor Marie (1802-85), a great French writer, born at Besançon, the son of General H., an officer in Napoleon's army. His childhood was full of change, as the family usually followed their father and the army, and he was educated at the Feuillantines in Paris (1809-11, and 1813-15), at Madrid (1812), and at the Ecole Polytechnique. His poetical genius asserted itself very early. In 1816 he produced a tragedy; the next year was nearly successful in an Académie competition; in 1819 began to contribute to the newly founded *Conservateur Littéraire;* and was several times the victor at the floral games of Toulouse. In 1822 he made his real literary début with *Odes et Poésies Diverses*. This volume contains no great innovations, but is remarkable for strength and beauty of diction and great dexterity in the handling of difficult rhythms. In

1823 he published anonymously *Han d'Islande*, a fantastic and extravagant prose romance, dealing with much force, but an utter disregard of possibilities, with a northern bandit. It was followed by *Bug Jargal*, a similar production (1826). His second volume of poems *Odes et Ballades* (1826), and his third, *Orientalis*, 1829, definitely mark the trend of his tastes and opinions. They are 'romantic' in the extreme, the subjects being barbaric and fantastic, the metre varied and irregular, and the language glowing and exotic, but the matter is still rather empty and puerile. His first attempt at drama

VICTOR HVGO

appeared in 1828. *Cromwell*, which was never acted, is more a romance in dramatic form than a true drama, but is of some importance in literary history. It was preceded by a somewhat paradoxical and incoherent preface, which served as a manifesto of the new romantic school, asserting the dramatist's independence and emancipation from all the old conventions. Its publication made H. the recognised head of the new movement, a position in which he took himself and his mission very seriously. In 1830 *Hernani*, the first of his typical dramas, was acted at the Théâtre Français. Its subject is the suicide of a noble Spaniard at the moment of his marriage, on account of a point of honour. Its style is in direct antithesis to all the traditions of the French stage. The language, though gorgeous, has none of the old classical periphrasis; the Alexandrine metre is completely changed in character by constant overlapping; and the old dramatic laws are set at nought. The play was the text of long and violent contention between the Classicists and the Romanticists, and this circumstance has given it a fictitious importance, since, in spite of the splendid march of the verse and the gorgeous diction, *Hernani* is lacking in some of the principles of dramatic art.

In 1831 a correspondingly revolutionary production in the realm of prose romance appeared in *Notre Dame de Paris*, a pretentious but picturesque novel of mediæval Paris, which shows the influence of Sir Walter Scott. Its failings are a lack of proportion and humour, and an incompleteness of construction, but to the average reader these are, at any rate at first, completely outweighed by the wonderful faculty of description, the command of passion, and the splendid and poetical language, which is displayed. In the same year H. published *Les Feuilles d'Automne*, a volume of lyric and contemplative verse, which contains some very fine poetry.

The next few years were occupied in the production of dramas on the lines of *Hernani*. *Marion de Lorme*, which appeared in 1831, is usually considered his best. The next year saw *Le Roi s'amuse*, interdicted after the first night, which has gained a world-wide reputation as *Rigoletto*. They were followed by *Lucrèce Borgia*, 1833, a melodrama; *Marie Tudor*, 1833; *Angelo*, 1835, a prose melodrama; *Ruy Blas*, 1838, which stands second among his plays; and *Les Burgraves*, 1843, a kind of sentimental epic clumsily put into dramatic form, which contains, however, some wonderful writing. All these dramas show an unparalleled command of language, mastery of passion, and fertility of invention, but are lacking in constructive art, which probably accounts for the waning of their popularity. Their production was interspersed with that of several volumes of charming verse, viz. *Chants du Crépuscule*, 1835; *Les Voix Intérieures*, 1837; and *Les Rayons et les Ombres*, 1840; and he also issued during this decade *Claude Gueux*, 1834; *Littérature and Philosophie Mêlées*, 1834, a collection of juvenilia; and *La Esmeralda*, 1836, an opera for Mdlle. Bertin.

H.'s political opinions had in the meantime been undergoing considerable changes. Previous to 1830 he had been an ardent legitimist, but during the reign of Louis Philippe

he became a constitutional royalist,
sitting in the Assemblée Constituante
as a representative of Paris, later an
extreme Liberal, and finally, on his
election to the Assemblée Législative
in 1848, a democratic republican.
After the *coup d'état* of 1852 he was
banished for opposition to Louis
Napoleon, and fled to Brussels and
then to Jersey. During this time his
literary output was mainly confined
to journalism and pamphleteering,
but he soon began more serious work
again in exile. The first to appear was
Napoléon le Petit, the least literary of
all his works. In 1853 he issued *Les
Châtiments*, giving vent to his anger
against the Second Empire. The book
is notable as a rare example of lyric
satire, *i.e.* a combination of true
poetry with invective. After three
years of silence, he next emerged in
an entirely different light with *Les
Contemplations*, 1856, a collection of
lyrics remarkable for beautiful expression, simple diction, and breadth,
and profundity of thought. In 1859
appeared the *Légende die Siècles*, a
collection of narrative and pictorial
poems dealing with different periods
of the world's history, which, though
somewhat unequal, contains some of
his masterpieces. The matter is
wonderfully varied, and the style is
marked throughout by a mastery of
language and versification. Among
the best of the poems are *Argmerillot*,
Le Petit Roi de Galice, and *Eviadmus*.
This volume shows H. at his best; the
medium being well adapted to his
powers and kind to his defects.

In 1862 H. issued *Les Misérables*, a
long and unequal prose romance,
dealing with modern life. Its descriptive portions are remarkable, and
much of the writing is touching and
sincere, but the style is full of mannerisms, and the plot abounds in
absurdities. *William Shakespeare*,
1864, was a strange and rhapsodical
volume of criticism, containing some
fine passages of ornate prose. In 1865
there appeared *Chansons des Rues et
des Bois*, a collection of light lyric
verse, notable for its achievements in
style. It shows H. in rather a new
light, and the grace, daintiness, and
wit of some of these poems, though
not always free from a suspicion of
laboured mannerism, proves the extraordinary adaptability of his genius.
Las Travailleurs de la Mer, another
prose romance, is a tale of passionate
adventure and self-sacrifice, and contains some exquisite passages. Another
romance, historical in nature, was
published in 1869, under the title of
L'Homme qui rit. Though full of
power, it is rather extravagant, and
the general effect is overwhelming
and almost wearisome.

After the revolution of 1870, H.
returned to France and again entered
politics, though not with very happy
results. His first action was to order
the Germans to leave France and set
up a German republic. He was
elected to the National Assembly at
Bordeaux as representative for the
Seine, but resigned on account of an
interruption by the Right during one
of his speeches. He remained through
the rule of the Commune and defended the Vendôme Column as long
as possible, and then retired to
Brussels. He was expelled from
Belgium on account of an im-
prudent speech in favour of the
Communists, and returned to France
where he unsuccessfully stood for
Paris. He lived in France till his
death, in considerable literary and
general popularity.

The writings of this last part of his
life are of comparatively little importance. They include: *L'Année
Terrible*, 1872, almost his weakest
book, a series of eloquent pictures of
the war, full of praises of France
and invective against Italy; *Quatre-
Vingt-Treize*, another historical romance ; a collection of speeches and
addresses in 1875-76 ; *Seconde Légende
des Siècles* (1876), which, though not
equal to its predecessor, is still full
of vigour; *Histoire d'un Crime*, 1877,
described as ' the apotheosis of the
Special Correspondent '; *L'Art d'être
Grand-père*, containing much that is
charming, but a good deal of ' sentimentalism '; *Le Pape*, 1878 ; *La Pitié
Suprême*, 1879 ; *L'Ane*, 1880 ; *Les
Quatre Vents de l'Esprit*, 1881, a remarkable last flash of genius ; and
Torquemada, 1882. He died on
May 22, and his funeral was marked
by a great display of public feeling.

His position in French literature is
important in that he not only bestowed on French romanticism a
peculiarly ' decorative ' character,
but actually kept the romantic spirit
alive in France for some thirty years
after its apparent decease. As a
writer his powers were wonderful. To
name only a few of his characteristics,
he is notable for vitality and wide
scope of genius, graceful lyrical
power, rhetorical magnificence, the
ability to express pathos, awe, and
indignation ; wealth of colour and
light ; variety of style, and consummate skill in the handling of
metre and language. His main
defects are a lack of humour and
proportion, and an all-pervading
egoism, but despite these he stands
on a level with the great names of
international literature.

Huguenots, a name applied to the
French Protestants of the 16th and
17th centuries. The party grew up

during the reigns of Francis I. and Henry II., and under Francis II. developed into a religious-political organisation, headed by the Bourbons, especially the King of Navarre and the Duke of Condé, and opposed to the Catholic party, headed by the Guises. The strife between them developed into the long series of religious wars which began in 1562. Civil rights were granted to the H. by Henry IV. in the Edict of Nantes (1598), but this was revoked by Louis XIV. in 1685, and many Protestants were driven out of France. Perfect civil equality was secured to all denominations by the revolution of 1789.

Huia, the Maori name for *Heteralocha acutirostris,* a New Zealand species of passeriform birds belonging to the family Corvidæ. The male and female differ greatly in appearance, the bill of the one being strong and straight, and that of the other curved and pliable. They are found in woody districts, and nest in hollow trees.

Hui-chau-fu, a tn. in the Anhui prov. of China, 100 m. S.W. of Hang-chau, is famous for its teas.

Huila, a volcano in the Andes, Colombia, 60 m. N.E. of Popayan. It is 18,500 ft. high.

Huilla, a fortified tn. in the prov. of Angola, Portuguese W. Africa, 90 m. N.E. of Mossamedes. It is healthily situated and is the centre of a fertile agricultural district.

Huitzilopochtli, the name of the Mexican war-god whose feasts were formerly celebrated in May, July, and December, amid scenes of revolting savagery. Many thousands of human victims were sacrificed yearly in his honour. The idol is generally carved in wood and of huge proportions; the face is covered with a golden mask, and on the head is a plumed helmet, the shape of a bird's beak.

Hu-kwang, formerly a prov. of Central China, is now divided into the two provinces of Hu-peh and Hu-nan, and administered by a governor, resident at Wu-chang-fu.

Hulke, John Whitaker (1830-95), an English surgeon and geologist, born at Deal. He was educated at King's College School, and obtained his medical degree in 1852. During the Crimean War he served at Smyrna and Sebastopol. In 1883 he was appointed to the presidency of the Geological and Pathological societies, and in 1893 he became president of the Royal College of Surgeons.

Hull, or **Kingston-on-Hull,** a parl., municipal, and co. bor., and riverport of E. Riding of Yorkshire, England, at the confluence of the H. and the Humber, 34 m. S.E. of York. It

is about 20 m. from the mouth of the Humber estuary and has excellent docks (over 200 acres), ranking as the third port in the kingdom. It is the main outlet for the cotton and woollen manufactures of the Midlands, and has a large trade with Germany and Scandinavia. It is one of the centres of the deep-sea fishing industry, and is an important steam-packet station. The greater part of the town is modern, and the notable buildings include : Holy Trinity Church, St. Mary's, Lowgate, Church (1333), the Grammar School (1486), and Trinity House School (1716) for nautical education. H. was constituted a free borough by Edward I. in 1299. It is the seat of a suffragan bishop, and returns three members to parliament. There are large ship-building yards, manufactures of textiles, oil, machinery, ropes, and chains, chemicals, and sugar-refining, tanning, and milling industries. Pop. (1911) 278,024.

Hull, the cap. of Ottawa co., Quebec, Canada, on the Ottawa R., opposite Ottawa, with which it is connected by a suspension bridge over the Chaudière Falls. It has a large lumber trade and numerous mills. Pop. 18,222.

Hull, Edward (*b.* 1829), an Irish geologist, born in Antrim; educated at Trinity College, Dublin. In 1850 he was appointed to the staff of the Geological Survey of the United Kingdom; in 1867 Scottish district surveyor; in 1869 director of the Geological Survey of Ireland and professor of geology in the Royal College of Science, Dublin; in 1873 president of the Royal Geological Society of Ireland. In 1883-84 he conducted a geological expedition, under the auspices of the Palestine Exploration Fund, in S. Palestine and Arabia Petræa, and another in the Nile Valley in 1893. He was a member of the Royal Commission on coal reserves in 1891, and secretary to the Victoria Institute in 1900. He has written numerous valuable works.

Hull, Isaac (1773-1843), an American naval officer, born at Derby, Connecticut. From a cabin boy he rose to the position of captain of a W. Indian trading vessel, and entered the American navy in 1798. He was given command of squadrons in the Mediterranean and Pacific ; received a medal from the Congress, and the freedom of several towns was conferred on him. He died in Philadelphia.

Hull, William (1753-1825), an American soldier, born at Derby, Connecticut ; he studied law and was called to the bar in 1775. He fought with distinction in the War of

Independence, and received the personal thanks of Washington for his services. He was made governor of Michigan Territory by Jefferson in 1805, and held the office till 1812, when he was appointed commander of the north-western army during the war with Great Britain. He was sent with 1500 men to defend Detroit, a task which presented great difficulties and in which he failed. He was court-martialled for cowardice and sentenced to be shot, but the sentence was not carried out.

Hullah, John Pyke (1812-84), a musical reformer, born at Worcester. He entered the Royal Academy in 1832, and attained fame as the composer of the music to Dicken's opera, *The Village Coquettes.* In 1840 he started popular classes for vocal training in Exeter Hall. He was appointed professor of singing at King's College and afterwards inspector of training schools for the United Kingdom. In 1876 the Edinburgh University conferred on him the degree of LL.D. He always opposed the tonic sol-fa system. He is the author of a *History of Modern Music* and a *Grammar of Vocal Music.* His most popular songs are: *Three Fishers; The Storm;* and *O That we two were Maying.* He died in London.

Hulme, Frederick Edward (1841-1909), a botanist and author, born at Hanley, Staffordshire. He studied art at S. Kensington, and in his seventeenth year became art-master of Marlborough College. Later he was appointed lecturer at King's College, London; he also held the posts of examiner to the Science and Art Department of the London Chamber of Commerce and lecturer to the Architectural Association. He was a voluminous writer and illustrator, his best-known work being *Familiar Wild Flowers,* which he began in 1875.

Huls, a tn. of Rhenish Prussia in the government of, and 17 m. N.W. of, Düsseldorf; manufactures silk, velvet, and linen. Pop. 6868.

Hulsean Lectures, founded by John Hulse (1708-90), an English divine. Hulse graduated at St. John's College Cambridge in 1724, and took orders, but in 1753 he came into his father's property in Cheshire, to which he retired, and on his death he left the property to the Cambridge University to maintain two divinity scholars at £30 a year each at his old college, to found a prize for a dissertation, and to found the offices of Christian advocate and Christian preacher or Hulsean lecturer. In 1860, the former office was changed by statute into the Hulsean professorship of divinity. The original terms of the lectureship provided for twenty lectures or sermons in St. Mary's great church, Cambridge, but these were reduced to eight in 1830, and later they were further reduced to four. The value of the Hulse endowment is between £800 and £900 a year, one-tenth goes to the lectureship, and one-tenth to the Hulsean prize, and the rest to the professor of divinity. The first to hold the office was the Rev. Christopher Benson, who lectured in 1820, and the following well-known names may be found among the lecturers : R. C. Trench, 1845 ; Christopher Wordsworth, 1847 ; James Moorhouse, 1865 ; F. W. Farrar, 1870 ; F. J. A. Hort, 1871 ; W. Boyd Carpenter, 1878, and M. Creighton, 1893.

Hulton, Little, a par. and tn. of S. Lancashire, England, situated 4 m. S.E. of Bolton. There are extensive coal mines near. Pop. (1911) 8113.

Humacao, a tn. on the E. coast of the island of Porto Rico, W. Indies, 30 m. S.E. of San Juan. Pop. 15,000.

Humane Society, The Royal. This Society was founded in England in 1774 by Dr. William Hawes (1736-1808) and Dr. Thomas Cogan (1736-1818), the object being to save life from drowning and to restore those who appeared to be drowned by artificial means. The two doctors having made many experiments, collected a number of their friends at the Chapter Coffee-house in St. Paul's Churchyard, and there the society was founded. The Receiving House, Hyde Park, was their first depôt (there are now some 280), and there boats and boatmen with life-saving apparatus are kept, and icemen supplied during the skating season. Money rewards, medals, clasps, and testimonials are bestowed on those who save or attempt to save people from drowning, and the society has extended its scope to include ' All cases of exceptional bravery in rescuing or attempting to rescue persons from asphyxia in mines, wells, blasting-furnaces, or in sewers where foul gas may endanger life.' In 1873 the Stanhope gold medal was instituted, and is given to the ' case exhibiting the greatest gallantry during the year '; prizes are also given for swimming to public schools and training ships. The society is carried on by means of subscriptions and bequests; the head offices are at 4 Trafalgar Square, London.

Humanitarians, originally a name given to a certain school of theologians in the middle of the 18th century who did not believe in the Trinity and regarded Jesus Christ as merely human, the founders of the Unitarian churches in England. It was also applied to the followers of Pierre Leroux (*q.v.*), who taught the perfection of man apart from the divine. In a more general sense it is used in modern times of a set of people whose main object is to lessen as far as possible the physical pain and discomfort in the world of to-day, and who hold strong views with regard to modern warfare, corporal punishment, etc.

Humansdorp, a div. of Cape Colony, bordering on the Indian Ocean, and bounded on the N. by the Winterhoek Mts. The capital is Humansdorp, 50 m. W. of Port Elizabeth. Pop. 1500.

Humayun (1508-56), a Mogul emperor of Delhi. In 1530 he succeeded his father, Baber, in India, the kingdom of Kabul and Lahore going to his brother Kamran. For ten years he was engaged in fighting the Afghans under Sher Shah, and was at length defeated and fled to Persia. In 1545 Sher Shah was killed, and H. returned to India with his son Akbar, and again occupied Delhi, but six months later he was killed by a fall from the parapet of his palace (1556), and his son, Akbar the Great, succeeded him. It was at his tomb, one of the most magnificent Mogul monuments near Delhi, that Major Hodson captured the last of the Moguls, Bahadur Shah, 1857.

Humber, an estuary on the E. coast of England lying between Yorkshire on the N. and Lincolnshire on the S., and formed by the rivers Trent and Ouse. These rivers join near the village of Faxfleet, and from there the H. runs for 18 m. in an easterly direction, and then 19 m. in a southeasterly direction to the North Sea, widening from a mile at the head to 8 m. in the bay formed by a spur on the Yorkshire coast known as Spurn Head. The area drained by the H. is 9293 sq. m. It is an important commercial waterway, and has on its banks the ports of Hull and Grimsby.

Humbert, Ranieri Carlo Emanuele Giovanni Maria Ferdinando Eugenio (b. 1844), King of Italy (1878-1900), eldest son of Emmanuel II., born at Turin, Sardinia. He succeeded his father as Humbert I., having previously married his cousin, Margherita Teresa Giovanna, Princess of Savoy and daughter of the Duke of Genoa. He at once proceeded on a tour through his kingdom, and an attempt was made to assassinate him at Naples (Nov. 17, 1878) by a fanatic named Passanante. His reign was peaceful, and he secured for Italy a share in the Triple Alliance, his relations with Great Britain being always most friendly. He was a fine soldier, and won popularity by his generosity and munificence and his personal activity among his people, who called him ' Humbert the good.'

A second attempt was made on his life in April 1897 by an anarchist named Acciarito, and a third attempt, made by another anarchist named Bresci, proved successful, and he died at Monya, July 29, 1900.

Humble-bee, or **Bumble-bee,** the name given to all species of *Bombus*, a well-known genus of Hymenoptera belonging to the family Apidæ and sub-family Socialinæ, the social bees. Their habits bear closer resemblance to those of the wasps than is the case with the genus *Apis*. The workers do not differ externally from the queens, and the colonies perish at the end of each season, save for a few females which survive the winter, and each of which starts a new society in the spring ; these females are much less prolific than the queen honey-bees, and a well-filled community contains only two or three hundred individuals. The female of *B. lapidarius* builds its nest in cavities among stones, merely lining the sides with moss, but *B. terrestris* and other species form a habitation out of carded moss, deserted mouse-nests, holes in the soil, etc. The wax is secreted in the abdomen of the insect, and is then transferred to the legs and moulded into building material. After the construction of the first cell, the female deposits the eggs therein, closes up the cavity, and rests several days before proceeding to the construction of other cells. The larvæ expand and distend the cell in a curious, irregular manner, and when full-grown they pupate in the moss, each larva forming a cocoon of finest silk. The queen scrapes away the wax from the cocoon, to assist pupation, and as the brood becomes matured she gives up to them the labour of collecting pollen and confines herself to producing eggs. The first broods are formed almost entirely of workers, who collect the food, scrape the wax from the cocoons, and enlarge the nest to accommodate the ever-growing family. The females, which are smaller than the mother, assist her in the process of egg-laying, as also do the workers to a lesser extent. The species of *Psithyrus* also inhabit the nests of the humble-bees, and some of them bear a curious resemblance to their hosts: they are generally somewhat larger, however, and their cells may be distinguished by their greater size. There is not that symmetry of structure in the cell of the bumble-bee which is so marked in the cell of the honey-bee, and they vary considerably in size ; also, the old cells are never used a second time for rearing, though they may be adapted for storing honey and pollen. These nests are frequently destroyed by various small mammals, as mice, weasels, and even foxes; and many small insects live in and around them. Humble-bees display a great variety of colouring, which runs generally in bars of alternate light and dark. *B. terrestris, B. hortorum, B. lapidarius,* etc., vary even in the same species. The genus is widely-distributed in the S. hemisphere, but is unknown in the Ethiopian and Australian regions.

Humboldt, a river, rises in the N.E. of Nevada, flows W.S.W. through the Humboldt Lake, and is lost in the marshy district known as the Humboldt and Carson Sink. Length, 384 m.

Humboldt, Friedrich Heinrich Alexander, Baron von (1769-1859), a naturalist, born at Berlin. He studied at Frankfort-on-the-Oder and Göttingen, and having made an excursion up the Rhine in the vacation, published *Mineralogische Beobachtungen über einige Basalte am Rhein* (1790). He afterwards went to Freiberg to study geology and produced his *Floræ Fribergensis Specimen,* 1793. In 1799 he went to S. America with Aimé Bonpland, and the next five years were taken up with the exploration of Venezuela, Colombia, Ecuador, Peru, Cuba, and Mexico, an account of which was published in his *Voyages aux Régions Equinoxiales du Nouveau Continent,* 1807, which consisted of thirty folio and quarto volumes. In 1807 he paid a visit to Italy, but ultimately went to Berlin, where he was occupied from 1827 - 28 in giving lectures; the substance of which appeared later in *Cosmos,* 1845-58, one of the greatest scientific works ever published. In 1829 he made a journey with Rose and Ghrenberg through Central Asia, and explored the Ural and Altai Mts., Dzungaria, and the Caspian, the results of this expedition appearing in *Fragments de Géologie et de Climatologie Asiatiques,* 1831, and in *Asie Centrale* (an enlargement of the earlier work), 1843. See *Life* by Professor Bruhns, translated into English by the Misses Lassell, 1873.

Humboldt, Karl Wilhelm, Baron von (1767-1835), a philologist, elder brother of Alexander von H., born at Potsdam. He was educated at Berlin, Göttingen, and Jena, and in 1801 became Prussian minister at Rome. In 1808 he returned to Prussia, and the following year was appointed minister of Public Instruction, the Berlin University owing its existence to him. In 1813 he was Prussian plenipotentiary at the congress of Prague, and in 1815 was one of the signatories of the capitulation of Paris, and in 1818 was present at the congress at Aix-la-Chapelle. But he

retired from political life in 1819 and devoted himself to literature. He made a special study of the Basque language, and was practically the first to bring it before the notice of European philologists. He also studied the languages of the East and of the South Sea Is., the great work of his life being on the ancient Kawi language of Java. In 1821 he published *Researches into the Early Inhabitants of Spain by the help of the Basque Language,* the result of his visit to the Basque country, and in 1828 *Uber den Dualis.* His *Gesammelte Werke,* 1841-52, were published by his brother, and his correspondence with Schiller, of whom he was a great friend, appeared in 1830.

Humboldtine, a native oxalate of the protoxid of iron, taking its name from the German naturalist Humboldt.

Humboldtite, the same as **Datolite,** a name given to crystals from Tyrol by Lévy because their form was supposed to be different from the ordinary datolites.

Hume, Allan Octavian (1829-1912), the ' Father ' of the Indian National Congress, son of Joseph H., a doctor of the East India Company. He was educated at the East India College (now Haileybury College), passing from there to the Indian Civil Service (1849). When the Indian Mutiny broke out he was officiating collector of Etwah between Agra and Cawnpore, and his vigour and judgment procured for him the loyalty of the native officials. He was commissioner of customs in Upper India, secretary to the government in the Home, and afterwards in the Revenue and Agricultural, Department. In 1879 he was appointed member of the Board of Revenue in the N.W. Provinces. In Simla he formed an organisation which would further the aspirations of advanced Indians, this was the birth of the National Congress (see his *Andi Alteram Partem*). When H. returned to England (1894), he took great interest in the British Committee of the Indian Congress. In India H. made a valuable collection of botanical and ornithological specimens, and published *The Game Birds of India, Burma, and Ceylon.* He presented his collection of birdskins and eggs, etc., to the British Museum of Natural History (S. Kensington). See *Life* by W. Wedderburn.

Hume, David (1771-76), a philosopher and historian, was intended for the bar, but abandoned the intention of becoming a lawyer owing to ill-health. He went to France in 1734 to recuperate, and there wrote *The Treatise of Human Nature,* which was published anonymously in 1739, two years after his return. This book attracted little attention at the time, but a better fate attended his *Essays Moral and Political* (1741-42), and his subsequent works, *Philosophical Essays on Human Understanding* (1748), the famous *Enquiry concerning the Principles of Morals* (1751), and his *Political Discourses* (1752). He had failed in 1745 to secure the professorship of ethics at Edinburgh University, and later his application for the chair of logic at Glasgow University was not successful; but in 1752 he was appointed keeper of the Advocate's Library at Edinburgh and also secretary to the Edinburgh Philosophical Society, which latter post he resigned five years later. He

DAVID HUME

now worked steadily at his history, which was published, two volumes at a time, between 1754 and 1761. In 1763 he went to Paris with Lord Hertford, and held an official post at the embassy, and he became a noted and popular figure in the society of the capital. The last years of his life were spent at Edinburgh. His autobiography, *My Own Life*, was published two years after his death, and his *Correspondence* (ed. Birkbeck Hill) in 1888. Other posthumous works were, *Suicide and Immortality*, 1777, and *Dialogues on Natural Religion*, 1779. The value of his philosophical writings has never been questioned, although at one time his scepticism made him notorious among the orthodox, and he takes his place as one of the leading metaphysicians in this or any other country. His history suffers severely from inadequate research, and is best studied

in the abbreviated version, edited by Dr. William Smith, 1870. The best biography is by John Hill Burton, 1846.

Hume, Fergus (*b.* 1862), a novelist, born in England, but educated in Dunedin, New Zealand, and called to the bar there. He published *The Mystery of a Hansom Cab*, 1887, came to London, 1888, and became one of our most popular novelists.

Hume, James Deacon (1774-1842), a political economist, was in the service of the custom house from 1791 to 1828, and from 1828 to 1840 was joint secretary to the Board of Trade. His great work was the consolidation of the 1500 statutes of the customs laws into ten coherent and well-systematised enactments. His arguments for free trade were quoted by Sir Robert Peel, and he was a founder of the Atlas Assurance Company (1808).

Hume, Joseph (1777-1855), a British politician, born at Montrose; went to India as an army surgeon, 1797, and by his knowledge of languages and scientific acquirements obtained lucrative positions and returned in 1808 with a fortune. He entered parliament as a Tory in 1812 for Weymouth, but under the influence of James Mill became one of the Benthamite philosophic Radicals. He was successively member for the Border Burghs, 1818, Middlesex, 1830, Kilkenny, 1837, and Montrose, 1892. His parliamentary career was marked by his rigid insistence on financial regularity, and his services in checking expenditure were of great value. He constantly supported measures of philanthropic humanitarianism, such as the suppression of flogging, the press-gang, etc. See *Memoir* by his son, J. B. Hume, 1855.

Hume, Martin Andrew Sharp (1847-1910), an author, born in London. He was educated privately, and at an early age began the study of Spanish, paying his first visit to Madrid in 1860. In 1889 he published a *Chronicle of King Henry VIII. of England*, but this did not meet with much success. He, however, continued writing, and became famous in 1896 by the publication of *The Courtships of Queen Elizabeth*, and *The Year after the Armada, and other Historical Studies*. These were followed in 1897 by *Sir Walter Raleigh* and *Philip II. of Spain*. In 1898 he became editor of the *Spanish State Papers* at the Public Record Office, but continued his literary work, producing *The Great Lord Burghley*, 1898, and *Spain, its Greatness and Decay*, 1479-1788, completed the following year by *Modern Spain*, 1788-1898. The two latter appeared in 1901 under the title of *The Spanish People: their Origin, Growth, and Influence*. The same year saw the publication of *Treason and Plot; Struggles for Catholic Supremacy in the Last Years of Queen Elizabeth*. His latter years were devoted to the writing of less scholastic books, e.g. *The Wives of Henry VIII., Queen Elizabeth and her England*, 1910, etc. H. did much to popularise Spanish history and politics.

Hume (or Home), Sir Patrick, first Earl of Marchmont (1641-1724), born at Polwarth, Berwickshire. He was the son of Sir Patrick H. of Polwarth, and became a member of the Scottish parliament in 1665. His opposition to the policy of Lauderdale resulted in his imprisonment, and after his release he joined the Duke of Monmouth, but becoming suspect he hid in the family vault of Polwarth Kirk until he fled to the Netherlands. He returned to Scotland in 1685 with the Argyll expedition, and when that failed escaped to Utrecht, where he remained until William of Orange came to England, when he returned, and once more entered the Scottish parliament. In 1690 he was made Lord Polwarth, and six years later he became Lord High Chancellor of Scotland, being created Earl of Marchmont in 1697.

Humeral (from Lat. *humerus*, shoulder), a wrap for the shoulders, used as a vestment in the Western Church. It is the same as the Amice, the name humeral being adopted more particularly in Germany. In modern Roman use it must be made of linen or of a hempen material, and not of wool, and a small cross must be embroidered in the centre. It is worn under the alb, except at Lyons and Milan, where they put it on over it. See AMICE.

Humidity of the atmosphere, refers to the amount of moisture that it contains. It is high or low according as the air is damp or dry. The amount of moisture in the air at any given time has a great bearing on weather conditions. The amount varies in different localities, and is never constant even in any one place; and temperature, pressure, wind, and sunshine are all affected according as the H. is high or low. The warmth of the body and breathing even depend upon H. Thus when the air is dry much more water vapour is expelled with each respiration than when the H. is high. Cold and heat are much more easily resisted in places of low H. than in places where the air is damp. (For methods of finding the *absolute* and *relative* H. see HYGROMETERS.) When the air is fully saturated with moisture, the relative H. would be 100, and this is seldom reached in practice except in fogs or mists. Sea air naturally has a high H., over 90 per cent., but land air, particularly in dry winter weather, may be as low as 50 per cent., or even, over deserts, 20 per cent. The relative H. in the British Isles varies from 30 to over 80 per cent., but as a rule it is very high.

Humiriaceæ, an order of dicotyledonous plants containing eighteen species, all of which occur in Africa and tropical America. There are only three genera, *Humirium*, *Helleria*, and *Saccoglottis*, and of these the best-known species is *Humirium balsamiferum*, a tall tree with a thick bark which abounds with a red balsamic fluid.

Hummel, Johann Nepomuk (1778-1837), a pianist, and composer, born at Presburg. He was a pupil of Mozart and an inmate of his house. At the age of ten he started on a concert tour through Europe, and returned to Vienna (1795) to study under Albrechtsberger and Salieri. In 1804 he succeeded Haydn as capellmeister to Prince Esterhazy, in 1816 he was appointed musical director at Stuttgart, and in 1820 he filled the same position at Weimar, where he died. He conducted operas in the chief cities of England, Russia, France, and Holland. His chief works are sonatas and études for the piano.

Humming-bird Moth, see HAWK MOTH.

Humming-birds are members of the coraciiform family Trochilidæ, and are so called because of the vibrating sound produced by their wings; there are from 400 to 500 species, all of which are confined to America and the W. Indies. Among them are some of the smallest of living birds, *Mellisuga minima* measuring only 2⅜ in. in length. They are characterised by a long and awl-shaped bill, and a long, cleft tongue in the form of a double tube, which can be protruded to a considerable distance, and withdrawn again very rapidly ; the sternum is greatly developed, forming a suitable base for the strong wing-muscles, which assist the untiring flight; the plumage is generally exquisite in colouring, especially in the males, with a brilliant metallic lustre, whose effect is heightened by the crest, ear-tufts, and ruffs. The Trochilidæ are insectivores, and dart from flower to flower in search of food, pausing over the plant with the body suspended in a vertical position, and the wings whirring continuously, which gives a curiously indistinct and misty effect to the plumage. *Patagona gigas*, the largest species, reaches a length of 8½ in., and inhabits the

Andes from Ecuador to Chili; it is bronze-green, with reddish under-parts, and is characterised by the flapping movement of its wings, in place of the usual vibratory movement. *Trochilus colubris*, in addition to the green-and-white colouring, has a brilliant red throat, with a forked tail of bluish black; *T. alexandri* of N. America has the throat a deep purple. *Lophornis* is a beautiful genus, extending from Costa Rica to Mexico; *L. ornatus* has fawn-coloured tufts with green terminal spots on each side of the neck. *Lodigesia mirabilis* of Peru is one of the most gorgeous species; the upper plumage is a lustrous bronze-green, the under-parts white, the throat emerald-green, rimmed with black, and the head and crest a vivid blue; the female is green, with white below. *M. minima*, called the bee H. because of its tiny size, is found in Jamaica and San Domingo, and the male is characterised by its dusky throat-spots. *Docimastes ensifer*, the sword-bill, has a straight beak, 5 in. long, which is more than the length of body and head together. *Rhamphomicron*, the thorn-bills, have the smallest beaks, that of *R. microrhynchum*, measuring only ¼ in. The species of *Phaëlthornis* are sometimes termed the hermits, because of their more sombre green and brown plumage, and also from their habit of frequenting dark woods and forests; they examine the crevices of trees in search of spiders, which form their habitual diet, and, poised in mid-air, the hermit will pass his bill over the under-surface of leaves, swallowing any insects hidden there. The H. will rarely live in captivity, and few have been carried across the Atlantic alive.

Humperdinck, Engelbert (*b.* 1854), a German musician, born at Siegburg. He studied at Paderborn Gymnasium, Köln Conservatory, and the Royal School of Music, Munich, and 1880-81 assisted Wagner in the preparations for the production of *Parsifal*. He taught music in the conservatories of Barcelona and Cologne (1885-88), and acted as musical adviser to Schott & Sons, publishers (Mainz), 1888-89. In 1884 his popular choral work *Das Glück von Edenhall* was first sung, and the choral ballade *Die Wallfahrt nach Kevlaar* in 1887; but it was the appearance of his *Hänsel und Gretel*, a musical fairy play, which made him famous. This was followed by *Königskinder* (melodrama), 1896, and *Dornröschen*, 1902. He also composed *Königskinder* (opera), 1910; *The Miracle* (pantomime, Olympia), 1912, and *Moorish Rhapsody*, 1898.

Humphreys, David (1753-1818), a poet and patriot, born in Derby, Connecticut, U.S.A. He was a colonel in the American revolutionary army, was attached to the suite of George Washington, and later became a general. H. was equally good at wielding the sword and the pen on his country's behalf. After the American War of Independence he had a long European experience: was minister at Lisbon and Madrid (at the latter place he interested himself in the exportation to America of Spanish merino sheep). When he returned to America he founded woollen works at Seymour (then Humphreysville), Connecticut. Some of his poems are: *An Address to the Armies of the United States*, *The Widow of Malabar* (a tragedy), *On the Happiness of America; On Agriculture*, and a Life of General Putnam. He helped Barlow, Hopkins, and Trumbull in the compilation of *The Anarchiad*. *See* Griswold's *Poets and Poetry of America*.

Humphry, Sir George Murray, F.R.S. (1820-96), a surgeon, born at Sudbury, Suffolk, and studied medicine at Norwich Hospital, and at St. Bartholomew's, London. In 1840 he was made a member of the Royal College of Surgeons, and in 1642 he was appointed physician at Addenbrooke's Hospital, Cambridge. He did much to improve the medical school at Cambridge, and held many important positions in the University.

Humulus, a genus of Moraceæ, which contains only two species, both of which are herbaceous perennials of climbing habit. The plants are diœcious, with male flowers in panicles and female flowers in false catkins; the fruit is an achene. *H. lupulus* is the hop, useful alike in brewing and in medicine

Hu-nan, a prov. of Central China, bounded on the N. by Hu-peh, on the E. by Kiang-si, on the S. by Kwang-si and Kwang-tung, and on the W. by Kwei-chow and Szechuen. The province is hilly in character, the only plain lying around Lake Tung-ting. The N. of the province is higher than the S., and among the mountains there is Heng-shan, one of the five sacred mountains (Wu-yo) upon which the celebrated tablet of Yu was placed. The principal rivers are the Siang-kiang with a basin of 39,000 sq. m., the Tsze-kiang with a basin of 10,000 sq. m., the Yueng-kiang with 35,000 sq. m., and the Ling-kiang with 80,000 sq. m. The principal products are tea, hemp, cotton, rice, paper, tobacco, and coal, the whole of the south-eastern part of the province being one vast coal-field, 21,700 sq. m. in extent.

The principal towns are the capital, Chang - sha - fu, Siang - t'an on the Siang-kiang, and Chang-te-fu on the Yueng-kiang. Since the time of the Taiping rebellion the Hunanese have been noted for their pride and obstinacy in admitting outside control. Area 83,380 sq. m. Pop. 22,169,673.

Hun-Barrow, a term used in Wiltshire for the ' barrows ' or cairns, which are largely found there, and are opened for archæological purposes.

Hunchback, or **Humpback,** a deformed condition of the spinal column. Slight irregularities of the normal curvature of the spine may result from various causes, such as malformation of other portions of the body, or even a well-established habit of standing or walking causing irregular pressure. The presence of a definite hump, however, is generally due to the development of Pott's disease, or tuberculous ulceration of the spine. This disease is characterised by the lodgment of tubercle germs in the vertebræ, and the consequent disintegration of part of their tissue by ulceration. In many cases a fall or blow originates the trouble, the structure being weakened and becoming more liable to tubercular infection. If the disease is not checked, the body of several vertebræ may crumble away, there is a collapse of their structure, and the spine curves sharply inwards, forming a pronounced hump and causing disproportion in the body generally. Unfortunately, the early symptoms are often indefinite. The child, for the disease is characteristic of the developing period of the bony structure, does not perhaps feel actual pain in the spine, but is easily fatigued and avoids anything like vigorous action. What pains there are may be ascribed to indigestion or rheumatism. The more definite symptoms are an inability to bend the back in stooping, a continued stiffness in the neck if the trouble be situated in the upper part of the column, and a disposition to turn the whole body instead of the trunk only when looking backwards for an instant.

The treatment, when early diagnosis is possible, involves complete rest for the spinal column by providing the patient with a carriage in which he can lie at full length on his back. The upright posture should never be assumed, and the patient should spend as much time as possible in the open air. The period of rest must be prolonged until there is reason to suppose that the disintegrated structures have been built up again. Suitable splints should be provided to keep the parts quiet. Pure air and good food are necessary adjuncts to any such course of treatment. If the disease has run its course for some time without detection, and the deformity has actually set in, there is little hope for a permanent cure. A certain proportion of cases have responded favourably to operative measures, which involve removing some of the posterior parts of the vertebræ. This operation, known as *laminectomy*, is resorted to when there are indications that the curvature has caused serious compression of the spinal cord.

Hundred, one of the most ancient subdivisions of a shire, analogous to the *pagus* of Tacitus, being, according to Stubbs, the union of a number of townships for the purpose of judicial administration, peace, and defence. There are many diverse theories to account for the exact origin of the term, but the most generally accepted is that it was at first an association of one hundred persons for purposes of police and justice. The chief man of the H. was the *Hundred's ealdor*, and each H. originally had a court called the H. moot. The personal rather than topographical origin of the H.— which latter view is disproved by the inequality in size of the different Hs. — seems to be confirmed by the now obsolete action against the H. in case of any loss by robbery, the object of which, according to Blackstone, was to make the H. answer for the robbery unless it succeeded in capturing the felon. The term H. still exists, but is now of no significance for any local governmental purposes, though under an old statute the H., or any corresponding division, is still liable in certain circumstances for damage caused by riot. The H. as an ecclesiastical division is now replaced by the deanery, and the H. rate by the county rate. *See under* HIGH-WAYS as to repair of H. bridges.

Hungary. This ancient kingdom takes rank among the states of Europe both in respect of territory and population. Although its naval and military forces, with the exception of the Honveds, are united with those of Austria, yet H. remains an independent state, the head of which is His Majesty Francis Joseph, the apostolic king. Owing to a recent rectification of frontier, its area is now 125,430 sq. m., which is greater than that of Great Britain, Austria, or Italy. H. lies almost in the centre of Europe, and has a well-defined frontier formed on the N., N.E., and E. by the Carpathians, and on the S. by the rivers Danube and Save. The whole country is in the form of an ellipse, from which a neck of land extends to the Adriatic. The Carpathians scarcely rise to the level of permanent snow, as the highest peak in the N. is the Francis Joseph (8736 ft.), and in the S. Negoi (6813 ft.). Several peaks range between 5000 and 7000 ft. Those of the High Tátra being precipitous and without foot-hills on the southern side, there reveal their full altitude. At the southern extremity of the range the banks of the Danube offer a series of beautiful pictures. The lower reaches from Báziás to Orsova are unrivalled in their majestic wildness. It was to H. that Europe entrusted the work of overcoming the dangers to navigation in this stretch of whirling water. On the W. three branches of the Alps enter Hungarian territory. One near Visegrád faces the spurs of the Carpathians, which extend right down to the Danube. This part of the river, flanked by forest-clad mountains, also offers a magnificent panorama. In the gently undulating part of the country which extends along the right bank of the Danube, are found H.'s largest lakes, the Balaton and the Fertö. The former is 47 m. long, with an area of 266 sq. m., and contains abundance of fish, the largest and most remarkable of which is that known as the fogas. In addition to the Danube, the principal rivers of H. are the Tisza, Drave, and Save. Less important are the Körös, Maros, Gran Szamos, Temes, and the Vág. The principal canals are the Francis Joseph, between the Danube and the Tisza, and the Bega, between the river of that name and the Temes. The latter canal, cut by the Romans, was enlarged in 1777. The forests of H. occupy 35,000 sq. m. Of this large area 18,000 sq. m. are covered with beech, 9000 sq. m. with oak, and 7000 sq. m. with conifers. The state owns about 6000 sq. m. of forest land, and enforces excellent forest laws throughout the country. The Great Plain (Hungarian *Alföld*) occupies 35,000 sq. m. in the centre of the country, having a greater extension from N. to S. than from E. to W., and its surface undulates from 200 to 400 ft. above sea-level. The area of the Lesser Plain, near the western frontier, is about 5000 sq. m. Together they cover nearly one-third of the country, and nearly all the area is under successful cultivation. Cornfields now take the place of pasture lands, and on once sterile sandy wastes there are now flourishing vineyards. The change has been largely due to the introduction of the false acacia (*Robinia pseud-acacia*), which was the first tree to become acclimatised, and by its protection and its influence on the climatic conditions has made possible the growth of other trees. Although the whole of H. lies between 44° and 49°, yet there

are great divergences in different parts between the minimum, mean, and maximum temperatures. The mean annual temperature ranges between 41° F. and 57° F. The highest mean temperature is near Fiume on the Adriatic, and the lowest is in the N. and N.E. Carpathian districts. Those mountains, however, largely protect the Lowlands from northerly winds. The rainfall also shows great divergencies; at the base of the N.E. Carpathians the annual average is 59 in., in the mountain district near the Adriatic it is 79 in., while on the Lesser Plain it is 20 in., and on the Great Plain 24 in. The chief agricultural product of H. is wheat, from which is made the famous Hungarian flour. Other important products are maize, barley, oats, and other cereals, as well as tobacco. Rice is grown in the S., where also experiments are being made in the cultivation of the cotton plant. Vineyards occupy nearly 31,000 sq. m.; the most celebrated wine is made in the Tokay district in N. Hungary. Melons and other choice fruits are raised in great abundance. More than 800,000 fruit-bearing trees have been planted on the sides of the high-roads. The money obtained by the sale of the fruit is expended on the maintenance of the roads. Much red pepper, known as paprica, is grown in some counties. Nature has been very bountiful to H. in respect of valuable minerals. From the Bronze Age onward these have been extensively dug and smelted. In later periods the Romans did much mining in the country, and derived from it their chief supply of gold. At the present day many gold and silver mines are being worked both by the state and by private proprietors. Coal is very abundant, but much of it is of rather inferior quality. A plentiful supply of iron-ore keeps several large smelting works fully occupied. Copper, lead, antimony, and zinc are also found. H. possesses the only opal mine in Europe. Enormous quantities of rock-salt exist in E. Hungary. Having been worked for many centuries, some of the salt mines include subterranean excavations of great extent. The salt industry is a monopoly of the state. Asphalt and petroleum are also found. Strong springs of the latter have been tapped recently near Nagyvárad and Máramaros-Sziget. But the most remarkable treasure is natural gas, which during the last few years has been found by deep borings in many parts of the country. This gas is a rich hydrocarbon, and by its abundance, force, and wide distribution must before long lead to a great development of industry. Already it is being utilised in ploughing and other agricultural operations, and in separating nitrogen from the atmosphere. These Hungarian gas wells are equal in extent and value to those of Pittsburg and other places in America. Mineral waters of various kinds, both hot and cold, spring forth plentifully in many parts, and are found to be very efficacious in the treatment of disease. At Ránkhirlány, near Kassa, a geyser may frequently be seen uplifting a great column of water. The most famous baths are those of Budapest, Trencsénteplitz, Vizakna, the Baths of Hercules, and Pöstyén. At the last-named place radio-active mud is successfully used in the treatment of rheumatism and allied disorders. Mineral waters are exported from H. to all parts of the world. The population of H. at the end of 1910 was 20,886,487, of whom 10,050,575 (48 per cent.) were Magyars, who reside in greatest numbers on the Plain and in the cities. The others are chiefly Roumanians (2,949,032), Slovaks (1,967,970), Croatians (1,833,162), Servians (1,106,471), Ruthenes (472,587), who occupy the mountainous districts, and Germans (2,037,435), who are widely distributed. The population of Budapest in 1910 was 880,371, and if the suburbs had been included, the total would have been more than a million. Other large cities are Szeged (118,328), Szabadka (94,610), and Debreczen (92,729). Nine other towns have more than 50,000 inhabitants. In Szeben, Brassó, and other counties near the S.E. frontier there are many large villages occupied by Saxons whose forefathers settled there in the 12th century and received extensive grants of land, which having been retained as common property, has greatly contributed to the very remarkable prosperity of these communities. Saxons, like all the other sub-nationalities in H., have retained their own language, religion, and customs. The pastures of H. support a vast number of useful animals. The census of such in 1911 showed that there were then 7,319,121 horned cattle, including 155,000 buffaloes. Horses numbered 2,351,481, of which 31,000 were used for military purposes. Of pigs, there were 7,580,446, and the number of sheep was 8,548,204, including many of the merino breed.

Language.—Few languages offer more fascination to the philologist than Hungarian. Until the 17th century it seemed a pure anomaly, for it was clearly not even a distant cousin to the neighbouring German, Wallachian, or Russian. In 1769 an astronomer, John Sajnovics, visited the Laplanders in Norway, and was impressed by the similarity of their language to his own. So vivid was this impression that he forgot for the moment about his astronomy and wrote instead a book (in Latin) to demonstrate the affinity between the two tongues. Since his day many other facts have come to light which go to prove that Magyar belongs with Voguland Ostiak to the Ugric branch of the Finno-Ugric division of the Ural-Altaic family. Yet there are still a number of learned scholars, as, for example, Arminius Vámbéry, who refuse to accept this classification. In view of the number of words in common use which are clearly Turkish in origin, they are inclined to regard Magyar as a Turco-Tartaric tongue. For this reason they are called Orientalists. There follows a brief enumeration of the most striking peculiarities of Magyar: (1) It is a language of affixes. *Atyámért* means ' for my father,' *m* being ' my ' and *ert* ' for.' (2) The active verbs have definite and indefinite forms: *latom* means ' I see him, her, or it,' and *latok* merely ' I see.' (3) There is no gender: ' he,' ' she,' and ' it ' are not even distinguished. (4) Extra syllables give the verb a potential, causative, or frequentative sense: *verhet* means ' he can beat '; *veret*, ' he causes to beat '; *vereget*, ' he often beats.' (5) Nouns have possessive suffixes, which vary according to number: *tollunk*, ' our pen '; *tollaink*, ' our pens.' Magyar is, moreover, rich in verbal derivatives, has a copious vocabulary, and is decidedly musical —and therefore adapted to poetry— by reason of the harmony of its consonants and vowels.

Literature.—The national literature of H. is, comparatively speaking, young. Indeed, there was little life in it till well on in the 18th century. The cause of this is not far to seek. Ever since the priests from Germany and Italy had introduced Christianity in the 11th century, Latin had been the official language. It was spoken at the court and in the churches; it was taught in the higher schools, and so became the language of the educated classes, and finally it was introduced into the administration. Latin was not discontinued in the schools till 1790, and was talked in parliament as late as 1825. The oldest written fragment in Magyar belongs to a funeral oration dating from 1171. During the pre-Reformation and Reformation periods (1437-1606) men of letters were chiefly engaged either in translating portions of the Bible or in writing voluminous rhyming chronicles. King Matthias Hunyadi was a true Medici to his countrymen in that he made his court a centre of intellectual and artistic life, in that he gathered together a great library, and in that he invited to his kingdom men of learning from all parts. In 1473—during his reign, that is—the first book was printed in H., namely, *Budai Krónika*, a history of H. up to his day. During the 17th century many writers distinguished themselves in the fields of theology and philology, but none obtained to such high honour as the poets Nicholas Zrinyi (*d.* 1664) and Stephen Gyöngyössi (*d.* 1704). The former wrote a national epic, the *Zrinyiasz*, after the manner of Tasso, in which he sang of the powers of his ancestor. There is life in his character drawing, and his language is sincerely emotional, if unpolished. The *Venus of Murány* of Gyöngyössi, though spoilt somewhat by an excess of mythology and metaphor, is redolent with an Ovidian grace of melody and descriptive charm. In the 18th century, not unjustly called the ' age of decadence,' the only outstanding name is that of Francis Faludi (*d.* 1779), the Jesuit, who developed a singularly pure and refined style both in his translations and in his original songs and idylls. From 1772 to 1830 there was a revival in literature and also a conscientious effort to reform the language. George Bessenyei (*d.* 1811) and Benedict Virag (*d.* 1830) are both representative of the classical school, who took Latin poets as their model. The former dreamed of being the Voltaire of H., whilst Virag wrote epistles and odes which fully account for his proud title of ' the Magyar Horace.' Francis Kazinczy (*d.* 1831), who wrote readable didactic verse and good biography in prose, was the leader of the movement for language reform. Alexander Kisfaludy (*d.* 1844), the author of the famous lyrics, *Himfy's Love*, was brother to the more celebrated Charles Kisfaludy (*d.* 1830), who may truly be said to have regenerated, if not created, national drama. Two other notable poets of this period are Francis Kölcsey (*d.* 1838), the idealist, who composed the *Hymnus*, now a national anthem, and Joseph Katona (*d.* 1830), who wrote the fine tragedy of the *Palatine Bánk*. One of the foremost of H.'s poets is Michael Vörösmarty (*d.* 1855). Had he left only his translations of Shakespeare behind him, his name would have lived, but as it is there are many fine lyrics and epics, such as the woefully tragic *Two Castles*, which prove Vörösmarty to be a great original poet besides an excellent translator. In the splendour of his lyrics, however, he was sur-

passed by Alexander Petöfi (*d.* 1849), whose freshness, rapture, sincerity, and passionate love of nature have rarely been equalled in any nationality. And side by side with Petöfi will ever stand John Arany (*d.* 1882). In his immortal epics, *Toldi* and *The Death of Buda*, as in his ballads, he absorbed all that is best in the old Hun and Magyar legend, whilst in creating Nicholas Toldi he ' touched indeed the very depths of Hungarian character.' To-day Hungarian authors of distinction are found in every field of literature, in the natural sciences, philosophy, and history, as well as in the world of fiction. The earliest historical novelist was Baron Nicholas Josika (*d.* 1865), an enthusiastic admirer of Scott. The humour, spontaneous faculty for invention, and irrepressible delight in story-telling of Maurus Jokai (*d.* 1904) explain at once his unbounded popularity as a writer of fiction.

History.—H. was founded about the year 889 by the then savage Magyars and Ungri, who were pressing westward across the Carpathians. St. Stephen (997-1038) instituted the monarchy. It was he, too, who did all he could to encourage his people to embrace Christianity; for he established an ecclesiastical polity, and endowed the infant Church by founding many bishoprics and abbeys. And in other respects also he was a wise king, so that he may truly be called the King Alfred of his people; to his reign may be traced the germs of the city corporations and county councils, as well as of the National Diet and many of the fundamental laws of the realm. But above all, his countrymen cherish his name because of the refining influence his humanity exercised over their untamed and warlike ancestors, and because of the stimulus his practical good sense gave to mining and other peaceful industries. At this time the king only exercised his authority directly over certain privileged towns and the royal demesnes; nobility and church were largely self-governing, whilst the nation at large was, for the most part, at the mercy of the landowners. We may here notice the ' Golden Bull,' which King Andrew II. conceded in 1222 to his barons: by this charter he recognised their right to take up arms against the sovereign should he be guilty of any grave infringement of their privileges, and guaranteed that the Diet should be summoned annually. The bulk of this brief sketch will be occupied with an account of the wars with Turkey and of the relationship of H. with the sister kingdom of Austria. The Hungarians first waged war against the

Saxon kings, Henry the Fowler and Otto the Great, who gained a great victory over them in 954, and from 1241 onwards they were busily engaged in repelling the persistent advances of the Mongols or Tartars. It was under Louis the Great (1342-82) that they first gained a signal victory over the Turks by the banks of the Maritza. This Louis was king also of Poland, and the importance of such a victory will be appreciated when it is remembered that H. and Poland were the natural bulwarks against Mohammedan aggressions on Western Christendom. In 1396 the Sultan Bajazet defeated Siegmund of H. at the battle of Nikopolis, but the disgrace was soon blotted out by the triumphant victories of the soldier-patriot, John Hunyadi. Panic among the latter's troops, due to the king's death, accounts for the defeat of the Hungarians at Varna (1444), but in 1456, a few months before his death, Hunyadi succeeded in raising the siege of Belgrade and scattering a formidable Ottoman host. H. reached the summit of her glory under Matthias Corvinus (1458-90), the son of Hunyadi, who proved a noble patron of art and letters, besides an able statesman, diplomat, and general. His successors were weak, and the country, therefore, fell an easy prey to the Turkish invaders. In 1526 these latter, under the leadership of Sultan Suleyman, who had already captured Shabatz and Belgrade, overwhelmed the Hungarians at the battle of Mohacs and slew their king, Lewis II. Buda, the capital, was taken, and the splendid library of Matthias wantonly destroyed. Until the peace of Carlowitz (1699), which concluded a bitter struggle between Austria and the Porte, the greater part of H. remained in Turkish hands, and a Turkish pasha presided in Buda. By that peace the Ottomans were obliged to yield most of their Hungarian conquests, but it was not till 1716, when Prince Eugene defeated them, that H. finally became independent of their sway. Siegmund, who was king of H. from 1392 to 1437, and who was crowned emperor of the Holy Roman empire in 1433, is the first link between the crowns of H. and Austria. After Lewis's death (1526), to which reference has already been made, the sovereignty of his kingdom was conferred on Ferdinand, Archduke of Austria, who was elected emperor in 1558. Ever since this time it has remained with the Austrian archdukes; until 1687 it was elective, but in that year it was made hereditary in the Hapsburg family. It must not be thought that H. submitted to Austrian rule

without a struggle. The resentment naturally rising from the loss of a national king was aggravated by the folly of many of the emperors. Thus Leopold I. (1657-1705), in his ruthless attempt to re-catholicise the kingdom, was responsible for the wholesale massacre of Protestants and for their alliance in self-defence with their hereditary foe, the Turks, and Joseph II. (1780-90) committed a fatal error in endeavouring to ride rough-shod over all their most time-hallowed institutions. But national feelings and prejudices are fortunately hard to suppress, and Joseph was forced to restore the ancient constitution. The year of revolution (1848) witnessed an outbreak of intense patriotism. The Hungarians, under the famous Kossuth, Deak, and others, made a desperate attempt to regain their former independence. A new constitution was promulgated, and for a time Kossuth was acknowledged as supreme governor. But in the end the Austrians, who had summoned the Russians to their aid, prevailed, and the old despotic régime was resumed without any trial by jury or freedom of the press. It was not until 1867 that the dual monarchy was consolidated under Francis Joseph, who is to this day (1913) the Emperor of Austria-Hungary. Foreign affairs, the army, and finance are controlled by the Delegations—a body composed equally of Austrian and Hungarian deputies. Otherwise the two nations are distinct, and have their own parliament, executive, and laws. It cannot be said there is anything ideal in this compromise. That it still excites some lively discontent is shown by the demand in 1902 for the use in Hungarian regiments of the national flag and of Magyar for the words of command, and also by the demand in 1908 for a separate Hungarian bank. The chief obstacle in the way of electoral reform and universal suffrage is the jealousy with which the Magyars, who have always been the predominant race, not unnaturally cling to their position of supremacy. They resent sharing equally with the many Servians, Slovaks, Ruthenians, Wallachs, and Germans, who make up the nation, the full privileges and responsibilities of citizenship and government. The rapid economic and intellectual development of H. augurs well for its future importance among European powers.

Hunger, an indefinite sensation usually referred to the stomach, but also combined with a non-localised feeling of weakness or faintness. Normal H. is not of necessity strictly periodic, but training may result in its recurrence becoming regular. In its earliest stages no suffering accompanies it, but later a gnawing pain sets in at the epigastrium, followed by weakness, and finally by the delirium of starvation. The general faintness is normally removed by the introduction of solid or semi-solid nutriment into the alimentary tract, even though the stomach is not used as in the passage of easily assimilated food into the large intestine. The almost immediate alleviation of suffering may be caused by the free secretion of gastric juice which may be brought about by the ingestion of indigestible substances. Abnormal H. accompanies some diseases, particularly those associated with *marasmus*. Other diseases cause morbid appetites, as the craving for chalk and lime, etc.

Hungerford, a par. and tn. of Berkshire, England, on the Wilts border. The ancient name was Ingleford, meaning ' Ford of the Angles.' It is situated on the R. Kennet, 9 m. N.W. of Newbury and 27 m. S.W. of Reading, and is a noted hunting and fishing centre. Pop. (1911) 3040.

Hungerford, Margaret Wolfe (*c.* 1855-97), an Irish novelist, born in Ireland. Mrs. H. made a name for herself by her breezy Irish love-stories, of which the best known are: *Molly Bawn*, 1878 ; *Mrs. Geoffrey*, 1881 ; *April's Lady*, 1891 ; and *A Conquering Heroine*, 1892.

Hung-yen, a tn. of French Indo-China in Tong-king. It is the capital of the province of H., and is situated on the left bank of the R. Songkoi, about 30 m. S.E. by S. of Hanoi.

Huningen (Fr. *Huningue*), a tn. and former fortress of Alsace - Lorraine, Germany, situated on the l. b. of the Rhine, 3 m. N. of Basel. It was once one of the principal ports on the E. French frontier. Pop. 3000.

Hünnen-Betten, or **Hunne Beds,** the name of a collection of megalithic cairns in the prov. of Drenthe in the Netherlands. Their date is not known, the Franks asserting that they belonged to a period long before the Christian era, while such authorities as Fergusson say they belong to a far later date. They resemble dolmens or the ' giants' graves ' that are found in other places in N. Europe.

Huns (Lat. *Hunni*, Gk. Οὖννοι), a wild nomadic people who were busily engaged in the early centuries A.D. in sweeping away old boundaries and in over-running the territories of nations which time had long since hallowed. Gibbon lays emphasis on their ' broad shoulders, flat noses, and small black eyes deeply buried in the head,' and other authorities speak of their swarthy complexions, rude manners, high-pitched voices, and frequent deformities. From the confused narratives of the Dark Ages, historians can distinguish four migratory tribes to which the name of H. has been applied : (1) The Magyars were Hunnish invaders of Hungary from 898 A.D., whilst the race of modern Hungarians was probably formed by these Magyars coalescing with the Kumans and other hordes, who had preceded them in the march westward. (2) The White H., or Ephialites, inhabited Bactria and the tracts between the Oxus and the Caspian in the days of Attila's conquests. In 484 they inflicted a crushing defeat on their Persian neighbours under Peroz, who was slain in battle, but during the following century their power was broken by the aggressive Turks. (3) The Hûnas, who made inroads into India, were contemporary with the Ephialites, and undoubtedly belonged to the same wave of barbarian migration. (4) But history has most to say about those savage hordes of H. who contributed so largely to the disintegration of the Roman empire, and who from 372 A.D. to 453 were continually threatening, nay thrusting back, imperial confines. An army of H., under Balamir, overcame the Alani, who dwelt between the Volga and the Don, completely disorganised the empire of the Ostrogoths (' Greutungi '), and finally routed the Visigoths (' Tervingi '). These tribes were driven to seek new homes between the Pruth and Danube, but in time their ferocious conquerors wrested even these lands from them and obliged them to retreat still farther, this time beyond the Danubian frontier. Two facts show that Roman supremacy was already on the wane: Emperors had begun to enlist the arms of the Hunnish invaders against other foes, and in 432 Theodosius II. agreed to buy peace from Rhuas or Rugulas, their king, by an annual payment of 350 pounds of gold. But the peace was hollow, and the death of Rhuas alone staved off the inevitable humiliation of Rome. Attila and Bleda succeeded Rhuas, their uncle, and were so formidable as to secure a double tribute. Under these chiefs the H. laid waste Scythia and Media, threatened Persia, sacked the Roman city of Margus in the East (441) and Sirmium in the West. In 445 Attila stood with his victorious armies before the walls of Constantinople; in 451 his progress westward across the Rhine was only stayed after a terrible battle on the Catalaunian plains (near Mery-sur-Seine), and in the following year, after raising

Aquileia and the cities of Venice, Attila was confronted with Pope Leo I. on the banks of the Mincio—an interview which ended in a retreat of the H. beyond the Alps. Next year Attila died, and in 454 the Goths, Gepidæ, and Suevi avenged his insolent victories near the R. Netad in Pannonia, where 30,000 H. were slain. The Hunnish nation never survived this calamitous defeat; their tribes dispersed, some settling in the Dobrudzha, others in Dacia, and others, again, returning to their old haunts—the southern steppes of modern Russia. Perhaps the Bulgarians are at the root a Hunnish people.

Hunstanton, a watering-place of Norfolk, England, situated on the Wash, 15 m. N.E. of Kings' Lynn. New H. stands about 1 m. from the old village, and possesses a pier, a wide expanse of sand, and a lighthouse with a fixed light, visible for 16 m. Pop. (1911) 2510.

Hunt, Alfred William (1830-90), an English painter, born in Liverpool, son of Andrew H., a landscape painter. He was educated at Corpus Christi College, Oxford, of which he became a fellow, 1858. He won the Newdigate Prize poem in 1851. He exhibited landscapes in oil and water-colour at the Royal Academy, and received encouragement from Ruskin, and took up painting professionally in 1861, when he married. His best pictures are in water-colour. Fine examples are in the Tate Gallery, London, and the Walker Art Gallery, Liverpool. See F. Wedmore, in *Magazine of Art,* 1891.

Hunt, Arthur Surridge (*b.* 1871), an English scholar and archæologist, educated at Queen's College, Oxford, of which he was a scholar and is now a fellow; won the Craven travelling studentship and joined Bernard Pyne Grenfell (*q.v.*) in exploration, for the Egypt Exploration Fund, of the ancient site of Oxyrhynchus, modern Belonesa. Their work here from 1896 onward resulted in most valuable discoveries of Greek papyri, the chief finds being *The Logia,* or ' Sayings of Christ,' large sections of the lost poet Bacchylides, etc.

Hunt, Henry (1773-1835), a political agitator, the son of a Wiltshire farmer, on whose land he worked from the age of sixteen. He soon began to interest himself in local politics, and he was always on the side of the reformers. For some years he worked in conjunction with Cobbett, and in 1810 they shared the same room in gaol, to which they had been committed for their political opinions. He more than once stood for parliament, but he never secured his object.

He was an active member of the Hampton Club, and he presided over the meeting in St. Peter's Field, Manchester, in August 1819, which, owing to the intervention of the soldiery, is known as the Peterloo Massacre. There is no doubt that he was of value to the cause of which he was an advocate. He published his *Memoirs* in 1820, and his *Correspondence* appeared in the same year. There is a worthless biography by Huish (1836).

Hunt, Henry Jackson (1819-89), an American soldier, born at Detroit, Michigan. He served throughout the Mexican War under Scott, and distinguished himself at Contreras, Churubusco, and Chapultepec. He fought at Bull Run (1861), and became chief of artillery in the Washington defences, and later held a similar post in the army of the Potomac. At the close of the war he assisted in the reorganisation of the United States army, and was made president of the permanent Artillery Board. In 1883, after holding various commands, he retired, and became the governor of the Soldier's Home, Washington, D.C. He wrote *Instruction for Field Artillery,* 1860.

Hunt, Leigh (James Henry Leigh-) (1784-1859), an author, was educated at Christ's Hospital School, London, to which he went from 1792. He was a shy, nervous, sensitive lad, and far happier wandering about the fields with a chosen companion than in taking part in the games and amusements of rougher and hardier boys. At a very early age he read poetry and began to write verses, which his father collected and published in 1801 under the title of *Juvenilia, or A Collection of Poems written between the ages of twelve and sixteen, by J. H. L. Hunt.* Owing to the elder Hunt's energy, a large subscription was obtained, and the little book passed through four editions in three years. The quality of the verse was not such as to merit much success. In 1805 H. began to contribute dramatic criticism to the *News,* and a selection of his articles were reprinted in book form two years later. In 1808 H. and his brother John started a newspaper, the *Examiner,* and for thirteen years wrote largely in its columns on many subjects, taking part not only in its literary direction, but also contributing political leaders. His persistent attacks on the character of the Prince Regent led to a government prosecution in 1812 of the brothers, who were sentenced to two years' imprisonment. It was while he was in prison that Thomas Moore brought Byron to him, which was the beginning of the famous friendship between these men.

At this time, too, he made the acquaintance of Keats, and introduced him to Shelley. He published several volumes of poems, including *The Story of Rimini*, 1816. In 1822 H. went to Italy to join Byron, with whom later he quarrelled. In 1825 he returned to England, and three years later he published *Lord Byron and some of his Contemporaries*, which brought a hornet's nest about his ears. All this time he was working very hard, contributing to the newspapers, editing periodicals, writing dramatic criticism and book-reviews, and every now and then issuing a book. He wrote a novel, *Sir Ralph Esher*, 1832, and a volume on *Christianism*, and he reprinted the best of his papers which had appeared in the *Indicator* and the *Companion*, 1830. His play *A Legend of Florence* was produced at Covent Garden in 1840. Four years later appeared one of his best-known books, *The Town*, and in 1855 appeared the most delightful of all his books, *The Old Court Suburb, or Memorials of Kensington* (reprinted 1902, when it was edited by Austen Dobson). He had earlier, in 1850, published his delightful *Autobiography*, which is certainly, and deservedly, the most popular of all his works, and won high praise from Carlyle. It was as a poet that H. desired to achieve fame, but it cannot be said that his ambition was ever satisfied. His verse was easy and agreeable, but it lacks dignity; he had not the lyrical gift, and has never taken the place he desired to fill in the roll of English poets. It is as an essayist that he has his claim to remembrance. In this branch of letters he does not, of course, rank with Lamb or Hazlitt, but he has undoubtedly, on a humbler plane, an individuality and charm of his own. His wide reading and his knowledge of the world gave him ample scope for finding suitable subjects for his innumerable papers, but he is never happier than when writing of 'My Books,' or discoursing about London, or describing the country. His *Autobiography* is the principal authority for his life, but this has been supplemented by his *Correspondence*, edited by his eldest son (1862).

Hunt, Richard Morris (1828-95), an American architect, born at Brattleborough, Vermont. He went to Europe to study, chiefly in Paris, where, in 1854, he was appointed inspector of works on the buildings connecting the Tuileries with the Louvre, and where he designed the Pavillon de la Bibliothèque. Returning to New York in 1855 he designed the Lennox Library, the Stuyvesant, and Tribune buildings; also public buildings in Princeton and Yale. He obtained the gold medal of the Institute of British Architects for his Administration Building at the Chicago Exhibition (1893). He did much to raise American architecture in the opinion of other countries, and helped to found the American Institute of Architects. There is a fine memorial to him in the wall of Central Park.

Hunt, Thomas Sterry (1826-92), an American chemist and geologist, born at Norwich, Connecticut. In 1845 he became a member of the Association of American Geologists and Naturalists of Yale, which became later the American Association for the Advancement of Science. A year later he was appointed assistant to Professor B. Silliman, Jun., at Yale, and became chemist to the Geological Survey of Vermont, afterwards filling the same appointment to the Canadian Geological Survey at Montreal. He was elected F.R.S. in 1859, and was president of the Royal Society of Canada. He wrote a remarkable 'Essay on the History of the names Cambrian and Silurian' (*Canadian Naturalist*, 1872), and his works include *Chemical and Geological Essays*, 1875; *Mineral Physiology and Physiography*, 1886; *A New Basis for Chemistry*, 1887; and *Systematic Mineralogy*, 1891.

Hunt, William Henry (1790-1864), an English water-colour painter, born in London, and studied with John Varley. He was a prominent member of the Society of Painters in Water-Colours, and may be regarded as one of the chief figures in the great English school. His principal pictures were of interiors, figures, and still life. Many fine examples are in the Victoria and Albert Museum, S. Kensington.

Hunt, William Holman (1827-1910), an English painter, born in London, joined the Royal Academy schools (1844), gaining admission to the exhibition with ' Hark ' in 1846. In 1848 the Pre-Raphaelite Brotherhood was started with Rossetti, Millais, and others, inspired by the technique of Ford Madox Brown. H.'s earlier pictures include ' Rienzi,' 1848; ' Valentine and Sylvia,' 1851 (greatly praised by Ruskin); ' A Hireling Shepherd,' ' Claudio and Isabella,' and ' Strayed Sheep,' 1852. In 1854 came, perhaps, his greatest and certainly most successful religious picture, ' The Light of the World,' presented to Keble College, Oxford, by the purchaser, Mr. Combe, of which a modified replica was painted in 1904 and exhibited in the chief cities of the British empire. A visit to Palestine produced ' The Scapegoat,' 1856, a meticulous study of the scenery of the Dead Sea; ' The Finding of Our

Saviour in the Temple,' 1860, now at Birmingham; 'The Shadow of Death' (exhibited 1873), representing a shadow of the Crucifixion thrown on the workshop wall by the stretched arms of Jesus, is at Manchester; 'The Triumph of the Innocents,' of which there are two pictures, at Liverpool and Birmingham, begun in 1875, was not finished till 1885. His best known later picture is 'May Day on Magdalen Tower, Oxford,' 1891. H. remained to the last a fervent adherent to the principles of the pre-Raphaelites. The best statement of his ideals and of the inner history of the movement is in his *History of Pre-Raphaelitism*, 1907. He received the Order of Merit, and was buried in St. Paul's.

Hunter, Sir Archibald (b. 1856), a British general; made D.S.O., 1886; K.C.B., 1898; served with distinction during the Egyptian campaign in the Sudan, 1884-85, and the Nile expedition, Toski, 1889, where he was wounded, and at Dongola, 1896. He was one of Kitchener's principal generals, and on the outbreak of the Boer War commanded the tenth division, being Sir G. White's chief of the staff at Ladysmith. He shared in the relief of Mafeking, and defeated Prinsloo at Caledon. His later appointments include the command in Scotland (1903), S. India, and Gibraltar (1910-13).

Hunter, Sir David, K.C.M.G. (b. 1841), a member for Durban first Union Parliament, born at Broxburn, Linlithgowshire, and educated at Kirkliston Free Church School. In 1853 he entered the service of the North British Railway Company as apprentice and served successively in the several departments. In 1879 he was nominated general manager of Natal Government Railways, and in 1881 became a member of the Natal Government Board. He was mentioned in several despatches in connection with the Transvaal War (1899-1902). In 1906 he retired from the general managership of railways. In 1907 he was a member of the Durban Town Council, and in 1910 M.P. for Central Durban.

Hunter, John (1728-93), a surgeon and anatomist, the brother of William H. whom he assisted in dissection (1748). He was house-surgeon at St. George's in 1756, and surgeon in 1768. He took part in an expedition to Belleisle in 1761, where he studied the conditions of the coagulation of the blood and served with the British army in Portugal in 1762, acquiring knowledge of gunshot wounds and inflammation. In 1763 he started a practice in London, but devoted his spare time to dissection and experiment. His chief works

were: *Treatise on the Blood, Inflammation and Gunshot Wounds,* 1794; *On the Venereal Disease,* 1786; *Observations on certain parts of the Animal Economy,* 1786; *Proposals for the Recovery of People apparently drowned,* 1776. H. made a notable surgical advance in the tying of the artery about the seat of disease in aneur'sm; indeed, he has been called by some the founder of scientific surgery.

Hunter, John (1738-1821), a British admiral, born at Leith, Scotland. He took part in the Rochefort expedition in 1757, and was present at the capture of Quebec in 1759. He was also at the Dogger Bank in 1781 and at Gibraltar the following year. In 1786 he was with Admiral Phillip, and helped to found the colony of New South Wales, of which he afterwards became governor (1795-1800). He also took a settling party to Norfolk Is., and made a survey of Port Jackson.

Hunter, William (1718-83), a doctor and anatomist, born in Lanarkshire. He studied at Glasgow, Edinburgh, and St. George's Hospital, London, and was assistant-dissector to Dr. James Douglas (1675-1742). In 1748 he was elected surgeon-accoucheur to the Middlesex, and to the British Lying-in Hospitals in 1749. He became the leading obstetrician of his time, and was consulted by Queen Charlotte, to whom he was appointed physician extraordinary in 1764. He was the first professor of anatomy in the Royal Academy (1768), and president of the Medical Society (1781). His chief work is *On the Human Gravid Uterus* (1774, Latin), the material for which took him twenty-five years to collect. It has been edited by Baillie (1794) and Rigby (1843). He also published *Medical Commentaries* (1762-64), and important papers on *Medical Observations and Inquiries.*

Hunter, William Alexander (1844-98), a lawyer, born in Aberdeen. He was educated at King's College, Aberdeen, where he greatly distinguished himself, and was called to the bar in 1867. In 1869 he was appointed professor of Roman law at University College, London, and of jurisprudence in 1878. He was an advocate for the higher education of women, and in 1890 secured free elementary education for Scotland. He published legal writings.

Hunter, Sir William Wilson (1840-1900), an Indian civilian and historian, was educated at Glasgow. He entered the Indian civil service in 1861 as assistant magistrate and collector in the district of Birbhum, but in 1869 was appointed by Lord Mayo to organise a statistical survey of the Indian empire, the new post of director-general of statistics being created for him in 1871. This work occupied him for twelve years, the compilation reaching 128 vols., but the whole was condensed into *The Imperial Gazetteer of India* (9 vols., 1881), his article on ' India ' being reissued in 1895 as *The Indian Empire: its Peoples, History, and Products*. He also published a *Comparative Dictionary of Non-Aryan Languages of India and High Asia* (1868), and made extensive collections for a history of India, one volume of which only appeared in his lifetime.

Hunter River, Coquon, or Coal River, a river of New South Wales, Australia, which rises in the Liverpool range. Its basin is an immense coal-field, and it flows into the Pacific at Port Hunter after a winding course of 300 m.

Hunting, *see* BIG GAME, FOX HUNTING, DEER STALKING, and SHOOTING.

Huntingdon, a bor. and co. seat of H. co., Pennsylvania, U.S.A., on the R. Juniata, 150 m. E. of Pittsburg. It is built on ground sloping to the river, which is used for water-power. The manufs. include: stationery, flour, furniture, radiators, and drain pipes; the surrounding country is rich in coal, iron, limestone, and fireclay. The town was named after the Countess of H. in 1767. Pop. (1911) 6861.

Huntingdon, a market tn. and municipal bor., and the co. tn. of Huntingdonshire, situated on the l. b. of the Ouse, 59 m. N. of London. Among the public buildings of the town are the town hall, dating from 1745, the county gaol and barracks, the county hospital, the Montagu Institute (1897), and All Saints Church, which contains several monuments of the Cromwell family. There is a racecourse at the bend of the Ouse to the S. of the town, where meetings are held in August. The town is governed by a mayor, four aldermen, and twelve councillors. The industries are not important, the principal being brewing, carriage-building, and iron-founding; the town is the centre of an agricultural district. H. is an ancient town, was destroyed by the Danes in 1010, and several times occupied by the Royalists in the Civil War. Pop. (1911) 4003.

Huntingdon, Selina Hastings, Countess of (1707-91), a daughter of Washington Shirley, second Earl Ferrers, and married, in 1728, Theophilus, ninth Earl of H., of Donington Park, Leicestershire. She was converted to Methodism by her sister-in-law, Lady Margaret Hastings, and henceforth devoted most of her time and energy to religion and religious work. She became intimate with George Whitefield, and later with the Wesleys, and was a member of the first Methodist society founded in Fetter Lane, London, in 1739. She erected a chapel in Brighton in 1761, and afterwards at such other fashionable resorts as Bath and Tunbridge Wells, in the hopes of attracting to her ' connection ' members of the upper classes. In 1767 she rented Trevecca House, in N. Wales, as a training institute for members of her religious conviction, and subsequently extended her operation to America, though she never visited that continent. There is an anonymous biography.

Huntingdonshire, or Hunts, an inland co. of England, an archdeaconry in the diocese of Ely and the prov. of Canterbury. The surface of the county, which is all below 500 ft., is gently varied in the W., the South, and the centre, whilst the E. and N.E. form part of the flat Fen district. The principal rivers are the Ouse and the Nen. The chief industries are agriculture and grazing; there are no minerals of importance, and other industries, which are also not very important, include brick-making, paper-making, brewing, malting, leather, and iron-founding. From a geological point of view the whole county, save for a small portion in the N.E., belongs to the Oölite rocks. Area of administrative county 233,984 acres. Pop. (1911) 55,577.

Huntington, the name of several places in the United States: 1. The co. seat of H. co., Indiana, on the R. Little, 25 m. S.W. of Fort Wayne. It has a public library, a business college and a central college, and limestone quarries and manufs. of wooden articles. Pop. (1910) 10,272. 2. A city and co. seat of Cabell co. in the state of W. Virginia, on the S. bank of the Ohio R., 50 m. W. of Charleston. Among the principal buildings are the state asylum for incurable lunatics, the county hospital, and a Carnegie library. It has car and railway waggon-repairing shops, machine shops, steel rolling mills, breweries, and gas-works. Pop. (1910) 31,161. 3. A township of Suffolk co., New York, on the N. side of Long Is. The southern part is occupied in market gardening, but along the Sound are the villages of H., Cold Spring Harbour, Centreport, and Northport, where many New York business men have residences. Pop. (1910) 12,004. 4. A tn. in Fairfield co., Connecticut, 15 m. W. of New Haven. Pop. (1910) 6545.

Huntington, Daniel (1816-1906), an American artist, born in New York. After studying under S. F. B. Morse, he produced ' A Bar-room Politician,' and ' A Toper Asleep ' (1837), one of his best-known works. After painting some landscapes on the Hudson R., he went to study at Rome in 1839, and on his return began portrait painting. In 1844 he again went to Rome, but returned in 1846 to New York. His best work has been done in portraiture, though he has also painted many religious and historical subjects, and landscapes. He was president of the National Academy from 1862 to 1869, and again from 1877 to 1891. Amongst his works may be mentioned, ' Queen Mary signing the death-warrant of Lady Jane Grey ' ; ' Mercy's Dream,' 1850 ; ' Sowing the Word,' 1869; ' St. Jerome,' 1870; and amongst his portraits, those of President Lincoln, W. C. Bryant, John Sherman, President van Buren, J. A. Dix, etc.

Huntington, Robert, D.D. (1636-1701), an English divine and Orientalist, was educated at Bristol Grammar School and Merton College, Oxford. He took his B.A. in 1657, and his M.A. in 1662; in 1670 he obtained the post of chaplain to the Levant Company and went to Aleppo. Here, until 1681, he passed his time in the study of Oriental languages and the collection of rare MSS. On his return home he received the degrees of B.D. and D.D. in 1683, in which year he was also made Provost of Trinity College, Dublin, on office which he held until 1692. He quitted Ireland in 1688, but returned after the battle of the Boyne. Shortly before his death he was made Bishop of Raphoe.

Huntingtower and Ruthvenfield, united villages of Perthshire, Scotland, situated in Tibbermore parish. The castle, which belonged to the earls of Gowrie, was the scene of the ' Raid of Ruthven ' in 1582, when James VI., then a boy, was kidnapped. There are bleachfields, which were established in 1774; these are fed with water from a Roman aqueduct, from the little river Almond.

Huntly, a market tn. of Aberdeenshire, Scotland. situated at the junction of the Bogie and Deveron, 9 m. S.E. of Keith, and 40 m. N.W. of Aberdeen. The ruins of Huntly, or Strathbogie castle are in the vicinity. H. is a prosperous town, lying in a rich agricultural district, with a trade in farm produce, and manufs. of farm implements. Pop. (1911) 4937.

Huntsville, the cap. of Madison co., Alabama, U.S.A. It is situated near the northern boundary of the state, 10 m. N. of the Tennessee R. Indian corn, cotton, and fruit are cultivated, and cotton is extensively manufactured. Iron and coal are found, and marble is quarried. Pop. (1910) 7611.

Hunucma, a small tn. of Mexico, situated in Yucatan, about 20 m. N.W. by W. of Mirida. Pop. 9000.

Hunyadi Janos, the name of a spring of mineral waters, situated in the neighbourhood of Budapest. The waters have considerable medicinal value, containing 15·9 per cent. sulphate of soda, 16 per cent. sulphate of magnesia, 1·3 per cent. chloride of sodium, and ·5 per cent. carbonic acid.

Hunyadi Janos, or **John Corvinus Hunyadi** (c. 1387-1456), an eminent Hungarian soldier, born at Hunyad in Transylvania. At an early age he entered the service of King Sigismund and distinguished himself in the Hussite wars. After the death of Albert in 1439, he aided in the election of Ladislaus III., who made him voivode of Transylvania, and captain of the fortress of Belgrade. In subsequent struggles with the Turks he won victories at Szendo (1441), at Szentimne, and the Iron Gates of the Danube (1442), but was defeated in 1444 at Varna, where the king met his death. H. was made governor of the country during the minority of Ladislaus V., but had continually to contend against the jealousy of Gara and the Czillei. In 1453 the king was declared of age, and H. organised a Turkish crusade, during which he won his last victory at Mendor Fehara in 1456, dying of plague in the camp three weeks after the battle. He was the first great Hungarian general in a modern sense, as he was the first to depend chiefly on strategy and tactics for his victories. His great personal influence was due to his natural genius allied with conspicuous nobility and integrity of character.

Hunza (also **Kanjut**) and **Nagar,** two small states on the N.W. frontier of Kashmir. The two states, though peopled by the same Dard race, were always at war, and when the Gilgit agency was established they turned their attention to the British agent. This led to the Hunza-Nagar expedition (1891) under Colonel A. Durand, the storming of Fort Nilt, and the subsequent occupation of the two states by British troops.

Huo-lu, or **Huai-lu,** a tn. of China, in the prov. of Chi-li, in 38° N. and 114° 26′ E. It is at the foot of the pass which leads from Chi-li to Shan-si, with which a trade in coal, iron, and pottery is carried on.

Huon Gulf, an extensive inlet, in the E. of German New Guinea, situated between lat. 6° 45′ and 7° 30′ S.; it possesses several fine harbours.

Huon of Bordeaux, the central

figure or hero of a 13th-century French *chanson de geste* called after his name. The poem is a mixture of the older historical epic and the later romances, and contains historical and purely legendary matter, the latter being marked by the character of the fairy Oberon or Auberon. It was printed in a prose version in 1516, and was translated into English by Lord Berners, 1540. *See* Gaston Paris' ed., 1898; Guissard and Grandmaison, *Anciens Poètes de la France*, 1860, and Sidney Lee's edition of Berners' trans., 1883.

Hupa, or **Hoopa,** the name of an Indian tribe who inhabit the Hoopa valley, California, and who formerly lived in villages by the Lower Trinity R.

Hu-peh, a prov. of Central China, bounded on the N. by Ho-nan, S. by Hu-nan, E. by Ngan-hui, and W. by Shen-si and Szechuen. The main portion of the province is a plain through which flows the Han R. Agriculture is the chief industry, cotton, wheat, rape-seed, tobacco, and beans being grown; vegetable tallow also forms one of the principal exports. A small quantity of gold is found in the Han R.; and some coal is worked. Cap., Wu-chang-fu. Chief port, Hankow. The area is 70,450 sq. m., and the pop. 35,280,685.

Hura, a genus of Euphorbiaceæ, is a native of tropical America. The best-known of the very few species of *H. crepitans*, the sand-box tree or monkey's dinner-bell. The fruit of the tree is a depressed woody capsule, and when ripe it explodes to scatter the seeds. The juice is acrid and causes blindness, the seeds contain a purgative oil.

Hurd, Richard (1720-1808), an English divine and writer, born at Congreve, Staffordshire. He was ordained in 1742, and in 1750 was appointed preacher at Whitehall, through the influence of his friend William Warburton. In 1765 he was made preacher at Lincoln's Inn, and two years later archdeacon of Gloucester. In 1774, he was appointed to the see of Lichfield and Coventry, and became tutor to the Prince of Wales and Duke of York, being made bishop of Worcester in 1781. His residence, Hartlebury Castle, contained a magnificent library. His works include: *Moral and Political Dialogues*, 1759; *Letters on Chivalry and Romance*, 1762; *Uses of Foreign Travel*, 1763; *Collected Works* (8 vols.), 1811.

Hurdis, James (1763-1801), an English man of letters, took holy orders, and in 1791 became vicar of Bishopstone. Such merits as his poems, *The Village Curate*, etc., possess may be traced to his friendship with Cowper,

Hurdoi, India, *see* HARDOI.

Hurdwar, India, *see* HARDWAR.

Hurdy-gurdy, a musical instrument, akin to the ' organistrum ' of which, indeed, it was a later development. In appearance it was something between a lute and a guitar. There were four or six strings in all, but only the first, called the ' chanterelle,' was reached by the movable frets or keys, so that it was possible to play a diatonic melody. The other strings were tuned as drones and were made to vibrate by the friction of a leather-covered and well-rosined wooden wheel turned by a handle with the right hand. This quaint instrument was invented by the Old French school (13th century), when it was developing polyphony over a pedal base.

Hurlford, a tn. of Ayrshire, Scotland, situated on the Irvine, 2 m. S. of Kilmarnock. The manuf. of fireclay is carried on, and there are coal mines and iron works. Pop. (1911) 4400.

Hurlingham Park, a fashionable resort of Fulham, London. The organisation of polo in England dates from its adoption by the Hurlingham Club in 1873, and the game is still played there. In 1867 the Hurlingham Pigeon-Shooting Club was formed, and the sport was carried on until its suppression in 1906.

Huron, a city of S. Dakota, U.S.A., co. seat of Beadle co. It stands on the r. b. of the James R., 103 m. E. of Pierre. Pop. (1910) 5791.

Huron, Lake, in point of size (23,200 sq. m.) the second of the five Great Lakes between Canada and the United States in N. America. It is bounded by Ontario except on the W. and S.W. where it adjoins Michigan. Grand Manitoulin Is., one of three thousand, and the peninsula of Cabot's Head divide the lake into two unequal sections, the northern consisting of North Channel and Georgian Bay. At the N. St. Mary's R. carries down water from Lake Superior, which is 20 ft. higher, whilst at the S. the St. Clair R. discharges into Lake Erie, which is 9 ft. lower; on the N.W. the Strait of Mackinac makes a connection with Lake Michigan. Lake Huron is 581 ft. above the sea and reaches a depth of 802 ft. It is subject to violent storms, and supplies plentiful salmon, trout, etc., to fishermen. Its trade facilities will be greatly increased on the completion of the ship canal connecting Georgian Bay with Montreal (begun in 1910).

Huronian, the name of a class of rocks which belong to the pre-Cambrian group; the H. rocks are divided into three subdivisions, upper, middle, and lower, each having marked unconformity from the rocks lying below and above. They consist of more or less metamorphosed sedimentary rocks, and, in Canada especially, valuable deposits of most of the important metals are found therein. Generally speaking, the H. rocks comprise quartzite, and slate, limestone, and igneous rocks, in addition to the above ores. They are well developed in the following districts : In the Marquette region of N. Michigan, with quartzites, slates, and conglomerates, and schists or ferruginous cherts; in the Menominee district of Michigan and Wisconsin, and in the Perokee Gogebic district of the same states, with quartzite, shales, and limestones, having beds of diabase and olivine-gabbro; in the Mesabi and Vermilion districts of Minnesota, with valuable iron ores.

Hurons. The word comes from the French *Huré*, bristled, and was used as a word of contempt in the sense of 'lout'; it was applied by the French in Canada to the Indian tribes occupying a part of the country in Ontario which was called Huronia. The tribes were of Iroquoian descent, and formed a confederacy called 'Wendat' (islanders), corrupted by the English into Wyandot (*q.v.*). The name is still found in the 'Hurons of Lorette' in Quebec and in the great Lake Huron.

Hurricane, a wind-storm. The word was borrowed in the 15th century by the Portuguese navigators from the Caribbeans, who described such a phenomenon by the word 'huracan.' H. has no special technical significance and is popularly used of any violent tempest, though, of course, it primarily referred to the sudden storms to which the West Indies are subject. Thus tornadoes, cyclones, and typhoons are all species of H. The tropical Hs. are whirling storms, the diameter of their circular motion being often as great as 300 m. Usually they travel in a westerly direction from the equatorial belt of calms which is their base, but in the Atlantic they sweep northward over the West Indies and then skirt the shores of the States in a north-easterly course. The winds blow spirally inward with a tremendous velocity, often 60 m. an hour, towards the centre of the swirl, which is also the centre of low pressure. The spiral movement does not reach the innermost circle, which is called the 'eye of the storm' and which extends for 10 m. or more. It should be noted that the direction of these inward-blowing air currents is counter-clockwise in the northern and in the opposite direction in the southern hemisphere. Above the circle of calm the skies are clear, but outside they are very overcast and torrential rains not infrequently descend. The duration of such a wind-storm may be only a few days or it may last many weeks. Fortunately, perhaps, they form mostly on the sea, where they are a great source of danger to ships, but if they pass, as sometimes, over an inhabited island they scatter the most wanton destruction in their path, and even when this does not happen they often cause great damage by heaving up huge waves against the continental shores. 'Typhoons' is the specific name for similar wind-storms in Oriental seas. *See* CYCLONES and TORNADOES.

Hursley, a par. and vil. of Winchester, Hampshire, England, in the Andover div. John Keble, author of the *Christian Year,* was vicar here and is buried in the churchyard. There are also memorials to the Cromwell family. Pop. (1911) 940.

Hurst, Hal (*b.* 1865), an English painter, born in London. He started as an illustrator and did black-and-white sketches for newspapers and magazines in London, Paris, New York, and Philadelphia. He eventually settled in London and took up painting. He is especially successful as a portrait painter, and painted 'The First Court of King Edward VII., by command of King Edward. His portraits also include a fine picture of Mrs. Hal H. (1896). He has frequently exhibited in the Royal Academy, his best-known pictures being: 'Caught '; 'Entangled '; 'The Siren,' 1896; 'An Incantation '; 'Faith,' 1897; 'The Capture,' 1898; and 'On the Sands,' 1905.

Hurst Castle, a par. and castle of Hampshire, England, situated about 4 m. S.W. of Lymington. The castle was erected by Henry VIII. for the purpose of defending the Solent. Charles I. was imprisoned here (1648).

Hurstmonceaux, a vil. of Sussex, England, in the Eastbourne parl. div., 9 m. from Eastbourne. The name is derived from Waleran de Monceux, who was lord of the manor in the 11th century. There are interesting castle ruins in the village. Pop. (1911) 1438.

Hurstpierpont, a par. and tn. of Sussex, England. 8 m. N. of Brighton. Pop. (1911) 3112.

Hurtado de Mendoza, Diego (1503-75), a Spanish diplomatist, poet, and historian, born at Granada, and educated at the University of Salamanca, also attending lectures at Bologna, Padua, and Rome, whilst serving under Charles V. He was sent as ambassador to England in 1538, to

Venice in the following year, acted for some time as military governor of Siena, and represented the diplomatic interest of Spain at the Council of Trent. From 1547 to 1554 he was special plenipotentiary at Rome; being obliged in 1568 to leave the court on account of a quarrel with Philip II., he settled at Granada and devoted himself to the study of Arabic poetry and to the production of his best work, the *Guerra de Granada*, a history of the revolt of the Moors of Alpujanas under Philip II. This history, although written in 1572, was not published until 1627. His talents as a poet were of no mean order, and he popularised the classical Italian hendecasyllabics. He is generally allowed to be the author of that great picaresque novel, *Lazarillo de Tormes*. *See* A. Senán y Alonsa, *Diego Hurtado de Mendoza apuntes biográfico críticos,* 1886.

Husband and Wife. The consideration of the essentials to a validly celebrated marriage, and the various recognised forms, past and present, of the ceremony or contract of marriage itself, are not dealt with in this article, and will be found dealt with under MARRIAGE; and the subject of the dissolution of marriage will be found under ALIMONY, DIVORCE, JUDICIAL SEPARATION, and MARRIAGE. This article will be restricted to the rights and obligations arising from the relationship of husband and wife. The older theory of Roman law contemplated the wife as a mere chattel of the husband, and gave her no superior rights to those of her own daughters. The later Roman law went to the opposite extreme, allowed the relationship of husband and wife to be contracted and dissolved by the slenderest forms, and left the parties all but independent of each other. This evolution has found its parallel in the social systems of many modern states, both as regards the personal freedom of the wife and the immunity of her separate property from the dominion of her husband. In the light of the latter-day Feminist movement, nothing could well be more extraordinary than the complacent platitudes of mediæval lawyers to the effect that the whole of a wife's personal property automatically passed to her husband on marriage, together with the rents and profits of her estates of inheritance, while her person was so far subjected to his will that he enjoyed the ancient privilege of administering moderate chastisement. This last-mentioned privilege according to Blackstone, had only begun to be ' doubted ' in the ' polite reign of Charles II.,' although, adds the classic commentator, the lower

classes still exert it. The lamentable facts of police court proceedings prove that they continue to do so at the present day, even without the saving grace of a shadowy privilege.

Theoretically each spouse has a legal right to the society and presence (*consortium*) of the other, but neither the petition for restitution of conjugal rights nor any other proceeding will avail to enforce that right. A husband has no legal right to restrain his wife from leaving him, and will even be ordered by the court to abstain from molesting her if she choose to stay away. Indeed, any physical compulsion put upon a wife is illegal, and in many cases would amount to cruelty so as to found a claim for judicial separation (*q.v.*). On the other hand, if a wife choose to leave her husband without adequate cause he is entitled to refuse to admit her into his home again; and the converse probably also applies. The suit for restitution of conjugal rights is now no more than a formal condition precedent to the subsequent formulation of a charge of desertion. The practical value of *consortium* lies in the right of the husband to bring an action of damages against a third party who has ' enticed away ' his wife, though the archaisms of the law still survive in the denial to a wife of a corresponding action. The action of *crim. con.* (criminal conversation), as it was called, for damages in trespass against another man who has committed adultery with his wife, was abolished on the establishment of the Divorce Court in 1857, and probably damages can only be obtained against an adulterer by giving him as co-respondent in a divorce petition; for it seems to be the better opinion that even the above-noticed action for enticing away is competent only to the case of one who is deprived of the services of his employees (*see* further on this. Jenks, *Husband and Wife in the Law* (Dent & Sons), 1909, and Pollock, *On Torts*). But each spouse may sue for damages for the loss of the ' comfort and society ' of the other spouse where the latter has been physically injured by the negligence or intentional wrongdoing of a third party. By a legal anomaly, however, the claim for damages when death results is restricted to the actual pecuniary loss sustained.

By the old common law the father, as the legal guardian by nature and nurture, has the complete control over the person, the education, and religious upbringing of his children during his lifetime; but covenants in separation deeds not to insist on the custody of children will bar the right, as, of course, will an order of the

Divorce Court with respect to the custody of children. But either parent convicted of cruelty to a child under sixteen may be deprived of the custody of it.

Rights of husband and wife in one another's property, and obligations arising from marriage.—The ancient maxim of the common law, and one eminently in accordance with feudal principles, was that husband and wife were one in the eye of the law. But this unity on its proprietary side was entirely for the benefit of the husband. The wife's freeholds became vested in the husband and herself jointly during coverture (*q.v.*); but the husband had the sole management and took the rents and profits, while if the wife predeceased him, he had a life estate in the wife's freeholds called a tenancy by curtesy (*see* under CURTESY). Further, the wife's personal property comprising leaseholds, and choses in action when reduced into possession (*see* under CHOSE IN ACTION), passed to the husband on marriage or became his if and when subsequently acquired by the wife. First equity (*q.v.*), and then statute law encroached upon, and finally whittled away, practically all these marital rights. Equity modified the common law by the doctrine of the ' separate use,' by which any property expressly given to the wife before or after marriage ' for her separate use ' was free from the husband's control, subject to the husband's claim to any part of it undisposed of by her at her death, and by the ' restraint or anticipation ' which, when attached to a gift of property to her, effectually kept that property free from her husband's persuasive influence, so far as prospective income was due, by the simple fact that she herself could not anticipate it. The Married Women's Property Act, 1882, effected a radical change in the wife's proprietary position, though the old law, as modified by equity and statute law prior to 1882, still applies to women married before Jan. 1, 1883. The Act of 1882 makes a married woman as free to enter into contracts as a *feme sole* (*i.e.* an unmarried woman) and her contracts will bind her separate estate so far as not restrained from anticipation; and, generally speaking, the Act puts a married woman in the same position as an unmarried woman with respect to all her property. But the husband still has the right to her property by survivorship if she dies intestate. Further the Act applies to all women married before Jan. 1, 1883, *as regards all property acquired by them since that date.* It is to be noted that notwithstanding the existence of a clause restraining the wife from anticipation, the court may, under the Conveyancing Act, 1881, bind her interest for her benefit and with her consent, and in any case the clause will not save her property from liability for her ante-nuptial debts, except to the extent of any part of her property that had not actually reached her hands when the debt was incurred. By an Act passed in 1893 a married woman's contracts bind not only her property in her possession at the time of making the contract, but all property she may acquire subsequently. With this enfranchisement of the wife's property there have been corresponding augmentations of such rights as she had in the property of her husband. At common law a widow was entitled to a dower or a life income of one-third of her husband's freeholds of inheritance, whether he had disposed of them prior to his death or not. This right was illusory by reason of the conveyancing device known as ' uses to bar dower,' and the Dower Act, 1833, made her claim subject to the husband's debts or dispositions, and even to any expression of his intention in his will or in a deed that any land should be exempt from dower. But equity gave her a right to dower out of her husband's equitable estates of freehold so far as not disposed of by him. The wife is still legally entitled to dower, but in practice settlements usually contain declarations against dower. (Jointure (*q.v.*) also bars dower.) But on the other hand, a wife now has stronger claims on her husband's personalty, assuming he dies intestate (*see* DISTRIBUTIONS, STATUTES OF). There is nothing to prevent the husband, any more than the wife, from willing away the whole of his personalty from his wife.

Husbands generally make their wives a periodical allowance for housekeeping. Strictly the wife can be called upon to account for every penny of this expended by her. If she saves any of it, the balance belongs to her husband, and if she invests such savings or puts them into her banking account the husband can get an order of the court summarily transferring such investment or savings into his own account, though if the wife disputes his title, he must prove that he had no intention of giving her any surplus. Each spouse can sue the other and bring criminal proceedings against the other for the protection of his or her separate property. But by the Married Women's Property Act, a married woman may not proceed criminally against her husband while they are living together, nor after they are separated, as to wrongs to her property committed before separation, except in respect of property wrongfully taken by the husband on leaving or deserting her.

It is a dogma of English law that the husband has the right to choose the house, and if the house is in his name, it follows, not from the matrimonial relationship, but as an ordinary result of the law of contract, that the husband has the right to allocate the rooms for various purposes, and, generally speaking, regulate the domestic arrangements. It need hardly be said that a husband who made an oppressive use of his contractual right might not only lose his wife, but would not even have the doubtful consolation of proceeding against her for desertion. If, of course, the wife leased or bought the house, or if it stands in her name, she can legally exclude the husband from entering it.

Each spouse is assumed to have undertaken the maintenance of the other and of the children of the marriage (including such illegitimate or other children as the wife may have had in marriage). But apart from payments ordered by a magistrate to be made for the support of a deserted wife on a separation order, the only means of enforcing the undertaking to maintain is through the Poor Law officers, if and when the children or wife become chargeable to parish relief. But the wife may pledge her husband's credit for necessaries for herself and the children, even where she has separate property of her own. The wife's liability for maintenance apparently only arises on the entire failure of the husband. But the law is by no means clear as to the exact circumstances when the wife's property can be resorted to for this purpose. Apart from the purchase of necessaries, the wife has no right to pledge her husband's credit, and it is unwise for tradesmen to assume that she has, for the reason that the husband can rebut the presumption that he has authorised his wife to pledge his credit, by proving either that he has expressly or impliedly forbidden her to do so, or that he makes her a sufficient allowance. If the husband by paying bills leads a particular tradesman to believe his wife has authority, he must give the tradesman express notice that he gives no further authorisation, if he desires to prevent the wife from further pledging his credit with that tradesman. The mere fact that a tradesman enters purchases in the wife's name and that she invariably pays with her own cheques, and that the tradesman did not know she was a married woman,

will not make her separate property liable if, in fact, she did not contract otherwise than as her husband's agent (Paquin *v.* Beauclerk, 1906, Appeal Cases, 148).

The husband is liable for the wife's ante-nuptial debts only to the extent of any property he may have acquired through her; but the wife is liable to the full extent of her separate property. A married woman can only be made *personally* liable on her debts so as to be amenable to the bankruptcy laws, if she trades apart from her husband. For his wife's antenuptial civil wrongs the husband's liability is similarly restricted, but he is liable without limitation jointly with the wife for civil wrongs (torts) committed by her during marriage, provided the parties were cohabiting at the time. But the wife incurs no liability in respect of her husband's debts or civil wrongs. As to the presumption that a married woman's crimes are presumed to have been committed under the coercion of her husband, and as to the criminal liability generally of married women, *see* under CRIMINAL LAW. Neither spouse can give evidence against the other when the latter is charged with a criminal offence; but by the Criminal Evidence Act, 1898, such spouse can give evidence on behalf of the other if requested so to do by the accused spouse. But in all civil proceedings both husband and wife can, generally speaking, be compelled to give evidence for and against each other (*see* EVIDENCE). In the absence of fraud a policy taken out by the husband and expressed to be for the benefit of his wife or children or both, can never be touched by his creditors. A husband is liable for his wife's income tax, and apparently if she refuses to pay and he cannot, he can be kept in prison until she does pay.

The Scots law of husband and wife is not now markedly dissimilar to the English, since the passing of the Married Women's Property (Scotland) Act, 1881. The wife has a separate estate in her movables, and the rents and profits of her heritable property belong to her. Parties married before the Act can come under its operation by mutual deed, and in any case come under the Act unless the husband, before marriage, has by irrevocable deed made reasonable provision for his wife in the event of her surviving him. The wife is not entitled to assign her prospective income from movables or dispose of her movables without her husband's consent. The husband has a right of succession to his wife's movables if she die intestate. *See* E. Jenks, *Husband and Wife in the Law* (J. M. Dent & Sons), 1909;

Lush, *Law of Husband and Wife*, 1910; Pollock, *On Torts*.

Husi, Hushi, or **Husch,** a tn. of Roumania, Moldavia, situated 9 m. W. of the Russian border. Wine is largely produced, and there is a noted yearly fair. The treaty of Pruth, between Turkey and Russia, was here signed in 1711. Pop. 16,000.

Huskisson, William (1770-1830), a statesman, after a preliminary grounding in affairs as private secretary to Lord Gower, the British ambassador at Paris, and then as secretary to the Admiralty, took his seat in parliament in 1796. From 1804 he held various minor offices, and in 1827 became Colonial Secretary, and leader of the House of Commons under Goderich, and retained these positions under Wellington, with whom, however, he presently disagreed, and from whose ministry he then retired. He was run over by an engine at the opening of the Manchester and Liverpool Railway on Sept. 15, 1830, and died in great agony the same day. There is a biography by J. Wright (1831).

Huss (or Hus), John (c. 1373-1415), a Bohemian religious reformer, born at Hussinecz in Bohemia. Hus was the name which he adopted himself, about 1396, as before then he was known as Johann Hussinecz, or de Hussynecz. He was educated at an elementary school, and the University of Prague, where he became B.A. in 1393; Bach. of Theol. in 1394, and M.A. in 1396. In 1400 he was ordained, and in 1402 was made rector of the University of Prague. The pro-Wyclif sentiments of H. gradually made him suspected of heresy, and his protest against the burning of Wyclif's books by the Archbishop of Prague in 1410 caused his excommunication. His support of the king in his policy to the papal schism, made him exceedingly popular, and although in 1411 the whole city of Prague was laid under an interdict, H. still preached and carried on his duties as usual. In the following year however, he was obliged to quit Prague, and whilst in seclusion, he wrote his *De Ecclesia*, his greatest work. In 1414 he was summoned to attend the council at Constance between King Sigismund and Pope John XXIII., and was granted a ' safe-conduct ' by the former. Nevertheless, he was imprisoned soon after his arrival, and, on his appearance before the council in 1415, was ordered to recant all his doctrines which were held to be heretical. On his refusal he was condemned to the stake, and met a martyr's death with exemplary fortitude on July 6. H. was a scholar of deep erudition, as

is proved by his *Super IV. Sententiarum*, but his principal glory was his spiritual teaching and his great influence for freedom. His works may be divided into four classes: (1) Dogmatical and polemical; (2) homiletical; (3) exegetical; (4) epistolary. See *Joannes Hus Opera Omnia*, edited by Flajshans (1904). *See also* Count Lützow, *Life and Times of John Huss*, 1909; W. Berger, *Joannes Hus and Konig Sigismund*, 1871.

Hussars, originally the name of the Hungarian cavalry raised by Matthias I. in 1458. The word is derived from the Hungarian *husz*, meaning twenty, as every twentieth house had to furnish a man for the corps. The arms and dress of this cavalry were imitated, and the word borrowed by other nations. The dress of a H. consisted of a busby, a heavily braided jacket, and a loose coat worn on the left shoulder. The regiments so-called in the British army are the 7th, 8th, 10th, 11th, 13th, 14th, 15th, 18th, 19th, 20th Hussars.

Hussites, War of, the name given to the struggle between the Bohemian followers of Huss and King Sigismund, which began in 1419. The popular feeling was stirred up by the news of the martyrdom of Huss, and in 1415 the nobles of Bohemia and Moravia sent the *protestatio Bohemorum*, couched in very strong terms, to the Council at Constance ; the contemptuous attitude of Sigismund, who declared that he would ' drown all Wycliffites and Hussites,' finally brought on the war. The Hussites were victorious at Ziskaberg in 1420 Deutsch Brod in 1422, Aussig in 1426, and Taus in 1431, and invaded Silesia, Saxony, and Franconia many times with success. After Taus negotiations were begun, and by the compact of Prague the moderate party of the Hussites gained their ends. There were, however, two opposing parties in the Hussite movement, the Utraquists and the Taborites. The former, who were also known as Calixtenes (Lat. *calix*, chalice), derived their name from the fact that their demand was for the communion in both kinds (*sub utraque specie*). The Taborites (from Tabor, their headquarters) were more advanced in their views and rejected most of the ceremonial of the Roman Church. The latter party refused to accept the compact of Prague, but was totally defeated by the Utraquists at Lipan in 1534. The Utraquist creed was that of the established Church of Bohemia, until all non - Roman creeds were prohibited in 1620. For a later development of the Taborites see *Bohemian Brethren*. *See also* E. Denis, *Huss et la guerre des Hussites*, 1878; H. Toman,

Husitské Valecnictor, 1878; L. Krum-
mell, *Utraquisten und Taboriten*,
1871, etc.

Husum, a tn. of Prussia, in Schleswig-Holstein, situated on the Husumer
Au, about 3 m. from the North Sea.
There is a steamboat service with
the N. Frisian Islands, and a trade
in cattle with England. The oyster
fisheries are important. Pop. 9429.

Hutcheson, Francis (1694-1746), an
Irish philosopher, born at Drumalig,
co. Down, and educated at Glasgow,
where he studied philosophy, classics,
literature, and theology. On leaving
Glasgow he was ordained and was on
the point of accepting a Presbyterian
ministry when he was persuaded to
start a private academy in Dublin.
While employed here, he published an
*Inquiry into the Original of our Ideas
of Beauty and Virtue*, 1725, followed
by an *Essay on the Passions and
Affections*, 1728. These writings
probably led to his election to the
chair of moral philosophy at Glasgow
in 1729, where he spent the remainder
of his life lecturing on a variety of
subjects. H.'s ethical writings constitute his chief claim to recollection,
and the best account of his teaching
is in Prof. Fowler's *Shaftesbury and
Hutcheson*. His greatest work is *A
System of Moral Philosophy*, 1755.
He adopted Lord Shaftesbury's views
in this direction, and exercised a
great influence upon the Scottish
philosophy of the modern school. *See*
Leechman, *Life*.

Hutchinson, a city of Kansas,
U.S.A., in Reno co. It is situated on
the R. Arkansas, and has salt works,
sugar factories, and meat-packing
works. Pop. (1910) 16,346.

Hutchinson, Anne (c. 1590-1643),
an American religious enthusiast,
daughter of a Lincolnshire clergyman
named Marbury. She married in 1634
and emigrated to Boston, Massachusetts, where she lectured, and was
a follower and admirer of the Rev.
John Cotton. She denounced the
Massachusetts clergy, and was tried
for heresy and sedition, and banished.
She then established a settlement on
Rhode Island, and set up a democracy (1638). Four years later, after
the death of her husband, she settled
on Long Island Sound in what is now
New York State, and was killed in
an Indian rising. A. H. and her
followers were known as Anti-
nomians. *See* C. F. Adams, *Anti-
nomianism in the Colony of Massachusetts Bay*.

Hutchinson, John (1615-64), an
English Puritan statesman, born at
Nottingham. Educated at Nottingham and Lincoln free schools and
later at Peterhouse, Cambridge. He
entered Lincoln's Inn in 1637 to study

law, but devoted himself rather to
music and divinity. In 1642 he entered the army of parliament with
the rank of lieut.-colonel, and was
appointed governor of Nottingham
castle and town. In 1646 he was returned to parliament as member for
Nottinghamshire. He was elected
member for the first two councils of
state of the commonwealth, but with
the expulsion of the Long Parliament
in 1653, retired into private life. After
the Restoration he was falsely accused of treasonable conspiracy and
confined to the Tower and Sandown
Castle from 1662 till 1664, dying at
the latter place.

Hutchinson, John (1674-1737), an
English theological writer, born at
Spennithorne, Yorkshire. He first
served as steward to the Duke of
Somerset, and other families of position, but ultimately devoted himself
to religious studies. In 1724 he published *Moses Principia* (Part I.), followed in 1727 by Part II., and by
many other works, including *Moses
Sine Principio, Power Essential and
Mechanical, Glory or Gravity, The
Religion of Satan*, etc. According to
H., the Bible contained the elements
of all rational philosophy as well as of
true religion. *See* Life by Spearman
in H.'s *Works*.

Hutchinson, John (1832-1910), a
Scottish sculptor, born in Edinburgh.
He first took to wood-carving, at the
same time attending an art school,
and then went to Rome for a time,
finally graduating as a sculptor. He
exhibited at the London Gallery in
1862, and became an academician in
1867, and librarian and treasurer in
1877 and 1886 respectively. His
principal work consists of statues of
Robert Bruce, John Knox, Queen
Victoria, the Prince Consort, etc.

**Hutchinson, Sir Jonathan, F.R.C.S.,
M.D., LL.D., F.R.S.** (1828-1913), an
English surgeon, born at Selby,
Yorkshire, where he was educated,
and afterwards entered St. Bartholo-
mew's Hospital. In 1884 he was
elected a member of the Royal Com-
mission on Smallpox Hospitals, and
in 1890-96 was on the Vaccination
Committee. In 1889 he was president
of the Royal College of Surgeons.
Amongst his publications are: *Rare
Diseases of the Skin; Illustrations of
Clinical Surgery; The Pedigree of
Disease; Fish-eating and Leprosy;
Syphilitic Affections of the Eye and
Ear;* and a *Lesser Atlas of Clinical
Illustrations*.

Hutt, Lower, a tn. of New Zealand,
in North Is., situated in Hutt co.,
10 m. N.E. of Wellington. Pop. 3400.

Hutten, Philip von (c. 1515-46) a
German adventurer, born at Birkenfeld, and a relative of Ulrich von

H. He joined a band of 600 adventurers from all parts of Europe in 1535, who went out to conquer the province of Venezuela granted to the Welsers of Augsburg by Charles V. In 1541 he set out at the head of an expedition to seek the mythical El Dorado, and after wandering about for some years returned to Venezuela to find the viceroyalty usurped by Juan de Caravajal, who seized H. and treacherously put him to death. See *Zeitung aus India Junkher Philipps von Hutten,* 1785.

Hutten, Ulrich von (1488-1523), a German poet and author, born at the castle of Steckelberg in Hesse. He was the eldest son of a noble but undistinguished family and was destined by his father for the cloister, being of feeble health. He was sent to the monastery of Fulda, but greatly disliked the life there, and in 1505 fled, going first to Cologne and afterwards to Erfurt and Frankfort-on-Oder, where he took his master's degree and published his first poem. He went from there to Wittenberg and Leipzig, and then passed into Italy, where he was plundered in the war of 1812 at the siege of Pavia, and later took service in the emperor's army. In 1517 he returned to Germany and had bestowed upon him, by the Emperor Maximilian, the laureate crown. While in Italy H. became imbued with a hatred of the papacy, and on his return to his native land he established a small printing press of his own, and issued pamphlets in German, violently denouncing the Roman clergy. He in turn was denounced at Rome by the Archbishop Albert, and availed himself of the protection of Franz von Sickingen, the champion of the knightly order. He was, however, soon forced to flee from the latter's castle and went to Basle, where he quarrelled with Erasmus, who did not approve of his extreme measures. From this time onwards till his death, which occurred at Zurich, he lived a wandering life. His chief works were : *Ars versificandi; Nemo; Vadisimus; Epistolæ,* and many admirable poems in Latin and German. See D. F. Strauss, *Ulrich von Hutten.*

Hutter, Leonhard (1563-1616), a German Lutheran theologian, born at Nellingen, near Ulm. He studied at various universities and then lectured for some years at Jena, afterwards becoming professor at Wittenberg, where he died. H. was a resolute defender of Lutheran orthodoxy, and attacked Calvinist doctrines in his *Concordia Concors.* His chief work was the *Compendium Locorum Theologicorum* (reprinted 1863).

Hutton, Charles (1737-1823), an English mathematician, born at Newcastle-on-Tyne. He was educated chiefly at a school in Jesmond, where he eventually became master. In 1760 he opened a school at Newcastle, amongst his pupils being John Scott, afterwards Lord Eldon, Chancellor of England. In 1764 he published his first work *The Schoolmaster's Guide,* followed in 1770 by a *Treatise on Mensuration both in Theory and Practice.* In 1778 appeared *Philosophical Transactions.* His *Mathematical and Philosophical Dictionary,* published in 1795, was a valuable contribution to scientific biography. *See* John Bruce, *Charles Hutton,* 1823.

Hutton, Sir Edward Thomas Henry (b. 1848), an English general, born at Torquay, educated at Eton, and in 1867 joined the 60th Rifles. In 1879 he served in the Zulu War, and in 1881 in the first Boer War. In 1882 he commanded an infantry corps in the Egyptian War and took part in operations at Alexandria. From 1893-96 he was in command of the military forces in New South Wales and subsequently, in the Eastern Transvaal, commanded the mounted troops on the flank of Lord Roberts' advance. He has published numerous pamphlets on military matters.

Hutton, Frederick Wollaston (1836-1905), a scientist and geologist, born at Gate Burton, Lincolnshire; educated at Southwell and the Naval Academy, Gosport, afterwards serving for three years in the Indian mercantile marine. In 1866 he emigrated to New Zealand and was appointed assistant-geologist to the Geological Survey there. In 1873 he became curator of the Otago Museum, and four years later professor of biology at the New Zealand University. Besides numerous scientific papers, H. was the author of *Darwinism and Lamarckism; The Lesson of Evolution;* and ' What is Life?' (*Hibbert Journal*), 1905.

Hutton, James (1726-97), a Scottish geologist, born at Edinburgh, and educated at the university there. He took up successively law, medicine, and agriculture. In 1768 he established himself in Edinburgh, where he devoted his life to literary and scientific research. In 1785 he published his *Theory of the Earth,* followed in 1792 by *Dissertations on Different Subjects in Natural Philosophy,* and *An Investigation of the Principles of Knowledge and of the Progress of Reason.* For biography of H., *see* Playfair, vol. v. of *Transactions of the Royal Society of Edinburgh.*

Hutton, Maurice, M.A., M.B.

(b. 1870), a professor of Greek and principal of University College, Toronto, educated at Glasgow Academy and Glasgow and Edinburgh Universities, graduating at the former as M.B. and O.M. with honours. He was the most distinguished graduate of the year in 1898, and obtained the Brunton Memorial prize. In 1899 he was resident physician at the Western Infirmary, Glasgow, and from 1900 to 1908 senior demonstrator of anatomy and lecturer in regional anatomy at Glasgow University. He has published several papers on anatomy in different medical journals.

Hutton, Richard Holt (1826-97), an English journalist and critic, born at Leeds. The son of a Unitarian minister, he was educated at University College School with a view to following in his father's footsteps, but finding no adequate sphere in the ministry, he became principal of University Hall. In 1861 he became joint-editor, with Meredith Townsend, of the *Spectator*, and in this capacity influenced a wide circle of readers by his weekly religious and literary contributions. His best work is shown in *Essays, Theological and Literary*, and he also wrote *Lives of Scott and Newman*. *See* Hogben's *Richard Holt Hutton of the Spectator* 1900.

Hutton, William (1723-1815), an English historian and topographer, born at Derby. He received a very poor education, and in 1749 opened a small bookshop at Southwell, Notts. The following year he settled in Birmingham and began contributing to magazines, and in 1781 published his *History of Birmingham*. Other of his publications are : *History of Derby; Edgar and Elfrida*, a poem; *Remarks upon N. Wales; Poems, Chiefly Tales; The Barbers, or The Road to Riches*, a poem, etc. *See* Phillip's *Annual History of Public Characters*, 1802.

Huxley, Thomas Henry (1825-95), an English scientist, born at Ealing. He matriculated at London University in 1842, and afterwards obtained a scholarship at the Charing Cross Hospital. Here he accomplished a great deal of work, and in 1845 announced his discovery of that layer of cells in the root-sheath of hair which now bears his name. The same year he graduated M.B. in London University, and from 1846-50 was assistant - surgeon on H.M.S. *Rattlesnake*. During the voyage he devoted himself to the study of animals, and established a morphological plan, dividing Hydrozoa into Radiata and Nematophora. In 1851 he was made F.R.S., became lecturer on natural history at the Royal School of Mines in 1854, and

naturalist to the geological survey the following year. From 1855-59 he published works chiefly dealing with fossil forms, the most important of which are his memoirs on Cephalaspis and Pteraspis (1858), the accounts of the Eurypterina (1856-59), and the description of Dicynodon, Rhamphorhynchus, and other reptiles. But one of his most brilliant successes was his *Theory of the Vertebrate Skull*, 1858, which was read before the Royal Society. In 1859 he published the *Origin of Species*, and in 1863 *Zoological Evidences as to Man's Place in Nature*, as well as *On the Causes of the Phenomena of Organic Nature*, both of which were widely read and discussed. In 1866 appeared his *Elementary Lessons in Physiology*, his *Manual of the Comparative Anatomy of Vertebrated Animals*, 1871, and *Elementary Biology* (with Martin) in 1875. But H's. publications do not represent all his work. He also filled many important posts. He was an active member of four royal commissions, including that of the sea-fisheries of the United Kingdom (1864-65), Hunterian professor at the Royal College of Surgeons (1863-69), Fullerian professor at the Royal Institution (1863-67), president of the Royal Society (1883-85), inspector of fisheries (1881-85), and rector of Aberdeen University (1872-74). Besides this he took a great interest in education, and was one of the original members of the School Board for London (1870-72).

Huy, a tn. in the prov. of Liège, Belgium. It stands on the Meuse, about 17 m. S.W. of the town of Liège, and is engaged in distilling and the manufacture of paper. H. possesses a citadel, and near by are the ruins of the abbey of Neufmoustier, the burial-place of Peter the Hermit, its founder. Pop. about 14,600.

Huygens, Christian (1629-95), a Dutch mathematician and physicist, born at the Hague. He studied at Leyden and Breda, and from 1649-55 resided alternately at Denmark, Holland, France, and England. He soon developed a strong mathematical bent, and his future greatness was predicted by Descartes. In 1651 he entered the lists of science, and his first essay, *Exetasis quadraturæ circuli*, was quickly followed by *Theoremata de quadratura hyperboles, ellipsis, et circuli*. In 1655 he discovered a satellite of Saturn, and in 1659, the ring of Saturn. H. was one of the first to apply the circular pendulum to the construction of clocks in 1656. In 1690 he published important treatises on light and weight. He also improved the telescope and developed the wave theory of light. His *magnum opus* was the *Horologium Os-cillatorium*, 1673, containing innumerable original discoveries. His researches in physical optics, however, constitute his chief title-deed to immortality. *See* P. Harting, *Christiaan Huygens in zijn Leuen en Werken geschetzl*, 1868.

Huygens, Constantijn (1596 - 1687), a Dutch poet, was born at the Hague. He devoted a great part of his time to politics, and was employed on one or two diplomatic missions. He has written works in Latin as well as in his own language, all of which testify to his originality. Among his works may be mentioned, *Momenta Desultoria*, 1644, and *Korenbloemen*, 1658.

Huysmans, Joris Karl (1848-1907), a novelist, of Dutch descent, but French by birth and culture. His early works are strongly realistic, but in middle age, after studying impressionism and mysticism, he gradually veered round to fervent religious idealism. His progress from the influence of Bandelaire and later of the French realists to devout Catholicism is evident in his works, from the realistic *En Menage*, 1881, through the transitional *A Rebours*, 1884, and *En Route*, 1895, to the great climax *La Cathédrale*, 1898, the epic of Chartres. This last work is scarcely a novel—it is too devoid of incident, too purely introspective; but it is full of beautiful writing and delicate insight into Christian symbolism, and is one of the greatest pieces of mystic literature ever penned. *L'Oblat*, 1905, and *Les Foules des Lourdes*, 1906, are his chief later works.

Huysum, Jan van (1682-1749), a Dutch painter, was born at Amsterdam. His best pictures are those of flowers and fruits, in which the exquisite colouring and truth of detail produce a close imitation of nature herself. His works are to be found in many of the continental galleries, and also in London.

Huyton with **Roby**, a par. and tn. of Lancashire, Eng., 5 m. E. of Liverpool, with coal-mines. Pop. (1911) 4559.

Huzara, India, *see* HAZARA.

Hven, or **Hveen,** an island of Sweden, situated in the Sound, 5 m. N.W. of Landskrona. Tycho Brahé lived here in his observatory until 1597.

Hwang-ho, *see* YELLOW RIVER.

Hwen-thsang, or **Hiouen-thsang** (*c.* 505-664), a Buddhist monk of China, born near Ho-nan. Between 629 and 645 A.D. he visited 110 different countries and places in India, studying the sacred books and districts. His *Memoirs of the Countries of the West* are an invaluable source for the history of the times. This work and a bibliography were translated into French by Stanislas Julien (1853-58). See *Hiouen Tsiang* (Trübner's Oriental Library, 1888).

Hyacinth, also called **Jacinth** (It. *giācinto*), in mineralogy, a variety of zircon. It is an uncommon mineral, and is found in the gem-gravels of Ceylon—some fine stones having been found in the form of pebbles in parts of New South Wales. The jacinth is described by some ancient writers as a yellow stone, whilst others refer to it as blue, which would appear to be our sapphire. Many of the gems sold as Hs. are in reality garnets, orange-brown hessonite, or cinnamon-stone. Optically it is simple to tell the difference, as the garnet has a single, and the H. a double power of refraction.

Hyacinth, the name applied to various plants of the order Liliaceæ, especially to those of the genus *Hyacinthus*. There are thirty species of this group, and all occur in Africa and round the Mediterranean; in Britain *H. orientalis*, with all its numerous varieties, is a favourite cultivated plant of the springtime, and the soil and climate of Holland seem peculiarly adapted to it. The wild H., well-known to British woods, called at times the English bluebell, is *Scilla nutans*, another liliaceous plant. It is bulbous, and the flowers are borne in graceful racemes. The grape-hyacinth, which also occurs in Britain, is *Muscari racemosum*.

Hyacinthe, Père (Charles Jean Marie Loyson) (*c.* 1872), an eminent French pulpit orator, born at Orleans. He entered the order of Carmelite monks and preached for some time at Lyons, going from there to Paris, where he attracted great crowds at the churches of St. Sulpice and Notre Dame. In 1869 he was excommunicated from his order for denouncing the abuses of the Church, but obtained a dispensation from his monastic vows and became l'Abbé Loyson. In 1871 he became a member of the Old Catholic Congress at Geneva, and the following year he married in London. In 1879 he established a Gallican congregation at Paris, having resigned his curacy in the Old Catholic Church at Geneva some years previously. *See* Puaux's *Le Père Hyacinthe et son église*, and L. W. Bacon's *Father Hyacinthe*, 1871.

Hyacinthus, in ancient mythology, the youngest son of the Spartan king Amyclas and Diomede; a youth of extraordinary beauty, beloved of Apollo and Zephyrus (Boreas). He returned the love of the former, but was indifferent to the latter, who, jealous of his rival, drove the discus of Apollo against the head of H. when they were playing quoits. The youth was killed by the blow, and from his blood there sprang the flower of the same name (hyacinth). H. was worshipped at Amyclæ as a hero, and the Hyacinthia, the second most important of Spartan festivals, was held in his honour.

Hyades (Gk. Ὑάδες, the rainy), in Greek mythology, were seven nymphs who were supposed to have nursed and protected Dionysus, and for their reward were placed in the constellation of the Bull. Their name is probably derived from the fact that their rising foretold wet weather, though other derivations have been suggested.

Hyæna, the name applied to the species of carnivorous mammals belonging to the family Hyænidæ, which range over Africa and Asia. They are massive animals, cat-like in appearance, with coarse, shaggy fur marked with irregular vertical stripes or large black spots; there are generally four toes, furnished with non-retractile claws; the hind limbs are shorter than the fore which adds to the ungainliness of their movements. The only living genus is *Hyæna*, whose species are mainly carrion-eaters, and are regarded by the Arabs with superstitious hatred; they produce a wailing, almost human-sounding, howl. *H. crocuta*, the spotted H., is limited to S. Africa, and *H. striata*, a striped species, is found in N. Africa and S. Asia. *Proteles cristatus*, the aard wolf of S. Africa, is sometimes included in this family.

Hyæna Dog, or Cape Hunting-dog, the name given to *Lycaon pictus*, a species of carnivorous mammals belonging to the family Camidæ and ranging over a large portion of S. Africa. It is remarkably hyæna-like in the markings of its fur and its long ears.

Hyalæidæ, the name of a family of gasteropod molluscs, commonly called the glass-shells, and synonymous with Cavoliniidæ. The principal genera are *Hyalea*, or *Cavolinia*, *Cuvierina*, *Cllo*, *Crescio*, *Hyalocylix*, and *Styliola*.

Hybla, the name of three ancient Sicilian cities: 1. *Hybla Major*, situated on the southern slope of Mt. Etna, and probably the site of the modern Paterno. 2. *Hybla*, called 'the Little,' and called Megara from the fact that the latter was built on nearly the same spot. 3. *Hybla Herœa*, on the route from Agrigentum to Syracuse. The famous Hyblæan honey was obtained from one of these towns.

Hybodus, the name of a genus of fossil elasmobranch fishes, belonging to the sub-order Squali and the

family Cestraciontidæ, or bull-headed sharks. They are found from the Triassic to the Cretaceous periods.

Hybrid (' an insult '), the progeny of two distinct varieties, as in the mongrel; of two distinct species, the common acceptance of the term ; or, much more rarely, of two different genera. Early investigators declared that Hs. were sterile, but Darwin's experiments clearly demonstrated the inaccuracy of this, as he was able to rear healthy young from a pair of Hs. between the domestic goose and the Chinese goose, which represent distinct species. The production of Hs. does not appear to be possible, between widely differing parents. In the animal kingdom many variety-hybrids have been obtained, and rather less species-hybrids. Genus-hybrids are rare, though the he-goat and ewe have been successfully crossed, as also have the star-fish, and sea-urchin. In the case of species, possibly the commonest examples are the production of the *mule* from the male ass and mare, and of the *hinny* from the horse and female ass, other examples occur in the case of the dog and fox; lion and tiger; hare and rabbit; canaries and finches, etc. Hybridism is spoken of by Broca as being (*a*) *natural*, when it occurs in the undisturbed natural conditions (the relatively few cases of this quoted are open to suspicion); (*b*) *incited*, when it is under direct human control; and (*c*) *artificial*, as in the mixing of the male elements with eggs, as in the case of fish and frogs. Hybridism has become of importance to florists, and their successful experiments date back to the 17th century. Genus-hybrids, which are rare, occur, as in the rhododendron and azalea. The other forms are more common. *Graft hybridism* has been chronicled as in the case of Adam's laburnum, and in the bizzarria from the bitter orange and citron. Usually H. resemble the male parents, and are generally unstable; in many cases the experiment results in definite economic gain as in the case of the hybrid Eur-American vine, which is more capable of resisting phylloxera than either of its parents.

Hydaspes, Punjab, India, *see* JHELUM.

Hydatid Cyst, *see* TAPE-WORMS and BLADDER WORM.

Hydatid Disease, or Echinococcus Disease (Gk. ὑδατὶς, a watery vesicle). Certain immature forms of tape-worms—in particular of *Tœnia echinococcus*—are sometimes present in the body, and it is from these that H. arises. Cysts are formed and the brain, liver, lungs, and kidneys are liable to this disease. This cyst may vary in size from the size of a hazel nut to that of a child's head; and of course the danger depends upon the size and the position of the cyst. The disease can only be treated surgically. H. arises in man through dogs being kept too much about a person, for the adult worm, being small, lives socially in the intestines of the dog, jackal, and wolf. The disease is most prevalent in Iceland, although it is found in most European countries. *See* TAPEWORMS.

Hyde, a municipal bor. in the co. of Cheshire, England, about 4 m. N.E. of Stockport. Its principal industry is the manuf. of cotton goods, but coal mining and engineering are also carried on. Pop. (1911) 33,444.

Hyde, Douglas (*b.* 1860), an Irish scholar and writer, known as ' an Craoibhin Aoibhiun,' born at French-park, co. Roscommon, and educated at Trinity College, Cambridge. Early in life he took up the study of Irish literature, Gaelic songs, and folktales, his *Literary History of Ireland* being the first attempt to write a comprehensive and systematic history of Gaelic literature. He also wrote: *Love Songs of Connaught; The Story of the Early Irish Literature; The Lad of the Ferule,* etc.

Hyde, Edward, *see* CLARENDON, FIRST EARL OF.

Hyde, Sir Nicholas (*c.* 1572-1631), the uncle of Edward H., first Earl of Clarendon, and in 1626 was appointed chief justice of the King's Bench. During his term of office he presided at the trial of several well-known men, among them Sir John Eliot and others.

Hyde, Thomas (1636-1703), an English Orientalist, a native of Billingsley in Shropshire. He was a student at Cambridge, and in 1658 became Hebrew lecturer at Queen's College, Oxford, afterwards chief librarian at the Bodleian Library. He was also made canon of Salisbury and archdeacon of Gloucester, and eventually canon of Christ Church. He helped Walton with the Persian and Syriac texts of the *Polyglot Bible,* and wrote *Historia Religionis Veterum Persarum,* 1700.

Hyde Park, an enclosed space of about 360 acres, situated between Whitehall and Kensington, London. It belonged originally to the Manor of Hyde, the property of the Abbey of Westminster, but was appropriated by Henry VIII. after the dissolution of the monasteries and is now a royal park. In times gone by duels were fought there, but in the 17th century it became a meeting-place of fashionable people, and during the London season is still used for this purpose. It is also a favourite

place for various political meetings. Among its points of interest may be mentioned the Marble Arch, now isolated from it, the Gateway at Hyde Park Corner, and the Serpentine.

Hyde Park, U.S.A.: 1. A tn. in Norfolk co., Massachusetts, U.S.A., on the Neponset R., 8 m. from Boston. The town includes Readville, Clarendon Hills, Hazlewood, and Fairmount, and is engaged in the manuf. of cotton, paper, and rubber goods, chemicals, machinery, and dyestuffs. Pop. (1910) 15,507. 2. A suburb of Chicago, U.S.A., was annexed to the city in 1889. In H. P. is situated Jackson Park, the scene of the Columbian Exposition.

Hyderabad, *see* HAIDARABAD.

Hyder Ali, *see* HAIDAR ALI.

Hydra, in Greek legend, a celebrated monster with a number of heads, inhabiting the marshes of Lerna in the Peloponnesus. Hercules had to destroy this monster, as one of his twelve labours, and he accomplished the feat with the aid of Iolaus. The middle head was immortal, and they managed to sever it and bury it under a huge rock.

Hydra, the name of the single genus of fresh-water polyps belonging to the cœlenterate order Hydrida. The species are widely distributed, being found in Europe, N. America, New Zealand, Australia, and tropical Africa. In Britain they are found attached to weed or plant stalks in still fresh water; these solitary polyps have a tubular body-wall, and the generative products are developed in the ectoderm; the mouth is placed at the summit of the hypostome, and there is a crown of long, slender, hollow tentacles, varying in number from six in *H. vulgaris* and *H. oligactis* to eight in *H. viridis*. All species are carnivorous, and will swallow Entomostraca of considerable size, until the body-wall expands to twice its usual dimensions.

Hydra, an island in the Grecian Archipelago, forming with the neighbouring island of Dokos the Bay of H. It has an area of about 21 sq. m., and its greatest length is 11 m. Its surface consists of barren rocks, only a few trees growing in favoured spots. H., the chief town, is built round the principal harbour and practically the entire population of the island is centred in this town. There is a fairly active trade in weaving, tanning, and shipbuilding.

Hydra, The Water-Snake, one of the old constellations, being mentioned by both Aratus and Ptolemy. From the time of the former it has always been a triple figure : a long snake, represented as trailing upon the ground, bears upon his back a cup (Crater), and near to his tail is seated a crow (Corvus). The mythological meaning is altogether unknown. *Hydra* must be distinguished from *Hydrus*, the Southern Snake, a southern constellation of Lacaille, which is situated between the bright star Achernar and the S. pole.

Hydracids are acids which consist of hydrogen united to an element or group of elements which do not contain oxygen. Hydrochloric acid (HCl) and hydrocyanic acid (HCN) are examples of H. Oxyacids, on the other hand, may be regarded as compounds of water with a non-metallic oxide, *e.g.* sulphuric acid ($H_2SO_4 = H_2O + SO_3$).

Hydragogues, *see* APERIENTS.

Hydrangea, a genus of Saxifragaceæ, contains about two dozen species which flourish in N. lands. These are hardy shrubs with opposite leaves, and some are of a climbing habit. They require a rich soil, protection from the cold, and a great deal of water; when in full bloom they are covered by numerous large cymose corymbs of brightly-coloured flowers. *H. hortensis* is the commonest example found in Britain.

Hydrant, *see* WATER SUPPLY.

Hydrate, a term applied to compounds of water with elements or with other compounds. The term *hydroxide* is one which is sometimes used as a synonym of H., and indeed we have no certain method of distinguishing the one from the other. In the H. the water is supposed to be present as such, and may be driven off by heating without affecting the characteristic properties of the substance (*e.g.* crystallised copper sulphate, $CuSO_4.5H_2O$). In the *hydroxide,* the water has apparently undergone rearrangement with the rest of the molecule, and cannot be removed without altering the characteristic properties of the substance (*e.g.* sulphuric acid, H_2SO_4 or $SO_2(OH)_2$, from SO_2 and H_2O).

Hydraulic Machinery includes all machines which depend upon water power. They may be divided up into two classes: (1) Motor machinery and (2) pumps. Water falling from a high to a low level can obviously be used to drive machines which are thus deriving their energy from water, and these are typical of the first class. The second class would include steam pumps for raising water from a low to a high level, or from a low to a high pressure. Thus, under the term H. M., is included several branches of engineering, and these branches are perhaps best dealt with separately; therefore *see* ACCUMULATOR, CRANE, LIFT, PUMP, TURBINES, WATER WHEELS, WATER

ENGINES, POWER TRANSMISSION, HYDRAULIC PRESS, INJECTOR, and HYDRODYNAMICS.

Most hydraulic machines depend upon the principles explained in hydrodynamics, and typified by the hydraulic press (*q.v.*), while Lord Armstrong's hydraulic accumulator (*see* ACCUMULATOR) established the success of storage and power transmission machinery. Pipes for carrying water under pressure are made of cast iron or steel, and the thickness and diameter vary with the average pressure of the water transmitted. A

HYDRAULIC MAIN

6-in. pipe, 1¼ in. thick, will carry water at 750 lbs. per sq. in. If P represent the pressure of water in lbs. per sq. in., *d* the internal diameter of the pipe, then the thickness of the pipe can be calculated from the formula :

$$t = \cdot 000125 \; Pd + x,$$

where *t* equals thickness of the pipe ; and $x = \cdot 37$ in. for pipes less than 12 in. in diameter, ·5 in. for pipes from 12 to 30 in., and ·6 in. for pipes from 30 to 50 in.

Hydraulic power is utilised in many directions because of its convenience for occasional use, and because of its freedom from smoke and noise, its capability of being transmitted and used without any attention, and because of its practical freedom from danger. *See* Blaine, *Hydraulic Machinery ;* Marks, *Hydraulic Power Engineering ;* Williams and Hazen, *Hydraulic Tables ;* Box, *Practical Hydraulics ;* Rogers, *Pump and Hydraulics.*

Hydraulic Press, invented by Joseph Bramah (*q.v.*) in 1785, and therefore known as 'Bramah's press.' The principle used in this machine is a well-known one in hydrostatics (*q.v.*), viz. that a pressure on any part of the surface of any liquid is transmitted equally in all directions through the mass.

As will be seen from the accompanying diagram, a force pump G can force water from the tank H, by way of a strong pipe E into a strong cast steel cylinder D. C, the plunger or ram, is thus forced upwards. On the top of the plunger is a table B, between which and the plate A— sometimes known as the entablature —anything, *e.g.* a bale or a number of books, can be pressed. The power of the press is calculated as follows: Let D and D_1 be the diameters of the

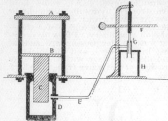

BRAMAH'S OR HYDRAULIC PRESS

pump plunger G and the ram C respectively. Then, if W be the pressure exerted on the pump, $W.\dfrac{D_1^2}{D^2}$ will be the pressure exerted by the ram. As an example: if a pressure of 50 lbs. be exerted on the pump plunger of diameter 1 in., then, if the diameter of the ram be 10 in., the pressure exerted will be $50 \times \dfrac{10^2}{1^2} = 5000$ lbs.

It is thus a very efficient machine, and it is used for pressing cotton and wool bales, bending iron plates, lifting weights, and raising bridge girders into place (hydraulic jacks); the pump G being either worked by hand by a lever F as shown, or by a steam engine.

Hydraulic Ram, *see* PUMPS.

Hydraulics, *see* HYDROMECHANICS.

Hydrazine (H_2N-NH_2), a colourless strongly alkaline liquid (boiling-point 114° C.) obtained by heating H. hydrate with barium oxide. Its salts are prepared from ammonia and hypochlorite; if the product is evaporated down with sulphuric acid, the sparingly soluble sulphate separates out. H. forms many derivatives in which hydrogen is replaced by alkyl groups, the most important being phenyl H. ($C_6H_5-NH-NH_2$), an oily liquid, which forms crystalline compounds with aldehydes and ketones.

Hydrea (modern *Hydra*), a small island off the E. coast of the Morea, Greece, having an area of about 20 sq. m. It is rocky and barren in character, and Hydra, a seaport town, is situated on the N. coast. During the Greek War of Independence the inhabitants of the island were very much to the fore. Pop. about 7000.

Hydrides, compounds containing hydrogen, combined with a single other element, but the term is gener-

ally restricted to such compounds where the element is a metal. Thus H_2O and HCl would be regarded as oxide and chloride, repectively, rather than as H. Compounds of hydrogen with metals such as arsenic, antimony, sodium, calcium, etc. (AsH_3, SbH_3, Na_2H, CaH_2 respectively), may be regarded as true H. in the limited sense of the term. With acids or water H. evolve hydrogen, use being made of this in the preparation of the gas for military balloons.

Hydriodic Acid, or **Hydrogen Iodide** (HI), a colourless gas, fuming strongly in moist air, and easily soluble in water to a solution, which, when saturated has a sp. gr. of 1·70, and contains about 52 per cent. of HI. Light turns it brown with deposition of iodine. It may be obtained by distilling potassium iodide with phosphoric acid, but is more easily prepared by acting on red phosphorus and iodine with water, or by passing sulphuretted hydrogen into water containing iodine in suspension. On heating, H. A. is decomposed into its elements. The salts of H. A., the iodides, are crystalline, and as a rule soluble in water. Silver iodide is used in photography, and potassium iodide in medicine to lessen secretions and absorb the products of inflammation.

Hydrobromic Acid, or **Hydrogen Bromide** (HBr), a colourless, fuming gas with a pungent smell, forming a fuming solution with water, which acts as a strong acid. In the presence of light it is decomposed with separation of bromine. H. A. is formed by the action of phosphoric acid on potassium bromide; it is most conveniently prepared, however, by dropping bromine on to a paste of red phosphorus and water, the gas evolved being passed into water. The bromides, or salts, derived from the acid are crystalline, and, as a rule, soluble in water. They are employed in photography, silver bromide being one of the most important salts that are sensitive to light. Potassium, sodium, and ammonium bromides are also used in medicine, and act as powerful hypnotics and depressants. If taken habitually they are apt to set up a variety of poisoning known as 'bromism.'

Hydrocarbons, the compounds of hydrogen with carbon, and may be regarded as the parent substances of all organic compounds. There are many classes of H., of which the following are the most important: (1) the paraffins, of general formula C_nH_{2n+2}, which are 'saturated' compounds, with the carbon atoms in an open or branched chain; (2) 'unsaturated' H. of the ethylene, acetylene, and other series, which will unite with elements, such as chlorine or bromine, without undergoing re-arrangement of the molecule; (3) H. containing a ring structure, such as benzene, naphthalene, anthracene, in which the carbon atoms are arranged in one or more closed rings. Com-bination of the above types is pos-sible, giving rise to an enormous number of H., derivatives of many of them being found in nature. Petroleum and other mineral oils consist almost entirely of H., those of the paraffin series being usually the most plentiful.

Hydrocele, a dropsy of the serous membrane surrounding the testis. It may occur as the result of inflamma-tion, or from a blow, but its cause is commonly unknown. It forms a smooth, elastic, pearshaped swelling, which although painless, may cause discomfort owing to its weight, since the quantity of fluid may be as much as 40 ounces. It can be distinguished from other disorders in the same position by reason of the fact that when the tumour is held between the observer and the light it is seen to be translucent. It can be distinguished from rupture since it gives no impulse when the sufferer coughs. It usually occurs in middle age, in persons of weak power, or with a tendency to gout. It does occur in children either as described above or as *congenital hydrocele.*

Palliative treatment consists in using suspending bandages, and tap-ping frequently. The *curative* treat-ment consists in setting up inflam-mation by injecting iodine, or by excision of the whole or part of the sac. Injection of chloride of zinc is sometimes used, as causing no pain or inflammation.

Hydrocephalus, means, literally, ' water on the brain,' but includes three distinct diseases—

(1) *Acute hydrocephalus,* or rather *tubercular meningitis,* is due to in-flammation of the membranes of the brain because of the presence of tubercles (*q.v.*). Fluid frequently forms within the brain, and it is a fatal disease, which is common in childhood, although it does occur less frequently among adults.

(2) *Chronic hydrocephalus* is distinct from acute H. since it is a dropsy. A watery fluid forms in the skull, before the bones have united to form the brain case, and by pressing outwards it increases the size of the head enormously, by forcing the bones apart. This may commence before birth, but is more usual in early child-hood. It has been known to occur at about the eighth or ninth year, and the fontanelles and sutures have been forced open under the pressure. If

they do not yield death quickly re-sults. Children suffering from H. usually die in infancy ; some may survive but they carry their com-plaint with them through life. Not a few cases of blindness, deafness, palsy, and idiocy are due to this, although the sufferer is not always so affected. Since the skull enlarges and the face only grows at the usual rate, cases can be diagnosed by the disproportion between the head and face which ensue.

(3) *Spurious hydrocephalus,* re-sembles acute H., and is often mis-taken for it. It is, however, due to a poor supply of blood to the brain, and is a disease of debility. As a result of this disease, the little patient will have a pale cool cheek, half shut regardless eye, interrupted sighing re-spiration, and an unclosed fontanelle. It can be distinguished from acute H. by the fact that in acute H. the sur-face of the fontanelle will be convex, while in spurious H. it will be concave or depressed because it lacks support, and originates in emptiness. Spurious H. readily yields to treatment, by means of nourishing diet and small doses of wine, ammonia, etc.

Hydrocharitaceæ, a natural order of monocotyledonous plants contain-ing thirteen genera and about fifty species. All occur as water-plants in tropical and temperate lands, and a few are marine; they usually inhabit ditches, lakes, and rivers. Nearly all have ribbon-like, submerged leaves, and some have floating leaves; the male and female flowers usually occur on different plants. They are gener-ally in parts of three, with a two-whorled perianth; the stamens are in from one to five whorls; the carpels form an inferior ovary, are united, and vary in number from two to fifteen; the ovary is unilocular, with numerous ovules. The chief genera are *Vallisneria, Elodea, Hydrocharis,* and *Halophila.*

Hydrochloric Acid, or **Hydrogen Chloride** (HCl), a colourless gas, closely resembling hydrobromic and hydriodic acids. It is readily soluble in water to a fuming, strongly acid solution which is known under the name of ' spirits of salt ' or muriatic acid. H. A. is formed by the direct union of hydrogen and chlorine, but is most conveniently obtained by heating common salt with sulphuric acid, *i.e.* as a by-product in the first stage of the Leblanc soda process, thus : $NaCl + H_2SO_4 = NaHSO_4 + HCl$, the acid sodium sulphate formed being capable of decomposing another molecule of salt at a higher tempera-ture, thus : $NaHSO_4 + NaCl = Na_2SO_4 + HCl$. The H. A. evolved is passed up towers, or ' scrubbers,' down which a stream of water trickles and dissolves the gas. A concentrated aqueous solution of H. A. has a sp. gr, of 1·2, and contains nearly 40 per cent. of the pure acid. The acid is very stable, being unaffected by heat or light; with most metals it reacts with liberation of hydrogen, the chloride of the metal being formed. In the presence of nitric acid, manganese dioxide, and other oxidising agents, chlorine is produced. The chlorides, or salts of H. A., are, as a rule (exceptions : silver, lead, and mercurous chlorides), soluble substances. Common salt, or sodium chloride (NaCl) is the most important of the chlorides, and is the substance from which all chlorine containing compounds, such as bleaching powder, potassium chlorate, etc., are prepared. H. A. is largely used as a cleaning and scouring agent for metals, e.g. iron before galvanising, etc., and for the production of chlorine. Common salt is used as a preservative, and is a necessary article of food with all animals living on a vegetable diet. Medicinally, it is used internally as an emetic, externally in baths for the relief of sciatica, rheumatism, etc.; and it is injected, in solution, to replace loss of blood.

Hydrochœrus, the name of a genus of Lystricomorphous rodents belonging to the family Caviidæ, and consisting of the single species H. capybara, the capybara. This is the largest of all rodents, and attains a length of 4 or 5 ft. It is aquatic, having webbed digits furnished with hoof-like nails, and is a native of S. America.

Hydrocotyle, a genus of umbelliferous plants, is indigenous to temperate and tropical lands. Only one species is British; this is H. vulgaris, the white-rot or pennywort, which is found in boggy places.

Hydrocyanic Acid, or **Prussic Acid** (HCN), was first obtained by Scheele in 1782 from the substance known as Prussian Blue. It is formed in the decomposition of the glucoside amygdalin, which is present in almonds, and other plants. A solution of the acid is best prepared by distilling potassium ferrocyanide with dilute sulphuric acid. The anhydrous acid may be prepared by the action of sulphuric acid on potassium cyanide, or by depydrating an aqueous solution of the acid with calcium chloride. When pure, H. A. is a light colourless liquid, freezing at -15° C. and boiling at 26° C., having the odour of bitter almonds. It is extremely poisonous, a single drop taken internally causing instantaneous death, due to paralysis of the heart. Smaller doses cause pain in the head, giddiness, and

nausea, accompanied by paralysis of respiration and of the spinal cord. In cases of poisoning, emetics, followed by injections of ether or alcohol, inhalation of ammonia, and artificial respiration may be of service. Chemically, H. A. is a feeble acid, faintly reddening litmus. Its salts, the cyanides, resemble the halides, but are poisonous, and enter into complex acid radicles, such as the ferrocyanides and ferricyanides. Potassium cyanide is used as a flux and reducing agent in metallurgical work, as a fixing agent in photography, but chiefly as a solvent for gold in the working of low grade ores. It is prepared commercially either from the ferrocyanide, or sulphocyanide, or, more recently, from barium cyanide formed in the electric furnace from barium carbide and the nitrogen of the air. Medicinally, H. A. is used in very dilute solution, externally to diminish itching in skin diseases, and internally as a sedative, and to allay vomiting and relieve coughing.

Hydrodynamics, see HYDROKINETICS.

Hydro-extractor, or Centrifuge, a machine for separating liquids from solids, by whirling the mixture in a perforated or wire cage, surrounded by a casing to collect the liquid that flies out through the openings.

Hydrofluoric Acid, or **Hydrogen Fluoride** (HF), a colourless liquid, boiling at 19° C. and giving off irritating and dangerous fumes. It is obtained in aqueous solution by heating calcium fluoride (fluor spar) with concentrated sulphuric acid in a leaden retort, and passing the gas evolved into water ($CaF_2 + H_2SO_4 = CaSO_4 + 2HF$). To obtain the pure acid, hydrogen potassium fluoride HF, KF is distilled in a platinum retort, the H. A. being collected in a cooled receiver of the same material. H. A. is an extremely active acid, and is especially valuable on account of its solvent action on silica and silicates, being used to etch glass. For this purpose the article is covered with wax, and the marks or other designs required are cut upon the wax with a steel tool; on exposing to the acid, the parts laid bare are etched, and the rest of the article is untouched. The fluorides, or salts of H. A., with the exception of those of the alkali metals, are insoluble in water. Of these calcium fluoride is the most important.

Hydrofluosilicic Acid (H_2SiF_6) is obtained, together with silicic acid, by passing silicon fluoride (prepared by the action of concentrated sulphuric acid on a mixture of fluor spar and fine sand) into water. H. A. is only known in aqueous solution, which is colourless. It behaves as a dibasic acid, and forms sparingly soluble potassium and barium salts. It is used in hardening objects made of gypsum.

Hydrogen (symbol H ; atomic weight 1), derived from the Gk. ὕδωρ, water, and γεννάω, to produce, is a gaseous element discovered by Cavendish in 1776, that occurs in nature chiefly in combination with oxygen, as water, H_2O. It is the lightest element known, and is taken as the standard for measuring gas density and atomic weights. H. is most conveniently prepared on a small scale by the action of sodium on water, or by the action of zinc on sulphuric acid, $Zn + H_2SO_4 = ZnSO_4 + H_2$. On the large scale, scrap-iron is used in place of zinc, or the gas is prepared by passing steam over red-hot iron, or by electrolysing water. When pure, H. is a colourless, odourless gas, which condenses at a low temperature, and under great pressure to a liquid boiling at - 253° C., and freezing at - 259° C. The liquid, which was first produced by Dewar in 1898, has a density only $\frac{1}{14}$th that of water, whilst the gas has a density $\frac{1}{15}$th that of air. H. is very insoluble in water, and is incapable of supporting respiration, although not actually poisonous. It burns in air with a non-luminous flame, water being formed; if mixed with air or oxygen and ignited a violent explosion is produced. H. is a powerful reducing agent, combining with the oxygen, chlorine, etc., of bodies with which it is heated. It unites with many elements to form hydrides of very varying properties, such as water, hydrochloric acid, sulphuretted hydrogen, and ammonia. The metal palladium has the power of absorbing about 900 times its volume of H., use being made of this property in purifying and storing small quantities of the gas. H. is present in all acids, in fact, the acids may be regarded as the salts of H. It is also present in hydrocarbons, oils, fats, starch, and, in fact, in almost all natural and artificial compounds of organic chemistry. Commercially, H. is used as a reducing agent, as a means of producing high temperatures in the oxy-hydrogen flame, and for filling balloons. For this latter purpose the gas is made, for military balloons at any rate, by heating aluminium with caustic soda solution, or by the action of calcium hydride (Hydrolith), CaH_2, on water, the weight of materials being an important consideration where transport is necessary. In fact 1 lb. of ' hydrolith ' will give as much H. as $7\frac{1}{4}$ lbs. of iron and sulphuric acid. Although H. was originally taken as the standard for atomic weights, it has been customary of late to take oxygen = 16 as

the basis, owing to the fact that the compounds of the elements with oxygen are more numerous and more readily analysed than those with H. On this arrangement H = 1·008, instead of unity.

Hydrogen Peroxide, or Dioxide (H_2O_2), is, when pure, a colourless, slightly viscid liquid having a sp. gr. of 1·45, freezing on cooling to a solid, having a melting-point of - 2° C. It is readily soluble in alcohol or water. The aqueous solution is obtained by the action of dilute sulphuric acid on hydrated barium peroxide, barium sulphate being precipitated. $BaO_2 + H_2SO_4 = BaSO_4 + H_2O_2$. Sodium peroxide, Na_2O_2, is often used in place of BaO_2. The aqueous solution obtained may be concentrated by evaporation, followed by distillation, under reduced pressure. The pure substance has a bitter taste, a faint odour resembling nitric acid, and is unstable, decomposing explosively under various conditions into oxygen and water. The aqueous solution is more stable, especially in the presence of a mineral acid, and may be kept for a considerable time. It is usually sold in ' volumes,' ' 20 vols.' for instance indicating that 1 volume of the solution will liberate 20 volumes of oxygen on decomposition. H. P. is a powerful oxidising agent, liberating iodine from potassium iodide, oxidising sulphides and sulphites to sulphates, and bleaching by oxidation. It also has the property of setting free the oxygen, together with its own available oxygen, from certain metallic oxides and highly oxidised salts. thus apparently acting as a reducing agent. H. P. is largely used in the arts for bleaching ivory, feathers, hair, etc. ; as a disinfectant, and also for restoring old oil paintings, by oxidising the black lead sulphide (formed by the action of sulphur compounds in the air on the lead contained in the paints) to the white sulphate. Sodium carbonate and barium percarbonate, prepared electrolytically, have recently been used with success for the manufacture of H. P.

Hydrography, a scientific description of the waters of the globe. The subject will include : (*a*) Marine surveying, or the measurement and mapping of the water areas; this will result in the preparation of maps and charts showing the position of seas, lakes, and rivers. Navigation demands from the nautical surveyor some knowledge of the contour of the ocean bed and an accurate outlining of all shallows, deeps, and reefs. The Hydrographic Department of the British Admiralty, which was established in 1795, undertakes the making of such charts under the charge of the Hydrographer to the Admiralty. (b) Physical properties of the water masses. The actual composition of the waters must be ascertained, and their varied and varying salinities introduce the wide question of oceanic circulation, to which is related the identification of thermal areas in both horizontal and vertical distributions. The tidal circulation has important bearings on questions of navigation, and the hydrographer is concerned in the preparation of tables showing the 'establishments of ports.' An important economic study in H. has for its objective the analysis of the distribution and movements of those myriads of micro-organisms plankton and nekton, which play so great a part in the life-history of the various food fishes. Not only does the subject cover the investigation of the salt water areas, but rivers and fresh water lakes also demand special treatment. To realise some of the classes of investigation comprised under this heading, reference should be made to the Official Reports of the Scientific Results of the Voyage of H.M.S. ' Challenger ' (50 vols.).

Hydrokinetics, or Hydrodynamics, the science dealing with fluids in motion, and forms a theoretical introduction to the practical subject of hydraulics. Fluids at rest are dealt with in hydrostatics (q.v.). A fluid may thus be defined as that which yields to the slightest tangential stress, if it be continued long enough. Thus, though a piece of pitch may be easily smashed into small fragments by a blow of a hammer, in course of time, if left to itself, it will spread itself out over a surface and flow like a liquid by virtue of its weight alone. Hence pitch is a fluid, but since its change of form takes place gradually, it is termed a viscous fluid. All fluids are viscous to some degree, and as the molecules move over one another, friction forces exist which tend to generate heat. But in the case of water, and, in fact, in most liquids, especially alcohol and ether, the viscosity is so small that actual results coincide very closely with the action of a perfect fluid—the ideal fluid, which is inviscid, i.e. which cannot sustain any tangential stress. So the theory of hydrokinetics deals almost entirely with perfect fluids. Fluid motion may be rotational (sometimes called vertical) or irrotational. Again, it may be steady or unsteady. By steady motion is meant that at any point fixed in space the motion of successive particles of fluid is always the same in magnitude and direction, though it may vary from

point to point. If the motion is the same at all points of the fluid, so that the fluid moves like a solid body, it is termed uniform. Thus rotational motion may be steady but not uniform. Moving masses of fluid, bounded partially or completely by solid boundaries, form a stream. A stream bounded by the same fluid moving differently is termed a current, and when bounded by different fluid is termed a jet. An eddy or vortex is formed by fluid with a circular or spiral motion. It is proved that a vortex must be endless or have its ends on the free surface of the liquid. The actual path of any particle of fluid is called a stream line, and if the stream lines are drawn through all points of a closed curve a tube of flow is formed. Thus there can be no flow across the lateral boundaries of a tube of flow. A line of flow is such that at any point of its length the tangent coincides with the direction of motion of the point. Stream lines and line of flow are coincident when the motion is steady.

The usual methods for forming the general equations of fluid motion are by means of differential and integral calculus and will be given later, but certain particular cases may be dealt with in a more elementary way. Thus the equation of continuity is obtained from the principle that the amount of incompressible fluid flowing into any completely bounded space, supposed continuously filled with liquid, must be equal to the amount that flows out. If a_1 and a_2 are the areas of any two cross sections of a stream, and v_1, v_2 the components of the velocity of the fluid normal to the cross sections, then the amounts of fluid flowing across the sections in a unit of time are a_1v_1 and a_2v_2. Hence $a_1v_1 = a_2v_2$, and these velocities are inversely proportional to the areas. Again, consider a liquid moving in a horizontal straight line uniformly, that is like a solid body, with no relative motion of its parts, and suppose a small portion of the liquid in the shape of a circular cylinder with its axis along the line of motion to become solidified. Let a be the area of its cross section, l its length, p_1 and p_2 the fluid pressures at its ends, m the mass of a unit volume of the fluid, and f its acceleration. Then mal is the mass of the cylinder and $(p_1 - p_2)a$ is the component of the resultant force on it in the direction of motion, since the ends are considered so small that the pressure over them may be taken as constant. Hence, by Newton's second law, $(p_1 - p_2)a = malf$, and thus so long as there is an acceleration the pressure varies along a horizontal straight line. Now if p_1 and p_2 are the pressures due to depths h_1 and h_2 below the free surface, it follows that $p_1 - p_2 = mg(h_1 - h_2)$, since the principle established in hydrostatics for pressure at given depths holds in this case.

$$\therefore h_1 - h_2 = \frac{p_1 - p_2}{mg} = \frac{mlf}{mg}.$$

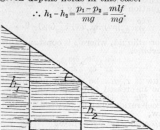

FIG. 1

Therefore the free surface of the liquid slopes downwards in the direction of motion at an angle to the horizon

$$\tan^{-1}\frac{h_1 - h_2}{l} = \tan^{-1}\frac{f}{g}.$$

Hence the free surface of a liquid in a vessel carried along at an acceleration, makes an angle with the horizontal, and this angle increases if the acceleration increases. If there is no acceleration, the surface is horizontal.

Again, if a vessel, in the form of a right circular cylinder with vertical axis, and the liquid within it rotates about the axis with a constant angular velocity ω, then any particle of liquid distant x from the axis will have an acceleration $\omega^2 x$ towards the axis. This increases as x increases. The pressure is therefore least on the axis of rotation and gradually in-

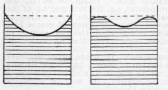

FIG. 2

1. Liquid and vessel rotating
2. Liquid only rotating

creases further from the axis. Hence the free surface will be lowest in the middle and will gradually rise towards the side of the vessel. It is found that a section of the surface by a plane through the axis of rotation gives a parabola, and the whole sur-

face is a paraboloid of revolution. When the liquid only, and not the vessel, rotates, the outer layer of the liquid in contact with the vessel is at rest. The next layer rotates slowly, and for a time each successive layer has a bigger angular velocity. As in the previous case, the velocity in the middle is zero, and gradually increases outwards, and hence the layer of greatest velocity is somewhere intermediate between the axis and the side of the vessel. The free surface then takes the form shown in the figure. The accumulation of mud near the inner bank of a river at a bend may be accounted for by continuing the argument.

The same general principle of the pressure gradient, as it is called, has been used to correct the common mistake that as a fluid passes through a pipe of varying cross section, it exercises greater pressure on the sides where the pipe is narrower. In fact, the opposite is true. Let AL,

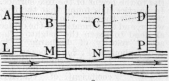

FIG. 3

BM, CN, DP be small vertical pipes let into such a pipe. Then the height to which the liquid rises in each of these gives the pressure. It is found that at L and P where the cross section is largest, the heights AL and DP are greatest. Account has to be taken in this experiment of the action of friction, which tends to lessen the height of the columns, and has a bigger effect the further the water travels along the pipe. This principle has a practical use in the Venturi water meter.

The principle of the conservation of energy gives a simple proof of an important equation of motion. Let a_1, p_1, v_1 and a_2, p_2, v_2 be the area of the cross section, the pressure, and the velocity respectively at two ends of a thin tube of flow, a being so small that p and v may be considered constant for the area. Since there is no flow across the boundaries, the equation of continuity gives $a_1 v_1 = a_2 v_2$. By the conservation of energy, the difference between the work done by the fluid crossing the two sections is equal to the total difference between the energy in the two cases. In a unit of time the difference between the work done is $p_1 a_1 v_1 - p_2 a_2 v_2$, the difference between the potential energy in the two cases is $m(a_2p_2V_2 - a_1p_1V_1)$, where m is the mass of a unit volume and V_1, V_2 the potential energy at the two sections, and the difference of kinetic energy is

$$\tfrac{1}{2}ma_2v_2 \times v_2{}^2 - \tfrac{1}{2}ma_1v_1 \times v_1{}^2$$

$$\therefore\ p_1a_1v_1 - p_2a_2v_2 = m(a_2p_2V_2 - a_1p_1V_1)$$
$$+ \tfrac{1}{2}ma_2v_2{}^3 - \tfrac{1}{2}ma_1v_1{}^3$$

$$\therefore\ p_1 + mV_1 + \tfrac{1}{2}mv_1{}^2 = p_2 + mV_2 + \tfrac{1}{2}mv_2{}^2$$

and this is the same for any two points of the tube of flow.

An important consideration in hydrokinetics is that of the escape of liquids from orifices. Consider a vessel with a very small orifice so made as to throw a jet vertically upwards, filled with water to a height h feet above the orifice. It is then said that the *head of water* is h feet. If the velocity of the escaping liquid is v feet per second, it follows at once that $v_2 = 2gh$, since the loss of kinetic energy equals the gain of potential energy. Thus water escaping should rise to the height of the free surface. In practice it is found that the friction with the air, the viscosity of water, and the formation of the orifice all tend to lessen the height. The actual velocity of discharge is in reality about $\cdot 97 + \sqrt{2gh}$ ft. per second for well-formed orifices, and $\cdot 97$ is called the coefficient of velocity. The area of the cross section of the jet from a sharp-edged orifice is considerably less than that of the orifice itself, and the ratio between the two (about $\cdot 64$) is called the coefficient of contraction. This may be measured experimentally by means of screws fixed at A and B just outside the orifice. If, further, the jet is horizontal initially a measurement of the parabolic path of the water will determine the velocity of discharge.

FIG. 4

The general equations of motion in hydrokinetics are formed by considering a small parallelopiped of sides δx, δy, and δz drawn through the point x, y, z and parallel to the axes of co-ordinates. If u, v, and w are the components of the velocity parallel to the axes, the amounts of fluid crossing the faces parallel to the plane of yz in time δt are $\rho u\delta y\delta z\delta t$ and $\rho u\delta y\delta z\delta t + \frac{\delta}{\delta x}(\rho u)\delta x\delta y\delta z\delta t$. Therefore the gain is $-\frac{\delta}{\delta x}(\rho u)\delta x\delta y\delta z\delta t$. Hence, considering the other faces in the same way, the

total gain may be found. But this gain is also the difference between $\rho\delta x\delta y\delta z$ and $\left(\rho + \frac{\delta\rho}{\delta t}\delta t\right)\delta x\delta y\delta z$, the increase of fluid in time δt. Hence the equation of continuity is

$$\frac{\delta\rho}{\delta t} + \frac{\delta}{\delta x}(\rho u) + \frac{\delta}{\delta y}(\rho v) + \frac{\delta}{\delta z}(\rho w) = 0.$$

For a liquid, where ρ is constant, this becomes

$$\frac{\delta u}{\delta x} + \frac{\delta v}{\delta y} + \frac{\delta w}{\delta z} = 0.$$

Now if x, y, z be the components of the impressed forces per unit mass, fx, fy, fz the components of the acceleration, then by Newton's second law,

$$fx\rho\delta x\delta y\delta z = x\rho\delta x\delta y\delta z + p\delta y\delta z$$
$$- \left(p + \frac{\delta p}{\delta x}\delta x\right)\delta y\delta z$$
$$\therefore\ \frac{1}{\rho}\frac{\delta p}{\delta x} = x - fx = x - \frac{\delta u}{\delta t} + u\frac{\delta u}{\delta x} + v\frac{\delta u}{\delta y} + w\frac{\delta u}{\delta z}$$

Two similar equations may also be formed, and there are now four equations to determine the five unknown quantities, p, ρ, u, v, w. But by Boyle's law $p = k\rho$, and hence the quantities may be determined.

For elementary work *see* chs. xi., xii., xiii. in Edwin Edser's *General Physics for Students*, and for more advanced work Basset's *Elementary Treatise on Hydrodynamics and Sound*, and Besant's *Treatise on Hydrodynamics*.

Hydrolysis (literally splitting by water), the term applied to those chemical reactions in which decomposition is brought about by the action of water, and must not be confused with hydration, in which water is taken up without causing disruption of the molecule, *e.g.* as in the conversion of quicklime into slaked lime. Examples of H. are numerous, *e.g.* the splitting up of the salts of weak acids by solution in water, the conversion of esters into acid and alcohol, the 'inversion' of cane sugar, and the formation of ammonium salts from nitriles. In some cases H. takes place by mere addition of water, but more usually heat is required, and in addition a small quantity of acid or alkali to hasten the reaction.

Hydromechanics, a term usually used to define those portions of the sciences of Hydrokinetics (*q.v.*) and Hydrostatics (*q.v.*), which are concerned with the principles of machinery. It is thus included in the wider term Hydraulics.

Hydromel, a beverage composed of honey and water. It may be either fermented, when it is known as vinous H., or mead or unfermented.

Hydrometer, an instrument for finding the densities of liquids. By density is meant the weight of a unit volume, usually the weight in grammes, per cubic centimetre. The relative density of any substance is the ratio of its density to that of water. The most elementary form of hydrometer consists in a thin glass tube AB (Fig. 1) ending in two spheres C and D. D is loaded so that the instrument floats in a vertical position. By Archimedes' principle, if any body floats in a liquid, its weight is equal to the weight of the liquid displaced. Hence the hydrometer will sink deeper in lighter liquids, and the density of a liquid is inversely proportional to the volume immersed. Since the tube AB is thin, only a very small additional volume is immersed where the hydrometer sinks lower, and hence the instrument is open to the objection that only liquids whose densities are nearly equal can be compared by means of any one hydrometer. Thus a hydrometer constructed for heavy liquids will sink entirely in light liquids. Let the hydrometer sink to the mark X in water, and to Y in any given liquid; then, if V and V¹ respectively be the volumes immersed in the two cases, the relative density of the given liquid is $\frac{V}{V^1}$.

FIG. 1

In practice a graduated scale is usually fixed to the stem AB, and the reading opposite the surface of any liquid in which the hydrometer is immersed is the density of the liquid. A common form of hydrometer in general use is the lactometer for finding the density of milk, and hence testing its quality. For scientific work, densities of liquids may be found most accurately by means of specific gravity bottles, but fairly accurate results may also be found by means of Nicholson's hydro-

meter which may be used for solids also. It consists of a hollow metal cylinder A (Fig. 2), generally brass, a thin stem with a well-defined mark C, and two cups B and D for weights. The whole is so loaded that it floats in an upright position. In finding the density of any liquid, the principle is to add weights in the cup B till the instrument sinks to the mark C. Let M be the weight of the hydrometer, m_1 and m_2 respectively the weights required to be added in B to make the hydrometer sink to the mark in water and in some given liquid. Then the water displaced weighs $(M+m_1)$, and the same volume of liquid displaced weighs $(M+m_2)$. Hence the relative density of the liquid is $\frac{M+m_2}{M+m_1}$. To find the density of a solid heavier than water, place it successively in the cups B and D, and add weights in B as before. If m_3 and m_4 respectively be the weights required to sink the hydrometer to the mark when the solid in B and in D, then (m_1-m_3) is the weight of the solid, and (m_1-m_4) is its apparent weight in water. By Archimedes' principle, the difference between these weights, viz. (m_4-m_3), is the weight of the water displaced by the solid. Hence the relative density of the solid is $\frac{m_1-m_3}{m_4-m_3}$. In practice it is found to be very difficult to get an extremely accurate result with a hydrometer, because of the surface tension and capillarity of liquids, which gives the surface of the liquid a curved form where it touches the stem. The possibility of error is diminished, however, by making the stem as thin as possible, and by keeping the instrument clean. In finding the density of a liquid to some degree of accuracy, attention must be paid to its temperature, as a rise in temperature lowers the density. There are many other forms of hydrometers, but the general principles involved are the same. *See* HYDROSTATICS.

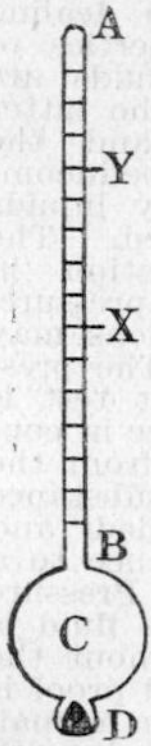

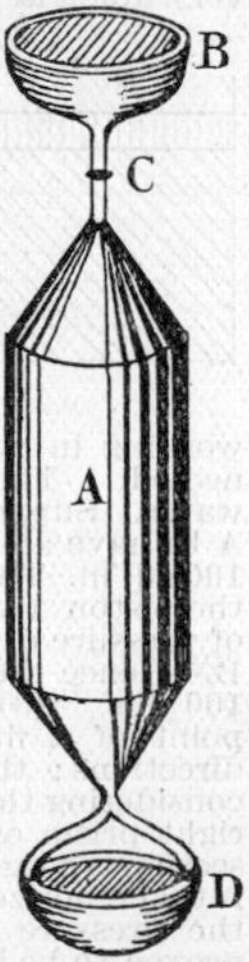

FIG. 2

Hydrometridæ, the name given to a family of hemiptera-heteropterous insects, often called pondskaters or water-striders. They live on the surface of water and feed on insects and aquatic débris. *Hydrometra, Velia,* and *Mesovelia* are common British genera.

Hydromys, the generic name of certain species of rodents belonging to the sub-order Simplicidentatæ and the family Muridæ. *H. chrysogaster,* the best-known species, is limited to Australia, and is aquatic in habit; it is a foot or so in length, with a somewhat long tail and yellowish fur; the limbs are webbed, and there are only two molars in each half of either jaw. *Xeromys* is an allied genus confined to Queensland.

Hydropathy, the name of a curative system in which the external and internal use of water is the chief remedial measure. The value of water applications of various kinds is recognised by all types of physicians, and the name hydrotherapy or hydrotherapeutics is applied to measures involving the use of water. H. is by common consent held to mean a definite theory of cure in which the value of water transcends all else, and, *per contra*, the administration of other drugs is looked upon as generally deleterious. The fame of H. originated with the work of Vincent Priessnitz (1801-51), a farmer of Grafenberg in Silesia. Priessnitz had administered cold-water bandages to sick and injured animals with marvellous success, and extending his practice to human beings, including himself, wrought such wonderful cures that the water system became the vogue, and establishments for the direction of the cure were instituted in England, Germany, France, and America. The new practitioners and the orthodox school of physicians denounced the others as quacks for many years ; but in course of time ordinary medical practice has absorbed many ideas of the water curers, while the more rigid hydropathic establishments of a former generation are now less extreme in their regulations.

Hydrophilidæ, the name of a family of polymorphous coleoptera, which are widely-distributed and chiefly aquatic. *Hydrophilus*, the typical genus, contains the species *H. piceus*, one of the largest of British beetles.

Hydrophobia, *see* RABIES.

Hydrophyllaceæ, an order of dicotyledonous plants, most of which occur in N. America. All are herbs or small shrubs and are generally hairy in appearance. The flowers are regular and hermaphrodite and are generally in parts of five; the sepals and petals are five in number and united, the stamens are five and are epipetalous ; the ovary is superior, and consists of two united carpels, usually with numerous ovules in each loculus; the fruit is often a loculicidal capsule. The chief genera are *Hydrophyllum* and *Nemophila*.

Hydroquinone, or **Para-dihydroxy Benzene** ($C_6H_4(OH)_2$), a colourless, odourless, crystalline substance (melting point, 169° C.) having a slightly sweet taste, and is readily soluble in alcohol, ether, and hot water. It is prepared by the oxidation of aniline to quinone by means of potassium bi-chromate and sulphuric acid, followed by reduction of the product with sulphur dioxide and extraction with ether. It acts as a reducing agent, being used for that purpose in photographic developers.

Hydrostatics, the science dealing with the mechanical properties of fluids in equilibrium. Fluids are either liquids or gases. The latter are easily compressible, and the former may be assumed to be incompressible, though in reality liquids may be slightly compressed. The most important consideration in hydrostatics is that of fluid pressure, and the following propositions may easily be established : (1) The pressure exerted by a fluid at test is always normal to the surface in contact with it ; this follows from the definition of a fluid as a substance which may be easily divided, and offers no permanent resistance to a change of shape. (2) Pressure applied to the surface of a fluid is transmitted equally throughout the fluid ; a rough experimental proof is obtained by pricking holes in a small india-rubber ball and filling it with water. If the ball is squeezed, the water will squirt out equally from all the holes. This principle is used in the Bramah press, which consists of two pistons A and B (Fig. 1), one of very much larger area than the other,

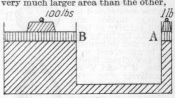

FIG. 1

working in cylinders which are connected. The vessel is filled with water. Suppose the cross section of A to have an area of 1 sq. in., and B 100 sq. in. Then a pressure of 1 lb. on the piston A will result in an increase of pressure of 1 lb. on every sq. in. of B. Hence the total pressure on B is 100 lbs. (3) The pressure at any point of a fluid is the same in all directions ; this may be proved by considering the equilibrium of a small right prism of the fluid, whose cross section is a right-angled triangle. This is taken horizontally on the fluid, and the pressure on the sloping face is proved to be independent of its angle to the horizon. (4) The pressure at any depth in a liquid at rest is the same for all points in the same horizontal plane. Consider the equilibrium of a thin horizontal right circular cylinder of the liquid. The pressures on the two vertical circular ends may be considered constant over each since they are small. By resolving the acting forces in the direction of the length of the cylinder it is seen that the horizontal pressures

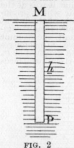

FIG. 2

on the ends are equal. From this proposition it follows that the free surface of any liquid is a horizontal plane. (5) The pressure at any depth in a liquid at rest apart from the pressure of the atmosphere is proportional to the depth below the surface. Let P be any point in a liquid (Fig 2) at depth h below the surface. Consider again a thin circular cylinder extending vertically from P to the surface M. The faces on the curved surface are all horizontal. Hence the upward pressure at P supports the weight of the cylinder. If κ be the area of the small horizontal end at P and w the weight of a unit volume of the liquid, then the upward pressure is $w\kappa h$. Hence the total pressure on any horizontal area is equal to the weight of a column of liquid on the area as base, and of height equal to the depth of the area below the free surface. An elementary experiment for testing the pressure at various depths of a liquid may be made as follows. Take a metal disc D (Fig. 3) supported by a string S and a hollow glass cylinder open at both ends A and B. Pass the string through the cylinder and pull it tight so as to hold the disc firmly against the lower end B. Lower this into a vessel of water. It will be found that when the end B is sufficiently low, the string may be let go, and the upward pressure of the water alone will be sufficient to hold the disc in position. By using discs of various weights and measuring the depth at which each is just held in position by the water, the law may be verified. In actual practice the reservoir supplying water to a

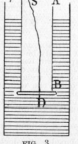

FIG. 3

town is placed on a high level in order to obtain an adequate pressure on the water main. Similarly canal banks and dock gates are made stronger towards the bottom to stand greater pressures.

Seing that the pressure in a liquid due to the liquid varies as the depth below the surface, the total pressure on any plane surface is best found by methods of integral calculus. But certain cases are simple. The total pressure on a horizontal plane area has been mentioned above. Thus if a number of vessels of varying shapes have bottoms of the same area and are filled with water to the same depth, the total pressures on the bottoms AB (Fig. 4) are all the same,

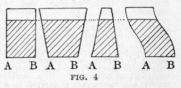

A B A B A B A B

FIG. 4

no matter how much water is put into each vessel; for each is the weight of a column of water of the same height and on the same base. In a similar way the resultant vertical pressure on a portion of any surface is the weight of the liquid enclosed by vertical lines drawn through all points bounding the portion of surface up to the level of the free surface of the liquid. To determine in general the total normal pressure on one side of a plane figure immersed in a liquid, by means of integral calculus, the figure is divided into a large number of very thin horizontal strips; the pressure at all points of the same strip may be considered constant. Let θ be the angle the plane makes with the vertical, x the vertical distance of any strip whose corresponding length is y. Then the total pressure is $\int_{x_1}^{x_2} wxy \sec \theta dx$, where x_1 and x_2 are the depths of the top and bottom strips respectively. The centre of pressure of any plane area immersed is the point of action of the resultant pressure, and this also is best found by means of integral calculus. In the case of a rectangular area with one side in the surface of the liquid, the centre of pressure is two-thirds of the way down.

Atmospheric pressure.—The earth is surrounded by a limited atmosphere which gets less dense at higher altitudes. It may be proved that air has weight by weighing a flask from which the air has been exhausted, and weighing it again when full of air. So, as in the case of liquids, the weight of a column of air is supported by the surface on which it rests, and this weight at the surface of the earth is known as atmospheric pressure. It amounts to about 15 lbs. on every sq. in. Since, in general, vessels contain air at atmospheric pressure inside as well as outside, this pressure is apt to be unnoticed. A common experiment is performed by means of the Magdeburg hemispheres, which consist of two metal hemispheres made to fit exactly together. They may easily be pulled apart by means of handles provided. If, however, the air is exhausted from the interior when they are fitted together, a very large force is necessary to overcome the atmospheric pressure and to separate them. The atmospheric pressure is measured by means of the barometer (q.v.) in which the column of air is balanced by a column of mercury, about 30 in. high. When much water vapour is present in the air it is lighter, and sometimes a column of mercury 28·5 in. high is sufficient to balance it. In a similar way if the barometer is carried up a mountain, and thus the column of air diminished in height, the mercury falls. A barometer constructed with water would be about 33 ft. high. The suction pump depends on the same principle as the water barometer, viz. that the pressure of the air on the surface of the water outside the pipe drives the water up the pipe where the air pressure is less. Since the air pressure is only equivalent to a column of 33 ft. of water, water cannot be raised by means of a suction pump through a height greater than 33 ft.

Though the weight of a column of air may be measured in this way, the pressure of gases in general is more usually dependent on their volume and temperature. Boyle's law, usually proved experimentally by means of a U-tube, states that the temperature of a gas being constant, the product of the volume and the pressure is always the same. A change of temperature also has an effect on volume and pressure, and it is found that if the pressure be kept constant an increase of 1° C. increases the volume of air by a times its volume at 0° C., where a is a constant calculated approximately at ·003665. Thus, if V_t and V_0 are the volumes at t° C. and 0° C. respectively, $V_t = V_0(1 + at)$, and hence $p = k\rho_t(1 + at)$, where p is the constant pressure and ρ_t the density at t° C. When $t = -273$ about $1 + at = 0$, and in this case the pressure is zero. It is convenient on occasions to use this mark (-273° C.) as zero, and temperature so measured is known as the absolute temperature. Boyle's law is well illustrated in the case of a diving bell. At the surface of water, at depths 33 ft., 66 ft., etc., the pressures are one, two, three, etc., atmospheres. Hence at a depth of 33 ft. the pressure of the air in a diving bell is twice what it was at the surface, and hence air which originally occupied the whole of the bell at one atmosphere pressure is now compressed to occupy half the volume at a pressure of two atmospheres (Fig. 5). Similarly at a depth of 66 ft. the water will have risen two-thirds of the way up into the bell.

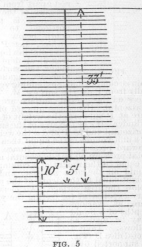

Archimedes' principle states that if a body be immersed in a liquid its apparent loss of weight is equal to the weight of the liquid displaced ; so the weight of a floating body equals the weight of the liquid displaced. Thus, a piece of cork totally immersed in water will rise to the surface because it displaces more than its own weight of water. In a similar way a balloon rises because its total weight is less than that of the air displaced. An iceberg whose specific gravity (q.v.) is about ten-elevenths will float in water with about ten-elevenths of its volume beneath the surface (for density and specific gravity *see* HYDROMETER). A most important practical application of the question of floating bodies occurs in shipbuilding. A ship will not be safe unless its shape and the arrangement of its cargo are such that it will right itself after a considerable roll to either side. The first thing then is to ensure that its vertical position is one of stable equilibrium, that is, that the forces at work will restore it to the vertical after a small roll to either side. In Fig. 6 let G be the centre of gravity of the ship and cargo, H that of the water displaced in a vertical position, and H^1 that of the water displaced after a small roll.

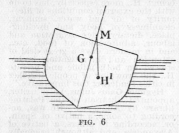

FIG. 6

Let the vertical through H^1 meet the centre line of the ship through G at the point M. Then M is called the *metacentre.* The equilibrium is not stable unless M is above G. It may be shown that M is the centre of curvature at H of the locus of H which is known as the curve of buoyancy. See Besant's *Elementary Hydrostatics. See also* CAPILLARITY and SURFACE TENSION.

Hydrotherapy, or Hydrotherapeutics, a system of cure which involves the internal or external administration of water. It may to an extent be distinguished from hydropathy as being a department of ordinary medical practice, the latter involving a doctrine in which the use of water is claimed as the supreme general cure for disease. The internal administration of water is of course necessary for the maintenance of life, but there are many reasons for supposing that fairly copious drinking of water is calculated to help the normal processes of metabolism. By supplying the body with abundance of fluid, the carrying away of waste products is facilitated, and the morbid effects of poisonous waste matter is thus avoided. If the practice of water-drinking is indulged in without consideration for times and seasons, the results are apt to be unsatisfactory, as undue dilution of certain secretions is bound to impair their efficiency. Good general rules for a person in ordinary health are the following: A glass of cold water on rising, one about an hour before each meal, and one before retiring at night. By so doing the dilution of the gastric juices

is avoided, the water is supplied when the body needs fluid for the preparation of gastric juices, and the action of the bowels is likely to be complete and easy.

The external application of water has two general purposes: that of skin cleansing, as in the ordinary soap and hot-water bath, and the application in a convenient form of a certain required temperature. To these may be added the more doubtful effects of substances in solution being absorbed by the skin, of possible radium emanations, and the stimulating effects of water containing gases dissolved under pressure. (*See* BALNEOLOGY.) By far the greater number of water applications for curative purposes are simply temperature applications. Among them may be mentioned cold packs and poultices, hot and vapour baths, and shock baths. The ordinary wet pack consists of a sheet wrung out of cold water and wrapped closely around the body; on this are superposed a number of dry blankets, the patient being kept practically immovable for an hour, when the packing is removed and the patient subjected to a bath at a little above body-temperature. The effect is soothing and provocative of increased cutaneous excretion. The cold pack aims at a lower temperature still; the body is surrounded somewhat loosely with a wet sheet, and the other coverings are loosely arranged so as to allow evaporation as uniformly as possible. The cold pack is used in cases of hyperpyrexia, that is, in extreme fever. The Turkish bath is really a hot-air bath; it consists of a number of chambers heated to different temperatures, so that the patient is exposed to a temperature gradually rising to 150° F. or higher, and is then allowed to regain the ordinary temperature of the air by gradations. The effect is to relieve internal congestion by bringing blood to the surface and to excite the peripheral excretory organs to increased activity. A prolonged application of heat locally is sometimes resorted to in order to cause congestion, and thus lead to a greater activity of disease-fighting corpuscles. Shock-baths, such as shower-baths, douches, wave-baths, etc., depend upon the sudden application of a particular temperature or the rapid alternation of two different temperatures. The effect is stimulating.

Hydrothorax (water on the chest), a collection of serous fluid in one or both of the pleural cavities, associated with disease of the heart, kidneys, and other organs.

Hydroxylamine (NH_2OH), an unstable substance forming colourless deliquescent needles (melting point,

33° C.). It may be prepared by the action of sodium nitrite on sodium bisulphite, followed by hydrolysis, or by the action of nascent hydrogen, from tin and hydrochloric acid, on ethyl nitrate or nitric oxide. It is also prepared electrolytically by the reduction of nitric acid. H., which is usually prepared in the form of its salts, is a powerful reducing agent, and forms compounds (oximes) by condensation with aldehydes and ketones.

Hydrozoa, the name given to a class of Cœlenterata belonging to the sub-phylum Cnidaria ; it is coincident with Hydromedusæ or Craspedota, with the addition of the Acalephæ. This class includes polyps, colonies of polyps which produce medusæ by budding, and medusæ which rise directly from the egg. The polyps, which are small in size, are generally attached permanently to foreign bodies, but sometimes, as in Siphonophora, the whole colony may be free-swimming. The first polyp assumes an upstanding position termed the hydranth, which lengthens and buds until it forms a colony or hydrosome. The generative cells, which are always ripening and discharging, may arise in a variety of places, but always migrate to the ectoderm of the gonophore. H. feed chiefly on animal substances, and with few exceptions are marine organisms. The class is divided into the orders Hydridæ, Hydrocorallinæ, Tubulariæ, Campanulariæ, Trachomedusæ, Narcomedusæ, and Siphonophora.

Hydrus, a fabulous water-snake or sea-serpent, formerly the name of a genus of venomous sea-snakes, now called Hydrophis. The hinder part of the body and tail is much compressed and raised vertically to facilitate swimming.

Hydrus (constellation), *see* HYDRA.

Hyères, or Hières, a tn. of the Riviera, Var, S. France, 11 m. E. of Toulon. Like its suburb Costebelle, it is a noted winter health-resort, facing the Mediterranean (about 2¼ m. away). H. Island (ancient *Stœchades*), including Port Cros, Porquerolles. Ile du Levant, form a roadstead. The town hall has a bust of Massillon (1663-1742), and the church of St. Louis and old ruined castle are interesting. Silk twist, essences, brandy, and oil are manufactured, and there is much trade in fruit, flowers, and salt. Pop. about 18,000. *See* Lentheric, *La Provence Maritime ancienne et moderne*, 1880.

Hygieia, the goddess of health, was in Greek mythology the daughter of Asclepius, and was worshipped at Corinth, Athens, and other places.

She is represented as a virgin wearing a long robe, and having by her side a snake which drinks from a cup in her hand.

Hygiene (Fr. *hygiène*), the science of health, its aim being to preserve health and prolong life by proper attention to physical laws. The subject has a wide aspect, and embraces the numerous agencies affecting man's physical and mental well-being. H., more especially, has to do with the external conditions of life— purity of air and water, sunlight, cleanliness of body and dwelling-place, dietary rules, recreation and labour, adulteration of food, etc., and in modern days a great deal of attention and investigation is bestowed on both public and private H., the crowding of people together in cities rendering this imperative.

Hyginus, Gaius Julius, Latin writer, appointed librarian of the Palatine library by Augustus. He was, according to some, a native of Spain, or, according to others, a native of Alexandria, and although originally a slave was freed by the emperor. His works are mostly lost, but the *Fabularum Liber* (*see* Schmidt's ed., 1872) and *Poeticon Astronomicon Libri IV.* (*see* Bunte's ed., 1875) are assigned to him. *See* Suet., *De Illust. Gramm.*; Van Steveren, *Mythographi Latini*, 1742 ; Bunte, *Dissertatio de vita Hygini . . .*, 1846.

Hygrometer, an instrument for measuring the relative or absolute amount of aqueous vapour in the air.

Principles of hygrometry : (a) Properties of vapours.—It is a matter of common observation that water exposed to the air disappears more or less quickly. The floors of shops, sprinkled with water in the hot weather quickly dry. A damp cloth exposed to the air becomes quite dry; on some days it dries rapidly, on other days very slowly, so that laundresses speak of a ' good drying day ' and a ' poor drying day.' The scientific term for the disappearance of the water is evaporation. The water becomes a gas which mixes with the air. This gas is called aqueous vapour. To elucidate the laws governing the evaporation of liquids, Dalton caused them to evaporate under the simplest possible conditions, viz. in a vacuous space, by introducing them into the vacuum above the mercurial column in a barometer. If a small globule of water is allowed to ascend to the top of the column it disappears very rapidly, filling the space above the mercury and producing a depression of the column. Another globule will also evaporate and produce a further depression, and so on. A point is reached, however, at which a globule does not evaporate but forms a thin layer of water on the top of the mercury. The introduction of more liquid is not attended by a depression of the mercury column if the temperature is kept constant. The liquid merely floats on top of the mercury, showing that evaporation has ceased. The space above the mercury cannot take up any more vapour; it is therefore said to be saturated, and the vapour in the saturated space is called a saturated vapour. The pressure of a saturated vapour is called the maximum vapour pressure. It increases with the temperature, but is quite independent of the volume of the space occupied by the vapour. If the vapour pressure at a given temperature is less than the maximum vapour pressure for that temperature, the vapour is said to be unsaturated. It has been proved by Regnault that the presence of a gas does not affect the quantity of vapour which a space can contain. The rate of evaporation is affected by the presence of the gas, but ultimately the quantity of vapour in a given space at the saturation point is the same whether the space is vacuous or contains air or any other gas which does not react chemically with water. Regnault determined the maximum vapour pressure of water vapour at various temperatures by observing the depression produced by the vapour in a barometer tube. Since the quantity of vapour required to saturate a given space depends solely on the temperature, the pressure exerted by saturated water vapour in a space containing air can be found from the tables of saturated vapour pressures compiled by Regnault. (b) *Relative humidity.*—If a space is not saturated with water vapour, the vapour pressure is less than the maximum value for the corresponding temperature. The ratio of the actual vapour pressure in a space to the saturation pressure for the same temperature, is called the relative humidity. The value of this ratio determines our estimate of the dampness or dryness of the atmosphere. The air is said to be damp when it is saturated or nearly saturated with aqueous vapour. The absolute quantity of aqueous vapour in the air does not determine its dampness but merely the proximity to saturation. For example, suppose that, on a summer's day, the temperature is 25° C. and that the pressure of the aqueous vapour is 11 millimeters, the air would feel dry because the saturation pressure at 25° C. is 23·55 millimetres. On the

other hand, suppose that, on a cold winter's day when the temperature is 5° C., the aqueous vapour pressure is 6·7 millimetres, the air would feel very damp because the saturation pressure is 6·998 millimetres at 5° C. The weight of aqueous vapour in a cubic metre of air in the former case is low, in the latter case high. The fraction of saturation or relative humidity may also be expressed by the ratio of the weight w of vapour contained in a given volume of air to the weight W which would saturate the same space at the same temperature. If the vapour obeys Boyle's law up to the point of saturation (which is approximately the case), then the weight of vapour contained in a given volume is simply proportional to the pressure, so that $\dfrac{w}{W} = \dfrac{p}{P}$, where p and P are, respectively, the corresponding actual vapour pressure and the saturation vapour pressure. There are thus two methods available for determining the fraction of saturation or humidity of the air. The first method consists in determining the actual pressure p of the vapour in the air and then ascertaining from the tables of maximum vapour pressure the maximum pressure P at the same temperature. This is the method practised in all dew-point instruments. In the second method the weight w of vapour in a measured volume of air is determined by the chemical H., and the weight W which would saturate the same volume at the same temperature is obtained from Regnault's tables.

Dew-point hygrometers.—If an atmosphere containing aqueous vapour is gradually cooled, a temperature will be reached at which the vapour will condense. This temperature is called the dew-point. At this temperature the quantity of vapour in the air is just sufficient to saturate it. In an unconfined atmosphere the pressure of the vapour will not change during the cooling, hence the actual pressure of the vapour in the air is equal to the maximum vapour pressure at the temperature of the dew-point. If, therefore, the dew-point is determined, the maximum vapour pressure for this temperature is found from the tables of vapour pressures, and this is the actual pressure f of the vapour in the air.

Regnault's hygrometer. — In this instrument (see Fig. 1) air is aspirated through ether contained in the silver thimble which closes the lower end of the glass tube E. Cooling is produced by the evaporation of the ether; when the temperature of the silver surface reaches the dew-point, the polish of the surface becomes dimmed owing to the deposition of moisture. The temperature at which this happens is read on the thermometer T. The moment at which the dew appears on the thimble attached to

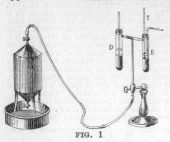

FIG. 1

E can be ascertained with great delicacy by comparing its surface with that of the surface of a similar thimble attached to the end of the glass tube D which contains nothing but air.

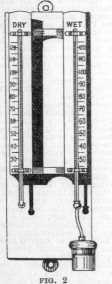

FIG. 2

Wet and dry bulb hygrometers.— This consists of two delicate thermometers attached to a wooden stand (*see* Fig. 2). One of the bulbs is covered with muslin and is kept

moist by being connected with a reservoir of water by means of cotton wick. Evaporation takes place more or less rapidly from the wet muslin, and the bulb of the thermometer which it covers is more or less cooled according to the hygrometric state of the air. If the air is quite saturated no evaporation will take place, and the temperature of the wet bulb is the same as that of the dry bulb. The drier the atmosphere the greater will be the difference in temperature between the two bulbs. The indications of this instrument depend on so many complex circumstances that it is impossible to deduce any theoretical formula connecting the difference in temperature of the two thermometers and the relative humidity of the air. Glaisher deduced empirically from a large mass of observations certain factors for computing the dew-point, and the indications of the instrument are interpreted by means of Glaisher's tables, which give the dew-point corresponding to any difference of reading between the two thermometers. These tables are not to be relied on when the wet bulb is greatly depressed below the dry bulb and the atmosphere is correspondingly dry. In its modern form the wet and dry bulb H. has become an instrument of comparatively great precision. To secure this accuracy the following conditions must be satisfied: (1) The two bulbs must be of the same size and sensitiveness; (2) the wet bulb must be covered with thin muslin saturated with pure water; (3) both thermometers must be whirled or ventilated rapidly and be protected from disturbing radiations.

Hygroscope, an instrument used to indicate whether the air is more or less moist. It gives no indication as to the quantity of moisture present. Its action depends on the property which organic substances have of elongating when moist and contracting as they dry. In one of the most common forms, a male and female figure are so suspended (by catgut) with reference to the doors of a toy-house that when the air is moist the man comes out of one door while the woman goes in at the other, the converse taking place when it is dry. As these Hs. change slowly their indications are always behind-hand with the state of the weather.

Hyksos, or 'shepherd kings,' a people from the East who conquered Egypt 'without a battle.' According to the historian Manetho, 'In the days of King Timæus (of whom we know nothing) Egypt, being convulsed with a terrible civil war, was suddenly invaded by an ignoble race who came from the East, and fell "without a battle." The conquerors destroyed cities and temples, and enslaved the inhabitants.' Manetho describes how ' when they had our rulers in their hands, they burnt our cities and demolished the temples of our gods, and reduced our wives and children to slavery.' Who these people were, we are not at present able to prove; certain it is that they came from the East and that to the cultured Egyptian they were ' the loathed and despised barbarian.' Authorities on the history of Egypt place the arrival of the H. at the end of the 12th dynasty, and their expulsion at the beginning of the 18th dynasty. The Egyptians were not by nature warlike; they were lovers of home and of peace; necessity at times drove them to extremes, but the whole nature of the country was ' to live and let live.' Some of the greatest of their soldier kings were blamed by their allies for want of ferocity and barbarity. This lack of military spirit must have caused the yoke of the barbarian to be very heavy; it had, however, the desired effect upon the country. At the final expulsion of the H., when the Egyptians at last rose and learnt to combine, no fate was vile enough for the barbarian, and no Egyptian who was able to bear arms refused to enlist. Of the many theories concerning the H., one assumes that, after the downfall of the 13th dynasty, a confederation of Semitic tribes from the Eastern Syrian desert migrated into the Delta during the internal trouble of the country, combined and then assumed the mastery of Lower Egypt. It is a more attractive theory to believe they were non-Semitic, and may have been related to, or formed part of, the Kheta or Hittite people (*q.v.*). These H. having established themselves, elected a king called Salatis, who reigned at Memphis and made all Egypt tributary to him. The great fortress at Avaris in the Sethroite nome or district, E. of Bubastis and close to Tanis, became their stronghold. Very few records or monuments of the H. have come down to us. Josephus gives us a few names of the H. kings, such as Salatis, Beon, who succeeded him, Apachnas, Apophis, Jonias, and Assis. Another king, Apopi, or Apepa I., whose name is inscribed on a granite slab at the Temple of Bubastis, appears to have tried to suppress the worship of the ancient gods of Egypt and struggled to force the country to pay homage to Set (the wicked one). A King Khyan, whose headless statue was found at Bubastis, seems to have spread his authority widely, and been either known or recognised as far as Bagdad, and also at Cnossus in Crete, where his name occurs on the lid of a jar. The scarabs of the H. have been found chiefly at Tell-el-Yehudiyeh, From the ruins of the fortifications of these people, authorities have argued that they were an uncivilised desert people, but we cannot yet, with any definite proof, say who they were or from whence they came. Their rule in Egypt may have lasted 500 years, or, as other authorities say, 100 years. Correct dates are still impossible to obtain.

Hylactes, the name of a genus of passeriform birds belonging to the family Pteroptochidæ and ranging over S. America.

Hylæosaurus (Gk. ὑλαῖος, of the wood, and σαῦρος, lizard), the name of a genus of fossil dinosaurs belonging to the Stegosauria, whose remains were discovered in the Wealden formation of Tilgati forest; the spine of these huge lizards was about 25 ft. long.

Hylobates, the name of a genus of mammals belonging to the Primates, family Anthropomorphidæ or Simiidæ, and commonly known as the gibbons. *H. syndactylus*, the siamang, is the best-known species.

Hylton, or **Hilton**, a vil. in the co. of Durham, England. It stands on the R. Wear, about 3 m. W. of Sunderland, and the people are engaged in shipbuilding and the manuf. of iron goods. Pop. (1911) 2000.

Hymen, in Greek mythology, the god of marriage, though originally the marriage song. He is generally supposed to be the son of Apollo and one of the Muses, and is represented as a beautiful youth carrying a bridal torch.

Hymenæa, a genus of leguminous plants found in tropical America. There are eight species in all, the commonest being *H. courbaril*, the locust or gum-anime tree. The wood is very heavy and takes a fine polish; the resin known as gum-anime exudes from the stem; the seeds are enveloped in a sweet mealy substance eaten by the Indians.

Hymenomycetes, a group of fungi belonging to the Basidiomycetes, which are the most highly organised of the fungi. The group is distinguished by the fact that in the fructification the hymenium or sporebearing layer is exposed before maturity, and does not remain enclosed as in the Gasteromycetes. *Clavaria*, *Polyporus*, and *Agaricus* (mushrooms) are among the principal genera.

Hymenoptera, the name given to a large order of Insecta which includes the bees, ants, wasps, etc.; its members are characterised by four membranous wings with few nervures, well-developed mandibles, movable abdomen, bearing, in the case of the female, an ovipositor which may or may not be retractile; certain families are furnished with a sting, and others with sawing or boring appendages; in the honey-bees, the subordinate mouth-parts are produced into a long, tongue-like proboscis, with which the insect extracts honey from flowers. The head is globular in shape, and mobile, with compound eyes and several occelli on the crown. The larvæ are cruciform and have a distinct head. There are over 30,000 species of H., which are grouped into two sub-orders, the Sessilventres and the Petiolata. To the first belong Tenthredinidæ, the saw-flies; Siricidæ, the wood-borers, etc. The Petiolata comprise the series Parasitica, with Cynipidæ, the gall-wasps; Ichneumonidæ, the larvæ-wasps, etc; the series Tubulifera, consisting of Chrysididæ, the burnished wasps, and the series Aculeata, containing Apidæ, the bees, Formicidæ, the ants, and many other important families.

Hymettus, an ancient mountain range of Attica, Greece, over 3000 ft. high, about 5 m. from Athens, now called Trelo Vuni (Vouni). It has always been famous for its honey. The ancients quarried a much-prized bluish-grey marble.

Hymns (Gk. ὕμνος). The word was employed among the Greeks to denote songs or poems in honour of gods or of heroes, or composed for some special occasion, and in Greece the number of H. was legion. Hesion, Homer, Pindar, Euripides, all make use of the term and testify to the frequency with which the compositions are used. Oldest among these are the Homeric H., a series of brief addresses to the gods. Among the latest pagan Greek productions are the Orphic H., which deal with the rites of initiation into the Hellenic mysteries. It is not certain whether these H., which share the characteristics of the Alexandrian school, are pre-Christian or not. In considering the question of hymnology from a Christian point of view, however, the early Hebrew poetry is especially valuable. It shows, indeed, the greatest heights to which poetry had risen before the beginning of the Christian era, and it may well be said that its best work has never since been excelled. The unique position which the Davidic psalter has ever held in the worship of Christendom shows the recognition of this fact by all nations. It must not be forgotten, moreover, that exquisite poetry is to

be found in many other portions of the O.T. The last great burst of Hebrew hymnody is closely connected with the Incarnation, and as such have always held a high place in the services of the church. For centuries the song of Zacharias (Luke i. 68-79), ' Blessed be the Lord God of Israel,' and the song of the Blessed Virgin Mary (Luke i. 46-55), ' My soul doth magnify the Lord,' have been used daily in the choir offices, the former in the morning, the latter in the evening.

As we consider the question of Christian hymnody, it will be well to begin with a definition, that of St. Augustine of Hippo: A H. 'is singing with the praise of God. If you praise God and do not sing you utter no hymn. If you sing and praise not God you utter no hymn. If you praise anything which belongs not to the praise of God, though in singing you praise, you utter no hymn.' This definition gives the distinction characteristic to the H. which belong to the four centuries preceding it.

Eastern hymnody.—The preface to the hymnary of the Mozarabic Breviary tells us that as Christianity itself came from the East, so also did the custom of hymn-singing. The words of Pliny, in the famous letter to Trajan (c. 110 A.D.), carry us further than this by showing at how early a date the custom was established in Bithynia. It is interesting also to note that this singing of H., for which the Christians were accustomed to meet before daybreak, was probably antiphonal, for this seems the most natural interpretation of the phrase *secum invicem.* Early Greek H. must be divided into two classes, the first consisting of those written in the rapidly dying classical metres, the second, and more important, of H. written in a more oriental and often Hebraic type. To the first class belongs the oldest of all Christian H., the Στόμιον πώλων ἀδαῶν, ascribed to Clement of Alexandria. This H. is simple and childlike, containing nothing but what could be found in the pages of Scripture. A higher mystical level is shown in the H. of St. Gregory of Nazianzus (also classical in form) in the 4th century, dealing chiefly with the doctrines of the œcumenical symbol and the contemplation of the Most Holy Trinity. Translations of all may be found in A. W. Chatfield's *Songs and Hymns of the Earliest Greek Christian Poets.* To the same school belong Synesius (375-430), Sophronius, and St. John of Damascus. Of all their works only three canons by St. John of Damascus have received a place in the Greek service-books. This saint also wrote many H. in opposition to the Arians, who carried on vigorous propaganda by this means. The later Greek H. are to be found chiefly in the various church service books, viz. the twelve volumes of the *Menœa*, giving the Prayer of Saints; the *Greater Octœchus* or *Paraclitice*, containing the Ferial office; the *Lesser Octœchus*, containing the ordinary Sunday services; the *Triodion* (Lenten season); the *Pentecostarion Charmosynon* (Easter and Pentecost); the *Euchologion*, containing the occasional offices; and the *Horologion* or *Hours of Prayer*. These books contain a vast number of H. of which the best selection is to be found in Christ and Paramkas's *Anthologia Grœca*, etc. They are best known in England by the translations of J. M. Neale of which mention may be made of ' Christian, dost thou see them? ' (St. Andrew of Crete, 660-*c.* 732), ' 'Tis the day of Resurrection ' (St. John Damascene), ' Jesus, Lord of life eternal ' (Joseph the Hymnographer), ' Jesus, Name all names above ' (Theoctistus of the Studium). But numbers may be found in any modern hymnal.

Syriac.—From the 2nd century until almost the close of the middle ages, the churches of Syria, Mesopotamia, and Western Persia produced many excellent H., which are, unfortunately, almost unknown in the West. The names of Bardesanes (Bar-Daisan, *b.* 154), and Ephraem Syrus (*d.* 378) must be mentioned. The H. of this writer still hold an important position in the service books of the Syriac churches.

Latin hymnology cannot be traced further back than the beginning of the 4th century, the earliest name with which any H. can be connected being that of Hilary of Poitiers, of whom Isidore of Seville says that ' he was the first who flourished in composing hymns in verse.' Several H. in the Mozarabic Breviary are ascribed to him. Contemporary with Hilary was Pope Damasus, to whom two extant H. are ascribed, but the real founder of Latin hymnody comes somewhat later. This title is unanimously given to St. Ambrose (*d.* 397), to whom a large number of extant H. is attributed. The twelve which the Benedictine editors give as genuine include some of the best known office H. Among them are ' Æterna Christi munera ' (The eternal gifts of Christ the King), for apostles and evangelists; ' O Lux beata Trinitas ' (O Trinity of blessed light), Saturdays in Trinitytide; and ' Splendor Paternæ gloriæ ' (O splendour of God's glory bright), Mondays from Epiphany to Lent. The many followers of St. Ambrose in his style of composing are often grouped as the Ambrosiani. From the 4th to the 11th century we have a regular stream of religious poets and hymn-writers, mostly of considerable merit. Only one or two of the most famous can now be mentioned. At the end of the 4th century comes Aurelius Clemens Prudentius, a Spaniard, from whose poems many of the Ferial H. (*e.g.* ' Lux ecce surgit aurea ') were taken. But his best-known H. is that for the Nativity, ' Corde natus ex parentis ' (Of the Father's love begotten). In the 5th century we have the layman Sedulius, the author of the well-known Christmas H., found in almost all the breviaries, ' A solis ortus cardine ' (From east to west, from shore to shore). The latter part of this, ' Hostis Herodes impie ' (Why, impious Herod, should'st thou fear?), forms the office H. for the Epiphany. Venantius Fortunatus, bishop of Poitiers (*d. c.* 609), is far better known. To him belongs the glorious Passiontide H., ' Vexilla Regis prodeunt ' (The royal banners forward go), and ' Pange lingua gloriosi ' (Sing, my tongue, the glorious battle), both of which occur in the Roman Breviary, but in a mutilated form. St. Gregory the Great, from whom the Gregorian melody takes its name, wrote much, but is less known. Some twelve H. are attributed to the one English Father, the Venerable Bede (673-735). In the next century Fulbert of Chartres wrote the triumphal Easter H., ' Chorus novæ Hierusalem ' (Ye choirs of New Jerusalem). From the 8th century dates also the *Urbs beata Hierusalem*, which became the H. throughout Europe for the dedication of a church. This, too, received very bad treatment at the hands of the revisers of the Roman Breviary. This period closes with the mention of St. Bernard of Clairvaux, the representative of the later mystic school, whose ' Jesu dulcis memoria ' (Jesu, the very thought of Thee) is known to all. By the end of the 11th century the liturgical use of H. was well established throughout Western Christendom, and such H. found a place in all service books. The next few centuries are important for the spread of the Sequence, a H. sung before the Gospel at mass, which was developed from the Alleluia by Notker of St. Gall (*d.* 912). Among writers of this kind Adam of St. Victor was the most important. The greatest of the mediæval sequences, however, is the ' Dies iræ, dies illa ' (Day of wrath, O day of mourning), the authorship of which is ascribed to Thomas of Celano, the friend of St Francis of Assisi. In the later centuries much was done both in the

writing of new H. and the classicalis-
ing of the old by the brothers San-
teuil in Paris, and by others who
wrote for the French and monastic
breviaries, but none rank as high as
those which have been already mentioned.

English hymnody.—It would be
possible to trace the beginnings of
English hymnody to the time of
Cædmon (7th century), but this
would lead us by too long a path. It
will be well to take the history up at
the Reformation. When the translations and adaptations of the old service books were made for the new
Book of Common Prayer, it was
Cranmer's intention that the old H.
should be translated likewise. But he
had not himself the poetic ability for
this task, and the work remained un-
done until the 19th century, when
several translations of the whole
body of the ancient Sarum H. were
made. Many of these are now coming
into great favour with English churchmen. During the couple of centuries
that followed the beginnings of the
Reformation there was then no book
of H. for use in the English Church.
In the Prayer Book itself there was
but one translation, that of the *Veni
Creator* in the Ordinal. Their place
was taken, however, to some extent
by the metrical paraphrases of the
Psalms, which generally supplanted
the Prayer Book versions. Until
almost the end of the 17th century
the most popular was the version by
Sternhold and Hopkins, commonly
known as the 'Old Version.' This later
gave way to the 'New Version' of Tate
and Brady. Several from this latter
work still find their place in hymnals,
such as, for example, the H. ' As
pants the hart for cooling streams.'
Many religious poems appeared in
private collections, and magnificent
devotional poetry was produced by
many of the metaphysical poets,
notably by George Herbert in *The
Temple.* In 1623 appeared George
Withers' *Hymns and Songs of the
Church*, the first attempt at a comprehensive hymn-book, but it never
secured any measure of success.
Many excellent H. were written also
by Bishops Taylor and Ken. But the
first hymn-book definitely designed
for use with the services of the Church
of England appeared in 1737, with
the title *Collection of Psalms and
Hymns*. It was compiled by John
Wesley, chiefly from the writings of
Isaac Watts, and published at
Charlestown in Georgia. Two years
later came the official foundation of
Methodism, and all later editions of
the book must be classed as Methodist.
The next step was taken by M.
Madan, whose indebtedness is more

to Whitefield than to Wesley, owing
to his sympathy with the former's
Calvinism. In 1760 he published *A
Collection of Psalms and Hymns extracted from various Authors*, etc.,
containing 170 H. It is noteworthy
that during the rest of the century
all the Church hymn-books that
appeared were built on the foundation of the various Nonconformist
collections, and that no great hymn-
writer arises within the church until
the production of the *Olney Hymns*
by Newton and Cowper. At the beginning of the 19th century there was
a great outburst of hymn-writing and
collecting, which had seen considerable advance even during the first
twenty years. The productions of this
period are characterised by a striving
for uniformity and harmony with the
Book of Common Prayer, and by a
desire to secure official recognition
which presages the later general return to the old Greek and Latin H.
and their translations. Meanwhile,
the thirty years which bring us to the
middle of the century saw an even
greater increase in the number of
hymn-books produced. Seventy-four
of these are quoted in Julian's *Dictionary*, and these are but a selection
of the most important. Bishop
Heber's *Hymns* (1827), containing
the hymns of H. H. Milman, was an
extremely influential collection, and
E. Bickersteth's *Christian Psalmody*
(1833) was also important. This last
collection surpassed all that had previously been produced both in breadth
and scholarship, but it was later supplanted by the *Hymnal Companion*
by the Rev. E. H. Bickersteth, son
of the above-named. The period immediately following 1850 was marked
chiefly by the large number of translations made not only from the Latin
and Greek but also from German and
other continental languages. Translations from the ancient service books
had already been made by Bishop
Mant, and his work was carried on by
J. M. Neale, Blew, and others. The
name of Miss Catherine Winkworth
stands above all others as a translator from the German. The influx of
these H., more definite in doctrine
and more robust in style, led to a
gradual exclusion of the Nonconformist and Calvinistic element which
had hitherto bulked so large. Moreover, the standard of religious poetry
had been raised considerably by the
influence of Keble's *Christian Year*.
The *Hymnal Noted* of 1852 and 1854
confined itself entirely to Latin
hymns, their excellence being enhanced by the beauty of Neale's
translations. But the hundreds of
hymnals which had now issued from
the press had left English hymnody in

great confusion, and an attempt was made by several of the most influential publishers to secure the withdrawal of many of the smaller books in favour of a new and broader collection. This resulted in the publication of *Hymns* (later *Hymns Ancient and Modern*), 1861, a collection which at first contained only 130 H., but which rapidly increased in size and in popularity until it almost entirely supplanted all other collections. At the beginning of the 20th century several new hymn-books, all aiming at a higher level of scholarship, were produced. The most important of these are the *English Hymnal* (1906) and the *Oxford Hymnal*.

Nonconformist hymnody. — Reference has already been made to the fact that Nonconformist H. formed for long the bulk of those in use in the Established Church. Though they did not share to so large an extent in the revival of the 19th century, yet the H. of the various dissenting bodies are still very important. The Baptists long resisted the practice of singing H. Their first hymn-writer was B. Keach, about 1673. The names of J. Stennett (1663-1713), S. Stennett, grandson of the former (1728-95), and W. Noel (1799-1873) are also worthy of mention. Both the Particular Baptists and the General Baptists now have official hymnbooks. The Congregationalists have produced many hymn-writers of great merit. Greatest of these is Isaac Watts (1674-1748), the importance of whose influence on the later development of English hymnody in general it is almost impossible to over-estimate. The names of Doddridge and Conder are also well known. In 1859 was published officially the *New Congregational Hymn Book*, to which a somewhat inferior supplement was added in 1874. Since that date, however, several other Congregational hymnals have been issued. Mention has already been made of the way in which Methodism was connected with the beginnings of the English hymnal. The idea was taken by John Wesley from the Moravian Brothers, from whom also he got the text of some German H. The greatest hymn-writer of Methodism is Charles Wesley, to whom several thousand H. of varying merit are ascribed. Many of them are among the most popular of H., both in the Church of England and among the various Methodist bodies. Finally, it may be said that the singing of H. now forms a larger part of the service among the anti-liturgical bodies than it has ever done within the Church.

Mention may now be made of the H. known as carols. The word was originally applied not to a song, but to a dance. The song was later added, and the name included both. Finally the dance was dropped, and the song retained the name. Carols, secular and religious, both in the vernacular, were very popular during the middle ages, being sung at festivals both in and out of church. Their history is especially connected with the miracle and mystery plays. Odd scraps of Latin, which seemed to link these popular songs to the liturgical service of the church are frequently found in them. From the Reformation to the 19th century we have almost an entire blank in the history of the carol. Then collections of modernised versions of the old carols were made and new ones were written. To this period belongs *Good King Wenceslas*, by J. M. Neale. The most popular collections are those by Chope and Woodward. *See* Julian's *Dictionary of Hymnology*, 1892 (last ed., 1907), to which this article is much indebted; J. M. Neale's *Hymns of the Eastern Church*, 1863; J. Pauly's *Hymni Breviarii Romani*, 1868-70; C. A. G. Chevalier's *Poésie liturgique du moyen-âge*, 1893; Norman's *Hymnarium Salisburiense*, 1851, and Daniel's *Thesaurus Hymnologicus*, 1853, with J. M. Neale's dissertation.

Hyndford, John Carmichael, third **Earl of** (1701-67), a Scottish diplomatist, sent as ambassador to Prussia during the War of the Austrian Succession, and instrumental in bringing about the treaty of Breslau (1742). He was envoy to Russia (1744-49), and helped on the peace of Aix-la-Chapelle. He was also sent to Vienna (1752-64). He succeeded to his father's title and estate in Lanarkshire (1737), became vice-admiral of Scotland (1764), privy councillor (1750). *See* Douglas, *Scottish Peerage*, ii.; Carlyle, *Life of Frederick II.*; Irving, *Upper Ward of Lanarkshire*, i.

Hyndman, Henry Mayers (*b.* 1842), a leading English socialist, and first chairman of the British Socialist Party. He graduated at Trinity College, Cambridge, and in 1866 acted as correspondent to the *Pall Mall Gazette* in the Italian war, becoming acquainted with Mazzini, Garibaldi, and Saffi. From 1869-71 he travelled in Australia, New Zealand, Polynesia, and America, and from 1871-74 occupied himself with journalistic work. In 1881 he founded the Social Democratic Federation. He was always an active agitator for social remedies, and in 1887 was tried with John Burns and others at the Old Bailey in connection with West End riots, but acquitted. He was a vigorous agitator against the war in South Africa (1899-1902) and is a stern critic of British rule in India. Amongst his numerous publications are: *Indian Policy and English Justice; Historical Basis of Socialism ; Socialism and Slavery*, a reply to Herbert Spencer ; *England for All*, etc.

Hyne, Charles John Cutcliffe Wright (*b.* 1866), an English novelist and traveller, born at Bilbury, Gloucestershire. He was educated at Bradford Grammar School, and graduated at Clare College, Cambridge, in 1887 rowing in the winning University Trial Eight. He travelled widely in search of literary material, visiting Europe, the Canary Islands, Congo Free State, Russian Lapland, Algeria, Morocco, Mexico, etc. Besides contributions to various magazines, he published the following: *The New Eden; Honour of Thieves, or the Little Red Captain; Adventures of Captain Kettle; Through Arctic Lapland; The Lost Continent; Kate Meredith; McTod; Atoms of Empire; Mr. Horrocks, Purser; Thompson's Progress; Empire of the World; The Escape Agents*, and *The Marriage of Kettle*, all of which are the outcome of his journeyings abroad. H. is also greatly interested in mining in Mexico, and an enthusiasitic big-game and cave-hunter.

Hyogo, or **Hiogo**, a seaport tn. on the island of Hondo, Japan. In 1868 it was opened to foreigners, and in 1892 was united to Kobé to form one town with it. It is a trading centre of considerable importance, and is easily accessible from Osaka and other towns of interest. It also possesses shipbuilding yards. Pop. about 300,000 (with Kobé).

Hyoid Bone, a U-shaped bone lying immediately above the thyroid cartilage of the larynx, and near the root of the tongue, to the muscles of which it gives attachment. It consists of a more or less rectangular body (*basihyal*), and two pairs of unequal *cornua* or horns ; the greater curve upwards and backwards, the smaller, about ⅓ in. in length, are attached to the basihyal near its junctions with the *great cornua*. The five distinct portions in youth have cartilaginous connections, but after middle age the whole may become ossified into a single bone.

Hypatia (*c.* 370-415), a famous female ancient philosopher, and mathematician, daughter of Theon, born in Alexandria. She lectured for a time in her native city, and then became the head of the Neoplatonic school there. Her deep erudition, sound judgment, and fine elocution, gained for her the admiration of all her hearers, and her house became the resort of all the great learners and distinguished men in Alexandria, amongst others, Orestes, the prefect of the city, with whom she was accused of being too intimate, and barbarously put to death by the savage Nitrian monks and fanatical Christian mob. For the little authentic knowledge about H., *see* Socrates, *Hist. ecclesiastica*, vii. 15.

Hyperæsthesia, an excessive sensibility of the nervous system, due to diseased conditions; it is particularly characteristic of hysteria. The sensory nerves are extremely sensitive to the slightest impressions, and may react without the presence of any external stimulus at all. H. is sometimes induced by rheumatism, sciatica, or any acute nervous complaint. In this condition the slightest irritation may give rise to a paroxysm of intense pain. In hysteria the sensations may be so exaggerated as to destroy all sense of proportion for the time being, and imaginary sensations may be accepted by the patient as real. The treatment involves removal of the cause; local applications of heat, cold, or electricity often afford temporary relief.

Hyperbola, the plane figure obtained by cutting a right circular cone by a plane inclined to the horizon at an angle greater than that of a generating line (*see* GEOMETRY). Hence it is known as a conic section. It is a symmetrical figure of two branches, each extending to infinity.

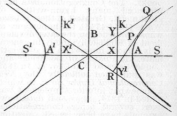

Any point on an hyperbola is such that its distance from a fixed point, known as the *focus*, always bears a constant ratio to its distance from a fixed straight line called the *directrix;* and this ratio, which is greater than unity, is called the *eccentricity* of the hyperbola. A second focus and directrix also exist, for which the same property is true. In the figure S, S[1] are the foci, KX and K[1]X[1] the directrices. SS[1] is the transverse axis, and CB the conjugate axis. C, the middle point of SS[1], is the centre, and A, A[1] are the vertices. The straight lines CY, CY[1] through the centre, known as *asymptotes*, gradually approach the curve, but actually only meet it at points infinitely distant. If the tangent at any point P on the curve cut the asymptotes in Q and R, the area of the triangle CQR is the same for all positions of P. An hyperbola is thus sometimes defined as the envelope of the line which forms with two given straight lines a triangle of constant area. In analytical conics the equation of an hyperbola referred to its axes is $\frac{x^2}{a^2} - \frac{y^2}{b^2} = 1$, and referred to its asymptotes is $xy = c^2$. When the asymptotes are at right angles to one another, the hyperbola is called *rectangular*.

Hyperbole (ὑπερβολή, overshooting, excess), a figure of rhetoric which 'lies without deceiving,' consisting of exaggerated and extravagant statements, used through excitement, or to express strong feeling and arrest the attention, and not intended to be taken literally. Formal compliments are often Hs. They form the basis of many metaphors, and occur frequently in high-flown or poetic language. The exact opposite is Litotes, or Meiosis.

Hyperbolic Functions, the name given to a set of six functions which are closely connected with the six trigonometrical ratios. The hyperbolic *sine* is written sinh, and may be defined by $\sinh\theta = \frac{e^\theta - e^{-\theta}}{2}$. Similarly the hyperbolic *cosine* is given by $\cosh\theta = \frac{e^\theta + e^{-\theta}}{2}$. The remaining four are obtained from the equations, $\tanh\theta = \frac{\sinh\theta}{\cosh\theta}$, $\coth\theta = \frac{\cosh\theta}{\sinh\theta}$, $\operatorname{sech}\theta = \frac{1}{\cosh\theta}$, and $\operatorname{cosech}\theta = \frac{1}{\sinh\theta}$. Since $\sin\theta = \frac{e^{\theta\iota} - e^{-\theta\iota}}{2\iota}$ and $\cos\theta = \frac{e^{\theta\iota} + e^{-\theta\iota}}{2}$ where $\iota = \sqrt{-1}$, ∴ $\frac{\sin\theta\iota}{\iota} = \frac{e^\theta - e^{-\theta}}{2} = \sinh\theta$ and $\cosh\theta\iota = \frac{e^\theta + e^{-\theta}}{2} = \cosh\theta$, and thus the connection with the trigonometrical ratios may be established. A series of formulæ parallel with the ordinary trigonometrical formulæ can be deduced, e.g.—

$\cosh^2\theta - \sinh^2\theta = 1$.
$\sinh(\theta+\phi) = \sinh\theta\cosh\phi + \cosh\theta\sinh\phi$.
$\sinh 2\theta = 2\sinh\theta\cosh\theta$, $\cosh 2\theta = \cosh^2\theta + \sinh^2\theta$, etc.

Hyperboloid, the name given in solid geometry to two surfaces belonging to the general class of conicoids, which in three-dimensional analytical geometry are represented by equations of the second degree in x, y, and z. The two forms of hyperboloids are known as the hyperboloid of one sheet (shown in the figure)

and the hyperboloid of two sheets. The simplest form of their equations are respectively $\frac{x^2}{a^2} + \frac{y^2}{b^2} - \frac{z^2}{c^2} = 1$ and $\frac{x^2}{a^2} - \frac{y^2}{b^2} - \frac{z^2}{c^2} = 1$. Both may be generated by a variable ellipse moving parallel to itself; and both are intersected by three mutually perpendicular planes in two hyperbolas and one ellipse. The hyperboloid of two

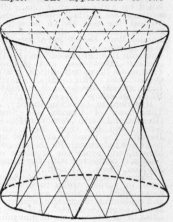

sheets is formed by two distinct surfaces extending to infinity, and each is touched at infinity by an asymptotic cone, in the same way as the hyperbola has two branches and a pair of asymptotes. The hyperboloid of one sheet is a ruled surface, and is such that through every point of it two straight lines, called generators, may be drawn so as to lie wholly on the surface. It may also be defined as the locus of the intersection of corresponding planes of two homographic pencils of planes.

Hyperborei (Gk. Ὑπερβόρεοι, Hyperboreans, 'beyond the North wind '), a mythical race supposed by the Greeks to dwell in the far N. They enjoyed perpetual youth, and lived in constant sunshine and unclouded happiness. The Rhipæan Mts. separated them from the rest of the world. The name was transferred to any people who lived far N. *See* Pindar, *Pyth.,* x.; Herod. iv.; Crusius, ' Hyperboreer ' in Roscher's *Lexikon,* 1884-97.

Hyperchlorhydria, *see* DYSPEPSIA.

Hyperides, or Hypereides (c. 395-322 B.C.), an Athenian orator, one of the ten of the Alexandrian canon, ranking next to Demosthenes. After studying under Plato and Isocrates, he became an advocate at Athens. H. warmly supported the Athenian opposition to Macedon, headed by Demosthenes and Lycurgus, and was a staunch friend of the former until they fell out over the case of Alexander's absconding treasurer, Harpalus. In the Lamian War that followed H. shared in the defeat at Crannon (322), and was captured and killed by Antipater at Ægina. His writings are witty, graceful, and ironical, the best known being the funeral oration over the dead in the Lamian War. *See* edition of speeches and fragments by Blass (1894); Churchill Babington's edition (1853); *Against Athenogenes*, and *Against Philippides* (Kenyon's edition, 1893). Consult Jebb's *Attic Orators*, ii., 1880; Blass, *Attische Beredsamkeit*, iii.,1898; Hager, *Quæstiones Hyperideæ*, 1870.

Hyperion, in Greek mythology, a Titan, son of Uranus and Gæa (Heaven and Earth), father of Helios, Selene, and Eos (Sun, Moon, and Dawn). The name is also used by poets as a patronymic for the sun-god himself, and hence the attribute of beauty is connected with the name. *See* Hes., *Theog.;* Apollod., i.

Hyperite, a name which has been given at various times to different rocks, allied to diabase, and diorite, and containing plagioclase, iron ores, biotite, hypersthene, etc. It is closely allied to the latter; if the hornblendic constituent of labradorite is a dark lamellar variety of either hornblende or pyroxene, a species of hypersthene, the rock is H. According to its present classification, H. may be interposed between diorite and gabbro. The volcanic belt encircling the Pacific is rich in hypersthene andesite, which is akin to H. It is especially abundant in the Rocky Mts, the Andes, Japan, Java, and the Philippines, and may be observed in the volcanoes of Hungary and the old volcanic systems of the Lake District, North Wales, the Ochils, etc.; whilst it issues from the more or less active volcanoes of Le Soufrière of St. Vincent, Krakatoa, and Pelée in Martinique.

Hypersthene, a rock-forming mineral consisting of silicates of iron and magnesium; formula (Fe, Mg) SiO_3. It belongs to the pyroxene group of metasilicates, and differs from the other members of the orthorhombic series of pyroxenes in possessing more iron. Thus *enstatite* is a magnesium silicate, *bronzite* contains more magnesium than iron, while in H. part of the magnesium of bronzite is replaced by iron. H. crystallises in the orthorhombic system, and has a prismatic cleavage, the angle between the planes being 87°. Well-developed crystals are rare, and the material usually forms the ground mass of igneous and metamorphic rocks of wide distribution.

Hypersthenite, a rock whose chief constituent is hypersthene (*q.v.*). It is a member of the pyroxenite group, and different species are named according to the other minerals present. Hs. are of igneous origin and occur in great abundance in the N. of Scotland, New Zealand, Saxony, the eastern states of America, and elsewhere. Closely allied are websterite, containing diallage and hypersthene, and the hypersthene-andesites, which consist essentially of plagioclase felspar, set in a ground mass of hypersthene.

Hyperthyroidea, a condition of the body caused by excessive activity of the thyroid gland. The thyroid gland is situated between the skin and the front of the windpipe, and has important functions, though their exact nature is not known. In certain districts, such as the Alpine regions of France, an enlargement of the gland is liable to occur, progressing to the formation of a large tumour or goitre, which may hang down as far as the breast. Ordinary goitre appears to be accompanied by interference with the functions of the thyroid gland, and is often improved by small doses of thyroid extract. A variety known as *exophthalmic* goitre, from a protrusion of the eyeballs which is characteristic of the disease, appears to be associated with increased activity of the thyroid gland. The symptoms, which include palpitation of the heart and excessive nervous irritability, are similar to those produced by an overdose of thyroid extract, and the treatment of the disease includes the administration of an anti-thyroid serum prepared from the blood of animals.

Hypertrophy, an abnormal growth of an organ or tissue, generally due to increased nutrition, *e.g.* well developed muscle. *Protective hypertrophy* occurs in the formation of a callus or hard covering, or in the case of local super-development of tissue in the neighbourhood of an embedded bullet or tumour. H. of the heart (*q.v.*) occurs as the result of the heart's effort to increase its efficiency which has been otherwise impaired, frequently a diseased condition of one organ causes H. in another, as in the case of disease of one kidney. The condition may be either congenital or acquired, and may be accompanied by an increase in the number of constituents of any particular texture (*hemiplasia*) and it may occur without any increase in bulk of the complete organ. Other examples of H. are *obesity, goitre, elephantiasis. See* ATROPHY.

Hypnerotomachia, a fantastic work probably written by Francesco Colonna (*c.* 1435-1527) under the pseudonym ' Poliphilus ' (Venice, 1499), in ' macaronic ' Latin, produced later by the Aldine Press. It contains fables, architectural and historical antiquities, and teaches that all human passions are only dreams. *See* 2nd ed. (1545, English trans. 1592); Lang's ed. ; reproduction in facsimile, 1904. Consult *Nouvelle Biog. Générale,* under ' Colonna.'

Hypnotics are used to induce sleep, by lowering the excitability of the nerve cells, or by producing temporary anæmia of the brain, the latter being induced in natural sleep. Thus warmth applied to the feet, a warm bath, a full meal, or various drugs, by diverting the blood from the brain, act as H. Drugs which dull the brain cells are known as narcotics (*q.v.*), and neither H. nor narcotic drugs should be used except on medical advice.

Hypnotism, a term applied to an abnormal condition of the brain usually of a temporary harmless character. It includes the series of phenomena which from time to time have been termed animal magnetism, mesmerism, induced somnambulism, odylic force, etc.

History.—From time immemorial forms of H. appear to have been known, *e.g.* somnambulism, or sleepwalking, has been noticed in all ages. Accounts of Egyptian conjurers and sorcerers imply a knowledge and use by them of this cerebral condition. Certain states of ecstasy which are more or less self-induced in types of fanatics are obviously related to H., and while affected, the individuals appear capable of resisting what would be pain and fatigue under normal circumstances (*cf.* accounts of Mount Athos monks). Imitativeness, as seen abnormally developed in the ' jumpers,' half-bred French-Canadians of the forest areas of Canada, is often of such a nature that they are incapable of resisting their inclinations; people similarly affected are found in the Malay Archipelago, and Central Africa. Definite investigations of the state have been made since the 16th century: Paracelsus at the end of this century established to his own satisfaction the existence of a sympathetic system between the human and the stars and other objects. Greatrakes of London (*b.* 1628) claimed an ability to cure diseases by a stroke of the hand, and he was credited with success in many cases of scrofula. Gassner, a Roman Catholic priest of Swabia, in the middle of the 18th century stated that disease was due to demoniacal possession and a supernatural power, with which he claimed to be invested, could be used to expel all forms of disease. In 1774 Mesmer, a Vienna physician, gained a large measure of success in the treatment of certain disorders. He proceeded to Paris in 1778, and by continued successes he gained a large following, and his suggestion of the actual transference of a ' magnetic fluid ' continued in vogue until within quite recent times. His treatment necessitated much apparatus, magnets, connecting wires, etc., with usually a central tub of water or other liquid round which the patients were seated. A pupil, Marquis de Puységar, in 1780, proved that the accessory magnets, etc., were unnecessary, and the claims of ' mesmerism ' became so insistent that a French commission was appointed in 1785 to investigate the matter fully; their report was unfavourable, and this, coupled with its later association with the notorious Cagliostro, brought it into disrepute. In 1831 Bertrand established the affinity of magnetic sleep to somnambulism, and suggested its use as a therapeutic agency, and a second French commission of this year reported rather more favourably. In 1841 Dr. Braid, a Manchester physician, discovered that a subject could be entranced by gazing at a bright object, and he suggested the name ' hypnotism,' from Greek ὕπνος, sleep. On the Continent schools of H. were established under the direction of the distinguished physiologist, Richet of France, and such physicians as Charcot (Salpêtrière), Liebault, Bernheim, Preyer and Heidenhain. In Britain Dr. Elliotson (editor of *Zoist*) supported H., and his advocacy resulted in his being driven out of the profession. Esdaile, a Calcutta surgeon, successfully carried out major operations and amputations while his patients were in the hypnotic state, but the discovery of chloroform in 1848 meant the possession of an anæsthetic of wider application and more certain results, and, in consequence, H. tended to become neglected. In 1882 Mr. Gurney carried out investigations in the subject, and the British Medical Association, after a long period of doubt and vacillation, reported favourably on its use in 1892. The names of Drs. Bramwell and Tuckey are associated with recent valuable work, and in 1907 the Medical Society for the Study of Suggestive Therapeutics was founded.

Methods.—The usual methods employed to bring about the hypnotic condition are either (*a*) peripheral, as in the gazing at a bright object so placed as to cause some slight muscular eye strain, flashing of mirrors, slow, monotonous ' mesmeric' passes, and even the ticking of a watch in very sensitive persons; (b) central stimulations as by verbal suggestions. Frequently there is a combination of these methods (Braid and Bernheim) as when the operator places a bright object slightly above the level of the subject's eye and suggests to him the idea of sleep, at the same time making hand passes before the face. It is found in practice that about 90 per cent. of persons are susceptible to H., and the proportion always appears to be higher in individuals trained to obey, *e.g.* soldiers, sailors, school children, etc., than in others. Liebault had some 1700 successes in 1756 persons treated. Bramwell had but two failures in his first 500 subjects, and no less than 240 became somnambules.

Symptoms.—There are three well-marked stages of hypnosis, first, *slight*, in which the voluntary muscles are affected, without loss of consciousness in the patient and without amnesia on returning to the normal condition; second, *deep*, in this the symptoms vary greatly; the sensory system is affected, there may be tonic contractures of the muscles (induced catalepsy of Heidenhain), or marked flexibility, there is frequently an increase of muscular strength, or a maintenance of an awkward attitude without muscular fatigue; there may be paralysis of one side, or one organ, by open or overt suggestion, or suggestion may be used to cause alterations of sensation. Visible symptoms include: change in pulse beat and in rate of respiration, dilated pupils, drooped eyelids, protruding eyeballs, and frequently flushed face and highly increased perspiration. This stage is usually marked by amnesia on waking, though a second hypnotic state will generally contain memories of the first. No satisfactory explanation has been given of post-hypnotic suggestion by which the subject can be made to carry out some action (not foreign to his nature) after the lapse of a given interval, as for example, the hypnotised person may be told to write his name, note the time, purchase some article, etc., after the expiration of, say, 5000 minutes, and although on waking he may have no cognition of the command, yet punctually to time he will endeavour to carry out the suggestion, usually doing so with some more or less plausible explanation. The third stage is *somnambulism*, in which the subject rarely makes any response to suggestions; this con-

dition can seldom be reached during the first experiments with a new subject.

Uses.—Although *psycho-therapeutics* are extensively used on the Continent, as in hospitals at Nancy, etc., and are now used in Britain, yet the treatment does not fulfil all the claims of its early exponents. There is no doubt that H. can be made to yield sleep without the use of drugs, which of itself is a valuable property, and during this sleep the subject is peculiarly open to suggestion, so that definite advantage follows its use in cases of hysteria, epilepsy, rheumatism, sea-sickness, etc. Few cases of authenticated cures in organic complaints are recorded, but even here considerable alleviation of pain can be induced. Its use has been suggested as an educational agent, even for the reformation of criminals on the Continent, as considerable improvements have followed its application in dipsomania, morphinomania, etc. Its properties as an anæsthetic have been referred to previously. Legislative control is necessary in its application as considerable danger may result from unqualified and unscrupulous exponents. In certain cases there is a danger of inducing insanity and, although no person can be hypnotised without his own consent, yet this consent can be induced in its turn in certain individuals. Exaggerated statements have been circulated as to the extent of control consequent on H., and experiments show that it is extremely difficult, in many cases impossible, to command an individual to carry out actions which are normally abhorrent to his character, *i.e.* H. cannot make a normal individual carry out a criminal campaign, though an unbalanced or pernicious mind may be rendered criminal.

Theories.—Mesmer assumed a vital fluid, while modern opinion is very unsettled. The chief theories of H. are (a) the pathological; (b) the physiological, and (c) the psychological. In (a), as enunciated by Charcot, it is classed with the other neuroses, and possibly this brief-lived theory gained attention rather on account of Charcot than for its own intrinsic value. In (b) it is regarded by Heidenhain as due to a temporary abolition of cerebral functions. (c) This is termed the Nancy school of opinion as expounded by Bernheim, Liebault, and Beaunis, and by it H. is explained as due to increased susceptibility, or the establishment of ' rapport ' based on a secondary consciousness between operator and subject. For further reading *see* J. M. Bramwell's *Hypnotism, its History, Practice, and Theory*, 1906, with full bibliography.

Hypnum, the largest genus of mosses, belongs to the series Pleurocarpi and its distribution is universal. The species are found both in living and fossil forms.

Hypocaust, an arrangement used by the Romans for heating their baths and villas. The furnace (hypocausis) was placed below the room to be heated, and the H. was a hollow space under the ' caldarium,' where the hot air was accumulated, and thence distributed round the walls, and to other rooms by means of pipes and passages (' cuniculi '). *See* Vitruvius, *De Architectura* (Schneider's ed., vol. ii., 1807-8; Rose's ed., 1889); Pliny, *Nat. Hist.*, ix., Winckelmann's works ; Smith's *Dict. of Classical Antiq.*, also Harper's, under ' Balneæ.'

Hypochæris, a genus of composite plants, contains over fifty species, all of which occur either in N. lands or in S. America. There are three British species, known popularly as cat's-ear, and they are found on dry, gravelly waste places. *H. radicata,* the common cat's-ear, has a long root, radical leaves, and bears heads of large yellow flowers.

Hypochlorous Acid (HClO) is only known in aqueous solution, and may be obtained by distilling bleaching powder with dilute nitric acid, or by dissolving chlorine monoxide in water. The solution obtained has a peculiar ' chlorous ' smell, and strong bleaching properties, the H. A. being readily resolved into hydrochloric acid and oxygen. Its salts, the hypochlorites, are almost unknown in the pure state, and are obtained, together with the chlorides, when chlorine is passed into a cold solution of the hydroxide of an alkali or alkaline earth. Bleaching powder (*q.v.*), or ' chloride of lime,' is prepared by passing chlorine over slaked lime, and consists of a compound of the chloride and hypochlorite. It is used in large quantities for bleaching in the textile trade. With small quantities of acid, H. A. is set free from hypochlorites, and with larger quantites, chlorine is evolved.

Hypochrondriasis (a name obtained by its supposed connection with the hypochrondriæ regions of the abdomen (*q.v.*), a mental disorder connected with, and perhaps caused by, disorder of digestive and biliary functions. It is characterised by palpitations, extreme sensibility, morbid feelings that simulate the disease, and great uneasiness about the health. In extreme cases it develops into melancholia. It is more frequently met with amongst the rich than the poor, and the best cure consists in getting more physical and mental exercise, and interests outside one self.

Hypocycloid, *see* EPICYCLOID.

Hypodermic Injection (ὑπό, under, δέρμα, skin), the introduction of a drug beneath the skin. It is effected by means of a hypodermic syringe, which is armed with a sharp hollow needle, so that the tissues underlying the skin can be reached without much inconvenience to the patient. The advantages of H. I. are that a drug can be introduced more directly to the tissues than by way of the stomach, the quantity required is therefore less, the treatment can be made local if required, and the operations of a possibly deranged stomach are not further interfered with. The method is used chiefly in connection with the group of drugs known as alkaloids, notably morphia and cocaïne.

Hypogene, a term applied in geology to rocks ' netherformed,' or crystallised, at depths beneath the earth's surface, also called primary or metamorphic rocks, such as granite, gneiss, diorite, etc. The term almost equals ' plutonic,' and is opposed to epigene.

Hyponitrous Acid (HNO), a colourless, crystalline substance, soluble in water, readily decomposing into nitrous oxide and water. Its salts, the hyponitrites, are formed by reduction of the nitrites by means of sodium amalgam. The silver salt is a yellow insoluble substance.

Hypophosphorous Acid (H_3PO_2), a colourless, crystalline compound, melting point 17° C., formed by the action of sulphuric acid on the barium salt, which is obtained by boiling phosphorus with a solution of baryta. On heating strongly, H. A. is decomposed into orthophosphoric acid, and gaseous phosphoretted hydrogen. It is a powerful reducing agent, precipitating gold, silver, and mercury in the metallic state, and copper in the form of its hydride, from solutions of their salts. The hypophosphites are largely used in medicine as tonics.

Hypostasis (ὑπόστασις, subsistence), a Greek term meaning substantial existence, much used in the Trinitarian controversies of the 4th and 5th centuries. At first used as equivalent to οὐσία (divine essence), its meaning in theology has changed considerably. It was regarded as synonymous with πρόσωπον or *persona* (person) at the council of Alexandria, 362 A.D., and is used to denote the distinct personal existence of each Person in the Trinity. *See* Loop, *Hist. of Doctrine,* 1893; Fisher (1896), Harnack (iv.), 1898; ' De orth. fid.,' iii., in Ottley's *Doctrine of the Incarnation,* ii.

Hypotenuse (ὑποτείνουσα, subtending), the longest side of a right-angled triangle, which lies opposite the right angle. The middle point of the H. is the centre of the triangle's circumscribed circle, and hence equidistant from the angles. The square described on the H. equals the sum of the squares on the other two sides. See *Euclid*, i. 47.

Hypothec, in Scots law, a security over any part of a debtor's property, the property being allowed to remain in the possession of the debtor; hence distinct from both a mortgage and a pledge. The idea is borrowed directly from civil law (*q.v.*), but in practice, Scots law allows of few Hs. Hs. are either implied (legal Hs.), or based upon express contract (conventional Hs.). The latter class is restricted to bottomry (*q.v.*), and respondentia (*q.v.*) bonds. The former include the Hs. of (*a*) a landlord over movables (*invecta et illata*) brought on to the leased premises, for rent current and due (but not for arrears); over produce and perhaps machinery and implements; for royalties payable under a lease of minerals; and over crops for current feu duties due in respect of agricultural land; (*b*) a law agent over his client's writs and title deeds, for his expenses (properly a lien), and (*c*) of seamen, who have a tacit H. over the ship, and the freight due to the shipowner, for their wages; of a shipowner over the cargo for freight due, and of cargo-owners over the ship for loss by improper stowage. Generally speaking, the creditor enforces his security by getting the subject of the H. assigned to him. *See* Abbot, *Shipping* (14th ed.); Gloag and Irvine, *Rights in Security.*

Hypothesis (ὑπόθεσις, foundation), in general, a supposition, proposition, or principle assumed as true for the purpose of argument, in order to draw conclusions or inferences for proof of some point in question, or to account for some occurrence. In science a conjecture or tentative theory adopted provisionally as a guide in investigating phenomena. If this conjecture is found after careful tests and examination entirely satisfactory in explaining the phenomena in accordance with known facts and principles, it is accepted as a scientific theory. *See* Naville, *La logique de l'hypothèse,* 1880; Logic text-books by Jevons, Bosanquet, Joseph; Jevons, *Principles of Science.*

Hypsipyle, daughter of Thoas of Lemnos, in Greek legend. She saved her father when the women of the island slew all the rest of the men. When the Argonauts landed and united with the Lemnian women, H. bore Jason twin sons. Driven from Lemnos when her father's escape was discovered, she became the nurse of Opheltes, son of King Lycur-

gus of Arcadia. While directing the heroes of the siege of Thebes to a spring in the Nemean forest, she left her charge, who was killed by a serpent. The funeral games instituted for Opheltes were the origin of the Nemean games.

Hyracotherium, the name of the best-known form of Hyracotheriidæ, a family of extinct ungulate mammals belonging to the order Perrisodactyla and considered to be the ancestors of the horse. The fossil form is confined to the Eocene strata of Europe and N. America, and shows a small animal 3 ft. or so in length, with a complete dentition, a well-marked coracoid process on the shoulder-blade, four digits on the fore limbs, and three on the hind limbs and orbits not enclosed by bone; the radius and ulna are separate, as also are the tibia and fibula.

Hyrax, the generic name of certain small species of mammals forming the order Hydracoidea; *Procavia* is an alternative term. These animals are popularly known as coneys, and somewhat resemble rodents in appearance, owing to the long, curved, front teeth, adapted for gnawing, the short ears, and reduced tail; in the structure of the molar teeth, however, they are nearer the ungulates. Their bodies are covered with short, close fur, uniformly coloured, and the sharply-pointed snout is split; the digits are furnished with nails, with the exception of the middle toe of each hind-foot, which has a long, curved claw. *H. syriaca,* the coney of the Bible, ranges over Syria, Palestine, and Arabia; it is of a dull yellow or fawn colour, with a small oval spot on the back; it is noted for its wariness and cannot be caught in traps; the nest is of dried grass and fur, in which the young are buried like those of a mouse. *H. capensis,* the rock-rabbit, daman or klip-das, is confined to Cape Colony and Natal.

Hyrcania, an ancient district of Persia, S. and S.E. of the Caspian (*Hyrcanum Mare*), separated from Parthia by the Sariphi Mts. (S.E.), with Media on W. It corresponded to the modern Astrabad and Mazanderan.

Hyrcanus, a name of two Jewish high-priests and princes of the Hasmonean family: 1. *John* (*Johanan*) *Hyrcanus I.* (*c.* 175-104 B.C.), son of Simon Maccabæus, early won fame as a general against the Syrians under Cendebæus. He became high-priest and governor of Judæa (135), and founded the Jewish monarchy, which continued in his family until Herod seized Judæa. There was much warfare during his reign. At first a Pharisee, he later joined the ranks of the Sadducees. *See* Josephus, *Ant.*, xiii., xiv. ; Werner, *Joh. Hyrcan,* 1877 ; Grätz, *Gesch.*, ii.,xiii., 1854-75 ; Schürer, *Gesch.*, i. 2. *Hyrcanus II.*, grandson of above, high-priest (*c.* 79-40 B.C.). His brother Aristobulus disputed the throne with him till his death (49 B.C.). Antipater and later Pompey (63) supported H. as a less formidable foe, and Judæa lost her independence. In 40 H. was captured by the Parthians, and lived in Babylonia till his invited back by Herod (36), who had him executed on a charge of treason (30). *See* Josephus, *Bellum Jud.*, i.; Jost, *Gesch. des Judeuthums und Seiner Sekten,* i. ; Holtzmann, *Judenthum und Christenthum.*

Hyslop, James (1798 – 1827), a Scottish poet. While acting as a shepherd near Airdsmoss (1812-16), the covenant associations of the district inspired his famous poem, ' The Cameronian's Dream ' (*Edinburgh Magazine,* 1821), set to music by Hamish M'Cunn, 1889. Through Lord Jeffrey's influence, H. became tutor on board a man-of-war (the *Doris,* and later the *Tweed*). He published accounts of his three years' voyage to S. America in the *Edinburgh Magazine. See* Mearns' ed. of *Poems,* 1887.

Hysmine and Hysminias, The Drama of, a romance written by a Greek author named Eumathius or Eustathius (probably not Eustathius the critic) of the 12th century. The work is conventional and artificial, and has little real merit. It was edited with a Latin version *De Ismeniæ et Ismenes Amoribus* by Gaulmin (1617-18). Editions appeared in 1634, 1644, and 1792, and a French translation and introduction by Lebas (1828).

Hyssop, or *Hyssopus officinalis,* a species of Labiatæ which forms a genus in itself and is a native of Europe, Asia, and the Mediterranean shores. It is a hardy plant, with stems which are shrubby near the ground but herbaceous above. The flowers are blue and were formerly used in medicine when dried ; the leaves are oblong and sessile, and are used in salads and in the manufacture of absinthe; the whole plant is bitter and aromatic.

Hystaspes, a name often occurring in Persian history. The father of Darius I. (521-486) was so named, and was a member of the royal house of the Achæmenidæ. He was governor of Parthia or satrap under Cambyses (*d.* 521) and Darius, and is sometimes erroneously confused with Zoroaster's patron (Vishtāspa).

Hysteria (Gk. ὑστέρα, womb), a

nervous disease, which was at one time erroneously supposed to be peculiar to women and to be due to disorders of the womb. It is more frequently met with in the female sex, particularly at or before the age of puberty. It is not, however, uncommon among boys. It seems to be developed from some emotional shock, *e.g.* a fright, or an unhappy love affair, although it may follow from certain diseases. It is never met with among savages, and some civilised races seem to be more subject to it than others, *e.g.* the French are more hysterical than the English. The symptoms of nervous diseases in general are all simulated by varying conditions of H., but H. popularly and usually represents those conditions from which the patient suffers temporary paroxysms or ' fits.' For these there is often no apparent or adequate cause, and at the end of the attack the patient rocks herself to and fro, tears being mingled with laughter, which is followed by a headache relieved by sleep. Digestive disorders are common in H., and the recorded cases of ' fasting-girls ' and of trances are very often due to H. The treatment consists in firm but sympathetic treatment, the patient being placed among strangers so that she will not be ' spoiled,' and encouraged to use self-restraint. Then when attacks occur care should be taken to prevent the patient hurting herself, but the efforts to attract attention should be disregarded. The Weir-Mitchell treatment is resorted to when the patient is not sent away. In this the patient is isolated and kept in bed, where she is fed with an abundance of easily digested food, and given daily massage and electric treatment. Drugs, *e.g.* morphia, iron, and valerianate of zinc are sometimes used to prevent the paroxysms, while a popular and effective method of cutting an attack short is to douche the head with cold water, although closing the mouth and nose for a few seconds with a towel is the most effective. In severe cases the injection of apomorphine is resorted to.

Hythe (A.-S. port, haven), a parl. bor. and watering-place of Kent, England, one of the Cinque Ports, on the S. coast, 4½ m. W. of Folkestone. It is in the diocese of Canterbury on the South-Eastern Railway. The market-house was rebuilt in 1794, an old cruciform church has been restored, and the Royal School of Musketry is here. The beach and golf-course are fine, but the sea's encroachments have destroyed the harbour. Pop. (1911) 6387.

I, the ninth letter of the English alphabet, called in Greek *iota*, and in Phœnician *yōd*. The symbol came to be written very small in Hebrew, hence our words jot (*cf.* Matthew v. 18) and jottings, little notes. In early Greek inscriptions it resembled a Z or S; later the symbol was straightened to **I**. It was first written with a dot in the 5th century A.D., especially for the sake of distinction when written in conjunction with *m, u,* or another *i*. In Phœnician I had the consonant value of *y* in yet, but in Greek it had only the vowel sound. In Latin it denoted *y* or *j* initially, *e.g.* index, judge; otherwise it had two sounds, *ĭ* and *ī*, the latter resembling the sound of *i* in machine, often written in English *ee,* as in meet. The O.E. *i* has remained practically unchanged in sound, *cf.* O.E. *sittan,* N.E. *sit.* O.E. long *ĭ* had the continental value (as in machine), but was later diphthongised, and in 16th-century MSS. is often written *ei ; cf.* O.E. *lîf, mîn,* N.E. *life, mine.* Consult the article in Sir James Murray's *New English Dictionary.*

Iacchus (Ἴακχος), the solemn title of Bacchus used in the Eleusinian mysteries. As the son of Demeter he is usually distinguished from the older Dionysus, son of Semele. He was a divinity peculiar to Athens. *See* Dyer, *Gods in Greece,* 1891. *See* Dionysus, Eleusinia.

Iambic Verse, in prosody, is applied to verses consisting of a foot, called an *iambus,* of two syllables, of which the first is short and the second long (˘ ‾). It is supposed to have been invented by Archilochus. It is particularly suited to the English language, which falls naturally into short and long syllables. It has, perhaps, most frequently been employed in blank verse of five feet, the beauty of the rhythm depending largely upon the cæsura, which falls in the third or fourth foot.

Iamblichus, or **Jamblichus Chalcidenus :** 1. A Syrian Neoplatonic philosopher of the 3rd and 4th centuries (*c.* 283 - *c.* 330 A.D.). But few of his philosophical and mathematical works are extant. The *Life of Pythagoras* and *Exhortation to Philosophy* were edited by Kiessling (1813-15), Nauck (1884), Pistelli (1888, 1894), Festa (1891), Parthey (1857), Ast (1817), and Friès (1790) also edited selections from his works. *See* Zeller, *Philosophie der Griechen.*

iii., 1889; Vacherot, *Hist. Crit. de l'Ecole d'Alexandrie,* ii., 1851 ; Chiagnet, *Hist. de la psychologie des Grecs,* v., 1893; Whittaker, *Neo-Platonists,* 1901. (For other details see under Jamblichus.) 2. A Syrian Greek writer of the 2nd century A.D., flourished under Trajan. He was author of Βαβυλωνικά, describing the adventures of the lovers Rhodane and Sinonis. Photius gives an epitome of the romance which is itself not extant (see *Bibliotheca,* chap. xciv.). *See* Chassang, *Hist. du Roman dans l'Antiquité,* 1862.

Ianthina (Gk. ἰάνθινος, violet-coloured), the name of a genus of gasteropod molluscs, belonging to the family Ianthinidæ, or oceanic violet-snails; they inhabit warm or tropical seas, and live below the surface during the day, rising to the top at night. The shell is thin and bluish in colour, the head comparatively large, and the floating appendage remarkably long and attached to the foot. When irritated, the animal emits a violet secretion. *I. fragilis* is the best-known species.

Iapetus, a Titan, of Greek mythology, the son of Uranus and Gæa. He was the father of Atlas and Prometheus, and the grandfather of Deucalion, and was accordingly regarded as the ancestor of the human race. He revolted against the new order under Zeus, and was consequently imprisoned in Tartarus.

Iapetus, the eighth satellite of Saturn, discovered by Cassini in 1671. It has the peculiarity of always appearing brighter when seen to the W. of the planet than when seen to the E.

Iapygia, in ancient geography, the name applied by the Greeks to Messapia or Apulia, S.E. Italy.

Ibadan, a walled, native city of Yoruba country, S. Nigeria, W. Africa, 83 m. N.N.E. of Lagos. Cap. of one of the Yoruba states, it is partly autonomous. There is a British resident, and Hausa troops are established here. Pop. about 150,000. See *Proc. Roy. Geog. Soc.,* 1891.

Ibagué, or **San Bonifacio de Ibagué,** a cap. of Tolima dept., Colombia, 60 m. W. of Bogota, in a rich agricultural district. There are warm springs and sulphur and silver mines near. Guataquisito on the Magdalena is its port. Pop. about 12,000.

Ibajay, a tn. on the N. coast of

Panay Is., Philippines, in Capiz prov. It is a military station near the mouth of the Rio de Ibajay, which rises in Bacalan Mt. and flows N.W. and N. to the sea. Amber is found near the Point of Potol. Pop. about 18,000.

Ibañez, Vicente Blasco (b. 1867), a Spanish statesman and novelist, studied at Valencia University. His advanced views roused opposition, and he retired to Paris for a time. He published *Cuentos valencianos*, 1893, and founded the journal *El Pueblo*, where his first novels, *Arroz y Tartana* (1894), *Flor de Mayo* (1895), and *La Barraca* (1896), appeared. During the troubles of the Cuban War he took refuge in Italy, writing *En el pais del arte*, 1897. Other works are: *Cañas y barro*, 1902 (French, *Boue et roseaux*, 1905); *El Intruso*, 1903; *La Bodega*, 1904; *La Horda*, 1905.

Ibarra, a cap. of Imbabura prov., Ecuador, S. America, about 50 m. N.N.E. of Quito. Founded in 1606, it was almost destroyed by earthquake in 1868. It is a bishop's see, and has woollen and cotton mills. It stands at the N. foot of Imbabura volcano. Pop. about 12,000.

Ibbenbüren, a com. and tn. of Westphalia prov., Prussia, 14 m. from Osnabrück, with glass, leather, and linen manufs. There are coal, iron, and lead-ore mines. Pop. 6008.

Iberia: 1. The Greek name for Spain, probably derived from Iberus, the Ebro. 2. The name by which Georgia in the Caucasus was known in ancient times.

Iberian Sea, the name given to the Mediterranean, between Spain and the N. African coast of Morocco and Algiers.

Iberis, *see* CANDYTUFT.

Ibex, the name of several species of *Capra*, a genus of Bovidæ, which includes the goats. The Alpine ibex, *Steinbok*, or bouquetin, was formerly abundant in Europe, but it is now rare, and almost extinct through hunting. *C. ibex*, as it is technically called, is larger than common goats, with no beard, long, thick horns curving backwards, and brown hair. It lives on shrubs and lichens and such vegetation as it can obtain on the hill sides, and leaps for extraordinary distances. In captivity it is generally vicious, but if caught young it can be tamed. From the milk butter and cheese are made, the hair is clipped and made into ropes, the horns are used for handles, and the skin is dressed and made into shoes and gloves. The I. is very destructive to vegetation and especially to vines, and on this account was freely offered in sacrifice to Bacchus.

Ibiqui, or **Ibicui**, a port in Argen-

tina, S. America, is near the confluence of the Uruguay and Parana.

Ibis, the generic name of several members of Ibididæ, wading birds related to the storks. They have large bodies with long curved bills, rather blunt at the end, with the upper mandible grooved, long necks and legs, and generally black and white plumage. The most famous species, *I. œthiopica* (or *religiosa*), the sacred I., was formerly worshipped by the Egyptians. It always appeared in Egypt at the rise of the Nile, and was supposed to preserve the country from plagues and serpents. It could not live out of Egypt, and there it was zealously preserved in temples. Numerous mummied remains of ibisis have been found at Thebes and Memphis, wrapped in linen in the ordinary way. *I.* (or *Eudocimus*) *Alba*, the white I., is a pure white species found in Florida. *I.* (or *Eudocimus*) *ruber*, the scarlet I., an American species, is brilliant scarlet with a few black patches. *I. falcinellus* is an African species sometimes strays to Britain and N. America.

Ibn Batûta, or **Abu Abdullah Mohammed** (1304–78), an Arab traveller, born in Tangier. He traversed Persia, Mesopotamia, Arabia, E. African coast, Asia Minor, the shores of the Caspian, Bokhara, Afghanistan, and India, China, Sumatra, and Southern Spain. On his return he settled at Fez, and wrote a most descriptive and graphic account of his adventures, valuable for their shrewd original observations. It was translated into English by S. Lee (1829), and into French by Defrémery and Sanguinetti (1859). He died at Fez, Morocco.

Ibn Ezra, or **Abraham ben Meir ibn Ezra** (1092–1167), a Jewish scholar and Bible commentator, born at Toledo. He was also a poet, mathematician, and astronomer. He wrote a Hebrew grammar, numerous poems used in the Jewish liturgy, a work on Jewish philosophy, and important commentaries on the O.T. He lectured in France, England, Italy, and Egypt, on astronomy and theology.

Ibn Gabirol, *see* AVICEBRON, SALOMON BEN GABIROL.

Ibn Haukal, Mohammed (d. 976), an Arabian geographer and traveller of the 10th century, born at Bagdad. He spent thirty years travelling in Islamic countries, and published a *Book of Roads and Kingdoms*, containing an instructive account of each land, accompanied by a map. A MS. copy is in the Bodleian Library.

Ibn Khallikan, Abbas Ahmed (1211-82), an Arabian historian and scholar, born at Arbela. He travelled in Syria and Egypt, and held the offices of cadi at Cairo, grand cadi at Damascus, and professor in one of the colleges, Cairo. He was a poet and compiler. His principal work is a biographical dictionary, *Deaths of Eminent Men.* He died in Damascus.

Ibn-Tofail, Abû Bakr Mahommed ibn Abd-ul Malik (*d.* 1188), an Arabian philosopher, born at Guadix in Spain. He studied medicine as well as philosophy, and became physician and vizier to the caliph Abu Ya qûb Yûsuf. His chief work was a philosophical romance, *Hajj ibn Yokdhân,* translated into English by Ockley (1708) and by Pecock (1674).

Ibn Zohar, *see* AVENZOAR.

Ibo, a seaport in Portuguese East Africa, on one of the Querimba Is. Exports ivory, rubber, and wax.

Ibrahim Pasha (1789–1848), an Egyptian viceroy, born at Cavalla, Rumelia, was the adopted son of Mehemet Ali Pasha of Egypt. He reorganised the army on European plans, and helped the Turks against the Greeks. In 1831, supporting his father against the sultan, he conquered Syria and became governor of the province. Mehemet Ali once more revolted against the sultan and Ibrahim inflicted a severe defeat on the Ottoman army at Nezib. The European powers now interfered, and he had to retire before the British troops, losing all he had gained. He went to his private estate at Heleopolis and lived there for several years. In 1848 he was appointed viceroy, as Mehemet Ali had become imbecile, but he died shortly afterwards at Cairo.

Ibrox, a S.W. suburb of Glasgow on the Clyde, Scotland.

Ibsambul, *see* IPSAMBUL.

Ibsen, Henrik (1828-1906), born at Skien, a small southern Norwegian timber port. At sixteen he became an apothecary's assistant, intending to study medicine. The effete puritanism and social prejudices of the Norwegian provincial life, in which his unhappy early years were passed, were rich material for the bitter satires on civilisation with which he subsequently stung Europe into fury. His earliest work, *Catilina* (1850), was purely historical, and was inspired by his reading of Sallust and Cicero for the examination at Christiania University. Whilst continuing his studies there, under the celebrated Heltberg, he associated with Jonas Lie, Vinje, Björnson, Botten-Hansen, and others. Thanks to Ole Bull, the violin virtuoso, he became director of Bergen Theatre from 1851-57, and wrote for its productions, but practically all the MSS. have since been destroyed, with the

notable exception of the vigorous historical drama, *Lady Inger of Ostrat.* In 1857 he was appointed manager to the National Theatre at Christiania. A year later appeared his first saga-drama, the splendid *Warriors of Helgeland. The Pretenders* followed in 1864, and 1873 saw the completion of *Emperor and Galilean,* his greatest historical prose-drama. I., the cynic, pessimist, and iconoclast, made his début in 1862 with *Love's Comedy,* cleverly written in epigrammatic verse. In the same style there followed *Brand* (1866), an attack on pietism, and *Peer Gynt* (1867), his most influential and

HENRIK IBSEN

popular dramatic poem, called by many 'the Scandinavian Faust.' It was, however, in the scathing satirical prose dramas which constituted his third period that the I. of European significance found mature expression. In the *League of Youth* (1869), *Pillars of Society* (1877), and *An Enemy of the People* (1882), he attacked the whole fabric of modern politics—as he terms it, 'government by geographical formula.' I.'s studies in femininism are of equal interest and power; *Rosmersholm* (1886) being the best, and the *Doll's House* (1879), in which he discusses the problems of modern marriage, being next in merit. *The Lady from the Sea* (1888) is an elegant poetic conception, essentially the same in idea as the *Doll's House.* In *Ghosts* (1881) I. exploits to the fullest the possibilities of hereditary disease as a dramatic motif. *The Wild Duck* (1884), an unsatisfactory piece of symbolism, is, like *Brand*, an attack on unpractical idealism. His later works are : *Hedda Gabler*, 1890; *The Master Builder*, 1892, the zenith of his powers; *Little Eyolf*, 1894; *John Gabriel Borkman*, 1896 ; and *When We Dead Awaken*, 1900; all of which are chiefly developed from the ideas contained in his earlier works. All his writing is pre-eminently suited for the stage, and consummately skilful in technique.

Ibstock, a vil. in Leicestershire, 5 m. N. of Market Bosworth. Archbishop Laud was rector of the parish church. The inhabitants are chiefly occupied in mining and manufacturing tiles and bricks. Pop. (1911) 4946.

Ibycus, a Greek lyric poet of about 540 B.C., born at Rhegium, Italy, and spent most of his life at the court of Polycrates of Samos. According to tradition he was murdered at sea near Corinth. The crime was traced, by means of cranes, which had followed the ship, and ' the cranes of Ibycus ' became a proverbial expression for divine revelation of crime. The story is the subject of one of Schiller's poems.

Içá, a dept. of Peru, bounded N. by Lima, S. by Arequipa, E. by Ayacucho, and W. by the Pacific ; covers an area of 8718 sq. m. Much of the surface is sandy desert, but the valleys of the Chincha, Condor, and I. are fertile, and yield fruits, cotton, and indigo. Wine and brandy is made from the fruit, and a considerable amount of copper is mined. The chief town is I. which was ruined by an earthquake in 1647. Pop. 90,962.

Içá, or **Putumayo,** a river in Ecuador, S. America, rises in the Andes, flows S.E., and at São Antonio, in Brazil, joins the Amazon. It is navigable for small craft for 750 m.

Icarius (Gk. Ικαριος), or **Icarus: 1.** An Athenian, was taught the art of cultivation of the vine by Dionysius in return for hospitably entertaining him. I. distributed his new gift freely, and the shepherds of the neighbourhood becoming intoxicated, thought they had been poisoned by him and slew him, throwing his body in a well. Erigone, his daughter, hung herself in despair on learning the news of her father's death. According to tradition, Erigone is the Virgo in the zodiac, Icarus is Boötes, and Icarus's dog, Maira, is the smaller Procyon. 2. A Lacedæmonian, was the father of Penelope, whom he tried to dissuade from accompanying her husband, Odysseus, to Sparta. She insisted on carrying out her intention with such modest firmness

that her father erected a statue of modesty in her honour.

Icarus, *see* DÆDALUS.

Ice (a word common to the Teutonic languages), the name given to the substance into which water changes when subjected to a sufficiently low temperature. It is a colourless crystalline solid, generally assuming forms belonging to the hexagonal system; its habit of twining is the origin of the ' ice-flowers ' and designs assumed by hoar-frost. In the form of hoar-frost, snow, and hail, I. is often precipitated. The temperature at which water freezes into I. is very easily determined, and for this reason is employed as one of the standard temperatures in the measurement of the scales of a thermometer. In the Centigrade system this temperature is zero, as in the Réaumur, whilst in the Fahrenheit system it is 32°. In the act of freezing, I. undergoes a noteworthy expansion, so that I. at 0° C. is not so dense as water, as is proved by the fact that it floats thereon. In the converse process of melting, I. contracts, and the water formed contracts under heat till the point of maximum density, about 4° C., is reached. Above this temperature the expansion of water is continual, and at no temperature is less dense than I. The density of I. at 0° C. is ·9175; of water at 0° C., ·99988; at 4° C., 1 ; at 10° C., ·99976 ; and at 100° C., ·95866. The coefficient of cubical dilatation of I. at moderately low temperatures, has been calculated as ·0001585, and its specific heat as ·505, or about half that of water. When I. is melted, although no rise of temperature takes place, a definite quantity of heat is absorbed, amounting to 80 calories per gram, and the same when water becomes I. This is expressed as the latent heat of fusion of I. Since water expands on freezing, its freezing point must be lowered by any increase of pressure, and it has been ascertained that for every additional atmosphere of pressure, the freezing point of water is lowered ·0075 degrees. This discovery was theoretically worked out by James Thomson in 1849, and verified experimentally by his brother William Thomson (Lord Kelvin) in the following year. Many of the properties of I. are explained by this, among others that of regelation, by which two blocks of I. laid side by side in contact gradually fuse into one. The pressure at the point of contact melts the I., the water thus formed escapes, and the I. freezes again, until in time the two surfaces coalesce. The motion of glaciers is also probably due to this process. I. forms on fresh water if the temperature of the air is below freezing point for sufficient time, but not until the whole mass of water is cooled down to the point of maximum density. Sea-water will not freeze, under the most favourable conditions, until a temperature of $-2°$ C. is reached; in the I. formed four-fifths of the salt originally present is rejected, so that water melted from sea-ice has less salinity than the surrounding sea. Ice exists on a gigantic scale in the glaciers and snows of mountainous regions, especially in the seas and lands of both Polar regions. From a physiographical point of view, I. is an important agent in the denudation and configuration of the land. Many traces, for instance, are left by glacial action which serve to show that the whole of Europe was at one time much more exposed to such action than now. (See GLACIAL ACTION, DENUDATION, BOULDER-CLAY, etc.) In the Upper Provinces of India, water is made to freeze at nights by being placed in porous vessels, wrapped round with a wet cloth. In Bengal, pits are dug 2 ft. deep and filled for three-quarters of the depth with dry straw. The water is then placed on this straw in flat porous jars; it evaporates at the expense of its own heat and the cooling is rapid enough to neutralise the slow influx of heat through the cool air above, or the badly conducting straw below. The uses of I. are many, and its consumption in civilised countries is growing; large quantities are imported from Norway into this country. I. is also largely made by artificial means, especially in the United States of America. For details as to methods, etc., see REFRIGERATING.

Ice Age, see GLACIAL PERIOD.

Iceberg (Ger. *Berg*, mountain), a hill of ice rising often as much as 270 ft. above the sea. It is a floating mass which has broken away from some glacier or ice-sheet in the Polar regions, and which sails away from its frozen home into warmer and navigable waters. When the I. first breaks away, the fracture is green or blue, but when it comes within view of whalers and other vessels, its cliff-like faces and graceful pinnacles glisten in the sunshine with a dazzling white. During its first flight, an I. strews the sea with pebbles and rocks and other detritus—the remnant of its glacier days. As it enters warmer zones, it melts, disintegrates, tilts, and often overturns. From the specific gravity of ice, it is calculated that only one-ninth of ice mountains appears above the ocean surface and, as their speed is often considerable,

it is clear that they are a grave source of peril to passing ships : it was collision with an I. which caused the wreck of the *Titanic* (1912).

Ice-breaker. Many of the harbours of Northern Europe are frozen over for a great part, or the whole, of the winter, to a depth of several feet, so rendering navigation impossible. The only method of keeping a channel open is to prevent the ice from freezing too thickly, and this is done by the continuous passage up and down of a specially-designed vessel. Such vessels are known as Is., and naturally present some peculiarities in construction. They must be both weighty and powerful, of exceptional strength, and capable of travelling at sufficient speed to break the ice by their momentum. In addition to cracking the ice into pieces of some score tons, they are constructed to slide up on to the ice and break it down with their weight. The *Ermak*, built for the Russian government, is a very good specimen of such boats. She has a length of 320 ft., a breadth of 71 ft., depth to upper deck 42 ft. 6 in.; her displacement is 8000 tons, and her engines, of 8000 I.H.P., develop a speed of 15 knots. As first built she had four screws, one at the bow and three at the stern, but the extra screw was not of so much service as had been anticipated, and a few years after was removed and a fresh bow built to the ship. The *Ermak* will break her way through 12 or 13 ft. with ease, and has rammed through 34 ft. She rescued on one occasion eight out of nine vessels which had been caught in the ice, the last one sank before the *Ermak* could reach her. A smaller I., built on the same lines, the *Sampo*, has been built for the government of Finland. Many Canadian and American ports are only kept open by the use of ice-breaking ferry steamers, such as the *Scotia*, built by Armstrong, Whitworth & Co. to carry railway trains across the Straits of Canso to and from Port Mulgrave, Nova Scotia. The *Scotia* is 282 ft. long, and has two sets of triple - expansion engines each of 1200 I.H.P., which give a speed of 12 knots. In 1906 the I., *Lady Grey*, was built for the Canadian government by Vickers, Maxim & Co., and in 1909 the *Earl Grey*, on the same lines, but modified for extra speed, was built by the same firm. This vessel engages in passenger traffic across the Northern Straits, and is used as the official yacht of the governor-general; with her cut-water stem, short bowsprit, elliptical stern, and two steel schooner-rigged masts, she resembles a yacht, but is nevertheless well adapted for her ice-breaking work. The hull is extra strong, and the outer skin is double right fore and aft along the water-line and to the bottom of the keel, where the friction of the ice is apt to wear away the material. Tanks are fitted in the fore part which can be filled at the rate of 250 tons an hour in order to give the required weight. The counter is specially strengthened so that she can break ice when going astern, and the rudder is built into the form of the ship to escape injury. The *Earl Grey* has a length of 250 ft., a beam of 47 ft. 6 in., a depth of 17 ft. 7 in., a displacement of 3400 tons, and accommodation for 50 first and 20 second-class passengers.

Iceland (Dan., island), an island situated in the North Atlantic Ocean, belonging to Denmark. It is 250 m. from the S.E. coast of Greenland and 600 m. W. of Norway. Its area is over 40,000 sq. m., length 298 m., and breadth 194 m. The total length of its coast-line is about 3730 m., about one-third of which belongs to the north-western peninsula. In shape it is a rough oval, its narrowest point being at the S. The coast-line pre-sents a continued succession of deep bays or fjords, penetrating far in-land except for a considerable por-tion extending along the S.E., which is almost unbroken. I. is an ice-covered plateau or tableland built up of volcanic rocks and pierced on all sides by fjords and valleys. The low-lands cover about one-fourteenth of the whole area, and are almost the only part of the island which is in-habited, the central tableland being absolutely uninhabitable on account of the rigour of the climate. The habitable area of I. is about one-fourth, glaciers, lava-streams, and elevated deserts making up the rest. The two bays, Hunafloi and Breithi-fjord, separate the N.W. peninsula from the main mass of the island, thus forming two tablelands—a large and small. The isthmus connecting the two is scarcely 5 m. wide, but has an altitude of 748 ft. The N.W. penin-sula has an elevation of 2000 ft. The interior of the island has a wild and desolate appearance and is covered by lofty mountain-masses of volcanic origin, many of them crowned with perpetual snow and ice. The glacier fields cover over 5000 sq. m., and glaciers exist in all the mountains above 4000 ft. in elevation. In several of the mountains the volcanic agency is still active, and terrible eruptions have repeatedly occurred within the last four centuries. The best known volcanoes are Hecla, Katla, and Askja. A large portion of

I. is covered by lava, and the hot springs or geysers scattered through-out the island are other specimens of volcanic agency. These are specially found in the S.W., where one of the main geysers throws up at intervals jets of water, stones, and mud to a height varying from 100 to 200 ft. In Mt. Hecla (5095 ft. high) are best exhibited the general effects of vol-canic agency. The scenery of the island is of great natural beauty, the climate is mild for the latitude, and the weather is extremely variable, storms and hurricanes often occurring. The vegetation is tolerably uniform throughout the island, presenting the characteristics of an Arctic-European type. Heath and bilberry cover large stretches of the surface, and grasses are of great importance to the in-habitants, who are dependent on them for supplying their live-stock. The de-velopment of forest-trees is insigni-ficant, the birch being almost the only tree found, and this in a very stunted form—3 ft. to 10 ft. in height. The wild flora of I. is small and delicate, with bright bloom, saxifrages, sedums, and heaths being especially admired. As regards the fauna, species are few. The polar-bear is an occasional visitant, and reindeer were intro-duced in 1770. The seas abound in seals and whales, and there are numerous species of birds, notably the wild-fowl and eider-duck. The cod-fisheries, too, are valuable, trout are plentiful in the lakes and streams, and salmon abound in many of the rivers.

History.—I. received the greatest portion of its population from Nor-way between 860 and 870, when it was colonised by Norsemen or Scandi-navian Vikings, though some settle-ments of Irish monks had been made about the end of the 8th century. The first Norwegian settlement was made in 870 by Ingolf on the S. coast, and was established permanently four years later at what is now Reik-javik. Other settlers soon followed, and in the course of sixty years all the habitable parts of the coast were settled. The government was at first in the hands of the overseer of the temple in each settlement, but latterly, when the separate juris-dictions were joined together, a kind of aristocratic republic was formed. Christianity was introduced in 981, and adopted by law in 1000, and schools and bishoprics were estab-lished. I. was a dependency of the Danish crown from 1388, but in 1902, national self-government (though still under Danish control) was secured, and the governor had his quarters in Reikjavik, the capital of the island. The principal exports of I. are salt and cod-fish to Spain, the Mediterranean, and the British Isles, and cod liver oil to the British Isles, and in 1909 they amounted to £714,046. The pop. numbers 85,089.

Language.—The Icelandic is the most northerly of all cultivated tongues. It is free from gutturals and excess of hissing sounds, soft and sonorous to the ear, and rich in roots and grammatical forms. There are twenty-eight letters in the alphabet, all the English except *w ;* also *œ,* ·o· (the German *ä* and *ö*), and a character for the English *th.* The present-day language is almost precisely the same as that spoken and written at the date of I.'s colonisation in the 9th century.

Literature. — Icelandic literature may be divided into two periods, the ancient, extending to the fall of the republic, and the modern, from that date to the present time. The literature of the ancient period may be divided into three groups, viz. the ancient, mythical, and heroic songs ; the scaldic poetry; and the sagas. I. has always borne a high renown for song, although it never produced a poet of a high order. Among the most important works in Icelandic literature is the collection of ancient heathen songs called the Elder or poetic Edda, compiled soon after the introduction of Christianity. Songs of victory, elegies, and epigrams also belong to the ancient period of the literature. Among the mythical songs may be mentioned the *Völuspa, Hämarsheimt, Hymiskavida,* etc. Of the writers of scaldic poems may be cited : Egil Skallagrimsson, who wrote a fine lament for his son; Eyvind, Kormak, etc. The crowning product of Icelandic genius, however, is the prose saga. This is, in its purest form, the life of a hero, composed in regular form and governed by fixed rules, and intended for oral recitation. The saga grew up in the quieter days that followed the change of faith (1002), when the deeds of the great families' heroes were still cherished by their descendants, and the exploits of the great kings handed down. At all feasts and gatherings the telling of stories was a great feature, and the reciter was obliged to work them into regular form. The Irish influence did much to perfect this form, and it is to the West that the best sagas belong. Besides the sagas, consisting chiefly of local and family histories, they also comprised a large number of histories and romantic works, amongst them being: the *Völsunga Saga ;* the *Gunnlaugs Saga;* the *Saga of Hrolf Kraka and his Companions; Frithiof's Saga,* etc. Of the larger and more important class of sagas referred to may be mentioned : the *Islendingabók ;* the *Landnamabók* (an account of the settlement of the island); the *Kristni Saga ;* the *Njál's Saga ; Viga-Glum's Saga ; Egil's Saga* (the biography of a celebrated poet and chief); the *Sturlunga Saga;* the *Knytlinga Saga;* the *Fœreyinga Saga ;* the *Eyrbyggja Saga* (an abstract of which was published by Sir Walter Scott), etc., etc. *See* J. C. Poestion, *Isländische Dichter der Neuzeit,* 1897; C. Küchler, *Geschichte der isländischen Dichtung der Neuzeit,* 1896 ; Ph. Schweitzer, *Island, Land, und Leute,* 1885; Alexander Baumgartner, *Island und die Farœr,* 1889.

Iceland Moss, or *Cetraria Islandica,* a lichen found in the N. hemisphere, frequently in Britain, and in great abundance in Iceland. It contains a bitter principle which is removed by steeping it in water, when it forms a valuable article of diet especially suitable for invalids.

Iceland Spar, a clear, colourless variety of calcite ($CaCO_3$), found in Iceland. It forms large rhombohedra having a specific gravity of 2·7 and a hardness=3. The value of I. S. lies in its having a strong double refraction, which makes it pre-eminently suited for polariscopes, Nicot's prisms, and other optical purposes. The supply from Iceland, where crystals of very large size are found, is nearly exhausted, and no substitute has been found to compare with it.

Iceni was the name of an ancient British people who inhabited that part of England where now exist the counties of Norfolk, Suffolk, Cambridge, and Huntingdon. Their queen, Boadicea, headed a revolt against the Romans, 61 A.D.

Ice-Plant, or *Mesembryanthemum crystallinum,* a species of Aizoaceæ found in S. Africa and cultivated in Britain. It is an annual plant with succulent leaves covered with glistening hairs, and bears white flowers.

Ichaboe, an island, half a mile in circumference, off the S.W. coast of Africa ; it belongs to the Cape of Good Hope and exports guano.

Ichang, a treaty port in the Chinese prov. of Hu-peh ; it is situated on the left bank of the Yang-tse R., about 15 m. below the entrance to the great Yang-tse gorges. The hilly country round is rich in rice, cotton, wheat, and barley fields, and in many kinds of fruit. I. is an important shipping centre, being the gate to the immense coalfields of Sze-chuen ; and its steamer traffic is in the hands of the British and the Chinese. Pop. 55,000.

Ich Dien (Ger., I serve), the motto adopted by the Black Prince after the battle of Crecy, along with a plume of three upright ostrich feathers, which since that time has been the crest of the Princes of Wales.

Ichneumon (Gk. ἰχνεύειν, to track or trace out), the name given to a species of *Herpestes*, a genus of small carnivorous mammals belonging to the Viverridæ; they have elongated weasel-shaped bodies, small heads, rounded ears, and short legs. *Herpestes ichneumon* ranges over S. Asia and all Africa, and *H. ichneumon*, var. *Widringtonii*, is found in the S. of Spain. The former was regarded as sacred by the Egyptians, who gave it the name of Pharaoh's rat;

ICHNEUMON PHARAONIS

the embalmed bodies of Is. were often preserved by priests in the temples. They will eat the eggs of serpents and swallow smaller vermin, and are sometimes domesticated for this purpose.

Ichneumon-flies, the name applied to the Ichneumonidæ, a family of insects containing nearly 6000 species, and belonging to the order Hymenoptera. They are found in almost all parts of the world, and in the larval state are generally parasitic in, and occasionally on, Lepidoptera; and other orders of insects; the Ichneumon larvæ thus destroy thousands of caterpillars, and are even inimical to spiders. The distinguishing features of the Ichneumonidæ are the long, jointed antennæ, closely compacted at the extremities. The females of the genera *Rhyssa* and *Thalessa* have ovipositors 3 or 4 in. in length, which are serrated so as to form an effective boring apparatus; by the aid of these organs the insects can deposit their eggs under the skins of species of Siricidæ, which live in solid wood. Having completed its metamorphoses, the I. pierces a way out with its mandibles; the genus *Pezomachus*, or wingless Ichneumons, are somewhat ant-like in appearance, and are very common in Britain. *Agriotypus armatus* is a remarkable British

species which goes under water for the purpose of depositing its eggs in the larvæ of Trichoptera; this insect belongs to Agriotypides, one of several sub-families of Ichneumonidæ, others being Ichneumonides, Cryptides, Tryphonides, Pimplides, and Ophionides. The species of this remarkable family existing in N. America and the tropics have yet to be investigated. Fossil Ichneumonidæ have been found in the Tertiary strata of America and Europe.

Ichor, was the ethereal fluid which, according to Greek mythology, flowed in the veins of the gods, instead of blood. The word is still used in the poetical sense. In pathology it signifies the watery, acrid discharge from ill-conditioned wounds.

Ichthyodorulites (Gk. ἰχθύς, fish, δόρυ, spear, and λίθος, stone) are the fossil spines of sharks, which are often found isolated in ancient strata, the rest of the skeleton having rotted away. The phosphatic nature of these vertebræ has preserved them to some degree of perfection, though they are the earliest fish-spines discovered, being first seen in the Upper Silurian rocks. Over forty genera of I. are recognised, as *Onchus, Ctenacanthus, Lepracanthus, Edestus,* etc.

Ichthyology (Gk. ἰχθύς, a fish), the term applied to that branch of zoology which treats of fishes (q.v.).

Ichthyornis (Gk. ἰχθύς, fish, and ὄρνις, bird), the name given to an extinct genus of Casinatæ or flying birds with a keeled breast-bone, which are only found in the Cretaceous strata of N. America. They form a group called Odontornithæ, because of their having rows of reptile teeth fixed in distinct sockets; they were birds of powerful flight, as shown by the construction of their wings. In shape, they resembled modern birds very closely, and they were about the size of a pigeon. Most of the specimens of I. are preserved in Yale University, and in the University of Kansas.

Ichthyosaurus, or **Ichthyopteri** (Gk., fish - lizard), a name applied by König in 1818 to a kind of porpoise-shaped marine reptile, with a fish-like body, from its outward appearance. They belonged to the Mesozoic period, becoming extinct after the deposition of the chalk. Nearly complete skeletons have been obtained from the lias of England and Germany. Remains also occur in the Rhætic, Jurassic, and Cretaceous strata of Europe, Australia, Africa, and S. America, those of the Lower Cretaceous age being distributed also in the East Indies and New Zealand. They varied in length from about 3 ft. to 10 yds. The *I. Trigonodon* from

Banz, Bavaria, is the largest known species, the head measuring over 2 yds. The English *I. platyodon* was about the same size. The commonest English species, *I. intermedius* and *I. communis*, were about 3 to 4 yds. long. Probably originally descended from land or marsh animals, the earliest known Ichthyosaurians (Mixosaurus) were very small, and occur in the Trias. They had large heads with a slender, pointed snout, huge eyes surrounded by a ring of overlapping 'sclerotic plates,' and jaws with a row of conical teeth, much of a size, firmly set in a continuous groove. As many as 400 teeth have been counted in a single mouth. They breathed air, and were carnivorous, feeding on fishes and molluscs.

tology, ii., 1902 ; Fraas, *Die Ichthyosaurier der süddeutschen Trias- und Jura-Ablagerungen*, 1891 ; *British Museum Guide to Fossil Reptiles and Fishes*, and *Catalogue* by Dr. Woodward ; Gadow, *Amphibia and Reptiles*, 1901 ; Hawkins, *The Book of the Great Sea-Dragons*, 1840.

Ichthyosis, *see* SKIN DISEASES.

Icilius, the name of a distinguished Roman family. Lucius I. was tribune of the plebs, 456 and 455 B.C., and a leader in the revolt against the Decemviri, 449 B.C. Spurius I. was one of the three envoys sent by the people to treat with the senate at the time of the succession to the Sacred Mount, 494 B.C.

Icolmkill, *see* IONA.

Iconium (modern *Konia*, or *Konieh*),

ICHTHYOSAURUS

Their bones and coprolites have supplied quantities of phosphate of lime for preparing artificial manures. The reptiles were apparently viviparous. The bones of the skeleton show numerous short vertebræ, deeply biconcave, making the backbone very flexible. There is scarcely any neck, the head passing directly into the fusiform body, which tapered to a bifurcate tail. Two pairs of paddle-like limbs or swimming flippers encased in skin are always found—the pectoral and pelvic fins. The hinder are often small, but never absent altogether. The skin is smooth, forming two triangular median fins, one in the middle of the back (dorsal), and one at the end of the tail. Examples are in the museums of Stuttgart, Tübingen, Budapest, and Chicago. The terminal vertebræ passed into the *lower* lobe of the tail-fin, which was expanded in a vertical plane. Behind the dorsal fin was a row of smaller, finer fins, as seen in a specimen from Würtemberg (1892). The resemblance between the I. and the whale is a curious example of convergence between two distinct races—reptiles and mammals—resulting from adaptation to aquatic life. The Baptanodon, Shastasaurus, and Ophthalmosaurus are allied Ichthyosaurians. Consult Owen, *A Monograph of the Fossil Reptilia of the Liassic Formations*, iii., 1881 (Mon. Palæont. Soc.); Zittel-Eastmann, *Textbook of Palæon-*

a tn. in Asiatic Turkey, situated in the principal military and commercial highway, in the centre of an extensive plain. It was orginally a Phrygian city, and was added to the Galatian country about 165 B.C. It appears to have been an important centre of Christianity, and was three times visited by Paul and Barnabas. It fell into the hands of the Turks about 1079, who made it the capital of their kingdom; and it also played a prominent part in the Crusades. The appearance of I. from a distance is imposing, being surrounded with Saracenic walls, from 2 to 3 m. in circuit, flanked with towers 30 ft. high. The interior, however, is desolate, and in a state of ruin. The most remarkable buildings are the ancient mosque, and several handsome modern ones ; and the old Turkish prison, with ruined towers and keep. The inhabitants are chiefly employed in making carpets, and preparing woollen and leather goods. Pop. 60,000.

Iconoclasts (Gk. εἰκονοκλάστης, image-breaker), a name applied to the Christian party in the church of the 8th and 9th centuries, who refused to tolerate the use of images in places of worship. In the early Christian church, only symbols like the fish, palm-branch, or dove, were used, but by the 4th century sacred pictures were apparently common, and denounced by the Spanish

Council of Eliberis (306). The sixth General (Trullan) Council of Constantinople (692) sanctioned the representation of Christ as a Man, and the second Council of Nicæa (787) allowed sacred images in the churches. Distinction was made between προσκύνησις τιμητική or δουλεία, veneration, and προσκύνησις λατρευτική or λατρεία, worship due to God alone. The Byzantine Emperor Leo III. (the Isaurian) issued an edict (726) forbidding honours to be paid to images. Another decree of 730 prohibited image-worship as idolatrous. Constantine V., Leo IV., and Michael Balbus, were also I., while Popes Gregory II. and III., and Germanus, patriarch of Constantinople, were like the Empress Irene, supporters of the iconolatræ (image-worshippers). One result of the quarrel between the iconolatræ and I., was the scission between E. and W. Rome became linked with the Carlovingian house, and the pope crowned Charlemagne in 800. The Roman church emphasised the utility of pictures and statues for teaching the illiterate (Council of Trent, sess. xxv.). Image-worship was restored in the East under Theophilus and Theodora (842). Records of the reforming I. of the 17th century prove that image-worship had been practised considerably in Britain. See ' Acts of the Iconoclast Council of 815 ' in Séances Acad. des Inscriptions, 1903 ; Theophanes' Chronographica (de Boor's ed., 1883-85); Krumbacher, Hist. of Byzantine Literature (2nd ed., p. 674); Bréhier, La Querelle des images, 1904 ; Tertullian, De Idololatria; Marin, Les moines de Constantinople, iv., 1897.

Icosandria (Gk. εἴκοσι, twenty ; ἀνήρ, male), the term used in Linnæan classification to indicate those plants which bear twenty or more stamens inserted on the calyx, e.g. the rose.

Ictinus, a famous Greek architect who lived towards the end of the 5th century B.C., and was thus a contemporary of Pericles and Phidias. His name will always be associated with the Parthenon at Athens, which he designed in conjunction with Callicrates (444-439 B.C.). I. was also the architect for the temple of Eleusis, where the mysteries were celebrated, and for the temple dedicated to Apollo Epicurius, near Phigalia in Arcadia. Portions of all these buildings still exist.

Ida (547-59), the first king of Bernicia, was in the prime of life when he assumed power. His rule probably did not extend S. of the Tees, the kingdom of Deira, between that river and the Humber, being founded after his death. He built a fortress called by the Angles Bebbanburch, now Bamborough. Six of his sons reigned in succession over Bernicia.

Ida, or Idda, a tn. of W. Africa, situated on the l. b. of the Niger, near the boundary of Northern and Southern Nigeria. Pop. about 8000.

Ida (Turkish Kaz-Dagh), a mountain range in Asia Minor, which extends through Phrygia and Mysia, and commands the ancient plain of Troy. Mount Gargarus (5748 ft. high), its loftiest peak, was the seat of the temple erected to Cybele, the Idœa Mater.

Ida, Mount, or Psilorati, in Crete, was famous for the worship of Zeus, the god being nurtured, according to mythology, in one of its caverns. This celebrated peak is situated almost in the centre of the island, and rises to a height of 8060 ft.

Ida, Mount, New Zealand, situated in the S. Island, about 70 m. N. of Dunedin ; gold-fields have been discovered in its neighbourhood.

Idaarderadeel, a vil. in the Netherlands, prov. of Frise. Pop. 5628.

Idaho (Indian, mountain-gem), a Rocky Mt. state of U.S.A., largely in the basin of Columbia R. It is bounded N. by British Columbia and Montana, E. by Montana and Wyoming, S. by Utah and Nevada, W. by Oregon and Washington. These limits were fixed in 1868, five years after formation of the territory, which was admitted to the American union in 1890. Area about 83,354 sq. m. The Snake (Shoshone or Lewis) R. is on the W., noted for its cañon and numerous cataracts. Goose Creek and Bear River Mts. come S. and S.E. of Salmon River Mts., which divide the state into N. and S. Idaho, and separate Snake R. valley from Great Salt Lake basin. Besides the mountainous regions there are desert and sage-plains and fields of basalt. All geological ages from the Silurian to the Pliocene are represented, especially the Tertiary and post-Tertiary periods. Gold has been found on Pend d'Oreille R., since 1852. The Cœur d'Alène mines of gold, silver, and lead are famous. Coal, salt, sulphur, and iron-ore are also found. The land is more suited for grazing than agriculture, but wheat, oats, barley, and potatoes are produced. There are twenty-three counties, the chief towns being Boisé (capital), pop. (1910) 17,358; Pocatello (1910), 9110; Cœur d'Alene (1910), 7291 ; Moscow (with state university); Lewiston (1910), 6043; Wallace, and Weiser. There are numerous schools and denominational colleges. The state has a governor, and sends one representative to Congress. Pop. (1910) 325,594. See Onderdonk, Idaho, Facts and Statis-

tics . . ., 1885; Hepburn, *Idaho Laws and Decisions*, 1900; Bancroft, *Washington, Idaho, and Montana*, 1890; Russell, ' Geology . . . of Snake River Plains of Idaho ' for *U.S. Geol. Survey, Bulletin* 199, 1902.

Idaho Springs, a banking tn. and resort of Clear Creek co., Colorado, U.S.A., on Colorado and S. Railway, 30 m. W. of Denver. Situated in the plateau regions of the Rockies, it has hot and cold soda-springs, and gold and silver are found. There are concentrating-mills, machine-shops, and lumber-yards. Pop. 2154.

Idalium (Gk. Ἰδάλιον), an ancient tn. of Cyprus, was situated almost in the centre of the island, on the site now occupied by the village Dalin or Idalion. It was sacred to the worship of Aphrodite, who was hence named Idalia. The town was destroyed by earthquake before the time of Pliny.

Idar, in Germany, a small tn. on the Idarbach; it is contained in the principality of Birkenfeld, grand-duchy of Oldenburg. Pop. 6892.

Idas (Gk. Ἴδας), in Greek mythology, was the son of Aphareus and Arené, and brother to Lynceus; he wooed Marpessa, daughter of the river-god Euenus, and carried her off from Apollo, who also sought her favour. They fled in a winged chariot given by Poseidon, but were overtaken by Apollo at Messenia, where god and mortal fought for the nymph. Zeus, interposing, told her to choose between her suitors, and she chose I. She became the mother of Cleopatra and Alcyoné, and having incurred the wrath of Apollo, they died young. I. and his brother both took part in the Argonautic expedition ; they were killed whilst engaged in a raid into Arcadia with their cousins Castor and Pollux. Zeus came upon them as they were quarrelling about the plunder and slew I. by lightning.

Iddesleigh, Sir Stafford Henry Northcote, first **Earl of** (1818-87), a statesman, began his political life in 1842, when he became private secretary to Gladstone. He succeeded as eighth baronet in 1851, and four years later entered parliament in the Conservative interest. A good speaker, Disraeli soon marked him as a coming man, and in 1866 appointed him president of the Board of Trade, and in the following year promoted him to the India Office. When his party returned to office in 1874 he became Chancellor of the Exchequer, and in 1876, when Disraeli went to the House of Lords, he became leader of the House of Commons. Created Earl of Iddesleigh in 1884, he went to the Foreign Office in 1886, but resigned after six months, so as to facilitate the arrangements between the Conserva-

tives and the Liberal-Unionists. An unselfish man, always putting party before himself, he was an admirable and much-loved statesman, though scarcely of the first rank, being lacking in initiative. Biography by Andrew Lang (1890).

Idea (Gk. ἰδέα, from ἰδεῖν, to see ; Lat. *species*), a term widely used both in philosophy and in common parlance for a mental image of any external object or for the abstract conception of a class of objects. It is also used in a wider sense for any product of intellectual action. Plato made use of the term in metaphysics to define the absolute realities eternally existing in the mind of God, on the model of which all the objects which can be perceived are made. These vary in detail, but the one archetype or ' idea ' remains constant, and can be apprehended only by the action of the intellect. Empirical thinkers, who insist on the reality of external objects have never accepted this usage. Locke, at the beginning of his *Essay on the Human Understanding*, defines the term ' idea ' as ' whatsoever is the object of the understanding when a man thinks,' including, that is to say, all objects of consciousness—percepts, images, and concepts. Hume limited the term to the mentally reconstructed images of perceptions, while he introduced the term ' impression ' for the direct perception. This use of the term is still common in popular language. Kant defined Is. (called by him Transcendental Is.) as the product of the Reason (*Vernunft*), of which they are the highest concepts, transcending the understanding, and therefore incapable of verification by experience. In the language of Hegel and the Idealists, the term almost returned to its Platonic significance, being used for the Absolute, which is the beginning and end of all things.

Idealism, the type of philosophy which holds the conception of the co-ordination of human and divine, or of object and subject. I. is based on the premiss that appearances are purely the perceptions, the ideas, of subjects. Zeno of Elea and, later, Plato anticipated modern I.; other systems were those of Locke, Descartes, and Spinoza, and also the Immaterialism of Berkeley. At the present time the term is generally held to signify the great German schools of Fichte, Schelling, and Hegel, respectively subjective, objective, and absolute, and their descendants, the transcendentalists. In subjective I. it is held that ideas and perceptions are determined wholly by the human mind. The objective, on the other hand, contends that they are of divine origin and inspiration.

Absolute I., such as Hegel's, identifies object and subject; it is a logical examination of neither, but of their identity, their correlation—an examination, not of the form which an idea takes, but of the idea itself. The word I. has also taken another meaning, of a purely literary nature—the expression of beautiful or optimistic temperament; in its results, it is analogous to the more general æsthetic idealogy of Cousin and Lessing. In this sense, such writers as Fogazzaro, Maeterlinck, Shelley, etc., are idealists, apart from any consideration of their purely philosophical sympathies. *See* FICHTE, HEGEL, SPINOZA, etc.

Identity, a question which is regarded variously according as it relates to questions of logic or of metaphysics. The logical law of I. is usually expressed by the formula $A = A$, or A is A. It is a necessary law of self-conscious thought, being, in fact, merely the positive expression of the law of contradiction which states that a judgment cannot be true and untrue at various times, and that the same attribute cannot at the same time be affirmed and denied of the same subject. Without such a law no thinking would be possible. The philosophical question of I. is concerned largely with the various ways in which I. can be predicated, and to the exact connotation of the term. The question as to whether or no I. excludes difference is an important one. Many have held that so far from excluding difference, it actually implies it, in other words, that I. is not undifferentiated, but differentiated, likeness. The question, however, is one of the conceptions of philosophical atomism. (*See* James, *Principles of Psychology*, 1890, and Bosanquet's *Essays and Addresses*, 1889.) The question of personal I., that is to say, of ' the continuity of personal experience in the exercise of intelligent causal energy, the results being associated in memory,' was first brought into prominence by Locke (*Essay*, bk. ii., ch. xxvii.), and soon occupied the attention of Hume and Butler. The fact is that which distinguishes each person from other thinking beings, and with which the preservation of sanity is closely bound up.

Ides, *see* CALENDS.

Idiocy, or ' mental deficiency or extreme stupidity depending upon malnutrition or disease of the brain occurring either before birth or before the evolution of the mental faculties in childhood, while imbecility is generally used to denote a less decided degree of such mental in-

capacity.' Thus I. differs from insanity in that one in the former condition never has been sane, while one in the latter has. Idiots vary from those having no power of speech, of care -for themselves, of distinction between two persons, with no feelings of love or hate, pleasure or pain, who are usually dwarfish, ugly, and misshapen, and who sometimes cannot even walk, to those who are often beautiful and normally developed physically, but who lack some mental faculty or intelligence, affection, or control. The large majority of mentally deficients are, however, physically unfit in some way or another, and are liable to certain diseases, such as consumption, rickets, and scrofula. Idiots are not all alike in being incapable of education, and perhaps the most wonderful of strides within recent years in education have been made in the methods of dealing with mentally deficient children. Many, under proper conditions, can be taught to earn their own living and to look after themselves, in fact, in many cases mentally deficient children have been brought well up to the average standard of intelligence. Dr. Maria Montessori first earned fame for her system, by its astonishing success among such children. Schools with specially trained teachers are being set up over England, and under the guidance of school medical officers children who before were hindrances and worries to teachers, and who, by reason of the fact that they were mocked and ridiculed by other children, used to become more confirmed in their imbecility, are now educated and improved both physically and mentally. Those who pioneered the work of educating and treating idiots and cretins, *e.g.* Read, Howe, and Seguin, started on a task which seemed almost impossible, and the value of their work and of those still engaged upon it is inestimable, and those teachers who have given themselves up to the work to-day, are engaged in probably the noblest and certainly the most arduous of all branches of the teaching profession. I. has been classified into ten divisions, and from these, pathological causes would seem to have a deal to do with the state, but the general cause has yet to be discovered. Undoubtedly in many cases it is hereditary, and consanguine marriages may cause it, but only in those cases where the stock is bad. It has been suggested that consumption in parents may cause the state to arise, and it is known that frights to mothers when pregnant sometimes results in the birth of an idiot. On the other hand, I. does occur in what otherwise appear to be healthy families. Special notice is taken of idiots and imbeciles in the law, and they are regarded as being irresponsible for their actions, and are treated as children, while at the present time special efforts are being made to secure the passing of another Bill dealing with the mentally deficient, which will still further increase the control of the state over such people. *See* Dr. Ireland, *Idiocy and Imbecility. See also* CRETINISM.

Idiosyncrasy, the converse of antipathy (*q.v.*), being a strong disposition towards certain things.

Idle, a tn. of the W. Riding of Yorkshire, England, situated near the Aire, 9 m. from Leeds. It manufactures woollen goods. Pop. 7552.

Ido, or **Revised Esperanto,** is, as its name indicates, the offspring of Esperanto (*q.v.*), the international auxiliary language. The origin of I. is, according to its partisans, to be found in the Delegation for the Adoption of an Auxiliary International Language, founded in 1901. The committee of this delegation, say the Idists, after examining all past and present schemes for an international language, adopted Esperanto with a few alterations, and I. grammars and dictionaries were first published in 1908. I., therefore, does not claim to supersede Esperanto as that tongue superseded Volapük, but merely to simplify, regularise, and improve it. The two chief alterations effected are the doing away with all accented letters and the suppression of a few grammatical rules (*e.g.* accusative case, agreement of the adjective), which the partisans of I. consider unnecessary. Orthodox Esperantist criticism falls mainly under two heads, viz. (1) That the alterations are too small and unimportant to make the change worth while; that the pulling out of a brick here and there imperils the whole structure of the language, at the same time confusing the indifferent public. (2) That the revised language was the jerrybuilt product of a gerrymandered committee. The following is the Lord's Prayer in I., which may be contrasted with the same in Esperanto (vol. v. page 524): 'Nia patro, qua esas en la cielo, tua nomo esez santigita; tua regno venez; tua volo facesez, quale en la cielo, tale sur la tero. Donez a ni hodie nia omnadia pano. E pardonez a ni nia debi, quale ni anke pardonis a nia deberi. E ne duktez ni en tento; ma liberigez ni de malo. Car tua esas la regno, la povo, e la glorio, sempre e sempre.'

Idocrase, or **Vesuvian,** a mineral consisting essentially of silica (37 to 39 per cent.), alumina (13 to 16 per cent.), and lime (33 to 37 per cent.), together with a small percentage of oxide of iron, magnesia, and water. It occurs in the form of short tetragonal crystals, which show a large number of faces (sp. gr. 3·4, h. 6·5). The mineral has a vitreous lustre and varies in colour from brown to green. It was first found in dolomitic blocks ejected from Vesuvius, but occurs also in granular limestone, serpentine, gneiss, and other metamorphic rocks. The finest specimens come from Siberia, Piedmont, and Norway, and are cut, polished, and sold as chrysolite or jacinth.

Idolatry (Gk. εἴδωλον and λατρεία, idol-worship), the worship paid to images or other objects supposed to be the abode of a superhuman personality. The term is sometimes used generically to denote all forms of worship of visible and concrete, as opposed to unseen, existences, thus including litholatry, pyrolatry, zoolatry, and the like. St. Paul uses it to express worship of false gods, and the whole heathen cultus (*see* Gal. v. 20 ; 1 Cor. x. 14 ; 1 Pet. iv. 3). Regarded by the early church as a degeneration from a higher primeval faith, it has since been shown rather to mark a stage of upward movement and progress in religious growth. While absent among Hottentots, Fuegians, Veddahs, Bushmen, and others, I. was extensively practised among the great civilisations of old, by Egyptians, Chaldeans, Indians, Greeks, Romans, Mexicans, and Peruvians. Relics of this worship remain in the ' nirgalli ' (images of monsters), common outside Chaldean palaces. Into these it was believed that malignant spirits, such as those of disease, would enter. Statues and idols connected with the worship of the dead were common among many peoples. The Maori ' atua,' or ancestral deity, was supposed to enter his carved wooden image on the incantations of a priest, and to deliver oracles. The earliest stages of I. are Naturism and Animism. Fetichism, a degraded form of the latter, is often the direct antecedent of I. Private and personal idols or fetiches, like the Hebrew teraphim (*see* Gen. xxxi. 19, 34 ; 1 Sam. xix. 13), are early adopted, but public, tribal, and national idols are a late development. The human figure came to be the predominant model. Images were probably introduced among Christians in the 2nd century, and are often found in Christian tombs in the Roman catacombs. In the 6th and 7th centuries abuses crept in. A reaction arose against I. in the East, culminating in iconoclasm (*c.* 726). A characteristic of I. is its tendency to revive even after the introduction of purer spiritual ideas. Thus the Israelites were often in danger of relapsing from monotheism (*see* Exod. xxxii.; 1 Kings xi. 5; xii. 28; xiv. 15, 23; xvi. 32). The Roman Catholic and Greek Churches still revere images of the Virgin and saints. The Reformers and Calvinists repudiated all relics of I., but Luther allowed idols as possibly helpful to devotion. Printed pictures of saints and icons are worshipped in Russia. *See* works of Voss, van Dale, Spencer, Tylor, Waitz, Schultze, Réville; Bingham, *Antiquities*, xvi. 4; Lubbock, *Origin of Civilisation*, 1902; d'Alviella, ' Les Origines de l'Idolâtrie ' in *Revue de l'histoire des Religions*, xii., 1885; Kraus, *Roma sotteranea*, 1879; Lippert, *Culturgeschichte*. See IMAGE-WORSHIP, RELIGION.

Idomeneus, son of Deucalion, king of Crete, and grandson of Minos. As king of Crete, he led eighty ships to Troy and played a leading part in the battle, being described in Homer's *Iliad* as one of the mightiest of the heroes. In later writers he is represented as vowing in a storm, provided he arrived safe home, to sacrifice to Poseidon whatever he first met on landing. The victim was his son, whom he accordingly sacrificed, and his subjects, in consequence, drove him forth. He wandered in Calabria and Italy, where he established a shrine of Apollo near Colophon; here he died and was buried.

Idria, a tn. and com. of Austria in the prov. of Carniola, situated on the Idrizza, about 30 m. N.N.W. of Trieste. There are quicksilver mines in the vicinity, which have been worked since the 16th century. Pop. 6090.

Idris, a mythical figure in Welsh tradition who had his rock-hewn chair on the summit of Cader Idris. He was supposed to have the power of conferring poetic inspiration, and of inducing madness or death.

Idrisi, *see* EDRISI MOHAMMED.

Idumæa, the ancient name for Edom, applied to the country extending from the Dead Sea southwards to the Gulf of Akabah, about 100 m. in length from N. to S. After the destruction of Jerusalem (70 A.D.), the name of I. disappeared from history, and the country was merged in Arabic Petræa.

Idun, or Iduna, the name of a goddess in Norse mythology. She was the daughter of the dwarf Svald, and became the wife of Bragi. She personified the reviving year, being imprisoned in the nether world by Thiassi (winter), from whom she escaped, and appeared again in the shape of a bird in the springtime.

Idyll (Lat. *idyllium*, a little image), a word used to describe a species of poem representing simple scenes of a pastoral life, not however exclusively used for poems of a pastoral character. Tennyson, for example, in his *Idylls of the King*, presents an epic style and treatment, the incidents portrayed being of a romantic and tragic nature. Theocritus, too, previously, in his *Eidyllia* (thirty in number), wrote less than half in the pastoral form.

Iesi, or Jesi, a tn. of Italy in the prov. of Ancona, situated on the l. b. of the Esino, 17 m. S.W. of Ancona. It is noted as the birthplace of the Emperor Frederick II., and possesses a fine cathedral. Pop. 23,000.

If, an islet of Bouches-du-Rhône dept., off the S. coast of France, opposite Marseilles in the Gulf of Lyons. It was once covered with yews (' ifs '). Its fortress, Château d'If, built by Francis I. (1529), is famous. It was used as a state prison later, Mirabeau and Philippe Egalité being imprisoned there. In Dumas' *Count of Monte Cristo* the hero is confined there.

Iffland, August William (1759-1814), a German actor and dramatist, born at Hanover, and educated for the ministry. He had a leaning for the stage, however, at an early age, and went to Gotha, where he studied under good teachers. In 1779 he went to Mannheim, and here he gained his reputation. In 1796 he became director of the Berlin National Theatre, and subsequently superintendent of all the royal theatres, the Berlin stage reaching its highest point under his management. Amongst the best of I.'s plays are: *The Bachelors, The Foresters, The Nephews, The Lawyers, Crime from Ambition,* and *Conscience*. His dramatic criticism is to be found in his *Almanach fur Theater und Theaterfreunde*, and his *Theorie der Schauspielkunst*. See *Iffland in seinen Schriften* (Düncker), 1859, and *Iffland's Berliner Theaterleitung*, 1896.

Ifni, a seaport tn. of W. Morocco, Africa, 35 m. from Aguilon, opposite the Canary Is., ceded to Spain by Morocco in 1883. Pop. about 6000.

Ifrit, Ifreet, Afrit, or Afreet, an ogre in Arabic folklore of an evil disposition.

Igel, a vil. of Rhenish Prussia, 3 m. S.W. of Treves. It contains the celebrated I. obelisk, or Heidenthurm, a sandstone monument 75 ft. high, one of the most remarkable Roman relics N. of the Alps. This was a funeral monument of the Secundini family. Pop. about 500.

Iggdrasil, *see* YGGDRASIL.

Iglau, a tn. on the Bohemian frontier of Moravia, Austria - Hungary, 123 m. N.N.W. of Vienna, on the Iglawa. Manufs. include tobacco, plush, woollens, cloth, glass, and pottery. It was a mining centre in the middle ages, silver being worked from the 8th century, but the industry is now approaching extinction. A treaty ending the struggle between Sigismund and the Hussites was signed here (1436). In 1805 the Austrians defeated the Bavarians here. Pop. 25,915.

Iglesias, a tn. and episcopal see of Cagliari prov., W. Sardinia, Italy, 32 m. from Cagliari. The chief mining centre of Sardinia, it has zinc and lead mines. There is a cathedral (1285), an old castle, and a bishop's palace. The town is partly surrounded by walls, and its citadel dates from 1325. Malaria is prevalent. Pop. about 21,000.

Iglesias de la Casa, José (1748-91), a Spanish poet, a native of Salamanca. He first wrote satiric ballads, epigrams, and ' letrillas ' directed against contemporary society and morals. He entered the church (1783), becoming priest of Larodrigo, and then of Carbajosa de la Sagrada. His later works contained much theological discussion. I. is often ranked with Quevedo (1580-1645). His *Collected Poems* first appeared in 1798. In 1802 some of them were put on the Index. *See* Ticknor, *Hist. of Spanish Lit.*, 1849; Longfellow, *Poets and Poetry of Europe.*

Iglo, a tn. of Hungary, in the co. of Zips, situated on the Hernad. It has iron and copper smelting works, and a trade in linen and flax. Pop. 9000.

Igloolik, a small is. of N. Canada, situated in the Arctic Ocean, in Fury and Hecla Strait, in lat. 69° 21′ N., and long. 81° 53′ W.

Ignatiev, Nikolai Pavlovitch (1832-1906), a Russian general and diplomatist, born in St. Petersburg, and the son of General Paul I., a favourite officer of Alexander II. He was educated in the corps of pages and exchanged from the military to the diplomatic service in 1856, having served in the Crimean War, and been made a colonel and majorgeneral. In 1858 he was made diplomatic attaché to General Muravieff, governor of E. Siberia, and negotiated the treaty of Aigun with China, by which the region of the Amur came into the possession of Russia. Two years later, he was sent as plenipotentiary to Peking. In 1863 he was placed at the head of the Asiatic department of the Ministry of Foreign Affairs, and made adjutant-general of the Czar. He was an active agent at the outbreak of the Russo-Turkish War in 1877, and the treaty of Stefano was chiefly owing to him. At the close of the war he fell into disfavour and retired from office. On the accession of Alexander III., however, he was made Minister of the Interior, but was dismissed in 1882 for permitting the persecution of the Jews.

Ignatius, Bishop of Antioch, one of the Apostolic Fathers, perhaps the most remarkable of all the figures of the century immediately following the Apostles. Very little, however, is known about his life, and about his birth and parentage nothing is known. A late tradition says that he was the little child whom Our Lord placed as a pattern in the midst of the disciples. More reliance is to be placed on the earlier tradition which speaks of him as the disciple ˆof St. John the Apostle. Eusebius also tells us that he was the second successor of St. Peter in the see of Antioch. Later traditions are so untrustworthy that we are forced to rely entirely on the internal evidence of the letters which I. wrote. These were sent from various cities at which the saint stopped as he was being hurried to Rome for martyrdom (115-117 A.D.) during a persecution which arose at Antioch in the reign of Trajan. The letters themselves present a most difficult critical problem, which now, however, after the labours of Zahn, Lightfoot, Harnack, and others, seems to have reached a satisfactory solution. The difficulty is brought about by the fact that three widely-different recensions of the letters exist. The *short* or Vossian recension, consists of seven letters, the number which Eusebius ascribes to I. They are written to the Ephesians, Magnesians, Trallians, Romans, Philadelphians, Smyrneans, and to Polycarp, respectively. This recension occurs in Greek, Latin, Armenian, and fragments in Syriac and Coptic forms. The *long* recension contains these seven in an expanded form and several others in addition, six in the Greek form, and ten in the Latin. Finally there is the *Syriac* or *Curetonian* recension, containing only three epistles, viz. those to the Romans, the Ephesians, and Polycarp, all in a shortened form. Much controversy has taken place as to which of these recensions was to be regarded as the genuine work of I. The arguments against the long recension are conclusive, and scholars are now generally united in upholding the claims of the Vossian recension. The Syriac recension is to be regarded as an abbreviated edition of the seven epistles, and not as the original and unexpanded form. The letters are directed against Gnostic and Docetic heresy, laying great stress on the duty of adherence to episcopal authority, and the essential nature of the episcopal office. *See* works by Zahn, Lightfoot, Funk, Harnack, etc.

Ignatius, Father (1837-1908), the name, as a religious, of Joseph Leycester Lyne, an Englishman who devoted his life to an attempt to revive the Benedictine life in the Church of England. In 1870 he founded a community at Llanthony Abbey, near Abergavenny, but his attempt having been made without any reference to ecclesiastical authority, it came to an end after his death, the property passing to the Benedictine community of Caldey, of which the greater number seceded in 1913 to the Church of Rome. F. I. was a great preacher, and his mission sermons in London attracted large numbers. In 1890 he made a tour through Canada and the United States, on which he was very well received. He was also engaged in writing against the schools of rationalism and the higher criticism.

Ignatius, St. (*c.* 790-878), Patriarch of Constantinople, was the son of Michael I., Emperor of the East. He was compelled to enter a monastery, whence he rose to the patriarchate through the favour of the Empress Theodora. He was an opponent of the iconoclasts. The influence of his brother Bardas, whom he had excommunicated led to his being forced to abdicate in 866, but he was restored in the following year.

Ignatius Loyola, *see* LOYOLA, IGNATIUS DE, and JESUITS.

Ignatius's Beans, St., or *Strychnos Ignatii,* a species of Loganiaceæ found in the tropics, and like others of its genus it contains strychnine. The beans are the bitter and horny seeds, and the name was given to the plants by Jesuits in honour of St. Ignatius.

Igneous Rocks include all those which at some time in their history have been in a molten condition. Their differing physical characters, which are largely dependent on their rate of cooling, suggest one form of classification into : (*a*) *Volcanic,* in which the rate of cooling has been comparatively rapid, so that the crystallisation is by no means perfect, hence this kind contains large quantities of glassy material ; (*b*) *plutonic,* in which the cooling has been extremely slow, so that the crystallisation is almost perfect, hence there is little, if any, glassy material present ; between these two in nature there is seldom any strongly marked line of separation, for they

merge into one another, and the *dyke* rocks may be defined as of the intermediate type. In the diagram P represents the deep-seated plutonic rocks, D the *intrusive* dyke rocks, later in age than the rocks they penetrate, and forming dome-shaped laccoliths L in certain areas. V indicates the volcanic *lavas, effusive* or *eruptive rocks.* These form *sills* which are contemporaneous with the sedimentary rocks they overlie. Examples of such sills occur in the North-Western territories of N. America, in Iceland, Færos, Deccan, Abyssinia, and fragments in Ireland and Scotland. Large shapeless masses (*bosses*) of plutonic rocks become exposed through the denudation of overlying rocks. These out-

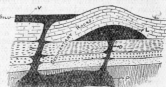

DIAGRAM TO SHOW VARIOUS IGNEOUS ROCKS

standing masses may be several miles in diameter. Other prominent rock-masses may be left by the weathering removal of surrounding material from the solidified lava in the neck of a volcano. Many such *necks* or *cores* remain, *e.g.* in Scotland, as relics of past volcanic activity. I. R. are chiefly composed of oxides, as silica, alumina, iron oxide, lime, magnesia, etc.; in consequence a frequent classification of such rocks depends on their chemical composition and more particularly on the percentage of silica present. A brief summary of such a grouping follows :

1. *Acid igneous rocks,* containing from 66 to 80 per cent. of silica. The plutonic example is *granite,* a holo-crystalline rock containing the essential minerals, quartz, felspar, and mica (generally muscovite). The glassy rapidly-cooled volcanic representative is *obsidian* which resembles bottle glass in appearance. The hemicrystalline variety is called *rhyolite.* The latter two have roughly the same chemical composition as that of granite.

2. *Sub-acid intermediate rocks* containing from 60 to 66 per cent. of silica. The essential constituents of these are orthoclase and hornblende, the latter of which may be replaced partly by augite or mica. Representatives in the same order as those of

the first group are *syenite, trachytic pumice*, or *trachyte glass*, and *trachyte*. The trachytes bear much the same relation to the syenites that the rhyolites do to the granites.

3. *Sub-basic intermediate rocks*, containing from 55 to 60 per cent. of silica. The essential mineral constituents are plagio-clastic felspar (usually oligoclase or labradorite) and hornblende which may be replaced by augite or mica as in the case of the syenites. Representatives in order are *diorite andesite glass* and *andesites*. The andesites occur in enormous masses in the Andes Mts., and are perhaps the most abundantly found of all the I.R.

4. *Basic rocks*, containing from 45 to 55 per cent. of silica, *i.e.* the acid-forming oxide is less in amount than the basic oxides. In this case the essential mineral constituents are plagioclastic felspar (usually labradorite or anothite), augite, and olivine. Magnetite is always present as an accessory. *Gabbro* is the holocrystalline plutonic representative. The glassy example is *tachylite* or *basalt glass*, while the hemicrystalline rock is *basalt*. In this group rocks called *dolerites* are intermediate in position between the gabbros and basalts.

5. *Ultra-basic rocks*, containing only 35 to 45 per cent. of silica, are very rich in olivine, which readily decomposes and causes the rocks to change quickly into some variety of the serpentines. Members of this class of ultra-basic rocks are also called *Peridotites*, e.g. *Picrites, Cherzolite*, and *Dunite*. Chemical analysis is, of course, impossible in the field, so that if it be necessary to classify the rock on the spot, it is usual to adopt some form of mineralogical grouping. Several systems have been proposed, one which is worked out very fully by Harris Teall is described in his *British Petrography*, a very brief summary of crystalline rocks would include: (*a*) Rocks of ferromagnesian minerals, *e.g.* olivine, augite, hornblende, biotite. Felspar is not present as an essential. (*b*) Rocks in which the felspar is essentially plagioclastic. (*c*) Rocks in which orthoclase is abundant; (*d*) Rocks containing nepheline and (or) leucite, both of which are absent in classes (*b*) and (*c*); (*e*) Other rocks not in the above four classes. Special classes are reserved for *vitreous* or glassy rocks, and also for *fragmental volcanic rocks* which may vary in texture from fine dust to large masses of scoriæ.

Distribution of igneous rocks.— The older I. R. occupy but a small aliquot part of the whole surface of the earth, nor are the existing masses of great extent. This will be more readily understood when it is remembered that the exposure of plutonic rocks can only be brought about by immense earth movements and fractures, or by denudation removing the overlying strata so that the crystalline rocks may be exposed. In the case of the younger I. R. of the lava and fragmental types, these are being produced at the present day along the lines of volcanic activity, as, for example, in the *Pacific girdle*. Regions of extinct volcanoes also contain varying amounts of eruptive rocks, as in the case of the Auvergne plateau of France and the Eifel mountains of W. Germany. By reference to a geological map the reader will readily identify the very numerous and widely scattered small masses of these rocks which exist on the surface of the globe.

Disintegration of igneous rocks.— Notwithstanding the hardness and compact character of these rocks yet they are particularly subject to weathering agencies. Chemical and mechanical analysis proves that all the materials building up the sedimentary rocks can be produced by the disintegration of the I. R., and, undoubtedly, *many* of the sedimentary rocks have been formed from such disintegration products. Chemical action takes place between the carbon dioxide of the atmosphere and certain compound silicates which results in the production of soluble carbonates and free silica, which latter may also be in a soluble form; rain water removes these products, and a mechanical disintegration follows. In the case of granite, the quartz is a simple compound, insoluble and consequently but little altered; on the breaking up of the granitic mass it is generally removed bodily by weathering agencies, and re-deposited to give a series of siliceous sedimentary rocks, *e.g.* sands, gravels, sandstones. The felspar is subject to the chemical changes outlined above, which is termed *kaolinisation* on account of the product kaolin or China clay which is composed of hydrated aluminium silicate separated from the felspar. The decomposition of the felspar results in the production of argillaceous sedimentary deposits, *e.g.* muds, clays, shales, together with soluble silica which may be extracted by plants and animals, *e.g.* diatoms and radiolaria, to build up their framework ; the resulting carbonate in each case will be dependent on the particular felspar which is decomposing, anothite will yield calcium carbonate, which in its turn may be extracted from its solution, and deposited to form new strata of corals, chalk, limestone, etc. The mica suffers but little decomposition, and is usually re-deposited almost unaltered.

Ignis Fatuus (Lat., foolish fire), a luminous appearance occasionally seen in marshy places and churchyards. It is usually visible shortly after sunset in autumn, and has been recorded in many countries. The light, which resembles a flame, is seldom pure white, and may be red, green, blue, or yellow. Accounts differ greatly, some observers speak of it as being fixed, and others as moving. Experiments have proved that it is not due to true combustion. Theories explaining its occurrence have been in turn discredited. These include the burning of marsh gas, phosphuretted hydrogen, and phosphorescent vapour. Many local names are given to the phenomenon, *e.g.* Will-o'-the-Wisp, Jack-a-lantern, etc. and its manifestations have given rise to a wealth of story and legend.

Ignoramus : 1. The word formerly written on a bill by a grand jury (*see* INDICTMENT, JURY) to signify that they ' ignored ' the bill on the ground that there was not sufficient evidence to authorise them in finding a ' true bill.' At the present day they indorse the bill in English ' Not Found,' ' No Bill,' or with similar words. 2. An ignorant person; especially an ignorant pretender to knowledge. In this connection the word was probably an extension of its appropriate legal meaning. Many writers, notably Beaumont and Carlyle, are fond of using the word in a personified sense. Dryden in his *Duke of Guise* puns on the legal sense, thus: ' Let ignoramus juries find no traitors, and ignoramus poets scribble satires.' The idea of Dryden's satire called *The Medal*, which appeared in 1682, is said to have been suggested to him by Charles II. as a reply to the striking of a medal in honour of the I. of the grand jury in throwing out a bill against Shaftesbury, always a butt of the poet-laureate.

Ignorance, in law. It is a legal maxim that I. of a law is no excuse for breaking it, however praiseworthy the motives of the lawbreakers. This maxim is said to rest on the legal presumption that every man knows the law. It would be truer to say that grounds of public policy have dictated the necessity of adhering to such a maxim. I. of fact is different. For example, if a man, whose wife was living, married another woman under the impression that it was lawful to have two wives, he would be guilty of bigamy: but if he did so under the impression that his first wife was dead, he would in

all probability be excused. There are, however, dicta to the effect that the rule is not universally applicable, at all events where no crime has been committed, or damages inflicted, and that a judge in a court of equity will be influenced by a plea of I.

Ignorantines, the name of a religious fraternity in the Roman Catholic Church, founded at Rheims (1679), its aim being the gratuitous instruction of poor children in both sacred and secular learning. It was organised (1683) by Jean Baptiste de la Salle. The order has now spread over the whole world. The brethren take vows of chastity, obedience, and poverty, but do not enter holy orders. They are more frequently called the ' Brothers of the Christian Schools.'

Igualada, a tn. of Barcelona prov., Spain, on the Noya, 32 m. N.W. of Barcelona. There are textile and other manufs., and it yields wines and agricultural produce. Its fortifications are now in ruins. Pop. about 10,000.

Iguana, a genus of tropical American lizards, of the family Iguanidæ, comprising about fifty genera, and 300 species. Nearly all the genera belong to the New World, occurring as far S. as Patagonia, and in a northward direction, as far as California and British Columbia, and most of them are arboreal, though some live on the surface of the sand and stones of the desert. They are characterised by the peculiar form of their teeth, which are round and blade-like at the root, with serrated edges towards the tip. One of the most common species is the *Iguana tuberculata*, with a large dew-lap and high, dorsal, fringed ridge. Their prevailing colour is green, and they differ greatly in size, from a few inches to several feet in length. During the warm hours, they bask on the limbs of trees, when they are easily caught by the natives, by means of a noose thrown over the head, their flesh being esteemed as food. To the same family belong the basilisk, and the ' horned toad.' *See* Gadow, *Amphibia and Reptiles,* 1901.

Iguanodon (*Iguana,* and Gk. ὁδούς, tooth), a genus of ornithopod dinosaurs, found fossil in Jurassic and Lower Cretaceous rocks of Europe. The I. was described by Mantell in 1825, from specimens found in Kent, England. It was from 15 to 25 ft. long ; the head large and narrow, and the massive body terminated in and long and very strong tail. The fore-limbs were small and adapted for grasping the leaves and branches of plants on which it fed. All the bones were hollow. The structure of the skeleton is altogether very remarkable. The front parts of both upper and lower jaws are without teeth, and suggest a hollow, beak-like arrangement. The I. walked on its hind legs, and sat on a tripod formed by these and its tail, after the manner of the kangaroo. Its fore-feet had four toes and a spur, and were much shorter than the three-toed hind limbs. It lived in the swampy regions of England and Belgium, and other parts of Europe during the Jurassic period. Several species of the I. are known, mostly from the Wealden and Purbeck beds. Twenty-nine fossil skeletons of the reptile were found at one time in Upper Jurassic sand-stones of the coal regions at Bernis-sart in Belgium. *See* Mantell's *Petri-factions and their Teachings* (London), 1851; Woodward, *Outlines of Verte-brate Palæontology for Students of Zoology*, 1898; Hutchinson's *Extinct Monsters*, 1892; Owen's *Fossil Rep-tiles* (4 vols.), 1849-84, etc.

Ihre, Johan (1707-80), a Swedish scholar and philologist, educated at Upsala University. After travelling in England and France, he became professor of poetry and theology at Upsala, and later (*c.* 1738) of belles-lettres and political science. His chief work is the *Glossarium Suio-gothicum* (1769), the foundation of Swedish philology. He was an excellent critic, and wrote valuable academical dissertations. *See* Flo-derus, *Parentation öfver J. Ihre*, 1781; Gezelius, *Biographiskt-Lexicon öfver namnkunnige Svenska Män.*

Ijssel, or **Yssel** (ancient *Isala*) : 1. A river of the Netherlands, Gelder-land, and Overijssel provinces, the northernmost arm of the Rhine delta, leaving it near Arnhem and flowing N. into the Zuyder Zee (E.), past Zutphen, Deventer, Zwolle, and Kampen. The upper part was originally a Roman canal made (*c.* 12 B.C.) to unite the Rhine with the Oude Ijssel, which joins the Nieuwe at Doesburg. Length about 70 m., all navigable. 2. A river of Utrecht and S. Holland provinces, connected by canal at Utrecht with the Oude Rijn, and entering the Nieuwe Maas, 3 m. above Rotterdam.

Ijsselmonde, or **Ysselmonde,** an island of the Netherlands, S. Holland, between two branches of the Meuse (Maas), the Oude and Nieuwe Maas, opposite Rotterdam. It is 15 m. long by 5 m. broad. There is a town of the name on the island. Pop. 4755.

Ijuvium, *see* GUBBIO.

Iki, an island belonging to Japan, lying off the north-western coast of Kiushiu. There is a harbour at Gonoura in the S.W. Area 57 sq. m. Pop. 36,530.

Ikuno, a tn. of Hondo, Japan, 35 m. N.W. of Kobé. Its silver mines, the second in size in Japan, are worked by the government. Pop. (estimated) 3000.

Ilagan, the cap. of the prov. of Isabela, Luzon, Philippine Is., about 200 m. N.N.E. of Manila. It is in a great tobacco growing district. Pop. 16,008.

Ilbert, Sir Courtenay Peregrine (*b.* 1841), an English statesman, educated at Marlborough and Oxford, clerk of the House of Commons since 1902. He was a barrister of Lincoln's Inn (1869), president of the Council of the Governor-General of India (1886), vice-chancellor of Calcutta University (1885-86), parliamentary counsel to the Treasury (1899-1901). He is on the Board of Governors of the London School of Economics, and vice-president of the London Library. Among his publications are : *The Government of India*, 1898; *Legislative Methods and Forms*, 1901; *Parliament*, 1911.

Ilchester, a market tn. in the southern parl. div. of Somersetshire, England, on the R. Yeo, 5 m. N.W. of Yeovil. It is supposed to be the Ischalis of Ptolemy; was an impor-tant Roman station and a flourishing Saxon town. Pop. (1911) 564.

Ildefonso, Saint (607-667), a Spanish prelate and theologian, born at Toledo; was a pupil of St. Isidore, became abbot of Agali, and attended the ninth council of Toledo in 653. In 658 he succeeded his uncle Eugenius as Archbishop of Toledo. He added fourteen lives to St. Isidore's *De Viris illustribus*, and wrote several theological works.

Ile-de-France, an old prov. of France, forming a kind of island bounded by the rivers Seine, Marne, Beuvronne, Thève, and Oise, and with Paris as its capital. Under the Revolution redistribution of pro-vinces it was divided into the depart-ment of the Seine with the greater part of Seine-et-Oise, Seine-et-Marne, Oise, and Aisne, and a small part of Loiret and Nièvre In the middle of the 9th century I. was made a duke-dom and its second duke, Odo, be-came King of France in 888, and was the ancestor of Hugh Capet. I. was the former name of Mauritius (*q.v.*).

Ile-du-Diable, one of the Iles du Salut off the coast of French Guiana, S. America, on which Captain Dreyfus (*q.v.*) was imprisoned in 1894.

Ilerda, the cap. of the Ilergetes in Hispania Tarraconensis. It stood upon an eminence on the r. b. of the R. Sicoris. It was used by the legates of Pompey as their base against Cæsar in the first year of the Civil War (49 B.C.).

Iletsk, a tn. in the Russian gov. of Orenburg near the confluence of the Ilek with the Ural. It is famous for its salt, mud, and brine baths and koumiss cures. Pop. about 12,000.

Ileum, the lower part of the small intestine. The small intestine is a tube about 23 ft. long ; the first 10 or 11 in. forms the duodenum, the next 9 ft. form the jejunum, and the remainder is the I. There is no definite line of division between the two main portions, but the jejunum occupies the upper and left part of the abdomen, while the I. occupies the lower and right. It terminates in the ileocæcal valve leading to the large intestine.

Ileus, a severe form of colic. It usually begins as a simple attack of ordinary colic, but rapidly becomes more painful. There is usually severe vomiting and the pain is spasmodic in character. Medical aid is necessary.

Ilex, a cosmopolitan genus of plants in the order Aquifoliaceæ, which consists of between one and two hundred species. *I. aquifolium,* the common holly, is found chiefly in Central Europe; it is valued as an ornamental tree and for its fine-grained, heavy, compact timber; the berries are poisonous and have violent emetic effects. *I. Paraguayensis,* the maté plant, is valued for its leaves, which are dried and used like common tea, under the name of Paraguay tea. The I. so frequently mentioned by classical authors is *Quercus Ilex,* the holm- or holly-oak, a species of Fagaceæ found round the Mediterranean.

Ilford : 1. Great Ilford, a par. and tn. on the Roding in S.W. Essex, 7 m. E.N.E. of London. The hospital of St. Mary and St. Thomas, originally founded in the 12th century as a leper hospital, is now composed of alms-houses and a chapel. It has photographic material factories and paper mills. Pop. (1911) 78,188. 2. Little Ilford, on the opposite bank of the Roding.

Ilfracombe, a seaport, market tn., and watering-place in N. Devon, England, 11 m. N.N.W. of Barnstaple. The beauty of its scenery and the temperate climate make it a favourite resort both in winter and summer. In the 14th century it was a place of some importance and supplied six ships and ninety-six men for the siege of Calais. It was besieged twice during the Civil War. Pop. (1911) 8935.

Ilhavo, a seaport in the dist. of Aveiro, Portugal, 40 m. S. of Oporto. Its chief industry is fishing, but there are famous glass and porcelain works at Vista Alegre. Salt is also exported. Pop. about 13,000.

Ili, one of the chief rivers of Central Asia in the Russian prov. of Semiryechensk. It rises at an altitude of 11,600 ft. on the western slopes of Mt. Kash-katur, E. of Lake Issyk-kul, and flowing in a twisted course past Kulja, through the Trans-Ili Ala-tau and Borokhoro Mts., to Iliysk and thence to Lake Balkash, into which it falls by seven mouths after a total course of 900 m. Its chief tributaries are the Kash, Chilik, and Charyn. Its valley is rich in coal, gold, and silver. *See* KULJA.

Iliad, *see* HOMER.

Iliamna, a volcano in Alaska, N. America, at the head of the Alaska Peninsula, W. of Cook Inlet. It was in eruption in 1901 and 1902. Alt. 12,000 ft.

Iligan Bay, on the N. coast of Mindanao, Philippine Is. The R. Iligan flows into it at the S.E. corner and here lies the town of Iligan with a large trade in rice, spices, and hemp. Pop. 6000.

Ilion, a vil. of Herkimer co., New York, U.S.A., on the S. bank of the Mohawk R., 12 m. S.E. of Utica. Its chief industry is the manuf. of Remington typewriters and fire-arms, notably the Remington rifle. Pop. (1910) 6588.

Ilissus, a small river of Attica, flowing into the sea near the Piræus. It was immortalised for its beauty by Plato in *Phœdrus,* but the beauty has vanished and the scenery become barren and sun-scorched.

Ilium, *see* TROY.

Ilk (A.-S. *ilc, ylc,* the same) is used in the phrase ' of that ilk,' added to a person's surname to denote that this name and the name of his ancestral estate are the same.

Ilkeston, a market tn. and municipal borough of Derbyshire, England, 9 m. E.N.E. of Derby. It is on a hill commanding the fine valley of the Erewash. It manufs. hosiery, lace, and earthenware. Coal and iron are found in the neighbourhood and an alkaline mineral spring. Pop. (1911) 31,657.

Ilkeston, Sir Balthazar Walter Foster, Baron (1840-1913), an Irish physician, educated at Trinity College, Dublin. He was professor of medicine at Queen's College, Birmingham (1868-90), and parliamentary secretary to the Local Government Board (1892 - 95). He was M.P. for Chester (1885-86) and for the Ilkeston division of Derbyshire from 1887-1910, in which year he was raised to the peerage. He has published : *Method and Medicine,* 1870 ; *Clinical Medicine,* 1874 ; *Political Powerlessness of the Medical Profession,* 1883 ; and *Public Aspects of Medicine,* 1890.

Ilkley, a health resort in the W. Riding of Yorkshire, England, on the R. Wharfe, 16 m. N.W. of Leeds. There are several hydropathic establishments. It was an ancient Roman station and possesses three curious Saxon crosses. Bolton Abbey (*q.v.*) is 5 m. N.W. Pop. (1911) 7992.

Illampu, or **Sorata,** a peak in the Cordillera Real, a mountain range of Bolivia. Alt. 21,275 ft.

Illawarra, a district of New South Wales, Australia, extending from a point 33 m. S. of Sydney, along the coast southwards for 40 m. to Shoalhaven. Industries: dairy produce, collieries. The I. Lake is a salt lagoon where fish are plentiful and fowls abundant.

Illecebraceæ, the name which was given by Bentham and Hooker to a group of plants known to other botanists as Paronychiaceæ, and it is now included in the order Caryophyllaceæ (*q.v.*).

Illecebrum verticillatum, or the whorled rush-grass, is the single species of its genus, and belongs to the Caryophyllaceæ. It is a small trailing shrub with opposite leaves having membranous stipules at the base. It occurs in bogs and wet marshy places of Europe and Africa, and may be found in Cornwall and Devon.

Illcoillewaet, a celebrated glacier in British Columbia, Canada, lying near Glacier House, on the Canadian Pacific Railway, having its origin in the snows and ice of Sir Donald Mt. It is in a condition of recession.

Ille-et-Vilaine, a maritime dept. of N.W. France, bordering Mt. St. Michel Bay and the English Channel. It formed part of the old province of Brittany, and is now bounded W. by the departments of Côtes-du-Nord and Morbihan, S. by Loire-Inférieure, E. and N.E. by Mayenne and Manche. The rivers Ille and Vilaine flow from N. and E., uniting at Rennes, the capital. The surface is mostly flat, with forests and marshes in the N. The former forest of Brocéliande in the W. is now represented by the far less extensive forest of Paimpont. The Marsh of Dol is a fertile region once engulfed by the sea. Grain (wheat and barley), tobacco, flax, and potatoes are among the chief crops. Honey, cider, and fruit are plentiful. The oysters of Cancale are exported. The chief minerals are granite (round Fougères), slate, and argentiferous galena at Bruz. St. Servan and St. Malo are the chief ports. Area 2697 sq. m. Pop. 608,098.

Illegitimacy, the status of a child born out of wedlock. The status is especially important in all legal systems from the consequences entailed by it in regard to the right to succeed to property. Socially, the prevalence or otherwise of I. may be an instructive commentary on national morality, though the conducing circumstances vary so greatly in different countries that what might be immorality in one nation would be no more than current morality in another. In this context it may be pertinent to recall an observation of Lecky in the *History of European Morals,* to the effect that a man is only immoral who does not practise the morality of his own country. The whole question, however, of the relation of I. to morality is notoriously a matter of controversy. It is, at least, arguable that a high degree of I. points to a correspondingly lower degree of prostitution, and inferentially, perhaps, to a comparatively higher national morality.

The greater the number of artificial hindrances to marriage, whether economical or social, the greater, as a rule, will be the I. In some countries like France, the term of military service must be completed before a man may marry. Again, in some legal systems a marriage would be illegal where the spouses had not first obtained the consent of their parents; while in France, again, the dowry system, tending as it does to the *mariage de convenance,* tends equally surely to a morganatic union. Some have supposed that I. is more rampant among the hot-blooded races of the S. of Europe, and S. America, or in other warm climates. But there is little statistical warranty for the assumption, although, so far as mere figures are concerned, two observations are material. First, that in most of those countries whose legal systems are based upon the Civil Law (*q.v.*), subsequent marriage, or even a less formal act will legitimate offspring otherwise illegitimate; and, secondly, statistics of any reliable kind are not forthcoming for the majority of Oriental races.

In England and other Christian nations there can be no doubt that the Christian religion acts powerfully as a deterrent of I., and that chastity is intimately involved in the age-long institution of monogamy. Whether religion or utilitarian considerations had more to do with the difference between the status of legitimate and illegitimate offspring, is open to doubt. Most Aryan nations acknowledged illegitimate children as part of their families, and gave them a right to share in the patrimony, though in the Roman law of succession illegitimate children were in a less favourable position in this respect than legitimate. According to Westermarck (*Origin and Development of the Moral Ideas*), it was nothing less than monogamy that gradually deprived the bastard of nearly all proprietary rights, and led up to the universal maxim that the bastard was *filius nullius aut filius populi* (the son of no man, or the son of the people). Christianity may well have done no more than throw the ægis of religion over what had long been a social commonplace; but the stigma it attached to infidelity to the marriage vow, and its doctrine that monogamous marriage was the only form of marriage that could exculpate intercourse, may well have gone far to stereotype the unenviable position of the bastard. Although ecclesiastical ideas of marriage and legitimacy were slow in permeating the ruder Celtic nations, they soon induced the Anglo-Saxon law-giver to deny to the bastard any claim of blood relation-

lation for the quinquennial period (1876-80), and 14 per cent. decrease as against the proportion to total births for the same period. The statistics show a progressive decrease for the five intervening quinquennial periods between 1880 and 1906, although in one individual year (1909) the rate went up beyond what it had been in 1906. For the whole of England and Wales in the census period of 1900-2 the proportion of illegitimate births to 1000 unmarried and widowed females aged fifteen to forty-five years was 8·5. In the same table the figures for the different registration counties show that Middlesex and Surrey have the lowest illegitimate rate per 1000, viz. 5·9; while next in order come Somerset 6·0, Gloucester 6·3, Devon 6·7, and London 6·9. The highest rate prevails in the Welsh counties, in Anglesey the rate being no less than 16·1. The eastern and

TABLE SHOWING MORTALITY (PER 1000 BIRTHS) OF LEGITIMATE AND ILLEGITIMATE INFANTS FROM ALL CAUSES IN ENGLAND AND WALES IN 1910

AGE	ENGLAND AND WALES			URBAN COUNTIES			RURAL COUNTIES		
	All infants	Legit.	Ill'git.	All infants	Legit.	Ill'git.	All infants	Legit.	Ill'git.
Under 1 year	105·44	101·64	194·84	115·31	111·35	213·27	87·43	84·15	145·55
Under 3 months	58·56	56·34	109·67	61·55	59·36	115·71	53·18	51·20	88·55
3 to 6 months	18·77	17·88	39·49	21·12	20·18	44·36	14·72	14·03	26·75
6 to 12 months	28·17	27·42	45·68	32·64	31·81	53·20	19·53	18·92	30·25

ship with the *Mægth* or family. Some have even attributed the curious custom of Borough-English (*q.v.*) to the doubts that were supposed to surround the birth of older children. The loss of social caste does not seem to have attached to the degradation of status incident to I. until somewhat later. Some medieval heroes of aristocratic if spurious birth, appear to have prided themselves on their title of 'Bastard.' The Conqueror was known as William the Bastard, without any connotation of shame, but rather as a distinctive appellation. But apart from exceptional instances, social inferiority gradually followed as a necessary corollary to deprivation of proprietary rights.

According to the 1910 *Annual Report of the Registrar of Births and Deaths*, there were 36,635 illegitimate births out of a total number of 896,962 registered births, giving 1·1 per 1000 of the total population. These figures show a decrease of 41 per cent., as against the proportion to total popu-

agricultural counties also retain their proverbially high rate. Suffolk, Norfolk, and Lincolnshire, all showing a rate over 12·0. Consistently high, too, is the rate in the three northern counties, Durham, Northumberland, and Cumberland. The Report also contains an instructive comparative table of international vital statistics. According to this table England and Wales, Scotland, and New Zealand, far outstrip the rest of the world in the rate of decrease of I. during the twenty years between 1880 and 1900, the figures being 39·7, 37·4, and 33·6 per cent., respectively. Next comes The Netherlands 29·9 per cent. decrease, and Italy 23·6 per cent. Practically all the other countries, the figures of which are forthcoming, also show a decrease: Ireland 13·6, Norway 12·7, Belgium 11·0, Denmark 10·0, Switzerland 9·3, Australia 9·0, Prussia 8·1, Austria 7·6, Germany 7·4, and Spain 3·1; but France and Sweden show an increase of 8·5 and 7·5 respectively. The table of statistics of infantile mortality make instructive and painful reading, and justify the increased stringency of legislation on the subject of cruelty to children (*see* CHILDREN ACT, 1908; CHILDREN, SOCIETY FOR PREVENTION OF CRUELTY TO). It will be noticed that in the rural counties the rate of mortality among illegitimate children, on the whole, more closely approximates to that of legitimate children. But, in all cases, the mortality is suggestively high in the case of illegitimate children under one year of age. The Registrar states that the excess of mortality of illegitimate children over legitimate is greatest in the case of diarrhœal, tuberculous, and wasting diseases. This last statistical fact, if true, allays to an appreciable extent the suspicion of death from overlaying, or other violent causes, but, of course, can hardly lessen suspicion of death from sheer neglect, though poverty may go far to excuse such neglect. See *Annual Reports of Registrar of Births and Deaths ;* Hooper, *The Law of Illegitimacy*, 1911.

Illicium, a small genus of Magnoliaceæ, flourishes in Asia and America. *I. verum* is the star-anise which occurs in China and contains an aromatic oil used in flavouring.

Illimani Mountain, one of the loftiest mountains of the Bolivian Andes, in the Eastern Cordillora Range, S. America.

Illinois (*Illini*, men), a group of N. American Indian tribes of the Algonquin linguistic family. They lived formerly in I. and the adjacent parts of Wisconsin, Iowa, and Missouri. The chief tribes were Cahokia, Peoria, Kaskaskia, Tamaroa, Michegamea, and Moingwena. As allies of the French they came into conflict with the Iroquois (1678). They now number under 200, and are situated on a reservation at the Quapaw Agency, Indian Territory. *See* La Salle's account of his explorations (1670-82); Catlin, *N. American Indians.*

Illinois, a river of U.S.A., formed by the union of the Kankakee and Des Plaines rivers in Grundy co., about 10 m. from Morris, Illinois. Rising near Lake Michigan, it flows S. and S.W. through La Salleco., entering the Mississippi about 20 m. above Alton and the Missouri's mouth. Length about 500 m., navigable for steamers 250 m. to La Salle, whence a ship canal connects it with the Chicago R. and the Chicago Drainage Canal, and hence with the Great Lakes. Ottawa and Peoria are the chief cities on its banks.

Illinois, one of the N. central states of the American Union, known as ' the Prairie State,' situated in the valley of the Mississippi and the basin of the Great Lakes. It is bounded N. by Wisconsin, E. by Lake Michigan and Indiana, S.E. by Kentucky, S.W. by Missouri, W. by Missouri and Iowa. The Mississippi R. is on the W., the Ohio on the S., and the Wabash on the E. frontier. The surface is a vast plain, with an average elevation of 500 ft., sloping slightly towards the S. and S.W. Cairo is the lowest point (267 ft. above the Gulf of Mexico), Silver Creek one of the highest (1145 ft.). There is a low, fertile plateau in the S. known as Egypt. The Great Prairie (200 m. long) is in the centre. The Illinois is the chief river, and there are saline, sulphur, and chalybeate springs in the S. The Illinois and Michigan Canal, connecting Lake Michigan and the Great Lakes with the Mississippi, was constructed between 1830-50. There is a difference of about 11° F. in the temperatures of N. and S. The soil is very fertile, but an underlying stratum of clay which retains the rainfall, necessitates elaborate drainage systems. Trees have been extensively planted, and I. ranks next to Iowa as an agricultural state. Wheat, corn, hay, and various other cereals are grown. Fruit is much cultivated, especially in the hilly belt of the S. There are good vineyards, the centre of the liquor industry being Peoria, which produces whiskies and high wines. Live stock are reared, and fine dairy produce is obtained. Slaughtering and meat-packing is the most important industry, centred at Chicago. Fisheries are also carried on largely, pike, bass, salmon - trout, carp, sturgeon, and paddle-fish being plentiful in the rivers and lakes. Bituminous coal is the chief mineral, the coal-field covering about 42,900 sq. m. Pig-iron, petroleum, natural gas, sandstone, and limestone are valuable also. Building-stone is quarried chiefly in Monroe, Lawrence, and Decatur counties. Zinc, fluor-spar, Portland cement, gypsum, and marble are found. Machinery, vehicles, soap, candles, and pottery are among the chief manufactures. Some of the most important towns are Chicago (pop. (1910) 2,185,283), Springfield (capital), Peoria, Quincy, Rockford, Joliet, E. St. Louis, Aurora, Galesburg, Jacksonville, Freeport, Lasalle, Ottawa. There are over 100 counties. Communication is excellent both by rail and water. The Sangamon and Morgan Railway was the first opened (1839). The N.W. University at Evanston was founded about 1851, Chicago University in 1892, and there are many other fine educational and charitable institutions. Area 56,650 sq. m. (650 q. m. water). Pop. (1910) 5,638,590.

History and constitution.—In 1673 Joliet explored I., and in 1675 Father Marquette founded a Jesuit mission among the Kaskaski Indians. La Salle gave the state its present name (1679), from the Indian tribes settled there, and built Fort Crèvecœur. Tonty continued his explorations. French traders settled in I. between 1683 - 90. In 1763 I. passed to England on the cession of Canada. It became part of the North-West American Territory in 1787, and of Indiana Territory in 1800. In 1818 it was admitted to the Union. The Mormon troubles culminated here (1840-44). The present constitution was adopted in 1870. There is a Senate of 51 members, and a House of Representatives of 153 members, elected for four and two years respectively. Twenty-seven representatives are sent to the Lower House of the Federal Congress. *See* Breese, *Histories of Illinois*, 1884 ; Wallace (1893), Moses (1893), Greene (1904), Perrier (1906); Mather, *The Making of Illinois*, 1900.

Illiterates. It is not easy to obtain reliable returns either in England or elsewhere of the average number of persons who are unable to read or write. Although the census returns suggest themselves as the natural mode of getting the information, there can be, even through this channel, no means of compelling persons to disclose their illiteracy, nor, unless they sign returns themselves, any direct evidence of such illiteracy. Voters at parliamentary elections may not sign by proxy in England, and I. voters before being allowed to record their votes by a mark in lieu of signature, must first make a declaration of their inability to read. The name of the I. voter is then entered by the returning-officer on a list with other voters who from some incapacity record their votes in a particular manner, and such list must contain the reasons for such particular mode of signature. The returns of the election officers for the last general election showed that in England, Wales, and Scotland less than 1 per cent. in each case were I. In Ireland, however, over 10 per cent. declared their inability to read. Of course the largest class of persons unable to read would be found among non-voters, and no certain method exists of finding out how large that percentage is of the total population. In countries where universal conscription is in vogue it is easy to get at the percentage of I. from the registration of recruits. In Germany, Sweden, and Switzerland over 99 per cent. are able to read and write,

but in Holland somewhat over 1 per cent. are I. In France and Belgium the percentages of I. are higher, being about 5 per cent. and 10 per cent. respectively. Nearly one-third of the Greek and Italian conscripts are I.; while in the Russian army the traditional privilege of soldiers to make valid ' nuncupative,' or oral, wills by reason of illiteracy is amply justified from the fact that those who read form the exceptions. Less than one-quarter of the Russian conscripts are able to read and write, and it is probable, from the notorious intellectual darkness in which the masses of that nation still live, that this percentage of I. is the average for the whole population as well. The marriage registers, where they exist, betray the proportion of I. spouses, and in Italy the proportion of I. husbands corresponds to that of the conscripts, while of the number of women married annually nearly one-half are I. From these registers it appears that the lowest percentage of I. is to be met with in England and Wales, Scotland, Germany, and Australia, and the highest, excluding Italy, in Ireland and S. Africa. It may be noted here that an incumbent (*q.v.*) may be deprived of his living for illiteracy.

Ilkirch-Grafenstaden, a vil. of Germany in Alsace, 5 m. S. of Strassburg. Pop. 6522.

Illo (or Ilow), Christian, an Austrian general during the Thirty Years' War and intimate friend of Wallenstein (*q.v.*). He was implicated in Wallenstein's desertion, and was assassinated a few hours before his friend, on Feb. 25, 1634, in the banquet-hall at the castle of Eger.

Illogan, a mining dist. in Cornwall, situated on the E. coast.

Illora, a tn. in Granada, Spain, on the R. Charcon (including six adjacent hamlets). Pop. 10,000.

Illorin, a walled native tn. of Nigeria, cap. of an administrative prov., and former cap. of an association of states of the Yoruba country, W. Equatorial Africa, about 170 m. N.N.E. of Lagos. It lies on the Asa, a tributary of the Niger. Pop. about 80,000.

Illuminati, the enlightened ones, the name assumed at various times by religious sects and secret societies. The Spanish 'illuminati' (*aluminados*) seem to have been in origin akin to the various mystic Gnostic heresies which flourished in the early middle ages, though their appearance in Spain is later. They were stamped out with ruthless severity by the Inquisition during the 16th century. They also established themselves in Picardy and elsewhere in France during the 17th century, and lasted in isolated bodies till the end of the 18th century. The Rosicrucian Illuminati are quite distinct; their tenets are mixed with alchemy and occultism (see ROSICRUCIANS). Finally, in 1776 a secret masonic society with republican and free-thinking views was formed by Adam Weishaupt, an ex-Jesuit and professor of Canon Law at Ingolstadt, Bavaria. It was anti-Jesuit, and was suppressed in 1785.

Illumination (term used in connection with the 'Enlightenment' period of philosophy). Scientific reason, or the appeal to reason as opposed to the reliance on external authority, marked the metaphysical systems from Descartes to Leibniz. The evolution of existing beliefs and institutions was completely ignored and their value denied, save in so far as they were consistent with abstract principles set up by the rationalists as the ultimate criterion of truth. With the rationalists the pure reason became opposed to all emotions and enthusiasms which failed to satisfy its dogmatic tests, and the net result of rationalist inquiry was the truly barren substitution of a natural deism for revealed religion of all kinds. This sterile and unimaginative philosophy was paradoxically, as it must seem to us, known as the Enlightenment, but the success that the scepticism of Pascal and others might well have had in confounding the principle of pure *a priori* reason was checked for a time by the remarkable progress of science. It was the shifting of the ground of metaphysical inquiry from the exclusive ground of deism to the analysis of knowledge that eventually sounded the death-knell of rationalism. Locke taught that knowledge was wholly empirical, and denied the existence of those innate ideas of reason upon which the rationalists had consciously or unconsciously rested their theories; and later Rousseau's emotional polemics restored the balance in favour of the feelings as against the intellect in the realms of speculative inquiry. Before the period of the Enlightenment had closed, and long before Rousseau, Spinoza's system of quasi-naturalism, which made God the beginning and end of philosophy, had checked the tendency of rationalism to remove God to the position of a mere far-off observer to all intents and purposes, and entirely unrelated to the mundane, by his insistence as a religious and ethical requirement of the essential *unity* of things. Voltaire introduced the results of the English Enlightenment into France, and the French Enlightenment took the form of a thoroughgoing materialism in which truth and religion were dia-

metrically opposed. Within this circle flamed the light of Rousseau, who beginning as an Encyclopédist of the French Enlightenment ended by being bitterly hostile to the whole principle of the rationalists, which in its apotheosis of the logical reason and condemnation of mysticism attained the conception of man as a self-centred unit entirely independent of the arbitrary environment in which he found himself. The cardinal fact in the Enlightenment is individualism and its corollary, the assumption that institutions could be cast off at will and a fresh start made. It ignored the fact that all institutions have their roots in the depths of time, and though this assumption was eminently favourable to the aims of the leaders of the French Revolution, Rousseau's doctrines, however unconsciously they may be susceptible of bare expression in terms of rationalism, departed from rationalism in that they denied the value to human welfare of all the sciences. Later it was the German empiricism begun by Lessing and Herder, and continued in the idealism of Hegel, Kant, and others that swept the so-called Enlightenment from the field of philosophy. Rousseau's demand for a return to nature ignored the social life in a way inconsistent with practical experience, and even with his own maturer views. The German philosophy also claimed the realisation of the abstract freedom of man, but in the endeavour to find again the value of the inner life of the individual insisted on shaping that freedom in forms of real worth and beauty, in some way commensurate with the obvious potentialities of life and feeling. With the earlier German empiricists God ceases to be a cold intellectual obstruction, and is regarded as immanent in nature, human affairs, and all spiritual experience. The smallness of the ambit of reason finds expression in Kant's transcendentalism, which looks upon it as an instrument utterly useless to fathom the realities of God and the soul. Perhaps Kant's critical philosophy is the last word on the subject, when it denies the claims of rationalism to comprehend reality, on the ground that thought and the material of sense are indissolubly connected, and that no sense-experience can possibly be an ultimate reality.

Illumination of MSS. The art of embellishing MSS. either by pictorial ornamentation or with decorated letters and designs in gold and colours was much practised in the middle ages, and especially applied to devotional works. The art appears to have evolved itself from the classical methods of decorating or illustrating the books of the 2nd and 3rd centuries with pictures either in outline or with gilt shading to enhance the light effects, and intended to represent scenes spoken of in the text; through the florid Byzantine art of adorning MSS. of the Gospels with brilliantly painted ornamental designs, gilt or silver lettering, and finely executed miniatures enhanced by highly gilt backgrounds; to the ornamentation of the Franco-Lombards of the so-called Carolingian school, the characteristics of which were a liberal use of gold and large and profusely embellished initial letters on most of the pages. A fragmentary copy of the *Iliad* on vellum, now in the Ambrosian Library of Milan, is said to be the earliest extant example of an illuminated MS. Its sobriety of decoration is in striking contrast with the brilliant miniatures (a technical term from Latin *minio*, to colour with red lead, meaning a picture in an illuminated MS. and not a ' small portrait ') of such MS. as the homilies of Chrysostom and various fragments of the Eusebian canons to be seen in the British Museum. The faults in the Byzantine art appear to be that, while the inherited Oriental splendour of colouring in gold and vermilion gave character to the general scheme of decoration, the drawings themselves, or miniatures, though classical in style, are not only dull and flat in colouring, but the whole form of the figures of the saints or other personages represented is constrained and unprepossessing. The reaction set in with the development of the art in Italy in the 9th and 10th centuries, and later in the Frankish empire. The Carolingian or Frankish art owed its attractiveness largely to the independent Celtic element originating in Ireland. The Irish art dispensed almost entirely with the use of gold, and relied for its effect on its designs and borders of intertwined ribbons, tangled knots, and intricate patterns and spirals, and legendary animals, the whole being executed with marvellous precision and minuteness. The celebrated Lindisfarne Gospels in the Cotton Collection in the British Museum is one of the finest examples of the Celtic style, though these were really productions of Scottish monastic settlements. The colouring of the Celtic style is less bizarre than the Byzantine, but the drawing of figures and objects, probably because being native-born it proceeded independently of all classical models, is crude. The Franco-Lombard art combined the best elements of the Celtic and Byzantine; a return was here made to the abundant use of gold. The pure ornament outweighs the illustrations or miniatures, which latter, as before, generally related to scenes or characters from the Gospels, and were executed in freehand in the later Roman or so-called ' debased classical ' style. Examples of Carolingian art are Lothair's Gospels, Charles the Bald's bible, and an evangeliarium to be seen in the British Museum Harleian MSS. A radical change came over the art of illumination at the end of the 12th century, and the conventional style then elaborated subsisted for something like 300 years. Almost the chief feature of bibles of this period is the border which generally takes the form of a frame of fanciful foliage or other device. Greater prominence is given to the characters or manuscript itself during this period, and in consequence the double-column pages are occupied mainly with the closely written characters, the ' miniatures ' having become nothing more than large initials containing in actual miniature a pictorial representation of some act or scene relating to the corresponding text. Numerous examples may be found in the small bibles of the period. By the 14th century greater skill in drawing had been attained, not only in the more agreeable delineation of the human form, whenever that was chosen, but in the representation of ornamental foliage. Scenery begins to appear, and the stiff and even grotesque contortions of the Byzantine figures yield to a free and dramatic arrangement or grouping, while the tawdry gold background disappears altogether. Skill in realistic drawing, however, tended to the destruction of illumination as an art in itself, and from the perfection attained in the middle ages the decorative execution declined to a style characterised by miniatures treated with admirable skill, bordered with gold, and interspersed with cleverly painted flowers and insects, while the text assumed a place of merely secondary importance. One of the best examples of 15th century illumination is the *Bedford Hours* now in the British Museum. With the Renaissance and the return to classic models the art of illumination attained its zenith in minute delicacy of colouring and perfection of drawing, and, furthermore, an official recognition by both the republican princes and the various popes and doges. Ultimately, it was the invention of printing, however, that destroyed the art and reduced it to the mere pastime of painting miniatures in spaces left for the purpose rather by way of subsequent adornment than as an art in itself.

Bibliography.—Bradley, *Manual of Illumination;* Shaw, *Handbook of the Art of Illumination of the Middle Ages;* Delamotte, *Primer of the Art of Illumination;* Westwood, *Facsimiles of Miniatures and Ornaments of Anglo-Saxon and Irish MSS.;* Tymms and Wyatt, *Art of Illuminating.*

Illuminations, see PYROTECHNICS.

Illusion, a term loosely applied both to delusions and hallucinations, or, in other words, to pervertions of the senses and perverted ideas. Psychologists differ as to the more appropriate application of the term. Esquirol, the celebrated French alienist (1772-1842), in classifying mental diseases, distinguished the two states by referring hallucinations to an excited state of the brain affecting the *remembrance* of the sensations of sight and causing the subject to see what is commonly termed visions or apparitions, and defining I. as the false interpretation of a sensation actually perceived. Dr. Ferrier, while including both under the generic name of Is., differentiates between an I. of the senses and a delusion of the mind. He defines Is. generally as sensations without a corresponding external object, giving the names *spectral illusion,* phantom, or phantasm, where the eye is or seems to be the seat of sensation, and the term *vivid idea* or *conception* when the I. is due to an act of ideation. The whole distinction is sharply drawn by regarding an I. as a mockery, false show, or deceptive appearance, and an hallucination, delusion, or ' illusive transformation ' (Ferrier) as a chimerical thought. Popularly, any transformed appearance of a real object, any appearance without a corresponding physical or external object, and any distorted, exaggerated, or misconceived notion or idea constitute Is. The distinction is important according to Dr. Tuke in regard to insanity, because, while the sane may easily transform a real object into something else than it is, the perception of an object externally projected without the slightest corresponding reality indicates some serious disturbance of the nervous system. Both Is. and delusions, however, are consistent with sanity. A scientist closely concentrating his mind and senses on some experimental work may well have visual and auditory Is. conjured up by a subtle interaction of some external object upon strained or expectant senses, without thereby being mentally diseased. Is. may occur quite early in life, and are more common to males than females. According to Dr. Ferrier some who have experienced Is. have been remarkable for active memories, great ability, and extreme sensitiveness, while others were by no means so endowed; and, again, some are in perfect health, while others are suffering at the time from either trifling indispositions curable by dieting or from serious inflammatory and febrile diseases. In the criminal law (*q.v.*), the term delusional insanity appears to embrace Is. and hallucinations indifferently, provided the reason is involved. *See* Tuke, *Dictionary of Psychological Medicine;* Beck's *Medical Jurisprudence;* Guy and Ferrier, *Principles of Forensic Medicine.*

Illustrated London News, founded by a small printer and newsagent of Nottingham named Herbert Ingram, and generally said to be the first illustrated newspaper ever published. The first number was brought out in May 1842, but although successful almost from the start, it was defective in that none of the pictures were executed from actual life. This defect, however, was counterbalanced by the reputation of its artists, among whom were John Gilbert, John Leech, and Birket Foster, and its proprietors were probably justified in their proud boast in 1887 that during a period of nearly half a century the I. L. N. had retained its position as the most widely circulated illustrated newspaper in the world. Later, the paper began to send out special artists into all parts of the world, to depict from life events of a topical nature, and the pictures of campaigns in various parts of Africa and elsewhere by Mr. Melton Prior were for years quite the feature of the paper. Its first notable editor was Charles Mackay, and its present editor is Mr. Bruce Ingram, a descendant of the founder. Among its most distinguished contributors have been Mark Lemon, George Augustus Sala, Clement Scott, and Andrew Lang. The brilliant paradoxes of perhaps the foremost freelance journalist of the day, Mr. G. K. Chesterton, have now, for some years, regularly appeared in the shape of causerie under the title of ' Our Note Book.' Another salient feature is the series of ' Portraits and Personal Notes.' In the early nineties, the half-tone block process of producing pictures reached a high pitch of excellence in the I. L. N., and in recent years the application of photography has become the dominant mode of reproduction.

Illustrations are as old as art itself. Two or three thousand centuries before Christ, and earlier still, the

Egyptians adorned the walls of sepulchral chambers and the pillars of temples with the exploits of their kings, and the Assyrians told the story of their great wars and sieges on the friezes of their monuments, but in the modern sense I. is the complement of expression in the medium of letters, or, in other words, the pictorial presentment of an idea already expounded in the printed text, to which, like accompaniment to song, I. itself is only an accessory. The reader, therefore, is referred elsewhere for the illuminated MSS. of mediæval times : this article only attempts to deal cursorily with book-illustration.

I. in this restricted sense followed close on the heels of the invention of printing. In 1499 outline I. were printed at Venice in the *Poliphili Hypnerotomachia*, and not long afterwards Botticelli executed his admirable designs of Dante's *Divina Commedia*. In these days, and indeed until well on in the 19th century I. were almost wholly line-engravings on wood or metal, the only notable exception being the mezotints and other similar processes, which were a device for expressing washes and broad tone surfaces in print.

Broadly speaking I. experienced the same ups and downs as painting, and whenever an important school of the greater art arose, then, too, the lesser art flourished. Thus the Italians, Pollajuolo and Mantegna not only painted but executed a number of excellent line-engravings, and the same is true of the German Dürer and of Holbein. In the 17th century I. was practised, or at least, directly encouraged by the school of Rembrandt in Holland and of Watteau and Fragonard in France, and in the following age bands of distinguished illustrators were gathered round Hogarth and Reynolds, whilst Millais, Rossetti, Arthur Hughes, and Burne-Jones, like the old masters before them, expressed their artistic ideals in line as well as brush-work. These Pre-Raphaelites were the leading spirits of the school of facsimile engraving, for they actually drew on the wood itself, and although they sometimes set the engraver an almost impossible task, yet they were responsible for a return to that close and ideal union between artist and engraver which in times past had so largely accounted for the excellence of the work done. Their I. figure in such contemporary magazines as *Good Words*, *Cornhill*, and *The Leisure Hour*, and a study of these will at once reveal their reverence for bygone eras, their emulation of old masters, their loving attention to detail, their naturalism and their passion for symbolical interpretation. The pictorial conviction of Millais' designs for Trollope's *Framley Parsonage* links the Pre-Raphaelite brotherhood with Houghton, Pinwell, Frederick Walker, and even Whistler, who represent ' the " sixties " period.' The broad characteristics of their drawings are idyllic delineation of the charms of country and home life and delight in open-air effects, freedom, and movement—a delight expressed partly by large clear spaces, and partly by loose, but nervously sensitive outlines. One of the most recent schools of illustrators was a group, who sketched for the *Dial* (1889-1897), and who are called neo-Pre-Raphaelites by those who avail themselves of names to trace transition and advance. Their magazine was an artistic protest against the indiscriminate issue of books, whose cheapness was the single apology for their careless binding, common paper, and inferior photographic I. A much more effectual protest was made by William Morris, when, in 1891, he set up his Kelmscott Press. Profit was a secondary consideration, and he printed a series of choice editions, which are an ornament to the shelves of the most fastidious of book collectors. Like his paintings and his tapestries his illustrated volumes are one and all animated with a true decorative sense and the sturdy spirit of romance and mediævalism. His influence gave rise to the ' Birmingham school,' and without exaggeration, may be said, even to-day, to inspire all workers in applied arts. And with Morris must be associated Ruskin, who gave such substantial and timely encouragement to the struggling artists of the day. His *Modern Painters* and *Stones of Venice*, for which the services of the best engravers were engaged, still remain models for all who aspire to making beautiful books. During the last thirty years there have been many fine illustrators, but in their conception of art, method, and choice of subject, they are too individualistic to make any effort at grouping or association expedient or even possible. The somewhat conventional grace of du Maurier, and the clever cartoons of Phil May long delighted the readers of *Punch*, whilst the pen and ink drawings of E. A. Abbey and Harry Furniss found a wide circle of admirers. In colour Walter Crane has expressed his delightful fancies in a number of the daintiest decorative designs. Kate Greenaway has again and again drawn her charming children in mob cap and long skirt; and Randolph Caldecott has made his name by his cheerful hunting scenes. The original Aubrey Beardsley has at the same time pleased and shocked his countrymen with his brilliant black and white portrayal of crime and vice. Two notable colour artists of to-day are Arthur Rackham and Edmund Dulac.

It only remains to note how photography has ousted drawing from much of the field it formerly occupied. Books of travel and topography in general, illustrated periodicals like the *Graphic*, and newspapers like the *Daily Mirror*, depend almost entirely on photographs for I., and as ' process ' allows these to be reproduced at a minimum expense, engraving and lithography, which demand manual skill, have now hardly any commercial use. The discovery of how to reproduce drawings on blocks by mechanical means has led to an enormous increase in pictorial literature, and although the very facility of reproduction has undoubtedly reduced the labour and pains which designers are willing to lavish on their work, yet by increasing competition it has as certainly raised to a high level its average efficiency.

Illyria, the name of a vaguely defined mountainous district on the western coast of the Adriatic running from Durazzo in Albania up to Fiume. Inland the line was still more indefinite, but it may be regarded as including the northern parts of Albania, Montenegro, the sanjak of Novibazar, part of Servia W. of the Morava, the Austrian provinces of Dalmatia and Bosnia - Herzegovina, and part of Croatia-Slavonia. The Roman province of Illyricum varied in area from time to time, and no strict geographical limits can be assigned to it. In early Greek history we only know of the barbarian ' Illyrians,' whose legendary ancestor was descended from Cadmus and Harmonia; archæological research shows that the primitive peoples spoke a Venetic dialect, also Meroapian, akin to modern Albanian. Greek colonies were settled all along the coast during the whole of the 6th century B.C., and coins and inscriptions have been found at Durazzo (Epidamnus), Spalato (Salona), Ragusa (Epidaurum), etc. The inter-tribal warfare seems to have been checked by Celtic pressure in the 4th century, and a confederation was formed which pressed on Macedonia. Under a chief, Bardylis, and his son Clitus, Amyntas was defeated, and later Perdiccas. Philip of Macedon finally crushed them. The tribes turned to piracy, and harried both Greek and Roman trade. Their queen Teuta insolently refused terms, and murdered the

Roman ambassador. In 180 B.C. an independent republic of Dalmatia was established, and the kingdom of the Illyrian Genthius was annexed to Rome, 168; Dalmatia continuing aggressive and powerful till 9 A.D., when the whole country became a Roman province. It furnished some of the best soldiers for the Roman armies, and many of the emperors were Illyrian by birth. In 379 A.D. Eastern Illyricum went to the Byzantine empire. The ethnological character of the district was modified by the Hunnish invasion in the 5th century, and in the 7th century by the Slavonic immigration of Croats and Serbs, though the coast towns still remained Italian in civilization. The primitive races remain in Albania alone. In 1809 the Illyrian provinces were formed and ceded to Italy; they were conquered by Napoleon and ceded to Austria in 1813, and till 1849 formed a kingdom of the Austrian empire.

Ilmen, a lake of Russia in the gov. of Novgorod, 30 m. in length from E. to W., by 24 m. in greatest breadth. Its chief tributary is the Lovat. It discharges its surplus waters by the Volkhov northward into Lake Ladoga.

Ilmenau, a tn. in the grand duchy of Saxe-Weimar, Germany, lying at the N. foot of the Thuringian Forest on the R. Ilm, 30 m. by rail S. of Erfurt. The town is a favourite watering-place, and was visited by Goethe who wrote his *Iphigenia* here.

Ilmenite, a titaniferous iron ore found in many localities, more particularly at Krageroe in Norway, where good crystals occur, in the United States, and in Canada. It has been found as sand on the banks of the Mersey, and at Helston in Cornwall. The name is derived from the Ilmen Mts. (Urals), where it is found in magnificent crystals. Its formula is generally given as $FeTiO_3$, but in many cases the mineral contains magnesium, so that it may be written $(Fe,Mg)TiO_3$. It is not isomorphous with hæmatite, but belongs to the parallel-faced hemihedral class of the rhombohedral system.

Ilminster, a market tn. of Somerset on the Isle, England, $10\frac{1}{2}$ m. from Taunton. Alt. 140 ft. Pop. (1903) 2287.

Il Obeid, *see* EL OBEID.

Ilobu, a native tn. of W. Equatorial Africa in the Yoruba country. Pop. 60,000.

Ilocos Norte, a mountainous coast prov. of North-Western Luzon, Philippine Is. Its peaks are in part volcanic. The valleys are watered by the Pagstan and other streams. Capital Laoag. Pop. 180,000.

Ilocos Sur, a coast prov. of North-Western Luzon, Philippine Is. Area 644 sq. m. It is rather flat and very fertile. Medicinal plants grow in the mountains. Pop. 190,000.

Iloilo, a Spanish settlement, and the chief port after Manila in the Philippine Is. It is the capital of Iloilo province, Panay, in Iloilo Strait, opposite Guimaras Is. It is an open port and commercially important, exporting sugar, rice, tobacco, coffee, hides, and abaca, and manufacturing fabrics, hats, carriages, etc. It has a cathedral, seminary, *casa real*, and court-house. The anchorage is good. Pop. about 20,000.

Ilsenburg, a tn. and watering-place of Prussian Saxony, 16 m. W. of Halberstadt. Pop. 4911.

Ilsley, a market tn. of England in Berkshire, 15 m. W.N.W. of Reading. Has sheep markets and fairs.

Ilus, son of Tros and Callirrhoë, and great-grandson of Dardanus. He was supposed to be the founder of Ilion, which he called Troy after his father. His son was Laomedon, and he was the grandfather of Priam.

Ilversgehofen, a tn. of Prussia in Saxony, situated in the circle of Erfurt and 2 m. N. of that place. Pop. 12,085.

Image, Selwyn (*b.* 1849), an English artist, educated at Marlborough and at New College and Slade School, Oxford. He took holy orders, and for some time was curate of St. Anne's, Soho. In 1910 he was appointed Slade professor of fine art. He is an artist in stained glass; his best work of this description may be found in St. Luke's, Camberwell, and at Morthoe Church, Devon. In 1894 he published a book of *Carols and Poems*.

Image - worship (Gk. εἰδωλολατρία the use for private or public devotions of graven or painted representations of sacred persons or things, to which honour and reverence are given, instead of to the invisible Godhead. The term is sometimes taken for the use, as in the Roman Church, of pictures or images which are only designed to convey to the worshippers an idea of that which they worship, but it is more often limited to the sense of meaning the actual worship of the image itself, not of that which it represents. I. was a comparatively late development of primitive religion, and grew out of the earlier 'fetish-worship,' in which a stone or a wooden post was worshipped with the idea that the spirit of a god had entered there to receive sacrifice (*cf.* Asherah, Ex. xxxiv. 13). The making of images in some definite form marks a definite advance in religious thought and shows the birth of conceptions of the Divine character and attributes.

Varro affirms that for more than 170 years from the foundation of Rome there was in the city no image of a god either in human or animal form, and historians have proved that neither in Greece, Persia, or Egypt, were there temples or idols in the earliest times. The Decalogue begins with the command to reverence the one true God and to recognise no other deities, but the lamentations and the denunciations of the prophets show how thoroughly the cults of other deities were rooted in the hearts of the Israelites, how hard it was to root out the idol-worship traditions of their Semite ancestors, and how easy it was for them to adopt the gods and the graven images of their Canaanitish neighbours (1 Kings xi. 8; Jer. xii. 18). The Jewish worship of idols was checked but not eradicated during the Exile, and various passages in the Talmud demonstrate the tendency of the Jews to adopt the gods of the Greeks and Romans, and more especially those of their Oriental neighbours. To prevent such relapses all association of Jews and Gentiles was rendered difficult, and by degrees the former were weaned from idolatrous worship. Neither in the N.T. nor in any genuine secular history of the first century of Christianity can any trace be found of the use of images in the worship of the Christians, and it was not until after the establishment of Christianity under Constantine that the practice became common. For the use of images in the Roman Church, *see under* ROMAN CATHOLIC RELIGION.

Imago (Lat., likeness, an image), in entomology, is the term applied to the final or perfect stage of insect development, following the larval and pupal stages; little growth occurs during this period, the insect being given over to reproduction.

Imam-Dour, a vil. of Asiatic Turkey, 70 m. N.W. of Bagdad on the Tigris, nearly opposite Tekrit.

Imandra, a lake of European Russia in the gov. of Archangel, 35 m. S. of Kola. Length 50 m., greatest breadth 10 m. Area 350 sq. m. It drains into the White Sea.

Imatra Falls in Finland, on the Vuoxen, a short distance from its exit from Saima Lake, 39 m. N. of Viborg.

Imaus, the ancient name for a part of the Himalaya Mts.

Imbecility, *see* IDIOCY.

Imbros, an island in the N.E. of the Ægean Sea, S. of Samothrace. It belongs to Turkey and is joined with Samothrace to form an administrative district of the sanjak of Lemnos. It is the seat of a Greek bishopric. It is extremely fertile. Principal town, Kastron. Pop. 9000.

Imeritia, a former div. of Western Asia, Transcaucasia, forming a part of the ancient Colchis, now included within the Russian government Kutais.

Imitation, a term in music referring to the repetition of a melody or a phrase, generally at a different pitch in another part of the composition. ' Exact ' I. is the repetition with the same intervals, motion, and rhythm, etc. ' Free ' I. is the repetition with these more or less modified. A marked example of musical I. is to be found in the Scherzo which immediately precedes the *Marcia Funebre* of Beethoven's sonata, No. 12, Op. 26. Another instance is to be found in Prelude III. of *Forty-eight Preludes and Fugues* by Bach.

Immaculate Conception (Lat. *in*, not ; *maculare*, to stain), the dogma of the Roman Catholic Church that the Virgin Mary was conceived without original sin. It probably arose from the desire to honour the Incarnation by raising the Blessed Mother herself above the taint of original sin, and it was contended that she was either sanctified before birth (*see* Jer. i. 5) or was entirely exempt from the stain of sin before the embryo was formed. The doctrine was the subject of bitter and strenuous controversy in the Church for nearly 700 years. In 1131 St. Bernard uttered the opinion that though sanctified before birth, the Virgin was not conceived without original sin. In 1307 Duns Scotus maintained the complete exemption from sin, and his school was backed by the Franciscan order. The Thomists, or followers of St. Thomas Aquinas, and the Dominicans took the opposite view. The Council of Basel (1431-43), without the Pope's sanction, declared the doctrine of the I. C. to be a dogma of the Catholic Church. Pope Sixtus IV. in 1470 commanded by a constitution that the disputants should observe charity and tolerance towards one another. The University of Paris at the same time refused degrees to those who did not defend the doctrine. The Council of Trent (1545-63) left the question unsettled, and the dispute waxed hotter until the end of the 16th century, when the pope forbade, except under certain conditions, all public discussion of the subject, and prohibited disputants from branding each other as heretics. Successive popes were requested to make a decision, but beyond adding importance to the feast of the conception and permitting the word immaculate to be used in connection therewith, the matter was not finally decided until the dogma was proclaimed by solemn decree by Pope Pius IX. on Dec. 8, 1854. The Greek Church celebrates the feast on Dec. 9. under the title of ' The Conception of St. Anne,' the Virgin's mother.

Immanence, or Immanent (Lat. *im*, in, and *manere*, to remain), a philosophic term used to denote the conception that the Deity pervades the universe itself, and that His activity and existence are expressed solely by the unrolling of the natural cosmos. It is in opposition to the doctrine of transcendentalism, which teaches that the Deity has an existence apart from the universe, which is in effect only a subsidiary expression of His activity. I. is, therefore, a fundamental conception of Pantheism, and becomes synonymous with the latter when applied in its narrowest sense. Immanent is also a philosophic term to express that kind of causality, the effects of which are not transmitted from the agent into other objects, but are produced in the agent itself. In contradistinction, that causation which goes beyond the agent into other objects is designated as ' transient.' *See* Lotze, *Metaphysic* (Bosanquet's ed., 1884), bk. i., ch. iv.-vi.

Immanuel, or Emmanuel, a Hebrew proper name meaning ' God (is) with us.' It first occurs in the Bible in the prophecy of Isaiah (vii. 14) to a child that was to be born as a sign from God that Judah would not be destroyed by Syria and Ephraim. The name occurs again in the Gospel of St. Matthew (i. 23), when it is applied to Jesus, the birth of the Messiah being taken as a fulfilment of the prophecy of Isaiah.

Immermann, Karl Leberecht (1796-1840), a German author, born at Magdeburg, studied law at Halle, fought at Ligny and Waterloo. On his return to Halle his inspiring friendship with the Countess von Ahlefeldt, Elise von Lützow, began He was a judge at Magdeburg (1823) and Düsseldorf (1827). In 1839 he managed the Düsseldorf Theatre. His first dramatic success was with the historical tragedies, *Das Frauer-spiel in Tirol* 1827, and *Kaiser Friedrich II.*, 1828. In 1831 appeared the mystic poem, *Merlin.* Of his novels, *Epigonen* (1836), the last imitation of Goethe's romanticism, and his modern realistic satire *Münch-hausen* (1838) are the best known.

Immigration, the act of moving into a country for the purpose of settling there. It is the converse of emigration, under which heading the causes of transference of population from one country to another, have already been dealt with. I. is an individual act, although sometimes determined indirectly by the government. Thus the governments of the British colonies offer special inducements in order to attract suitable British subjects to settle in their territories by affording assisted passages, making grants of land, establishing information bureaus in London and elsewhere, and advertising the resources of the colony. On the other hand, the immigrant may have been forced to leave his native land on account of government despotism. The *Mayflower*, for example, left England with settlers for America fleeing from religious persecution. The revocation of the Edict of Nantes (1685) by Louis XIV. of France, withdrew religious freedom from the French Protestants, and as a consequence many thousands left the country. Many of them went to Prussia, where they were hospitably received by the King Frederick William and established at Berlin, then quite recently planned, to the subsequent prosperity of which they largely contributed by their skill and industry. Others came to England and settled notably at Spitalfields and Bethnal Green, where they carried on silk-weaving, watch-making, and other industries. From that time there has been no great collective I. into the United Kingdom, although the statistics show a steady increase of general I. The number of immigrants per annum rose from 175,747 in 1900 to 350,429 in 1911, more than one half of the immigrants being British and Irish subjects returning to the homeland. From 1880 there commenced a great influx of poorer class Jewish immigrants from Russia, Poland, and the countries of S.E. Europe. They were mainly intending to proceed to the United States in order to escape from the anti-Semitic legislation of their native countries, and from the onus of compulsory military service. The American I. laws, which were passed in 1882, deterred many whom poverty or disease prevented from entertaining any hope of being allowed to land there. London had, in consequence, to absorb the worst type of refugee, and before long a feeling of resentment was aroused. It was found that these alien immigrants caused a displacement of British born workers, lowered the standard of living, and housed together in unsanitary conditions. A Committee of the House of Commons was appointed in 1889 to inquire into the question of this foreign pauper I., and a Royal Commission was

appointed in 1902 to report upon the same question. The recommendations of the latter body led to the introduction of the Criminal Aliens Bill of 1904 and to the Aliens Act of 1905, which came into effect on Jan. 1, 1906. By this Act an immigrant is held to be undesirable and to be repatriated if he cannot show that he is able to support himself and his dependants, if he is an idiot, a lunatic, or a criminal, or if he has any disease or infirmity likely to cause him to become a charge upon the rates. In the case of persons fleeing from religious or political persecution, admission is not to be refused on account of want of means. After once having been admitted, aliens are still liable to be repatriated upon certain specific accounts. Appeal is allowed from the I. officer to a board appointed by the Secretary of State. The country which has to cope with the question of I. upon the largest scale is the United States. Statistics which have been kept from 1820 show that the number of immigrants rose from 143,000 in 1821-30 to 2,812,000 in 1871-80, 5,246,000 in 1881-90, 3,687,000 in 1891-1900, and 3,833,000 for the five years 1901-5. In the earlier part of the century the immigrants came mainly from Great Britain and Ireland. The political unrest in Germany and the revolution of 1848 led to many Germans going over to America, and a steady flow continued throughout the latter half of last century. The development of the railway system and the consequent opening up of farm lands gave a great impetus to emigration from all parts of Western Europe. Towards the end of the century, however, the immigrants from the eastern and southern countries of Europe began to preponderate, and Austria-Hungary, Italy, and Russia now furnish more than half the total number. This great influx of new-comers, mostly of an inferior social status, has always caused considerable uneasiness in the minds of the native American. Even in the early part of the century the Irish were objected to as lowering the standard of living, ousting the native-born workman, and having an undue percentage of paupers, criminals, and diseased persons. How much truth there is in these charges is not easily determined, and one must bear in mind that there is always a tendency for the native-born inhabitant to despise the new arrival, while even to-day the descendants of the old Dutch families affect to despise the descendants of the newer English settlers. It appears on investigation, that the new arrivals speedily adapt themselves to the social conditions of their adopted fatherland and insist upon as high a standard of living as the American workman. With the gradual change of nationality of the bulk of the immigrants came the additional fear that the American national character would be submerged and the objections against the unrestrained entry of foreigners increased in vigour. I. into the United States has consequently been dealt with by the Act of 1882 and by the Undesirable Persons Act of 1891, which provides that any passenger from abroad shall be examined on arrival and not allowed to land if found to be a convict, lunatic, or idiot, epileptic, or suffering from contagious disease, pauper liable to become a public charge, or to be either a professional beggar, polygamist, anarchist, or prostitute. Each steamboat company must pay a tax of two dollars per head for all immigrants brought over, and the money so raised forms an I. fund to defray the expenses of administering the Acts. Furthermore, a series of Alien Contract Labour Laws were passed in 1885, 1887, 1888, and 1891, which prevented any person coming to the United States to perform any service under contract made previous to emigration. All such contracts are held void in law. Certain exceptions are, however, made, notably in the case of authors, lecturers, singers, and persons employed by foreigners in temporary residence. Prepayment of passage money is also illegal except in the case of friends or relatives.

The increase of Chinese into America was also regarded with intense jealousy. This I. grew in volume as the completion of the trans-continental railway system and the discovery of gold in California led to the development of the Pacific coast. The Chinese were found to work for wages far below those that would support a European in comfort, and the agitation against them led Congress to pass an Act in 1882 suspending Chinese I. for ten years. This Act has been renewed from time to time, and is still in force. It is enforced with extreme rigour, and persons bringing Chinese, not legally entitled to enter, into the country, are subject to imprisonment for a term not exceeding one year. Apart from the question of undue competition with the native workmen, the Chinese immigrant was regarded as never likely to become a permanent settler, and was accused of not being amenable to the laws of the white races, of evading payment of taxes, of desecrating graveyards, and of being governed by habits opposed

to the well-being of the community. The I. of the Japanese was also restricted by measures taken by the Japanese government in 1908.

The British colonies have generally found it necessary to pass Acts in order to control the type of immigrant arriving on their shores. In Australia, by the Act of 1901, a language (or educational) test is imposed, and all idiots, lunatics, diseased persons, criminals, and prostitutes are refused admission. An attempt has also been made to protect the native-born worker by refusing admission to all persons coming to fulfil contracts made prior to emigration. Rigorous regulations have also been made, governing the employment of the Chinese coolie, once engaged largely in Queensland to cultivate the sugar-cane, and ultimately the system was abolished, coolies found in Australia after Dec. 31, 1906, being liable to deportation. In New Zealand similar laws are in force.

The British South African colonies have also passed similar laws to those which hold in Australia, but allow the contract labourer. The question of the Chinese immigrant became of great political importance, owing to the report of a committee in 1903 that the native labourers were insufficient to supply the requirements of the mining industries. The British government in 1904 passed an ordinance allowing for the importation of Chinese labour, which was strongly opposed by the Liberal party. The government of Cape Colony in the same year prohibited Chinese labour in its territory. In 1906 some 55,000 Chinese coolies were employed in the Rand mines. In 1907, however, the Transvaal parliament resolved by a large majority to abolish the system, and by March 1910 all the Chinese had been repatriated.

The Canadian government offers great inducements, especially to farmers, to settle in Canada, and in 1911 some 185,000 persons left the British Isles to settle there. Considerable I. also takes place from the United States. The Canadian government has also passed laws excluding paupers, criminals, and diseased immigrants, and refuses to allow the entry of Chinese.

I. takes place on a large scale to the countries of S. America. The immigrants are chiefly Italians and Spanish, though numbers of British, Russians, Germans, and French also go. In Argentina one quarter of the population is Italian, while the immigrants to Brazil were mainly Italians, until the Italian government was induced to stop the emigration of Italians to that country on account of their unsatisfactory treatment. *See* ALIEN, and CHINESE LABOUR QUESTION.

Bibliography.—For the question of I. as it affects London, *see* Major W. Evans Gordon's *The Alien Immigrant*, 1903; Whelpley, *The Problems of the Immigrant*, 1905; *The Report of the Royal Commission on Alien Immigration*, 1903-4. For United States I., see *United States Industrial Commission Reports*, vol. xv., 1901; B. Brandenberg's *Imported Americans*, 1904; P. Robert's *Anthracite Coal Communities*, 1904; C. S. Bernheimer's *The Russian Jew in the United States*, 1905; and Bryce's *American Commonwealth*, 1911.

Immingham Dock, 5 m. N.W. of Grimsby, was constructed (1906-12) by the Great Central Company on the S. shore of the Humber. It has a capacity of 1,215,000 cubic ft., and an acreage, with adjoining property, of about 1000 acres.

Immortality (Lat. *in*, not, and *mortalis*, mortal, connected with *mors*, death), the continued existence of the human soul after the death of the body. In some form or other, the belief in human I. is practically universal. In even the most primitive animistic cults its influence is clearly discernible, while in all the higher cults it forms an important section of their philosophy. In the more primitive cults we have the provision made for the journeys and sustenance of the departed ' soul,' the after-life being looked upon as little more than a continuation of the earth-life. An elaborate philosophy of the after-life is found in Egypt, and lengthy accounts are given in the Books of the Dead, telling of the descent of the spirits to the judgment-hall of Osiris. Reproductions of many of the pictures of these scenes are well known. Among the Indian peoples of the East a different view of the journeys after death gave rise to the belief in the transmigration of souls. After death the soul passed into the body of some fresh being, higher or lower in the social scale, according as the life had been good or bad. Buddhism made no alteration in this doctrine, except that it furnished a final goal in the attainment of Nirvana, which, involving as it does the annihilation of personality, can hardly be described as I. It has been disputed whether the Hebrews had any idea of I. before the exile, and there is much in the biblical books which would lead one to suppose that they had not (for varying conceptions of Sheol, *see* HELL), and it is certain that they considered the after-life as at most only a shadow of this life. Among the Hebrews, the Persians, and the other Semitic tribes, the idea of I. is generally associated with the resurrection of the body. The Greeks, while many of them (*e.g.* Socrates, Plato) held the I. of the soul, the resurrection of the body was entirely foreign to their thoughts. The Christian faith teaches both the I. of the soul and the resurrection of the body. St. Paul (1 Cor. xv. 44, etc.), teaches this clearly, and he also lays stress on the important fact that the resurrection-body is not carnal, but spiritual. *See* Salmon's *Christian Doctrine of Immortality* (4th ed.), 1901 ; Charles's *Critical Hist. of the Doctrine of a Future Life*, 1897.

Immortality. Corporations (*q.v.*) (including the king who is legally a corporation sole) are, in law, incapable of dying. This is one of the reasons for the old mortmain statutes which were directed against the conveyance of lands to ecclesiastical corporations, it being against the policy of the law to allow land so to be tied up in perpetual ownership as to restrict the probability of its free circulation. The death of the reigning monarch is constitutionally merely an event which results in the immediate demise of the crown, though formerly there was a real interregnum between the death of one king and the election and coronation of his successor; with the result that the state had, in the interval, no one to represent it for the purpose of maintaining order. But this fictitious I. of the king did not get rid of the rule that parliament was necessarily dissolved by the death of the king, although it was appreciated that the consequences of a sudden and automatic dissolution were highly inconvenient, especially in regard to taxes, the collection of which could not be enforced in the absence of a proper authorisation. It was not till 1837 that an Act was passed, providing for the continued existence of parliament for six months after the death of the king, unless sooner dissolved by his successor. For the other legal and constitutional effects of this attribute of I. in the king, *see* CROWN.

Immortelles, *see* EVERLASTING FLOWERS.

Imola, a tn. of Italy in the prov. of Bologna, situated on the R. Santerno. It has a considerable trade in wine. Pop. 12,500.

Imola, Innocenzio da (*b. c.* 1490), also called **Francucci,** an Italian painter of the 16th century, born at Imola. The latest date on his works is 1549. He was a pupil of Francia and lived in Bologna, decorating the churches of that city with frescoes. His masterpiece is the picture entitled 'Archangel Michael and Satan.' See Vasari, Lives of the Painters.

Imoschi, Imoski, or **Imotski,** a frontier tn. of Austria, situated in Dalmatia, 30 m. N.W. of Mostar. Pop. (com.) 41,895.

Impact, the collision between bodies. The mathematical theory of the subject is not concerned with cases in which the I. results in the destruction of either of the bodies. When two bodies impinge, the time of I. may be divided into two parts—the first known as the time of *compression,* during which even the hardest bodies suffer temporary loss of shape at the point of impact; and the second, the time of *restitution,* during which the natural shape is regained. The more elastic bodies are those which exert a greater effort to recover their shape; hence they rebound further. An *inelastic* body is one which makes no effort to regain ts shape, which is permanently altered by I. In actual practice, no perfectly inelastic bodies have been found; but a lump of putty is an approximate example. A common experiment to illustrate this loss of shape in the case of a hard body is made by dropping an ivory ball on to a greased marble surface. A circle of distinct size is found to be made, and a still larger circle, if the ball is dropped from a greater height, thus showing that the surfaces touched over an area during I. Newton found that the relative velocity of two bodies after a direct I. is in a constant ratio to the relative velocity before I., and is in the opposite direction. This ratio has been found experimentally for various pairs of substances in contact. It is known as the *coefficient of restitution,* and in mathematical formulæ is denoted by *e.* Thus for two glass solids $e = ·94$, for two ivory solids ·8, and for one of iron and one of lead ·13. The example given first approximates as nearly as anything else in practice to a state of perfect elasticity. The mathematical theory is based in the first place on considerations of the I. of smooth spheres and planes. When the surfaces in contact are rough, and the I. is not direct, rotations are set up, and the results have to be modified. First consider the direct I. of two spheres (that is, two spheres which impinge in such a way that their line of centres is the same as the then two lines of motion). Let m, m_1 be their masses, u, u_1 their velocities before I., and v, v_1 their velocities after I. All velocities are measured in the same direction, and if the spheres are moving in opposite directions u or u_1 will be negative. Since at I. the impulse received by one body is equal and opposite to that received by the other, the momenta received are equal and opposite. Hence the total momentum in either direction in the line of motion is unaltered by I. Hence follows the equation $mu + m_1 u_1 = mv + m_1 v_1$. Again, Newton's Experimental Law states that the relative velocity after I. is equal to $-e$ times the relative velocity before. Hence $v - v_1 = -e(u - u_1)$. These two equations are then sufficient to determine v and v_1, the velocities with which the bodies move off after I. Thus, in particular, a ball falling to the ground with velocity u, rebounds with velocity eu. It will rebound a second time with velocity $e^2 u$, and so on. When the I. is oblique, the components of the initial velocities perpendicular to the line of centres at I. are unaltered. This gives two equations. The two equations stated above hold equally for the components of the initial velocities resolved along the line of centres, and hence there are four equations which will determine the two new velocities and the new directions after impact. In the former case, the kinetic energy before impact is $\frac{1}{2}mu^2 + \frac{1}{2}m_1 u_1{}^2$, and after impact is $\frac{1}{2}mv^2 + \frac{1}{2}m_1 v_1{}^2$. The two equations give $(\frac{1}{2}mu^2 + \frac{1}{2}m_1 u_1{}^2)$
$$-(\tfrac{1}{2}mv^2 + \tfrac{1}{2}m_1 v_1{}^2) = \frac{1 - e^2}{2} \frac{mm_1}{m + m_1}(u - u_1)^2.$$
Hence this expression represents the kinetic energy lost by the I. It chiefly reappears in the form of heat.

Impanation, literally embodiment in bread (Lat. *panis*), a theological or ecclesiastical term used in the controversies in regard to the Real Presence of Christ's body in the bread of the Eucharist. It is applied to a local presence or inclusion of Christ's body in the bread after consecration, 'an hypostatical and personal union of the bread with Christ's body.' It differs from Transubstantiation (*q.v.*), and has sometimes been used loosely as equivalent to Consubstantiation.

Impatiens, a large genus of balsaminaceous plants which occurs in warm and tropical countries, and is so called from the sudden and elastic force with which the species burst their capsules. *I. balsamina,* the common balsam, is well-known in British conservatories, and *I. Noli-me-tangene,* the touch-me-not, is also a common plant. The valves of the capsule roll inwards when touched, or fully ripe, jerking out the seeds, and the plant emits an unpleasant odour.

Impeachment, the arraignment before the High Court or parliament of a minister of state for high crimes and misdemeanours. The first recorded exercise of the power was

in the reign of Edward III., when
Latimer and Neville were impeached
for the fraudulent purchase of crown
debts and for removing the staple
from Calais. I. is a judicial proceeding in which Commons act as accusers
and the Lords, in pursuance of the
long settled rule that the judicial
powers of parliament are vested exclusively in the Upper Chamber, as
judges. A member of the House of
Commons moves the I. in the first
instance, and if the motion is carried
the accused is impeached by a deputation of members at the bar of the
House of Lords. Articles of I. are
drawn up and copies submitted to
the Lords and to the accused. The
latter is then arrested and detained
in the custody of Black Rod. The
prosecution is conducted by certain
of the commoners who are styled
managers. The Lords deliver a
verdict ' upon their honour,' and
where a verdict of guilty is found,
sentence is not passed until the
accusers demand it. The prisoner may
move the court in arrest of judgment.
The Act of Settlement provides that
no pardon from the crown can be
pleaded to an I. Where the accused
is a peer, the Lord High Steward pre-
sides, where a commoner, the Lord
Chancellor. I. is now virtually
obsolete. Public opinon has for years
been a far stronger inducement to
ministers not to abuse their powers
than the terrors of an I. Formerly,
however, it was a valuable weapon in
the hands of the Commons for controlling the actions of the crown
ministers. But there is no doubt
whatever that the power was grossly
abused. Ministers were often impeached for reasons which in these
days would merely form ground for
strong party differences. Perhaps the
most famous case of I. was that of
Lord Chancellor Bacon on a charge
of receiving bribes. This I. was important in that it re-affirmed the
right of the Commons to hold
ministers responsible for their acts to
the nation. The Is. of Geo. Villiers,
Duke of Buckingham, Thomas Wentworth, Earl of Strafford, and Arch
bishop Laud in 1626, 1640, and 1640
respectively, seem in modern eyes to
do no more than exemplify the varying fortunes of party warfare. One of
the specific charges against Buckingham was that of accumulating offices.
In these days patronage in one form
or another is a frequent subject of
hostile party and press comment, but
the law officers of the crown would
hardly suggest an I. Both Wentworth
and Laud were accused of trying to
subvert the fundamental laws of the
realm, but the comprehensiveness of
the charge does not alter the fact that

Wentworth's foreign policy and
Laud's papist views and sympathies
did not happen to meet with the
approval of a stern Puritan parliament. The last Is. were those of
Warren Hastings in 1788 and Lord
Melville in 1806 for alleged malversation of office. But even before that
time the principle of ministerial responsibility (see CABINET, GOVERN-
MENT) to parliament had become
what it now is—the fundamental safeguard of the whole principle of
representation.

Impenetrability is generally accepted as one of the properties of
matter, viz. that two different
portions of matter cannot occupy the
same space at the same time. When
a nail is knocked into a piece of wood,
it takes up its new position by dis-
placing certain particles of the wood.
Many experiments were made to disprove the theory, notably one, in
which a metal globe was completely
filled with water and then compressed
until the outside was seen to be
covered with moisture. But this was
explained as merely proving that
particles of water could be forced
between the particles of metal. A
pint of water and a pint of alcohol
make up a mixture of less than two
pints, but this is due to the fact that
in the mixture the molecules are
closer to one another. On the other
hand, the many theories recently
advanced of the composition of atoms
make it doubtful whether they
possess the property of I.

Imperator, a passenger and mail
steamer of the Hamburg-American
Line, launched by the Kaiser Wilhelm in 1913. It is the largest vessel
in the world, and has a length of 919
ft., 98 ft. beam, 62 ft. deep, speed
$22\frac{1}{2}$ knots, 72,000 horse-power, displacement of 70,000 tons. It is pro-
pelled by quadruple screws.

Imperial Institute, The, was founded
in 1887 as a national memorial of the
Jubilee of Queen Victoria. The buildings in S. Kensington, London, were
erected after designs by Mr. T. E.
Collcult. The objects of the Institute
are to display and illustrate the
natural resources, arts, and industries
of the colonies and India, to investigate scientifically and technically its
commercial and other resources with
a view to the use of its raw materials,
and to give every information in
regard to the British empire and its
resources. Its spacious galleries contain a wonderful collection of art
treasures from India, many of them
gifts from the feudatory native
princes to Queen Victoria. These and
the rich Colonial exhibits are open
free to the public. There is also a
Scientific and Technical Department,

with fully equipped laboratories for research work, while the Reference Library and Reading-rooms contain a full collection of necessary works and all colonial and Indian papers, periodicals, blue-books, maps, etc. The Institute languished from public inattention to its valuable work and collections, and in 1902 was transferred to the control of the Board of Trade; in 1909 it was attached to the Colonial Office, under the management of an advisory committee, on which the India Office and Board of Trade are represented. The University of London occupies a portion of the buildings.

Imperialism. In a general sense I. means merely a system of government under an emperor, a definition which, however orthodox, is either a truism, or, in view of the totally different politics and constitutions that in different states may happen to fall under the denomination of empire, contradictory or even false. Germany till comparatively recently was a loose union of neighbouring kingdoms in a federation formed primarily for customs' purposes; the British empire a small compact central state with a great number of dependencies scattered over the face of the globe; China an agglomeration of peoples utterly incapable of cohesive and organised action as a whole. Yet all three are called empires. The United States are a federation markedly similar in form to Germany, Holland possesses dependencies in the remotest corners of the world, yet neither are designated empires. The term also connotes imperial state or authority, in which sense it serves to contrast the ultimate authority of a mother state with the delegated powers of its outlying dependencies, *e.g.* we say that the constitutions of the British self-governing colonies depend directly or indirectly on imperial statutes. Similarly, the ancient Roman empire consisted of two distinct parts: Rome or, later, Italy and its provinces, the latter comprising the foreign possessions of Rome. I. in this sense reached its highest expression in or about the time of Augustus. Cæsarism spelt the well-nigh absolute autocracy of the imperator over a servile senate and a humbled people. After the death of the elder Theodosius, 395 A.D., when the division between the East and the West became permanent, each part continued to be called an empire. The Eastern empire ended ingloriously under Turkish rule, but the Western, after the vicissitudes of the Gothic dynasty, developed under Charlemagne into the Holy Roman empire, with the pope as lord of the

Roman duchy or imperial feudatory, though the allegiance paid to the papal see varied at different times with the strength of the particular German or Italian emperors.

But the term I. as used in England has a narrower but much more pregnant sense, as meaning the policy of those who aim at a closer knitting together of the countries forming the British empire. To latter-day imperialists, ' the spirit of empire,' sounds an inspiring note and conjures up dreams of an Anglo-Saxon federation or confraternity of states which, for solidarity, material and moral progress, the like of which the world has never seen. But in its beginnings I. had no such heroic foundation. It was an antidote to the doctrines of the ' Manchester school,' and a movement frankly initiated rather in the interests of mere national safety. It is clear to any one contemplating the heterogeneous compound of the British empire that Great Britain, its hub, may be compared to the central offices of a vast business concern. It can create of its own motion next to nothing of the material wealth that goes to make its strength; its life-sap is drawn largely from its self-governing dependencies, and it is a mere platitude to say that once these are gone Great Britain would sink to the level of a fourth-rate power. In its way the secession of the N. American colonies from allegiance to the English crown was a blessing in disguise. One lesson it taught has only really been appreciated in the last few years, and that is that the great colonies with representative institutions are worthy of consideration on an equal footing with the mother country. But another lesson it taught was of more immediate importance; it seemed to many that the grant or acquisition of self-government was but a step in the direction of final emancipation, and that it must inevitably follow that one great colony after another would eventually be lopped away from the trunk of the empire. Of a gratuitously artificial nature, too, was the commercial policy between the mother country and the colonies. It was hoped to keep the colonies intact by restricting the importation and exportation of colonial goods to British ships manned for the most part by Englishmen, and this policy enacted by the Navigation Act of 1660, was continued up to the time of the repeal of the Corn Laws in 1846, and the laying of the corner-stone of Free Trade in 1849 by the repeal of the Navigation Act. That this stunting of colonial trade hampered the material progress of the empire was amply demonstrated by Adam Smith and a host of other economists of the period. That a policy of free trade, with its consequent expansion of colonial power, accelerated the final dismemberment of the empire seemed no less probable. The optimism of the ' Manchester school,' therefore, expressed itself in the paradox that the empire was really in a better position without colonies that were no longer compelled to open their markets exclusively to the mother country, and that it was unnecessary to retain them at all. There followed after the middle of the 19th century a period of more or less complete mutual indifference. The colonies fostered their manufactures with the help of tariffs directed largely against British goods, while Great Britain consistently ignored colonial trade. The continuance of such a policy might well have been indefinite but for the sudden and lively perception of danger to the whole fabric of the empire from a hitherto unlooked for source. The astonishing rise and progress of the German empire, and its steady policy of naval and military aggrandisement awoke English statesmen to the realisation of the comparative ease with which a state of not much inferior fighting strength could, by shutting out food supplies, cripple the British empire. However alarmist such fears may have tended to become there was, and is even now, a strong element of justification for entertaining them, and their direct outcome was the Imperialist movement, which found concrete expression in the Imperial Federation League and the inauguration of colonial conferences (q.v.). The Imperial Federation League was founded in 1884 with the avowed object of bringing about a federation of the British empire, and was itself the outcome of a colonial conference held in that year under the presidency of Mr. W. E. Forster. Lord Rosebery became its second president, and in 1887, following on its energetic propagandist work, a number of representatives of many of the colonies came to London to confer with each other and with English statesmen on the question of maintenance and defence of common imperial interests, consistently with the retention by the colonial parliaments of their existing autonomy in local matters. This movement in the direction of imperial federation has gathered strength with the progress of time and received a fresh impetus from the vigorous administration of the colonial office under Mr. Joseph Chamberlain, with whose name, and

that of Mr. Cecil Rhodes, the spirit of I. in later years became primarily associated. Mr. Chamberlain, inheriting the dictum of Beaconsfield, that colonial constitutions far from being steps towards disintegration, formed part of a great policy of imperial consolidation, encouraged the cordial relations with the colonies by organising further conferences and invited their co-operation during the darker days of the Boer War of 1900. The enthusiasm and loyalty of the colonial representatives on the occasion of Queen Victoria's Diamond Jubilee, and the prompt military aid rendered by such troops as Strathcona's Horse, may be regarded as indications of the final and complete reversal of the above-noticed doctrines of the ' Manchester school ' of Cobden and Bright. But the change was slower and far more recent than might be imagined. Without doubt the so-called ' Little Englander ' policy of the ' Manchester school ' was checked years before the later conferences by the almost simultaneous rush of the Powers for protectorates and ' spheres of influence ' in Africa. In this race for territory Cecil Rhodes in S. Africa, and Sir George Goldre in W. Africa, augmented the empire within the space of twenty years by a total area exceeding that of the whole of Europe. But even late in Rhodes' career something was lacking in the direction of a proper confidence in and reciprocity with this as well as other growing limbs of the empire. Possibly Mr. Chesterton strikes the true note in saying that ' While from the point of view of a Victorian aristocrat like Palmerston, Socialism might be the cheek of gutter snipes, imperialism would be the intrusion of cads.' Rhodes, indeed, on one occasion threatened to secede altogether unless the mother country altered her policy towards S. Africa. It is here that the work of the Imperial Federation did so much good; for its aim was to replace dependence by association and by such association or co-ordination to lead up to a united empire or federation, a union different from a mere hegemony on the one hand and on the other an autocratic I. like that of the Cæsars or Napoleon Bonaparte. In the purely fiscal part of its doctrines the ' Manchester school ' of thought was and, of course, is very far from extinct. It is claimed by many of the present Unionist party that Mr. Chamberlain's Tariff Reform project of giving preference to colonial goods and protecting the trade of the empire by retaliatory duties on foreign goods was no more than a natural evolution of the idea of I. Colour may conceivably be lent to this assumption by the fact that at the Conference of 1907 all the colonial premiers advocated tariffs. I. may well require a more substantial basis than mere ' Jingoism ' if it is to be more than a dream. But whether a free trade or a protective policy will ultimately prove to be its economic foundation is a question the answer to which seems to be referable to individual judgment or prejudice. The legacy of ' Little Englanderism ' left by the ' Manchester school ' has borne interest in the shape of a very general denial of all imperialist ideas to any who favour a continuance of a free trade policy. But apart from purely economic arguments, followers of that policy may well reply that whatever may have happened in such federations as the zollverein of the German states, the dream of a world-powerful Saxon empire should look for its fulfilment not to the notoriously unequal operation of tariff duties, but to the sentiment of national destiny fostered by the knowledge of a common ancestry. Intellectually, at all events, the fervour of this vision of I. has received a tremendous blow at the hands of the revived Socialism, the more so in that the newer Socialism attacked the existing social scheme not by any appeal to the emotions, but by a cold analysis of the mechanical crudities of the industrial system. To the Socialist neither the cynicism of a protective tariff nor what Mr. Chesterton calls the ' brutal optimism ' of the ' Manchester school ' is a whit more commendable than the ' rightly articulated might ' of Carlyle (*French Revolution*) in his or any other philosopher's heroics against universalistic hedonism or the greatest-happiness principle of the utilitarians, or against any other theory or doctrine consistent with a callous egoism in ethics and, in religion or metaphysics, a deity ranged on the side of the strong. Socialism cares nothing for huge colonial extensions of empire if the economic analysis shows that land in the colony is not really freer than in the home country. As Mr. Bernard Shaw says, the United States and the colonies have been ' peopled by fugitives from the full-blown individualism of Western Europe, pre-empting private property ' precisely as in the old economic conditions of cultivation. Whether, however, the negations of Socialism are likely to prevail over the tangible offerings of the great self-governing colonies is a question that so far belongs rather to the sphere of pure conjecture. The practical value

of such an inquiry is lessened by reflecting that the little headway made by Socialism in actual politics although in the form of a mitigation of the extreme asperities of undiluted individualism, has so far been in favour not of the world generally but of the labouring masses of the particular state concerned. If, therefore, in its political expression Socialism becomes as parochial as the egoism it affects to displace, I. or something as inspiring will probably take its place.

Imperial Nursing Service was formed after the S. African War under the title of Queen Alexandra's Imperial Military Nursing Service. It supplies the nursing staff for the whole army, and is managed by a board of which Queen Alexandra is president, and the director-general Army Medical Service is chairman. Candidates for admission must be of British parentage, and must possess certificates of three years' training and service in medical and surgical nursing in a civil hospital.

Imperial Service Order, the name of a decoration confined to members of the Civil Service. Long and meritorious service in either a clerical or administrative capacity is the qualifications for the order, the members of which are limited in number to 425. King Edward VII. founded the order in 1902.

Impetigo Contagiosa, an acute, inflammatory, contagious disease of the skin, characterised by the formation of vesicles or pustules that dry into flat straw - coloured crusts; from beneath the crust a thick discharge oozes and the skin beneath is tender and raw. The head and face are the parts usually affected, and the disease is generally found amongst ill-nourished and neglected children, though adults may contract it. The treatment consists of the application of poultices to remove the crust, followed by a dressing of zinc ointment to heal the skin. The general health should at the same time be improved by attention to cleanliness, good food, and suitable tonics.

Impey, Sir Elijah (1732-1809), Chief-Justice of Bengal, India, born at Hammersmith, educated at Westminster School with Warren Hastings, the beginning of a life-long intimacy. In 1773 he was made the first chief-justice of the newly-established supreme court of Bengal in Calcutta, and was in close connection with Warren Hastings, the governor-general. In 1775 a native, Nuncomar or Nanda Kumar, who had succeeded Hastings as collector of Burdwan, brought a charge of peculation against the governor-general, supported by France's and Hastings' opponents on the Council. Nuncomar was arrested on a charge of forgery, tried by I., condemned, and hanged. In 1777 he decided in favour of Hastings over the ratification of the governor's resignation. He was recalled in 1783 and impeached in the House of Commons for his sentence on Nuncomar but was acquitted. Macaulay's charges of a conspiracy with Hastings to contrive a judicial murder have been entirely disproved by Sir James Fitzjames Stephen in *The Story of Nuncomar*, 1885.

Imphail, the native name of Manipur (*q.v.*).

Imphee, the name applied to the variety *Saccharatum* of the species *Sorghum vulgare*, or common millet. It is a native of Africa, and sugar is often prepared from its stems.

Implacable, a British battleship of 15,000 tons' displacement, class B. She was launched at Devonport in 1899 and completed in 1902. Speed 18 knots. The French *Duguay Trouin*, captured in 1805, was also so called, and served as a training-ship.

Implement, in Scots law, means performance of a contract or obligation. If at the proper time an obligation is not implemented according to the true meaning of its terms and it has not been extinguished (discharged) in a legal manner, the debtor is said to be in breach (*q.v.*), and the creditor may sue for damages or for specific performance according to the nature of the contract.

Implements and Machinery, Agricultural, present a greater variety at the present time than they did in ancient times, though the great advance has been not so much in the form of the various implements as in the adaptation of mechanical power (steam or petrol, etc.) to their use. About the year 1870, owing to the increased cost of horses and the scarcity of labour, the question of steam-driven agricultural implements was placed in prominence. The hopes that horse labour could be entirely superseded by mechanical power proved to be unfounded, as although a greater quantity of work could be done, the quality suffered somewhat. It would appear, therefore, that steam is most useful as an auxiliary to horse tillage. So used, its value is very great, as large areas of land can be treated in a very short time. The horses are thus set free for lighter operations, and the amount of time saved by the use of steam is particularly noticeable in a wet season. The steam working of bastard fallows in summer, for instance, is very advantageous, and after the harvest a great amount of the autumn cultivation can profitably be done by steam-driven instruments. The various implements required may be classified under six heads: (1) Those used in preparing the soil before the seed is sown, (2) those used in sowing seeds, (3) those used in cultivating crops whilst still growing, (4) those used in harvesting crops, (5) those used in preparing the crops for market, (6) those used in preparing crops required for home consumption.

In the first class come various classes of ploughs, grubbers, harrows, rollers, land pressers, etc. The surface of the ground is broken up into furrows by the action of the plough, and so exposed in fresh places to the action of the atmosphere. The ordinary form of plough drawn by horses is still used on most farms, but some very good examples of steam ploughs have been invented, some ploughing as many as eight furrows at a time. The function of grubbers, or cultivators, is to rend the soil by means of their curved teeth, and if they are very powerful they may serve instead of a plough. The heavier varieties of harrow serve a similar purpose to the grubbers, the light forms are used to render the service ready for the seed, and to cover the latter when sown. Rollers are used to break up the clods and to smooth the surface after sowing. They are either plain, toothed, or formed of rings, and vary in weight from light wooden to heavy iron varieties. A presser consists of one or more iron wheels mounted on a frame, which follows the plough or ploughs and presses the furrows as they are formed.

In the second class come drills of various kinds, seed-sowers, and machines for the distribution of manure. Seed-sowing machines scatter the seed on the surface of the land, either broadcast or in furrows, according to the class of seed sown and the crop required. Manure-distributors act on much the same principles. The seed is deposited below the surface of the ground in rows by means of special knives in the drilling machines. These are of many varieties, such as corn-drills, clover drills, turnip-drills, water-drills, dry-drills, etc.

In the third class come the various varieties of hoes. Ordinary hoes for use by hand are still the most largely employed, but various kinds of horse-hoes are on the market, both simple and multiple.

In the fourth class are the binding machines, reaping and mowing machines, machines for loading and stacking the hay, rakes drawn by horses, swathe-turners, etc. It was in the first years of the 20th century that self-binding harvesters first came into popularity; at the same time potato-planting and potato-lifting machines were more used. Thirty sheaves a minute are tied up by the harvesters, and as much as an acre of corn can be cut and tied up in an hour.

In the fifth class the threshing-machine is the most noteworthy, as it combines many operations formerly performed by different machines, or by manual labour. The straw, the chaff, the head-corn, and the tail-corn are all separated and delivered at the same time by a good threshing-machine. Other operations are also performed in some varieties, such as delivering the cut straw into bags, tying the straw into bundles, or de-livering the correct weight of corn into sacks ready for delivery.

In the sixth class are the various machines which are necessary to pre-pare the food for the different ani-mals during the winter, etc. Such are chaff-cutters, root-pulpers, boilers, machines for slicing and shredding roots, breaking oilcake, etc. They can all be connected with a steam engine. Any single-cylinder, horizontal or vertical engine may be taken and mounted on a wheeled truck; thrash-ing, grinding, and also all the opera-tions carried out by machines of the last class can be carried out by its aid. The fly-wheel, or pulley, ad-jacent is simply belted up to the machine which it is required to oper-ate. Many operations on a large estate, such as brick and tile making, wood sawing, lime burning, etc., are performed by the aid of various machines not included in the above category. The engine above de-scribed can often be used in connec-tion with such machines also. For the operation of threshing, in particular, as well as many other operations, an agricultural engine is used. This is a variety of the multitubular loco-motive boiler, together with an engine. Two kinds of agricultural engines are in use, the first being called 'portable' and requiring horses to haul it; the second or 'traction' type has its own motive power. On farms of moderate size, it is usual to hire engines of this class for a brief period in the year, as it is only on very large estates that suffi-cient work could be found to com-pensate for their cost.

See the separate articles on the implements mentioned; for the special implements, etc., for a dairy, see DAIRYING and CHURNS. See also Malden's *Farm Buildings and Eco-nomical Agricultural Appliances*, 1876;

Martin's *Farm Appliances*, 1903; and Malden's *Tillage and Implements*, 1891.

Imponderable Substances, a name formerly applied to hypothetical substances contained in other matter, and responsible for the phenomena of heat, light, electricity, magnetism, etc. As no difference of weight could be detected when a body varied as regards heat, electricity, etc., such substances were called imponderable. After being abandoned for several years, the hypothesis that energy is a form of matter, or that matter and energy are ultimately identical, is again being put forward by reputable physicists.

Imports and Exports. Nothing affords so striking a commentary on the uncertainties of the science of political economy than the fact that the controversies that raged from the time of Adam Smith to the middle of the 19th century, on the relation of exchange values of commodities be-tween countries to national wealth, revived at the end of the century with altogether unabated vigour—long after they were commonly deemed finally determined—in the movement for Tariff Reform. Theoretically, the exports of a country exchange for imports at such values as that the former will pay for the latter, and it is probably true that exports and imports constantly tend to an equality. But it was long uncertain whether it was more advantageous to have a surplus aggregate value of imports over exports, or *vice versâ*. According to Mill this uncertainty arose primarily from the traditional habit of looking rather to the profits of merchants than the price of com-modities to the consumer, a habit which, in its turn, rested on the long-discarded belief that money alone was wealth. At the time of Mill it had become generally settled that the profit of foreign trade consists in the difference between the price at which the goods are bought and carried, and the price at which they are sold. The difference between the gross money-value of the exports and imports of a country will give a rough idea of the amount of this profit. In England in 1863, 1864, and 1865, for example, the ratio of imports to exports was about 5 to 4. This fact would have excited alarm before Adam Smith's time. The assumption would have been that England was buying more than it sold. But, according to Mill, and to Pro-fessor Ashley, and others of the 'Free Trade' school of thought ('free im-ports' would more accurately ex-press the doctrine), the only direct advantage accruing to a country from foreign trade consists in the imports;

because, after paying with exports for the things it cannot itself produce, except at a greater expense of capital and labour than the cost of the exports, there is *ex hypothesi* a surplus of labour and capital for the production of other things. Mill expresses this categorically by pointing out that the opposite theories assume that what a country parts with, and not what it obtains, constitutes its gain; and adversely criticises Adam Smith's doctrine that the benefit of foreign trade was that it afforded an outlet for surplus produce and enabled a portion of the capital of the exporting country to replace itself with a profit. His criticism may be summarised in his deduction: that a country produces an exportable article in excess of its own wants from no inherent necessity but as the cheapest mode of supplying itself with other things. The inference drawn from this theory of Mill's, is that the only alternative to exporting in excess of wants would be the employment of the capital and labour thus set free in producing things previously imported, with a corresponding loss to consumers by reason of higher prices. And this strife between the capitalist, or producer, and the consumer is to be observed in all the fiscal arguments of the present day, though it may as yet be too early to say what that policy will be in England during the next decade, especially seeing that during the last two centuries demands for a protective policy have constantly recurred. Of course, the process of interchange of commodities is not necessarily as simple as the statement of its fundamental principle. There is the element of the cost of carriage, and it by no means follows that any particular imports can be allocated as the price of any particular exports, since any one given country trades with so many other countries. Moreover, exchange values are continually fluctuating, or, as it is termed, the market is always 'higgling' within the limits of the ratios of the costs of production in each country, although they tend to an ultimate equality in accordance with Mill's law of the equation of international demand—a law which experience shows is in no wise affected by improvements in the process of manufacture of any given article, because that improvement will eventually enure to the reciprocal benefit of all countries concerned in trading in that article. Similarly, the cost of carriage only complicates, but does not affect the above law, unless it be true that a country with an over-whelming advantage in transport must have the ultimate advantage in exchange. One, at all events, of the

principal causes of England's adherence to the principle of free imports has been stated by Liberal ministers to be the extent of its carrying facilities, or the fact that so great a quantity of imports is carried in British ships.

The most important items of British imports are foodstuffs and raw materials, while about one-half the total exports are articles wholly or mainly manufactured. The aggregate value of imports (merchandise) to the United Kingdom in 1911 was £680,157,527; exports, £556,878,432, being far in excess of that of any other nation; the next in order being Germany with about £500,000,000 imports and £400,000,000 exports; the United States about £350,000,000 and £450,000,000 respectively, and France somewhat over £300,000,000 for both imports and exports. *See* Annual Parliamentary Papers and Board of Trade Blue Books; Bowley's *Elements of Statistics;* Mayo Smith's *Statistics and Economics,* 1899; Bastable's *International Trade,* 1903. *See also* INTERNATIONAL TRADE; FREE TRADE; PROTECTIVE FREIGHT; CUSTOMS DUTIES; EXCISE.

Impost, in architecture, the name of the upper portion of a door-post from which the arch springs; these may project with mouldings, or take the form of a complete capital with an abacus, or repeat on a smaller scale the entablature of the larger portions of the building.

Impotency, which may be caused by malformation, by general weakness due to overwork, sexual excesses, old age, anxiety, certain diseases such as diabetes, or by an affection of the spinal cord, is a condition of the male generative organs which either temporarily or permanently prevents sexual intercourse. Quack remedies, if not useless, are irritant and harmful, but as a rule an active open-air life and liberal feeding, sexual rest, tonics, and cold baths will effect a cure. *See* MARRIAGE.

Impound: 1. To place in a pound goods or cattle distrained for rent due or for damage done respectively. The things impounded are detained until *replevied* or redeemed. A person at whose instance cattle are impounded is liable if the cattle be not properly tended while in the pound. (As to pound breach *see under* BREACH.) 2. Where a judge during a civil trial is of opinion that the evidence discloses the commission of a criminal offence and orders the documents in the case to be retained and sent to the director of public prosecutions, he is said to I. the documents.

Impregnable, a British gun-ship

(6557 tons), launched in 1860, serving at Devonport as a training-ship for boys (1910). Vessels of this name have existed since 1786.

Impregnation in the higher plants is preceded by pollination. The pollen grain then germinates on the stigma and puts out a small tube which penetrates the style until it reaches an ovule. Then one nucleus of the pollen grain, called the generative nucleus, which is the male elements, fuses with the female nucleus of the ovule.

Impressionism, the somewhat vague and indiscriminate name given to a certain type of modern painting which is most strongly represented by the French schools of Manet on the one hand and Claude Monet on the other. The former is purely realistic in its ideals; the latter, for which the name ‘luminism,’ or, as Camille Mauclair suggests, ‘chromatism,’ would be more correct, aims at the study of atmospheric effects, the play of light, and similar chromatic values. The term I. arose through the exhibition of Monet’s ‘Impressions,’ a sunset which aroused particular ridicule at the Salle des Réfusés (1863), and four years later a phrase in the catalogue of the exhibition of Manet’s work established it still more firmly. It was Whistler who introduced the word into English art-vocabulary by his exhibition at the Grosvenor Galleries (1878). Since those days, in the teeth of opposition which is unparalleled in the history of art—except perhaps in the somewhat analogous case of Wagner’s music-dramas—the movement has spread over the whole of Europe. The French element is discussed below in some detail; it will be sufficient to mention the chief foreign representatives : (German) Max Liebermann and Knehl; (Belgian) Van Rysselberghe, Verheyden, and Heymans; (Swiss) Félix Vallotton; (Dutch) Matthys Marys; (Italian) Pietro Fragiacomo, Boldini, Segantini, and Michetti; (Spanish) Zuloaga, Francisco Pradilla, y Bastida, and Rusiñol; (Danish) Viggo Johansen and Kroyer; (Swedish) Anders Zorn; (Norwegian), Thanlow; (Russian) Ilya Repin. In Britain, apart, of course, from Turner and Constable, the movement is chiefly represented by the Glasgow school, John Lewis Brown, Guthrie, and Lavery; whilst Whistler, Sargent, Harrison, and Mary Cassatt are responsible in America.

The sources from which I. was evolved are of the widest. It was in spirit akin to the Romantic Movement, as a revolt against the classical or academic schools, but technically it was no less a revolt against Romanticism also. In technique Watteau, Monticelli, and Delacroix are the chief forerunners of I. as far as the division of tones is concerned; Lorrain, Vernet, Ruysdael, and Poussin are its progenitors in the matter of landscape treatment and composition. The movement was also very strongly influenced by the exhibition of Japanese paintings of Hokusai, Outamaro, and Hiroshige at the International Exposition in 1867, both as regards its realism (e.g. Manet) and ‘luminism’ (e.g. Monet). But it might be claimed with no small degree of truth that I. was chiefly of English origin, although it has taken its headquarters in France, so to speak. According to Wynford Dewhurst, 90 per cent. of the theory of I. was clearly embodied in Ruskin’s *Elements of Drawing*. And it was from Turner and Constable that Monet, Pissarro, and the others took their chief inspiration, especially in the matter of landscape treatment—the ideal style of subject for impressionist treatment, and the one in which the greatest results have been achieved.

In the first place, I. centred round Manet, who was virtually the president of a little club that used to meet at the Café Guerbois, in the Guartier Batignolles; the circle included Monet, Pissarro, Cézanne, Dégas, Jongkind, Berthe Morisot, Fantin Latour (whose life-sized painting of a group of the principal members now hangs in the Luxembourg), Renoir, Desboutins, Bazille, Legros, and Whistler (at that time a student). They also found sympathetic support in Gautier, Baudelaire, the Goncourts, Zola, Mallarmé, and other men of letters, at different periods. It is therefore justifiable to regard Manet as the first great painter to lead the revolt of modern art against the symbolists and Romantics; and his protest took the form of an uncompromising realism—a realism more psychological and delicate than that of Courbet, analogous to the literary realism of the Goncourts and Flaubert. In the realist-impressionists, as the chief of whom we may name Manet, Courbet, Bastien-Lepage, and Dégas, we find the artistic criterion of truth or character—*vérité vraie*—substituted for that of beauty. But this was only one of the ideals of the new art; there were two others, respectively the study of the mystery and beauty of light, and the study of ‘impression,’ i.e. the catching and reproduction of a momentary vivid glimpse of a scene, as opposed to the systematic reproduction of the details which are unseen in such glimpses. The impressionists were the first to learn the art of presenting a *tout ensemble*, wherein details were either deleted or subordinated to the summarised effect of the whole. A blurred vision of things which encircle a central object on which the gaze is focussed, is correct optically. To a realist painter it is also correct artistically. And not only the focal principle, but brilliant sunlight, mist, or perspective are capable of blurring the definition of objects. Of the luminists, *i.e.* those whose main concern was the study of the mystery and beauty of light, as mentioned above, Monet was the leader; they may be considered as the direct descendants of Delacroix. Of the other school, Renoir and Dégas may be taken as most typical. With Monet and his group, the whole technique of I. is thoroughly investigated for the first time; before them only tentative experiments had been made, if we except the discarding of bitumen— an idea sympathetic with the English Pre-Raphaelite movement, as a reaction against the heavy canvasses of the obscurantists. They ostracised the conventional tonality of brown, and the use of all browns, blacks, and ochres; by the majority all palette mixtures were abandoned and only the pure colours of the spectrum, in addition to white, were accepted.

It is particularly with Monet, who has been well called the 'lyrical pantheist of I.,' that the art of chromatism is developed to a state bordering on perfection; his series of hayricks, cathedrals, water-lilies, and Thames scenes are marvellous investigations of colour values. Light, when playing on an object, more or less dissolves the tones, according to its strength; thus the true value of sunlight can be reproduced only by the juxtaposition of touches of pure, or prismatic, colours on canvas in such a manner that, at the right focal distance, an optical recomposition similar to the result of actual sunlight will be effected. Wynford Dewhurst considers that in the right hands the following palette is capable of doing anything, and of 'rendering the shimmer and palpitation of dazzling sunlight': cadmium or chrome (three tints), madder (three tints), vermilion, cobalt, cobalt violet, French ultramarine, emerald oxide of chromium, and blanc d'argent.

Side by side with the juxtaposition of touches of pure colour are the principles of : (1) The simplification of light and shade in the presentation of mass rather than outline; (2) the investigation of shadow, which is not absence of light, but light of diminished intensity; and (3) the separation of local colour and reaction. By the employment of these means the impressionists succeed in a marvellous degree in the portrayal of motion—the sway of shadow, the passage of light, the heaving movement of water, the sensation of wind. However much of this may be credited to such painters as Géricault and Fromentin, the combined value of light and of movement in relation to one another reaches its supreme expression on the canvasses of Monet, Renoir, Dégas, Cézanne, Pissarro, and Sisley. Berthe Morisot, one of the three brilliant women who were amongst the earliest disciples of I.—the two others being Eva Gonzales and Mary Cassatt—used to say that 'before one of Monet's pictures, I always know which way to incline my umbrella.'

Two types of I. have so far been discussed—the realism of Courbet ad Manet, and the chromatism of Monet. With it we must also associate the visionaries, or spiritualists — Gustave Moreau for his symbolism, Puvis de Chavannes for his fine decorative treatment, and Carrière for psychic insight. The last named, like Whistler, Harrison, and Pointillin, belongs to a distinct school, whose technique differed from that of Monet in so far as, instead of employing the principle of juxtaposition of pure colour, they applied flat tints in a broad style, using not only the pure, radiant prismatic colours, but also palette mixtures. It remains only to refer to the method known as 'Pointillism,' whereby the colour is transferred to the canvas in spots instead of in mass, as in the case of the chromatists already discussed. The inception of this method, which is associated rather with the Neo-I. of which Ganguin, Denis, and Van Rysselberghe are the leaders, is attributed to M. Henry, who conceived the æsthetic expression of the newly discovered scientific theories on colour-waves and spectral analysis in the works of Helmholtz and Chevreul about 1880. The idea concerned itself especially with complementary colours and the reaction of tones. Its chief practical application is ascribed to Geo. Seurat, who incidentally stated that the principle was employed by Delacroix theoretically although not practically—the grounds for such an assertion are weak—but it is probable that the theory owes more of its development to Signac, whose landscapes are for the most part elaborate studies the new method. Van Gogh has also used this technique, and Van Rysselberghe employs it constantly. There are also some efforts from the brush of Pissarro, who, however, soon discarded the manner. The gifted mystic Henri Martin is pre-eminently a Pointillist, whilst Denis, Angrand, and Henri-Edmond Cross might also be mentioned. But the method is obviously alien to the spirit of art; it is charmless, devoid of character, too purely theoretical and removed from inspiration. Whatever there may be in the generous claims made for it as a means of mural decorative work, *e.g.* ceilings, friezes, etc., it certainly leaves much to be desired as a medium for easel work.

Although I. is scientific rather than artistic, in the accepted sense of the words, it does not smell of the lamp. It is a boast of the impressionists that they worship character rather than beauty or æsthetic idealism. As such, the appreciation of I. does not demand genius or culture, but rather temperament, the sense of *joie-de-vivre.* ' The principal object in any picture,' it was once said, ' is the Light.' Many painters of the school are guilty of making it the *only* object, and no amount of eagerness to explore new technique, however perfect its promise, can excuse the bald vulgarity of the subjects which, it must be conceded, have too often been chosen for experiment. But the future possibilities of chromatism, which it is safe to assume have only been suggested so far, promise a new and glorious lease of life for art.

The first success of I. was the exhibition of Manet in 1884, consisting of some forty pictures—less than ten years after the first public sale, when such frantic hostility was shown that it was necessary to organise police precautions! In 1897 the collection of Caillebotte, a wealthy amateur who had befriended I. from the onset and had even gained some small notoriety for his own work, was accepted with reluctance, and after considerable hesitation, by the Ministry of Fine Arts and exhibited in the Luxembourg. The same year at the Vever sale, and two years later at the Choquet sale, the once despised canvasses changed hands for enormous sums. Manet's portrait of Monet in his studio, for instance, which realised about 150 francs in 1884, went for 10,000 francs. And at the last important impressionist sale, the Pellerin, Paris, 1910, even greater prices were offered. For a general outline of I., consult Camille Mauclair's *French Impressionists* (Duckworth's Pop. Library of Art); Wynford Dew-

hurst's ' What is Impressionism ? ' (*Contemp. Review*, March 1911); and *Impressionist Painting* (Newnes, 1904). An excellent bibliography is given in this last-named volume.

Impressment, the act of forcibly taking persons or goods for the public service ; but generally restricted to the work of press-gangs in compelling persons to serve as soldiers or sailors in time of war. I. of sailors differed from that of soldiers. I. of sailors was regarded as a prerogative right of the crown, given by the common law and recognised by statute. This is explained by constitutional historians by the fact that the feudal tenure of land made provision for land but not for sea service. I. of soldiers was declared illegal by the Long Parliament of 1641, but was occasionally resorted to subsequently, *e.g.* during the American Civil War, under special parliamentary authority. I. of soldiers is to be distinguished from *conscription*, which although also a state-regulated method of compulsory enlistment, applies to all able-bodied persons alike. Probably no attempt to revive the degrading practices of naval press-gangs would now be made, although theoretically the crown still retains its prerogative. It may be observed here that during the Boer War of 1900 the I. of goods was commonly known by the term ' commandeering.'

Imprisonment, *see* PRISONS.

Impropriation, the grant of a benefice or parsonage to a layman or lay corporation as opposed to ' appropriation,' or the ' annexing of a benefice to the proper and perpetual use of some religious body politic.' The terms have, however, been used synonymously both by text writers and in statutes. Both terms imply the endowment of vicarages consequent on the rise of parish churches by the consent of the bishop who alone had the care of souls in his diocese, together with the title to all ecclesiastical revenues. But as the practices of appropriation and I. originally prevailed, there was an essential difference ; for a layman, not having care of souls, applied the temporalities of the benefice to his own use. Before the Reformation, appropriation and I. prevailed extensively, the monasteries furnishing the most numerous examples of the religious corporations that obtained grants of benefices. After the suppression of monasteries the crown was vested with all such rights as related to the grant of benefices ; but the crown freely transferred its rights to laymen. In practice the spiritual duties of rectories, the tithes or whole property of which have descended to laymen, are always discharged by a vicar (Lat. *vicarius*, delegated), who receives a certain portion of the emoluments of the living (*see* GLEBE). *See* Phillemore's *Ecclesiastical Law;* Blackstone's *Comments.*

Improvisatori, or Improvisation, the art of composing verses, whether accompanied to music or not, on the spot without preparation, and on subjects suddenly proposed, is distinctly Italian in origin, though the Provençal troubadours, in spite of the elaborate versification of their poems, are credited with the power. Silvio Antonio (1540-1603) was made a cardinal through his power of composing verses on any subject; Perfetti (1681-1747), to the accompaniment of a guitar, astonished the whole of Italy by his skill. He was crowned with laurel by Pope Benedict XIII. Corilla Olimpica, Madame de Staël's Corinne, was also crowned. Outside Italy, the Swedish poet, K. M. Bellman (1740-95), the French Joseph Méry (1798-1865), and the English humorist Theodore Hook (1788-1891) may be mentioned. Many of the great musicians and instrumentalists have exhibited their power of improvisation.

Imputation, the attribution to another of some quality or character, especially of a charge of guilt. The term is used technically in theology of the attribution to all faithful believers in Christ of His righteousness, by vicarious substitution, of man's sin to Him, and of Adam's sin and its consequences to all mankind as Adam's descendants. The term thus plays a part in the doctrines of original sin, of predestination, and especially of the orthodox view of the Atonement (*q.v.*).

Ina, or Ine, king of the W. Saxons, or Wessex, succeeded Ceadwalla in 688. He forced compensation for the death of Ceadwalla's brother from Kent in 694, conquered Geraint of W. Wales in 710, and fought in Wiltshire against the Mercians, and in 725 crushed a revolt of the S. Saxons. He drew up a still extant code of laws for Wessex, and abdicated in 726, and retired to Rome where he died, the date not being known. He is said to have built Glastonbury.

Inaccessible Islands, *see* TRISTAN DA CUNHA.

Inagua, Great and **Little,** two islands in the archipelago of the Bahamas in the British W. Indies, situated at the southern end of the group. Great Inagua has an area of 530 sq. m. and contains salt ponds. Pop. 1453.

In Articulo Mortis (literally, at the point of death). In Roman theology the absolution of penitents is competent only to confessors of the regular orders of priesthood who have obtained episcopal approval, and to secular priests who have acquired jurisdiction from their bishops. But a simple priest even if degraded or apostate may extend absolution to a penitent *in articulo mortis* in all cases, including those of grievous sins, which are ordinarily reserved for absolution by some ecclesiastical superior, like the ordinary of a diocese. As to the admissibility in evidence of the declaration of a deceased person relative to the cause of his death, *see under* DECLARATIONS OF DECEASED PERSONS.

Inca, a tn. in the Balearic Islands in the Mediterranean, 17 m. E.N.E. of Palma, Majorca, belonging to Spain. Oil, wine, and almonds are its chief products, and it gives its name to one of the five judicial districts into which the islands are divided for the purpose of administration. Pop. 7579.

Incandescence, the term applied to the state bodies are in when they give out light through being highly heated and yet are not undergoing chemical change. It is usually associated with solids, although the oxy-hydrogen flame is an example of its appearance in gases. *See* GAS LIGHTING, and ELECTRIC LAMPS.

Incandescent Light is produced when a 'mantle,' consisting of a conical hollow gauze of certain metallic oxides, is placed in a hot but non-luminous flame produced by a burner of the Bunsen type. In fact, all practical methods of illumination depend on the incandescence of solid bodies (particles of carbon in the case of candle and gas flames; the filament in the case of electric light), heated either by chemical action or by electricity. In the case of candle and gas lighting, the proportion of energy evolved as light is but a small fraction of that given out as heat. Welsbach was the first to improve this ratio, by substituting certain metallic oxides for the carbon as the incandescent body. The 'mantle' is made by impregnating a cotton or ramie 'stocking,' with a solution of various salts, the usual mixture being 99 parts thorium nitrate and 1 part cerium nitrate. On ignition a skeleton of the oxides of the metals remains, giving out a brilliant light by virtue of its incandescence. Mantles are also made for use in an inverted position, and with gas under greater pressure.

Incantation (Lat. *incantatio*, from *incantare*, to enchant; from *in* + *cantare*, to sing repeatedly), the use of a set form of words, spoken or sung, to produce a magical and super-natural effect. The use of the word *incantare* in Latin is very early, for it appears in a passage quoted by Pliny from the Twelve Tables, and from it is derived, through the French, our word ' enchant.' It is almost certain that the use of magic spells must be traced to an Akkadian source, for many ancient examples of Baby-lonian and Assyrian formulæ have been discovered. An interesting side-light on the important position which the Magi or magicians, generally Chaldæans, held at an Eastern court, is given in the Book of Daniel. Ulti-mately we are told that Daniel him-self became their head. An almost unbounded power was given in ancient times to the power of magic rimes, to which the gods and the powers of nature were believed to be subject. Many of these could be used by any individual, but others were the property of the priest or magician, whose influence was due to his sup-posed power for good or evil. In Christian times, the use of enchant-ments has by no means ceased, even in the countries commonly named Christian. It can easily be traced through the centuries. In the middle ages the sacred ceremonies and rites of the church were often conceived of by the ignorant as charms. An allu-sion to the use of the first fourteen verses of St. John's Gospel as a kind of incantation is given in Chaucer's *Prologue* in the lines on the Friar beginning ' So plesaunte was his *In Principio*.' Many of the old nursery rhymes now dying out were formerly used as incantations against rain, and the powers of nature, *See* Lenor-mant's *Chaldean Magic* (translated 1878). Maury's *La Magic et l'astro-logie* (4th ed.), 1877; Frazer's *Golden Bough* (enlarged ed.), 1900.

Incarnation (from Lat. *incarnari*, to be made flesh ; from *in*+*caro*, flesh), in Christian theology, the act by which the Second Person of the Blessed Trinity assumed human form and human nature. In many other religions, and especially in those of India, are there accounts of the tak-ing of human flesh by the gods in order to secure a fuller revelation to the world, but these differ essentially from the orthodox Christian belief in the I. of Jesus Christ, which lays stress on the fact that the Logos, eternally divine, then became also essentially human, so that Christ was ' perfect God and perfect Man ; one not by conversion of the Godhead into flesh, but by taking of the man-hood into God.' *See* Wilberforce's *Doctrine of the Incarnation*, 1882 ; Orr's *Christian View of God and the World*, 1893 ; Gore's Bampton

Lecture, 1891 ; Eck's *Incarnation*, 1902.

Incarvillea, a genus of Bignoniaceæ, which flourishes in Asia. There are only five species, and all are plants with alternate leaves and bright-coloured flowers. *I. sinensis* is culti-vated in British conservatories, and bears scarlet flowers.

Ince-in-Makerfield, a tn. and urban dist., Lancashire, England, in parl. div. of Ince. It stands on the Leeds and Liverpool Canal, 1 m. S.E. of Wigan. It has collieries, iron, and waggon works, cotton mills, etc. Old Hall is a fine specimen of half-timbered work. Pop. (1911) 22,038.

Incendiarism, *see* ARSON.

Incense (Lat. *incensum*, from *in-cendere*, to burn), a perfume arising from the fumigation of resins, gums, balsams, etc., used in public worship from a very early date, and prevailing in many ancient religions. There is no regular formula for the preparation, but the ingredients, after having been well mingled, are placed in the censer or thurible and sprinkled over the hot charcoal contained therein, when they at once become volatilised, and diffuse their odour through the edifice. In the Catholic Church, I. is chiefly used in the eucharistic service, being regarded as a sacrifice. In the last half century its use was abolished in the Reformed churches, but has been restored to a certain extent in the Anglican communion. Writers are not agreed as to the exact date at which the use of I. was introduced, but it was not generally adopted till the 6th century, in the time of Gregory the Great.

Incest, sexual intercourse between persons prohibited from marrying, by reason of kinship or affinity. For-merly I. was not a crime by English law, except in so far as the spiritual courts took cognisance of the offence. But by the Incest Act, 1908, inter-course by a male with his grand-daughter, daughter, sister, or mother, is a misdemeanour, punishable with penal servitude. Consent of the female is no defence, and a consenting female is liable to the same punish-ment. ' Brother ' and ' sister ' as used in the Act include half-brother and half-sister. No prosecution may take place without the sanction of the Attorney-General. The Act does not extend to Scotland, because I. was already a crime in Scots law. Al-though marriage with a deceased wife's sister is now lawful (*see* DE-CEASED WIFE'S SISTER) intercourse with a wife's sister will enable a wife to obtain a divorce on the ground of incestuous adultery. In primitive tribes the prohibition of consangui-nial marriages is a slow development.

Mr. Frazer, in dealing with totemism, in relation to exogamy, is too prone to dogmatising on the origin of the aversion to incestuous unions. Whether that aversion sprang from religious or merely ethical sentiments, or from a perception of disastrous effects on racial developments, is a question the answer to which depends mainly on conjecture. (For an exhaustive discussion, see Herbert Spencer on 'Punaluan Groups,' in the *Principles of Sociology;* Frazer, *Totemism;* and Morgan, *Ancient Society*). That inquiry into the evolution of thought on the subject of I. is fraught with difficulty, seems almost to follow from the extraordinary mythology of the ancient Greeks. That the Greek gods could be so strangely associated with I. argues a mode of thought to which moderns have apparently lost the key, and doubtless justifies Mr. H. G. Wells' satirical comments on the typical English classical education, which lays so much store by a mythology replete with traditions of 'unaccountable Incests' (*Tono Bungay*).

Inch, from the Gaelic word *innis,* meaning a small island, or a land by a river, found in the geographical names of Scotland and Ireland. It is also used locally of a meadow by a river as the 'Inches of Perth,' and sometimes in the sense of rising ground in the midst of a plain.

Inchbald, Elizabeth (*née* Simpson) (1753-1821), married, at the age of nineteen, Joseph Inchbald, an actor. She now was able to fulfil her desire and go on the stage. She made her début in the provinces, as Cordelia to her husband's *Lear*. Until her husband's death in 1779, they toured the country, but then she secured an engagement in London, where she remained until her retirement in 1789. She never achieved any great fame as an actress. Mrs. Inchbald began writing plays at an early age, but the first piece that was produced was *The Mogul Tale*, at the Haymarket in 1784. In all she wrote, or adapted, some twenty plays, but none met with any great success. Better known than these is her romance *A Simple Tale* (1791), which attracted much attention, and is her best work. In 1806 she began to edit *The British Theatre*, in twenty-five volumes, and this is a collection of considerable value to students of the drama. There is a biography by James Boaden, 1833.

Inchcape Rock, see BELL ROCK.

Inchcolm, or **Island of Columba,** an island in the Firth of Forth, forming part of the parish of Aberdour, Fifeshire, Scotland. It contains a fine Augustinian monastery founded in 1123 by Alexander I.; the church, chapter house, refectory, cloisters, and a square tower being still preserved. There is also an ancient stoneroofed oratory, supposed to have been a hermit's cell. From the island the earls of Murray take their title of Lord St. Colme (1611).

Inchgarvie, a rocky islet in the Firth of Forth off the coast of Fifeshire, Scotland. It possessed at one time a fine old castle that was used as a state prison, but the ruins were cleared in order to build one of the piers of the Forth Bridge. It is in the royal burgh of Inverkeithing.

Inchkeith, an island in the Firth of Forth, forming part of the parish of Kinghorn in Fifeshire, Scotland. It is a barren rock and has now become government property on which a fine lighthouse has been built, which can be seen for a distance of 21 m. Henry VIII. fortified it after the battle of Pinkie, but in 1549 it was recaptured by the Scottish and French troops. In 1881 forts were built on the different headlands and linked up by military roads. St. Adamnan was the founder of a monastery on the island in 700.

Inchmahome (' the Isle of Rest '), an island in the Lake of Menteith, in Perthshire, Scotland. It contains the ruins of an Early English Augustinian priory built in 1238 by Walter Comyn, and possessing a very fine W. doorway. Queen Mary is said to have spent some months on the island when a child before going to France (1548).

Incidence, Angle of, is a term used for the angle made by the direction of a disturbance infringing on the surface of a medium with the normal to the surface.

Incledon, Charles Benjamin (1763-1826), an English tenor, born in Cornwall, was a choir boy, and then entered the navy. In 1783 he took up singing professionally, and appeared with great success at Covent Garden, 1790; ranking as the first tenor of his day. Though successful in opera and oratorio his greatest popularity was achieved by his ballad singing, as in *Sally in our Alley,* the *Arethusa, Black-eyed Susan,* etc. He made one of the earliest tours in America, 1827.

Inclination of one line to another, which meets it, but is not in the same straight line, is Euclid's definition of an angle.

Inclination, see DIP OF THE MAGNETIC NEEDLE.

Inclined Plane, a rigid plane inclined at an angle to the horizon. It is a mechanical instrument used to facilitate the lifting of heavy bodies. In the case of an incline of 1 in 6, a power of 1 lb. will support a weight of 6 lbs., thus giving a mechanical advantage of 6.

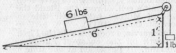

INCLINED PLANE

Inclosures, *see* COMMONS AND ENCLOSURES.

In Cœna Domini, a papal bull, the commencing words of which were ' In Cœna Domini,' formerly issued every year in Holy Week. Its object was to publish the papal censure of all heresies, schisms, and infractions of papal privileges, and various temporal crimes. It was first published in 1363, and was only discontinued in 1770, when the pope yielded to the opposition of European kings who objected to the bull as a limitation of their sovereign authority.

Income Tax, a tax on income from whatsoever source derived, graduated according to the amount of income and with a differentiation in certain cases between earned and unearned income. The I. T. as a general tax on property and employments was first imposed by Pitt in 1799 as a war tax. It was a temporary imposition on income from land, personal property, trades, professions, offices, pensions, stipends, and employments, and also upon incomes arising out of Great Britain, and was graduated on all incomes ranging from £60 to £200 a year, with a tax of 10 per cent. on incomes above £200. When the war with France broke out again in 1803, Addington re-imposed the tax at the rate of 5 per cent. on incomes of £150 a year and over. But the Income Tax Act of 1803 did not require a general return of income from all sources, as had the Act of 1799, but only particular returns of income from particular sources. In 1805 Pitt, having returned to power, continued the tax, and added one-fourth to all the rates. The coalition ministry after the death of Pitt augmented the rate to 10 per cent., and from that year the tax was continued and increased from time to time, until its abrogation in 1815. Even in these earlier Acts there was some principle of differentiation, *e.g.* in the Act of 1806 the exemption of incomes not over £50 was only allowed where the income was derived from labour, viz. from professions, trades, and offices. The principle of exemption by way of allowance for children was adopted in the earliest

Act, but discontinued in 1806. In the first year of its imposition the I. T. produced over £6,000,000; in 1815 £14,320,000. Regarded at first and even now in theory, as essentially a war tax, it was not revived again till Peel, for merely fiscal purposes, in 1842, imposed it at the rate of 7d. in the pound, or about 3 per cent., adopting in his Act the groundwork of the Act of 1806. But the limit of exemption rose to £150 and was made irrespective of the mode of derivation. Farmers were taxed on a lower estimate of their profits, and gasworks and railway companies were brought in. Although in 1842 it was imposed for three years only it has been continued ever since, and has now definitely lost all semblance of a temporary war tax. Mr. Gladstone in 1853 extended its operation to Ireland, and so made it universal in the kingdom. Numerous changes in detail have been effected from time to time by way of extension of limits of exemption and abatement, allowances for various purposes, such as deductions for repairs by landlords and in the requirements as to filling up returns. But the principal change was the democratic one of granting relief in respect of ' earned income ' up to £2000, and imposing a super-tax on incomes over £5000.

The provisions relating to the rate, collection, and assessment of the I. T. immediately prior to the changes introduced by the Finance Act of 1909 will be conducive to a clearer appreciation of those changes, and may be summarised. For the most part, of course, the provisions as to administration and incidence have undergone no alteration. It was divided into five schedules according to the different sources of income. Schedule A formed the charge on the owners of land and houses; B on the benefit arising out of the use or occupation of land, which benefit was measured by a proportion of the rent or annual value; C related to income from any public revenue, imperial, colonial or foreign; D, income from professions, trades, and other occupations, together with all such incomes as were not included in any of the other schedules; and E was a charge on persons employed by the state, or engaged in any other office of profit in a public corporation or company. Incomes not exceeding £160 were totally exempt; real property exempt included public parks and recreation grounds, prisons, public offices, or other crown property, and canals, mines, quarries, etc., from which no income or benefit is derived, beyond the general profits of the concern to which they belong. Other exemptions were incomes from property held on trust for charitable purposes in so far as applied to such purposes; the stock dividends or other income of friendly societies (q.v.), and of industrial and provident societies (see under FRIENDLY SOCIETIES). Incomes of individuals not exceeding £400 were allowed an abatement of £160; not exceeding £500, of £150; not exceeding £600, of £120; and not exceeding £700, of £70. An abatement for premiums for life assurance, not exceeding one-sixth of the income was also allowed. The relief to ' earned ' incomes was a reduction of 3d. in the pound upon the rate paid on unearned incomes. The general rate was 1s. in the pound, and 9d. in the case of earned incomes not exceeding £2000. The tax was granted for a year only (but, of course, annually renewed). tThe assessment and collection of the tax was entrusted for the most part to local commissioners, known as general or district commissioners, appointed by the Land Tax Commissioners out of their own body, and not in any way subject to the control of the government. These commissioners received no remuneration, although exempted from parochial offices and jury service. Their duties consist in signing and allowing I. T. assessments, and hearing appeals. They also appoint local officers for I. T. purposes. There are also special salaried commissioners appointed by the crown to make assessments under schedule C, and where the tax-payer elects, under Schedule D, also to assess railway companies and dividends out of foreign and colonial stocks, funds or other revenues. Special commissioners may hear appeals from their own or the assessments of local commissioners. The assessment of the salaries under Schedule E are made by the commmissioners for public offices. The local officials are the clerks to the local or general commissioners, who are paid by poundage on the assessments, and who being generally solicitors act as legal advisers to the commissioners; the assessors for each parish, and parochial collectors. The assessors' chief duties are to serve forms on tax-payers and enter particulars of the value of the property to be taxed after the tax-payers send back their forms filled in. Where the assessors object to the tax-payers estimate, they may put their own valuation on the property, subject to the owner's right of appeal. The duty of a collector is to obtain payment of the I. T. from the persons on whom it is imposed, and for this purpose he is supplied with warrants to enforce payment. As indicated above most of these provisions are re-enacted annually, and to ensure collections in due time, these provisions and all enactments relating to I. T. not specifically repealed, have full force as soon as the tax is granted in any Finance Act (see Section 18 (2) of the Finance Act, 1907). A Select Committee was appointed in 1906 to inquire into and report on the question of graduating the I. T., and differentiating between permanent and precarious incomes. The committee recommended a partial graduation by an extension of the existing system of abatements, even up to incomes of £1000 or more. They also recommended graduation by a super-tax, and a differentiation between earned and unearned incomes to be limited to incomes not exceeding £3000 a year. Some of these recommendations found expresson in the Finance Act, 1909-10. One shilling remains the rate on incomes between £2000 and £3000, and 9d. on incomes below £2000. But the rate on all unearned incomes and on the earned portions of incomes exceeding £2000 from all sources was raised to 1s. 2d. A supertax of 6d. in the pound was imposed on persons whose incomes exceeded £5000, the first £3000 not to be charged with such tax. To obtain relief in respect of earned income a person must put in a claim before Sept. 30, in the financial year ending April 5, for which the tax is charged. Persons whose total incomes do not exceed £500 may claim an abatement of £10 for each child under sixteen years of age. The other exemptions and abatements remain as before 1909. Where the total income of a husband and wife does not exceed £500, and the husband is assessable under Schedule D, on an income in no way connected with the wife's business, the wife can separate her claim for exemption or abatement from that of her husband, on account of the profits of her business produced by her own personal labour. The owners of lands and houses (provided the annual value of the house does not exceed £8) may claim an abatement not exceeding one-eighth of the annual value of the land, or one-twelfth of the house or houses, for the average cost of maintenance, repairs, insurance and managements; the average generally being taken for the five years preceding the date of assessment.

The table in the Fifty-Fifth Report of the Inland Revenue Commissioners shows a curious irregularity in the net receipts from I. T. For the eleven financial years from 1901-2 to 1911-12 the total receipts for the United Kingdom were as follows:—

1901-2	.	£35,378,700
1902-3	.	38,659,846
1903-4	.	30,500,450
1904-5	.	31,263,654
1905-6	.	31,294,752
1906-7	.	31,891,949
1907-8	.	31,860,380
1908-9	.	33,708,541
1909-10	.	12,752,098
1910-11	.	60,505,094
1911-12	.	41,315,655

The low figures for 1909-10 were due to delay in passing the now historic Finance Bill of that year, and the figures for the ensuing year really include a large part of the over-due tax of the previous year, and further, £500,000 for super-tax was included in the returns for 1909-1910, and the commissioners state that it is not possible to furnish complete statistics for any year in regard to the super-tax because they continue to receive returns for 1909-10, 1910-11, and 1911-12. The yield for 1909-10 was up to the time of their report £2,575,000.

The fiscal systems of most other countries, except France and Hungary, provide for some form of I. T. In Germany the income is classified for the purpose of taxation into four sources: (1) Capital; (2) land; (3) trade and industry; and (4) employment for gain. The limit for exemption is £150 a year. There is a graduated I. T. in Italy dating from 1864, but income derived from land is not subject to I. T. In Spain the primary classification of incomes is into those derived from personal exertion, and those from property with a graduation according to the nature of the employment. In most countries where income derived from capital is made a fundamental head of classification, the rate of the tax is higher than for incomes derived from other sources. In Austria the I. T. imposed on net income is in a graduated percentage from 0·6 per cent. of an income of £52 up to 4 per cent. on £4000, with a further complicated progression on incomes above that amount. The endeavour to impose an I. T. in the United States has in the past met with fluctuating success. As in England it began as a war tax when it was imposed by the Federal Government after the Civil War. It was not abrogated till 1872, but when revived in 1895 the courts declared it to be unconstitutional, with the result that the constitution had to be amended to vest in Congress the necessary authority to impose the tax, and the amendment is now before the states legislatures for their consideration.

But in Massachusetts, and in a few other states, an I. T. is levied for local purposes on all professional incomes over £400, and in Pennsylvania on a few particular businesses.

Bibliography.—*Annual Reports of the Commissioners of Inland Revenue* ; Palgrave, *Dictionary of Political Economy;* Ely's *Taxation in American States and Cities ;* Dowell's *Income Tax Laws,* and *History of Taxation in England ;* Robinson, *The Law relating to Income Tax.*

Incommensurable, *see* COMMENSURABLE.

Inconvertible Paper Currency. Where notes or other recognised instruments for the payment of money are not convertible into money on demand, such paper currency is said to be inconvertible. England enjoys a convertible paper currency, and by English law the Bank of England must always pay gold on demand for its notes, and a private bank must always give gold or Bank of England notes, on demand, in exchange for its own notes.

Incorporated Law Society, a society of solicitors established in 1825 to exercise a general control over the interests of solicitors. Any solicitor practising in Great Britain, or who has ceased to practise, is elegible for membership. The present membership is upwards of 9000. The society is composed of a president and vice-president annually elected, and an elective council of forty ordinary and ten extraordinary members. The society examines students for all the solicitors' examinations, and makes arrangements for lectures. It is authorised by statute to inquire into all cases of alleged misconduct on the part of solicitors, and to report the result of its inquiry to the High Court; the High Court may in its discretion either strike the name of the offending solicitor off the rolls or suspend him from practice. In cases of suspected criminal offences by solicitors the society may report to the Public Prosecutor. The society has a building in Chancery Lane, London, and a splendid library.

Incorporated Society of Authors, The, *see* AUTHORS, THE INCORPORATED SOCIETY OF.

Incorporeal Chattels and Hereditaments. Incorporeal chattels are the rights or interests incident to personal property, *e.g.* copyrights, patent rights, annuities, debts, cash at a bank, government stocks, debentures of companies. Such property is said to be incorporeal because it has only a notional existence as opposed to corporeal chattels, or those having a physical existence. Incorporeal hereditaments are rights over or in connection with the enjoyment of land, as opposed to the right of immediate or future possession of the land itself, *e.g.* rights of way, advowsons (right of presentation to a vacant living), rents, commonable rights (*see* COMMON, RIGHTS OF). Formerly the term incorporeal hereditament included future estates or interests in land or the right to the future possession by way of reversion, or remainder (*see* ESTATE, GRANT); such incorporeal hereditaments were said to ' lie in grant ' (by deed) while corporeal lay in livery, *i.e.* transfer of possession was necessary effectually to pass them to another. As both incorporeal chattels and hereditaments now pass by deed, the distinction between them has no practical importance.

Increment, Unearned (and **Decrement**). The Finance Act, 1909, introduced the novel principle of taxing the increased site value of land where such accretion of value can be said in any case to have been due to some cause not specially connected with, or referable to the merits of the owner, such as the general progress in wealth of the community. The I. value duty is at the rate of £1 for every £5 of I. value accruing after April 30, 1909, and is levied on certain occasions (noticed below) upon the amount, if any, by which the site value of the land on the occasion on which the duty is to be collected, exceeds the original site value of the land as ascertained in accordance with the general provisions of the Act as to valuation. The original assessable site value or starting-point as on April 30, 1909, is fixed by the general valuation to be made under the Act, which valuation appears to be the estimated market price of the freehold (if sold free from any mortgage charges, and subject to such fixed payments as rent, rates, tithe, taxes, and such burdens as easements and restrictive covenants), minus certain deductions representing the value of the buildings, cost of capital expenditure on improvements, and the increment in site value *by reason of the presence of the buildings upon the land*. The difference thus given is the basis upon which the owner is to be taxed, and the four occasions on which the duty is leviable are : (1) Sale of any interest in the land; (2) Passing of any interest on death; (3) Grant of a lease for a term exceeding fourteen years; (4) At fixed periods in respect of land held by a body corporate or unincorporate. Agricultural land is exempt so long as it has no higher value than its market value for purely agricultural purposes. Small houses and properties in the occupation of the owner, lands used for games and recreation, flats, and crown lands, are also exempt. The Act gives no right to claim the refunding of duty on subsequent occasions when the land may have decreased in value by analogy, *e.g.* to the compensation payable under the Lands Clauses Act, 1845, in respect of land ' injuriously affected ' by the execution of works under statutory powers. *See* Casson and Ridgway's *Housing, Town Planning, etc., Act,* 1909 (3rd ed., 1912).

Incubation and **Incubators** (from Lat. *incubare,* to brood; *incumbere,* to lie on or within). I. is strictly the action of a bird in sitting on her eggs to hatch them, but the term is also used of the development of the germs of disease, within the body, and especially in connection with the artificial machines ('fostermothers,' or ' incubators '), employed in hatching eggs artificially, or for similar purposes in bacteriological laboratories. In nature, incubation is often the task of the female only, but sometimes the male takes his share, as in the case of ostriches, and most passerine and running birds. In other cases, again, the eggs are laid among rotting vegetation, the high temperature thus afforded making brooding unnecessary. The period of incubation varies considerably in length, from three weeks with ravens and common fowls, to six or seven with swans and ostriches, and two weeks or less with swallows. The habit of brooding over their young is not infrequently found in other creatures as well as in birds, for example, in earwigs, centipedes (*Scolopendra*), and pythons. Two of the chief factors in maintaining the spark of life are heat and moisture, and therefore provision must be made first and foremost for these essentials. Artificial incubation was known from the earliest times, and practised among the Chinese and Egyptians by means of huge egg-ovens, types of which are in use by primitive people to the present day. The two main classes of incubator are those in which hot air is used for keeping up a uniform high temperature, and those in which hot water secures the same end. Of the hot-air incubators, one of the best known is enclosed in a double-walled metal case, the space between the walls being packed with a non-conducting material. The egg-chamber is warmed by a circular heating-box, itself heated by a lamp. There are flues for the passage of the hot air, and tubular channels by which fresh air enters. The heat is regulated by an apparatus, and the necessary moisture obtained by the evaporation of water in a vessel. Among the earliest recorded types of hot-water incubators are Brindley's (1845), which never became generally used ; Colonel Stuart Wortley's (1866) ; and Mr. Thomas Christy's, which has passed through several forms. The most recent (1894) is double-walled, with non-conducting material between the walls. The hot-water tank, consisting of two chambers, is above the incubation drawer containing the eggs. A ventilating shaft passes through the tank, and under the perforated bottom of the drawer is an enclosed air-space, while fresh air can be let into the drawer from a few apertures at its top. The ventilating shaft can be regulated, and the water in the tank is heated by an external boiler, the particular form of which ensures a continual circulation of water. The next improved form was that of Mr. Charles Hearson (1880), which had a new type of thermostatic capsule, ensuring better regulation of the heat than the hot-water system, and which was also simpler, as it needed no boiler. The principle underlying the design of this capsule is that the boiling-point of a liquid depends, not only upon temperature, but also upon pressure. A fluid was compounded which would boil at 100° F., and enclosed in an air-tight capsule with flexible sides. These sides expanded when the temperature of the air round the capsule had reached 100°, and this expansion raised a lever and set working the apparatus for allowing the escape of the heat, generated by a lamp or gas-jet. A sliding weight also helped to keep up a regular temperature. This system works admirably, and the incubator requires no adjustment for months at a time in spite of the variations of our climate. Modern improvements have led to a large variety of forms being introduced. They aim at simplifying the process to the greatest possible extent and making it more dependable while saving labour by such devices as mechanical egg-turners, automatic lamp - fillers, etc. All these well - known, up - to - date incubators are of relatively small size, and can take only a strictly limited number of eggs. The size will probably greatly increase in the future for commercial purposes, and may contain as many as 30,000 eggs at a time. The mammoth incubators, as these large structures are called, are well advanced in the experimental stage, and an interesting possibility is that they may be used co-operatively by a number of poultry traders, especially in a district of smallholders. Subject to the efficient control in them of temperature and ventilation,

the cost of working, both as regards fuel and labour, is reduced to a minimum, and one experienced man would be likely to have considerably better results if his whole time were given to the charge of the incubators than would a number of busy men or women of less experience. Artificial incubation has the following advantages over the natural process : (1) A much larger number of eggs are able to be successfully hatched ; (2) The chickens are free from vermin ; (3) They are free from the danger of being trodden to death by the hen. On the other hand, eggs that have had to be kept some little while and are not quite fresh, always hatch better under the hen, whose bodily warmth seems to exert some favourable influence on the germ that artificial methods fail to supply. Loss of chickens, through their inability to escape from the shell, is sometimes very heavy in incubators. For a single sitting or two of eggs the broody hen is naturally more convenient. Game-keepers use incubators largely for rearing pheasants, and, of course, on large poultry-farms they are indispensable. Various forms of foster-mothers, artificially warmed by lamps or hot water, have also been contrived in which the chickens can be successfully reared after they are hatched. In due course they are moved to cold brooders, and finally to poultry-houses. Young chicks are capable of picking up food as soon as they require nourishment, and specially prepared foods can be easily introduced.

Bacteriological incubators differ from those for birds in that the heating surface generally surrounds all sides of the incubation chamber, and there is usually no special apparatus for keeping the air moist. There are various forms, some heated by warm water, others by warm air. They are mostly square or rectangular in shape but some bacteriologists prefer cylindrical forms. One of the best known cylindrical types is that of Dr. d'Arsonval ; and among the square forms the best are Dr. Hüppe's and Hearson's.

Human incubators have also been designed for rearing children, too weak to survive under ordinary conditions. The first was that of Dr. Tarnier (1880), used in Paris, and an improvement was made in Hearson's, which is used at various hospitals and workhouses throughout Great Britain.

See T. Christy, jun., *Hydro-Incubation;* L. Wright, *The Book of Poultry;* J. H. Sutcliffe, *Incubators and their Management;* H. H. Stoddard, *The New Egg Farm.* For bacteriological incubators, *see* catalogues of Hearson of London; Camb. Scientific Instrument Co., Cambridge, and P. Lequex, Paris.

Incumbent (Lat. *incumbo*, I bend or lean), a word which is said variously to signify 'diligent residence,' or 'assiduous application to duties.' In ecclesiastical law it includes such rectors, vicars, and perpetual curates as have been duly instituted in their offices. Every I., or holder of a parochial benefice, has care of souls in his own parish (*see* IMPROPRIATION), and it is a spiritual offence for any other clergyman to preach, read prayers, or otherwise officiate in the parish of another I., without authorisation of the diocesan bishop. An I. is *ex officio*, chairman of the vestry, and upon him devolves the duty of keeping the local register of marriages, baptisms, and burials. Two Is. may in certain circumstances effect an exchange of livings (*see also* GLEBE, as to extending poor livings) by deed. An I. may be deprived of his living for illiteracy, minority, sermoniacal offences (trafficking in benefices), lack of holy orders, conviction for felony, and other crimes, and such spiritual offences as affirming doctrines contrary to the Thirty-nine Articles, heresy, schism, and demanding payment for administering a sacrament. An I. may resign by application to the ordinary, but a resignation is invalid unless assented to by the bishop.

Incunabula, the term used for books printed before the year 1500. *See* A. J. Bernard, *De l'origine et des debuts de l'imprimerie en Europe*, 1853.

Indecency. Indecent exposure of the person in public is a common law misdemeanour, punishable by fine or imprisonment with hard labour or both, whether there be an intention to violate the canons of decency or not. The public exhibition of obscene writings, pictures, or photographs, is punishable by fine and imprisonment, and magistrates have power to issue search warrants for the seizure and destruction of obscene books or pictures, in places where such articles are suspected to be sold or dealt with for profit. Advertisements dealing with venereal diseases also come within the Acts prohibiting the exhibition of indecent writings or prints, and are punishable on summary conviction with one month's imprisonment or a fine of 40s. Sending indecent prints, books, etc., through the post, is punishable either on indictment with twelve months imprisonment with hard labour, or summarily by a fine of £10. An indecent assault upon any female is punishable by imprisonment not exceeding two years, under the Of-

fences against the Person Act, 1861. Sodomy or bestiality is a felony punishable by penal servitude for life, or imprisonment, not exceeding two years, with or without hard labour. The Criminal Law Amendment Act, 1885, provides a punishment of not more than two years' imprisonment with or without hard labour, in the case of any male person publicly or privately committing, or being a party to the commission of any act of gross I., by any male with any other male person. Scots law is practically similar in all respects.

Indefinite, in mathematics, was originally used for infinite, but at the present time is generally only to be found in the phrase I. integral, to denote the process of integration, without reference to limits. $\int x^n dx$ and $\int_o^a x^n dx$ are respectively I. and definite integrals.

Indemnity, a contract, express or implied, to keep a person immune from liability under a contract into which he has entered, or intends to enter. Contracts of fire, marine, and accident insurance (but not life assurance), are instances of such contracts. An I. differs from a contract of guarantee or suretyship, because the liability of a guarantor or surety depends upon a third person, the principal debtor, making default, whereas the person under a liability to indemnify another is bound to do so, irrespective of the default of other persons. A contract of I. is not, but a guarantee is, within the Statute of Frauds (*see* CONTRACT, and FRAUDS, STATUTE OF), and, therefore, the form of an I. is immaterial. Other familiar examples of Is. are the implied contracts by principals to indemnify their accredited agents from all liability properly incurred in relation to the agency. This principle in the law of agency also applies as between partners. A contract to indemnify a person against liability for an unlawful Act is void. In a wider sense I. connotes that unwritten principle of our law which enjoins the obligation of the state to compensate a person whose private property has been compulsorily taken for public purposes : a principle which, in particular cases, finds statutory expression in various private Acts of parliament supplemented by the Lands Clauses Acts.

Indenture, practically synonymous with a deed (*q.v.*), since the requirement of 'indenting' the edges became unnecessary to the validity of an instrument. An I. was an instrument made between two or more persons with distinct interests, as opposed to a deed poll or instrument made by one person or set of persons having identical interests. Formerly, copies of an instrument were always made on the same parchment, or paper, and then cut into as many parts as there were copies, with a wavy or scalloped line, so that the genuineness of any part could at any future time be established by merely fitting the edges together. Other formalities having taken the place of ' indenting ' the designation of a deed as an I. is now mere surplusage.

Independence : 1. The cap. of Buchanan co., Iowa, U.S.A., It is situated on the Illinois Central, and on the Chicago Rock Island and Pacific Railroads, also on the Wapsipinicon R. The town is noted for farming, and possesses the State Hospital for the Insane. Pop. (1910) 3517. 2. The cap. of Montgomery co., Kansas, U.S.A. It is situated on the Verdigris R., and on the Atchison, Topeka and Santa Fé, and the Missouri Pacific Railroads. The chief public building is the court-house. It is the centre of a natural oil and gas region. The chief industries are agriculture, and the manuf. of cotton, paper, crackers, sugar, and flour. Pop. (1910) 10,480.

Independence Day, a day observed in the United States on July 4. It is a legal holiday, and is kept up by various celebrations, such as patriotic speeches and meetings. It commemorates the Declaration of Independence on July 4, 1776.

Independent Labour Party (the ' I.L.P.'), the largest and most influential of British Socialist organisations. The I.L.P., which must not be confused with its offspring the Labour Party, was founded at a conference held at Bradford in 1893 over which Mr. J. Keir Hardie, M.P., presided, and as illustrative of the close connection of the man with the party, it may be mentioned that Mr. Hardie was elected in 1913 to the chairmanship, so that he might preside over the coming-of-age conference, also to be held in Bradford. Other distinguished chairmen have been Mr. J. Ramsay MacDonald, M.P., and Mr. Philip Snowden, M.P. The fortunes of the I.L.P. are intimately bound up with those of the Labour Party which it has created and to a certain extent dominated, but the party, as a party, has been steadily declining in membership during the period 1910-13. At present there are seven members of the Labour Party in the House of Commons returned under the auspices of the I.L.P. The party is represented on the board of the *Daily Citizen* (q.v.), and publishes the *Labour Leader* (weekly) and the *Socialist Review* (monthly). Secre-

tary, Mr. F. Johnson ; address, Salisbury Square, Fleet Street, London, E.C.

Independent Order of Oddfellows. see ODDFELLOWS.

Independents, or Congregationalists, see CONGREGATIONALISTS.

Indeterminate, in mathematics, used in several connections. Simultaneous equations are called I., when an insufficient number of such equations is given. Thus the equation $5x +3y=21$, where x and y are independent unknown quantities, is I., and has an infinite number of solutions. In the differential calculus, the name Indeterminate is given to such expressions as the limit of $\dfrac{a^2-x^2}{a-x}$ when $x=a$, which take the form $\dfrac{0}{0}$, or similar forms, such as $\dfrac{\infty}{\infty}$, $0\times\infty$, etc.

Index, in mathematics, that number placed after a quantity to denote the power to which the quantity is to be raised. Thus $a^4=a\times a\times a\times a$. It follows that $a^6\times a^7=a^{6+7}=a^{13}$, and, more generally, $a^m\times a^n=a^{m+n}$, where m and n are positive whole numbers. This is one of the fundamental laws of algebra, and is known as the Index Law. So also $a^m\div a^n= a^{m-n}$, and $(a^m)^n=a^{mn}$. It has been found convenient to make use also of fractional and negative indices, which at first sight seem unintelligible. To ensure that the Index Law $a^m\times a^n=a^{m+n}$ shall be true for all values of m and n, integral and fractional, positive and negative, we therefore give to such quantities as $a^{\frac{1}{2}}$ and a^{-6} those meanings to which the formula leads us. Thus $a^{\frac{1}{2}}\times a^{\frac{1}{2}}=a^{\frac{1}{2}+\frac{1}{2}}=a$, $\therefore\ a^{\frac{1}{2}}=\sqrt{a}$, and more generally $a^{\frac{p}{q}} =\sqrt[q]{a^p}$, also $a^0\times a^4=a^{0+4}=a^4$, $\therefore\ a^0=\dfrac{a^4}{a^4}$ $=1$, and $a^6\times a^{-6}=a^{6-6}=a^0=1$, $\therefore\ a^{-6} =\dfrac{1}{a^6}$, and more generally $a^{-n}=\dfrac{1}{a^n}$.

See LOGARITHM.

Index Librorum Prohibitorum, the title of a list of books prohibited by the Roman Church on doctrinal or moral grounds. The origin of ecclesiastical prohibitions dates from a very early period in the history of the church, and the earliest known instance is the *Notitia Librorum Apocryphorum qui non recipiuntur,* a catalogue of forbidden apocryphal works, issued by Pope Gelasius (494). What may be regarded as the first Roman Index was published by Pope Paul V. (1557-59) through the Inquisition at Rome, and was confirmed by Clement VIII. in 1595. When the books in the list or catalogue are allowed to be read after correction or alteration, with the approval of the orders of the papal authorities, the list is termed *Index Expurgatorius*. The preparation of the Index was, in the first instance, committed to the care of the congregation of the Roman Inquisition, but later Pope Sixtus V. organised a special congregation, consisting of a prefect, cardinals, consulters, and examiners of books, the proceedings being governed by rules laid down by Pope Benedict XIV. in a constitution issued in 1753. All books that animadvert upon Roman doctrine and all versions of the Bible by unauthorised persons, are placed on the Index. *See* T. Hurley, *Commentary on the Present Index Legislation,* 1908.

India, an extensive peninsula of Southern Asia; after China the most populous country of the world. The population of the country approaches 300,000,000, and is composed of a heterogeneous mass of various nations, having different languages, faiths, and customs. Since the beginning of the 17th century, the history of I. has been closely connected with that of Great Britain. Since that time it has become a dependency of the British empire and affords a huge market for her produce and also a great field for British capitalists. The name by which the country is known, ' India,' is derived from the Persian name *Hind,* which has been handed down to us through the Greeks and Romans. This name is derived from the Sanskrit name given to the R. Indus (*Sindhus*). At times the name Hindustan has been applied to the whole peninsula, but this is incorrect, since the name applies only to a particular region of that country. The natives of I. are so mixed that they have no *one* name for the country, but since the British occupation the official native form of the name has been fixed as Hind and the Anglicised form as India.

The country.—I. is a large peninsula which juts out southward from the mainland of Southern Asia. It is a triangle in form, the huge mountain ranges of the Himalayas forming the base of the triangle, whilst the apex runs far out into the Indian Ocean. On its western coast it is washed by the waters of the Arabian Sea, whilst on the E. is found the Bay of Bengal. The extreme length of I. is about 1900 m., and its breadth, at its widest part, is about 1600 m., but the peninsula tapers down almost to a fine point, its southern extremity being Cape Comorin. The southernmost point is in the very centre of the tropical region, its latitude being about 8°, whilst the most northerly point is found well within the limits of the temperate zone, *i.e.* 37° N. Thus the peninsula experiences extremes of weather. The official designation I. includes not only the peninsula already described, but also Burma, on the E., together with the islands of the Arabian Sea, and the Bay of Bengal, and Aden and Perim, all of which are politically administered as I. On the other hand, Ceylon, an island adjacent to the S.W. coast of I., is treated and administered separately. In former days— the days of the great companies—I. was by no means altogether under the sway of the British, but the Dutch, Portuguese, and French had settlements on the coast also. The remains of these settlements may be traced in the various towns which belong to the French and Portuguese even at the present day, *e.g.* Goa (Portuguese), Pondicherri (French). The chief boundaries of I. are : On the N., the Himalaya Mts., which separate I. from Tibet and China : on the W., the Suliman Mts., which separate it from Afghanistan and Baluchistan; on the S. and S.W., the Arabian Sea and the Indian Ocean; on the E., the spurs of the Himalayas, which separate it from Burma, and the Bay of Bengal, an inlet of the Indian Ocean. The geography of I. can be the more easily examined and followed if we divide the whole country up into the three natural divisions into which it falls : (1) The mountain ranges, *i.e.* the Himalayas ; (2) the river plains ; (3) the peninsula real, or the southern plateau of I., which goes by the name of the Deccan. (1) *The Himalayas :* This series of mountain ranges is the loftiest mountain system of the world. The range extends for a distance of 1500 m. round the northern boundary of I., and sweeps round in a half bend. The most precipitous face of the mountains faces S. and forms an almost but not altogether impassable boundary. In two places the mountain range is severed by streams bursting through, the Dihang R. in the E., and the Indus in the W. The mountains soar to a height in places of nearly 30,000 ft. and are continually snow covered. Nevertheless, since time immemorial distinct and well-known trade routes have been known and communications kept up with the countries N. of the Himalayas in spite of the barrier of the mountains. The Himalayas form a double boundary to the N. of I. and send out also spurs and offshoots which fill the country between the Ganges and the parent mountains themselves. On the W. this offshoot is known by the name of the Suliman Mts; on the N.E. it forms the boundary between Assam and I., being known as the Naga Mts. The boundary between I. and Baluchistan is also formed by the offshoots of the Himalayas, but these latter offshoots by no means attain the elevation of the others mentioned. The chief passes of the mountainous division of India are the Khyber Pass, the Kurram Pass, the Gemal Pass, and the Bolan Pass. These form the chief means of communication between I. and the N.W. (2) *The river plains:* This division of I. is the richest and most populous part. It extends in a broad belt across practically the widest part of I., running from E. to W. From the beginning of history we find this part of I. the continual prey of marauding tribes, who sweep down from the hills to plunder. The chief provinces of this part of I. are Bengal, the United Provinces, the Punjab, and Rajputana. The importance of the mountain system, the Himalayas, may be judged when we see the effect of it on the well watered plains. The river system of I. consists of three great rivers: the Indus, the Ganges, the Bramaputra. The Indus rises on the northern slopes of the Himalayas, sweeps round and enters at the W. extremity of the range, and waters the Punjab. The Ganges is formed by the amalgamation of the streams which drain the southernmost slopes of the Himalayas, whilst the Bramaputra rises also within easy distance of the Indus in the northern slopes of the Himalayas, flows E. N. of the Himalayas for some considerable distance, and then enters I. at the extreme eastern point of the Himalaya Mts. It is therefore to be noticed that the river system, of such vast importance to the people of I., is the drainage of both the northern and the southern slopes of the Himalaya Mts. (3) *The peninsula proper, the southern plateau of India:* This comprises the presidencies of Bombay and Madras, together with the Central Provinces, Hyderabad, and Mysore. The name of the Deccan was formerly applied to it. Its northern boundary is the Vindhya Mts., a range which stretches for about 800 m. from E. to W., and which has two great peaks at each extremity. In earlier days this formed a fairly effective barrier between the N. and the S. of I., since the range varies in height from 3000-4000 ft. The range is now, however, pierced by both road and railway, and communication between N. and S. firmly established. The two

sides of this triangular plateau, which has the Vindhya Mts. for a base, are formed by the Eastern Ghats and the Western Ghats. The Western Ghats are on an average a much loftier range of mountains than the Eastern. The three chief rivers of this district are the Godavari, the Kistna, and the Cauvery. These rise in the Western Ghats but discharge into the Bay of Bengal on the eastern coast. The Western Ghats, in fact, form such a severe barrier on the western coast that the line of mountains is unbroken by a river gorge, the rivers which rise in the Western Ghats discharging, as already pointed out, in the Bay of Bengal, and the rivers which drain the Vindhya Mts. discharge in the Gulf of Cambay. Chief amongst the rivers of the latter class may be mentioned the Nerbudda and the Tapti. The three geographical divisions of I. form divisions in almost every other department also —in speech, language, race, and characteristics. The three main divisions of I. already referred to, correspond also to the differences in geological structure. The oldest of these three divisions is the peninsular division which was, and has been, land for many, many centuries. This part of I. was land at a time when the mountainous portion, *i.e.* the Himalayas, was overrun by the sea. It is in this part that we find the oldest strata, in fact, the age of the Vindhya Mts. cannot be determined. The deposits found on the Himalayan Mts. are marine deposits, and from the Palæozoic period to the Eocene period these mountains were overrun by the sea. The Himalayan region is one of great compression, in which we find masses of Tertiary rocks of vast thickness, which are overthrust and folded in the most violent fashion. In peninsular I. the oldest rocks consist of gneiss, granite, and crystalline rocks. The rocks of this region are intersected by bands of transition strata of very ancient but undetermined age. The strata are generally found in an undisturbed state, and the Vindhyan formations, as already mentioned, are of great antiquity. In great contrast to these regions is the region which separates the two, and which is known by the name of the Indo-Gangetic plain. This plain is covered with alluvium and sand blown thither by the winds. There is no rise in level between the two great rivers, the Indus and the Ganges. The alluvial deposits of the plain have been subjected to frequent examination and prove to us that there has been a gradual depression of that region even within modern times. The chief deposits which are found in the Indo-Gangetic plain are gravel, sand, and clay, together with deposits of peat and forest beds. The Delta deposit has also been subjected to severe examination, but the depth of the deposit here cannot be exactly calculated. By boring, a depth of some 480 ft. was reached, but this was known not to approximate even the real depth. In one part of the Bay of Bengal, which washes the delta, the currents have apparently washed away the deposit brought down by the rivers. The depth of the bay here is over 1800 ft., so that allowing for the fact that the rest of the soundings which are taken in the immediate neighbourhood only give, at most, 10 fathoms, we can come to the conclusion that the deposit from the river has filled up the bay in that part, and that therefore the alluvial deposit equals the depth of the bay, *i.e.* about 1800 ft. The alluvial deposit of the plain has been proved by boring to be over 1000 ft. in thickness. We are able to gather from the examination of the alluvial deposits that the depression of the Indo-Gangetic plain is of recent date, and that it is probably connected with the elevation of the northern mountainous district, the Himalayas.

Climate.—Not unnaturally, in a country which stretches from the tropical regions to well into the temperate zone, many differences will be experienced in the climate of such a country. Any extreme of climate, then, either of the tropics or of the temperate zone, will be found in I. Its geographical situation has great influence on this, especially the huge mountain barrier of the N., which prevents any influence of the plateaux of Central Asia, and its peninsular points surrounded by the sea in the S. The whole country experiences three well-marked and well-defined periods—the cool, the hot, and the rainy seasons. The cool months are experienced during Nov., Dec., Jan., and the early part of Feb. The weather is then at its pleasantest, dry and cool. The hot season which follows belongs, at any rate officially, to March. From this time until the middle of June there is a continual rise of temperature which is experienced with greatest severity in Central and Southern I. The contrast in temperature during the cool months is between N. and S., but during the hot months the contrast is between the interior and the coast. It is in the interior of Northern I. (Punjab) that the greatest temperatures are experienced during this period. The monsoons or the rainy season usually begins about the middle of June. These monsoons are caused by the absorption by the sun of moisture from the ocean, and if the monsoons fail then follows one of those famines which periodically do so much harm to I. The rainy season lasts for about three months, and during that period rain is generally experienced all over I. The rainfall is by no means, however, equal in all parts of I. Parts of I., especially in the Deccan, are left after the rains with a very small supply of water, hence arises the necessity for a good system of irrigation and canals. At one place in I. the average rainfall for the year is 500 in. (Cherrapunji). The season which immediately follows the rains is the most unhealthy season of all in I. The monsoons cease about the middle of September, and the months which follow, October and November, may be regarded as the Indian autumn. During this period malaria and malarious diseases are usually rife in I., especially in the N.

Fauna.—The lion, although at one time threatened with extinction in I., is now found fairly plentiful. A variety of lion peculiar to I., *i.e.* maneless, is found here. The chief beast of prey of I., however, is the tiger, which is found in practically every part of I. The advance of civilisation and the attacks made on this animal by sportsmen have caused the tiger to become rarer than formerly, but he is by no means exterminated. The man-eating tiger is usually an old animal that has become too enfeebled to be able to catch his ordinary prey. He kills often from sheer desire to destroy, and is a real curse to the country in which he is found. It is no unusual thing to hear of a man-eating tiger destroying over 100 persons. The favourite method of tiger shooting is from the backs of elephants. The leopard is also found in even greater numbers than the tiger in all parts of I. The destruction to life and property caused by this animal is enormous. The cheetah is another type often confused with the leopard proper. Amongst the other wild animals to be found are the bear, the boar, the wolf, the bison, the elephant, and the rhinoceros. Wild goats and wild sheep are found on the highest slopes of the Himalayas. The wild ass is also to be found in parts of I., but is practically unapproachable owing to its timidity and speed. The domesticated animals of I. are chiefly the cow, the ox, and the buffalo. The two latter are used principally as beasts of burden, the cow being regarded as a sacred animal by the Hindus. Horses are bred in I., and but recently the breed has been improved by the importation of foreign horses; they are used but little amongst the working native population. Donkeys and mules are used very considerably. Sheep and goats are plentiful, as is also the pig, but this latter animal is of little use, since by the majority of the native population the pig is despised and loathed. Monkeys abound in the country, but they are regarded as sacred, and are therefore in perfect security. They are also very tame. Deer of all kinds abound throughout the whole of the country, and they are of use chiefly in providing sustenance for the animals of prey. The rivers are all infested with crocodiles and alligators. Poisonous snakes abound also in all parts of the country, the worst of all these reptiles being the Cobra dâ Capello (the hooded cobra), which is the most deadly of all. Another specimen of great danger is the Russelian snake; specimens of these latter kind are usually carried about by the native showmen, who cause them to assume a position as if dancing whilst they charm them with music. Many of the snakes found in I., however, are innocuous, and the dangerous ones are gradually receding before the march of civilisation, since the government offer a reward for every one which is killed. The birds of I. are of the usual variety found in tropical countries. The birds of prey include the vulture, the eagle (many specimens of which are to be found), and falcons of all kinds. Herons and kingfishers abound, and are much sought after on account of their plumage. Waterfowl are particularly numerous, and almost all the game birds found in Europe abound in I. Amongst the specimens to be found are pigeons, partridges, quail, plover, ducks, and varieties of each kind are found in abundance. It is interesting to note that the jungle fowl of I., which are supposed to be the ancestors of the domestic fowl so frequently seen in this country, abound in the jungles of I. The supply of fish in I. is exceedingly abundant, and, indeed, forms a very great proportion of the food of the poorer classes. The lakes, the rivers, and the sea all abound equally in fish, and the art of fishing is very extensively cultivated by all. Lately, however, the supply of fish throughout the country has shown some sign of decreasing in quantity. There seem to be two reasons for this : (1) that the methods of irrigation have led to a decrease, and (2) the fry of the fish is not properly preserved, but taken indiscriminately. Since fish forms such an important article of diet, it is necessary to take measures to prevent such a disaster as the diminution of fish in I. would be.

Flora.—I. has no peculiar botanical features of its own. Its geographical position, as in many other respects, however, cause its vegetation to be various and plentiful. Its products are those of the tropics and of the temperate zone. Rice forms the staple product of I., and has done so ever since anything has been known of I. at all. The products of the tropical regions are very much those which one would be led to expect to find in such a country—tobacco, sugar cane, and spices. Tea is grown on the slopes of the E. Himalayas, and has become one of the main products of I. In Assam the tea plant is found growing wild. Coffee has been grown in the southern parts of the peninsula, but with somewhat indifferent success. The chief trees which are found are the mango, the orange, the banyan, and the bamboo. The teak and various other trees useful for timber are produced in the more hilly districts, whilst on the slopes of the Himalayas are found the cedar, the fir, and the pine. But within recent times a Forestry Department has been set up for I., and the forests, which previously had suffered much owing to wanton destruction, are now more carefully preserved. The most indigenous flower is the waterlily, and European flowers are found in the greatest profusion at the present time. The whole of the vegetation of I., however, may be regarded as an extension of the vegetation to be found in the principal districts which immediately border on the peninsula, *i.e.* of China, Persia, and Malaysia.

Political divisions.—I. has a total area of 1,789,154 sq. m., and a population which was returned in 1911 at 315,132,537, showing an increase on the previous census (1901) of 20,771,481. This can be subdivided again into British territory and native states, which are more or less under the control of· British officials. The area and population of the British territory is 1,097,901 sq. m. and 244,267,542 (1911); of the native states, 691,253 sq. m., with a population of 70,864,995. The population to the square mile in 1901 was, in British territory, 211 persons, and in the native states 91 persons, working out for the whole of I. at an average of 165 persons per square mile. The native states all recognise the suzerainty of the British crown, but are directly governed by a native chief, who is usually helped by a British resident. The British provinces are as follow : Burma, Assam, Bengal, Bihar and Orissa, the United Provinces, Ajmer - Merwara, Punjab, N.W. Frontier Provinces, Baluchistan (British), Bombay, Central Provinces and Berar, Coorg, Madras, Andamans, and Nicobars. The chief native states are: Hyderabad, Baroda, Mysore, Kashmir, Rajputana, Central India, Bombay States, Madras States, Central Provinces States, Bengal Provinces States, Bengal States, United Provinces States, Punjab States, Baluchistan, Sikkim, and N.W. Frontier. All these states are ruled over by a native prince, who exercises supreme control, and has the power of life and death. Each native state has an army and revenues of its own, but the power of the ruler is limited by treaty arrangements by the presence of the British resident and by the fact that the British government refuse to allow the native states to make inter-alliances to go to war or to misgovern the subject population. Any oppression or misgovernment speedily receives the attention of the official authorities. The census of 1911 returned the following populations for the three largest towns: Calcutta, 1,222,313; Bombay, 979,445; Madras, 518,660. It returned twenty-nine cities with a population of over 100,000.

Racial types.—The whole population of I. may be divided into at least seven distinct racial types. The following is a list of the types, and the districts in which those types most frequently prevail : the Turko-Iranian type, Baluchistan and N.W. Frontier; the Indo-Aryan type, Punjab, Rajputana, and Kashmir ; the Scytho-Dravidian type of Western I. ; the Aryo-Dravidian type, United Provinces and Behar; Mongolo-Dravidian type, Bengal and Orissa; Mongoloid of the Himalayas, Assam, Burma; the Dravidian type, which extends practically throughout the whole of the peninsula proper.

Religion.—The chief religions of I., with the population which belongs to each one, is given by the 1911 census, as follows: Hindu, 217,586,920 ; Sikh, 3,014,466; Jain, 1,248,182 ; Parsee, 100,100; Buddhist,10,721,449; Mohammedan, 66,623,412; Christian, 3,876,196 ; Jew, 20,980 ; Animist, 10,295,168. The oldest and most primitive of all these religions is that of the Animist. From the Animist to the Hindu is but a step, the chief characteristics of the Hindu faith being the acceptation of a large number of gods, of the caste system, and of the cow as a sacred animal. Buddhism, Jainism, and the religion of the Sikhs, can be held to be almost offshoots of the original Hindu faith, and, in fact, other beliefs which can be held to differ far more than Buddhism from Hinduism are regarded simply as sects or offshoots of the original Hindu faith. Of recent years the hostility between the Hindu and the Mohammedan has been noticed to be considerably on the decrease. Whereas, however, there are innumerable sects and schisms amongst the believers in the Hindu faith, there are but two sects amongst the Mohammedans—the Sunnis and the Shiaks. The Sunnis in I. are greatly in the majority. The original Mohammedan population was found amongst the Mongols and Pathans who invaded I. as conquering races, and even to the present time it is possible to mark distinctly the descendants of these conquering races who were originally Mohammedan, and the converts of the conquered race, who followed the faith of the conquerors, less from religious conviction than from the desire to better their lot, and whose descendants since have become as fanatical and as fervid in their faith as the descendants of their previous conquerors. The majority of the Buddhists in I. are to be found in Burma, and not in I. Proper. The total for the whole of I. is 10,721,449 ; of these, 10,384,579 are to be found in Burma; 80,000 out of 100,000 Parsees are to be found in the Presidency of Bombay; of the Sikhs in I., out of a total of 3,000,000, 2,800,000 are to be found in the Punjab Province and the Punjab States. And of the nearly 4,000,000 Christians in I., over 2,500,000 are to be found in the province of Madras, or in the native states of Madras. The Christian population of the Bombay Presidency is 233,246, and the number of Jews to be found in the same place, 15,081, out of a total of 20,980.

Language.—The following are the chief linguistic families of I. The numbers given are in millions of the population. Indo-Chinese family : Pwo-Karen, 0·43 ; Tibeto-Burman, 9·56; Siamese-Chinese, 1·72; Dravido-Munda family: Munda, 3·18, Dravidian, 56·51; Indo-Aryan, 221·16; Semitic, 0·01 ; Unclassed, 0·35 ; European languages, 0·27 ; Unrecognisable, 0·10 ; the whole being completed by two returns, Vernaculars of other Asiatic countries, 0·08; and language not returned, 0·95. Of languages more prevalent than English in the peninsula 24 were returned.

Education.—The system of education which exists in I. at the present time owes its existence entirely to the British government, but it has always been found to be most successful when, as far as the natives are concerned, it has been based upon some system previously set up by tradition, or by the efforts of the natives themselves. From the earliest days I. cannot be said to have been a primitive country; it had its system of education in its own peculiar literature, at a time when its future European conquerors were wrapped in the mists of ignorance themselves. We find traces of Indian literature and education as far back in the history of that country as we can go, and many of the institutions which we find traces of are similar to the early educational institutions of Eastern Europe and Western Asia. The real impetus to education, *i.e.* modern education in I., came from the missionaries, who had studied the vernacular in order the more easily to continue their work, and who aimed also at the teaching of English to the natives, in order that they might attain to the culture of the West. After a number of colleges had been established in I., the government, after a long report had been made to them, established three universities—one at Calcutta, another at Madras, and a third at Bombay. This was also accompanied by a scheme of local education which was, in principle, very thorough, and which extended throughout every province. Schools receiving government aid were set up everywhere, and a properly graduated system of education, which extended from the elementary school to the university, was established. Recently, the whole system has been thoroughly overhauled, and it appears obvious that something must be done to increase the amount of elementary education, since the primary schools were very badly attended. The desire for secondary education and a university course was, amongst a certain class, very great, but in the primary schools less than 5,000,000 attended, out of a total population of 300,000,000. Some steps have already been taken, and a permanent grant of nearly £4,000,000, is now made annually for primary schools. Technical schools and industrial schools have been set up all over the country. Engineering, veterinary, and agricultural colleges have done much good work, and have been very largely attended, and, on the whole, education in I. may be said to be distinctly on the upward grade. The returns made in the census of 1901 were as follows:—

	Able to read and write	Unable to read and write
Males	14,690,080	134,752,026
Females	996,341	142,976,459

The educational outlay in the year 1909-10 was £4,588,082. There are at present five universities: Calcutta, Madras, Bombay, Allahabad, and the Punjab, and these all have a number of affiliated colleges. In each province there is a normal school, and there are eight schools of art. In the year 1908-09, 11,885 students matriculated. Altogether there are in British India 170,469 educational institutions, with a total attendance of 6,211,918 scholars. But of the total number of boys of school-going age, less than 29 per cent. attend school, and less than 5 per cent. girls.

History.—In a country of the area, the population, and the diversity of language and race, such as I., not unnaturally history becomes a matter of some conplexity and ⁴difficulty. To do more than summarise the main movements in such a history is impossible, and it is only with the widest movements that this sketch of the history of I. is concerned. The earliest account of I. goes back, according to the Hindu, to a time some 3000 years before the beginning of the Christian era, but it is wellnigh impossible to place any confidence in the legendary accounts which we have of those periods. The first invasion of I. was that of the Aryans, who came from the N.W. and lived for some time on the southern slopes of the Himalayas before they finally entered the great Indo-Gangetic plain and drove back the Dravidian population into the real peninsula to the S. These invaders had a settled system of civilisation and a fixed religious system. They were well acquainted with the various arts, and above all they brought with them the *Rig Veda*, the Hindu hymnal that established the antiquity of their origin. They formed states in the great plain, and they built great towns, the sites of many of these remain down to the present day (*e.g.*, Benares, Aryan Baranesi). This social system divided them definitely up into four divisions : the Brahmans, or the priests ; the Kahatrigas, or nobles ; the Varsigas, almost the modern milddle class, and the Sudras, or serf class, composed principally of non-Aryan peoples who were the slaves of their conquerors. Even during this early period some communications and commerce seems to have taken place between the people of I. and the Western peoples especially with the inhabitants of Babylon. Gradually the civilisation and the religion of this people became corrupted, and about the year 500 B.C. there lived the great reformer Buddha (*q.v.*). His life and works have been shrouded in mystery ; nevertheless, there is no doubt but that he was a real personage, and that he established a new and simplified faith, which his disciples spread over the greater part of I. At the same time we get the rise of Jainism, a religion which was founded by Vardhamana Mahavira, and which has often been regarded as an offshoot of Buddhism. Buddhism may be said to have been established as a state religion by Asoka, king of Behar, who helped the Buddhist missionary, built many monasteries, and caused the religion to be promulgated throughout the country. But in spite of the fact that Buddhism quickly took root and rapidly spread throughout the whole country, it is necessary to keep in mind the fact that it never superseded entirely the older faith of the Hindu. The Brahmanism which had been introduced with the coming of the Aryans, and although for a time Buddhism appeared to have gained the upper hand, ultimately the original religion became the more prominent, But, again, although as a religion of India Buddhism has failed to hold its own, nevertheless it has in other countries of the East spread with astounding rapidity, and at the present time well over one quarter of the inhabitants of the globe are followers of the tenets of Buddha. Nor has it been without definite effect upon the ruling religion of I. at the present time—Brahmanism.

Although some knowledge of I. had been obtained previous to the Greek invasion, it is with the invasion of Alexander the Great (*q.v.*) that the real history of I. with relation to the outside world may be said to begin. The detailed knowledge of the Indo-Gangetic plain were only obtained by the men of learning who followed in the train of Alexander's army. Alexander's campaign was confined, however, to the Punjab and to Sind, and although he made no definite settlement we know that he planted cities and left Greek garrisons behind him. He had evidently determined to return, but died before he was able to. On his death I. passed to Seleucus. Seleucus found by the time that he had definitely established his Syrian kingdom, that a new power had arisen in I., and this time a power that had to be reckoned with. From far E. of the Indus there had arisen a certain Chandragupta, who by the time that Seleucus had established himself in Syria, had also consolidated his own kingdom which brought him face to face with the Greek monarch. An alliance was made between them, and for a time the relation between the Greek and the native kingdoms were cordial and well established. Our knowledge of the system of government of Chandragupta is due to the fact that the ambassador sent to his court by Seleucus, Magasthenes, wrote an account of the court, government, and institutions of I. The grandson of this great king was Asoka, the champion of Buddhism. Many traditions concerning his conversion to Buddhism have been handed down, and certainly his grandfather had been a strong upholder of Brahmanism, but these stories may to a very great extent be disregarded. From the inscriptions and rock edicts which Asoka caused to be placed throughout the length and breadth of his empire we are able to learn that he ruled practically the whole of I. with the exception of the extreme S. of the peninsula. During his reign Buddhism became the predominant religion of I., but after his death, although the empire did not at once decay, nevertheless the decay began, and near the beginning of the 2nd century B.C., the Mauryas dynasty came to an end. Two other dynasties may be here noticed, the Sunga dynasty and the Andhra dynasty, but of both very little is definitely known. The Greek provinces of I. had in the meantime become independent kingdoms under Greek rulers, and in the middle of the 2nd century B.C. the Western Punjab became for a time part of the Parthian empire. In the middle of the 2nd century B.C., tribes from Central Asia began to invade I., and to move S. and W. in search of new homes and pasturage. The first race of invaders was known as the Sakas, who established themselves W. of Kandahar, and gave to the country the name of Sakastan. Another tribe of invaders was known by the name of the Kushan, and in the 1st century A.D. the chief of this tribe established a great kingdom in the N.W. of I., and made himself master of it. On this kingdom his successor Kaniskha, seems to have been successful in building up a great empire, which extended probably over the whole of Northern I. The year 78 A.D. is usually given as the date of the establishment of the Saka satraps, but there is great dispute on this particular point. The empire of the Kushans does not seem to have come to an end until the beginning of the 4th century of the Christian era, but the details of this dynasty towards its end are but little known, since the history of the 3rd century in I. is probably the last known of all since the invasion of the Aryans. Towards the beginning of the 4th century the Gupta dynasty was established, and almost immediately began to prosper. It was founded by Chandragupta, who extended his kingdom along the valley of the Ganges, and was increased by his son, Samudragupta, who conquered all the provinces of the Ganges, and established himself in Southern I. as well. Under Chandragupta II. fresh additions were made to the empire, but finally, about the year 480, the Huns from Central Asia broke up the empire and brought the Gupta dynasty to an end. The Huns established themselves in N. India, which they annexed to the Hun empire, which now extended from Persia to Khotan, and finally, at the beginning of the 6th century, the Huns were beaten by a Gupta king. The 5th and 6th centuries, however, seem to have been periods of terrific warfare in the history of I. The last native prince of Northern I. was Harsha, who ruled with a strong hand the whole of Northern I., but after whose death confusion reigned in the land practically to the conquest by the Mohammedans. Much of the knowledge which we have of I. during these periods is due to the journeys and the works of the Chinese pilgrims, who came to visit the shrines made sacred to them by their religion. Perhaps the greatest of all these was Juan Chwang, who came in the time of Harsha, and who has left a book in which he gives the experience of his travels throughout practically every part of I. After the death of Harsha, the history of I. is a confusion of dynasties and kings, whom it is impossible to mention in detail. But gradually in Northern I. the provinces began to find some shape and form under the government of the Rajputs, or members of the ruling families. At the end of the 9th century the most important kingdom was that of Panchala, whilst the Pala kings ruled in Bengal, and another important dynasty was the Chaurel dynasty. Until the end of the 3rd century the Andhra dynasty ruled the Deccan, and this dynasty was succeeded by the Chalukya Rajputs, which lasted until the beginning of the 7th century, and was then merged in the Chola dynasty. The chief kingdoms of the very S. were the Pandya, the Chera, and the Chola. These kingdoms suffered in many essential points from the kingdoms of the N. The chief power of the S. passed into the hands of Chola, but finally, in the 13th and 14th centuries, the invading Mohammedans found the kingdoms of the S. a very easy prey.

The close of the 10th century witnessed the beginning of the incursions of the Mohammedans. The great Mohammedan empire originated in the setting up of two small independent Mohammedan states in the N. of I. The founders of both these states were originally slaves,

and they were bitterly opposed by the Rajputs of the N. of I. At the end of the 10th century (987) the Sultan Mahmud of Ghazni ascended the throne of the Amir of Sabuktigin, and commenced a holy war against the inhabitants of I. In a great number of campaigns he gradually increased his power until it extended practically to the Deccan. The history of the Mohammedan conquest cannot here be traced out in detail, since long before the Mohammedan empire was set up, and before even the Mohammedans claimed for one of their dynasties the title of emperor, many Mohammedan settlements had been made. Dynasty after dynasty settled themselves at Delhi, and gradually spread into the Deccan itself; amongst the Mohammedan states formed in the Deccan, the more important ones were Golconda and Bagapur. Traces of the extent of the Mohammedan invasion can be found at the present time in the many architectural remains, and by this means we are able to learn that practically the whole of I. gradually passed into their hands. The beginning of the 13th century witnessed the outrages of the Mongol chieftain, Chinghiz Khan (Genghis Khan). The Mongol hordes, however, although they attained considerable power in the N.W. of India, were, nevertheless, unsuccessful in their attempts to penetrate into I. itself, and these attempts were beaten back principally by the Mohammedans of Northern I. In 1398 came the great invasion from Central Asia of Taimur the Lame (usually spoken of as Tamerlane), who, sweeping down from the mountains, penetrated to Delhi, swept all opposition before him, and after perpetrating a fearful massacre before Delhi caused himself to be proclaimed emperor of I. Quickly, however, he passed out of I., and for a time the title passed with him, and I. again remained merely a collection of states with no real head. At the beginning of the 16th century, however, appeared the greatest of all the conquerors of I. in the person of Baber. Baber was a Mongol descended from the great Taimur and from the equally ferocious Chinghiz Khan, both of whom had made attacks upon I. with varying success. He had spent the greater part of his youth in a vain attempt to restore the empire of Taimur, and failing in this object he turned his attention to I. In 1526 he defeated the army of the Sultan Ibrahim in a battle fought to the N. of Delhi, and was proclaimed emperor of I. From this time dates the succession of Grand Moguls who ruled, at least nominally, from the time of Baber to the middle of the

19th century (1857). Still for a time Delhi alone remained in the hands of the conqueror, but gradually the whole of Northern I. was conquered. The son of Baber, however, was forced for a time into exile by a usurper, but again returned and restored the dynasty. The descendants of Baber ruled at Delhi until the break-up of the Mogul empire in 1878. They conquered the Mohammedan states of Northern I., and then made their empire real, whilst they also exercised some control over the Mohammedan states of the Deccan. The greatest of all the Mogul emperors was in all probability Akbar the Great to whom the whole of I. with the exception of the very S. owed allegiance. The laws of his period, the brilliance of his court, and the magnificence of the architecture of his reign, are all worthy of note. The splendour and brilliance of Akbar's reign were continued by his immediate successors. The last of the great Mogul emperors was Aurunzeb, who died in 1707. This date is usually accepted as the date of the final break-up of the Mogul empire, on whose ruins the Mahrattas formed an empire which was the greatest and most important in I. during the middle of the 18th century, when the great and important European movements in that century began. On the break-up of the Mogul empire, the following practically independent states sprang into existence, that of the Nabob of Oudh, the Nizam of Hyderabad, the Nabob of the Carnatic, and Hyder Ali at Seringapatam. The Mahrattas who came from the Western Ghats were led by Sivaji, who began his career as a brigand chief, and finally made himself master of considerable territory in the neighbourhood of Poona. On the death of Sivaji for a time the Mahratta power declined, but the whole of the last twenty years of Aurunzeb's reign was occupied in a vain attempt to finally crush this power. On the death of Aurunzeb the power of the Mahrattas began slowly to increase, and the decline of the Mogul line became more marked with the rise of the Sikhs, a sect of Hindus who followed a reformed faith, and who had originally been but a religious body. They had, however, met with persecution, and had finally become a political power. At the beginning of the 18th century they were a power to be reckoned with in India. Little by little the provinces of the great Mogul empire fell away from their allegiance. The Deccan became independent, Oudh followed suit, Bengal, Behar, and Orissa, though nominally still dependent, became to all intents and purposes independent. A general revolt of the provinces took place, and to make the confusion worse confounded a foreign invader in the person of Nadir Shah, ruler of Persia, appeared in the land also. The power of the Mahrattas had increased, and they were now the greatest power in I. The throne at Delhi was still occupied by descendants of the Mogul dynasty, but they were weaklings, and were only nominal kings. The Shah of Persia, having plundered Delhi, returned to Persia, and I. was again free of foreign invaders, but, nevertheless, she was now but a conglomeration of independent states. The Punjab was annexed by the Mahrattas, who finally were badly defeated by a coalition of the Mohammedan princes in I. who feared that the power of the Hindus was becoming too great (1761). For a time the Mahratta power fell, but was revived, though never to the extent that it had attained under various independent princes.

The first European settlements and the power of the British in India.— Europeans had known of the existence of the trade route to I. *viâ* the Red Sea far away back in the earliest days of history, but the establishment of a Moslem power in Egypt had effectually closed that route to trade, the result was that it had been necessary to seek out some new way of approaching I. Towards the end of the 15th century many attempts were made to 'double the Cape,' and finally the task was accomplished by Vasco da Gama, who arrived by that route at Calicut in 1498. He stayed here for a short time, traded, and then returned to Lisbon. After this many important Portuguese settlements were made on the western coast, the most important of all being Goa, and they administered their Indian possessions for a time well, but towards the end of the 10th century the power in the East began to pass from their hands into the hands of the Dutch. They were driven from Ceylon, and the Dutch also established themselves firmly in the Malay Peninsula. The next great struggle which ensued was that between the British East India Company and the Dutch, and finally the Dutch were driven out of I. England first appeared to claim a share in the spoils of the East in 1600, when she obtained a charter for her East India Company (*q.v.*), and her first factory was established at Herat in 1608. In 1639 the site of Madras was bought, and in 1661 Bombay passed as the dowry of the queen of Charles II. into the hands of the Company. In 1690, after many failures, a settlement was made on the Hugli which developed into the city of Calcutta. The French appeared in I. later than the English. A company with somewhat similar objects to that of the East India Company was founded in 1664. Their most important settlement in I. was Pondicherri, which they retain even to the present day, but although, as will be shown, they made a great struggle for political power in I., they failed very largely because of the lack of interest of the home government. Up to the middle of the 18th century I. was important only in the eyes of the Company as a trading station; British I. had not yet been established, and although the Mogul dynasty had ended, yet the power of the British had not been increased by that fact. Taking into consideration the fact that in 1761 the Mahratta power had been overthrown, and the previous year the battle of Wandewash had finally broken the French power, we may safely accept as the date for the beginning of the British empire in I. the year 1761. The Mogul empire, as has already been pointed out, continued to survive until after the Indian Mutiny, but during the whole of that time it was practically purely nominal. The life struggle for supremacy in I. between the French and the British had been commenced during the War of the Austrian Succession (1740-48). During this war the French had been the more successful, and had, in fact, captured Madras. The treaty which ended the war, however, ordered the restoration of all conquests, and so Madras again passed into British hands. With the outbreak of the Seven Years' War (1756-63) rivalry between France and England continued. A series of succession questions in the Deccan had given both a pretext for joining in the native quarrels, and now the attention of the English commander, Clive, was called from the Deccan to the N. The succession of the Surajah Dowlah to the throne of Bengal had brought about the Black Hole of Calcutta, and Clive came N. with Watson to revenge the massacred English. The battle of Plassey (1757) ensued, and with the victory of the British Company troops at that battle began the final supremacy of the British in I. Four years later, at Wandewash, Sir Eyre Coote finally broke the power of the French in the Deccan. The throne of Bengal had passed into the hands of the nominees of the British Company, and from sheer gratitude favour after favour was heaped upon them. But for a time the British Company still regarded the victory which they had won as merely a means of definitely

establishing a monopoly and *not* an empire. Clive, when he returned to I. in 1765, realised that it was possible to build up a great British empire on the ruins of the fallen Mogul empire, but he advised against taking the risk which was necessary. The Company collected the revenues of Bengal, Behar, and Orissa, but as the vassals of the nominal emperor at Delhi. Clive during his administration pressed on many reforms which were necessary, but was sadly hampered by the fact that any reform which entailed a diminution of dividend was not popular with the board of directors who still ruled I. Finally, in 1767, he returned to England, and was later bitterly attacked. The House of Commons, however, recorded its appreciation of the services which he had rendered, but Clive, worn out by the attacks and by ill-health, committed suicide in 1774. He may well be regarded as the founder of British greatness in I., and had witnessed the Company become the sovereign of Bengal, Behar, and Orissa. In the meantime the English had been left with a clear field in the other parts of I. after the treaty of Paris (1763). The Portuguese, the Dutch, and now the French, had all disappeared as rivals to the power of the English. Henceforth the English had to consolidate their power with little fear of interference from any of the European Powers. The English power was threatened by Hyder Ali of Mysore, but the victory of Coote at Porto Novo again asserted the power of the British, which had seemed to fail at the end of the first Mysore War.

Between the years 1767-72 the British government of I. may be regarded as in a state of flux. It took the Company some time to realise that it was a sovereign power, but finally, in 1772, it appointed Warren Hastings as governor of Bengal. Warren Hastings had already been proved in the service of the Company, and had shown real and outstanding ability. There are many points which are debatable in the career of Warren Hastings, but here it is necessary only to mention the events without discussing the ethics of them. Hastings certainly reformed the revenue collecting system, established civil and criminal courts, and made large economies. He sold certain territory to the Nabobs of Oudh, but by so doing set up Oudh as a buffer state between the British and the Mahrattas, and later, when he gave the Nabobs of Oudh help in the Rohilla War, he did so because he realised that the Rohillas were a real menace to the British. In 1773 the Regulating Act was passed by Lord North's government, and this gave the home government certain powers over the officials of the Company, instituted a supreme court of justice, and a council of four. Warren Hastings became the first governor-general. For a time the hostility of his councillors prevented the operation of his schemes, but he was finally able to overcome even this difficulty. It is possible to pass many strictures on the conduct of Warren Hastings, but we must admit that whilst he made mistakes, on the whole his main ideas were for the ultimate good of the British, and he did much to establish British power on a firm footing. As governor-general he was supreme in I., and he gave help both to the Madras and Bombay Presidencies when they needed it. When he returned from I. in 1785 he was impeached, and after a trial of seven years was acquitted in 1795, and died in 1818. During his period of power hardly any annexations had been made. Some territory had been gained round Bombay, but on the whole he had been opposed to annexation, otherwise he would probably have annexed the territory which he sold to the Nabobs of Oudh. Orissa still remained nominally the Company's, but was in reality in the possession of the Mahrattas. In the interval that elapsed between the departure of Hastings and the arrival of Cornwallis I. was governed by Mr. Macpherson, senior member of the council. In 1784 Pitt's India Bill was passed, which created a council for I. on which sat certain of the directors and the board of control, nominated by the crown. The real power was now in the hands of the crown, although nominally it still remained with the Company, a state of affairs which existed until 1858. Cornwallis was both governor-general and commander-in-chief, and had power of veto to an extent never enjoyed by Warren Hastings. He employed himself at first with internal reform, and established a proper system of civil service for the servants of the Company. He was responsible in 1793 for the permanent settlement of Bengal, Behar, and Orissa; by this the assessment of the revenue was declared perpetual. The system was a good one, but was open to one or two obvious criticisms. Whilst on the whole fair, it could and did in some cases appear to be harsh. Legal reform also occupied his serious attention, and many reforms which enabled justice to be obtained more easily and quickly were made. The British policy was still directed against any attempt at systematised

annexations. The attack by Tipoo Sahib on Travancore, however, necessitated the interference of Cornwallis, and the war ended by the cession of half of Mysore to the Company. The territory acquired by the Company went to form the beginning of the Presidency of Madras. Cornwallis left India in 1793, and was succeeded for a time by Sir John Shore. He, however, did not have the courage of his convictions, and allowed the Nizam to be defeated by the again rising power of the Mahrattas, and during his administration, also, the power of Tipoo Sahib again increased, whilst for a short time an Afghan invasion also threatened Northern I. In 1798 Shore (created Lord Teignmouth) was succeeded by Lord Wellesley, probably the greatest of all the governors-general of I. In 1799 the fourth Mysore War broke out, being definitely undertaken by Wellesley with definite aims. The war was short; in the course of it Tipoo Sahib was killed. His territories were divided between Madras, the Nizam (who acted as an ally), and the representative of the ancient rulers of Mysore who had been dispossessed by Hyder Ali. The overthrow of Tipoo Sahib, who had been intriguing with Bonaparte, was of great importance to British prestige in I., and the news of it was received with acclamation everywhere. Wellesley was an open advocate of a policy of annexation, and by his system of setting up subsidised princes did much to extend the power of Britain throughout the whole peninsula. The subsidised princes were entirely dependent upon the British, and had to dismiss any officers of any other nationality from their courts. In 1803 the second Mahratta War broke out, and General A. Wellesley (brother of the governor-general) won the battle of Assaye against overwhelming odds and practically broke the power of the Mahrattas. Almost at the same time Lake defeated another army and entered Delhi. The troops of Sindia were utterly defeated, and the prince accepted a subsidy from the hands of the British. The aggressive policy of Wellesley, however, led to his recall, and Cornwallis was sent out for a second time to reverse this particular part of his policy. Wellesley had also been instrumental in causing many reforms in I., in establishing a school for civil servants, and in bringing the finances of the country into a sound condition in spite of the expenses of his numerous campaigns. Cornwallis had barely reached the country in 1805 when he died. He was immediately succeeded by Sir

George Barlow, and finally by Lord Minto. During Barlow's short administration he continued, in spite of his promises to the contrary, the spirit of Wellesley's policy. He did not attempt to reverse the treaty arranged with the chief of the Mahrattas, and he continued the British resident in attendance on the Nizam. In 1806 a mutiny of Sepoys took place at Vellore, and in 1809 the officers of the army of Madras seemed on the point of mutiny also. Lord Minto, on his arrival, recognised that it was well-nigh impossible to carry out the desired policy of nonintervention. He interfered in order to keep order in Travancore. During the 18th century the power of the Sikhs had been increasing continually in the Punjab, and they now, under their leader, Ranjit Singh, put forward claims, that could not for one moment be admitted by the British, to territory in the Punjab itself. A British army was sent against Ranjit Singh, but no fighting took place, the menace being sufficient. In 1809 peace was made between the ruler of Lahore and the British, but the British frontier had advanced to the Sutlej. Under Lord Minto's governorship missions were despatched to Persia and Afghanistan to combat French influence, whilst at the same time attacks were made on the French colonies of Mauritius and Ile de Bourbon, whilst the Dutch colonies in Java were attacked and captured also. The monopoly of the East India Company was abolished in 1813, save as far as trade in the China seas was concerned. The period between the departure of Wellesley and the arrival of Lord Hastings was one of stagnation as far as events in I. were concerned. Hastings, however, reverted to the policy of Wellesley. During his proconsulship the Gurkhas were defeated and part of their territory of Nepal annexed, whilst the war against the Pindaris widened into a war with the Mahrattas, much of whose territory in the neighbourhood of Poona was annexed. The next result of the work of Wellesley and Hastings was that the power of the British was definitely established as the paramount power of I., and much territory, especially in Central I., passed into British hands. The power of the Great Mogul had been definitely supplanted by the power of Great Britain.

Lord Hastings finally left I. in 1823. British supremacy over the native states was finally established, and the whole peninsula of I. was ruled by the British. But an independent kingdom had been set up in Burma, Afghanistan had developed into a really strong state, and under Ranjit Singh the state of the Punjab had been unified and strengthened. Almost immediately troubles occurred with these Powers. Burma was the first to come to blows, and the war resulted in the loss of some territory to the British. Afghanistan, regarded as an important buffer state between Russia and British I., became for a time the centre of the storm. The Persians, influenced by the Russians, interfered in Afghanistan; the British, to protect their interests, were also forced to interfere, and were at first successful, but a later Afghan rising drove them out of Afghanistan, and of the 4000 British who left Kabul only one arrived safely at Jellahbad. An expedition was sent to Afghanistan to avenge this disaster. Kabul was stormed, the prisoners released, and the British evacuated the country. The Afghan affair was unfortunate, and did little good and a great amount of harm. In 1843 Scinde was annexed by Sir C. Napier, and the next great war took place on the death of Ranjit Singh, the lion of the Punjab. He had promised peace to the British and had kept his promise, but on his death war again broke out. Two wars were fought with the Sikhs, the first in 1845, the second in 1848-49. The Sikhs of the Punjab were the most formidable enemies the British had yet met in I., but the victory at Gujerat (1849) finally delivered the Punjab to the British. In 1852 Lower Burma was annexed, this annexation taking place whilst Lord Dalhousie was governor-general, and in 1856 Oudh was also annexed. Nagpur and Ghansi also passed into the possession of the British about the same time. Between 1823 and the outbreak of the Mutiny many social reforms had taken place under British rule in I. The country had been developed, the *suttee* had been abolished, the education of the natives had been encouraged, canals had been developed, the telegraph and railways introduced, and a system of cheap postage had also been initiated. These reforms had been especially noticeable during the administration of Lord Dalhousie, and must be regarded as one of the causes of the outbreak of the Mutiny in 1857. The various inventions such as the telegraph were *not* understood by the native mind, and railway travelling upset the ideas of caste. Other causes were the distrust of the British policy of annexation, and especially great were the military causes. The Sepoys believed themselves the essential part of the British military power in I. The campaign in Afghanistan and the later Crimean War had shaken their faith in British power, and above all the report spread that the new cartridges were smeared with the fat of the cow and the pig, thus defiling both Hindoo and Mohammedan. The Mutiny broke out on May 10 at Meerut, and from Meerut spread to Delhi. Within three weeks the whole Ganges basin was aflame with mutiny, and at Delhi the representative of the royal line had again been proclaimed emperor of I. There were less than 40,000 British soldiers to hold in check a population of well-nigh 100,000,000. Cawnpore and Lucknow were besieged, and the mutineers were growing in numbers every day. It is interesting to note that the recently annexed Punjab remained loyal. The most horrible episode of the whole mutiny was the massacre at Cawnpore (July 1857). The greatness of the British was never shown to better advantage. Lawrence held the Punjab in check, a small British force advanced against Delhi, Havelock marched to the relief of Cawnpore with a small force, and Lucknow held out under the greatest difficulties. Attention must also be drawn to the loyalty of various of the Sepoy regiments, and those natives who did remain loyal rendered invaluable services to the British. In September the turn of the tide came. Delhi was stormed, Lucknow was reinforced by Havelock and Outram, and was relieved by Campbell in November, although the city was not finally taken until the following year. In 1858 the Mutiny may be said to have ended, although the Central Provinces were not pacified until the following year. The chief results of the Mutiny were the rule of the East India Company came to an end, and in 1877 Queen Victoria was proclaimed empress of I. I. itself was thoroughly pacified, and in the reforms of the future due regard was paid to the feelings of the natives. The artillery in I. also became practically an entirely British section of the Indian army.

After the Mutiny I. settled down to a period of peace, broken only by the constant suspicion of Russian intrigue in Afghanistan. This led in 1878 to the second Afghan War. The Amir was deposed, and his successor promised to receive a British resident, who was in a short time murdered, as was also his escort. This resulted in the famous march of Roberts from Kabul to Kandahar, and eventually an Amir who was favourable to the British was set up. This Amir reigned until 1901, and his successor remained friendly to the British. Finally, in 1907, a convention between Russia and Britain was signed, and later an agreement as to the line of delimitation of their respective spheres of influence in Persia was arrived at in 1912. Quetta and the south-eastern districts of Afghanistan were annexed after the second Afghan War, and the purchase of the Suez Canal was of great use in the defence of I. Our supremacy over the Afghan tribes was also recognised, and although numerous campaigns have been necessary in order to keep the hill tribes in order, on the whole our suzerainty has been fully recognised. In 1885 Upper Burma was annexed as a result of the third Burmese War, and our Indian empire was practically completed. On the whole, since the Mutiny, British statesmen have been occupied in attempting to better the lot of the native. The plague, which so frequently occurs in I., has been combatted, railways have been fully developed, and, above all, education has been well looked after. Legislative councils have been adopted for each province, and the electoral system has been developed in the constitution of the Legislative Council of the Viceroy. Finally, after his coronation in 1911, George V. visited I. and held a Coronation Durbar at the beginning of 1912 in I. itself, this being the first visit of an English Raj to the Indian empire. Many results followed from this. The loyalty of the empire was fully displayed, and Bengal was again divided into *two* divisions, and the capital of I. was officially proclaimed as Delhi.

Occupations of the people.—The great mass of the population of I. is occupied in agricultural work. This is not to be wondered at in a country where the accidents of birth and birthplace combine to make it difficult for the people to do anything other than follow the chosen occupation in the chosen place. Each Indian village is practically self-contained, and as far as possible the government provides that the land shall be held by peasant proprietors. The bulk of the population lives in the villages, and the caste system tends to crush any natural ambition which a native may have. Further, the differences of race and religion tend to make it increasingly difficult for any native to emigrate from place to place as his ambition dictates. The vast majority of the natives are contained in the villages, and are self-supporting. They engage in cattle and sheep breeding and the occupations of the country. The material and the implements used are usually manufactured by the natives in the villages themselves. The present age has seen, however, a great change come over some parts of I. In the W., for example, large cotton factories have been set up, whilst the manufacture of jute is one of the staple industries of Calcutta. This has necessitated the founding of factories, and both industries have taken a strong hold on the natives. In Assam and the lands of the lower Himalayas many of the natives are devoted to the industry of tea-growing. Agriculture, however, still remains, and probably will remain, the greatest of all the industries of I. The Indian merchant is occupied chiefly in disposing of the produce of the land, and in his usual occupation of a money-lender. The trade of I. is rapidly increasing each year. The development of the seaports and the increased demand has caused a very great change to come over the I. that in the pre-British days exported only the spices, cottons, fabrics, and other luxuries which the West demanded. Wheat and rice are exported nowadays in huge quantities, raw cotton, oil seeds, raw jute, tea, opium, hides, and indigo are amongst the next most important of all the exports of I. As far as indigo is concerned, however, the export trade of that article, owing to the competition of the artificial article, has fallen off from 50,000,000 to less than one-eighth of that quantity. Raw wool also forms an important part of the exports of I. But it is to be noticed particularly that the export of manufactured jute and cotton goods is rapidly increasing. Up to a few years ago scarcely any of the raw jute and cotton were manufactured in I. itself; nowadays it forms an essential feature of Indian trade. It is exported principally to the East. The chief imports of I. are manufactured cotton goods, hardware, machinery, clothing, and coal.

Communications. — The development of the communications of I. have had a very marked effect upon the increased trade. The improved system of roads, the increased use of the natural and artificial waterways, and the building of good and reliable railways has been of the greatest importance to industrial I. The great towns are linked together by good roads which are utilised for short-distance traffic and even for places some hundreds of miles distant. The rivers, especially the Ganges, the Brahmaputra, and the Irawadi, are used by the natives to take the produce of the interior to the seaports, whilst the canals also are well utilised. The most important development of all, however, is the development of the railways. All the large towns are linked up together, this having been done by means of good trunk systems for military purposes, and they are now used for purposes of trade. Every district of I. is served by a railway, and the thinly populated districts have specially narrow-gauge light railways. More than 500,000 men are employed, and the whole system has within recent days been thoroughly overhauled and linked up properly.

Indiana, a N. central state of the U.S.A., generally known as the 'Hoosier State,' the second to be erected from the old N.W. territory. It covers an area of 36,350 sq. m., 440 of which are water-surface; and its greatest length and breadth are respectively 277 m. and 145 m. It is bounded on the N. by Michigan, on the S. by Kentucky, on the E. by Ohio, and on the W. by Illinois. The state lies in the Mississippi valley and in the basin of the Great Lakes, and is well watered by several streams, of which the most important is the Wabash, dividing the state into two unequal parts—N. and S. The greater part of the surface is undulating prairie land. In the N. there is a range of sandhills and a number of lakes of glacial origin, and in the S. there is a chain of picturesque rocky hills known as 'Knobs.' The fertility of the soil is largely increased by a system of under-draining. Agriculture is the principal industry, the chief crops being wheat, rye, barley, oats, maize, potatoes, and tobacco, and dairy produce is exported. The chief mineral productions are coal, petroleum, limestone, sandstone, building-stones, etc., and natural gas, the chief field of which is in Delaware county. The manufs. include iron, glass, encaustic tiles, carriages, railroad cars, woollens, etc. The climate is remarkably equable. Pop. (1910) 2,700,876. Consult W. H. Smith, *History of Indiana*, 1897.

Indianapolis, the cap. and the largest city of Indiana, U.S.A., 195 m. S.S.E. of Chicago by rail, and 824 m. W. of New York. It is one of the best built and most attractive inland cities of America. Many of its streets are 100 ft. wide and diagonally intersect the four main avenues of Massachusetts, Indiana, Virginia, and Kentucky, which radiate from the Central Park, Monument Place. The city is encircled by a railway, connecting all the great trunk lines, thus facilitating traffic. The chief buildings and institutions are the state capitol, county court-house, Board of Trade building, public library, Masonic Temple, Central Hospital, Blind and Deaf and Dumb asylums. As a centre of education, I. is of considerable importance, the most noted institutions being the

University, the Central College of Physicians and Surgeons, Technical Institute, etc. The city is built on a level plain, surrounded by gently sloping, beautifully wooded hills, and the surrounding country is fertile and rich in mineral wealth. The manufs. comprise iron goods, furniture, carriages, waggons, etc. Pop. (1910) 233,650. *See* B. R. Sulgrove, *History of Indianapolis and Marion County*, 1884.

Indian Archipelago, *see* EAST INDIES.

Indian Architecture, *see* ARCHI-TECTURE—*India.*

Indian Army and Defence. After the Mutiny of 1857, and when the Indian empire was taken over by the crown, it was decided that the European army in India should be amalgamated with that of the crown. Many schemes were put forward, but finally the whole European army was transferred to the crown. The proportion of Europeans to natives in the army was theoretically supposed to be not more than three of native troops to one of European troops, but in practice this often failed, since the European army was seldom up to its full numerical strength. Since that time the European army has been treated on the same basis as the other British armies which serve in other parts of the British empire. Many changes, however, have been made in the army systems of organisation in recent years. Formerly the army was organised on a presidential basis, a staff corps being formed in 1861 for each of the presidencies. This system for a time worked well, but finally the old presidential system of organisation was done away with, and the whole Indian army was reorganised under the command of one single commander-in-chief. The staff corps became the staff of the Indian army, and the basis of organisation was one northern and one southern command, together with a separate command for Burma, all under the control of a commander-in-chief of the Indian army. Previous to this, and during the government of Lord Dufferin, the incident usually known as the Penjdeh scare took place, and led incidentally to the formation of the Imperial Service Corps. The princes of India volunteered to give pecuniary aid to the government, this was at the time rejected, but they were later informed that a proposal to place a certain number of native troops in each state at the disposal of the government, to be trained, drilled, and officered by British officers, would be welcomed. This was done, and gave rise to the Imperial Service

troops, whose value and efficiency have already been tested and proved. The present strength of the Imperial Service troops is about 18,000, of whom one half is infantry and the other cavalry. The division is by no means exact, since the Imperial Service troops also have some artillery and some camel corps. The present strength of the army in India amounts roughly to 74,000 British troops and 160,000 native troops. The total establishment in India at full strength is about 230,000 men and officers, the expenditure annually amounting to nearly £18,000,000. These figures do not include the reserve, the Imperial Service troops, the levies in the N.W., nor the militia of the Khyber. In the native army the composition of the regiments is very varied indeed. The troops consist of men of all races and religions, and these vary naturally with the position of the command. In the ranks of the native army in India is found Pathans, Sikhs, Punjabis, Mahrattas, Hindus, Gurkhas, together with representatives from almost every race to be found in India. The terms of enlistment are general, and although the native troops seldom serve beyond the seas, nevertheless they enlist for service within or without the British empire, and can be taken overseas if necessary. The qualifications for enlistment varies in the branch of the service and in some cases the tribe of the man enlisting. The infantry and cavalry are organised into double companies, each commanded by a British officer, together with a British junior officer. The native officers, risaldars in the cavalry, and subahdars in the infantry, issue all orders to the native troops. The senior officer is called the risaldar-major, whilst to each half company is usually attached a junior native officer who is called a jemadar.

Indian Civil Service. The Public Works, Forest, and Telegraph departments in India do not, strictly speaking, belong to the I. C. S. proper, although sometimes referred to as branches thereof. The I. C. S. is limited in number to about 1000 members. Vacancies are filled by open competition in England, the examination being the same as for the Class I. of the Civil Service of England (*q.v.*). Candidates who are successful in this examination must subsequently spend one year in England, during which time they receive £150 if in residence at one of the universities or colleges approved by the Secretary of State for India. They must then pass a thorough examination in riding and an examination in the Indian Penal Code and Code of Criminal Procedure, the principal vernacular language of the province to which they are assigned, and the Indian Land Act; these three subjects are compulsory. In addition the optional subjects are Hindu and Mohammedan law, Sanskrit, Arabic, Persian, and Burmese. The commencing salary in India is 400 rupees per mensem. One quarter of the time spent on active service may be taken as leave. After twenty-five years' service, of which twenty-one years must have been active service, the Indian civil servant may retire on an annuity of £1000 per annum. The unit of administration in India is the district, at the head of which is a collector-magistrate, or acting-commissioner. There are two main branches of the service, the executive and the judicial; after a man has spent four years in each department, he must choose into which he will enter. Nearly all the most important administrative and judicial appointments in India are appropriated by statute to Indian civil servants; in the administrative department the highest post is that of lieutenant-governor of a province, and in the judicial, that of a judge of the high court (who may receive a pension of £1200 a year).

Indian Corn, see MAIZE.

Indian Cress, see NASTURTIUM.

Indian Fig, see BANYAN TREE.

Indian Fire, a white signal light, composed of seven parts of sulphur to two of realgar and twenty-four of nitre.

Indian Hemp, see BHANG and HEMP.

Indian National Congress, a congress of educated natives to discuss political aspirations, etc. As a result of a movement which began nearly forty years ago, the first I. N. G. was held in Bombay in December 1885. The chairman of the British Committee is Sir W. Wedderburn, Bart., a retired Indian civil servant; an official report of the various sessions of the congress is published by the committee, which is situated in Palace Chamber, Westminster, London, S.W. A weekly journal entitled *India*, giving a record and review of Indian affairs, is also published by the committee.

Indian Ocean, The, is bounded on the N. by the territories of India and Persia in Asia Minor, and is divided from the Pacific Ocean by the Asiatic Archipelago and Australia in the E., and from the Atlantic Ocean by the continent of Africa in the W. It attains to its greatest breadth of 6000 m. between the two extreme southern points of Africa and Australia, viz. Cape Agulhas and Tas-

mania, and these two points mark the boundaries of the I. O. on the S., forming an imaginary dividing line from the Antarctic Ocean. Two arms surrounding the peninsula of India, the Arabian Sea on the W., and the Bay of Bengal on the E., form part of the I. O. But the Red Sea and Persian Gulf, which communicate with the Arabian Sea by means of the Gulfs of Aden and Oman respectively, are separate seas. The Pacific Ocean can be approached from the I. O. by means of the channels between the Sunda Islands and the Timor Sea, whilst the Mediterranean Sea in the N.W. communicates with the I. O. by means of the Suez Canal and Red Sea. There are two important straits, Mozambique Channel in the W., separating Africa from Madagascar Island, and Palk Strait in the E. separating India from Ceylon. The I. O. is dotted about with thousands of islands, some of which are of coral formation, as the Maldive, Chagos, and Cocos groups; others, such as the Crozet Islands and St. Paul's Island, are volcanic. The chief islands in the W. are Madagascar, Mauritius, Bourbon, the Seychelles, and Socotra, belonging to Africa, whilst the principal islands in the E. are the Laccadives, Maldives, Ceylon, the Andaman Isles, and Nicobar, belonging to Asia. In spite of these innumerable islands, the I. O. is most navigable. The principal large rivers discharging themselves into this ocean are the Zambesi, Indus, Ganges, Brahmaputra, Irawadi, Godaveri, and Kistna. The bed of the I. O. attains to a depth of about 2000 fathoms in some parts. The mean temperature of the surface water is over 80° F. in all parts N. of 13° S. There are two warm currents moving southwards, the Mozambique and Aghuilas currents, whilst a colder current in the E., called the West Australian current, crosses the I. O. moving northwards.

Indian Orders of Knighthood are two in number, the most excellent Order of the Star of India, and the most eminent Order of the Indian Empire. The first was established in 1861, and besides the king and a grand master, who is the viceroy of India for the time being, is divided into three classes: Knights Grand Commanders, Knights Commanders, and Companions. The first class (G.C.S.I.) is 44 in number, the second (K.C.S.I.) is 100, and the third (C.S.I.) is 200 in number. The badge is worn pendent from a light blue ribbon, with white stripes edgewards; the collar is composed of alternate links of lotus flowers, red and white roses, and palm branches enamelled in gold, with an imperial crown in the centre. The mantle worn is of light blue satin, lined with white. The motto is ' Heaven's light our Guide.' The Order of the Indian Empire was instituted in 1877. In addition to the sovereign and the viceroy for the time being, who is grand master, there are three classes in the order : Knights Grand Commanders (G.C.I.E.), Knights Commanders (K.C.I.E.), and Companions (C.I.E.). The members of the first class number 40, of the second 120, to the third there is no limit, but only 40 are allowed to be created annually. The badge is hung from a purple riband, and the collar is composed of elephants, peacocks, and Indian roses. The motto is *Imperatricis Auspiciis.*

Indian Shot, or *Canna indica,* the best-known species of the order Cannaceæ, and is to be found in all tropical countries. The plant receives its name from the resemblance of its seeds to shot.

Indian Territory, formerly a territory of the United States, is about the size of Ireland. It lies W. of Arkansas, and the state of Oklahoma bounds it on the right. It is separated from Texas by the Red R. This country has been especially reserved for the Indian tribes by the government of the United States, and was assigned to them by Act of Congress in 1830. The territory contains fertile prairies and rich valleys, and is crossed by a broad belt of forest about 40 m. wide called ' Cross Timbers.' The climate is pleasant and salubrious, and agriculture and cattle-rearing form the chief occupations. I. T. is occupied by five tribes: the Cherokees, the Creeks, the Chocktows, the Chickasaws, and the Seminoles. The Indians have the right of self-government, subject to the suzerainty of the United States. Each tribe has its principal and second chief, who are elected for a period of two to four years. The Cherokees inhabit the region N. of the Arkansas capital, Tahlequah. The Creeks occupy the land S. of the Cherokees, between the R. Arkansas and the N. fork of the Canadian River. The Chocktows occupy the S.E. corner between the Red, Arkansas, and Canadian rivers. The Chickasaws occupy the territory bordering on Texas, whilst the Seminole tribes inhabit the land lying between the N. and S. forks of the Canadian River. All the tribes, with the exception of the Seminoles, are in a high state of civilisation, and possess a written code of laws. Coal, iron, and petroleum springs abound. Pop. (1910) 1,657,155.

Indiarubber, Rubber, or **Caoutchouc,**

the principal constituent of the coagulated milky juice, or latex, which is furnished by several species of plants and trees. I. is so called because of its usefulness in rubbing out pencil and other marks, and because the first specimens came from the Indies. Caoutchouc is a name derived from *cahuca,* the name for rubber in Ecuador, or *caucho,* the name in Peru. The laticiferous system of a tree is a special cell system, not to be confused with the sap. The latex is chiefly secreted in small sacs lying in the cortical tissue between the outer bark and the wood, though it is also in some cases present in the leaves or roots. By cutting through the outer bark in an appropriate manner into the latex cells, the latex is made to flow out in the shape of a whitish, more or less viscous, fluid. This process is known as ' tapping ' the tree. Different methods, both of tapping and coagulating the latex, and of preparing the rubber for export and later for the market, are practised in different regions. A brief account of the principal varieties of rubber-bearing trees and plants and their relative commercial importance may first be given.

Rubber-bearing trees and plants are numerous, and fall into four main orders: Euphorbiaceæ, Apocynaceæ, Urticaceæ, and Compositæ.

A. *Euphorbiaceæ.*—(1) The chief tree belonging to this order, and, in fact, the most important rubber-bearing tree in the world, is *Hevea basiliensis,* from which 60 per cent. of the world's supply is obtained. It is indigenous over large tracts of S. America, principally in areas watered by the Amazon and its tributaries, *i.e.* in the states of Para, Amazonas, and Brazil. The tree grows to a height of 100 ft. and has a diameter, when fully grown, of about 40 in. There is no doubt that vast tracts of land bearing this tree have not yet been touched for the purposes of rubber producing, but a start in the direction of tapping this ' hinterland ' has been made with the Madeira-Maniove Railway. (2) An other important rubber-producing tree is the Manihot, of which the two main varieties are *Manihot glaziovii* and *Manihot dichotoma.* The noteworthy point about Manihot is that it will thrive at higher altitudes and in a poorer soil than Hevea, and can consequently be grown for rubber where the latter cannot. The latex of Manihot coagulates very rapidly, and the rubber obtained therefrom is consequently often impure, but when properly prepared the rubber is of exceptional strength and high quality. Generally speaking, for tyre covers and articles subjected to great mechanical strain the rubbers produced from Manihot and *Ficus elastica* (to which reference will be made) cannot be surpassed. The Maniçoba or Ceara rubber, from the provinces of Ceara in Brazil, is the most important commercial variety of rubber obtained from Manihot. (3) Some species of the Sapium tree, *e.g. Sapium tolimense*, from which the rubber known commercially as Colombia Virgen, grow to a considerable height, and the rubber is of a fair quality if properly prepared. (4) The Micandra tree, of which the principal variety is the *Micandra syphonoides*, is found on the Upper Amazon, and it is believed that the latex is mixed with that of Hevea in the preparation of such rubbers as Scrappy Negroheads, but no certain facts are known.

B. *Apocyneæ.* — The bulk of African rubber belongs to this order, the most important species being *Funtumia, Landolphia, Clitandra, Hancornia,* and *Dyera*. (1) The only species of Funtumia of commercial importance is the *Funtumia elastica*, the latex of the other species being only used for adulterating purposes. The rubber is known as ' silk rubber ' on account of the peculiar sheen of the freshly-cut surface of recently coagulated rubber, or from the silky hairs which are attached to the seeds. Funtumia occurs on the Gold and Ivory Coasts, Uganda, etc.; it grows to a height of 40 or 50 ft., with a diameter of 30 to 40 in., though specimens in the Matiora forest reach a height of 800 ft. and a diameter of 80 in. When properly prepared the rubber is of high quality and special mechanical strength. (2) Landolphia vines of considerable size are found in the Congo district, the E. and W. coasts of Central Africa, Abyssinia, etc., *Landolphia owariensis, L. Hendelotii, L. Thollonii*, and in Madagascar, *L. sphærocarpa*, and *L. Pierrei* are the principal species. The most diverse methods of coagulating the latex are practised. The vines are not easily tapped, and are consequently, in most cases, cut down and bled to death, the residue of latex remaining in the fibres, etc., being afterwards extracted by mechanical means. (3) The Clitandra is another species of creepers found in great quantities in the Gold Coast and Congo, the preparation of rubber from which is carried on in much the same way as from Landolphia. (4) In certain Brazilian provinces the *Hancornia speciosa* yields rubber known as Maryabeira, of medium quality, the coagulation of which is produced by the use of alum. (5)

Dyera costulata produces Jelutong rubber. It was formerly thought that the rubber obtained from Jelutong was not a pure rubber, but this view is erroneous; it had its origin in the fact that most of it has heretofore been prepared by methods which have failed to separate from the raw material certain substances which exercise a deleterious effect on the stability and vulcanising capacity of the finished product. The Jelutong tree grows to a large size, with a diameter of from 48 to 70 in.

C. *Urticaceæ.* — There are two main species of Urticaceæ, *Ficus* and *Castilloa*. (1) *Ficus elastica*, or Ramborg rubber, is found in Burma, Ceylon, Malaya, Java, India, etc. The latex has a tendency to coagulate rapidly, and hence the proportion of ' scrap ' in the rubber is rather high. The rubber when properly prepared is of very good quality, but the yield is poor. The principal commercial varieties obtained from *Ficus elastica* are Assam, Rangoon, Java, and Penang. (2) The *Castilloa* species, of which the main varieties are *Castilloa elastica* and *C. Ulei*, represents the indigenous rubber tree of Mexico and Central America. Most Peruvian *caucho* (whence caoutchouc) rubber is obtained from *C. Ulei*, whilst Mexican Strips and the different West Indian varieties are obtained from *C. elastica*. The coagulating methods vary, but when properly prepared high-class rubber is obtained.

D. *Compositæ.* — The principal species of this order is the Guayule shrub (*Parthenium argentatum*), which is found in a belt of land, varying in width from 1 to 100 m., from Fort Stockton in Texas to the Tropic of Cancer in Mexico. The industry in connection is very interesting, as the rubber from the Guayule shrub does not flow in the form of latex, but is dispersed through the mass of woody fibre in the plant. From 6 to 18 per cent. is rubber, the same quantity resin, about 10 per cent. extractives, and the remainder wood fibre, water, etc. The shrubs are either pulled up by the roots or cut off close to the ground, the latter process being preferable, as then lateral shoots are afterwards put out by the plant. Both chemical and mechanical processes are used for obtaining the rubber, the latter being the more common. The shrubs are crushed to a pulp in a machine and then left in settling tanks, when the bark, etc., sinks to the bottom. The rubber so obtained is a useful rubber for low-grade goods, containing from 17 to 25 per cent. of resin. The future of the Guayule shrub is doubtful; the present supply will be exhausted by about 1915, and whereas Lloyd thinks that two-fifths of the former yield can then be obtained if the shrubs are cut, C. P. Fox is of the opinion that the plant is doomed. 12,000 tons of rubber were obtained from Guayale in 1910.

With regard to the collection and preparation of rubber, from the latex to the state in which it is exported, there are two main systems. The Para rubber, the market price of which regulates those of the other varieties, is prepared in quite a different manner from the rubber which is grown on the plantations of Ceylon, the Malay Peninsula, Java, etc., the rise of which has been the chief feature of the rubber industry in recent years. The former is known as ' wild ' rubber, the latter as ' plantation rubber. A brief account of the methods employed in each case follows :

Preparation of wild rubber.—The land in the Amazon district is divided up into ' concessions ' or *seringals*, which are sub-let to *seringueiros*. An *estrada* is a path running through the seringal and passing close to as many trees as possible; one seringueiro can manage two estradas. It is estimated that in order to start and run an estate of from 10,000 to 15,000 trees, an expenditure of £5000 is required. This includes the advances made to the seringueiros, which are repaid at a high rate of interest. The death or illness of a seringueiro, however, precludes repayment, as owing to the absurdly inflated cost of living in the rubber districts the seringueiro rarely does more than support himself. The trees are tapped by means of a small iron hatchet called a *machadinha*, having a blade about an inch broad. The incisions take the form of either V-shaped cuts or of oblique lines. Two days before the tapping proper begins, a cut is made at the height of about 10 ft. The phenomenon, known as ' wound response,' has been known for many years ; it is more marked in the Hevea than in any other tree. The first tapping is made at a height of from 6 to 7 ft., and the subsequent tappings are made at intervals of from 1½ to 2 in. until the base of the tree is reached. About 35 consecutive daily tappings are thus necessary to complete a ' tapping line,' or *arracao*. The next tapping line is commenced at a horizontal distance of 17 or 18 in. from the first. The usual practice is for one incision to be made each day, but sometimes four or five cuts are made at the same time. The collecting cups are fixed to the tree by means of a lump of moist clay, or some similar method. After the

seringueiro has completed the round of the estrada to tap the trees, he goes over the same to collect the latex. Trees having a less circumference than 9 in. should not be tapped. The latex is transferred from the collecting tins to pails, and thence to a flat basin. The coagulation is brought about by a smoking process, which ' cures ' the rubber at the same time. A fire is made in a small brazier from materials which give a dense smoke, rich in such products of the dry distillation of woody matter as creosote, acetic acid, etc. The nuts of the urucuri palm (*Attalea excelsa*) are very suitable and are largely used, as they abound in the rubber districts. A mandril consisting of a long wooden rod, or of a paddle, is disposed with one end on a cross piece and the other on the operator's knees, so that it can be rolled either over the top of the brasier, and so exposed to the full volume of smoke, or over the basin which contains the latex. The operator then pours a small quantity of the latex over the wooden paddle, or rod, forming a thin film of liquid, which is rotated in the smoke until it sets. This process is repeated with successive films until a ' biscuit ' or ' ball ' of rubber of the required size is obtained. Large balls or biscuits are made on the circular rod, small balls on the paddle ; the weight of the biscuit or ball varies from 20 to 100 lbs. The mass of rubber when removed from the mandril is ready for export, forming the ' fine Para ' of commerce. ' Extra-fine Para ' is the name given to rubber which is treated as above, but the operator, by omitting to remove any already coagulated ' clots ' of rubber, dirt, etc., from the latex, causes the rubber obtained to be of irregular shape, and somewhat inferior quality. The scraps of rubber which adhere to the bark of the trees, or coagulate in the collecting cups, etc., are compressed, unsmoked, into irregular masses known as ' Negroheads.' In the general characteristics of wild rubbers as a whole there are very marked differences, which are partly due to the inherent properties of the various latices, and partly to the different methods of collection and preparation which are practised. Two main factors determine the value of a rubber, its chemical purity and its physical properties. Chemical impurities in rubber are either natural or adventitious; to the former class belong water, resin, ash, and matter insoluble in rubber solvents and to the latter such things as earth, bark, stones, etc. The chief physical properties to be considered are mechanical strength, elasticity, etc., and vulcanising capacity. The experiments lately carried out serve to show that the differences in latices is small, and may be lessened by scrupulous care in preparation. It is possible to prepare all rubbers so that not more than 5 per cent. of foreign substances is left. As regards mechanical strength, *Funtumia elastica*, *Landolphia*, and *Manihot* are best, then *Hevea* and *Ficus elastica*, and then *Castilloa* and *Sapium*. All wild rubbers contain a considerable percentage of moisture and a varying amount of mechanical impurities; the following table shows the loss on washing of several brands :—

Name.	Loss on washing. per cent.
Fine Para	12-20
Negroheads . . .	20-40
Manicoba	28-30
Borneo	25-50
Matto Grosso . . .	15-30
Mangabeira . . .	30-35
Upper Congo (red and black Kassai Equateur, better quality) . . .	6-12
African Niggers . .	15-40
Madagascar Pinky . .	18-20
Madagascar Niggers . .	40-50
Assam	15-40

Plantation rubber.—The most important occurrence in the rubber industry since the discovery of vulcanisation has been the foundation and rise of the Eastern plantations. The first large batch of seeds was planted in Ceylon in 1876, but for twenty years the industry was in an experimental stage. The rise of the industry may be gauged from the fact that in 1890, 300 acres were under planted rubber in Ceylon; in 1904, 11,000 acres; and in 1910, 190,000 acres. The total acreage under planted rubber in 1911 was estimated at 980,000, made up as follows :—

Ceylon	200,000
Malay Peninsula . .	400,000
Java, Sumatra, and Borneo . . .	200,000
S. India and Burma .	35,000
German colonies . .	45,000
Mexico, Brazil, Africa, and West Indies .	100,000

The production of rubber in the Malay Peninsula in 1906 was 935,056 lbs.; in 1907, 2,278,870 lbs.; in 1908, 3,539,922 lbs.; and in 1909, 6,741,509 lbs. The exports of rubber from the Federated Malay States in 1909 was 6,087,815 lbs., and in 1910, 12,212,526 lbs., whilst from the whole of the Malay Peninsula the exports in 1908 were 1575 tons; in 1909,

3330 tons; and in 1910, 6504 tons. The basic idea underlying the plantation industry is that of producing the maximum amount of good rubber in a limited area and a favourable locality, by means of native labour under skilled white superintendence.

Climate and locality.—A tropical or sub-tropical region is best suited for rubber, with a moist but equable climate, no excessive temperatures, heavy night dews, and a moderate rainfall. Malaya is thus an ideal district, as the day temperature is 85° to 87°F., the night temperature 77° to 79° F., the rainfall varies from 80 to 120 in. per annum, the humidity is 80 to 90 per cent., and the night dews are heavy and regular. The land should be readily drained and gently undulating. Hevea does not flourish at a height of over 1000 ft., but other species can be grown at a greater height, especially Manihot. A comparatively poor soil will grow rubber trees, a light to medium sandy loam being the best; the soil should be in a fine state of mechanical division. The procedure in preparing, starting, and equipping a rubber plantation is briefly as follows : The ground must first of all be cleared of all existing timber ; and when the undergrowth is well withered, it should be burnt out. All tree-stumps, etc., should be removed, and time allowed for everything in the nature of decaying vegetable matter to be destroyed or absorbed by the soil. As regards spacing the trees, if they are planted too close, although a yield good of rubber may be obtained at first, after a time it will decrease very rapidly. Then if inter-crops are grown, as in some plantations, a wide space must, of course, be left. Twenty feet between each tree and between the rows, appears to be the best from many points of view. When the question of spacing has been decided, the ground is marked out in lines, and holes dug for the young plants. The plants are generally raised from seed in pots, though occasionally the seeds are planted in their destined site from the first. The question of weeding is a somewhat vexed one. Clean weeding is the best course from a theoretical point of view, but is not always possible practically. The ideal inter-crop is one which will prevent weeds, and at the same time give a return large enough to compensate for the loss caused by the slower growth of the rubber tree ; in the present (1913) inflated condition of the rubber market such a crop cannot be found. As regards tapping, in some species the removal of a small quantity of the bark enables all the latex to be collected. Thus from two to six tappings per annum suffice for *Funtumia elastica* and *Castilloa elastica*, but Hevea requires from 100 to 150 tappings; in spite of this, Hevea gives a greater amount of rubber for each tree, owing probably in large part to the phenomenon of 'wound response.' It is not advisable to tap immature trees, although from commercial reasons it is often done, as the latex is of poor quality, and the tree is weakened. Some districts appear to favour the production of larger trees than others, but it may safely be said that Hevea should not be tapped before four or five years old. In some regions trees can be tapped all the year round, as in Malaya, Western Java, Sumatra, and Borneo, whilst in Ceylon and E. Java, as on the Amazon, there are distinct seasons. The trees are tapped at a height of from 6 to 10 ft.; high tapping produces poor latex and causes the tree to run dry. An ordinary gouge, either plain or wry-necked, is used, one of the innumerable varieties of patent knives being very rarely employed. The Amazon method of tapping is now almost abandoned on plantations, and many different systems are in vogue, such as the full herring-bone, the whole or half-spiral, the quarter herring-bone, etc. Of these the last mentioned is, perhaps, the best, and one quarter of the tree should be tapped one year, and the opposite one in the following year. The use of the pricker and the drip-tin, a tin containing water or ammonia, so arranged as to drip down the cuts in the bark with the latex, and prevent it coagulating, is largely discontinued. Many varieties of collecting cups are used, metal, cocoa-nut husk, and glass, of which the last is best, where its use is possible. It is usual to put a little water, diluted ammonia, or formalin solution into each cup to prevent premature coagulation of the latex. The trees are generally tapped in the early morning, and the latex collected, taken to the factory, and strained as soon as possible, in order to prevent the formation of scrap. There are several systems of coagulation, but probably 99¾ per cent. of the plantation rubber is coagulated by means of acetic acid, which is added to the strained latex. The Da Costa system coagulates in bulk by the simultaneous application of steam and smoke to the latex, and appears to produce a very strong rubber. The rubber is treated by one of two processes after coagulation; it is either merely made into sheets by the action of washing rollers, or made into crêpe, and then relieved of as many of the non-rubber constituents as possible. If the former method be adopted, the rubber must be anti-septicised and cured by smoking in order that it may not become tacky or mouldy. Plantation rubber, broadly speaking, is now generally shipped in a dry condition, whilst Para rubber, as described, is shipped wet. Drying should be carried out at as low a temperature as possible.

The increase in the rubber industry as a whole may be seen from the fact that the imports of rubber into the United Kingdom were in 1830, 23 tons; in 1850, 381 tons; in 1870, 7656 tons; in 1890, 13,200 tons; in 1907-8, 29,889 tons; in 1909, 35,000 tons; and in 1910, 43,848 tons. The most important rubber-consuming country is the United States of America, which takes about half of the total, the United Kingdom and Germany each take one-sixth, whilst the rest of the world takes the remaining one-sixth. The following figures give a few facts concerning the industry in different countries.

United States of America:—

	Years 1907-8	Years 1908-9	Years 1909-10
Imports of crude rubber (lbs.)	62,233,160	88,359,895	101,044,681
Import value ($) .	36,613,185	61,709,723	101,078,825
Average price per lb. (cents.) .	58·8	69·8	100

Other imports of different classes of rubber during the same period were as follows:—

	Years 1907-8	Years 1908-9	Years 1909-10
	lbs.	lbs.	lbs.
Balata	584,552	1,157,018	399,003
Gutta-percha . . .	188,610	255,559	784,501
Waste rubber . . .	16,331,033	20,497,695	37,364,671
Gutta-jelutong . . .	22,803,303	24,826,296	52,392,444

The value and quantity of crude rubber imported and re-exported into the United Kingdom was:—

Years	Imports		Re-Exports	
	Quantity	Value	Quantity	Value
	cwts.	£	cwts.	£
1904-8 (average)	587,781	9,302,990	334,129	5,858,488
1907 . .	667,294	10,934,759	—	—
1909 . .	700,062	14,138,204	397,924	9,118,084
1910 . .	876,968	26,096,988	467,872	14,853,063

In Germany the imports for 1909 were 15,500 tons, of which 4000 tons were re-exported; in 1910, 18,700 tons were imported, and 4900 tons re-exported. In France in 1909, 13,184 tons were imported, and 8243 re-exported; in 1910, 16,850 tons were imported, and 12,217 re-exported. As regards the future of the rubber industry, no definite facts or figures can, of course, be given, but increases may be looked for in the following directions in the next few years. Unless unforeseen calamities occur by 1915 or 1916, the rubber plantations will be yielding about 70,000 tons more than they do now; an increase of about 10,000 tons may be looked for from Jelutong and vine rubbers, and a small increase from selected forest areas worked on plantation lines. Against this, there will be a decrease of about 10,000 tons of low grade and impure African and S. American rubber, so that in 1915 the total production will probably be between 145,000 and 160,000 tons. Then, or shortly after, the consumption will approximately equal the production, with the result that prices will become lower, and the demand consequently greater. It is often said that either the plantation or the wild rubber industry is doomed to extinction, but this will certainly not happen for a long time to come, if ever. The main factors in the future of both the industries are the quality of the rubber produced, the cost of production, and competition. Taking into account the enormous and increasing demand for rubber, it seems probable that both good and bad plantations and wild rubber estates will have some time of grace before failure. But the unfit will gradually be weeded out, and only the well-managed plantations and well-managed wild rubber estates survive, whilst the ill-managed of both kinds will die out.

Chemistry of rubber.—Rubber is chiefly composed of the soft, solid, elastic substance known as caoutchouc. The phenomenon of coagulation would seem to consist of the change of the globules in the latex into solid caoutchouc through polymerisation or condensation, in which process a liquid passes into a solid without alteration of composition, or by condensation with the elimination of the elements of water. In the best rubbers the percentage of caoutchouc is as high as 90. The composition of a few brands of rubber and of *Para latex* is as follows :—

	Para Latex (Ceylon)		Para R. (Ceylon)	Ceara R. (Ceylon)	Castilloa R. (Ceylon)	Ficus elastica (Bengal)	Landolphia Kirkii (E. Africa)
Water .	55·15	Caoutchouc	94·6	76·25	86·19	84·3	80·1
Caoutchouc .	41·90	Resin .	2·66	10·04	12·42	11·8	6·9
Proteids .	2·18	Proteids .	1·75	8·05	·87	2·3	5·3
Sugar, etc. .	0·36	Ash .	0·14	2·46	·20	·8	7·7
Ash-salts .	0·41	Moisture .	0·85	3·2	·32	·8	—

Vulcanisation. — The rise and present dimensions of the rubber industry are entirely due to the discovery of the process known as vulcanisation, of which there are two main varieties: Hot vulcanisation consists in exposing the rubber to the action of sulphur as such, and of heat. Cold vulcanisation consists in exposing the rubber to the action of dilute sulphur-chloride (S_2Cl_2). The main principles for the manufacture of rubber goods are very much the same as for the last ten years, though great improvements have been made in machinery, etc. The crude rubber is first purified by washing, and then dried. The necessary quantity of sulphur (if any) is then mixed with the rubber by means of a mixing machine. The next step is ' calendering,' that is rolling out the well-mixed ' dough ' to sheets of the required thickness. The calendered material is then sent to the ' making-up ' table, where it is cut in suitable sizes for the hydraulic or vulcanising press, or prepared for moulds, etc. In many classes of goods, such as solid tyres, and ' squirted ' tubing, the rubber is not calendered, but forced through a die. In the case of elastic thread articles, the rubber is mixed with flowers of sulphur, and ' let down ' with a solvent, and then spread on to the cloth. All articles in which the layer of rubber is thin, are treated by the cold vulcanising method, and larger articles by the hot. The reason for this is that, as the action of sulphur chloride is so strong, in a thick layer of rubber the outside would be over-vulcanised before the inside was finished. A ' combination ' of the rubber and sulphur must take place, not only a mixture, before vulcanisation occurs. At 120° C. rubber will absorb about one-tenth of its weight in sulphur, but is not vulcanised ; if raised for an hour to 140° C., vulcanisation takes place. The heat for hot vulcanisation is obtained either by high - pressure steam, heated glycerin, or a sulphur bath. In cold vulcanisation the goods are either placed in a leaden cupboard, and exposed to the vapour of chloride of sulphur, or are dipped for a few seconds into a mixture of one part of chloride of sulphur to forty parts of carbon di-sulphide, or purified light petroleum. Then they are subjected to a temperature of 40° C. for a short time to dry them, and then treated with a warm alkaline solution to remove any traces of the hydrochloric acid generated in drying. Macintoshes are prepared by layers of I. paste made with benzol or coal-naphtha; if the material is cotton or linen, hot vulcanisation; if silk or wool, cold is employed. The percentage of sulphur in vulcanised rubber is about 1 to 2, of mineral matter from - 25 to 70, and of rubber from 12 to 60, according to the class of goods. When vulcanisation is carried too far, from too much sulphur being added, and the rubber being heated for an unduly long time, a hard, horn-like, and often black substance is produced called ebonite

or vulcanite. It is made by incorporating 40 per cent. of sulphur to purified Borneo rubber, shaping the mass required, and heating it for six, eight, or ten hours at a temperature of 135° to 150° C. Ebonite is valuable to the electrician for its insulating properties, and to chemists and photographers, because it is unaffected by most chemical re-agents. The search for an artificial substitute for rubber, that is to say a synthetic rubber, has occupied the attention of many, but up to now the production of such an article has not been achieved; synthetic rubber to be useful, must, of course, be cheaper than natural rubber. For an account of the atrocities and cruelties in connection with the collection of Congo rubber, *see* Morel's *Red Rubber*, and of Amazon-rubber, *see* PUTUMAYO. *See also* Henri Jumelle's *Les plantes à caoutchouc et à gutta* ; H. Wright's *Hevea trasiliensis, or Para Rubber*, 1908 ; *Le caoutchouc dans l'Afrique occidental française*, 1906 ; B. Schidowitz, *Rubber*, 1911 ; H. L. Terry, *India-rubber and its Manufacture*, 1907.

Indicator, in engineering, *see* VACUUM AND STEAM GAUGES.

Indicator, a term used in chemistry to denote a substance used for the detection of minute amounts of materials. Commonly, the word is applied to those bodies which ' indicate ' an acid or alkaline reaction. One of the most frequently used Is. is litmus, a substance prepared from certain lichens. This with alkalies gives a blue, and with acids a red coloration, and in most cases the colour-change is sharply defined. In titrating acids and alkalies, care has to be exercised in the choice of I. For example, in the case of carbonates, litmus may not be used (unless the titration be performed, so that all the carbon dioxide is expelled, since the latter has a distinct effect upon the I.). Similarly, the Is. prepared synthetically require discretion in their use, *e.g.* phenol phthalein is an excellent I. for strong acids and bases, but may not be used for the titration of a weak acid by a base, since the end-point is not sharp. Another frequently used I. is methyl orange, which is the sodium salt of an acid, helianthine. This is a sodium salt of an organic acid, which in presence of alkalies is yellow, and in acid solution red. It is, however, necessary that the acid should be ' strong,' otherwise no sharp end point can be obtained. Of other natural Is. may be mentioned cochineal and extracts of red cabbage, and other vegetables, but the greater number of the more recent products belong to the benzine series. Much has been written concerning the 'theory of indicators' with a view to explaining the change of colour that occurs according to the reaction of the solution. The first adequate explanation was offered by Ostwald, who based his views upon the ionic theory of solution (*q.v.*). According to this view, an acid is a substance which, in aqueous solution, yields free hydrogen ions, and conversely an alkali is one which yields free hydroxide ions. Consequently a solution which contains ions of hydrogen and of hydroxyl in equivalent amounts may be regarded as neutral. This condition is most nearly realised in the case of pure water, which is only slightly dissociated into its component ions. Further, a 'strong' acid or a 'strong' base is one which, in aqueous solution, is strongly dissociated. On the other hand, a 'weak' acid or base is one which in solution is not dissociated to any great extent, but remains *non-ionised*. The assumption made by Ostwald in his theory to account for the behaviour of Is. is that the latter are either weak acids or weak bases, and that the change of colour is due either to the presence of the non-ionised substance or of a coloured ion. In the case of phenol phthalein, it is supposed that we are dealing with a weak and colourless acid. In the terms of the dissociation hypothesis, this is only dissociated to a slight extent, and any increase in the concentration of hydrogen ions, such, for example, as takes place if a strong acid be present, tends to diminish the dissociation. In consequence, there is no colour change. If, however, an alkali such as sodium hydroxide be added, the hydroxyl ions associate or combine with the hydrogen ions of the I., leaving cations of sodium, and the anions of the I. The latter, in this case, are supposed to be coloured, and, therefore, the colour change is manifest. In the case of methyl orange, a difference is noticeable. Here the free acid is red and the anion yellow. On addition of a 'strong' acid, the undissociated acid helianthine is formed, which has a red colour. Alkalies containing free hydroxyl ions turn the red to a yellow colour, because the hydroxyl ions combine with the hydrogen ions of the helianthine, setting free the anions of the I. which possess a yellow colour. In addition to the above theory there has been proposed a so-called chemical explanation depending upon the structural differences existing between the 'lactoid' or colourless form and the 'quinonow' or coloured form. It has been assumed that all coloured sub-

stances possess the quinonow structure (*see* QUINONE), and one view of the change of colour of Is. is based upon the change into the quinone type. Phenol phthalein, in the free state, is represented by the formula

$$C_6H_4\diagdown C \diagup C_6H_4 \cdot OH$$
$$C \diagup O \diagdown C_6H_4 \cdot OH$$
$$\diagdown O$$

its acidic properties being due to the presence of a phenolic (*i.e.* OH) group. On treatment with alkalies, a change in structure occurs, and the salt is regarded as having the following constitution:—

$$C_6H_4\diagdown C \diagup C_6H_4 \cdot OH$$
$$C \diagup O \diagdown (a) \diagdown C_6H_4 \diagup (b) O$$
$$\diagdown O.M^1$$

(where M^1 is a monovalent metal. The double-bonds (*a*) and (*b*) present in the molecule are characteristic of the quinonoid structure.) This latter view is in agreement with Hautzsch's theory of pseudo-acids, and pseudo-bases, and is not entirely antagonistic to Ostwald's dissociation hypothesis.

Indiction, a term used in chronology to denote a period of fifteen years. The meaning of the word originally signified 'the imposition of a tax,' but it gradually crept into the calendar of historians, principally ecclesiastics, to mark time; thus, in the middle ages the dates of charters were expressed in Is. as well as in years of the Christian era. The Papal Indiction, which has alone survived, was reckoned as starting Jan. 1, 313.

Indictment, in criminal law, is a written accusation against one or more persons of a crime preferred to. and presented upon oath by, a grand jury. All treasons and felonies, misprisions of either, and misdemeanour of a public nature at common law (*e.g.* seditious riots) are punishable on I. The following is an example of an I. for larceny: 'Kent to wit: The jurors for our Lord the King upon their oath present that Richard Jones on the 1st day of May, in the year of our Lord, 1901, four sacks of coal, of the goods and chattels of William Hirst, feloniously did steal take and carry away: against the peace of our Lord the King, his crown and dignity.' The formal parts are: (1) the *commencement*, the principal feature of which is the venue or place from which the grand jury is drawn, and, generally, where the crime was committed; (2) the name of the accused; a misnomer will be cured by the defendant pleading to the I.; (3) the time when the offence was committed, but time is not material except where of the essence of the offence, as *e.g.* burglary, which must be between 9 p.m. and 6 a.m. ; (4) description of the facts and circumstances essential to constitute the crime : an omission of an essential ingredient of crime is not cured by plea or verdict ; (5) the places may, in some cases, be required to be stated ; in others the venue in the margin (*see* the form), or county, or other division, is deemed to be the place for all facts set forth in the I. ; (6) conclusion—errors in the formal conclusion will not vitiate an I. An I. may contain any number of counts, but not more than one offence can be charged as a rule in the same count. The object of including more than one count is to charge the accused either with different offences, or a previous conviction, or with being an habitual criminal (*see* CRIMINAL LAW), or to describe the facts of one transaction by different terms, so that if on the evidence they do not sustain one charge they may another. For example, a count for larceny is very often accompanied by a count for receiving. As a rule, it is against the policy of our criminal law to charge *different* felonies in *different* counts, *i.e.* as opposed to charging different species or aspects of the same offence or transaction : and as a rule, a count for a *felony* is never joined with a count for a *misdemeanour*. Different misdemeanours may be charged in different counts, provided all the acts were substantially one transaction, or constituted transactions essentially similar.

Indies, East and West, *see* EAST INDIES and WEST INDIES.

Indigestion, *see* DYSPEPSIA.

Indigirka, a river rising in the Stanovoi highlands of Yakutsk, a prov. in Eastern Siberia, and flowing into the Arctic Ocean. Length nearly 1000 m.

Indigo, a naturally-occurring dyestuff obtained from various plants. Chief among these are species of *Indigofera* (e.g. *I. sumatrana*, from which the Bengal I. is prepared). I. is also present in the juices of *Isatis tinctoria*, or the woad plant, which is still cultivated in England for the preparation of a fermentation vat used in I. dyeing. I. occurs in the form of a glucoside, known as *indican*, and this latter, on exposure to the influence of atmospheric oxygen and a ferment present in the leaves of the indigo-bearing plant, is converted into the insoluble blue, *indigotine*, which is the essential prin-

ciple of I. The preparation of natural I. is carried out as follows: the plant is cut down, steeped in vats for about twelve hours, and the extract, which is of a greenish colour, separated and run into fresh vats, where it is stirred vigorously, so as to bring the indican into contact with the atmospheric oxygen. Insoluble I. is precipitated as a mud, which is collected, pressed, dried, and cut into cubes. Various components other than indigotine are present, the most important being indirubine, or indigo red, indigo green, and indigo brown. The importance of natural I. as a dyestuff has greatly diminished during the last decade owing to the perfection of various synthetic processes for its manufacture. The success of these has been in large part due to the work of Von Bæyer, who, by a series of masterly researches elucidated the constitution of the dyestuff, and showed that it could be correctly represented by the formula

$$C_6H_4 \underset{NH}{\overset{CO}{\diagup\diagdown}} C = C \underset{NH}{\overset{CO}{\diagdown\diagup}} C_6H_4$$

The earlier methods for the manufacture of I. have not proved entirely successful on a commercial scale, but one process has attained such a degree of success as to enable it to introduce a synthetic product, which can compete in the open market with the natural material. This is the Neumann synthesis, which is at present worked by the Badische Anilin- und Soda Fabrik. The steps in the process are given in the diagram on the following page. Owing to the great rise in price of naphthalene, it is possible that Sandmeyer's synthesis of I. from theocarbanilide may yet prove a successful rival to the above-described method.

Indigo Bird (*Cyanospiza cyanea*), a small bird of the finch family, native of the U.S.A. It is about $5\frac{1}{2}$ in. long, the adult male of a beautiful blue colour, whilst the female and young are of a bluish grey. It has a sweet song, something like a canary, and frequents open spaces.

Indium (In = 114), a rare metallic element which occurs in certain specimens of zinc-blende, and resembles aluminium and thallium in its properties. It is a soft white metal, unacted on by air or water at ordinary temperatures, but on heating it burns to its sesquioxide with a blue-violet flame, which gives two characteristic lines in the indigo part of the spectrum; hence its name.

Individual (Late Lat. *individualis*, that which is not divided), originally denoted a thing that is indivisible in substance; thus Milton in his *Animadversions* speaks of the 'individual' Catholic Church. Hence, it also meant inseparable; *cf. Paradise Lost,* iv., 406, 'an individual solace.' Later it was used, as opposed to the word collective, to mean pertaining to a single person, as in the phrase 'individual effort,' or to anything of a striking and original character. In colloquial speech it is often used as a noun to denote man or person.

Individualism, *see* ANARCHISM and SOCIALISM.

Order is preserved throughout Indo-China by a force of about 27,500 soldiers, half of whom are French and half native. The most important products are sugar, tea, rice, silk, zinc, and lumber, and in 1909 the total value of the imports was £10,000,000, and of the exports, £11,000,000. It was owing to the work of missionaries that French influence began in S.E. Asia. Siam was the first place in which it was felt, and from there it gradually spread to Tongking and Annam in the 17th century. It was

NAPHTHALENE — Oxidation with fuming Sulphuric acid and mercury — COOH / COOH (PHTHALIC ACID) — ammonia — CO / CO > NH (PHTHALIMIDE)

ANTHRAMILIC ACID — COOH / H / NH — Monochloracetic acid ClCH$_2$.COOH — COOH / NH·CH·COOH (PHENYL GLYCINE CARBOXYLIC ACID)

INDOXYLIC ACID — C(OH) = C·COOH / NH — Loss of CO$_2$ — C(OH) / CH / NH (INDOXYL)

CO / C = C / CO / NH ... NH OR C$_6$H$_4$ / CO / C = C / CO / C$_6$H$_4$ / NH ... NH

INDICOTINE
INDIGO

Indo-China, French, a name which have been incorporated to a certain extent the French dependencies of Cochin-China, Tong-king, Annam, Cambodia, and Laos. In 1887 Annam, Tong-king, and Cambodia were united into a customs-union. From 1893 to 1896 the French gradually annexed portions of Siam E. of the Mekong R., and in 1900 the territory of Kwangchi-wan, on the coast of China, was placed under the authority of the governor-general of Indo-China. Hanoi is the seat of the governor-general, under whose authority is the whole region, with the exception of Cochin-China, which is still administered by a lieutenant-governor directly responsible to the French Minister of the Colonies.

not, however, till 1861 that the principal part of Cochin-China fell under French influence and that they established a protectorate at Cambodia (of recent years considerably added to at the expense of China). The Revolution more or less retarded progression, but in 1882, the third republic assumed a very aggressive policy, and from that time onwards they steadily pressed their conquests until they obtained possession of the whole of the country E. of the Mekong. Area 300,000 sq. m. Pop. (estimated)16,500,000. *See* Doumer's *L'Indo-Chine Française,* 1904.

Indo-China, or **Farther India,** also known as **Chin-India,** the southeastern peninsula of Asia, extending southwards into the Indian Ocean.

It comprises Tongking, Annam, French Cochin - China, Cambodia, Laos, Siam, the Shan country, Burma, and Malacca. It is washed on the E. coast by the gulfs of Tonquin and Siam and the Chinese Sea, and on the W. by the Bay of Bengal. The region differs entirely in character from India proper. The northern part of the interior is very mountainous, and is occupied by Shans. It belongs partly to British and partly to Siamese and French territory, but is in a large measure practically independent. The greater portion of the area is sparsely peopled almost entirely by the Mongolian stock, who employ languages of monosyllabic character closely allied, except in the Malay sub-peninsula, to the Chinese. The prevailing religion is Bhuddism, but in the Malay Peninsula Mohammedanism is prevalent. The paucity of population is in a great measure due to the mountainous nature of a large part of the country and to the existence of numerous and extensive swamps in the more level districts of the interior, and the defectiveness of communications. The need of strong government, inroads of robber bands from the mountains, and devastating wars are also attributable causes of the low population. The staple food of the inhabitants everywhere is fish and rice.

Indo-China, like Hindustan, has a history of primitive cultivation, foreign conquests, and indigenous culture evolutions. Older half-civilisations of the more primitive tribes, whose remains are of great antiquity and considerable importance, lie beyond the modern civilisation of Indo-China, and earlier even than these are the monuments of prehistoric man, especially the chipped implements discovered by Noetling near Yenangyoung on the Irawadi in Upper Burma in 1894.

Politically and historically, Indo-China is divided between two European states (England and France) and the state of Siam. England possesses Burma, the Straits Settlements, and the protectorates of the Malay Peninsula. France has Cochin-China, Tongking, Cambodia, Annam, and Haut et Bas - Laos; while Siam has a population of about 6,320,000. Roughly speaking, the respective populations of English and French Indo-China are 11,108,000 and 24,434,000.

Europeans arrived in the peninsula in 1508; the Portuguese, Siqueira, went to Malacca, and three years later Albuquerque built a fort there. In 1596 the Dutch appeared on the scene and occupied Cambodia and Malacca, and in the 18th century the English and French arrived. None of these, however, definitely established themselves in the peninsula till the 19th century.

Sometimes the names Annam and Cochin-China are used as interchangeable, or the whole region is considered as Annam, with the subdivisions of Tongking and Cochin-China, or, conversely, Cochin-China has Tongking and Annam for its northern and southern sections. The early navigators gave the name of Cochin-China to the whole coast from Siam to China, and the name of Annam was adopted by the Annamese as the official name for the whole country in the 3rd century A.D. Though Annam lies in the torrid zone, Tongking on the whole enjoys an excellent climate. The heats, however, in June and July are sometimes almost intolerable. Tigers, buffaloes, rhinoceroses, and elephants abound in the mountains of Annam, and much fishing is carried on.

The greater part of Cambodia, nominally a French protectorate, but practically a dependency, consists of alluvial plains completely inundated during the rainy season. There are schistose forest-clad tracks in the N.E., and in the N. and W. there are mountains containing iron, limestone, sandstone, and some copper.

Siam occupies the central portion of the Indo-China Peninsula, its present area being about 250,000 sq. m., of which 60,000 are in the Malay Peninsula. Its chief production is rice, the national food. The Chinese have the principal commerce of the capital, and the labour market is supplied by Chinese coolies. Siam produces hemp, tobacco, cotton, and coffee, and tropical fruits are abundant, the banana especially being cheap and plentiful. Gold has been produced in Siam for many years past, and the country has lately been a field for the researches of mining prospectors, and several concessions, mostly for gold and gems, have been granted to European speculators.

The Laos and the Shans, a number of tribes of common origin living on the borders of Burma, Siam, and China, are one and the same people, and closely akin to the Siamese. Their country is a succession of wide river-valleys, separated by high ridges. There are extensive forests of teak; and iron, rubies, and silver are extracted.

Indo-European, see ARYAN.

Indomitable, a British armoured cruiser (17,250 tons), built at Govan, launched 1907, and completed 1908. It is fitted with turbine engines, has eight 12-in. and sixteen 4-in. guns.

Its speed is 26-27 knots. When Prince of Wales, King George V. returned in the *Indomitable* from Quebec to Cowes, 1908.

Indore, a native state of Central India in the dominions of the Maharajah Holkar. It covers an area of 9500 sq. m., and is surrounded S. and W. by the territories of the Bombay Presidency, and N. and E. by those of Scindia and the rajah-ships of Dhar and Dewass. It is traversed in the S. by the Satpura range, and in the N. by the Vindhya Mts., and between these are the districts watered by the Nerbudda. There are some fertile plains, and most of the country is well wooded. The chief products consist of wheat, timber, tobacco, raw cotton, and opium. The chief tn. and cap. is Indore, situated in a fine undulating plain, and other places of note are the British garrison towns of Mhan and Mehidpur, Mheysur and Mandle-sar, and the ruined city of Mandu. Pop. about 850,690.

Indorsement, writing on the back of an instrument something relative to and affecting the transaction evidenced by the instrument, *e.g.* the I. of a bill of exchange or cheque payable to order operates to transfer the right to payment to the indorsee or person to whom the indorser hands the bill or cheque. The I. of a negotiable instrument may be in ' blank,' *i.e.* where the name of the indorser only is written on the instru-ment, the effect being that the instru-ment becomes payable to bearer; or ' conditional,' *i.e.* the property in the instrument is transferred subject to some contingency being fulfilled; or ' qualified,' *i.e.* which enlarges, restricts, or otherwise qualifies the liability of the indorser; or ' special,' where the name of the indorsee is inserted; or ' restrictive,' *i.e.* which restricts the negotiability of the instrument to some particular purpose or person. Mortgage deeds are often ' indorsed ' with a statement of the discharge of the mortgagor's liability, where there has been such discharge.

Indra, in Indian mythology, the ruler of the bright firmament who stands at the head of the heaven of the gods. In Vedic poetry he is re-presented as performing wonderful deeds for the benefit of good men, at the same time possessing all the attributes of a warlike god. *See* Hopkin's *Religions of India*, 1895.

Indre, a dept. of Central France, lying S. of the dept. of Cher, and covering an area of about 2666 sq. m. It was formed in 1790 from parts of the old provinces of Berry, Orléannois, Marche, and Touraine, and is named from the river flowing through it.

The surface consists of a vast plateau divided into three districts, viz. the Boischant, a well - wooded plain abounding in marshes in the S., com-prising nearly seven-tenths of the entire area; the Champagne, a fertile district in the N. producing cereal crops; and the Breune in the W., between the Cher and Creuse, a region of moors, marshes, and ponds, formerly unhealthy, but now con-siderably improved by means of drainage and afforestation. The Champagne district affords excellent pasturage for sheep, which produce first-rate wool. The chief products are chestnuts, grain, the vine, sugar-beet, wheat, oats, potatoes, turnips, etc. Much poultry is also reared. Amongst the principal manufactures are paper, leather, cloth, and pottery. The dept. is divided into the arrons. of Châteauroux, Le Blanc, Le Châtre, and Issoudun. Châteauroux is the chief town. Pop. 290,216.

Indre-et-Loire, a dept. of central France, comprising small parts of Anjou, Poitou, and Orléannois, and nearly the whole of the old prov. of Touraine. It is drained by the Loire and its tributaries, the chief of which are the Indre, Cher, and Vienne. The chief districts of the dept. are the Gâtine, a plateau region, diversified by woods and plains, to the N. of the Loire; the Champeigne, a chain of vine-clad slopes between the Cher and the Indre; the Veron, a district of orchards and vines between the Loire and Vienne; the hilly and un-productive plateau of Ste. Maure; and the marshy territory of the Breune. The chief products are grapes, apples, beetroots, grain, and hemp, and there are manufactures of paper, silk, rope, and bar-iron. Mega-lithic monuments are numerous in the dept. The chief tn. is Tours. Pop. 341,205.

Indri (*Indris brevicaudata*), a sub-family of the Lemuridæ, large monkey-like lemurs inhabiting Mada-gascar, especially the E. coast forests, first discovered 1780. They are black and white in colour, of diurnal habits, and live chiefly on fruit. *See* LEMUR.

Induction, an English Church cere-mony for giving possession of a benefice to a clergyman. The I. is performed after a mandate from the bishop to the archdeacon (or dean and chapter). The inductor takes the clergyman by the hand and lays it on the key of the church door. The clergyman is then admitted, and tolls a bell as a public notification to his parishioners. The incumbent's possession is completed by ' reading himself in,' reading the Thirty-nine Articles, and making formal vows to accept them and conform to the rules of the Church. Scottish ministers are ordained by the Presbytery without further ceremony.

Induction, in logic, the process of real inference, or the proceeding from the known to the unknown. This operation of *discovering* and *proving* general propositions is contrasted with deduction, which is the method of *applying* general propositions once discovered to such particular cases as are considered to be within the scope of the established propositions. The great exponent of deductive principles, Aristotle, neglected I., and only identified it with a complete enumeration of facts. Bacon's *Novum Organum* contains little true I., though it contains directions for drawing up the various kinds of lists of instances. Whewell's *Philosophy of the Inductive Sciences* (1840) marks a distinct advance, and shows a due appreciation of the cardinal point neglected by Bacon—the function of theorising in inductive research. He shows that science advances only in so far as the mind of the inquirer is able to suggest, organising ideas whereby experiments and observations are made to dovetail into an intelligible system. J. S. Mill in his *System of Logic* (1843) ignores the constitutive work of the mind, and regards knowledge as the merely passive reception of impressions. Recent advances in mental science have established the great importance of I., and clearly show that the most valuable faculty in scientific inquiry is that of suggesting new and valuable hypotheses.

Induction and **Induction Coil**, *see* ELECTRICITY—*Electro-magnetic Induction.*

Indulgence. This term, in Roman Catholic theology, signifies the remission of the temporal penalty of sin, granted to a repentant sinner by Church authority. The I., however, is never considered a sacramental remission of the sin itself. In the early centuries a stringent course of penetential observance was exacted by all who fell into grievous fault, such as apostasy, murder, and adultery. Such offenders were excluded from Church communion for various periods, and it is to these public penances that the historical origin of Is. is traced. When ecclesiastic discipline became less severe, these punishments were computed into fines for the benefit of the Church. Although the first recorded instance of the use of the word ' indulgence ' was in the 11th century by Alexander II., the institution was found in full development during the wars of the Crusades, the serving in which was accounted an equivalent substitute for penance,

provided always the service was from motives of devotion and not from pure greed or love of glory. The only source of Is. in the first instance was Rome, and pilgrims had to resort there to obtain them.. In this way they eventually became the objects of the meanest traffic, for when the number of pilgrims began to decrease, Is. were put in the hands of foreign archbishops and bishops and even of agents, who were sent about to trade in them. The last extreme in the lavish dispensation of Is. took place at the beginning of the 16th century, when the then pope, Leo X., published an I., the principal condition for the gaining of which was the subscribing of funds necessary for the erection of St. Peter's of Rome.

Indulgence, The Declaration of, issued by James II. in 1687. It had for its object the suspension of all laws tending to force the consciences of the king's subjects—its real object being to relieve the Roman Catholics. It was very unpopular, and the culminating point of the universal dissatisfaction was testified in the refusal of the seven bishops to order their clergy to read it aloud from their pulpits.

Indus, a southern constellation between Grus and Pavo, published by Bayer, 1603. The chief star (of 3·2 magnitude) gives a solar spectrum. Near by are the clusters of Tucana and Telescopium.

Indus, a great river of northern India, rising in the Kailas mountain group, near the sources of the Brahmaputra, Sutlej, and Gogra. It takes a north-westerly direction in the upper part of its course, past the foot of the Himalayas, through the Kashmir territories and through Middle Tibet. It then follows a north-westerly direction for about 230 m. between the chains of Ladakh to the N. and Zanskar to the S., passing through mountain scenery unmatched by any in the world. Here it receives the waters of the Shyok, its largest tributary, and after a course of about 180 m. leaves the mountain regions, and at Attock in the Punjab is joined by the Kabul R. from Afghanistan. For the remainder of its course, some 930 m., it follows a south-westerly direction till it enters the Indian Ocean. It loses much water from passing through desert regions, but is navigable at all seasons. During the melting of the mountain snows, from May to August, destructive floods often occur. It is spanned by several bridges, even in its upper mountain courses—the iron railway bridge at Attock, and the cantilever ' Lansdowne Bridge ' at Sukkur being triumphs of engineering skill.

The total length of the I. is nearly 2000 m., its minimum width is 500 ft., and depth 9 to 10 ft. *See* Haij, *The Indus Delta Country,* 1894.

Industrial Property Convention, a convention between Belgium, Brazil, France, Guatemala, Italy, Netherlands, Portugal, Salvador, Servia, Spain, and Switzerland for the protection of industrial property, signed at Paris, March 20, 1883. Industrial property according to the articles of the Convention includes patents, designs, and industrial models, trade marks, trade names, and, of course, such industrial products as are the subjects of such patents, designs, etc. To these were added by the final protocol, agricultural products, viz. wines, grain, fruit, cattle, etc., and mineral products, including mineral waters. The object of the Convention was to guarantee the citizens of each of the contracting states such advantages in respect of their industrial property as were accorded by the legal systems of each of those states to their own subjects. These advantages were also extended to persons dominated in one of the contracting states, although such persons were citizens of a non-contracting state. The Convention provided for the organisation of an international office or central bureau to be called ' Bureau International de l'Union pour la Protection de la Propriété Industrielle,' the expenses of which were to be defrayed by the administrations of the respective contracting states. The bureau is situated at Berne, and the protocol casts upon the Swiss administration the duty of superintending its expenses, making the necessary advances, and rendering the proper accounts for communication to the other administrations. *See State Papers,* vol. 74.

Industrial and Provident Societies. Societies which can be registered under the Industrial and Provident Societies Acts of 1893 and 1894 are those formed to carry on any industry, business, or wholesale or retail trade authorised by its rules, including dealings in land. To a certain extent the rules of registration and general statutory regulation of these societies are assimilated to those of friendly societies (*see under* Friendly Societies). Though in their original purpose and constitution all I. and P. S. were more or less of one kind, the process of development necessitates a division of modern I. and P. S. into: (1) Co-operative societies, or associations of labourers, or small capitalists formed with the object of getting necessaries at lower than market prices by means of co-operative stores, or for carrying on various businesses, including lending money and banking; and (2) building and land societies (*see also* Building Societies). The majority of these societies lend money on mortgage or other security, or act as savings banks. The primary characteristics of an I. and P. S. are indicated by the description : ' Industrial ' connotes the making of a profit by the mutual personal exertions of the members, while ' provident ' emphasises the providing for the future of the members by the distribution of the profits. But societies which combined the function of actual production with that of providing members with the necessaries of life were at first comparatively rare. But in later years the development of co-operative societies has been phenomenal. The history of I. and P. S. shows that it was long before they gained public confidence, or even met with legal recognition. According to Brabrook, they were viewed with mistrust because they became associated with ever wider schemes enunciated by promoters who probably looked upon them as socialistic organisations. Robert Owen's projects were especially illustrative of this idea. The first legal recognition of co-operative societies was in the Friendly Societies Act of 1846, which extended the benefits of registration to societies formed for the frugal investment of the savings of the members for better enabling them to purchase food, firing, clothes, or other necessaries, or tools, implements, or materials of their trade or calling, or to provide for the education of their children or kindred. The basis of the law of I. and P. S. is now to be found in the Consolidated Industrial and Provident Societies Act, 1893, as amended by the Act of 1894. To be entitled to registration, an I. and P. S. must consist of at least seven members. The Treasury may appoint public auditors, determine their remuneration, and fix the fees and make regulations as to registry and procedure. No member of an I. and P. S., other than a registered society, may hold more than £200 in shares. The society must make an annual return of its receipts and expenditure, funds and effects to the registrar of friendly societies. On the application of one-tenth of the members or of 100 where the membership is 1000 or more, the registrar may appoint an inspector to investigate the affairs of the society. A society, if registered, may sue and be sued in its registered name.

Industrial Schools, properly the name for schools in England established, usually by voluntary contributions, for the industrial training of children. The term is often applied to ragged schools, where mechanical arts are taught, or to ordinary 'elementary' schools. They are chiefly for vagrant and neglected children, who are often lodged, clothed, and fed up to the age of fourteen, or sometimes sixteen. They are regulated by the Children Act, 1908, and various Elementary Education Acts. *See* EDUCATION, REFORMATORY SCHOOLS, TECHNICAL EDUCATION.

Indy, Paul Marie Théodore Vincent d' (*b.* 1851), a French musical composer, born at Paris. He studied at the conservatoire, and was a pupil of Diémer, Lavignac, and César Franck. He then became organist of the church of Saint Ler. I. is one of the leading composers of the day, though his works are not noted for their originality so much as for their fine construction. Amongst them may be mentioned: *La Forêt enchantée*, a symphonic legend; *Wallenstein*; *Attende-moi sous l'orme*; *Le Chant de la Cloche*; *Fervaal*; *Sainte Marie-Magdeleine*, a cantata for female voices; *Antoine et Cléopâtre*, an overture; *Lied*, for violin and orchestra; *Tableaux de Voyage*, an orchestral suite in six parts, etc.

Ineboli, or Ainabol, a seaport of Asia Minor, situated on the Black Sea, about 70 m. S.W. by W. of Sinope. It possesses a safe roadstead, and does an export trade in wool, mohair, etc. Pop. 9000.

Inebriates and Inebriates Acts. The term inebriate is generally used to denote an habitual drunkard. Clinically, drunkenness is no more than a temporary cerebro-spinal disorder induced by the absorption of much alcoholic drink in a short space of time. It varies in form according to such circumstances as the amount of alcohol taken, the state of the stomach, the climatic conditions, and the reactions of the individual, and in its psychical effect on the individual there may be many degrees of perversion of the senses, vertigo, and confusion of the intellect. But when long persisted in, it may result in a diseased condition of the nervous system popularly termed inebriety. The symptoms are a craving for alcohol or an irresistible obsession and impulse to drink (dipsomania), which may be either chronic or periodical mental disorder of a depressive nature characterised by an undefined sadness, uneasiness, and apathy. These symptoms no doubt vary in intensity, and, of course, the quantity of alcohol absorbed varies according to the degree of resistance, but from the moment the subject succumbs to the temptation he can no longer fight against it, and it is only a question of time when alcoholic insanity follows on disintegration of the cells of the brain. The only chance of cure is to protect the subject against himself by enforcing total abstinence and by suitable treatment with alkaline bromides or other sedatives. Dr. Tuke speaks of moral treatment during convalescence, but obviously to seek to point out to the patient that his dipsomania was a disease and not a vice, while it may conceivably do good to the ill-educated can hardly have much effect on the educated inebriate. If, however, as some assert, dipsomania is largely confined to the naturally degenerate or hereditarily predisposed moral treatment (in the above sense) seems wasted labour. There are a considerable number of voluntary compulsory institutions for the cure of inebriates, but the several results appear to be discouraging. The Inebriates Acts allow of two classes of institutions: (1) State and certified inebriate reformatories, and (2) licensed retreats. There are about two state and twelve certified inebriate reformatories, and a score of voluntary or licensed retreats. The great majority of patients are women.

Inebriates Acts, 1879-1898. — The object of these Acts is to make provision for the compulsory detention and special treatment of criminal 'habitual drunkards' in state or certified inebriate reformatories, and provides for the voluntary detention of non-criminal 'habitual drunkards' in licensed retreats. In connection with the Inebriates Acts it may be noted that by the English law drunkenness is no excuse for crime, though where intention is of the essence of the offence, it may well amount to an extenuating circumstance; but drunkenness so far persisted in as to produce *delirium tremens*, or any other species of alcoholic insanity, renders a person incapable of committing crime in the eye of the law, though he may be confined as a criminal lunatic. The Inebriates Act, 1898, which initiated the establishment of these reformatories, gives power to the court, where a person is convicted on indictment for an offence punishable with imprisonment or penal servitude, and who committed the crime while under the influence of drink, to order him to be detained in a state or certified inebriate reformatory provided: (1) The jury find, or the prisoner admits, that he is an habitual drunkard, and (2) the managers of the reformatory are willing to receive him. The committal may be either in addition to or in substitution for any other sentence. State reformatories are of a more penal character than the certified reformatories, and contain the more refractory prisoners. The Act of 1898 empowers the Home Secretary to establish and make regulations for state reformatories of his own motion, but he may only establish certified reformatories when a county or borough council make application to him. The Act provides for contributions by the Treasury, and by councils of counties and boroughs to defray the cost of maintaining inebriate reformatories. Expenses in individual cases may be recovered from the estate of the inebriate.

Retreats.—The Habitual Drunkards Act, 1879, the expressed object of which is the care and control of habitual drunkards, enables a county or borough council to grant to any person or persons jointly a licence to keep a retreat. One, at least, of the persons to whom a licence is granted must reside in the retreat and be responsible for its management, and the medical attendant of the retreat must be a duly qualified medical man. ' Habitual drunkard ' (a term now changed in the later Acts to ' inebriate ') in this Act is defined as a person who, not being amenable to any jurisdiction in lunacy, is, notwithstanding, by reason of habitual intemperate drinking of intoxicants, at times dangerous to himself or herself, or to others, or incapable of managing himself or herself, and his or her affairs. Every licence is subject to a duty and is impressed with a £5 stamp, and 10s. for every patient above ten in number which it is intended to take in. The Acts make ample provision for inspection. The inspector of retreats, appointed by the Home Secretary, must inspect every retreat at least twice a year. The Act of 1898 empowers the Home Secretary to regulate the procedure on application for admission into a retreat, the medical treatment, and other matters incidental to the due execution of the Acts.

Inequality, in astronomy. For the sake of convenience the average motion of a heavenly body (supposed to be made in a circle which has the average distance of that body from its primary for its radius) is the first object of calculation when the place of the body at some future time is to be predicted. All the alterations which are rendered necessary by the unequal motion of the planet are called inequalities.

Inertia. Newton's first law, ' That every body perseveres in its state of remaining at rest, or of moving uniformly in a right line, except in so far as it is compelled by impressed forces to change its state,' is sometimes called the law of inertia. It has always been easy to understand that force is required to set a body at rest in motion, and the property of I. was recognised from this standpoint by the ancients. It was not until the time of Galileo, however, that it was recognised that the same property held true of bodies in motion, and that it was understood that were it not for external causes, a body in motion would never of itself come to rest. The *Moment of Inertia* is found by summating the products of every particle of a mass into the square of its distance from a given point or axis of rotation, or expressed as a formula $I = \Sigma(mr^2)$. *See* MOMENTS.

Inez de Castro, *see* CASTRO, INES DE.

Infallibility, freedom from all error in the teaching of faith and morals claimed by the Roman Catholic Church. The question of the I. of the Church has been a subject of dispute for many centuries, the dispute centring not in the question as to whether or no the Church is infallible, but in the question as to how and where its infallible utterances were made. The view of the I. of the Church held by the Eastern Orthodox churches is retrospective, their teaching being that all the acts of the councils received in the East as œcumenical are infallible. In the West, the question has been one between the Gallican and Ultramontane parties (*see* GALLICANISM), and the latest decision of the Roman Church on the subject was made at the Vatican Council of 1870. This council teaches ' That when the Roman Pontiff speaks *ex cathedrâ*, that is, when he, using his office as pastor and teacher of all Christians, in virtue of his Apostolic office, defines a doctrine of faith and morals to be held by the whole Church, he, by the divine assistance, promised to him in the person of blessed Peter, possesses that infallibility with which the Divine Redeemer was pleased to invest His Church in the definition of doctrine on faith or morals, and that, therefore, such definitions of the Roman Pontiff are irreformable in their own nature and not because of the consent of the Church.' No attempt has yet been made, however, to say exactly when the pope is speaking *ex cathedrâ*, and there is no certainty among Roman Catholics as to whether certain utterances are to be regarded as infallible or not. It is quite agreed, however, that the I. does not extend to pronouncements on scientific and similar matters.

Infamy, not now a term of art in English law, but formerly used to denote the loss of status consequent on conviction for an offence involving dishonesty or inhumanity, which loss entailed disqualification as a witness or juror. The principal crimes which involved I. were treason, felony, all offences based upon fraud, piracy, subornation of perjury, and common law cheating. But neither past nor present moral heinousness now disqualifies any one as a witness, though the evidence of such a person may well be discredited by a jury, and conviction for crime does not disqualify as a juror unless, of course, the person convicted is actually in prison.

Infant, in law, means a person, male or female, under twenty-one years of age. In some legal systems, *e.g.* in those of Ohio, Kansas, and other of the United States, females cease to be Is. at eighteen. Infancy is an important status in the law, more especially in regard to contractual capacity, and responsibility for crime. (As to the effect of infancy on the validity of contracts, *see under* CONTRACTS.) An adult who has made a contract with an I. cannot make it void, though the I., generally speaking, can. In many of the United States a male I. may at fourteen, the age of legal ' discretion ' in an I., validly consent to marry or disagree to and annul a promise of marriage made before attaining fourteen. At fourteen an I. may also make a will of his personal property and choose a guardian, but he cannot act as executor until he has reached seventeen. A female at seven may be given in marriage, and at twelve she may assent to or dissent from a proposed marriage. In England an I., male or female, is, generally speaking, incapable of doing all the above things. But a male I. at fourteen may contract a valid marriage, and a female I. at twelve. If two Is. below fourteen and twelve respectively have married, they need not remarry after attaining those years, provided they agree to or affirm the marriage that has taken place. Where the consent of parents or guardians is required a publication of banns is void if any one parent or guardian publicly dissents. A licence cannot be obtained by an I. without swearing that he has obtained the necessary consent, and the consent required is that of the father if living, and if dead the guardian or guardians; if no guardians, then that of the mother, if unmarried, and if not, of some person appointed by the court. A marriage, however, is valid without consent although the parties

may incur penalties, *e.g.* for false swearing. An I. husband may be sued for his wife's debts contracted before marriage, but would not be liable to a greater extent than the property he may have acquired through or from his wife. For the responsibility of Is. for crimes, *see under* CRIMINAL LAW.

Infanta, the Spanish and Portuguese title given to the princesses of the royal family, the eldest princess being also called ' la princesa.' It corresponds to ' infante,' the title given to the princes of the royal house.

Infant Feeding, *see* CHILD.

Infanticide. The practice of I. was common to ancient nations, prevalent in India, especially among the high-caste families of Rajputana, and in China down to recent times, and probably largely practised among aboriginal peoples at the present day. In the history of society, at least so far as its evolution is inferred from the customs of savage races, I. is closely associated by scientists with exogamy, or the custom of marrying outside the tribal community. Female children especially suffered, for among savage tribes they were a source of weakness and danger, for they could not support themselves and were useless as fighting units. No more painful commentary on the genesis of human society is to be found than this mental attitude of the male towards the economic dependence of the female. With nations or peoples of a later date, especially the Hindus, the motives for I. were occasionally religious or superstitious, but far more often merely prudential. The belief in some tribes was that if a daughter remained without a husband the parents were disgraced. Principally, however, it was nothing less than the fact that propagation outran the means of subsistence that induced the abominable practice of I. India, before the stringent legislation of the British, furnished a flagrant illustration of the practical working out of the doctrines of Malthus. The virtual stamping out in India of this practice—only too glaringly evidenced by the extraordinary disproportion of the male to the female population, for again it was the females that chiefly suffered—is ever to be associated with the names of Jonathan Duncan and Major Walker, who initiated measures which culminated in Acts authorising districts whose percentage of female children fell below a certain average, to be placed under police supervision. No less terrible in all its incidents of callousness and a sordid inappreciation of any idea of destiny in the human race was the custom in China, and although mitigated by the influence of Christian missionaries, there is every reason to believe that it is still largely practised. But emotional condemnation of I. is apt to falter in the light of cold philosophical reasoning in its favour of such ancient classical writers as Aristotle and Terence. It is curious that the *jus vitæ necesique* (right of life and death) over his children which the Roman father had till late in the history of Roman jurisprudence, and the analogous right given to the Greek head of a family, should have prevailed as late as it did in societies otherwise so highly endowed intellectually. Among the Spartans, too, there were laws positively enjoining the exposure of deformed children, as, indeed, at an earlier date among the Romans. The combined effect of the legislation of Constantine, Valeus, and Valentinian, at a period strongly under the influence of the Christian fathers, put an end to the practice of exposure, took away the paternal right of life and death, and punished the practice with the penalties of parricide.

It is said by statisticians that I. among modern European nations shows no sign of diminution. It need hardly be said that it is universally punishable as a crime, whether, as in some legal systems, as a specific offence, or, as in others, under the general head of murder. In England intentional or other inexcusable I. is either murder or manslaughter, according to the circumstances. To amount to murder it must be proved that the infant was in the legal sense a human being, or, to adopt Coke's phrase, ' a reasonable creature and being.' This means that the child must have completely proceeded in a living state from the body of its mother, whether it has breathed or not, and whether the umbilical cord, or navel, is severed or not. Therefore, killing a child in the womb is not murder, although it may well be punishable under the Acts relating to abortion. But if a child die, after being born alive, as a result of drugs or wounds received while in the womb, such I. is murder. (*See also* ABORTION; CHILDREN, CRUELTY TO, SOCIETY FOR PREVENTION OF; CONCEALMENT OF BIRTH: and ILLEGITIMACY.) The Scots criminal law is not dissimilar to the English in this respect. All over Europe, and in some Oriental countries, through the exertions and pecuniary assistance of Europeans, a great deal has been done to prevent I. by the institution of foundling hospitals. In Belgium and other countries such institutions are supported by public funds, while elsewhere numerous private charities for destitute and orphan children have been founded.

Infantilism, a term applied to those conditions, when childish characteristics persist into later life. Where I. is myxœdematous, it is due to atrophy or inactivity of the thyroid gland, and is then identical with cretinism. The term 'infantilism' includes many other groups of cases which are with difficulty reduced to a type. The special characteristic is absence or modification of some of the secondary sexual features ; *e.g.* hair does not grow in the arm-pit, or the pubic region, and the voice may retain its childish pitch. The individual may be fully adult in other respects, possessing normal sexual functions, but usually shows malnutrition, either generally, or in some special direction. The cause is some constitutional derangement of metabolism, and the condition generally illustrates the tendency under such circumstances towards modification of the secondary sexual characteristics. Myxœdematous I., or cretinism, is due to the disturbance of a specific secretion, that of the thyroid gland. This gland, which was first described by Gall in 1873, and whose functions were investigated by Ord in 1878, excretes a waste product of proteid nature, though its exact constitution is uncertain. If the excretion is not performed efficiently, an accumulation takes place, which shows itself in a puffy and swollen condition of the subcutaneous tissue. This is accompanied by general weakness, physical and mental. If the gland is absent at birth, or is congenitally diseased, the sexual characters remain undeveloped during life, and the condition may not be observed until the time of puberty. The face retains the chubby appearance of childhood, the voice remains of childish pitch, the second dentition may be absent or abnormal, the genitals are rudimentary, and the mental outlook and intellectual activity remain those of a child. The connection between this condition and the state of the thyroid gland has been demonstrated by observation and experiment. In many cases the gland has been found to be atrophied or absent, and removal of the gland in animals has been followed by similar phenomena. When the thyroid gland is removed in adults, the resulting condition seems that of a partial reversion to childhood: the mental activities become slower, and less complex, the patient is childishly irritable, and there is a marked loss of hair. The treatment of myxœdema, whether occurring in adults, or as a congenital condition, includes administration of extract of the thyroid gland, which has been found of particular efficacy in many cases.

Infantry, the name given collectively to a body of troops who fight on foot and who are armed only with hand weapons. How the name I. came to be applied to them is not definitely known. Many conjectures have been made, but none with such degree of probability that it is possible to give definite credence to it. I. as an effective fighting force has existed since the beginning of all fighting, but not always with an equal degree of success. The Greek, Roman, and Gothic armies all had their supplies of I., but the I. in most cases was simply that part of the fighting force which could not be mounted. The mounted men were the chosen warriors, the I. the rank and file. The armies of Greece and Rome were usually composed of more I. than anything else, and the I. fought in close serried masses, and gave by their closeness an added strength and weight to their tactics. The period, however, between the fall of the Roman empire and the end of the 11th century does not add to the glory of the history of the I. Hastings itself is a typical example of what the I. of the time were worth. The period which follows is the period of the feudal armies, when battles were decided not by the I. but by the feudal cavalry. The charges of heavy cavalry decided the battle, and the unhappy I. of the defeated side were indiscriminately slaughtered. But it is interesting here to note the change which was brought about first by the introduction of the archer, and secondly by the introduction of I. tactics which were capable of overthrowing the feudal cavalry. The battle of Falkirk (1298), between Wallace and Edward I., although it was not a victory for the I., nevertheless illustrates very strongly the methods adopted to overthrow the old feudal method. The ' schiltrons ' of Wallace, i.e. the circles of spearsmen, did much to hold the cavalry at bay. The best example, however, was Courtrai (1302), where the burghers of Bruges overthrew the feudal army of Count Robert of Artois. Crecy followed, and Crecy was essentially a victory for the new I. tactics. The age of the feudal army was rapidly declining, the combination of the resistance of the I. and the shooting of the archers was its final deathblow. But the lessons which the I. had taught during the Hundred Years' War were speedily forgotten, and the cavalry again asserted its superiority. But from this time on-

wards the I. became a definite part of the army. No longer is it simply regarded as that part of the army which is inefficient and effete, but as an essential and important section. The introduction of firearms naturally increased this result. They had to defend themselves, they depended for their defence upon I., and they adopted, therefore, tactics which would overcome the resistance of cavalry. They went about always in dense masses, whilst their squares of pikemen were well-nigh unable to be broken. They massed themselves together and at the same time adopted missile tactics. It was necessary that the cavalry should adopt new tactics to meet those of the I.

The period which commences with the opening of the 16th century was to a great extent a period of experiment. During the 16th century many combinations of tactics were tried. The period immediately before had proved that the archer was no longer of any great value, and for a time the I., armed in Swiss fashion with long pikes, prevailed. Finally, a combination of the piked armed I. and the I. armed with guns was adopted, and as these tactics commanded the enemy both at a distance and at close quarters, for a time, at any rate, the problem seemed solved. The 16th and early 17th centuries was the age of the mercenary soldier. Against untrained rebels this type of soldier was invincible, and nowhere do we find a better example of this than in the Spanish wars in the Netherlands. The Thirty Years' War had great results in the tactics of the I. of Europe. The methods adopted by Gustavus Adolphus and the Swedes during that war were eagerly imitated by the rest of Europe. Especially noticeable is it that the arquebuse used by the Swede had been lightened and was now able to be fired without using a rest. The Civil War in England proved still further that the main arm of the victorious army was its cavalry, but with the end of the 17th century we find that the old pike tactics of the I. pass away altogether. The 18th century made great progress in the tactics of the I., the bayonet fixed to the muzzle of the gun took the place of the pike. Fire tactics were adopted by the I. The enemy were riddled with fire from the guns of the I. at as short a distance as possible, and then, when the opposing ranks had been disorganised, the bayonet charge completed the attack. The long wars of the 18th century brought in their train many changes. The tactics of Frederick the Great and his methods of training the I. were eagerly adopted throughout the military circles of Europe, and later these were superseded by the tactics of Napoleon in the long European wars. The revolutionary wars brought in their train many vital changes, in fact from the year 1798 can be dated the beginning of modern I. tactics. The change was due very largely to the methods of Napoleon, who, having poured an overwhelming artillery fire into the masses of the enemy, brought his I. up to complete the attack. It was a combination of the two methods of artillery fire and I. charges. The I. methods of the Peninsular War were on the British side somewhat different. They were modelled on the old tactics of Frederick the Great, but they combined mobility and an ability to use cover, with the massed strength of the former German type. The tactics consisted in reserving fire until the enemy were within easy striking distance, and then pouring in a murderous volley and following this up with a bayonet charge. The next great epoch-making war, as far as the I. were concerned, was the Franco-Prussian War of 1870. Much discussion took place as to the exact lessons to be learnt of that war, and the result was that a very much more extended order of attack was adopted by the I. The massed firing tactics were relegated to the artillery almost entirely, and the I., in extended order, and taking advantage of every inch of cover, slowly crept to the attack. These methods have undergone some change since that time, especially as a result of the South African War, and later of the Russo-Japanese War, but the changes have not radically altered the principle, and the attack in extended order for the I. is still the basis of I. tactics.

Organisation and equipment of British infantry.—The unit of the British I. is the battalion, which is divided up into eight companies. The battalion is commanded by a lieutenant-colonel. Each company is commanded by a captain, and has attached to it two lieutenants. In addition, the other officers of the battalion are an adjutant, usually with the rank of captain, and a quartermaster. Each company is divided in five sections, each of which is under the control of a sergeant, and each half company is under the control of a lieutenant. The sergeant-major, or colour-sergeant, assists the captain in the administrative duties. This officer is usually called a warrant officer, since he holds a warrant from the Secretary of State for War. The principal non-commissioned officer is the quartermaster-sergeant. There are two colours, the ' King's ' and the

' regimental.' The battalion consists of 1000 men, who are, as mentioned, divided into eight companies. It is interesting to note that the British lieutenant commands two sections of a battalion, each of which sections is under the control of a sergeant. In the armies of Europe it is customary for the half company to be under the control of the lieutenant, but the value of the British system lies in the fact that the non-commissioned officer must be capable of controlling and commanding his own section, so that under active service conditions, if the lieutenant is killed or disabled, he is able to continue in the command.

Infant Schools, *see* KINDERGARTEN and EDUCATION.

Infection, distinguished from contagion (*q.v.*) by reason of the fact that it signifies the transmission of a disease without direct contact. Thus infectious diseases are usually contracted by breathings. In malarial diseases, *e.g.* ague, the disease poison is taken from the soil, air, or water in some way, but there is no conclusive evidence that the disease can be transmitted directly from one person to another. Typhoid fever again is infectious, and is usually water-borne. The typical infectious diseases are, however, small-pox, measles, mumps, scarlet fever, whooping-cough, etc., and these are both infectious and contagious. I. depends upon the presence of a germ (*q.v.*), and prevention is best effected by isolation. *See* articles on the diseases mentioned, and HYGIENE, DISINFECTANTS, CONTAGION, and GERM.

Infeftment, or **Sasine,** in Scots law means both the act or symbolical ceremony of giving to another the possession of heritable land, and the writ or instrument of sasine in which such act or ceremony is expressed. I. being a feudal act, and the crown being the lord paramount of all Scottish feus or fiefs, an I. can only be under a grant from the crown. This is interpreted in practice to mean, that to constitute a valid I. the transferee must show a feudal chain of title going back ultimately to the crown. But there may be real rights without I. These exceptions include leases, servitudes (analogous to rights of way or other rights over the land of another), udal lands situate in the Orkneys and Shetlands, crown lands, and churches and glebe of the Church of Scotland. The methods of I. now in vogue are: (*a*) By direct registration. (*b*) By transmitted warrants, *i.e.* by a transferor who is not himself infeft and can only transmit through another. (*c*) By notarial instrument, used where the disponee does not wish to record the whole of the conveyance. The notarial instrument sets out the nature of the deed generally, and in detail only such portions as actually convey the lands. (d) *Ex propriis manibus* (little used), under the Consolidation Act of 1868, a short form by which a husband may give his wife I. (e) By warrant of registration under the Land Registers Act, 1868, and the Consolisation Act of 1868. (f) According to the clause of direction in a deed to record the deed in the Register of Sasines.

Inferior Courts comprise in England all those that are below the dignity of the High Court of Justice, and whose decisions are subject to review by the High Court. The principal I. C. exercising civil jurisdiction are the county courts, from the decisions in which an appeal lies to the High Court where the amount involved exceeds £20. Where the plaintiff in the High Court has no visible means of paying the defendant's costs, the defendant may, in swearing an affidavit to that effect, get an order remitting the case for trial in the county court. There are also certain local courts exercising a considerable civil jurisdiction, the most important being the Chancery Court of the County Palatine of Lancaster, the powers of which, within its local limits, are similar to those of the Chancery Division of the High Court; the Mayor's Court of London, the Court of Passage of Liverpool, and the Salford Hundred Court, all exercising within their local limits a full common law jurisdiction. The courts of the universities of Oxford and Cambridge have by ancient charters a jurisdiction in actions to which any member or servant of the university is a party, at least where the cause of action arose within the liberties of the university. Other I. C. called the Ecclesiastical Courts (*q.v.*) give redress in actions of an ecclesiastical or spiritual nature. So great an authority as Stephen states that their jurisdiction rests entirely on the tolerance of the municipal law. The criminal courts of inferior degree are : (1) The general county sessions or quarter sessions (*see* COUNTY SESSIONS), which is a court of first instance, and of appeal against summary convictions by petty sessional magistrates. An indictment (*q.v.*) may be removed to the King's Bench Division from quarter sessions by writ of *certiorari* (*q.v.*) in certain cases, such as where an impartial trial cannot be had in the I. C., or some more than ordinarily difficult point of law is involved ;

(2) borough quarter sessions, with judicial functions identical with those of the county quarter sessions, and presided over by a ' recorder ' who becomes a borough magistrate *virtute officii* ; (3) petty sessional courts consisting of at least two justices or a police or stipendiary magistrate, or the lord mayor or an alderman in the city of London. These courts have a limited jurisdiction to try indictable offences under the Summary Jurisdiction Acts. The King's Bench Division can grant a *certiorari* to transfer a case to the High Court where the magistrates exceed their jurisdiction or there is some manifest informality, and on a *special case* stated by the justices can decide any point of law submitted for the decision of the High Court. Again, the High Court may issue a writ of prohibition to stop proceedings where the magistrates have no jurisdiction, and generally speaking any I. C. which attempts to exceed the limits of its jurisdiction may be prevented by such a writ, and conversely a writ of *mandamus* may be issued to compel any I. C. to exercise its jurisdiction, at all events in cases where relief is sought in respect of the infringement of some *public* right or duty. In some rare instances, ancient courts of *Piepowder* still survive, *e.g.* in Barnet during the time when the fair is being held. (On this curious revival *see* the article in the *Law Times*, Sept. 21, 1912.)

Infernal Machines, a name given to mechanical contrivances with a dangerous explosive and used for a nefarious purpose. Such machines are generally made to look quite harmless and frequently have some clockwork arrangement by which the explosive is fired after a certain lapse of time. They are frequently used by political agitators. In 1883-85 Irish agitators made many attempts to blow up public buildings by such machines, including the House of Commons and the Tower, while other instances include the assassination of Alexander II. of Russia (1881), Orsini's attempt to kill Napoleon III. (1858), and the Chicago outrage of 1886.

Inferobranchiata, the term formerly applied to a group of gasteropod molluscs whose gills are situated under a projecting mantle, as in the Phyllidiidæ, and afterwards extended to include allied forms without gills.

Infidel, a term popularly used to describe a person who rejects Christianity as a divine revelation. The word does not properly apply to heathens or heretics. Moslems employ a similar term (' giaour,' ' kaffir,' etc.) to describe Christians.

Infinite, connotes chiefly the attributes of the Deity or Absolute Being, but is also used to describe the boundlessness and immeasurableness of space, time, or the universe. The use of the word in the Milesian school of Greek philosophers, *e.g.* by Anaximander, marks, however crudely, the beginning of an attempt to give a scientific statement of the universe. It is often assumed by modern thinkers that the Greek philosophers, and even such modern philosophers as Hobbes and Hegel, confounded the idea of the ' immeasurable ' with that of the ' unbounded,' because, according to the methods of elliptic non-Euclidean geometry, it is at least plausible to argue that space is as ' measurable ' as the surface of any *unbounded* spherical body, or the necessarily unbounded circumference of a vast circle, and, again, because geometry can conceive of an immeasurable and unbounded right line becoming bounded by merely cutting off a small part and leaving the line bounded by the two terminals so formed. Whether these methods which attempt to apply the rigid exactness of mathematical science to philosophical theories of the space are valid, depends on the extent to which they may be said themselves to postulate such arbitrary assumptions as that space is in any way analogous to a sphere or that an I. line becomes finite by imagining a point of section.

Infinite and **Infinity** are perhaps the most difficult conceptions mathematicians have to make. Infinity is defined as being that quantity which is greater than every assignable quantity, and it is denoted by the sign ∞. It is most easily conceived as a imit, *e.g.* as the quantities $\frac{1}{2}$, $\frac{1}{3}$, $\frac{1}{4}$, $\cdots \frac{1}{n} \cdots$ get smaller and smaller, so *n* gets larger and larger, and the limit to which *n* tends, as the infinitesimal $\frac{1}{n}$ tends to zero, is ∞. In higher geometry parallel lines are those which meet at infinity, and the asymptotes of an hyperbola are the tangents to the curve at points on it infinitely distant. All points at infinity are on the line at infinity, whose equation in areals is $x + y + z = 0$, and all circles pass through two imaginary points known as the circular points at infinity.

Infinitesimal, in mathematics, is defined as a quantity smaller than every assignable quantity. The idea of an I. is obtained by supposing a quantity to decrease indefinitely but yet never actually to become zero. In calculations in general an I. may be neglected in comparison with ordinary magnitudes. If ϵ is an I., ϵ^2 is an I. of the second order, and ϵ^2 similarly may be neglected in comparison with ϵ. A practical conception is obtained in astronomical problems. The distance of most fixed stars from the earth is very great, and the radius of the earth so small in comparison that it may be regarded as an I. and neglected in the calculations without any loss of accuracy.

Infirmary, *see* HOSPITAL.

Inflammation, a term used to denote certain tissue-changes which are accompanied by the symptoms of redness, swelling, pain, and heat-sensations. I. is primarily a protective process by which the body attempts to get rid of some irritating or injurious substance, and is a feature of almost every disease and injury. Like many other natural processes, however, the I. is apt to carry on its work without regard for the comfort of the individual, and the duty of the physician is often to guard against I. killing the patient while it removes the cause of his disease. Modern theories tend to attribute the symptoms known as I. to reactions between microbes and the white corpuscles. Where the tissues are injured and no germs are present, the process of repair goes on without undue swelling or pain, while any invasion of bacteria is attended by the characteristic symptoms of I., sometimes followed by suppuration or the formation of abscesses. The process of I. begins with the presence of an excess of blood. The blood stream is retarded in the region of irritation; this gives the red appearance and also accounts for the sensation of heat. The blood vessels become dilated and there is considerable effusion of white corpuscles through the walls of the vessels. The continuance of the irritating stimuli causes more and more blood to flow to the part with still greater effusion of lymph and white corpuscles, so that the part swells, the feeling of heat becomes more intense, and the pain takes on a throbbing character owing to the communication of the motion of the heart to the dilated arteries. The white corpuscles are busy destroying germs, dead tissue is being detached, and new tissue built up ; the products of I. are carried away in the blood or discharged from abscesses, etc. The treatment of I. is based on the need for expediting the work of the inflammatory process and relieving the body of the strain caused by the purely natural procedure. It is therefore necessary to remove or destroy the microbes or agents which cause irritation, to

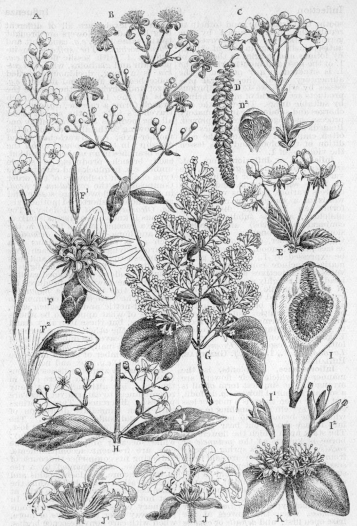

TYPES OF INFLORESCENCE

A. Raceme—Bird Cherry. B. Panicle—Traveller's Joy. C. Corymb—*Pyrus sorbus*. D¹. Catkin—Hazel. D². Single male flower of Hazel Catkin. E. Umbel—Dwarf Cherry. F. Capitulum or Head—*Olearia Haastii*. F¹. Stamens and pistil of inner florets. F². A single ray floret. G. Thyrsus—Lilac. H. Dichasium—Euonymus. I. Hypanthodium—Fig. I¹. Single female flower. I². Single male flower. J. Verticillaster—Jerusalem Sage. J¹. Longitudinal section of same. K. Glomerule—Box.

soothe that irritation, and to help to repair the injury caused by the germs. Microbes are destroyed by antiseptic dressings in case of skin I., by lotions and gargles in the case of I. of the nose and mouth, while if the I. is situated in any portion of the alimentary canal, the natural processes by which waste and injurious products are got rid of may be helped by suitable drugs. To lessen the discharges and subdue the inflammatory process astringents are employed. Remedies called *antiphlogistics* are often employed to change the condition of the blood and thus lessen the violence of I.

Inflection, or **Inflexion** (from Lat. *inflectere*, to bend), in grammar, the variations, changes, or modifications of form which words undergo to express various relations with other words of a sentence or clause. It forms an important division of philology, and is subdivided into conjugation (verbs) and declension (nouns, pronouns, adjectives). Gender, number, and voice, as well as case, tense, mood, and person may be expressed by I., and some grammarians include comparison of adverbs and adjectives also under this head. I. is, roughly speaking, a mark of Indo-Germanic and Semitic languages as opposed to agglutinative or analytic. It may be internal, initial, or final in Semitic, but is usually final in Indo-Germanic words, except in cases of reduplication. Modern English has comparatively few Is. left. *See* Jespersen, *Progress in Language . . .*, 1894. *Cf.* GRAMMAR, PHILOLOGY.

Inflorescence, in plants, is the manner in which their flowers are arranged. The simplest form of all is a solitary terminal flower, *e.g.* daffodil, but more often there is a more or less complex system of branching (*q.v.*) in which the branches do not develop into foliage-shoots but bear flowers. The stalk upon which the flowers are borne is known as the *peduncle* or *rachis;* if the flowers spring directly from the peduncle they are said to be *sessile*, but if they depend from a secondary stalk they are said to possess *pedicels*. An I. found at the apex of a shoot is *terminal*, if found in the axils of leaves it is *axillary*. There are two distinct types of I.: *indefinite* or *racemose*, when the flowers at the base open first; and *definite* or *cymose* when the flowers at the apex first become mature. One of the commonest forms of the indefinite I. is the *raceme*, in which the flowers are connected to the peduncle by pedicels, *e.g.* lily-of-the-valley and bird-cherry. The *corymb* resembles the raceme in being stalked, but the pedicels, produced at different levels, are all of different lengths and the flowers are brought to the same level, *e.g.* candytuft and *Pyrus sorbus*. The *spike* is an indefinite I. with sessile flowers, *e.g.* plantain and gladiolus, while the *catkin* is a long, deciduous crowded spike bearing unisexual flowers, *e.g.* hazel and birch. In the *panicle* the axis of the I. branches, and each branch forms a raceme, *e.g.* oats and traveller's joy ; in the *simple umbel* all the pedicels are given off at one level owing to the abbreviation of the mother-axis, *e.g.* dwarf-cherry and cowslip ; in the *compound umbel* the axis branches in an umbellate fashion, each branch producing a simple umbel, *e.g.* hemlock and carrot. The type common to flowers of the order Compositæ is the *capitulum* or *head*, in which the flowers are sessile and are borne on a shortened mother axis, *e.g. Olearia Haastii* and daisy. The curious I. known as a *thyrsus* is mixed, being a raceme, and is found in the lilac and horse-chestnut. A *dichasium* such as is seen in *Euonymus* is a biparous cyme in which each axis produces two daughter axes and ends in a flower. The I. of the fig is a peculiar, hollow, pear-shaped capitulum, and the flowers are produced internally; this is called a *hypanthodium*. The *verticillaster* common to the dead-nettle and Jerusalem sage, consists of what appear to be whorls of flowers, but these in reality stand one above the other and are borne in the axils of leaves on opposite sides of the stem. Finally, a *glomerule* consists of a number of cymes united to form a head, *e.g.* box and nettle.

Influenza, a zymotic disease, popularly confused with a severe cold in the head, but although it has many resemblances to catarrh yet there are points of difference. Thus I. brings with it an immediate depression of spirits, and sudden debility. The sense of taste and appetite are lost, the tongue becomes white and creamy; while sneezing and running of the eyes are frequent accompaniments. Shivering fits commence the course of the disease, accompanied by a rise in temperature, headache, pains and soreness all over the body, while the pulse becomes weak, and the skin, at first hot and dry, becomes moist. In ordinary cases the acute symptoms pass away after three days or more, when with care convalescence begins. There are always dangers of relapse, and premature exertion may easily bring on heart disease or even wreck the nervous system. I. is an epidemic disease, and spreads very rapidly. The atmospheric condition with which it is connected is not known. It may occur in all kinds of weather. It is known, however, to travel generally westwards or from S.E. to N.W. Thus the great epidemic of 1889-90 started in the Far East and spread rapidly over all Europe, and became the worst epidemic experienced for forty years in Britain. Since then it has appeared epidemically annually in some part of the British Isles.

In treating for I., the patient is immediately put to bed in a warm room, and fed with light food frequently. Complete rest is the main point, the remainder of the treatment being symptomatic. Thus warm bags of salt ease the aching limbs, while drugs such as phenacetin and antipyrin are sometimes used with great care. Stimulants are used, but only in small quantities *after* food has been taken. Purgatives are used at the commencement of the attack, and in cases where cardiac irregularity occurs, heart tonics are administered. Then in the convalescent stage, rest and the moderate use of stimulants, together with nerve tonics like preparations of iron, quinine, and strychnine, or hypophosphites, etc., are the best means of overcoming the resultant debility. A sea voyage or a few weeks at a watering-place is, however, the best cure. *See* EPIDEMIC, GERM.

In Formâ Pauperis (' in the character of a poor man '). Any person may sue or defend an action as a pauper on proof that he is not worth £25, his wearing apparel and the subject matter of the cause only excepted. Before being allowed to appear *in formâ pauperis* as a *plaintiff* a person must lay a case before counsel for his opinion as to whether or not he has reasonable grounds for suing as a pauper ; and no person may sue as a pauper unless the statement of the case laid before counsel for his opinion, together with the counsel's opinion, and an affidavit by himself or his solicitor that the statement of the case sets out fully and truly all the material facts to the best of his knowledge and belief, are produced to the court or judge to whom the application to sue *in formâ pauperis* is made. No court fee is payable by a person admitted to sue or defend *in formâ pauperis.* Where a person is admitted to sue or defend *in formâ pauperis,* the court may, if necessary, assign him counsel or solicitor, or both, to assist him, and these latter may not refuse assistance, except for good reason shown. Any person who agrees or endeavours to take or obtain any fee or reward from a person admitted to sue or defend *in formâ pauperis* for the conduct of the business as to which he has been so

admitted is guilty of contempt of court (*q.v.*); and if the pauper litigant agrees to give any fee, he will be at once disentitled to sue or defend in the same case as a pauper. It is the duty of the solicitor assigned to a pauper litigant to take care that no notice is served, or summons issued, or petition presented without good cause.

Information: 1. A mode of proceeding against persons accused of crimes other than felonies. It is a speedy process, which brings an offender to trial without a previous finding by a grand jury. Such criminal Is. are of two kinds : (*a*) Is. *ex officio*, and (*b*) Is. by the Master of the Crown office. The former may be used in certain cases of misdemeanour, such as seditious libels, or riots, oppression, and bribery by magistrates or other officers, or other misdemeanours tending to the disturbance or danger of the government, where the circumstances are such that the ordinary delays incidental to legal process must be avoided. In form an *ex officio* I. is a formal written charge of an offence filed by the Attorney-General in the King's Bench Division. A crown office I. is filed in the King's Bench Division by the Master of the Crown Office on the application of a private individual. Leave of court must first be obtained. Such Is. are only granted in the case of suggestions of the commission of misdemeanours of a gross and notorious kind, *e.g.* aggravated libel, bribery at elections. In practice Is. for libel are only granted where the person libelled occupies a public office or position. After a criminal I. of whatever kind has been filed, the accused is tried in the usual way by a petty jury. 2. A charge made to a justice of the peace or stipendiary or other magistrate of some offence punishable on summary conviction. A justice cannot issue a warrant for arrest in the first instance, except upon an I., or complaint in writing made on the oath of the informant or other person on his behalf. Where a summons only is issued in the first instance the I. need not be on oath or in writing. *See* Archbold's *Criminal Pleading, Practice, and Evidence,* 1910 ; Russell, *On Crimes.*

Informer, a common I. is one who prefers an accusation against another, with the object of recovering a statutory reward for so doing. Any person may bring criminal proceedings on behalf of the crown in the absence of express statutory provisions to the contrary. *Civil* proceedings for penalties can only be brought by Is., where a statute expressly allows them to do so, and in any case must be brought within a year of the alleged offence. In another sense, the term I. is used to denote an accomplice in crime who has turned king's evidence. An Act of 1400 provides for punishing false Is. *See* Russell, *On Crimes.*

Infusion, a process of extracting the active principles of vegetable substances without boiling. The product of the process is also termed an I. The general method is to digest the parts containing the substance to be extracted in water. If the substance is volatile and is soluble in cold water, it is better to digest the material in cold water, as it can then be extracted without admixture of other substances. Many active principles are, however, more readily soluble in hot water, and the temperature should be regulated according to the degree of volatility of the substance. When it is necessary to boil the mixture the process is known as decoction; this is often accompanied by chemical changes in some of the substances concerned.

Infusoria, a term applied to numerous classes of active Protozoa, appearing in stagnant infusions of animal or vegetable matter. The majority of them occur in great numbers, and are provided with vibratile locomotor processes of their living matter, which are practically permanent, and express the predominantly active constitution of these cells. When dirty water is held in a glass vessel between the eye and the light, the I. are generally quite visible, though most of them are microscopic. They occur both in fresh and salt water.

Infusorial Earth, a deposit of a siliceous nature, formed principally of the frustrates of diatoms. In making dynamite it is employed as an absorbent of nitro-glycerine, and it is also used under the name of ' Tripoli Powder ' for polishing purposes.

Inge, Very Rev. William Ralph (*b.* 1860), an English divine, Dean of St. Paul's since 1911. He had a brilliant career at Eton and Cambridge, was assistant master at Eton (1884-88), fellow and tutor of Hertford College, Oxford (1889-1904), select preacher at Oxford and Cambridge frequently between 1893-1910, Lady Margaret Professor of Divinity, Cambridge (1907-11). His writings include: *Society in Rome under the Cæsars,* 1886 ; *Eton Latin Grammar* (with Rawlins), 1889 ; *Christian Mysticism,* 1899 ; *Faith and Knowledge,* 1904 ; *Speculum Animæ,* 1911 ; *The Church and the Age,* 1912.

Ingelheim, two small market tns. of Germany adjoining each other in the grand - duchy of Hesse - Darm-

stadt, about 8 m. W. of Mainz. At one time they were celebrated for the palace of Charles the Great. Pops. 3500 and 3853.

Ingelmunster, a tn. of Belgium in W. Flanders, situated 7½ m. N. of Courtrai, with manufs. of carpets, linen, and salt. Pop. 6500.

Ingelow, Jean (1820-97), an English novelist and poetess, born in Boston, Lincolnshire. She published her first poems, *A Rhyming Chronicle of Incidents and Feelings,* 1850, anonymously. Her poems are characterised by their novelty and charm, and her novels also are worthy of attention. Among her works are *Poems,* 1863, which contained ' The High Tide on the Coast of Lincolnshire, 1571,' one of her best ; ' A Story of Doom,' 1867 ; ' Deborah's Book and the Lonely Rock,' 1867 ; ' The Grandmother's Shoe,' 1867. Among her novels are : *Mopsa the Fairy,* 1869 ; *Off the Skelligs,* 1872 ; *Don John,* 1876 ; *Fated to be free,* 1875. See *Some Recollections of Jean Ingelow and her Early Friends* (London), 1901.

Ingemann, Bernhard Severin (1789-1862), a Danish writer, born at Thorkildstrup in Falster. From 1822 till his death, he was a lecturer at the academy of Sorö. He wrote many poems and also various other kinds of works, among them being : *Reinald Underbarnet,* 1815 ; *Valdemar den Store og hans Mœnd,* 1824 ; *Erik Menveds Barndom,* 1828 ; *Samlede Skrifter,* 1843 - 44 ; *Guldœblet, et sventyrdigt i tolo Sange,* 1856. *See* H. Schwanenflügel, *Ingemanns Liv og Digtning,* 1886.

Ingenhousz, Johannes (Johan or Jan) (1730-99), a Dutch physician, chemist, and scientist. Coming to London about 1765, he became intimate with Dr. Pringle, and was recommended by him as aulic councillor and physician to Maria Theresa and Joseph II. (*c.* 1769). After travelling abroad I. settled in London (*c.* 1779), becoming F.R.S. He conducted researches in electricity, inventing an electrophorus and the plate electrical machine. His works include : *Experiments on Vegetables, discovering their Power of Purifying Air in Sunshine* . . ., 1779 ; *Essay on the Food of Plants* . . ., 1796 ; *Anfangsgründe der Electricität,* 1781. See *Biographie Médicale.*

Ingersoll, a tn. of Oxford co., Ontario, Canada. It stands on the Grand Trunk and Canadian Pacific Railways, and on the Thames R. It manufactures agricultural implements and furniture. Pop. 5000.

Ingersoll, Charles Jared (1782-1862), a son of Jared I., was for fourteen years district-attorney for Pennsylvania, and from 1841-47 a prominent leader of the Democrats. Previous to this he sat in Congress for two years (1813-15), when he advocated the principle that ' free ships make free goods.' He published a political satire entitled, *Inchiquin's Letters*, and a *Sketch of the War of* 1812, also some poems and a drama.

Ingersoll, Jared (1749-1822), an American jurist, born in Connecticut. He became one of the most prominent lawyers and judges in Philadelphia. From 1780-81, he was a member of Congress, and six years later he became a delegate to the convention that framed the Federal constitution. His son, Charles Jared, more or less followed in his footsteps.

Ingersoll, Robert Green (1833-99), an American lecturer and lawyer, born at Dresden, New York, and was the son of a Congregational minister. He practised law in Illinois, and in 1857 went to Persia. In 1862 he became a colonel in a cavalry regiment, and not long after was made attorney-general of Illinois. He became known by reason of his lectures directed principally against Christianity. Among his writings are : *The Gods and Other Lectures*, 1876 ; *Some Mistakes of Moses*, 1879 ; *Great Speeches*, 1887. *See* Edward G. Smith, *The Life and Reminiscences of Robert G. Ingersoll*, 1904.

Inghirami, Tommaso (surnamed ' Fedra ' from his success as Phædra in Seneca's *Hippolytus*) (1470-1516), a poet, orator, and humanist of an Italian noble family. Seven of his Latin orations were published (Rome, 1777), and Erasmus says he was called ' the Cicero of his age.' Julius II. made him keeper of the Vatican library. He left MSS. of a *Commentary on Horace's 'Ars Poetica,'* and *Abstract of Roman Hist.*

Ingleborough, a hill in the W. Riding of Yorkshire, England, about 17 m. S.E. of Kendal. On the S. is Ingleborough Cave containing stalagmites and stalactites, and on the top of the hill are the remains of an old camp. Alt. 2373 ft.

Ingleby, Clement Mansfield (1823-86), a Shakespearean scholar, born at Edgbaston, Birmingham. He was educated at Cambridge, and afterwards joined his father as a solicitor. He gave up this profession, however, and spent his time in writing, chiefly works on Shakespeare, among them being : *The Shakespeare Fabrications*, 1859 ; *A Complete View of the Shakespeare Controversy*, 1861 ; *Shakespeare's Hermeneutics*, 1875 ; *Shakespeare's Bones*, 1883.

Ingleton, a vil. of the W. Riding of Yorkshire, England, situated on the Greta, about 10 m. N.W. of Settle. In the vicinity are situated limestone caves. Pop. about 1800.

Inglis, Sir James Charles (*b.* 1851), the general manager and consulting engineer of the Great Western Railway since 1903. He has taken a leading part in the construction of numerous railway and harbour works and is president of the Institute of Civil Engineers. He was knighted in 1911.

Inglis, John (**Lord Glencorse**) (1810-91), born in Edinburgh. From 1867 till his death he was Lord Justice-General of Scotland and Lord President of the Court of Session. He is remembered for his brilliant defence of Madeline Smith in 1857. In 1863 he published an *Historical Study of Law*. *See* Watt's *Life*, 1893.

Ingoldsby, Sir Richard (*d.* 1685), an English soldier, born in Buckinghamshire. Originally on the parliamentary side, and instrumental in bringing about the death of Charles I., he eventually ranged himself on the side of Charles II., and captured General Lambert. He was successful in obtaining a pardon from the king for his former actions.

Ingoldsby, Thomas, *see* BARHAM, RICHARD HARRIS.

Ingolstadt, a fortified tn. of Bavaria, standing on the l. b. of the Danube, 45 m. N.W. of Munich. It contains an old castle and was famous for its university, founded in 1472, where many great scholars were students. In 1800 it was moved to Landshut, and in 1826 to Munich. The town dates from the 9th century ; it was fortified early in the 16th century, and again in the 19th after the French had destroyed its former fortifications. Pop. 23,760.

Ingraham, Joseph Holt (1809-60), an American writer and clergyman of the American Episcopal Church. He went to sea and served in S. American revolutions; became a teacher, 1832; finally taking orders, 1855. He wrote the novels, *Lafitte . . . ; Captain Kyd; The Dancing Feather; The Hunchback and the Roué*, 1843, and *The South-west, by a Yankee,* 1836; and the popular religious series, *The Prince of the House of David*, 1855; *The Pillar of Fire*, 1859; *The Throne of David*, 1860.

Ingrain Colours, those which are dyed in the material before it is manufactured, and are thus rendered fast and able to resist the action of water when washed.

Ingram, Arthur Foley Winnington (*b.* 1858), Bishop of London, born in Worcestershire, the fourth son of the Rev. E. Winnington Ingram, of Stamford Rectory. Educated at Marlborough College and Keble College, Oxford, obtaining a first-class Mods. and a second-class Greats. From 1881-84 he acted as private tutor, and then held a curacy in St. Mary's,

Shrewsbury, for one year, leaving it to become private chaplain to the Bishop of Lichfield, which position he continued to fill till 1889. In that year, he became head of Oxford House, Bethnal Green, and chaplain to the Archbishop of York, and Bishop of St. Albans. In 1895 he became rector of Bethnal Green, and in the following year, rural dean of Spitalfields. From 1897 to 1901 he was canon of St. Paul's Cathedral and Bishop of Stepney (suffragan to Bishop of London). He has published *Church Difficulties* ; *Work in Great Cities* ; *Christ and His Friends* ; *Banners of the Christian Faith*, etc.

Ingram, Herbert (1811-60), born at Boston, Lincolnshire. In 1842 he founded the *Illustrated London News*, in conjunction with Nathaniel Cooke. In 1856 he became M.P. for Boston, his native town. He was drowned in a collision on Lake Michigan, while on a tour in America.

Ingram, John H. (*b.* 1849), an English traveller, linguist, and author; editor of the Eminent Women Series. His works include: *Poems by Dalton Stone*, 1863; *Flora Symbolica*, 1868; *Memoir of Poe*, 1874; *Haunted Houses of England*, 1883-84 ; *Life of O. Madox-Brown*, 1884 ; *Poe's Works*, 1888; *E. B. Browning's Works and Memoir*, 1888; *Darley's May Queen*, 1892; *C. Marlowe and his Associates*, 1904; *Chatterton*, 1910.

Ingram, John Kells, Dr. (1823-1907), an Irish author and economist, educated at Dublin. He was long connected with Trinity College, becoming fellow in 1846, professor of oratory and English literature in 1852, regius professor of Greek in 1866, librarian in 1879, and vice-provost in 1898. As an undergraduate he produced *The Memory of the Dead*, or *Who fears to speak of 'Ninety-Eight?* 1843, a poem adopted as the anthem of the Irish nationalisation movement. His *Political Economy*, contributed to the *Ency. Brit.*, was published separately in 1888, and translated into eight European languages and into Japanese. Other works are: *On the Present Position and Prospects of Political Economy*, 1878; *History of Slavery and Serfdom*, 1888; *Sonnets . . . ; Outlines of the History of Religion*, 1900; *Human Nature and Morals according to A. Comte*, 1901; *Practical Morals*, 1904; *Final Transition*, 1905. He wrote papers on geometrical analysis and classical etymology, and edited the *Imitation of Christ*, 1893 (from Dublin and Cambridge MSS.). *See* Falkiner, *Memoir*, 1907; Palgrave's *Dict. of Polit. Econ.* (App. 1908); *Positivist Review* (June 1907, Beesly and Swinny).

Ingram, Sir William James (*b.* 1847), an English editor, educated at Winchester and Cambridge, son of the founder of the *Illustrated London News* (1842), now managing director of the Illustrated London News and Sketch, Ltd. He became a barrister of Inner Temple in 1872, and was three times M.P. (L.) for Boston in 1874-95.

Ingres, Jean Auguste Dominique (1781-1867), a French painter, born at Montauban. In 1796 he became a pupil of David, and in 1801 was successful in obtaining the Grand Prix. In 1806 he proceeded to Rome where he studied and worked until 1820, leaving in that year for Florence. Here he stayed four or five years and then returned to Paris. While in Italy he had carefully studied Raphael, and he brought the latter's influence to bear upon David's teaching. He again visited Rome and finally returned to Paris in 1841, having been made grand officer of the Legion of Honour. Among his pictures are : ' The Vow of Louis XIII.'; ' Apotheosis of Homer '; ' Stratonice '; ' Œdipus and the Sphinx '; ' The Odalisque.' See *Life* by Raymond Balze, 1880.

Ingulph (*d.* 1109), an abbot of Crowland, an honour conferred on him by William of Normandy, having previously been his secretary. He had before this visited the Holy Land on a pilgrimage and on his return had joined a monastery in Normandy. The *Historia Monasterii Croylandensis*, printed by Henry Savile (1596), and of which there is a translation by Riley in Bohn's Antiquarian library (1854), once attributed to him, is now considered to be the work of some later writer and merely a romance.

Inhalation, used in medicine of that treatment which aims at affording some relief by causing the patient to inhale or breathe in certain drugs dissolved in warm water. The nature of the relief sought varies with the disease. Thus I. may serve as an antiseptic or stimulant, or, again, as a remedy for spasms or other respiratory irritation.

Inhambane, a seaport standing on the bay of the same name and situated in Portuguese East Africa. It does a large trade in wax, india-rubber, and copal. Population about 3400.

Inheritance, in a general sense means the act of inheriting, whether the thing, quality, or otherwise inherited be the property of a deceased person, a tradition, a predisposition to disease, or mental or moral qualities. In a narrower sense restricted to the legal right to property by descent, or, by extension, to the property inherited. Roman law differed radically from English law in two important respects : (1) In English law the word ' heir ' (and its derivatives) is confined exclusively to the person entitled on an intestacy to real estate, and any title or dignity and heirlooms passing with the estate; (2) the maxim *Nemo esthœres viventis* (no one is the heir of living person) is rigidly applied so as to exclude a prospective heir or possible heir from any rights in the property until the death of the ancestor. As a corollary of (1), it is to be observed that a person named in a will of realty is by English law a *devisee* and not an heir ; in Roman law the term ' heir ' applied indiscriminately to all who, being in the power of the head of the family, had a natural claim on his property, irrespective of whether they took under a testament or on intestacy, which he took by descent or under a testament. Roman testaments were originally made by public proclamation in the *Comitia Curiata* (or Council of Roman Family Heads), or by means of a fictitious sale, in which the testator handed over his property to the *familiœ emptor* or person destined either to be the heir or trustee for the ultimate beneficiaries. There was, as in every legal system, a prescribed order of succession to property, the first claimants being called the *sin heredes*, *i.e.* all persons in the power of the deceased who on his death became *sin juris*. After these came the *agnati* or members of the same civil family in a definite progression. To exclude effectually his own heirs, the testator had to do so by name in the will. But it was essential to institute an heir of some kind, for a Roman testament was of no effect unless there was such a person to succeed to the *persona* of the testator, *i.e.* to continue his legal existence after death, hence the necessity of the old practice of a fictitious sale above noticed and later the institution by will. To effect such institution where the testator desired to exclude the natural claimants, a slave could be nominated as *heres necessarius*, *i.e.* he could not decline the burden of the property. Later, excluded children were given the right to impugn the will if omitted in it, and recover a certain share of the property. In English law the fundamental difference in the canons of descent to real property from the Roman and civil systems founded on the civil law is that the rule of primogeniture has prevailed from remote feudal times. The rules of descent to freeholds of I. are these : (1) Descent is traced

from the last ' purchaser ' (a technical term meaning the person who last took in any other way than by descent); (2) descent is to the lineal issue *in infinitum;* (3) males are preferred to females; primogeniture determines the male entitled, but females succeed equally as co-parceners (*q.v.*). (4) Remoter lineal issue ' representing ' their own parents (who would if not deceased have succeeded to the property) take *per stirpes*, *i.e.* as opposed to taking *per capita* or in their own right (for a detailed explanation of this, *see under* DISTRIBUTIONS, STATUTES OF); (5) the nearest ancestor takes on failure of lineal issue; (6) paternal ancestors and their issue are preferred to maternal, and male maternal to female maternal ancestors and issue; (7) the issue of ancestors represent such ancestors, and half-blood take next after the common male ancestor and issue, but next after common female ancestor. A posthumous child takes by descent only from his birth; hence to obviate his exclusion it is necessary to constitute him devisee by anticipation. All the above canons apply to copyhold land, save where varied by custom. *See* BURGAGE, GAVELKIND, BOROUGH ENGLISH.

Inhibition, used in a technical sense of the sentence passed upon a clergyman, by which he is prevented from the exercise of his ecclesiastical functions. It can therefore be used as a weapon for enforcing the laws of the church.

Inia (*Inia geoffrensis*), a toothed fresh-water dolphin, found in the lakes near the Cordilleras and in some of the upper tributaries of the Amazons, where it is regarded with superstition by the Indians. It is about 8 ft. in length, has a long cylindrical snout with stiff hairs, and only the merest rudiment of a dorsal fin. It is generally found in troops of three or four and is hunted on account of the oil it yields. It feeds chiefly on fish.

Inisfail, used in poetry as a synonym for Ireland, and means ' the island of the Fall.' The ' Fail ' or ' Lia-fail ' is the stone which, since the days of James VI. of Scotland, has rested under the coronation chair in Westminster Abbey. Legend tells that it was on this stone that Jacob fell asleep when he dreamt of the flight of stairs reaching to heaven, and the Dedennans carried it to Ireland and set it up as the ' inauguration ' stone at Tara.

Inishkeel, an island of Ireland, belonging to co. Donegal, and situated in Gweebarra Bay, with a capacious harbour.

Inishmacsaint, a par. of Ireland on the Erne, partly in co. Donegal and partly in Fermanagh. It is named from an abbey founded by St. Nenn in the 6th century.

Inishmore, an island of Ireland, situated at the mouth of Galway Bay. It is 9 m. in length and 2½ m. in breadth, possessing two natural harbours on the N. coast.

Initials. In some cases signature by I. constitutes a good signature in law. Section 12 of the Civil Procedure Act, 1883, provided that in all actions upon written instruments, it should be sufficient to designate any of the parties by their initials, but the section is now obsolete. There are decisions to the effect that signature by I. is allowable in the case of memoranda and agreements comprised under the Statute of Frauds (*see* FRAUDS, STATUTE OF). By the Wills Act, 1837, a will or codicil may be validly signed by I. only. Probably there are no documents which in the eye of the law must be signed in full, although it is clearly unwise from the point of view of identification not to do so. A deed certainly requires no signature, the traditional essentials of every deed being no more than sealing and delivery. In Scots law I. also constitute a good signature to a deed, but the genuineness of the I. must be proved. In American law it seems that I. are no part of a name, and that no middle name or I. is recognised by law.

Initiative. It is a commonplace of political science that very few constitutions are really so framed as to ensure the representation of the views of the majority of the electorate upon any one particular issue. Some deny that a Representative Chamber like the English House of Commons is returned for the purpose of effectuating the will of the majority upon every single issue, on the ground that legislative authority and omnipotence rest with parliament and not with the electorate, and it is further asserted that any relation of agency as may subsist between the electorate and its representatives, subsists only so far as the latter can be said to be entrusted with a mandate for carrying out a general party policy. Sir A. Dicey points out that it is inconsistent with the legal notion of English parliamentary sovereignty to suppose that parliamentary electors have any legal means of initiating, sanctioning, or repealing the legislation of parliament, because the opinion of the electorate can only be expressed through parliament. Not that this view of the functions of the electorate is by any means essential to a representative policy, for in Switzerland all parliamentary deliberation is regarded as purely preliminary, and by the process of the Obligatory Referendum of legislative proposals, even after being passed by the Federal Assembly, must on the demand of a certain number of citizens be submitted to the electors for formal approval before they can become laws. This, indeed, was done in the times of ancient Rome in the question literally asked of the people 'Jubetisne?' Some of the Swiss cantonal constitutions go even further than this, by the device of the right of I. This right makes it incumbent on the legislature to publish proposals advocated by a certain proportion of the electorate, and cause them to be voted on at the local polling stations. It must be conceded that the I. ensures the literal observance of the will of the majority, but it is questionable whether it is a sound political expedient to cast on the people at large the actual business of law-making. Practised politicians must almost of necessity be better able to formulate the general aims of the majority in detailed proposals than the people themselves. Moreover, the people are apt to be so blended by prejudice or party passion as to be incapable of weighing up all that can be said for and against a proposed law, and certainly it must hamper indefinitely the work of legislation if every important amendment suggested at any stage of a bill had to be referred to the electorate for approval. Sidgwick, inspired by Bentham, advances the ingenious solution of making a member's election annually renewable with a view to deferring the final ratification of the legislative measures of the year until the annual election, so that in the interim the people might have an opportunity for cancelling any unpopular legislative innovation. For a full discussion of the question of the control of the people over government, *see* Sidgwick's *Elements of Politics,* ch. xxvii.

Injection, the act of throwing a substance into one or other of the cavities of the body; or the substance so injected. The substance is generally employed as an aqueous solution and is intended to have a curative effect by direct action on the organ into which it is injected or to which it is readily conveyed by the natural processes of the body. Hypodermic Is. are made by piercing the skin and introducing the active substance into the subcutaneous tissues by means of a small syringe. Intravenous I. is the introduction of a solution directly into a vein. Intramuscular I. is the introduction of a solution into the substance of a muscle. Vaginal, urethral, and rectal Is. are introduced into the vagina, urethra, and rectum respectively.

Injector, an apparatus for forcing water into a boiler against the pressure of the steam. M. Henri Giffard invented an I. in 1858 which is now in general use. Steam from the boiler passes into a conical pipe, the size of the opening of which can be regulated by an adjustable cone. As the steam rushes out of this, it meets the feed water, and is condensed, so creating a partial vacuum, which causes the water to rush in with a very great velocity, and to pass down another conical pipe. The escaping steam behind helps to drive it down this pipe. As it emerges from the narrow end of this conical pipe, it passes into the narrow end of another one. So, as it passes on down this expanding cone, its velocity slackens and the pressure increases. So the water is forced into the boiler through a non-return valve. This I. may be worked either by exhaust steam from the engine, or by steam from the boiler.

Injunction, in English law, a remedy given as a rule by a court of equity (q.v.) to restrain one or more of the parties in an action from doing or allowing their agents or servants to do an act which the court holds to be inequitable in regard to the rights of the other party. The I. was one of the modes by which the Chancellor built up his whole equity jurisdiction (see CHANCELLOR, CHANCERY, COURT, EQUITY). By this weapon the equity courts could override the common law whenever the latter was in conflict with the dictates of good conscience. The I. in such cases was issued in the form of a prohibition commanding the plaintiff not to go on with his action at common law on pain of imprisonment for contempt of court if he disobeyed. Is. are either (a) interlocutory or preliminary, or (b) final or perpetual. An interlocutory I. is granted on merely prima facie evidence, and for the purpose of preventing further damage to the plaintiff pending the ultimate decision of the dispute; it is usually only granted on the plaintiff giving an undertaking to pay damages if he does not succeed at the trial in making good his claim. Final or perpetual Is., as the name implies, definitely settle the rights of the parties. Is. as a rule are negative, i.e. they command a person to forbear from doing an act. But a mandatory I. is one which enjoins a positive act, e.g. to pull down a building erected in contravention of the rights of another. But even an I. which is negative in form may have an indirectly positive effect, e.g. an I. restraining A from performing, in breach of his contract with B, for any other manager than B will usually have the effect of making A stick to his contract rather than be out of employment. Is. may be granted to restrain the continued or threatened infringement of almost all kinds of rights.

Ink, a material used for producing records on paper and similar substances. The earliest varieties appear to have been prepared by suspending some carbonaceous material such as soot in a sticky solution (gum or varnish), but later the secretion of the cuttle-fish, or Sepia, was used. In the middle ages there first came into use an I. composed of a decoction of gall-nuts or other tannin-yielding substance, mixed with an iron salt. The use of these depended upon the formation of a bluish substance, which on oxidation (that is, exposure to the air) was converted into a black substance. The modern ' blue-black ink ' consists essentially of the same ingredients, but a ferrous salt is used and the development of the black colour only takes place after a shorter or longer exposure to the air. In order that the writing may be visible before oxidation a colouring matter (usually some indigo derivative) is added. This causes the blue appearance first noticed and the subsequent oxidation causes the black to appear. In the preparation of such Is. either China or Turkey galls are usually employed. These are ground, steeped in water, and to the aqueous extract a solution of ferrous sulphate (green vitriol or copperas) is added. At first a clear solution of a dark blue colour is obtained, but from this there gradually separates a black insoluble precipitate. In order to keep this in suspension gum arabic or some other viscid material is added. The I. soaks into the paper and is there oxidised, but the presence of the gum gives to the writing a ' shiny ' appearance. In order to avoid this certain Is. are made by using indigo - sulphonic acid (prepared by dissolving indigo in strong sulphuric acid) to which is added metallic iron. Ferrous sulphate is thus formed, and when the excess of acid is neutralised by means of chalk, the clear supernatant liquid obtained on allowing the mixture to stand, yields on mixing with a tannin solution a clear freely-flowing I. Certain conditions require to be fulfilled before an I. can be described as satisfactory. It should be non-corrosive, non-poisonous, permanent, not easily erased, and non-fermentable. The last requirement is usually fulfilled by the addition of some antiseptic, such as phenol or thymol.

Coloured inks.—These are usually aqueous solutions of the soluble coaltar colours. Thus, solutions of the eosins and rhodamines give red Is.; brilliant green and indigo preparations, etc., are used for the manufacture of green and blue Is., respectively. Further, blue I. is made from Prussian blue dissolved in oxalic acid. So-called gold and silver Is. are obtained by mixing the finely divided metals or their substitutes with gum and a solution of a soluble silicate.

Copying inks are made by the addition of glycerine, gum, or dextrin to a concentrated soluble tannin I. The addition of these materials greatly retards the oxidation of the tannate of iron by forming a film over the surface of the writing. This dissolves when the damp tissue paper is applied and an impression is thereby obtained.

Printers' ink usually consists of a varnish-like material made from resin, soap, and a drying oil in which is suspended a colouring matter. For black a mixture of lamp-black and indigo (the latter in small amount) is used. Reds, blues, and yellows are obtained by means of carmine, Prussian blue, and lead chromate, respectively. Other colours may be prepared by suitable mixtures of the above.

Marking inks nearly always contain some silver salt as a basis. A solution of the salt mixed with gum gives in contact with organic matter, such as cotton or linen, a stain which on exposure to light or heat or both gradually becomes black. The stain is indelible, but in course of time fades to a brownish colour.

Sympathetic inks are those which become visible only after suitable treatment. Thus a solution of galls may be used for writing. Thereby is produced a writing which on drying is invisible, but which on washing over with a weak solution of an iron salt becomes dark. If a solution of a cobalt salt be used for writing, no characters are visible until the paper on which the writing has been made is warmed. The characters then appear blue. Such inks are of no practical use but figure as of importance in fiction.

There are further cases of I. which belong to a special class. Some compounds appear to have the property of functioning, as though they possessed a certain structure, but also possess the property of easily modifying this. So, *e.g.* isatin (*q.v.*) exists in two modifications, the one stable and the other labile. Similarly acetoacetic ester can be represented either as $CH_3.CO.CH_2.COOC_2H_5$ (the keto form), or as $CH_3.C(OH):CH.COOC_2H_5$ (the enol form). Each is convertible the one into the other under certain ascertained conditions. This phenomenon is designated as *desmotropy* or *tantomerism*. In addition to the above-mentioned cases there are many in which the isomerism is due, not to a difference in the molecule itself, but to the arrangement of the atoms within the molecule. This form of I. is spoken of as *spatial-* or *stereo-isomerism* (*q.v.*).

Inkerman, a vil. in the Crimea, lying E. of Sebastopol. Here on Nov. 5, 1854, the English met the Russians in battle, and after a brave resistance, and when defeat seemed imminent, were reinforced by the French and gained the victory.

Inland Revenue, *see* EXCISE AND CUSTOMS DUTIES, TARIFF AND TAXATION.

Inland Sea, a sea of Japan, situated between the main island on the N., and the islands of Shikoku and Kiushiu on the S. It is about 240 m. in length, and its greatest breadth is 40 m. Its shores are exceedingly beautiful, and the waters are very calm.

END OF VOL. VII

THE TEMPLE PRESS, PRINTERS, LETCHWORTH

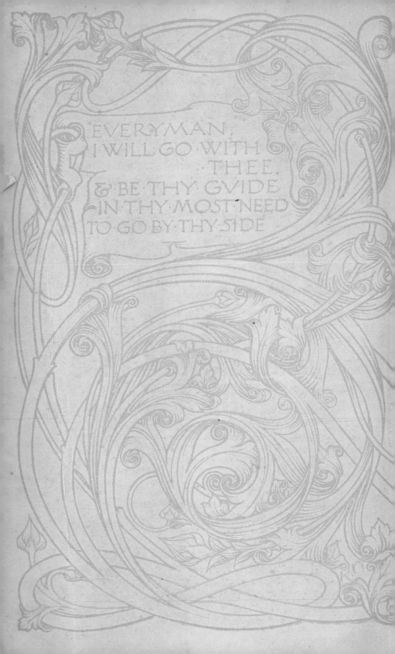

EVERYMAN,
I WILL GO WITH
THEE,
& BE THY GVIDE
IN THY MOST NEED
TO GO BY THY SIDE